IRISH CONVEYANCING LAW

Second Edition

by

Professor J.C.W. WYLIE
LL.M. (Harvard), LL.D. (Belfast),
Consultant, A&L Goodbody, Solicitors,
Dublin, Belfast, London, New York, Brussels

Consultant Editor:
Deborah H. Wheeler
BA (Mod), Barrister-at-law, Lecturer in
Land Law and Conveyancing at the Kings Inns

Butterworths

Ireland	Butterworth (Ireland) Ltd, 26 Upper Ormond Quay, **Dublin** 7
United Kingdom	Butterworths a Division of Reed Elsevier (UK) Ltd, Halsbury House, 35 Chancery Lane, **London** WC2A 1EL and 4 Hill Street, **Edinburgh** EH2 3JZ
Australia	Butterworths Pty Ltd, **Sydney, Melbourne, Brisbane, Adelaide, Perth, Canberra** and **Hobart**
Canada	Butterworths Canada Ltd, **Toronto** and **Vancouver**
Malaysia	Malayan Law Journal Sdn Bhd, **Kuala Lumpur**
New Zealand	Butterworths of New Zealand Ltd, **Wellington** and **Auckland**
Puerto Rico	Butterworths of Puerto Rico Inc, **San Juan**
Singapore	Reed Elsevier (Singapore) Ltd, **Singapore**
South Africa	Butterworth Publishers (Pty) Ltd, **Durban**
USA	Michie, **Charlottesville,** Virginia

© J.C.W. Wylie 1996

First Edition 1978
Second Impresssion 1980
Third Impression 1983

A CIP Catalogue record for this book is available from the British Library.

ISBN 1 85475 1816

Printed in Ireland by ColourBooks Ltd, Dublin.

Preface

I consider that I ought to begin the Preface to the second edition of this work with an apology! Alas, it is nearly 20 years since the first edition was published and I readily concede that this has been too long a gap. I am afraid that the pressure of other commitments (including, it must be said, publishing ones) rendered it impossible to undertake the major task of revision at an earlier stage. Readers will quickly discover that the long interval since publication of the first edition has resulted in numerous changes and it is these to which I must first draw attention.

This edition has involved some major restructuring of the work and much rewriting. It no longer seeks to cover the law of Northern Ireland. When the first edition was being written there were very few modern texts on Irish law and my then Consultant Editor, the late Mr Justice John Kenny, was most insistent that we should do our best to serve lawyers in the two jurisdictions. However, we both recognised that the result was always likely to be a somewhat unhappy compromise. The publishing world in Ireland has now changed out of all recognition and so my new Consultant Editor and I decided that this edition should confine its scope to the law in the Republic of Ireland. Even with that the book remains very substantial in size.

It has been necessary, of course, to reflect the large number of legislative changes and many judicial decisions which have had an impact on conveyancing law and practice over the past couple of decades. Regrettably, most of the former seem to make life even more complicated for the hard-pressed conveyancer. The first edition warned that the Family Home Protection Act, 1976, however laudable its policy aims, was likely to cause all sorts of problems for conveyancers. I was criticised by some for doing so, but it gives no sense of satisfaction to record that a fraction only of the difficulties was anticipated. Notwithstanding the belated attempt at some amelioration made by the Family Law Act, 1995, this and other legislation will continue to need careful attention by conveyancers.

The overall aims of this edition remain the same as set out in the Preface to the first edition, which is reproduced in the ensuing pages. It must be emphasised that a book of this nature has to meet needs which are not easily reconciled. One of its primary aims is an educative one, which necessitates explaining things to the less experienced which the more experienced know thoroughly and may feel do not need telling. Every effort is also made to address the more difficult points of law and practice, but no book can purport to deal with every point. The publication since the first edition of many other texts, which deal with topics of relevance to conveyancing, has enabled us to reduce the coverage in this edition and to concentrate on the conveyancing aspects. The hope remains that all those involved in, or interested in, conveyancing law and practice will find the book of some use. One of the remarkable features of recent decades has been the tireless efforts of the Law Society's Conveyancing Committee in providing support and guidance to conveyancers. Just how active the Committee has been was constantly reiterated as the revision work was being done. A new version of the *General Conditions of Sale* was published in 1995 and a new version of the *Objections and Requisitions on Title* was published in 1996. This edition takes both fully into account and I am most grateful to the Committee for giving permission to reproduce the forms themselves, and other forms referred to throughout the book, in the appendices.

As with the first edition, many have provided most welcome assistance. In the past few years it has been my privilege to be a consultant to A&L Goodbody, Solicitors (Dublin, Belfast, London, New York and Brussels). It has, indeed, been a most rewarding experience to work in the firm's Property Department and I am grateful for the most useful comments on draft chapters provided by members of the Private Client and Property Departments. Paddy Fagan, Solicitor, one of the longest-serving members of the Law Society's Conveyancing Committee, commented on the entire draft manuscript and provided much help and guidance. In Cardiff Jackie Jones, B.Sc.Econ, M.Phil, LL.B (Wales), Barrister-at-law, and Warren Palmer, LL.B (Wales) did most of the initial research into caselaw since the publication of the first edition. However, none of these people bears any responsibility for the text.

Special thanks must go to my new Consultant Editor, Debby Wheeler, Barrister-at-law. For many years the Lecturer in Land Law and Conveyancing at the King's Inns, and with long experience of practice at the Bar, she brought to bear on the manuscript a vast knowledge of Irish conveyancing law and practice. Our almost weekly meetings over the past couple of years have certainly been most productive and this edition has benefited much from her watchful eye.

Finally, I must pay tribute to Butterworth's Legal Editor in Dublin, Louise Leavy, who co-ordinated the production of this edition in a splendid fashion, and to Marian Sullivan for her wonderful keyboard skills.

Every effort has been made to state the law according to materials available up to 1st May 1996.

JCW Wylie

June 1996

Preface to First Edition

In the Preface to *Irish Land Law* (1975), I expressed the view, somewhat rashly, perhaps, that that book should be regarded as a beginning only and that a comprehensive book on conveyancing law was needed. The Incorporated Law Society of Ireland evidently took the same view, and this book is the result. It was commissioned by the Society in 1976 and, like *Irish Land Law,* has been sponsored by the Arthur Cox Foundation, whose chairman, Mr Justice Kenny, again very kindly agreed to act as Consultant Editor for the law of the Republic of Ireland.

The general aims of this book are the same as those which were expressed in the preface to *Irish Land Law*. Like the earlier book, it covers the law of both the Republic of Ireland and Northern Ireland. Thus, though integrated treatment of the law in both jurisdictions has been possible for the most part, there have been occasions when separate treatment has been necessary. This book has also been written for both students and practitioners.

So far as I am aware, this is the first textbook which seeks to provide comprehensive coverage of Irish conveyancing law. Its timing is particularly propitious in view of recent developments in both parts of Ireland. In the Republic, the Law Society issued a new contract for sale form, incorporating revised general conditions of sale, in 1976. At the time of writing, this form is in the process of being amended slightly and, when printed, will be known as the 1978 edition. However, throughout this book reference is made to the 1976 edition, the substance of which is exactly the same, except for an amendment to condition 17(2). This amendment is indicated on the form which is reproduced in Appendix A at the end of the text, and for its significance readers are referred to paragraphs 7.026-7 and 7.041 in the text. The Law Society in Northern Ireland has also been revising its general conditions of sale and the new edition is in the final stages of printing at the time of writing. I am most grateful to both Societies for giving me permission to reprint their new forms in Appendix A and, of course, the new conditions of sale are discussed in detail throughout the book. And for ease of cross-reference to the new conditions, I have included in the preliminary pages a table of references to the conditions in the text. There have also been important legislative developments which have had, or will have, considerable effect on conveyancing practice. Apart from the introduction of new taxes in recent years to which conveyancers must have regard, 1976 saw the enactment in the Republic of the Family Home Protection Act and the Local Government (Planning and Development) Act, both of which have required urgent reconsideration of day-to-day practice. In Northern Ireland, the Land Registration Act (NI), 1970, came finally into force on October 1st, 1977, along with the new Rules made under it. Important changes were also introduced by the Solicitors (NI) Order, 1976. All these matters are considered in detail in the text.

Perhaps a few more words may be said about the contents of this book. First, it has been written very much as a companion volume to *Irish Land Law* and this has had several consequences. One is that every effort has been made to avoid unnecessary duplication. Readers must bear this in mind, for it explains why a fuller discussion of certain topics is not to be found in this book. Where this occurs, the reason is usually that such discussion will be found in *Irish Land Law* and an appropriate cross-reference has been inserted instead. This has, of course, enabled me to make a considerable reduction in the size of the text, a matter which is so important in these days of escalating printing and publishing costs. It should also be mentioned that I have resisted the temptation to use this book as a method of updating *Irish Land La*w, for that will be done by a supplement which is being planned for the near future. Indeed, the intention is that in future years both books will be kept up-to-date by regular supplements. For this reason, the projected landlord and tenant legislation in the Republic, to which attention is drawn in several places in this book, will be dealt with in more detail in a supplement to *Irish Land Law*.

The absence of any 'rival' has, of course, meant that I have had to concentrate on stating the law as it is. However, I hope that I have not failed to point out areas where reform is necessary and to draw attention to those areas of conveyancing law and practice which seem to excite so much public comment nowadays. But the book remains primarily a text written by a lawyer for lawyers.

Many people have given me assistance in the writing of this book, but three in particular must have a special mention. First, its writing has resulted in continuation of the most happy working relationship between Mr Justice Kenny and myself which began several years ago when *Irish Land Law* was being planned. Once again he has acted as Consultant Editor for the law of the Republic of Ireland and he has also agreed again to accept joint responsibility for statements of that law. He has read the entire text and made numerous amendments and additions which I have been only too happy to accept. He was also primarily responsible for the writing of chapter 8. His invaluable contributions to the project have been made when other calls on his time have been most pressing and I am most grateful for all his efforts, as I am for the very kind hospitality he and his family provided during trips to Dublin.

Mr John F Buckley, Solicitor and Member of the Council of the Incorporated Law Society of Ireland, has also seen the entire text and has provided much counsel and advice on law and practice in the Republic. He has also assumed the burden of organising consultations with other solicitors, distributing parts of the text to others for comment and collating replies, tasks which he has had to fit in along with his very busy practice and work on committees of the Law Society. The interest in the project which he has shown, and his encouragement, have been most welcome, as has been the hospitality he and his family have provided in Dublin on numerous occasions in recent years. Mr Jack Pinkerton, Solicitor and former President of the Incorporated Law Society of Northern Ireland, has provided me with much useful information about practice in Northern Ireland and has commented on several parts of the text. In recording my special thanks to Messrs Buckley and Pinkerton, I must emphasise that neither of them should be held in any way responsible for the text of the book. Nor should various other bodies or persons who have commented on particular sections of the text or provided information. So far as the Republic is concerned, I am particularly grateful for the comments and advice of the following Dublin solicitors: Messrs. Eric Brunker, Patrick V Fagan, Ernest B Farrell, Garrett P Gill and Rory O'Donnell. I would also like to thank Mr James J. Ivers, Director-General of the Law Society, and his staff for their co-operation and Mr Colum Gavan Duffy, the Society's librarian, for help in relation to research material. In Northern Ireland, various members of the Law Society's Conveyancing and the Law of Property Committee commented on parts of the text and the Society's Assistant Secretary, Mr H Wynn Evans. provided much useful information and dealt with numerous queries. I am also grateful for the help of the following: Mr Bill Leitch, Solicitor, former First Parliamentary Draftsman of Northern Ireland and now Law Reform Consultant; Ms Liz Madill, Law Librarian in the Queen's University of Belfast; Mr. W. Bowden of the Registry of Deeds for Northern Ireland; Mr. Brian McAleenan, Solicitor.

Finally, special mention must be made of my mother who has been responsible for the typing of various drafts of the manuscript and my wife who has helped with preparation of the tables and index. The publishers and printers must also be thanked for their efforts in recent months.

Every effort has been made to state the law as on January 1st, 1978 .

J.C.W. Wylie

University College, Cardiff
February, 1978

I think that elementary justice requires that I should state that the entire of the first draft of this book (except that of chapter 8) was written by Mr Wylie who has also, without any assistance from me, prepared the index to the book and (most tedious and time consuming work) the table of cases and other tables.

Until I read the first draft I did not realise how much conveyancing law is to be found in the nominate Irish Reports and Mr Wylie's great industry has enabled him to give numerous references to early Irish cases which are never cited in Court.

Ours has, indeed, been a very happy partnership.

Conveyancing law is not taught in any of the university law schools in the Republic of Ireland though there are courses in the subject in King's Inns and in the Incorporated Law Society. One of the excuses frequently offered for this omission is the absence of a suitable text book. That excuse has now been removed and I hope that in the near future conveyancing law will become an optional subject in the four university law schools in the Republic of Ireland.

I have not been in practice as a conveyancer since February 1961 and I know that the practice in that field changes rapidly. In 1961, when I was appointed to the High Court, the sale of flats was unknown. If there are any errors in relation to current practice in the Republic, I am solely responsible.

John Kenny

The Supreme Court
Dublin
February, 1978

The Arthur Cox Foundation

Arthur Cox, classical scholar, senator and former President of the Incorporated Law Society of Ireland, was associated both as director of and solicitor to many industries which have become great enterprises. He was a specialist in company law and conveyancing and was Chairman of the Company Law Reform Committee. He made many outstanding contributions to our community. When he decided to retire from practice, a number of his clients, professional colleagues and other friends thought that the most appropriate tribute to him would be a fund to help the publication of legal textbooks. The market in Ireland for these is so small that very few of them have been written and their absence is a severe handicap to lawyers and law students. There was a generous response to our appeal.

After his retirement he was ordained a priest and went to Zambia to do missionary work. He died there as a result of a motor car accident.

He often spoke to me about the importance of having textbooks on Irish law and their vital role in the education of students in the practice of the law. As Mr. Wylie and I had co-operated in the writing of *Irish Land Law* and as our relationship was such a happy one, I was glad to accept his invitation to act as Consultant Editor for this book. The Trustees of the Foundation (Mr C Russell Murphy FCA, the Incorporated Law Society and I) are glad to have been able to sponsor the publication of this book.

John Kenny

The Supreme Court
Dublin
May, 1978

Contents

Preface v
Preface to First Edition vii
The Arthur Cox Foundation xi
Contents xiii
Table of Statutes xvii
Table of Cases xlv

Chapter 1 Nature of Conveyancing

I.   Nature of Conveyancing 1
II. Conveyancing in Ireland 6
III. Role of Professional Persons 18

Chapter 2 Sale By Public Auction

I.   Auctioneers 25
II. Vendor's Solicitor 51
III. Purchaser's Solicitor 60

Chapter 3 Sale By Private Treaty

I.   House or Estate Agents 63
II. Vendor's Solicitor 85
III. Purchaser's Solicitor 88

Chapter 4 Caveat Emptor

I.   Introduction 95
II. Caveat Emptor 99

Chapter 5 Pre-Contract Enquiries or Requisitions

I.   Enquiries or Requisitions 121
II. Remedies for Inaccurate replies 130

Chapter 6 Formation of the Contract

I.   Introduction 141
II. Statute of Frauds (Ireland) 1695 145
III. Exchange 191
IV. Registration 195

Chapter 7 Conditional Contracts

I.   General Principles 200

II.   Illustrations 203

Chapter 8   Other Special Cases

I.   Sale by Public Auction 223
II.   Option to Purchase 224
III. Acquisition of the Freehold 227
IV.   Court Sales 232
V.   Compulsory Purchase 232

Chapter 9   Contents of the Contract

I.   Memorandum of Sale 244
II.   Particulars and Tenure 245

Chapter 10 Conditions of Sale

I.   Statutory Regulation 285
II.   General Conditions 287
III. Special Conditions 310

Chapter 11 Special Contracts

I.   Court Sales 313
II.   Building Agreements 319

Chapter 12 Position of Parties Pending Completion

I.   Vendor as Trustee 333
II.   Purchaser as Beneficiary 356
III. Registered Land 369

Chapter 13 Remedies for Enforcement of the Contract

I.   General Principles 373
II.   Vendor and Purchaser Summons 392
III. Forfeiture and Recovery of Deposit 395
IV.   Specific Performance 403
V.   Rescission 419
VI.   Damages 427

Chapter 14 Deduction of Title

I.   Introduction 437
II.   Deduction of Title 451

Chapter 15 Investigation of Title

I.   Perusal of Title 506
II.   Requisitions on Title 510

III. Searches 524
IV. Acceptance of Title 531

Chapter 16 Requisitions on Title

I. Introduction 535
II. The Standard Form 536

Chapter 17 Drafting and Construction of Deeds

I. Drafting the Conveyance 611
II. Construction of Conveyances 617

Chapter 18 Form and Contents of Deeds

I. Documents for Registered and Unregistered Land 625
II. Contents of Deeds 627

Chapter 19 Documents for Particular Transactions

I. Sales 695
II. Leases 708
III. Fee Farm Grants 715
IV. Mortgages 718
V. Wills and Assents 723
VI. Settlements and Trusts 727

Chapter 20 Completing the Transaction

I. Preparation for Completion 729
II. Completion 741
III. After Completion 750

Chapter 21 Post-Completion Remedies

I. Merger 757
II. Remedies 760

Appendix I

Pre-contract documentation 777

Appendix II

Standard Contract for Sale 789

Appendix III

Objections And Requisitions On Title 817

Appendix IV

Land Act, 1965, Section 45
(Exempted "Towns") 873

Index... 877

Table of Statutes

(i) Republic of Ireland

Acquisition of Land (Assessment of Compensation) Act 1919 (9 & 10 Geo 5 c 57)
   s   2 .... 8.14, 8.22
     79(2) 8.18
Administration of Estates Act 1925 (15 & 16 Geo 5 c 23) 1.27
   s 36(1) 18.82
     (7) 15.19
Administration of Estates Act 1959 (No 8) 14.66, 15.46, 16.54
Age of Majority Act 1985 (No 2) 2.02, 16.69
Air Pollution Act 1987 (No 6) 1.21
Apportionment Act 1814 (54 Geo 3 c 32) 20.06
Apportionment Act 1870 (33 & 34 Vict c 35)
   s   2 .... 20.06
     3 .... 20.06
     7 .... 20.06
Arbitration Act 1954 (No 26) 10.66
   s 26 .... 10.66
     32 .... 20.50
Arbitration Act 1980 (No 7) 10.66
Auctioneers and House Agents Act 1947 (No 10) 2.01, 2.26, 3.01
   .... 3.15, 3.17-3.19
   s   2(1) 3.01
     6(1) 2.02
     (2) 2.02
     (3) 2.02
     7(1) 3.02
     (2) 3.02
     (3) 3.02
     8 .... 2.02
     9 .... 2.02
     10 .... 3.02
     11 .... 2.02
     12 .... 2.02
     13 .... 2.02
     14 .... 2.02-2.03
     (a) 2.03
     17 .... 2.03
     18 .... 2.02

20(2)...2.02
   (3)...2.02
20(1)(a)..2.02
22...2.02
23...2.02
24...2.02
Auctioneers and House Agents Act 1967 (No 9) .. 2.01, 2.26, 3.01, 3.15, 3.17-3.19
  s   2...2.03
      3...2.03
      4...2.04
      5...2.04
      6...2.04
      7...2.04
      8...2.04
      9...2.04
     11...2.03
     12...2.02, 3.02
Auctioneers and House Agents Act 1973 (No 23) 2.01, 2.26, 3.01
     ....3.15, 3.17-3.19
  s   1(2)..2.35
      2...2.35, 3.32
      (1)...2.35, 10.10
      (2)..2.35
      3...2.03
Bankruptcy Act 1988 (No 27)..14.67
  s 14...12.28-12.28
     44...12.28
      (2)...12.28
     46...15.47
     56..12.27, 17.02
      (5)...12.27
      (6)...12.27
     57...12.28-12.28
     58...12.28
     59...16.24
Building Control Act 1990 (No 3) 1.22, 3.42, 5.09, 5.12, 9.28, 16.74
  s   3...16.79
      6...16.79
      (2)...16.79
      8...16.80
      9...16.80
     12...16.80
     22(7)...10.55, 10.69, 16.77, 16.81
     23(1)...16.95

Building Societies Act 1989 (No 17)
s   22.. 20.32
     27... 17.02, 19.55
        (2) 18.43
     35.. 19.53
     36.. 19.53
     84.. 19.56
Capital Acquisitions Tax Act 1976 (No 8) 19.61
s   3(1)(c)... 16.25
     7.. 18.91
     10.. 16.25
     14.. 18.91
     41.. 12.20
     47.. 16.25
Capital Gains Tax Act 1975 (No 20)
s   14(6) 19.69
     Sch 4 para 11 .... 16.25
Central Bank Act 1942 (No 22).. 20.31
Central Bank Act 1971 (No 24).. 20.31
Chancery Amendment Act 1858 (21 & 22 Vict c 35) 13.54
s   2.. 13.54
Coinage Act 1950 (No 32).. 20.31
Coinage (Amendment) Act 1966 (No 5) 20.31
Companies Act 1963 (No 33)
s   99.. 15.48
    101.. 15.48
    103.. 15.48
    230.. 12.29
    231... 11.04, 11.07
       (2) 11.06
          (b).. 12.29, 18.130
    276.. 18.130
       (1)(b).. 12.29
    290.. 12.29
    Table A 18.128
Companies Act 1990 (No 33)
s   29.. 16.28, 18.113
     31.. 16.28
Companies Clauses Consolidation Act 1845 (8 & 9 Vict c 16) 8.14
Consumer Credit Act 1995 (No 24)... 2.40, 19.49
Conveyancing (Ir) Act 1634 (10 Chas 1, sess 2 c 3)
s   1.. 14.67
     3.. 14.67
     10.. 16.24
     14.. 16.24

Conveyancing Act 1881 (44 & 45 Vict c 41) 19.33, 19.52, 21.28

s   2 ....14.70, 15.19

   (ii) 19.13

   (v) 2.42, 18.82

   (vii) 18.33

   3(1) 14.69, 14.70

   (3) 14.59, 15.11, 15.24, 16.69, 18.29

   (4) 14.75

   (5) 14.75

   (6) 14.18, 14.48-14.50, 15.42, 18.102

   (9) 14.49

   (11) 15.24

   6 .... 9.18, 18.54, 18.57, 18.71

   (1) 18.10, 18.54

   (2) 18.54

   (3) 18.54

   (4) 18.54

   (5) 18.54

   7 .... 15.19, 18.49, 18.82, 18.100

   .... 19.26, 19.31, 19.46, 21.05, 21.07, 21.14-21.15

   (1)(A) 21.27

   (B) 21.15

   (D) 21.24

   (C) 21.24

   (2) 21.16

   (3) 21.16

   (5) 19.26

   (6) 21.22

   (A) 21.16

   (C) 21.16

   (D) 21.16

   8(1) 18.134

   9 ....18.102

   (2) 18.104

   (3) 18.104-18.105

   (4) 18.104

   (5) 18.104

   (8) 18.104

   (9) 18.105

   13(1) 14.69

   14 ....16.93, 19.45

   (3) 19.45

   19 ....19.02

   21(2) 15.19

   24 ....18.131

46.. 18.131
49(1) 18.48
50(1) 18.85
54(1) 18.43
55(1) 12.16, 18.45
56... 20.27, 20.33
   (1) 18.46
58... 18.105, 21.22
59... 18.98
60(1) 18.97
62(1) 18.77
63...18.33, 18.82-18.83
   (1) 18.82
   (3) 18.82
66(1) 14.73
   (2) 14.73
70(1) 11.07
3rd Sch 17.09
4th Sch 17.09
Pt IX 18.129
Pt V 17.09

Conveyancing Act 1882 (45 & 46 Vict c 39)
  s   3... 16.62
      (1) 4.02
        (i).. 4.21

Conveyancing Act 1911 (1 & 2 Geo 5 c 37)
  s   5(1) 15.19

Currency Act 1927 (No 32) 20.31

Currency (Amendment) Act 1930 (No 30).. 20.31

Decimal Currency Act 1969 (No 23).. 20.31

Decimal Currency Act 1971 (No 21).. 20.31

Documentary Evidence Act 1868 (31 & 32 Vict c 37) 18.31

Documentary Evidence Act 1882 (45 & 46 Vict c 9) 18.31

Documentary Evidence Act 1895 (58 & 59 Vict c 9) 18.31

Environmental Protection Agency Act 1992 (No 7)............................ 1.21

Family Home Protection Act 1976 (No 28) 1.25, 1.35, 2.40, 2.47, 3.36
.... 4.02, 4.06, 5.08, 7.22, 9.23, 13.27
.... 14.11, 14.27, 16.23, 16.61, 16.69
.... 16.70, 16.72, 18.04, 18.115, 21.20
  s   1.. 3.39
      (1) 9.06
   2.. 16.69
      (1) 16.62

(2)..16.62
3 ....3.39, 16.63, 16.69, 16.79
(1)..5.29, 16.62, 16.69, 16.70-16.71
(2)..16.62
(3)(a) 15.01, 16.62-16.62
(b) 15.01, 16.62-16.62, 16.70
(4)..16.62
(5)..16.62
(6)..16.62
(8)(a) 16.70
(i)..16.70
(ii)..16.71
(b)(i) 16.70
(ii) 16.70-16.71
(c) 16.70
(d) 16.70
(9)..16.69
4 ....16.63
(1)..16.69
(2)..16.69
(4)..16.69
5(2)..16.71
14 ....16.62, 18.91, 18.110, 20.39-20.41
15 ....5.29
Family Law Act 1981 (No 22) 1.25, 3.36, 5.08, 16.66
s   3 ....16.72
4 ....16.72
10 ....16.69
(1)..5.08
Family Law Act 1995 (No 26) 3.36, 16.62, 16.62, 16.70, 16.72
s   3(2)(a) 16.73
(c) 16.73
35 ....16.73-16.73
36 ....16.72
48 ....16.72
54 ....1.25, 4.06, 5.08
(1)..16.69
(a)..16.62
(b)..16.69
(ii) 16.70
69 ....16.71
Pt II 16.66, 16.73
Finance (Miscellaneous Provisions) Act 1968
s   20 ....16.26

Finance Act 1902
  s   9... 20.40
Finance (1909-10) Act 1910
  s   4... 16.25
      74(6) 20.40
Finance Act 1928 (No 11)
  s   6... 14.48
Finance (No 2) Act 1947 (No 33)
  s 13... 16.38
Finance Act 1949 (No 13)
  s 26... 16.40
     27... 16.40
Finance Act 1956 (No 22)
  s 30... 16.42
Finance Act 1969 (No 21)
  s 49... 11.09
Finance Act 1970 (No 14)
  s 40... 20.40
    1st Sched 20.40
Finance Act 1978 (No 21)
  s 43... 12.20
Finance Act 1981 (No 16)
  s 21(2) 16.26
     29... 16.26
Finance Act 1982 (No 14)
  s 34(1) 16.25
Finance Act 1983 (No 15)
  s 94... 11.10
     95... 16.25
     110A 16.25
       (9) 16.25
      (10) 16.25
Finance Act 1984 (No 9)
  s 105... 16.25
    106... 16.25
    109... 16.25
Finance Act 1985 (No 10)
  s 64... 16.25
Finance Act 1990 (No 13)
  s 112... 11.10, 18.03, 18.111
      (5) 18.111
    120... 18.112
    204(b) 20.40

Finance Act 1991 (No 13)
s   5 ....18.42
     94 ....18.10, 20.38
     96 ....20.38
     97 ....20.38
     100 ....18.10
     Pt IV 20.38
Finance Act 1992 (No 9)
ss109-119 ....19.61
Finance Act 1993 (No 13)
s   79 ....2.02
     100 ....11.10
     107 ....16.25
     109-119 ....16.25
Finance Act 1994 (No 13)
s   93 ....5.12
     107 ....16.25, 20.41
     146 ....14.49, 14.82, 16.25
Finance Act 1995 (No 8)
s   76 ....16.25
     122 ....11.11
     149 ....16.25, 20.41
Fire Services Act 1981 (No 30).......................5.03, 5.09, 5.14, 16.74, 16.79, 16.83
Fisheries (Consolidation) Act 1959 (No 14) 16.13
Forestry Act 1946 (No 13) 16.12
Forestry Act 1988 (No 26) 16.12
Forgery Act 1913 (3 & 4 Geo 5 c 27) 18.10
Guardianship of Infants Act 1964 (No 7)
s   11 ....16.69
Health Act 1947 (No 28) 9.47, 16.91
Housing (Miscellaneous Provisions) Act 1931 (No 50)
s   31(1)..4.13
Housing (Miscellaneous Provisions) Act 1992 (No 18) 16.17
s   8 ....20.41
Housing (Private Rented Dwellings) Act 1982 (No 6) 5.13, 16.02, 16.16
s   11(2)..16.18
Housing (Private Rented Dwellings) (Amendment) Act 1983 (No 22)...5.13, 16.02
                                                                                16.16-16.18
Housing Act 1966 (No 21) 4.16, 4.23
s   39 ....4.16
     55 ....8.16
     76 ....8.15

77 .... 8.16
78
   (1) 8.17
   (2) 8.17
     (a) 8.17
     (b) 8.17
   (3)(a)(i) 8.17
       (ii) 8.17
     (b) 8.17
   (4) 8.17
   (5) 8.17
79(1) 8.18
80(1) 8.19
81(1) 8.20
   (2) 8.20
   (3)(a) 8.20
     (b) 8.20
82(1) 8.21
   (2) 8.20
   (3) 8.21
84 .... 8.22
86 .... 8.15
90 .... 8.08
114 .... 4.13
3rd Sch 8.16
art 1 .... 8.16
art 2(a) 8.18
   (b) 8.18
   (c) 8.18
   (g) 8.18
   (k) 8.22
   (l) 8.22
art 4 .... 8.16
   (a) 8.16
   (b) 8.16
art 5(1)(a) 8.16
   (b) 8.16
4th Sch 8.22

Housing Act 1970 (No 21)
  s   6 .... 8.18

Housing Act 1988 (No 28)
  s 18 .... 17.02, 19.55, 20.18
   (2) 18.43

Housing of the Working Classes Act 1890 (53 & 54 Vict c 70)
  Sch 2 .... 8.14

Improvement of Land (Ir) Act 1864 (27 & 27 Vict c 72) 13.40
Income Tax Act 1967 (No 6)
   Sched 19, Pt II 14.48
Insurance Act 1936 (No 45) 2.03
Interpretation Act 1937 (No 38) 8.08
   s 11 ....17.17
      (c)..16.50
     12 ....8.05, 16.44, 17.17
   Pt III 10.15
Interpretation Act 1889 (52 & 53 Vict c 69)
   s 20 ....6.27
Intoxicating Liquor Act 1927 (No 15) 16.104
Intoxicating Liquor Act 1960 (No 18) 16.105
Intoxicating Liquor Act 1988 (No 16)
   s 8 ....16.106
Irish Bankrupt and Insolvent Act 1857 (20 & 21 Vict c 60)
   s 115 ....12.28
     328 ....12.28
     332 ....12.28
Irish Church Act 1869 (32 & 33 Vict c 42) 9.26, 14.44
Irish Land Act (3 Edw 7 c 37)
   s 54(1)...16.30
Irish Land Commission (Dissolution) Act 1992 (No 25).....1.13, 3.02, 16.20, 16.30
Judgment Mortgage (Ir) Act 1850 (13 & 14 Vict c 29) 15.45, 16.44
   s 5 ....15.45
     6 ....12.09
Judgments Registry (Ir) Act 1871 (34 & 35 Vict c 72)
   s 12 ....15.45
Judicial Separation and Family Law Reform Act 1989 (No 6)................1.25, 3.36
   ....5.08, 16.72
   s 29 .... 16.73-16.73
      (4)..16.73
     35 ....16.66
     46(2)...16.73
   Pt II 16.66, 16.73-16.73
Land Act 1923 (No 42)
   s 24(2)(c)...1.16
     29 ....16.20
     40(6)...16.36
     65 ....16.30
     66 ....16.31
Land Act 1927 (No 19)
   s 3 ....16.30
     4 ....16.30

Land Act 1939 (No 26)
s 23... 16.30
   39... 16.20
Land Act 1946 (No 12)
s 3... 16.30
   6... 16.30
Land Act 1965 (No 2) 16.29
s 12.................................5.08, 5.18, 10.69, 16.30-16.31, 16.49, 18.56, 18.114
   (1) 1.13, 16.31
   (2) 1.13
   (3) 1.13, 16.31
   (4) 16.32
      (a)... 16.32
      (b)... 16.32
   (6) 16.31
   (7) 10.12
   (8) 16.31
   13.. 16.31, 16.36
   (2) 16.36
   18... 16.14
   25... 16.31
   42... 16.20
   45...5.08, 5.18, 7.23, 10.48, 10.69, 16.34-16.37
       ....16.43-16.51, 18.03, 18.114
   (1) 1.13
   (2)
      (b)
       (iii) 16.50
   (3) 16.52
    (a)(i)... 16.50
      (ii).. 16.50
      (iv)... 16.50
   (5) 16.51
   (6) 16.51
Land Act 1984 (No 24).. 19.36
s 7(3) 9.26, 14.44
Land Clauses Consolidation Act 1845 (8 & 9 Vict c 18)
s 6-15 .... 8.14
   18-20 .... 8.14
   24... 8.14
   69-75 .... 8.18
   73-75 .... 8.18
   76-79 .... 8.18
   81-83 .... 8.14
   85-91 .... 8.19
   Sch A and B 8.14

Landlord and Tenant Act 1931 (No 55) 13.83
  s 62 ....15.02
Landlord and Tenant Law Amendment Act, Ireland 1860 (23 & 24 Vict c 154)
                               ....14.12, 19.12, 19.39
  s   1 ....18.53
      3 ....6.09, 19.37
      4 ....6.34, 17.02
    16 .... 18.15, 18.98, 19.31
    19 ....19.32
    21 ....19.32
    41 ....19.26, 21.05
    42 ....19.29
    50 ....20.06
Landlord and Tenant (Amendment) Act 1980 (No 10)..........................14.73, 16.16
Landlord and Tenant (Amendment) Act 1984 (No 4)......................................8.10
  s 17 ....13.41, 13.47
Landlord and Tenant (Amendment) Act 1994 (No 20).....................................16.16
  s   4 ....16.17
Landlord and Tenant (Ground Rents) Act 1967 (No 3) 1.19, 5.13, 8.08
                              ....8.11, 14.70, 16.94
  s   2(1)...8.10
      (3)...8.10
    3(2)...8.07
    4 ....8.08
    5(3)...8.08
    6 ....8.09
      (2).. 8.10-8.11
    7 .... 5.30, 8.08-8.10
      (1)...5.30
    8 ....8.08
      (2)...5.30
    11-6 ....8.08
    12 ....8.08
    14 ....8.08
    17(1) 8.10
    20 ....8.10
    21(1)(a) 8.10
        (b) 8.10
      (2)...8.10
      (3)...8.10
    22 ....8.10
    23 ....5.30
      (1)...8.08
    32 ....10.11, 17.04
    33 ....8.12

Landlord and Tenant (Ground Rents) (No 2) Act 1978 (No 16) .. 1.19, 11.09, 14.75
.... 16.97, 19.10, 19.13, 19.15
   s   1 .... 19.12
      4 .... 8.08
     16(2)(a) 19.15
     26 .... 8.08
     27(1) 19.45
     28 .... 8.12, 14.70
  Pt II 8.08
  Pt III 16.94
Landlord and Tenant (Ground Rents) (Amendment) Act 1984 (No 15) ... 5.13, 8.07
Landlord and Tenant (Ground Rents) (Amendment) Act 1987 (No 12) . 1.19, 14.70
Law of Distress and Small Debts (Ir) Act 1889 (51 & 52 Vict c 70) 2.31
Law of Property Amendment Act 1859 (22 & 23 Vict c 35) 14.66
   s 21 .... 18.85
     24 .... 9.31, 14.61
Law of Property Amendment Act 1860 (23 & 24 Vict c 38)
   s   8 .... 9.31, 14.61
Legal Practitioners (Ir) Act 1876 (39 & 40 Vict c 44)
   s   3 .... 20.50
Licensing (Ireland) Act 1902 (2 Edw 7 c) 16.105
Local Government (Dublin) Act 1930 (No 27)
   s 18 .... 16.47
Local Government (Dublin) Act 1993 (No 31) 16.47
Local Government (Financial Provisions) Act 1978 (No 35)
   s   3 .... 20.07
     5 .... 20.07
   Local Government (Multi-Storey Buildings) Act 1988 (No 24)
.... 1.22, 3.42, 5.09, 5.12
   s   1(1) 16.95
     2 .... 16.96
      (1) 16.96
     3 .... 16.95
      (2)(c) 16.95
     4 .... 16.95
  Sch 1 .... 16.95
  Sch 3 .... 16.95
Local Government (Planning and Development) Act 1963 (No 28) 1.21, 5.09
.... 16.46, 16.74
   s   8 .... 16.78
     26 (2) 7.17
      (9) 7.17
     69(1) 8.22
    386-88 .... 16.79
  4th Sch 8.22

Local Government (Planning and Development) Act 1976 (No 20) 16.74
Local Government (Planning and Development) Act 1982 (No 21) 16.74
Local Government (Planning and Development) Act 1983 (No 28) 16.74
Local Government (Planning and Development) Act 1990 (No 11) 16.74
Local Government (Planning and Development) Act 1992 (No 14) 16.74
   s   19 ....10.69, 16.77, 16.81
Local Government (Planning and Development) Act 1993 (No 12)
   ....1.21, 5.09, 16.74
Local Government (Water Pollution) Act 1977 (No 1) 1.21
Local Government Act 1925 (No 5) 16.48
   s   25 ....18.59
Local Government Act 1953 (No 12)
   s   2 ....18.59
Local Government 1960 (No 2) Act (No 23)
   s   10 ....8.15
Local Government Act 1991 (No 11)...16.74
Local Registration of Title (Ir) Act 1891 (54 & 55 Vict c 66) 1.02, 14.25, 18.69
   s   19 ....18.70
       21 ....18.70
       22 ....1.15
       25 ....14.13
       44(2)...12.05
       55 ....9.13
       57 ....9.13
       59(1)...18.70
       64 ....18.70
Married Women's Status Act 1957 (No 5)
   s   12 ....16.72
Public Dance Halls Act 1935 (No 2)...16.107
Public Health (Ireland) Act 1878 (41 & 42 Vict c 52) 9.21
   s   41 ....16.79
Public Health Acts (Amendment) Act 1890 (53 & 54 Vict c 59)
   s   51 ....16.107
Railway Clauses Consolidation Act 1845 (8 & 9 Vict c 20) 8.14
Railways (Ir) Act 1851 (14 & 15 Vict c 70)
   s   3 ....8.14
        4 ....8.14
       5-15...8.14
        8 ....8.14
       16 ....8.14
       17 ....8.14

19...8.14
25...8.14

Railways (Ir) Act 1860 (23 & 24 Vict c 97)
  s   2...8.14

Railways (Ir) Act 1864 (27 & 28 Vict c 71)
  s   13...8.14

Real Property Act 1845 (8 & 9 Vict c 106)
  s   2..17.02, 18.48
     3...17.02
     4...18.49
     5..18.07-18.08, 18.13

Registry of Deeds (Ir) Act 1832 (2 & 3 Will 4 c 22)
  s   32..14.52

Registration of Deeds Act (Ir) 1707 (6 Ann c 2) 1.16
  s   6..18.136

Registration of Title Act 1964 (No 16) 1.02, 1.27, 14.24
  s   2...16.55
      (1)...21.06
     3(1)..12.06
     9(10)..18.105
     23(1)(a)..1.15, 14.25
     24(2)...20.42
     25...14.13, 18.10, 20.42
     28...14.31
     30...14.27
     31...14.27, 14.33, 16.70
      (1)..18.70
     32
      (1)..18.70
     35...14.37
     38..18.106
     50...14.26
     51(2)...18.127
      (3)..14.32
      (4)...14.32, 20.35
     52...14.59
      (1)...18.83, 21.06
     52-8 ....18.83
     61(2)...18.26
      (3)..14.66
     65...18.43
     67..9.02
     68(2)...12.05
     69(1)(j)..18.81
      (s)..16.70

71(4)..12.06
72 ....16.23
72(1)(j)...9.23, 16.23
85 ....9.13, 18.55, 18.81
86 ....9.13
87 ....9.13
88(1)...9.13
(2)..9.13
92(1)...18.92
(2)..18.92
97 ....6.66
105(1)..14.32
(2)..18.106
(4)...14.31
107(1)...14.30, 15.41
(2)...15.41
108(1)...15.41
(2)...15.41
115 ....10.12, 14.41, 14.59
117 ....10.12, 20.18
123 ....18.88
(1)...18.88
(2)...18.88
(3)...18.88

Renewable Leasehold Conversion Act 1849 (12 & 13 Vict c 105) 19.39
s   1 ....14.11, 14.56
7 ....14.11, 14.56
37 ....14.76

Safety, Health and Welfare at Work Act 1989 (No 7) 16.79

Sale of Goods Act 1893 (56 & 57 Vict c 71)
s   12 ....9.15
55(4)..9.15
62 ....6.09

Sale of Goods and Supply of Services Act 1980 (No 16)
s   22 ....9.15

Sale of Land by Auction Act 1867 (30 & 31 Vict c 48) 2.14, 2.18, 10.16
s   4 ....2.15
5 ....2.15-2.17
6 ....2.15
7 .... 2.25, 11.06, 11.07

Sales of Reversions Act 1867 (31 & 32 Vict c 4) 21.35

Sea Pollution Act 1991 (No 22) 1.21

Settled Land Act 1882 (45 & 46 Vict c 38) 1.27, 14.65, 14.77-14.78
....15.19, 18.14, 19.02, 19.07, 19.33
s   4(1)..18.42

Settled Land Act 1890 (53 & 54 Vict c 69) 1.27, 14.65, 14.77-14.78
....15.19, 18.14, 19.02, 19.07, 19.33
Solicitors (Ir) Act 1898 (61 & 62 Vict c 17)
   s   4.. 20.15
Solicitors Remuneration Act 1881 (44 & 45 Vict c 44) 18.54, 20.49, 21.05
Solicitors Act 1954 (No 36) 1.12
   s   58.. 1.04
Solicitors (Amendment) Act 1960 (No 37) 1.12
   s   8.. 20.15
Solicitors (Amendment) Act 1994 (No 27)
   s   18.. 20.15
        38.. 20.15
        68.. 3.45
        73.. 2.45
        94.. 20.49
Stamp Act 1891 (54 & 55 Vict c 39) 20.40
   s   1.. 20.38
         (3) 18.10
          (b)... 20.38
        5.. 18.42, 20.38
        14.. 15.13, 16.25
        15(2) 18.10
        62.. 20.40
        114.. 15.13
        117.. 10.09
Statutory Declarations Act 1835 (5 & 6 Will 4 c 62) 9.11, 14.80
Statute of Frauds (Ir) 1695 (7 Will 3 c 12) 1.31, 3.33, 6.04, 6.07-6.09
....6.12, 6.14-6.19, 6.22, 6.27, 6.33
.... 6.34-6.37, 6.43-6.51, 6.55-6.56
.... 6.59-6.62, 7.01, 7.03, 7.06, 7.08,
....7,12, 8.02-8.04, 8.06, 9.01-9.02,
.... 9.05, 10.01, 10.50, 13.47, 18.121
   s   2...3.07, 3.25, 3.35, 6.03-6.07, 6.09-6.10
....6.13, 6.16, 6.32, 6.34, 6.47, 13.44-13.46
Statute of Limitations (Amendment) Act 1991 (No 18)................................... 4.17
Statute of Limitations 1957 (No 6).......................... 4.17, 9.11, 14.10, 14.27, 14.54
   s   2(1) 12.09
        11(2) 4.17
        (5) 12.09
Statute of Uses (Ir) 1634 (10 Chas 1 sess 2 c1) 18.77, 18.86, 18.90
Statutory Declarations Act 1938 (No 37) 9.11
Succession Act 1965 (No 27) 1.27, 15.46, 16.72, 19.60
   s   10.. 16.54
        52(1)(b)(i) 18.85

(2)...16.54, 18.85
(5)...17.02, 19.68
(6)...21.18
53 ....15.19
(1)...16.54
54
(2)...14.66
78 ....6.27
90 ....17.20
121 ....14.59
Pt IX 16.62
Supreme Court of Judicature (Ir) Act 1877 (40 & 41 Vict c 57) .. 5.23, 6.51, 13.54
s   28(7)...13.11
(11)...18.44
78 ....20.15
Tenantry (Ir) Act 1779 (19 & 20 Geo 3 c 30) 14.76
Towns Improvement (Ir) Act 1854 (17 & 18 Vict c 103) 16.44, 16.48
Trustee Act 1893 (56 & 57 Vict c 53) 18.30
s   17...18.47
20 ....18.36
30 ....8.13
31 ....8.13, 13.56
33 ....8.13, 13.56
Value-Added Tax Act 1972 (No 22)..10.68
s   4(5)..11.11
4A 5.12
Vendor and Purchaser Act 1874 (37 & 38 Vict c 78)
s   1 .... 14.54, 14.69-14.70
2 .... 14.54, 14.69-14.70, 14.70-14.74
(2)..14.50, 18.28
9 .... 10.66, 13.02, 13.26, 13.29, 13.36
13(1)...14.70
Voluntary Conveyances Act 1893 (56 & 57 Vict c 21) 14.67

(ii) Northern Ireland

Administration of Estates Act 1955 (c 24)
s   35(3)..15.19
Criminal Injuries Act 1956 (c 10)
s   4(4)..6.12
Criminal Injuries to Property (Compensation) Act 1971 (c 38)
s   4(4)..6.12

Defective Premises Order 1975 (SI 1039 (NI 9) 4.15
Housing Executive Act 1971 (c 5) 4.15
Interpretation Act 1954 (c 33)
   s 45(1)(a).. 18.70
      46(2) 6.12
Land Registration Act 1970 (c 18)
   s 11(1) 18.70
Perpetuities Act 1966 (c 2)
   s   9(1) 18.72
Roads Act 1948
   s 42(1) 6.12
Solicitors Act 1922 (12 & 13 Geo 5 c 19) 1.12
Solicitors Act 1938 (2 Geo 6 c 14) 1.12
Solicitors Act 1943 (c 4) 1.12
Solicitors Act 1948(c 27) 1.12
Solicitors Order 1976 (SI 582 (NI12) 1.12
Trustee Act 1958 (c 23)
   s 35... 18.30
      37(1) 18.30

(iii) England and Wales

Auctions (Bidding Agreements) Act 1927 (17 & 18 Geo 5 c 12)
   s   4(2) 2.24
Auctions (Bidding Agreements) Act 1969 (c 56) 2.24
Charging Orders Act 1979 (c 53) 6.11
Compulsory Purchase Act 1965 (c 56) 8.14
Defective Premises Act 1972 (c 35) 4.15
Estate Agents Act 1979 .... 3.01
Housing Act 1974
   s 125.. 13.41, 13.47
Land Charges Act 1925 (15 & 16 Geo 5 c 22) 1.27, 4.06
   s 15.. 1.29
Landlord and Tenant (Covenants) Act.. 18.98
Land Registration Act 1925 (15 & 16 Geo 5 c 21) 1.27
   s 70.. 14.27
        (1)(g).. 16.23
    110.. 14.29
    112.. 14.30

Land Registration Act 1988 (c 3)
s   1 .... 14.30
Law of Property Act 1925 (15 & 16 Geo 5 c 20) 1.27
s 23 .... 14.77
    33 .... 14.77
    34 .... 6.11
    35 .... 6.11
    36 .... 6.11
    40 .... 1.31, 6.04, 7.08
     (1) 6.06, 6.09, 6.11
     (2) 6.48
    44(1) 14.54
     (5) 14.72
    45(1) 14.59, 16.69
     (4)(a) 14.49
     (6) 18.28
     (9) 18.102
     (10) 18.102

    48(1) 10.08
     (2) 10.08
    49(1) 13.26
     (2) 13.35
     (3) 13.26
    51 .... 17.02
    56(1) 18.08, 18.13
     (2) 18.07
    57 .... 18.07
    58 .... 18.39
    61 .... 10.15, 17.17
    63 .... 18.82
    65 .... 18.77-18.78
    68 .... 18.45
    73 .... 18.120
    74 .... 18.128
    76 .... 21.05, 21.08, 21.28
    77 .... 18.98, 19.31
    78 .... 21.22
   115 .... 19.56
   183 .... 14.61
   198(1) 14.72
   205(1)(ii) 6.09, 18.82
       (ix) 6.11, 19.13
  Sch 2 .... 21.05

Law of Property Act 1969 (c 59)
   s   23.. 14.54
       25.. 14.60
Law of Property (Miscellaneous Provisions) Act 1989 (c 34)
   s   1.. 18.120
       (4) 18.120
       2............................... 1.31, 6.04-6.05, 6.28, 6.33, 6.48, 6.63, 8.05
       3.. 13.79
Law of Property (Miscellaneous Provisions) Act 1994 (c 36) 21.14
Leasehold Reform Act 1967 (c 88)
   s   5.. 8.09
       8.. 8.09
Local Land Charges Act 1975 (c 76) 1.29, 4.06
Mock Auctions Act 1961 (9 & 10 Eliz 2 c 12) 2.24
Northern Ireland (Temporary Provisions) Act 1972.. 1.12
Powers of Attorney Act 1971 (c 27) 18.129
Property Misdescriptions Act 1991 (c 29).. 3.01, 5.29
Settled Land Act 1925 (15 & 16 Geo 5 c 18) 1.27, 14.77
Statute of Frauds 1677 (29 Chas 2 c 3) 6.06, 6.10
   s   4.. 1.31, 6.09
Town and Country Planning Act 1968 (c 72)
   s   30.. 8.14
      Sch 3 .... 8.14
Trustee Act 1925 (15 & 16 Geo 5 c 19) 1.27
   s   38.. 18.30

TABLE OF STATUTORY INSTRUMENTS

(i) Republic of Ireland

Auctioneers and House Agents Act 1947 (Accounts Examination and Certificate)
Regulations 1968 (SI 10/1968) 2.02

Building Control Regulations 1991 (SI 305) 16.79

Building Control Regulations 1994 (SI 153) 16.79

Building Regulations 1991 (SI 306) 16.79

Building Regulations 1994 (SI 154) 16.79

Compulsory Registration of Ownership (Carlow, Laois and Meath) Order 1969
(SI 87) 16.55, 20.42

European Communities (Milk Quotas) Regulations 1994 (SI 70) 1.14, 5.19, 16.101

European Communities (Milk Quotas) Regulations 1995 (SI 266) 5.19, 16.101

European Communities (Safeguarding of Employees' Rights on Transfer
of Undertakings) Regulations 1980 (SI 306) 5.15
Reg 5(1) 5.15

Family Law Act 1995 (Commencement) Order 1996 (SI 46) ... 16.66, 16.69, 16.70

Food Hygiene Regulations 1950 (SI 205) 9.47, 16.91

Food Hygiene Regulations 1961 (SI 24) 16.92

Food Hygiene Regulations 1971 (SI 322) 16.92
Reg 32 .... 16.105
Reg 42 .... 16.105

Housing Act (Acquisition of Land) Regulations 1966 (SI 278)
Sch
Form 1 .... 8.16
Form 2 .... 8.16
Form 4 .... 8.17
Form 5 .... 8.21
Form 7 .... 8.16
Form 8 .... 8.16
Form 9 .... 8.16
Form 10 .... 8.17
Form 11 .... 8.21
Form 12 .... 8.18

Housing (New House Grant) Regulations 1990 (SI 24)
para 8 .... 11.10

Housing (New House Grants etc) Regulations 1990 (Amendment
Regulations 1996 (SI 88) 11.10

Housing (Private Rented Dwellings) Regulations 1982 (SI 217) 16.18

Housing (Registration of Rented Houses) Regulations 1996 (SI 30) 16.17

Housing (Private Rented Dwellings) Regulations 1983 (SI 286) 16.18

Housing (Rent Tribunal) Regulations 1983 (SI 222) 16.18

Housing (Rent Tribunal) Regulations 1988 (SI 140) 16.18

Housing (Rent Books) Regulations 1993 (SI 146) 16.17

Ground Rents Registers Regulations 1967 (SI 152)
   1st Sch Pt I and II 8.10
   2nd Sch 8.10
   reg 4 ....8.10

Land Act 1965 (Additional Category of Qualified Person) Regulations 1970
   (SI 40) 16.46

Land Act 1965 (Additional Category of Qualified Persons) Regulations 1972
   (SI 332) 16.50

Land Act 1965 (Additional Category of Qualified Persons) Regulations 1983
   (SI 144) 16.50

Land Act 1965 (Additional Category of Qualified Person) Regulations 1994
   (SI 67) 16.47

Land Act 1965 (Additional Category of Qualified Persons) Regulations 1995
   (SI 56) 16.50

Landlord and Tenant (Ground Rents) Act (Forms) 1967 (SI 43) 8.08
   Form 1 ....8.08
   Form 2 ....8.08
   Form 5 ....8.08

Land Registry Rules 1910
   Order IV r 30-31 ....14.14

Land Registration Rules 1972 (SI 230) 17.11, 20.44
   Form 1 ....20.45
   Form 2 ....20.45
   Form 17 ....20.44
   Form 19 ....18.55, 18.101, 19.06
   Form 21 ....19.06
   Form 22 ....18.56, 18.118
   Form 24 ....19.07
   Form 29 ....18.81
   Form 31 ....18.101
   Form 37 ....19.68
   Form 48 ....14.66, 19.68
   Form 49 ....19.68
   Form 58 ....19.68
   Form 67 ....19.47
   Form 68 ....19.47
   Form 71A 19.55
   Form 71B 19.55

Form 72 .... 19.47

Form 106 .... 15.41

r   3 .... 18.55

    3(3)(a)... 18.22

    14 .... 20.45

    15 .... 20.45

    16 .... 20.45

    19 .... 14.54

    25(b) 18.81

    30(1)(a).. 19.13

       (b)... 19.13

    52... 17.10

     (1) 17.10

    53... 17.11

    54.. 18.135

    55(1) 18.135

    56.. 18.56, 18.132

    58... 18.122, 18.132

    63... 14.14

    69... 17.03

    77(4) 18.136

   130(1) 18.81

     (2) 18.81

     (3) 18.81

      .... rules 148-50 18.70

   159.. 14.31

   161.. 14.31

   162.. 14.32, 20.44

   164.. 20.44

   165.. 20.44

   170.. 14.53

   174(3) 18.69

   188.. 14.30

     (1) 14.30

     (2) 14.30

   190-4 .... 15.41

   195.. 15.41

   196(1) 15.41

     (3) 15.41

     (4) 15.41

   197(1) 15.41

(2)..15.41

198 ....14.30, 15.41

(1)..14.34

Sched of Forms 18.04, 18.08, 18.11, 18.22-18.26

.... 18.41, 18.48, 18.88, 18.106, 18.116, 18.132-18.135, 19.01

Land Registration Rules 1986

r   3 ....18.69

Land Registration (Open Register) Rules 1991 (SI 122) 14.30

Land Registration Fees Order 1991 (SI 363) 20.44

Local Government (Multi-Storey Buildings) Act 1988 (Commencement) Order
(SI 285) 16.95

Local Government (Multi-Storey Buildings) Regulations 1988 (SI 286) 16.95

Local Government (Multi-Storey Buildings) Regulations 1990 (SI 95) 16.95

Local Government (Planning and Development) Regulations 1994 (SI 86)
Art 10(1)(a)(viii) 16.77

Professional Indemnity Insurance Scheme Regulations 1995 (SI 312) 10.31

Rules of the Supreme Court 1905
Order 55 rr 66-8 ....12.20

Rules of the Superior Courts 1986
Order 3(12) 13.26

20 r 1 ....13.26

38 ....13.26

51 ....11.04

r 4 ....11.04

5 ....11.06

8 ....11.06

9 ....11.04

84 ....8.17

Safety Health and Welfare at Work (Construction) Regulations 1995 (SI 138)
.... 16.79, 16.84-16.85

Solicitors (Interest on Client's Moneys) Regulations 1995 (SI 108).........2.10, 2.45
.... 10.25-10.26, 20.49

Stamp Duty (Particulars to be Delivered) Regulations 1995 (SI 144) ..16.25, 20.41

Trustee (Authorised Investments) Order 1967 (SI 285) 19.70

Trustee (Authorised Investments) Order 1969 (SI 241) 19.70

Trustee (Authorised Investments) Order 1974 (SI 41) 19.70

Trustee (Authorised Investments) Order 1983 (SI 58) 19.70

Trustee (Authorised Investments) Order 1985 (SI 224) 19.70

Trustee (Authorised Investments) Order 1986 (SI 372) 19.70

(ii) Northern Ireland

Land Registration Rules 1977 (SR & O No 154)
  r 50 .... 14.14

(iii) England and Wales

Land Registration Rules 1925 (SR & O No 1093)
  r 77 .... 21.06

Table of Cases

A

Abbeyford Estates Ltd, Re (HC) unrep, 29 October 1993 .... 12.27, 12.29
Abbott v Ryan (1901) 1 NIJR 75 .... 13.40, 13.55
Abdulla v Shah [1959] AC 125; [1959] 2 WLR 12; 103 Sol Jo 15 .... 12.22
Aberaman Ironworks v Wickens (1868) 4 Ch App 101 .... 12.44
Aberfoyle Plantations Ltd v Cheng [1960] AC 115; [1959] 3 WLR 1011;
    [1959] 3 All ER 910; 103 Sol Jo 1045 .... 7.03
Ackroyd & Sons v Hasan [1960] 2 QB 144; [1960] 2 WLR 810;
    [1960] 2 All ER 254 .... 3.29
Acrey, Re [1897] 1 Ch 164 .... 14.50
Adair v Carden (1892) 29 LR Ir 469 .... 18.99, 21.02-21.03
Adams v McKeown (1892) 26 ILT 504 .... 2.34
Aga Khan v Firestone [1992] ILRM 31 .... 8.04, 16.53
Airey, Re [1897] 1 Ch 164; 66 LJCh 152; 76 LT 151; 41 Sol Jo 128;
    45 WR 286 .... 18.134
Airlie v Fallon [1976-7] ILRM 1 .... 2.12-2.15, 2.19
Ajit v Sammy [1967] AC 255; [1966] 3 WLR 983; 110 Sol Jo 790 .... 13.17
Alan Estates Ltd v WG Stores Ltd [1982] Ch 511; [1981] 3 WLR 892;
    [1981] 3 All ER 481; 125 Sol Jo 567 .... 18.125-18.127
Allen & Co Ltd v Whiteman (1920) 89 LJ Ch 534; 123 LT 773;
    64 Sol Jo 727 .... 6.20
Allen & Driscoll's Contract, Re [1904] 2 Ch 226; 73 LJCh 614; 91 LT 676;
    48 Sol Jo 587; 20 TLR 605; 52 WR 680; 68 JP 469; 2 LGR 959 .... 14.75
Allhusen v Whittell (1867) LR 4 Eq 295; 36 LJCh 929; 16 LT 698 .... 19.63
Allied Irish Banks plc v Finnegan [1996] 1 ILRM 401 .... 15.01, 16.23, 16.62
    .... 16.67, 16.69
Allied Irish Banks plc v Griffin [1992] 2 IR 70; [1992] ILRM 590 .... 12.09
Allied Irish Bank plc v O'Neill [1996] ICLC 36 .... 16.31, 16.62, 16.69
Allingham v Atkinson [1898] 1 IR 239 .... 20.06
Allman v McDaniel [1912] 1 IR 467 .... 10.04-10.05, 10.67, 20.08
Allot, Re [1924] 2 Ch 498; 94 LJCh 91; 132 LT 141 .... 18.90
Altlham's Case (1610) 8 Co Rep 150b; 77 ER 701 .... 18.87
Aluminium Shop Fronts Ltd, Re [1987] IR 419 .... 12.17
Alvanley v Kinnaird (1849) 2 Mac & G 1; 16 LT (os) 165; 14 Jur 897;
    42 ER 1 .... 9.35
Anderson (WB) & Sons Ltd v Rhodes Ltd [1967] 2 All ER 850 .... 5.27
Anderson v Higgins (1844) 1 Jo & Lat 718 .... 14.76
Anderson v Ryan [1967] IR 34 .... 9.15
Andrade (Cyril) Ltd v Sotherby & Co (1931) 47 TLR 244; 75 Sol Jo 120 ...... 10.18
Angel v Jay [1911] 1 KB 666; 80 LJKB 458; 103 LT 809; 55 Sol Jo 140 .... 5.26

Angell v Duke (1875) LR 10 QB 174; 44 LJQB 78; 32 LT 25; 39 JP 247;
23 WR 307 ....6.13
Anglia Television Ltd v Reed [1972] 1 QB 60; [1971] 3 WLR 528;
[1971] 3 All ER 690; 115 Sol Jo 723 ....13.78, 13.85
Annesley v Muggridge (1816) 1 Madd 593; 56 ER 218 ....10.27
Anns v Merton London Borough Council [1977] 2 WLR 1024;
[1977] 2 All ER 492; 75 LGR 555 ....4.15
Anom Engineering Ltd v Thornton (HC) unrep, 1 February 1983 ....6.07, 6.18
Antrim (Earl of) v Gray (1875) IR 9 Eq 513 .... 14.52-14.52, 14.56, 18.74-18.75
Antrim County Land, Building & Investment Co Ltd, Re (1909) 43
ILTR 120 ....13.28
Appah v Parcliffe Investments Ltd [1964] 1 WLR 1064; [1964] 1 All ER 838;
108 Sol Jo 155 ....6.12
Aquis Estates Ltd v Minton [1975] 1 WLR 1452; [1975] 3 All ER 1043 ....7.20
Arbib & Class's Contract, Re [1891] 1 Ch 601; 60 LJCh 263; 64 LT 217;
39 WR 305 ....15.29
Archbold v Lord Howth (1866) IR 1 CL 608; 1 ILT 760 ....6.51-6.52, 6.57
Archer v The Earl of Calidon [1894] 2 IR 473 ....16.44
Arenson v Casson, Beckman, Rulle v & Co [1975] 3 All ER 903;
3 WLR 815; 119 Sol Jo 810; 1976 1 LLoyd's Rep 179 ....5.27
Armstrong & Holmes Ltd v Holmes [1994] 1 All ER 826 ....6.64, 8.05
Armstrong v Courtney (1863) 15 Ir Ch R 138 ....13.41
Arnold v Veale [1979] IR 342n 6.16
Ashburner v Sewell [1891] 3 Ch 405; 60 LJCh 784; 65 LT 524; 7 TLR 736;
40 WR 169 ....9.22
Ashe, Re (1855) 4 Ir Ch R 594 ....2.24
Ashe & Hogan's Contract, Re [1920] 1 IR 159; 54 ILTR 97 ....13.27, 14.12
....14.42, 14.81
Astra Trust Ltd v Adams [1969] 1 Lloyd's Rep 81 ....7.19
Atkins v Delmege (1847) 12 Ir Eq R 1 ....11.05
Atkinson & Horsell's Contract, Re [1912] 2 Ch 1; 81 LJCh 588;
56 Sol Jo 324 ....13.68, 14.10-14.12, 14.58, 14.61, 14.81
Atkinson v Pillsworth (1787) 1 Ridgw PC 449 ....17.15
Att-Gen for NSW v Dickson [1904] AC 273; 73 LJPC 48; 90 LT 213 ....18.73
Att-Gen v Manorhamilton Co-operative Livestock Mart Ltd [1966] IR 192 .....2.02
Auerbach v Nelson [1919] 2 Ch 383; 88 LJCh 493; 122 LT 90; 35 TLR 655;
63 Sol Jo 683 ....6.23
Avard, Re [1948] Ch 43; [1947] 2 All ER 548; [1948] LJR 354; 63 TLR 567;
91 Sol Jo 613 ....8.05
Avon Finance Co Ltd v Bridges [1985] 2 All ER 281; 123 Sol Jo 705.............21.38

B

Babacomp Ltd v Rightside Properties Ltd [1974] 1 All ER 142; 26 P & CR 526;
231 Est Gaz 237 ....13.21
Bagnell v Edwards (1876) IR 10 Eq 215 ....6.51, 13.39

Bain v Fothergill (1874) LR 7 HL 158; 43 LJ Ex 243; 31 LT 387; 23 WR 261;
  39 JP 228 ....9.31, 13.09, 13.54, 13.62, 13.79-13.80, 13.85, 16.75
Baines v Tweddle [1959] Ch 679; [1959] 3 WLR 291; [1959] 2 All ER 724;
  103 Sol Jo 563 .... 15.31
Baker v Denning (1838) 8 Ad & El 94 .... 6.33
Baker v Dewey (1823) 1 B & C 704; 107 ER 259 .... 18.44
Balkis Consolidated Co Ltd, Re (1888) 58 LT 300; 4 TLR 204;
  36 WR 392 .... 18.122
Ball v Cullimore (1835) 2 Cr M & R 120; 1 Gale 96; 5 Tyr 753;
  4 LJ Ex 137 .... 12.33
Ballard v Shutt (1880) 15 Ch D 122; 49 LJCh 618; 43 LT 173;
  29 WR 73 .... 12.34
Ballen v White (1960) 12 P & CR 66 .... 7.16
Ballyowen Castle Homes Ltd v Collins (HC) unrep, 26 June 1986 .... 7.08
Baltimore Extension Rly Co, Re [1895] 1 IR 169; 29 ILTR 54 .... 8.14
Bamford v Shuttleworth (1840) 11 A & E 926; 113 ER 666 .... 2.26
Banco Ambrosiano v Ansbacher & Co [1987] ILRM 669 .... 5.23
Banco Exterior International v Mann [1995] 1 All ER 936 .... 16.23, 16.69
Bank of Baroda Ltd v Punjab National Bank Ltd [1944] AC 176;
  [1944] 2 All ER 83; 114 LJPC 1; 60 TLR 412; 88 Sol Jo 255 .... 20.31
Bank of Ireland v Hanrahan (HC) unrep, 10 February, 1987 .... 16.62
Bank of Ireland v Purcell [1989] IR 327 .... 16.62, 16.69
Bank of Ireland v Slevin (HC) unrep, 16 February 1989 .... 16.69
Bank of Ireland v Smith [1966] IR 646; 102 ILTR 69 ... 1.38, 2.13, 2.27, 5.26, 5.27
  ....9.29, 9.44, 11.02-11.04
Bank of Ireland v Smyth [1993] 2 IR 102; [1996] 1 ILRM 241;
  [1996] ICLC 1 .... 1.35, 4.02, 9.23, 15.01, 16.23-16.23
  .... 16.62, 16.67, 16.69
Bank of Ireland v Waldron [1944] IR 303; 78 ILTR 48........................... 2.27, 10.44
  .... 11.02-11.04, 12.21, 12.23, 16.15
Bank of Ireland Finance Ltd v Daly Ltd [1978] IR 79 .... 12.15, 12.16
Bank of Nova Scotia v Hogan (HC) unrep, 21 December 1992 .... 16.23
Bankes v Small [1887] 36 Ch D 716; 56 LJCh 832; 57 LT 292; 3 TLR 740;
  35 WR 765 .... 21.33
Bannon v EAT & Drogheda Town Centre (HC) unrep, 5 October 1992 .... 5.15
Banque Bruxelles Lambert SA v Eagle Star Insurance Co Ltd [1995] 2 All
  ER 769 .... 1.38
Banter v FW Capp & Co Ltd [1938] 4 All ER 457 .... 3.13
Barber v Cricket [1958] NZLR 1057 .... 7.15
Barber v Wolfe [1945] Ch 187; [1945] 1 All ER 399; 114 LJCh 149;
  172 LT 384; 89 Sol Jo 176; 61 TLR 249 .... 13.29, 13.60-13.61
Barclay v Messenger (1874) 43 LJ Ch 449 .... 13.14
Barclays Bank Ltd v Carroll (HC) unrep 10 September 1986 .... 14.27, 16.62, 16.70
Barclays Bank Ltd v Stasek [1957] Ch 28; [1956] 3 WLR 760;
  [1956] 3 All ER 439; 98 Sol Jo 145 .... 14.63

Barclays Bank plc v Estates & Commercial Ltd London Times,
  13 March 1996 .... 12.17
Barclays Bank plc v Eustice [1995] 4 All ER 511 .... 12.29
Barclays Bank plc v O'Brien [1993] 3 WLR 786;
  [1993] 4 All ER 417 .... 1.35, 16.23
Barclays Bank plc v Weeks Legg & Dean [1996] EGCS 29 .... 14.11, 15.05
Barclays Bank v Breen (1962) 96 ILTR 179 .... 13.40
Barker's Estate, Re (1879) 3 LR Ir 395 .... 21.05
Barkworth v Young (1856) 4 Drew 1; 26 LJCh 153; 28 LT (ns) 199;
  5 WR 156; 62 ER 1; 3 Jur (ns) 34 .... 6.06
Barnewall's Estate, Re (1867) IR 1 Eq 304; 1 ILT 349 .... 9.26
Barnwell v Harris (1809) 1 Taunt 430; 127 ER 901 .... 14.54
Barr's Contract, Re [1956] Ch 551; [1956] 1 WLR 918;
  [1956] 2 All ER 853; 100 Sol Jo 550 .... 13.17
Barratt v Costelloe (1973) 107 ILTSJ 239 .... 6.07, 6.18, 6.25, 6.28
Barrett Apartments Ltd, Re [1985] IR 350; [1985] ILRM 679................... 3.10, 3.15
.... 4.25, 10.31, 11.17, 12.02, 12.08, 12.12, 12.44, 15.48
Barrett v Brahms (1967) 111 Sol Jo 35 .... 18.105
Barrington, Re (1834) 3 LJ Bey 122; 4 Deac & Ch 693; 2 Mont & A 146 ...... 12.34
Barrington v Lee [1972] 1 QB 326; [1971] 3 WLR 962;
  [1971] 3 All ER 1231; 115 Sol Jo 833 .... 2.10, 3.11, 3.16
Barron v Cowan (1930) 64 ILTR 168 .... 3.22
Barry v Buckley [1981] 1 IR 306 .... 7.07
Barry v O'Grady (1846) 9 Ir Eq R 550 .... 6.28
Barsht v Tagg [1900] 1 Ch 231; 69 LJCh 91; 81 LT 777; 44 Sol Jo 133;
  16 TLR 100; 48 WR 220 .... 12.18, 20.06
Barton v Lord Downes (1842) Fl & K 505; 4 Ir Eq R 607 .... 9.26
Basildon District Council v J E Lesser (Properties) Ltd [1985] QB 839;
  [1984] 3 WLR 812; [1985] 1 All ER 20; 128 Sol Jo 330.............................. 4.13
Bastable, Re [1901] 2 KB 518; 70 LJKB 784; 84 LT 825; 49 WR 501;
  17 TLR 560; 45 Sol Jo 576 .... 12.27
Baumann v James (1868) 3 Ch App 508; 18 LT 424; 32 JP 643;
  16 WR 877 .... 6.30
Bayley v Conyngham (1863) I5 ICLR 406 .... 18.74
Bayly's Estate, Re (1860) 12 Ir Ch R 315; 6 Ir Jur (ns) 25 .... 20.50
Baynes & Co Ltd v Lloyd & Sons [1895] 2 QB 610; 64 LJQB 787;
  73 LT 250; 11 TLR 560; 44 WR 328; 59 JP 710 .... 21.30
Beard v Porter [1948] 1 KB 321; [1947] 2 All ER 407; [1947] LJR 77;
  177 LT 570; 91 Sol Jo 544; 63 TLR 543 .... 10.44, 13.87
Beauclerk v Hanna (1888) 23 LR Ir 144; 23 ILTR 26 ....6.53, 6.55-6.57
Beauman v Kinsella (1858) 8 ICLR 291; (1859) 111 ICLR 249 .... 18.60
Beaver v McFarlane [1932] LJ Ir 128 .... 4.08
Bechal v Kitsford Holdings Ltd [1988] 3 All ER 985;
  [1989] 1 WLR 105.. 13.20-13.20
Becker v Partridge [1966] 2 QB 155; [1966] 2 WLR 803;
  [1966] 2 All ER 266; 110 Sol Jo 187 ....9.17, 14.70, 14.73-14.75

Beckett v Nurse [1948] 1 KB 535; [1948] 1 All ER 81; LJR 450;
 92 Sol Jo 54; 64 TLR 95 .... 6.14
Beesly v Hallwood Estates Ltd [1961] Ch 105; [1961] 2 WLR 36; [1961] 1 All ER
 90; 105 Sol Jo 61 .... 18.126-18.128
Behzadi v Shaftesbury Hotels Ltd [1991] 2 WLR 1251; [1991] 2 All ER 477
 .... 13.12, 13.17, 13.18
Belfast Bank v Callan [1910] 1 IR 38 .... 11.04, 20.07
Belfast Water Commissioners, Re (1884) 12 LR Ir 13 .... 8.14
Bell v Balls [1897] 1 Ch 663; 66 LJCh 397; 76 LT 253; 41 Sol Jo 331;
 13 TLR 274; 45 WR 378 .... 6.38
Bell v Lever Bros Ltd [1932] AC 161; 101 LJKB 129; 146 LT 258;
 76 Sol Jo 50; 48 TLR 133 .... 13.66
Bellamy v Debenham [1891] 1 Ch 412; 60 LJCh 166; 64 LT 478; 7 TLR 199;
 39 WR 257 .... 13.78
Bellew v Bellew [1982] IR 447; [1983] ILRM 128 .... 12.33
Belshaw v Rollins [1904] 1 IR 284; 4 NIJR 105; 38 ILTR 90 .... 12.11
Belton v Kirwan [1943] IR 525 .... 6.12
Bennett v Bennett (HC) unrep, 24 January 1977 .... 17.20
Bennett v Brumfitt (1867) LR 3 CP 28; Hop & Ph 407; 37 LJCP 25;
 17 LT 213; 31 JP 824; 16 WR 131 .... 6.33
Bennett v Ingoldsby (1676) Cas Temp Finch 262 .... 21.33
Bennett Walden & Co v Wood [1950] 2 All ER 134; 66 TLR 3 .... 3.27-3.29
Bentall Horsley & Baldry v Vicary [1931]1 KB 253; 100 LJKB 201;
 144 LT 365; 47 TLR 99; 74 Sol Jo 862 .... 3.13
Bentham v Hardy (1843) 6 Ir LR 179 .... 6.13
Bentray Investments Ltd v Vennar Time Switches Ltd (1985) 274 EG 43 .... 18.125
Beresford v Clarke [1908] 2 IR 317; 42 ILTR 136 .... 20.09
Berkowitz v MW (St John's Wood) Ltd [1993] 48 EG 133 .... 5.27
Bernard v Meara (1861) 12 Ir Ch R 389; 7 Ir Jur (ns) 333 .... 13.41
Bernstein (Lord) of Leigh v Skyviews & General Ltd [1978] QB 479;
 [1977] 2 All ER 902; [1977] 3 WLR 136; 121 Sol Jo 157; 241 EG 917 ..... 19.13
Berry Ltd v Brighton & Sussex BS [1939] 3 All ER 217 .... 7.12
Beswick v Beswick [1968] AC 58; [1967] 3 WLR 932; [1967] 3 All ER 1197;
 111 Sol Jo 540 .... 13.41, 18.08, 18.13
Bexwell v Christie (1776) 1 Cowp 395; 98 ER 1150 .... 2.14
Beyfus v Lodge [1925] Ch 350; 95 LJCh 27; 133 LT 265; 69 Sol Jo 507;
 41 TLR 429 .... 9.11, 13.35, 14.75
Bigg v Whisking (1853) 14 CB 195; 2 CLR 617 .... 6.13
Biggs-Atkinson & Ryan's Contract, Re [1913] 1 IR 125 .... 20.06
Billings (AC) & Son Ltd v Riden [1958] AC 240; [1957] 3 WLR 496; [1957] 3 All
 ER 1; 101 Sol Jo 645 .... 4.15
Billyack v Leyland Construction Co Ltd [1968] 1 WLR 471; [1968] 1 All ER 783
 4.13
Bingham v Bingham (1748) 1 Ves Sen 126; 27 ER 934 .... 21.37
Binks v Rokeby (1818) 2 Swanst 222; 36 ER 600 .... 10.18

Bird v Fox (1853) 11 Hare 40; 68 ER 1178 ....9.11
Birmingham Canal Co v Cartwright (1879) 11 Ch D 421; 48 LJCh 552;
   40 LT 784; 27 WR 597 ....8.03
Birmingham, Re [1959] Ch 523; [1958] 3 WLR 10; [1958] 2 All ER 397; 102 Sol Jo
   454 ....12.16, 12.46
Black v Grealy (HC) unrep, 10 November 1977 ....6.07
Black v Kavanagh (1974) 108 ILTR 91 ....3.33, 6.14-6.19, 6.25, 6.28, 6.31
   ....6.42, 6.45, 7.01, 7.03, 7.06, 7.09, 7.12
Blackburn v Smith (1848) 2 Exch 783; 18 LJ Ex 187; 154 ER 707 ....13.58
Blackhall v Gibson (1878) 2 LR Ir 49 ....18.32, 18.38
Blackwood v Gregg (1831) Hayes 277; Gasc 292 ....13.48
Blaiberg & Abrahams, Re [1899] 2 Ch 340; 68 LJCh 578; 81 LT 75;
   43 Sol Jo 625; 47 WR 634 ....15.19
Blaibery v Keeves [1906] 2 Ch 175; 75 LJCh 464; 95 LT 412; 54 WR 451 ......9.07
Blake v Marnell (1811) 2 Ba & B 35 ....17.19, 18.25
Blakeney v Hardie (1874) IR 8 Eq 381 ....6.02, 17.27
Blennerhassett v Day (1813) Beat 468 ....18.120, 18.125-18.126
Bligh v Martin [1968] 1 All ER 1157; [1968] 1 WLR 804; 112 Sol Jo 189;
   19 P & CR 442 ....21.37
Blore v Sutton (1817) 3 Mer 237; 36 ER 91 ....6.50
Blount v GS & W Rly Co (1851) 2 Ir Ch R 40 ....8.14, 12.18, 12.34
Bluck v Gompertz (1852) 7 Exch 862; 155 ER 1199 ....6.33
Blumberg v Life Interests & Reversionary Securities Corp [1898] 1 Ch 27;
   66 LJCh 127; 75 LT 627; 41 Sol Jo 130; 45 WR 246 ....20.31
Blunden v Desart (1842) 5 Ir Eq R 221; 2 Dr & War 405; 2 Con & L 111 ......20.50
Boggs, Re (1951) 85 ILTR 1 ....20.49
Bolton Partners v Lambert (1889) 41 Ch D 295; (1889) 41 Ch D 302;
   58 LJCh 425; 60 LT 687 ....6.36
Bolton v London School Board (1878) 7 Ch D 766; 47 LJCh 461; 38 LT 277; 26 WR
   549 ....14.54, 15.53
Bond v Hopkins (1802) 1 Sch & Lef 413 ....6.48, 6.51
Bonnewell v Jenkin (1878) 8 Ch D 70; 47 LJCh 758; 38 LT 581; 26 WR 294 ..7.12
Bonomi v Backhouse (1858) El Bl & El 622; 120 ER 642 ....19.13
Boobyer v Thorville Properties, Ltd (1968) 19 P & CR 768 ....7.16
Boothman v Brown (1900) 1 NIJR 41 ....13.58
Boothman v Byrne (1923) 57 ILTR 36 ....2.10, 10.24
Boots v Christopher & Co [1952] 1 KB 89; [1951] 2 All ER 1945;
   [1951] 2 TLR 1169; 95 Sol Jo 788 ....3.29
Borrowes v Borrowes (1871) IR 6 Eq 368 ....18.25, 18.32-18.34, 18.82
Bottomley v Bannister [1932] 1 KB 458; 101 LKJB 46; 146 LT 68;
   48 TLR 39 ....4.15
Bourke v Grimes (1929) 63 ILTR 53 ....13.04, 13.55, 14.42, 14.45
Bousfield v Hodges (1863) 33 Beav 90; 55 ER 300 ....2.07
Bowen v Duc d'Orleans (1900) 16 TLR 226 ....6.43
Bowes v Dublin Corporation [1965] IR 476 ....21.05

Bowman v Hyland (1878) 8 Ch D 588; 47 LJCh 581; 39 LT 90; 26 WR 877 . 15.32

Bown v Stenson (1857) 24 Beav 631; 53 ER 501 .... 12.34, 15.53

Boyce v Greene (1826) Batty 608 .... 6.10, 6.20, 6.29

Boyd v Dickson (1876) IR 10 Eq 239 ....2.54, 9.02, 9.38, 10.04-10.05
.... 12.34, 13.52-13.53, 14.17, 14.19, 14.42

Boydell v Drummond (1809) 11 East 142; 103 ER 958 .... 6.51

Boyle v Lee [1992] 1 IR 555; [1992] ILRM 65................6.02-6.03, 6.15, 6.18-6.18
.... 6.25, 7.06, 7.08-7.10, 13.44-13.46

Boyle v Mulholland (1860) 10 Ir Ch R 150 .... 17.19, 18.66

Boyle v Olpherts (1841) 4 Ir Eq R 241; 1 Long & Town 320 .... 18.75

Bradford v Dublin & Kingstown Rly Co (1858) 7 ICLR 624 .... 17.19, 18.66, 18.75

Bradley v Donegal County Council (HC) unrep, 14 November 1989 ... 12.25, 12.36

Braithwaite's Settled Estate, Re [1922] 1 IR 71 .... 8.04

Brakspear & Sons Ltd v Barton [1924] 2 KB 88 .... 19.27

Bramwell's Contract, Re [1969] 1 WLR 1659; 113 Sol Jo 875;
     20 P & CR 889 .... 9.11

Branca v Cobarro [1947] KB 854; [1947] 2 All ER 101; 177 LT 332;
     63 TLR 408 .... 7.12

Brennan v Bolton (1842) 2 Dr & War 354 .... 6.49, 6.56, 6.58

Brennan v O'Connell [1980] IR 13 .... 2.09, 3.07, 3.12, 6.36, 6.41

Breslin v Hodgens (No 2) (1874) IR 8 Eq 397; 8 ILTR 110 .... 14.51

Brett & Ors v Niall Collins Ltd (HC) unrep, 3 May 1995 .... 5.15

Brewer & Hawkin's Contract, Re (1899) 80 LT 127 .... 9.43

Brewer Street Investment Ltd v Barclay's Woollen Co Ltd
     [1953]1 All ER 1330.. 12.21

Bridge v Campbell Discount Co Ltd [1962] AC 600; [1962] 2 WLR 439;
     [1962] 1 All ER 385; 106 Sol Jo 94 .... 13.32

Bridges v Mees [1957] Ch 475; [1957] 3 WLR 215; [1957] 3 All ER 577;
     101 Sol Jo 232 .... 12.02

Bridgwater's Settlement, Re [1910] 2 Ch 342; 79 LJCh 746; 103 LT 552 ...... 18.33

Brien v Dwyer (1979) 141 CLR 378 .... 10.22

Brien v Swainson (1877) 1 LR Ir 135 .... 7.03, 7.11

Brine & Davies' Contract, Re [1935] Ch 388; [1935] All ER Rep 871;
     104 LJCh 139; 152 LT 552 .... 9.17, 9.26

Bristol & West Building Society v Christie [1996] EGCS 53 .... 1.36

Britain v Rossiter (1879) 11 QBD 123 .... 6.48

British Railways Board v Glass [1965] Ch 538; [19664] 1 WLR 294;
     [1964] 3 All ER 418; 108 Sol Jo 673 .... 18.73

Brohan v Crosspan Developments Ltd [1985] ILRM 702 .... 11.21

Brook Cottage Ltd, Re [1976] NI 78 .... 11.06

Brookes v Drysdale (1877) 3 CPD 52; 37 LT 467; 26 WR 331 .... 18.94

Broughton v Snook [1938] Ch 505; [1938] 1 All ER 411; 107 LJCh 204;
     158 LT 130; 54 TLR 301; 82 Sol Jo 112 .... 6.07, 6.53, 6.58

Brown & Mitchell's Contract, Re (1902) 2 NIJR 106 .... 13.28

Brown v Armstrong (1873) IR 7 CL 130 .... 14.52

Brown v Chadwick (1857) 7 ICLR 101 ....18.73-18.75
Brown v Gould [1972] Ch 53; [1971] 3 WLR 334; [1971] 2 All ER 1505;
    115 Sol Jo 406; 22 P & CR 871 ....8.04
Brown v IRC [1965] AC 244; [1964] 3 WLR 511; [1964] 3 All ER 119;
    108 Sol Jo 636; 42 TC 60; 43 ATC 224; SLT 202; SC (HL) 10.26
Brown v Norton [1954] IR 34; 88 ILTR 102 ....4.12, 4.13, 4.15, 11.15
Browne v Burton (1847) 17 LJKB 49; 5 Dow & L 289; 2 Saund & C 220;
    12 Jur 97 .... 18.09
Browne v Mulligan [1976-7] ILRM 327 ....12.37
Browne's Estate, Re [1913] 1 IR 165; 47 ILTR 58 ....13.50
Browning v Wright (1799) 2 Bos & P 13; 126 ER 1128 ....21.28
Brownlee v Duggan [1976] 5 NIJB 11 ....13.54
Brownlow v Keatinge (1840) 2 Ir Eq R 243 ....20.50
Bryant & Barningham's Contract, Re (1890) 44 Ch D 218; 59 LJCh 636;
    63 LT 20; 38 WR 469 .... 14.61
Bryant v Busk (1872) 4 Russ 1 ....14.51
Bryant v Taylor (1867) IR 2 QB 161 ....14.54
Bryce v Fleming [1930] IR 376 ....16.24
Buckler's Case (1597) 2 Co Rep 55; 76 ER 537 ....18.82
Buckley v Dawson (1854) 4 ICLR 211; 6 Ir Jur (os) 374 ....13.82
Buckley v Irwin [1960] NI 98 ....6.13, 13.48-13.48, 21.35
Buckley v Lynch [1978] IR 6 ....4.18
Buckmaster v Harrop (1807) 13 Ves 456 ....6.38
Bunny v Hopkinson (1859) 27 Beav 565; 29 LJCh 93; 1 LT 53;
    [1950] WN 50...21.32
Burgess v Cox [1951] Ch 383 ....6.07, 6.29
Burke v Dublin Corporation [1991] 1 IR 341 ....4.16
Burke v Lynch (1814) 2 Ba & B 426 ....13.50
Burnett v Lynch (1826) 5 B & C 589 ....15.11
Burns v Langford (1901) 35 ILTR 148 ....2.29, 3.22
Burrough v Skinner (1770) 5 Burr 2639 ....2.10, 2.26
Burroughs v Oakley (1819) 3 Swanst 159 ....15.52
Burrowes v Hayes (1834) Hay & Jon 597 ....17.19
Burt v Claude Cousins & Co Ltd [1971] 2 All ER 611; [1971] 2 QB 426;
    [1971] 2 WLR 930 ....2.10, 2.45, 3.11, 3.16, 10.26
Burton v Barclay (1831) 7 Bing 745; 5 Moo & P 785; 9 LJ (os) CP 231 ....18.82
Butcher v Nash (1889) 61 LT 72 ....6.20
Butler & Selmon's Contract, Re [1907] 1 Ch 238 ....14.61
Butler v Gilbert (1890) 25 LR Ir 230 ....17.18, 18.25, 18.35, 18.58
Butler v Mountview Estates Ltd [1951] 2 KB 563; [1951] 1 TLR 524;
    [1951] 1 All ER 693 ....12.22, 21.10
Butwick v Grant [1924] 2 KB 483 ....2.10
Byrne v Lafferty (1845) 8 Ir Eq R 47 ....11.05
Byrne v Revenue Commissioners [1935] IR 664; 68 ILTR 235 ....18.125-18.127

C

C v C [1976] IR 254 .... 16.23
Caballero v Henty (1874) LR 9 Ch 447; 43 LJCh 635; 30 LT 314;
    22 WR 446 .... 9.23
Cahill v Sutton [1980] IR 269 .... 4.17
Calcraft v Roebuck (1790) 1 Ves 221 .... 12.20
Callaghan v Pepper (1840) 2 Ir Eq R 399 .... 6.34, 6.56
Callon v Flynn (1890) 26 LR Ir 179 .... 8.14
Calvert, Re [1898] 2 IR 501 .... 6.10
Caney v Leith [1937] 2 All ER 532; 156 LT 483; 53 TLR 596;
    81 Sol Jo 357 .... 7.12
Capital & Counties Bank Ltd v Gordon [1903] AC 240; 72 LJKB 451;
    88 LT 574; 19 TLR 402; 51 WR 671 .... 20.31
Carbin v Somerville [1933] IR 276 .... 5.23-5.26, 13.48, 13.58, 13.64
Carew v Jackman [1966] IR 177 .... 16.31, 21.05
Carew's Estate, Re (1858) 26 Beav 187; 28 LJCh 218; 32 LT (os) 154;
    4 Jur (ns) 1290; 7 WR 81 .... 2.24
Carew's Estate, Re (1887) 19 LR Ir 483 .... 14.56
Carlill v Carbolic Smoke Ball Co [1893] 1 QB 256; 62 LJQB 257; 67 LT 837;
    57 JP 325; 41 WR 210; 9 TLR 124 .... 2.20
Carling v GN Rlys Co (1869) 21 LT 17 .... 12.20
Carlish v Salt [1906] 1 Ch 335; 75 LJCh 175; 94 LT 58; 50 Sol Jo 157;
    54 WR 244 .... 9.21
Carncross v Hamilton (1890) 9 NZLR 91 .... 6.20
Carney v Fair (1920) 54 ILTR 61 .... 3.07, 6.41
Carolan & Scott's Contract, Re [1899] 1 IR 1 .... 13.28
Carpenter's Estates v Davies [1940] Ch 160 .... 13.41
Carr v Lynch [1900] 1 Ch 613; 69 LJCh 345; 82 LT 381; 48 WR 616 .... 6.20
Carr v Phelan [1976-7] ILRM 149 .... 6.24, 8.06, 13.45
Carrigan v Carrigan (HC) unrep, 3 May, 1983 .... 16.62
Carrige & McDonnell's Contract, Re [1895] 1 IR 288 .... 15.22
Carrigy v Brock (1871) IR 5 CL 501 .... 2.09, 6.17, 6.38, 21.04
Carrington v Roots (1837) 2 M & W 248; Murph & H 14; 6 LJ Ex 95;
    1 Jur 85 .... 6.07, 6.09
Carritt v Real & Personal Advance Co (1889) 42 Ch D 263; 58 LJCh 688;
    61 LT 163; 37 WR 677 .... 14.65
Carrodus v Sharp (1855) 20 Beav 56; 52 ER 523 .... 20.06
Carroll v Keayes (1873) IR 8 Eq 97; 8 ILTR 47 .... 4.21, 9.23
Carson v Jeffers [1961] IR 44 .... 20.06
Carter's Trusts, Re (1869) IR 3 Eq 495 .... 17.18
Carthy v O'Neill [1981] ILRM 443 .... 6.13, 6.19, 6.32, 7.08
Casey v Irish Intercontinental Bank [1979] IR 364 ; 114 ILTR 18 ... 6.15, 6.33, 7.08
Cassidy v Baker (1969) 103 ILTR 40 .... 8.03, 8.05
Castellain v Preston (1883) 11 QBD 380; 52 LJQB 366; 49 LT 29;
    31 WR 557 .... 12.38

Cato v Thompson (1882) 9 QBD 616; 47 LT 491 .... 9.35
Caton v Caton (1867) LR 2 HL 127; 36 LJCh 886; 16 WR 1 .... 6.50
Caulfield v Maguire (1856) 5 Ir Ch R 78 .... 17.16
Cellulose Processors Ltd v Flynn & O'Flaherty Ltd
   (HC) unrep, 28 April 1986 .... 12.19
Central London Rly Co v City of London Land Tax Commrs [1911] 1 Ch 467;
   [1913] AC 365 .... 18.59
Chadburn v Moore (1892) 61 LJ Ch 674; 67 LT 257; 41 WR 39;
   36 Sol Jo 666 .... 3.07, 3.08
Chafer & Randall's Contract, Re [1916] 2 Ch 8; 85 LJCh 435; 114 LT 1076;
   60 Sol Jo 444 .... 15.19, 18.36
Chamberlain v Farr [1942] 2 All ER 567; 112 LJKB 206 .... 12.33
Chambers v Betty (1815) Beat 488 .... 6.28
Chaney v Maclow [1929] 1 Ch 461; 98 LJCh 345; 140 LT 312; 73 Sol Jo 26;
   45 TLR 125 .... 6.38
Chaproniere v Lambert [1917] 2 Ch 356; 86 LJCh 726; 117 LT 353;
   33 TLR 485; 61 Sol Jo 592 .... 6.48, 6.53, 6.59
Cheapside Land Development Co Ltd v Messels Service Co
   [1977] 2 All ER 62; [1977] 2 WLR 806 .... 19.34
Cheese v Thomas [1994] 1 All ER 35 .... 13.58, 13.64
Chelmsford Auctions Ltd v Poole [1973] QB 542; [1973] 2 WLR 219;
   [1971] 1 All ER 810; 117 Sol Jo 219 .... 2.34
Chelsea & Walham Green BS v Armstrong [1951] Ch 853; [1951] 2 TLR 312;
   [1951] 2 All ER 250 .... 18.08
Cherry Court v Revenue Commissioners [1995] 2 ILRM 228 .... 18.48, 21.03
.... 21.05, 21.09
Cherry v Anderson (1876) IR 10 CL 204 .... 2.28, 2.34, 3.32
Chesterfield's (Earl of) Trusts, Re (1883) 24 Ch D 643 .... 19.63
Chichester v Hobbs (1866) 14 LT 433 .... 6.33
Child v Stenning (1879) 11 Ch D 82 .... 21.32
Chillingsworth v Esche [1924] 1 Ch 97; 93 LJCh 129; 129 LT 808;
   68 Sol Jo 80; 40 TLR 23 .... 7.11, 10.18
Chinnock v Sainsbury (1869) 3 LT 258; (1869) 30 LJ Ch 409 .... 2.32
Chipperfield v Carter (1895) 72 LT 487 .... 7.12
Chism v Lipsett [1905] 1 IR 60; 38 ILTR 259 .... 14.52
Chiverst & Sons Ltd v Air Ministry [1955] Ch 585; [1955] 3 WLR 154;
   [1955] 2 All ER 607; 99 Sol Jo 435 .... 21.30
Christie Owen & Davies Ltd v Rapacioli [1974] 2 All ER 311;
   [1974] 2 WLR 723; 188 Sol Jo 167 .... 3.29
Christopher & Co v Essing [1948] WN 461 .... 3.13
CIBC Mortgages plc v Pitt [1993] 4 All ER 433; [1994] 1 AC 200;
   [1993] 3 WLR 802 .... 1.35, 16.23
CIF Holdings Ltd v Barclays Bank (Ir) Ltd (HC) unrep, 25 July 1986 .... 17.22
City & Westminster Properties Ltd v Mudd [1959] Ch 129;
   [1958] 3 WLR 312; [1958] 2 All ER 733; 102 Sol Jo 582 ....5.26, 6.13, 17.19

City of Glasgow Friendly Society v Gilpin Ltd (1971) 22 NILQ 196 ...... 3.33, 6.15-
   6.16, ... 6.19, 6.31, 7.12
City of Kamloops v Neilsen (1984) 10 DLR (4th) 641 .... 4.17
City of London Land Tax Commrs v Central London Rly Co [1913] AC 364 18.59
Clare v Dobson [1911] 1 KB 35 .... 19.32
Clark Boyce v Mouat [1993] 3 WLR 1021; [1993] 4 All ER 268 .... 1.34, 1.35
Clarke v Callow (1876) LJQB 53 .... 6.07
Clarke v Early [1980] IR 229 .... 17.25
Clarke v Hall (1888) 24 LR Ir 316 .... 18.32, 18.38
Clarke v Moore (1844) 7 Ir Eq R 515; 1 Jo & Lat 723 .... 13.40, 13.50
Clarke v Ramuz [1891] 2 QB 456; 60 LJQB 679; 65 LT 657; 7 TLR 626;
   56 JP 5 .... 12.21-12.22, 21.03
Clarke v Taylor [1899] 1 IR 449 .... 14.06, 14.10, 14.11, 14.19, 14.42, 14.56
Clarke v Wallis (1966) 35 Beav 460 .... 13.60
Clarke's Will Trusts, Re [1920] 1 IR 47 .... 8.04
Clayton (Joseph) Ltd, Re [1920] 1 Ch 257; 89 LJCh 188; 122 LT 517;
   36 TLR 109; 64 Sol Jo 176 .... 11.07
Clayton v Ashdown (1714) 2 Eq Ca Abr 516; 9 Vin Abr 393 .... 13.47
Clayton v Leech (1889) 41 Ch D 103; 61 LT 69; 37 WR 663 .... 14.73
Clea Shipping Corporation v Bulk Oil International Ltd
   [1984] 1 All ER 129 .... 13.06
Cleary, Re [1922]1 IR 94; 56 ILTR 163 .... 16.31
Clegg v Wright (1920) 54 ILTR 69 .... 13.12, 14.17-14.19, 15.26
Clements v Conroy [1911] 2 IR 500 .... 9.23, 9.37, 15.26
Clements v Henry (1859) 10 Ir Ch R 79 .... 17.16
Clibborn v Horan [1921] 1 IR 93; 55 ILTR 49 .... 13.07, 13.57, 13.68, 14.10
   .... 14.12, 14.81
Clinan v Cooke (1802) 1 Sch & Lef 22 .... 6.26, 6.29-6.31, 6.50, 6.56, 6.59, 13.45
Clinton, Re [1988] ILRM 80 .... 17.20
Clitheroe v Simpson (1879) 4 LR Ir 59 .... 13.44
Cloncurry (Lord) v Laffan [1924] 1 IR 78; 58 ILTR 57 .... 6.28, 6.42-6.43
Coates v Boswell (1886) 11 App Cas 232; 55 LJCh 761; 55 LT 32 .... 9.35
Cockcroft, Re (1883) 24 Ch D 94; 52 LJCh 811; 49 LT 497; 32 WR 223 .... 12.46
Cockwell v Romford Sanitary Steam Laundry Ltd [1939] 4 All ER 370 .... 8.05
Coffey v Brunel Construction Co Ltd [1983] IR 36 .... 12.50
Cohen v Nessdale Ltd [1981] 3 All ER 118; [1982] 2 All ER 97 .... 6.59, 7.08
Cohen v Roche [1927] 1 KB 169; 95 LKJB 945; 136 LT 219; 42 TLR 674;
   70 Sol Jo 942 .... 2.24
Cole v Rose [1978] 3 All ER 1121 .... 13.20, 13.35
Coleman v Dundalk Urban District Council (SC) unrep, 17 July 1985 .... 4.16
Coleman v Fry (1873) IR 7 CL 247 .... 13.67
Coleman v Upcott (1707) 5 Vin Abr 527; 2 Eq Cas Abr 45 .... 6.14
Coles v Trecothick (1804) 9 Ves 234; 1 Smith KB 233 .... 2.11, 3.12, 6.38-6.40
Colgan v Connolly Construction Co (Ir) Ltd [1980] ILRM 33 .... 4.16
Colhoun v Trustees of Foyle College [1898] 1 IR 233 .... 13.27

Collingridge v Royal Exchange Assurance Corp (1877) 3 QBD 173;
   47 LJQB 32; 37 LT 525; 26 WR 112; 42 JP 118 .... 12.38
Collins v Prosser (1823) 1 B & C 682; 3 Dow & Ry KB 112;
   1 LJ (os) KB 212; 1107 ER 250 .... 21.13
Collins v Stinson (1883) 11 QBD 142; 52 LKJB 440; 48 LT 828;
   31 WR 920; 47 JP 439 .... 2.26, 10.26, 12.47
Collis's Estate, Re (1864) 14 Ir Ch R 511; 9 Ir Jur (ns) 177 .... 9.33
Combe v Swaythling [1947] Ch 623; [1947] 1 All ER 838; [1948] LJR 392;
   177 LT 76 .... 10.25, 12.44, 13.34
Commane v Walsh (HC) unrep, 2 May 1983 .... 13.21
Commins & Hanafy's Contract, Re (1905) 39 ILTR 85 .... 10.18, 13.34, 13.64
Commission for New Towns v Cooper (GB) Ltd [1995] 2 All ER 929 .... 1.31, 6.09
Commonage at Glennamaddoo, Re [1992] IR 297 .... 16.30
Compton v Bagley [1892] 1 Ch 313; 61 LJCh 113; 65 LT 706 .... 14.45, 14.47
Computastaff Ltd v Ingeldew Brown Bennison & Garrett (1983) 268 EG 906 .5.28
Conaty v Ulster Development Ltd (1966) 17 NILQ 162 .... 6.26, 6.29
Conlon & Faulkener's Contract, Re [1916] 1 IR 241 .... 14.18, 14.42, 14.48
Conlon v Murray [1958] NI 17 .... 13.38, 13.43, 13.48, 13.49
Connell v O'Malley (HC) unrep, 28 July 1983 .... 17.22
Connolly v Keating (No 2) [1903] 1 IR 356 ....11.02, 12.04, 12.23-12.24
.... 13.76, 15.52
Connor, Re (1894) 28 ILTR 67 .... 8.14
Connor v Fitzgerald (1883) 11 LR Ir 106 .... 6.48-6.49, 6.53, 6.55-6.57
Connor v Potts [1897] 1 IR 534 .... 5.26
Connswater Properties Ltd v Wilson (HC) (NI) unrep, 8 July 1986 .... 5.26
Conolly v Parsons (1797) 3 Ves 625n 2.14
Containercare (Ir) Ltd v Wycherley [1982] IR 143 .... 16.62
Cook v Taylor [1942] Ch 349; [1942] 2 All ER 85; 111 LJCh 214;
   167 LT 87; 86 Sol Jo 217; 58 TLR 278 .... 9.08, 10.44
Cooke v Tombs (1794) 2 Anst 420 .... 6.60
Coombs v Wilkes [1891] 3 Ch 77; 61 LJCh 42; 65 LT 56; 40 WR 77;
   7 TLR 592 .... 6.20
Cooper, Re (1882) 20 Ch D 611 .... 18.10
Cooper v Cartwright (1860) John 679; 70 ER 592 .... 17.07
Cooper v Critchley [1955] Ch 431; [1955] 2 WLR 510; [1955] 1 All ER 520;
   99 Sol Jo 148 .... 6.11
Cooper v Emery (1844) 1 Ph 388; 13 LJCh 275; 2 LT (os) 437; 8 Jur 181;
   41 ER 679 .... 14.54, 18.104
Cooper v Phibbs (1867) LR 2 HL 149; 16 LT 678; 15 WR 1049 .... 13.67
Cooper & Crondace's Contract, Re [1904] 90 LT 258 .... 13.27
Co-operative Insurance Society Ltd v Argyll Stores (Holdings) Ltd
   [1996] 09 EG 128 .... 13.41
Copelin's Contract, Re [1937] 4 All ER 447; 45 TLR 130 .... 14.56, 14.59, 16.69
Corbett v Hill (1870) IR 9 Eq 671 .... 18.61
Cordell v Second Clanfleld Properties Ltd [1969] 2 Ch 9; [1968] 3 WLR 864;
   [1968] 3 All ER 746; 112 Sol Jo 841 .... 18.78

Corder v Morgan (1811) 18 Ves 344; 34 ER 347 .... 18.13
Cork & Youghal Rly Co v Harnett (1871) LR 5 HL 111 .... 8.14
Corless v Sparling (1874) IR 8 Eq 335 .... 13.40, 14.19, 14.42, 14.56, 15.51
Cornwall v Henson [1900] 2 Ch 298; 69 LJCh 581; 82 LT 735; 49 WR 42;
    16 TLR 422; 44 Sol Jo 514 .... 12.44
Corrigan v Crofton [1985] ILRM 189 .... 4.12
Corrigan v Woods (1867) IR 1 CL 73; 1 ILT 102 .... 12.33
Corrigan v Woods (1883) 11 LR Ir 106 .... 6.56
Costelloe v Maharaj Krishna Properties (Ir) Ltd (HC) unrep, 10 July 1975 ...... 7.04
    .... 7.14, 7.23, 16.53
Cottrell v Watkins (1839) 1 Beav 361; 3 Jur 283; 48 ER 980 .... 14.58
Cottrill v Steyning & Littlehampton BS [1966] 1 WLR 753;
    [1966] 2 All ER 295; 106 Sol Jo 736 .... 13.85
County Estates Ltd v Aco Ltd (1955) 89 ILTR 8 .... 7.22
Courcier & Harold's Contract, Re [1923] 1 Ch 565; 92 LJCh 563;
    81 LT 104; 43 Sol Jo 484; 39 TLR 283 .... 9.08
Courtney, Re [1981] NI 58 .... 15.12, 18.86, 19.42
Cowley v Watts (1853) 17 Jur 172; 22 LJCh 591; 21 LT (os) 97; 1 WR 218 ..... 6.23
Cox & Neve's Contract, Re [1891] 2 Ch 109; 64 LT 733;
    39 WR 412 .... 14.55, 14.59, 14.71, 15.24
Coyle v Central Trust Investment Society Ltd [1978] ILRM 211 .... 13.13, 13.27
    .... 15.19-15.22
Craig v Elliott (1885) 15 LR Ir 257 .... 6.30-6.31
Crane v Naughten [1912] 2 IR 318 .... 6.09, 6.16, 6.26, 6.29, 6.31
Crawford v Boyd & Co (1935) 69 ILTR 65 .... 5.28, 15.03
Crawford v Toogood (1879) 13 Ch D 153; 49 LJCh 108; 41 LT 549;
    28 WR 248 .... 13.17
Crean v Drinan [1983] ILRM 82 .... 7.04
Cricklewood Property & Investment Trust Ltd v Leighton's Investment
    Trust Ltd [1945] AC 221; 114 LJKB 110; 172 LT 140; 89 Sol Jo 93;
    61 TLR 202 .... 12.37
Croft Inns Ltd v Scott [1982] NI 95 .... 8.05, 13.03, 13.40, 13.54
Croly v O'Callaghan (1842) 5 Ir Eq R 25 .... 2.27, 12.16, 12.20, 18.44
Crongliton v Blake (1843) 12 M & W 205 .... 14.50
Crosby's Contract, Re [1949] 1 All ER 830; 65 TLR 456 .... 8.05
Crowley v Allied Irish Banks Ltd [1987] IR 282;
    [1987] ILRM 400 .... 1.38, 3.41, 4.18
Crowley v Flynn [1983] ILRM 513 .... 13.27
Crowley v O'Sullivan [1900] 2 IR 478 .... 6.51, 6.55, 13.40
Crumlish v Registrar of Deeds & Titles [1990] 2 IR 471;
    [1991] ILRM 37 .... 18.70
Cubitt v Gamble (1919) 35 TLR 223; 63 Sol Jo 28 .... 20.31
Cuckmere Brick Co Ltd v Mutual Finance Ltd [1971] Ch 949;
    [1971] 2 WLR 1207; [1971] 2 All ER 633; 115 Sol Jo 288 .... 2.12, 3.13
Cuddon v Tite (1858) 1 Giff 395; 31 LT (os) 340; 6 WR 606;
    4 Jur (ns) 579; 65 ER 971 .... 12.14

Culhane v Hewson [1979] IR 8 .... 2.07-2.10, 10.22

Culhane v O'Maoileoin (HC) unrep, 17 November 1988 .... 1.37, 3.44

Cullen v O'Meara (1869) IR 4 CL 537 .... 9.25, 9.31-9.32, 9.34, 13.64

Cumberland Consolidated Holdings Ltd v Ireland [1946] KB 264;
    [1946] 1 All ER 284; 115 LJKB 301; 174 LT 257; 62 TLR 215
    .... 10.44, 12.21, 13.87

Cumberland Court (Brighton) Ltd v Taylor [1964] Ch 29; [1963] 3 WLR 313;
    [1963] 2 All ER 536; 107 Sol Jo 594 .... 13.16, 13.19, 14.64, 18.33, 19.56

Cumming v Reid (1874) IR 8 CL 166 .... 12.26

Cummins & Hanafy's Contract, Re (1905) 39 ILTR 85 .... 15.26

Cundy v Lindsay (1878) 3 App Cas 459; 38 LT 573; 42 JP 483;
    26 WR 406; 14 Cox CC 93 .... 13.66

Cunningham & O'Connor v Oasis Stores Ltd (HC) unrep, 12 May 1995 .... 5.15

Curley v Mulcahy (HC), unrep, 21 December 1977 .... 5.27

Curling v Austin (1862) 2 Dr & Sm 129; 10 WR 682; 62 ER 570 .... 9.11

Curling v Walsh (1988) 6 ILT 184 .... 4.07-4.11

Curran v NI Co-Ownership Housing Association Ltd [1987] NI 80;
    [1987] 2 All ER 13; [1987] 2 WLR 1043; 131 Sol Jo 506 .... 3.41, 4.15, 4.23

Currie v Consolidated Kent Collieries Corp Ltd [1906] 1 KB 134; 75 LJKB 199; 94
    LT 148; 13 Mans 61 .... 12.29, 12.48

Curtin v O'Mahoney [1991] 2 IR 562; [1992] ILRM 7.................................... 17.20

Curtis Moffat Ltd v Wheeler [1929] 2 Ch 224; 98 LJCh 374; 41 LT 538 .... 18.18

Cussack v Bothwell (1943) 77 ILTR 18 .... 3.25

Cussack v Hudson (1880) 6 LR Ir 309 .... 14.56

Cutts v Thodey (1842) 13 Sim 206; (1842) 6 Jur 1027; (1844) 1 Coll 223 ..... 15.37

D

D(MP) v D(M) [1981] ILRM 179 .... 14.59, 16.61

D & F Estates Ltd v Church Commissioners for England & Wales
    [1988] AC 177 .... 4.15

D'Silva v Lister House Development Ltd [1971] Ch 17; [1970] 2 WLR 563;
    [1970] 1 All ER 858; 113 Sol Jo 921 .... 6.61, 18.126

Dale v Hamilton (1846) 5 Hare 360; 16 LJCh; 11 Jur 163; (1847) 2 Ph 266;
    16 LJCh 397; 11 Jur 574 .... 6.59

Dalton v Angus (1881) 6 App Cas 740; 30 WR 191; 46 JP 132 .... 19.13

Dames & Wood, Re (1885) 29 Ch D 626; 54 LJCh 771; 53 LT 177;
    33 WR 685 .... 15.28-15.30

Damon Cia Naviera SA v Hapag-Lloyd International SA [1985] 1 All ER 475
    .... 10.19, 10.22, 13.31

Dances Way, Re [1962] Ch 490; [1962] 2 WLR 815 .... 18.73

Daniel v Adams (1964) Ambl 495 .... 2.07

Daniel, Re [1917] 2 Ch 405; 87 LJCh 69; 117 LT 472; 61 Sol Jo 646;
    33 TLR 503 .... 13.85

Daniels v Trefusis [1914] 1 Ch 788; 83 LJCh 579; 109 LT 922;
    58 Sol Jo 271 .... 6.43, 6.45, 6.56

Dardis & Dunns Seeds Ltd v Hickey (HC) unrep, 11 July 1974 .... 15.44, 16.44
Darlington Borough Council v Wiltshire Northern Ltd [1995] 3 All ER 895 .. 11.22
Darlington v Hamilton (1854) Kay 550; 2 Eq Rep 906; 23 LJCh 1000;
   24 LT (os) 33; 69 ER 233 .... 15.25
Darville v Lamb, English Law Society Gazette, 27 March 1996 .... 5.23, 16.07
Daulia Ltd v Four Millbank Nominees Ltd [1978] 2 All ER 557;
   [1978] Ch 231; [1978] 2 WLR 621 .... 6.09, 6.54, 6.59
Davey v Harrow Corp [1958] 1 QB 60; [1957] 2 WLR 941; [1957] 2 All ER 305; 101
   Sol Jo 405 .... 18.62
David v Sabin [1893] 1 Ch 523; 62 LJCh 347; 68 LT 237; 37 Sol Jo 248;
   9 TLR 240; 41 WR 398; 2 R 342 .... 21.08, 21.15, 21.22-21.23, 21.28
Davidson & Torrens, Re (1865) 17 Ir Ch R 7 .... 8.05
Davies v Hilliard (1965) 101 ILTR 50 .... 12.33
Davies v Sweet [1962] 2 QB 300; [1962] 2 WLR 525; [1961] 1 All ER 92;
   105 Sol Jo 1083 .... 6.20
Davis v Fitton (1842) 4 Ir Eq R 612; 2 Dr & War 225 .... 17.19
Davis v Gallagher [1933] LJ Ir 26 .... 6.29, 6.31
Davis v Hone (1805) 2 Sch & Lef 341; (1807) 2 Sch & Lef 741 .... 13.39
Davis v Town Properties Investment Corp Ltd [1903] 1 Ch 797; 72 LJCh 389;
   88 LT 665; 47 Sol Jo 383; 51 WR 417 .... 21.31
Davison's Estate, Re (1893) 31 LR Ir 249; [1894] 1 IR 56 .... 18.17, 18.32
.... 18.38-18.40
Davitt's Estate, Re (1936) 70 ILTR 53 .... 6.55
Davy, Re [1908] 1 Ch 61; 77 LJCh 67; 97 LT 654 .... 12.20
Davys & Verdon & Saurin's Contract, Re (1886) 17 LR Ir 334 .. 9.38, 15.04, 15.25
Dawson v Baxter (1886) 19 LR Ir 103 .... 14.56
Dawson v Brinckman (1850) 3 M & G 53 .... 9.14
Day v Singleton [1899] 2 Ch 320; 68 LJCh 593; 81 LT 306; 43 Sol Jo 671;
   48 WR 18 .... 13.34, 13.80, 13.86
Day v Woolwich Equitable BS (1889) 40 Ch D 491 .... 18.46
Day's Estate, Re (1876) 10 ILTR 18 .... 2.27, 12.20
De Lassalle v Guildford [1901] 2 KB 215; 70 LKJB 533; 84 LT 549;
   17 TLR 384; 49 WN 467 .... 4.11, 5.26, 6.13
De Vesci v O'Kelly (1869) IR 4 CL 269; 3 ILT 528 .... 14.56
De Voeux v Mara (1963) 15 Ir Ch R 16 .... 20.06
Dean v Wilson (1878) 10 Ch D 136; 48 LJCh 148; 27 WR 377 .... 11.05
Deansrath Investments, Re [1974] IR 228 .... 8.22
Dease v O'Reilly (1845) 8 Ir LR 52 .... 20.06
Debenham v Mellon (1880) 6 App Cas 24; 50 LJQB 155; 43 LT 673;
   45 JP 252; 29 WR 141 .... 6.37
Debenham v Sawbridge [1901] 2 Ch 98; 70 LJCh 525; 84 LT 519;
   49 WR 502; 17 TLR 441; 45 Sol Jo 466 .... 21.37
Deighan, Re (1897) 31 ILTR 45 .... 9.33, 9.34
Deighton & Harris's Contract, Re [1898] 1 Ch 458; 67 LJCh 240;
   78 LT 430; 42 Sol Jo 324; 46 WR 341 .... 13.68, 15.28

Delany & Deegan's Contract, Re [1905] 1 IR 602 .... 13.27, 15.36
Delany (Blanchardstown Mill Ltd) v Jones [1938] IR 826 .... 12.33
Delany v Keogh [1905] 2 IR 267; 5 NIJR 161 ...... 2.12-2.13, 5.24-5.25, 9.31, 13.04
Delgado v Crean (HC) unrep, 28 May 1978 .... 6.18
Dellafiora v Lester [1962] 3 All ER 393; [1962] 1 WLR 1208; 106 Sol Jo 570 3.29
Delmer v McCabe (1863) 14 ICLR 377; 8 Ir Jur (ns) 236 .... 17.15
....18.32-18.40, 21.05
Delta Vale Properties Ltd v Mills [1990] 2 All ER 176; [1990] 1 WLR 445
....13.21-13.24
Dempsey v Tracy [1924] 2 IR 171 .... 19.27
Dennehy v Corrigan [1902] 2 IR 63n 18.64-18.67
Denny v Hancock (1870) 23 LT 686; 6 Ch App 1 .... 9.22
Des Reaux & Setchfield's Contract, Re [1926] Ch 178; 95 LJCh 338;
    134 LT 623; 70 Sol Jo 137 .... 15.31
Desmond v Brophy [1985] IR 449; [1986] ILRM 547 .... 1.36, 3.10, 3.15, 3.17
....3.44, 4.25, 10.23-10.25, 10.31, 11.17, 15.05
Devenport v Charsley (1886) 54 LT 372 .... 9.27
Devlin v Northern Ireland Housing Executive [1982] NI 377 .... 7.11
Devoy v Hanlon [1929] IR 246; 63 ILTR 61 .... 12.05, 12.50, 12.52, 18.124, 18.132
Dewar v Mintoff [1912] 2 KB 373; 81 LJKB 885; 106 LT 763;
    28 TLR 324 .... 6.20, 10.19, 13.31
Dewell v Tuffnell (1855) 1 K & J 324 .... 11.07
Di Munro v Childs (HC) unrep, 14 December 1979 .... 17.15
Diamond v Campbell-Jones [1961] Ch 22; [1960] 1 All ER 583;
    104 Sol Jo 249 .... 13.85
Dibbins v Dibbins [1896] 2 Ch 348 .... 8.05
Dickie v White (1901) 1 NIJR 128; 35 ILTR 52 .... 10.29, 10.44, 13.30, 13.34
....13.57, 13.62, 13.67-13.68
Dickinson v Barrow [1904] 2 Ch 339; 73 LJCh 701; 91 LT 161 .... 6.58
Diligant Finance Co Ltd v Alleyne (1972) 23 P & CR 346 .... 18.19
Dimmock v Hallett (1866) 2 Ch App 21 ....2.17, 9.27
Dimsdale Developments (South East) Ltd v De Haan (1983) 47 P & CR 1 ..... 13.35
District Bank Ltd v Luigi Grill Ltd [1943] Ch 78; [1943] 1 All ER 136;
    112 LJCh 127; 168 LT 53; 59 TLR 125 .... 14.61
District Bank Ltd v Webb [1958] 1 WLR 148; [1958] 1 All ER 126;
    102 Sol Jo 107 .... 18.33
Doe d Kearns v Sherlock (1824) 1 Fox & Sm 79 .... 18.42
Doe d Oldham v Walley (1828) 8 B & C 22; 108 ER 951 .... 14.50
Doherty v Gallagher (HC) unrep, 9 June 1975 .... 6.07, 6.16, 6.25, 13.48
Doherty v Waterford & Limerick Rly Co (1850) 13 Ir Eq R 538;
    2 Ir Jur (os) 285 .... 13.47
Doherty's Contract, Re (1884) 15 LR Ir 247 .... 13.27, 14.75, 18.99
Dolan v Nelligan [1967] IR 247 .... 16.33
Domb v Isoz [1980] Ch 548; [1980] 2 WLR 565; [1980] 1 All ER 942;
    123 Sol Jo 838 .... 6.61

Domville, Re (1879) 3 LR Ir 282; 9 ILTR 204 .... 12.28
Donegall v Templemore (1858) 9 ICLR 374 .... 14.50-14.51, 17.19, 18.32, 18.60
Donnellan v Dungoyne Ltd [1995] 1 ILRM 388 .... 1.38, 3.14, 5.26, 5.27, 15.37
Donnelly v O'Connell (1924) 58 ILTR 164 .... 6.63, 7.01, 7.13, 10.02
Donoghue v Stevenson [1932] AC 562; [1992] All ER Rep 1 .... 4.15
Doran v Delaney [1996] 1 ILRM 490 .... 1.37, 5.28, 9.10, 15.02-15.03
 .... 15.05, 15.37, 16.07, 16.22
Dorene Ltd v Suedes (Ireland) Ltd [1981] IR 312;
    [1982] ILRM 126 .... 7.03, 7.07, 13.44
Douglas v Allen (1842) 2 Dr & War 213; 1 Con & L 367 .... 17.19
Dowdall v McCartan (1880) 5 LR Ir 642 .... 12.16, 12.46
Dowling v Ireland [1991] 2 IR 379 .... 16.101
Doyle v Hearne [1987] IR 601; [1988] ILRM 318.. 12.08
Doyle v Hort (1880) 4 LR Ir 455; 12 ILTR 172 .... 21.05
Doyle v Kinsley (1864) 9 Ir Jur (ns) 26 .... 21.05
Doyle v Ryan [1981] ILRM 374 .... 10.18, 13.22, 13.30, 13.31-13.33
Doyle v Youell (1938) 72 ILTR 253 .... 4.12, 11.15
Doyne v Harvey (1816) 1 Hog 2 .... 12.17
Doyne's Traverses, Re (1888) 24 LR Ir 287 .... 8.14
Draisey v Fitzpatrick [1981] ILRM 219 .... 7.04, 7.14, 9.11, 10.05, 13.30
Drakeford v Piercey (1866) 7 B & S 515 .... 2.10
Drapers' Co v McCann (1878) 1 LR Ir 13; 12 ILTR 21 .... 13.26
Drew v Earl of Norbury (1846) 3 Jo & Lat 267;
    (1846) 9 Ir Eq R 524 .... 18.82, 18.119
Drewrey v Ware-Lane [1960] 3 All ER 529; [1960] 1 WLR 1204;
    104 Sol Jo 933; 176 Est Gaz 297 .... 3.28, 3.29
Drive Yourself Hire Co (London) Ltd v Strutt [1954] 1 QB 250;
    [1953] 3 WLR 1111; [1953] 2 All ER 1475; 97 Sol Jo 874 .... 14.70, 18.08
Driver v Broad [1893] 1 QB 744; 63 LJQB 12; 69 LT 169; 9 TLR 440;
    41 WR 483; 4 R 411 .... 6.09
Drought v Jones (1841) Fl & K 316 .... 11.05
Drummond v Attorney-General (1849) 2 HLC 837 .... 17.15, 17.19
Drummond v Tracey (1860) John 608; 29 LJCh 304; 1 LT 364; 8 WR 207;
    6 Jur (ns) 369; 70 WR 562 .... 14.64
Du Sautoy v Symes [1967] Ch 1146; [1967] 2 WLR 342; [1967] 1 All ER 25;
    111 Sol Jo 133.. 8.04
Dublin (South) City Markets Co, Re (1888) 21 LR Ir 245 .... 8.14
Dublin Corporation v Barry [1897] 1 IR 65 .... 20.06
Dublin Corporation v Trinity College, Dublin [1986] ILRM 283 .... 16.33
Dublin Laundry Co Ltd v Clarke [1989] ILRM 29 .... 6.35, 13.20, 14.10, 14.11
 .... 14.14, 14.18, 15.36, 15.38, 16.68
Dublin, Wicklow & Wexford Rly Co, Re (1891) 27 LR Ir 79 .... 8.14
Duce & Boots Cash Chemists (Southern) Ltd Contract, Re [1937] Ch 641;
    [1937] 3 All ER 788; 106 LJCh 387; 157 LT 477; 81 Sol Jo 651;
    53 TLR 1000 .... 14.56, 15.19, 18.36

Duckett v Gordon (1860) 11 Ir Ch R 181 .... 18.94
Duddell v Simpson (1866) 2 Ch App 102; 36 LJCh 70; 15 LT 305;
   15 WR 115; 12 Jur (ns) 969 .... 15.28
Duffield v McMaster [1896] 1 IR 370 .... 12.11
Duffy v Duffy [1947] Ir Jur Rep 39 .... 21.35
Duggan v Allied Irish BS (HC) unrep, 4 March 1976 .... 13.40, 13.54
Duggan v O'Connor (1828) 1 Hud & Br 459 .... 18.32, 18.38
Duncuft v Albrecht (1841) 12 Sim 189 .... 6.10
Dunn v Blackdown Properties Ltd [1961] Ch 433; [1961] 2 WLR 6618;
   [1961] 2 All ER 62; 105 Sol Jo 257; 125 JP 397 .... 18.72
Dunne v Revenue Commissioners [1982] ILRM 438 .... 11.10
Dunning (AJ) & Sons (Shopfitters) Ltd v Sykes & Son (Poole) Ltd
   [1987] 1 All ER 700 .... 21.28
Dunthorne & Shore v Wiggins [1943] 2 All ER 678; 168 LT 381 .... 12.33
Durrow Brick & Tile Works Co, Re [1904] 1 IR 530 .... 12.15
Duthy & Jesson's Contract, Re [1898] 1 Ch 419; 67 LJCH 218;
   78 LT 223; 42 Sol Jo 269; 46 WR 300 .... 14.48, 18.102
Dutton v Bognor Regis United Building Co Ltd [1972] 1 QB 373;
   [1972] 2 WLR 299; [1972] 1 All ER 462; 136 JP 201; 116 Sol Jo 16;
   70 LGR 57; [1972] 1 Lloyd's Rep 227 .... 4.15
Dwyer v Rich (1871) IR 6 CL 144 .... 18.59
Dwyer, Re [1901] 1 IR 165; 34 ILTR 168 .... 12.21
Dyas v Cruise (1845) 8 Ir Eq R 407; 2 Jo & Lat 460 .... 3.08, 6.36, 6.41
Dyas v Rooney (1890) 27 LR Ir 4 .... 13.13-13.14, 13.25
Dyas v Stafford (1881) 7 LR Ir 590; (1882) 9 LR Ir 520 .... 2.09, 2.11, 3.12
   .... 6.02, 6.14, 6.33, 6.40, 7.21
Dykes v Blake (1838) 4 Bing NC 463; 6 Scott 320; 7 LJCP 282;
   132 ER 866 .... 9.22
Dyster v Randall & Sons [1926] Ch 932; 95 LJCh 504; 135 LT 596;
   70 Sol Jo 797 .... 13.67

E

Eagon v Dent [1965] 3 All ER 334 .... 21.03
Earl v Mawson (1973) 228 Est Gaz 529 .... 7.16, 7.18
East London Union v Metropolitan Rly Co (1869) LR 4 Exch 309;
   38 LJ Ex 225 .... 13.78
Eastern Counties Rly v Hawkes (1855) 5 HLC 331 .... 13.47
Eastwood v Ashton [1915] AC 900; 84 LJCh 671; 113 LT 562;
   59 Sol Jo 560 .... 18.58, 21.28
Eaton v Midland Great Western Railway Co (1847) 10 Ir LR 310 .... 8.14
Ebworth & Tidy's Contract, Re (1889) 42 Ch D 23; 58 LJCh 665; 60 LT 841;
   37 WR 657; 54 JP 199 .... 14.49
Eccles v Bryant [1948] Ch 93; [1974] 2 All ER 865; LJR 418;
   98 Sol Jo 53 .... 6.61, 6.63
Ecclesiastical Commrs v Pinney [1899] 2 Ch 729; 69 LJCh 844; 83 LT 384;
   49 WR 82; 16 TLR 556; 44 Sol Jo 673 .... 12.21

Ecclesiastical Commrs for England's Conveyance, Re [1936] Ch 430;
105 LJCh 168; 155 LT 281 .... 18.13
Edgell v Day (1865) LR 1 CP 80; 35 LJCP 7; 13 LT 328; 14 WR 87;
12 Jur (ns) 27 .... 10.25, 10.30
Edler v Auerbach [1950] 1 KB 359; [1949] 2 All ER 692;
65 TLR 645 .... 4.07, 5.12, 16.75
Edmonds v Peake (1843) 7 Beav 239; 13 LJCh 13; 49 ER 1056 .... 10.26
Edwards v Hodding (1814) 5 Taunt 815; 1 Marsh 388 .... 2.26
Edwards v McLeay (1815) G Coop 308; (1818) 2 Swan 287; G Coop 308;
36 ER 625 .... 9.31
Edwards v Wickwar (1865) LR 1 Eq 68; 35 LJCh 48; 13 LT 428;
29 JP 820; 14 WR 79 .... 9.27
Edwards' Will Trusts, Re [1982] Ch 30; [1981] 3 WLR 15;
[1981] 2 All ER 941; 125 Sol Jo 258 .... 16.54
Ee v Kakar (1979) 40 P & CR 223 .... 7.04, 7.19
Egan, Re (HC) unrep, 16 June 1989 .... 17.20
Egan v Ross (1928) 29 SR (NSW) 382 .... 3.16
Egmont (Earl of) v Smith (1877) 6 Ch D 469 .... 12.22
Elliot & H Elliot (Builders) Ltd v Pierson [1948] Ch 452;
[1948] 1 All ER 939; LJR 1452; 92 Sol Jo 271 .... 13.68
Elliott v Pierson [1948] Ch 452; 1948] 1 All ER 939; [1948] LGR 1452;
92 Sol Jo 271 .... 14.61, 15.38
Ellis v Goulton [1893] 1 QB 350; 62 LJQB 232; 68 LT 144; 9 TLR 223;
41 WR 411; 4 R 267 .... 2.26, 10.25-10.27, 10.30
Ellis v Rogers (1885) 29 Ch D 661; 53 LT 377 .... 14.08
Ellis v Rowbotham [1900] 1 QB 740; 69 LJQB 379; 82 LT 191; 44 WR 423;
16 TLR 258 .... 20.06
Ellis v The Lord Primate (1864) 16 Ir Ch R 184 .... 18.75
Elliston v Reacher [1908] 2 Ch 655 .... 19.10
Else v Barnard (1860) 28 Beav 228; 29 LJCh 729; 2 LT 203; 6 Jur (ns) 621 .... 2.07
Embankment Properties Ltd v Calaroga Ltd (HC) unrep, 28 January &
24 October 1975 .... 15.36
Embourg Ltd v Tyler Group Ltd (SC) unrep, 5 March 1996 .... 1.32, 6.02, 6.61-6.62
.... 7.03, 7.06-7.07, 7.08-7.11
Engell v Fitch (1869) LR 4 QB 659; 38 LJQB 304; 17 WR 894; 10 B & S 738
.... 13.80, 13.85
Englefield Holdings Ltd & Sinclair's Contract, Re [1962] 1 WLR 1119;
[1962] 3 All ER 503; 106 Sol Jo 721 .... 9.21, 9.27
Enraght v Fitzgerald (1842) 2 Dr & War 43; 2 Ir Eq R 87 .... 12.18, 12.35
Erlanger v New Sombrero Phosphate Co (1878) 3 App Cas 1218;
39 LT 269; 27 WR 65 .... 13.58
Errington v Rorke (1859) 7 HLC 618 .... 18.66
Erskine v Adeane (1873) 8 Ch App 756; 42 LJCh 849; 29 LT 234;
38 JP 20; 21 WR 802 .... 6.13
Erskine v Armstrong (1887) 20 LR Ir 296 .... 6.26

Esdaile v Stephenson (1823) 1 Sim & St 122; 57 ER 49 .... 20.09
Essex v Daniel (1875) LR 10 CP 538; 32 LT 476 .... 13.78
Esso Petroleum Co Ltd v Mardon [1976] 2 All ER 5; [1976] QB 801;
    [1976] 2 WLR 583; 120 Sol Jo 131 .... 5.27
Establissement Bandelot v RS Graham & Co [1953] 2 QB 271;
    [1953] 2 WLR 180; [1953] 1 All ER 149; 87 Sol Jo 45 .... 18.19
Etchingham v Downes (1946) 80 ILTR 73 .... 2.28, 3.25
Evans v Glasgow District Council 1978 SLT 17 .... 12.40
Evans v Grey (1882) 9 LR Ir 539 ....18.123-18.124, 18.133
Evans v Hoare [1892] 1 QB 593; 61 LJQB 470; 66 LT 345; 56 JP 664;
    40 WR 442; 8 TLR 441 .... 6.33
Evans v Roberts (1826) 5 B & C 829; 8 Dow & Ry KB 611; 4 LJ (os) KB 313 6.09
Eyre v Sadlier (1863) 15 Ir Ch R 1; 14 Ir Ch R 12.15
Eyston v Simonds (1842) 1 Y & C Ch Cas 608 .... 13.68
Ezekiel v McDade [1995] 47 EG 150 .... 1.38, 4.23

F

Fain v Ayers (1826) 2 Sim & St 533; 57 ER 450 .... 18.103
Fairbairn, Re (1940) 74 ILTR 4 .... 14.30
Fairweather v St Marylebone Property Co Ltd [1963] AC 510;
    [1962] 2 WLR 1020; [1962] 2 All ER 288; 106 Sol Jo 368 .... 14.12, 14.81
Fallon v Gannon [1988] ILRM 193 .... 1.36, 5.27
Farm Fresh Foods Ltd, Re [1980] ILRM 131 .... 2.43, 12.16
Farmer v Casey (1898) 32 ILTR 144 .... 2.05, 2.12
Farquhar v Farley (1817) 7 Taunt 592 .... 2.26
Farr, Smith & Co v Messers Ltd [1928] 1 KB 397; 97 LJKB 126;
    138 LT 154; 72 Sol Jo 14; 44 TLR 48 .... 6.14, 6.42
Farrer v Lacy, Hartland & Co (1885) 31 Ch D 42; 55 LJCh 149;
    53 LT 515; 34 WR 22; 2 TLR 11 .... 2.10, 10.24
Faruqi v English Real Estates Ltd [1979] 1 WLR 963; 38 P & CR 318;
    123 Sol Jo 321; 251 EG 1285 .... 9.02, 13.35
Fay v Miller, Wilkins & Co [1941] Ch 360; [1941] 2 All ER 18;
    110 LJCh 124; 166 LT 33; 85 Sol Jo 213; 57 TLR 423 .... 6.20, 21.08
Fennelly v Anderson (1851) 1 Ir Ch R 706; 4 Ir Jur (os) 33 .... 13.47
Fenton v Browne (1807) 14 Ves 144 .... 2.26
Fenton v Schofield (1966) 100 ILTR 69 .... 5.23-5.25
Fenwick v Macdonald, Fraser & Co Ltd 1904 6 F 850 .... 2.20
Ferguson v Merchant Banking Ltd [1993] 3 IR 382;
    [1993] ILRM 136 .... 12.29, 13.66
Field v Boland (1837) 1 Dr & Wal 37 .... 6.37
Finkielkraut v Monohan [1949] 2 All ER 234; LJR 1378; 93 Sol Jo 433 .... 13.13
    .... 13.20, 13.35
Finlay v Murtagh [1979] IR 249 .... 1.36, 4.18
First National Bank plc v Thompson [1996] 1 All ER 140 .... 18.33
First National Building Society v Ring [1992] 1 IR 375 .... 12.09

First National Commercial Bank plc v Humberts [1995] 2 All ER 673 .... 1.36
First National Securities Ltd v Hegarty [1985] 1 QB 850; [1984] 3 WLR 769;
    [1984] 3 All ER 641 .... 6.11
First National Securities Ltd v Jones [1978] Ch 109; [1978] 2 WLR 475;
    [1978] 2 All ER 221 .... 18.122
Firstpost Homes Ltd v Johnson [1995] 4 All ER 355 .... 6.28, 6.33
Firth v Midland Rly Co (1875) LR 20 Eq 100; 44 LJCh 313; 32 LT 219;
    23 WR 509 .... 6.24
Fischer v Parry & Beveridge Pty Ltd [1963] VR 97 .... 3.16
Fischer v Winch [1939] 1 KB 666; [1939] 2 All ER 144; 108 LJKB 473;
    160 LT 347; 83 Sol Jo 192; 55 TLR 553 .... 18.62
Fishbourne v Hamilton (1890) 25 LR Ir 483 .... 18.73-18.75
Fishguard & Rosslare Rlys, Re [1908] 1 IR 321 .... 8.14
Fison's Will Trusts, Re [1950] Ch 394; [1950] 1 All ER 501; 66 TLR 475;
    94 Sol Jo 238 .... 8.05
Fitzgerald v Browne (1854) 4 ICLR 178; 7 Ir Jur (os) 90 .... 13.83
Fitzgerald v McCullagh (1858) 7 ICLR 457; 3 Ir Jur (ns) 220 .... 14.47
Fitzgerald, Re [1925] 1 IR 39; 59 ILTR 53 .... 14.30
Fitzpatrick v Collins [1978] ILRM 244 .... 17.15
Fitzpatrick v DAF Sales Ltd [1988] IR 464 .... 20.50
Fitzpatrick v Dublin Corporation [1971] IR 169 .... 8.19
Flanagan & McGarvey & Thompson's Contract, Re
    [1945] NI 32... 9.22, 9.26, 18.80
Flanagan v Griffith (HC) unrep, 26 January 1985 .... 4.18
Fleetwood v Green (1809) 15 Ves 594.. 15.51
Fleming v Bank of New Zealand [1900] AC 577; 69 LJPC 120; 83 LT 1;
    16 TLR 469 .... 6.36
Flexman v Corbett [1930] 1 Ch 672; 99 LJCh 370; 143 LT 464 ... 9.25, 9.39, 15.50
Flight v Barton (1832) 3 My & K 282; 40 ER 108 .... 9.25, 9.40
Flight v Bolland (1828) 4 Russ 298; 38 ER 817 .... 13.47
Flight v Booth (1834) 1 Bing NC 370; 1 Scott 190; 4 LJCP 66;
    131 ER 1160 .... 9.32-9.33, 9.44
Flood v Finlay (1811) 2 Ba & B 9 .... 17.19
Flower v Hartopp (1843) 6 Beav 476; 12 LJCh 507; 1 LT (os) 384;
    7 Jur 613; 49 ER 910 .... 9.11
Flureau v Thornhill (1776) 2 Wm Bl 1078; 96 ER 635 .... 13.80-13.81
Flynn & Newman's Contract, Re [1948] IR 104 .... 4.04, 9.19-9.22
    ....9.24, 9.27, 9.32-9.33, 9.43, 10.03, 10.05, 13.27
    ....13.34, 13.36, 13.62, 13.68, 14.03-14.08, 15.04
Flynn v Buckley [1980] IR 423 .... 15.45
Foley, Re (1951) 85 ILTR 61 .... 20.44
Foley's case [1957] NI 130 .... 16.30
Ford & Ferguson's Contract, Re [1906] 1 IR 607 .... 13.27, 13.29
Ford & Hill, Re (1878) 10 Ch D 365; 48 LJCh 327; 40 LT 41; 27 WR 371;
    43 JP 334 .... 15.18, 15.36

Forrer v Nash (1865) 35 Beav 167; 6 New Rep 361; 11 Jur (ns) 789;
  14 WR 8 .... 13.68
Forster v Rowland (1861) 7 H & N 103 .... 6.45
Forster v Silvermere Golf & Equestrian Centre Ltd (1981) 42 P & CR 255 .... 13.78
Foster, Re (1883) 22 Ch D 797; 52 LJCh 577; 48 LT 497; 31 WR 774 .... 6.56
Foster v Cunningham [1956] NI 29 .... 20.06
Foster v Deacon (1818) 3 Madd 394 .... 12.22
Foster v Lyons [1927] 1 Ch 219; 96 LJCh 79; 137 LT 372; 70 Sol Jo 1182 .... 18.78
Foundling Hospital v Crane [1911] 2 KB 367; 80 LJKB 853; 105 LT 187 .... 18.127
Fox v Bannister King & Rigbeys [1987] 1 All ER 737 .... 20.15
Fox v Clarke (1874) IR 9 QB 565; (1957) 21 Conv 164 .... 18.61
Fox v Mackreth (1788) 2 Bro CC 400; (1791) 4 Bro PC 258;
  2 Cox Eq Cas 320 .... 9.35
Francis v Cowliffe Ltd (1976) 33 P & CR 368 .... 13.41
Fraser v Pape (1904) 91 LT 340; 20 TLR 798 .... 6.07
Freer v Rimmer (1844) 14 Sim 391 ....2.20-2.22
Friends Provident Life Office v Doherty [1992] ILRM 372 .... 4.02
Fuller v Abrahams (1821) 3 Brod & Bing 116; 6 Moo PC 316 .... 2.24
Fuller v Dublin CC [1976] IR 20 .... 8.17
Fung Ping Shan v Tong Skun [1918] AC 403; 87 LJPC 22; 118 LT 380 .... 18.19
Furlong & Bogan's Contract, Re (1893) 31 LR Ir 191 .... 12.50, 14.13
Furlong & Sheehan, Re (1889) 23 LR Ir 407 .... 14.42
Furtado v Lumley (1890) 6 TLR 168; 54 JP 407 .... 2.10, 2.26, 10.26

G

Gaby v Driver (1828) 2 Y & J 549 .... 2.26, 10.29
Gaelcrann Teo v Payne [1985] ILRM 109 .... 7.03
Gaggin v Upton (1859) Dru temp Nap 427 .... 12.38
Gahan v Boland (SC) unrep, 20 January 1984 .... 5.26
Gainsborough (Earl of) v Watcombe Terra Cotta Clay Co Ltd
  (1885) 54 LJ Ch 991; 53 LT 116; 1 TLR 486 .... 18.36
Galdan Properties Ltd, Re [1988] IR 213; [1988] ILRM 559 .... 2.43, 20.17, 20.50
Gale & Wright v Buswell (1961) 178 Est Gaz 709 .... 3.29
Gallagher v McDowell Ltd [1961] NI 26 .... 4.15
Gallie v Lee [1969] 2 Ch 17; [1968] 1 WLR 1190; [1969] All ER 322 .... 21.38
Galton v Emuss (1844) 1 Coll 243 .... 2.24
Galvin (GF) (Estates) Ltd v Hedigan [1985] ILRM 295 .... 3.05, 3.19-3.20
Games v Bonner (1884) 54 LJ Ch 517; 33 WR 64 .... 14.81
Garde Browne, Re [1911] 1 IR 205 .... 14.56
Gardiner, Re (1861) 11 Ir Ch R 519 .... 21.05
Gardiner v Irish Land Commission (1976) 110 ILTR 21 .... 20.44
Gardiner v Sevenoaks RDC [1950] 2 All ER 84; 94 Sol Jo 385;
  66 TLR 1091; 114 JP 352; 48 LGR 360 .... 18.41
Gardiner v Tate (1876) IR 10 CL 460 .... 2.09, 6.02, 6.38
Gardner v Coutts & Co [1967] 3 All ER 1064; [1968] 1 WLR 173 .... 8.04

Gardom v Lee (1865) 6 H & C 651; 34 LJ Ex 113; 12 LT 430; 13 WR 719;
11 Jur (ns) 393; 159 ER 687 ...... 15.29

Gartside v Silkstone & Dodworth Iron & Coal Co (1882) 21 Ch D 762;
47 LT 76; 31 WR 36 ...... 18.09, 18.128

Gavaghan v Edwards [1961] 2 QB 220; [1961] 2 WLR 948;
[1961] 3 All ER 477; 105 Sol Jo 405 ...... 6.42

General Finance, Mortgage & Discount Co v Liberator Permanent
Benefit BS (1878) 10 Ch D 15; 39 LT 600; 27 WR 210 ...... 18.33

Geoghegan v Connolly (1858) 8 Ir Ch R 598 ...... 9.37, 15.26

Geoghegan v Fegan (1872) IR 6 CL 139 ...... 18.54

Geoghegan, Re [1918] 1 IR 188; 52 ILTR 105 ...... 16.30

Geraghty & Lyon's Contract, Re (1919) 53 ILTR 57 ...... 13.27, 14.06-14.08
...... 14.17-14.19, 21.05-21.05, 21.10-21.12, 21.24-21.27

Geraghty v Minister for Local Government [1976] IR 153 ...... 8.16

Geraghty v Rohan Industrial Estates Ltd [1988] IR 419 ...... 9.13, 9.34
...... 9.45-9.46, 10.66, 18.55-18.59, 18.70

Geryani v O'Callaghan (HC) unrep, 25 January 1995 ...... 9.21, 9.24, 9.34
...... 9.44-9.47, 15.37, 16.91

Giddy & Giddy v Horsfall [1947] 1 All ER 460 ...... 3.29

Giffard v Hort (1804) 1 Sch & Lef 386 ...... 13.50

Giles v Brady [1974] IR 462 ...... 15.45

Gillen v Gibson (1910) 44 ILTR 17 ...... 2.34

Gillespie v Hogg [1947] Ir Jur Rep 51 ...... 9.13, 14.36, 18.70

Gilliat v Gilliat (1869) LR 9 Eq 60; 39 LJCh 142; 21 LT 522; 34 JP 196;
18 WR 203 ...... 2.17

Gillis v McGhee (1862) 13 Ir Ch R 48 ...... 13.41

Gilmore v The O'Connor Don [1947] IR 462; 82 ILTR 141 ...... 12.26, 15.01, 15.19

Gissing v Gissing [1971] AC 886; [1970] 3 WLR 255; [1970] 2 All ER 780;
114 Sol Jo 550 ...... 16.23

Glass v Patterson [1902] 7 IR 660; 2 NIJR 129 ...... 20.06

Glendinning v Orr [1989] NI 171 ...... 5.28, 15.02, 16.76

Gloag & Miller's Contract, Re (1883) 23 ChD 320; 52 LJCh 654;
48 LT 629; 31 WR 610 ...... 9.24, 12.34, 15.53

Gloucestershire CC v Richardson [1969] 1 AC 480; [1968] 3 WLR 645;
[1968] 3 ALL ER 1181; 112 Sol Jo 759; 67 LGR 15 ...... 4.13

Glow Heating Ltd v Eastern Health Board [1988] IR 110 ...... 11.22

Goddard's Case (1584) 4 Co Rep 46; 76 ER 396 ...... 18.120

Goding v Frazer [1967] 1 WLR 286; [1966] 3 All ER 234;
110 Sol Jo 870 ...... 3.11, 3.16

Godley v Power (1961) 95 ILTR 135 ...... 6.13, 6.15, 6.28, 7.09

Godwin v Francis (1870) LR 5 CP 295; 39 LJCP 121; 22 LT 338 ...... 3.14, 13.85

Golden Vale Co-Operative Creameries Ltd v Barrett (HC) unrep,
16 March 1987 ...... 5.27

Goodman v Eban Ltd [1954] 1 QB 550; [1954] 2 WLR 581;
[1954] 1 All ER 763; 98 Sol Jo 214 ...... 18.121

Goody v Baring [1956] 1 WLR 448; [1956] 3 All ER 11; 100 Sol Jo 320 .... 1.34, 5.12, 15.17
Gordon Hill Trust Ltd v Segall [1942] 1 All ER 379 .... 12.12
Gordon-Cumming v Houldsworth [1910] AC 537; 80 LJPC 47 .... 9.10
Gorman v Byrne (1857) 8 ICLR 394 .... 18.90
Gorringe v Land Improvement Society [1899] 1 IR 142 .... 13.40
Gosford v Robb (1845) 8 Ir LR 217 .... 18.129, 18.133
Gosling v Woolf [1893] 1 QB 39; 68 LT 89; 41 WR 106; 5 R 81 .... 14.70
Gourley v Duke of Somerset (1815) 19 Ves 429 .... 6.24
Gowan v Tighe (1835) L1 & G temp Plunk 168 .... 11.07, 12.14
Grafton Court Ltd v Wadson Sales Ltd (HC) unrep, 17 February 1975 .... 5.26
Graham & Scott (Southgate) Ltd v Oxlade [1950] 2 KB 257;
   [1950] 1 All ER 856; 95 Sol Jo 269; 66 TLR 808 .... 3.27-3.29, 7.19
Graham v Graham (1791) 1 Ves 272; 30 ER 339 .... 18.127
Graham v Pitkin [1992] 2 All ER 235; [1992] 1 WLR 403 .... 7.15
Gran Gelato Ltd v Richcliff (Group) Ltd [1992] 1 All ER 865;
   [1992] 2 WLR 867 .... 1.37, 5.27-5.28, 9.47
Grange Developments Ltd, Re [1987] ILRM 733 .... 12.02, 12.35
Grangeford Structures Ltd v SH Ltd [1990] 2 IR 351 .... 11.24
Grant v Dawkins [1973] 1 WLR 1406; [1973] 3 All ER 897; 117 Sol Jo 665 . 13.54
Gray v Fowler (1873) LR 8 Ex 249; 42 LJ Ex 161; 29 LT 297; 21 WR 916 ... 15.29
Gray v Smith (1889) 43 Ch D 208; 43 Ch D 217; 59 LJCh 145; 62 LT 335;
   38 WR 310; 8 TLR 109 .... 6.11
Grealish v Murphy [1946] IR 35; 80 ILTR 111 .... 16.69, 21.35
Greaney Ltd v Dublin Corporation (HC) unrep, 7 March 1994 .... 16.83
Great Torrington Commons Conservators v Moore Stevans [1903] 1 Ch 347;
   73 LJCh 124; 89 LT 667; 68 JP 111; 2 LGR 397 .... 18.60
Green Dale Building Co v Dublin CC [1977] IR 256 .... 8.18, 8.22
Green v Bartlett (1863) 14 CBNS 681 .... 2.07, 2.29
Green v Hall (1848) 12 LT(os) 151 .... 2.29
Green v Sevin (1879) 13 Ch D 589; 49 LJCh 166; 41 LT 724;
   44 JP 282 .... 13.16-13.17
Greene v Quinn (1941) 75 ILTR 107 .... 12.18, 12.20, 12.34
Greenwood v Turner [1891] 2 Ch 144; 60 LJCh 351; 64 LT 261;
   39 WR 315 .... 12.33
Gregg v Kidd [1956] IR 183 .... 16.23
Gregg v Richards [1926] 1 Ch 521; 95 LJCh 209; 135 LT 75;
   70 Sol Jo 433 .... 18.87
Grey v Pearson (1857) 6 HLC 61 .... 17.16
Greyhill Property Co Ltd v Whitechap Inn Ltd (HC) unrep, 5 October 1993 .... 5.23, 5.27, 15.37, 16.83
Griffith v Pelton [1958] Ch 205; [1957] 3 WLR 522; [1959] 3 All ER 75;
   101 Sol Jo 663; 170 Est Gaz 189 .... 8.03
Griffiths v Young [1970] Ch 675; [1970] 3 WLR 246; [1957] 3 All ER 601; 114 Sol
   Jo 571; 21 P & CR 770 .... 6.15, 7.08

Grigsby v Melville [1973] 3 All ER 455; [1974] 1 WLR 80; 117 Sol Jo 632 .. 19.13
Grindell v Bass [1920] 2 Ch 487; 89 LJCh 591; 124 LT 211; 36 TLR 867 .... 6.14
.... 6.34, 6.42
Grist v Bailey [1967] Ch 532; [1966] 3 WLR 618; [1968] 2 All ER 875;
    110 Sol Jo 791 .... 13.67, 21.37
Guardian Assurance Co v Viscount Avonmore (1872) IR 6 Eq 391 ..... 18.32, 18.38
Guardian Builders Ltd v Kelly [1981] ILRM 127 ....6.19-6.20, 6.22, 13.50
Guardian Builders Ltd v Sleecon (HC) unrep, 18 August 1988 .... 6.10
Guardians of Limerick Union v Heffernan (1877) IR 11 Eq 302 .... 15.45
Guckian v Brennan [1981] IR 478 .... 13.27, 14.27, 16.63, 16.68, 16.70
Guerin v Heffernan [1925] 1 IR 57 .... 10.44, 13.15
Guerin v Ryan (HC) unrep, 28 April 1977 .... 6.33
Gun v McCarthy (1883) 13 LR Ir 304 .... 5.23, 13.48, 13.64-13.67, 21.35
Gunter v Halsey (1739) Amb 586; West temp Hard 681 .... 6.53
GW Rly Co v Fisher [1905] 1 Ch 316; 74 LJCh 241; 92 LT 104;
    53 WR 279 .... 21.12, 21.29

H

H(J) v H(WJ) (HC) unrep, 20 December 1979 .... 13.50
H & L v S [1979] ILRM 105 .... 16.62-16.63
Hadgett v IRC (1877) 37 LT 612; (1877) 3 Ex D 46............................. 15.19, 20.40
Hadley v Baxendale (1854) 9 Exch 341; 23 LJ Ex 179; 23 LT (os) 69;
    2 WR 302; 18 Jur 358; 156 ER 145 .... 13.77
Hadley v London Bank of Scotland Ltd (1865) 3 De GJ & Sm 63;
    12 LT 747; 11 Jur (ns) 554; 13 WR 978 .... 12.14
Haedicke & Lipski's Contract, Re [1901] 2 Ch 666; 70 LJCh 811; 85 LT 402;
    45 Sol Jo 738; 17 TLR 772; 50 WR 20 .... 9.25, 9.39
Hagarty v Nully (1862) 13 ICLR 532 .... 18.87
Haire-Foster v McIntee (1889) 23 LR Ir 529; 24 ILTR 44 .... 6.57, 13.50
Halifax Commercial Banking Co Ltd & Wood, Re (1898) 79 LT 536;
    43 Sol Jo 124; 15 TLR 106; 47 WR 194 .... 14.51, 14.58
Halifax Mortgage Services Ltd v Stepsky [1996] 2 All ER 277 .... 4.02
Halkett v Dudley [1907] 1 Ch 590; 76 LJCh 330; 96 LT 539; 51 Sol Jo 290
.... 13.68, 14.51
Hall v Betty (1842) 4 Man & G 410; 5 Scott NR 508; 11 LJCP 256 .... 14.08
Hall v Burnell [1911] 2 Ch 551; 81 LJCh 46; 105 LT 409; 55 Sol Jo 737 ...... 10.30
.... 13.31, 13.55, 13.60
Halley v O'Brien [1920] IR 330 .... 6.33
Halsall v Birizell [1957] Ch 169; [1957] 2 WLR 123; [1957] 1 All ER 371;
    101 Sol Jo 88 .... 19.10, 19.15
Halter v Ashe (1696) 3 Lev 438 .... 18.09
Hamer v Sharp (1874) LR 19 Eq 108; 44 LJCh 53; 31 LT 643; 23 WR 58 .... 3.07
Hamilton v Bates [1894] 1 IR 1; 28 ILTR 184 .... 9.26, 9.34
Hamilton v Hamilton [1982] IR 466; [1982] ILRM 290.. 12.02, 12.08, 12.40, 16.62
.... 16.62-16.63, 16.69, 16.69

Hamilton v Musgrove (1871) IR 6 CL 129 .... 14.56
Hammond v Allen [1993] 08 EG 122 .... 13.41
Hanbury v Bateman [1920] 1 Ch 313; 89 LJCh 134; 122 LT 765 .... 18.82
Hancock v BW Brazier (Anerley) Ltd [1966] 1 WLR 1317;
   [1966] 2 All ER 901; 110 Sol Jo 368 .... 4.12, 4.13, 21.03
Handman & Wilcox's Contract, Re [1902] 1 Ch 599 .... 13.52
Hanly v Shannon (1834) Hay & Jon 645; 2 L Rec (ns) 111 .... 18.61
Hanslip v Padwick (1850) 5 Exch 615; 19 LJ Ex 372; 16 LT (os) 416 .... 13.86
Harding v Metropolitan Rly Co (1872) 7 Ch App 154; 41 LJCh 371;
   26 LT 109; 20 WR 321; 36 JP 340 .... 8.14
Harding's Estate, Re (1860) 11 Ir Ch R 29 .... 14.52-14.52
Hardman v Child (1885) 28 Ch D 712; 54 LJCh 695; 52 LT 465 .... 15.28
Hardy v Elphinck [1974] Ch 65; [1973] 2 WLR 824; [1973] 2 All ER 914;
   117 Sol Jo 373; 226 Est Gaz 1957 .... 6.14, 6.42
Hargreaves & Thompson's Contract, Re (1886) 32 Ch D 454; 56 LJCh 199;
   55 LT 239; 2 TLR 681; 34 WR 708 .... 13.29
Hargreaves Transport Ltd v Lynch [1969] 1 All ER 455; [1969] WLR 215;
   113 Sol Jo 54; 20 P & CR 143 .... 7.17
Harman & Uxbridge & Rickmansworth Rly Co, Re (1883) 24 Ch D 720;
   52 LJCh 808; 49 LT 130; 31 WR 708 .... 14.65, 15.19
Harmer v Jumbil (Nigeria) Tin Areas [1921] 1 Ch 200; 90 LJCh 140;
   124 LT 418; 65 Sol Jo 93; 37 TLR 91 .... 21.31
Harnett v Yielding (1805) 2 Sch & Lef 549 .... 13.39, 13.43-13.45, 13.52
Harrington v Hoggart (1830) 1 B & Ald 577 .... 2.10, 2.26, 10.25-10.29, 10.32
Harris v Nickerson (1873) LR 8 QB 286; 42 LJQB 171; 28 LT 410;
   37 JP 536; 21 WR 635 .... 2.19-2.20
Harris v Swordy (No 2) (HC) unrep, 16 June 1975 .... 12.21-12.22
Harris v Wyre Forest District Council [1990] 1 AC 831; [1989] 2 All ER 514;
   [1989] 2 WLR 790; 133 Sol Jo 597; 87 LGR 685; 21 HLR 424
   .... 1.38, 3.41, 4.23
Harrop v Thompson [1975] 2 All ER 94; [1975] 1 WLR 545; 118 Sol Jo 753 ..2.24
Hart v Hart (1841) 1 Hare 1; 11 LJCh 9; 5 Jur 1007 .... 14.51
Hart v Swaine (1877) Ch D 42; 47 LJCh 5; 37 LT 376; 26 WR 30 .... 5.26, 9.31
Harte v Sheehy (HC) unrep, 14 March 1986 .... 1.37, 3.44
Harvey v Pratt [1965] 2 All ER 786; [1965] 1 WLR 1025; 109 Sol Jo 474 .... 6.26
Hasham v Zenab [1960] AC 316; [1960] 2 WLR 374;
   104 Sol Jo 125 .... 12.37, 13.10, 13.42
Hastingwood Property Ltd v Saunders Bearman Anselm [1990] 3 All ER 107;
   [1990] 3 WLR 623 .... 3.17, 20.15
Hatten v Russell (1888) 38 Ch D 334; 57 LJCh 425; 58 LT 271; 36 WR 317 .14.18
Hatton v Waddy (1837) 2 Jon 541; Hay & Jon 601 .... 18.99
Haverty v Brooks [1970] IR 214 .... 1.34
Hawkesworth v Turner (1930) 46 TLR 389 .... 6.13
Hawkins v Price [1947] Ch 645; [1947] 1 All ER 689; LJR 887; 117 LT 108;
   91 Sol Jo 263 .... 6.07, 6.25

Haydon v Bell (1838) 1 Beav 337; 2 Jur 1008; 48 ER 970 .... 12.34
Hayes Estate, Re [1920] 1 IR 207 .... 6.32
Haynes v Haynes (1861) 1 Drew & Sm 426; 30 LJCh 578; 42 WR 56;
  3 R 715 .... 8.14
Healy Ballsbridge Ltd v Alliance Property Corp Ltd [1974] IR 441 .... 13.12
  .... 13.16-13.17, 13.20
Healy v Farragher (SC) unrep, 21 December 1972 .... 9.10, 9.12, 9.17, 9.23, 9.27
Healy v Healy (HC) unrep, 3 December 1973 .... 7.04, 7.15-7.16, 10.32
  .... 10.67, 13.53
Heard v Cuthbert (1851) 1 Ir Ch R 369 .... 12.26
Heaseman & Tweeedie's Contract, Re (1897) 69 LT 89 .... 14.63
Heath v Chilton (1844) 12 M & W 632 .... 6.37
Heath v Crealock (1874) IR 10 Ch 22 .... 14.64
Heatley v Newton (1880) 19 Ch D 326; 51 LJCh 225; 45 LT 445;
  30 WR 72 .... 2.18
Hedley Byrne & Co Ltd v Heller & Partners Ltd [1964] AC 464;
  [1963] 3 WLR 101; [1963] 3 All ER 515; 107 Sol Jo 454 .... 5.27, 15.37
Heffer v Martin (1867) 36 LJ Ch 372; 31 JP Jo 375; 15 WR 390 .... 2.24
Hegarty & Sons Ltd v Royal Liver Friendly Society [1985] IR 524 ...... 11.14-11.16
  .... 11.22
Hegarty v Morgan (HC) unrep, 15 March 1979 .... 16.62, 16.65
Hegarty v O'Loughran [1990] 1 IR 148; [1990] ILRM 403 .... 4.17
Hellings v Parkes Breslin Estates [1995] 29 EG 119 .... 1.38
Helsham v Langley (1841) 1 Y & C Cas 175; 11 LJCh 17 .... 6.33
Heneghan v Davitt [1933] IR 375; 67 ILTR 134 .... 13.40
Heneken v Courtney (1967) 101 ILTR 25 .... 2.31, 2.34, 3.19, 3.22, 3.31
Hennessy v Kiernan (1904) 38 ILTR 250 .... 13.39
Henniker v Howard (1904) 90 LT 157 .... 18.62
Henthorn v Frazer [1892] 2 Ch 27; 61 LJCh 373; 66 LT 439; 40 WR 433;
  8 TLR 459; 36 Sol Jo 30; 49 JP 100 .... 6.61
Heppenstall v Hose (1884) 51 LT 589 .... 15.32
Hermann v Hodges (1873) LR 16 EG 18 .... 13.40
Heron Garage Properties Ltd v Moss [1974] 1 All ER 421; [1974] 1 All ER 421; 117
  Sol Jo 697; 28 P & CR 54 .... 7.04, 7.16
Heron v Ulster Bank Ltd [1974] NI 44 .... 17.16
Hetling & Merton's Contract, Re [1893] 3 Ch 269; 62 LJCh 783; 69 LT 266; 37 Sol
  Jo 617; 9 TLR 553; 42 WR 19 .... 18.46
Hewitt's Contract, Re [1963] 3 All ER 419; [1963] 1 WLR 1298; 107 Sol Jo 1003
  20.09
Hext v Gill (1872) IR 7 Ch 699; 41 LJCh 761; 27 LT 291; 20 WR 957 .... 18.75
Hibernian Bank Ltd v Harrington (1912) 46 ILTR 27 .... 10.44
Hibernian Bank v Cassidy (1902) 36 ILTR 156 9.22, 9.24, 9.26, 9.33, 10.05, 11.02
Hibernian Transport Companies Ltd, Re [1972] IR 190 .... 2.25, 2.27, 7.07, 11.06
Hickey v Broderick [1931] LJ Ir 136 .... 9.13
Hickey v Keating (HC) unrep, 25 January 1980 .... 13.27

Hickey v Tipperary (South Riding) CC [1931] IR 621 ....6.12

Higgins v ILC [1960] IR 277 ....14.06

Highett & Bird's Contract, Re [1903] 1 Ch 287; 72 LJCh 220; 87 LT 697; 47 Sol Jo
   204; 51 WR 227 ....12.22, 14.75

Highland Finance Ireland Ltd v Sacred Heart College of Agriculture Ltd
   [1992] 1 IR 472; [1993] ILRM 260..12.15, 12.16

Hill & Grant Ltd v Hodson [1934] Ch. 53 ....2.18

Hill v Harris [1965] 2 QB 601; [1965] 2 WLR 1331; [1965] 2 All ER 358;
   109 Sol Jo 333 ....4.08, 5.12, 9.41, 14.73, 16.75

Hillas & Co Ltd v Arcos Ltd (1932) 147 LT 503; 38 Com Cas 23 ....6.24

Hillingdon Estates Co v Stonefield Estates Ltd [1952] Ch 267;
   [1952] 1 All ER 853; [1952] 1 TLR 1099; [1952] WN 224;
   80 LGR 587; 2 P & CR 415 ....12.37

Hinton v Sparkes (1868) LR 3 CP 161; 37 LJCP 81; 17 LT 600;
   16 WR 360 ....10.24, 13.33

Hipwell v Knight (1835) 1 Y & C Ex 401; 4 LJ Ex Eq 52;
   160 ER 163 ....12.28, 14.47

Hissett v Reading Roofing Co Ltd [1970] 1 All ER 122; [1969] 1 WLR 1757;
   113 Sol Jo 815; 20 P & CR 924 ....21.03

Hoare v Kingsbury UC [1912] 2 Ch 652; 81 LJCh 666; 107 LT 492;
   76 JP 401; 56 Sol Jo 704; 10 LGR 829 ....6.51

Hobhouse v Hamilton (1803) 1 Sch & Lef 207 ....14.52-14.52

Hobson v Bell (1839) 2 Beav 17; 8 LJCh 241; 3 Jur 190; 48 ER 1084 ....9.11

Hodder v Ruffin (1830) Taml 341 ....11.07

Hodge, Re [1940] Ch 260 ....16.54

Hodgens v Keon [1894] 2 IR 657 ....2.10, 2.34, 10.24

Hodges v Earl of Litchfield (1835) 1 Bing NC 492 ....13.86-13.86

Hogan & Marnell's Contract, Re [1919] 1 IR 422 ....13.28, 13.52, 14.10, 14.15

Hogan v Healy (1876) IR 11 CL 119 ....13.58

Hoggart v Scott (1830) 1 Russ & M 293; Taml 500; 9 LJ (os) Ch 54 ....13.47

Hollier v Eyre (1842) 2 Dr & War 590; 9 Cl & F 1 ....17.19

Hollis' Hospital & Hague's Contract, Re [1899] 2 Ch 540; 68 LJCh 673;
   81 LT 90; 43 Sol Jo 644; 47 WR 691 ....14.15

Holliwell v Seacombe [1906] 1 Ch 426; 75 LJCh 289; 94 LT 186;
   54 WR 355 ....15.33

Holmes & Cosmopolitan Press Ltd Contract, Re [1944] Ch 53;
   [1943] 2 All ER 716; 113 LJCh 14; 87 Sol Jo 414.....................................14.56

Holohan v Ardmoyle Estates (HC) unrep, 5 March 1966, (SC), unrep 1 May 1967
   ....13.16

Holohan v Friends Provident & Century Life Office [1966] IR 1 2.12, 11.06, 13.22

Holroyd v Marshall (1862) 10 HLC 191; 33 LJCh 193; 7 LT 172;
   9 Jur (ns) 213; 11 WR 171; 11 ER 999 ....12.02, 12.12

Holt v Payne Skillington, London Times, 22 December 1995;
   [1995] EGCS 201 ....4.18

Homsey v Searle [1996] EGCS 43 ....8.04, 8.06

Hooker v Wyle [1973] 3 All ER 707; [1973] 1 WLR 235; 117 Sol Jo 545 ..... 13.19
Hoon v Nolan (1967) 101 ILTR 99 .... 6.07, 6.14, 6.25
Hooper v Ramsbottom (1815) 6 Taunt 12; 1 Marsh 414; 128 ER 936 .... 18.127
Hope v Harman (1847) 16 QB 751; 8 LT (os) 554; 11 Jur 1097; 117 ER 1069
.... 18.133
Hope v Lord Cloncurry (1874) IR 8 Eq 555; 9 ILTR 58 .... 6.48, 6.50, 6.58
Hopkin's Lease, Re [1972] 1 WLR 372; [1972] 1 All ER 248; 23 P & CR 15 17.15
Hopkins v Geoghegan [1931] IR 135 .... 10.05, 13.17, 14.18, 14.42
.... 14.48-14.49, 20.41
Hopwood v Brown [1955] 1 WLR 213; [1995] 1 All ER 550; 99 Sol Jo 168 .. 18.68
Horgan v Deasy [1979] ILRM 71 .... 13.08, 13.50, 16.36
Hornby v Cardwell (1881) 8 QBD 329 .... 19.32
Horner v Walker [1923] 2 Ch 218; 92 LJCh 573; 129 LT 782 .... 6.31
Horton v Kurzke [1971] 1 WLR 769; [1971] 2 All ER 577; 115 Sol Jo 287;
22 P & CR 661 .... 13.20
Hoskins v Woodham [1938] 1 All ER 692 .... 4.12
Hounslow London Borough v Twickenham Gardens Developments Ltd
[1971] Ch 233; [1970] 3 WLR 538; [1970] 3 All ER 326;
114 Sol Jo 603 .... 13.06, 13.41
House of Spring Gardens Ltd v Point Blank Ltd [1984] IR 611 .... 13.57
Household Fire & Carriage Accident Insurance Co v Grant (1879) 4 Ex D 216;
48 LJQB 577; 41 LT 298; 27 WR 858; 44 JP 152 .... 6.61
Howard v Hopkins (1742) 2 Atk 371 .... 2.24
Howard v Maitland (1883) 11 QBD 695; 53 LTQB 42; 48 JP 165 .... 21.22, 21.30
Howard (John) & Co (Northern) v Knight [1969] 1 Lloyd's Rep 364 .... 7.19
Howe v Hall (1870) IR 4 Eq 242 .... 6.53, 6.54-6.57
Howe v Lord Dartmouth (1802) 7 Ves 137 .... 19.63
Howe v Smith (1884) 27 Ch D 89; 53 LJCh 1055; 50 LT 573; 32 WR 802;
48 JP 773 .... 10.18, 13.61
Howell v Howell [1992] 1 IR 290 .... 17.16
Howell v Kightley (1856) 21 Beav 331; 25 LJCh 866; 52 ER 887 .... 14.75
Howlin v Power (Dublin) Ltd (HC) unrep, 5 May 1978 .... 6.29, 6.48, 6.59
Hoyle, Re [1893] 1 Ch 85; 62 LJCh 182; 67 LT 674; 37 Sol Jo 46; 41 WR 81;
2 R 145 .... 6.15
Hucklesby v Hook (1900) 82 LT 117; 44 Sol Jo 277 .... 6.33
Hudson v O'Connor [1947] 1 Jur Rep 21 .... 3.08, 6.33
Hudson v Temple (1860) 30 LJ Ch 251; 29 Beav 536; 31 LT 495; 9 WR 243;
7 Jur (ns) 248; 54 ER 735 .... 13.15
Hughes v Fanagan (1891) 30 LR Ir 111 .... 15.19
Hughes v Kearney (1803) 1 Sch & Lef 132 .... 12.17
Hughes, Dickson & Co Ltd v Hughes Ltd [1924] 1 IR 113 .... 13.40, 13.53
Hume v Bentley (1852) 5 De G & S 520; 21 LJCh 760; 16 Jur 1109 .... 14.59
Hume's Estate, Re (1905) 5 NIJR 196 .... 18.82, 21.05
Humphries v Broglan (1850) 12 QB 739 .... 19.13
Humphries v Humphries [1910] 2 KB 531; 79 LJKB 919; 103 LT 14 .... 6.07

Hungerford v Bechier (1855) 5 Ir Ch R 417 .... 18.32
Hunt v Luck [1902] 1 Ch 428; 71 LJCh 239; 86 LT 68; 46 Sol Jo 229;
    18 TLR 265; 50 WR 291 .... 9.23
Hunt v Silk (1804) 5 East 447; 2 Smith KB 15 .... 13.58
Hunt (Charles) Ltd v Palmer [1931] 2 Ch 287; 100 LJCh 356; 145 LT 630;
    75 Sol Jo 525 .... 9.40, 13.35
Hunter v Martin (1903) 37 ILTR 91 .... 3.20
Husband v Grattan (1833) Alc & Nap 389 .... 13.32
Hussey v Horne-Payne (1879) 4 App Cas 311; 48 LJCh 846; 41 LT 1;
    27 WR 585; 43 JP 814 .... 7.13
Hutchinson v Mains (1812) Alc & Nap 155 .... 18.61
Hynes Ltd v Independent Newspapers Ltd [1980] IR 204 .... 13.11, 14.45, 19.34

I

Imray v Oakshette [1897] 2 QB 218; 66 LJQB 544; 76 LT 632;
    41 Sol Jo 528; 13 TLR 411; 45 WR 681 .... 14.71-14.73
Inchiquin (Earl of) v Burnell (1795) 3 Ridgw PC 376 .... 18.73-18.74
Incorporated Law Society of Ireland v Browne (1961) 95 ILTR 6 .... 7.14
Industrial Development Authority v Moran [1978] IR 159 .... 12.29, 18.131
Industrial Yarns Ltd v Greene [1984] ILRM 15 .... 13.57
Ingram v Gillen (1910) 44 ILTR 103 .... 2.13, 2.24, 5.25
Inman v Stamp (1815) 1 Stark 12 .... 6.12
Innisfail Laundry Ltd v Dawe (1963) 107 Sol Jo 437; 186 Est Gaz 879 .... 13.19
International Securities Ltd v Portmarnock Estates Ltd (HC) unrep,
    9 April 1975; (1975) 69 Gaz ILSI 176 .... 7.16, 10.18, 10.32, 13.17, 13.30
Interview Ltd, Re [1975] IR 382 .... 12.06
Invercargill City Council v Hamlin [1996] 1 All ER 756 .... 4.15, 11.22
Irani Finance Ltd v Singh [1971] Ch 59; [1970] 3 WLR 330;
    [1970] 3 All ER 199; 114 Sol Jo 636; 21 P & CR 843 .... 6.11
IRC v Maple & Co (Paris) Ltd (1907) 77 LJKB 55 .... 10.09
Irish Bank of Commerce Ltd v O'Hara (HC) unrep 10 May 1989 .... 12.09
Irish Civil Service Building Society & O'Keeffe, Re (1880) 7 LR Ir 136 .... 15.19
Irish Industrial Benefit Building Society v O Brien [1941] IR 1 .... 9.34, 11.04
Irish Land Commission v Maquay (1891) 28 LR Ir 342 .... 5.26, 9.07, 9.29, 10.44
Irish Leisure Industries Ltd v Gaiety Theatre Enterprises Ltd (HC) unrep
    12 February 1975 .... 13.76, 13.80, 13.81, 13.83
Irish Life Assurance Co Ltd v Dublin Land Securities Ltd [1986] IR 332;
    [1989] IR 253 .... 13.66
Irish Life Assurance Co Ltd v Dublin Land Securities Ltd [1989] IR 253 .... 21.38
Irish Mainport Holdings Ltd v Crosshaven Sailing Centre Ltd (HC) unrep,
    16 May 1980 .... 7.11, 7.13
Irish National Insurance Co Ltd v Scannell [1959] Ir Jur Rep 41 .... 2.03
Irish Permanent Building Society v O'Sullivan [1990] ILRM 598 .... 2.13, 3.14
    .... 3.41, 15.03
Irish Sailors' & Soldiers' Land Trust v Donnelly [1944] IR 464 .... 12.33

Irish Shell & BP Ltd v Costello [1984] IR 511; [1985] ILRM 554 .... 12.33
Irish Telephone Rentals Ltd v Irish Civil Service Building Society Ltd
    [1992] 2 IR 525; [1991] ILRM 880 .... 13.32
Irons v Douglas (1841) 3 Ir Eq R 601 .... 18.75
Irvine v Deane (1849) 2 Ir Jur (os) 209 .... 6.20, 6.29, 6.31, 9.02
Irwin, Re (1856) 5 Ir Ch R 290 .... 9.34
Isaac, Re [1894] 3 Ch 506 .... 12.11
Isaacs v Towell [1898] 2 Ch 285; 67 LJCh 508; 78 LT 619; 42 Sol Jo 469 .... 15.29
Isitt v Monaghan CC (1905) 5 NIJR 118; 39 ILTR 112 .... 6.12

J

Jackson v Bishop (1979) 48 P & CR 57 .... 21.28
Jackson & Haden's Contract, Re [1906] 1 Ch 412; 75 LJCh 226; 94 LT 48;
    50 Sol Jo 254; 54 WR 434 .... 15.31
Jackson & Oakshott, Re (1880) 14 Ch D 851; 28 WR 794 .... 15.28
Jackson & Woodburn's Contract, Re (1887) 37 Ch D 44 .... 13.27
Jackson (Francis) Developments Ltd v Stemp [1943] 2 All ER 601 .... 12.33
Jacobs v Revell [1900] 2 Ch 858; 69 LJCh 879; 83 LT 629; 49 WR 109 .... 13.34
.... 14.58, 14.80
Jacques v Lloyd D George & Partners Ltd [1968] 2 All ER 187;
    [1968] 1 WLR 625 .... 3.28
Jaggard v Sawyer [1995] 1 WLR 269; [1995] 13 EG 132 .... 13.54
James v Litchfield (1869) LR 9 Eq 51; 39 LJCh 248; 21 LT 521;
    18 WR 158 .... 9.23
James v Smith [1931] 2 KB 317; 100 LJKB 585; 145 LT 457 .... 3.30
Jameson v Kinmell Bay Land Co Ltd (1931) 47 TLR 593 .... 6.10
Jameson v Squire [1948] IR 153; 87 ILTR 46 .... 8.04, 13.40
Janmohamed v Hassam (1976) 241 EG 609 .... 7.04
Jared v Clements [1903] 1 Ch 428; 72 LJCh 291; 88 LT 97; 47 Sol Jo 435;
    19 TLR 219; 51 WR 401 .... 14.65
Jarmain v Egelstone (1813) 5 C & P 172 .... 13.86
Jarrett v Hunter (1886) 34 Ch D 182; 56 LJCh 141; 55 LT 727; 51 JP 165;
    35 WR 132; 3 TLR 117 .... 6.20
Jeakes v White (1851) 6 Exch 873 .... 14.09
Jelbert v Davis [1968] 1 All ER 1182; [1968] 1 WLR 589; 112 Sol Jo 172 ..... 18.72
Jenkins & Commercial Electric Theatre Co's Contract, Re
    (1917) 61 Sol Jo 283 .... 18.103
Jenkins v Jones (1882) 9 QBD 128; 51 LJQB 438; 46 LT 795; 30 WR 668 ... 21.29
Jenkins v Jones (1888) 40 Ch D 71 .... 21.30
Jennings v Travener [1955] 2 All ER 769; [1995] 1 WLR 932; 99 Sol Jo 543... 4.12
Jennings & Chapman Ltd v Woodman, Matthews & Co [1952] 2 TLR 409 ... 12.21
Jennings' Trustee v King [1952] Ch 899; [1952] 2 TLR 469;
    [1952] 2 All ER 608; 96 Sol Jo 648 .... 12.47
Jessop v Smith [1895] 1 IR 508 .... 13.40, 18.125
Jeune v Queen's Cross Properties Ltd [1974] Ch 97; [1973] 3 WLR 378;
    [1973] 3 All ER 97; 117 Sol Jo 680; 26 P & CR 98 .... 13.41

Johnson v Agnew [1980] AC 367; [1979] 2 WLR 487; [1979] 1 All ER 883;
  123 Sol Jo 217 .... 10.19, 10.59, 13.03, 13.04, 13.54, 13.78
Johnson v Dodgson (1837) 2 M & W 653; Murph & H 271; 6 LJ Ex 185;
  1 Jur 739 ....6.33
Johnson v Longleat Properties [1976-7] ILRM 93 ....4.12
Johnson & Tustin, Re (1885) 30 Ch D 42; 54 LJCh 889; 53 LT 281;
  1 TLR 579; 33 WR 737 ....14.48
Johnston v Boyes [1899] 2 Ch 73; 68 LJCh 425; 80 LT 488; 43 Sol Jo 457;
  47 WR 517 ....2.10, 2.13, 2.20, 10.24, 20.31
Johnston v Holdway [1963] 1 QB 601; [1963] 2 WLR 147; [1963] 1 All ER 432;
  107 Sol Jo 55 ....18.78
Johnston v Johnston (1869) IR 3 Eq 328; 3 ILT 154 .... 12.14, 12.18, 12.34
Johnston v McAllister (1835) 1 Jon 499 ....6.09
Joliffe v Blumberg (1870) 18 WR 784 ....6.45
Jones v Flint (1839) 10 Ad & El 753; 2 Per & Dav 594; 9 LJQB 252 ....6.09
Jones v Lipman [1962] 1 WLR 832; [1962] 1 All ER 442; 106 Sol Jo 531 ..... 14.61
Jones v Quinn (1878) 2 LR Ir 516; 13 ILTR 16 ....2.15
Jones v Read (1876) IR 10 CL 315 ....18.61
Jones v Rimmer (1880) 14 Ch D 588; 49 LJCh 775; 43 LT 111; 29 WR 165 ...9.27
Jones, Re [1893] 2 Ch 461; 62 LJCh 996; 69 LT 45; 3 R 498 ....21.33
Jopling-Pursar v Jackman (SC) unrep, 31 March 1995 ....13.44
Joseph v National Magazine Co [1959] Ch 14; [1958] 3 WLR 366;
  [1958] 3 All ER 52; 102 Sol Jo 602 ....13.41
Joyce v Liverpool Corporation [1995] EGCS 77 ....13.41
JPR, Re (1940) 74 ILTR 11 ....14.51
Judd v Donegal Tweed Co (1935) 69 ILTR 117 ....2.07, 2.29, 3.20-3.22, 9.03
Judd v Doyle's Motors Ltd (1938) 72 ILTR 100 ....3.22
Julian, Re [1950] IR 57 ....17.20

K

Kavanagh & Balfe's Contract, Re (1898) 32 ILTR 6 ....9.34, 13.81
Kavanagh Ltd, Re [1952] Ir Jur Rep 38 ....20.50
Kavanagh v Cuthbert (1874) IR 9 CL 136 ....2.08, 2.12, 6.38
Keane v Irish Land Commission [1979] IR 429 ....16.36
Kearns v Manresa Estates Ltd (HC) unrep 25 July 1975 ....13.27
Keating v Bank of Ireland [1983] ILRM 295 ....9.32, 9.34, 9.46, 13.20, 13.29
Keck v Faber (1915) 60 Sol Jo 253 ....13.78
Keen v Mear [1920] 2 Ch 574; 89 LJCh 513; 214 LT 19 ....3.08-3.09, 6.32
  .... 13.80, 13.82, 13.86
Keenan Bros, Re [1985] IR 401; [1985] ILRM 641 ....12.06
Kehoe v Louth & Son [1992] ILRM 282 ....15.02
Keighley, Maxstead & Co v Durant [1901] AC 240; 70 LJKB 662; 84 LT 777; 17
  TLR 527; 45 Sol Jo 536 ....6.36
Kelly v Crowley [1985] IR 212 ....1.36, 4.02, 5.28
Kelly v Duffy [1922] 1 IR 62; 56 ILTR 129 ....13.80-13.84

Kelly v Irish Nursery & Landscape Co Ltd [1983] IR 221;
[1981] ILRM 433 .... 6.62, 7.11
Kelly v Park Hall School Ltd [1979] IR 340 .... 6.15, 7.08
Kelly v Power (1812) 2 Ba & B 236 .... 18.32
Kempston v Butler (1861) 12 ICLR 516; 6 Ir Jur (ns) 410 .... 18.61
Kempthorne, Re [1930] 1 Ch 268; 99 LJCh 177; 142 LT 111; 46 TLR 15 .... 6.11
Kendal v Micfield (1740) Barn Ch 46; 2 Eq Cas Abr 615 .... 18.87
Kennaway, Re [1889] WN 70 .... 20.40
Kennedy v Hayes (1840) 2 Ir LR 186 .... 18.84
Kennedy v McMaster [1935] Ir Jur Rep 2 .... 2.34
Kennedy v Wrenne [1981] ILRM 81 .... 5.26, 6.13, 13.27, 15.30-15.31
Kenny v La Barte [1902] 2 IR 63 .... 17.19, 18.66-18.67
Kenny's Trusts, Re [1906] 1 IR 531; 40 ILTR 102 .... 8.13
Keppel v Wheeler [1927] 1 KB 577; 96 LJKB 433; 136 LT 203 .... 6.15, 7.08
Kerns v Manning [1935] IR 869 .... 6.25, 6.42
Kerr v Kerr (1854) 4 Ir Ch R 493; 7 Ir Jur (os) 76 .... 18.41, 18.87
Khodaram Irani v Burjorji Dhunjibai (1915) 32 TLR 156 .... 13.15
Kidd v O'Neill [1931] IR 664; 66 ILTR 47 .... 11.03
Kiely v Minister for Social Welfare [1977] IR 267 .... 8.16
Killiney & Ballybrack Development Association v Minister
for Local Government (1978) 112 ILTR 69 .... 8.16
Killner v France [1946] 2 All ER 83; 175 LT 377; 90 Sol Jo 543 .... 20.25
Kilmer v British Columbia Orchard Land Ltd [1913] AC 319; 82 LJPC 77;
108 LT 306; 29 TLR 319; 57 Sol Jo 338 .... 13.33
Kimber Coal Co v Stone & Rolfe Ltd [1926] AC 414 .... 6.35
Kine v Balfe (1813) 2 Ba & B 343 .... 6.32, 6.53, 6.55-6.56
King v Victor Parsons & Co [1972] 1 WLR 801; [1972] 2 All ER 625;
[1973] 1 WLR 29; 116 Sol Jo 901; [1973] 1 Lloyd's Rep 189;
225 Est Gaz 611 .... 4.13
King v Wilson (1843) 6 Beav 124; 49 ER 772 .... 13.17
King's Settlement, Re [1931] 2 Ch 294; 100 LJCh 359; 145 LT 517 .... 18.32
King's Will Trusts, Re [1964] Ch 542; [1964] 2 WLR 913; [1964] 1 All ER 833;
108 Sol Jo 335 .... 16.54
Kingsnorth Trust Ltd v Bell [1986] 1 All ER 423; [1986] 1 WLR 119;
130 Sol Jo 88 .... 1.35
Kingston v Ambrian Investment Co Ltd [1975] 1 All ER 120;
[1975] 1 WLR 161; 119 Sol Jo 47 .... 18.125-18.127
Kingswood Estate Co Ltd v Anderson [1963] 2 QB 169; [1962] 2 WLR 1102;
[1962] 3 All ER 593; 106 Sol Jo 651 .... 6.53
Kissock & Currie's Contract, Re [1916] 1 IR 376; 49 ILTR 8 .... 12.03, 12.13
.... 12.16, 13.28, 15.42
Kissock & Taylor, Re [1916] 1 IR 393; 50 ILTR 100 .... 20.09
Kitchen v Palmer (1877) 46 LJ Ch 611 .... 15.28
Knight Sugar Co Ltd v Alberta Rly & Irrigation Co [1938] 1 All ER 266;
82 Sol Jo 132 .... 21.02

Knight v Cockford (1791) 1 Esp 190 ...... 6.33
Knight v Williams [1901] 1 Ch 256; 70 LJCh 92; 83 LT 730; 45 Sol Jo 164;
    49 WR 427 ...... 14.63
Koenigsblatt v Sweet [1923] 2 Ch 314; 92 LJCh 598; 129 LT 659;
    67 Sol Jo 638; 39 TLR 237 ...... 6.33, 6.36
Kreditbank Cassel v Schenkers Ltd [1927] 1 KB 826; 96 LJKB 501;
    136 LT 716; 71 Sol Jo 141; 43 TLR 237 ...... 18.10
Kwei Tek Chao v British Traders & Shippers Ltd [1954] 2 QB 459;
    [1954] 2 WLR 365; 98 Sol Jo 163 ...... 18.10
Kyne v Tiernan (HC) unrep, 15 July 1980 ...... 16.62

L

L(B) v L(M) 2 IR 77; [1992] ILRM 115 ...... 16.23
Lac Minerals Ltd v Chevron Mineral Corporations of Ireland
    [1995] 1 ILRM 161 ...... 8.04
Lacon v Mertins (1743) 3 Atk 1 ...... 6.59
Ladenbau (G & K) Ltd v Crawley & De Reya [1978] 1 All ER 682;
    [1978] 1 WLR 266 ...... 5.28
Lahey v Bell (1843) 6 Ir Eq R 122 ...... 9.02, 11.04, 14.71-14.71
Laird v Pym (1841) 7 M & W 474; 10 LJ Ex 259; 8 Dowl 860; H & W 11;
    171 ER 852 ...... 13.78
Lake v Bushby [1949] 2 All ER 964; 94 Sol Jo 82 ...... 5.28, 16.76
Lally v Concannon (1853) 3 ILR 557; 6 Ir Jur (os) 26 ...... 20.07
Lamb v Camden London Borough Council [1983] 3 All ER 161 ...... 12.40
Lambert v Dublin, Wicklow & Wexford Rly Co (1890) 25 LR Ir 163 ...... 8.14
Langen & Wind Ltd v Bell [1972] Ch 685; [1972] 2 WLR 170;
    [1972] 1 All ER 296; 115 Sol Jo 966 ...... 12.16
Langford v Mahoney (1843) 3 Jo & Lat 109; 5 Ir Eq R 569; 4 Dr & War 81;
    2 Con & L 317 ...... 15.42
Lanyon v Martin (1884) 13 LR Ir 297 ...... 6.49, 6.57
Lapedus v Glavey (1965) 99 ILTR 1 ...... 21.05
Larkin v Lord Rosse (1846) 10 Ir Eq R 70 ...... 9.26, 9.33, 9.34, 13.52
Last v Hucklesby (1914) 58 Sol Jo 431 ...... 6.31
Lauder v Alley (1867) IR 1 CL 82 ...... 14.56
Laurence v Lexourt Holdings Ltd [1978] 2 All ER 810; [1978] 1 WLR 1128;
    122 Sol Jo 681 ...... 21.37
Lavan v Walsh [1964] IR 87; 99 ILTR 147 ...... 6.15, 6.28, 6.31, 6.34-6.35, 13.49
Laverty v Purcell (1888) 39 Ch D 508; 57 LJCh 570; 58 LT 846; 4 TLR 353;
    37 WR 163 ...... 6.10, 13.54
Law v Jones [1974] Ch 112; [1973] 2 WLR 994; [1973] 2 All ER 437;
    117 Sol Jo 305; 26 P & CR 42 ...... 6.04, 6.15, 7.08
Law v Roberts & Co [1964] IR 292 ...... 3.08, 6.02, 6.15, 6.18, 6.20-6.24
    ...... 6.28, 6.31, 6.41, 7.12
Law v Roberts & Co (No 2) [1964] IR 306 ...... 2.27, 11.04, 12.20
Lawes v Bennett (1785) 1 Cox CC 167 ...... 12.11

Lawrence v Cassel [1930] 2 KB 83; 99 LJKB 525; 143 LT 291;
74 Sol Jo 421 .... 4.12, 21.03
Lawrenson v Butler (1802) 1 Sch & Lef 13 .... 13.47
Lawrie v Lees (1881) 7 App Cas 19; 51 LT Ch 209; 46 LT 210;
30 WR 185 .... 14.75
Layburn v Grindley [1892] 2 Ch 13; 61 LJCh 352; 36 Sol Jo 363;
40 WR 474 .... 18.61
LB v HB (HC) unrep, 31 July 1980 .... 16.62
Leachman v L & K Richardson Ltd [1969] 1 WLR 1129; [1969] 3 All ER 20;
113 Sol Jo 405; 20 P & CR 647 .... 18.63
Leader v Tod-Heatly [1891] WN 38 .... 13 78
Leathem v Allen (1850) 1 Ir Ch R 683; 3 Ir Jur (os) 73 .... 14.59, 14.71, 15.25
Leathley v Dublin Corp [1942] Ir Jur Rep 20 .... 20.07
Lecky v Walter [1914] 1 IR 378 .... 5.26
Lecky & Aiken's Contract, Re (1906) 40 ILTR 65 .... 13.27
Lee v Mann (1817) 8 Taunt 45; 1 Moore CP 481 .... 2.10, 10.29
Lee v Rayson [1917] 1 Ch 613; 86 LJCh 405; 116 LT 536; 61 Sol Jo 368 .... 9.33
Leeds Industrial Co-Operative Society Ltd v Stack [1924] AC 851;
93 LJCh 436; 131 LT 710; 40 TLR 745; 68 Sol Jo 715 .... 13.54
Leeds, Re [1902] IR 339; 2 NIJR 113; 36 ILTR 74 .... 20.06
Leek & Moorlands BS v Clark [1952] 2 QB 788; [1952] 2 TLR 401;
[1952] 2 All ER 492; [1952 WN 414; 96 Sol Jo 561 .... 6.37
Leemac Overseas Investments Ltd v Harvey [1973] IR 160 .... 2.10, 2.26, 3.10,
....3.15-3.17, 10.18, 10.26-10.32
Leeman v Stocks [1951] Ch 941; [1952] 2 TLR 662; [1951] 1 All ER 1043;
[1951] WN 258; 95 Sol Jo 368 .... 6.33, 6.38
Lee-Parker v Izzet [1971] 3 All ER 1099; [1971] 1 WLR 1688; 115 Sol Jo 641;
22 P & CR 1098 .... 7.04, 7.15, 10.25, 12.34
Lee-Parker v Izzet (No 2) [1972] 1 WLR 775; [1972] 2 All ER 800;
116 Sol Jo 446 .... 7.04, 7.15
Legal Practitioners (Ir) Act 1876, Re [1951] Ir Jur Rep 1 .... 20.50
Legge v Croker (1811) 1 Ba & B 506 .... 9.31, 13.64, 21.35
Lehmann v McArthur (1868) 3 Ch App 496; 37 LJCh 625; 32 JP 135;
18 WR 877 .... 14.75
Leigh v Jack (1879) 5 Ex D 264; 49 LJQB 220; 42 LT 463; 44 JP 488;
28 WR 452 .... 18.59
Leitch v Simpson (1871) IR 5 Eq 613 .... 13.53
Lennon, Re [1928] NI 195 .... 16.31
Leppington v Freeman (1891) 66 LT 357; 40 WR 348 .... 12.14
Leslie v Crommelin (1867) IR 2 Eq 134; 1 ILT 745 .... 5.26, 13.52
Lever Finance Ltd v Needleman & Krentzer's Trustee [1956] Ch 375;
[1956] 3 WLR 72; [1956] 2 All ER 378; 100 Sol Jo 400 .... 20.25
Lever v Koffler [1901] Ch 543; 70 LJCh 395; 84 LT 584; 49 WR 506;
45 Sol Jo 326 .... 6.14
Levingston v Somers [1941] IR 183 .... 15.02

Levy v Stogdon [1898] 1 Ch 478; 67 LJCh 313; 78 LT 185; [1899] 1 Ch 5;
68 LJCh 19; 79 LT 364 .... 13.31
Lewcock v Bromley (1920) 127 LT 116; 37 TLR 48; 64 Sol Jo 75 ....3.07-3.08
Lewis v Campbell (1819) 8 Taunt 715 .... 21.32
Lewis, Re (1908) 42 ILTR 210 .... 9.21, 9.34, 11.02
Leyland & Taylor's Contract, Re [1900] 2 Ch 625; 69 LJCh 764; 83 LT 380;
16 TLR 566; 49 WR 17 .... 9.21
Lift Manufacturers Ltd v Irish Life Assurance Co Ltd [1979] ILRM 277 .... 11.22,
13.41
Linden Gardens Trust Ltd v Lenesta Sludge Disposals Ltd [1994] 1 AC 85;
[1993] 3 All ER 417; [1993] 3 WLR 408; 137 Sol Jo 183......................... 11.22
Lindsay & Forder's Contract, Re (1895) 72 LT 832 .... 9.35
Lindsay v Lynch (1804) 2 Sch & Lef 1 ....6.03, 13.40, 13.45
Lindsey v GN Rly v Co (1853) 10 Hare 644; 22 LJCh 995; 17 Jur 522;
1 WR 257... 6.51
Linehan v Cotter (1844) 7 Ir Eq R 176 .... 9.33, 13.58
Linggi Plantations Ltd v Jagatheesan [1972] 1 MLJ 89 .... 13.33
Linton v Royal Bank of Canada (1967) 60 DLR (2d)398 .... 18.122
Lipkin Gorman v Karpanale Ltd [1991] 2 AC 548; [1991] 3 WLR 10;
[1992] 4 All ER 512; 135 Sol Jo 36 .... 16.33
Lipmans Wallpaper Ltd v Mason & Hodgron Ltd [1969] 1 Ch 20;
[1968] 2 WLR 881; [1968] 1 All ER 1123 .... 14.75
Listowel v Gibbings (1858) 9 ICLR 223; 4 Ir Jur (ns) 64 .... 17.16, 18.73, 18.75
Lloyd v Stanbury [1971] 1 WLR 535; [1971] 2 All ER 267; 115 Sol Jo 264;
22 P & CR 432 .... 12.21, 12.34, 13.85
Lloyd v Sullivan (HC) unrep, 6 March 1981 .... 16.69
Lloyd's Bank v Bullock [1896] 2 Ch 192; 65 LJCh 680; 74 LT 687;
40 Sol Jo 545; 12 TLR 435; 44 WR 633 .... 18.128
Lloyd's Bank v Rossett [1991] 1 AC 107; [1990] 2 WLR 867 .... 16.23
LNW Rly v Mayor of Westminister [1902] 1 Ch 269 .... 18.59
Lock v Bell [1931] 1 Ch 35; 100 LJCh 22; 144 LT 108 .... 13.15, 13.25
Lockett v Norman-Wright [1925] Ch 56; 94 LJCh 123; 132 LT 532;
69 Sol Jo 125 .... 7.11
Lockharts v Bernard Rosen & Co Ltd [1922] 1 Ch 433; 91 LJCh 321;
127 LT 18; 66 Sol Jo 350 .... 12.22
Loftus v Roberts (1902) 18 TLR 532 .... 6.24
Lombank Ltd v Kennedy [1961] NI 192 .... 13.32
Lombard & Ulster Banking Ltd v Kennedy [1974] NI 20 .... 6.10
London & Cheshire Insurance Co Ltd v Laplagrene Property Co Ltd
[1971] Ch 499; [1971] 2 WLR 257; [1971] 1 All ER 766; 114 Sol Jo 912;
22 P & CR 108 .... 18.45
London Corp & Tubb's Contract, Re [1894] 2 Ch 524; 63 LJCh 580;
7 R 265 .... 20.09
Lonergan v McCarthy [1983] NI 129 ....6.24, 8.06, 13.45
Long v Millar (1879) 4 CPD 450; 48 LJQB 569; 41 LT 306; 43 JP 797;
27 WR 720 ....6.30-6.31

Longlands Farm, Re [1968] 3 All ER 552; 20 P & CR 25 .... 7.04, 7.17-7.18
Longvale Brick & Lime Works Ltd, Re [1917] 1 IR 321; 51 ILTR 117 .... 2.14
.... 2.24-2.25
Lonsdale & Thompson Ltd v Black Arrow Group plc [1993] 3 All ER 648 ... 12.39
Lord v Stephens (1835) 1 Y & C Ex 222; 160 ER 90 .... 12.22
Lotteryking Ltd v Amec Properties Ltd [1995] 28 EG 100. .... 1.31
Louis v Willson [1949] IR 347 .... 7.03
Lowe v Ashmore Ltd [1971] Ch 545; [1970] 3 WLR 998; [1971] 1 All ER 1057;
      114 Sol Jo 866; 49 ATC 224 .... 6.09
Lowe v Hope [1970] Ch 94; [1969] 3 WLR 582; [1969] 3 All ER 605;
      113 Sol Jo 796; 20 P & CR 857 .... 10.19, 13.31, 13.60
Lowe v Swift (1814) 2 Ba & B 529 .... 6.50, 13.45
Lowes v Lush (1808) 14 Ves 547 .... 12.28
Lowis v Wilson [1949] IR 347 .... 6.15, 7.11
Lowry v Reid [1927] NI 142 .... 6.48, 6.49-6.51, 6.53, 6.54, 6.60, 13.40
Luby's Estate, Re (1909) 43 ILTR 141 .... 18.86
Lutchmunsing v Rapp (1967) 204 Est Gaz 1119 .... 13.20
Luttrell v McCreery (1850) 1 ICLR 7 .... 18.94
Luxor (Eastbourne) Ltd v Cooper [1941] AC 108; [1941] 1 All ER 33;
      110 LJKB 131; 164 TLR 213; 85 Sol Jo 105 .... 3.13, 3.19, 3.24-3.27, 3.29
Lydon v Lydon (1874) 8 ILTR 85 .... 13.50
Lynch Monahan & O'Brien Ltd, Re (HC) unrep 14 October 1986 .... 13.40
Lynch v O'Meara (SC) unrep, 8 May 1975 .... 7.13
Lynch v Thorne [1956] 1 WLR 303; [1956] 1 All ER 744; 100 Sol Jo 225 ...... 4.13
Lyons v Murphy [1986] IR 666 .... 13.29
Lyons v Thomas [1986] IR 66 .... 12.21-12.22, 12.36, 13.27, 15.28-15.32
Lyons & Carroll's Contract, Re [1896] 1 IR 383; 30 ILTR 3 .... 13.36, 14.06
Lysaght v Edwards (1876) 2 Ch D 449; 45 LJCh 554; 34 LT 787;
      24 WR 778 .... 12.02, 12.12, 12.16

M

Macara (James) Ltd v Barclay [1944] 2 All ER 31; [1944] 3 All ER 589;
      114 LJKB 188; 172 LT 8; 61 TLR 78; [1945] KB l48 .... 13.14, 13.35
MacBryde v Weekes (1856) 22 Beav 533; 28 LTOS 135 .... 13.15, 13.17
Mackey v Jones (1959) 93 ILTR 177 .... 6.02
MacLean v Fitzsimon (1845) 3 Cr & Dix 381 .... 3.20
Macnamara v Carey (1867) IR 1 Eq 9; 9 ILT 24 .... 17.18-17.19, 18.35
Maconchy v Clayton [1898] 1 IR 291 .... 6.28, 6.31, 13.03, 13.57
.... 13.68, 14.10-14.11, 14.56, 15.50
Maddison v Alderson (1883) 8 App Cas 467; 52 LJQB 737; 49 LT 303;
      47 JP 821; 31 WR 820 .... 6.48, 6.53, 6.60
Madill v Blakely (1900) 34 ILTR 28 .... 9.26
Magee v Pennine Insurance Co Ltd [1969] 2 QB 507; [1969] 2 WLR 1278;
      [1969] 2 All ER 891; 113 Sol Jo 303 .... 21.37
Magennis v Fallon (1830) 2 Mol 590 .... 9.34

Maguire v Armstrong (1814) 2 Ba & B 538 ....21.05, 21.33
Maguire v Conway [1950] IR 44 ....6.02, 13.48
Mahon v Irish National Insurance Co Ltd [1958] Ir Jur Rep 41 ....3.15
Mahony v Davoren (1892) 30 LR Ir 664 ....9.26, 14.44
Main v Melbourne (1799) 4 Ves 720 ....6.59
Mainprice v Westley (1865) 6 B & S 420 ....2.20
Malcolm (Roger) Developments Ltd Contract, Re (1960) 176 Est Gaz 1237; (1961)
    25 Conv 260 ....13.17
Malhotra v Choudhury [1980] Ch 52; [1978] 3 WLR 825; [1979] 1 All ER 186;
    122 Sol Jo 681 ....13.78, 13.80, 13.84
Malone v Henshaw (1891) 29 LR Ir 352 ....12.22, 12.30
Malone v Malone (HC) unrep, 9 June 1982 ....13.77
Maloney v Elf Investments Ltd [1979] ILRM 253 ....13.27
Malzy v Eichholz [1916] 2 KB 308; 85 LJKB 1132; 115 LT 9; 60 Sol Jo 511;
    32 TLR 506 ....19.15, 21.30
Manchester Diocesan Council for Education v Commercial & General
    Investments Ltd [1970] 1 WLR 241; [1969] 3 All ER 1593; 114 Sol Jo 511;
    21 P & CR 38 ....13.42
Manchester Ship Canal Co v Manchester Shipping Co [1901] 2 Ch 37;
    70 LJCh 468; 84 LT 436; 49 WR 418; 17 TLR 410; 45 Sol Jo 394 ....8.04
Manifold v Johnston [1902] 1 IR 7; 1 NIJR 166 ....9.26, 9.33, 9.34, 10.05, 11.02
Manning, ex p (1727) 2 P Wms 410 ....12.35
Mansfield v Doolin (1869) IR 4 CL 17 ....11.24, 17.15
Manton v Mannion [1958] IR 324 ....12.18, 12.20, 20.09
Mappin Bros v Liberty & Co Ltd [1903] 1 Ch 118; 72 LJCh 63; 87 LT 523;
    47 Sol Jo 71; 19 TLR 51; 67 JP 91; 51 WR 264 ....18.59
March Properties Ltd v Commissioners of Public Works in Ireland
    (SC) unrep 11 November 1993 ....13.29
Marine Investment Co v Haviside (1872) LR 5 HL 624; 62 LJCh 173 ....14.51
Markey v Coote (1876) IR 10 CL 149 ....12.33-12.34
Marks v Board (1930) 46 TLR 424; 74 Sol Jo 354 ....7.19
Marks v Lilley [1959] 1 WLR 749; [1959] 2 All ER 647;
    103 Sol Jo 658 ....13.10, 13.42
Marsh & Earl Granville, Re (1882) 24 Ch D 11; 52 LJCh 189; 47 LT 471;
    31 WR 239; (1883) 24 Ch D 20; 53 LJCh 81; 48 LT 947;
    31 WR 845 ....14.56, 14.57, 18.28
Marsh v Collnett (1798) 2 Esp 665 ....14.50
Marsh v Jeff (1862) 3 F & F 234 ....2.29
Marsh v Joseph [1897] 1 Ch 213 ....20.15
Marshall v Green (1875) 1 CPD 35; 45 LJQB 153; 33 LT 404; 24 WR 175 .....6.09
Marshall v Parsons (1841) 9 C & P 656 ....2.32
Marshall v Taylor [1895] 1 Ch 641; 64 LJCh 416; 72 LT 670; 12 R 310 ....18.62
Martin v Cotter (1846) 9 Ir Eq R 351; 3 Jo & Lat 496 ....9.26-9.27, 9.32
    ....9.33-9.34, 10.05, 13.50, 15.17, 15.51
Martin v Irish Industrial Benefit Society [1960] Ir Jur Rep 42 ....4.23

Martin v Irish Permanent Building Society (HC) unrep, 30 July 1980 .... 13.26
.... 16.65, 16.68
Martin v Lysaght (1850) 2 Ir Jur (os) 184 .... 18.17
Maskell v Ivory [1970] Ch 502; [1970] 2 WLR 844; [1970 1 All ER 488;
   114 Sol Jo 189; 21 P & CR 360 .... 12.33
Mason v Armitage (1806) 13 Ves 25 .... 2.24
Mason v Clarke [1954] 1 QB 460; [1955] 2 WLR 853; [1955] 1 All ER 914;
   99 Sol Jo 274 .... 18.74
Massarella v Massarella (HC) unrep, 10 July 1980 .... 7.04, 8.04
Massereene (Viscount) v CIR [1900] 2 IR 138; 33 ILTR 114 .... 20.40
Massereene (Viscount) v Finlay (1850) 13 Ir LR 496 ....6.20-6.22, 6.28
Massey v Midland Bank plc [1995] 1 All ER 929 .... 1.35, 16.23, 16.69
Massy v O'Dell (1859) 9 Ir Ch R 441; 3 Ir Jur (ns) 360 .... 17.15, 18.99
Matthews v Baxter (1873) 28 LT 669; 21 WR 741 .... 6.38
Mauser v Back (1848) 6 Hare 443 .... 9.35
Mawson v Fletcher (1870) 6 Ch App 91; 40 LJCh 131; 23 LT 545;
   19 WR 141; 35 JP 391 .... 15.28
May v Belleville [1905] 2 Ch 605; 74 LJCh 678; 93 LT 241;
   49 Sol Jo 651 .... 15.11, 18.77
May v Platt [1900] 1 Ch 616; 69 LJCh 357; 83 LT 123; 48 WR 617 ... 21.11, 21.28
Mayer v Pluck (1971) 223 Est Gaz 33 .... 2.24
Mayfield v Wadsley (1824) B & C 357; 5 Dow & Ry KB 224;
   LJ (os) KB 31 .... 6.09
Mayson v Clonet [1924] AC 980; 93 LJPC 237; 131 LT 645; 40 TLR 678 .... 13.60
McAnarney v Hanrahan [1993] 3 IR 492; [1994] 1 ILRM 210
   .... 1.37, 2.08, 2.13, 3.14
   .... 5.24, 5.27, 5.28, 15.03, 15.37
McArdle v Irish Iodine Co (1864) 15 ICLR 146 .... 18.08, 18.13, 18.128
McArthur (J Albert) Co Ltd, Re [1959] Ir Jur Rep 59 .... 2.03-2.04
McC v McC [1982] ILRM 27 .... 14.27
McC v McC [1986] ILRM 1 .... 16.23
McCallum v Hicks [1950] 2 KB 371; [1950] 1 All ER 864; 66 TLR 747;
   94 Sol Jo 210 .... 3.25, 3.29
McCambridge v Winters (HC) unrep, 28 May 1984 .... 5.26, 13.27
McCann v Pow [1975] 1 All ER 129; [1975] 1 WLR 1643; 118 Sol Jo 717 ..... 3.12
McCann v Valentine (1901) 1 NIJR 28 .... 9.21, 9.27, 9.34, 13.27
McCarthy v McCarthy (HC) unrep, 1 May 1984; 30 ILT 216 .... 16.62
McCarthy v Voluntary Health Insurance Board (HC) unrep, 24 July 1984 .... 3.21
McCausland v Murphy (1881) 9 LR Ir 9 .... 6.09
McClenaghan v Bankhead (1874) IR 8 CL 195. .... 14.56
McClure & Garrett's Contract, Re [1899] 1 IR 225; 33 ILTR 49 .... 14.10-14.12
   .... 14.80, 15.25
McCormick v Duke [1907] 1 IR 339 .... 18.32
McCoubray v Thompson (1868) IR 2 CL 226 .... 13.44
McCrystal v O'Kane [1986] NI 123 .... 13.40, 13.43, 13.48

McCullagh v Lane Fox & Partners Ltd [1994] 08 EG 118; [1996] 18 EG 104 .. 1.37
.... 3.14, 5.27
McCullough v Ministry of Commerce (NI) [1960] NI 75 .... 6.12
McDermott & Kellett's Contract, Re (1904) 4 NIJR 89 .... 9.17, 9.33, 9.34
.... 13.28-13.29, 13.52, 13.81-13.84, 14.10, 14.16, 17.24
McDonnell & Branigan's Contract, Re (1922) 56 ILTR 143 .... 13.27
McDonnell v Kenneth (1850) 1 ICLR 113 .... 18.75
McDonnell v McGuinness [1939] IR 223; 73 ILTR 80 .... 5.26, 13.80-13.84
McDonnell v McKinty (1847) 10 Ir LR 514 .... 18.75
McDonnell v Stenson [1921] 1 IR 80; 56 ILTR 61 .... 12.11
McFarlene v McFarlene [1972] NI 59 .... 16.23
McGeary v Campbell [1975] NI 7 .... 4.12, 4.13, 4.15, 11.15
McGillycuddy v Joy [1959] IR 189 .... 6.02, 6.09, 6.17
McGirr v Devine [1925] NI 94 .... 12.50, 14.14
McGowan v Harrison [1941] IR 331; 75 ILTR 163 .... 4.11, 4.12, 4.15, 8.04
McGrory v Alderdale Estate Co Ltd [1918] AC 503; 87 LJCh 435; 119 LT 1;
    62 Sol Jo 518 .... 14.08
McGuill v Aer Lingus Teo (HC) unrep, 3 October 1983 .... 12.37
McGuire v Conwell (1932) 66 ILTR 213 .... 10.18, 13.04, 13.57-13.60
McIlvenny v McKeever [1931] NI 161 .... 21.03
McInerney Properties v Roper [1979] ILRM 119 .... 7.08
McKay v McNally (1878) 4 LR Ir 438; 13 ILTR 130 .... 14.52
McKee v McMahon (1935) 69 ILTR 180 .... 11.16, 11.24
McKenna v Herlihy (1920) 7 TC 620 .... 6.09
McKillop v McMullen [1979] NI 85 .... 7.04, 7.16
McKinty v Belfast Corporation [1973] NI 1 .... 6.12
McLean (In b) [1950] IR 180; 86 ILTR 86 .... 17.25
McLean v McErlean [1983] NI 258 .... 12.50
McLoughlin & McGrath's Contract, Re (1914) 48 ILTR 87 .... 14.10
McLoughlin v Alexander (1910) 44 ILTR 253 .... 6.32, 13.40, 13.45
McMahon v Gaffney [1930] IR 576; 64 ILTR 87 .... 2.28, 2.34, 3.32, 9.38, 13.62
.... 13.81-13.85, 15.30-15.35
McMahon v McIlroy (1869) IR 5 Eq 1 .... 1.34
McManus v Cooke (1887) 35 Ch D 681; 56 LJCh 662; 56 LT 900; 51 JP 708;
    35 WR 754; 3 TLR 622 .... 6.51
McManus v Fortescue [1907] 2 KB 1; 76 LJKB 393; 96 LT 444; 23 TLR 292;
    51 Sol Jo 245 .... 2.19-2.21
McManus v Kiernan [1939] IR 297 .... 9.13, 12.50-12.51, 14.36
McMeekin v Stevenson [1917] 1 IR 348; [1992] ILRM 776.... 2.09, 6.16, 6.31, 6.38
McMullen v Farrell [1993] 1 IR 123 .... 1.36, 4.02, 5.28, 14.73, 15.02
McNally v Donnelly (1894) 28 ILTR 85 .... 19.27
McNeill v Crommelin (1858) 8 ICLR 61; 3 Ir Jur (ns) 279 .... 17.16
McNulty v Hanratty (1918) 52 ILTR 43 .... 2.07, 2.29, 2.34, 3.32, 13.82
McParland v Conlon [1930] NI 138 .... 12.50-12.51
McPherson v Watt (1877) 3 App Cas 254 .... 9.35

McQuaid v Lynam [1965] IR 564 ....6.14, 6.15-6.16, 6.26-6.29
....6.31-6.33, 13.81-13.82, 13.86
McQuillan v Maguire [1996] 1 ILRM 394 .... 14.67
McQuirk v Branigan (HC) unrep, 9 November 1992 .... 16.69
McSweeney v Bourke (HC) unrep, 14 November 1980 .... 5.27
McVicker's Contract, Re (1890) 25 LR Ir 307 .... 9.26, 9.33, 9.34
Meacock (John) & Co v Abrahams [1956] 3 All ER 660 .... 2.30-2.32
Meadows v Tanner (1820) 5 Madd 34 .... 2.14
Meagher v Mount [1984] ILRM 671 .... 12.19
Meara v Meara (1858) 8 Ir Ch R 37 .... 13.49
Meara v Rogers (1858) 3 Ir Jur (ns) 108 .... 1.34
Meath v Winchester (1836) 4 Cl & Fin 445; 3 Bing NC 183; 10 Bli (ns) 330;
    3 Scott 568; 132 ER 380 .... 14.50
Meehan v Jones (1982) 56 ALJR 813 .... 7.15
Melzak v Lillienfield [1926] Ch 480; 95 LJCh 305; 135 LT 145;
    70 Sol Jo 487; 42 TLR 364 .... 9.25, 9.39
Mendoza & Co v Bell (1952) 159 Est Gaz 372 .... 3.13
MEPC Ltd v Christian-Edwards [1981] AC 205; [1973] 3 WLR 713;
    [1979] 3 All ER 752; 123 Sol Jo 786 .... 14.10
Mersey Steel & Iron Co v Naylor Benzon & Co (1882) 9 QBD 648 .... 13.07, 13.57
Mespil Ltd v Capaldi [1986] ILRM 373 .... 6.02
Mesure v Britten (1796) 2 Hy Bl 717 .... 10.65
Metropolitan Properties v O'Brien [1995] 1 IR 467;
    [1995] 2 ILRM 383 .... 1.18, 8.08, 19.13
Meyler v Meyler (1883) 11 LR Ir 522 .... 17.17
Midgley Estates Ltd v Hand [1952] 2 QB 432; [1952] 1 All ER 1394;
    [1952] 1 TLR 1454; 96 Sol Jo 375 .... 3.28
Midland Bank plc v Cameron, Tong, Peterkin & Duncans 1988 SLT 611
    .... 5.28, 15.37
Midland Bank plc v Cooke [1995] 4 All ER 562 .... 16.23
Midland Bank Trust Co Ltd v Hett, Stubbs & Kemp [1979] Ch 384;
    [1978] 3 WLR 167; [1978] 3 All ER 571; 121 Sol Jo 830 .... 6.64
Midland Business Agency v Apted (1971) 218 Est Gaz 1727 .... 3.13
Miley v Carty [1927] IR 541 .... 12.11
Millard v Harvey (1864) 34 Beav 237; 11 LT 360; 10 Jur (ns) 1167;
    13 WR 125 .... 6.37
Miller v Cannon Hill Estates Ltd [1931] 2 KB 213; 100 LJKB 740; 144 LT 567; 75
    Sol Jo 155 .... 4.11
Miller v Wheatley (1891) 28 LR Ir 144 .... 14.52-14.52
Miller & Aldworth v Sharp [1899] 1 Ch 622; 68 LJCh 322; 80 LT 77;
    47 WR 268; 43 Sol Jo 245 .... 6.57
Miller & Pickergill's Contract, Re [1931] 1 Ch 511; 100 LJCh 257;
    144 LT 635 .... 14.56
Millichamp v Jones [1983] 1 All ER 267; [1982] 1 WLR 1422; 126 Sol Jo 726
    .... 10.19-10.22, 13.31

Mills v Healy [1937] IR 437 ....13.04, 13.08, 13.16-13.17, 13.25
....13.57, 13.62, 13.68
Milner & Organ's Contract, Re (1920) 89 LJ Ch 31; 123 LT 168;
    64 Sol Jo 468 ....15.31
Ministery of Housing & Local Government v Sharp [1970] 2 QB 223;
    [1970] 2 WLR 802; [1970] 1 All ER 1009; 134 JP 358; 114 Sol Jo 109;
    68 LGR 187; 21 P & CR 166 ....5.27
Miscampbell v McAlister [1930] NI 74 ....18.70
Mitchell & McElhinney's Contract, Re [1902] 1 IR 83; 2 NIJR 171;
    36 ILTR 53 ....2.53, 9.17, 9.37-9.38, 10.05, 13.27, 14.10, 14.13
Mohan v Roche [1991] 1 IR 560 ....13.27, 14.56, 14.66, 14.81, 16.54
Molesworth v McCreith (1845) 8 Ir Eq R 1 ....20.50
Moloney v Elf Investments Ltd [1979] ILRM 253 ....7.04, 7.16, 7.18
Molphy v Coyne (1919) 53 ILTR 177 ....9.25-9.26, 9.32-9.34, 9.38, 9.43-9.44
....13.29, 13.40, 13.52-13.53, 14.17, 15.31
Molyneux v Hewtry [1903] 2 KB 487; 89 LT 350; 72 LJKB 873;
    52 WR 23 ....9.25
Monaghan CC v Vaughan [1948] IR 306 ....13.48, 13.64
Monnickendam v Leanse (1923) 39 TLR 445; 67 Sol Jo 706 ....6.07
Monro v Taylor (1848) 8 Hare 51; (1852) 3 Mac & G 713; 21 LJCh 525;
    19 LT (os) 97; 42 ER 434 ....12.14
Montgomery & Rennie v Continental Bags (NZ) Ltd [1972] NZLR 884 ....21.02
Montgomery v Fleming (1905) 39 ILTR 229 ....2.28, 2.34, 3.32
Moody & Yates' Contract, Re (1885) 30 Ch D 344; 54 LJCh 886; 53 LT 845;
    33 WR 785 ....14.48
Moody v Cox [1917] 2 Ch 71 ....1.34
Mooney v McMahon [1911] I IR 125; 45 ILTR 41 ....12.05, 12.50
Moore v Blake (1808) 1 Ba & B 62 ....13.50
Moore v Crofton (1946) 9 Ir Eq R 344; 3 Jo & Lat 438 ....13.40, 13.48
Moore v Merrion Pier & Baths Co (1901) 1 NIJR 184 ....6.10
Moorehead's Estate, Re (1861) 12 Ir Ch R 371 ....9.34
Moorhead v Kirkwood [1919] 1 IR 225 ....8.13, 13.56
Moorhead's Estate, Re (1861) 12 Ir Ch R 371 ....13.64
Moran v Dublin Corporation (1975) 109 ILTR 57 ....8.16
Morgan v Griffith (1871) LR 6 Exch 70; 70 LJ Ex 46; 23 LT 783;
    19 WR 957 ....6.13
Morgan v Milman (1853) 3 De GM & G 24; 22 LJCh 897; 1 WR 134;
    17 Jur 193 ....6.24
Morgan v Park Developments Ltd [1983] ILRM 156 ....4.17
Morgan v Russell & Sons [1909] 1 KB 357; 78 LJKB 187; 100 LT 118;
    25 TLR 120; 53 Sol Jo 136 ....6.10
Moroney, Re (1887) 21 LR Ir 27 ....16.24
Morris v Allan (1957) 91 ILTR 52 ....20.49
Morris v Duke-Cohan & Co (1975) 119 Sol Jo 826 ....10.19
Morris v Redmond (1936) 70 ILTR 8 ....4.12, 11.15

Morris, Re (1940) 74 ILTR 235 .... 16.30
Morrissey (Daniel) & Sons Ltd v Nalty [1976-7] ILRM 269 .. 2.07, 2.19, 2.28, 2.32
.... 3.07, 3.13, 3.21, 3.24, 6.38
Morrow v Carty [1957] NI 174 .... 2.10, 10.18, 10.21, 10.24
.... 13.30-13.31, 14.45, 20.31
Mortal v Lyons (1858) 8 Ir Ch R 112 .... 3.08, 6.41, 6.56
Mortgage Express Ltd v Bowerman & Partners [1996] 04 EG 126;
    [1996] 2 All ER 836 .... 15.05
Mortimer v Bell (1865) 1 Ch App 10; 35 LJCh 25; 13 LT 348; 29 JP 803;
    11 Jur (ns) 897; 14 WR 68 .... 2.14
Moulton v Edmonds (1859) 1 De GF & J 246; 29 LJCh 181; 1 LT 391;
    6 Jur (ns) 305; 8 WR 153 .... 14.51
Mountain (Alexander) & Co v Rumere [1948] 2 KB 436; [1948] 2 All ER 482;
    92 Sol Jo 540; 64 TLR 493 .... 18.19
Mountford v Scott [1975] 1 All ER 198; [1975] 2 WLR 114; 118 Sol Jo 755 .. 8.03
Mowall v Castle Steel & Iron Works Co (1886) 34 Ch D 58; 55 LT 645 ...... 18.128
Moxhay v Inderwick (1847) 1 De G & Sm 708 .... 18.99
Mulhall v Haren [1981] IR 364 .... 6.15, 6.32, 6.62, 7.08
Mulholland v Corporation of Belfast (1859) Dru temp Nap 539;
    9 Ir Ch R 292 .... 14.17, 14.71
Mullens v Miller (1882) 22 Ch D 194; 52 LJCh 380; 48 LT 103; 31 WR 559 .. 3.12
Mulligan v Dillon (HC) unrep, 7 November 1980 .... 13.26-13.27, 16.68
Mumford v Bank of Scotland, The Times 1 July 1994 .... 1.35
Munro v Taylor (1850) 8 Hare 51 .... 12.21
Munro v Taylor (1852) 3 M & G 713 .... 9.14
Munster & Leinster Bank Ltd v McGlashan [1937] IR 525; 71 ILTR 123
    .... 12.15-12.17, 12.44, 18.32, 18.40
Munster & Leinster Bank v Munster Motor Co [1922] 1 IR 15 .... 2.25, 11.06
Murdoch Lownie Ltd v Newman [1949] 2 All ER 783; 65 TLR 717;
    93 Sol Jo 711 .... 3.25-3.26
Murnaghan Bros v O'Maoldomhnaigh [1991] 1 IR 455 .... 12.02
Murphy, Re [1957] NI 156 .... 8.04
Murphy, Re [1977] IR 243 .... 8.22
Murphy & Griffin's Contract, Re [1919] 1 IR 187; 53 ILTR 100 .... 13.27
.... 14.10-14.10
Murphy v A-G [1982] IR 241 .... 13.50
Murphy v Brentwood District Council [1991] AC 398; [1990] 3 WLR 414;
    [1990] 2 All ER 908; 22 HLR 502; 134 Sol Jo 1076; 89 LGR 24 .... 4.15
Murphy v Corporation of Dublin [1972] IR 215 .... 8.16
Murphy v Forde (1943) 77 ILTR 130 .... 16.31
Murphy v Harrington [1927] IR 339 .... 2.37, 6.15-6.16, 6.21
.... 6.34, 13.04, 13.47, 13.50, 13.54
Murphy v Harte (1912) 46 ILTR 197. .... 2.34
Murphy v Quality Homes (HC) unrep, 22 June 1976 .... 4.13, 13.54, 13.77
Murphy & McCormack, Re [1939] 1 IR 322 .... 12.04, 12.50-12.52

Murphy (Daniel) Ltd, Re [1964] IR 1 .... 6.02
Murphy d Wray v Morrisson (1831) 2 Hud & Br 406 .... 18.32
Murphy, Buckley & Keogh Ltd v Pye (Ir) Ltd [1971] IR 57 .... 2.30, 3.05, 3.19
Murray v Diamond [1982] ILRM 113 .... 16.62
Murray v Mace (1872) IR 8 CL 396 .... 4.08, 4.12
Murray v Murray (HC) unrep, 15 December 1995 .... 16.23
Murray v Palmer (1805) 2 Sch & Lef 474 .... 21.35
Murray v Two Strokes Ltd [1973] 1 WLR 823; [1973] 3 All ER 357;
    117 Sol Jo 447; 26 P & CR 1 .... 8.04
Murray & Hegarty's Contract, Re (1885) 15 LR Ir 510 .... 15.42
Musgrave v McAvey (1907) 41 ILTR 230 .... 12.33
Musgrave v McCullagh (1864) 14 Ir Ch R 496 .... 9.38, 15.04, 15.25
Mutual Life & Citizens Assurance Co Ltd v Evatt [1971] AC 793;
    [1971] 2 WLR 93; [1971] 1 All ER 150; 114 Sol Jo 932;
    [1970] 2 Lloyd's Rep 441 .... 5.27
Myers v Burke (1892) 26 ILT 306 .... 18.53
Mynn v Joliffe (1834) 1 Moo & R 326 .... 2.10
Myton Ltd v Schwab Morris [1974] 1 WLR 331; [1974] 1 All ER 326;
    118 Sol Jo 117; 228 Est Gaz 333 .... 10.18, 10.22

N

Nagle v Baylor (1842) 3 Dr &War 60 .... 13.48
Nagle v Shea (1875) IR 9 CL 389 .... 18.31
Nally v Nally [1953] IR 19 .... 20.44
Napier v Williams [1911] 1 Ch 361; 80 LJCh 298; 104 LT 380;
    55 Sol Jo 235 .... 18.96
Napper v Lord Allington (1700) 1 Eq Cas Arb 166 .... 21.33
National Bank Ltd v O'Connor (1969) 103 ILTR 73 .... 13.48, 13.67
National Bank v Beirne (1901) 35 ILTR 9 .... 9.16, 9.33-9.34, 11.04
National Carriers Ltd v Panalpina (Northern) Ltd [1981] AC 675;
    [1981] 2 WLR 45; [1981] 1 All ER 161; 125 Sol Jo 46 .... 12.37
National Irish Bank Ltd v Graham [1994] 2 ILRM 109 .... 16.62
National Provincial Bank of England & Marsh [1895] 1 Ch 90; 71 LT 629;
    39 Sol Jo 43; 43 WR 186 .... 13.35, 14.59
National Provincial Bank v Jackson (1886) 33 Ch D 1; 55 LT 458;
    34 WR 597 .... 18.122, 18.133
National Provincial Building Society v Ahmed [1995] 38 EG 138 .... 15.19
National Westminster Bank plc v Morgan [1985] 1 AC 686;
    [1985] 2 WLR 588; [1985] 1 All ER 821; 129 Sol Jo 205 .... 1.35
Neighbourhood Public House Ltd v McInerney & Co Ltd (HC) unrep,
    21 June 1983 .... 10.67
Neilson v Poole (1969) 20 P & CR 909 .... 18.67-18.68
Nelson & Co v Rolfe [1950] 1 KB 139; [1949] 2 All ER 584; 65 TLR 494;
    93 Sol Jo 576 .... 3.29
Nelthorpe v Holgate (1844) 1 Coll 203; 8 Jur 551; 63 ER 384 .... 9.23

Nestor v Galway Corporation (HC) unrep, 17 April 1983 .... 8.19
Nestor v Murphy [1979] IR 326 .... 16.62
Neville & Sons Ltd v Guardian Builders Ltd [1990] ILRM 601;
    [1995] 1 ILRM 1 .... 12.37, 16.53
Neville v Slattery Estates Co Ltd (HC) unrep, 15 February 1984 .... 7.04, 12.14
New Forest Estate Co Ltd v Revenue Commissioners [1965] IR 172;
    99 ILTR 78 .... 16.39, 20.38
New Hart Builders v Brindley [1975] 1 All ER 1007; [1975] Ch 342; [1975] 2 WLR
    595; 119 Sol Jo 256; 29 P & CR 476 .... 6.33
Newbigging v Adam (1886) 34 Ch D 582; 56 LJCh 275; 55 LT 794;
    3 TLR 259; 35 WR 597; (1888) 13 App Cas 308 .... 13.61
Newman v Maxwell (1899) 80 LT 681 .... 12.22
Nicholl v Chambers (1852) 11 CB 996; 21 LJCP 54; 18 LT (os) 243;
    138 ER 770 .... 9.11
Nichols & Van Joel's Contract, Re [1910] 1 Ch 43 .... 13.28, 13.49, 13.52, 14.15
Nisbet & Port's Contract, Re [1906] 1 Ch 386; 75 LJCh 238; 94 LT 297;
    50 Sol Jo 191; 22 TLR 233; 54 WR 286 .... 14.58, 14.60, 14.71
Nives v Nives (1880) 15 Ch D 649; 49 LJCh 674; 42 LT 832; 29 WR 302 .... 12.16
Nixon v Albion Marine Insurance (1867) LR 2 Exch 338; 36 LJ Ex 180;
    16 LT 568; 15 WR 964 .... 10.09
Noble v Edwardes (1877) 5 Ch D 378; 37 LT 7 .... 13.78
Nolan v Feely (1899) 33 ILTR 132 .... 13.81-13.82
Nolan v Nolan (1958) 92 ILTR 94 .... 13.64
Nolan, Re [1963] IR 341; 98 ILTR 178 .... 2.03, 3.15, 14.30
Norfolk (Duke of) v Worthy (1808) 1 Camp 337. .... 2.26
Norris v Cooke (1857) 7 ICLR 37; 2 Ir Jur (ns) 443 .... 6.34, 6.37
Norta Wallpapers (Ir) Ltd v John Sisk & Son Ltd [1987] IR 114 .... 4.13, 11.22
North v Drinan [1931] IR 468 .... 2.31, 3.22, 3.31
North v Loomes [1919] 1 Ch 378; 88 LJCh 217; 120 LT 533 .... 6.07, 6.42, 6.45
Northern Bank Finance Corporation Ltd v Charlton [1979] IR 149 .... 13.04
    .... 13.57-13.58
Northern Bank Ltd v Duffy [1981] ILRM 308 .... 12.18-12.19, 20.09
Northern Bank Ltd v Henry [1981] IR 1 .... 4.02, 14.27, 15.01, 16.23
Northern Banking Co v Devlin [1924] 1 IR 90; 58 ILTR 118 .... 12.52
Norwich & Peterborough BS v Steed (No 2) [1993] 1 All ER 331;
    [1992] 3 WLR 669 .... 21.38
Norwich Union Life Insurance Society v Preston [1957] 1 WLR 813;
    [1975] 2 All ER 418; 101 So Jo 534; 169 Est Gaz 587 .... 10.44
Nottingham Patent Brick & Tile Co v Butler (1886) 16 QBD 778;
    55 LJQB 280; 54 LT 444; 2 TLR 391; 34 WR 405 .... 14.15, 14.59, 15.24
NW Investments (Erdington) Ltd v Swani (1970) 214 Est Gaz 1115 .... 7.18
Ny Molle Kro [1987] ECR 5465 .... 5.15

O

O'Brien v Bord na Mona [1983] IR 255; [1983] ILRM 3146 .... 8.16
O'Brien v Ireland [1991] 2 IR 387; [1990] ILRM 46 .... 16.23, 16.101

O'Brien v Kearney [1995] 2 ILRM 232 .... 9.22, 9.26, 9.32, 9.34
.... 9.46, 13.20, 13.29, 13.40, 13.53, 16.101
O'Brien v Murray (1864) 17 ICLR 46 .... 15.46
O'Brien v Seaview Enterprises Ltd (HC) unrep, 31 May 1976 .... 13.14
O'Brien v White-Spunner [1979] ILRM 240 .... 12.14
O'Connor v Faul (1957) 91 ILTR 7 .... 2.10, 2.32, 3.31, 10.24
O'Connor v First National Building Society [1991] ILRM 208 ......1.37, 3.41, 4.22-
    4.24, ...5.10
O'Connor v Foley [1906] 1 IR 20 .... 21.06
O'Connor v Harvey (1910) 44 ILTR 242 .... 20.07
O'Connor v McCarthy [1982] IR 161; [1982] ILRM 201 .... 6.03-6.04
.... 6.65, 12.29, 13.54
O'Donnell v Ryan (1854) 4 ICLR 44; 6 Ir Jur (os) 327 .... 14.56, 17.15, 17.19
O'Donoghue & Co Ltd v Collins (HC) unrep, 10 March 1972 .... 4.11, 4.13
.... 5.26, 11.23
O'Fay v Burke (1858) 8 Ir Ch R 511 .... 6.50
O'Flaherty v Arvan Properties Ltd (SC) unrep, 21 July 1977 .... 6.26, 7.12
O'Flanagan & Ryan's Contract, Re [1905] 1 IR 280; 39 ILTR 87 ....9.34-9.38
.... 14.06, 14.17
O'Hanlon v Belfast Inns Ltd [1962-63] Ir Jur Rep 25 ....3.20-3.22
O'Hara v Flint [1979] ILRM 156 .... 13.40
O'Leary v Buckley (1922) 56 ILTR 14 .... 16.30
O'Loghlan v O'Callaghan (1874) IR 8 CL 116 .... 16.33
O'Mahony v Gaffney [1986] IR 36 .... 6.09
O'Mullane v Riordan [1978] ILRM 73 .... 7.04, 7.16, 13.08
O'Neill, Re [1967] NI 129 .... 11.03, 12.27
O'Neill, Re [1989] IR 544 .... 12.47, 14.67, 16.24
O'Neill (Hugh) & Co Ltd v Roche (HC) unrep, 19 January 1972 ....4.13, 11.14
O'Neill v Ryan (No 3) [1992] 1 IR 166; [1991] ILRM 672 .... 13.38, 13.43
.... 13.49, 13.67
O'Neill v Ryan [1944] Ir Jur Rep 9 .... 9.34
O'Regan v White [1919] 2 IR 339 .... 13.47
O'Reilly v Fineman [1942] Ir Jur Rep 36 .... 9.15
O'Reilly v Gleeson [1975] IR 258 .... 9.10, 9.12
O'Rourke v Copeland (1892) 26 ILTR 126 .... 15.45
O'Rourke v Percival (1811) 2 Ba & B 58 .... 13.43
O'Shea v Lister House Development Ltd [1971] Ch 17 .... 18.128
O'Sullivan v Weekes (1903) 4 NIJR 153 .... 17.18
O'Toole v Palmer [1943] Ir Jur Rep 59 ....3.19, 3.24-3.25
Oak Co-Operative BS v Blackburn [1968] Ch 730; [1968] 2 WLR 1053;
    [1968] 2 All ER 117; 112 Sol Jo 172 .... 18.19
Oakden v Pike (1865) 34 LJ Ch 620; 12 LT 527; 13 WR 673; 11 Jur (ns) 666
.... 14.42, 15.37
Ockenden v Henly (1858) 1 B & E 485 .... 13.78
Ogilvie v Foljambe (1817) 3 Mer 53 ....6.23, 6.33, 14.08

Oliver v Hinton [1899] 2 Ch 264; 68 LJCh 583; 81 LT 212; 43 Sol Jo 622;
    15 TLR 450; 48 WR 3 .... 14.71
Oliver v Hunting (1890) 44 Ch D 205 .... 6.30
Oliver v Rooney [1895] 2 IR 660; 30 ILTR 105 .... 14.56
Ormond (Lord) v Anderson (1813) 2 Ba & B 363 .... 13.45-13.47
Otto v Bolton [1936] 2 KB 46; [1936 1 All ER 960; 105 LJKB 602;
    154 LT 717; 52 TLR 438; 80 Sol Jo 896 .... 4.15
Otway's Estate, Re (1862) 13 Ir Ch R 222 .... 13.58, 13.76, 21.02

P

Page v Midland Rly [1894] 1 Ch 11; 68 LJCh 126; 70 LT 14; 38 Sol Jo 41;
    42 WR 116 .... 21.12
Pagebar Properties Ltd v Derby Investments Ltd [1972] 1 WLR 1500;
    [1973] 1 All ER 65; 116 Sol Jo 844; 24 P & CR 316 .... 9.40, 13.20
Paine v Meller (1801) 6 Ves 349; 31 ER 1088 .... 12.38, 20.06
Palmer v Coates (1905) 39 ILTR 221 .... 9.34
Palmer v Greene (1856) 25 LJ Ch 841 .... 12.22
Palmer v Johnson (1884) 13 QBD 351; 53 LJQB 348; 51 LT 211; 33 WR 36 21.03
Palmer v Lark [1945] Ch 182; [1945] 1 All ER 355; 144 LJ 222; 172 LT 367;
    89 Sol Jo 188; 61 TLR 276 .... 20.25, 20.29
Pape v Westacott [1894] 1 QB 272; 63 LJQB 220; 70 LT 18; 42 WR 130;
    10 TLR 51; 38 Sol Jo 39 .... 2.10, 10.24, 20.31
Parfitt v Jepson (1877) 46 LJQB 529; 36 LT 251; 41 JP 600 .... 2.18
Park Hall School Ltd v Overend [1987] IR 1; [1987] ILRM 345 ... 1.36, 6.15, 15.05
Parker v Clark [1960] 1 WLR 286; [1960] 1 All ER 93; 104 Sol Jo 251 .... 6.14
Parker v Judkin [1931] 1 Ch 475; 100 LJCh 159; 144 LT 662 .... 18.82, 21.08
Parker v Staniland (1809) 11 East 362 .... 6.09
Parkes v Irish National Insurance Co Ltd [1962] IR 50 .... 2.03
Parkes v Parkes [1980] ILRM 137 .... 16.39, 16.52, 17.19
Parkgrange Investments Ltd Shandon Park Mills Ltd (HC) unrep, 2 May 1991
    .... 6.35
Parkin v Thorold (1852) 16 Beav 59 .... 13.14
Parkinson, Re [1898] 1 IR 390 .... 8.14
Parnell, Re (1875) 10 Ch App 512; 44 LJ Bey 138; 33 LT 115; 23 WR 846 .. 12.47
Parr v Lovegrove (1858) 4 Drew 170; 31 LT (os) 364; 4 Jur (ns) 600;
    6 WR 201 .... 14.06, 14.56
Parvis v Rayer (1821) 9 Price 488 .... 14.08
Patel v Ali [1984] Ch 283; [1984] 2 WLR 960; [1984] 1 All ER 978;
    128 Sol Jo 204 .... 13.49
Patent Ivory Manufacturing Co, Re (1888) 38 Ch D 156; 57 LJCh 878;
    58 LT 395; 36 WR 801 .... 6.51
Patman v Harland (1881) 17 Ch D 353; 50 LJCh 642; 44 LT 728;
    29 WR 707 .... 14.60, 14.71-14.73
Patrick v Milner (1877) 2 CPD 342; 46 LJQB 537; 36 LT 738; 41 JP 568;
    25 WR 790 .... 13.14

Payne v Cave (1789) 3 Term Rep 148 ....2.20
Peacock v Freeman (1888) 4 TLR 541 ....2.28
Pearce v Gardner [1897] 1 QB 688; 66 LJQB 457; 76 LT 441; 45 WR 518 ......6.31
Peilow v O'Carroll (1972) 106 ILTR 29 ....2.38, 5.26, 6.31, 9.07
....9.16-9.18, 9.29, 9.37, 9.44
....13.03, 13.34-13.34, 18.71
Pengall (Lord) v Ross (1709) 2 Eq Cas Abr 46 ....6.59
Penn v Bristol & West Building Society London Times, 19 June 1995 ....1.35
Pennett & Partners v Millett [1949] 1 KB 362 ....3.29
Penny v Watts (1849) 1 Mac & G 150; 2 De G & Sim 523; H & Tw 266;
    19 LJCh 212; 14 LT (os) 82; 13 Jur 459 ....9.23
Pentland v Stokes (1812) 2 Ba & B 68 ....13.45
Perks v Stern (1972) 222 Est Gaz 1441 ....4.13
Perrin v Roe (1889) 25 LR Ir 37 ....5.26, 9.26, 9.34
Perry v Woodfarm Homes Ltd [1975] IR 104 ....14.12, 14.81
Perryman's Case (1599) 5 Co Rep 84a 18.127
Peyton v McDermott (1838) 1 Dr & Wal 198 ....14.52
Phelan v Tedcastle (1885) 15 LR Ir 169 ....6.26
Phelps v White (1881) 7 LR Ir 160 ....5.26, 14.42
Phillips v Caldcleugh (1886) IR 4 QB 159; 9 B & S 967; 38 LJQB 68;
    20 LT 80; 17 WR 575 ....13.58, 13.68
Phillips v Homfray (1871) 6 Ch App 770 ....9.35
Phillips v Lambin [1949] 2 KB 33; [1949] 1 All ER 770; [1949] LJR 1293;
    93 Sol Jo 320 ....12.21, 13.17
Phillips v Miller (1875) LR 10 CP 420; 44 LJCP 265; 32 LT 638; 23 WR 834 .9.23
Phillips v Silvester (1872) LR 8 Ch 173; 42 LJCh 225; 27 LT 840; 21 WR 176 ......
    12.13, ...12.21
Phipps & Co Ltd v Rogers [1925] 1 KB 14 ....17.17
Pierce v Corf (1874) LR 9 QB 210 ....6.29
Piers v Piers (1847) 11 Ir Eq R 358 ....12.34
Pilkington v Wood [1953] Ch 770; [1953] 3 WLR 522; [1953] 2 All ER 810;
    97 Sol Jo 572 ....21.08
Pim v Coyle [1903] 2 IR 457 ....12.50
Pim v Coyle [1907] 1 IR 330; 41 ILTR 109 ....12.05
Pips (Leisure Production) Ltd v Walton (1980) 43 P & CR 415; 260 EG 601 ..13.68
Pirelli General Cable Works Ltd v Oscar Faber & Partners
    [1983] 2 AC 1 ....4.15, 4.17
Pitt v PHH Asset Management Ltd [1993] 4 All ER 961 ....6.04, 8.04
Plews v Samuel [1904] 1 Ch 464; 73 LJCh 279; 90 LT 533; 52 WR 410;
    48 Sol Jo 276 ....12.14, 20.06
Poole v Clarke & Co [1945] 2 All ER 445 ....3.25
Poole v Coates (1842) 2 Dr & War 493; 4 Ir Eq 497; 1 Con & L 531 ....13.52
Poole v Griffith (1865) 15 ICLR 239 ....18.71
Poole v Hill (1840) 6 M & W 835; 9 Dowl 300; 10 LJ Ex 81 ....17.04
Poole & Clarke's Contract, Re [1904] 2 Ch 173; 73 LJCh 612; 91 LT 275;
    53 WR 122; 20 TLR 604; 48 Sol Jo 588 ....18.99

Pooley, Re (1878) 8 Ch D 367; 48 LJ Bey 15; 38 LT 663; 27 WR 646 .... 12.27
Popham v Exham (1860) 10 Ir Ch R 440 .... 2.14, 11.03-11.04
Postmaster-General & Colgan's Contract, Re [1906] 1 IR 287;
    40 ILTR 112 .... 10.44, 12.18, 20.09
Potter v Duffield (1874) LR 18 Eq 4; 43 LJCh 472; 22 WR 585 .... 6.20
Potters v Loppert [1973] 1 All ER 658; [1973 Ch 399; [1973] 2 WLR 469;
    115 Sol Jo 862; 224 Est Gaz 1717 .... 2.10, 2.26, 2.45, 10.26
Potts v Nixon (1870) IR 5 CL 45 .... 18.44
Powell v Dillon (1814) 2 Ba & B 416 .... 6.14, 6.28
Powell v Hemsley [1909] 1 Ch 680; 78 LJCh 741; 101 LT 262;
    25 TLR 649 .... 18.98
Powell v Jessop (1856) 18 CB 336; 25 LJCP 199; 4 WR 465 .... 6.10
Powell v London & Provincial Bank [1893] 2 Ch 555 .... 18.124, 18.129
Powell v Marshall, Parkes & Co [1899] 1 QB 710; 68 LJQB 477; 80 LT 509;
    42 WR 419; 15 TLR 289; 43 Sol Jo 382 .... 12.28
Power v Barrett (1887) 19 LR Ir 450; 21 ILTR 221 .... 5.23, 9.25-9.26, 9.31, 9.40
Power v Coates (1905) 39 ILTR 221 .... 9.17
Powers v Fowler (1855) 4 E & B 511; 3 WR 166 .... 6.14
Pratt v Barker (1828) 1 Sim 1 .... 18.42
Prebble & Co v West (1969) 211 Est Gaz 831 .... 3.13
Price v Strange [1978] Ch 337; [1977] 3 WLR 943; [1977] 3 All ER 371;
    121 Sol Jo 816... 13.47, 13.68
Priestley & Davidson's Contract, Re (1892) 31 LR Ir 122 .... 13.27-13.29, 13.82,
    14.19, ... 14.42, 15.35
Priestley's Contract, Re [1947] Ch 469; [1947] 1 All ER 716; [1947] LJR 974;
    176 LT 418; 91 Sol Jo 325 .... 10.06
Prior v Moore (1887) 3 TLR 624 .... 3.08
Pritchard v Briggs [1980] Ch 338; [1979] 3 WLR 868; [1980] 1 All ER 294;
    123 Sol Jo 705... 8.04
Proctor v Pugh [1921] 2 Ch 256; 91 LJCh 1; 127 LT 126 .... 13.68, 15.33
Property & Bloodstock Ltd v Emerton [1968] Ch 94; [1947] 3 WLR 973;
    [1967] 3 All ER 321; 111 Sol Jo 414 .... 7.16, 7.22, 10.02
Provincial Bank of Ireland Ltd v Farris [1944] IR 150 .... 2.25, 11.06
Provincial Bank of Ireland Ltd v Goulding [1942] IR 108 .... 2.27-2.28
    .... 2.33-2.34, 11.04
Provincial Bank of Ireland v McKeever [1941] IR 471 .... 13.64
Pryde & Metson's Contract, Re (1968) 19 NILQ 214 .... 9.33, 14.07
Public Trustee v Pearlberg [1940] 2 KB 1 .... 15.29
Puckett & Smith's Contract, Re [1902] 2 Ch 258; 71 LJCh 666; 87 LT 189;
    50 WR 532 .... 9.43
Pulbrook v Lawes (1876) 1 QBD 284; 45 LJQB 178; 34 LT 95; 40 JP 452 ...... 6.07
Pursell & Deakin's Contract, Re [1893] WN 152; 37 Sol Jo 840 .... 18.103

Q

Quadrangle Development & Construction Co Ltd v Jenner [1974] 1 WLR 68;
    [1974] 1 All ER 729, 117 Sol Jo 912; 229 Est Gaz 1341;
    27 P & CR 441 .... 13.13, 13.20
Quigley & McClay's Contract, Re [1918] 1 IR 347 .... 15.29

Quinion v Horne [1906] 1 Ch 596; 75 LJCh 293; 54 WR 344;
  50 Sol Jo 272 .... 15.30
Quinn v McCool [1929] IR 620 .... 12.05, 12.50
Quinn v Quality Homes Ltd [1976-7] ILRM 314 .... 1.38, 4.18
Quinn v Shields (1877) IR 11 CL 254 .... 17.15, 18.73, 18.75

R

R (Montgomery) v Belfast Corporation [1915] 2 IR 36 .... 8.14
R (Moore) v Abbott [1897] 2 IR 362 .... 8.14
R (Proctor) v Hutton [1978] NI 139 .... 13.64, 16.23
R (Secretary of State for War) v County Cork JJ [1900] 2 IR 105 .... 8.14
R v Kitson (1869) LR 1 CCR 200 .... 18.10
R v Wells [1939] 2 All ER 169 .... 18.10
Radcliff v Hayes [1907] 1 IR 101 .... 18.74
Radford v De Froberville [1977] 1 WLR 1262; [1978] 1 All ER 33;
  121 Sol Jo 319 .... 13.78
Rae v Joyce (1892) 29 LR Ir 500; 26 ILT 324 .... 21.35
Rafferty v Schofield [1897] 1 Ch 937; 66 LJCh 448; 76 LT 648;
  45 WR 460 .... 8.05, 12.22
Raineri v Miles [1981] AC 1050; [1980] 2 WLR 847; [1980] 2 All ER 145;
  124 Sol Jo 328 .... 13.12, 13.15
Raingold v Bromley [1931] 2 Ch 307; 100 LJCh 337; 145 LT 611 .... 7.12
Ranelagh (Lord) v Melton (1864) 2 Drew & Sin 278; 5 New Rep 101;
  34 LJCh 227; 11 LT 409; 28 JP 820; 10 Jur (ns) 1141; 13 WR 150 .... 8.05
Rawlings v General Trading Co [1921] 1 KB 365; 90 LJKB 404;
  124 LT 562; 37 TLR 252; 65 Sol Jo 220; 26 Com Cas 171 .... 2.24
Rawlinson v Ames [1925] Ch 96; 94 LJCh 113; 132 LT 370; 69 Sol Jo 142 .... 6.58
Ray, Re [1896] 1 Ch 468; 65 LJCh 316; 73 LT 723; 60 JP 340;
  44 WR 353; 40 Sol Jo 238 .... 21.18
Rayner v Paskell & Son (1948) 152 Est Gaz 270 .... 3.11, 3.16
Rayner v Preston (1881) 18 Ch D 1; 50 LJCh 472; 44 LT 787; 45 JP 829;
  29 WR 547 .... 12.02, 12.38
Reading Trust Ltd v Spero [1930] 1 KB 492; 99 LJKB 186; 142 LT 361;
  74 Sol Jo 12 .... 20.26
Record v Bell [1991] 1 WLR 833; [1991] 4 All ER 471; (1991) P & CR 192
  .... 1.31, 6.05
Redding v Wilkes (1791) 3 Bro CC 400 .... 6.60
Reed (Dennis) Ltd v Goody [1950] 2 KB 277; [1950] 1 All ER 919;
  66 TLR 918; 94 Sol Jo 270 .... 3.25, 3.29
Reed (Dennis) Ltd v Nicholls [1948] 2 All ER 914 .... 3.29-3.30
Reeve v Berridge (1888) 20 QBD 523; 57 LJQB 265; 58 LT 836; 52 JP 549;
  36 WR 617 .... 9.26, 9.40, 14.02
Regalian Properties plc v London Dockland Development Corporation
  [1995] 1 All ER 1005 .... 6.24
Regina Coeli [1976] 5 NIJB 40 .... 13.40

Reid v Miller [1928] NI 151 .... 12.05, 17.25
Reidy v Pierce (1861) 11 ICLR 361 .... 14.52
Renwick v Daly (1877) IR 11 CL 126; 9 ILTR 96 .... 17.18
Retail Parks Investments Ltd v Royal Bank of Scotland plc
    London Times 18 July 1995 .... 13.41
Revell v Hussey (1813) 2 Ba & B 280 .... 13.38
Revenue Commissioners v Moroney [1972] IR 372 .... 17.19, 18.42, 18.44, 18.86
Reynold v Kingman (1587) Cro Eliz 115 .... 18.87
Reynolds v Waters [1982] ILRM 335 .... 13.27, 16.65, 16.68
Rhodes v Baker (1851) 1 ICLR 488 .... 6.09
Rhone v Stephens [1994] 2 All ER 65 .... 19.10
Rich's Wills Trusts, Re (1962) 106 Sol Jo 75 .... 7.15
Richards v Hill [1920] NZLR 724 .... 3.16
Richards v Phillips [1969] 1 Ch 39; [1968] 3 WLR 33; [1968] 2 All ER 859;
    112 Sol Jo 460 .... 2.08, 2.21-2.23, 6.38
Richardson v Chasen (1847) 10 QB 756; 16 LJQB 341; 11 Jur 890 .... 13.86
Richardson v Mahon (1879) 4 LR Ir 486 .... 11.16, 11.24
Richardson v McCausland (1817) Beat 457 .... 12.16
Rickards (Charles) Ltd v Oppenheim [1950] 1 KB 616; [1950] 1 All ER 420;
    66 TLR 435; 94 Sol Jo 161 .... 13.24
Ridgway v Wharton (1857) 6 HLC 238; 27 LJCh 46; 29 LT (os) 390;
    4 Jur (ns) 173; 5 WR 804 .... 6.30, 7.03
Ridley v Oster [1939] 1 All ER 618 .... 9.33
Riley v Troll [1953] 1 All ER 966 .... 7.11
Rishton v Whatmore (1878) 8 Ch D 467; 47 LJCh 629; 26 WR 827 .... 6.31
Riverplate Properties Ltd v Paul [1979] 2 All ER 656 .... 13.66
Robb & Spillane's Contract, Re (1901) 1 NIJR 206 .... 9.17, 9.34
Roberts v Berry (1853) 3 De GM & G 284; 22 LJCh 398; 20 LT (os) 215 ..... 14.47
Roberts v Church Commrs for England [1972] 1 QB 278; [1971] 3 WLR 566;
    [1971] 3 All ER 703; 115 Sol Jo 792; 220 Est Gaz 189 .... 18.09
Roberts v O'Neill [1983] IR 47 .... 13.40, 13.48-13.49, 13.54
Robertson v Skelton (1849) 12 Beav 260; 19 LJCh 140; 14 LT (os) 542;
    14 Jur 323 .... 12.37
Robertson's Application, Re [1969] 3 All ER 257; [1969] 1 WLR 109;
    112 Sol Jo 943; 20 P & CR 123 .... 21.08
Robinson v Wall (1847) 2 Ph 372; 16 LJCh 401; 9 LT (os) 389; 11 Jur 577 .... 2.14
Roche v Peilow [1985] IR 232 .... 1.36, 3.15, 4.02, 4.25
.... 5.28, 11.17, 15.05, 15.48
Rochfort v Ennis (1861) 13 ICLR 324 .... 17.24
Rockeagle Ltd v Alsop Wilkinson [1991] 4 All ER 659 .... 3.17, 10.26
Rodger v Harrison [1893] 1 QB 161 .... 6.65
Rodwell v Phillips (1842) 9 M & W 501; 1 Dowl (ns) 885; 11 LJ Ex 217 .... 6.09
Roe v Lidwell (1860) 11 ICLR 320 .... 17.24, 18.66
Rogers v Challis (1859) 27 Beav 175 .... 13.40
Rohan Construction Ltd v Antigen Ltd [1989] ILRM 783 .... 11.14-11.16, 11.22

Rohan v Molony (1905) 39 ILTR 207 ....2.28, 2.34
Rolph v Crouch (1867) IR 3 Exch 44 ....21.32
Ronayne v Sherrard (1877) IR 11 CL 146 ....6.09
Rooks Rider v Steel [1993] 4 All ER 716 ....20.15
Rooney & McParland Ltd v Carlin [1981] NI 138 ....21.38
Rooney v Byrne [1933] IR 609; 67 ILTR 66; [1933] LJ Ir 58 ....7.14, 7.15, 7.23
....10.18, 13.25
Rooney v Thomas (1947) 81 ILTR 64 ....2.07, 6.38, 9.03
Rorke v Errington (1859) 7 HLC 617 ....14.56
Rorke v Sherlock (1877) IR 11 Eq 510 ....21.05
Rose v Watson (1864) 10 HLC 672; 3 New Rep 673; 33 LJCh 385;
    10 LT 106; 10 Jur (ns) 297; 12 WR 585 ....12.02, 12.12, 12.44
Rosenbaum v Belson [1900] 2 Ch 267; 69 LJCh 569; 82 LT 658;
    48 WR 522; 44 Sol Jo 485 ....3.08
Ross v Caunters [1980] Ch 297; [1979] 3 WLR 605; [1979] 3 All ER 580;
    123 Sol Jo 605 ....1.36, 1.37, 5.27
Ross v Irish National Insurance Co Ltd (1958) 92 ILTR 92 ....2.04
Ross & Boal Ltd, Re [1924] 1 IR 129 ....6.10
Rossdale v Denny [1921] 1 Ch 57; 90 LJCh 204; 124 LT 294; 37 TLR 45;
    65 Sol Jo 58 ....7.11
Rossiter v Miller (1878) 3 App Cas 1124; 48 LJCh 10; 39 LT 173; 42 JP 804;
    26 WR 865 ....6.20, 7.12
Rowe v Law [1978] IR 55 ....17.20
Rowe v May (1854) 18 Beav 613 ....2.10, 2.26, 10.27
Royal Avenue Hotel Ltd v Richard Shops Properties Ltd [1985] 6 NIJB 52 .....7.04
Royal Bristol Permanent BS v Bomash (1887) 35 Ch D 390; 56 LJCh 840;
    57 LT 179 ....12.21
Rushbrooke v O'Sullivan [1908] 1 IR 232 ....13.39, 13.41-13.41
Russ & Brown's Contract, Re [1934] Ch 34; 103 LJCh 12; 150 LT 125;
    50 TLR 19; 77 Sol Jo 749 ....9.17
Russell v Minister for Local Government [1976] IR 185 ....8.16
Rutherford v Acton Adams [1915] AC 866; 84 LJPC 238; 113 LT 931 ....9.32
Rutherford's Conveyance, Re [1938] Ch 396; 108 LJCh 70; 158 LT 405;
    54 TLR 429; 82 Sol Jo 195 ....18.95
Ruthven's Trusts, Re [1906] 1 IR 236 ....8.13, 13.56
Rutledge v Hood (1853) 3 ICLR 447 ....14.56
Ryan, Re (1952) 86 ILTR 104. ....2.03
Ryan v Mutual Tontine Westminster Chambers Association [1893] 1 Ch 116 13.41
Ryan v Pilkington [1959] 1 WLR 403; [1959] 1 All ER 689; 103 Sol Jo 310;
    173 Est Gaz 487 ....3.11, 3.16
Rye v Rye [1962] AC 496; [1962] 2 WLR 361; [1962] 1 All ER 146;
    106 Sol Jo 94 ....18.96

S

Sadlier v Higgs (1853) 4 HLC 435 ....14.51-14.52
Safeera Ltd v Wallis (HC) unrep 12 July 1994 ....18.128

Sainsbury v Matthews (1838) 4 M & W 143; 1 Horn & H 459; 8 LJ Ex 1;
  2 Jur 946 .... 6.09
Sale v Lambert (1874) LR 18 Eq 1; 43 LJCh 470; 22 WR 478 .... 6.20
Sandilands, Re (1871) IR 6 CL 411 .... 18.122
Sansom & Narbeth's Contract, Re [1910] 1 Ch 741; 79 LJCh 374;
  102 LT 677; 54 Sol Jo 475 .... 18.52, 18.65
Saunders v Anglia BS [1971] AC 1004; [1970] 3 WLR 1078;
  [1970] 3 All ER 961; 114 Sol Jo 885; 22 P & CR 300 .... 21.38
Saunders v Edwards [1987] 2 All ER 651; [1987] 1 WLR 1116 .... 9.15
Saunders v Leslie (1814) 2 Ba & B 509 .... 12.16-12.17, 18.45
Savage v Canning (1867) 16 WR 133; IR 1 CL 434 .... 6.13
Savage v Carroll (1810) 1 Ba & B 265 .... 6.53-6.54, 6.56
Savage v Carroll (1815) 2 Ba & B 444 .... 13.45
Savage v Nolan [1978] ILRM 151 .... 17.19
Scarfe v Adams [1981] 1 All ER 843; 125 Sol Jo 32 .... 9.12
Scarlett, Re [1958] NI 28 .... 12.50-12.51
Schindler v Pigault (1975) 30 P & CR 328; 119 Sol Jo 273 .... 13.35
Scorell v Boxall (1827) 1 Y & J 396 .... 6.09
Scott, Re (1879) 13 ICLR 139 .... 13.27
Scott v Anderson (1857) 2 Ir Jur (ns) 422 .... 6.09, 14.56
Scott v Bradley [1971] Ch 850; [1970] 2 WLR 731; [1971] 1 All ER 583;
  114 Sol Jo 172; 22 P & CR 353 .... 6.07
Scott v Coulson [1903] 2 Ch 249 .... 13.67
Scott v McCombe (1965) 16 NILQ 122, 418; (1966) 17 NILQ 418 .... 6.16, 6.19
  .... 6.31, 7.12
Scott v Nixon (1843) 3 Dr & War 38; 6 Ir Eq 8; 2 Con & L 185 .... 14.81
Scott v Rains [1966] NZLR 527 .... 7.15
Scott's Estate, Re (1854) 7 Ir Jur (os) 329 .... 6.35
Scott & Alvarez's Contract, Re [1895] 2 Ch 603; 64 LJCh 821; 73 LT 43;
  43 WR 694; 11 TLR 471; 39 Sol Jo 621; 12 R 474 .... 13.35, 14.10
Scully v Corboy [1950] IR 488; 83 ILTR 188 .... 6.09
Seal v Claridge (1881) 7 QBD 516; 50 LJQB 316; 44 LT 501 .... 18.134
Securities Trust Ltd v Hugh Moore & Alexander Ltd [1964] IR 417 .... 5.27
Seddon v North Eastern Salt Co Ltd [1905] 1 Ch 326; 74 LJCh 199;
  49 Sol Jo 119 .... 5.26
Sefton (Earl of) v Tophams Ltd [1967] AC 50; [1966] 2 WLR 814;
  [1966] 1 All ER 1039; 110 Sol Jo 271 .... 18.98
Selkirk v Romar Investments Ltd [1963] 1 WLR 1415; [1963] 3 All ER 994;
  107 Sol Jo 907 .... 6.24, 13.52, 15.30-15.31
Sepes Establishment Ltd v KSK Enterprises Ltd [1993] 2 IR 225;
  [19993] ILRM 46 .... 17.22
Sepia Ltd v O'Hanlon Ltd [1979] ILRM 11 .... 7.04, 7.16, 7.18, 13.04, 13.07, 13.17
Sergie, Re [1954] NI 1 .... 17.02, 19.47
Seven Seas Properties Ltd v Al-Essa [1993] 3 All ER 577 .... 13.77
Seymour, Re [1913] 1 Ch 475 .... 18.129

Shannon Ltd v Venner Ltd [1965] Ch 682; [1965] 2 WLR 718;
[1965] 1 All ER 590 .... 18.72
Shannonside Holdings (US) v Associated Mortgage Investors
(HC) unrep 12 March 1980 .... 13.40
Shardlow v Cotterell (1881) 20 Ch D 90; 51 LJCh 353; 45 LT 572;
30 WR 143 .... 6.23
Sharman & Meade's Contract, Re [1936] Ch 755; [1936] 2 All ER 1547; 105 LJCh
286; 155 LT 277; 80 Sol Jo 689 .... 9.10, 18.65
Sharman v Brandt (1871) LR 6 QB 720; 40 LJQB 312; 19 WR 936 .... 6.34
Sharneyford Supplies Ltd v Edge [1987] 2 WLR 363; [1987] 1 All ER 588;
131 Sol Jo 22 .... 5.28, 13.80, 13.84
Sharpe v ET Sweeting & Sons Ltd [1963] 2 All ER 455; [1963] 1 WLR 665;
107 Sol Jo 666 .... 4.15
Shaw v Foster (1872) LR 5 HL 321; 42 LJCh 49; 17 LT 281; 20 WR 907 ...... 12.02
Sheers v Thimbley & Son (1879) 76 LT 709; 13 TLR 451; 41 Sol Jo 558 .... 6.29
Sheggia v Gradwell [1963] 3 All ER 114; [1963] WLR 1049; 107 Sol Jo 572;
187 Est Gaz 329 .... 3.25-3.28
Sherbrooke v Dipple (1980) 41 P & CR 173; 255 EG 1203; 124 Sol Jo 345 ...... 7.08
Sheridan v Higgins [1971] IR 291 .... 2.09, 2.11, 3.12, 6.36, 6.40-6.41
.... 12.18, 13.12, 13.40, 20.09
Sherlock's Estate, Re [1899] 2 IR 561 .... 12.11
Shiels v Flynn [1975] IR 296 .... 13.27
Shoreditch Vestry v Hughes (1864) 17 CBNS 137 .... 15.29
Shuttleworth v Clews [1907] 1 Ch 176; 79 LJCh 121; 101 LT 708 .... 13.78
Sibbald v Lowrie (1853) 23 LJ Ch 593; 3 Eq Rep 485; 22 LT (os) 155;
18 Jur 141; 2 WR 89 .... 15.51
Sibel v Kent [1976-77] ILRM 127 .... 7.23, 13.48, 16.53
Signal v Kay-Stratton [1955] NZLR 1025. .... 6.12
Silkes v Wild (1861) 1 B & S 587; (1863) 4 B & S 421; 32 LJQB 375;
8 LT 642; 11 WR 954; 2 New Rep 456 .... 13.80, 13.84
Silver (Geoffrey) & Drake v Baines [1971] 1 QB 396; [1971] 2 WLR 187;
114 Sol Jo 865; [1971] 1 All ER 473 .... 20.15
Silver Wraith Ltd v Siuicre Éireann Cpt (HC) unrep, 8 June 1989 .... 6.53, 7.11
Simmons v Heseltine (1858) 5 CBNS 554 .... 13.58
Simmons v Pennington & Son [1955] 1 WLR 183; [1955] 1 All ER 240;
99 Sol Jo 146; 164 Est Gaz 580 .... 12.38, 15.37
Simmons v Woodward [1892] AC 100 .... 18.19
Simms v Sinclair (1884) 18 ILTR 60 .... 19.27
Simpson v Sadd (1854) 4 De GM 665; 3 Eq Rep 263; 24 LJCh 562;
24 LT (os) 205; 1 Jur (ns) 457; 3 WR 118 .... 12.34
Sims-Clarke v Ilet Ltd [1953] IR 39 .... 8.04, 13.27
Sindall plc v Cambridgeshire County Council [1994] 3 All ER 932 .... 9.47, 13.67
Sindall v Cambridgeshire County Council [1994] 3 All ER 932 .... 13.67
Siney v Dublin Corporation [1980] IR 400 .... 4.16
Sisk & Son Ltd v Lawter Products BV (HC) unrep, 13 November 1976 .... 11.16

Skeat's Settlement, Re (1889) 42 Ch D 522; 58 LJCh 656; 61 LT 500;
    37 WR 778 .... 18.103
Skinner v Andrews & Hall (1910) 26 TLR 340 .... 2.28
Skinner v Reed's Trustees [1967] Ch 1194; [1967] 3 WLR 871;
    [1967] 2 All ER 1286 .... 2.10, 2.26, 10.25-10.29
Slater, Re (1897) 76 LT 529 .... 18.09
Slator v Trimble (1861) 14 ICLR 342; 2 Ir Jur (ns) 255 .... 16.69
Smallman (JL) Ltd v O'Moore [1959] IR 220 .... 13.48, 13.67
Smelter Corporation of Ireland Ltd v O'Driscoll [1977] IR 305 .... 5.25, 13.38
Smith, Re (1892) 67 LT 64 .... 18.122
Smith, Re [1917] 1 IR 170; [1918] 1 IR 45 .... 14.25
Smith, Re [1939] IR 244 .... 16.31
Smith & Olley v Townsend (1949) 1 P & CR 28; 94 Sol Jo 332 .... 7.20
Smith v Chadwick (1882) 20 Ch D 27; (1884) 9 App Cas 187; 53 LJCh 873;
    50 LT 697; 48 JP 644; 32 WR 687 .... 6.29
Smith v Chichester (1842) 4 Ir Eq R 580; 2 Dr & War 393; 1 Con & L 486 ... 20.50
Smith v Colbourne [1914] 2 Ch 533; 84 LJCh 112; 111 LT 927;
    58 Sol Jo 783 .... 4.08
Smith v Eric S Bush [1990] 1 AC 831; [1989] 2 WLR 790;
    [1989] 2 All ER 514; 133 Sol Jo 597; 87 LGR 685;
    21 HLR 424 .... 1.38, 3.41
Smith v Hamilton [1951] Ch 174; [1950] 2 All ER 928; 66 TLR 937;
    94 Sol Jo 724 .... 2.10, 2.26, 10.26, 13.15, 13.17
Smith v Jackson (1816) 1 Madd 618 .... 10.26
Smith v Jones [1952] 2 All ER 907; [1952] WN 518; [1952 2 TLR 846 .... 6.24
Smith v Lynn [1951] NI 69 .... 9.16, 9.29, 13.40
Smith v MacGowan [1938] 3 All ER 447; 159 LT 278; 82 Sol Jo 605 .... 6.39
Smith v Mansi [1963] 1 WLR 26; [1962] 3 All ER 857; 106 Sol Jo 876;
    184 Est Gaz 723 .... 1.34, 6.22, 6.61-6.62
Smith v Marrable (1843) 11 M & W 5 .... 4.08
Smith v Robinson (1879) 13 Ch D 148; 49 LJCh 20; 41 LT 405;
    28 WR 37 .... 14.59, 14.61, 15.24
Smith v Surman (1829) 9 B & C 561; 4 Man & Ry KB 455;
    7 LJ (os) KB 296 .... 6.09
Smith v Wallace [1895] 1 Ch 385; 64 LJCh 240; 71 LT 814; 43 WR 539;
    13 R 201 .... 15.30
Smith v Webster (1876) 3 Ch D 49; 445 LJCh 528; 35 LT 44;
    40 JP 805 .... 6.43-6.44
Smith v Wheatcroft (1878) 9 Ch D 223; 47 LJCh 745; 39 LT 103;
    27 WR 42 .... 13.67
Smiths (Harcourt Street) Ltd v Hardwicke Ltd (HC) unrep, 30 July 1971 .... 8.08
Smyth v Lynn [1951] NI 69 .... 5.23, 5.26, 13.49
Smyth v Shaftesbury (1901) 1 NIJR 34 .... 14.56
Smyth v Smyth (1903) 37 ILTR 82 .... 11.07
Sneesby v Goldings [1995] 36 EG 136 .... 1.38, 4.23

Soden & Alexander's Contract, Re [1918] 2 Ch 258; 87 LJCh 529;
119 LT 516 .... 15.19
Solicitor (A), Re (1919) 53 ILTR 51 .... 20.15, 20.18
Solicitor (A), Re [1966] 1 WLR 1604; [1966] 3 All ER 52 .... 20.15
Solle v Butcher [1950] 1 KB 671; [1949] 2 All ER 1107;
66 TLR 448 .... 13.67, 21.37
Solomon v Estates Management & Development Agency Ltd
(HC) unrep 14 July 1980 .... 13.03, 13.55
Somers v Erskine (No 2) [1944] IR 368 .... 15.02
Somers v Nicholls [1955] IR 83 .... 2.08, 3.01, 3.19
Somers v W [1979] IR 94 .... 15.01, 16.62, 16.63-16.65, 16.69
Soper v Arnold (1889) 14 App Cas 429; 59 LJCh 214; 61 LT 702; 38 WR 449;
STLR 698 .... 10.18, 13.34, 21.05
Sorrell v Finch [1977] AC 728; [1976] 2 All ER 371; [1976] 2 WLR 833;
120 Sol Jo 353; 238 Est Gaz 639 .... 2.10, 3.11, 3.16-3.17
Souter v Drake (1834) 5 B & Ald 992 .... 14.08
South City Market Co, Re (1884) 13 LR Ir 245 .... 8.04
South Eastern Rly v Associated Portland Cement Co [1910] 1 Ch 12;
79 LJCh 150; 101 LT 865; 74 JP 21; 26 TLR 61; 54 Sol Jo 80 .... 18.78
Southby v Hunt (1837) 2 My & Cr 207; Donnelly 196;
1 Jur 100 .... 15.21
Sparkam-Souter v Town & Country Developments (Essex) Ltd [1976]
2 All ER 65; [1976] 1 QB 858; [1976] 2 WLR 493; 120 Sol Jo 216;
74 LGR 355 .... 4.15
Sparrow & James' Contract, Re [1910] 2 Ch 60; 79 LJCh 491 .... 18.65, 18.68
Spector v Ageda [1973] Ch 30; [1971] 3 WLR 498; [1971] 3 All ER 417; 115 Sol Jo
426; 22 P & CR 1002 .... 1.34
Spencer v Clarke (1878) 47 LJ Ch 692; 9 Ch D 137; 27 WR 133 .... 18.45
Spencer v Registrar of Titles [1906] AC 503 .... 18.87
Spencer & Hauser's Contract, Re [1928] Ch 598; 97 LJCh 335; 139 LT 287;
72 Sol Jo 336 .... 14.80
Spijkers v Gebroedeas Benedik Abattoir CV [1986] ECR 000 .... 5.15
Spindler & Mear's Contract, Re [1901] 1 Ch 908; 70 LJCh 420;
84 LT 295; 49 WR 410; 45 Sol Jo 361 .... 15.29
Spiro v Glencrown Properties Ltd [1991] 1 All ER 600 .... 1.31, 6.05, 8.05
Spiro v Lintern [1973] 1 WLR 1002; [1973] 3 All ER 319; 117 Sol Jo 584;
227 Est Gaz 2045 .... 6.36
Spollen & Long's Contract, Re [1936] Ch 713; [1936] 2 All ER 711;
105 LJCh 347; 155 LT 554; 80 Sol Jo 510 .... 14.10-14.11, 15.52
Spottiswoode, Ballantyne & Co Ltd v Doreen Appliances Ltd
[1942] 2 KB 32; [1942] 2 All ER 65; 111 LJKB 569; 167 LT 33 6.15, 7.08, 7.11
Sprague v Booth [1909] AC 576; 78 LJPC 164; 101 LT 211 .... 13.31
Spunner v Walsh (1847) 10 Ir Eq R 386;11 Ir Eq R 597 .... 9.23, 9.25, 9.32
.... 9.39-9.40
Spurrier v Hancock (1799) 4 Ves 667 .... 15.20
St Albans Investment Co v Sun Alliance & London Insurance Ltd [1983] IR 362
.... 12.39

St Edmondsbury & Ipswich Diocesan Board of Finance v Clarke (No 2)
[1973] 1 WLR 1572; [1973] 3 All ER 902; 117 Sol Jo 1793 .... 18.78
St Luke's & St Anne's Hospital Board v Mahon (HC) unrep, 18 June 1993 ... 17.22
St Thomas's (Governors of) Hospital v Richardson [1910] 1 KB 271;
79 LJKB 488; 101 LT 771; 17 Mans 129 .... 12.27
Stafford v Mahony [1980] ILRM 53 .... 1.38, 2.13, 5.27
Stamers v Preston (1859) 9 ICLR 351 .... 17.02, 18.43
Stanley v McGauran (1882) 11 LR Ir 314 .... 2.13
Staple of England v Bank of England (1887) 21 QB 160; 57 LJQB 418;
52 JP 580; 36 WR 880; 4 TLR 46 .... 18.128
Staples v Young [1908] 1 IR 135; 42 ILTR 17 .... 14.51, 18.73, 18.75
Starkey v Barton [1909] 1 Ch 284 .... 13.40
Starling Securities Ltd v Woods (HC) unrep, 24 May 1977 .... 6.35, 6.58
Starr-Bowkett Building Society & Siburn's Contract, Re (1889) 42 Ch D 386;
58 LJCh 651; 61 LT 346; 38 WR 1; 5 TLR 701 .... 15.28
Starside Properties Ltd v Mustapha [1974] 2 All ER 567; [1974] 1 WLR 816;
118 Sol Jo 388 .... 13.33
State (Callaghan) v Irish Land Commission [1978] ILRM 201 .... 16.36
State (Furey) v Minister for Defence [1988] ILRM 89 .... 8.17
State (Nicolaou) v An Bord Uchtála [1966] IR 567 .... 16.62
Steadman v Drinkle [1916] 1 AC 275; 85 LJPC 79; 114 LT 248; 32 TLR 231 13.33
Steadman v Steadman [1976] AC 536; [1974] 3 WLR 56; [1974] 2 All ER 977;
118 Sol Jo 480; 29 P & CR 46 ....6.48, 6.51, 6.53-6.54, 6.59, 6.60
Steele v Morrow (1923) 57 ILTR 89 .... 18.54
Steele v Steele [1913] 1 IR 292; 47 ILTR 241 .... 12.11
Steeven's Hospital v Dyas (1864) 15 Ir Ch R 405; 8 Ir Jur (ns) 411 .... 6.51, 6.56
Stevens v Guppy (1828) 3 Russ 171; 6 LJ (os) Ch 164 .... 15.53
Stevens v Hutchinson [1953] Ch 299; [1953] 2 WLR 545; [1953] 1 All ER 699;
97 Sol Jo 171 .... 6.11
Stevenson, Re [1928] NI 135 .... 16.31
Stewart v Eddowes (1874) LR 9 CP 31; 43 LJCP 204; 30 LT 333;
22 WR 534 .... 6.33
Stewart v Marquis of Conyngham (1851) 1 Ir Ch R 534 .... 9.26, 9.33-9.34, 14.51
Stewart, Re [1925] 2 IR 51; 59 ILTR 1 .... 12.17
Stickney v Keeble [1915] AC 386; 84 LJCh 259; 112 LT 664 .. 13.11, 13.15, 13.17
Stinson v Owens (1973) 24 NILQ 218 .... 3.08, 6.18, 6.19, 6.25
.... 6.28, 6.31, 6.41
Stirrup's Contract, Re [1961] 1 WLR 449; [1961] 1 All ER 805;
105 Sol Jo 206 .... 18.82
Stock v Meakin [1900] Ch 683; 69 LJCh 401; 82 LT 248; 48 WR 420;
16 TLR 284 .... 21.31
Stock v Urey [1955] NI 1 .... 9.15
Stockloser v Johnson [1954] 1 QB 476; [1954] 1 All ER 630; [1954] 2 WLR 439;
98 Sol Jo 178 .... 13.32, 13.33
Stokell v Niven (1889) 61 LT 18; 5 TLR 481 .... 6.20

Stokes & Quirke Ltd v Clohessy [1957] IR 84 .... 2.29-2.30, 3.22-3.25
Stokes v Whicker [1920] 1 Ch 411; 89 LJCh 198; 123 LT 23;
    64 Sol Jo 292 .... 6.20, 6.29
Stone & Saville's Contract, Re [1963] 1 WLR 163; [1963] 1 All ER 353;
    106 Sol Jo 1030 .... 9.02, 13.20, 13.68, 14.17, 15.36
Stoney v Eastbourne RDC [1927] 1 Ch 367; 95 LJCh 312; 135 LT 281;
    90 JP 173; 70 Sol Jo 690; 24 LGR 333 .... 21.22, 21.28
Strickland v Turner (1852) 7 Exch 208; 22 LJ Ex 115 .... 13.67, 21.37
Stromdale & Ball Ltd v Burden [1952] Ch 223; [1951] 1 All ER 59;
    [1951] 2 TLR 1192 .... 18.122, 18.133
Strong, Re [1940] IR 382; 74 ILTR 177 .... 12.04-12.05, 12.30, 12.50-12.51
Stuart v Ferguson (1832) Hayes 452 .... 12.15, 12.17
Stud Managers Ltd v Marshall [1985] IR 83 .... 13.22
Sudbrook Trading Estate Ltd v Eggleton [1983] 1 AC 444;
    [1982] 3 WLR 315; [1982] 3 All ER 1; 126 Sol Jo 512 .... 6.24, 8.06
Suleman v Shahsavari [1989] 2 All ER 460; [1988] 1 WLR 1181; 9 EG 69
    .... 13.78, 13.85
Sullivan v Bailli (1891) 65 LT 528 .... 21.32
Sullivan's Estate, Re (1889) 23 LR Ir 255 .... 3.08, 6.41, 6.58
Sun Fat Chan v Osseous Ltd [1992] 1 IR 425 .... 13.44
Sunderland v Louth Co Council [1990] ILRM 658 .... 4.16, 4.18
Sunderland v McGreavey [1987] IR 372 .... 1.38, 3.41, 4.18
Sunnybank Inn Ltd v East Coast Inns Ltd (HC) unrep, 11 May 1979 .... 8.05
Surrey County Council v Bredero Homes Ltd [1993] 3 All ER 705 .... 13.78
Sutcliffe v Thackral [1974] AC 727; [1974] 2 WLR 295; [1974] 1 All ER 859;
    118 Sol Jo 148; [1974] 1 Lloyd's Rep 318 .... 5.27
Svanosio v McNamara (1956) 96 CLR 186 .... 21.37
Swain (Frank) v Whitfield Corp Ltd (1962) 183 Est Gaz 479 .... 2.30
Swan v Kane unrep (NI) 20.06
Swan v Miller [1919] 1 IR 151 .... 6.02, 6.14
Sweeney v Dennis (1883) 17 ILTR 76 .... 6.57
Swinbanks, ex p (1879) 11 Ch D 525 .... 18.134
Syke v Giles (1839) 5 M & W 645; 9 LJ Ex 106 .... 2.10

T

Tailby v Official Receiver (1888) 13 App Cas 523 .... 12.12
Talbot v Talbot [1968] Ch 1; [1967] 3 WLR 438; [1967] 2 All ER 920;
    11 Sol Jo 278 .... 8.05
Taylor, Re [1901] 1 KB 562; 79 LJKB 610; 102 LT 84; 26 TLR 270;
    54 Sol Jo 271; 17 Mans 145 .... 12.27
Taylor v Brown (1939) 2 Beav 180; 9 LJCh 14 .... 13.17
Taylor v Gorman (1844) 7 Ir Eq R 259 .... 20.50
Taylor v London & County Banking Co [1901] 2 Ch 231; 70 LJCh 477;
    84 LT 397; 49 WR 451; 17 TLR 413; 45 Sol Jo 394 .... 18.82
Taylor v Smyth [1991] 1 IR 142; [1990] ILRM 377 .... 12.20, 13.04, 13.17
    .... 13.55, 13.57, 13.78

Taylor v Taylor [1968] 1 All ER 843; [1968] 1 WLR 378; 112 Sol Jo 111;
   19 P & CR 193 .... 6.11
TCB Ltd v Gray [1986] 1 All ER 58; [1988] 1 All ER 108; 130 Sol Jo 224 .. 18.122
Tempany v Hynes [1976] IR 101 ....5.06, 6.65, 12.02-12.04
.... 12.05-12.06, 12.07-12.10, 12.13-12.15
.... 12.21, 12.30, 12.36, 12.40, 12.42, 12.51, 15.45, 16.22
Temple Press Ltd v Blogh [1955-56] Ir Jur Rep 53 .... 20.50
Tennant v Clancy [1987] IR 15; [1988] ILRM 214... 18.60
Tennent v Robinson (1852) 2 ICLR 142; 4 Ir Jur (os) 147 .... 17.04
Terry & White's Contract, Re (1886) 32 Ch D 14; 55 LJCh 345; 54 LT 353;
   34 WR 379; 2 TLR 327 .... 13.29, 15.28
Tesco Stores Ltd v William Gibson & Son Ltd (1970) 314 Est Gaz 835 .... 7.17
Tevanan v Norman Brett (Builders) Ltd [1972] 223 EG 1945 .... 7.08
Thackeray v Wood (1865) 6 B & S 766; 6 New Rep 305; 34 LJQB 226;
   13 WR 996 .... 21.28
Thames Plate Glass Co v Land & Sea Telegraph Co (1870) LR 11 Eq 248;
   40 LJCh 165; 19 WR 303 .... 12.29, 12.48
Thellhuson v Liddard [1900] 2 Ch 635; 69 LJCh 673; 82 LT 743; 49 WR 10   18.82
Thirkell v Cambi [1919] 2 KB 90; 89 LJKB 1; 121 LT 532; 35 TLR 652;
   63 Sol Jo 723; 24 Com Cas 285 ....6.15, 6.45, 7.08
Thomas v Brown (1876) 1 QBD 714; 45 LJQB 811; 35 LT 237; 24 WR 821 .. 6.20
Thomas v Dering (1837) 1 Keen 729; 6 LJCh 267; 1 Jur 427 .... 13.49
Thompson & Cottrell's Contract, Re [1943] Ch 97; [1943] 1 All ER 169;
   112 LJCh 109; 168 LT 155; 59 TLR 1127; 87 Sol Jo 57 .... 9.17
Thompson v Hickman [1907] 1 Ch 550; 76 LJCh 254; 96 LT 454;
   23 TLR 311 .... 18.59
Thompson v King [1920] 2 IR 365; [1921] 2 IR 438 ....7.03-7.04, 7.07
Thompson v Lambert (1868) IR 2 Eq 433; 2 ILT 369 .... 9.20, 9.35, 13.64
Thompson v McCullough [1947] KB 447; [1947] 1 All ER 265; [1947] LJR 498;
   176 LT 493; 63 TLR 95; 91 Sol Jo 147 .... 18.125
Thompson v Thompson (1871) IR 6 Eq 113 .... 17.16, 17.26, 18.32-18.34, 18.82
Thomson v Guy (1844) 7 Ir LR 6 .... 5.23, 5.26, 9.16, 9.29
Thornett v Haines (1846) 15 M & W 367; 15 LJ Ex 230; 7 LT (os) 264 .... 2.14
Throckmerton v Tracy (1555) 1 Plow 145 .... 18.87
Tiernan Homes Ltd v Sheridan [1981] ILRM 191 ....7.04, 7.16-7.18
Tilley v Thomas (1867) LR 3 Ch App 61; 17 LT 422; 32 JP 180; 16 WR 166   13.15
Timmins v Moreland Street Property Co Ltd [1958] Ch 110;
   [1957] 3 WLR 678; [1957] 3 All ER 265; 101 Sol Jo 815 .... 6.22, 6.28-6.29
.... 6.31, 9.23-9.24, 14.08
Tisdall v Parnell (1863) 14 ICLR 1 .... 18.71
Tithe Redemption Commission v Runcorn UDC [1954] Ch 383;
   [1954] 2 WLR 518; [1954] 1 All ER 653; 118 JP 265; 98 Sol Jo 212;
   52 LGR 231; 163 Est Gaz 218 .... 18.59
Tiverton Estates Ltd v Wearwell Ltd [1974] 2 WLR 176; [1974] 1 All ER 209;
   117 Sol Jo 913; 27 P & CR 24; 228 Est Gaz 1213 .... 6.04, 6.14, 6.61, 7.08

Todd & Co v M & GW Rly (1881) 9 LR Ir 85 ....13.41
Todd & McFadden's Contract, Re [1908] 1 IR 213; 42 ILTR 78 .... 10.21, 14.42
....14.45-14.47, 15.20
Tomkin Estates Ltd v O'Callaghan (HC) unrep, 16 March 1995 ....9.13
Toole v Macken (1855) 7 Ir Jur (os) 385 ....18.61
Toole v Medicott (1810) 1 Ba & B 393 ....6.54, 6.58
Tootal Clothing Ltd v Guinea Properties Ltd [1992] 41 EG 117 ....1.31, 6.05
Torrance v Bolton (1872) LR 14 Eq 124; 41 LJCh 643; 27 LT 19; 20 WR 718;
    (1872) 8 Ch App 118; 42 LJCh 177; 27 LT 738; 21 WR 134 ....9.07
Tottenham v Byrne (1861) 12 ICLR 376; 7 Ir Jur (ns) 14 ....18.59, 18.73-18.75
Tottenham's Estate, Re (1869) IR 3 Eq 528; 3 ILT 134 ....14.56
Tourret v Cripps (1879) 48 LJ Ch 567 ....6.33
Towey v Ulster Bank Ltd [1987] ILRM 142 ....5.27
Towle v Topham (1877) 37 LT 308 ....6.20
Trainor, Re [1936] NI 197 ....18.70
Travers v Gloucester Corp [1947] KB 71; [1946] 2 All ER 506; 115 LJKB 517;
    175 LT 360; 62 TLR 723; 90 Sol Jo 556 ....4.15
Treacy v Dwyer Nolan Developments Ltd [1979] ILRM 163 ....11.23, 13.41
Trendex Trading Corporation v Credit Suisse [1982] AC 679;
    [1981] 3 WLR 766; [1981] 3 All ER 520; 125 Sol Jo 761...........................11.22
Trinder & Partners v Haggis (1951) 158 Est Gaz 4; [1951] WN 416;
    95 Sol Jo 546 ....3.29
Truckell v Stock [1957] 1 WLR 161; [1957] 1 All ER 74; 101 Sol Jo 108 ......18.61
TSB Bank plc v Camfield [1995] 1 All ER 951 ....16.23, 16.69
Tully v ILC (1963) 97 ILTR 174 ....2.20-2.23
Tulsk Co-Op Livestock Mart Ltd v Ulster Bank Ltd (HC) unrep, 13 May 1983
    ....5.27
Tuohy v Courtney (No 1) [1994] 2 ILRM 503 ....4.17
Tuohy v Courtney (No 2) [1994] 3 IR 1; (SC) unrep, 26 July 1994 ....4.17
    ....5.28, 9.34
Tupper v Foulkes (1861) 9 CBNS 797; 30 LJCP 214; 3 LT 741; 7 Jur (ns) 709;
    9 WR 349 ....18.123
Turner v Harvey (1821) Jac 169 ....9.35
Turner v Marriott (1867) LR 3 Eq 744; 15 LT 607; 15 WR 420 ....12.44
Turner v Moon [1901] 2 Ch 825; 70 LJCh 822; 85 LT 90; 50 WR 237
    ....21.28, 21.31
Turnley v Hartley (1848) 3 New Pract Cas 96 ....6.29
Turpin & Ahern's Contract, Re [1905] 1 IR 85 ....9.38, 13.36, 14.03, 14.52
    ....15.04, 15.25
Twaddle v Murphy (1881) 8 LR Ir 123 ....19.42
Twining v Morrice (1788) 2 Bro C C 326 ....2.24
Tyrell v Imperial Tobacco Co Ltd [1926] IR 285 ....15.13
Tyrell, Re (1900) 82 LT 675; 64 JP 665 ....21.37

U

Udall v Capri Lighting Ltd [1987] 3 All ER 262; 131 Sol Jo 443 .... 20.15
Ulster Bank Ltd v Shanks [1982] NI 143 .... 4.02, 9.23
Unidare Plc v Scott Ltd [1991] 2 IR 88 .... 6.02
United Bank of Kuwait Ltd v Hammoud [1988] 1 WLR 1051;
    [1988] 3 All ER 418 .... 20.15
United Bank of Kuwait plc v Prudential Property Services Ltd
    [1995] EGCS 190 .... 1.36
United Dominions Trust v Western [1976] QB 513; [1976] 2 WLR 64;
    [1975] 3 All ER 1017; 119 Sol Jo 792 .... 21.38
United Scientific Holdings Ltd v Burnley Borough Council [1978] AC 984;
    [1977] 2 WLR 806; [1977] 2 All ER 62; 75 LGR 407; 121 Sol Jo 223 ...... 13.11
    .... 14.45, 19.34
United Yeast Co Ltd v Cameo Investments Ltd (1977) 111 ILTR 13 ..... 6.35, 13.13
    .... 13.17, 13.20, 13.30, 13.34
Universal Corporation v Five Ways Properties Ltd [1979] 1 All ER 552 .... 13.35
Universal Steam Navigation Co v McKelvie & Co [1923] AC 492 .... 6.35
Upperton v Nickolson (1871) 6 Ch App 436; 40 LJCh 401; 25 LT 4;
    35 JP 539; 19 WR 733 .... 15.21
Usitravel Ltd v Freyer (HC) unrep, 29 May 1973 .... 3.33, 7.12

V

Vale of Neath County v Furness (1876) 45 LJ Ch 276 .... 6.23
Van Hool McArdle Ltd v Rohan Industrial Estates Ltd [1980] IR 237
    .... 11.02, 11.06
Van Nierop v Commissioners of Public Works [1980] 2 IR 189. .... 13.50
Vandeleur v Dargan [1981] ILRM 75 .... 12.20, 13.03, 13.04
    .... 13.54-13.55, 13.78-13.78
Vaughan v Irish National Insurance Co Ltd (1955) 89 ILTR 179 .... 2.04
Vesey v Elwood (1842) 3 Dr & War 74; Fl & K 667 2.14, 2.25, 11.06, 11.07, 12.35
Vian & Gaffney, Re (1877) IR 11 Eq 521 .... 13.26
Vickers v Vickers (1867) LR 4 Eq 529; 36 LJCh 946 .... 6.24
Vignolles v Bowen (1847) 12 Ir Eq R 194 .... 9.23, 9.25, 9.33, 9.34, 9.39
Vincent v Going (1841) 3 Dr & War 75 .... 11.07, 12.36
Vincent v Premo Enterprises Ltd [1969] 2 QB 609; [1969] 2 WLR 1256;
    [1969] 2 All ER 941; 113 Sol Jo 266; 20 P & CR 591 .... 18.125
Viscount Securities Ltd v Kennedy (HC) unrep, 6 May 1986 .... 10.44, 13.20
Von Hatzfeldt-Wildenburg v Alexander [1921] 1 Ch 284; 81 LJCh 184;
    105 LT 434 .... 7.03
Vone Securities Ltd v Cooke [1979] IR 59; 103 ILTR 40 .... 8.05, 10.15, 17.17
Vowles v Miller (1810) 3 Taunt 137 .... 18.62

W

W v Somers [1983] IR 122; [1983] ILRM 343 .... 16.62
Waddell v Wolfe (1874) LR 9 QB 515; 43 LJQB 138; 23 WR 44 .... 15.25

Wakeham v Mackenzie [1968] 1 WLR 1175; [1968] 2 All ER 783;
   112 Sol Jo 504; 19 P & CR 565 ....6.60
Waldron v Jacob (1870) IR 5 Eq 131 ....6.20, 6.22-6.25, 6.29, 6.31
Walker v Boyle [1982] 1 WLR 495; [1982] 1 All ER 634; 125 Sol Jo 724 ....5.28
Walker & Elgee's Contract, Re (1919) 53 ILTR 22 ....13.27-13.28, 14.10, 14.15
Walker & Oakhott's Contract, Re [1901] 2 Ch 383; 70 LJCh 666; 84 LT 809;
   50 WR 41; [1902] WN 147; 37 LJNC 388 ....13.29
Walker v Bartlett (1856) 18 CB 845; 25 LJCP 263; 27 LT (os) 299;
   2 Jur (ns) 643; 4 WR 681 ....6.10
Wall v Hegarty [1980] ILRM 124 ....1.36-1.37, 5.27
Wallace v Roe [1903] 1 IR 32 ....2.09, 6.17, 6.34, 6.38
Wallington v Townsend [1939] Ch 588; [1939] 2 All ER 225; 106 LJCh 305;
   160 LT 537; 55 TLR 531; 83 Sol Jo 297 ....18.67
Wallis & Barnard's Contract, Re [1899] 2 Ch 515; 68 LJCh 753; 81 LT 382;
   48 WR 57 ....13.27
Wallis & Grout's Contract, Re [1906] 2 Ch 206; 75 LJCh 519; 94 LT 814;
   54 WR 534; 22 TLR 540 ....14.54
Wallis v Smith (1883) 21 Ch D 243; 52 LJCh 145; 47 LT 389; 31 WR 214 ...13.33
Walpoles (Ir) Ltd v Jay (HC) unrep, 20 November, 1980 ....16.62
Walsh, Re [1916] 1 IR 40 ....14.27
Walsh v McGauran (HC) unrep 14 June 1977 ....18.56, 18.62
Walsh v Wightman [1927] NI 1 ....19.45
Walters v Morgan (1861) 3 De GF & J 718; 4 LT 758 ....9.35
Want v Stallibrass (1873) LR 8 Exch 175; 42 LJ Ex 108; 29 LT 293;
   21 WR 685 ....15.21
Ward & Jordan's Contract, Re [1902] 1 IR 73; 2 NIJR 38; 35 ILTR 249 ....9.34
Ward v Grimes (1863) 8 LT 782; 9 Jur (ns) 1097; 11 WR 794 ....15.21
Ward v McMaster [1985] IR 29; [1986] ILRM 43; [1988] IR 337 ....1.38, 3.41
   ....4.16, 4.23
Ward v Spivack Ltd [1957] IR 40 ....3.20
Ward's Estate, Re (1909) 43 ILTR 113 ....14.52
Warde v Dixon (1858) 28 LJ Ch 315; 32 LT (os) 349; 5 Jur (ns) 698;
   7 WR 148 ....15.22
Warlow v Harrison (1858) 1 E & E 295; 29 LJQB 14; 1 LT 211; 6 Jur (ns) 66;
   8 WR 95 ....2.13, 2.20
Warrington v Warrington (1849) 8 CB 134 ....12.34
Washbourn v Burrows (1847) 1 Ex Ch 107; 5 Dow & L 105; 16 LJ Ex 266 .....6.09
Waterpark (Lord) v Fennell (1855) 5 ICLR 120; 1 Ir Jur (ns) 45 ....17.19, 18.73
Watford Corporation's & Ware's Contract, Re [1943] Ch 82; [1943] 1 All ER 54;
   112 LJCh 94; 168 LT 153; 59 TLR 98; 87 Sol Jo 30 ....12.21
Watkins v Watkins (1849) 12 LT (os) 353 ....13.78
Watling v Lewis [1911] 1 Ch 414 ....21.10
Watson v Burton [1957] 1 WLR 19; [1956] 3 All ER 929; 101 Sol Jo 45;
   168 Est Gaz 613 ....9.29, 9.33, 9.47
Watson v Davies [1931] 1 Ch 455; 100 LJCh 87; 144 LT 545 ....6.36

Watson v Healy Lands Ltd [1965] NZLR 511 .... 10.22

Watson v Newton (1920) 96 Est Gaz 140 .... 2.29

Watts v Spence [1976] Ch 165; [1975] 2 WLR 1039; [1975] 2 All ER 528;
    119 Sol Jo 168 .... 13.80

Waucob v Reynolds (1850) 1 ICLR 142; 2 Ir Jur (os) 148 .... 6.12

Webb v Hughes (1870) IR 10 Eq 281; 39 LJCh 606; 18 WR 749 .... 13.25

Webster v Donaldson (1865) 34 Beav 451; 12 LT 69; 11 Jur (ns) 404;
    13 WR 515 .... 12.14

Weldman v Spinks (1861) 5 LT 385 .... 8.05

Weldon v Bradshaw (1873) IR 7 Eq 168 .... 21.05

Wells (Merstham) Ltd v Buckland Sand & Silica Ltd [1965] 2 QB 170;
    [1964] 2 WLR 453; [1964] 1 All ER 41; 108 Sol Jo 177 .... 6.13

Wells v Chelmsford Local Board of Health (1880) 15 Ch D 108 .... 8.18

Wells v Maxwell (1863) 331 1 Ch 44 .... 13.17

West (Richard) & Partners (Inverness) Ltd v Dick [1969] 2 Ch 424;
    [1969] 2 WLR 1190; [1969] 1 All ER 943; 113 Sol Jo 165;
    20 P & CR 293 .... 7.17

Weston & Thomas's Contract, Re [1907] 1 Ch 244; 76 LJCh 179;
    96 LT 324 .... 9.32, 15.30

Weston v Lawrence Weaver Ltd [1961] 1 QB 402; [1961] 2 WLR 192;
    [1961] 1 All ER 478; 105 Sol Jo 155 .... 18.62

Whaley v Bagnal (1765) 1 Bro Parl Cas 345 .... 6.60

Wharton v Kelly (1861) 14 ICLR 293; 7 Ir Jur (ns) 58 .... 17.15

Wheeldon v Burrows (1879) 12 Ch D 31; 48 LJCh 853; 41 LT 327; 28 WR 196 ....
    9.18, ... 18.71

Whelan v Cork Corporation [1991] ILRM 19 .... 1.17, 8.12

Whitbread & Co Ltd v Watt [1902] 1 Ch 835; 71 LJCh 424; 86 LT 395;
    50 WR 422; 18 TLR 465; 46 Sol Jo 378 .... 10.25, 13.62

White v Bateman (1891) 29 LR Ir 281 .... 15.46

White v Beck (1871) IR 6 Eq 63 .... 12.26

White v Bijou Mansions Ltd [1937] Ch 610; [1937] 3 All ER 269;
    107 LJCh 32; 157 LT 105; 53 TLR 818; 81 Sol Jo 498 .... 14.72

White v Grand Hotel, Eastbourne Ltd [1913] 1 Ch 113 .... 18.72

White v Jones [1995] 2 WLR 187; [1995] 1 All ER 691 .... 1.36-1.37, 5.27

White v McCooey [1976-7] ILRM 72 .... 13.48

White v McMahon (1886) 18 LR Ir 460 .... 6.26

White v Proctor (1811) 4 Taunt 209 .... 6.38

White v Spendlove [1942] IR 224 .... 6.07, 6.26, 6.29, 10.18, 13.34, 13.36

White v Taylor (No 2) [1969] 1 Ch 160; [1958] 2 WLR 1402;
    [1968] 1 All ER 1015; 112 Sol Jo 420; 19 P & CR 412; 205 Est Gaz 1315 17.19

White's Charities, Re [1898] 1 Ch 659; 67 LJCh 430; 78 LT 550; 46 WR 479;
    42 Sol Jo 429 .... 18.59

White & Carter (Councils) Ltd v McGregor Ltd [1962] AC 413;
    [1962] 2 WLR 17; [1961] 3 All ER 1178; 105 Sol Jo 1104 .... 13.06, 13.78

White & Hague's Contract, Re [1921] 1 IR 138; 55 ILTR 52 .... 9.37, 10.04
    .... 14.06-14.07, 14.10, 14.25, 14.38, 15.04, 15.26

White & Smith's Contract, Re [1896] 1 Ch 637; 65 LJCh 481; 74 LT 377;
44 WR 424; 42 Sol Jo 373 .... 9.26, 9.40
Whitham v Bullock [1939] 2 KB 81 .... 19.31
Whiting to Loomes (1881) 17 Ch D 10; 50 LJCh 463; 44 LT 721; 29 WR 435
.... 15.13
Whitney Moore & Keller v Shipping Finance Corporation Ltd [1964] IR 216
.... 20.49
Whittington v Seale-Hayne (1900) 82 LT 49; 16 TLR 181;
44 Sol Jo 229 .... 5.26, 13.61
Wiggins v Lord (1841) 4 Beav 30 .... 10.26
Wigginton & Milner Ltd v Winster Engineering Ltd [1978] 1 WLR 1462;
[1978] 3 All ER 436; 122 Sol Jo 826 .... 18.64, 18.68
Wilcox v Redhead (1880) 49 LJCh 539; 28 WR 795 .... 7.12
Wilde v Gibson (1848) 1 HLC 605; 12 Jur 527 .... 5.26, 9.31
Wilde v Watson (1878) 1 LR Ir 402 .... 3.07, 3.08-3.09, 6.41
Wilkes v Spooner [1911] 2 Ch 473 .... 15.36
Wilkinson Ltd v Brown [1966] 1 All ER 502; [1966] 1 WLR 195;
109 Sol Jo 955 .... 3.28-3.30
Wilkinson Ltd v O'Neill (1961) 181 Est Gaz 137 .... 3.29
Wilks v Davis (1817) 3 Mer 507 .... 6.24
Willes v Latham (1837) S & Sc 441 .... 14.10, 14.59, 14.71-14.71, 15.25
Willett & Argenti (1889) 60 LT 735; 42 Ch D 23; 5 TLR 476 .... 14.49
Williams v Evans (1866) LR 1 QB 352; 35 LJQB 111; 13 LT 753; 30 JP 692;
14 WR 330 .... 2.10, 10.24
Williams v Gabriel [1906] 1 QB 155 .... 21.30
Williams v Kenneally (1912) 46 ILTR 292 .... 6.26, 13.45
Williams v Kennedy (HC) unrep, 19 July 1993 .... 13.34, 15.30-15.31
Williams v Millington (1788) 1 H Bl 81 .... 2.34
Williams v Williams (1861) 12 Ir Ch R 507 .... 21.05
Williams & Glyn's Bank Ltd v Boland [1981] AC 487; [1980] 3 WLR 138;
[1980] 2 All ER 408; 124 Sol Jo 443 .... 16.23
Willis v Jermin (1590) Cro Eliz 167 .... 18.128
Willis v Latham (1837) S & Sc 441 .... 9.02
Willmott v Barber (1880) 15 Ch D 96. .... 13.49
Wills v Stradling (1797) 3 Ves 378 .... 6.56-6.58
Willson v Greene [1971] 1 WLR 635; [1971] 1 All ER 1098; 115 Sol Jo 206 . 18.68
Wilson (Builders) Ltd v NIHE [1989] NI 208 .... 11.24
Wilson v Bloomfield (1979) 123 Sol Jo 860 .... 5.28
Wilson v Clapham (1819) 1 Jac & W 36 .... 12.14
Wilson v Finch Hatton (1877) 2 Ex D 336 .... 4.08
Wilson v Hart (1866) IR 1 Ch 463 .... 14.71
Wilson v Keating (1859) 27 Beav 121 .... 18.44
Wilson v Thomas [1958] 1 WLR 422; [1958] 1 All ER 871;
102 Sol Jo 270 .... 13.26, 13.52
Wilson v Wilson (1854) 14 CB 616; 2 CLR 818; 23 LJCP 137; 23 LT (os) 158;
2 WR 421 .... 10.24

Wilson & Steven's Contract, Re [1894] 3 Ch 546 .... 13.29
Wimpey (George) & Co Ltd v Sohn [1967] Ch 487; [1966] 2 WLR 414;
  [1966] 1 All ER 232; 110 Sol Jo 15 .... 14.12, 14.58, 14.80, 21.11
Windsor Refrigeration Co Ltd v Branch Nominees Ltd [1961] Ch 88;
  [1960] 3 WLR 108; [1960] 2 All ER 568; 104 Sol Jo 526 .... 18.128
Windsor Securities v Loreldal London Times 10 September 1975 .... 13.33
Winn v Bull (1877) 7 Ch D 29; 47 LJCh 139; 42 JP 230; 26 WR 230 .... 7.11
Winter v Lord Anson (1827) 3 Russ 488; 6 LJ (os) Ch 7 .... 12.16
Wise v Leahy (1875) IR 9 CL 384 .... 18.63
Wise v Whitburn [1924] 1 Ch 460; 93 LJCh 235; 130 LT 655; 68 Sol Jo 302 21.08
Withy v Cottle (1823) Turn & R 78 .... 13.15
Witter Ltd v TBP Industries Ltd [1996] 2 All ER 573 .... 13.04
Wolverhampton Corp v Emmons [1901] 1 KB 515 .... 13.41
Wong (Edward) Finance Co Ltd v Johnson, Stokes & Master [1984] AC 29;
  [1984] 2 WLR 1; 127 Sol Jo 784 .... 19.56, 20.32
Wood Preservation Ltd v Prior [1968] 2 All ER 849; [1969] 1 All ER 364;
  112 Sol Jo 927 .... 7.03
Wood v Jagoe (1904) 4 NIJR 143 .... 2.34
Wood v Jamieson (1844) 6 Ir Eq R 420; 1 Jo & Lat 3 .... 21.05
Wood v Knox (1852) 3 Ir Ch R 109; 4 Ir Jur (os) 309 .... 18.126
WoodBrick (Harold) Co Ltd v Ferris [1935] 2 KB 198 .... 13.14
Woods v Brown [1915] 1 IR 29; 48 ILTR 133 .... 2.14, 2.25, 11.06, 11.07
Woods v MacKenzie Hill Ltd [1975] 2 All ER 170; [1975] 1 WLR 613;
  119 Sol Jo 187; 29 P & CR 306 .... 13.19
Woods v Martin (1860) 11 Ir Ch R 148 .... 12.44
Workers Trust & Merchant Bank Ltd v Dojap Investments Ltd
  [1993] 2 All ER 370 ; [1993] 2 WLR 702 .... 10.18, 13.33
Worthington v Warrington (1849) 8 CB 134; 18 LJCP 350; 13 LT (os) 303 .. 13.86
Wragg v Lovett [1948] 2 All ER 968 .... 3.08-3.09
Wright & Thompson's Contract, Re [1920] 1 Ch 191; 89 LJCh 66;
  122 LT 92; 38 TLR 37; 64 Sol Jo 52 .... 14.48
Wright v Chatteris (1846) 7 LT (os) 111 .... 13.86
Wright v Dannah (1809) 2 Camp 203 .... 6.38
Wright v Griffith (1851) 1 Ir Ch R 695; 3 Ir Jur (os) 138 .... 14.06, 14.19, 14.71
Wright v St George (1861) 12 Ir Ch R 226 .... 6.28
Wright v Stavert (1860) 2 El & El 721; 29 LJQB 161; 24 JP 405;
  6 Jur (ns) 867; 8 WR 413 .... 6.10-6.12
Wright v Tracy (1874) IR 8 CL 478; 8 ILTR 142 .... 17.02
Wroth v Tyler [1974] Ch 30; [1973] 1 All ER 897; [1973] 2 WLR 405;
  117 Sol Jo 90; 25 P & CR 138; 228 Est Gaz 1715 .... 13.49, 13.54
  .... 13.78, 13.80, 13.83
Wyld v Silver [1963] 1 QB 169; [1963] Ch 243; [1962] 3 WLR 841;
  [1962] 3 All ER 309; 106 Sol Jo 875; 60 LGR 461 .... 21.22
Wynne v Liverpool Corporation [1995] EGCS 77 .... 13.41
Wyse v Leahy (1875) IR 9 CL 384 .... 15.10

Wyse v Russell (1882) 11 LR Ir 173; 17 ILTR 31 ....6.26

X

Xenos v Wickham (1866) LR 2 HL 296; 36 LJPC 313; 16 LT 800; 16 WR 38;
    2 Mar LC 537 ....18.124

Y

Yandle & Sons v Sutton [1922] 2 Ch 199; 91 LJCh 567; 127 LT 783 ......9.23, 9.26
Yates v Farebrother (1819) 4 Madd 239 ....10.26
Yeilding & Westbrook, Re (1886) 31 Ch D 344; 55 LJCh 496; 54 LT 531;
    34 WR 397 ....12.44
Yianni v Edwin Evans & Sons [1982] QB 373; [1981] 3 WLR 843;
    125 Sol Jo 694 ....4.23
Young & Harston's Contract, Re (1885) 31 Ch D 168; 53 LT 837;
    34 WR 84 ....20.09
Young v Schuler (1883) 11 QBD 651 ....18.119

Chapter 1

NATURE OF CONVEYANCING

I. NATURE OF CONVEYANCING

[1.01] Conveyancing is concerned largely with the acquisition and transfer of estates and interests in land.[1] It has, therefore, a close connection with land law and, indeed, the two subjects are so intertwined that it is often difficult to see where the distinction lies between them. Generally it may be said that land law is more concerned with defining the various estates and interests which make up the ownership of land,[2] while conveyancing is more concerned with the procedures whereby the owners of those estates and interests may dispose of them, eg, by sale, lease or mortgaging, and what the purchaser, lessee or mortgagee must do to get a good title to what he is buying or acquiring.

[1.02] Ownership of land under our system of law is extremely complex and in respect of any particular piece of land it may be fragmented into numerous interests and sub-interests. This is especially so in the urban areas of Ireland, where the ownership may be split up amongst a great number of people holding under what are known as "pyramid" titles.[3] For this reason it is not surprising that the disposition of such land, or conveyancing, is also complicated. This is a basic fact which those who frequently call for a simpler and cheaper system would do well to remember.[4] It should also be emphasised that conveyancers are usually well aware of the difficulties of their branch of the law and considerable efforts have been made in recent

---

1. Among the leading English textbooks are Annand and Cain, *Modern Conveyancing* (1984); Barnsley, *Conveyancing Law and Practice* (3rd ed, 1988); *Emmet on Title* (19th ed, by Farrand); Farrand, *Contract and Conveyance* (4th ed, 1983). See also Wolstenholme and Cherry, *Conveyancing Statutes* (13th ed, by Farrand 1972); Wylie, *Irish Conveyancing Statutes* (1994).
2. See Wylie, *Irish Land Law* (2nd ed, 1986), especially paras 1.01-04. See also Coughlan, *Property Law* (1995) Ch 1; Lyall, *Land Law in Ireland* (1994) Ch 1.
3. *Ibid* paras 4.179-82. To some extent the position has been ameliorated by the ground rents purchase scheme: see Wylie, *Irish Landlord and Tenant Law* Ch 31; Fitzgerald, *Land Registry Practice* (2nd ed, 1995) Ch 17. See also para **[16.92]** *post*.
4. Arguably, modern developments have made matters even more complicated, see para **[1.20]** *et seq, post*.

decades to simplify the system, though it is fair to say that much remains to be done. Perhaps the greatest contribution towards simplification, and, of course, thereby the cost, of conveyancing was the introduction during the last century of a system of registration of title. As we shall see,[5] this system, where it applies, greatly reduces, though it does not abolish,[6] the scope of one of the major and time-consuming steps in the conveyancing process, investigation of title.[7] The significance of this is great in Ireland when one remembers that most agricultural land, which was vested in tenant farmers under the Land Purchase Acts (with fee simple titles),[8] became subject to compulsory registration under the Local Registration of Title (Ireland) Act 1891.[9]

[1.03] The complexity of conveyancing can, perhaps, be illustrated best by comparing the transfer of the ownership of a chattel, eg, a bicycle, with the conveyance of a piece of land.[10] In most cases the ownership of a chattel may be transferred with the minimum of formality and the utmost speed. One can hand over the purchase price to the seller and take immediate physical delivery of the chattel. Rarely does one have to query the right of the seller to sell or to consider the need to obtain legal or other expert advice before completing the transaction. Thus the costs involved in the transaction, apart from raising the purchase price, are usually minimal and the expenses are often non-existent. With a transfer of a piece of land, however, the reverse is true. One 'cannot assume that the purported seller is the owner of the land or, if he owns some estate or interest, that there are no other owners of estates or interests which are superior to his or, at least, would conflict with the estate or interest to be acquired by a purchaser from him so as to reduce its value and its saleability. Several enquiries and searches may be necessary to determine such matters and a full investigation of the title will

---

[5.] See especially Ch 14 *post*.

[6.] See para **[15.07]** *post*.

[7.] This is true, of course, only where the title to the land in question is already registered. Title to land which becomes subject to registration for the first time on the occurrence of the transaction in question will have to be investigated before the Land Registry will complete the process of registration, Ch 20 *post*. Furthermore, a registered land transaction is more complicated where it involves a disposition of part only of the parcel registered.

[8.] See *Irish Land Law,* paras 1.50-6 1.63-8 18.02-3 and 21.02.

[9.] Now replaced by the Registration of Title Act 1964. See Fitzgerald, *Land Registry Practice* (2nd ed, 1995).

[10.] See Lawson and Rudden, *The Law of Property* (2nd ed, 1982) Ch IV. Much useful learning is still to be found in Sugden, *The Law of Vendors and Purchasers* (14th ed, 1862). Sir Edword Sugden (later Lord St Leonards) was successively Lord Chancellor of Ireland and of Great Britain.

often be necessary if the title to the land is not already registered in the Land Registry.

[1.04] Caution is the watchword of the conveyancer and should be observed by every purchaser of land. The result is that most conveyancing transactions take several weeks to complete. It is well-established amongst conveyancers that each transaction ought to be conducted according to time-honoured procedures - many steps to be taken in stages at the right time and in the right order. If the well-worn paths are trod, the transaction should be completed to the satisfaction of all concerned. If one strays one courts disaster. To the lay person this often seems to be formalism, indeed, almost fetishism, but to the conveyancer it is an indispensable condition of the practice of the profession. That is not to say that there may not be room for improvements or that changes in conveyancing practice have not occurred and will not occur. These are matters which will be raised frequently throughout this book. For the moment it may be said with fairness that the past reputation of conveyancers for conservatism is justified, for a small mistake may have the result that the purchaser does not get a good title and when this happens he will not be able to borrow money on the security of the property or to sell it at a later date; this acknowledgement of the reputation for conservatism is not, of course, the same as saying that the conservatism was or is unjustified. The source of the criticism of conveyancing practice which seems to have been rising in strength on both sides of the Irish Sea in recent decades is not hard to see.[11] Despite this, conveyancers insist that there is a limit to how far they can simplify procedures and, therefore, reduce costs. From time to time it is even suggested that, if conveyancers will not co-operate by simplifying procedures, conveyancing should be handed over to those who will provide a cheaper service.[12] Controversy is inevitable and for the moment we are content to draw attention to it. It is better to suspend judgment until a full study of what precisely is involved in the process of conveyancing, as conducted by the conveyancers of today, has been made.

[1.05] By way of introduction we summarise the main stages of a typical conveyancing transaction.[13] *First*, there is the stage before a binding contract for the sale or other disposition of the land in question is entered into.[14] This

---

11. In more recent times the criticism has been muted, no doubt partly because of the property slump which has hit the market in England in particular.
12. The issue of the solicitors' "monopoly" (within the terms of s 58 of the Solicitors Act 1954) has been raised from time to time but has never been removed by the Oireachtas.
13. The remaining chapters of the book follow this order.
14. See Chs 2-5 *post*.

stage may include pre-contract negotiations involving an estate agent or auctioneer and questions may arise concerning such matters as deposits paid at this stage[15] and entitlement to fees and commissions.[16] Other matters which may be relevant at this stage include the raising of finance for the transaction (eg, a loan for purchase of the property in question),[17] arranging an independent survey of the property,[18] planning applications and searches[19] and, perhaps, increasingly nowadays *pre*-contract enquiries or "requisitions".[20] It should be noted that often, perhaps too often, solicitors are not instructed at this stage of the transaction and so find themselves later trying to get their clients out of ill-considered commitments which they have entered into.

[1.06] The *second* major stage is completion of the formalities for a binding contract for the sale or other disposition of the land in question, in particular compliance with the Statute of Frauds.[21] Here solicitors usually do play the dominant role, at least so far as the fixing of the terms of the contract is concerned.[22] In most cases this will be done by using the standard form contract issued by the Law Society of Ireland.[23]

[1.07] Once the parties are committed to a binding contract, the *third* stage arises which in most cases is handled by the solicitors for the two sides to the contract. This stage is traditionally referred to as the investigation of title. In the case of a sale, this involves the vendor's solicitor in deducing or showing evidence of the vendor's title to the property[24] and the purchaser's solicitor in examining that title and satisfying himself as to its validity and value,[25] if necessary by raising queries and additional questions with the vendor's solicitor, ie, requisitions on title.[26] As has already been mentioned, this stage

---

15. See paras **[2.26]** and **[3.15]** *post*.
16. See paras **[2.28]** and **[3.18]** *post*.
17. See para **[3.44]** *post*.
18. See para **[4.21]** *post*.
19. See para **[3.42]** *post*.
20. On the different practices which have traditionally operated as between Ireland and England with respect to pre-contract or preliminary enquiries, see paras **[1.29-30]** *infra*.
21. (Ir) 1695, s 2. See Ch 6 *post* and the recent comprehensive treatment in Farrell, *Irish Law of Specific Performance* (1994).
22. *Cf* sales by private treaty with sales by public auction, and note also special cases such as court sales and compulsory purchase by a public authority. See Chs 2-3, 8 and 11, *post*.
23. See Ch 9 and Appendix II *post*.
24. Note, however, that increasingly the vendor's solicitor deduces title *before* the contract is entered into, at least to the extent of furnishing *prima facie* evidence of the title: see paras **[5.02]** and **[14.02]** *post*.
25. See Ch 15 *post*.
26. See Ch 16 *post*.

in the conveyancing process is greatly simplified where the title to the land in question is registered in the Land Registry.[27] Connected with the investigation of title is the need to make important searches relevant to the title to try to ensure that the purchaser will not be affected by some undisclosed or unforeseen transaction, but such searches are usually made shortly before completion.[28] The logic of making these searches at this stage, after rather than before the parties commit themselves to a binding contract, is examined later.[29]

[1.08] Once the purchaser's solicitor (or barrister retained to give an opinion on the matter) is satisfied with the title and accepts it on his client's behalf, the *fourth* stage arises, the drafting of the conveyance for the transaction in question; though it is often the case that the purchaser's solicitor will furnish the draft conveyance with his requisitions on title, taking care to specify that this is done without prejudice to the requisitions.[30] The purchaser's solicitor (or barrister asked to settle the form of conveyance) normally performs this task, again frequently using or adapting a standard form document which may be found in one of the well-known books of precedents[31] or, in the case of registered land, a form prescribed or suggested by Land Registration Rules. Correspondence may take place (though this is rare) between the purchaser's solicitor and the vendor's solicitor before the final draft is agreed, and engrossed.[32] The engrossed conveyance is then sent, together with, in the case of unregistered land,[33] a memorial for registration in the Registry of Deeds, to the vendor's solicitor for execution by the vendor.[34] Arrangements for completion are then made (if not already agreed) and, some days before that, the vendor's solicitor sends the purchaser's solicitor an "apportionment" account showing the amounts due for rates and rent (if any) by one to the other, the amount of interest payable (if any) and the amount of the purchase money payable on the completion date after making provision for these items and after crediting the deposit. It is called an apportionment account because any rent, rates or other annual outgoings are apportioned on a from-day-to-day basis by reference to the completion date.[35]

---

27. See also Chs 14 and 15 *post.*
28. See para **[15.39]** *et seq, post.*
29. Paras **[1.29]** *infra* and **[5.01]** *et seq, post.*
30. Otherwise he may be deemed to have waived his client's right to object to title and to have accepted the title, see para **[15.52]** *post.*
31. See chs 17-19 *post.* Of particular use in Ireland is Laffoy, *Irish Conveyancing Precedents.*
32. Para **[17.06]** *post.*
33. See para **[18.136]** *post.*
34. See para **[18.119]** *post.*
35. See para **[20.03]** *post.*

[1.09] The *fifth* stage is completion.[36] In the case of unregistered land the executed deed for the transaction, together with the documents of title, are handed over in return for the balance of money shown on the apportionment account. Any points arising from searches are explained and dealt with[37] and the purchaser also usually receives the keys to the property. This completion process will be rather more complicated if other parties are involved, eg, a building society, which is often so in the typical case of a house purchase transaction.[38] The deed for the current transaction will be taken to the Stamp Office for stamping[39] and then, in the case of unregistered land, registered in the Registry of Deeds.[40] In the case of registered land, or if the land is in an area of compulsory registration and the transaction is the first conveyance on sale,[41] registration in the Land Registry will be necessary to complete the formalities and to ensure that the legal title passes to the purchaser.[42] Finally, each solicitor furnishes his client with his Bill of Costs[43] and discharges any undertakings given to third parties, such as a building society or a bank.[44]

[1.10] It cannot be emphasised too much that this summary gives the barest outline of the conveyancing process. Many matters are not mentioned[45] and numerous variations occur depending upon the nature of the transaction. This should become clearer from the discussion in the remaining parts of this book, which follow the order of the main stages in the conveyancing process mentioned above. Before that, however, something further must be said of conveyancing law and practice in Ireland.

II. CONVEYANCING IN IRELAND

There are several major factors to be kept in mind when considering the discussion in the remaining chapters of this book.

[36.] See Ch 20 *post.*

[37.] It was common to provide that the vendor was to furnish only such searches as were already in his possession and for the purchaser to make further searches on his own behalf. However, in 1978 the Law Society's Conveyancing Committee recommended that the vendor should, in addition, requisition and furnish a negative search against himself and other parties immediately on the title. See further, para **[15.43]** *post.*

[38.] Para **[20.01]** *post.*

[39.] Para **[20.38]** *post.*

[40.] Para **[20.43]** *post.*

[41.] Para **[16.55]** *post.*

[42.] Para **[20.44]** *post.*

[43.] Para **[20.49]** *post.*

[44.] Para **[20.14]** *post.*

[45.] See further, Chs 2-3 *post.*

A. Historical Background

[1.11] Just as the land law of Ireland is rooted in the history of the island, so is conveyancing law and practice. It could not be otherwise, for the one subject is complementary to the other. This historical background has been considered in detail elsewhere[46] and so it is proposed here simply to highlight those features which have had a lasting influence on modern conveyancing.

1. Two Jurisdictions

[1.12] One obvious factor to be borne in mind is the fact that since 1920 there have existed two quite separate jurisdictions in Ireland, the Republic of Ireland (previously Saorstát Éireann) the law and practice of which is the subject-matter of this book, and Northern Ireland. This has inevitably resulted in variations in the statute law applicable in the field of conveyancing as in other areas of law,[47] and, of course, there is the further complication in Northern Ireland of its remaining part of the United Kingdom and, therefore, also subject to much Westminster legislation.[48] So far as practice is concerned, solicitors are now governed by the rules and regulations of two separate professional bodies, the Law Society of Ireland in the Republic[49] and the Law Society of Northern Ireland.[50] We return later to the special role of solicitors with respect to conveyancing.[51]

2. Agricultural Land

[1.13] As a result of the operation of the Land Purchase Acts during the last hundred years or so,[52] most agricultural land in both parts of Ireland is held in fee simple by the occupying landowners. There is very little leasehold agricultural land because of restrictions against subletting or sub-division of land.[53] An agricultural or pastoral holding could be let, sublet or sub-divided without the consent in writing of the Land Commission,[54] unless the land

---

46. See *Irish Land Law*, Ch 1.
47. *Cf* eg, Wallace, *Land Registry Practice in Northern Ireland* (2nd ed, 1987).
48. Since 1974 all legislation has been passed by Orders-in-Council made under the Northern Ireland (Temporary Provisions) Act 1972.
49. See Solicitors Acts 1954 1960 and 1994.
50. See Solicitors (NI) Order 1976, which replaced the Solicitors Acts (NI) 1922, 1938, 1943 and 1948.
51. Para **[1.34]** *infra*.
52. See *Irish Land Law*, paras 1.51-6 and 1.63-8.
53. *Ibid*, paras 18.03 and 20.27.
54. Land Act 1965, s 12(1). The Commission may exercise their power to withhold consent "solely to prevent the creation or continuance of holdings, which, in the opinion of the Land Commission, are not economic holdings." *Ibid*, s 12(2). See para **[16.30]** *post*. The Commission continues to function until the Irish Land Commission (Dissolution) Act 1992 is brought into effect by an appropriate statutory instrument.

purchase annuity[55] had been paid off and the land was within an urban area or certified by the Commission as being required for urban development by reason of its proximity to an urban area.[56] It is still true that there is very little leasehold conveyancing in respect of agricultural land in Ireland, despite attempts from time to time to stimulate modern leasing.[57] The standard method of expansion of a holding for the Irish farmer, which also avoided the restrictions just mentioned,[58] was the taking of conacre and agistment lettings.[59] These arrangements, however, are often made informally without the aid of a conveyancer.[60]

[1.14] There is one special feature of agricultural land which has arisen in recent times and about which conveyancers should take precautions. This is the "Milk Quota" system introduced by the EEC in the early 1980s.[61] Such a quota is a valuable asset for the farm in question and its existence or not is clearly an important consideration for anyone acquiring an interest in the farm.[62] The Law Society has recommended the use of special requisitions to check on such matters.[63]

[1.15] Perhaps the most significant feature of agricultural land in Ireland is the fact that all land which was vested in tenant farmers under the Land Purchase Acts became subject to compulsory registration of title under the Local Registration of Title (Ireland) Act 1891.[64] Since most agricultural land is, therefore, already registered freehold land, investigation of title may be a simple matter and conveying or charging it thereby a straightforward process. However, the slight qualification has to be entered partly because

---

[55.] See *Irish Land Law*, paras 1.51-3 and 1.55.

[56.] Land Act 1965, s 12(3). Note, however, the "general" consent to such sub-division issued in 1977: see para **[16.34]** *post*. Note also that the Land Commission consent is required for the vesting of an interest in non-urban land in a person who is not a qualified person within s 45(1) of the 1965 Act (eg not being an Irish citizen or a resident in the State continuously for seven years). See **[16.37]** *post*.

[57.] See Wylie, *Irish Landlord and Tenant Law*, para 1.12.

[58.] Apart from dealing with Land Act consents, the Land Commission's activities were until recently largely concerned with relief of congestion, especially in the Western counties, and enlargement of uneconomic holdings.

[59.] *Irish Landlord and Tenant Law,* para 3.20 *et seq.*

[60.] Note the criticisms quoted in *Irish Land Law,* para 20.27.

[61.] See the discussion at para **[16.101]** *post*.

[62.] In certain circumstances the farmer may be able to retain the quota after a transfer.

[63.] See the Society's *Conveyancing Handbook* issued in 1990, Ch 6, but note the new recommendations issued in February 1995 to take account of changes made by the European Community (Milk Quota) Regulations 1994.

[64.] Section 22. The 1891 Act is now replaced by the Registration of Title Act 1964 (see now s 23(1)(a) of that Act). On its operation, see Fitzgerald, *Land Registry Practice* (2nd ed, 1995).

many titles registered under the 1891 Act were registered subject to a "note as to equities" preserving rights and interests vested in third parties and remaining protected without registration,[65] and partly because of the propensity of Irish farmers to execute home-made wills leaving ill-defined rights in their farms to surviving relatives, eg, "rights of residence".[66] Another problem results from the emigration of younger people from the poorer rural areas, so that it is common for there to be a failure to prove farmers' wills or to take out letters of administration to their estates. Often the widow and one of the sons continue to farm the land without attention to the formalities of the law and many years may pass before a nest of conveyancing problems turns up. The widow or son, or both, may wish to enter into some transaction with respect to the land and it is only then that it is discovered that the title is still registered in the deceased farmer's name. Or some of the other members of the family may return and lay claim to shares in the farm under the deceased farmer's will or as intestate successors. Indeed, the farm may pass informally through the hands of more than one generation of the deceased farmer's family before the problems come to light. In the end the rights of the various claimants are usually determined according to the doctrine of adverse possession,[67] which illustrates how the register in the Land Registry can for many years cease to "mirror" the true state of the title to the land.[68]

3. Urban Land

[1.16] The conveyancing position with respect to urban land in Ireland was, until recently, a complete contrast to that applying to agricultural land. Here, for the most part, there prevailed a system of *unregistered leasehold* conveyancing instead of *registered freehold* conveyancing. The Land Purchase Acts did not apply to urban land and the registration of title system was not extended compulsorily to urban land when it was introduced in the nineteenth century. This concept has been introduced only recently[69] and very little voluntary registration has occurred in the meantime. However, in recent years some of those developing what was agricultural land[70], the title

---

65. See *Irish Land Law,* para 21.07 and para 13.25; see also para **[14.38]** *post.*

66. See *ibid,* paras 20.13-24.

67. *Ibid*, paras 23.40-2. See the discussion in Brady and Kerr, *The Limitation of Actions* (2nd ed, 1994), Ch 5 and Brady, *Succession Law in Ireland* (2nd ed, 1995), Ch 10. Note the need now for a tax clearance certificate before the Land Registry will register a possessory title: see para **[14.82]** *post.*

68. *Ibid,* para 21.01.

69. See Fitzgerald, *Land Registry Practice* (2nd ed, 1995), Ch 1.

70. Some voluntary registration has also been effected by developers in urban areas, especially by institutions used to the widespread compulsory registration in England and Wales.

to which was not registered, or demesne lands (which were not subject to the Land Purchase Acts[71]) have voluntarily registered the titles. This expedites conveyancing and may reduce expense in future dealings with the land as lower solicitors' scale fees apply in the case of registered land.[72] Urban land is instead largely subject to the Registry of Deeds system introduced by the Registration of Deeds Act (Ireland) 1707.[73] This is simply a system of registration of documents dealing with land and is not a system of registration of title. It does not simplify investigation of title in the way that a title system does; its main function is the securing of priority for registered dealings over unregistered ones.[74] However, since the system applies to all land not subject to the Land Registry system, the making of Registry of Deeds searches[75] is a standard feature of conveyancing with respect to unregistered land, which is, as has already been explained, mostly urban land.

[1.17] The other very significant feature of conveyancing with respect to urban land in both parts of Ireland is the complexity of so many of the titles. It is common to find that a particular plot of land forms part of a large sub-division scheme, whose origin may date back to a grant made decades, if not centuries, ago. A series of fee farm and sub-fee farm grants,[76] leases and sub-leases has usually been employed to create further sub-divisions of the original plot. The result is that the occupier of any one part of that original plot holds under a "pyramid" title in common with his neighbours and is often subject to a bewildering number and variety of rights created by exceptions and reservations in earlier conveyances.[77] Then the conveyancing complications can be considerable, eg, if a prospective purchaser intends to develop the plot which he wishes to buy. Failure to investigate the pyramid title thoroughly in such a case could expose the purchaser to conflicting

---

71. See Land Act 1923, s 24(2)(c).
72. See para **[20.49]** *post.*
73. See *Irish Land Law,* Ch 22.
74. *Ibid*, para 3.086-9 and 13.141-50.
75. See para **[15.42]** *post.*
76. Which, though passing the fee simple to the grantee, in most instances creates the relationship of landlord and tenant between the grantor and grantee - hence the relevance of leasehold law in urban land in Ireland. See the discussion of fee farm grants in *Irish Land Law,* Ch 4, especially at paras 4.057-111.
77. See on pyramid titles, *Irish Land Law,* paras 4.179-82. Fortunately, much simplification has resulted from the operation of the ground rents legislation, which enables the occupying lessee to buy out the superior interests and to acquire an unincumbered fee simple. See *Irish Landlord and Tenant Law,* Ch 31.

claims by superior owners, eg, grantees or lessees claiming the right to enforce restrictive covenants against the plot in question.[78]

[1.18] Another complexity of conveyancing in urban areas which is a comparatively recent development in Ireland is the growth of flat and apartment schemes, ie, where self-contained flats or apartments are built in a block in such a way that they are totally dependant on each other for support and the use of common facilities, such as gas and electricity installations, water and sewerage pipes, stairways and lifts. Catering for the rights and needs of the developer and builder of such schemes on the one hand, and of the various flat owners on the other, poses some intricate problems for the conveyancer.[79] Until recently the prevalence of leasehold conveyancing tended to confine such schemes in Ireland to leasehold schemes which create fewer problems from the conveyancing point of view. However, in recent years conveyancers have found themselves faced with the problems which arise if any of the flatowners subsequently acquire the freehold to particular flats or apartments.[80]

[1.19] Finally, it should be noted that, while most conveyancing in the urban areas of Ireland remains concerned with leasehold law, recent legislation is rapidly bringing about a change. Under this legislation,[81] residential occupiers holding under long leases have been given the right to buy out the freehold of their homes.[82] As the terms created by leases such as those granted under the Settled Land Acts of the late nineteenth century[83] approached expiry, more and more lessees have felt the need to exercise their rights under this legislation. And, since so much urban residential property in Ireland was held under such leases, the pattern of the past decade has been a steady rise in the amount of urban freehold property. This may

---

78. See *Irish Land Law,* Ch 19, especially at paras 19.46-47. One of the advantages of acquiring the fee simple under the ground rents scheme is the fact that most covenants cease to have effect: see *Whelan v Cork Corporation* [1991] ILRM 19 (an appeal was dismissed by the Supreme Court orally on 15 November 1990). Note that this may be so even though the fee simple is acquired outside that scheme: see *Irish Landlord and Tenant Law,* p 1031.

79. See further, para **[19.11]** *et seq, post.* Also Aldridge, *The Law of Flats* (2nd ed, 1989);Cawthorn and Barraclough, *Sale and Management of Flats* (2nd ed, 1996); George and George, *The Sale of Flats* (5th ed, 1984).

80. See the recent Supreme Court decision in *Metropolitan Properties v O'Brien* [1995] 1 IR 467, especially the judgment of O'Flaherty J. See also Andrae-Jones, 'A Concurrent Lease to Secure Flat Maintenance' (1962) 26 Conv 348; Scamell, 'Legal Aspects of Flat Schemes' (1961) 14 CLP 161; Tolson, 'Land without Earth: Freehold Flats in English Law' (1950) 14 Conv 350.

81. The Landlord and Tenant (Ground Rents) Acts 1967-1987.

82. See *Irish Land Law,* paras 18.26-8 and 18.40-1. Also *Landlord and Tenant Law,* Ch 31.

83. *Ibid,* Ch 8 and paras 18.21-5.

bring about a long-term and, perhaps, the only solution to the problem of pyramid titles.[84]

4. Some Modern Developments

[1.20] One of the major features of the twentieth century has been the development of new branches of the law and the great expansion of existing ones. Land law has seen much of this development[85] and this has inevitably influenced conveyancing law and practice. In the next few paragraphs we outline some of these new influences, most of which will be discussed in greater detail later in the book.

(i) Planning and Environmental Law

[1.21] One of the most significant developments of the twentieth century has been the growth of planning law and concern about the environment.[86] The concept of the regulation by the State of the use of land by private landowners was first introduced in Ireland during the 1930s. There is now in force comprehensive legislation dealing with planning and control of the impact of land use and development on the environment[87] and its application to the transaction in question must always be borne in mind by the parties and their conveyancers.[88] This is especially so where one of the parties proposes to change the existing use of the land or to build on it (both of which are included in the definition of "development" for the purposes of the planning legislation[89]) in such a way that the permission of the relevant planning authority is required. If the question of planning permission is not resolved as between the parties during the preliminary negotiations,[90] it will in most cases be raised at later stages of the conveyancing process, eg, as one of the terms or conditions of the contract[91] or as a requisition on title.[92]

[1.22] Quite apart from the central question of planning permission for development, numerous other, but related matters may concern the modern conveyancer. One is the enormous scope of public authority activities

---

[84.] *Ibid*, para 21.27. And note the prohibition of new ground rents contained in the Landlord and Tenant (Ground Rent) Act 1978.

[85.] See further *Irish Land Law*, paras 1.63-83. Also Lyall, *Land Law in Ireland* (1994), Ch 17.

[86.] See Scannell, *Environmental and Planning Law in Ireland* (1995).

[87.] Eg the Local Government (Planning and Development) Acts 1963-1993; Local Government (Water Pollution) Acts 1977-1990; Air Pollution Act 1987; Sea Pollution Act 1991; Environmental Protection Agency Act 1992.

[88.] See further para **[16.74]** *et seq, post.*

[89.] See para **[16.74]** *post.*

[90.] See paras **[3.42]** and **[5.09]** *post.*

[91.] Para **[7.16]** *post.*

[92.] Para **[16.74]** *post.*

nowadays in the fields of housing, public health, roads and drainage. The degree of regulation has been greatly extended by recent legislation like the Local Government (Multi-Storey Buildings) Act 1988 and the Building Control Act 1990. One of the great problems for the conveyancer today is discovering quickly and easily to what extent any of these sorts of matters may affect the piece of land with which he is currently dealing.[93] Failure to discover, for example, the existence of a closing or demolition order or proposed compulsory purchase order relating to that land may have disastrous consequences for his client. The financial burden which the client might face in complying with most of the new statutory regime could be enormous; the penalties under the new environmental protection legislation can be severe indeed. The result has been the growth in the number of requisitions on title made nowadays[94] and increasing use of pre-contract enquiries or requisitions.[95] The difficulties faced by conveyancers in these matters has resulted in a flood of recommendations and advice to practitioners issued by the Law Society's Conveyancing Committee.[96] These include standard form documents such as the *Pre-Contract Check List on Acquisition of Private Dwellinghouse* and *Pre-Lease Enquiries or Check List.*[97]

(ii) Compulsory Purchase

[1.23] Part of the development of public authority activities just mentioned has been the rapid growth during the twentieth century of powers of compulsory purchase. All sorts of State and Semi-State bodies, central government departments and local authorities have been given extensive statutory powers of compulsory acquisition of land. The result is that many transactions relating to land do not involve the traditional concept of two parties free to negotiate on a voluntary basis the terms and conditions of their agreement, which will then be executed according to time-honoured conveyancing procedures. Instead, the landowner may find himself forced to part with his land and often by use of procedures designed specifically to short-circuit normal conveyancing practice. We shall discuss these different procedures by way of comparison in later chapters.[98]

---

93. Note also the matters mentioned in Chs 4 and 5 *post.*
94. See Ch 16 *post.*
95. Paras **[1.29-30]** *infra.*
96. Many of these were collected together in the *Conveyancing Handbook* published in 1990. It is important to note that this has become increasingly out-of-date and practitioners should have regard to later items published in or issued with the Society's *Gazette.*
97. See *Conveyancing Handbook*, paras 4.19 and 12.11. For discussion see paras **[5.06]** *et seq* and para **[5.12]** *et seq post.* Set out in full at Appendix I *post.*
98. See, eg, para **[8.14]** *post.* See also the extensive treatment in McDermott and Woulfe, *Compulsory Purchase and Compensation in Ireland: Law and Practice* (1992).

(iii) Taxation

[1.24] Land has always been a primary source of wealth and so has usually attracted a substantial incidence of taxation. Today this is particularly the case and there are few conveyancing transactions which do not have some tax implications. The past decade or so has seen a rapid expansion in the number of taxes applicable and every conveyancer has a duty to advise his client as to their relevance to the transaction being contemplated or entered into. This is no easy duty to perform, for some of the new taxes are extremely hard to master conceptually and have been introduced by legislation containing some bewildering terminology. This is not a book on taxation, but an attempt will be made throughout to draw attention to the more important tax considerations, where they are relevant.

(iv) Family Property

[1.25] A subject with which conveyancers have had to grapple in recent decades has been legislation relating to family property. The Family Home Protection Act 1976 created many conveyancing difficulties and has proved to be one of the most litigated statutes of modern times.[99] Other legislation of which account must be taken includes the Family Law Act 1981[100] and the Judicial Separation and Family Law Reform Act 1989.[101] Again the Law Society's Conveyancing Committee has issued recommendations for the guidance of practitioners.[102]

B. Comparison with English Practice

[1.26] Throughout the ensuing chapters attention will be drawn to the many areas where English conveyancing practice differs substantially from that in Ireland. For the moment it may be useful to summarise some of the major points of difference. It must be emphasised that some of the traditional differences are not as great as they once were.

1. Substantive Land Law

[1.27] The first obvious point to make is that, since substantive land law differs between Ireland on the one hand and England[103] on the other,[104] it is

---

[99.] See para **[16.61]** *post*. Note the important amendments made by s 54 of the Family Law Act 1995, para **[16.69]**, sub-para (h) and **[16.70]** *post*.

[100.] See para **[16.72]** *post*.

[101.] As amended by the Family Law Act 1995, see para **[16.73]** *post*. For fuller discussion of the pre-1990 legislation, see Duncan and Scully, *Marriage Breakdown in Ireland* (1990).

[102.] See *Conveyancing Handbook*, Ch 1.

[103.] It should, of course, be noted that in this context "England" really means "England and Wales" which form one jurisdiction and share a common conveyancing system.

[104.] See *Irish Land Law*, especially at para 1.05 *et seq*. See also Lyall, *Land Law in Ireland* (1994).

inevitable that conveyancing law and practice differs in many respects. One crucial factor is that both parts of Ireland still do not have any equivalent of much of the 1925 Birkenhead legislation. There is no equivalent of the central core of that scheme, namely the Law of Property Act 1925, and in the field of settlements the pre-runners of the Settled Land Act 1925, are still in force, ie the Settled Land Acts 1882-90. There is no equivalent either of the Land Charges Act 1925,[105] and arguably these are the three Acts of 1925 which had the greatest impact on English conveyancing practice after 1925;[106] the last one has probably caused more problems than any of the others.[107] And, whereas England had only a few local deeds registries, the Registry of Deeds has operated throughout both parts of Ireland since the early eighteenth century.[108] Thus of the six major Birkenhead Acts, it may be said that in Ireland there are equivalents only of the Trustee Act,[109] the Land Registration Act,[110] and the Administration of Estates Act.[111] It must be stressed that they are equivalents only and that there are numerous important differences in the Irish legislation.

[1.28] Apart from the 1925 legislation, there are many areas where, largely for historical reasons, the law has developed differently and different concepts have been employed. The consequences of the "Irish Land Problem" have been discussed elsewhere.[112] This led to the passing of the Land Purchase Acts and the significant effect they had on conveyancing in the rural parts of Ireland.[113] The prevalence of leasehold conveyancing in urban areas has also been mentioned earlier,[114] as have the problems caused by pyramid titles.[115] One of the concepts used in this context is a fee farm grant, which can take several different forms, most of which are not met at all in English conveyancing practice.[116] Other concepts commonly found in

---

[105] Now the Land Charges Act 1972 and Local Land Charges Act 1975. But note that contracts for the sale of land are treated as registrable in the Registry of Deeds in Ireland, see para **[6.65]** *post.*

[106] See Grove, 'Conveyancing and the Property Acts of 1925' (1961) 24 MLR 123; Hargreaves, 'Modern Real Property' (1956) 19 MLR 14; Withers 'Twenty Years of the 1925 Legislation" (1972) 36 Conv 325.

[107] *Cf* the Statutory Charges Register in Northern Ireland, see *Irish Land Law,* para 21.57 *et seq.*

[108] See further, paras **[15.42-4]** *post.*

[109] Though the pre-runner, the Trustee Act 1893, is still largely in force. However, the 1925 Act did not make many substantive changes in the earlier Act. See *Irish Land Law,* Ch 10.

[110] Registration of Title Act 1964. See Fitzgerald, *Land Registry Practice* (2nd ed, 1995).

[111] See Succession Act 1965. See Brady, *Succession Law in Ireland* (2nd ed, 1995).

[112] See *Irish Land Law,* Ch 1.

[113] See para **[1.13]** *supra.*

[114] See para **[1.16]** *supra.*

[115] See para **[1.17]** *supra.*

[116] See *Irish Land Law,* paras 4.057-111. Also *Irish Landlord and Tenant Law,* para 4.40 *et seq.*

Irish, but not English, practice include leases for lives renewable for ever,[117] leases for lives combined with a term of years,[118] judgment mortgages,[119] rights of residence[120] and conacre and agistment lettings.[121]

2. Pre-Contract Enquiries and Searches

[1.29] One of the most striking developments in English conveyancing practice in recent decades was the growth in the use of pre-contract or preliminary enquiries before the parties commit themselves to a binding agreement for the transaction in question. Over the years these enquiries became quite extensive, with most solicitors using a standard form or list. While this appeared to be a quite logical development, in the sense that the complications of modern legislation[122] suggest a need to take such precautions before allowing one's client to commit himself to a contract, the practice aroused considerable controversy in England,[123] as we shall discuss later.[124] Until recently it had not been adopted to any significant extent in Ireland. It is only in very recent times that the Law Society's Conveyancing Committee has felt obliged to recommend the use of *pre*-contract enquiries in certain circumstances,[125] in addition to the traditional *post*-contract requisitions on title.[126] Nor had there been adopted in Ireland the system in England of making detailed searches of local authorities prior to the contract, though enquiries on planning matters are fairly common in Ireland at this stage. Lack of any extensive practice in this area is not really very surprising, because, of course, local authorities in Ireland are not obliged to keep local land charges registers as they have been in England since 1925.[127] However, it has come to be recognised increasingly in recent years that, such are the complexities of legislation and related regulations which may affect land nowadays, pre-contract enquiries may be appropriate in many cases.[128] Indeed the Law Society's Conveyancing Committee has now issued a

---

[117.] See *Irish Land Law,* paras 4.167-76.

[118.] *Ibid,* paras 4.177-8.

[119.] *Ibid,* paras 13.163-90.

[120.] *Ibid,* paras 20.13-24.

[121.] *Ibid,* paras 20.25-7. See also Wylie 'The "Irishness" of Irish Land Law' (1995) 46 NILQ 332.

[122.] See para **[1.20]** *supra.*

[123.] See, eg, Adams, 'Enquiries before Contract' (1970) 120 NLJ 610 and 630; Wickenden and Edell, 'The Practitioners' Inquisition' (1961) 25 Conv 336.

[124.] Ch 5 *post.*

[125.] See *ibid.*

[126.] See Ch 16 *post.*

[127.] See Land Charges Act 1925, s 15. See now Local Land Charges Act 1975.

[128.] See the Law Society's *Conveyancing Handbook,* para 12.11. For discussion see Ch 5 *post.*

Purchaser's Solicitor's Pre-Contract Check List on Acquisition of Private Dwellinghouse.[129]

[1.30] Subject to the recent changes in practice mentioned in the previous paragraph, it remains the position in Ireland that many of the enquiries made in England at the pre-contract stage are generally made after the contract has been entered into, as part of the investigation of title. They are usually raised in the form of requisitions on title.[130] The same is generally true of searches, eg, in the Registry of Deeds.[131]

3. Formalities for Contracts

[1.31] There is now a clear divergence between Irish law and English law on the formalities for creation of an enforceable contract for the sale or other disposition of land. Here the position remains governed by the Statute of Frauds,[132] but in England the law was altered substantially[133] by s 2 of the Law of Property (Miscellaneous Provisions) Act 1989.[134] It is questionable whether the new provision in England has brought the improvements to law and practice which were anticipated.[135] A number of questions of interpretation has already arisen.[136]

[1.32] In England it has long been standard conveyancing practice that a binding contract for the transaction in question does not come into force until an "exchange" has taken place. Each party signs his own copy of the agreed form of the contract and these copies are then exchanged, usually by post.[137] In Ireland, however, there was no such general practice and normally what happened was that the purchaser signed the contract and this was then

---

[129.] *Ibid. Cf* the *Pre-Lease Enquiries or Check List, ibid,* para 4.19. For discussion see para **[5.12]** *post.*

[130.] See para **[15.17]** *et seq, post.*

[131.] See para **[15.39]** *et seq, post*

[132.] Statute of Frauds (Ir) 1695. For a comprehensive discussion of the operation of this statute, see Farrell, *Irish Law of Specific Performance* (1994). See also Wylie, *Irish Conveyancing Statutes* (1994), p 23 *et seq*; Ch 6 *post.*

[133.] The English Statute of Frauds 1677, s 4 of which was the equivalent of s 2 of the Irish statute, governed the matter there until it was replaced, without substantive amendment, by s 40 of the Law of Property Act 1925.

[134.] Section 2 now requires the contract to be in writing and signed by or on behalf of both parties. It also abolishes the doctrine of part performance.

[135.] The new provision was based on recommendations made by the Law Commission: see *Report on Formalities for Contracts for Sale, etc, of Land* (Law Com No 164; 1987).

[136.] See, eg, *Spiro v Glencrown Properties Ltd* [1991] 1 All ER 600; *Record v Bell* [1991] 4 All ER 471; *Tootal Clothing Ltd v Guinea Properties Management Ltd* [1992] 41 EG 117; *Commission for New Towns v Cooper (GB) Ltd* [1995] 2 All ER 929; *Lotteryking Ltd v Amec Properties Ltd* [1995] 28 EG 100.

[137.] This system is not without its problems, see paras **[6.61]-[6.63]** *post.*

sent to the vendor for his acceptance and signing. This remains common practice but in recent times solicitors have, on occasion, adopted an "exchange" system. We shall discuss later the advantages and disadvantages of the two systems.[138]

4. Abstracts of Title

[1.33] In the case of unregistered land in particular,[139] one of the most important stages of the conveyancing process is the investigation of title. The purchaser's solicitor must be supplied with documentary evidence of title and it was the practice prior to this century on both sides of the Irish Sea for this to be done by giving him an "abstract" of title. In essence this is a summary of the relevant documents of title and of relevant events, such as births, deaths and marriages, from which the purchaser's solicitor can decide whether to accept the title on his client's behalf and to proceed further with the transaction.[140] The practice survived in England, though by the 1960s some had suggested that good abstracting was a dying art which would eventually succumb to modern techniques, such as photocopying of the title deeds.[141] In both parts of Ireland abstracts were almost unknown in modern practice and for decades the standard practice was to send the bundle of original deeds to the purchaser's solicitor and to leave it to him to wade through them. Fortunately the advent and use of photocopying machines has greatly reduced the risk of vital title documents being mislaid. We shall return to this subject later.[142]

III. ROLE OF PROFESSIONAL PERSONS

[1.34] Most conveyancing transactions involve the employment of professional persons. A central role is played by solicitors, usually at least two - one acting for the vendor and the other acting for the purchaser. The courts tend to discourage the same solicitor acting for both parties in the same transaction, because of the dangers of that solicitor facing a conflict of interest. During the course of most transactions, several points of potential conflict may arise and it may prove extremely difficult for one solicitor to hold the balance fairly between the various parties. For example, such matters as fixing the terms and conditions of the contract for sale or drafting the conveyance involve numerous decisions which necessarily tend to favour one party at the expense of the other and, if one solicitor acts for both

---

138. See *ibid*. See also the recent discussion by the Supreme court in *Embourg Ltd v Tyler Group Ltd*, Supreme Court, unrep, 5 March 1996 (223/95).

139. See Ch 14 *post*.

140. See paras **[14.42]-[14.44]** *post*.

141. See the English Law Society's Working Party Group on Conveyancing's *Second Interim Report* (1966) paras 40-43, also (1969) 66 L Soc Gaz 492.

142. Paras **[14.42]-[14.53]** *post*.

parties, he may find himself unavoidably drawn into a position where the interest of one of his clients conflicts with the interest of his other client. If there is a conflict of interest, there is a conflict of duties which a solicitor should take care to avoid. Moreover, a solicitor who acts for vendor and purchaser in the same transaction thereby fixes the purchaser with notice of everything of which he has acquired knowledge as solicitor for the vendor and thus deprives the purchaser of the defence of *bona fide* purchaser for value without notice. It is true, of course, that there may be occasions when acting for both parties may be justified, eg, where both parties clearly opt for this despite being warned of the risks, whether because they wish to save time in completion or because they are close friends or, perhaps, even relations who have always employed the same solicitor or, live in a locality where there are few solicitors in practice and the same solicitor has been used by both parties for many years. Apart from such exceptional cases, however, the general view of judges seems to have been that the practice of acting for both parties to a conveyance ought to be discouraged. Indeed, such a view was being expressed by Irish judges over a century ago,[143] and it has been repeated in recent times.[144] Similar comments have been made by English judges.[145] The Law Society some time ago drew solicitors' attention to the possibility of an opinion arising in the public mind that certain transactions are an "inside affair" which benefit solicitors more than their clients. In particular, reference was made to reports that builders or their agents had been known to make a suggestion to a prospective purchaser such as: "Our solicitor will look after your side of the business too; it'll be cheaper for you." It was pointed out that many of the recent causes for complaint raised in the public media turned out, on investigation, to have their base in situations where a solicitor had been acting for both parties, particularly in housing transactions.[146]

[1.35] More recently the issue arose as to the propriety of a solicitor acting both for a client and the client's lending institution, or for a lending institution and its customer. The Law Society's Conveyancing Committee became concerned about the implications of some English decisions

---

[143.] See, eg, *McMahon v McIlroy* (1869) IR 5 Eq 1 at 10: "I have never seen a case which illustrates more forcibly the evils which result from the same solicitor being employed for both seller and buyer." (*Per* Chatterton VC). See also *Meara v Rogers* (1858) 3 Ir Jur (ns) 108.

[144.] See, eg, *Haverty v Brooks* [1970] IR 214 at 218: "Although I do not attach any blame to [the solicitor], I do emphasise that this is another example of the undesirability of one solicitor acting for both parties in a transaction of this kind." (*Per* McLoughlin J).

[145.] See, eg, *Moody v Cox* [1917] 2 Ch 71 at 91 (*per* Scrutton LJ); *Goody v Baring* [1956] 1 WLR 448 at 450 (*per* Danckwerts J); *Smith v Mansi* [1963] 1 WLR 26 at 30 (*per* Danckwerts J); *Spector v Agenda* [1973] Ch 30 at 47 (*per* Megarry J). *Cf Clark Boyce v Mouat* [1993] 4 All ER 268, para **[1.35]** *infra*.

[146.] See the *Gazette* March 1976 p 26 and June 1975 p 148.

suggesting that in certain circumstances the lending institution's right to enforce its security could be at risk if, eg, the borrower's spouse, who was joining in the mortgage or giving consent under the Family Home Protection Act 1976, did not have independent advice.[147] This is particularly so where the other spouse may have misrepresented the nature of the transaction or have exercised undue influence.[148] In due course the Committee drew a distinction between the situation where the other spouse is a "third party" obtaining no direct benefit from the transaction and one where that spouse does obtain such benefit.[149] The latter applies in the typical house purchase mortgage, since the purpose of the transaction is to provide a home for both spouses. In such cases the Committee took the view that there was no necessity for separate solicitors to act for the lending institution and the borrowers provided the "common" solicitor is the borrowers'.[150] This distinction has recently been recognised by the House of Lords in England in cases where a spouse joined in the transaction as surety for a loan designed to provide funds primarily for the other spouse's benefit, eg, to meet debts or to finance a business venture.[151] The Law Lords have held that, while a lending institution's security is generally at risk only if it has *actual* knowledge of wrongdoing affecting one of the borrowers (eg undue influence), where it knows that one of them is acting as a surety for the other's benefit, it may be fixed with constructive notice of the wrongdoing.[152] It must, therefore, take precautions to ensure that the innocent party is made aware of the nature of, and risks involved in, the transaction, by, eg, suggesting that independent advice is sought by that party.[153] It is suggested that the somewhat broader statement of Geoghegan J in *Bank of Ireland v Smyth*[154] should be viewed in the light of these developments, especially since his judgment was largely based on earlier

---

[147.] See, eg, *Kingsnorth Trust Ltd v Bell* [1986] 1 All ER 423. Note the Committee's views published in the *Gazette* December 1983 and May 1986.

[148.] See, eg, *National Westminster Bank plc v Morgan* [1985] 1 All ER 821.

[149.] See the *Gazette*, December 1986.

[150.] *Ibid. Cf* the views expressed by the Privy Council in *Clark Boyce v Mouat* [1993] 4 All ER 268.

[151.] *Barclays Bank plc v O'Brien* [1993] 4 All ER 417; *CIBC Mortgages plc v Pitt* [1993] 4 All ER 433. Note also *Penn v Bristol and West Building Society* London Times, 19 June 1995, where it was suggested that a solicitor may be liable for breach of warranty of authority even though he is unaware of a fraud being perpetrated by his client: see the discussion by Worsley in the English Law Society's *Gazette* 21 June 1995.

[152.] The Scottish courts are not convinced that even constructive notice arises in such cases: see *Mumford v Bank of Scotland*, London Times 1 July 1994.

[153.] The English courts seem to accept that making that suggestion is enough, ie, there is no need to provide the independent advice: see *Massey v Midland Bank plc* [1995] 1 All ER 929. *Cf* para **[16.69]** sub para (c) *post*.

[154.] [1993] 2 IR 102. On appeal the Supreme Court did not address this issue, deciding the case instead on the application of the doctrine of notice to the Family Protection Act 1976: see [1996] 1 IR 241 and para **[16.69]** sub para (b) *post*

decisions in the lower courts in England.[155] The views expressed by the Conveyancing Committee probably hold good, *viz*, that there is nothing improper in the same solicitor acting for both the borrower and the lender in the same transaction. Where, however, one spouse is being asked to join in or to give consent to a transaction designed for the benefit of the other spouse, a solicitor acting also for the lending institution, *a fortiori* if that institution employs or retains him, should at the very least ensure that the joining or consenting spouse is advised[156] of the desirability of obtaining independent legal advice. A failure to do so may not only put at risk the enforceability of the transaction but also open the solicitor to a claim for negligence.

[1.36] Mention of a claim for negligence draws attention to one of the most significant developments in conveyancing law in recent years. This is the increasing recognition by the courts that professional persons and others who hold themselves out as possessing particular skills or expertise in providing services connected with conveyancing transactions run the risk of having a claim for negligence succeed if they fall below the standard of care to be expected.[157] This remains the primary area where the courts are quite prepared to impose liability for pure economic loss.[158] The result has been that numerous cases have come before the courts, in which it has been recognised that a duty of care arose in the conveyancing transaction, which, if it had been breached with consequent loss to the person owed the duty, would have involved substantial liability in damages.[159] It must further be recognised that in many cases liability for breach of contract may also arise, because, of course, the service is usually being provided under a contractual arrangement.[160] Examples of solicitors being held liable in conveyancing

---

155. In particular, the Court of Appeal decision in the *O'Brien* case, *op cit*, the reasoning of which was largely rejected by the House of Lords. See Sanfey 'Consenting Adults: The Implications of *Bank of Ireland v Smith*' (1996) 3 CLP 31.

156. It is wise to give this advice in writing, for evidentiary reasons should a dispute arise.

157. See generally, McMahon and Binchy, *Irish Law of Torts* (2nd ed, 1990), Ch 14.

158. *Ibid*, Ch 10.

159. Reliance on counsel's "expert opinion" probably remains a good defence in most instances for a solicitor: see *Park Hall School Ltd v Overend* [1987] ILRM 345. *Cf* adhering to a universal practice which is, nevertheless, risky to the client's interest: see *Roche v Peilow* [1985] IR 232; *Desmond v Brophy* [1985] IR 449. See also *Wall v Hegarty* [1980] ILRM 124 (following *Ross v Caunters* [1980] Ch 297, which has recently been reaffirmed by the House of Lords in *White v Jones* [1995] 1 All ER 691); *Kelly v Crowley* [1985] IR 212; *Fallon v Gannon* [1988] ILRM 193; *McMullen v Farrell* [1993] 1 IR 123.

160. See the discussion of such coincidental liability by the Supreme Court in *Finlay v Murtagh* [1979] IR 249. There are, of course, important differences between contractual and tortious claims, eg, different limitation periods (see *First National Commercial Bank plc v Humberts* [1995] 2 All ER 673) and defences, such as contributory negligence in tort (*United Bank of Kuwait plc v Prudential Property Services Ltd* [1995] EGCS 190; *Bristol and West Building Society v Christie* [1996] EGCS 53).

transactions will be referred to at various points in the ensuing text, as appropriate. It is, however, important to stress that liability may arise in respect of any aspect of the transaction, wherever the solicitor fails to carry out that part in accordance with the requisite standard of care. In considering the requisite standard, the courts are not impressed by a defence that the solicitor was only following the client's instructions. In a recent case,[161] Barron J made the following salutary remarks:

> "A solicitor cannot in my view fulfil his obligations to his client merely by carrying out what he is instructed to do. This is to ignore the essential element of any contract involving professional care or advice. The professional person is consulted by the client for the very reason that he has specialist or professional skill and knowledge. He cannot abrogate his duty to use that skill and knowledge. To follow instructions blindly is to turn himself into a machine."[162]

[1.37] It must always be borne in mind that most conveyancing transactions involve substantial consideration. Even a straightforward purchase of a residential house will often involve the largest transaction from the financial point of view that the parties are likely to enter into during their lifetime. It is imperative then that their professional advisers take steps to ensure that the clients' financial interests are safeguarded.[163] Increasingly in recent times the courts have come to recognise that solicitors owe a duty in this respect, both a contractual duty to carry out their instructions in the transaction and a duty of care in tort, which, if breached, may result in liability for negligence. Nowadays a solicitor is not just under a duty to carry out the conveyancing process in a proper manner,[164] he is also expected to ensure that his client is given appropriate financial advice about the transaction in question and to warn the client of the financial risks involved. The conveyancing process itself must be carried out in such a way that the client is not exposed to unnecessary costs or expenses. Thus in *Harte v Sheehy*[165] a case involving the sale and purchase of valuable farms, Costello J held that the vendor's solicitor had been guilty of negligence on a number of counts, including failure to honour undertakings relating to charges on the property being sold and to discover the number and amount of these charges.[166] In *Culhane v*

[161.] *McMullen v Farrell* [1993] 1 IR 123.

[162.] *Ibid*, p 142.

[163.] The Law Society recognised the need for solicitors to provide independent financial advice to clients by establishing in 1989 Solicitors Financial Services, a non-profit making organisation to which subscribing solicitors' clients have access for advice on mortgage and other loans, insurance, tax planning and so on.

[164.] Which, eg, would usually include advising purchasers to have an independent inspection or survey made of a property which is obviously in a poor state of repair: see *O'Connor v First National Building Society* [1991] ILRM 208. See para **[4.24]** *post*.

[165.] High Court, unrep, 14 March 1986 (1982/10930P).

[166.] As to the importance of compliance with undertakings, see para **[20.14]** *post*.

O'Maoileoin[167] Murphy J held that the solicitor acting for the purchasers of a substantial residence at an auction was negligent in not ensuring that his clients had the funds necessary to meet the deposit of £95,000. While there is no doubt as to the duty owed to the solicitor's own client, it is very doubtful whether any duty or assumption of responsibility arises in respect of the other party to the transaction.[168] The well-recognised exception to this is, of course, a disappointed beneficiary under a will, or intended will, drawn or to be drawn up by a solicitor.[169]

[1.38] It is also important to realise that it is not only solicitors who are open to claims for breach of contract or negligence in respect of how they carry out conveyancing transactions. It has long been recognised by the courts that professional persons involved in the building industry, like architects, engineers and surveyors, are at risk if they fall below the appropriate standard of care.[170] With respect to services more directly connected with conveyancing transactions, auctioneers[171] and estate agents[172] must act with due care in providing the services undertaken. There have been numerous cases in recent years, especially in England,[173] holding surveyors and valuers liable in respect of valuations made for loan purposes.[174]

[167.] High Court, unrep, 17 November 1988 (1979/8161P).

[168.] Responsibility to the other party may arise in special circumstances: see *Doran v Delaney* [1996] 1 ILRM 490 (see para **[15.37]** *post*. *Cf* the view of the English Court of Appeal: *Gran Geloto Ltd v Richcliff (Group) Ltd* [1992] 1 All ER 865. For a similar divergence of views *re* an estate agent's or auctioneer's duty to a prospective purchaser *cf McAnarney v Hanrahan* [1993] 3 IR 492 and *McCullagh v Lane Fox and Partners Ltd* [1996] 18 EG 104: see para **[5.27]** *post*.

[169.] See the discussion of the principles involved, including their application in various parts of the world, by Lord Goff of Chieveley in *White v Jones* [1995] 1 All ER 691. The majority decision in *White* approved the earlier decision of Megarry VC in *Ross v Caunters* [1979] 3 All 580, which was followed by Barrington J in *Wall v Hegarty* [1980] ILRM 124.

[170.] See *Quinn v Quality Homes Ltd* [1976-7] ILRM 314; *Crowley v Allied Irish Banks Ltd* [1987] IR 282; *Sunderland v McGreavey* [1987] IR 372.

[171.] See *Stafford v Mahony* [1980] ILRM 53. *Cf Bank of Ireland v Smith* [1966] IR 646.

[172.] See *McAnarney v Hanrahan* [1993] 3 IR 492; *Donnellan v Dungoyne Ltd* [1995] 1 ILRM 388. See also *Hellings v Parkes Breslin Estates* [1995] 29 EG 119; *McCullagh v Lane Fox and Partners Ltd* [1996] 18 EG 104.

[173.] Note, in particular, the extent to which the English courts have extended liability for losses partly attributable to the dramatic fall in the property market in the late 1980s and early 1990s. See *Banque Bruxelles Lambert SA v Eagle Star Insurance Co Ltd* [1995] 2 All ER 769.

[174.] See the House of Lords decisions in *Smith v Eric s Bush* [1987] 3 All ER 179; *Harris v Wyre Forest District Council* [1989] 2 WLR 790. See also *Sneesby v Goldings* [1995] 36 EG 136; *Ezekiel v McDade* [1995] 47 EG 150. The principles enunciated in these cases probably apply in Ireland: see *Ward v McMaster* [1988] IR 337: see para **[4.21]** *et seq, post*.

Chapter 2

SALE BY PUBLIC AUCTION

In this chapter we are concerned primarily with the respective roles of the auctioneer, the vendor's solicitor and the purchaser's solicitor in the preliminary stages of a sale by public auction.

I. AUCTIONEERS

A. Statutory Regulation

[2.01] Auctioneers are subject to the scheme of regulation imposed by the Auctioneers and House Agents Acts 1947 1967 and 1973.[1] The following are the main features of the scheme.

1. Licences and Auction Permits

[2.02] It is an offence for a person to carry on the business of auctioneer without an auctioneer's licence and to conduct an auction unless he has such a licence or an auctioneer's permit.[2] Licences are granted by the Revenue Commissioners subject to compliance with certain conditions,[3] eg, that the applicant has already obtained a certificate of qualification from a district justice with jurisdiction in the relevant court area[4] and a certificate of the Accountant of the Courts of Justice to the effect that the applicant maintains in the High Court a deposit in the form of money, authorised securities or a guarantee bond.[5] A licensed auctioneer may apply to the Revenue Commissioners for an auction permit to enable a nominee to conduct auctions on the applicant's behalf or on behalf of an applicant which is a company or unincorporated association.[6] A certificate of qualification may

---

[1.] See the discussion in Mahon, *Auctioneering and Estate Agency in Ireland* (1990).
[2.] 1947 Act, s 6(1) and (3). See *Att-Gen v Manorhamilton Co-operative Livestock Mart Ltd* [1966] IR 192.
[3.] 1947 Act, s 8. Where an appeal is lodged against a refusal to grant a licence, a temporary licence may be issued, s 24. As to the need now for tax clearance certificates, see Finance Act 1993, s 79.
[4.] 1947 Act, ss 11 and 12, as amended by the 1967 Act, s 12. See the Auctioneers and House Agents Act 1947 (Accounts Examination and Certificate) Regulations 1968 (SI 10/1968).
[5.] 1947 Act, s 14. See further para **[2.03]** *infra*.
[6.] 1947 Act, s 9.

be refused on any of a number of grounds, eg the applicant is not a "fit and proper person," is an undischarged bankrupt or under the age of 18 years.[7] A person holding an auction must, throughout the auction, display in a conspicuous position at the place where the auction is being held a placard bearing the name under which he is licensed and the address of his principal place of businesss.[8] If he holds only an auction permit to conduct auctions on behalf of a licensed auctioneer, the placard must bear the licensed auctioneer's name and principal place of business.[9] Any licensed auctioneer convicted of an offence involving fraud, dishonesty or breach of trust is liable to be disqualified for a specified period by the Court and, or as an alternative, to have his licence and every auction permit granted to him or his nominee cancelled or suspended for a specified time.[10] These restrictions and regulations do not apply in certain special cases, eg, auctions conducted by certain officials such as a sheriff or county registrar, a rate collector or an officer of customs and excise.[11]

2. Deposits or Guarantee Bonds

[2.03] An essential part of the protection afforded the general public by this scheme of regulation is the requirement that an auctioneer must lodge a deposit in the High Court and obtain a certificate to this effect as one of the conditions of the granting of a licence. The deposit must be of a certain value, currently fixed at £10,000,[12] and must be maintained in the High Court for the period for which the licence is in force. The deposit may be in the form of money, securities authorised by the High Court rules as to investment of money under the control of the Court or a guarantee bond issued by a licensed[13] assurance company.[14] The depositor may now substitute subsequently one form of deposit for another.[15] A register of depositors is kept by the Accountant of the Courts of Justice.[16] The High

---

7. 1947 Act, s 13. The age of majority was, of course, reduced from 21 to 18 by the Age of Majority Act 1985.
8. 1947 Act, s 20(1)(a). This does not apply where a notice of intention of the auction, containing the relevant information, has been published in a newspaper circulating in the area where the auction is held or displayed in a conspicuous position in the area, s 20(3).
9. Section 20(2). Again a notice published in a newspaper or displayed in the area will suffice, see fn 8, *supra*.
10. 1947 Act, s 18. On cancellation, the licence or permit must be surrendered to the Revenue Commissioners and a notice of cancellation is published in *Iris Oifigiúil,* ss 22 and 23.
11. 1947 Act, s 6(2).
12. 1973 Act, s 3, raising the previous figures of £2,000, fixed by s 14(a) of the 1947 Act, and £5,000, fixed by s 2 of the 1967 Act.
13. Ie under the Insurance Act 1936.
14. 1947 Act, s 14. See *Irish National Insurance Co Ltd v Scannell* [1959] Ir Jur Rep 41.
15. 1967 Act, s 3. *Cf Re Ryan* (1952) 86 ILTR 104.
16. 1947 Act, s 17.

Court may order, on application by *ex parte* motion, that the deposit be used to pay a judgment debt found due to the applicant in any proceedings against the licensed auctioneer, in discharge of a liability incurred in relation to the receipt or payment of money or the safe custody of property.[17] However, in the case of a deposit in the form of a guarantee bond, it is a condition of the granting of any such Court order that the relevant assurance company were given notice of the institution of the proceedings against them *before* the hearing of the proceedings.[18] The insurance company must also have been given notice of the institution of proceedings against the auctioneer *after* the proceedings were brought but *before* the hearing.[19] Failure to do this will deprive the plaintiff of any subsequent claim against the guarantee bond, should any judgment debt declared in the proceedings against the auctioneer be left undischarged.[20]

3. Accounts

[2.04] An auctioneer is under a statutory duty to keep at all times properly written up accounts, which should show all his dealings with money received or held by him for, or paid by him to or on behalf of, each client.[21] He must also open and keep one or more client bank accounts into which he must pay, without unnecessary delay, clients' money, which can then be withdrawn only for restricted purposes, eg, to repay the client or to meet proper fees or commission due to the auctioneer.[22] Though the client has priority generally over other claimants against the auctioneer in respect of money in such an account,[23] the sums to the credit of every client account kept by the auctioneer vest in the Official Assignee whenever the auctioneer is adjudicated bankrupt or, being an arranging debtor, he vests his estate in the Official Assignee on filing a petition for arrangement.[24] The Official Assignee, the liquidator of an insolvent auctioneer company or any interested person in other cases can apply to the High Court for an order

---

[17] 1967 Act, s 11. See *Parkes v Irish National Insurance Co Ltd* [1962] IR 50. *Cf Re McArthur (J Albert) Co Ltd* [1959] Ir Jur Rep 59 (bond not part of company's assets and so not transferring to liquidator on a winding up).

[18] *Ibid* s 11(3)(b). The assurance company may waive the requirement as to notice, *Bergin v Shield Insurance Co Ltd* (1956) 90 ILTR 141. If the company pays out under its bond it may recoup the sums paid from the auctioneer, *Irish National Insurance Co Ltd v Scannell* [1959] Ir Jur Rep 41.

[19] See the discussion by the Supreme Court in *Re Nolan* [1963] IR 341.

[20] See *Mahon v Irish National Insurance Co Ltd* [1958] Ir Jur Rep 41; *Re Nolan* [1963] IR 341. Also *Leemac Overseas Investments Ltd v Harvey* [1973] IR 160.

[21] 1967 Act, s 4.

[22] 1967 Act, s 5.

[23] 1967 Act, s 6.

[24] 1967 Act, s 7.

directing that the deposit or guarantee bond maintained in the Court be used to pay costs, fees and expenses incurred in connection with the client account and to make good any deficiency in the account.[25] As between themselves, claimants against the deposit generally rank in priority according to the date of their judgments against the auctioneer, though it has been held that the best criterion for this purpose is the date of the order giving leave to enter judgment rather than the date when judgment is actually given.[26] These provisions do not deprive an auctioneer of any recourse or right against money in a client account, whether such right arises by way of lien, set-off, counter-claim, charge or otherwise.[27]

B. Conduct of Auction

There are several rules which govern the conduct of a sale of land by auction.[28]

1. Instructions

[2.05] The first obvious rule is that the auctioneer must carry out the vendor's express instructions, as must any agent defer to his principal. Failure to comply with these may result in the auctioneer being held liable to the vendor for any loss suffered by the latter.[29] The starting point must always be the instructions given by the vendor or his solicitor. In *Daniel Morrissey and Sons Ltd v Nalty*[30] Gannon J concluded with respect to the contract between the auctioneers and owners of the property in question:

> "The plaintiffs [auctioneers] were expressly employed in terms stated by themselves to sell the property by public auction at a specified place on a specified date at a specified time upon conditions of sale which were to be furnished to them in advance with the further information that they would require from the accountants for the information of persons attending the auction ... This contract between the plaintiffs and the defendants was of such a nature as to make them the sole agents of sale in this manner and no other method of sale could be engaged in without a notice thereof to and agreement of the other party."[31]

---

25. 1967 Act, s 8. *Cf Re McArthur (J Albert) Co Ltd* [1959] Ir Jur Rep 59 (fn 17 *supra*).
26. *Ross v Irish National Insurance Co Ltd* (1958) 92 ILTR 92. See also *Vaughan v Irish National Insurance Co Ltd* (1955) 89 ILTR 179.
27. 1967 Act, s 9.
28. See Mahon, *Auctioneering and Estate Agency in Ireland* (1990) Ch 6. See also Murdoch, *The Law of Estate Agency and Auctions* (3rd ed, 1994) especially Chs 9-11.
29. *Farmer v Casey* (1898) 32 ILTR 144.
30. [1976-7] ILRM 269.
31. *Ibid*, p 273. See also para **[2.07]** *infra*.

To some extent the auctioneer is usually governed by the conditions of sale drawn up by the vendor's solicitor. Thus the standard conditions issued by the Law Society lay down rules as to such matters as fixing a reserve price,[32] bidding by the vendor[33] and withdrawal of the property before it has been sold.[34]

2. Implied Authority

[2.06] Apart from any express instructions, whether given through the medium of conditions of sale or otherwise, an auctioneer has implied authority to do various things in relation to the sale of land.

(i) To Sell

[2.07] There is no implied authority to sell *by private treaty*,[35] though express authority may be given in his instructions[36] or possibly inferred from a custom of the trade.[37] And, of course, unauthorised acts may be subsequently ratified by the vendor.[38] In *Daniel Morrissey and Sons Ltd v Nalty*[39] Gannon J amplified the position under the terms of the auctioneers' contract under consideration in that case in this way:

> "Under the terms of this contract there was no obligation on the plaintiffs [the auctioneers] to convey to the defendants any offers which they might have received prior to the auction nor was there any obligation on the defendants to accept any offers which might have been received prior to or otherwise than at the auction in the presence of other contending purchasers. The parties agreed upon a particular remuneration for the plaintiffs for the work for which they were engaged, namely, a percentage amount calculated upon the basis of the sum at which the property might be knocked down at auction. The plaintiffs were at the risk of no response to their inducement to purchasers to attend the auction, or at the risk of lack of finance in the hands of potential purchasers, or at the risk of inadequacy of bids at the auction, or at the risk that the conditions as to title or other terms of sale might be unacceptable to its potential purchasers, and also at the

32. *General Conditions of Sale* (1995 edition) cond 4(b): see para **[2.14]** *infra*.
33. Cond 4(c)(i): see para **[2.15]** *infra*.
34. Cond 4(c)(ii): see para **[2.19]** *infra*.
35. *Daniel v Adams* (1964) Ambl 495. See also *Rooney v Thomas* (1947) 81 ILTR 64; *Daniel Morrissey and Sons Ltd v Nalty* [1976-7] ILRM 269 (para **[2.05]** *supra*); *Culhane v Hewson* [1979] IR 8.
36. *Green v Bartlett* (1863) 14 CBNS 681.
37. *Sed quaere*, see *Judd v Donegal Tweed Co* (1935) 69 ILTR 117. See also *Williams on Title* (4th ed, by Battersby 1975) p 125 fn 13.
38. See *Else v Barnard* (1860) 28 Beav 228; *Bousfield v Hodges* (1863) 33 Beav 90. *Cf McNulty v Hanratty* (1918) 52 ILTR 43.
39. [1976-7] ILRM 269.

risk that the defendants might withdraw their instructions for the auction. The contract contains no provision for remuneration in the event of no auction being held but the provision for the payment to the plaintiff of the expenses of advertising appears to be consistent with the position that there would be no remuneration if there were no auction."[40]

(ii) To sign a contract

[2.08] It is settled that an auctioneer has not only authority to sell the property by auction but also authority[41] to render that contract enforceable as required by statute in the case of land, ie, by signing the note or memorandum in writing required by s 2 of the Statute of Frauds (Ireland) 1695.[42] This matter was discussed by the Irish Court of Exchequer in *Kavanagh v Cuthbert*,[43] wherein Dowse B stated:

> "An important part of an auctioneer's work, when he sells real estate, on the very lowest estimate of his legal obligation to his employer, is to use reasonable care to have a binding contract, under the Statute of Frauds, entered into by the person who purchases the property at the auction. It may be that he does not undertake without any qualification to make a binding contract. It cannot be seriously disputed that he undertakes to bring the same amount of care to this part of his work that he undertakes to bring to other parts of it."[44]

In the same case Fitzgerald B stated:

> "It seems to me to be clear that it is not by law a duty implied from the employment of an auctioneer, and his acceptance of such employment, that a binding contract shall be made with a person to whom a lot is knocked down, but only that due care and skill shall be used on the part of the auctioneer, in order that such person shall be bound by contract ..."[45]

In *Culhane v Hewson*,[46] where a contract resulting from a public auction was later rescinded by the vendor for failure by the purchaser to pay the deposit required by the conditions of sale, McWilliam J rejected the argument that the auctioneer had authority to waive the notice of termination or to renew or revive the contract.

[2.09] Not only has an auctioneer authority to sign on behalf of his principal, the vendor, but he also has implied authority to sign on behalf of the highest

---

40. *Ibid* pp 273-4. As to commission see para **[2.28]** *infra*.
41. Unless restricted by express instructions, see *Somers v Nicholls* [1955] IR 83.
42. This subject is discussed in detail in Ch 6, especially para **[6.38]** *post*.
43. (1874) IR 9 CL 136.
44. *Ibid* p 140.
45. *Ibid* pp 143-4. *Cf Richards v Phillips* [1969] 1 Ch 39 at 63 (*per* Pennycuick J).
46. [1979] IR 8. *Cf McAnarney v Hanrahan* [1993] 3 IR 492.

bidder at the auction, the purchaser, though an Irish judge has remarked: "I think from the very nature of the case the authority of the auctioneer as agent for the vendor is of a more permanent character than his authority as agent for the purchaser".[47] In another case, Fitzgerald J remarked:

"... the auctioneer is agent for both parties, and is authorised by them to affix his name to the contract; ... his signature binds both parties, and is a compliance with the Statute of Frauds ..."[48]

However, an auctioneer's implied authority in this regard is confined to the salesroom and may not extend to his employees or agents,[49] though once again there may be subsequent ratification of an unauthorised signing by the auctioneer's principal.[50] It would also seem to be the case, on principle, that an auctioneer's authority to sign on behalf of the purchaser does not apply where the auctioneer is auctioning his own property, ie, he is the vendor. There is no suggestion in the caselaw that the courts contemplated that the vendor could be regarded as having authority to sign on behalf of the purchaser.

(iii) To receive money

[2.10] On a sale of land by auction it is usual for a deposit to become payable immediately by the purchaser.[51] The standard conditions of sale require the deposit to be paid to the vendor's solicitor rather than the auctioneer.[52] Furthermore, in the absence of an express provision or of circumstances indicating otherwise, it seems to be the modern view that an auctioneer probably has no implied authority to receive a deposit in the case of a sale of land by auction.[53] If he does have authority to receive a deposit, the general rule seems to be that he may accept payment in cash only and not by cheque, bill of exchange or IOU.[54] Though it has been suggested in England that the

---

[47.] *McMeekin v Stevenson* [1917] 1 IR 348 at 354 (*per* Ross J). *Cf Dyas v Stafford* (1881) 7 LR Ir 590 at 601 (*per* Chatterton VC) para **[2.11]** *infra*.

[48.] *Gardiner v Tate* (1876) IR 10 CL 460 at 474; see also at 464 (*per* Whiteside CJ). And see *Carrigy v Brock* (1871) IR 5 CL 501; *Wallace v Roe* [1903] 1 IR 32.

[49.] See however *Dyas v Stafford* (1881) 7 LR Ir 590 (auctioneer's clerk held authorised to sign as part of the sale) (reversed on different ground, (1881) 9 LR Ir 520). *Cf Sheridan v Higgins* [1971] IR 291.

[50.] *Sheridan v Higgins, op cit; Brennan v O'Connell* [1980] IR 13.

[51.] Failure to pay the deposit may entitle the vendor to rescind the contract: see *Culhane v Hewson* [1979] IR 8.

[52.] *General Conditions of Sale* (1995 edition), cond 4(d).See further para **[10.16]** *post*.

[53.] *Mynn v Joliffe* (1834) 1 Moo & R 326; *Drakeford v Piercey* (1866) 7 B & s 515; *Butwick v Grant* [1924] 2 KB 483.

[54.] See the discussion in *Hodgens v Keon* [1894] 2 IR 657. Also *Boothman v Byrne* (1923) 57 ILTR 36; *O'Connor v Faul* (1957) 91 ILTR 7. And see *Williams v Evans* (1866) LR 1 QB 352; *Pape v Westacott* [1894] 1 QB 272.

circumstances of the case may justify acceptance of a cheque nowadays,[55] this was not the view of McVeigh J in *Morrow v Carty*.[56] As in the case of all agents, auctioneers are under a duty to account to their principals for all money received on their principals' behalf.[57] However, if an auctioneer receives a deposit from the purchaser, he is presumed by law to receive it as stakeholder and not, as in the case of a solicitor,[58] as agent of the vendor.[59] As such, the auctioneer has a personal responsibility for its safe-keeping and must not part with it until one or other of the parties to the sale becomes entitled to it,[60] ie, the vendor on the transaction's completion or the purchaser if the transaction falls through.[61] And, pending this occurrence, it seems that as stakeholder the auctioneer is not a trustee for either party and is, therefore, not liable to account for any interest on the deposit which may be earned by him by placing it in a deposit account at a bank.[62] However, it appears to be settled that the vendor is liable for any default on the part of a stakeholder-auctioneer with respect to a deposit held by him, the crucial point being that in this case the purchaser is required to pay it to him under the conditions of sale imposed by the vendor.[63] This sort of case must be distinguished from one which often arises in sales by private treaty, ie where a deposit is paid to an estate or house agent before the contract for sale is entered into.[64] In practice the auctioneer often deducts his expenses and

---

[55.] See *Farrer v Lacy, Hartland & Co* (1885) 31 Ch D 42, especially at 46 (*per* Baggallay LJ) and 48 (*per* Bowen LJ). *Cf Johnston v Boyes* [1899] 2 Ch 73. See also *Syke v Giles* (1839) 5 M & W 645.

[56.] [1957] NI 174 at 177-8 (following *Johnston v Boyes op cit*).

[57.] And note the statutory duty to pay such money into a client's bank account, para **[2.04]** *supra*.

[58.] See para **[10.30]** *post*.

[59.] See the discussion in *Leemac Overseas Investments Ltd v Harvey* [1973] IR 160. See also *Furtado v Lumley* (1890) 6 TLR 168. Note, however, that the Law Society's *General Conditions of Sale (1995 ed)* require the deposit to be paid, in the case of both an auction and private treaty sale, to the vendor's solicitor "as stakeholder": see para **[10.28]** *post*.

[60.] Or consents to the parting, *Skinner v Reed's Trustees* [1967] Ch 1194 at 1200 (*per* Cross J).

[61.] *Burrough v Skinner* (1770) 5 Burr 2639. See also *Leemac Overseas Investments Ltd v Harvey* [1973] IR 160 at 164 (*per* Kenny J).

[62.] *Lee v Mann* (1817) 8 Taunt 45; *Harrington v Hoggart* (1830) 1 B & Ald 577; *Smith v Hamilton* [1951] Ch 174; *Potters v Loppert* [1973] 1 All ER 658. *Cf* a solicitor-stakeholder, para **[10.32]** *post* and the requirements of the Solicitors (Interest on Client's Moneys) Regulations 1995 (SI 108/1995).

[63.] See *Leemac Overseas Investments Ltd v Harvey* [1973] IR 160 at 165 (*per* Kenny J). Also *Rowe v May* (1854) 18 Beav 613.

[64.] *Burt v Claude Cousins & Co Ltd* [1971] 2 QB 426 at 450 (*per* Sachs LJ); *Barrington v Lee* [1972] 1 QB 326 at 335 (*per* Lord Denning MR); *Sorrell v Finch* [1976] 2 All ER 371 at 381 (*per* Lord Edmund-Davies) and 384 (*per* Lord Russell of Killowen). *Cf Leemac Overseas Investments Ltd v Harvey* [1973] IR 160. See generally, para **[3.11]** *post*.

commission from the deposit before remitting the balance to the vendor or his solicitor, and there would appear to be no sanction against this.

(iv) To Delegate

[2.11] The traditional view is that an auctioneer has no authority to delegate the performance of his duties to anyone else, including his clerk and other persons in his employment[65] - in essence the maxim *delegatus delegare non potest* applies.[66] However, there is some authority in Ireland for saying that this general principle is subject to the qualification that the normal practice of auctioneers in a sale by auction is to make use of their clerks. In *Dyas v Stafford*,[67] it was held that the signing of a memorandum of sale by an auctioneer's clerk was done as part of the sale and was in that case to be regarded as authorised by the vendor. Chatterton VC stated:

> "The auctioneer, being himself an agent, cannot delegate his authority, and his clerk cannot by any act of his be constituted an agent of the vendor. The authority of the clerk must, therefore, be derived directly from the vendor; and that he has such authority for certain purposes is, I think, well established ...
>
> ...the clerk of an auctioneer is an agent for both the vendor and purchaser to enter a minute of the sale at the time and as part of the transaction of the auction, and by his signature to such minute to constitute it a note or memorandum of the agreement signed by an agent thereunto lawfully authorised, within the terms of the statute ... There is, I think, a difference between the agency of the clerk in the case of a vendor from that of a purchaser. In the latter case the agency is only constituted on the moment by the bid of the purchaser, who thus authorises the clerk to enter his name and bidding, and to bind him by his signature. The agency for the vendor is of a more deliberate character and arises from the employment of the auctioneer which by the usages and mode of such sales carries with it the employment of his clerk. The vendor must be presumed to have been aware of and to have adopted these usages, and thus to have given an authority to the clerk, when the occasion should arise, to act as his agent directly in doing those acts which it was necessary for the clerk to do ... This implied authority must, however, be restricted to the circumstances from which it is implied, and cannot, in my opinion, be fairly extended beyond the auction, including therein the signature, as part of the transaction of the auction, of any agreement so constituted by the terms and conditions of sale."[68]

---

[65] *Coles v Trecothick* (1804) 9 Ves 234 at 251 (*per* Lord Eldon LC). *Cf Sheridan v Higgins* [1971] IR 291.

[66] See *Irish Land Law,* (2nd ed, 1986) para 10.030.

[67] (1881) 7 LR Ir 590 (reversed on different ground, (1882) 9 LR Ir 520). *Coles v Trecothick, supra* was distinguished on the ground that it involved a sale by private treaty.

[68] *Ibid*, pp 600-1.

3. Duty of Care

[2.12] As Dowse B said in *Kavanagh v Cuthbert*:

> "An auctioneer differs in no respect from any other person who holds himself out to the world as ready to undertake any work which he may be employed to do. He impliedly, by undertaking a work, undertakes to bring reasonable care, skill, and diligence to the doing of it."[69]

That case concerned an auctioneer's duty to the vendor to secure an enforceable contract for the sale of the property auctioned.[70] Other cases illustrate his duty to use care in advertising the property and in making oral or written descriptions of it,[71] and to see that he does everything reasonable to secure the best price possible for the property.[72] And, of course, he must carry out his instructions and abide by the conditions of sale, eg, as to the amount of deposit to be accepted.[73]

[2.13] In addition to his duty to the vendor, the auctioneer may owe a duty to the purchaser. Under the general law of negligence it is clear that an auctioneer owes a duty of care in respect of the auction he conducts to all those who attend the auction.[74] It seems clear now that this includes liability for negligent misstatements about the property being sold.[75] If he fails to comply with the conditions upon which the auction is held, he may find himself liable for breach of warranty of authority, eg, where he withdraws property from a sale expressed to be "without reserve".[76] He will also, of

---

[69] (1874) IR 9 CL 136 at 139-40.

[70] See para **[2.08]** *supra*.

[71] *Delany v Keogh* [1905] 2 IR 267; *Airlie v Fallon* [1976-7] ILRM 1. See generally on misrepresentations at the pre-contract, stage, para **[5.23]** *et seq, post.*

[72] *Cuckmere Brick Co Ltd v Mutual Finance Ltd* [1971] Ch 949. *Cf Holohan v Friends Provident and Century Life Office* [1966] IR 1; see *Irish Land Law* (2nd ed, 1986) para 13.036.

[73] *Farmer v Casey* (1898) 32 ILTR 144. But these may require the deposit to be paid to someone else, eg, the vendor's solicitor, see para **[2.10]** *supra* and para **[10.16]** *post.*

[74] See *Kavanagh v Cuthbert* (1874) IR 9 CL 136, especially at 139 (*per* Dowse B). See also para **[5.27]** *et seq, post.*

[75] *Airlie v Fallon* [1976-7] ILRM 1. See also the discussion in *Bank of Ireland v Smith* [1966] IR 646; *Stafford v Mahony* [1980] ILRM 53; *Irish Permanent Building Society v O'Sullivan* [1990] ILRM 598; *McAnarney v Hanrahan* [1993] 3 IR 492. These latter cases involved auctioneers making statements outside the auction room: see para **[5.27]** *post.*

[76] Presumably on the basis of an implied contract made by the purchaser with the auctioneer, by making a bid on the faith of the statement or condition that the sale was "without reserve", see *Warlow v Harrison* (1858) 1 E & E 295; *Johnston v Boyes* [1899] 2 Ch 73. See the discussion in *Gower*, (1952) 68 LQR 457.

course, be liable for any false statements made or other form of fraudulent conduct.[77]

4. Reserve Price and Vendor's Right to Bid

[2.14] These matters concern two long-established practices on the part of vendors whereby they have sought to secure a sale at the highest price possible. By fixing a reserve price the vendor can ensure that the property is sold for at least a set minimum price, if it is sold at all. By reserving a right to bid, on his own behalf or through an agent (sometimes referred to as a "puffer"), he can participate in the auction of his own property and, perhaps, force up the bidding of third parties by entering his own bid at appropriate times. From early times the courts became concerned about such practices, especially where it appeared that insufficient notice or warning of their use was given by the vendor or auctioneer. Eventually the rule was laid down by the common law courts that any bid by the vendor or his agent was a fraud on the other bidders, unless the right to bid was *expressly* reserved.[78] The courts of equity did not go quite as far as this: there the rule developed that a vendor could appoint one agent to bid for him, without disclosing this, provided this was not "inequitable" and provided the sale was not expressed to be "without reserve".[79] It was this conflict between the common law and equity that the Sale of Land by Auction Act 1867 sought to resolve.[80]

[2.15] Section 4 of the 1867 Act provides:

And whereas there is at present a conflict between Her Majesty's courts of law and equity in respect of the validity of sales by auction of land where a puffer has bid, although no right of bidding on behalf of the owner was reserved, the courts of law holding that all such sales are absolutely illegal, and the courts of equity holding under same circumstances giving effect to them, but even in courts of equity the rule is unsettled; and whereas it is expedient that an end should be put to such conflicting and unsettled opinions: Be it therefore enacted that from and after the passing of this Act whenever a sale by auction of land would be invalid at law by reason of the

---

77. *Delany v Keogh* [1905] 2 IR 267; *Ingram v Gillen* (1910) 44 ILTR 103. See also *Stanley v McGauran* (1882) 11 LR Ir 314.

78. *Bexwell v Christie* (1776) 1 Cowp 395; *Thornett v Haines* (1846) 15 M & W 367.

79. *Conolly v Parsons* (1797) 3 Ves 625n; *Meadows v Tanner* (1820) 5 Madd 34; *Robinson v Wall* (1847) 2 Ph 372; *Mortimer v Bell* (1865) 1 Ch App 10. *Re* court sales, see *Popham v Exham* (1860) 10 Ir Ch R 440, para **[11.05]** *post*.

80. The Act does not apply generally to court sales, see s 8. *Cf* s 7 (relating to discontinuance of the practice of re-opening biddings in court sales unless there is fraud or other improper conduct), see *Woods v Brown* [1915] 1 IR 29, especially at 36-7 (*per* Palles CB); *Re Longvale Brick and Lime Works Ltd* [1917] 1 IR 321. As to re-opening biddings, see *Vesey v Elwood* (1842) 3 Dr & War 74 at 78-80 (*per* Sugden LC).

employment of a puffer, the same shall be deemed invalid in equity as well as at law.

It is clear from this section that the intention was to make the common law rule as to the use of puffers prevail,[81] ie, that the right to bid had to be expressly reserved to the vendor or his agent. Unfortunately, the draftsman of the Act did not leave the matter there and, instead, provided in ss 5 and 6 what appears to be an attempt at a restatement of the common law on the subject. Section 5 provides:

> And whereas as sales of land by auction are now conducted many of such sales are illegal, and could not be enforced against an unwilling purchaser, and it is expedient for the safety of both seller and purchaser that such sales should be so conducted as to be binding on both parties: Be it therefore enacted by the authority aforesaid as follows: that the particulars or conditions of sale by auction of any land shall state whether such land will be sold without reserve, or subject to a reserved price, or whether a right to bid is reserved; if it is stated that such land will be sold without reserve, or to that effect, then it shall not be lawful for the seller to employ any person to bid at such sale, or for the auctioneer to take knowingly any bidding from any such person.

Section 6 then provides:

> And where any sale by auction of land is declared either in the particulars or conditions of such sale to be subject to a right for the seller to bid, it shall be lawful for the seller or any one person on his behalf to bid at such auction in such manner as he may think proper.

[2.16] The drafting of these provisions is not as precise as it might have been and it has given rise to some questions of construction. One query raised has been whether it is vital to stipulate a reserve price or to reserve a right to bid *in the particulars or conditions of sale*, as apparently required by s 5, or whether it is enough for the auctioneer to declare this to be the case orally at the auction. The Act does not lay down an express sanction for failure to comply strictly with its provisions and it has been argued that such a failure should not be treated as invalidating the sale altogether, but rather as converting the sale into one "without reserve".[82] The point may be of little practical significance because the standard conditions of sale do contain express provisions on the matter. Thus condition 4(b) of the Law Society's *General Conditions of Sale (1995 Edition)* provides:

[81.] See *Jones v Quinn* (1878) 2 LR Ir 516. See also *Airlie v Fallon* [1976-7] ILRM 1.

[82.] In *Airlie v Fallon* [1976-7] ILRM 1, the reserve was lifted during the bidding and Hamilton J held that this rendered a subsequent sale illegal as the only other bidder was acting as agent for the vendor.

"... there will be a reserve price for the subject property whether the same shall comprise the whole or any part of the property set forth in the particulars and the Auctioneer may refuse to accept any bid."

Condition 4(c)(i) provides that the vendor may "bid himself or by an agent up to the reserve price".

[2.17] Another query that has been raised from time to time is whether the conditions of sale must state both that there is a reserve price and that a right to bid is reserved. It has been argued that reservation of the latter may be enough and that it implies automatically the existence of a reserve price.[83] And it has been pointed out that s 5 is worded in alternative form, so that it does not seem to require inclusion of both provisions. However, the traditional view is that both matters ought to be mentioned expressly in the conditions of sale,[84] and, as we have seen, the standard form in general use in Ireland does so.

[2.18] It seems that the courts will construe express reservations strictly against the vendor. Thus it has been held that, where the conditions of sale reserve a right to bid once only,[85] the purchaser was entitled to refuse to complete where the auctioneer in fact bid three times on behalf of the vendor.[86] It also appears that a right to bid *beyond* the reserve price[87] must be expressly reserved.[88] However, it has been suggested that it is not necessary strictly to use, eg, the words "with reserve" or "without reserve" in the conditions of sale, so long as whatever words or expressions are used they make it clear what the position is as required by the 1867 Act.[89]

5. Right to Withdraw Property

[2.19] It is clearly settled that an advertisement or other intimation that an auction is to be held does not bind the vendor or auctioneer to hold the auction. The property in question may be withdrawn from sale at any time before the auction is held without incurring any liability to prospective purchasers.[90] The question remains, however, whether the property may be

---

83. *Dimmock v Hallett* (1866) 2 Ch App 21 is often cited in support of this argument, but the case was decided before the 1867 Act came into force.

84. See *Gilliat v Gilliat* (1869) LR 9 Eq 60 at 62 (*per* Lord Romilly MR). Also *Williams on Title* (4th ed, 1975), p 121, fn 14.

85. *Cf* cond 4(c)(i) of the Law Society's *General Conditions* (para **[2.16]** *supra*) which does not seem to limit the number of bids.

86. *Parfitt v Jepson* (1877) 46 LJQB 529.

87. *Cf* again cond 4(c)(i), fn 85 *supra*.

88. *Heatley v Newton* (1880) 19 Ch D 326.

89. See *Hill & Grant Ltd v Hodson* [1934] Ch. 53, especially at 61 (*per* Luxmoore J).

90. *Harris v Nickerson* (1873) LR 8 QB 286. Nor will the vendor normally incur any liability to the auctioneer, but this obviously depends on the terms of the agreement with him: see *Daniel Morrissey and Sons Ltd v Nalty* [1976-7] ILRM 269 (*per* Gannon J), see para **[2.07]** *supra*.

withdrawn once the auction begins and before it is knocked down to the highest bidder. The law on this point is far from clear and has given rise to considerable controversy.[91] It seems to be agreed that, where the sale is subject to a reserve price, the property can be withdrawn at any time before the reserve is reached.[92] The Law Society's *General Conditions of Sale (1995 Edition)* in fact provide that the vendor may:

> "withdraw the whole of the property set forth in the Particulars or, where such property has been divided into lots, withdraw any one or more of such lots at any time before the same has been sold without disclosing the reserve price."[93]

[2.20] It is not so clear whether the property may be withdrawn when the sale is "without reserve". Though there is some authority supporting the view that property cannot be withdrawn in such a case without incurring liability,[94] the view is difficult to support according to traditional principles of the law of contract. It is difficult to see how the vendor or his agent, the auctioneer, can be held bound not to withdraw when it is clearly accepted law that a bidder at an auction is not bound by his bids, until he is declared the highest bidder and becomes the purchaser on the fall of the hammer. Up to that point the bidder can in law retract his bid[95] and it is arguable that the vendor should have a reciprocal right of withdrawal.[96] In this respect the recognised law relating to bidders at auctions would seem to exclude application of another principle of the law of contract, namely that, where an offer is made to the general public, it may be accepted so as to conclude a contract by the first person to perform the conditions of the offer.[97] On the other hand, if the vendor is allowed to withdraw in the case of a sale "without reserve", he can so exercise his right as to achieve in effect a sale "with reserve". It remains to be seen whether the courts will accept another suggested solution to this problem, namely that a "collateral" contract may

---

91. See the discussion in (1952) 68 LQR 238 and 457; (1953) 69 LQR 21.
92. *McManus v Fortescue* [1907] 2 KB 1. *Cf* withdrawing the reserve during the bidding: see *Airlie v Fallon* [1976-7] ILRM 1, para **[2.16]** fn 82 *supra*.
93. Cond 4(c)(ii).
94. See especially the discussion in *Warlow v Harrison* (1858) 1 E & E 295, especially at 316 (*per* Martin B). *Cf Mainprice v Westley* (1865) 6 B & s 420; *Harris v Nickerson* (1873) LR 8 QB 286; *Johnston v Boyes* [1899] 2 Ch 73. See also the Scottish case, *Fenwick v Macdonald, Fraser & Co Ltd* 1904 6 F 850. And see *Tully v ILC* (1963) 97 ILTR 174.
95. *Tully v ILC* (1963) 97 ILTR 174. See also *Payne v Cave* (1789) 3 Term Rep 148, *Freer v Rimmer* (1844) 14 Sim 391. Note, however, that the standard conditions of sale provide expressly that "no accepted bid shall be retracted". See *General Conditions of Sale (1995 ed)*, cond 4(b). See further paras **[2.21]-[2.22]** *infra*.
96. See *Fenwick v Macdonald, Fraser & Co Ltd* 1904 6 F 850 at 854 (*per* Lord Trayber).
97. See *Carlill v Carbolic Smoke Ball Co* [1893] 1 QB 256. See Clark, *Contract Law in Ireland* (3rd ed, 1992) pp 7-9.

be created by the offer to sell "without reserve" and acceptance by anyone who bids in reliance on that offer.[98] Yet not every bidder will suffer by withdrawal of the property; in effect it is only the highest bidder at the point of withdrawal who suffers loss. [99]

6. Bidding

[2.21] The general rule is that a bid at an auction constitutes an offer to buy rather than an acceptance of an offer to sell.[100] Under the general law of contract, an offer is not effective unless communicated to the offeree and so the auctioneer must be made aware of the bid.[101] Again under the general law, the bid is not accepted so as to create a binding contract until the property is knocked down to the bidder at the price bid.[102] Though this is not the case where the sale is subject to a reserve price which has not been reached. In that situation the sale to the highest bidder is invalid even though the auctioneer has knocked the property down to him.[103] However, it should be noted that the Law Society's *General Conditions of Sale (1995 Edition)* specify that, subject to the reserve price and the right of the auctioneer to refuse to accept any bid, "the highest accepted bidder shall be the Purchaser".[104]

[2.22] It was common for standard form conditions to provide that no bid should be retracted[105] and this gave rise to some controversy. Since such a provision ran contrary to the general law of contract as applied to auctions, which states that a bid is an offer only and is thus retractable at any time until accepted by knocking down the property to the bidder,[106] it was thought by many to be unenforceable.[107] It is arguable, however, that the parties should be free to determine the basis upon which they will conduct their bargaining and it seems that such a condition may be enforced in the case of a court sale.[108] Since 1976 the standard forms of conditions have adopted a

---

[98]. See *Johnston v Boyes* [1899] 2 Ch 73. *Cf Tully v ILC* (1963) 97 ILTR 174.

[99]. See Gower, (1952) 68 LQR 457.

[100]. *McManus v Fortescue* [1907] 2 KB 1.

[101]. *Richards v Phillips* [1969] 1 Ch 39.

[102]. Either by using the traditional hammer or giving some other indication to the public attending the auction that the property has been sold, see the discussion in *Tully v ILC* (1963) 97 ILTR 174.

[103]. *McManus v Fortescue* [1907] 2 KB 1.

[104]. Cond 4(b). See *Tully v ILC* (1963) 97 ILTR 174.

[105]. See the Law Society's 1968 *Public Auction Conditions of Sale*, cond 2.

[106]. See para **[2.21]** *supra*, but see also para **[2.20]** especially fn 97, *supra*.

[107]. See Dart, *Vendors and Purchasers* (8th ed, 1929), vol 1, p 122; *Williams on Title* (4th ed, 1975), pp 123, fn 6 and 124.

[108]. See *Freer v Rimmer* (1844) 14 Sim 391. See further on court sales, paras **[2.27]**, *infra* **[8.13]** and **[11.01]** *post*.

different position. The provision is qualified by attaching the epithet "accepted" to the word "bid" in the clause in question.[109] It is not clear that this creates any substantive change in that no bid can be "accepted" in the sense of creating a binding contract until, at the very least, it constitutes the "highest" bid[110] and the reserve price, whose existence is also specified by the standard form, is reached. If the new qualification means accepted in this sense, rather than simply any bids received and announced by the auctioneer during the course of the auction, then, of course, it does make the condition conform substantially with the common law.

[2.23] The standard conditions, in addition to conferring upon the auctioneer the right to refuse to accept any bid,[111] give him power to deal with any dispute which arises as to bidding, eg, as to whether any bid was communicated to him and therefore became effective.[112] He is given the option either to determine the dispute or to put the property up again at the last undisputed bid.[113] Prior to 1976 the standard forms provided only for the latter.[114] The vendor is also given the right to divide the property being sold into lots and to sub-divide, consolidate or alter the order of sale of any lots.[115]

[2.24] It has been a matter of some controversy over the years as to what extent secret agreements may be made as between bidders themselves and as between the vendor or auctioneer and one or more bidders at the auction. As a general rule the courts will strive to protect the public in general and other bidders in particular against practices which constitute fraud.[116] Even if fraud is not proved, the court may in its discretion refuse to grant a purchaser specific performance on the ground that he has acted in an improper manner[117] - "he who comes into equity, must come with clean hands."[118] There have been several cases where the court has refused to recognise a sale as valid because it has been "damped", ie, the property has been

---

[109.] See now *General Conditions of Sale (1995 ed)*, cond 4(b).

[110.] As also specified by cond 4(b), see para **[2.21]** *supra*.

[111.] *General Conditions of Sale (1995 ed)*, cond 4(b). The *Conditions* specify also that no person "shall advance at a bidding a sum less than that fixed by the Auctioneer", *ibid*.

[112.] See *Tully v ILC* (1963) 97 ILTR 174. See also *Richards v Phillips* [1969] 1 Ch 39.

[113.] Cond 4(b).

[114.] 1968 *Public Auction Conditions of Sale*. See *Tully v ILC* (1963) 97 ILTR 174.

[115.] *General Conditions of Sale (1995 ed)*, cond 4(a).

[116.] See *Re Ashe* (1855) 4 Ir Ch R 594, especially at 601(*per* Brady LC) and 602 (*per* Monahan CJ); *Ingram v Gillen* (1910) 44 ILTR 103.

[117.] See *Twining v Morrice* (1788) 2 Bro C C 326; *Mason v Armitage* (1806) 13 Ves 25. See also para **[13.48]** *post*.

[118.] See *Irish Land Law*.(2nd ed, 1986) paras 3.058 and 3.151.

prevented from reaching its true price by some artificial means such as a secret arrangement between the vendor or auctioneer and one of the bidders.[119] Nor may a bidder seek to deter other bidders by making misrepresentations or disparaging remarks about the property.[120] On the other hand, the vendor or auctioneer must not seek to secure an inflated price by fraud or misrepresentations, eg, that bogus bids were genuine.[121] However, it appears that there is nothing to prevent two or more bidders making an agreement not to bid against each other in an attempt to secure a cheap sale.[122] Indeed, the courts have even enforced such "knock-out" agreements as between the parties to them,[123] and have ensured that a division of the spoils between the parties takes place subsequently.[124] As has been pointed out by judges[125], the vendor's means of protection against this sort of practice is to make sure that he fixes a reserve price.[126] There is no equivalent in Ireland of the English legislation relating to "dealers' rings".[127] The English Auctions (Bidding Agreements) Acts 1927 and 1969,[128] render illegal "knock-out" agreements made or "rings" operated by "dealers", ie, persons who in the normal course of business attend sales by auction for the purpose of purchasing goods with a view to reselling them.[129] Nor is there any equivalent of the English Mock Auctions Act 1961, which makes it illegal to conduct "mock" auctions[130] of certain goods as a means of promoting the sale of other goods for more than their real value.

[2.25] Finally, it should be noted that s 7 of the Sale of Land by Auction Act 1867, puts an end to the former practice[131] of the courts of equity of re-

---

119. See *Re Ashe* (1855) 4 Ir Ch R 594.
120. *Fuller v Abrahams* (1821) 3 Brod & Bing 116. See also *Howard v Hopkins* (1742) 2 Atk 371; *Mayer v Pluck* (1971) 223 Est Gaz 33.
121. *Ingram v Gillen* (1910) 44 ILTR 103; *Re Longvale Brick & Lime Works Ltd* [1917] 1 IR 321.
122. *Re Carew's Estate* (1858) 26 Beav 187; *Heffer v Martin* (1867) 36 LJ Ch 372.
123. See *Galton v Emuss* (1844) 1 Coll 243.
124. *Rawlings v General Trading Co* [1921] 1 KB 365; *Cohen v Roche* [1927] 1 KB 169.
125. See *Heffer v Martyn* (1867) 36 LJ Ch 372 at 373 (*per* Lord Romilly MR); *Harrop v Thompson* [1975] 2 All ER 94 at 98 (*per* Templeman J).
126. See para **[2.14-18]** *supra*.
127. This legislation resulted originally from the publicity that followed McCardie J's decision in *Cohen v Roche* [1927] 1 KB 169.
128. Their application to NI is expressly excluded by s 4(2) of the 1927 Act.
129. The Acts were clearly aimed at practices prevalent in auctions of works of art and antiques and seem to be confined in operation to the sale of goods as opposed to the sale of land.
130. Eg, by giving a refund or credit after the goods are knocked down or by making the purchase of cheap goods a pre-condition to bidding in the sale of other goods.
131. See the discussion in *Vesey v Elwood* (1842) 3 Dr & War 74 at 79-81 (*per* Sugden LC).

opening biddings in court sales on the ground that the property was being sold at an undervalue.[132] But the section made an express exception to cover cases where fraud or other improper conduct in the management of the sale exists.[133]

7. Deposits

[2.26] As we have seen,[134] the standard conditions of sale in use require that the purchaser of land at an auction should pay the stipulated deposit[135] immediately after the sale to the vendor's solicitor rather than the auctioneer. And, apart from express authority to the contrary, it seems that an auctioneer has no implied authority to receive such a deposit on the vendor's behalf.[136] If a deposit is in fact paid to the auctioneer and it is subsequently lost, eg, through bankruptcy of the auctioneer or misappropriation by him, difficult questions can arise as to the purchaser's remedies.[137] Clearly the purchaser can sue the auctioneer personally[138] if he has not disappeared, and in Ireland he has a chance of recovering because of the protection afforded by the Auctioneers and House Agents Acts.[139] Apart from such statutory protection, which is, of course, dependant upon the auctioneer following the statutory requirements in respect of, eg, client accounts, a question which is often raised is whether the vendor may be held responsible for the loss of the deposit in such circumstances. The answer to this question would seem to depend upon the capacity in which the auctioneer received the deposit. If he received it as the *authorised* agent of the vendor, the vendor will be liable under the ordinary law of agency.[140] However, the general presumption in

---

[132.] See *Woods v Brown* [1915] 1 IR 29 at 36 (*per* Palles CB). This rule against re-opening biddings in court sales has been extended in Ireland to cover private tenders accepted after an abortive auction, see *Munster & Leinster Bank v Munster Motor Co* [1922] 1 IR 15; *Provincial Bank of Ireland Ltd v Farris* [1944] IR 150; *Re Hibernian Transport Companies Ltd* [1972] IR 190.

[133.] *Ibid*, p 37 (*per* Palles CB). See also *Re Longvale Brick & Lime Works Ltd* [1917] 1 IR 321. See further para **[11.06]** *post*.

[134.] Para **[2.10]** *supra*.

[135.] 10% of the purchase price, see *General Conditions of Sale (1995 ed)* cond 4(d).

[136.] See para **[2.10]** *supra*.

[137.] See further on this point in relation to house or estate agents, paras **[3.15-17]** *post*.

[138.] *Sed quaere* where the auctioneer is simply holding the money as agent for the vendor, see *Bamford v Shuttleworth* (1840) 11 A & E 926; *Ellis v Goulton* [1893] 1 QB 350.

[139.] See the discussion in paras **[2.01-4]** especially para **[2.03]** *supra*. However, if the auctioneer is a member of one of the professional bodies, members of the public suffering loss may be protected. Thus the Irish Auctioneers and Valuers Institute (IAVI) has a compensation fund, which supplements the statutory bond, as does the Institute of Professional Auctioneers and Valuers (IPAV). The Society of Chartered Surveyors, the Irish branch of the RICS, has a compulsory professional indemnity insurance scheme. See Mahon, *Auctioneering and Estate Agency in Ireland*, (1990) Ch 8.

[140.] *Leemac Overseas Investments Ltd v Harvey* [1973] IR 160, especially at 165 (*per* KennyJ). See also *Duke of Norfolk v Worthy* (1808) 1 Camp 337.

the case of an auction is that any deposit received by the auctioneer is held by him as "stakeholder" rather than as agent for the vendor.[141] A stakeholder is a person whose duty it is to hold money in his hands not for one or other of the parties to a transaction, but for *both*, until some event occurs upon the happening of which it becomes his duty to hand over the money to one or other of the parties, eg, to the vendor if the sale goes through or to the purchaser if it does not. Pending that event, he must hold on to the money and not release it to one of the parties without the consent of the other.[142] If he releases the money before it is due, he is personally liable for its return.[143] Unless there is some express provision to the contrary, a stakeholder so long as he properly holds on to the "stake" is not liable to pay interest on the money held,[144] nor is he liable to account for any interest earned by putting the money in a deposit account.[145] Though a stakeholder-auctioneer is not agent for the vendor, it seems to be settled now that nevertheless the vendor is liable for the loss of any deposit held by him. As Kenny J said in *Leemac Overseas Investment Ltd v Harvey*:

> "When the sale is by public auction, the stakeholder will be nominated by the vendor who drafts the conditions of sale and who is therefore liable for his default."[146]

As the judge said later, though the auctioneer is a stakeholder, he is in essence "agent for the vendor so far as the vendor is liable for the loss of the deposit caused by his insolvency or misconduct."[147] In this respect an auctioneer receiving a deposit after a contract for sale has arisen from the auction should be distinguished from a house or estate agent receiving a deposit before a contract for sale by private treaty is entered into.[148]

---

141. *Edwards v Hodding* (1814) 5 Taunt 815; *Furtado v Lumley* (1890) 6 TLR 168. Note, however, that the Law Society's standard contract form requires the deposit to be paid to the vendor's *solicitor* as stakeholder. See para **[2.10]** *supra*.

142. *Leemac Overseas Investments Ltd v Harvey* [1973] IR 160 at 164 (*per* Kenny J). See also *Collins v Stinson* (1883) 11 QBD 142; *Skinner v Reed's Trustees* [1967] Ch 1194.

143. *Burrough v Skinner* (1770) 5 Burr 2639, *Edwards v Hodding* (1814) 5 Taunt 815, *Furtado v Lumley* (1890) 6 TLR 168.

144. *Gaby v Driver* (1828) 2 Y & J 549. *Cf Farquhar v Farley* (1817) 7 Taunt 592 (purchaser recovering loss of interest on deposit held by the auctioneer in suit against vendor for breach of contract).

145. *Harrington v Hoggart* (1830) 1 B & Ald 577. See also *Smith v Hamilton* [1951] Ch 174 especially at 184; "The stakeholder is not bound to pay interest: he retains the benefit of it: that is his reward for holding the stake." (*Per* Harman J). *Cf re* estate agents, *Potters v Loppert* [1973] 1 All ER 658.

146. [1975] IR 160 at 165. *Cf Fenton v Browne* (1807) 14 Ves 144 at 150 (*per* Grant MR).

147. *Ibid*, p 165. *Cf Rowe v May* (1854) 18 Beav 613 at 616 (*per* Romilly MR).

148. See paras **[3.15-17]** *post*.

8. Court Sales

[2.27] A public auction is the standard method of carrying out a sale under a court order, eg, an application by a mortgagee of land seeking to realise his security because of a default on the mortgage by the mortgagor.[149] It must be emphasised that in such a case the sale is conducted under the control of the court.[150] Though the vendor is the mortgagee, not the court,[151] the auctioneer is engaged and the conditions of sale, including the reserve price, are fixed under the control of the court.[152] Thus the auctioneer will be paid expenses and remuneration according to scales laid down for court sales.[153] And in *Law v Roberts & Co (No 2)*,[154] a case involving a suit for specific performance against a purchaser who had failed to complete on the day fixed for closing the sale, Kenny J insisted on fixing a rate of interest to be paid by the purchaser which related to current bank interest rates, so as to deter such purchasers from delaying completion for the longest possible period as, in effect, a cheap form of borrowing.[155]

C. Fees and Commission

Perhaps one of the most controversial aspects of the law relating to auctioneers has been the general subject of their remuneration, including both fees or commission and expenses. There are three main questions to be answered: (i) when does the auctioneer become entitled to payment; (ii) how much does he become entitled to; (iii) who is responsible for paying it?

1. Entitlement

[2.28] The general rule is that the auctioneer's entitlement to payment is governed by the terms of his contract with the vendor in the case of a private sale,[156] and by the terms of his appointment by the court in the case of a court sale.[157] Thus it may be a matter of construction whether he is entitled as soon

---

[149.] See *Irish Land Law* (2nd ed, 1986), paras 13.040-1.

[150.] See *Re Hibernian Transport Companies Ltd* [1972] IR 190. See further, paras **[11.01-09]** *post.*

[151.] *Bank of Ireland v Waldron* [1944] IR 303; *Bank of Ireland v Smith* [1966] IR 646, especially at 656 (*per* Kenny J). See also para **[11.03]** *post.*

[152.] *Bank of Ireland v Smith* (*op cit*) p 650 (*per* Kenny J). See also *Law v Roberts & Co (No 2)* [1964] IR 306; para **[11.04]** *post.*

[153.] *Provincial Bank of Ireland Ltd v Goulding* [1942] IR 108 at 109: "It is a term of the auctioneer's appointment in these cases that he shall abide by any order of the court as to his remuneration ..." (*Per* Gavan Duffy J).

[154.] [1964] IR 306.

[155.] *Ibid*, p 307. The rate was fixed at 6% instead of the 4% suggested by some earlier authorities, see, eg, *Re Day's Estate* (1876) 10 ILTR 18; though the higher rate seems to have been the court rate prior to 1834, see *Croly v O'Callaghan* (1842) 5 Ir Eq R 25.

[156.] *Cherry v Anderson* (1876) IR 10 CL 204; *Montgomery v Fleming* (1905) 39 ILTR 229.

[157.] *Provincial Bank of Ireland Ltd v Goulding* [1942] IR 108 para **[2.27]** *supra.*

as the auction is completed and the purchaser enters into a binding contract to buy the property auctioned or whether he must wait until the sale is completed by the subsequent conveyance of the property to the purchaser.[158] But it is important to note that often there is no formal agreement drawn up between the vendor and auctioneer, though some auctioneers write a letter to the vendor advising him as to the fees and advertising expenses. In *McMahon v Gaffney*,[159] Meredith J commented:

> "... payment of auctioneers' fees in Ireland is generally disposed of before, or independently of the contract of sale. The consideration for payment, by whomsoever made, is the work done by the auctioneer ... And the payment is disposed of as a matter *dehors* the contract of sale itself, and is in no way dependent on its completion."[160]

Even if completion is the general rule, it seems clear that the auctioneer may still be able to claim payment though no sale is actually completed, provided he has done all that was required of him and the non-completion is not due to any action of his, eg, a repudiation of the agreement made at the auction either by the vendor[161] or the purchaser.[162]

[2.29] The position is, perhaps, not quite so clear where the auction proves to be abortive but, as often happens, a private sale is concluded afterwards. Often the ultimate purchaser is someone who attended and may even have bid at the auction, and who may have first become aware of the property being for sale through the efforts of the auctioneer, eg, by his advertising. To some extent the auctioneer's entitlement to commission pursuant to a private sale depends on the scope of his original authority to sell. As we have seen,[163] the general law treats him as having authority to sell by auction only and so, in the absence of express authority to sell by private treaty as well,[164] a claim for commission on such a sale after an abortive auction may fail[165] This will be especially so where the purchaser at the subsequent private sale

---

[158.] See discussion in *Cherry v Anderson* (1876) IR 10 CL 204. See also *Peacock v Freeman* (1888) 4 TLR 541; *Skinner v Andrews and Hall* (1910) 26 TLR 340.

[159.] [1930] IR 576.

[160.] *Ibid* p 585.

[161.] *Rohan v Molony* (1905) 39 ILTR 207. *Cf* where the vendor calls off the auction before it is due to be held: see *Daniel Morrissey and Sons Ltd v Nalty* [1976-7] ILRM 269, para **[2.29]** *infra*.

[162.] *Provincial Bank of Ireland Ltd v Goulding* [1942] IR 108. *Cf Etchingham v Downes* (1946) 80 ILTR 73.

[163.] Paras **[2.05-7]** *supra*.

[164.] See *McNulty v Hanratty* (1918) 52 ILTR 43. *Cf Green v Bartlett* (1863) 14 CBNS 681.

[165.] See *Burns v Langford* (1901) 35 ILTR 148. *Cf Stokes and Quirke Ltd v Clohessy* [1957] IR 84. See also *Daniel Morrissey and Sons Ltd v Nalty* [1976-7] ILRM 269, para **[2.07]** *supra*.

is not introduced by the auctioneer[166] for then he is not the "effective cause" of the sale.[167] In *Judd v Donegal Tweed Co*,[168] decided some forty years ago, in the High Court, it was alleged that there was a custom amongst Irish auctioneers that, after an abortive auction, the auctioneer remained the exclusive agent for the sale for a reasonable period determined by the value of the property and was entitled to commission on a sale occurring within that period no matter by whose agency it was effected. It was held that the existence of such custom had not been proved so as to bind the vendors in that case. In practice, prudent solicitors never allow their clients in a private sale to pay the commission until the sale is closed. If it is paid before then and the sale is not completed, because, eg, the title is bad or the purchaser cannot raise the purchase price, great difficulty may be experienced in recovering the commission. Apart from this, solicitors take the view that in most cases the auctioneer is not entitled to the commission until the sale is closed.

[2.30] If no sale of any kind results, whether from the auction or otherwise, it is doubtful if an auctioneer is entitled to any payment except his outlay, in the absence of an express clause to this effect in his contract with the vendor. Thus a claim for a reasonable sum for an auctioneer's trouble and expense in preparing for and holding an abortive auction, essentially based on the *quantum meruit* principle, has been rejected by the English Court of Appeal.[169] Such a claim may be allowed, however, where the lack of a sale by the auctioneer results from the vendor disposing of the property himself before the auction or through another agent,[170] though again the validity of such a claim depends largely on the interpretation of the contract between the auctioneer and the vendor.[171]

[166.] *Burns v Langford, op cit.*

[167.] *Judd v Donegal Tweed Co* (1935) 69 ILTR 117. *Cf Green v Hall* (1848) 12 LT(os) 151; *Watson v Newton* (1920) 96 Est Gaz 140. See para **[3.22]** *post.*

[168.] *Ibid. Cf Marsh v Jeff* (1862) 3 F & F 234, especially at 252: "Auctioneers could not among themselves make such a custom to bind the rest of Her Majesty's subjects" (*Per* Keating J).

[169.] *John Meacock & Co v Abrahams* [1956] 3 All ER 660. But *cf Frank Swain v Whitfield Corp Ltd* (1962) 183 Est Gaz 479, especially at 479 (*per* Upjohn LJ). *Cf Stokes and Quirke Ltd v Clohessy* [1957] IR 84.

[170.] In *John Meacock & Co. v Abrahams, op cit*, there was a standard clause, included in the Chartered Auctioneers' and Estate Agents' Institute's scale of charges, entitling the auctioneer to the scale commission in the event of any sale, whether arranged by the auctioneer or not, effected between the date of acceptance of instructions and the date of the auction.

[171.] See *Murphy Buckley & Keogh Ltd v Pye (Ir) Ltd* [1971] IR 57. Also see para **[3.20]** *post.*

2. Amount

[2.31] Apart from a few special cases where a statutory scale may be laid down,[172] the amount of commission to which an auctioneer is entitled in a private sale by auction depends on the terms of his contract with the vendor. This will usually state the amount of commission due and indicate whether or not advertising costs and other out of-pocket expenses are included. Often the contract will incorporate a scale of charges issued by a relevant professional body, eg, the Irish Auctioneers and Valuers Institute.[173] If the auctioneer wants a professional scale to apply, he must heed the warning given by Hanna J in *North v Drinan*[174]:

> "This is an association scale, framed to prevent the members of the profession from undercutting one another, but it is clear law that it is not binding on clients unless it is expressly brought to their notice, and agreed to by them, or established by convincing proof of some universal custom. If this is not done the Court has to determine for itself what is a reasonable remuneration for the services rendered."[175]

[2.32] If the contract does not specify the amount of commission, it is settled that an auctioneer, like any professional person, is entitled to reasonable remuneration for his services.[176] What is reasonable obviously depends upon the circumstances of each particular case, but the courts usually have reference to what is the custom of the trade and, of course, to any scale charges laid down by professional bodies for such cases.[177] It seems, however, that, if no express stipulation is made as to out-of-pocket expenses, these are to be taken as being paid for out of the commission.[178] Though, if no commission is earned, eg, because no sale results, arguably the auctioneer should still be entitled to claim for any expenses nevertheless incurred.[179] In *Daniel Morrissey and Sons Ltd v Nalty*[180] where the agreement with the auctioneers was held to entitle them to commission on a sale by auction only, Gannon J held that they were not entitled to commission on a sale

---

[172.] Eg, sales of goods seized by a landlord under a distress for rent, in accordance with regulations made under the Law of Distress and Small Debts (Ir) Act 1888. However note that the remedy of distress for rent is never invoked these days: see Wylie, *Irish Landlord and Tenant Law,* para 12.14 *et seq.*

[173.] See para **[2.26]** fn 139 *supra.*

[174.] [1931] IR 468.

[175.] *Ibid* p 473.

[176.] *North v Drinan op cit.* See also *Heneken v Courtney* (1967) 101 ILTR 25.

[177.] See *O'Connor v Faul* (1957) 91 ILTR 7 (alleged local custom in Co Louth held unreasonable).

[178.] *Marshall v Parsons* (1841) 9 C & P 656.

[179.] Some English authority exists to support this view, see, eg, *Chinnock v Sainsbury* (1869) 3 LT 258 at 259 (*per* Romilly MR; *Cf* (1869) 30 LJ Ch. 409 at 411), *John Meacock & Co v Abrahams* [1956] 3 All ER 660 at 663 (*per* Denning LJ).

[180.] [1976-7] ILRM 269.

arranged by private treaty after the vendors called off the auction, as they were entitled to do.[181] However, he held that they were entitled to their advertising expenses relating to the aborted auction, holding that the separate provision for those in the agreement was consistent with the provision that there would be no remuneration if no auction was held.[182]

[2.33] In the case of a court sale, the general rule is that laid down by Gavan Duffy J in *Provincial Bank of Ireland Ltd v Goulding*[183]:

> "It is a term of the auctioneer's appointment in these cases that he shall abide by any order of the Court as to his remuneration."[184]

In fact scale fees for auctions conducted under a court order for sale have been laid down from time to time so as to govern auctions in court sales.[185]

3. Payment

[2.34] Perhaps one of the most controversial subjects relating to auctioneers and house or estate agents in Ireland was the issue of responsibility for payment of their fees and commissions.[186] For many years it was the standard practice in both parts of Ireland that the *purchaser* rather than the vendor was responsible for payment of the fee or commission.[187] As Johnston J explained in *McMahon v Gaffney*:[188]

> "The liability for the auctioneer's fees is a matter of contract between the vendor and purchaser, and in Ireland the almost invariable arrangement is that the purchaser should be the person responsible. That is the well-recognised and established practice, and a condition to that effect is customarily set out in the conditions of sale. There is nothing harsh or oppressive in such an arrangement. The bidder knows beforehand that he

---

[181.] See paras **[2.05-7]** *supra*.

[182.] The terms were set out in a letter sent by the auctioneers to the vendors as follows: "Referring to your recent conversation with our Mr J Young concerning the above, we wish to thank you for your instructions to offer this property for sale by auction at 3 pm on Wednesday 28th May 1975 in our salesrooms, Lower Merrion Street, Dublin 2 and you may be assured that we shall do everything possible to achieve a successful result ... We confirm that our auction fees are at the rate of 2½% payable by the vendor, and your liability for advertising will not exceed £400. We shall endeavour to keep these expenses as low as possible."

[183.] [1942] IR 108.

[184.] *Ibid* p 109.

[185.] See *ibid*.

[186.] See the discussion in the *Survey of the Land Law of Northern Ireland* (1971), Ch 6.

[187.] *Rohan v Molony* (1905) 39 ILTR 207; *Kennedy v McMaster* [1935] Ir Jur Rep 2. However, in the Dublin area it was common for the vendor to pay the estate's agent fees on a sale by *private treaty*.

[188.] [1930] IR 576.

will have to pay the auctioneer's commission, and he regulates his bidding accordingly."[189]

This was invariably made a condition of sale, whether the sale was arranged privately or by public auction,[190] and whoever drew up the formal conditions of sale, eg, the vendor's solicitor, included an appropriate clause to this effect in the conditions.[191] Thus the purchaser became bound to pay the fee or commission by the terms of his contract with the vendor and the vendor's solicitor regarded it as his duty to see that this condition was complied with. This meant, of course, that the auctioneer could not sue the purchaser directly for failure to pay, because there was no contract between the auctioneer and the purchaser. As Palles CB explained in *Cherry v Anderson*:[192]

> "Upon the sale of real estate the auctioneer has no right to sue in his own name, analogous to his right on the sale of goods. In the latter case he has, or is deemed to have, a possession of the goods and a qualified property in them.[193] On the sale of real property the right to sue depends on the written contract alone; and unless that contract be so framed as to render the auctioneer the ostensible vendor ... he cannot on the sale of real estate maintain in his own name an action against the purchaser."[194]

Thus the auctioneer's remedy for non-payment of commission was to sue the vendor on the basis of his contract with the vendor, and the vendor could then recoup the amount by suing the purchaser on the basis of the contract for sale.[195] If the purchaser actually paid the commission but the sale subsequently fell through, it seems that the purchaser could recover his commission from the vendor, but not from the auctioneer.[196] There may have been rare cases, however, where the auctioneer could sue the purchaser directly, eg, where he also acted for the purchaser in the sale.[197] In *Hodgens v Keon*,[198] the purchaser gave the auctioneer an IOU for the deposit on the

---

[189] *Ibid*, p 585.

[190] *Provincial Bank of Ireland Ltd v Goulding* [1942] IR 108.

[191] See the 1968 edition of the Law Society's *Public Auction Conditions of Sale*, especially the memorandum of agreement incorporated therein.

[192] (1876) IR 10 CL 204.

[193] See *Williams v Millington* (1788) 1 H Bl 81 at 84 (*per* Lord Loughborough CJ); *Chelmsford Auctions Ltd v Poole* [1973] QB 542.

[194] (1876) IR 10 CL 204 at 209; see also *McMahon v Gaffney* [1930] IR 576 at 585 (*per* Meredith J) and 586 (*per* Johnston J). *Cf Montgomery v Fleming* (1905) 39 ILTR 229.

[195] See *Kennedy v McMaster* [1935] Ir Jur Rep 2.

[196] *Adams v McKeown* (1892) 26 ILT 504; *McNulty v Hanratty* (1918) 52 ILTR 43; *McMahon v Gaffney* [1930] IR 576; *Kennedy v McMaster* [1935] Ir Jur Rep 2. *Cf Murphy v Harte* (1912) 46 ILTR 197.

[197] See *Wood v Jagoe* (1904) 4 NIJR 143. *Cf Heneken v Courtney* (1967) 101 ILTR 25.

[198] [1894] 2 IR 657.

property knocked down to him and it was held that the auctioneer could sue the purchaser on this.[199] Palles CB took the view that the auctioneer in such a case could sue the purchaser whether or not he was authorised by the vendor to receive an IOU.[200] Finally, it should be noted that, in sales by the court, the auctioneer's fees were never payable by the purchaser but were paid out of the purchase money at a lower rate than that which usually applied to sales by auction.

[2.35] The position with respect to responsibility for payment of an auctioneer's fees was radically changed by s 2(1) of the Auctioneers and House Agents Act 1973. This provides:

> ... any provision (whether express or implied) in an agreement entered into after the commencement of this Act[201] and relating to the sale, lease or letting of property (not being personal chattels), whereby the purchaser, lessee or tenant is required to pay or bear the cost of auctioneers' or house agents'[202] fees or expenses in respect of the sale, lease or letting, shall be void, and any moneys paid under or on foot of such a provision shall be recoverable as a simple contract debt in a court of competent jurisdiction.

Thus the rule is now firmly established that in respect of sales by auction an auctioneer's[203] fee or commission and expenses must be paid by the person who employs him to do the work in question, ie, normally the vendor. This point is emphasised by s 2(2) of the 1973 Act which provides that nothing in the provision just quoted "shall affect the liability of a person to pay fees or expenses to an auctioneer or house agent in respect of the acquisition of any property in a case where the auctioneer or house agent had been retained by the person to acquire such property and does not also act, in relation to such acquisition, on behalf of the person from whom the property is acquired". It should be noted, however, that s 2 of the 1973 Act would not seem to apply to certain transactions in land with which auctioneers and estate agents are familiar, eg, conacre and agistment lettings. The reference to "sale, lease or letting" and, in particular, to the corresponding "purchaser, lessee or tenant" suggests that it does not apply to arrangements which do not create an interest like a tenancy, but rather something falling short of that like a licence to use land.

[199.] See also *Gillen v Gibson* (1910) 44 ILTR 17 (auctioneer recovering on IOU given to him by the purchaser for the amount of the auction fees).

[200.] See also *Montgomery v Fleming* (1905) 39 ILTR 229. And see *McMahon v Gaffney* [1930] IR 576 at 585 (*per* Meredith J) and 586 (*per* Johnston J).

[201.] Ie, 12 December 1973, see s 4(3).

[202.] See further, para **[3.32]** *post*.

[203.] The 1973 Act relates, of course, only to licensed auctioneers, see s 1(2) and para **[2.02]** *supra*.

II. Vendor's Solicitor

[2.36] We must now consider further the role of the vendor's solicitor in the preliminary stages of a sale by public auction.[204] As a general rule, the vendor usually consults his solicitor before the auction takes place, if only because the auctioneer requires information, eg, as to the title to the property or as to the conditions of sale to be incorporated in the contract for sale. In the early stages of a sale by auction, the vendor's solicitor is concerned with two matters primarily, apart from enquiries as to the property. The first is the taking of detailed instructions as to the sale from the vendor and the second is the drawing up of the conditions of sale governing the auction itself, along with any other instructions to the auctioneer.

A. Taking Instructions

[2.37] The importance of taking detailed instructions from the client at the earliest opportunity cannot be emphasised too often.[205] It is vital for the solicitor to secure all the information at the beginning of the transaction which he is going to use at the various stages in the conveyancing process which occur later. It will cause him and his client all sorts of difficulty later on, and possibly further expense through delays, if this guiding rule of practice is not adhered to assiduously. For this reason it is wise to adopt the practice of always using a written "instructions form", which may be varied according to whether the solicitor is acting for the vendor or the purchaser and whether it is a sale or purchase by public auction or private treaty. And it need hardly be said that the value of such forms depends upon the care used to see that the items referred to are all raised with the client and the information obtained filled in on the form. In addition, a solicitor may find it useful to keep a "progress sheet", listing all the steps to be carried out, in the appropriate order, for the transaction in question. If each step is marked off as it is taken and the sheet is kept to hand, eg, pinned to the cover of the client's file, the solicitor, who may have dozens of transactions currently in hand, can tell at a glance the state of progress in that particular transaction. The use of such a check-list should also guard against the possibility of some vital step in the process being missed out, with resultant loss to the client and liability for the solicitor. The following is a brief outline of the various matters which should be covered in taking instructions from the client, especially in the case of the vendor's solicitor.

[204.] His role in the case of a sale by private treaty is considered later, see para **[3.33]** *post.*

[205.] See the discussion in *Murphy v Harrington* [1927] IR 339.

1. Particulars of Parties

[2.38] It is essential that the client's full name, address. telephone and fax number, marital status and, probably, his occupation be obtained. His full name must be obtained because this will have to be checked with his name as it appears in the title deeds or, in the case of registered land, the name under which his title is registered in the Land Registry. His name will also have to be inserted correctly in the contract for sale[206] and the ultimate conveyance or transfer document.[207] Failure to obtain strictly accurate information on these points from the beginning can lead to infuriating snags later on in the transaction. It is also wise to have a note as to where the client can be contacted, in a hurry if necessary, should further consultation with him become essential at some later stage. In addition to particulars relating to one's client, it is also wise to obtain from him any information he can give as to other parties involved in the transaction and with whom one is going to have dealings before the transaction is completed. In the case of a sale by auction, it is essential to obtain the name and address of the auctioneer, if only to be able to confirm with him the date and venue of the auction. The auctioneer should consult the vendor's solicitor on the question of the conduct of the auction, in particular in relation to the drawing up of the conditions of sale and their incorporation in the contract of sale to be concluded with the purchaser at the auction.[208] It is important that the particulars describing the property in the contract drawn up by the vendor's solicitor coincide with any description given by the auctioneer in his advertising.[209] Of course, in this case particulars relating to the purchaser and his solicitors will not be available until the auction takes place and the highest bidder becomes known.[210]

2. Particulars of the Property

[2.39] It is equally essential that full particulars relating to the property to be sold should be obtained. This includes both a physical and a legal description, ie, the full address of the property as shown by the title deeds which the client may have or Land Registry description (including the folio number)[211] and the title held by the vendor (freehold, leasehold, etc). Once again this information is needed for documents to be drafted later, such as the contract for sale.[212] It is also important at this stage to determine clearly

---

[206.] See para **[9.05]** *post.*

[207.] Para **[18.12]** *post.*

[208.] See para **[2.45]** *infra.*

[209.] See the discussion in *Peilow v O'Carroll* [1972] 106 ILTR 29. Also para **[9.07]** *et seq, post.*

[210.] *Cf* the case of a sale by private treaty, para **[3.39]** *post.*

[211.] See para **[9.10]** *post.*

[212.] See para **[9.07]** *post.*

what is included in the sale of the property. This is particularly the case with fixtures and fittings, such as curtain rails and pelmets in the case of residential property, and other items which the vendor may agree to leave for the purchaser, such as carpets and curtains, refrigerators, washing machines and cookers.[213] If this matter is determined from the beginning unpleasant disputes which can so often arise in practice may be avoided.

[2.40] In addition to determining precisely the vendor's interest in the property being sold and whether his title is registered in the Land Registry or not, it is important to discover whether the sale is subject to any rights or interests held by third parties. This is particularly so where the property is leasehold property, as is often the case in the urban areas of Ireland,[214] in which case there may be sub-tenants subject to whose interests the purchaser is to take. Apart from that problem, the vendor's interest may be subject to a mortgage or charge which is still undischarged. It must be determined whether this is to be discharged out of the purchase money raised by the current sale, which is usually the case, or left out-standing so as to bind the purchaser when he becomes owner of the property. If there is such a mortgage or charge, full details as to the mortgagee or chargee and as to the debt outstanding must be obtained. If an extra charge or penalty is payable for early redemption,[215] the sooner notice of any intended redemption on conclusion of the current sale is given the better. Where the sale involves a family home, the vendor's spouse's prior consent to the sale must be obtained for both the contract for sale and the conveyance to be valid under the Family Home Protection Act 1976.[216] In such circumstances, it may be wise to obtain that consent prior to the auction and to insist upon the spouse attending the auction so as to be able to endorse the consent on the contract entered into with the highest bidder. This is just one example of the matters upon which the purchaser's solicitor will wish to be satisfied and which will be raised as enquiries or requisitions on title, either before or after the auction is held.[217]

[213.] See para **[9.15]** *post*.

[214.] Paras **[1.16-7]** *ante*.

[215.] Eg, lending institutions frequently require a set period of notice of redemption or payment of interest for that period in lieu of notice: see *Irish Land Law* (2nd ed, 1986) para 13.101. Note, however, that under the Consumer Credit Act 1995, mortgage lenders will not be able to charge early redemption fees on home loans except in the case of fixed-rate interest loans.

[216.] See para **[16.61]** *post*.

[217.] See para **[2.47]** *infra* and Chs 15 and 16 *post*.

3. Title Deeds and Other Relevant Documents

[2.41] The vendor's solicitor must, in the case of a sale of unregistered land, discover at the earliest possible stage the whereabouts of the title documents relating to the property being sold. In the case of a sale by public auction, he will need these to check the vendor's title so as to be able to frame the conditions of sale properly, ie, to determine the precise terms of the contract for sale.[218] Whether the sale is by public auction or private treaty he will again have to refer to the title documents in deducing title to,[219] and answering any requisitions on title raised by,[220] the purchaser's solicitor. And, of course, on completion the title documents will normally have to be handed over to the purchaser as the new owner of the property.[221]

[2.42] The nature of the title documents will vary from case to case. For example, in the case of unregistered land, they will consist of the traditional form of title deeds or conveyances,[222] eg, conveyances of the freehold, fee farm grants and sub-grants, leases of various kinds and sub-leases, mortgages and charges. In the case of registered land, however, traditional title deeds are replaced on registration of the title in the Land Registry by the entries on the folio relating to the land in question maintained by the Registry.[223] Where the registered owner creates a mortgage on the land, this is effected by means of a registered charge, in respect of which the chargee may be issued with a certificate of charge.[224]

[2.43] It is often the case that the vendor does not have the relevant title documents in his possession, in which case his solicitor will have to make arrangements to obtain them. They may be lodged with the vendor's bank. If this is simply for safe custody, there is little problem, unless, as is often the case, the documents are lodged in a sealed box or envelope, in which case the bank may be unaware of the precise contents. Thus a request for their production may produce a reply by the bank manager that he does not have them. Another problem may arise if the vendor has lost the receipt for the box or envelope issued by the bank. Also they may be deposited with the

---

[218.] See Chs 9 and 10 *post*.

[219.] See Ch 14 *post*.

[220.] See Ch 15 *post*.

[221.] See para **[20.34]** *post*.

[222.] Note the definition of "conveyance" in s 2(v) of the Conveyancing Act 1881. which includes: "assignment, appointment, lease, settlement and other assurance, and covenant to surrender, made by deed, on a sale, mortgage, demise, or settlement of any property, or any other dealing with or for any property."

[223.] See para **[14.33]** *post*. The registered owner may be issued with a "land certificate" showing these entries, see paras **[14.31-32]** *post*. See generally Fitzgerald, *Land Registry Practice*, (2nd ed, 1995).

[224.] See Fitzgerald *op cit*, Ch 9.

bank as security for an overdraft or other loan[225] not yet cleared by the vendor. The bank will obviously be reluctant to release deeds held as security for a loan still unrepaid and will facilitate the vendor's solicitor only on his giving a personal undertaking as to their safe keeping and that the loan will be discharged out of the proceeds of sale. Similarly, in the case of a mortgage of unregistered land,[226] the title deeds will usually be held by the mortgagee, eg, a building society, until the mortgage is discharged.[227] Once again the title deeds will not usually be released unless the vendor's solicitor gives a personal undertaking to the mortgagee.[228] These examples of what is very common practice serve to illustrate how solicitors' personal undertakings help to "oil" the machinery of conveyancing. Yet they also indicate how essential it is that solicitors recognise the importance of honouring such undertakings.[229] If the various institutions inevitably involved in land transactions ever lost confidence in the value of such undertakings, conveyancing would be made a much more difficult process. For this reason it is vitally important that the vendor's solicitor should take a note of any undertakings given by him to third parties, eg, by entering it on his instructions form or on his sales progress form,[230] so as to remind him to carry them out at the appropriate time. In passing it may be mentioned that documents of title are sometimes lost or mislaid. If the solicitor who formerly acted for the vendor has ceased to practice, the documents may be untraceable, or they may have been destroyed by fire. If the originals cannot be produced, it is essential that the purchaser should be bound by the conditions of sale not to require production of the originals, but to accept certified or plain copies or even memorials registered in the Registry of Deeds as conclusive evidence of their contents.[231] It is of the greatest importance, therefore, that the vendor's solicitor should find out before drafting the contract or conditions of sale which original documents of title are missing. The absence of originals is certain to create the suspicion that

---

[225.] Thereby creating an equitable mortgage on the land - a very common practice in Ireland, see *Fitzgerald, op cit*, p 354. See *Re Farm Fresh Foods Ltd* [1980] ILRM 131.

[226.] In the case of registered land, the chargee is strictly entitled to the charge certificate only and not the land certificate as well, see *Fitzgerald, op cit*, p 215, but usually insists in practice on holding the land certificate (if one has been issued to the mortgagor).

[227.] See *Irish Land Law*, (2nd ed, 1986) paras 13.005-6.

[228.] A solicitor who obtains the title deeds on accountable receipt, and thereby holds them on trust for the mortgagee, does not hold them for his client and so cannot claim a lien over them for, eg, unpaid fees: see *Re Galdan Properties Ltd* [1988] IR 213; para **[20.50]** *post*.

[229.] See generally the Law Society's *Conveyancing Handbook*, Ch 2 and para **[20.24]** *post*.

[230.] See para **[2.37]** *supra*.

[231.] For discussion of the difficulties lost documents create on an application for first registration of the title, see Fitzgerald, *Land Registry Practice* (2nd ed, 1995), p 375 *et seq*.

they have been deposited as security and, whenever possible, an explanation for their absence should be given. Indeed, it sometimes happens that all the documents of title furnished consist of memorials and in such a case the purchaser's solicitor may insist upon an insurance company bond being furnished by way of indemnity. Even if he does not insist on this, it is likely that the lending institution from whom his client may be borrowing a substantial proportion of the purchase price will insist upon it. Furthermore, if the vendor is selling part of the property only and so is not handing over the originals on completion, this should be stated in the conditions of sale and an inspection of the originals and a covenant for their production and safe-keeping should be offered.[232]

[2.44] Apart from title documents, there will usually be other documents relating to the vendor's property which his solicitor will need. Thus there will come a point when he and the purchaser's solicitor will have to settle how financial charges incurred during the year of the sale are to be apportioned as between the vendor and purchaser, eg, in respect of the rates payable on the property and any rent such as fee farm rents and leasehold rents.[233] The purchaser's solicitor will usually require production of the latest demand for rates in respect of commerical property and receipts in respect of any rents paid by the vendor. The purchaser's solicitor may also request information as to current insurance covering the property, for, as we shall see,[234] the position of the purchaser once the contract to purchase has been entered into may still need consideration.[235]

4. Terms of Sale

[2.45] In the case of a sale by public auction, it is particularly important that the vendor's solicitor settles with his client the position with regard to the conduct of the auction. In particular, he must check that the standard conditions relating to such items as fixing a reserve price, bidding by the vendor himself or an agent and withdrawal of the property before or during the auction, are agreeable to him.[236] Even if the standard conditions are acceptable, the figure for the reserve price must be determined. It is also important that the amount of the deposit and the person to whom it is payable should be decided. A solicitor who receives a deposit should, in general, place it immediately on deposit in his client account, especially if

---

[232.] See also para **[18.102]** *post*.

[233.] See para **[20.03]** *post*.

[234.] See para **[12.36]** *post*

[235.] Notwithstanding the position now under the Law Society's standard contract form, see para **[12.40]** *post*.

[236.] See the discussion at paras **[2.14-18]** *supra*.

the money is received on behalf of the vendor.[237] Though if the solicitor holds the money as stakeholder there may be a question as to who is the client as regards the deposit money.[238]

[2.46] Apart from these matters, the vendor's solicitor must determine whether there are any special terms relating to the present sale which are not usually present. Thus the vendor may not be selling with vacant possession, but subject to the occupational rights of third parties, eg, tenants or sub-tenants. He may not intend to discharge a mortgage or charge on the land out of the proceeds of sale, but instead wishes the purchaser to take it over when he becomes the owner, subject to the latter's and the mortgagee's agreement on this, which will rarely be forthcoming. The sale may be subject to the landlord's consent if the property is leasehold and a special condition dealing with this may be inserted in the contract.

5. Anticipation of Purchaser's Enquiries

[2.47] Though, as we shall see,[239] the vendor's solicitor is more likely to be concerned with this matter at an early stage in the case of a sale by private treaty, arguably it is prudent to pay some attention to it even in the case of a sale by public auction. Essentially the vendor's solicitor is concerned with eliciting information from his client about items likely to be raised at some stage by the purchaser's solicitor. Increasingly, nowadays, many matters relating to the property are raised *before* the purchaser enters into the contract.[240] Thus some query is likely to be raised about the existence of the usual public services, eg, mains water supply and sewerage disposal, drainage, gas and electricity supply. If the property being sold is part of a larger property, eg, one flat in a block of flats, the question of common

---

237. See Solicitors (Interest on Clients' Money) Regulations 1995 (SI 108/1995), made under s 73 of the Solicitors (Amendment) Act 1994. *Cf* the Law Society's recommendations published in the *Gazette*, November 1980, and its views on the use of individual Deposit Receipts as opposed to a general client account published in the *Newsletter*, April/December 1986; see *Conveyancing Handbook*, pp 13.4 and 13.19.

238. Generally a stakeholder is entitled to keep any profit made from holding the stake: see *Potters v Loppert* [1973] 1 All ER 658; *cf Burt v Claude Cousins & Co Ltd* [1971] 2 All ER 611 at 622 (*per* Sachs LJ). Arguably, in the spirit of the interest regulations, the stake money, unless the agreement provides otherwise, should be put in the client account and treated like client's money, the interest to be accounted for to the person who becomes entitled to the stake money in due course. See the Solicitors (Interest on Clients' Moneys) Regulations 1995 (SI 108/1995).

239. See para **[3.36]** *post*.

240. See the Law Society's *Pre-Contract Check List on Acquisition of Private Dwelling House* (reproduced in Appendix 1 *post* and on p 12.11 of the *Conveyancing Handbook*). It is pointed out that additional enquiries or requisitions will usually have to be made in respect of commercial property, licensed premises, agricultural land, flats and other multi-storied buildings.

services, including additional items like stairways and lifts, becomes of paramount importance.[241] Another matter likely to be raised is whether the street or road which the property abuts has been taken in charge or adopted by the local authority and so is maintained at public expense.[242] If the property does not abut a public road, it will be necessary to establish what rights of access to such a road exist. The purchaser will also be concerned about the boundaries of the property, especially about any recent disputes as to them, and about any party walls and fences.[243] The vendor's solicitor ought also to check with his client whether any alterations or extensions have been made to the property and, if so, whether any requisite planning permission[244] or landlord's consent was obtained and relevant building regulations complied with.[245] If the property to be sold is the vendor's family home, the question of consent required under the Family Home Protection Act 1976, arises.[246] The question of Land Act consent may also arise.[247]

6. Financial Matters

[2.48] Though advice on financial matters may be more important for a purchaser,[248] there are some matters which ought to be considered by the vendor's solicitor. One is that the vendor may be involved in more than one transaction, eg, he may be buying another property. In that case it is quite possible that the net[249] proceeds of sale of this existing property will not be sufficient to meet the total purchase price of the new property. So he may need advice on how to raise the balance, eg, by taking out a loan secured by a mortgage on the new property being bought. If the vendor is short of ready cash he may have difficulty in meeting the deposit on his new property before he receives the proceeds from the sale of his old property. A prospective bidder at an auction must bear in mind the fact that if he is successful in having the property knocked down to him at the auction, the deposit is payable immediately. His solicitor should be able to advise him on this problem, eg, a bridging loan may be arranged with the vendor's bank. Alternatively, a special arrangement may be made whereby the deposit paid by the purchaser of his existing property can be released for immediate use

---

[241.] See para **[16.97]** *post.*

[242.] See para **[16.09]** *post.*

[243.] As to the complications of ownership of these, see *Irish Land Law* (2nd ed, 1986), paras 7.53-62.

[244.] See para **[16.74]** *post.*

[245.] See para **[16.79]** *post.*

[246.] See para **[16.61]** *et seq, post.*

[247.] See para **[16.29]** *post.*

[248.] See para **[1.37]** *ante.*

[249.] Ie, after discharge of any outstanding liabilities such as a mortgage loan charged on the property sold, and payment of fees and commissions arising from the sale.

by the vendor instead of being held until completion.[250] This is very rarely agreed to.

[2.49] It may, of course, be the case that the proceeds of the sale are not needed for some immediate purpose such as the purchase of a new property. In that case the vendor may require advice from his solicitor as to a suitable short or long-term investment for the money. This may involve the solicitor in a close examination of the vendor's family circumstances and raises the complex subject of estate planning, which the modern taxation system has made so important. Any advice as to investment of capital must take account of the immediate and future incidence of taxation.[251] This examination may also reveal, eg, that the vendor has not yet made a will or that his will was made many years ago when his family and financial circumstances were quite different, in which case he should be advised to consider making a new will. Quite apart from the investment of the proceeds of sale, the vendor should be advised as to any liability to tax which may arise from the sale itself, eg, capital gains tax.[252]

7. Completion

[2.50] One of the most important matters for both parties is the fixing of a closing date, ie, the date when the conveyancing process is to be completed by, *inter alia*, the vendor handing over the title deeds and keys to the property in return for the balance of the purchase money due.[253] One of the primary tasks of the parties' respective solicitors is to conduct their conveyancing activities in such a way as to meet that date. Failure to do so may result in the party in default incurring extra liabilities, eg, the purchaser may be faced with interest charges.[254] Thus the solicitors must take into account in fixing the closing or completion date, which is invariably specified in the contract for sale,[255] the various steps to be taken in carrying out the conveyancing process for the transaction in question and agree on a realistic date. However, it is important to realise that each party may have a considerable stake in how early or late that date is, especially if, as is so often the case, that party is also involved in another transaction. For this reason each solicitor ought to discuss the question of the closing date to be specified in the contract with his client and any ancillary matters, eg, whether time should be made of the essence of the contract[256] and what rate

---

[250.] See para [10.25] *post.*

[251.] For the relevant taxes, see the annual *Butterworths Tax Guide.*

[252.] *Ibid*, Pt 3.

[253.] Completion is somewhat more complicated in the case of registered land, see para [20.44] *post.*

[254.] See para [20.09] *post.*

[255.] See para [9.05] *post.*

[256.] See para [13.10] *post.*

of interest should be charged in the event of delay in completion.[257] Also, if there is going to be a long delay in completion because, eg, some problem about the title has arisen, provision may be made for putting the balance of the purchase money on joint deposit in the names of the vendor's and purchaser's solicitors while the problem is being sorted out. Finally, there is the question of whether the purchaser should be allowed into possession before completion, if he requests this, and, if so, upon what terms.[258]

B. Drafting Particulars and Conditions of Sale

[2.51] Apart from taking instructions from his client, and attending to matters which necessarily arise therefrom, the primary task of the vendor's solicitor in the early stages of a sale by auction is to draft the particulars and conditions of sale. This is usually done by using the standard form issued by the Law Society, a matter we discuss in detail in a later chapter.[259] In addition to drawing up what will constitute the terms of the contract to be entered into by the vendor and the purchaser, the vendor's solicitor may have to issue instructions to the auctioneer on a variety of other matters, eg, advertising of the sale.

[2.52] It is also possible that the vendor's solicitor may become involved in negotiations about the sale, especially the conditions of sale, prior to the auction. Thus the auctioneer's advertisements may have indicated that the conditions were available for inspection at the vendor's solicitor's office and an interested prospective purchaser may have instructed his solicitor to examine them with a view to trying to secure any amendments thought desirable before the auction is held.

III. PURCHASER'S SOLICITOR

[2.53] The purchaser's solicitor usually has a very minor role to play in the case of a sale by public auction. Indeed, frequently he is not instructed until after the auction is held and his client has entered into the contract to purchase on being declared the highest bidder.[260] His role then is largely the completion of the post-contract stages of the conveyancing process,[261] which

---

[257.] Note the rate stipulated in the Law Society's standard contract form, see para **[10.14]** *post.*

[258.] See para **[12.32]** *post.*

[259.] See Ch 9 *post.*

[260.] See *Re Mitchell and McElhinney's Contract* [1902] 1 IR 83 at 86-7 (*per* Porter MR). On more than one occasion the Law Society has warned against the practice of furnishing auctioneers with copies of the contract, thereby enabling the auctioneer to procure a purchaser's signature to it before his solicitor may have had a chance to vet it: see the *Gazette*, July/August 1979 and April 1983; *Conveyancing Handbook*, p 12.5.

[261.] See Ch 14 *et seq, post.*

in some respects are the easier stages. This is not a very satisfactory position for a solicitor to find himself in, ie, acting for a client who has committed himself to a contract in the fixing of whose terms the solicitor has had no say at all. If the terms turn out to be operating harshly against his client, there may be very little that his solicitor can do to mitigate them. In this respect, the purchaser's solicitor's role should be contrasted with his role in the case of a sale by private treaty where generally he is instructed at an earlier stage.[262]

[2.54] If a prospective bidder at a sale by public auction does decide to instruct his solicitor before the auction is held, the latter's function is not much different from that in the case of a sale by private treaty, a matter we discuss in detail later.[263] The one qualification which he is likely to bear in mind in deciding what action to take in the preliminary stages is the fact that, until the auction is held,[264] his client is at most a potential purchaser only, whose likelihood of becoming the actual purchaser depends on several unknown quantities, eg, the existence of other bidders. Thus, apart from taking instructions from his client, the solicitor may decide that there is little point in doing much else prior to the auction.[265] If, however, the conditions of sale are, as is usual, available for inspection prior to the auction, the purchaser's solicitor ought in his client's interest to examine them and, if necessary, ought to try to persuade the vendor's solicitor to introduce appropriate amendments. However, it is likely that the vendor's solicitor will be reluctant to do this because several other potential bidders may have already consulted them and may have decided to bid at the auction subject to the conditions as they stand. Furthermore, advertisements relating to the sale may have been published incorporating express references to the conditions now being objected to. This illustrates how a potential purchaser's solicitor is at a disadvantage in the case of a sale by public auction and has a more restricted scope for negotiation over the terms of the contract ultimately entered into by his client.[266] If the client intends to develop the property, his attention should be drawn specifically to the restrictions imposed by planning legislation.[267] If the client wishes to buy agricultural land the possible need for Land Act consent should be discussed.[268] In the case of

---

[262.] This is discussed at para **[3.47]** *post.*

[263.] See para **[3.37]** *et seq, post.*

[264.] Unless of course, a private sale to his client can be negotiated prior to the auction.

[265.] It is, of course, not uncommon for a solicitor to represent his client at the auction and to bid on his behalf: para **[2.55]** *infra.*

[266.] See *Boyd v Dickson* (1876) IR 10 Eq 239 at 241-2 (*per* Sullivan MR); also fn 262 *supra.*

[267.] See para **[16.74]** *post.*

[268.] See para **[16.29]** *post.*

industrial property the implications of environmental protection legislation must be considered as part of a "due diligence" exercise.[269]

[2.55] Finally, it is not uncommon for a prospective bidder at a public auction to instruct his solicitor to bid for him at the auction. In such a case, not only must the solicitor familiarise himself with the conditions of sale governing the auction, he must also make sure that he has obtained clear instructions from his client on such matters as to whether there is a limit beyond which the client does not wish him to bid and as to whether he has authority to sign the contract for sale on behalf of the client.[270] It is also essential to obtain funds from the client for the deposit which will be payable immediately upon the property being knocked down in his favour.

[269.] See para **[5.14]** *post.*
[270.] See para **[6.42]** *post.*

Chapter 3

SALE BY PRIVATE TREATY

As in the previous chapter, here we are concerned with the respective roles of the house or estate agent, the vendor's solicitor and the purchaser's solicitor in the preliminary stages of the sale.

I. HOUSE OR ESTATE AGENTS

A. Statutory Regulation

[3.01] As in the case of auctioneers,[1] house agents are subject to the scheme of regulation imposed by the Auctioneers and House Agents Acts 1947, 1967 and 1973.[2] For the purposes of these Acts a "house agent" means a "person who, as agent for another person and for or in expectation of reward, purchases, sells, lets or offers for sale or letting, or invites offers to purchase or take a letting of, or negotiates for the purchase, sale or letting of a house otherwise than by auction or attempts to effect such purchase, sale or letting."[3] A "house" is defined as including "part of a house" and also includes "a building of any kind and part of any building".[4]

1. Licences

[3.02] As in the case of auctioneers[5] it is an offence for a person to carry on the business of a house agent without a licence[6] granted by the Revenue Commissioners.[7] This restriction does not apply, however, to licensed auctioneers, qualified solicitors or agents of state bodies, eg, the Commissioners of Public Works and the Land Commission.[8] An applicant

---

1. See para [2.01] *ante*.
2. See Mahon, *Auctioneering and Estate Agency Law in Ireland* (1990), Ch 1. *Cf* the English Estate Agents Act 1979 and Property Misdescriptions Act 1991: see Murdoch, *Law of Estate Agency and Auctions* (3rd ed, 1994), Chs 6 and 7.
3. 1947 Act, s 2(1). See the discussion in *Somers v Nicholls* [1955] IR 83, especially at 87-8 (*per* O'Daly J).
4. *Ibid.*
5. See para [2.02] *ante*.
6. 1947 Act, s 7(1) and (3). See *Somers v Nicholls* [1955] IR 83.
7. 1947 Act, s 10.
8. 1947 Act, s 7(2). The Irish Land Commission (Dissolution) Act 1992, provides for its dissolution and transfer of its various functions to different bodies, but the Act has yet to be brought into effect.

for a licence must satisfy qualifications similar to those applicable to an applicant for an auctioneer's licence.[9]

2. Deposits

[3.03] The provisions relating to deposits or guarantee bonds lodged in the High Court as a means of protection against loss of money apply to licensed house agents just as they apply to licensed auctioneers.[10]

3. Accounts

[3.04] The provisions relating to the keeping of accounts also apply equally to house agents.[11]

B. Conduct of Sale

As in the case of auctioneers,[12] there are several matters to be considered in relation to the role of a house or estate agent in the case of a sale by private treaty.

1. Instructions

[3.05] Like any agent, a house or estate agent must comply with any express instructions given to him by the vendor. These instructions fix the terms of the contract between the vendor and the estate agent and determine the scope of his authority in relation to the matters dealt with by them.[13] Often, of course, the agent will insist upon the vendor signing a standard form contract recommended by a professional body to which the agent belongs, or one drawn up by his firm for general use. Needless to say it is in the vendor's own interest to see that the terms of the contract, or his instructions, cover the points of particular concern to him, eg, whether the agent is given a sole right to sell the property or a sole agency,[14] what his commission is going to be, when he is to become entitled to it and whether the rate specified is inclusive or exclusive of other expenses (eg, in respect of advertising),[15] and whether his authority extends to entering into a contract with the purchaser on the vendor's behalf.[16] Failure to give proper instructions on these matters,

---

[9.] 1947Act, ss 10-4, as amended by the 1967 Act, s 12. See para **[2.02]** *ante.*
[10.] See para **[2.03]** *ante.*
[11.] See para **[2.04]** *ante.*
[12.] See para **[2.05]** *et seq, ante.*
[13.] See *Murphy, Buckley & Keogh Ltd v Pye (Ir) Ltd* [1971] IR 57; *G F Galvin (Estates) Ltd v Hedigan* [1985] ILRM 295.
[14.] Note the difficulties caused by the use of the expression "sole selling agency" in *G F Galvin (Estates) Ltd v Hedigan* [1985] ILRM 295: see para **[3.20]** *infra.*
[15.] See para **[3.18]** *et seq, infra.*
[16.] See para **[3.08]** *infra.*

or to see that the terms of any contract entered into cover them, may cause unpleasant disputes later on, which may have to be resolved in accordance with the general law, a subject to which we now turn.

2. Implied Authority

[3.06] It is now settled that, in the absence of express instructions, a house or estate agent acting in a sale by private treaty has implied authority to do certain things. As a general rule, however, his authority is less extensive than that of an auctioneer,[17] which no doubt is due to the special circumstances surrounding a sale by public auction. There the contract is concluded immediately upon a prospective purchaser being declared the highest bidder and having the property knocked down to him.[18] It is essential, therefore, to complete the necessary formalities for rendering that contract enforceable as quickly as possible, hence the auctioneer's extensive implied authority in this regard.[19] In the case of a sale by private treaty, however, the fixing of the terms of the contract is usually the subject of negotiation for a period of time after the prospective purchaser makes a firm offer to buy which the vendor or his agent accepts. And it is for this reason that the purchaser's solicitor usually has a greater role to play in pre-contract negotiations in the case of a sale by private treaty.[20]

(i) To Sell

[3.07] It has long been settled that, in the absence of explicit instructions to the contrary, a house or estate agent has no authority to sell the property.[21] His function is generally confined to effecting an introduction between the potential purchaser and the vendor, so that the vendor may eventually decide whether to enter into a contract with the purchaser, both parties then being advised usually by their respective solicitors. This is the way in which courts have tended to construe express instructions or terms of contracts authorising agents to do such things as, eg, "procure an offer",[22] "procure a purchaser"[23] and "find a purchaser".[24] However, later cases have decided this point more on the basis of the agent's lack of authority to sign a contract for

---

17. See paras **[2.06-10]** *ante.*
18. See para **[2.21]** *ante.*
19. See paras **[2.08-9]** *ante.*
20. *Cf* in a sale by public auction, para **[2.53]** *ante.*
21. See *Wilde v Watson* (1878) 1 LR Ir 402, which applied one of the leading English authorities on the point, *Hamer v Sharp* (1874) LR 19 Eq 108.
22. *Wilde v Watson, op cit.* See also para **[3.27]** *infra.*
23. *Hamer v Sharp, op cit.*
24. See *Daniel Morrissey and Sons Ltd v Nalty* [1976-7] ILRM 269 at 274 (*per* Gannon J). See also *Chadburn v Moore* (1892) 61 LJ Ch 674. See also para **[3.25]** *infra.*

sale on the vendor's behalf,[25] eg, the note or memorandum in writing necessary to render the contract enforceable under s 2 of the Statute of Frauds (Ir) 1695. It is also important to remember that unauthorised acts by the estate agent may subsequently be ratified, with retrospective effect, by the vendor, so as to render the contract specifically enforceable against him. However, in *Brennan v O'Connell*[26] the Supreme Court emphasised that for ratification to have this effect, the vendor's actions must be done with knowledge of material facts known to the agent which it was *objectively* necessary for him to know in order to decide whether to approve the agent's actions. In that case the court rejected the argument that lack of knowledge of an enquiry from another potential purchaser vitiated the ratification. As Henchy J explained:

"If information which, merely by the subjective standards of a particular vendor, is thought necessary to be disclosed before a sale can be approved, the contract of agency should provide for such disclosure. If that were not the law, a vendor could avoid an otherwise valid ratification, on which the estate agent may have acted by claiming that the estate agent had withheld from him information which he (the vendor), for private and unpredictable reasons, considered necessary - such as the identity of the purchaser; or the nature of his race, religion or politics; or the way in which the property is to be used by the purchaser; or other purely personal or idiosyncratic considerations which would not reasonably be expected to be material to a decision to reject or to accept an offer to purchase.

The contract of agency should, expressly, or by necessary implication, authorise the property owner to do so before he can avoid an otherwise valid ratification by relying on non-disclosure of a circumstance which, according to ordinary business standards, could not be said to be material to a decision to accept or reject a particular offer. No such term can be read into the agency here. As the mere fact that someone had made an inquiry about the terms on which the property might be sold could not, without more, be held to be a consideration which might be expected in the ordinary course of business to affect a decision to assent to an otherwise acceptable offer, the non-disclosure of that inquiry cannot be held to avoid the ratification."[27]

---

25. See *Carney v Fair* (1920) 54 ILTR 61. Also *Chadburn v Moore* (1892) 61 LJ Ch 674; *Lewcock v Bromley* (1920) 127 LT 116.
26. [1980] IR 13.
27. *Ibid*, pp 17-18.

(ii) To Sign a Contract

[3.08] This matter was discussed at length in *Law v Roberts & Co*[28] and, after a survey of the relevant authorities, Kenny J[29] concluded:

"These cases seem to establish the following propositions:

1. When a contract for sale is made between a purchaser and an estate agent retained by the owner, the onus of proving that the estate agent had authority to make the contract is on the purchaser.[30]

2. An estate agent as such has no implied authority to conclude a contract for sale.[31]

3. An owner who puts his property on the books of an estate agent and authorises him to find a purchaser and to negotiate a sale does not thereby authorise him to conclude a contract.[32]

4. An owner who puts his property on the books of an estate agent and informs him of the lowest price which he will accept does not thereby authorise him to conclude a contract.[33]

5. An estate agent who is instructed to sell at a defined price has authority to conclude a contract for sale at that defined price[34] if the contract is an open contract.[35]

6. An estate agent may be expressly authorised to accept on behalf of the owner an offer made to the agent, and, in that event, has authority to conclude a contract.

7. If an offer is made to an estate agent and if he communicates it to the owner and is authorised to accept it or if the owner states that he will accept it,[36] the agent has authority to make an open contract with the purchaser."[37]

In the *Law* case, the estate agent received an offer below the selling price stipulated by the company vendors which he communicated to the managing director of the company. The latter then instructed the agent to accept the offer, which he did, and later a director of the agent's firm wrote to the

---

[28.] [1964] IR 292.

[29.] His decision was affirmed by the Irish Supreme Court, *ibid.*

[30.] "It seems to me that proof of an authority so far extending the ordinary authority of such agents should be clear and conclusive;" *per* Chatterton V-C. in *Wilde v Watson* (1878) 1 LR Ir 402 at 405. See also *Dyas v Cruise* (1845) 8 Ir Eq R 407.

[31.] As to a land agent, see *Mortal v Lyons* (1858) 8 Ir Ch R 112.

[32.] See *Chadburn v Moore* (1892) 61 LJ Ch 674. *Cf Hudson v O'Connor* [1947] 1 Jur Rep 21.

[33.] See *Prior v Moore* (1887) 3 TLR 624.

[34.] See *Rosenbaum v Belson* [1900] 2 Ch 267; *Keen v Mear* [1920] 2 Ch 574. *Cf Lewcock v Bromley* (1920) 127 LT 116; *Wragg v Lovett* [1948] 2 All ER 968. See also *Re Sullivan's Estate* (1889) 23 LR Ir 255; *Stinson v Owens* (1973) 24 NILQ 218.

[35.] For the meaning of "open contract", see para **[14.05]** *post*. Also para **[3.09]** *infra*.

[36.] *Cf Carney v Fair* (1920) 54 ILTR 61.

[37.] [1964] IR 292 at 302.

vendors' managing director and solicitor and the purchaser confirming the sale. It was held that the estate agent had authority to accept the offer and that the correspondence written and signed by the director of his firm constituted a note or memorandum of the agreement signed by an agent of the vendors, sufficient to render the contract enforceable against them.

[3.09] As Kenny J indicated in the *Law* case, the courts have generally confined an agent's authority in such cases to conclusion of an "open" contract, ie, one where the terms are generally left to be implied by the general law, especially those relating to the title to be deduced to the purchaser by the vendor.[38] In other words, the courts are reluctant to sanction house or estate agents drawing up complicated terms relating to matters better left in their view to solicitors.[39] This may, of course, cause considerable trouble because, under an open contract, 40 years' title, beginning with a good root of title, must be shown. So it has been suggested from time to time that, where the agent has in fact been furnished with a draft contract by the vendor's solicitor, he should be regarded as having implied authority to sell on the terms contained in it.[40]

(iii) To Receive Money

[3.10] A matter of considerable controversy some years ago on both sides of the Irish Sea was the question of the authority of house or estate agents to receive money on behalf of the vendor, eg, a deposit paid by the purchaser. The reason for much of the controversy is that in the case of a sale by private treaty, unlike in the case of a sale by public auction,[41] such money is often paid before the contract for sale is entered into by the vendor and purchaser. Thus it is not a "deposit" in the usual sense of that word, ie, a sum paid by the purchaser as a guarantee of his performance of the contract, which the contract requires him to pay and which may be forfeited by the vendor on his default.[42] Rather it is what is sometimes referred to as "earnest money", ie, money paid by the purchaser to show his good faith in making his offer for the property and to persuade the vendor or his agent to conclude negotiations for the sale of the property. Since, however, there is as yet no contract in force between the vendor and the agent, there is no legal obligation upon the purchaser to pay it and, if he does pay it and later changes his mind before

---

[38.] See para **[14.05]** *post*. See also the discussion in *Wilde v Watson* (1878) 1 LR Ir 402.

[39.] See *Keen v Mear* [1920] 2 Ch 574, especially at 579 (*per* Russell J); *Wragg v Lovett* [1948] 2 All ER 968 at 969-70 (*per* Lord Greene MR).

[40.] Note, however, the Law Society's strictures about furnishing auctioneers with contracts: see para **[2.53]** fn 260 *ante*.

[41.] See para **[2.10]** *ante*.

[42.] See paras **[10.16-32]** and **[13.30-36]** *post*.

any contract is entered into, he is entitled to demand return of the money without incurring any liability.[43] The recent controversy centred around the liability, if any, of the vendor to repay such money to the purchaser if the agent cannot do so because, eg, the agent had disappeared or had been declared bankrupt. This is a subject we discuss in detail later,[44] but for the moment we are concerned with the authority of the agent which is obviously a relevant factor in determining the vendor's, ie, his principal's, liability.

[3.11] In view of the courts' reluctance to hold that a house or estate agent has implied authority to sign a contract on behalf of the vendor, one would have expected them to hold that there is no implied authority to receive money on the vendor's behalf, at least not at the pre-contract stage. Yet this point was not finally decided in England until the House of Lords in 1976 decision in *Sorrell v Finch*[45] dealt with a series of confusing Court of Appeal decisions.[46] The House laid down emphatically that the engagement of an estate agent by a prospective vendor does not confer on the estate agent any implied or ostensible authority to receive as agent of the vendor a pre-contract deposit from a would-be purchaser. The only reported authority in Ireland on the point is the decision of Kenny J in *Leemac Overseas Investment Ltd v Harvey*,[47] but this decision was based largely upon the then English authorities[48] and to that extent should be reconsidered after *Sorrell v Finch*. The *Leemac* case in fact related to a pre-contract deposit, and it was admitted in argument that the same law applied to it as to a deposit paid under a contract. Subsequent events have, of course, suggested that that admission should not have been made. This is a matter to which we return later.[49]

(iv) To Delegate

[3.12] By analogy with the position of an auctioneer,[50] the general rule is probably that a house or estate agent has no implied authority to delegate the performance of his duties to someone else. This was certainly held to be the

---

43. See *Leemac Overseas Investment Ltd v Harvey* [1973] IR 160; *Re Barrett Apartments Ltd* [1985] IR 350; *Desmond v Brophy* [1985] IR 449.

44. See paras **[3.15-17]** *infra*.

45. [1976] 2 All ER 371.

46. Ie *Ryan v Pilkington* [1959] 1 WLR 403; *Rayner v Paskell & Son* (1948) 152 Est Gaz 270; *Goding v Frazer* [1967] 1 WLR 286; *Barrington v Lee* [1972] 1 QB 326; *Burt v Claude Cousins & Co Ltd* [1971] 2 QB 426.

47. [1973] IR 160. *Cf* pre-contract deposits paid to the vendor's solicitor, *Desmond v Brophy* [1985] IR 449.

48. Especially *Goding v Frazer* [1967] 1 WLR 286.

49. See para **[3.16]** *infra*.

50. See para **[2.11]** *ante*.

case by the English Court of Appeal, which held that an estate agent, especially one appointed as sole agent, had no authority to employ a sub-agent without express authorisation.[51] As Lord Denning MR remarked:

> "The reason is because an estate agent holds a position of discretion and trust. Discretion in his conduct of negotiations. Trust in his handling of affairs. It is his duty, certainly in the case of a sole agent, to use his best endeavours to sell the property at an acceptable price to a purchaser who is satisfactory and who is ready and willing and able to purchase the property. It is his duty also to take care to prepare particulars of the property accurately, and to make no misrepresentation about it. It is his duty to receive applications, to make appointments to view, and to negotiate the best price that can be obtained in the circumstances. Furthermore, he is at liberty in the course of the negotiations to receive a deposit as stakeholder, but not as agent for the vendor. Those functions and duties of an estate agent, certainly of the sole agent, require personal skill and competence. So much so that I think an estate agent has no authority to delegate his responsibilities to a subagent, unless he is expressly authorised so to do."[52]

Of course, any unauthorised delegation, like any unauthorised act by an agent, may be ratified subsequently by the vendor so as to bind him as principal.[53]

3. Duty of Care

[3.13] The dictum of Lord Denning MR quoted in the previous paragraph is an illustration of how English judges have come round to the view that an estate agent, especially one who is a sole agent, does owe certain duties.[54] Thus it is arguable that a house or estate agent owes a duty to his client, the vendor, to take some action to bring about a sale, perhaps to use his best endeavours to do so if he has the sole right to sell or a sole agency agreement.[55] Unfortunately there is little authority on the point, though some English cases make it clear that sole agents must beware of failing to provide

---

51. *McCann v Pow* [1975] 1 All ER 129. See also *Mullens v Miller* (1882) 22 Ch D 194.
52. *Ibid*, pp 131-2. *Cf Dyas v Stafford* (1881) 7 LR Ir 590 (*affd* (1882) 9 LR Ir 520). See also *Coles v Trecothick* (1804) 9 Ves 234.
53. *Sheridan v Higgins* [1971] IR 291. See also *Brennan v O'Connell* [1980] IR 13, para **[3.07]** *supra*.
54. *Cf* the views expressed in *Luxor (Eastbourne) Ltd v Cooper* [1941] AC 108, especially at 117 (*per* Viscount Simon LC), 124 (*per* Lord Russell of Killowan) and 153 (*per* Lord Romer). See also *Daniel Morrissey and Sons Ltd v Nalty* [1976-7] ILRM 269 at 373 (*per* Gannon J).
55. See *Mendoza & Co v Bell* (1952) 159 Est Gaz 372; *Prebble & Co v West* (1969) 211 Est Gaz 831.

the consideration given in return for the sole agency.[56] It is also clear that, once the agent begins to act for his client, he owes the basic duty of all agents to their principals to use reasonable care and skill in his dealings and to have regard to his principal's interest.[57]

[3.14] So far as prospective purchasers are concerned, any duty which a house or estate agent owes generally lies in tort only, eg, not to make negligent misstatements,[58] for usually there is no contractual relationship between the agent and the person who ultimately enters into the contract to buy the land. If, however, the agent receives a pre-contract deposit from a prospective purchaser, he will, of course, be liable for its safe-keeping and, depending upon the capacity in which he received it,[59] will have to account for it. He may also be liable to the purchaser in damages if he has purported to act for the vendor without the latter's authority, eg, in entering into a contract for sale, ie, for breach of warranty of authority.[60]

4. Deposits

[3.15] As mentioned earlier in this chapter,[61] one of the most controversial areas of conveyancing in recent decades relates to the common practice of house or estate agents receiving a "deposit" from the prospective purchaser before the contract for sale is entered into. In theory, of course, there is no obligation upon the purchaser to pay such a deposit at the pre-contract stage, but he often feels under pressure to do so to convince the agent of his good faith in making an offer, especially if he has been told by the agent that several other people have expressed an interest in the property. Also, since vendors became, by statute, responsible for payment of house or estate agents' fees, it has become common for agents to require the purchaser to pay a form of "booking deposit". The reason is that the agent wishes to deduct his fees and expenses from the deposit rather than wait for the vendor to furnish payment. There would appear to be no direct sanction against such a practice. There is no doubt as to the agent's personal liability in respect of

---

[56.] See *Bentall Horsley & Baldry v Vicary* [1931]1 KB 253; *Christopher & Co v Essing* [1948] WN 461; *Midland Business Agency v Apted* (1971) 218 Est Gaz 1727.

[57.] *Banter v FW Capp & Co Ltd* [1938] 4 All ER 457; *Cuckmere Brick Co Ltd v Mutual Finance Ltd* [1971] Ch 949.

[58.] See *McAnarney v Hanrahan* [1993] 3 IR 492; *Donnellan v Dungoyne Ltd* [1995] 1 ILRM 388 and para **[5.27]** *et seq, post. Cf McCullagh v Lane Fox and Partners* [1996] 18 EG 104 (no duty owed to prospective purchaser). Note that a building society may be liable to a purchaser where an auctioneer or estate agent acts on its behalf: see *Irish Permanent Building Society v O'Sullivan* [1990] ILRM 598.

[59.] See further, para **[3.15]** *et seq, infra.*

[60.] *Godwin v Francis* (1870) LR 5 CP 295.

[61.] Paras **[3.10-11]** *supra.*

such deposit money, and the purchaser is usually assured of its repayment, if the purchase falls through, because of the protection afforded by the Auctioneers and House Agents Acts 1947 1967 and 1973.[62] But even this scheme does not always guarantee protection as *Leemac Overseas Investments Ltd v Harvey*[63] illustrated. In that case a prospective purchaser, who had paid a deposit in respect of a proposed purchase which fell through *before* any contract for sale was entered into, recovered only part of his deposit from the estate agent to whom he had paid it. He had made the mistake of thinking that the agent was solvent and failed to notify the insurance company, which had issued the guarantee bond lodged in the High Court by the agent under the Acts, *before* the hearing of his proceedings against the agents. Thus under settled law he could not claim the balance of the deposit from the insurance company[64] and was forced into trying to reclaim it from the agent's principal, the vendor.[65] Similar risks to a prospective purchaser arise in respect of other forms of "booking deposits", such as those commonly paid to builders. In *Re Barrett Apartments Ltd*[66] the Supreme Court reiterated that, if no contract for sale is entered into, the "purchaser" has acquired no estate or interest in the land to which a lien could attach,[67] and so remains an unsecured creditor left to claim alongside other such creditors if the builder goes into liquidation. In *Desmond v Brophy*[68] Barrington J held that purchasers' solicitors were negligent in failing to put builder's solicitors on notice that their clients booking deposit, paid to the builder's solicitors, to reserve a site on a proposed development, was to be held by them as stakeholders and *not* as agents for the builder. The builder's solicitors paid the pre-contract deposit over to the builder in accordance with their standing instructions. When the builder subsequently went into receivership the purchasers succeeded in recovering the lost deposit, plus interest, from their solicitors. Clearly, if instructed before any such deposit is paid, the purchaser's solicitor must now advise his client as to the risks involved in paying such pre-contract deposits to a vendor or builder or to his agent.[69]

[62.] See para **[3.03]** *supra*. He may also be able to claim against a compensation fund if the agent belongs to a professional body operating a scheme covering members, eg, the IAVI.

[63.] [1973] IR 160.

[64.] *Mahon v Irish National Insurance Co Ltd* [1958] Ir Jur Rep 41; *Re Nolan* [1963] IR 341.

[65.] As to which claim, see para **[3.16]** *infra*.

[66.] [1985] IR 350.

[67.] See para **[12.44]** *post*.

[68.] [1985] IR 449. As to the need to make pre-contract searches against the builder company see *Roche v Peilow* [1985] IR 232, para **[11.17]** *post*.

[69.] Note that the National House Building Guarantee Scheme was extended in 1990 to cover lost deposits and see now on the HomeBond Scheme, para **[4.25]** *et seq, post*.

[3.16] Unfortunately, the attitude of the courts on both sides of the Irish Sea has been somewhat inconsistent on the extent of these risks in recent decades, especially in England where several conflicting views were expressed until the matter was finally dealt with by the House of Lords in *Sorrell v Finch*.[70] Clearly if the estate agent receives the deposit as "agent" of the vendor, and this is within the scope of his authority, the vendor is liable.[71] What caused the controversy was what the position was where the capacity in which the money was received was either not specified or, if it was, was specified as being something else, eg, as "stakeholder". One view put forward in England was that an estate agent had implied or ostensible authority to receive such a pre-contract deposit on behalf of the vendor, and so the latter should still be responsible even if nothing was said as to the agent's capacity in receiving it.[72] Lord Denning MR dissented from this proposition and insisted that at most the agent in such a case received the deposit as a "stakeholder" for both parties.[73] But his brother judges took the view that, even in cases where the agent received the money as "stakeholder", the vendor was still liable because he had put the agent into the position of being able to receive it by appointing him in the first place.[74] This view was accepted by Kenny J in *Leemac Overseas Investments Ltd v Harvey*,[75] where he held that the vendor was liable to return the part of the deposit received by the estate agent as stakeholder which the prospective purchaser had failed to recover from the agent himself. As Kenny J remarked, he had to decide a dispute which related to the question "as to which of the two innocent parties is to bear the loss".[76] However, at the same time as this case was being decided in Ireland, Lord Denning MR was pointing out the dangers of such a proposition for unwary vendors.[77] He noted that an unscrupulous estate agent might deal with several prospective purchasers, take a deposit from each of them and then disappear, leaving the vendor with liability to return several deposits amounting in total to more

---

[70.] [1976] 2 All ER 371. See Kovats, 'Estate Agents Holding Deposits' (1971) 121 New LJ 431; Macintyre, 'Loss of the Deposit' (1958) 22 Conv 258; Murdoch, 'The Lost Deposit' (1972) 36 Conv 5.

[71.] *Ryan v Pilkington* [1959] 1 All ER 689.

[72.] See, eg, *Burt v Claude Cousins & Co Ltd* [1971] 2 QB 426. See also *Goding v Frazer* [1967] 1 WLR 286; *Barrington v Lee* [1972] 1 QB 326.

[73.] See his judgments in the *Burt* and *Barrington* cases, fn 72 *supra*.

[74.] See *Goding v Frazer* [1967] 1WLR 286 at 297 (*per* Sachs J); *Burt v Claude Cousins & Co Ltd* [1971] 2 QB 426 at 450 (*per* Sachs LJ) and at 452 (*per* Megaw LJ).

[75.] [1973] IR 160. See para **[3.15]** *supra*.

[76.] *Ibid*, p 168.

[77.] See again his judgments in *Burt v Claude Cousins & Co Ltd* [1971] 2 QB 426; *Barrington v Lee* [1972] 1 QB 326.

than the full value of the property being sold![78] He also reiterated the basic point that, so long as the estate agent held the deposit as a stakeholder, the vendor had no right to demand its payment to him[79] - that would presumably not arise until the sale had gone through, ie, not until the contract had been entered into at the very least. If the vendor had no right to the money, the Master of the Rolls could not see how he could be made liable for its return.[80]

[3.17] This, then, was the state of the authorities which faced the House of Lords in *Sorrell v Finch*.[81] Though the law lords had, in the words of Lord Edmund-Davies, "deep misgivings ... that innocent purchasers should, through absolutely no fault of theirs, find themselves in their present unfortunate plight,"[82] they held unanimously that the engagement of an estate agent by a prospective vendor does not confer on the agent any implied or ostensible authority to receive as agent of the vendor a pre-contract deposit from a would-be purchaser. In the absence of such express authority from the vendor, they held that the purchaser is at all times until the contract is entered into the only person with any claim or right to the deposit moneys and this was a right on demand. Thus, Lord Edmund-Davies went on:

> "... I fail to see that the justice of the case demands that the vendor, however personally innocent, should be held liable to repay the deposit in the event of the agent defaulting. It is not open to the prospective purchaser to deny knowledge of his unfettered legal right to get his money back at that stage, and if, with that actual or imputed knowledge, he chooses to pay a deposit and leave it in the estate agent's hands, while one must naturally have sympathy with him, such intuitions of justice as I possess do not demand that he should be recouped by a vendor who shares his innocence and differs from him only in engaging someone to find a purchaser for his house."[83]

This decision is, of course, not strictly binding in Ireland, but, in the absence of any reported authority at all on the point here, it must be regarded as of persuasive authority. To the extent that Kenny J's decision in *Leemac Overseas Investments Ltd v Harvey* was based on views expressed in some

---

78. *Cf*, Lord Russell of Killowen in *Sorrell v Finch* [1976] 2 All ER 371 at 384.
79. *Cf*: Kenny J in *Leemac Overseas Investments Ltd v Harvey* [1973] IR 160 at 167.
80. Support for this view may be found in *Rayner v Paskell & Son* (1948) 152 Est Gaz 270 and in some Australian and New Zealand cases, see *Egan v Ross* (1928) 29 SR (NSW) 382; *Fischer v Parry & Beveridge Pty Ltd* [1963] VR 97; *Richards v Hill* [1920] NZLR 724.
81. [1976] 2 All ER 371.
82. *Ibid*, p 382.
83. *Ibid*, pp 379-80.

of the earlier English cases and on admissions made in the case, his decision must be reconsidered in the light of the criticism of those views by the House of Lords.[84] Fortunately, the point should arise rarely in Ireland because of the protection afforded would-be purchasers by the Auctioneers and House Agents Acts. Nevertheless, the moral of the story remains that a prospective purchaser in Ireland should beware of paying a pre-contract deposit to a house or estate agent without first obtaining legal advice on the matter. All too often the purchaser will not know for certain whether the agent has express authority from the vendor to receive it on the latter's behalf and, even if he is fairly sure of this, there may be difficulty in proving it if the point is disputed later. There is also the risk that the estate agent will not belong to one of the professional bodies, like the IAVI, which operates a compensation fund or indemnity scheme to protect members of the public. Cases such as these support the view that most purchasers would be well advised to consult their solicitors at an early stage even in cases of sales by private treaty. If that is done, the deposit money held by the purchaser can be paid to his solicitor and the vendor's house or estate agent can be informed of its availability in the solicitor's hands. Any query as to the purchaser's good faith can then be dealt with as between the vendor's agent or solicitor and the purchaser's solicitor.

C. Fees and Commissions

[3.18] Over the years the subject of house or estate agents' fees and commissions has been litigated on numerous occasions on both sides of the Irish Sea. As in the case of auctioneers,[85] there are three main questions to be considered: (1) when does the agent become entitled to payment; (2) how much does he become entitled to, (3) who is responsible for paying it?

---

84. Note the discussion of the *Leemac* case and the English cases by Barrington J in *Desmond v Brophy* [1985] IR 449 at 454-456. Barrington J was of the view that the reasoning relating to estate agents does not necessarily apply to solicitors. The point is that in most cases the vendor's solicitor, or, as in the *Desmond* case, a builder's solicitor, will be acting as agent for the vendor or solicitor, whether in receiving money or otherwise. The mistake the purchaser's solicitors made in that case was in not making it clear that the booking deposit was to be held by the builder's solicitors as stakeholders: see para **[3.15]** *supra*. If they had done so, the builder's solicitors would have been obliged to hold the money on deposit and would not have been entitled to hand it over to the builder. To the extent that this was contrary to the arrangement with the builder, this would have been a matter for negotiation, initially between the builder's solicitors and their client. As to the position of a solicitor stakeholder see *Hastingwood Property Ltd v Saunders Bearman Anselm* [1990] 3 All ER 107; *Rockeagle Ltd v Alsop Wilkinson* [1991] 4 All ER 659.
85. See para **[2.28]** *ante*.

1. Entitlement

[3.19] It cannot be emphasised too often that the basic principle governing entitlement to commission, fees and expenses is that it depends largely upon the terms of the contract between the vendor and his house or estate agent.[86] All the other so-called rules or principles must be read subject to this overriding general principle.[87] Unfortunately, the terms of contracts made between vendors and their agents, or of instructions issued by the vendors to their agents, have exhibited enormous variation and the courts have found themselves faced with many difficult questions of construction.[88] The following is an attempt to extract from the cases some general principles.

(i) Sole Right to Sell and Sole Agency Agreements

[3.20] It is fairly common practice for an agent to seek to protect himself from doing work in respect of selling a property only to find later on that the actual sale is achieved through someone else's efforts, thereby normally depriving him of any claim to commission.[89] This is usually done by insisting that his agreement with the vendor includes a term conferring upon him the sole right to sell the property or a sole agency for the sale. It is important to realise that these two concepts are not the same thing and that in each case it is a question of construction which of them has been incorporated in the agreement. The distinction between the two was recently explained by Henchy J in *Murphy, Buckley & Keogh Ltd v Pye (Ir) Ltd*,[90] when he said in relation to the contract between the vendors and their estate agents:

> "... there was nothing in the contract which gave the plaintiffs the sole right
> to sell; they were merely appointed sole agents to find a purchaser who
> would be ready to complete at a price acceptable to the defendants, and the

---

[86.] See *Heneken v Courtney* (1967) 101 ILTR 25; *Murphy, Buckley & Keogh Ltd v Pye (Ir) Ltd* [1971] IR 57; *GF Galvin (Estates) Ltd v Hedigan* [1985] ILRM 295. The leading English authority is the House of Lords decision in *Luxor (Eastbourne) Ltd v Cooper* [1941] AC 108. See also *O'Toole v Palmer* [1943] Ir Jur Rep.

[87.] Of course, there is the further overriding principle that an agent cannot legally enter into a contract for such commission unless he has a licence under the Auctioneers and House Agents Acts, see *Somers v Nicholls* [1955] IR 83.

[88.] See Bicknell, *Estate Agents' Right to Commission* (1966) 116 New LJ 603; Gower, *Estate Agents' Commission* (1950) 13 MLR 491; Kerr, 'Estate Agents' Commission in Northern Ireland' (1973) 24 NILQ 1; Maurice, 'Estate Agents' Commission' (1950) 14 Conv 274; Napley, 'Estate Agents' Commission' (1970) 67 Law Soc Gaz 461. See also Mahon, 'Auctioneering and Estate Agency in Ireland' (1990) Ch 2; Murdoch, *The Law of Estate Agents and Auctions* (3rd ed, 1994) Ch 5.

[89.] Generally on the ground that he is not the "effective cause" of the sale, see para **[3.22]** *infra*.

[90.] [1971] IR 57.

defendants were to have the right to revoke the agency. It is clear that the contract precluded the defendants from selling through another agent during the currency of the plaintiffs' agency; it is equally clear that the contract contained no express term which precluded the defendants themselves from selling."[91]

Thus a sole agency agreement merely prevents the vendor from depriving the sole agent of his commission by selling through another agent;[92] it does not preclude the vendor from selling the property himself.[93] If the agent wants to protect himself against that contingency as well, he must go further and make sure that the terms of the contract confer upon him the sole right to sell.[94] A failure to make the point crystal clear turns it into a matter of construction. In *GF Galvin (Estates) Ltd v Hedigan*[95] the estate agents were employed on a "sole selling agency" basis, but on the basis also that they would act as lobbyists to try to persuade the planning authority to rezone the land for industrial purposes. It was agreed that the land would not be marketed until after this hoped-for rezoning. In fact the owners sold the land without the assistance of the agents and before a motion for rezoning was passed. Costello J accepted that the agreement did not prevent the owners selling themselves without any obligation to pay commission to the agents, but held also that if must have been intended that such a sale would not deprive the agents of commission in respect of their efforts as lobbyists seeking rezoning. However, this latter point did not assist the agents in the case before him since the rezoning motion was passed some time after the sale by the owners and there was no basis for a claim based on a *quantum meruit*.

[3.21] In *Daniel Morrissey and Sons Ltd v Nalty*[96] the owners of the property cancelled the public auction arranged with a firm of auctioneers and subsequently sold the property themselves by private treaty to a purchaser who had initially contacted the auctioneer to make an offer on seeing the notice "postponing" the auction. Gannon J rejected the auctioneers' claim to commission on the basis that their agreement with the owner was to sell by

---

[91.] *Ibid*, p 65.
[92.] *O'Hanlon v Belfast Inns Ltd* [1962-63] Ir Jur Rep 25. See also *Ward v Spivack Ltd* [1957] IR 40; *Judd v Donegal Tweed Co* (1935) 69 ILTR 117. *Cf MacLean v Fitzsimon* (1845) 3 Cr & Dix 381.
[93.] This was the actual decision in the *Murphy* case.
[94.] *Cf Hunter v Martin* (1903) 37 ILTR 91.
[95.] [1985] ILRM 295.
[96.] [1976-7] ILRM 269.

auction only. At most they were entitled to reimbursement of their advertising expenses.[97]

(ii) Effective Cause

[3.22] It has been laid down in numerous cases that a pre-condition of an agent becoming entitled to commission is that he must establish that he was the "effective cause" of the sale.[98] This principle, however, must not be taken too literally, because ultimately the question of the agent's entitlement depends upon the precise terms of his contract with the vendor. As one Irish judge once said in a case involving a firm of auctioneers: "The plaintiffs, as auctioneers, and knowing their business better than the average property owner, could have made a contract express as to what they should be paid in any foreseeable eventuality.[99] What the principle does mean usually is that the courts generally adhere to the view that, in the absence of very special express terms in the agent's contract, he is going to have to establish that the sale was brought about by his efforts essentially and was not due to some other cause. Thus in a dispute between several agents to a claim for the commission on a sale, the court will generally award it to the agent who actually brought it about, eg, by effecting the introduction between the purchaser and the vendor.[100] If the agent's contract does not contain express terms as to his entitlement to commission, again the court will generally insist that he establishes that he was the effective cause of the sale[101] Though it must be emphasised that, to be entitled to commission at all, the agent must first establish the existence of a contract with the vendor requiring him to perform certain work in relation to the sale of the property in question.[102] However, so long as he can establish that he did eventually perform the vital act in bringing about the sale, it seems that the courts will not generally concern themselves with how diligent the agent was in performance of his duties. Thus Hanna J explained:

[97.] See para **[2.32]** *ante*. *Cf McCarthy v Voluntary Health Insurance Board* High Court, unrep, 24 July 1984 (1982/1959P) (estate agent employed by prospective purchaser to negotiate purchase of premises not entitled to commission on purchase ultimately negotiated by purchaser itself, but entitled to remuneration for services rendered prior to implied termination of his employment).

[98.] See eg *O'Hanlon v Belfast Inns Ltd* [1962-63] Ir Jur Rep 25; *Heneken v Courtney* (1967) 101 ILTR 25. See also *Burns v Langford* (1901) 35 ILTR 148.

[99.] *Stokes & Quirke Ltd v Clohessy* [1957] IR 84 at 88 (*per* McLoughlin J).

[100.] See *Barron v Cowan* (1930) 64 ILTR 168. This, of course, is without prejudice to a claim for damages against the vendor for breach of a sole agency agreement with another agent, see para **[3.20]** *supra*.

[101.] *North v Drinan* [1931] IR 468; *Judd v Donegal Tweed Co* (1935) 69 ILTR 117; *Judd v Doyle's Motors Ltd* (1938) 72 ILTR 100.

[102.] *Heneken v Courtney* (1967) 101 ILTR 25.

"The law is rather favourable to the agent, but it is quite clear. It is that, if an agent employed for that purpose brings parties together or into touch with one another in the relation of buyer and seller, and a contract ensues upon it, the agent is entitled to remuneration. Delays and postponement or indifference to the result on the part of the agent does not disentitle him to his commission so long as, in the opinion of the Court, the relation of principal and agent has not, in fact. been broken, and the introduction was a vital element."[103]

(iii) Contract or Completion

[3.23] Perhaps the issue which has exercised the courts more than any other in this context is how far the conveyancing process must progress before the agent can claim his commission; in particular whether it is a pre-condition that the purchaser introduced by the agent should enter into a binding contract for the purchase of the property or, even further, whether that contract should be carried out by completion of the transaction and transfer of the title in the property to the purchaser, together with payment of the balance of the purchase money to the vendor. Clearly the answer in each case must depend again upon the terms of the agent's contract, but unfortunately the matter is not always made entirely clear and the courts have been faced with a variety of agreements over the years.

[3.24] The general rule adopted by the courts, ever since the House of Lords decision in *Luxor (Eastbourne) Ltd v Cooper*,[104] is that normally agents' contracts are to be interpreted as requiring at least that the purchaser introduced enters into a binding contract before the agent becomes entitled to commission. Prior to that event, the agent is not entitled to make a claim for services rendered on a *quantum meruit* basis and the vendor is entitled to refuse to enter into a contract with the would-be purchaser and can thereby deprive the agent of commission. As McLoughlin J stated in *Stokes & Quirke Ltd v Clohessy*:[105]

"It cannot, to my mind, be implied from the circumstances in this case that he [the vendor] undertook to pay them [the agents] a fee of any amount on their introduction of a possible purchaser whom he might be willing at the time to accept, or that he bound himself not to withdraw any acceptance of an offer made unless it were an acceptance which would be binding on him vis-à-vis a purchaser. Other than what did happen in this case, anything might have happened. He might have withdrawn from the bargain (if there

---

[103.] *North v Drinan* [1931] IR 468 at 472.

[104.] [1941] AC 108, followed in *O'Toole v Palmer* [1943] Ir Jur Rep 59; *Stokes & Quirke Ltd v Clohessy* [1957] IR 84. See also *Daniel Morrissey and Sons Ltd v Nalty* [1976-7] ILRM 269.

[105.] [1957] IR 84.

was a final one), as he was quite entitled to do. Had he done so, any services rendered by the plaintiffs to the defendant were of no value to him."[106]

It is clear then that if an agent wants to be assured of payment for services actually rendered, or wants to make commission payable or his entitlement to arise before any contract is entered into by the purchaser introduced by him, he must see that this is spelt out clearly and expressly in the terms of his contract with the vendor. This point may be emphasised by a brief consideration of the way in which the courts have interpreted clauses commonly used by estate agents.

(a) "Find a Purchaser"

[3.25] It is settled now that such an instruction, and similar ones such as "find a purchaser or someone to buy", require that there must be a legally binding contract in force between the vendor and the purchaser introduced by the agent before the agent becomes entitled to his commission.[107] Until that event, either of the principal parties may withdraw and thereby deprive the agent of his entitlement to commission.[108] Once the contract is entered into,[109] the vendor may not withdraw so as to deprive the agent of his commission, ie, he cannot rely upon non-completion of the transaction brought about by his own default.[110] However, it also seems to be the case that if the purchaser fails to complete the transaction, and this is not due to any default on the part of the vendor, the latter will not be liable to pay commission, ie, though the agent may become entitled to his commission upon the contract being entered into, the vendor does not become obliged to pay it until completion and receipt of the balance of the purchase money.[111]

[106.] *Ibid.*, p 89.

[107.] *Luxor (Eastbourne) Ltd v Cooper* [1941] AC 108 and *McCallum v Hicks* [1950] 2 KB 371, both approved in *Stokes & Quirke Ltd v Clohessy* [1957] IR 84.

[108.] *O'Toole v Palmer* [1943] Ir Jur Rep 59.

[109.] Arguably "legally binding contract" in this context means one sufficiently evidenced in writing as required by s 2 of the Statute of Frauds (Ir) 1695, or at least otherwise enforceable in equity due to acts of part performance (see Ch 6, *post*). See *Murdoch Lownie Ltd v Newman* [1949] 2 All ER 783 at 789 (*per* Slade J); *McCallum v Hicks* [1950] 2 KB 371 at 274 (*per* Denning LJ); *Dennis Reed Ltd v Goody* [1950] 2 KB 277 at 283 (*per* Bucknell LJ). *Cf Sheggia v Gradwell* [1963] 3 All ER 114.

[110.] *Cussack v Bothwell* (1943) 77 ILTR 18; *Cf Etchingham v Downes* (1946) 80 ILTR 73. See also *Dennis Reed Ltd v Goody* [1950] 2 KB 277 at 285 (*per* Denning LJ).

[111.] "I think it must be taken that in the ordinary way the meaning of 'purchaser' in such a document is a purchaser who is willing and able to complete." *Per* Singleton J in *Poole v Clarke & Co* [1945] 2 All ER 445 at 448. See also *Dennis Reed Ltd v Goody* [1950] 2 KB 277 at 285 (*per* Denning LJ).

(b) "In the Event of Business Resulting"

[3.26] An agreement containing a clause that the agent was entitled to commission "in the event of business resulting" has similarly been interpreted as requiring at least that the purchaser introduced by the agent should enter into a binding contract for purchase.[112]

(c) "On Securing for You an Offer"

[3.27] It has been held that an agreement entitling an agent to commission "on securing for you an offer" was not carried out where the offer made was one "subject to contract", ie, at the very least the offer had to be a firm and unconditional one, which, once accepted, would create a contract.[113] If, however, the offer made had not been so qualified and had been a firm one, arguably the agent would then have become entitled to his commission, even though the vendor decided not to accept the offer and no contract came into force.[114]

(d) "Introduce a Person Who Signs a Legally Binding Contract"

[3.28] This is a rather clearer formula, and it has been held that, once a purchaser signs such a contract to purchase the land, the agent becomes entitled to his commission, even though the purchaser later withdraws and the sale is never completed.[115] However, for this formula to succeed in the agent's favour, the courts have emphasised that it must be clearly drafted, otherwise it runs the risk of being held to be too uncertain to be enforceable.[116] Furthermore, there has been a marked tendency, certainly amongst English judges, to construe such formulae as using the words "purchaser" or "person signing a contract" in a special sense. Such expressions have often been taken to mean a purchaser "ready, willing and able to purchase", so that a signing or offer subject to a qualification which is inconsistent with those characteristics will not be enough.[117] We consider this point further in the next paragraph.

[112.] *Murdoch Lownie Ltd v Newman* [1949] 2 All ER 783.

[113.] *Bennett Walden & Co v Wood* [1950] 2 All ER 132. *Cf Graham & Scott (Southgate) Ltd v Oxlade* [1950] 2 KB 257.

[114.] See *Luxor (Eastbourne) Ltd v Cooper* [1941] AC 108 at 120 (*per* Lord Simon LC).

[115.] *Midgley Estates Ltd v Hand* [1952] 2 QB 432. *Cf Sheggia v Gradwell* [1963] 3 All ER 114; *Wilkinson v Brown* [1966] 1 All ER 502; *Jacques v Lloyd D George & Partners Ltd* [1968] 2 All ER 187.

[116.] *Jacques v Lloyd D George & Partners Ltd op cit. Cf Drewrey v Ware-Lane* [1960] 3 All ER 529.

[117.] See *Graham & Scott (Southgate) Ltd v Oxlade* [1950] 2 KB 257 (offer "subject to contract" and subject to satisfactory survey).

(e) "Introduce a Purchaser Ready, Willing and Able to Purchase"

[3.29] This formula, and similar ones such as "willing and able to purchase", "ready and willing to purchase" and "prepared and able to purchase", has often been used by estate agents for the purpose of making commission become due even though no contract is entered into. Their main argument has been that introduction of such a purchaser is all that can be reasonably expected of an agent who, having achieved this, ought not to be deprived of his commission because of some factor entirely outside his control, eg, the vendor refusing to accept the prospective purchaser's offer. And, indeed, at one time the English courts seemed to interpret such clauses in this way, so that agents were held to be entitled to commission without any contract being signed.[118] Later decisions, however, seemed to have cast doubt on this approach and the courts in England for a time took a much stricter view of these clauses.[119] However, the balance was restored by the Court of Appeal in *Christie Owen & Davies Ltd v Rapacioli*,[120] where the Court rejected *dicta* in some of the earlier cases and reiterated that an estate agent is entitled to commission where he introduces a purchaser able to purchase, who makes his readiness and willingness clear by making an unqualified offer within the terms indicated as acceptable by the vendor. This remains so where the sale does not proceed because the vendor rejects the offer on other grounds, eg, because he receives a better offer. It has been emphasised that the burden lies upon the agent to prove that the purchaser introduced by him was "ready, willing and able to purchase". Though it is doubtful whether the concept of being "ready" adds anything to being "able,"[121] several cases have held that a prospective purchaser's "willingness" is negatived if his offer is made subject to a qualification or condition,[122] eg, "subject to contract"[123] or "subject to satisfactory survey".[124] Indeed, it was even argued that the prospective purchaser's "willingness" could be effectively proved

---

[118.] See *Giddy & Giddy v Horsfall* [1947] 1 All ER 460; *Dennis Reed Ltd v Nicholls* [1948] 2 All ER 914; *Pennett & Partners v Millett* [1949] 1 KB 362; *Nelson & Co v Rolfe* [1950] 1 KB 139.

[119.] The change in attitude became particularly apparent in the Court of Appeal decision in *Graham & Scott (Southgate) Ltd v Oxlade* [1950] 2 KB 257. See also *McCallum v Hicks* [1950] 2 KB 271; *Dennis Reed Ltd v Goody* [1950] 2 KB 277; *Bennett Walden & Co v Wood* [1950] 2 All ER 132.

[120.] [1974] 2 All ER 311.

[121.] See the discussion in *Wilkinson Ltd v Brown* [1966] 1 All ER 509.

[122.] *Cf* where the qualification is introduced by the vendor to an unqualified offer by the purchaser.

[123.] *Bennett Walden & Co v Wood* [1950] 2 All ER 132. See also *Gale & Wright v Buswell* (1961) 178 Est Gaz 709. And see para **[7.06]** *post*.

[124.] *Graham & Scott (Southgate) Ltd v Oxlade* [1950] 2 KB 257. See para **[7.19]** *post*.

only by his entering into a contract for purchase.[125] The point is taken that, until the contract is entered into, the vendor is free to reject any offer made or to negotiate the terms of the contract, and so the purchaser's offer is really relevant only if it is made on terms acceptable to the vendor. The terms which are acceptable only become clear when the final draft of the contract is approved and the contract is signed by both parties in this form. Hence the argument that the agent should not be regarded as being entitled to commission until that event happens.[126] However, the majority of English judges have taken a rather broader view, for an interpretation such as that just outlined would clearly defeat the whole object of including the formula in the agent's contract with the vendor. Thus it has been stated that the agent would still be entitled to commission under the formula, though no contract was entered into, where the prospective purchaser made an offer on terms which were acceptable to the vendor and remained willing on that basis up to the time when the vendor changed his mind as to the terms and refused to enter into a contract on the original terms.[127] In other words, a purchaser "willing to purchase" is a different concept from a purchaser "who does in fact enter into a contract to purchase" the property.[128] The "willingness" of the purchaser in a particular case is largely a question of fact and the court may still find it present in a case where the only reason for no contract being entered into lies in the actions of the vendor.[129]

[3.30] As regards the prospective purchaser's being "able" to purchase, the courts have been concerned primarily with his financial resources.[130] However, clearly other considerations may be relevant in a particular case, eg, the vendor's inability to obtain the landlord's consent to an assignment of leasehold property.[131]

---

125. This view was championed by Lord Denning in particular, see *McCallum v Hicks* [1950] 2 KB 271 at 276; *Dennis Reed Ltd v Goody* [1950] 2 KB 277 at 287-8. See also *Luxor (Eastbourne) Ltd v Cooper* [1941] AC 108 at 139 (*per* Lord Wright). *Cf Gale & Wright v Buswell* (1961) 178 Est Gaz 709.

126. Indeed, it has even been suggested that the purchaser's willingness must remain until the purchase is completed, see *Boots v Christopher & Co* [1952] 1 KB 89; *Dellafiora v Lester* [1962] 3 All ER 393.

127. *Dennis Reed Ltd v Goody* [1950] 2 KB 277 at 283 (*per* Bucknell LJ). See also *Nelson & Co v Rolfe* [1950] 1 KB 139.

128. *Ackroyd & Sons v Hasan* [1960] 2 QB 144 at 163 (*per* Ormerod LJ). *Cf* where the agent's contract refers expressly to a "prospective" purchaser, *Drewery v Ware-Lane* [1960] 3 All ER 529.

129. *Trinder & Partners v Haggis* (1951) 158 Est Gaz 4; *Wilkinson Ltd v O'Neill* (1961) 181 Est Gaz 137; *Christie Owen & Davies Ltd v Rapacioli* [1974] 2 All ER 311.

130. *James v Smith* [1931] 2 KB 317 at 322 (*per* Atkin LJ). See also *Dennis Reed Ltd v Nicholls* [1948] 2 All ER 914.

131. *Dellafiora v Lester* [1962] 3 All ER 393. *Cf Wilkinson Ltd v Brown* [1966] 1 All ER 502.

2. Amount

[3.31] Normally the amount of commission to which a house or estate agent is entitled is specified in the contract with the vendor, often by incorporation of a scale recommended by one of the professional bodies, eg, the Irish Auctioneers' and Valuers' Institute. It is common for this contract to specify that payment of advertising expenses and other out-of-pocket expenses incurred on behalf of the vendor is in addition to commission. If it is intended to adopt a professional scale, this must be made clear as the remarks of Hanna J in *North v Drinan*[132] emphasised:

> "This is an association scale, framed to prevent the members of the profession from undercutting one another, but it is clear law that it is not binding on clients unless it is expressly brought to their notice, and agreed to by them, or established by convincing proof of some universal custom. If this is not done the Court has to determine for itself what is a reasonable remuneration for the services rendered."[133]

In the absence of an express provision in the agent's contract, what is "reasonable remuneration" must depend upon the circumstances of each particular case.[134]

3. Payment

[3.32] As in the case of sales by public auction, it was, until recently, the practice in both parts of Ireland in sales by private treaty for the house or estate agents' fees or commission and expenses to be paid by the purchaser rather than the vendor who employed the agent.[135] A provision to this effect was usually included in the agent's contract with the vendor and, in theory, if the purchaser refused to pay the commission, the agent's sole remedy was to sue the vendor, as he had no contract with the purchaser.[136] However, in practice this problem did not arise because a clause requiring the purchaser to pay was usually inserted as a special condition in the contract for sale between the vendor and the purchaser.[137] Thus the vendor's solicitor collected the commission to be paid to the vendor's agent in addition to the purchase money due to the vendor. Though this practice had obvious

---

[132.] [1931] IR 468.

[133.] *Ibid*, p 473. See further on an alleged custom as to payment of an agent, *O'Connor v Faul* (1957) 91 ILTR 7.

[134.] *Heneken v Courtney* (1967) 101 ILTR 25.

[135.] See the discussion in the *Survey of the Land Law of Northern Ireland* (1971), paras 192-200.

[136.] See *Cherry v Anderson* (1876) IR 10 CL 204; *Montgomery v Fleming* (1905) 39 ILTR 229 (auction cases). See also para **[2.34]** *ante*.

[137.] See also *McNulty v Hanratty* (1918) 52 ILTR 43.

advantages for agents, eg, it usually assured payment of their commission without having to sue for it, provided the sale went through, it did have serious drawbacks. One was that it actively discouraged vendors from trying to sell privately and, therefore, tended to be inflationary by forcing purchasers in every case to pay the full purchase price plus commission.[138] Furthermore, arguably it is usually less burdensome for a vendor to pay the commission out of the purchase price than for the purchaser to have to pay it in addition to the purchase price. Apart from that, as a matter of general principle, the person who decides to employ an agent to perform services for him ought to pay for them rather than a person who has had no choice in the matter. The previous practice was reversed in due course and now a house or estate agent's fees or commission and expenses must in general be paid by the vendor and any express or implied provision to the contrary is void. The statutory provision in question, ie, s 2 of the Auctioneers and House Agents Act 1973, was considered earlier in relation to auctioneers.[139]

II. VENDOR'S SOLICITOR

[3.33] We considered the role of the vendor's solicitor in the early stages of sale by public auction in the previous chapter,[140] and for the most part what was said there is equally applicable to the case of a sale by private treaty. However, the major qualification must be stated that often the vendor does not consult his solicitor until preliminary negotiations are completed between him and the purchaser, usually with the aid of a house or estate agent. This is an important point to bear in mind because it sometimes results in the parties reaching an agreement without the prior advice of their respective solicitors, and the danger exists that the written evidence which is the only item left to render that agreement enforceable under the Statute of Frauds (Ir) 1695, may be brought into existence inadvertently by one or other solicitor after he is instructed, but before he intends to commit his client.[141] In other words, a solicitor may find that the parties have pre-empted his usual role of negotiating the terms of the contract on behalf of his client and have reduced his function to the purely technical one of completing the formalities required by the Statute of Frauds to render the contract enforceable. Thus some years ago, Gannon J warned:

[138.] See *McMahon v Gaffney* [1930] IR 576 at 586 (*per* Johnston J), quoted at para **[2.34]** *ante*.
[139.] See para **[2.35]** *ante*.
[140.] See paras **[2.36-52]** *ante*.
[141.] See further, para **[7.06]** *post*.

"In my opinion solicitors are not entitled to arrogate to themselves authority to negotiate or to make a contract for their clients when, as in this case, the clients themselves have bound themselves by their own agreement. More usually the authority of solicitors to negotiate and conclude a contract on behalf of their clients may be implied from the circumstances, but in my view of the facts in this case no such circumstances arise as to imply such authority in these solicitors. Undoubtedly each solicitor could, and the interests of his client required that he should, ensure that the agreement is made legally enforceable. On the evidence before me, I am satisfied that no negotiations for the conclusion of a contract were entered into by the solicitors, nor had they any authority to do so, nor was there any necessity for further negotiations on their part. The contract was made verbally by the plaintiff and the defendant and one term -namely as to the closing date - was varied verbally by them and all the essential terms of it as so varied were set out in a sufficient written memorandum thereof to make the agreement enforceable against the defendant."[142]

Bearing this point in mind, some further remarks may be added to the earlier discussion of the vendor's solicitor's role.[143]

A. Taking Instructions

[3.34] The importance of taking detailed instructions from the vendor at the earliest opportunity applies equally in the case of a sale by private treaty. Since the property is likely to have been put in the hands of a house or estate agent for sale, it is wise to contact him and to ask for a copy of the sale particulars prepared by him. Since it is likely that the purchaser's solicitor will also obtain a copy of these and the purchaser has made his offer on the basis of them, any discrepancy between them and the particulars in the contract for sale drawn up by the vendor's solicitor is likely to give rise to some awkward queries. It is also important to check with the agent whether he has received any pre-contract deposit from the purchaser.[144]

B. Drafting Particulars and Conditions of Sale

[3.35] As in the case of a sale by public auction,[145] one of the main tasks of the vendor's solicitor in a sale by private treaty is to draw up the contract to

---

[142.] *Black v Kavanagh* (1974) 108 ILTR 91 at 96. See also *City of Glasgow Friendly Society Ltd v Gilpin Ltd* (1971) 22 NILQ 196; *Usitravel Ltd v Freyer* High Court, unrep, 29 May 1973, para **[6.42]** *post*.

[143.] See para **[2.37]** *et seq, ante*.

[144.] In the light of recent case law, arguably this is more important now for the purchaser's solicitor, see paras **[3.15-17]** *supra*.

[145.] See para **[2.51]** *ante*.

be entered into by the parties. At the very least, his responsibility in this regard involves making sure that the "memorandum or note" in writing required by s 2 of the Statute of Frauds (Ireland) 1695, comes into existence, so as to render the contract enforceable between the parties.[146] Though, as we have seen,[147] this is all that the vendor's solicitor may be required to do in a particular case, usually he is expected to negotiate the terms of the contract with the purchaser's solicitor. Initially he will draw up the contract in draft form, usually using the standard form issued by the Law Society,[148] and checking the vendor's title against the title documents. This draft[149] is then sent to the purchaser's solicitor for his approval and, if that is given, for signing by the purchaser and return of the copy signed. As we shall see later,[150] it is essential that care is taken in wording any letter accompanying the draft contract, and any subsequent correspondence. Though not strictly necessary at this stage, it is fairly common practice for the vendor's solicitor to send copies of the title documents to the purchaser's solicitor at the same time as he sends the draft contract. If this is done, it is unwise to send the originals, if only because the vendor's solicitor will probably have given a personal undertaking as to their safekeeping and will be holding them on accountable receipt.[151]

C. Searches and Enquiries

[3.36] Because there is usually a delay of some weeks between the date when the vendor instructs his solicitor and the date when a binding contract is entered into with the purchaser, it is arguable that the most economic and efficient system of conveyancing would require that the vendor's solicitor uses that time to obtain further information which the purchaser's solicitor is going to need in due course. However, this practice is rarely adopted, partly because the making of such searches is generally regarded as the responsibility of the purchaser, the expense of which, though limited, few vendors are prepared to incur.[152] And it is no doubt significant that the practice is rarely adopted in England and Wales where pre-contract searches and enquiries have been common practice for much longer. Having said that,

---

[146.] This matter is discussed in detail in Ch 6, *post*.

[147.] See para **[3.33]** *supra*.

[148.] *General Conditions of Sale (1995 Edition)*. This is discussed in detail in Chs 9-10 *post*.

[149.] Preferably in duplicate to enable the purchaser's solicitor to use one as a working copy for amendment and correction and keeping in his file.

[150.] See para **[7.06]** *post*.

[151.] See para **[14.43]** *post*.

[152.] Such searches should not be confused with other searches, eg, in the Registry of Deeds, which may be requisitioned from the vendor under the terms of the contract and supplied at the post-contract stage, see para **[15.43]** *post*.

a sensible vendor's solicitor should anticipate that in certain cases, because of the nature of the property being sold or the circumstances surrounding the sale, various *pre*-contract enquiries or requisitions are likely to be raised by the purchaser's solicitor. Thus the purchaser's solicitor may be concerned about compliance with planning or building regulations or the impact of environmental protection legislation.[153] If the property is a family home there arises the issue of consent under the Family Home Protection Act 1976.[154] The vendor's solicitor should be prepared to deal with such *pre*-contract enquiries or requisitions,[155] because, although technically there is no obligation to answer them, since no contract as yet exists between the vendor and the purchaser, a failure to do so may result in the prospective purchaser being advised by his solicitor to end negotiations for the purchase.[156]

III. PURCHASER'S SOLICITOR

[3.37] In contrast with a sale by public auction,[157] the purchaser's solicitor generally has a major role to play in a sale by private treaty. If he is not instructed before the purchaser makes an offer for the vendor's property, eg, to the vendor's house or estate agent, he is usually instructed shortly afterwards and requested to "complete the formalities". Though it is possible that the purchaser has already entered into a contract to buy the property, and may even have signed a written one provided by the vendor's agent, most purchasers are aware of the dangers of this and will have made it clear that the offer was a tentative one or one "subject to contract".[158] The most that the purchaser may have done is to pay a pre-contract "deposit"[159] to the vendor's agent as a sign of his good faith in making the offer. Thus the purchaser's solicitor will usually find himself involved in negotiating the terms of the contract with the vendor's solicitor and, perhaps, carrying out other tasks before his client is finally committed to the purchase.

A. Taking Instructions

[3.38] As in the case of the vendor's solicitor,[160] the purchaser's solicitor must take care that he receives full detailed instructions from his client at the earliest opportunity. Once again it is good practice to get into the habit of

---

[153.] See paras **[5.09]** and **[16.74]** *post*.

[154.] See para **[16.61]**. Note also the impact of the Family Law Act 1981 and Judicial Separation and Family Law Reform Act, 1989 (as amended by the Family Law Act 1995), see para **[16.72]** *et seq, post*.

[155.] See Ch 5 *post*.

[156.] See para **[5.02]** *post*.

[157.] See para **[2.53]** *ante*.

[158.] See further, para **[7.06]** *post*.

[159.] As to the dangers of this, see paras **[3.34-5]** *supra*.

[160.] See para **[3.34]** *supra*.

using a detailed instructions form,[161] which can be filled in at the first interview and then pinned to the purchaser's file for further reference. If used in conjunction with a purchase "progress sheet",[162] on which each step in the conveyancing process is marked off as it is taken, there is less chance of some vital facts being missed to the client's detriment. The following is an outline of the matters upon which the purchaser's solicitor will usually seek to obtain instructions at an early stage.

1. Particulars of Parties

[3.39] It is, of course, just as essential for the purchaser's solicitor to obtain full details as to the parties to the transaction as it is for the vendor's.[163] One point of considerable importance now in Ireland about which the purchaser's solicitor will want information, though the purchaser may not be able to help, is whether the vendor is married and, if so, whether his or her spouse is willing to give the consent to the sale required by statute. The reason for this is that under the Family Home Protection Act 1976, a conveyance of any interest in the family home by one spouse to any person except the other spouse is void unless done with the prior consent of that other spouse.[164] Since a "conveyance" is defined by the Act as including "an enforceable agreement (whether conditional or unconditional)" to make a conveyance,[165] the purchaser's solicitor must consider the question of consent at the contract stage of the conveyancing process and not leave it to the post-contract stage. Some years ago the Law Society recommended that solicitors should ensure that the "other" spouse signs a form of consent to the sale to be endorsed on the contract and the conveyance.[166]

2. Particulars of Property

[3.40] It is also essential for the purchaser's solicitor to check with the purchaser the details of the property being bought. These may then be checked with the particulars provided by the vendor's solicitor in the draft contract. A further check may be made by writing to the vendor's house or estate agent and asking him to furnish a copy of the sale particulars prepared by the latter. Particular care should be taken to discover if extra items are included in the sale of the property, eg, fixtures and fittings.[167]

---

161. See para **[2.37]** *ante.*
162. *Ibid.*
163. See para **[2.38]** *ante.*
164. Section 3. See further, para **[16.61]** *post.*
165. Section 1.
166. See further, para **[16.69]** *post.*
167. See para **[2.39]** *ante* and **[9.15]** *post.*

3. Survey

[3.41] A matter which should always be raised with the purchaser for his consideration, in the light of advice given by his solicitor, is whether an independent survey should be obtained of the property being bought. Each case must obviously be considered in the light of its own circumstances, but some general rules may be stated. One is that it should not be assumed that an independent survey is unnecessary because the purchaser is borrowing most of the purchase price from a lending institution, eg, a building society, which will insist on arranging its own survey, ie, on the ground that, if the institution decides to lend the amount sought by the purchaser, the assumption can be made that the survey was satisfactory. The point is that the objects which the lending institution has in mind in arranging a survey do not necessarily coincide with those which the purchaser might have in mind. The former is primarily concerned to see that the property is of sufficient value to be adequate security for the loan being made, which will normally be only a percentage of the valuation put on the property by the institution's expert valuer, ie, not necessarily the selling price of the property. Thus the lending institution may ignore minor matters which do not in its view reduce the property's security value sufficiently for it to be concerned,[168] but these may be matters which will nevertheless seriously inconvenience the purchaser. It is true that the courts on both sides of the Irish sea have increasingly recognised the fact that members of the public tend to rely on the lending institution's "survey" and so have been prepared to hold that a duty of care arises sufficient to justify a claim in negligence against the lender[169] or its valuer.[170] However, it is small comfort to a purchaser of a defective property to be told that he may have a claim in negligence, with all the delay and expense its pursuit will involve, especially when the precaution of having an independent survey by an expert before the contract to purchase was entered into would have forewarned him of the problem. In *O'Connor v First National Building Society*[171] Lynch J held that

---

[168.] Though in some cases the lending institution may make the repair of these items within a set period a condition of making the loan, or even make a "retention" until they are fixed, i.e., keep back a proportion of the loan amount agreed.

[169.] See *Ward v McMaster* [1988] IR 337; *Irish Permanent Building Society v O'Sullivan* [1990] ILRM 598. *Cf Curran v NI Co-Ownership Housing Association Ltd* [1987] 2 All ER 13. Note that most lending institutions will seek to absolve themselves from such liability by, eg, a notice in the loan application form and, provided it is clearly enough drafted, the courts are likely to enforce it: see *O'Connor v First National Building Society* [1991] ILRM 208.

[170.] See *Smith v Eric s Bush* and *Harris v Wyre Forest District Council*, both reported at [1989] 2 All ER 514. *Cf Sunderland v McGreavey* [1987] IR 372; *Crowley v Allied Irish Banks Ltd* [1987] IR 282 (both cases involving architects).

[171.] [1991] ILRM 208. See further on surveys at para **[4.21]** *post.*

there is a *prima facie* duty on the purchaser's solicitor to advise his client that he ought to have an independent survey by a suitably qualified person and the onus is on the solicitor to show why this duty should not apply in the particular case.

4. Planning and Environmental Matters

[3.42] The purchaser's solicitor should check with his client the purposes for which the property is being bought. The point is that if he intends to "develop" the property within the meaning of the planning legislation, eg, engage in building operations or change the existing use of the property,[172] he will usually have to obtain the permission of the relevant planning authority, if this has not been granted already. The question of existing planning permission will have to be checked with the vendor's solicitor.[173] If it has not been granted for the development the purchaser has in mind, the question then arises as to whether he should be advised to obtain this before he enters into the contract to purchase or whether he can enter into the contract but make it subject to a condition as to planning permission. The client should also be made aware of the need for compliance with building regulations under the Building Control Act 1990 and with other legislation such as the Local Government (Multi-Storey Buildings) Act 1988. Where commercial and industrial property is being considered for purchase, the impact of the plethora of legislation now protecting the environment must be borne in mind. These thorny questions are considered in later chapters.[174] It should also be mentioned that the question of physical suitability of the property in question for the sort of development the purchaser has in mind is another important factor in favour of the purchaser arranging his own independent survey of the property.[175] Though in this sort of case it may be necessary to arrange a rather more comprehensive survey than might otherwise be required.

[3.43] There may be other questions which are worth raising with the purchaser at this stage, because he has probably inspected the property being sold or has had some dealings already with the vendor or his agent. He may know that, in the recent past, alterations, such as reconstruction work or extensions, were made to the property. If he so informs his solicitor, it immediately raises in the latter's mind the question of whether the appropriate planning permission was obtained, whether any relevant

---

172. See paras **[16.74]** *post*.
173. Usually, as a pre-contract enquiry or requisition, para **[5.09]** *post*, rather than a requisition of title, para **[16.74]** *post*.
174. See Chs 5 and 16 *post*.
175. See para **[3.41]** *supra*.

building regulations were complied with and, if the property is leasehold, whether any necessary consent of the landlord was obtained. If the alterations were made in breach of any of these matters, the purchaser could be seriously prejudiced if he goes ahead in buying the property without their being rectified beforehand. Clearly these are matters which will have to be raised with the vendor's solicitor at some stage.[176]

5. *Financial Matters*

[3.44] It is crucial that the purchaser's solicitor should discuss with the client the various financial matters which are necessarily involved in the transaction. Thus it must be made clear to him that he will usually be required to pay a substantial deposit once he enters into the contract,[177] and, if he does not have the cash to hand, arrangements must be made to see that he does by the time the contract is concluded, if necessary by arranging a temporary loan.[178] Then there is the question of the balance of the purchase money due on completion, which is usually going to be financed out of the sale of the purchaser's existing property or raised through a mortgage loan secured on the property being bought, or, often, a combination of both. It is now accepted by the courts that it is the duty of the purchaser's solicitor to advise his client on these matters and to see that the conveyancing process is properly co-ordinated so as to ensure that the client incurs no unnecessary expense or loss.[179]

[3.45] In addition to these matters, it will do no harm to mention to the client the other financial charges he may be obliged to meet, eg, survey fees,[180] search fees,[181] insurance costs,[182] stamp duty,[183] and, of course, his solicitor's fees.[184]

[176.] See paras **[5.09]** and **[5.12]** *post*.

[177.] See para **[10.16]** *post*.

[178.] See para **[2.48]** *ante*.

[179.] *Desmond v Brophy* [1985] IR 449; *Harte v Sheehy* High Court, unrep, 14 March 1986 (1982/10930P); *Culhane v O'Maoileoin* High Court, unrep, 12 November 1988) (1988/8161P).

[180.] See para **[3.41]** *supra*.

[181.] See paras **[5.03]** and **[15.39]** *post*.

[182.] See paras **[3.46]** *infra* and **[12.42]** *post*.

[183.] See para **[20.38]** *post*.

[184.] See para **[20.49]** *post*. Under s 68 of the Solicitors (Amendment) Act 1994, a solicitor is obliged to inform the client of the charges, or to give an estimate or the basis of charging, at the time of taking instructions, or as soon as is practicable thereafter.

6. Insurance

[3.46] It is also essential that the purchaser's solicitor should discuss with his client the various insurance matters which are relevant to the transaction. One crucial point used to be that it is a general principle of our law that the risks relating to the property pass, at least to some extent, to the purchaser, not on completion of the transaction by transfer of the title to him, as one might expect at first sight, but as soon as the contract for sale is entered into.[185] This common law rule is mitigated now by the Law Society's standard contract form,[186] but there may be cases, eg, where the standard form is not used, where the purchaser's solicitor must see that his client has adequate insurance cover from the date of the contract in relation to the property itself. Insurance of the contents, of course, is a less pressing matter since normally the purchaser's belongings will not be moved into the property until after completion.[187]

[3.47] Apart from insurance relating to the property itself, there may be other insurance matters to be considered. Thus the mortgage scheme being arranged for the purchaser may be linked to insurance policies, in which case advice may be needed on the various types of policy available. Even if the mortgage is a standard repayment mortgage, it is wise for the purchaser to arrange life insurance cover for the term of the mortgage, to ensure that his dependants are not saddled with the mortgage repayments after his death. Frequently, lending institutions insist upon such cover and a failure to put it in place in time will cause delays in the issue of the loan cheque.

7. Completion

[3.48] Finally the purchaser's solicitor ought to discuss with his client the date to be fixed in the contract as the closing date for completion of the transaction. Various factors may have to be taken into consideration, eg, the various financial arrangements mentioned earlier.[188] Considerable time may be needed to complete these satisfactorily, and then there are the additional complications which arise if the purchaser is involved in another transaction linked to the present one, eg, sale of his existing house. Clearly sufficient time must be allowed for these and other matters to be carried out by the purchaser's solicitor, such as his investigation of the title,[189] but the

---

[185.] See para **[12.36]** *et seq.*

[186.] *General Conditions of Sale (1995 Edition)*, conds 43-45. See para **[12.40]** *et seq, post.*

[187.] *Cf* however, fixtures and fittings included in the sale, if the Law Society's contract form is not used.

[188.] See paras **[3.44-5]** *supra.*

[189.] See Ch 15 *post.*

purchaser should also be warned that the fixing of the completion date will have to be a matter for negotiation with the vendor and his solicitor and that a compromise not wholly to either party's liking may have to be reached.[190]

B. Preliminary Enquiries and Searches

[3.49] The extent to which the purchaser's solicitor will become involved with these matters is considered in detail in a later chapter.[191]

C. Negotiation of Terms of Contract

[3.50] Just as the vendor's solicitor usually prepares the draft contract to be entered into by the vendor and purchaser, the purchaser's solicitor is usually given the opportunity to consider this draft and, if he thinks this is necessary in his client's interest, to suggest amendments to be made before the parties sign it. This is also a subject which is considered in detail in a later chapter.[192]

[190.] See further para **[13.10]** *post.*
[191.] See Ch 5 *post.*
[192.] See Ch 9 *post.*

Chapter 4

CAVEAT EMPTOR

I. INTRODUCTION

[4.01] In this and the next chapter we are concerned with further matters which may arise during the pre-contract stage of the conveyancing process. However, it must be emphasised at the outset that these matters constitute one of the most controversial aspects of modern conveyancing and recent decades witnessed the development of a considerable divergence between Irish and English practice.[1] Though in recent years practice in Ireland has been coming closer to that prevailing in England.

[4.02] The central point at issue is the extent to which the purchaser or his solicitor ought to make preliminary enquiries in respect of the property being bought and searches in registers[2] *before* the purchaser commits himself to a binding contract for sale. The traditional answer to this question is that it depends upon whether or not the purchaser would be fixed with notice[3] of, and, therefore, would take subject to, rights and interests which such enquiries and searches would reveal. On this s 3(1) of the Conveyancing Act 1882, provides:

"A purchaser shall not be prejudicially affected by notice of any instrument, fact, or thing unless -

(i) It is within his own knowledge, *or would have come to his knowledge if such inquiries and inspections had been made as ought reasonably to have been made by him*; or

(ii) In the same transaction with respect to which a question of notice to the purchaser arises, it has come to the knowledge of his counsel, as such, or of his solicitor, or other agent, as such, *or would have come to the knowledge of his solicitor, or other agent, as such, if such inquiries and inspections had been made as ought reasonably to have been made by the solicitor or other agent.*" (Italics added.)

---

1. As to English practice, see Barnsley, *Conveyancing Law and Practice* (3rd ed, 1988), Ch 7.
2. There is, of course, the allied question of how far the vendor's solicitor ought to make searches in anticipation of being asked to supply them to the purchaser's solicitor at a later stage in the transaction, eg, in the requisitions on title, see para. **[15.43]** *post.*
3. The doctrine of notice is discussed in *Irish Land Law* (2nd ed, 1986), paras. 3.069-93.

It is clear that a purchaser is affected by notice of matters which he would have discovered by reasonable "inquiries and inspections", ie, "constructive" notice on his part, or which his solicitor would have discovered in the same way, ie, constructive notice on the part of his solicitor which is "imputed" to the purchaser.[4] A failure by the purchaser's solicitor to ensure that the appropriate inquiries and inspections are made or, at the very least, that the client is warned of the need to make them and of the risk run if they are not made, exposes the solicitor to a successful claim for negligence.[5] The questions remain, however, as to what are such "reasonable" enquiries and inspections which the purchaser or his solicitor ought to make and as to when they ought to be made.

[4.03] So far as the physical state of the property being purchased is concerned, the basic rule of conveyancing is *caveat emptor*, ie, "let the buyer beware".[6] It is not the vendor's duty to disclose defects in the physical condition of his property but rather it is the duty of the purchaser to protect himself by making an inspection of the property and, if necessary, commissioning a survey of the property. Though the application of the general rule may be modified in cases of fraud on the part of the vendor,[7] or even where he volunteers inaccurate information without realising its inaccuracy.[8] The carrying out of an inspection and of any survey thought necessary is something which should normally be done before the contract is entered into. Unless some safeguarding provision is inserted in the contract,[9] failure to do so may result in the purchaser being left without an adequate remedy in the event of some defect coming to light later. The scope for providing a safeguard in the contract is usually very limited, for it would be almost impossible to draw up a clause covering every potential physical defect. Apart from that, the contract is usually drawn up by the vendor's

---

4. On "constructive" and "imputed" notice, see *ibid*, paras 3.072-3. See also the discussion in *Northern Bank Ltd v Henry* [1981] IR 1; *Ulster Bank Ltd v Shanks* [1982] NI 143; *Bank of Ireland v Smyth* [1996] 1 ILRM 241. Generally the client has notice imputed to him of information gained by his solicitor while acting for him in the transaction ("as such"): see *Halifax Mortgage Services Ltd v Stepsky* [1996] 2 All ER 277. *Cf* under the Family Home Protection Act 1976: see para **[16.22]**, sub-para (h) *post*.

5. *Roche v Peilow* [1985] IR 232; *Kelly v Crowley* [1985] IR 212; *McMullen v Farrell* [1993] 1 IR 123. *Cf Friends Provident Life Office v Doherty* [1992] ILRM 372.

6. This rule is considered in detail later, see para **[4.07]** *infra*.

7. See para **[5.23]** *post*.

8. See para **[5.26]** *post*. Note also the remedies the purchaser may have for misdescription and non-disclosure of defects under the contract for sale, see paras **[9.23-48]** *post*.

9. One possibility is to make the contract subject to a condition as to a satisfactory survey, see para **[7.19]** *post*.

solicitor and it would be very unlikely that he or his client would agree to such a clause.

[4.04] So far as the title to the property is concerned, an element of the concept of *caveat emptor* applies here too, in that under traditional conveyancing theory it is the duty of the purchaser to investigate the title of the property.[10] However, to some extent this duty is qualified by the vendor's correlative duty to deduce title, though it is usually circumscribed by the terms of the contract for sale,[11] and his duty to disclose latent defects in title known to him.[12] But according to traditional conveyancing theory the duty of investigating title does not arise until after the contract has been entered into. One practical reason for this is that the contract usually defines precisely the extent of the vendor's duty in relation to showing title, eg, by specifying what title documents he is obliged to produce and the length of title to be shown[13] and the statutory provisions governing the matter become relevant only after the contract fails to provide for these matters, ie, is "open" as to title.[14] The result is that the various tasks performed by the purchaser's solicitor in relation to investigation of title, eg, perusal of the title documents, the making of requisitions on title and searches in the Land Registry or Registry of Deeds,[15] take place during the post-contract stage of the conveyancing process.

[4.05] What has caused practitioners on both sides of the Irish Sea to re-examine the traditional processes in recent decades has been the extensive growth this century in the number of interests and charges affecting land which are not easily discoverable by an inspection or survey of the physical state of the property or by an investigation of the title in the traditional sense, ie, interests or charges not revealed by the title documents or searches in the Land Registry or Registry of Deeds. Most of these interests and charges are the creation of statute law, eg, public health and housing legislation, roads and highways legislation, planning and environmental legislation.[16] Many of the interests and charges are created in favour of public bodies, eg, central and local government departments, but in most cases they are burdens on the

---

10. See chs 15 and 16, *post*.
11. See para **[14.05]** *post*.
12. See para **[9.24]** *post*. See also *Re Flynn and Newman's Contract* [1948] IR 104 at 109-10 (per Kingsmill Moore J).
13. See para **[14.03]** *post*.
14. See para **[14.05]** *post*.
15. Though, in practice, such searches as are already in his possession are furnished by the vendor's solicitor, as may be required by the terms of the contract for sale, see para **[15.43]** *post*.
16. See further Ch 5 *post*.

land which will affect successive owners, hence the need to make enquiries and searches in respect of them. Yet the difficulty has often been that many of these interests and charges have not been registered in a central registry which is easily searched and some have not been registered at all and have to be sought by written enquiries to several different departments or bodies.

[4.06] In Ireland, until recently, there was little support for the introduction of a system of preliminary enquiries and searches such as that in use in England and Wales for decades. So far as searches are concerned, one obvious reason is the lack of any registers such as the local authority land charges registers introduced by the English Land Charges Act 1925.[17] So far as pre-contract enquiries of the vendor's solicitor are concerned, most of the information which would be sought by this means in England and Wales was instead sought in Ireland at the post-contract stage by requisitions on title.[18] The standard form in general use in Ireland[19] covers a wide range of matters, not all of which may be strictly described as queries about the title to the property.[20] Thus the requisitions cover general information about the vendor and the property[21] and more particular matters relating to leasehold property,[22] registered land,[23] planning matters[24] and licences for hotels or restaurants.[25] Many of the requisitions relate to the supply of documentation by the vendor's solicitor[26] and in practice he will often have obtained this at an early stage (if the vendor did not already have the items when he first instructed his solicitor) in anticipation of receiving requisitions to this effect at a later stage. Thus in practice the vendor's solicitor, though he may not be called upon to produce the documents until the post-contract stage, may procure some of them while the contract itself is still being negotiated. In this way much of the burden of procuring documentation is put on the vendor's solicitor and the purchaser's solicitor may find that his role is often restricted to a traditional investigation of the title.[27] In every case he should

---

17. See now the English Local Land Charges Act 1975.
18. See generally, Chs 15 and 16, *post.*
19. Ie the Law Society's *Objections and Requisitions on Title* (1996 ed), which was revised following introduction of the Society's new *General Conditions of Sale (1995 ed).*
20. See Ch 14 *post.*
21. Eg, relating to particulars of the vendor and the property, its facilities (drainage etc) and public charges on it.
22. Reqs Nos 9-10 and 33-34.
23. Req No 21.
24. Req No 27.
25. Req No 41-42.
26. There will usually also be provisions in the contract relating to documentation to be produced by the vendor's solicitor, see para **[9.11]** *et seq, post.*
27. See Ch 15 *post.*

consider the need for an independent survey of the property[28] and in many cases he may consider it wise to make planning and environmental enquiries before allowing his client to enter into the contract.[29] The complexity of modern planning and environmental protection systems is such that most properties may be affected by current restrictions or planning proposals,[30] or exposed to the substantial sanctions introduced in recent years under the environmental protection legislation[31] and care must be taken to see that a purchaser is made aware of these. It must not be assumed that the terms of the contract for sale and the requisitions on title will always elicit this information, in which case it is the purchaser's solicitor's duty to discover it. And complications have arisen because of the restrictions imposed by the Family Home Protection Act 1976, on the power of one spouse to dispose of the family home without the consent of the other spouse. Since the Act covers contracts for sale as well as transfer deeds, the question of the need for an appropriate consent arises during the pre-contract stage.[32] The result is that increasingly enquiries (or "requisitions")[33] are made *before* the contract is entered into, a subject we return to in the next chapter.[34]

II. CAVEAT EMPTOR

[4.07] As we mentioned earlier,[35] one of the first principles of our conveyancing system is the maxim *caveat emptor* - let the buyer beware.[36] This has particular significance so far as the physical condition of the property is concerned and raises the issue of the respective positions of the vendor and purchaser at the pre-contract stage of the conveyancing process.[37] It arises at that stage because to the extent that the law imposes a

---

[28.] See para **[4.21]** *infra.*

[29.] See para **[5.06]** *post.* Another solution maybe to make the contract subject to a planning condition, see para **[7.16]** *post.*

[30.] See para **[16.74]** *post.*

[31.] See para **[1.21]** *ante.*

[32.] See para **[16.62]** *post.* Note also the effect of the Family Law Reform Act 1995, s 54: see para **[16.70]** *post.*

[33.] Usually by extracting the relevant part of the Law Society's *Objections and Requisitions on Title* form. The 1996 revised edition is considered in Ch 16 *post.*

[34.] Ch 5 *post.*

[35.] See para **[4.03]** *supra.*

[36.] The whole subject was studied in depth by the Law Reform Commission's Working Paper No 1, *The Law Relating to the Liability of Builders, Vendors and Lessors for the Quality and Fitness of Premises* (1977). See also McMahon and Binchy, *Irish Law of Torts* (2nd ed, 1990), Ch 13.

[37.] Their positions with respect to the title to the property, especially the vendor's duties of showing a good title and disclosing defects, relate more to the post-contract stage and are, therefore, considered later, see paras **[9.20]** and **[14.06]** *post.*

burden of self-protection on the purchaser he, or his solicitor, must consider what steps to take for protection *before* the purchaser is committed to a binding contract to buy the property in question.[38] In the next few paragraphs we consider the scope of the *caveat emptor* principle and how a purchaser may obtain protection from its application.

A. Scope of the Principle

[4.08] The general rule is that the vendor is under no duty to disclose defects in the condition of the property and so, eg, is not to be taken as giving any warranty as to the habitability of the property[39] or its fitness for the use to which the purchaser intends to put it.[40] It is true that the common law recognised some limited exceptions to this rule, eg, in the case of a letting of furnished accommodation, there may be an implied covenant or warranty on the part of the landlord that the premises are fit for human habitation at the commencement of the tenancy.[41] Apart from such exceptions, the onus lies upon the purchaser to discover defects in the condition of the property by, eg, making his own inspection before entering into the contract.[42] Failure to do this might leave the purchaser without a remedy for a defect discovered after the contract has been entered into.[43] A few years ago the Law Society's Conveyancing Committee warned purchaser's solicitors of the need to advise the purchaser *in writing* to have the structure of the property checked out by a qualified engineer or architect.[44] Failure to do so opens the solicitor to a claim for negligence if the client subsequently has to pay for structural work to correct defects which a survey would have brought to light.[45]

---

38. Especially when the contract itself may, by its terms, seek to restrict the purchaser's remedies even further than is done by the general law, see para **[9.28]** *post*.
39. *Edler v Auerbach* [1950] 1 KB 359. See also *Curling v Walsh* (1988) 6 ILT 184.
40. This has been extended in England to cases where the unfitness was due legal restrictions, eg, user prohibited by a head-lease, see *Hill v Harris* [1965] 2 QB 601; see also *Smith v Colbourne* [1914] 2 Ch 533. *Cf* the vendor's duty to disclose defects in title, para **[9.24]** *post*.
41. *Smith v Marrable* (1843) 11 M & W 5; *Wilson v Finch Hatton* (1877) 2 Ex D 336. *Cf Murray v Mace* (1872) IR 8 CL 396; *Beaver v McFarlane* [1932] LJ Ir 128 (unfurnished accommodation). See Wylie, *Irish Landlord and Tenant Law*, para 12.08.
42. See further on this subject, para **[4.21]** *infra*.
43. Ie, unless the vendor was guilty of a misrepresentation (see para **[5.23]** *post*), entered into a collateral warranty (see para **[5.26]** *post*), misdescribed the property in the contract (see para **[9.29]** *post*), or failed to disclose a defect in title he ought to have disclosed (see para. **[9.24]** *post*).
44. *Gazette*, March 1992, p 71.
45. See para **[4.24]** *infra*.

[4.09] There is one situation where precautions such as commissioning a survey will not protect a purchaser from the dangers of the *caveat emptor* principle. This is where the property being purchased includes a building which is not yet erected or works not yet completed, ie, the transaction involves a building contract whereunder the vendor undertakes to erect a building or to execute other works on the land in question.[46] The point is that no amount of inspection of the land up to the date of the contract will protect the purchaser against defects in the building or works completed after the contract is entered into.[47] The application of the principle of *caveat emptor* to such contracts has been the subject of considerable controversy on both sides of the Irish Sea. This situation involves a "contract" builder and should be distinguished from one involving a "spec" builder, ie, where a builder builds a property on his land and sells it after it has been completed, or, at least, substantially completed.[48]

B. New Buildings

1. Common Law

[4.10] In considering the position of a purchaser of a new building it is important to consider the position both at common law and under any agreement entered into with the vendor. In most cases, the purchaser will be able to claim protection under both, but it has to be said that the law is not as clear as it might be. This imposes a considerable burden on the purchaser's solicitor to give clear advice to his client and to see that every effort is made to maximise protection of his client's position.

[4.11] At common law a "spec" builder, ie, one who builds a property on his own land and then sells it, was generally entitled to the full protection of the *caveat emptor* principle.[49] In the absence of an express warranty or some misrepresentation, the purchaser would usually find himself without a remedy,[50] but it would now seem that even a "spec" builder may find himself liable in negligence.[51] On the other hand, a "contract" builder, ie one who

---

[46.] The form of the agreement, or agreements, entered into by the purchaser may vary, see para **[11.08]** *et seq, post.*

[47.] The alternative is to ensure that there are express provisions covering the vendor's liability in the contract, see para **[4.19]** *infra.*

[48.] The distinction may not be as significant, at least in respect of tortious liability, as it used to be: see McMahon and Binchy, *Irish Law of Torts* (2nd ed, 1990), Ch 13. See also paras **[4.16]** and **[4.18]** *infra.*

[49.] *McGowan v Harrison* [1941] IR 331 at 337 (*per* Maguire P).

[50.] *Curling v Walsh* (1988) 6 ILT 184. But note the criticism of this rule, para **[4.12]** *infra.*

[51.] See para **[4.15]** *infra.*

builds the property in question under an agreement entered into with the purchaser, has always been regarded at common law as being in a different position. In particular, the courts have long regarded such a builder as being subject to an *implied* warranty as to the condition of the property being built.[52]

(i) Implied Warranty

[4.12] The general common law rule applicable to a builder is that, where he agrees to sell a plot of land and to build a house on it, or simply agrees to build a house on a plot already owned by the other party to the building agreement, he impliedly warrants that the house when built will be reasonably fit for human habitation.[53] In the case of a sale of a house in the course of erection, a similar implied warranty exists,[54] for, as Davitt P explained in *Brown v Norton*,[55] the cases established the propositions:

> "... that there should be implied a warranty that the house in each case would be completed and when completed would be reasonably fit for immediate occupation; that this warranty covered the work already done on the houses[56] at the dates respectively of the agreement to sell and the work to be done thereafter; and as regards what was already done it was a warranty that the work and material used was such that the house when complete would be reasonably fit for immediate occupation; that as regards what was to be done it was a warranty that the work and material was of that same quality; that as regards what was to be done there was the further warranty implied that the work would be done in a good and workmanlike manner and with materials of good quality and description ..."[57]

As regards the question of work covered by the warranty, this matter arose in a Northern Ireland case, *McGeary v Campbell*,[58] where the purchaser entered into a contract to buy the house when it was nearly completed (only joinery and electrical work remained to be done). It was argued that the warranty did

---

[52.] Such warranty may also arise expressly from some representation or assurance made by the vendor of property. See *O'Donoghue & Co Ltd v Collins* High Court, unrep, 10 March 1972 (1970 No 2771P); see also *De Lassalle v Guildford* [1901] 2 KB 215; *Miller v Cannon Hill Estates Ltd* [1931] 2 KB 213.

[53.] *Lawrence v Cassel* [1930] 2 KB 83; *Hancock v BW Brazier (Anerley) Ltd* [1966] 1 WLR 1317.

[54.] *Miller v Cannon Hill Estates Ltd* [1931] 2 KB 213, cited with approval in *Brown v Norton* [1954] IR 34 at 44 (*per* Davitt P). See also *Morris v Redmond* (1936) 70 ILTR 8.

[55.] [1954] IR 34, applied by McMahon J in *Johnson v Longleat Properties* [1976-7] ILRM 93. See also *Corrigan v Crofton* [1985] ILRM 189.

[56.] *McGeary v Campbell* [1975] NI 7 at 8 (*per* Lowry LCJ), see *infra*. See also *Hancock v BW Brazier (Anerley) Ltd* [1966] 1 WLR 1317.

[57.] *Op cit* p 52.

[58.] [1975] NI 7.

not cover defective foundations already completed, but Lowry LCJ rejected the argument in these terms:

> "I do not accept the contention, and I hold that, if any work remains to be done, the implied warranty in regard to houses to be built and being built applies to the house in every respect. To hold otherwise would be tantamount to saying that, where a house the subject of an agreement to purchase is in the course of erection, the intending purchaser has to inspect it in order to satisfy himself on two points, first to see what work remains to be done, since it is only with regard to that work that the builder implies a warranty of fitness, and secondly to make sure that, as far as the work has gone, the house suffers and will suffer from no defects attributable to its construction. This is plainly an impracticable idea - to such an extent, that, to apply the well-known test ..., no one would say as between men of business that such a term 'goes without saying', much less that it is necessary in order to give business efficacy to the contract. Were such a gloss to be placed on contracts to buy uncompleted houses, the purchaser could never in practice complain about defects due to bad foundations.
>
> Neither is it practicable to apply a different test in the case of almost finished houses compared with those which are only half finished. The real and only contrast is between completed and uncompleted houses."[59]

However, it appears to have been accepted at common law, and Lowry LCJ agreed, that this tripartite warranty (ie., in respect of (a) fitness for human habitation, (b) doing the work in a good and workmanlike manner and (c) use of good quality materials) did not apply in the case of a sale of a house already built at the date of the contract, even though the house was newly built and unoccupied up to that date.[60] This is, of course, the typical situation where a "spec" builder is involved.[61] Presumably the reason for this restriction in the scope of the implied warranty was that the purchaser had an opportunity to inspect a house already completed and so the general principle of *caveat emptor* could be applied without the harshness that would occur in the case of a building still to be completed. But Davitt P criticised this restriction, again in *Brown v Norton*, in the following terms:

> "I confess that I am unable to appreciate any difference in principle between cases on the one hand of a sale of a dwelling-house in the course of erection and the letting of a furnished dwellinghouse,[62] and on the other hand cases of the sale of a dwellinghouse unfurnished, if in all cases it is

---

[59] *Ibid*, p 8. See also *Jennings v Travener* [1955] 2 All ER 769.
[60] *Murray v Mace* (1872) IR 8 CL 396; *Doyle v Youell* (1938) 72 ILTR 253; *McGowan v Harrison* [1941] IR 331. See also *Hoskins v Woodham* [1938] 1 All ER 692.
[61] See para **[4.11]** *supra*.
[62] See para **[4.08]** *supra*.

clearly the common though unexpressed will of the parties that what the purchaser or lessee is contracting to acquire and the vendor or lessor is contracting to supply is a dwelling-house for the purchaser or lessee to live in at the earliest opportunity ... I doubt if a general rule against implying a warranty in cases within the second category can be supported in principle and suspect that if it exists it must rest solely upon authority ... When these cases are closely examined they appear to me not to afford a very solid support for a rule of such a general nature ..."[63]

He then concluded, albeit *obiter*:[64]

"I am strongly inclined to the opinion that the only general proposition which can be safely derived from the earlier authorities is that there is no rule of law which provides that, on the mere sale or letting of an unfurnished but completely built house, there shall be implied a warranty that it is reasonably fit for habitation. To say that in no case of such a sale or letting, no matter how compelling the circumstances, can a Court hold that such a warranty is implied seems to me to be a wholly different and very much wider proposition."[65]

In an earlier case, *McGowan v Harrison*,[66] Maguire P had held that there was no implied warranty of reasonable fitness for human habitation on the part of a building contractor who demised a newly erected house to the plaintiff in the action for a term of 500 years.[67]

[4.13] It is also clear that at common law any implied warranty is displaced by an express provision in the building contract,[68] for then the builder's duty is to comply with the terms of the agreement.[69] Thus in *Brown v Norton*[70] the

---

[63.] [1954] IR 34 at 54.

[64.] The actual decision in the case was that an express covenant in the agreement negatived any implied warranty, see para **[4.13]** *infra*.

[65.] *Op cit* p 55.

[66.] [1941] IR 331.

[67.] This point was not appealed to the Supreme Court, which held that such a sale by lease or underlease did not constitute a "contract for letting for habitation" so as to attract the implied condition that the house was reasonably fit for human habitation, and the undertaking by the landlord to keep it that way during the tenancy, provided by s 31(1) of the Housing (Misc Provs) Act 1931 (see now s 114 of the Housing Act 1966). See generally Wylie, *Irish Landlord and Tenant Law*, para 15.07.

[68.] *McGeary v Campbell* [1975] NI 7 at 7 (*per* Lowry LCJ). See also *Lynch v Thorne* [1956] 1 All ER 744; *King v Victor Parsons & Co* [1972] 2 All ER 625 (*aff'd* [1973] 1 WLR 29). *Cf Gloucestershire CC v Richardson* [1969] 1 AC 480. And see *Norta Wallpapers (Ir) Ltd v John Sisk & Son Ltd* [1987] IR 114.

[69.] Failure to comply with the express terms of the agreement will, of course, involve the builder in liability, see *Hancock v BW Brazier (Anerley) Ltd* [1966] 1 WLR 1317. See also *Murphy v Quality Homes* High Court, unep, 22 June 1976 (1975/4344P).

[70.] [1954] IR 34.

agreement relating to a house in the course of erection contained a clause in the following terms:

"The purchaser having inspected the building as it now stands will be taken as satisfied therewith, but should the purchaser require any additions or alterations to be made or any work to be done that is not at present contemplated he agrees to pay the additional cost of such work."

Davitt P held that this express term negatived any implied warranty, in relation to work done at the date of the agreement, that the quality of that work and of the materials used was such that the house, when completed, would be reasonably fit for immediate occupation as a residence. Thus it would seem that a purchaser may be debarred from suing on the implied warranty where the contract contains express provisions as to how the house is to be built, and as to the materials to be used,[71] and the builder complies with these, even though a defect still results.[72] Though the English courts have construed the express terms of such building agreements very strictly and have held that the implied warranty may still be invoked by a purchaser where, eg, the builder adopts an improved, but different, specification from that in the contract.[73] They have also construed strictly exemption clauses in building agreements, so that, eg, a provision that a habitation certificate was to be "conclusive evidence" of completion of a house was held not to bar an action in respect of structural defects.[74] Similarly, a clause rendering the builder liable for defects notified within a specified time was held not to prevent the purchaser from relying on the implied warranty at a later stage, nor to prevent an action for damages with respect to defects discovered within the time limit.[75]

(ii) Negligence

[4.14] Quite apart from any remedy a purchaser of a new building may have under the warranties implied at common law, there is the possibility of a remedy in tort on the ground of negligence. This remedy may become vital where the building has been transferred before a defect comes to light, because it is clear that the original purchaser only can sue on an implied

---

71. See, eg, *O'Donoghue & Co Ltd v Collins* High Court, unrep, 10 March 1972 (1970\2771P). *Cf Hugh O'Neill & Co Ltd v Roche* High Court, unrep, 19 January 1972 (1970\722P). See further on the contents of building agreements, paras **[11.08-24]** *post*.
72. *Lynch v Thorne* [1956] 1 WLR 303. *Cf* where the builder designs the building: See *Basildon District Council v J E Lesser (Properties) Ltd* [1985] QB 839.
73. *King v Victor Parsons & Co* [1972] 1 WLR 801 (*aff'd* [1973] 1 WLR 29).
74. *Billyack v Leyland Construction Co Ltd* [1968] 1 WLR 471. *Cf Perks v Stern* (1972) 222 Est Gaz 1441.
75. *Hancock v BW Brazier (Anerley) Ltd* [1966] 1 WLR 1317.

warranty, since he alone is a party to the contract in which it is implied. Unfortunately the application of the tort of negligence to builders has been a very controversial issue in recent decades.[76]

[4.15] The original view of the judges was that a vendor was not liable in tort for defects in his property rendering it dangerous or unfit for habitation, even though the defects were due to his negligence.[77] In *Otto v Bolton*,[78] this principle was held not to be affected by *Donoghue v Stevenson*.[79] In the *Otto* case it was held that a builder of a new house was not liable when, after completion of the house, a ceiling collapsed and injured the purchaser's mother. However, a sign of a change of attitude on the part of the judges was given by the decision of the Northern Ireland Court of Appeal in *Gallagher v McDowell Ltd*.[80] In that case a dwelling-house was erected by the defendants, a firm of building contractors, for the then Northern Ireland Housing Trust[81] and on completion was inspected and passed by the Trust's architect. Six days later the plaintiff and her husband, the first tenant, went into occupation and eighteen months later the plaintiff was injured when the heel of an ordinary high-heeled shoe went through a hole in a floor. Expert evidence established that the hole had been repaired by insertion of a wooden plug, but that this was not a proper method of repair and that the plug had not been fitted in a workmanlike manner. The Court of Appeal held that the building contractors owed a duty of care in repairing the hole to the plaintiff as a lawful user of the house they had constructed.[82] However, the Court made clear that its decision was confined to cases where the builder was a contractor only and was not to be taken as disputing the immunity of a "spec" builder who was also the owner of the house sold or let.[83] This distinction between a builder and a builder-owner was accepted later in England,[84] but was much criticised by the English Law Commission in a Report issued in 1970 recommending abolition altogether of the immunity

---

76. See McMahon and Binchy, *Irish Law of Torts* (2nd ed, 1990), Ch 13.
77. *Bottomley v Bannister* [1932] 1 KB 458. See also *Travers v Gloucester Corp* [1947] KB 71.
78. [1936] 2 KB 46. The decision seems to have been recognised by Irish judges, see *McGowan v Harrison* [1941] IR 331; *Brown v Norton* [1954] IR 34.
79. [1932] AC 562, wherein cases like *Bottomley* were distinguished as relating to real property as opposed to chattels, see at pp 598 (*per* Lord Atkin) and 609 (*per* Lord MacMillan).
80. [1961] NI 26.
81. Since replaced by the Northern Ireland Housing Executive, see Housing Executive Act (NI) 1971.
82. They were also held not to be absolved on the ground of there being a reasonable possibility of intermediate examination or inspection of the property, since they could not reasonably have anticipated that the Trust's architect's inspection would expose the danger in question.
83. See espec [1961] NI 26 at 38 (*per* Lord MacDermott LCJ). See also para **[4.11]** *supra*.
84. *Sharpe v ET Sweeting & Sons Ltd* [1963] 2 All ER 455.

of builders from negligence liability.[85] This Report led to the enactment in England of the Defective Premises Act 1972.[86] As it happened, while the Bill which became the English 1972 Act was being considered in Parliament at Westminster, the English Court of Appeal held in *Dutton v Bognor Regis United Building Co Ltd*[87] by a majority of two to one,[88] that a builder who created a defect in property was not absolved from liability for negligence merely because he was the owner of the premises built.[89] And it seems that the majority took the view that the builder's duty was owed to successive purchasers of the property, unless the "proximity" was broken by an intermediate inspection or opportunity of inspection that ought to have disclosed the defect,[90] and extended to cover economic as well as physical loss, eg, diminution in the value of the premises due to the defects.[91] The Court as a whole held also that, where a local council's bye-laws required approval of the foundations of a building by its building inspector, the building inspector owed a duty of care to successive purchasers since any defect in the foundations might not come to light until damage appeared perhaps decades later, and the council were liable for his negligence in passing defective foundations. A similar ruling against a council was subsequently made in Northern Ireland in *McGeary v Campbell*,[92] where Lowry LCJ said:

"... once the Council assumes the responsibility of controlling building, it owes a general duty of care to those who may be affected by its decisions."[93]

And the *Dutton* case was approved by the House of Lords in *Anns v Merton London Borough Council*.[94] In the *Anns* case, the Lords held unanimously that a local authority exercising its statutory functions and duties under the public health legislation in respect of buildings may be held liable for

---

[85.] *Report on the Civil Liability of Vendors and Lessors for Defective Premises* (Law Com No 40), espec at paras 38-47. *Cf* the Law Reform Commissions Working Paper No 1, *The Law relating to the Liability of Builders, Vendors and Lessors for the Quality and Fitness of Premises* (1977) and *Report on Defective Premises* (LRC 3 - 1982).

[86.] It was followed in NI by the Defective Premises (NI) Order 1975.

[87.] [1972] 1 QB 373. *Cf* as regards a contractor doing work on another's land, *AC Billings & Son Ltd v Riden* [1958] AC 240.

[88.] Lord Denning MR and Sachs LJ, Stamp LJ dissenting on this point.

[89.] Thus overruling *Otto v Bolton* [1936] 2 KB 46 and refusing to follow *Bottomley v Bannister* [1932] 1 KB 458.

[90.] [1972] 1 QB 373 at 396 (*per* Lord Denning MR) and at 404-5 (*per* Sachs LJ).

[91.] *Ibid*, pp 396 (*per* Lord Denning MR) and at 403-4 (*per* Sachs LJ).

[92.] [1975] NI 7.

[93.] *Ibid*, p 9.

[94.] [1977] 2 All ER 492.

negligent inspection of foundations, or for failure to take reasonable care to see that its bye-laws are complied with. This duty of care is owed to all future tenants or assignees of the property in question. In *Sparkam-Souter v Town and Country Developments (Essex) Ltd*,[95] the English Court of Appeal held that in such an action against a council for negligent approval of foundations, the cause of action accrues and the limitation period begins to run only when the owner of the premises discovers the defects, or with reasonable diligence ought to have discovered them. This decision was also approved by the House of Lords in the *Anns* case, where it was held that causes of action in respect of damage which did not become apparent until more than six years after the negligent inspection by the council were not statute-barred. Since then the story in England has been one of retrenchment. In particular the House of Lords has reiterated the distinction between a claim for personal injury caused by the defective building and one for damage to or loss of value in the building itself, ie, pure economic loss. In respect of the latter, the English judges have now set their faces against recovery in tort for negligence, whether the claim is made against the builder or the local authority regulating building operations.[96]

[4.16] In Ireland the position of a purchaser of defective premises may be stronger, but it is difficult to be firm on this point because the courts have yet to consider the retrenchment which has recently occurred in England. So far as the builder is concerned, liability in tort for negligence in respect of economic loss was recognised by Costello J in *Ward v McMaster*.[97] On an appeal to the Supreme Court in that case, it was held that such loss could also be recovered against the housing authority which failed to carry out its statutory duty to make a proper valuation of the premises for loan purposes.[98] This followed the approach taken previously by the Supreme Court in *Siney v Dublin Corporation*[99] in relation to carrying out its statutory

---

95. [1976] 2 All ER 65. *Cf Pirelli General Cable Works Ltd v Oscar Faber & Partners* [1983] 2 AC 1.
96. *Murphy v Brentwood District Council* [1990] 2 All ER 908. See also *Curran v Northern Ireland Co-owner Housing Association Ltd* [1987] 2 All ER 13: *D & F Estates Ltd v Church Commissioners for England and Wales* [1988] AC 177. Note, however, that the Privy Council (comprising four Law Lords) has recently upheld the contrary view of the New Zealand courts, as applicable in that jurisdiction: see *Invercargill City Council v Hamlin* [1996] 1 All ER 756.
97. [1985] IR 29. This point was not appealed to the Supreme Court [1988] IR 337. Costello J had refused to follow *Colgan v Connolly Construction Co (Ir) Ltd* [1980] ILRM 33, where McMahon J held that damages for defects in the quality of the premises were not recoverable in negligence unless personal injury or damage to health was involved.
98. In accordance with s 39 of the Housing Act 1966. This is in line with the views of the New Zealand courts recently upheld by the Privy council in the *Inverscargill* case, fn 96 *supra*.
99. [1980] IR 400.

duties when letting premises to tenants.[100] However, in *Sunderland v Louth Co Council*[101] the Court held that this principle did not apply to a planning authority. The reason for holding that a duty of care did not arise in such cases was explained by McCarthy J in these terms:

> "The fundamental difference between what may be called planning legislation and housing legislation is that the first is regulatory or licensing according to the requirements of the proper planning and development of the area but the second is a provision in a social context for those who are unable to provide for themselves; if they are unable to provide for themselves then the duty on the provider reaches the role that would be taken by professional advisers engaged on behalf of the beneficiary. This is in marked contrast to the watchdog role that is created under the Planning Act, a watchdog role that is for the benefit of the public at large. This is emphasised by the existence of the appeals procedure, formally to the relevant minister of the government, assigned by him to a junior minister, and since 1976 carried out by the planning appeals board (An Bord Pleanala). The latter body has a national jurisdiction but must still deal with any planning appeal by the test of local standards - the proper planning and development of the area. It would follow from the plaintiffs' argument that there would be imposed upon the planning appeals board in the case of an application for retention of a dwelling house constructed without permission, a duty to carry out an examination of the drainage system including the suitability of the soil, presumably irrespective of whether or not the applicant for such permission had done so. Such a duty would lie upon the board as much in the case of a large scale housing development, and, presumably separately in respect of each house, as it would for a single development such as here. The liability, whether it be of the planning authority or of the planning appeals board, would remain indefinitely towards any occupier.
>
> I point to these consequences, not *in terrorem*, but rather to seek to identify on a reasonable approach the intention of the legislature in enacting the relevant parts of the Planning Act. That Act was to make provision, in the interest of the common good, for the proper planning and development of cities, towns and other areas, whether urban or rural; the Act permits the making of building regulations, which, if they had existed, might well enure to the benefit of the plaintiffs. There are no such regulations relevant to County Louth.

[100.] Again under the Housing Act 1966. *Siney* was followed by the Supreme Court in *Coleman v Dundalk Urban District Council* Supreme Court, unrep, 17 July 1985 (1980\6902P) and *Burke v Dublin Corporation* [1991] IR 341. See Wylie, *Irish Landlord and Tenant Law*, para 15.08.

[101.] [1990] ILRM 658.

Conclusion

The Act in conferring statutory powers on planning authorities imposed on them a duty towards the public at large. In my view, in conferring those powers, the Oireachtas did not include a purpose of protecting persons who occupy buildings erected in the functional area of planning authorities from the sort of damage which the plaintiffs have suffered. This being so, the Council, in the exercise of those powers, owed no duty of care at common law towards the plaintiffs. It follows that the claim must fail and the appeal be dismissed."[102]

[4.17] A particular problem which arises in respect of a defective buildings is the fact that the defect (eg in the original foundations) may lie hidden for many years, during which period the building may change ownership several times. When the defect comes to light (eg when cracks appear in walls) the owner at that time may find that his claim for negligence against the builder is met with the defence that it is statute barred.[103] Courts the world over have struggled with the problem of "latent" damage.[104] In Ireland, the problem was resolved where the claim is for *personal injuries* by Statute of Limitations (Amendment) Act 1991, which introduces a "discoverability" test[105] by which the limitation period runs from the "date of knowledge" of the cause of action if this is later than the date of accrual.[106] The 1991 Act does *not* apply to a claim for *property* damage and it is not clear whether the Irish courts will adopt the approach of other jurisdictions of applying a similar date of knowledge rule.[107] In *Morgan v Park Developments Ltd*[108] Carroll J stated, albeit *obiter*,[109] that in property damage cases a date of knowledge or date of discoverability rule was to be preferred, arguing that the presumption of constitutionality pointed to interpreting the Statute of Limitations in such a way as to avoid "harsh and absurd" results. However, this constitutional argument has not found favour with other judges[110] and the Supreme Court insisted on applying the statute strictly in *Hegarty v O'Loughran*.[111] Similarly, in *Tuohy v Courtney (No 1)*,[112] a purchaser of a

---

[102.] *Ibid* p 663.

[103.] See Statute of Limitations 1957, s 11(2) (6 year period for tort actions).

[104.] See the discussion in Brady and Kerr, *The Limitation of Actions* (2nd ed, 1994), Ch 3.

[105.] Following the Law Reform Commission's *Report on the Statute of Limitations: Claims in respect of Latent Personal Injuries* (LRC 21 - 1987).

[106.] See Brady and Kerr, *op cit* p 74 *et seq*.

[107.] Eg see the Supreme Court of Canada decision in *City of Kamloops v Neilsen* (1984) 10 DLR (4th) 641. *Cf* the English House of Lords decision in *Pirelli General Cable Works Ltd v Oscar Faber & Partners* [1983] 2 AC 1. See Brady and Kerr, *op cit* p 79 *et seq*.

[108.] [1983] ILRM 156.

[109.] The claim was held to be statute barred whatever rule was applied.

[110.] See, eg, Finlay J in *Cahill v Sutton* [1980] IR 269 (a personal injury case).

[111.] [1990] 1 IR 148. See also *Tuohy v Courtney (No 2)* [1994] 3 IR 1.

[112.] [1994] 2 ILRM 503.

house, who believed when he bought it in 1978 that he was acquiring a freehold interest, whereas it was in fact a leasehold interest with less than 30 years to run, had his action, based on a summons issued when he discovered the truth, in 1987, against his solicitor for negligence dismissed by Blayney J on the ground that the cause of action was barred by the Statute of Limitations 1957.[113]

[4.18] There is one further point to be emphasised about negligence claims by a purchaser or subsequent owner of a defective building. This is that the builder is not the only possible defendant. We saw earlier that the local authority may be open to a claim on the basis that it acted in breach of its statutory duties.[114] Apart from such a claim, it is, of course, possible that a claim may be made successfully against professional people involved in the building for breach of professional duty of care, such as architects, engineers and surveyors.[115] Such an action lies notwithstanding that a claim may also lie in contract.[116]

2. Building Agreement

[4.19] A purchaser's position will clearly be affected by any agreement he may have entered into with the builder of the property. The operation of building agreements is a subject which we consider later,[117] but a few points may be stressed at this stage. First, the purchaser's solicitor must scrutinise the agreement carefully to see to what extent it modifies the purchaser's common law rights.[118] He must also check the extent to which it incorporates or is intended to operate alongside the Law Society's *General Conditions of Sale*.[119] Care must be taken, especially in major developments, over collateral warranties intended to benefit subsequent purchasers, both in terms of ensuring that they are going to be procured from all appropriate parties and in terms of their scope.[120] Failure to attend to these matters

---

[113.] In subsequent proceedings, *Tuohy v Courtney (No 2)* (fn 111 *supra*) Lynch J held that time ran at the earliest from the date the plaintiff's solicitor returned the duplicate contracts for sale signed by him on the plaintiff's behalf or at the latest from the date of the closing of the sale. An appeal was dismissed by the Supreme Court, unrep, 26 July 1994 (338/345/1992).

[114.] See para **[4.15]** *supra*.

[115.] See *Quinn v Quality Homes Ltd* [1976-7] ILRM 314; *Buckley v Lynch* [1978] IR 6; *Flanagan v Griffith* High Court, unrep, 26 January 1985 (1981\12174P); *Crowley v Allied Irish Banks Ltd* [1987] IR 282; *Sunderland v McGreavey* [1987] IR 372 (*aff'd* on a different point by the Supreme Court, *sub nom Sunderland v Louth Co Council* [1990] ILRM 658).

[116.] *Finlay v Murtagh* [1979] IR 249. See also *Holt v Payne Skillington*, London Times, 22 December 1995, [1995] EGCS 201.

[117.] See para **[11.08]** *post*.

[118.] See para **[11.15]** *post*.

[119.] All too often these are not properly incorporated or there is an inconsistency in the provisions: see para **[11.13]** *post*.

[120.] See para **[11.22]** *post*.

adequately can greatly reduce the protection the original and subsequent purchasers may obtain from an express building agreement.

C. Protection of Purchaser

[4.20] In view of what has been said in the previous paragraphs about the scope of the *caveat emptor* principle, and, in particular, in view of present uncertainty in Ireland of the rules governing liability for defects in new buildings, something further should be said about securing protection for a prospective purchaser.

1. Inspection and Independent Survey

[4.21] The most obvious way in which a purchaser can seek to protect himself against defects in the physical condition of the property is to inspect it before he enters into a contract for its purchase. Failure to do this will not prevent him from being fixed with constructive notice of any "act or thing" which would have come to his knowledge if such "inspections had been made as ought reasonably to have been made by him."[121] Thus most conveyancers take the view that an inspection of the property by the purchaser, or someone on his behalf, prior to the contract is the very minimum of what ought to be done, for it will at least reveal obvious defects in the physical condition of the property.[122] The question remains, however, as to when something further ought to be done, such as the commissioning of an independent survey of the property.[123] The point is that the purchaser, as a layman, may well miss on his own inspection several signs of defects which would be obvious to an expert, such as a qualified architect, surveyor or engineer. This is a particular problem where the property in question is some decades old, for then problems relating to dampness in walls, dry and wet rot in woodwork, defective roof timber and weaknesses in foundations are fairly common.

[4.22] Conveyancers in the past have tended to adopt different views on the need for an independent survey according to the circumstances of each case. One generally accepted rule-of-thumb was that the older the property the more likely it was that a survey should be made on behalf of the purchaser. A survey should also usually be made in cases where the purchaser proposed to engage in building or reconstruction operations on the property. On the

---

[121.] Conveyancing Act 1882, s 3(1)(i), see para **[4.02]** *supra*.

[122.] It may also reveal the existence of occupants other than the vendor, about whom further enquiries may become necessary, see the discussion in *Carroll v Keayes* (1873) IR 8 Eq 97. See also para **[9.23]** *post*.

[123.] See para **[3.41]** *ante*.

other hand, a survey was often dispensed with where the property was comparatively modern, eg, built in the past twenty-five years, and the purchaser proposes to continue the existing use of the property. The classic example of such a case is a modern dwelling-house which has always been used as a private residence and which the purchaser proposes to use in the same way. Indeed, the view is often given that, since in such a case the purchaser is often borrowing the purchase money from an institution which will insist upon its own independent survey, the purchaser can rely, albeit indirectly, upon that survey, especially since he usually has to meet the cost of it! However, as we have pointed out before, care must be taken on this point, for a number of reasons.[124]

[4.23] A survey commissioned by a lending institution, eg, a building society, is made, primarily, for its purposes, ie, as a prospective mortgagee concerned about the value of its security rather than as a prospective purchaser concerned about the state of the property he intends to occupy as his home. Of course, defects discovered in the property will often affect both parties, but some may have a significance of a greater or lesser degree according to the different interests of the parties. However, increasingly in recent years the courts on both sides of the Irish Sea have taken the view that the position may be different where the lending institution makes its survey report available to a prospective purchaser and is aware that the latter is going to rely upon it. Thus in *Martin v Irish Industrial Benefit Society*[125] a Circuit Court Judge in Ireland held the Society liable in negligence to a purchaser[126] who had obtained, by arrangement with its secretary and on payment of a fee, an assessor's report of a house printed on the Society's form. She bought the house on the strength of this report, but it turned out to be structurally defective and she thereby incurred repair expenses. In *Ward v McMaster*[127] the Supreme Court held that a housing authority owed a duty under the Housing Act 1966 to ensure that, by a proper valuation by an expert, a house was adequate security for the loan it was making.[128] It should

---

[124.] In 1992 the Law Society's Conveyancing Committee recommended that *every* purchaser should be advised *in writing* to have not only the structure but also vital services like a septic tank checked out by a qualified engineer or architect: See *Gazette*, March 1992, p 71. *Cf O'Connor v First National Building Society* [1991] ILRM 208, para **[4.24]** *infra*.

[125.] [1960] Ir Jur Rep 42.

[126.] Though not a member of the Society, she had had money on deposit with it and withdrew it to purchase the house in question.

[127.] [1988] IR 337. *Cf Curran v Northern Ireland Co-Ownership Housing Association Ltd* [1987] NI 80.

[128.] The claim for negligence against the valuer employed by the authority failed on the ground that he was an auctioneer with no expertise in building construction; see [1985] IR 29 at 54 (*per* Costello J). *Cf Yianni v Edwin Evans & Sons* [1982] QB 373.

have anticipated that the purchaser/borrower would rely on this.[129] It should be noted, however, that the Supreme Court recognised that the housing authority could have excluded this duty by a suitably worded clause in its loan documentation,[130] similar to that commonly used by building societies.[131]

[4.24] The risk that the lending institution will seek to exclude its liability reinforces the duty of the purchaser's solicitor to advise his client of the need to consider having an independent survey made by an appropriate expert. A failure so to advise the client opens the solicitor to liability for negligence. In *O'Connor v First National Building Society*[132] Lynch J accepted the submission of counsel that:

> "... there can be no absolute rule of law that a solicitor must always advise a purchaser that he ought to have an independent inspection of the property by a suitably qualified person."[133]

However, having received evidence as to established practice from the Law Society's Conveyancing Committee, he concluded that:

> "such a duty *prima facie* arises and it is for a solicitor who contends that no such duty arose in any particular case to show circumstances such as those mentioned by counsel for the second defendants by way of illustration if he is to negative the existence of the duty."[134]

Those circumstances given by way of illustration were the case where the purchaser was himself an architect and had carried out his own inspection of the property.[135] However, the onus rests on the solicitor and the *O'Connor* case illustrates how heavy a one it is. The purchaser in that case appeared to be connected with the building trade and the solicitor mistakenly assumed it was not necessary to advise him of the desirability of an independent survey. In fact the purchaser was a retired CIE bus driver and no more than a DIY enthusiast, so Lynch J held the solicitor liable in negligence. It is suggested,

---

129. The English courts have taken a similar view in relation to building society loans: see *Smith v Eric s Bush* and *Harris v Wyre Forest District Council* [1989] 2 All ER 514. See also *Sneesby v Goldings* [1995] 36 EG 136; *Ezekiel v McDade* [1995] 47 EG 150.

130. *Op cit* pp 342 (*per* Henchy J) and 346 (*per* McCarthy J).

131. See *O'Connor v First National Building Society* [1991] ILRM 208, where Lynch J held the Society absolved from liability by the following clause in its loan application form:

> "(8) No responsibility can be accepted by the Society for the condition of the property."

132. *Ibid*.

133. Thus the recommendation made by the Law Society's Conveyancing Committee in 1992 (see para **[4.22]** fn 124 *supra*) may be said to go too far, but arguably it is better to be safe than sorry and should be followed unless there is clear justification for not doing so.

134. *Op cit* p 214.

135. *Op cit* p 213.

therefore, that the purchaser's solicitor ought, at the very least, in every case to advise his client in writing of the wisdom of having an independent survey done, unless he knows that his client has the necessary expertise to carry one out himself or one has already been put in hand.

2. HomeBond Scheme

[4.25] This is the latest version of the scheme introduced in 1978 by the Construction Industry Federation, with the approval of the Department of the Environment. The National House Building Guarantee Scheme (as it was called) was originally designed to give purchasers of new dwelling houses[136] a guarantee against "major structural defects" arising within six years of completion. Part of the protection lay in the inspection carried out by a DOE inspector during the dwelling's construction and the final survey report by such an inspector when it was completed, on the basis of which the NHBGS issued a Guarantee Certificate. This was a welcome attempt to protect purchasers of new houses and was given added force when in 1979 the Building Societies Association announced that, as from 1 January 1980, its members would not normally advance mortgage loans in respect of new dwellings unless they were covered by the Scheme.[137] Nevertheless, the Scheme was of limited value and its shortcomings were highlighted by a number of interested bodies.[138] Chief amongst these was the lack of cover for "minor" structural and non-structural defects, cover for 6 years only, no protection against insolvency of the builder during construction, protection under the scheme only if remedies against the builder had been exhausted and a low limit (originally £15,000) on recovery in respect of any one dwelling and in respect of any one builder (originally £250,000). Over time, some of these shortcomings have been addressed. For example, as from 1 October 1990 the Scheme was extended to indemnify purchasers against loss of deposits paid to builders[139] up to a maximum of £20,000 or 15% of the purchase price, whichever was the lesser. At the same time the limit of

---

136. Including bungalows, maisonettes and flats, plus any garage, an integral part of the structure.

137. Later the Association made it clear that this applied even to "once off" houses being built by builders or direct labour: see the *Gazette*, March 1983.

138. Eg Law Reform Commission in its Working Paper No 1, *The Law relating to the Liability of Builders, Vendors and Lessors for the Quality and Fitness of Premises* (1977). See also the Dublin Solicitor's Bar Association's warnings first issued in the *Gazette*, May 1978 and reproduced in the Law Society's *Conveyancing Handbook*, Ch 5.

139. The risk of loss of "booking" deposits was highlighted in para 10.134 of the 1st edition of this book (see para **[11.17]** *post*) and confirmed by the Supreme Court in *Re Barrett Apartments Ltd* [1985] IR 350; see especially McCarthy J at p 361. The need for solicitors to take steps to safeguard clients was highlighted by *Roche v Peilow* [1985] IR 232 (negligence not to make a companies search against the builder: see para **[15.48]** *post*); *cf Desmond v Brophy* [1985] IR 449: see para **[3.15]** *ante*.

recovery in respect of any one dwelling was extended to £30,000 and cover for serious non-structural defects was provided for 2 years, in addition to the 6 year guarantee for structural defects.

[4.26] As from 26 January 1995 the NHBGS has operated under the HomeBond mark and symbol, with some significant changes to the level of protection conferred on the purchaser. The 6-year structural guarantee has been extended to 10 years,[140] which incorporates the 2 years cover for non-structural defects first introduced in 1990.[141] A Stage Payment Bond replaces the old Deposit Cover Certificate and increases the indemnity to 50% of the purchase price or £35,000 (whichever is the lesser) *after* the Final Notice has been issued following a Main Structural Inspection found acceptable by HomeBond.[142] This extra protection in the later stages of construction is designed to cover things like stage payments made to the builder, as opposed to, eg, a booking deposit paid at the beginning of, or even prior to, construction. The 10-year structural guarantee runs from the date of the Final Notice (Form HB11), which is a vital document which should be kept with other title documents.

[4.27] The HomeBond Scheme also involves a number of changes in documentation and procedures. Under the NHBGS three major documents were issued to purchasers - the House Purchaser's Agreement (Form HG5), the Deposit Cover Certificate (Form HG4) and the Guarantee Certificate (Form HG6). These are now replaced by one document - the Guarantee Agreement (Form HB10) - issued as dwellings are registered by the builder. The Guarantee Agreement has two schedules, one containing the Stage Payment Bond and the other the 10-year Guarantee Certificate. So far as claims procedures are concerned it remains the case that the builder is primarily responsible for remedying major defects in the first two years. The purchaser can resort to HomeBond only if the builder fails to act. As regards years three to ten, the builder has the option within 60 days of remedying the defect, otherwise HomeBond is responsible. The claim must still be submitted to the builder to enable him to choose the option of remedying the defect and he must be allowed access to carry out the work.

[4.28] It must be reiterated that the HomeBond Scheme is no panacea for purchasers of new dwellings and many of the warnings issued in respect of the NHBGS remain valid. The Scheme still does not cover many non-structural defects which commonly can affect a new building or items installed, such as the central heating system or a lift or swimming pool. The

---

[140.] This period of cover has long been the cover provided by the English NHBC Scheme.

[141.] Eg water and smoke penetration.

[142.] Prior to this the previous indemnity limits still apply.

financial limits on recovery will often prove to be inadequate in these inflationary times. A trap which subsequent purchasers must avoid is the rule that no cover applies to any successor to the original purchaser in respect of a major defect which his predecessor knew or ought to have known about or which a reasonable examination by a competent surveyor, architect, or engineer would have disclosed. Solicitors acting for such a subsequent purchaser of a dwelling still covered by the 10-year guarantee should, therefore, ensure that enquiries are made of the existing owner[143] as to whether a defect exists in respect of which a claim should be made *before* his client acquires title.[144] Given the importance of this matter, it is considered that this is another reason why the purchaser should be advised to have his own independent survey done,[145] to ensure that he knows whether to insist upon a claim being lodged before he contracts to buy the property, or at the latest, before he closes the purchase.[146]

[143.] The questions on the Law Society's *Objections and Requisitions on Title* (1996 ed) form are arguably not detailed enough in this regard, since they simply ask whether the property is registered and, if so, request the furnishing of the Guarantee Certificate/Final Notice: see para **[16.08]** *post*.

[144.] Presumably, "shall have acquired title" refers to closing of the sale, which is the earliest date when the purchaser acquires a legal title (in the case of registered land, of course, the legal title is not acquired until the purchaser is registered as the new owner): see para **[20.44]** *post*). The purchaser will usually acquire an equitable interest from the date of the contract, see para **[12.02]** *post*.

[145.] See para **[4.23]** *supra* and para **[5.10]** *post*.

[146.] See fn 144 *supra*.

Chapter 5

PRE-CONTRACT ENQUIRIES OR REQUISITIONS

[5.01] It was stated in an earlier chapter that one of the most significant developments in conveyancing practice in Ireland in recent years has been a move towards *pre*-contract enquiries or requisitions.[1] This practice has been encouraged by the Law Society's Conveyancing Committee, but the Committee has held back from recommending a wholesale shift to *pre*-contract enquiries such as that which became evident in England some decades ago[2] and away from extensive *post*-contract requisitions on title. Instead, the Committee has recommended a more selective approach, which may involve bringing forward to the *pre*-contract stage requisitions which would otherwise be raised *post*-contract as part of the traditional investigation of title.[3] The extent to which this should be done, must remain a matter of professional judgment for the purchaser's solicitor. Much must depend upon the particular property being acquired by the client and the nature of the transaction being engaged in.

[5.02] It will be noted that the title of this chapter refers to enquiries *or* requisitions in the alternative. The point here is that the expression "requisitions" does have a technical meaning. According to traditional conveyancing theory it refers to the raising of queries as part of the *post*-contract investigation of title which "requires" a response from the vendor. That requirement stems from the fact that at this stage of the transaction a contract exists between the parties, under which the vendor has an obligation[4] to show good title to the property, the subject of the contract.[5] A failure by the vendor to provide an adequate response would, in most circumstances,[6] justify the purchaser rescinding the contract. For this reason,

---

1. See para **[1.29]** *ante*.
2. See Wickenden and Edell, 'The Practitioners' Inquisition' (1961) Conv 336. See also Annand and Cain, *Conveyancing Solutions 1: Enquiries Before Contract* (1986).
3. See Ch 15 *post*.
4. There is judicial uncertainty as to whether the obligation is an implied term in the contract or derives from a rule of law: see para **[14.08]** *post*.
5. See para **[14.09]** *post*. Note that the Law Society's standard contract form contains a definition of "Requisitions" for the purposes of the contract: see *General Conditions of Sale (1995 ed)*, cond 2.
6. Note, however, the vendor's right of rescission under cond 18 of the Law Society's *General Conditions of Sale (1995 ed)*: see para **[15.25]** *et seq, post*.

the vendor and his solicitor must treat such requisitions with the utmost care. On the other hand, enquiries or "requisitions" raised at the *pre*-contract stage of a conveyancing transaction are necessarily of a quite different order. At this stage, there is no contract between the parties, and therefore, no obligations owed to one another. Even though the purchaser's solicitor extracts parts of the Law Society's standard *Objections and Requisitions on Title* form and purports to furnish these to the vendor's solicitor as "requisitions", they are nothing of the sort. Since the vendor has no contract with the purchaser, he is under no obligation to respond. At this stage he has no duty to show good title to the property and may stand on the fundamental principle of *caveat emptor*, according to which he has no duty to disclose details of the property.[7] Indeed, as is discussed later,[8] the fact that a full response to such *pre*-contract enquiries or "requisitions" may result in, eg, some innocent misrepresentation which justifies the purchaser rescinding later any contract entered into,[9] suggests that the vendor and his solicitor should exercise extreme caution over any response. However, as with so much of conveyancing and commercial practice, common sense and a recognition of practical realities of the parties' position must come into play. The vendor and his solicitor must appreciate that the raising of *pre*-contract enquiries or requisitions is now considered "good practice" in appropriate circumstances. It is part of the process of deciding whether the purchaser ought to commit himself to a binding contract. If the vendor insists on standing on his strict legal position by refusing to respond to such enquiries or requisitions, the inevitable consequence in most cases will be that the purchaser will abandon negotiations and refuse to enter into the contract. Indeed, it would be negligent of the purchaser's solicitor in such circumstances at the very least not to advise his client of the dangers of proceeding.[10] The position in practice is, therefore, that the purchaser's solicitor must persist in making such enquiries and raising such "requisitions" as are appropriate in the particular case and the vendor's solicitor must see that a proper response is made in order to secure the sale or other transaction sought by his client, taking care to see that no inaccurate or misleading statements are made which may ultimately jeopardise the transaction or give rise to a claim for damages.

[5.03] The remaining paragraphs of this chapter deal with two matters. First, they discuss the various *pre*-contract enquiries or requisitions which are commonly made or should be made nowadays. It must be reiterated that

---

7. See Ch 4 *ante*.
8. Para **[5.20]** *et seq, infra*.
9. See para **[5.26]** *infra*.
10. See para **[1.34]** *et seq, ante*. Indeed, many solicitors would go further and seek warranties from the vendor on certain matters: see para **[5.26]** *infra*.

these vary according to the nature of the property and the transaction to be entered into. What is appropriate in the particular case is a matter to be considered by the purchaser's solicitor. It should also be noted that the discussion is largely confined to enquiries or requisitions and does not deal with "searches" in the sense of searches in registries, such as the Land Registry and Registry of Deeds. Such searches traditionally form part of the *post*-contract investigation of title.[11] However, as will be mentioned in later paragraphs, the purchaser's solicitor may consider it appropriate to make some searches prior to the contract in, for example, the Companies Offices, where the vendor is a company,[12] or the Sheriff's Office, where leasehold property is being acquired.[13] Planning searches should be made prior to the contract in any case where works may have been done to the property requiring planning permission or compliance with related legislation like the Fire Services Act 1981. It should also be remembered that many years ago[14] the Law Society's Conveyancing Committee recommended that the vendor should not only furnish with the draft contract any searches in the vendor's possession but also requisition a negative search against himself and other parties immediately on title. Failure by the vendor to lodge such a requisition at this stage will usually result in searches not being ready at closing and the need for hand searches to be made then, with the consequent risk of delays and additional expense.[15] The Society's standard contract form contains a "Searches Schedule" which refers to the recommended practice and should remind practitioners to comply with it. Regrettably it is all too often ignored.

[5.04] The other matter dealt with is the remedies available to the purchaser where inaccurate or misleading replies are given by the vendor or his solicitor acting on his behalf. As mentioned above, the existence of these should make the vendor and his solicitor deal with the enquiries or requisitions in a careful manner.

I. ENQUIRIES OR REQUISITIONS

[5.05] The enquiries to be made or requisitions to be raised in a particular case will vary according to its circumstances. As we shall see, use may be made of the form recommended and recently revised by the Law Society's

---

11. See para **[15.39]** *et seq, post. Cf* planning searches, para **[5.06]** *infra.*

12. See para **[15.48]** *post.* Such a search is also important where there is a management company involved in the building in which a flat, apartment, unit or other property being acquired is situated: see para **[16.97]** *post.*

13. See para **[15.46]** *infra.*

14. See the *Gazette*, July/August 1978, p 125.

15. See para **[15.43]** *post.*

Conveyancing Committee. In some instances, it may be appropriate to extract parts of the Society's *Objections and Requisitions of Title* form.[16] In other cases it will be appropriate to make enquiries or raise requisitions which are not part of any of the standard forms.

A. Residential property

[5.06] In 1990 the Law Society's Conveyancing Committee prepared and issued to practitioners[17] a purchaser's solicitor's *Pre-Contact Check List on Acquisition of Private Dwellinghouse.*[18] Apart from the fact that the *Check List* does not deal with matters relating to property other than residential property, it is important to emphasise that it is not designed for use as *pre*-contract requisitions. Rather it is more in the form of an *aide memoire* for the purchaser's solicitor, reminding him of matters which should be attended to by him and which may require making enquiries or raising requisitions with the vendor's solicitor or elsewhere. Some of the items, however, relate more to matters which the purchaser's solicitor should attend to without necessarily referring to the vendor's solicitor. Thus, the first item on the *Check List* is a reminder to the purchaser's solicitor to consider the question of insurance of the interest in the property[19] which the purchaser usually acquires when the contract for sale is entered into. To be taken into account in this connection are the provisions in the Law Society's *General Conditions of Sale (1995 Edition)*[20] dealing with the risk of loss or damage to the property during the intermediate period between the date of the contract and actual completion of the sale. This matter is considered in a later chapter.[21] The second item refers to a "survey" and mentions also "planning and new roads and road widening search, zoning as to amenities (eg, commercial/industrial developments, halting sites) etc and identity". This reminds the purchaser's solicitor of two important matters to be considered at the *pre*-contract stage. One is the need for the purchaser to consider the appropriateness of commissioning his own independent survey, rather then relying upon any valuation report obtained by his lending institutions.[22] The other is to make enquiries of and searches in the register

---

16. See the 1996 edition which is reproduced in Appendix III *post.*
17. It was issued with the July/August 1990 *Gazette.*
18. The *Check List* is reproduced in Appendix I *post.*
19. The extent of this interest is a matter of some controversy following the Supreme Court's decision in *Tempany v Hynes* [1976] IR 101; see para **[12.02]** *et seq, post.*
20. Conds 43-45.
21. Para **[12.36]** *et seq, post.*
22. See paras **[4.24]** *ante* and **[5.10]** *infra.*

maintained by the local planning authority. This matter is considered further later, and it should be noted that it is not confined to residential property.[23]

[5.07] Some of the items on the *Check List* relate to matters clearly within the knowledge of the vendor and so would justify enquiries or requisitions directed at him. Such matters include the services to the property, such as drainage, water supply, telephone line and cable television,[24] and fixtures, fittings and other contents included in the sale.[25] These and related matters, such as whether roads, footpaths, sewers and drains have been taken in charge by the local authority[26] and easements and rights or charges in respect of them,[27] are also the subject of requisitions in the Law Society's *Objections and Requisitions on Title*[28] which may, therefore, be extracted and sent to the vendor's solicitor *pre*-contract. The same applies to questions such as whether the property is registered under the old National House Building Guarantee Scheme or its recent replacement, the HomeBond Scheme,[29] and whether it is subject to leases or licences.[30]

[5.08] Other items on the *Check List* draw attention to matters which must be resolved if the purchaser is to acquire valid title to the property. One is the possible need for consent under the Land Act 1965;[31] another is the need for a spouse's consent to both the contract and the conveyance as required by the Family Home Protection Act 1976.[32] Since the 1976 Act renders "void" an "enforceable agreement" entered into without "prior consent" the need for *pre*-contract enquiries is particularly important. This point was emphasised in a letter from the President of the Law Society to members dated 23 July 1976 and the requisition in the Society's *Objections and*

---

23. Para **[16.17]** *et seq, post.*
24. See items 5, 8 and 9.
25. Item 10: see further para **[9.15]** *post.*
26. Item 6.
27. Items 7 and 12.
28. See Nos 1-4 in the 1996 edition. See para **[16.06]** *et seq, post.*
29. See item 4 on the *Check List* (which refers to the former only) and para **[4.25]** *et seq, ante.* See also Nos 1-4 and 22.2 of the *Objections and Requisitions* form: see para **[16.59]** *post.*
30. Item 11; *cf* Nos 9, 32 and 33 of the *Objections and Requisitions*, paras **[16.16]** and **[16.91]** *post.*
31. Item 13 on the *Check List* which refers to s 45 of the 1965 Act; *cf* consent under s 12, para **[5.18]** *infra.* See also No 19 of the *Objections and Requisitions*, para **[16.29]** *post.*
32. See No 24 of the *Objections and Requisitions*, para **[16.61]** *post.* Technically, consent to the contract will also cover the conveyance, but a second consent to be endorsed on the conveyance should also be obtained: see **[16.69]** *post.*

Requisitions on Title form may be used. The effect of the 1976 Act[33] and other family legislation,[34] is considered in a later chapter.[35]

[5.09] The *Check List* draws attention to the need to determine whether there has been any "development" to the property the subject of the contract, ie, a change of use or building work for which planning permission would have been required under the Local Government (Planning and Development) Acts.[36] Here again the matter can be raised with the vendor's solicitor by using the requisition covering this matter on the Law Society's *Objections and Requisitions on Title* form.[37] Since the *Check List* was issued the Society's Conveyancing Committee has advised practitioners to raise *pre*-contract requisitions in relation to the Local Government (Multi-Storey Buildings) Act 1988. An interim set was published in 1990[38] and a revised version is now contained in the new *Objections and Requisitions on Title* form.[39] In 1994 the Committee issued a set of *pre*-contract requisitions and requisitions on title relating to the Building Control Act 1990 and the regulations made under that Act.[40] This too is now contained in the *Objections and Requisitions on Title* form.[41]

[5.10] Finally, in relation to residential property these are two categories of such property in respect of which some *pre*-contract enquiries or requisitions should be made. One is a newly erected property, which may or may not be covered by the HomeBond Scheme.[42] It is imperative to determine what the position is on this matter and to elicit other details relating to the property, by, eg, adapting the requisitions in the *Objections and Requisitions on Title* form[43] The other category is where the dwelling is a new flat, apartment, townhouse or similar property which is part of a complex involving, eg, a management company. Again it would seem wise to elicit information *pre*-contract by adapting the requisition in the *Objections and Requisitions on Title* form.[44] Eliciting *pre*-contract information is also important with respect

---

[33.] As amended by s 10(1) of the Family Law Act 1981 and s 54 of the Family Law Act 1995: see para **[16.70]** *post.*

[34.] Eg, the Family Law Act 1981 and Judicial Separation and Family Law Reform Act 1989.

[35.] Para **[16.61]** *et seq, post.*

[36.] Item 15.

[37.] No 27: para **[16.74]** *post.*

[38.] See the *Gazette*, May 1990.

[39.] No 35: see para **[16.95]** *post.*

[40.] See para **[16.79]** *post.*

[41.] No 28; note also No 29 (relating to the Fire Services Act); see para **[16.83]** *post.*

[42.] See para **[4.25]** *et seq, ante.*

[43.] No 22; see para **[16.59]** *post.* Note also the need for a companies search against the builder/developer: see para **[11.17]** *post.*

[44.] No 36: see para **[16.97]** *post.*

to both categories in the case of subsequent sales. Thus, in the case of a relatively new house it is vital to determine whether it is still covered by the old NHBG Scheme or the new HomeBond Scheme. In either case, it is particularly important to determine whether a defect justifying a claim has already come to light and whether a claim has been made under the relevant scheme. The point is that it is a feature of these schemes that there is no liability to a subsequent purchaser who acquires title "after the owner of the Dwelling for time being knew or should have known of the Major Defect or whose reasonable examination by a competent surveyor, architect or engineer would have disclosed the Major Defect". At the very least an enquiry should be made of the vendor whether any such defect has been noticed and whether a claim has been lodged in respect of it. However, that puts reliance on the vendor which provides a purchaser with little comfort,[45] if he really wishes to remain the owner of the property in question but have any defects put right. The only safe way of ensuring that any defect covered by the Scheme is put right in favour of the purchaser is to have a *pre-contract* survey done and insist on the vendor lodging a claim for any major defect revealed by it before the sale is closed.[46] Clearly, the purchaser's solicitor should advise his client accordingly. It would be unwise to rely upon the valuation report commissioned by the purchaser's lending institution.[47]

[5.11] In the case of "second hand" flats and similar properties in managed complexes detailed information must be obtained relating to the development in question and, in particular, with respect to the operation of the management company and any form of management agents. A detailed requisition on these matters is contained in the *Objections and Requisitions* form.[48]

B. Leases

[5.12] In 1990 the Law Society's Conveyancing Committee issued "Guidelines on enquiries to be made when taking a Rack Rent lease or a renewal thereof".[49] The Committee recognised that there are severe statutory

---

45. Ie, the vendor may be guilty of a misrepresentation justifying rescission of the contract by the purchaser.
46. The Scheme refers to "acquired title", so that it is probably sufficient if the claim is lodged before completion. It is unlikely that the expression is intended to refer to the *equitable* interest which the purchaser usually acquires on entering into the contract for sale: see **[12.02]** *post.*
47. *O'Connor v First National Building Society* [1991] ILRM 208; see para **[4.24]** *ante.*
48. No 37: see para **[16.99]** *post.*
49. These were issued with the May 1990 *Gazette. Cf* the earlier 'Guidelines Re Lessor's Title, published in the January/February 1980 *Gazette*; see further *infra.*

restrictions on a tenant's right to investigate the landlord's title,[50] which are largely unaffected by the Law Society's *General Conditions of Sale (1995 Edition)*,[51] but was concerned that nevertheless it was prudent for a leasehold purchaser's solicitor to obtain *prima facie* evidence of the landlord's title and to make some *pre*-contract enquiries. Reference was drawn to the decision of the English Court of Appeal in *Hill v Harris*,[52] in which it was held that it is the duty of an incoming tenant to satisfy himself that the premises are "legally" fit for his purposes, ie, that there are no convenants in, eg, the head-lease restricting user of the premises. The duty of the incoming tenant's solicitor to protect his client was emphasised by the following comment by Russell LJ:

> "... although the matter is not for decision before us, I find it at the moment not easy to see what conceivable defence the solicitors then acting for him would have to a claim for equivalent damages for negligence, in that they did not take the ordinary conveyancing precaution, before allowing their client to take a sub-lease, of finding out by inspection of the head-lease what were the covenants, restrictive of user or otherwise, contained in the head-lease."[53]

The Committee furnished with the "Guidelines" a set of *Pre-Lease Enquiries or Check List*[54] which is designed primarily for transactions involving the taking of a new lease.[55] The "Guidelines" point out that it should not be necessary to raise all the matters listed where the transaction involves the renewal of an existing lease, eg, evidence of the landlord's title (unless this was not obtained when the original lease was granted or the landlord has changed since it was granted). Conversely, consideration should be given in particular cases as to whether amendments or additions should be made to the printed form. For example, where the landlord is a company a copy of the certificate of incorporation and of the memorandum and articles of association should be requested as part of the evidence of title to grant the lease.[56] The item relating to multi-storey buildings should be altered in accordance with the new requisition in the *Objections and*

---

50. See para **[14.68]** *et seq, post.*
51. Cond 9: see para **[14.74]** *post.*
52. [1965] 2 All ER 358. Similar views as to the need to check legal fitness for the new tenant's purpose were expressed by Devlin J in *Edler v Auerbach* [1949] 2 All ER 692 at 699.
53. *Ibid* p 363. See also Danckwerts J in *Goody v Baring* [1956] 2 All ER 11 and Browne-Wilkinson V-C in *County Personnel (Employment Agency) Ltd v Pulver & Co* [1987] 1 All ER 289.
54. Reproduced in Appendix I *post.*
55. *Cf* the assignment of an existing lease where requisition No 33 in the Law Society's *Objections and Requisitions on Title* deals with the matter: see para **[16.93]** *post.*
56. See further para **[16.27]** *post.*

Requisitions on Title form[57] to reflect the fact that the Local Government (Multi-Storey Buildings) Act 1988 does not apply to new buildings commenced after 1 June 1992, which came within the scope of the Building Control Act 1990, and regulations made thereunder. In the case of commercial leases, account should be taken of the recent provision allowing the landlord and tenant to shift responsibility for paying VAT from the landlord to the tenant.[58] An enquiry should be raised as to whether VAT will arise on the creation of the lease or the rents payable by the tenant and whether the landlord is willing to agree to shift responsibility.[59] If the lease is of part only of a multi-let building (eg, a suite of offices in a block or unit in a shopping centre), an enquiry should be made about service charges, including contributions to insurance premiums relating to any block policy maintained by the landlord.[60]

[5.13] Apart from such *pre*-contract enquiries, it should be noted that the *Objections and Requisitions on Title* form contains other requisitions relating to leasehold property. One deals with the case of a sale of the landlord's interest, ie, subject to existing tenancies;[61] another deals with the same situation where the Housing (Private Rented Dwellings) Acts 1982-1983, may apply;[62] another deals with assignment of property held under a lease or fee farm grant;[63] another raises the issue whether the vendor of such property has taken steps to acquire the fee simple under the Landlord and Tenant (Ground Rents) Acts 1967-1984.[64] In all these cases some of the questions in the requisitions in question relate to information which the purchaser ought to have before committing himself to the contract for sale and so they should be raised at the *pre*-contract stage. In particular, the purchaser and his solicitor ought to know at the very least whether the legislation in question applies in the particular case.

C. Commercial and Industrial Property

[5.14] The nature of commercial and industrial properties and of transactions relating to such properties suggests that some additional *pre*-contract

---

[57.] No 35: see para **[16.95]** *post.*
[58.] See the new s 4A inserted in the Value-Added Tax Act 1972, by s 93 of the Finance Act 1994.
[59.] Such agreement must be approved by the Revenue Commissioners on application by a form available from local VAT offices: see Laffoy, *Irish Conveyancing Precedents*, p L14.
[60.] See Laffoy, *ibid* p L11 and Precedent L2.5.
[61.] No 9: see para **[16.16]** *post.*
[62.] No 10: see para **[16.18]** *post.*
[63.] No 33: see para **[16.93]** *post.*
[64.] No 34: see para **[16.94]** *post.*

enquiries or requisitions should usually be made. Indeed, where, as is often the case, the transaction involves substantial investment by more than one party, eg, the acquisition of a substantial business operation, a "due diligence" exercise should be carried out by the solicitor or solicitors acting for the purchasing and other investing parties, ranging over both financial and property matters.[65] The object of this is to carry out a full "health check" on the operation, including a thorough investigation of the title, a full survey on the property, a check on compliance with planning, environmental and related legislation and, of course, a detailed examination of the business' financial state. For obvious reasons, this should be completed and the results discussed with the client or clients before any commitment is made to a binding contract.[66] Some of the matters already mentioned take on special significance in such cases, eg, checking out compliance with the planning legislation and that relating to building control and regulation. Particular care is needed over the operation of the condition governing development in the Law Society's *General Conditions of Sale (1995 Edition)*.[67] In the case of industrial properties great care must also be exercised over the myriad of legislation enacted in recent times for the protection of the environment.[68] The civil and criminal liabilities which can arise under this legislation are severe indeed and any purchaser of or investor in a property which is governed by it must proceed with great caution.[69] It has become increasingly clear in recent times that *pre*-contract environmental enquiries should be made by the purchaser's solicitor. A requisition covering environmental matters is now included in the latest version[70] of the Law Society's *Objections and Requisitions on Title* form[71] and this may form the basis of *pre*-contract enquiries.[72]

[65.] See Fanagan, 'Environmental Due Diligence' (1995) IPELJ 3.

[66.] Though in certain circumstances a conditional contract may be entered into: see para **[7.05]** *et seq, post.*

[67.] Cond 36: see para **[16.75]** *post.*

[68.] For a comprehensive discussion of this and planning legislation, see Scannell, *Environmental and Planning Law in Ireland* (1995).

[69.] See the paper given by Dr Scannell ('Civil Liability for Environmental Damage') at a Law Society CLE Seminar on 'Environmental Law and its Implications for Conveyancing Transactions' on 26 September 1995.

[70.] 1996 edition.

[71.] No 31: see para **[16.86]** *post.* Note also No 29 dealing with the Fire Services Act 1981: see para **[16.83]** *post.*

[72.] *Cf* the set of 'Pre-Contract Enquiries concerning Environmental Matters' appended to the paper delivered by Garrett Gill (of Matheson Ormsby Prentice, Solicitors) at the Law Society CLE seminar referred to in **[5.14]** fn 69 *supra.*

[5.15] Where business property is acquired with a view to continuing the same or a similar business on the property, it is important to bear in mind that the existing employees may be protected from dismissal in accordance with the EC Acquired Rights Directive.[73] If the business is going to "retain its identity"[74] after the purchase, the purchaser must ascertain what employees are involved. This particularly affects transfers of properties like shops and stores, factories, farms and other premises involving a substantial number of employees,[75] but it is important to note that the Directive applies equally to premises where only a few or even just one employee is involved, eg, a receptionist in a doctor's or dentist's surgery or an office of a professional person practising as a sole practitioner. The purchaser's solicitor should make *pre*-contract enquiries to ascertain what employees are currently involved in the business being acquired.[76]

[5.16] Another matter which may be of particular importance in transactions involving commercial property is the scheme of tax-based incentives which may be applicable, such as the urban renewal incentives operating in "designated areas" like the Custom House Docks Area and Temple Bar Area in Dublin.[77] The Law Society's *Objections and Requisitions on Title* form contains a requisition as to transfer of allowances to the purchaser,[78] but *pre*-contract enquiries should be made to determine what these are and it may be wise to have the replies checked by the purchaser's tax adviser.

[5.17] Finally, it must be borne in mind that certain types of commercial or business property are subject to various licensing systems.[79] The obvious

---

[73] See the European Communities (Safeguarding of Employees' Rights on Transfer of Undertakings) Regulations 1980 (SI 306/1980).

[74] See *Bannon v EAT and Drogheda Town Centre* High Court, unrep, 5 October 1992. See also *Spijkers v Gebroedeas Benedik Abattoir CV* [1986] ECR 1119; *Ny Molle Kro* [1987] ECR 5465; McMahon and Murphy, *European Community Law in Ireland* (1989), para 25.11.

[75] In *Cunningham and O'Connor v Oasis Stores Ltd* High Court, unrep, 12 May 1995 (the EAT) the purchaser of the lease of empty shop premises was held to be conducting substantially the same business as had previously been carried on not by the assignor of the lease, but by a licensee. In fact, the former employees of the licensee failed in their claim because the new lessee succeeded in its argument that the dismissals were "for economic, technical or organisational reasons entailing changes in the workforce" within the meaning of Regulation 5(1) of the 1980 Regulations.

[76] It would appear that an attempt to pay off the employees prior to the purchase is likely to be void if the cause of this is essentially the transfer of the business. In *Brett and Others v Niall Collins Ltd* High Court, unrep, 3 May 1995 the EAT declared as null and void a purported dismissal of the employees by the receiver of a business and payment of redundancy money to them prior to the sale of the business as a going concern.

[77] See *Butterworths Tax Guide 1995-96*, paras 5.30 *et seq* and 16.125 *et seq*.

[78] No 31: see **[16.86]** *post.*

[79] See McDonald, *Hotel, Restaurant & Public House Law* (1992).

ones are those which attach to pubs, hotels and restaurants, but other licences may be relevant such as public dancing, music and singing licences. These matters are also covered by comprehensive requisitions in the *Objections and Requisitions on Title* form.[80]

D. Agricultural Property

[5.18] Two matters in particular arise in respect of agricultural property, both of which should be raised at least in a preliminary fashion at the *pre*-contract stage. One is that Land Act consent[81] may be required for the transaction in question, either because it involves a letting, sub-letting or sub-division within s 12 of the Land Act 1965 (not covered by "general consent"), or a vesting of the land in a "person" who is not a qualified person within the meaning of s 45 of the 1965 Act, in which case again consent will be needed. These matters are covered by a requisition in the Law Society's *Objections and Requisitions* form.[82]

[5.19] The other matter which may be of crucial importance in a sale of agricultural property is the milk quota attaching to the land.[83] It is clearly important to determine the position with regard to any such quota prior to entering into the contract, so that appropriate provisions relating to it can be included in the contract for sale. In February 1995 the Law Society issued a News Sheet confirming this, which included recommended requisitions which were drafted so that they can be used as *pre*-contract enquiries in particular cases. These are reproduced in the latest version of the Society's *Objections and Requisitions on Title* form.[84]

II. REMEDIES FOR INACCURATE REPLIES

[5.20] At this point, it may be useful to consider the legal position if it is discovered that a reply to an enquiry or *pre*-contract requisition directed to the vendor or his solicitor is inaccurate. The possible remedies which may be invoked by the purchaser are matters which the vendor, or more particularly,

---

[80.] Nos 40-43: see para **[16.103]** *et seq, post.*

[81.] From the Land Commission until the Irish Land Commission (Dissolution) Act 1992, is brought into force and the Commission's powers under the 1965 Act devolve to the Minister for Agriculture, Food and Forestry: see s 4 of the 1992 Act.

[82.] No 19: see para **[16.29]** *post.*

[83.] The Law Society has published a number of items in the *Gazette* on this subject, now collected in Ch 6 of the *Conveyancing Handbook* (1990). See now the European Communities (Milk Quotas) Regulations 1994 (SI 70/1994) and 1995 (SI 266/1995). See also Ryan-Purcell, 'Law Relating to Milk Quota Transactions in Ireland' (1994) CLP 179.

[84.] 1996 edition, No 39: see para **[16.101]** *post.*

his solicitor, ought to take into account in making replies to *pre*-contract enquiries or requisitions.[85] The dangers of incurring liability are now considerable, as we shall discuss in a moment. However, while the vendor and his solicitor could probably claim that they are under no duty strictly to give replies according to traditional conveyancing theory, this attitude would run counter to what is becoming the conventional practice. Solicitors acting for purchasers generally take the view that the making of such enquiries is an important step in providing protection for the purchaser and in this they are encouraged by the Law Society.[86] If a solicitor makes such enquiries and expects replies when he is acting for a purchaser, many would say that it behoves him to make replies when he is acting for a vendor. Apart from that, there is always the risk that a point-blank refusal to reply may cause the purchaser's solicitor to advise his client to call the whole deal off and to refuse to enter into a contract of sale.

[5.21] In considering the purchaser's remedies for inaccurate replies it is important to draw a distinction between two periods of time when the inaccuracy is discovered. If it is discovered before the purchaser enters into the contract of sale, his remedies do not, in general, involve court proceedings. He can call the whole deal off without incurring any liability or can negotiate new terms. Since he is still in the negotiating stage, he has probably suffered no loss as a result of inaccurate statements on the vendor's part and so, even if he suspects fraud, there may be a little point in suing, eg, in tort for deceit. On the other hand, if the inaccuracy is discovered after the purchaser has committed himself to a contract of sale, he will probably be concerned with remedies enforceable by action in court. In this context we are concerned with remedies for misrepresentations or misstatements made at the *pre*-contract stage. The question of misdescription in the contract itself is considered in a later chapter.[87]

[5.22] Though we are considering the question of a purchaser's remedies for *pre*-contract misrepresentations in the context of statements made by the vendor or his solicitor in reply to enquiries or requisitions made by the purchaser or his solicitor, it should be noted that these remedies may also be relevant in respect of misrepresentations made by other agents of the vendor, eg, an auctioneer, house or estate agent.[88]

---

85. See para **[5.02]** *supra*.

86. See para **[5.06]** *supra*.

87. See para **[9.29]** *post*. Note that Cond 33 in the Law Society's *General Conditions of Sale (1995 ed)* applies not only to misdescriptions in the contract, but also to misstatements and misrepresentations made in the course of any "negotiations leading to the sale": see paras **[9.44]** and **[9.46]** *post*.

88. See Chs 2 and 3 *ante*.

A. Fraudulent Misrepresentation

[5.23] It is settled that a fraudulent misrepresentation of fact[89] made by or on behalf of the vendor and inducing the purchaser to enter into the contract of sale entitles the purchaser to rescind the contract before completion.[90] As FitzGibbon J said in *Carbin v Somerville*[91]:

"To sell a leaky house or a leaky ship on a fraudulent misrepresentation that it is sound entitles the party defrauded to rescind the contract..."[92]

This right of recission is not necessarily lost because the property may have been altered in the meantime, for as FitzGibbon J stated in the same case:

"We have not been referred to any decision of any Court, or to any opinion of any reputable text-writer, to the effect that when a party to a contract has been induced to enter into it by fraudulent misrepresentation he loses his right to repudiate it on discovery of the fraud because the subject-matter cannot be restored to the defendant in the identical condition in which it was at the date of the contract, where the alteration is due to the nature of the subject-matter itself and cannot be attributed to any act of the plaintiff"[93]

If the fraud is not discovered until after completion, the purchaser may apply to have the transaction set aside,[94] or may seek damages, eg, on the basis of the difference between what the purchaser was induced to pay for the property as a result of the misrepresentation and what it was actually worth at the date of the contract.[95]

---

[89] "Exaggerated representations, as puffing advertisements. are not to he taken into consideration ..." *Per* Crampton J, *Thomson v Guy* (1844) 7 Ir LR 6 at 15. See also re mere expressions of opinion, *Smyth v Lynn* [1951] NI 69. And see Devlin, 'Fraudulent Misrepresentation' (1937) 53 LQR 344.

[90] *Carbin v Somerville* [1933] IR 276; *Smyth v Lynn, op cit*. See also *Greyhill Property Co Ltd v Whitechap Inn Ltd* High Court, unrep, 5 October 1993 (1990/2384P). *Cf* as regards non-disclosure of restrictive covenants which the vendor knows or ought to know will interfere with the purchaser's objects in buying the property, *Power v Barrett* (1887)19 LR Ir 450, especially at 457-8 (*per* Chatterton V-C), and see para **[9.25]** *post*. The onus of proof of fraud is the ordinary civil standard based on the balance of probabilities: see *Banco Ambrosiano v Ansbacher and Co* [1987] ILRM 669.

[91] [1933] IR 276.

[92] *Ibid*, p 288.

[93] *Ibid*, p 289.

[94] The Court may order the conveyance to be delivered up and cancelled, but it is questionable whether this is necessary since the Judicature (Ir) Act 1877. See *Gun v McCarthy* (1883) 13 LR Ir 304. See para **[21.35]** *post*.

[95] See the discussion in *Fenton v Schofield* (1966) 100 ILTR 69. *Cf Darville v Lamb*, English Law Society Gazette, 27 March 1996 (vendors, who resold property at a loss due to their disclosure of a long-standing dispute with a neighbour over noise created from his mending old cars, recovering damages form their previous owner for failure to disclose the dispute to them when they bought the property from him).

[5.24] The purchaser may also sue in tort for damages for deceit. Thus, in *Delany v Keogh*,[96] a purchaser of a public house at an auction succeeded in an action against the auctioneer for a statement made by the latter in advertisements, and at the auction itself, that the landlord of the premises had accepted for years a rent substantially lower than the rent specified in the lease (£18 instead of £25). These statements were made despite the fact that the landlord had written to the auctioneer some days before the auction, informing him that in future he would insist upon payment of the higher rent. The auctioneer took the precaution of consulting the vendor's solicitor and he advised him that in his opinion the landlord was estopped from claiming the higher rent and instructed the auctioneer to proceed. Though the auctioneer claimed that he believed this opinion was correct,[97] he made no mention of the matter at the auction and the Court of Appeal held[98] him liable for deceit on the ground that the actual statements made by him implied a representation that he had no reason to believe that the reduction in rent would be discontinued. Holmes LJ stated:

> "It is not necessary that the misrepresentation which will sustain an action of deceit should be made in actual terms. Words may be used in such circumstances, and in such connexion, as to convey to the person to whom they are addressed a meaning or inference beyond what is expressed; and if it appears that the person employing them knew this and also knew that such meaning or inference was false, there is sufficient proof of fraud."[99]

As the learned judge pointed out later,[100] the auctioneer should have said at least that the landlord had expressed an intention to insist upon the higher rent, but that the vendor's solicitor was of the opinion that he was estopped.

[5.25] It should also be noted that a fraudulent misrepresentation made by or on behalf of the vendor will give the purchaser a good defence to an action brought by the vendor for specific performance.[101] It must, of course, be instrumental in inducing the purchaser to enter into the contract,[102] but not necessarily the sole factor inducing the purchaser.[103] Such a

---

[96.] [1905] 2 IR 267. *Cf McAnarney v Hanrahan* [1993] 3 IR 492.
[97.] In fact the landlord subsequently sued the purchaser for the higher rent and recovered it.
[98.] Reversing the KBD (Palles CB and Johnson J, Andrews J dissenting).
[99.] [1905] 2 IR 267, 286-7. See also the discussion in Farrell, *Irish Law of Specific Performance* (1994), para **[9.12]** *et seq.*
[100.] *Ibid* p 289.
[101.] See *Farrell, op cit* para **[9.12]** *et seq.*
[102.] *Fenton v Schofield* (1965) 100 ILTR 69.
[103.] *Carbin v Somerville* [1933] IR 276.

misrepresentation made by the vendor's agent is still a good defence even through the vendor is unaware of the fraud.[104]

B. Innocent Misrepresentation

[5.26] It remains the position in Ireland[105] that a purchaser's remedies for innocent misrepresentation, especially one made at the *pre*-contract stage, are very restricted. The rules are as follows. First, the representation in question must be one of material fact rather than of law or mere opinion.[106] Secondly, if it induces the purchaser to enter into the contract,[107] he may seek rescission in equity, provided the contract has not been performed, eg, on completion of the transaction by conveyance of the property.[108] Thirdly, there is no right to damages unless the representation becomes a term of the contract or a collateral warranty.[109] If it becomes a term of the contract, in effect constituting a misdescription,[110] the purchaser may either rescind the contract or sue for damages, where the misrepresentation amounts to a condition. If it is a warranty only, he may seek damages only.[111] Alternatively, the purchaser may carry on with the contract subject to compensation by way of abatement of the purchase price.[112] If the

---

[104.] *Ingram v Gillen* (1910) 44 ILTR 103; *cf Delany v Keogh* [1905] 2 IR 267. See also *Smelter Corporation of Ireland Ltd v O'Driscoll* [1977] IR 305.

[105.] See Clark, *Contract Law in Ireland* (3rd ed, 1992), Ch 11. See also *Farrell, op cit*, para **[9.16]** *et seq.*

[106.] Nor must it be a mere "puffing" description of the property such as an auctioneer or estate agent commonly gives, see *Peilow v O'Carroll* (1972) 106 ILTR 29 at 47 (*per* Budd J). See also *Thomson v Guy* (1844) 7 Ir LR 6 at 15 (*per* Crampton J); *Phelps v White* (1881) 7 LR Ir 160 at 163 (*per* Palles CB).

[107.] See *Gahan v Boland* Supreme Court, unrep, 20 January 1984 (1983/37) (noted [1985] ILRM 218); *McCambridge v Winters* High Court, unrep, 25 August 1984 (1983/486 Sp). *Cf* where by the time the purchaser enters into the contract he knows the true facts: see *Grafton Court Ltd v Wadson Sales Ltd* High Court, unrep, 17 February 1975 (1964/269); *Donnellan v Dungoyne Ltd* [1995] 1 ILRM 388.

[108.] *Lecky v Walter* [1914] 1 IR 378, applying *Seddon v North Eastern Salt Co Ltd* [1905] 1 Ch 326. See also *Wilde v Gibson* (1848) 1 HLC 605; *Angel v Jay* [1911] 1 KB 666.

[109.] *Irish Land Commission v Maquay* (1891) 28 LR Ir 342 at 351-2 (*per* Palles CB); *Smyth v Lynn* [1951] NI 69 at 75-8 (*per* Curran J); *Bank of Ireland v Smith* [1966] IR 646 at 659 (*per* Kenny J). See also *Peilow v O'Carroll* (1972) 106 ILTR 29. However, the purchaser may be entitled to an indemnity in respect of liabilities necessarily incurred under the contract, eg, his costs, see *Hart v Swaine* (1877) Ch D 42; *Whittington v Seale-Hayne* (1900) 82 LT 49.

[110.] See further, para **[9.29]** *et seq, post.*

[111.] See *Carbin v Somerville* [1933] IR 276 at 289 (*per* FitzGibbon J); *Bank of Ireland v Smith* [1966] IR 646 at 659 (*per* Kenny J). See also *Thomson v Guy* (1844) 7 Ir LR 6. *Cf O'Donoghue & Co Ltd v Collins* High Court, unrep, 10 March 1972 (1970/2771P).

[112.] *Leslie v Crommelin* (1867) IR 2 Eq 134; *Perrin v Roe* (1889) 25 LR Ir 37; *Connor v Potts* [1897] 1 IR 534. See para **[9.34]** *post.*

misrepresentation does not become a term of the contract, it is possible that the court may construe it as amounting to a "collateral" warranty, in effect, constituting an agreement independent of the main contract, for which the purchaser may again seek damages.[113] The courts in recent times have shown increasing willingness to regard statements designed to induce a party to enter into a contract or some other transaction like taking a lease of a unit in a shopping centre as a collateral warranty.[114]

C. Negligent Misstatement

[5.27] There is another possible basis for liability for inaccurate replies to *pre*-contract enquiries. This stems from recent developments in the tort of negligence, for the courts on both sides of the Irish Sea have now firmly established that the tort extends to misstatements in certain circumstances.[115] There is now considerable authority for the view that a prerequisite duty of care is owed by persons who possess some special skill or competence, hence its application in cases involving accountants,[116] architects[117] and company auditors,[118] or because of some "special relationship," eg, a fiduciary or contractual one between the person making the statement and the person relying upon it.[119] This point was emphasised in the Irish case of *Bank of Ireland v Smith*,[120] which involved an innocent misrepresentation made in auctioneers' advertisement of land subject to a court order for sale

---

[113.] *Phelps v White* (1881) 7 LR Ir 160 at 165 (*per* Palles CB); *McDonnell v McGuinness* [1939] IR 223 at 229 (*per* Gavan Duffy J) (affd Sup Ct). See also *De Lassalle v Guildford* [1901] 2 KB 215; *City and Westminster Properties Ltd v Mudd* [1959] Ch 129.

[114.] See *Grafton Court Ltd v Wadson Sales Ltd* High Court, unrep, 17 February 1975 (1964/269); *Kennedy v Wrenne* [1981] ILRM 81; *Connswater Properties Ltd v Wilson* High Court (NI), unrep, 8 July 1986 (1985/161).

[115.] The starting point is the House of Lords decision in *Hedley Byrne & Co Ltd v Heller & Partners Ltd* [1964] AC 464 which has been approved in Ireland, see *Securities Trust Ltd v Hugh Moore & Alexander Ltd* [1964] IR 417. See generally McMahon and Binchy, *Irish Law of Torts* (2nd ed, 1989) Ch 10.

[116.] The *Hedley Byrne* case itself. See also *Golden Vale Co-Operative Creameries Ltd v Barrett* High Court, unrep, 16 March 1987 (1983/5120P).

[117.] *Sutcliffe v Thackral* [1974] AC 727. See also *Curley v Mulcahy* High Court, unrep, 21 December 1977 (1975/833); *Greyhill Property Co Ltd v Whitechap Inn Ltd* High Court, unrep, 5 October 1993 (1990/2384P).

[118.] *Arenson v Casson, Beckman, Rulle v & Co* [1975] 3 All ER 901. See also *McSweeney v Bourke* High Court, unrep, 14 November 1980 (1977/1728P).

[119.] *Mutual Life and Citizens Assurance Co Ltd v Levall* [1971] AC 793 (Lords Reid and Borthy-Gest, both parties to the *Hedley Byrne* decision, dissented from the proposition that the duty of care is limited to persons who carry on the business or profession of giving advice). See also *WB Anderson & Sons Ltd v Rhodes Ltd* [1967] 2 All ER 850. And see Brazier, 'The Innocent Purchaser and his Professional Advisers' (1976) 40 Conv 179.

[120.] [1966] IR 646.

made in a mortgage suit. Though it was accepted that the auctioneers were the agents of the vendors who had carriage of the sale,[121] Kenny J rejected the argument on behalf of the purchaser that an auctioneer ought to anticipate that any statements he makes will be relied upon by the purchaser and that, therefore, he owes a duty of care and will be liable in tort if it is made inaccurately and carelessly.[122] Kenny J stated:

> "... the relationship between the person seeking the information and the person giving it, if not fiducary or arising out of a contract for consideration, must be 'equivalent to contract' before any liability can arise ... Even if an auctioneer's fees are paid by the purchaser[123] (and in this case the vendors are liable for them), a contractual relationship between the vendors' auctioneers and the purchaser does not exist."[124]

However, more recent cases have doubted whether the principle should be so limited.[125] In *McAnarney v Hanrahan*[126] the plaintiffs arrived late for what had proved to be an abortive auction of licensed premises with living accommodation. During discussions with the auctioneer, in which it transpired that the lease was nearing the end of its term, the auctioneer told the plaintiffs that negotiations had taken place with the ground landlords and the freehold could be purchased for £3,000 or less. The representations were untrue and Costello J found that they were made to induce the plaintiffs to purchase the lease of the premises, which they did. When later they discovered that the landlord's price for the freehold was £40,000 they sued the auctioneer for negligence. Costello J distinguished *Bank of Ireland v Smyth*, holding:

> "Here [the auctioneer] took upon himself responsibility for giving his opinion about the purchase of the freehold. He should have known that the plaintiffs would place reliance on what he told them, particularly as he expressly stated that the negotiations had already taken place with the landlords. In my opinion a special relationship thus arose between [the

---

121. The court is not usually the vendor in the case of a court sale, see para **[11.03]** *post*.
122. The *Hedley Byrne* case was cited in support.
123. See on this, para **[2.34]** *ante*.
124. [1966] IR 646 at 660. These remarks were strictly *obiter* since it was held that negligence was not proved. Damages were awarded for breach of warranty.
125. It was doubted in England, see *Minister v of Housing and Local Government v Sharp* [1970] 2 QB 223 at 268-9 (*per* Lord Denning MR). See also *Ross v Caunters* [1980] Ch 297, approved by the House of Lords in *White v Jones* [1955] 1 All ER 691, and followed by Barrington J in *Wall v Hegarty* [1980] ILRM 124. Note, however, that the English Court of Appeal has more recently argued that neither the vendor's solicitor (see *Gran Gelato Ltd v Richcliff Ltd* [1992] 1 All ER 865) nor his estate agent (see *McCullagh v Lane Fox and Partners Ltd* [1996] 18 EG 104) should, in the course of ordinary conveyancing practice, be regarded as owing a duty of care to the purchaser.
126. [1993] 3 IR 492.

auctioneer] and the plaintiffs which imposed on him the duty of care in giving the information. He breached that duty in that before making the statement he took no care to see what price the landlords would require for their interest. This case is different from *Bank of Ireland v Smith* [1966] IR 646 in which Kenny J held that no duty of care towards prospective purchasers was imposed on an auctioneer when placing an advertisement which contained misleading information. In this case the particular circumstances of the negotiations and the express assumption of responsibility to which I have referred created a special relationship which was absent in the circumstances which Kenny J was considering."[127]

This decision was followed by O'Hanlon J in *Donnellan v Dungoyne*,[128] where letting agents falsely claimed that virtually all the units in a shopping centre were let and would be occupied and trading before Christmas. He held that a case had not been made for rescission, but awarded damages for breach of warranty[129] and negligent misrepresentation.[130]

[5.28] It is important to recognise the scope of the principle at play here. It is not suggested that the vendor's solicitor or estate agent owes a duty of care to the purchasers in the ordinary course of conveyancing. His primary duty is to his own client the vendor, on whose behalf he acts and against whom the purchaser's remedies should primarily lie.[131] Such enquiries as are sent to the vendor's solicitor by the purchaser or his solicitor are sent on the basis that he will see that they are replied to on his client's behalf, so that the purchaser and his solicitor may decide whether to proceed further in the light of those replies. Unless there are special circumstances suggesting that the vendor's solicitor has stepped outside his role as solicitor for the vendor and has undertaken a direct responsibility towards the purchaser, the purchaser's remedy for inaccurate statements or replies to *pre*-contract enquiries lies against the vendor on whose behalf they are made, ie, for misrepresentation by the vendor[132] rather than negligence by the vendor's solicitor.[133] That

---

[127.] *Ibid* p 497. *Cf Tulsk Co-Op Livestock Mart Ltd v Ulster Bank Ltd* High Court, unrep, 13 May 1983 (1981/3555P); *Towey v Ulster Bank Ltd* [1987] ILRM 142.

[128.] [1995] ILRM 388. He also cited *Esso Petroleum Co Ltd v Mardon* [1976] 2 All ER 5, where the oil company's expert falsely indicated the potential through put of petrol. *Cf Stafford v Mahony* [1980] ILRM 53. And see *Fallon v Gannon* [1988] ILRM 193.

[129.] See para **[5.26]** *supra*.

[130.] See also recent English decisions such as *Berkowitz v MW (St John's Wood) Ltd* [1993] 48 EG 133; *cf McCullagh v Lane Fox & Partners Ltd* [1996] 18 EG 104.

[131.] This is the purport of the English Court of Appeal's decisions in the *Gran Gelato* and *McCullagh* cases, fn 125 *supra*. But see *Wilson v Bloomfield* (1979) 123 Sol Jo 860; *Cf Walker v Boyle* [1982] 1 All ER 634.

[132.] See para **[5.23]** *et seq, supra*.

[133.] *Gran Gelato Ltd v Richcliff (Group) Ltd* [1992] 1 All ER 865 at 872-873 (*per* Nicholls V-C). Note, however, that no reference was made to the Court of Appeal decision in *Wilson v Bloomfield* fn 131 *supra*.

such "special circumstances" are needed was recognised by Hamilton J in *Doran v Delaney*,[134] in which he rejected any argument that the vendor's solicitors were liable to the purchaser for replies made to requisitions on title, pointing out that the purchaser "can reasonably be expected to rely upon his own solicitor to investigate title and similar matters".[135] It is suggested that the vendor's solicitor will only "step outside" his role as solicitor for the vendor where, eg, he enters into direct discussions or contact with the purchaser and in doing so says or does something to lead the purchaser reasonably to the view that he is assuming personal responsibility for what he says or does.[136] Apart from that, the vendor's solicitor owes a duty of care to his own client, the vendor, in respect of the various conveyancing steps to be taken *pre-* and *post*-contract, and this duty is, of course, founded on the contractual relationship between solicitor and client as well as on the basis that a solicitor is taken to possess a special skill or competence in conveyancing matters.[137] Thus, a vendor's solicitor who is negligent in making replies to *pre*-contract enquiries may find himself sued by his own client,[138] hence the importance of getting the client to check them before they are sent to the purchaser's solicitor. By the same token it is clear that the purchaser's solicitor may be liable in negligence to the purchaser if he does not carry out appropriate enquiries or searches or does not do so in a competent manner.[139] This includes a duty to disclose to his client any adverse or otherwise significant information gained thereby.[140] Indeed, it has been held in Ireland that a duty of care in making *pre*-contract enquiries may be owed by persons other than solicitors. In *Crawford v Boyd & Co*,[141] the Northern Ireland Court of Appeal held liable for negligence a property broker who was instructed by a prospective purchaser of a business to make enquiries about the property. Andrews LJ stated:

[134.] [1996] 1 ILRM 490. He did not refer to any English case, but cited the Scottish case *Midland Bank plc v Cameron, Tong, Peterkin and Duncans* 1988 SLT 611.

[135.] *Ibid*, p 510. He held the purchaser's solicitor liable in negligence: see para **[15.02]** *post*.

[136.] Ie adopting Costello J's approach in the *McAnarney* case, para **[5.27]** *supra*. *Cf* Lynch J in *Tuohy v Courtney (No 2)* [1994] 3 IR 1; on appeal the Supreme Court (*per* O'Flaherty J) upheld Lynch J's acceptance of the evidence of the vendor's solicitor that he had not made to the purchaser the inaccurate statements about the nature of the title which had been alleged: [1994] 2 ILRM 503.

[137.] See the discussion by Barron J in *McMullen v Farrell* [1993] 1 IR 123; *Doran v Delaney supra*; para **[1.36]** *ante*.

[138.] See *Sharneyford Supplies Ltd v Edge* [1985] 1 All ER 976.

[139.] *Kelly v Crowley* [1985] IR 212; *Roche v Peilow* [1985] IR 232; *Doran v Delany supra*. See also *G & K Ladenbau Ltd v Crawley & De Reya* [1978] 1 All ER 682; *Computastaff Ltd v Ingeldew Brown Bennison & Garrett* (1983) 268 EG 906.

[140.] *Lake v Bushby* [1949] 2 All ER 964. See also *Glendinning v Orr* [1989] NI 171.

[141.] (1935) 69 ILTR 65.

"It is our opinion that when an intending purchaser requires investigations to be made it is the duty of the person so instructed to make all enquiries that would enable him to give a reliable opinion on the subject."[142]

D. Statutory Sanctions

[5.29] Quite apart from the remedies discussed above, it is possible that there may be a special statutory sanction relevant to a particular case. Thus, s 15 of the Family Home Protection Act 1976, creates a special criminal offence under that Act of "knowingly" giving information which is "false or misleading in any material particular".[143] This applies where any person having an interest in any premises is required in writing by or on behalf of any other person proposing to acquire that interest to give any information necessary to establish if the conveyance of that interest requires a consent under s 3(1). Thus, if a prospective purchaser makes *pre*-contract enquiries of the vendor, such as those mentioned previously,[144] the latter runs the risk of committing a criminal offence if he refuses to reply or makes false replies. And it should be noted that s 15 states that such liability is without prejudice to any other liability, civil or criminal.

[5.30] Where a person serves a notice requiring information under the Landlord and Tenant (Ground Rents) Act 1967,[145] a statutory duty to give the information arises so far as the information required is within the possession or procurement of the person upon whom the notice is served.[146] The ultimate sanction is the power of the county registrar for the area to appoint an officer of the Court to execute a conveyance on behalf of a person who refuses or fails to execute a conveyance.[147]

---

[142] *Ibid* p 66.

[143] *Cf* the liability of estate agents in England under the Property Misdescriptions Act 1991: see Murdoch *Law of Estate Agency and Auctions* (3rd ed, 1994), Ch 7.

[144] Para **[5.08]** *supra*.

[145] Sections 7 and 23. See para **[16.94]** *post*.

[146] 1967 Act s 7(3). These provisions are designed to secure joinder of all necessary parties to a conveyance of the fee simple to a long lessee, see Wylie, *Irish Landlord and Tenant Law*, para 31.47. See also para **[16.92]** *post*.

[147] 1967 Act, s 8(2). See Wylie, *Irish Landlord and Tenant Law*, *op cit*, para 31.48.

Chapter 6

FORMATION OF THE CONTRACT

[6.01] In this part of the book we are concerned with the second major stage of the conveyancing process - the contract stage.[1] In this present chapter we discuss the formalities of the creation of a contract for the sale or other disposition of land.[2] In Chapters 9-11 we discuss the detailed contents of the contract, in Chapter 12 we discuss the position of the parties under the contract pending completion and in Chapter 13 we consider various aspects of enforcement of the contract. Throughout the discussion of these chapters it must be borne in mind that, while in the normal case the creation and the fixing of the details of the contract is done formally under the supervision of the parties' solicitors, all too often a contract comes into existence in an informal manner, sometimes with one or other, or both, of the parties not being advised by a solicitor. As we shall see, this can create considerable problems of interpretation as to the precise terms of the bargain made by the parties, and can give rise to equally difficult questions as to the parties' remedies for enforcement, should one or other of them refuse to abide by the informal agreement.

I. INTRODUCTION

[6.02] The first point that must be emphasised with respect to conveyancing contracts is that they must, like any other contract, comply with the general principles of the law of contract relating to formation of a contract.[3] Thus, the parties to the purported contract must have the legal capacity to enter into such a contract.[4] They must have had an intention to create legal relations,[5] and the terms of their agreement must be sufficiently certain that, if necessary, a court will be able to see precisely what it is they have agreed.[6]

---

1. See **[1.05-1.06]** *ante*.
2. Some special cases are considered in Chs 7 and 8.
3. See *Dyas v Stafford* (1882) 9 LR Ir 520. See also Farrell, *Irish Law of Specific Performance* (1994) Ch 3.
4. This subject is discussed in *Irish Land Law* (2nd ed, 1986), Ch 25.
5. See *Mackey v Jones* (1959) 93 ILTR 177. See also the discussion by the Supreme Court in *Boyle v Lee* [1992] 1 IR 555, para **[6.15]** *infra* and **[7.08]** *post*. See also *Embourg Ltd v Tyler Group Ltd* Supreme Court, unrep 5 March 1996 (223/1995), para **[6.62]** *infra*.
6. See *McGillycuddy v Joy* [1959] IR 189. See also *Gardiner v Tate* (1876) IR 10 CL 460, especially at 475 (*per* Fitzgerald J).

There must have been a proper offer and acceptance,[7] and the agreement must be supported by consideration.[8] These are all matters which lie strictly outside the compass of this book. We are concerned more with special rules applicable to conveyancing contracts.

[6.03] The one special requirement relating to formation of conveyancing contracts is that contained in s 2 of the Statute of Frauds (Ireland) 1695, which requires, *inter alia*,[9] that contracts for the sale of land should be evidenced in writing. The object of the Statute in making this provision was made clear by its preamble, which stated that it was passed for "prevention of many fraudulent practices which are commonly endeavoured to be upheld by perjury and subornation of perjury." The idea was that the requirement of written evidence of the contract would prevent a party from claiming that someone else had entered into an oral contract with him when he had not done so. But, as the courts have come to realise after centuries of litigation, the provision is something of a "two-edged sword," which is often as likely to facilitate the perpetration of "fraud" as it is to prevent it.[10] The requirement of written evidence will also prevent a party from claiming that someone else had not entered into an oral contract with him even though he has done so. So most of the cases in which the Statute was pleaded tended to be cases where the defendant was denying the existence of a contract and argued that the lack of written evidence supported him in this claim. Not surprisingly, the courts soon realised that a strict interpretation of s 2 would enable many defendants to break their word and to go back on firm bargains made by them, simply because the precaution had not been taken to ensure that the requisite written evidence was brought into existence. The Court of Chancery in particular was not prepared "to allow a statute to be used as an instrument of fraud."[11] The result has been the development of the doctrine of part performance,[12] under which a purely oral contract may be enforced by the court in certain circumstances, despite the absence of the written

---

7. See the discussion in *Mespil Ltd v Capaldi* [1986] ILRM 373; *Unidare Plc v Scott Ltd* [1991] 2 IR 88. See also *Blakeney v Hardie* (1874) IR 8 Eq 381; *Swan v Miller* [1919] 1 IR 151; *Law v Roberts & Co* [1964] IR 292. As regards auction sales, see paras **[2.21]** *ante* and **[8.02]** *post.*

8. *Maguire v Conway* [1950] IR 44. *Cf Re Daniel Murphy Ltd* [1964] IR 1. See generally Clark, *Contract Law in Ireland* (3rd ed, 1992), Part 1.

9. The section applied also to contracts of guarantee, contracts in consideration of marriage and contracts not to be performed within the space of one year. See Wylie, *Irish Conveyancing Statutes* (1994) p 24 *et seq*; Farrell, *Irish Law of Specific Performance* (1994), Ch 5.

10. See the remarks of Lord Redesdale in *Lindsay v Lynch* (1804) 2 Sch & Lef 1 at 5. See also Costello J in *O'Connor v McCarthy* [1982] IR 161 at 169-70 and McCarthy J in *Boyle v Lee* [1992] 1 IR 555 at 584-5.

11. See *Irish Land Law* (2nd ed, 1986), para 3.049.

12. Discussed in detail at para **[6.48]** *et seq, infra.*

evidence required by s 2 of the Statute of Frauds. Further relaxation of the Statute's requirements has been introduced by the readiness with which courts are now prepared to allow oral evidence to be given to explain the written evidence that does exist.[13] And, as we shall see, often the written evidence that is eventually accepted as sufficient by the courts has come into existence in a rather haphazard fashion, with little thought given to the Statute by the parties concerned - indeed, they may have given no thought to it at all, being unaware of it and its requirements, and have had no intention of creating the requisite written evidence.[14]

[6.04] In view of these developments, some have queried whether the Statute does not do more harm than good. It is argued that, as pointed out in the previous paragraph, the provisions of s 2 are as likely to prevent the enforcement of a true bargain as they are to prevent the enforcement of what was not a bargain at all.[15] To the counter argument that the courts in their interpretation of the provisions have considerably reduced this risk, the further argument is made that, as a result of the courts' efforts in this regard, the case law on the subject has become extremely complex - indeed, some would say so complex that at times it is difficult to predict the likely outcome of litigation. Some would say that this point was amply illustrated by the muddle created by the English Court of Appeal judges some years ago[16] in their efforts to combat the increasing instances of "gazumpin"[17] during the property boom of the late 1960s and early 1970s. Gazumping is a practice which becomes common when there is a sellers' market.[18] The vendor of a particular property may find that he receives several offers from prospective purchasers and can play one off against the other. Even if he "agrees" to sell to one, he is always free under the Statute of Frauds to disregard that and to accept a higher offer and thereby "gazump" the first

---

[13.] See para **[6.22]** *infra*.

[14.] Para **[6.15]** *infra*.

[15.] See, eg, Pritchard, 'An Aspect of Contracts and Their Terms' (1974) 90 LQR 55.

[16.] See *Law v Jones* [1974] Ch 112; *Tiverton Estates Ltd v Wearwell Ltd* [1974] 2 WLR 176. See Wilkinson, '*Law v Jones*: Problems for Conveyancers' (1973) 123 New LJ 941. See also English Law Commission's Report No 164, *Formalities for Contract for Sale etc of Land* (1987), which resulted in the replacement in England of the Statute of Frauds requirement (by then to be found in s 40 of the Law of Property Act 1925) by s 2 of the Law of Property (Miscellaneous Provisions) Act 1989. Section 2 requires the contract to be *made* (as opposed to evidenced) in writing, to incorporate *all* terms agreed and to be signed by or on behalf of *both* parties.

[17.] See Barnsley, *Conveyancing Law and Practice* (3rd ed, 1988), pp 206-7. *Cf* the use of "lock-out" agreements: *Pitt v PHH Asset Management Ltd* [1993] 4 All ER 961.

[18.] However, it is not uncommon for the vendor to be gazumped by a prospective purchaser who later withdraws, see (1972) 36 Conv 1; also (1972) 116 Sol Jo 110. See *O'Connor v McCarthy* [1982] IR 161.

prospective purchaser, so long as he has been careful not to allow the appropriate written evidence of the first "agreement" to come into existence. This may happen several times until the vendor is prepared to commit himself finally, leaving behind a string of outraged prospective purchasers, each of whom thought he had entered into a bargain for the purchase of the property in question.

[6.05] It is questionable, however, whether repeal of s 2 of the Statute of Frauds (Ireland) 1695, would effect a desirable solution to such problems. In the first place, it must be borne in mind that, so long as title to land in Ireland is complicated[19] purchase of land will remain a more complicated process than other purchase transactions and for their own protection the parties ought to enter into a detailed contract.[20] It hardly seems wise to leave the settling of such details to an oral agreement, about which the parties are likely to have different recollections later. Indeed, it has been argued that what is needed is not the removal of the requirement of written evidence and enforcement of oral agreements, but the strengthening of the requirement so that it relates not only to evidence of the agreement[21] but requires the agreement itself to be in writing, perhaps in a common statutory form.[22] Care would have to be taken over the drafting of such a provision to avoid the difficulties over interpretation which have recently come to light in England.[23] Secondly, quite apart from questions of title, the size and value of land usually dictates the exercise of care in checking its physical condition before commitment to its purchase,[24] so that a delay before that commitment is inevitable in most cases. A delay may be necessary for a variety of other reasons, eg, the purchaser has to arrange a loan for the purchase price or is dependent upon selling his existing property.[25] It is factors such as these which have led to the current practice of solicitors allowing several weeks to pass before their clients are committed to a written agreement.[26] It is difficult to see how else the clients can be protected, whatever the formalities for

---

[19] This point can still be made with respect to registered land, since our registration system is not exhaustive, see para **[14.22]** *post.*

[20] See Chs 9 and 10, *post.*

[21] See para **[6.06]** *infra.*

[22] The Law Society in England had suggested this, see (1966) 63 L Soc Gaz 171, but in due course the Law Commission opted for a full writing requirement but not in a statutory form: see para **[6.04]** *supra.*

[23] See on s 2 of the Law of Property (Miscellaneous Provisions) Act 1989, eg *Spiro v Glencrown Properties Ltd* [1991] 1 All ER 600; *Record v Bell* (1991) P & CR 192; *Tootal (Clothing) Ltd v Guinea Properties Ltd* [1992] 41 EG 117.

[24] See Chs 4-5, *ante.*

[25] See para **[1.37]** *ante.*

[26] *Cf* sales by public auction, see paras **[2.53]**, *ante* and **[8.02]** *post.*

creation of the contract,[27] unless one resorts to the use of "conditional" contracts, a practice which has become increasingly common in Ireland in recent years. However, as we shall discuss later,[28] conditional contracts give rise to their own problems. Thus, many solicitors take the view that, although the traditional delay in entering into a contract for sale may involve a risk of gazumping, the risks of a premature commitment to a binding contract may be even greater. And it is arguable that gazumping is only an intermittent problem, dependent upon market conditions, and even when such conditions are favourable for the practice, it may arise only in a minority of cases. If that is so, the old adage that "hard cases made bad law" may be apt! It is, perhaps, not without significance that the English Law Commission initially found it difficult to derive any satisfactory solution to the problem and its eventual solution has proved to be troublesome.[29]

II. STATUTE OF FRAUDS (IRELAND) 1695

A. Section 2

[6.06] So far as it relates to conveyancing contracts, s 2 provides:

> ... no action shall be brought whereby to charge ... , any person ... upon any contract or sale of lands, tenements, or hereditaments, or any interest in or concerning them ... unless the agreement upon which such action shall be brought, or some memorandum or note thereof, shall be in writing, and signed by the party to be charged therewith, or some other person thereunto by him lawfully authorized.[30]

In the next few paragraphs we consider each aspect of this provision, but first one crucial point must be emphasised. The section does not, as is sometimes thought to be the case, require a contract for the sale of land to be in writing. All it requires is that there should be at least written evidence (in

---

27. Greater use of the concept of an option to purchase has been suggested but this creates difficulties for the vendor, since he is bound so long as the option exists, whereas the purchaser is not and may in the end decline to exercise it (though, admittedly, at the risk of loss of the consideration for the option), see para **[8.03]** *post*.

28. See Ch 7 *post*.

29. See Seventh Annual Report (1971-72) (Law Com No 51), para [23].

30. The similar wording of s 4 of the English Statute of Frauds 1677, was replaced by s 40(1)of the Law of Property Act 1925, which read:

> "No action may be brought upon any contract for the sale or other disposition of land or any interest in land, unless the agreement upon which such action is brought, or some memorandum or note thereof, is in writing, and signed by the party to be charged or by some other person thereunto by him lawfully authorised"

Section 40 has been replaced by s 2 of the Law of Property (Miscellaneous Provisions) Act 1989; see **[6.04-5]** *supra*.

the form of a "memorandum or note") of the contract; the contract itself may be purely oral. Thus, the parties to the transaction may make an oral agreement, which under the general law of contract is a fully binding contract, but which does not become enforceable under s 2 until some time later when a written memorandum comes into existence.[31] This may be drafted by their solicitors and signed by the parties many weeks after they made their agreement.[32] Of course, in many, if not most, cases not only will the bare essentials of a memorandum or note[33] be prepared by the parties' solicitors, but a full written contract will be drawn up, probably based upon the standard form issued by the Law Society.[34] This may be desirable for the parties' protection, but it is not essential under s 2. The need for written evidence applies whether the sale is by public auction or private treaty[35] and whether the title to the land is registered or not.[36]

B. No action

[6.07] Section 2 requires written evidence only to render the contract enforceable by action. Lack of such evidence does not mean that there is no contract between the parties.[37] So long as it complies with the general principles of the law of contract,[38] an oral contract for the sale of land is perfectly valid. It may be enforced in any way other than by action.[39] Indeed, even this is not strictly true, because the contract will even be enforced by action unless the other party pleads the Statute of Frauds as a defence.[40] It

---

31. Thus, while the contract may precede the memorandum, the reverse is not normally true, for a memorandum or note under s 2 presupposes the existence of the contract; hence the word "thereof" after the word "note". See para **[6.14]** *infra*. *Cf* where a purchaser forwards a written signed proposal to the vendor to be accepted by the latter or not, as he pleases.

32. In *Barkworth v Young* (1856) 4 Drew 1, the memorandum came into existence fourteen years after the contract.

33. See para **[6.17]** *infra*.

34. This is discussed in detail in Chs 9 and 10 *post*.

35. See generally, Chs 2 and 3, *ante* and para **[8.02]** *post*.

36. On the question of contracts relating to registered land, see para **[6.66]** *infra*.

37. No less an authority than Baron Parke made this elementary error in *Carrington v Roots* (1837) 2 M & W 248 at 259!

38. See para **[6.02]** *supra*.

39. Eg, if the purchaser defaults, the vendor may forfeit any deposit he has paid, see para **[13.30]** *post*. Also *Monnickendam v Leanse* (1923) 39 TLR 445. If the vendor defaults, the purchaser may recover his deposit in a claim based on total failure of consideration, see *Pulbrook v Lawes* (1876) 1 QBD 284; also para **[13.34]** *post*.

40. It seems that the court may not give leave to amend the pleadings where the defence has been inadvertently omitted, see *Broughton v Snook* [1938] Ch 505 at 511. See also *Clarke v Callow* (1876) LJQB 53; *Fraser v Pape* (1904) 91 LT 340. Once the contract has been enforced in proceedings where the defence was not pleaded, its enforceability is *res judicata* in any further proceedings between the same parties and the defence cannot be pleaded in those proceedings, *Humphries v Humphries* [1910] 2 KB 531. *Cf* on the converse case, *White v Spendlove* [1942] IR 224.

also seems that a party may waive the benefit or submit to the performance of any term or condition[41] which may have been omitted from the memorandum and would, therefore, ordinarily not be enforceable - where such benefit or performance affects him exclusively.[42] Thus, the plaintiff may be able to enforce the contract as evidenced in the memorandum, provided that it is otherwise sufficient,[43] by foregoing the benefit of a term also agreed to but not included in the memorandum.[44] In *Barratt v Costelloe*,[45] Kenny J stated:

> "My view is that when parties conclude an oral contract which contains a term wholly for the benefit of one of them and there is a written memorandum which does not contain any reference to that term, the party for whose benefit the term was inserted may waive it and sue successfully on the contract of which there is a memorandum. The note in writing for the purpose of the Statute of Frauds has to be of the contract sued on, not the contract made and the plaintiff may waive a term which is wholly in his favour and which is not referred to in the memorandum."[46]

[6.08] Apart from these cases, there are some well-recognised exceptions to s 2. One is the doctrine of part performance, an equitable doctrine developed by the Court of Chancery, whereby an oral agreement for the sale of land may be enforced despite the absence of the written evidence required by the Statute of Frauds. We discuss this doctrine later in this chapter.[47] Another is that sales under a court order will be enforced, even if there is no written evidence,[48] on the ground that the court supervises the transaction and will ensure that no fraud is perpetrated. Court sales are considered in the next chapter.[49]

---

41. Formerly, it was thought that this rule was confined to terms "of no great importance," see *Hawkins v Price* [1947] Ch 645 (also *Fry on Specific Performance* (6th ed), p 243)). But this has recently been doubted in England, see *Scott v Bradley* [1971] Ch 850. *Cf Doherty v Gallagher* High Court, unrep, 9 June 1975 (1973/2830P). However, to be sufficient the memorandum must include all the essential terms of the agreement, see para **[6.17]** *infra*.

42. *Cf* a term or condition affecting both parties, see *Hawkins v Price* [1947] Ch 645.

43. See para **[6.18]** *post*.

44. See *North v Loomes* [1919] 1 Ch 378 (vendor waiving term that purchaser should pay his costs). *Cf Burgess v Cox* [1951] Ch 383; RE M(egarry) (1951) 67 LQR 299.

45. (1973) 107 ILTSJ 239, followed by Costello J in *Anom Engineering Ltd v Thornton* High Court, unrep, 1 February 1983 (1979/1988). The question of waiver of a term also arose in *Hoon v Nolan* (1967) 101 ILTR 99, but was dealt with in a most cursory way by the Supreme Court. It is submitted, with respect, that the decision is wrong on this point.

46. See transcript of judgment (13 July 1973) (1973/703P). Similarly, if the term was agreed but omitted from the memorandum, the party not to be benefited can submit to it and seek to enforce the agreement: see *Black v Grealy* High Court, unrep, 10 November 1977 (1977/244Sp).

47. Para **[6.48]** *infra*.

48. Though, of course, there usually is writing, see para **[8.13]** *post*.

49. *Ibid*. See also Ch 11 *post*.

C. Sale of Land

st. of Frauds

[6.09] Section 2 applies to "any contract or[50]sale of lands, tenements, or hereditaments, or any interest in or concerning them".[51] It is clear from the voluminous case law on the section that it applies to contracts for sale in the widest sense,[52] eg, sales of freehold interests (including contracts for the grant or assignment of fee farm grants[53]), contracts for the grant, assignment and surrender[54] of leases,[55] contracts for mortgages[56] and for the grant of easements and profits.[57] In *Crane v Naughten*,[58] a contract for exclusive grazing rights on freehold land for a period of six months was held to be a contract relating to an interest in land and, therefore, within the Statute of Frauds. However, the contract in that case was distinguished from the more usual agistment contract common in Ireland,[59] which, like a conacre "letting"[60] does not confer "possession" on the grantee and so, arguably, does not create an interest in land. Yet, in *McKenna v Herlihy*,[61] a case involving a dispute over assessment for income tax, the Irish King's Bench Division still held that an agistment contract[62] did involve a sale of lands rather than of goods. Thus, Gibson J stated:

[50.] Section 40(1) of the English Law of Property Act 1925, substituted the word "for," see para **[6.06]**, fn 30 *supra*.

[51.] See *Johnston v McAllister* (1835) 1 Jon 499.

[52.] Section 40(1) of the English Law of Property Act 1925, recognised the courts' wide interpretation by inserting the words "or other disposition" after the word "sale" (see para **[6.06]**, fn 30 *supra*) and "disposition" is defined in s 205(1)(ii). In *Daulia Ltd v Four Millbank Nominees Ltd* [1978] 2 All ER 557, the Court of Appeal held that s 40(1) even applied to a unilateral agreement to enter into a contract for the sale of land. As regards an agreement resulting from a compromise of proceedings: see *O'Mahony v Gaffney* [1986] IR 36.

[53.] See *Irish Land Law* (2nd ed, 1986), para 4.057 *et seq*.

[54.] See *Ronayne v Sherrard* (1877) IR 11 CL 146. See also a contract relating to options (eg a "put" option) to be included in a lease: *Commission for the New Towns v Cooper (GB) Ltd* [1995] 2 All ER 929.

[55.] Including leases for lives renewable for ever and leases for lives combined with a term of years, *ibid*, para 4.167 *et seq*. Note, however, that under s 4 of Deasy's Act 1860, the grant of certain leases or tenancy agreements (eg, periodic tenancies) may be made orally. A contract for such a grant must still comply with s 2 of the Statute of Frauds (Ir) 1695, see *McCausland v Murphy* (1881) 9 LR Ir 9; Wylie, *Irish Landlord and Tenant Law*, Ch 5.

[56.] Including a contract for the sale of debentures charged on land, even if only by way of floating charge, see *Driver v Broad* [1893] 1 QB 744.

[57.] *McGillycuddy v Joy* [1959] IR 189.

[58.] [1912] 2 IR 318.

[59.] See *Irish Land Law* (2nd ed, 1986), paras 6.113 and 20.25-7, *Irish Landlord and Tenant Law*, para 3.29 *et seq*.

[60.] *Irish Landlord and Tenant Law*, para 3.20 *et seq*.

[61.] (1920) 7 TC 620.

[62.] Gibson J stated that the contract was "for agistment, grazing or temporary depasturage; the lands were to continue to be in Lord Cloncurry's sole occupation; there was to be no contract of tenancy or relation of landlord and tenant; the land was to be used for grazing purposes only; McKenna was to undertake all herding; and Lord Cloncurry was to continue to pay all poor rate, county cess, and all other taxes which might be charged on the lands." *Ibid*, p 625.

"The contract was one concerning land within section 4 of the Statute of Frauds,[63] and not for sale of goods within section 17. McKenna was not the occupier, having only the eatage of the pasture; he was not rateable. Taking the grazing for a temporary purpose, measured by months,[64] he had not such use of the lands as would make him constructively an occupier ... He was not entitled to use the land as land. He only could take the herbage, his enjoyment of which, even if it could be protected by action against wrongful interference, did not vest in McKenna legal occupation for rating and Income Tax. Between *terra* and *vestura terra* there is a marked distinction ..."[65]

On the other hand, in *Scully v Corboy*,[66] Gavan Duffy J held that an oral contract for the letting of "meadowing," fit and ripe for cutting, was enforceable despite s 2 of the Statute of Frauds (Ireland) 1695, as a sale of goods under the Sale of Goods Act 1893. He pointed out that s 62 of the 1893 Act contains a very wide definition of "goods," including things attached to or forming part of the land which are agreed to be severed under the contract of sale. This question of severance has certainly been regarded as crucial by the English courts, even before 1893, in cases involving the sale of growing crops.[67] If the growing crops are sold with the intention that the property in them is not to pass to the purchaser until they are severed from the land, the sale is to be regarded as a sale of goods rather than a sale of an interest in land - especially where the vendor is to cut the crops and deliver them to the purchaser.[68] On the other hand, where there is an intention that the property in the crops is to pass before they are severed from the land, the English courts have drawn a distinction between the natural produce of land (*fructus naturales*), eg, timber[69]or growing grass,[70]

---

63. He should, of course, have referred to s 2! Section 4 in the English Statute of Frauds 1677, was the equivalent of s 2 in the Statute of Frauds (Ir) 1695. He was not the first Irish judge to make this slip, see *Ronayne v Sherrard* (1877) IR 11 CL 146 at 149 (*per* Palles CB); also *Scott v Anderson* (1857) 2 Ir Jur (ns) 422. Section 4 of the Irish Statute concerned trusts of land, see *Irish Land Law* (2nd ed, 1986), para 9.022.

64. Agistment and conacre are sometimes known as the eleven months "take" or eleven months system, see *Irish Land Law* (2nd ed, 1986), para 20.25.

65. (1920) 7 TC 620 at 625. Earlier, Gibson J had commented: "There is, or may be, a difference where the actual land for grazing is the subject of the agreement or where the mere grass is disposed of ...." *Ibid.*

66. [1950] IR 488. He refused to follow *Rhodes v Baker* (1851) 1 ICLR 488 (a usury case) which held that the sale of growing trees or underwood was a sale of an interest in land. But *McKenna v Herlihy* was not cited in *Scully*. See *infra*.

67. *Marshall v Green* (1875) 1 CPD 35. See the discussion by Hudson, 'Goods or Land?' (1958) 22 Conv 137. See also *Williams on Title* (4th ed, by Battersby; 1975), p 50.

68. See *Washbourn v Burrows* (1847) 1 Ex Ch 107.

69. Also growing fruit, see *Rodwell v Phillips* (1842) 9 M & W 501.

70. *Carrington v Roots* (1837) 2 M & W 248.

and produce dependent upon the work and labour of man (*fructus industriales*), eg, growing corn[71] and potatoes.[72] Sale of the former has been held to be the sale of an interest in land,[73] whereas the sale of the latter has been held to be a sale of goods or chattels only.[74] However, most of the English case law on this subject belongs to the nineteenth century and may be of questionable authority today,[75] quite apart from the doubt that must exist as to how far it is applicable in Ireland, especially in view of the prevalence of such informal arrangements as conacre and agistment "lettings".[76] The method of creation of such "contracts" or "lettings" in the rural parts of Ireland tends to blur the distinction between contracts and grants,[77] and s 2 of the Statute of Frauds (Ireland) applies to contracts only. In many cases in practice the conacre or agistment "contract" is in substance a grant and is, therefore, outside the scope of s 2.[78]

[6.10] It is clear that a contract for the sale of things attached to land may come within s 2. One obvious example is a contract relating to fixtures[79] unless it relates to "fixtures" which are removable, eg, a tenant's fixtures[80] or

---

[71.] *Jones v Flint* (1839) 10 Ad & El 753.

[72.] *Evans v Roberts* (1826) 5 B & C 829; *Sainsbury v Matthews* (1838) 4 M & W 143.

[73.] *Rhodes v Baker* (see fn 66 *supra*) is consistent with this principle. *Scully v Corboy* may also be explained on the ground that the fact that the meadowing was fit and ripe for cutting indicated that the parties contemplated its immediate removal, a factor which the English courts have held converts what would otherwise be a sale of an interest in land (in a case of *fructus naturales* like growing timber or grass) into a sale of chattels, see *Marshall v Green* (1875) 1 CPD 35 at 42. See also *Scorell v Boxall* (1827) 1 Y & J 396; *Smith v Surman* (1829) 9 B & C 561. In this respect, an agistment contract, as in *McKenna v Herlihy*, may be different in that the "severance" or "removal" is not so immediate, being spread over the time the animals in question are grazing. Thus in that case Gibson J stated with respect to the agistment contract: "It operated on an area growing grass and bears no resemblance to a purchase of roots, etc, as goods, which, in certain conditions, might make the occupier of a farm liable to an extra assessment [of income tax]."(1920) 7 TC 620 at 626.Yet, does not the act of grazing constitute an immediate "severance" of the grass in question?

[74.] *Parker v Staniland* (1809) 11 East 362; *Mayfield v Wadsley* (1824) B & C 357.

[75.] But see *Lowe v Ashmore Ltd* [1971] Ch 545 at 557, where Megarry J seems to have regarded a contract for the sale of turves as a contract for the sale of goods.

[76.] See *Irish Land Law*, paras [20-25-7]; *Irish Landlord and Tenant Law*, para [3.20] *et seq*.

[77.] This distinction survives in Ireland despite s 3 of Deasy's Act 1860. See *McCausland v Murphy* (1881) 9 LR Ir 9 and the discussion in Sheridan, 'Walsh v Lonsdale in Ireland' (1952) 9 NILQ 190; *Irish Landlord and Tenant Law*, para 5.01 *et seq*.

[78.] Though such lettings create rights similar to those created under a grant of a profit à prendre, they do not have to be granted by a deed, see *Irish Landlord and Tenant Law*, paras 2.18 and 2.25.

[79.] See *Irish Land Law* (2nd ed, 1986), para 4.155.

[80.] See *Lombard and Ulster Banking Ltd v Kennedy* [1974] NI 20. *Cf* fixtures on mortgaged premises, see *Re Ross and Boal Ltd* [1924] 1 IR 129. See also *Irish Landlord and Tenant Law*, Ch 9.

other fixtures which are not regarded as being part of the land, eg, trade, ornamental and domestic fixtures.[81] In England, the Statute of Frauds has been held to apply to a contract for the sale of building materials in a house to be demolished, which were to be removed within a specified time,[82] and to a contract for the removal of slag from land.[83] In *Boyce v Greene*,[84] the Irish King's Bench judges held that a contract for the sale of shares in the Mining Company of Ireland, which possessed mines and other land and whose shares were transferable by a private Act of Parliament, was a contract for the sale of an interest in land requiring a note or memorandum in writing under s 2 of the Statute of Frauds (Ireland) 1695. The more modern view, however, seems to be, at least in England, that such a sale of shares does not involve sale of an interest in land unless there is evidence that the shareholders take a direct interest in the land in question.[85]

[6.11] In Ireland a contract for sale of an individual share in land would clearly come within s 2,[86] as there is no statutory trust for sale in cases of co-ownership,[87] as is the case in England under the Law of Property Act 1925.[88] Even in England, the Court of Appeal, in a controversial decision,[89] stated that s 40(1) of the 1925 Act still applied to a contract for the sale of an undivided share held under the statutory trust for sale, despite the doctrine of conversion,[90] under which the interest would be classified as personalty rather than realty.[91]

[6.12] A contract for a mere licence to occupy land would not seem to involve an interest in land, unless at the very least exclusive occupational

---

[81.] *Re Calvert* [1898] 2 IR 501; *Moore v Merrion Pier and Baths Co* (1901) 1 NIJR 184.

[82.] *Lavery v Purcell* (1888) 39 Ch D 508.*Cf* a contract to build a house, *Wright v Stavert* (1860) 2 El & El 721; see also *Jameson v Kinmell Bay Land Co Ltd* (1931) 47 TLR 593.

[83.] *Morgan v Russell & Sons* [1909] 1 KB 357.

[84.] (1826) Batty 608.

[85.] See *Guardian Builders Ltd v Sleecon* High Court, unrep, 18 August 1988 (1987/7645P); see also *Duncuft v Albrecht* (1841) 12 Sim 189; *Powell v Jessop* (1856) 18 CB 336; *Walker v Bartlett* (1856) 18 CB 845.

[86.] See *Gray v Smith* (1889) 43 Ch D 208.

[87.] See generally, *Irish Land Law* (2nd ed, 1986), Ch 7.

[88.] See ss 34-6.

[89.] *Cooper v Critchley* [1955] Ch 431.

[90.] See *Irish Land Law* (2nd ed, 1986), para 3.094 *et seq*. Yet the definition of "land" in s 205(1)(ix) of the 1925 Act also expressly excluded "an undivided share in land".

[91.] *Cf Re Kempthorne* [1930] 1 Ch 268; *Stevens v Hutchinson* [1953] Ch 299; *Taylor v Taylor* [1968] 1 All ER 843; *Irani Finance, Ltd v Singh* [1971] Ch 59. Note, however, that the Charging Orders Act 1979 made it clear that an order charging land could be made against a beneficial interest in land held under a trust for sale: see *First National Securities Ltd v Hegarty* [1984] 1 All ER 139.

rights are to be conferred.[92] Thus, a contract for lodgings will not usually be within the section, since the lodger or boarder normally has no right to exclusive possession.[93] This test of whether or not rights of exclusive possession are intended to be conferred is also relevant with respect to a similar concept which is commonly met in Ireland, ie, a right of residence.[94] On the other hand, the Northern Ireland courts have taken divergent approaches, albeit in different contexts, to the position of a statutory tenant whose rights of occupation derive solely from the protection conferred by the Rent Acts.[95] In *McCullough v Ministry of Commerce (NI)*,[96] the Divisional Court held that a statutory tenant had a sufficient "estate or interest" in land to be entitled to compensation under compulsory purchase legislation.[97] However, in *McKinty v Belfast Corporation*,[98] McVeigh LJ held that a statutory tenancy was "movable property" within the definition of that expression in s 46(2)[99] of the Interpretation Act (NI) 1954, and was excluded from entitlement to compensation under the Criminal Injuries Act (NI) 1956. Section 4(4) of the 1956 Act[100] excluded compensation in respect of "an incorporeal hereditament (including an easement or profit or other right) or a loss of a mere pleasure or amenity," and the judge held that a statutory tenant had no estate or interest in land, but at most an "other right" within s 4(4). Thus, the courts in Northern Ireland have held that a statutory tenant is entitled to compensation if the property he occupies is acquired compulsorily to build a road, but not if it is bombed by a terrorist!

---

92. See *Isitt v Monaghan CC* (1905) 5 NIJR 118; *Hickey v Tipperary (South Riding) CC* [1931] IR 621; *Belton v Kirwan* [1943] IR 525. See generally on licences relating to land, *Irish Land Law* (2nd ed, 1986), Ch 20. Where there is occupation or other acts justifying application of the doctrine of estoppel (see *Irish Land Law* (2nd ed, 1986), paras 20.07-12), arguably there are sufficient acts of part performance to take the case out of the Statute of Frauds anyway, see para **[6.56]** *post*.

93. See *Waucob v Reynolds* (1850) 1 ICLR 142. See also *Wright v Stavert* (1860) 2 E & E 721; *Appah v Parcliffe Investments Ltd* [1964] 1 WLR 1064; Cullity (1965) 29 Conv 336. *Cf Inman v Stamp* (1815) 1 Stark 12.

94. For a discussion of the various possible constructions of the nature or such a right, see *Irish Land Law* (2nd ed, 1986), paras 20.13-24. See also Harvey, 'Irish Rights of Residence - The Anatomy of a Hermaphrodite' (1970) 21 NILQ 389.

95. See *Irish Land Law* (2nd ed, 1986), para 18.39.

96. [1960] NI 75. See Calvert, (1964) 15 NILQ 110. *Cf Signal v Kay-Stratton* [1955] NZLR 1025.

97. Ie, Roads Act (NI) 1948, s 42(1), which defined "land" as including "buildings and land covered by water, and any estate or interest in land and any easement or right in, to or over land or water."

98. [1973] NI 1.

99. Ie, "property of every description (including growing crops) except immovable property."

100. Replaced by the similar s 4(4) of the Criminal Injuries to Property (Compensation) Act (NI) 1971.

[6.13] Where the contract covers several matters, some relating to interests in land and others not so, eg, a contract for sale of farm land and of farm implements and tools,[101] and there is no written evidence of the contract as a whole, the question arises as to whether it is enforceable as to the matters not covered by s 2 of the Statute of Frauds (Ireland) 1695. The answer seems to depend upon whether, as a matter of construction, the agreement must be taken as one entire agreement or whether it can be severed into parts, with each part being able to stand on its own as a separate agreement.[102] If the former is the true construction, s 2 applies and written evidence of the entire agreement is required.[103] If, however, the contract can be severed into separate parts, those parts which do not relate to interests in land may be enforced without any written evidence.[104] Alternatively, part of the agreement may be construed as a collateral contract and enforceable as such.[105]

D. Written Memorandum or Note

[6.14] Section 2 of the Statute of Frauds (Ireland) 1695, provides that, if the contract itself is not in writing, there must be some written memorandum or note of the contract, ie, some form of written evidence of it.[106] It is important to realise that such a written memorandum or note is not the contract, but only evidence of the contract. Thus, in *McQuaid v Lynam*,[107] which involved, *inter alia*, the question of enforceability of an oral variation in the terms of a contract, Kenny J pointed out:

> "In any discussion of this problem it is essential to distinguish between the case in which the parties to an agreement intend that agreement to find expression in a written contract and that in which the parties make an oral contract which is intended to be binding. If in the latter case a memorandum or note in writing is required by the Statute of Frauds, that memorandum or note does not become the contract. This distinction appears in section 2 of the Statute of Frauds ... In the first type of case, that is, where the parties intend their agreement to find expression in a written document, a subsequent oral variation of the contract is not effective unless

---

[101.] See *Buckley v Irwin* [1960] NI 98.

[102.] *Bentham v Hardy* (1843) 6 Ir LR 179. See also *Bigg v Whisking* (1853) 14 CB 195.

[103.] *Bentham v Hardy, op cit.* See also *Hawkesworth v Turner* (1930) 46 TLR 389.

[104.] *Morgan v Griffith* (1871) LR 6 Exch 70; *Erskine v Adeane* (1873) 8 Ch App 756 (agreements for leases and to keep down game). Note the divergent views on agreements for the sale of land and for set-off against the purchase price, see *Archer v Hall* (1859) 7 WR 222 and *Savage v Canning* (1867) 16 WR 133.

[105.] See *Godley v Power* (1961) 95 ILTR 135; *Kennedy v Wrenne* [1981] ILRM 81; *Carthy v O'Neill* [1981] ILRM 443. See also *Angell v Duke* (1875) LR 10 QB 174; *De Lasalle v Guildford* [1901] 2 KB 215; *City of Westminster Properties Ltd v Mudd* [1959] Ch 129; *Wells (Merstham) Ltd v Buckland Sand and Silica Ltd* [1965] 2 QB 170.

[106.] See para **[6.06]** *supra.*

[107.] [1965] IR 564. *Cf Hoon v Nolan* (1967) 101 ILTR 99.

it is evidenced by a memorandum or note in writing ... But in the other type of case, where the oral agreement is intended to be the contract, evidence may be given of an agreed variation even if there is a memorandum or note of the contract but not of the variation."[108]

It is clearly settled that the memorandum or note does not have to be brought into existence at the same time as the contract.[109] It may come into existence much later, but must be in existence by the time the action on the contract is commenced.[110] On the other hand, s 2 clearly presupposes the existence of a contract when it speaks of a memorandum or note "thereof," so that normally the contract must precede the memorandum or note.[111] However, there is a line of authority that a written offer, which has been accepted orally, is a sufficient memorandum provided it is signed and containing all the relevant details - even though no contract can be said to exist until the offer is accepted.[112]

1. Intention

[6.15] It is also settled that the party or parties in question need not intend to create the requisite memorandum or note. As Meredith J put it in *Murphy v Harrington*[113]:

" ... a signature to a document which contains the terms of a contract is available for the purpose of satisfying the section, though put *alio intuito*, and not in order to attest or verify the contract ..."[114]

[108.] *Ibid*, p 573. See also *Beckett v Nurse* [1948] 1 KB 535.

[109.] See *Powell v Dillon* (1814) 2 Ba & B 416; *Black v Kavanagh* (1974) 108 ILTR 91.

[110.] Though the English courts seem to have held that a defence raised by a party not originally a party to the action, but subsequently joined, may constitute a sufficient memorandum against that party, see *Grindell v Bass* [1920] 2 Ch 487; *Farr, Smith & Co v Messers Ltd* [1928] 1 KB 397. *Cf. Hardy v Elphinck* [1974] Ch 65.

[111.] Thus, in *Dyas v Stafford* (1882) 9 LR Ir 520 at 523, Law C pointed out that, "in the case of a sale by auction, the written evidence which the statute requires is not itself the contract, but only a note of it; for the actual sale takes place when, in response to the highest bidder, the auctioneer's hammer goes down." See also FitzGibbon LJ at p 529: "Before any note or memorandum of a contract can be made, there must be a contract, complete and concluded, which, but for the Statute of Frauds, would bind and be enforced against the party to be charged".

[112.] *Swan v Miller* [1919] 1 IR 151. See also discussion in *Coleman v Upcott* (1707) 5 Vin Abr 527; *Powers v Fowler* (1855) 4 E & B 511; *Lever v Koffler* [1901] Ch 543; *Parker v Clark* [1960] 1 WLR 286; *Tiverton Estates Ltd v Wearwell Ltd* [1974] 2 WLR 176. And see *Dyas v Stafford* (1882) 9 LR Ir 520 at 524 (*per* Law C).

[113.] [1927] IR 339.

[114.] *Ibid*, p 342. *Cf Re Hoyle* [1893] 1 Ch 85 at 99 (*per* Bowen LJ). See also Kenny J in *McQuaid v Lynam*: "It is settled law that the memorandum or note required by the Statute of Frauds may consist of a document which was not intended to be such a note or memorandum but it must, however, be signed by the party to be charged and the signature must have been intended to authenticate the whole document of which it forms a part." [1965] IR 564 at 569. As regards the need for signature by the party to be charged, see para **[6.32]** *infra*.

This is a vitally important point to remember, for the law reports are littered with cases where a memorandum or note has been held to have come into existence inadvertently, so that the parties found themselves bound by a contract without intending this to happen and without realising at the time that it had happened.[115] As we shall see later, there have been numerous cases where solicitors' correspondence has been held to constitute a sufficient memorandum[116] and the dangers of inadvertently bringing such a memorandum or note into existence should never be ignored by solicitors. All too often draft contracts containing the details of what the parties may have already agreed orally are dispatched, accompanied by letters signed by solicitors without qualification. It is true that the solicitor's signature may not be enough to render the memorandum binding on his client, but this is a matter of construction and, as we shall see, there have been many cases where it has been held to be enough.[117] Apart from that, it is clear that most solicitors, and, no doubt, their clients intend that no contract should come into existence until the draft contract has been approved and the final form is signed by the parties themselves. If that is the case,[118] it cannot be emphasised too strongly that the greatest care should be taken to see that this is made clear in all correspondence, eg, by stating expressly that the matter is still "subject to contract".[119] After considerable controversy,[120] the courts seem to have reached the conclusion that such a qualification in the alleged memorandum, by negativing the existence of an agreement between the parties, renders it insufficient for the purpose of the Statute of Frauds.[121]

[115.] See, eg, *Murphy v Harrington* [1927] IR 339; *McQuaid v Lynam* [1965] IR 564.

[116.] See, eg, *Godley v Power* (1961) 95 ILTR 135; *Lavan v Walsh* [1964] IR 87; *Black v Kavanagh* (1974) 108 ILTR 91.

[117.] See para **[6.42]** *infra*.

[118.] *Cf* where it is not so, see *Black v Kavanagh* (1974) 108 ILTR 91. See also *City of Glasgow Friendly Society v Gilpin* (1971) 22 NILQ 196. See also where an "exchange" is contemplated: para **[6.61]** *infra*.

[119.] See *Lowis v Wilson* [1949] IR 347. *Cf Godley v Power* (1961) 95 ILTR 135; *Law v Roberts & Co* [1964] IR 292. See also *Keppel v Wheeler* [1927] 1 KB 577, especially at 584 (*per* Bankes LJ); *Spottiswood, Ballantyne & Co Ltd v Doreen Appliances Ltd* [1942] 2 KB 32, especially at 35 (*per* Lord Greene MR). See further on such conditional contracts, para **[7.06]** *post*.

[120.] See, eg, *Kelly v Park Hall School Ltd* [1979] IR 340; *Casey v Irish Intercontinental Bank* [1977] IR 364; *Park Hall School Ltd v Overend* [1987] IR 1; *Mulhall v Haren* [1981] IR 364. *Cf Thirkell v Cambi* [1919] 2 KB 90; *Griffiths v Young* [1970] Ch 675; *Law v Jones* [1974] Ch 112. See also Wilkinston, '*Law v Jones*: Problems for Conveyancers' (1973) 123 New LJ 941.

[121.] The leading decision in Ireland is that of the Supreme Court in *Boyle v Lee* [1992] 1 IR 555; see para **[7.08]** *post* and Farrell, *Irish Law of Specific Performance* (1994) Ch 4. *Cf Tiverton Estates Ltd v Wearwell Ltd* [1974] 2 WLR 176.

2. Form

[6.16] It should be clear from the preceding discussion that one of the difficulties about s 2 of the Statute of Frauds (Ireland) 1695, is that it does not specify exactly what form the requisite memorandum or note should take. The result is that, apart from the parties' or their solicitors' correspondence, which we mentioned above, a variety of documentation[122] has been accepted by the courts as a sufficient memorandum or note, eg, an entry in a solicitor's instruction book,[123] a note in an auctioneer's sale book,[124] a cheque for a deposit,[125] a receipt for a deposit together with an application to a building society for a loan[126] and a draft tenancy agreement.[127] Of course, in practice the written evidence usually takes the form of a detailed written contract drawn up by the vendor's solicitor and approved by the purchaser's solicitor before signing by their respective clients.[128] Such a contract is usually based on the standard form of contract, incorporating conditions of sale, issued by the Law Society,[129] and this standard form includes a section providing the memorandum required by the Statute of Frauds.[130]

3. Contents

[6.17] Though the courts have to recognise that no precise form of memorandum or note is required by the Statute of Frauds, they have made it clear that the evidentiary purpose of such a memorandum or note dictates that it must contain certain basic information about the agreement of which it is said to be evidence. It must, as Palles CB once said, "contain on its face all the essential elements of a contract."[131] The reason is clear, as was explained by Gibson J in *Crane v Naughten*.[132]

---

122. Though often as a result of joinder of two or more documents, see para **[6.28]** *infra*.
123. *Murphy v Harrington* [1927] IR 339.
124. *McMeekin v Stevenson* [1917] 1 IR 348. *Cf Crane v Naughten* [1912] 2 IR 318.
125. Though details of the sale were written at the bottom of it, see *Doherty v Gallagher* High Court, unrep, 9 June 1975 (1973/2830P).
126. *McQuaid v Lynam* [1965] IR 564.
127. *Scott v McCombe* (1965) 16 NILQ 122 and 418. *Cf City of Glasgow Friendly Society v Gilpin Ltd* (1971) 22 NILQ 196. See also *Arnold v Veale* [1979] IR 342n.
128. See Ch 9 *post. Cf* the case of a sale by public auction, see paras **[2.08]** *ante* and **[8.02]** *post*.
129. See the discussion in Chs 9 and 10 *post*.
130. See para **[9.05]** *post*.
131. *Carrigy v Brock* (1871) IR 5 CL 501 at 504. See also *Scott v McCombe* (1965) 16 NILQ 122 and 418; *McGillycuddy v Joy* [1959] IR 189 at 211 (*per* Budd J); *Black v Kavanagh* (1974) 108 ILTR 91 at 96 (*per* Gannon J).
132. [1912] 2 IR 318. See also *Wallace v Roe* [1903] 1 IR 32 at 35 (*per* Chatterton V-C).

"It is a memorandum of what the contract is. Accordingly, if the memorandum is not in accordance with the true contract, it is a bad memorandum ..."[133]

[6.18] As a result of centuries of case law on the subject, it has come to be recognised that the "essential elements" which must be included[134] for the memorandum or note to be effective are what are sometimes referred to as the four "P"s,[135] ie, specification of the parties, the property, the price, and any other essential provisions.[136] This fourth category is something of a vague "catch-all" requirement, the substance of which tends to fluctuate with each new decision.[137] What seems clear is that the courts are prepared to adopt a flexible approach to its application in particular cases, and Irish judges have recently emphasised that a subjective test should be adopted, ie what must be included, at least under this fourth category, is what the parties themselves regarded as essential or material to their agreement and not what the court, on a more objective basis, might regard as essential or material.[138] Thus, so long as the other three categories are included in the alleged memorandum or note, it will be sufficient for the purposes of the Statute of Frauds even though the court might consider that it should have included other terms - if those other terms were not regarded as important by the parties.[139] In *Black v Kavanagh*,[140] Gannon J concluded that neither of the parties to an agreement for the sale of a private house "attached any importance to the matter of the payment of a deposit or as to its amount".[141] In *Barratt v Costelloe*,[142] Kenny J took the same view of written correspondence which did not disclose the title being offered nor give an unequivocal date for the granting of possession to the purchaser. Needless to say, these matters would normally be covered by a formal agreement drawn up by a solicitor, especially if he used the standard form issued by the Law

---

[133.] *Ibid*, p 324.

[134.] In addition to the question of signature by the party to be charged, see para **[6.32]** *infra*.

[135.] See further, para **[6.20]** *et seq, infra*. More seems to be required in the case of agreements relating to the grant of a lease or tenancy, see para **[6.26]** *infra*.

[136.] Subject, of course, to the point that a party may waive a provision missing from the memorandum, see para **[6.07]** *supra*.

[137.] *Cf* in another context Lord Macnaughten's fourth category of charitable trusts, see *Irish Land Law* (2nd ed, 1986), paras 9.091 and 9.102-3.

[138.] *Barrett v Costelloe* (1973) 107 ILTSJ 239. See also *Anom Engineering Ltd v Thornton* High Court, unrep, 1 February 1983 (1987/198P).

[139.] *Stinson v Owens* (1973) 24 NILQ 218. See also *Delgado v Crean* High Court, unrep, 28 May 1978 (1977/1904P).

[140.] (1974) 108 ILTR 91.

[141.] *Ibid*, p 95. See also *Stinson v Owens* (1973) 24 NILQ 218. *Cf Law v Roberts & Co* [1964] IR 292 at 297 (*per* Kenny J); *Boyle v Lee* [1992] 1 IR 555.

[142.] (1973) 107 ILTSJ 239.

Society. And, it seems clear from the judgments of the Supreme Court in *Boyle v Lee*[143] that the absence of any reference to what most parties would regard as an important element in the agreement, eg, the deposit to be paid, will raise the question whether the parties had ever reached the stage of a concluded agreement.

[6.19] On the other hand, it also seems to be the case that inclusion of extra terms, not agreed by the parties, does not necessarily vitiate the memorandum or note. This emphasises once again the point that the memorandum or note required by the Statute of Frauds is not the contract itself and so need not mirror exactly what has been agreed[144] - it need contain the "essentials" of that agreement only to provide evidence of the parties' bargain. This point arises frequently where the alleged memorandum or note consists of a solicitor's correspondence and a draft agreement, which may have included in it terms not specifically agreed to by the parties themselves but which one or other, or both, of their solicitors consider ought to be included. Thus, in *Black v Kavanagh*,[145] Gannon J held that the parties' prior oral agreement was evidenced by letters written by the vendor's solicitor in connection with a draft written contract which contained many additional provisions,[146] but was never signed by the vendor. In *Scott v McCombe*,[147] on the other hand, Lord MacDermott LCJ had held that a draft tenancy agreement was a sufficient memorandum even though several amendments had been made to it, so that it did not conform exactly with what the parties originally agreed. The learned judge said:

> "If the party to be charged signs a memorandum containing the essentials of what has been agreed, he cannot be entitled to the protection of the Statute merely because he has added to the memorandum items which have not been agreed."[148]

[143.] [1992] 1 IR 555. For further discussion of the implications of this case see para **[7.08]** *post*.

[144.] See para **[6.17]** *supra*.

[145.] (1974) 108 ILTR 91.

[146.] He also held that the vendor's solicitor had no authority to vary the prior oral agreement made by his client, see para **[3.33]** *supra* and **[6.42]** *infra*.

[147.] (1965) 16 NILQ 122. See also *Guardian Builders Ltd v Kelly* [1981] ILRM 127; *Carthy v O'Neill* [1981] ILRM 443.

[148.] *Ibid*, p 123. See also *City of Glasgow Friendly Society v Gilpin* (1971) 22 NILQ 196, where Gibson J held that submission of a draft tenancy agreement in somewhat but not radically different terms from those contemplated by the parties in their original agreement did not constitute a repudiation of that agreement; nor did subsequent correspondence on the basis of the draft amount to mutual rescission of the earlier agreement, which was, therefore, enforceable as evidenced by the correspondence.

But the Northern Ireland Court of Appeal varied his judgment on this point, holding that the memorandum had to be found in the correspondence rather than in the draft tenancy agreement, since it was clear that this contained a note of a number of terms not agreed by the parties.[149] In *Stinson v Owens*,[150] Lord MacDermott, in holding that an oral agreement for sale of a farm was evidenced by a memorandum consisting of an estate agent's letter and draft contract enclosed therewith, drew a distinction between extra terms included in the memorandum which purport to be terms of the agreement made by the parties and those which are merely put forward for consideration. If the extra terms were not in fact part of the parties' oral agreement, then in the former case the memorandum is bad as a misstatement of the agreement, but in the latter case it may still be sufficient provided it does also include what the parties did agree. These cases reiterate the need for extreme caution to be exercised by solicitors in sending draft contracts along with signed correspondence.[151]

(i) Parties

[6.20] The memorandum or note must contain either the names of the parties to the contract in question or such description of them as enables them to be identified with certainty.[152] It must refer to both the vendor and purchaser and indicate which party is the vendor and which the purchaser.[153] If a party is not named, the description must be sufficiently precise to enable the court to identify him, if necessary by reference to other documents referred to.[154] Thus, it has been held that descriptions like "proprietor",[155] "owner",[156] "mortgagee",[157] "legal personal representative",[158] "tenant"[159] and even

---

[149.] (1965) 16 NILQ 418.

[150.] (1973) 24 NILQ 218.

[151.] See para **[6.16]** *ante* and **[6.47]** *supra*.

[152.] *Law v Roberts & Co* [1964] IR 292 at 297 (*per* Kenny J). See also *Irvine v Deane* (1849) 2 Ir Jur (os) 209; *Guardian Builders Ltd v Kelly* [1981] ILRM 127. *Cf Jarrett v Hunter* (1886) 34 Ch D 182 at 184-5 (*per* Kay J).

[153.] See *Boyce v Greene* (1826) Batty 608. See also *Dewar v Mintoff* [1912] 2 KB 373. *Cf Carncross v Hamilton* (1890) 9 NZLR 91 (clear from the surrounding circumstances which party was which). And see *Stokes v Whicker* [1920] 1 Ch 411.

[154.] A maxim often applied is - *id certum est quod certum reddi potest* (certain is that which can be rendered certain), see *Viscount Massereene v Finlay* (1850) 13 Ir LR 496; *Waldron v Jacob* (1870) IR 5 Eq 131. See also paras **[6.22]** *infra* and **[17.23]** *post*. In *Davies v Sweet* [1962] 2 QB 300, the English Court of Appeal held that a memorandum is sufficient if it identifies, instead of one of the parties to the contract, someone else who will be bound by it, eg an agent of that party who has incurred personal liability (see para **[6.35]** *infra*).

[155.] *Sale v Lambert* (1874) LR 18 Eq 1; *Rossiter v Miller* (1878) 3 App Cas 1124.

[156.] *Jarrett v Hunter* (1886) 34 Ch D 182; *Butcher v Nash* (1889) 61 LT 72.

[157.] *Allen & Co Ltd v Whiteman* (1920) 89 LJ Ch 534.

[158.] *Towle v Topham* (1877) 37 LT 308; *Fay v Miller, Wilkins & Co* [1941] Ch 360.

[159.] *Stokell v Niven* (1889) 61 LT 18. *Cf Coombs v Wilkes* [1891] 3 Ch 77 ("landlord").

"you"[160] and "I"[161] have in certain circumstances been sufficient.[162] On the other hand, other descriptions have been held to be too ambiguous or equivocal to be sufficient for identification purposes, eg, "vendor",[163] "client"[164] and "friend".[165]

[6.21] It does not seem to matter in what part of the memorandum the parties are named or identified, or the order in which the details are written down. In *Murphy v Harrington*,[166] Meredith J stated:

" ... it appears to me that if the document is one which the Court is of opinion must be taken as a whole, as in this case, it can make no difference at what point of time in the one entire transaction the names were actually written down: Whether, that is to say, they were put down last, as the names of the parties to the contract above written, or the particulars last, as the terms of the contract entered into between the parties whose names are written above. Where the document owes its origin to the parties giving to a solicitor instructions as to the contract entered into between them, with a view to his taking the usual steps preparatory to completion, the latter is the natural order. The names were in fact, as evidence showed, put down as the names of the parties who gave the instructions that followed, and that set forth the terms of the contract entered into between them -which contract the solicitor was to take the necessary steps to carry into effect ..."[167]

(ii) Property

[6.22] The property which is the subject-matter of the contract must also be so described in the memorandum as to be identifiable with certainty. The maxim *id certum est quod certum reddi potest*[168] is frequently invoked by the courts in this context and parol evidence will be admitted, if necessary, to establish the identity of the property referred to in the memorandum. As Blackburn CJ said in *Viscount Massereene v Finlay*:

" ... it is clear upon principle we do not trench upon the Statute of Frauds by admitting this evidence. Where there is a reference in the contract to

---

[160.] *Carr v Lynch* [1900] 1 Ch 613.
[161.] *Stokes v Whicker* [1920] 1 Ch 411.
[162.] See *Rossiter v Miller* (1878) 3 App Cas 1124 at 1141 (*per* Lord Cairns).
[163.] *Potter v Duffield* (1874) LR 18 Eq 4; *Thomas v Brown* (1876) 1 QBD 714. See also *Jarrett v Hunter* (1886) 34 Ch D 182 ("solicitor to the vendor").
[164.] *Jarrett v Hunter, op cit.*
[165.] *Ibid.*
[166.] [1927] IR 339.
[167.] *Ibid*, pp 342-3.
[168.] See *Viscount Massereene v Finlay* (1850) 13 Ir LR 496. Also *Law v Roberts & Co* [1964] IR 292 at 297 (*per* Kenny J). And see para **[6.20]** *supra.*

something *dehors*, it is settled law that that something is capable of proof."[169]

Thus, in *Waldron v Jacob*,[170] evidence was admitted which showed that a letter referring to "this place" was written at a certain place.[171] In that case, Chatterton V-C accepted the principle that the memorandum need contain a physical description of the property only; it need not refer to the vendor's legal title to it or interest in it. As he put it, a reference to the property "imports an agreement for the purchase and sale of the vendor's interest, whatever it was."[172] On the other hand, in *Viscount Massereene v Finlay*[173] there was an express reference in letters constituting the memorandum to the vendor's "interest" in the property and it was held that parol evidence could be resorted to to show what that interest was.

[6.23] Once again some expressions have been held to be insufficient, as too general eg, the words "the property"[174] on its own, as compared with "my house".[175] As we discuss later, further details are required where the property is leasehold.[176]

(iii) Price

[6.24] The memorandum or note must specify the consideration for the sale,[177] or at least some method of ascertaining it.[178] The memorandum may indicate that the price is to be arrived at by valuation.[179] If the valuer is named, it seems that the contract remains unenforceable until he makes his valuation.[180] If he is not named, it may be enforced as an agreement to sell at a "fair" valuation.[181] But it must be noted that a price to be fixed by valuation

---

[169.] *Ibid*, pp 504-5. See also *Guardian Builders Ltd v Kelly* [1981] ILRM 127.

[170.] (1870) IR 5 Eq 131.

[171.] *Cf Smith v Mansi* [1963] 1 WLR 26 at 30 (*per* Russell LJ).

[172.] (1870) IR 5 Eq 131 at 137.See also *Timmins v Moreland Street Property Co Ltd* [1958] Ch 110 at 118-21 (*per* Jenkins LJ) and 132 (*per* Romer LJ).

[173.] (1850) 13 Ir LR 496.

[174.] *Vale of Neath County v Furness* (1876) 45 LJ Ch 276. *Cf Shardlow v Cotterell* (1881) 20 Ch D 90.

[175.] *Cowley v Watts* (1853)17 Jur 172. *Cf Ogilvie v Foljambe* (1817) 3 Mer 53. See also *Auerbach v Nelson* [1919] 2 Ch 383.

[176.] See para **[6.26]** *infra*.

[177.] *Law v Roberts & Co* [1964] IR 292 at 297 (*per* Kenny J).

[178.] See *Smith v Jones* [1952] 2 All ER 907. The method must be effective, see *Carr v Phelan* [1976-7] ILRM 149, and see para **[8.07]** *post*.

[179.] See *Selkirk v Romar Investments Ltd* [1963] 1 WLR 1415.

[180.] *Vickers v Vickers* (1867) LR 4 Eq 529; *Firth v Midland Rly Co* (1875) LR 20 Eq 100.

[181.] *Wilks v Davis* (1817) 3 Mer 507; *Morgan v Milman* (1853) 3 De GM & G 24. Where the parties' mechanism, eg, arbitration breaks down, the court may substitute other machinery, but probably only where this is a subsidiary part of the agreement: see the House of Lords decision in *Sudbrook Trading Estate Ltd v Eggleton* [1983] 1 AC 444. *Cf Lonergan v McCarthy* [1983] NI 129.

is not the same as a price "to be agreed". In the latter case, the parties have made no agreement at all on the price and the contract is unenforceable.[182] The courts will not imply an agreement to sell at a reasonable price, if the parties have not agreed on a price.[183]

(iv) Other Provisions

[6.25] As to whether other provisions should be included in the memorandum or note depends upon whether the parties agreed to such other provisions and regarded them as being important. We saw earlier that the Irish judges have reiterated that the test is a subjective one - it depends upon whether the provisions in question were regarded by the parties as essential or material to their agreement.[184] Each case must depend upon the court's interpretation of the parties' view on the provision which is alleged to be missing from the memorandum.[185] Thus, the Irish courts have upheld a memorandum as being sufficient despite the absence of any statement of the deposit to be paid by the purchaser,[186] of a date for the purchaser taking possession of the property[187] or of the title being offered by the vendor.[188] Yet these are all matters which one would normally expect to be covered by any formal contract drawn up by a solicitor.[189] It should also be remembered, however, that the general law may imply terms into the contract in the absence of any express provision, eg, that the purchaser will be given vacant possession on completion[190] and that completion will take place within a reasonable time of signing the contract.[191]

(v) Leases

[6.26] It seems to be clear that a memorandum or note of a contract to grant a lease must contain some additional information.[192] There is a long line of

---

[182.] *Loftus v Roberts* (1902) 18 TLR 532. *Cf Hillas & Co Ltd v Arcos Ltd* (1932) 147 LT 503. See also *Regalian Properties plc v London Dockland Development Corporation* [1995] 1 All ER 1005.

[183.] *Gourley v Duke of Somerset* (1815) 19 Ves 429 at 431 (*per* Grant MR); *Morgan v Milman* (1853) 3 De GM & G 24 at 27 (*per* Lord Cranworth, LC).

[184.] See para **[6.18]** *supra*

[185.] See the discussion in *Hoon v Nolan* (1967) 101 ILTR 99.

[186.] *Stinson v Owens* (1973) 24 NILQ 218. *Cf Barratt v Costelloe* (1973) 107 ILTSJ 239 (figure for deposit stated in memorandum never communicated to vendor by his agent); *Boyle v Lee* [1992] 1 IR 555 discussed in para **[7.08]** *post*.

[187.] *Barratt v Costelloe, op cit*. See also *Doherty v Gallagher* High Court, unrep, 9 June 1975 (1973/2830P) (no reference in memorandum and only vague assurance given orally). *Cf Hawkins v Price* [1947] Ch 645. And see *Black v Kavanagh* (1974) 108 ILTR 91.

[188.] *Barratt v Costelloe, op cit*. See also *Waldron v Jacob* (1870) IR 5 Eq 131. *Cf Kerns v Manning* [1935] IR 869, especially at 880 (*per* Murnaghan J).

[189.] Hence their inclusion in the draft contract drawn up by the vendor's solicitor in *Black v Kavanagh* (1974) 108 ILTR 91. See *Boyle v Lee* [1992] 1 IR 555 and para **[7.08]** *post*.

[190.] See para **[10.44]** *post*.

[191.] See para **[13.11]** *post*.

[192.] The consideration (see para **[6.24]** *supra*) is normally the rent to be charged, but, of course, a fine (lump sum) may also be payable, see para **[19.25]** *post*.

authority in Ireland to the effect that the memorandum or note[193] must specify the date of commencement of the lease or tenancy, and, if it does not, the memorandum or note is insufficient.[194] The courts will not imply a term that it is to commence within a reasonable time of the agreement.[195] However, it seems that the memorandum will be sufficient if it does at least contain an express reference to circumstances from which the date of commencement can be clearly ascertained. Thus, in *Phelan v Tedcastle*[196] Chatterton V-C explained:

> "The agreement before me now, in my opinion, contains a sufficiently clear statement of the *terminus* from which the parties contracted that the lease should commence. It contains a description of two starting points, the first being that at which the defendant was to enter into possession for a temporary letting, which is defined by the words, 'I propose taking possession of said premises immediately after the execution of the *habere* in said ejectment, and continuing to hold same until the six months for redemption expires.' There is no more uncertainty in the terms of the agreement than there would be in an agreement to hold for a life."[197]

It is also established that the memorandum or note must specify the duration of the lease or the term for which the tenancy is granted.[198]

4. Writing

[6.27] It is of the essence of the requirements of the Statute of Frauds that the evidence of the contract for sale should be in writing. We saw earlier than no particular form of writing is necessary[199] and so, as is the case with analogous statutory requirements,[200] presumably writing includes typewriting, printing, lithography, photography and any other method of reproducing words in visible form.[201]

[193.] A *fortiori* the contract itself.

[194.] *Wyse v Russell* (1882) 11 LR Ir 173; *Phelan v Tedcastle* (1885) 15 LR Ir 169; *White v McMahon* (1886) 18 LR Ir 460; *Erskine v Armstrong* (1887) 20 LR Ir 296; *Williams v Kenneally* (1912) 46 ILTR 292; *Kerns v Manning* [1935] IR 869; *White v Spendlove* [1942] IR 224; *McQuaid v Lynam* [1965] IR 564; *Conaty v Ulster Development Ltd* (1966) 17 NILQ 162; *O'Flaherty v Arvan Properties Ltd* Supreme Court, unrep, 21 July 1977.

[195.] See *Harvey v Pratt* [1965] 2 All ER 786.

[196.] (1885) 15 LR Ir 169. See also *White v McMahon* (1886) 18 LR Ir 460.

[197.] *Ibid*, p 174.

[198.] *Clinan v Cooke* (1802) 1 Sch & Lef. 22; *Crane v Naughten* [1912] 2 IR 318.

[199.] See para **[6.16]** *supra*.

[200.] Eg, the requirement that wills be in writing, Succession Act 1965, s 78. Brady, *Succession Law in Ireland* (2nd ed, 1995), para [2.04] *et seq*.

[201.] See Interpretation Act 1889, s 20.

5. Joinder of Documents

[6.28] It is settled that the memorandum or note need not be contained in one document only, but may be made up from a number of documents.[202] A common example is where a sufficient memorandum is found to exist in correspondence,[203] whether written between the parties themselves,[204] or the parties and their agents,[205] or their agents themselves.[206] Thus, there have been numerous cases where the correspondence between the solicitors acting for the two parties to the transaction has been held to constitute a sufficient memorandum or note.[207] However, it must be emphasised that not every document written in the course of the transaction can be used necessarily, for the cases establish that certain conditions must be satisfied to justify joinder of two or more documents.[208] In *McQuaid v Lynam*[209] Kenny J stated:

> "I think that the modern cases establish that a number of documents may together constitute a note or memorandum in writing if they have come into existence in connection with the same transaction or if they contain internal references which connect them with each other."[210]

[6.29] It is clear that if each of the documents in question is signed by the party to be charged or his agent,[211] and if, when they are put side by side, they are obviously connected with the same transaction, either because they expressly refer to each other or to the same transaction, or by implication so refer, then they may be taken together to constitute a sufficient memorandum or note.[212] Greater difficulty arises, however, where only one of the documents is signed. The rule then seems to be that you must start

---

[202.] See *Chambers v Betty* (1815) Beat 488; *Viscount Massereene v Finlay* (1850) 13 Ir LR 496; *Barratt v Costelloe* (1973) 107 ILT 239. See Fridman, 'Joinder of Documents to Form a Memorandum' (1958) 22 Conv 275.

[203.] *Wright v St George* (1861) 12 Ir Ch R 226 at 233 (*per* Smith MR). See also *Powell v Dillon* (1814) 2 Ba & B 416.

[204.] See *Barry v O'Grady* (1846) 9 Ir Eq R 550; *Maconchy v Clayton* [1898] 1 IR 291; *Law v Roberts & Co* [1964] IR 292.

[205.] See *Stinson v Owens* (1973) 24 NILQ 218.

[206.] *Lavan v Walsh* [1964] IR 87.

[207.] For examples, see *Lord Cloncurry v Laffan* [1924] 1 IR 78; *Godley v Power* (1961) 95 ILTR 135; *Lavan v Walsh, op cit*; *Black v Kavanagh* (1974) 108 ILTR 91.

[208.] For examples, see para **[6.31]** *infra*

[209.] [1965] IR 564. See also the discussion in the leading English case, *Timmins v Moreland Street Property Co Ltd* [1958] Ch 110. *Cf* the position now under s 2 of the English Law of Property (Miscellaneous Provisions) Act 1989: see *Firstpost Homes Ltd v Johnson* [1995] 4 All ER 355.

[210.] *Ibid*, p 570.

[211.] See further para **[6.32]** *infra*.

[212.] *Irvine v Deane* (1849) 2 Ir Jur (os) 209. See also *Davis v Gallagher* [1933] LJ Ir 26; *Sheers v Thimbley & Son* (1879) 76 LT 709.

with the signed document and can connect with it only other documents which are referred to in it, either expressly or impliedly. Thus, in *Waldron v Jacob*,[213] Chatterton V-C refused to connect an advertisement for the sale of the property in question with a signed letter concerning the property. He said:

> "I do not think I can look to the advertisement for sale to construe this written memorandum, as it is neither expressly nor impliedly referred to in it, nor is it shown that the agreement was entered into on the basis of it ..."[214]

You cannot join other documents with the signed document without such a cross-reference, and you cannot establish a connection by parol evidence. As Gibson J put it in *Crane v Naughten*[215]:

> " ... documents relied upon as constituting the contract must refer to each other in such a way as to dispense with parol evidence of connection."'[216]

Thus, it is clear that there cannot be a cross-reference to a document not in existence when the first document was signed.[217] In *McQuaid v Lynam*,[218] Kenny J commented:

> " ... as the memorandum or note considered as a whole must be signed[219] it would seem to follow that the document which is signed must be the last of the documents in point of time, for it would be absurd to hold that a person who signed a document could be regarded as having signed another document which was not in existence when he signed the first."[220]

---

213. (1870) IR 5 Eq 131. See also *Boyce v Greene* (1826) Batty 608. *Cf Stokes v Whicker* [1920]1 Ch 411 *Burgess v Cox* [1951] Ch 383. And see *Howlin v Power (Dublin) Ltd* High Court, unrep, 5 May 1978 (1977/736P).

214. *Ibid*, p 137.

215. [1912] 2 IR 318. *Cf Peirce v Corf* (1874) LR 9 QB 210 at 218 (*per* Archibald J); *Long v Miller* (1879) 4 CPD 450 at 456 (*per* Thesiger LJ).

216. *Ibid*, p 327. Earlier he said: "If an auctioneer sells on his catalogue, he must refer to it in his auction-book." *Ibid*, p 326. See also *Clinan v Cooke* (1802) 1 Sch & Lef 22 at 33 (*per* Lord Redesdale) para **[6.30]** *infra*.

217. *Bolyce v Greene* (1826) Batty 608; *Crane v Naughten* [1912] 2 IR 318, especially at 326 (*per* Gibson J). See also *Turnley v Hartley* (1848) 3 New Pract Cas 96.

218. [1965] IR 564.

219. See further, para **[6.32]** *infra*.

220. *Op cit*, p 570. Further, terms added after the signing cannot normally be incorporated in the memorandum, see *White v Spendlove* [1942] IR 224. Though additions made in the presence of the party who has just signed, and accepted by him, may be incorporated, see *Conaty v Ulster Development Ltd* (1966) 17 NILQ 162. See also *Timmins v Moreland Street Property Co Ltd* [1958] Ch 110 at 123 (*per* Jenkins LJ). *Cf Smith v Chadwick* (1882) 20 Ch D 27 at 62 (*per* Jessel MR).

It is also clear that there cannot be a cross-reference in the signed document to another document of which, at the time of signing, the person signing was not aware, even though it was in existence at that time.[221]

[6.30] Once a connection is established between two or more documents, then parol evidence is admissible to explain them. In *Clinan v Cooke*,[222] a question arose as to whether an agreement for a lease could be connected with a public advertisement relating to the letting of the property and Lord Redesdale LC remarked:

> "Now if the agreement had referred to the advertisement, I agree parol evidence might have been admitted to show what was the thing (namely the advertisement) so referred to, for then it would be an agreement to grant for so much time as was expressed in the advertisement, and then the identity of the advertisement might be proved by parol evidence; but there is no reference whatever to the advertisement in this agreement ..."[223]

In *Craig v Elliott*,[224] Chatterton V-C explained further:

> "These cases[225] show that parol evidence may be received, not only to identify a particular writing referred to, but to prove that such a writing existed and must have been referred to by the writing signed by the party sought to be charged."[226]

That case involved the question of whether a signed letter which referred to a draft lease for the property in question was a sufficient memorandum, and Chatterton V-C said later:

> " ... the letter contained sufficient reference to the draft of the lease to admit parol evidence to show that there was such a draft and that there was nothing else to which the letter could refer, and thus to connect the draft with the letter signed by the defendant. These papers so connected constitute a sufficient writing to satisfy the requirements of the Statute."[227]

[6.31] Finally, it may be useful to note some examples of documents which have been held to be so connected that they could be joined to constitute a sufficient memorandum or note. The following have been connected: letters

---

[221.] See *Pierce v Corf* (1874) LR 9 QB 210.
[222.] (1802) 1 Sch & Lef 22.
[223.] *Ibid*, p 33.
[224.] (1885) 15 LR Ir 257.
[225.] Eg, *Ridgway v Wharton* (1857) 6 HLC 238; *Baumann v James* (1868) 3 Ch App 508; *Long v Millar* (1879) 4 CPD 450.
[226.] *Ibid*, p 263. *Cf Oliver v Hunting* (1890) 44 Ch D 205 at 208 (*per* Kekewich J).
[227.] *Ibid*, p 264.

between the parties[228]; letters between the parties' solicitors[229]; a letter and a draft lease or tenancy agreement[230]; conditions of sale and a completion notice[231]; a solicitor's letter and a draft contract[232]; an estate agent's letter and a draft contract[233]; an auctioneer's note and conditions of sale[234]; a receipt for the deposit and an application for a loan from a building society.[235] On the other hand, usually because of the lack of a cross-reference, the following have been held not to be connected: a letter and an advertisement for sale[236]; an auctioneer's agreement and an advertisement[237]; an auctioneer's book and catalogue.[238]

E. Signature

[6.32] The memorandum or note in writing required by s 2 of the Statute of Frauds (Ireland) 1695, must be signed, but the section does not require signature by both parties. It requires only signature by "the party to be charged therewith,"[239] ie, the defendant in the action to enforce the contract,[240] or by the party's authorised agent, ie, by "some other person thereunto by him lawfully authorised."[241] Where the defendants are co-owners, eg, vendors holding title to the property as joint tenants,[242] they must both sign if a decree of specific performance is to be granted to enforce the contract,[243] though a contract entered into by one joint tenant may cause a severance of the joint tenancy in equity.[244]

---

228. *Maconchy v Clayton* [1898] 1 IR 291; *Law v Roberts & Co* [1964] IR 292. *Cf* a letter and an envelope, see *Pearce v Gardner* [1897] 1 QB 688; *Last v Hucklesby* (1914) 58 Sol Jo 431.

229. *Lavan v Walsh* [1964] IR 87.

230. *Craig v Elliott* (1885) 15 LR Ir 257. *Cf Scott v McCombe* (1965) 16 NILQ 122 and 418; *City of Glasgow Friendly Society v Gilpin* (1971) 22 NILQ 196. And see *Horner v Walker* [1923] 2 Ch 218.

231. *Irvine v Deane* (1849) 2 Ir Jur (os) 209.

232. *Black v Kavanagh* (1974) 108 ILTR 91.

233. *Stinson v Owens* (1973) 24 NILQ 218.

234. *McMeekin v Stevenson* [1917] 1 IR 348. *Cf Rishton v Whatmore* (1878) 8 Ch D 467.

235. *McQuaid v Lynam* [1965] IR 564. *Cf Long v Millar* (1879) 4 CPD 450; *Timmins v Moreland Street Property Co Ltd* [1958] Ch 110.

236. *Waldron v Jacob* (1870) IR 5 Eq 131. *Cf Davis v Gallagher* [1933] LJ Ir 26.

237. *Clinan v Cooke* (1802) 1 Sch & Lef 22.

238. *Crane v Naughten* [1912] 2 IR 318. *Cf Peilow v O'Carroll* (1972) 106 ILTR 29.

239. See *Kine v Balfe* (1813) 2 Ba & B 343; *McLoughlin v Alexander* (1910) 44 ILTR 253. See also para **[6.49]** *infra*.

240. See para **[6.07]** *supra*.

241. See para **[6.06]** *supra*. See also Emery, 'Statute of Frauds: The Authenticated Signature Fiction - An Illogical Distinction' (1975) 39 Conv 336.

242. See *Irish Land Law* (2nd ed, 1986), Ch 7.

243. *Re Hayes Estate* [1920] 1 IR 207. See also *Keen v Mear* [1920] 2 Ch 574; *Carthy v O'Neill* [1981] ILRM 443; *Mulhall v Haren* [1981] IR 364.

244. See *Irish Land Law* (2nd ed, 1986), paras 7.29 and 7.32.

1. Mode of Signature

[6.33] As in other cases of a statutory requirement for signature,[245] the courts have interpreted the word "signed" in the Statute of Frauds fairly broadly.[246] Thus, it has been held to include signature by initials only[247] or by impression of a rubber stamp,[248] or even to be found in a printed heading on notepaper.[249] Lack of a signature in the conventional sense may not be fatal provided the person's name appears somewhere in the memorandum, eg, a hand-written document beginning with the words such as "I, John Doe, agree ..."[250] However, in every case it is essential, as Kenny J put it in *McQuaid v Lynam*,[251] that "the signature must have been intended to authenticate the whole document of which it forms a part."[252] It was argued in that case that an application to a building society for a loan constituted a sufficient memorandum and on this point Kenny J commented:

> "The writing of 'EJ Lynam' opposite the printed words 'name of builder' by the second defendant on the application to the Building Society was not a signature of that document by the defendants or by either of them as it was not intended to give authenticity to any part of it. The document was intended to be - and was - signed by the plaintiff and the writing of the name of the defendants was intended to give information to the Building Society. The application is not therefore a memorandum or note in writing of the contract ...'"[253]

It does seem to be settled, however, that the signature does not necessarily have to appear at the foot or end of the memorandum[254] so long as it can be

---

[245.] Eg in the case of wills, see Brady, *Succession Law in Ireland* (2nd ed, 1995), para [2.10] *et seq.*

[246.] See *Evans v Hoare* [1892] 1 QB 593 at 597 (*per* Cave J). The English courts are apparently going to take a more strict view under s 2 of the Law of Property (Miscellaneous Provisions) Act 1989: see *Firstpost Homes Ltd v Johnson* [1995] 4 All ER 355.

[247.] *Chichester v Hobbs* (1866) 14 LT 433. An illiterate's mark will also be sufficient, *Baker v Denning* (1838) 8 Ad & El 94; *Helsham v Langley* (1841) 1 Y & C Cas 175.

[248.] See *Hudson v O'Connor* [1947] Ir Jur Rep 21; also *Bennett v Brumfitt* (1867) LT 3 CP 28.

[249.] See *Casey v Irish Intercontinental Bank Ltd* [1979] IR 364; also *Tourret v Cripps* (1879) 48 LJ Ch 567; *Hucklesby v Hook* (1900) 82 LT 117. *Cf Dyas v Stafford* (1882) 9 LR Ir 520.

[250.] See *Halley v O'Brien* [1920] IR 330; also *Knight v Cockford* (1791) 1 Esp 190; *Johnson v Dodgson* (1837) 2 M & W 653. In *Leeman v Stocks* [1951] Ch 941 it was held that entering the defendant's name before the agreement was made (at an auction) was sufficient, see para **[6.38]** *infra*. If the document is not written by the defendant, it appears that it must be written at his dictation, see *Hucklesby v Hook* (1900) 82 LT 117.

[251.] [1965] IR 564.

[252.] *Ibid*, p 569. See also *Dyas v Stafford* (1882) 9 LR Ir 520 especially at 524 (*per* Law C), 528 (*per* Deasy LJ) and 529 (*per* FitzGibbon LJ).

[253.] *Ibid.* It was held, however, that a signed receipt for the deposit money authenticated the building society application, *Ibid*, p 571. See para **[6.31]** *supra*.

[254.] *Cf* in the case of a will, see Brady, *Succession Law in Ireland* (2nd ed, 1995), para [2.16] *et seq.*

regarded as authenticating the document as a whole, wherever it appears.[255] It also appears that, once the defendant has signed the memorandum, he may amend it or require alterations to be made, without the need for a further signature on his part or even, perhaps, the customary initialling of the amendments or alterations.[256] However, it has recently been held that this rule should apply only where the amendment or alteration is made before the parties finally conclude their agreement,[257] ie, it should not apply to allow an unsigned variation of a concluded agreement.[258] In such a case a fresh signature is needed, or, at least, a revival of the old signature by appropriate words or gestures specifically directed to it as a signature, whatever that means![259]

2. Authorised Agents

[6.34] Perhaps one of the most controversial areas of conveyancing law is the question of when another person may be said to have authority to act for one of the parties to the transaction. We have already touched on this matter in an earlier chapter.[260] Section 2 of the Statute of Frauds (Ireland) 1695,[261] requires that the other person[262] signing must be "lawfully authorised"[263] by the party to be charged and authorised "thereunto," ie, presumably to sign the contract or the memorandum or note, as the case may be. It is clear then that the authority to sign does not have to be given in writing, it may be given orally.[264] It is also clear that the agent need not sign expressly as agent,[265] nor necessarily intend that the signed document should operate as a

---

[255.] *Ogilvie v Foljambe* (1817) 3 Mer 53; *Evans v Hoare* [1892] 1 QB 593. See the discussion of such cases by Deasy LJ in *Dyas v Stafford* (1882) 9 LR Ir 520.

[256.] See *Stewart v Eddowes* (1874) LR 9 CP 31; *Koenigsblatt v Sweet* [1923] 2 Ch 314.

[257.] Unless, perhaps, it is done to correct a mistake in a statement of an existing agreement, see *Bluck v Gompertz* (1852) 7 Exch 862.

[258.] This was the view of Goulding J in *New Hart Builders v Brindley* [1975] 1 All ER 1007.

[259.] Goulding J did admit that counsel's arguments "do not commend themselves to my uninstructed reason," but felt compelled to accept his interpretation of the authorities (see fn 256 *supra*) despite his view that he thought it "equally right or equally wrong in all cases to treat the approval of the alterations as equivalent to going over the existing signature with a pen." There was, he felt, a "strong current of judicial opinion" to support counsel's view "even though it draws what I conceive (perhaps from some limitation of insight or of learning on my part) to be an illogical distinction." *Ibid*, p 1012. *Cf Guerin v Ryan* High Court, unrep, 28 April 1977 (1977/386P).

[260.] See paras **[2.06]** *et seq* and **[3.06]** *et seq, supra*.

[261.] See para **[6.06]** *supra*.

[262.] One party cannot sign as agent for the other party to the same agreement, *Sharman v Brandt* (1871) LR 6 QB 720.

[263.] It is not clear that the word "lawfully" adds anything, though this epithet is commonly used in statutes, *cf* s 4 of Deasy's Act 1860: see *Irish Landlord and Tenant Law* para 5.25.

[264.] *Callaghan v Pepper* (1840) 2 Ir Eq R 399 at 401 (*per* Pennefather B). See also *Norris v Cooke* (1857) 7 ICLR 37.

[265.] *Wallace v Roe* [1903] 1 IR 32. *Cf Lavan v Walsh* [1964] IR 87 (see para **[6.35]** *infra*).

memorandum or note for the purposes of the Statute of Frauds.[266] In *Wallace v Roe*,[267] an auctioneer signed a memorandum of a sale as "witness" and the vendor was held bound by it. Chatterton V-C stated:

"If he had not put in the word 'witness,' there could, in my opinion, have been no doubt as to its being a signature within the statute. I cannot hold that its meaning is to be thus confined. The document required no attestation. What was he to be witness of? I can only give it the meaning of an authentication of the whole contract, as stated in the paper he signed. I do not think that the otherwise unmeaning introduction of the word 'witness' is, under the facts of this case, sufficient to confine the effect of the signature accompanying it, and in fact to render the signature inoperative."[268]

[6.35] Where an agent signs a contract, or memorandum or note of it, on behalf of his principal, he should take care to make this clear, eg, by signing expressly "as agent" or "for" the principal.[269] The danger is that otherwise, ie, if he just signs in his own name without qualification, he may be held to be liable personally on the contract. This is a matter of construction, as Budd J explained in *Lavan v Walsh*:[270]

"The question as to whether an agent is to be deemed to have contracted personally in the case of a contract in writing depends on the intention of the parties as appearing from the terms of the written agreement as a whole. The construction of the document is a matter of law for the court ..."[271]

After a survey of the authorities, Budd J concluded that there was much support for one proposition:

"The proposition is to the effect that if the contract be signed by the agent in his own name, without qualification, he is deemed to have contracted personally, unless a contrary intention plainly appears from other portions of the document ..."[272]

---

[266]. *Murphy v Harrington* [1927] IR 339 at 342 (*per* Meredith J). *Cf Grindell v Bass* [1920] 2 Ch 487.

[267]. [1903] 1 IR 32

[268]. *Ibid*, p 35.

[269]. See *Universal Steam Navigation Co v McKelvie & Co* [1923] AC 492; *Kimber Coal Co v Stone & Rolfe Ltd* [1926] AC 414.

[270]. [1964] IR 87. See Reynolds, 'Personal Liability of an Agent' (1969) 85 LQR 92.

[271]. *Ibid*, p 96.

[272]. *Ibid*. See also *Dublin Laundry Co Ltd v Clarke* [1989] ILRM 29; *Parkgrange Investments Ltd v Shandon Park Mills Ltd* High Court, unrep, 2 May 1991.

In that case, a solicitor's letter referred to the sale of land to him "in trust" for a client and it was held on the facts of that case that, nevertheless, he had contracted personally.[273] However, Budd J did issue a warning:

> "I do not wish to be taken as saying, for example, that whenever a solicitor signs 'in trust' he is personally liable ..."

He explained his reasons earlier:

> "Since a solicitor, by virtue of the very nature of his profession, normally acts for other people it is not in the normal nature of things to expect that a solicitor would bind himself personally when acting for a client. It is a consideration that I feel should in many cases be borne in mind when approaching the question of deciding whether a solicitor has bound himself personally or not."[274]

Thus, Butler J held, in *United Yeast Co Ltd v Cameo Investments Ltd*,[275] that a solicitor who had signed "in trust" was not personally liable. He stated:

> "Where an agent, acting for an undisclosed principal, is clearly shown to have contracted merely as an agent then the true position and intention of the parties is recognised and the agent drops out of the transaction. I am satisfied that by common usage a solicitor who signs a contract to purchase in trust is clearly recognised as merely acting as agent and, in the absence of a clear stipulation to the contrary, incurs no personal liability."[276]

[6.36] If the agent signs without authority, then, under the general principles of the law of agency, the signature may become effective by being subsequently ratified by his principal.[277] Such subsequent ratification supplies retroactive authorisation of the signature so as to render the contract enforceable under the Statute of Frauds,[278] and so a withdrawal in the meantime by the other party, even before the ratification, is ineffective.[279]

[273.] *Ibid*, p 101.

[274.] *Ibid*, p 98.

[275.] (1977) 111 ILTR 13. *Cf Re Scott's Estate* (1854) 7 Ir Jur (os) 329.

[276.] *Ibid*, p 16. Note also the decision of McWilliam J in *Starling Securities Ltd v Woods* High Court, unrep, 24 May 1977 (1975/4044P). And see the special provision in the Republic's Law Society's *General Conditions of Sale (1995 Edition)*, para **[10.50]** *post*.

[277.] *Dyas v Cruise* (1845) 8 Ir Eq R 407, especially at 423 (*per* Sugden LC): "If an agent lets a property, and the principal being informed of it, adopts that letting, he is just as much bound as if he had given a previous authority."

[278.] See the discussion by the Supreme Court in *Sheridan v Higgins* [1971] IR 291. See also *Brennan v O'Connell* [1980] IR 13; Farrell, *Irish Law of Specific Performance* (1994), para [3.41] *et seq*.

[279.] *Bolton Partners v Lambert* (1889) 41 Ch D 295. But *cf Fleming v Bank of New Zealand* [1900] AC 577. And see *Watson v Davies* [1931] 1 Ch 455.

But subsequent ratification is effective only where the unauthorised act in question was done by an agent purporting to act for a principal,[280] though the principal may be estopped in certain circumstances from denying the agent's authority.[281] It also seems that an unauthorised alteration by an agent of a memorandum signed by his principal may be ratified by the principal.[282]

[6.37] In the absence of express authorisation, it is a question of construction whether the agent has authority to sign a memorandum for the purposes of the Statute of Frauds.[283] Thus, normally a wife is not the agent of her husband in this regard,[284] but implied authority may arise from the circumstances of the case, eg, where the husband stood by and let her sign.[285] There are some special cases which should be considered, though we have touched on them in an earlier chapter.[286] In each of these the courts have taken different attitudes to the question of the existence of implied authority to sign a contract, or a memorandum or note thereof, so as to render the contract enforceable under the Statute of Frauds.

(i) Auctioneers

[6.38] We saw earlier[287] that an auctioneer has implied authority to sign a memorandum on behalf of both parties to the transaction,[288] ie, both the vendor who employs him[289] and the person who becomes the purchaser by making the highest bid at the auction.[290] However, there is an important point of distinction. The authority to sign on behalf of the vendor arises from his contract of employment with the vendor and lasts for whatever period is to be implied from that,[291] whereas his implied authority in respect of the purchaser arises simply from the latter being declared the highest bidder at the auction.[292] Thus, his authority to sign on behalf of the purchaser is of a

---

280. *Keighley, Maxstead & Co v Durant* [1901] AC 240.
281. *Spiro v Lintern* [1973] 1 WLR 1002.
282. *Koenigsblatt v Sweet* [1923] 2 Ch 314.
283. *Field v Boland* (1837) 1 Dr & Wal 37; *Norris v Cooke* (1857) 7 ICLR 37.
284. *Debenham v Mellon* (1880) 6 App Cas 24; *Leek & Moorlands BS v Clark* [1952] 2 QB 788.
285. *Heath v Chilton* (1844) 12 M & W 632; *Millard v Harvey* (1864) 34 Beav 237.
286. Chs 2 and 3, *ante*.
287. See paras **[2.06]** *et seq.*
288. *Gardiner v Tate* (1876) IR 10 CL 460 at 474 (*per* Fitzgerald J). As to his duty of care, see *Kavanagh v Cuthbert* (1874) IR 9 CL 136 and para **[2.12]** *ante. Cf Richards v Phillips* [1969] 1 Ch 39 at 53 (*per* Pennycuick J).
289. *Carrigy v Brock* (1871) IR 5 CL 501; *Wallace v Roe* [1903] 1 IR 32; *Mc Meekin v Stevenson* [1917] 1 IR 348.
290. *Gardiner v Tate* (1876) IR 10 CL 460 at 464 (*per* Whiteside CJ).
291. Note the extent to which this was taken in the English case of *Leeman v Stocks* [1951] Ch 941.
292. *Coles v Trecothick* (1804) 9 Ves 234; *White v Proctor* (1811) 4 Taunt 209.

less "permanent" nature[293] and is generally confined to the time of the sale in the auction room.[294] As Ross J said in *McMeekin v Stevenson*;[295] the test is whether the memorandum was "in substance" made "at the time and as part of the transaction of sale".[296] The authority to sign on behalf of the vendor, however, is confined to a sale by auction and does not extend to a sale by private treaty after an abortive auction.[297]

[6.39] If the sale is in lots, the auctioneer must sign a separate memorandum for each lot, unless a special agreement is made or special consent is given.[298]

[6.40] We also saw earlier,[299] that an auctioneer, as agent, is governed by the general principle *delegatus delegare non potest*, so that in general his clerk or other employee may not sign so as to create a sufficient memorandum of the sale.[300] However, authority may be extended impliedly to such persons in special circumstances[301] and, of course, subsequent ratification may be made.[302]

(ii) House or Estate Agents

[6.41] As distinct from an auctioneer acting in a sale by public auction,[303] a house or estate agent acting in a sale by private treaty does not in general have implied authority to sign a memorandum,[304] though he may, of course,

---

[293.] See *Gardiner v Tate* (1876) IR 10 CL 460 at 474 (*per* Fitzgerald J); *Mc Meekin v Stevenson* [1917] 1 IR 348 at 354 (*per* Ross J). See also para **[2.09]** *ante*. It seems that there is no such authority if the auctioneer himself is the vendor, see *Buckmaster v Harrop* (1807) 13 Ves 456; *Wright v Dannah* (1809) 2 Camp 203.

[294.] See the leading English case, *Bell v Balls* [1897] 1 Ch 663 (signature one week after sale too late).*Cf Chaney v Maclow* [1929] 1 Ch 461 (signature). See also *Matthews v Baxter* (1873) 28 LT 669 (eight days later).

[295.] [1917]1 IR 348 (some particulars filled in auctioneer's book before sale and rest added the morning following the sale - held sufficient memorandum).

[296.] *Ibid*, p 354. See also *Chaney v Maclow* [1929] 1 Ch 461.

[297.] *Rooney v Thomas* (1947) 81 ILTR 64. See also *Daniel Morrissey and Sons Ltd v Nalty* [1976-7] ILRM 269. See para **[2.07]** *ante*.

[298.] *Smith v MacGowan* [1938] 3 All ER 447.

[299.] Para **[2.11]** *ante*.

[300.] See *Sheridan v Higgins* [1971] IR 291. See also *Bell v Balls* [1897] 1 Ch 663.

[301.] See the views of Chatterton V-C in *Dyas v Slafford* (1881) 7 LR Ir 590 at 600-1 (quoted in para **[2.11]** *ante*). *Cf Coles v Trecothick* (1804) 4 Ves 234.

[302.] *Sheridan v Higgins* [1971] IR 291. See para **[6.36]** *supra*.

[303.] *Cf* acting in a sale by private treaty, see *Rooney v Thomas* (1947) 81 ILTR 64, para **[6.38]** *supra*.

[304.] See the discussion in paras **[3.06]** *et seq, ante*, which quote the summary of the law given by Kenny J in *Law v Roberts & Co* [1964] IR 292 at 302.

be given express authority[305] or have his signature subsequently ratified.[306] One reason for this was given by Chatterton V-C in *Wilde v Watson*:[307]

> "A house or estate-agent has no implied or general authority to conclude a contract for sale, his duty is to find a purchaser or tenant, and communicate his offer to his principal ... It is common practice to place houses or estates on the books of a number of these agents at the same time, and if each had authority to conclude a contract for the owner the result would be, that he might become bound to let or sell the same premises to several different parties at the same instant ..."[308]

It also seems to be the case that a house or estate agent cannot in general delegate his functions to someone else,[309] so that, if he does have authority to sign a contract or memorandum, he must do so himself.

(iii) Solicitors

[6.42] The question of a solicitor's implied authority has been an extremely controversial one over the years and the case law is far from clear. What is at least clear is that solicitors should not always assume that they have no authority to conclude a contract, or to sign a memorandum so as to bind their clients, and should be aware of the risk that they may inadvertently commit their clients to contracts before they intended to do so.[310] It seems that a distinction should be drawn between concluding an agreement on behalf of the client and bringing into effect a written memorandum to render enforceable an oral agreement already concluded by the client. The different attitude of the courts to these two quite different processes was stressed by Meredith J in *Kerns v Manning*[311]:

> "Comparatively slight evidence would, in accordance with ordinary experience, be required to prove that a solicitor had authority to make a memorandum as the legal evidence of a concluded contract, but that a solicitor had authority to deal with the substance of the transaction in any manner which he thought fit, is a fact which should be clearly proved ..."[312]

---

[305]. *Dyas v Cruise* (1845) 8 Ir Eq R 407. *Cf Carney v Fair* (1920) 54 ILTR 61. See also *Re Sullivan's Estate* (1889) 23 LR Ir 255; *Stinson v Owens* (1973) 24 NILQ 218.

[306]. *Ibid*, p 423 (*per* Sugden LC); *Sheridan v Higgins* [1971] IR 291; *Brennan v O'Connell* [1980] IR 13.

[307]. (1878) 1 LR Ir 402.

[308]. *Ibid*, p 405. Similarly a land agent, see *Mortal v Lyons* (1858) 8 Ir Ch R 112.

[309]. See para **[3.12]** *ante*.

[310]. See para **[6.15]** *supra*. *Cf* as regards a barrister, eg, by signature to pleadings, *Grindell v Bass* [1920] 2 Ch 487; *Farr, Smith & Co v Messers Ltd* [1928]1 KB 397. See also *Hardy v Elphinck* [1974] Ch 65.

[311]. [1935] IR 869.

[312]. *Ibid*, p 881. *Cf Lord Cloncurry v Laffan* [1924] 1 IR 78 at 84 (*per* O'Connor LJ), para **[6.43]** *infra*.

The distinction was amply illustrated by the case of *Black v Kavanagh*.[313] In that case Gannon J found that the parties themselves had made a complete oral agreement for the sale of a house before they instructed their respective solicitors to prepare the necessary legal documents. At that stage he considered the parties' position to be as follows:

> "Both of them recognised and accepted that legal formalities, which to them were no more than formalities, were necessary and that the procedure of such a nature would be followed on their behalf by the named solicitors, and no further authority was given to either solicitor. They relied on their solicitors to prepare any documents necessary to give legal force and effect to their agreement, and each was willing and expected to put his hand to whatever documents his solicitor required for that purpose whether it be called a contract, or a draft contract, or a memorandum of agreement ..."[314]

Thus, Gannon J concluded that the solicitors had no authority to negotiate the terms of the contract - this had been done already by the parties.[315] But there remained the question of whether that contract had been sufficiently evidenced in writing for the purposes of the Statute of Frauds, for the parties themselves had put nothing in writing. Their solicitors, however, had done so, in that they had engaged in the usual correspondence about the transaction and a draft agreement (albeit containing terms the parties had not agreed to and which, Gannon J held, the solicitors had no authority to insert) had been drawn up. This correspondence was then held to be a sufficient memorandum of the parties' agreement, even though the solicitors still thought the matter was at the draft stage only or, as it is often put, still "subject to contract".[316] As Gannon J put it:

> "... the solicitors merely confirmed in writing the agreement reached. To me it is clear from the evidence that the solicitors had the authority of their respective clients to confirm and communicate in writing on their behalf the terms of the agreement made verbally and this they did ..."[317]

[6.43] The question of when a solicitor may be said to have authority to sign a memorandum for the purposes of the Statute of Frauds, as was held to be the case in *Black v Kavanagh*, has been a very controversial one over the years.[318] It gave rise to a dispute reported in 1924 amongst the judges of the

---

[313.] (1974) 108 ILTR 91. *Cf North v Loomes* [1919] 1 Ch 378; *Gavaghan v Edwards* [1961] 2 QB 220.

[314.] *Ibid*, p 95.

[315.] See his remarks quoted in para **[3.33]** *ante*.

[316.] See further, para **[7.06]** *post*.

[317.] (1974) 108 ILTR 91 at 96.

[318.] See the discussion in the leading English cases of *Smith v Webster* (1876) 3 Ch D 49; *Bowen v Duc d'Orleans* (1900) 16 TLR 226; *Daniels v Trefusis* [1914] 1 Ch 788. And see the discussion of these cases in *Lord Cloncurry v Laffan* [1924] 1 IR 78.

Court of Appeal of the then Irish Free State in *Lord Cloncurry v Laffan*.[319] In that case the vendor's agent agreed orally with the purchaser for the sale of freehold lands. No formal agreement was entered into, but the purchaser entrusted to his solicitor the carrying out of the contract. On the day of the oral agreement the vendor's solicitor wrote to the purchaser's solicitor in the following terms:

"[The vendor's agent] informs me that he has agreed with [the purchaser] for the sale to him of his holding ... in fee-simple for the sum of £10,000. Under these circumstances we think it would be possible to reasonably limit the title."

On the next day, the purchaser's solicitor, in acknowledging that letter, stated in his reply:

"The simple agreement arrived at herein appears in the first part of your letter, and I suggest that we can dispense with any further agreement."

The majority of the Court of Appeal,[320] affirming the decision of the Master of the Rolls below,[321] held that the letter by the purchaser's solicitor was within the general scope of his authority and constituted a memorandum or note sufficient to satisfy the Statute of Frauds - even though the solicitor had not been specifically authorised to sign such a memorandum and in writing the letter had had no intention of signing one. Ronan LJ firmly dissented from this majority decision, and it may be instructive to look at the two points of view more closely, if only as a warning to all solicitors to take care in how they word their correspondence.

[6.44] For the majority, Molony CJ accepted a general proposition which has been recognised by the English courts[322]:

"It is clear that a solicitor who is instructed to prepare a formal agreement between the parties is not an agent lawfully authorised to sign a memorandum under the Statute of Frauds ...; but the case may be different where a solicitor is entrusted with the carrying out and completion of a contract for the purchase of land."[323]

On his construction of the facts, Molony CJ concluded with respect to the position of the purchaser's solicitor:

"He had entrusted to him as a solicitor the carrying out of the contract for the purchase of land. That involved an authority to do everything that was

---

[319.] [1924] 1 IR 78.
[320.] Molony CJ and O'Connor LJ.
[321.] [1923] 1 IR 127.
[322.] *Smith v Webster* (1876) 3 Ch D 49.
[323.] [1924] 1 IR 78 at 81.

necessary and proper for the protection of his interests;[324] ... he was instructed to complete, and not merely to negotiate, the contract ..."[325]

[6.45] O'Connor LJ, who agreed with the Chief Justice, dealt with one further point raised in argument,[326] and, in doing so, reiterated the dangers to be borne in mind by solicitors in dealing with the day-to-day correspondence necessarily involved in a conveyancing transaction:

"It is sometimes said that an agent - in the absence of express authority to do so - has no power to bind his principal by signing a note or memorandum of a verbal contract already entered into by his principal. The proposition thus stated is, in my opinion, too wide. There is no doubt but that the signature by such an agent of a note or memorandum affixed merely for the sake of constituting such a note or memorandum will not bind the principal. The reason, of course, is obvious - namely, that the agent has no express authority to sign such a note or memorandum for the mere purpose of binding his principal, nor is it within the scope of his implied authority to do so. But it may be that the agent has implied authority to sign something, which, if signed by the principal, would be a note or memorandum within the Statute of Frauds - to sign it, not for the purpose of binding his principal (which is not within the scope of the agent's authority) but for other purposes which are within the scope of the agent's authority. Such a case may - and I think frequently does - arise where a solicitor is employed in reference to a contract for sale or purchase of land. The solicitor has no authority, for the sake of binding his principal, to sign a note or memorandum of the contract. But if, in the course of the transaction for which he is employed and in pursuance of the authority entrusted to him, the solicitor has to sign something which, if signed by the client, would be a note or memorandum within the Statute of Frauds, then the client is as much bound by the solicitor's signature as if it were his own. An example would be where a controversy arises as to the terms of the contract; the solicitor carrying on the correspondence on behalf of the client would or might not only be entitled, but bound to state the terms of the contract correctly. If he does so, I fail to see upon what principle his client is not bound by a transaction which he has himself, impliedly, of course, authorised.

In cases of this sort the question resolves itself into this - was it within the scope of the solicitor's authority to write and sign what he did write and

---

[324.] *Ibid*, p 81.

[325.] *Ibid*, pp 83-4, citing *Daniels v Trefusis* [1914] 1 Ch 788 (instructions to forward documents); *North v Loomes* [1919] 1 Ch 378 (instructions to carry out the agreement); *Thirkell v Cambi* [1919] 2 KB 90 (instructions to deny contract). See also *Forster v Rowland* (1861) 7 H & N 103 (instructions to settle agreement); *Joliffe v Blumberg* (1870) 18 WR 784 (instructions to settle terms of the agreement).

[326.] See also *Black v Kavanagh*, para **[6.42]** *supra*.

sign? As I believe that the statement of the contract relied upon in this case was within the solicitor's authority, I hold that the decision of the Master of the Rolls was right and that this appeal should be dismissed.

Of course, this does not mean that if a solicitor unnecessarily interjects into a correspondence a statement of the contract and signs it that it would bind his principal. It would not; for such statement would not be within the solicitor's authority at all; for it would not be a necessary and ordinary incident of the correspondence."[327]

[6.46] Ronan LJ dissented from the majority decision, and stated his contrary view firmly[328]:

"Authority to conduct correspondence qua solicitor with another solicitor is quite different from authority to sign a memorandum of a contract."[329]

In his opinion, the purchaser's solicitor was employed simply as a solicitor; there was "not a scrap of evidence" showing that he was given authority to sign a memorandum.[330] As regards the suggestion made in argument that the solicitor was akin to an agent "of necessity," a point not relied upon by the majority, he thought that this "very peculiar" doctrine (applying mainly to ship captains) had no application where communication can be had reasonably with the principal.

"The idea that a solicitor may on this principle render his client liable for £10,000, when the client lives quite close to him, is absurd. The doctrine of agency of necessity has no application in this case."[331]

[6.47] The lessons of these cases for solicitors seem to be clear. First, each solicitor should make a point in every case of getting explicit instructions from his client as to the precise scope of his authority, both as regards negotiating and concluding a contract and signing a memorandum of the contract for the purposes of the Statute of Frauds.[332] The general law on the subject of implied authority seems to be far too uncertain to leave the matter to be determined by it. Secondly, when first instructed, each solicitor should make every effort to determine whether his client has already concluded a contract, so that only the "formalities" are to be completed. Thirdly, if explicit instructions have not been obtained, the greatest care should be taken in dealing with all correspondence relating to the transaction. If it is

---

[327.] [1924]1 IR 78 at 84-5.

[328.] But note that the Irish Reports record that "This judgment was not revised by Ronan LJ". See [1924] 1 IR 78 at 85.

[329.] *Ibid*, p 87.

[330.] *Ibid*, p 89.

[331.] *Ibid*, p 89.

[332.] Arguably this should be put in writing to avoid disputes later.

intended that the matter should be regarded as still subject to negotiation, ie, in the pre-contract stage, this should be stated expressly in the correspondence, perhaps, all correspondence, eg, by entering a note that the matter is still "subject to contract".[333] This may be reiterated by stating after the signature of any letters, especially, eg, any letter detailing the terms of the agreement or enclosing a draft agreement, that the solicitor is not to be taken to be the agent of his client for the purposes of s 2 of the Statute of Frauds (Ireland) 1695.[334]

F. Part Performance

[6.48] As we mentioned earlier,[335] perhaps one of the most significant developments in relation to the Statute of Frauds was the doctrine of part performance.[336] This doctrine was devised by the Courts of Equity when they realised that the evidentiary requirements of the Statute of Frauds were as likely to facilitate fraud as they were to prevent it (as was intended).[337] The underlying principle was explained by Chatterton VC in *Hope v Lord Cloncurry*[338] in these words:

> "The principle upon which the rule in cases of part-performance was engrafted on the Statute of Frauds is, that it would be a fraud on the part of a person who had entered into an agreement by parol for a lease or sale, and had allowed expenditure to be made upon the faith of it,[339] afterwards to turn round and say that it did not legally exist ..."[340]

Andrews LJ gave a similar formulation in *Lowry v Reid*[341]:

[333.] This will probably be enough to prevent the correspondence from being regarded as a sufficient memorandum. ie., by denying the existence of an agreement, see para **[7.08]** *post*.

[334.] Unless, of course, he is an express agent in that case! See para **[7.10]** *post*.

[335.] Para **[6.03]** *supra*.

[336.] See Farrell, *Irish Law of Specific Performance* (1994) Ch 6; also Wallace, 'Part Performance Re-Examined' (1974) 25 NILQ 453. Note that the doctrine was given statutory recognition in England by s 40(2) of the Law of Property Act 1925 but can no longer operate since the enactment of s 2 of the Law of Property (Miscellaneous Provisions) Act 1989: see para **[6.04]** *supra*.

[337.] See para **[6.03]** *supra*.

[338.] (1874) IR 8 Eq 555.

[339.] Note that this is just one illustration of a typical act of part performance, see para **[6.58]** *infra*.

[340.] (1874) IR 8 Eq 555 at 557. *Cf Bond v Hopkins* (1802) 1 Sch & Lef 413 at 433 (*per* Lord Redesdale LC).

[341.] [1927] NI 142. This decision by the NI Court of Appeal remains the most comprehensive judicial discussion of the doctrine in Ireland. *Cf* the later discussion by the House of Lords in *Steadman v Steadman* [1974] 3 WLR 56. See also *Howlin v Power (Dublin) Ltd* High Court, unrep, 5 May 1978 (1977/736P).

"Thus, the doctrine is a purely equitable one. Its underlying principle is that the Court will not allow a statute which was passed to prevent fraud to be made itself an instrument of fraud.[342] In other words, the court disregards the absence of that formality which the statute requires when insistence upon it would render it a means of effecting, instead of a means of averting, fraud. The question in each case is, whether the plaintiff has an equity arising from part performance which is so affixed upon the conscience of the defendant that it would amount to a fraud on his part to take advantage of the fact that the contract is not in writing. The right to relief rests not so much on the contract as on what has been done in pursuance or in execution of it."[343]

This quotation from Andrews LJ in the *Lowry* case does emphasise one of the two main explanations for the operation of the doctrine,[344] which has received considerable judicial approval over the years. This is that the courts are not "charging the defendant"[345] upon a contract which fails to meet the evidentiary requirements of the Statute of Frauds, thereby disregarding a clear statutory provision, but rather are charging him upon the "equities" which arise from the acts of part performance in which he has acquiesced,[346] so that his conscience is affected in the eyes of equity and the courts will not allow him to plead the Statute as a defence.[347] The other main explanation is that the courts, in furtherance of the Statute of Frauds' purpose of requiring objective[348] evidence of the existence of the contract, are simply substituting for one form of evidence (ie, writing as specified by the Statute) another form (ie, acts of part performance), which may be equally objective and, therefore, should be accepted by the courts as sufficient for enforcement of the agreement.[349] The danger of this formulation is, however, that, in applying it, the courts may require as strict a standard of evidentiary proof as the writing required by the Statute of Frauds and this may have led to the restrictions or conditions imposed by the courts on the operation of the doctrine of part performance,[350] which judges in more recent times seem to

---

[342.] See *Irish Land Law* (2nd ed, 1986), paras 3.048 and 3.149.

[343.] [1927] NI 142 at 154-5.

[344.] See *Steadman v Steadman* [1974] 3 WLR 56 at 61-2 (*per* Lord Reid) and 78-9 (*per* Lord Simon).

[345.] See para **[6.32]** *supra*.

[346.] See the classic statement of this rationalisation by Lord Selborne LC in *Maddison v Alderson* (1883) 8 App Cas 467 at 475-6; and see Lord Blackburn at p 489. See also *Chaproniere v Lambert* [1917] 2 Ch 356 at 359 (*per* Swinfen Eady LJ).

[347.] See *Connor v Fitzgerald* (1883) 11 LR Ir 106 at 116 (*per* Chatterton V-C).

[348.] Ie, not dependent solely upon the personal testimony of the parties.

[349.] See *Britain v Rossiter* (1879) 11 QBD 123 at 130 (*per* Cotton LJ).

[350.] Most of which found expression in Fry's classic work, *Specific Performance* (1st ed, 1858; 6th ed, 1921).

have relaxed. It may, therefore, be useful to examine in a little more detail the conditions for the operation of the doctrine and then to give some common illustrations of its application.

1. Conditions

(i) Acts by Plaintiff

[6.49] The difference between enforcement of a contract under the Statute of Frauds and enforcement under the doctrine of part performance was succinctly stated by Andrews LJ in *Lowry v Reid*[351]:

> "Under the Statute the note or memorandum of the contract must be signed by the party to be charged.[352] Under the doctrine of part performance the equity must be possessed, not by the party to be charged, but by the plaintiff - the person who seeks relief; and this equity arises from his part performance of the contract ..."[353]

Thus, the order of events commonly is: the plaintiff seeks specific performance of the oral agreement[354]; the defendant resists this by raising the Statute of Frauds (ie, the lack of written evidence signed by the defendant) as a defence; the plaintiff counters this defence with the plea that he, the plaintiff, has performed acts of part performance sufficient to take the case outside the Statute.[355]

(ii) Fraud by Defendant

[6.50] As we saw above,[356] the underlying basis of the doctrine is that its application to a particular case prevents the defendant from committing fraud on the plaintiff. As Lord Redesdale LC said in *Clinan v Cooke*[357]:

> "I take it that nothing is considered as a part performance which does not put the party into a situation that is a fraud upon him, unless the agreement is performed ..."[358]

But if there is no fraud on the part of the particular defendant, the doctrine cannot be invoked by the plaintiff in his action against that defendant. This

---

[351] [1927] NI 142.

[352] See para **[6.32]** *supra*.

[353] [1927] NI 142 at 155. See also Flanagan J in *Lanyon v Martin* (1884) 13 LR Ir 297 at 303: "There is, in my opinion, great force in the argument ... that the act of part performance must be one of the plaintiff seeking relief, and not by the defendant against whom relief is sought ..."

[354] See para **[13.37]** *et seq, post*.

[355] See *Brennan v Bolton* (1842) 2 Dr & War 349 at 354-5 (*per* Sugden LC); *Connor v Fitzgerald* (1883) 11 LR Ir 106 at 116 (*per* Chatterton V-C).

[356] Para **[6.48]** *supra*.

[357] (1802) 1 Sch & Lef 22.

[358] *Ibid*, p 41. See also *Connor v Fitzgerald* (1883) 11 LR Ir 106 at 116 (*per* Chatterton V-C).

was clearly illustrated by the case of *Hope v Lord Cloncurry*,[359] where it was held that a parol agreement for the grant of a lease entered into by a tenant for life under a settlement[360] did not bind the remainderman,[361] despite part performance by the tenant during the life of the tenant for life, because the remainderman had neither acquiesced in the part performance nor known of the agreement. Chatterton V-C explained:

"... there is not, in cases like the present, that personal fraud which would exist if the person who stood by and permitted the expenditure were the person who had himself entered into the agreement. The agreement, in such a case, binds the party who stands by, because it would be a personal fraud on his part to defeat it; but that fails where the part-performance is not in the time of the tenant in remainder but of the tenant for life, as against whom it can be enforced. I have not here a case where part performance and expenditure are shown to have taken place after the remainder had become vested in possession, and after the remainderman had actual notice of the execution of an agreement ..."[362]

(iii) Specific Performance

[6.51] As we saw above,[363] the doctrine of part performance is usually pleaded by the plaintiff to counter the defence, based on the Statute of Frauds, raised by the defendant in an action for specific performance of an oral agreement. It is an equitable doctrine[364] and has often been said to be confined to cases involving actions for specific performance.[365] Indeed, it has even been suggested that its application is confined to the most common case for such action, ie., contracts relating to land,[366] but this suggestion has not been accepted in Ireland.[367] Thus, in *Crowley v O'Sullivan*[368] Palles CB

[359.] (1874) IR 8 Eq 555. *Cf Caton v Caton* (1867) LR 2 HL127; *Blore v Sutton* (1817) 3 Mer 237.

[360.] With leasing powers.

[361.] *Cf* the actual grant of a lease under statutory leasing powers, see *Irish Land Law* (2nd ed, 1986), para 8.071 *et seq*.

[362.] (1874) IR 8 Eq 555 at 557. See also *Lowe v Swift* (1814) 2 Ba & B 529; *O'Fay v Burke* (1858) 8 Ir Ch R 511.

[363.] Para **[6.49]** *supra*.

[364.] See *Bond v Hopkins* (1892)1 Sch & Lef 413 at 433 (*per* Lord Redesdale LC); *Archbold v Lord Howth* (1866) IR 1 CL 608 at 621 (*per* Christian J); *Lowry v Reid* [1927] NI 142 at 154 (*per* Andrews LJ). It was not recognised at common law, see *Boydell v Drummond* (1809) 11 East 142.

[365.] *Cf McManus v Cooke* (1887) 35 Ch D 681 at 697.

[366.] See *Irish Land Law* (2nd ed, 1986), para 3.144.

[367.] Nor, apparently, in England now, see *Steadman v Steadman* [1974] 3 WLR 56 at 60-1 (*per* Lord Reid), 72-3 (*per* Viscount Dilhorne), 80-1 (*per* Lord Simon). *Cf* at p 66 (*per* Lord Morris) and at p 86 (*per* Lord Salmond).

[368.] [1900] 2 IR 478.

warned that one should guard against the opinion that the doctrine was so limited.[369] In his opinion:

> " ... the true rule was ... that the doctrine of part performance is applicable to every case in which a Court of Equity would, before the statute,[370] have sustained a suit for specific performance, were the contract in writing ..."[371]

Thus, in that case specific performance was granted in respect of a partnership agreement, part of which involved the acquisition of business premises, along with stock-in-trade and book debts.[372] In *Lowry v Reid*,[373] where the suggestion was made that the doctrine did not apply to a contract for exchange of land, Andrews LJ was even more emphatic:

> " ... in my opinion, there could be no foundation for the suggestion that the doctrine does not apply to contracts for the exchange of lands, as in my judgment the doctrine applies to all contracts of which, before the Judicature Act, a Court of Equity would have granted specific performance if the alleged contract had been in writing; and these are not confined to contracts for the sale of land ... but include contracts for the exchange of lands ..."[374]

In *Steevens's Hospital v Dyas*,[375] Smith MR granted specific performance of a contract by a corporation for the grant of a lease, on the ground that there had been part performance.[376]

[6.52] To the extent that the doctrine is an equitable one, and since the plaintiff obtains the equitable remedy of specific performance if he is successful, it becomes irrelevant in any case where the court would refuse to exercise its discretion in favour of the plaintiff,[377] eg, on the ground of laches.[378]

---

[369] *Ibid*, p 489.

[370] Ie, the Judicature (Ir) Act 1877, which fused the administration of the courts in Ireland, see *Irish Land Law* (2nd ed, 1986) , paras 3.031-7.

[371] *Ibid*, p 490. See also at p 492. "... the doctrine of part performance is applicable to any case in which a Court of Equity would, before the statute, have decreed specific performance."

[372] *Cf Bagnell v Edwards* (1876) IR 10 Eq 215.

[373] [1927] NI 142.

[374] *Ibid*, p 157.

[375] (1864) 15 Ir Ch R 405.

[376] *Cf Lindsey v GN Rly v Co* (1853) 10 Hare 644; *Re Patent Ivory Manufacturing Co* (1888) 38 Ch D 156; *Hoare v Kingsbury UC* [1912] 2 Ch 652.

[377] For discussion of the "defences" to an action for specific performance, see Farrell, *Irish Law of Specific Performance* (1994), Ch 9 and para **[13.43]** *et seq, post*.

[378] *Archbold v Lord Howth* (1866) IR 1 CL 608 at 621 (*per* Christian J).

(iv) Reference to the Contract

[6.53] It is clear that the acts of part performance pleaded by the plaintiff must have some reference to the alleged oral contract of which he seeks enforcement, but the courts have taken different views over the years on the precise amount of reference required.[379] The traditional view was that the act or acts relied upon had to be unequivocally referable not only to a contract such as that alleged, but referable to no other contract.[380] There are numerous expressions in the Irish cases[381] to this effect, eg, "refer only to a Contract of Sale",[382] "distinctly referable to the Contract alleged in the Pleadings"[383]; "plainly referable to the alleged contract"[384]; "can only be referred to the agreement"[385]; "necessarily referable to the alleged agreement"[386] and "referable to the very agreement relied on by the plaintiff".[387] But later judges have taken the view that this imposed far too great a restriction on the doctrine, for it would be a very rare case where there might not be other possible, albeit unlikely, explanations for the acts in question. This latter view was put forward as long ago as 1927 by Andrews LJ in *Lowry v Reid*[388]:

> "I would add that I can find no authority to support [the] contention that it is not permissible even to consider the terms of the parol agreement until it is clearly established that the acts of part performance refer unequivocally to the contract relied upon, and to that alone. Indeed, it would be, in my opinion, impossible to apply the proposition as so stated in practice; for how, I ask, could it be said that the acts of part performance referred unequivocally to an agreement the terms of which were *ex hypothesi* not known, unless, indeed, they were acts of such clear, cogent, and conclusive character that they embodied and themselves proved the actual terms of the

---

[379.] It is upon this point in particular that there may be a difference between the two main explanations for the operation of the doctrine, see para **[6.48]** *supra*.

[380.] Or "to no other title," as it is commonly put. See (1963) 79 LQR 21.

[381.] See also the English cases, eg *Maddison v Alderson* (1883) 8 App Cas 467 at 479 (*per* Lord Selborne LC) and at 484 (*per* Lord O'Hagan); *Chaproniere v Lambert* [1917] 2 Ch 356 at 361 (*per* Warrington LJ).

[382.] *Savage v Carroll* (1810) 1 Ba & B 265 at 282 (*per* Manners LC).

[383.] *Kine v Balfe* (1813) 2 Ba & B 343 (*per* Lord Manners LC).

[384.] *Howe v Hall* (1870) IR 4 Eq 242 at 252 (*per* Sullivan MR).

[385.] *Connor v Fitzgerald* (1883) 11 LR Ir 106 (*per* Chatterton V-C).

[386.] *Beauclerk v Hanna* (1888) 23 LR Ir 144 at 149 (*per* Chatterton V-C).

[387.] *Ibid*, p 150.

[388.] [1927] NI 142. See also *Broughton v Snook* [1938] Ch 505 at 515 (*per* Farwell J); *Kingswood Estate Co Ltd v Anderson* [1963] 2 QB 169 at 189 (*per* Upjohn LJ, who described the "no other title" theory as "long exploded"). This view was also given general approval by the House of Lords in *Steadman v Steadman* [1974] 3 WLR 56.

agreement, in which case it would be wholly unnecessary for the plaintiff to make any reference to or to rely in any way upon the parol agreement ... If these words[389] are to be taken literally, and to be construed as deciding that the acts of performance must in themselves necessarily imply the existence of the contract, that is, the precise contract pleaded, I am not prepared to accept them as containing a correct statement of the law ... the true principle of the operation of the acts of part performance seems only to require that the acts in question be such as must be referred to some contract, and may be referred to the alleged one; that they prove the existence of some contract and are consistent with the contract alleged."[390]

This view has now been adopted by the House of Lords in England,[391] where it was emphasised by some of the law lords that the standard of proof required of the plaintiff was only that he should establish "on the balance of probabilities" that it was more likely than not that the acts were performed in reliance on a contract with the defendant which was consistent with the contract alleged.[392]

(v) Parol Evidence

[6.54] It was also the traditional view of the operation of the doctrine that the establishment of an act or acts of part performance justified the admission of parol evidence further to prove the precise terms of the contract ultimately to be enforced by the court.[393] As Manners LC put it in *Savage v Carroll*,[394] once an act of part performance is established, "the Party may go into

---

[389.] Ie in *Maddison v Alderson* (1883) 8 App Cas 467 at 485 (*per* Lord O'Hagan); "It must be unequivocal. It must have relation to the one agreement relied upon and to no other. It must be such, in Lord Harwicke's words, as could be done with no other view or design than to perform that agreement. It must be sufficient of itself, and without any other information or evidence, to satisfy a Court from the circumstances it has created and the relations it has formed that they are only consistent with the assumption of the existence of a contract the terms of which equity requires, if possible to be ascertained and enforced." Lord Hardwicke's words are to be found in *Gunter v Halsey* (1739) Amb 586 at 587.

[390.] [1927] NI 142 at 158-60. The last sentence of this quotation adopts a statement in Fry's *Specific Performance* (6th ed, 1921), p 278, para 582. See also *Silver Wraith Ltd v Siuicre Éireann cpt* High Court, unrep, 8 June 1989 (1987/6178P). *Cf* Moore CJ at p 151: "If such acts are not unequivocably referable to the performance of the contract, in whole or in part, then the evidence as to them is irrelevant and the necessary proof of part performance fails."

[391.] *Steadman v Steadman* [1974] 3 WLR 56, even by Lord Morris of Borth-y-Gest, who dissented from the actual decision in that case, see p 65.

[392.] *Ibid*, p 61 (*per* Lord Reid) and pp 81-2 (*per* Lord Simon).

[393.] Or as *Fry* put it, the parol evidence is "let in" by the acts of part performance, see *Specific Performance* (6th ed, 1921), p 277, para 5.70. Note the criticisms of this formulation by Viscount Dilhorne in *Steadman v Steadman* [1974] 3 WLR 56 at 74. See fn 398 *infra*.

[394.] (1810) 1 Ba & B 265.

Evidence of the Terms of that Contract".[395] But even this theory was challenged in *Lowry v Reid*,[396] by Moore LCJ who commented on the argument that parol evidence could not be admitted until it was first proved that acts of part performance established the existence of the contract:

> "If I have correctly stated this proposition, I can only say that I do not accept it. I think it is an inversion of the principle which should obtain. In my opinion, we must at some stage consider the contract and its effect, before we are in a position to judge, whether or not the acts relied on to take the case out of the statute are acts of part performance of the contract."[397]

Though Viscount Dilhorne seems to have taken a similar view in *Steadman v Steadman*,[398] the other law lords in that case accepted the traditional view. Thus, Lord Reid stated:

> "You must not first look at the oral contract and then see whether the alleged acts of part performance are consistent with it. You must first look at the alleged acts of part performance and see whether they prove that there must have been a contract and it is only if they do so prove that you can bring in the oral contract."[399]

2. Illustrations

[6.55] Whether or not the acts of part performance relied upon by the plaintiff are sufficient to take the case out of the Statute of Frauds depends upon the circumstances of each case.[400] There may be a single act which in itself is sufficient[401] or a series of acts which, taken together, substantiate a claim of part performance.[402] Indeed, in some cases there may be acts of part

---

[395.] *Ibid*, p 282. See also his comment in *Toole v Medlicott* (1810) 1 Ba & B 393 at 402: "he is, according to the best of my judgment, entitled to go into Parol Evidence to prove that Agreement; this appears to me to be the Result of all the Decisions on the Subject of Part-Performance." See also *Howe v Hall* (1870) IR 4 Eq 242 at 252 (*per* Sullivan MR).

[396.] [1927] NI 142.

[397.] *Ibid*, p 151.

[398.] With respect of Fry's statement that the acts of part performance "let in" the parol evidence of the contract, he commented that the use of these words "was a little unfortunate for it lends some support to the argument ... that acts of part performance are the key which opens the door to the contract. I do not think that that is so. They are the key to rendering the contract enforceable." [1974] 3 WLR 56 at 74.

[399.] *Ibid*, p 61. See also Lord Morris of Borth-y-Gest at p 65, Lord Simon at p 79 and Lord Salmon at p 84. And see *Daulia Ltd v Four Millbank Nominees Ltd* [1978] Ch 231.

[400.] *Kine v Balfe* (1813) 2 Ba & B 343 at 348 (*per* Lord Manners LC). See also *Savage v Carroll* (1810) 1 Ba & B 265 at 282.

[401.] See *Re Davitt's Estate* (1936) 70 ILTR 53.

[402.] See *Crowley v O'Sullivan* [1900] 2 IR 478.

performance executed by both parties to the contract so as to render it enforceable by each against the other.[403]

(i) Possession

[6.56] It has long been accepted as a general rule that the giving and taking of possession is an act of part performance of a contract for sale, ie, the alleged vendor vacating the property and the alleged purchaser taking over possession.[404] As Lord Redesdale LC put it in *Clinan v Cooke*[405]:

"... if upon a parol agreement, a man is admitted into possession, he is made a trespasser, and is liable to answer as a trespasser if there be no agreement ..."[406]

Where, however, the contract relates to leasehold property a distinction must be drawn between the case where a tenant takes possession of the property for the first time and where he continues in possession, eg, where the contract is for the renewal of the existing lease or for the purchase of the reversion. In the former case, the normal rule applies that taking possession is part performance.[407] As Chatterton V-C said in *Connor v Fitzgerald*: "In the case of giving and taking possession *de novo*, this is part performance on both sides ..."[408] In the latter case, on the other hand, continuing in possession is usually not enough in itself. In *Brennan v Bolton*,[409] Sugden LC explained as follows:

"... the rule is perfectly clear, that if a man is in possession of land as tenant, a mere parol agreement cannot have any operation in law, for the Statute of Frauds is in the way, and there is nothing, but the subsisting tenancy, to which this Court can refer any act, which may have been done, where it is consistent with his character as tenant. His remaining in possession is a mere continuance of the character, which he all along filled, and any act, which may be thus referred to a title distinct from the agreement, cannot be considered as operating to take the case out of the

---

[403.] See *Beauclerk v Hanna* (1888) 23 LR Ir 144 at 150 (*per* Chatterton V-C). See also *Connor v Fitzgerald* (1883) 11 LR Ir 106 at 116 (*per* Chatterton V-C); *Howe v Hall* (1870) IR 4 Eq 242.

[404.] See *Callaghan v Pepper* (1840) 2 Ir Eq R 399 at 401 (*per* Pennefather B). See also *Savage v Carroll* (1810) 1 Ba & B 265 at 282; *Kine v Balfe* (1813) 2 Ba & B 343 at 348; *Steeven's Hospital v Dyas* (1864) 15 Ir Ch R 405; *Corrigan v Woods* (1883) 11 LR Ir 106.

[405.] (1802) 1 Sch & Lef 22. See also *Daniels v Trefusis* [1914] 1 Ch 788.

[406.] *Ibid*, p 41. *Cf Re Foster* (1883) 22 Ch D 797 at 808 (*per* Jessel MR).

[407.] *Kine v Balfe* (1813) 2 Ba & B 343; *Callaghan v Pepper* (1840) 2 Ir Eq R 399; *Mortal v Lyons* (1858) 8 Ir Ch R 112.

[408.] (1883) 11 LR Ir 106 at 116.

[409.] (1842) 2 Dr & War 349.

Statute. I cannot, therefore, refer any act of the tenant after his possession as tenant to a new tenancy under a parol agreement ..."[410]

There must be some additional acts consistent with the new agreement and not explainable as merely a continuance of his position under the existing agreement. Thus, again Sugden LC explained in *Brennan v Bolton*:

"... the continuance on the part of the tenant to perform his duties as a tenant is not a ground, on which this Court could rest, as constituting an act of part performance. The improvements, which have been made on the farm, and the alleged expenditure by the tenant, are but what takes place in the ordinary course of husbandry ..."[411]

[6.57] There is, however, a line of Irish authority to the effect that payment and acceptance of an increased rent, as specified under the new tenancy agreement, is sufficient part performance.[412] Similarly, payment and acceptance of a reduced rent is sufficient.[413] In both such cases, there is usually part performance by the two parties to the agreement, as Chatterton V-C explained:

"I am of opinion that there has been part performance by both landlord and tenant - by the tenant, in availing himself of the benefit, of the reduction, and tendering the rent at the amount ascertained by the agreement, and accepting a receipt attributing the payment to the agreement itself; by the landlord, in accepting the reduced rent, and allowing the tenant to retain possession of his holding - and that such acts of part performance are referable to the very agreement relied on by the plaintiff."[414]

(ii) Alterations or Improvements

[6.58] There have been several cases where expenditure incurred in respect of making alterations or improvements to the property the subject of the alleged agreement has been held to be a sufficient act of part performance.[415]

[410.] *Ibid*, p 351. *Cf Wills v Stradling* (1797) 3 Ves 378.

[411.] *Ibid*, p 355.

[412.] *Archbold v Lord Howth* (1866) IR 1 CL 608; *Howe v Hall* (1870) IR 4 Eq 242; *Connor v Fitzgerald* (1883) 11 LR Ir 106; *Lanyon v Martin* (1884) 13 LR Ir 297. *Cf Sweeney v Dennis* (1883) 17 ILTR 76 (tenant continued to pay the old rent instead of the increased rent under the new parol agreement). As regards England, see *Miller and Aldworth v Sharp* [1899] 1 Ch 622.

[413.] *Beauclerk v Hanna* (1888) 23 LR Ir 144; *Haire-Foster v McIntee* (1889) 23 LR Ir 529.

[414.] *Ibid*, p 150. Similarly in a case involving an increase in rent, see *Connor v Fitzgerald* (1883) 11 LR Ir 106 at 116.

[415.] *Toole v Medlicott* (1810) 1 Ba & B 393 at 401-2 (*per* Manners LC); *Hope v Lord Cloncurry* (1874) IR 8 Eq 555 at 557 (*per* Chatterton V-C); *Re Sullivan's Estate* (1889) 23 LR Ir 255 at 256 (*per* Monroe J). See also *Dickinson v Barrow* [1904] 2 Ch 339; *Broughton v Snooke* [1938] Ch 505. As regards demolition work, see *Starling Securities Ltd v Woods* High Court, unrep, 24 May 1977 (1975/4044P).

Though in the case of a tenant continuing in possession, improvements taking place "in the ordinary course of husbandry" may not be sufficient.[416] It is doubtful if the taking of possession need accompany the making of alterations or improvements,[417] though it usually does so[418] and, when it does, obviously strengthens the plaintiff's claim.[419]

(iii) Payment of Money

[6.59] The established rule on this was stated by Lord Redesdale in *Clinan v Cooke*[420]:

> "Now it has always been considered that the payment of money is not to be deemed part performance to take a case out of the Statute ..."[421]

Later he gave his explanation for the rule:

> "Payment of money is not part performance; for it may be repaid; and then the parties will be just as they were before, especially if repaid with interest. It does not put a man who has parted with his money into the situation of a man against whom an action may be brought"[422]

Or, as it is sometimes put, payment of money is always an "equivocal" act, explainable on a variety of grounds, eg, making or repayment of a loan, other than as a payment made under a contract for sale of property.[423] Yet one of the most interesting features of the House of Lords decision in *Steadman v Steadman*[424] is the number of *dicta* by the law lords disputing this general rule.[425] Thus, Lord Reid stated:

[416.] *Brennan v Bolton* (1842) 2 Dr & War 349 at 355 (*per* Sugden LC), see para **[6.56]** *supra*.

[417.] See *Rawlinson v Ames* [1925] Ch 96.

[418.] See cases cited in fn 415 *supra*.

[419.] *Wills v Stradling* (1797) 3 Ves 378.

[420.] (1802) 1 Sch & Lef 22.

[421.] *Ibid*, p 40. This dictum may not be strictly accurate, see eg, the view of Lord Hardwicke in *Lacon v Mertins* (1743) 3 Atk 1 and *Main v Melbourne* (1799) 4 Ves 720. But there is much support for it, see, eg, *Lord Pengall v Ross* (1709) 2 Eq Cas Abr 46; *Dale v Hamilton* (1846) 5 Hare 360; *Chaproniere v Lambert* [1917] 2 Ch 356.

[422.] *Ibid*, p 41. *Cf Steadman v Steadman* [1974] 3 WLR 56 at 60 (*per* Lord Reid).

[423.] See *Steadman v Steadman* [1974] 3 WLR 56 at 83 (*per* Lord Simon).

[424.] [1974] 3 WLR 56.

[425.] It should be noted that there were several acts of part performance relied upon in that case, apart from the payment of £100 by the husband to his wife, eg announcement of the oral agreement to the justices, abandonment by the husband of his right to claim remission of arrears of maintenance and conveyancing steps, such as preparation and delivery to the wife for her signature of the form of transfer. Yet some law lords seem to have considered the payment of the £100 enough in itself, see *ibid*. p 60 (Lord Reid), p 72 (Viscount Dilhorne), p 83 (Lord Simon) and p 89 (Lord Salmon). *Cf* p 67 (Lord Morris).

"But to make a general rule that payment of money can never be part performance would seem to me to defeat the whole purpose of the doctrine and I do not think that we are compelled by authority to do that."[426]

Lord Salmon said:

"... I do not accept the line of authority which ... laid down that payment can never constitute such an act because it is impossible to deduce from payment the nature of the contract in respect of which the payment is made. It is no doubt true that often it is impossible to deduce even the existence of any contract from payment. For example, a payment by a parent to his child or a husband to his wife is in general no evidence of a contract; indeed, the presumption is to the contrary. Nevertheless the circumstances surrounding a payment may be such that the payment becomes evidence not only of the existence of the contract under which it is made but also of the nature of that contract. What the payment proves in the light of its surrounding circumstances is not a matter of law but a matter of fact. There is no rule of law which excludes evidence of the relevant circumstances surrounding the payment - save parol evidence of the contract on behalf of the person seeking to enforce the contract under which the payment is alleged to have been made."[427]

It remains to be seen whether the Irish courts will have second thoughts on this subject. In *Howlin v Power (Dublin) Ltd*,[428] McWilliam J, while accepting that the reasoning in *Steadman* was correct, emphasised that it is still necessary in part performance cases to establish that it would be fraudulent or inequitable to rely on the Statute of Frauds.

(iv) Other Acts

[6.60] Several other acts have been held to be sufficient. Thus, in *Lowry v Reid*[429] a mother undertook orally to make a will leaving her two farms to her son and thereby induced him to convey his own farm to his brother and to pay him £200. The Northern Ireland Court of Appeal held that the son's act in giving up his own farm on the faith of his mother's promise was a sufficient act of part performance, entitling him to specific performance.[430] A matter of some controversy has been the question of how far taking conveyancing steps can amount to acts of part performance. Thus, it has

---

[426.] *Ibid*, p 60. *Cf* p 83 (Lord Simon).

[427.] *Ibid*, p 88. See also *Daulia Ltd v Four Millbank Nominees Ltd* [1978] Ch 231; *Cohen v Nessdale Ltd* [1981] 3 All ER 118.

[428.] High Court, unrep, 5 May 1978 (1977/736P).

[429.] [1927] NI 142. See also *Wakeham v Mackenzie* [1968] 1 WLR 1175. *Cf Maddison v Alderson* (1883) 8 App Cas 467.

[430.] The mother had made a will to give effect to her undertaking but subsequently revoked it, leaving her son a life interest only in her farms.

been held that giving instructions to draw up a conveyance,[431] or delivery of an abstract of title or title deeds[432] are insufficient. On the other hand, in *Steadman v Steadman*[433] some of the law lords seem to have regarded preparation and delivery of a form of transfer to the other party for signature to be sufficient.[434]

III. EXCHANGE

[6.61] In England and Wales it has become the standard practice in recent decades to require one further step to be taken for the formation of a binding contract, namely, an "exchange" of contracts.[435] Indeed, the need for an exchange is usually regarded in England as being part of what is meant by saying that the transaction is still "subject to contract".[436] Under this system, the contract is drawn up in duplicate and, when finally approved by both sides, each solicitor gets his client to sign his copy. These two signed copies are then exchanged so that each party ends up with a copy signed by the other party, which is all that he needs for the purposes of enforcement under the Statute of Frauds.[437] It is rare nowadays for a ceremonial exchange to be made, eg, by the parties and/or their solicitors meeting together in the vendor's solicitor's office. Exchange was, until recently, usually conducted by post. Once the purchaser's solicitor has obtained his client's signature on his copy of the contract, he usually telephones the vendor's solicitor and informs him that his client's signed copy is being put in the post that day (or whenever he specifies), together with a cheque for the deposit required under the contract (or any balance still due). The vendor's solicitor then gets his client to sign his copy of the contract, if he has not already done so, but

---

431. *Redding v Wilkes* (1791) 3 Bro CC 400; *Cooke v Tombs* (1794) 2 Anst 420.

432. *Whaley v Bagnal* (1765) 1 Bro Parl Cas 345.

433. [1974] 3 WLR 56.

434. See Viscount Dilhorne, *ibid*, p 72: "I do not think the contention ... that the sending of the transfer for execution was an act preparatory to the performance of the contract and not in performance of it is well founded. It is well established that preparatory acts such as instructing a solicitor to prepare a lease or conveyance do not constitute sufficient part performance ... But here it went beyond mere preparation. In the absence of conditions it was the husband's duty to send the transfer for execution by the wife ... The transfer was thus sent in discharge of an obligation that rested on the husband by virtue of the contract."

435. The leading authority on the subject is the Court of Appeal decision in *Eccles v Bryant* [1948] Ch 93. See also *Smith v Mansi* [1963] 1 WLR 26. And Barnsley, Conveyancing Law and Practice (3rd ed, 1988), Ch 8; *Williams on Title* (4th ed, by Battersby; 1975), pp 24-5.

436. See, eg *D'Silva v Lister House Development Ltd* [1971] Ch 17; *Tiverton Estates Ltd v Wearwell Ltd* [1974] 2 WLR 176.

437. Ie, a copy signed by "the party to be charged," see para **[6.32]** *supra*. Note the somewhat unusual method of exchange adopted by the solicitors in *Embourg Ltd v Tyler Group Ltd* Supreme Court, unrep, 5 March 1996 (223/1995), whereby the vendor's solicitor sent two copies of the contract to the purchaser's solicitor, who returned *both* copies signed by the purchaser! See fns 447 and 449 *infra*.

he does not usually post it off (together with a receipt for the deposit) to the purchaser's solicitor until he receives the purchaser's signed copy.[438] It seems to be settled in England that there is no contract until the vendor's solicitor does at least put this signed copy in the post, even though prior to that time there may be two copies in existence, each signed by one or other of the two parties.[439] It is not yet settled, however, whether the exchange is completed and the contract is binding as soon as the vendor's copy is put in the post,[440] which is the normal postal rule in contract law,[441] or whether it must be received by the purchaser or his solicitor before the contract is binding.[442] Increasingly solicitors in England have adopted a system of telephonic exchanges and, following judicial recognition[443] of the practice, the Law Society recommended the use of procedures set out in formulae to regulate the practice.[444] These formulae also cover exchanges by telex and fax.

[6.62] It must be emphasised that, as yet, a system of exchange of contracts has not been adopted much in Ireland,[445] though there are some signs of its use in the Dublin area.[446] Normally what happens is that the purchaser's solicitor gets first his client to sign the contract in duplicate, as approved, and then sends these signed copies to the vendor or his solicitor for "acceptance".[447] This may be accompanied by a letter from the purchaser's

---

438. Again, as a matter of courtesy, he may telephone the purchaser's solicitor to tell him that this has been or is about to be done.

439. This is the actual decision in *Eccles v Bryant* [1948] Ch 93.

440. This was the view of Cohen LJ in *Eccles v Bryant, ibid* p 107. *Cf* Asquith LJ at p 108. The English *Standard Conditions of Sale* (3rd ed) now also adopt this view in cond 2.1.1 which provides:

"If the parties intend to make a contract by exchanging duplicate copies by post or through a document exchange, the contract is made when the last copy is posted or deposited at the document exchange."

441. *Henthorn v Frazer* [1892] 2 Ch 27. *Cf Household Fire & Carriage Accident Insurance Co v Grant* (1879) 4 Ex D 216.

442. See the English *Standard Condition of Sale* (3rd ed), cond 2.1.1, fn 440 *supra*.

443. See *Domb v Isoz* [1980] Ch 548.

444. See Silverman, *The Law Society's Conveyancing Handbook 1995* Ch 04 and Appendix VII.

445. See para **[1.32]** *supra*.

446. See *Kelly v Irish Nursery and Landscape Co Ltd* [1981] ILRM 433, especially at 438 (*per* Kenny J). See also *Mulhall v Haren* [1981] IR 364 at 377-8 (*per* Keane J) and the judgment of the Supreme Court in *Embourg Ltd v Tyler Group Ltd* 5 March 1996 (223/1995)

447. Technically, in so far as signature of the written contract or memorandum is merely completion of the formalities required by the Statute of Frauds, this may not be acceptance of an offer to purchase in the strict contractual sense - that may have already taken place, see paras **[6.06-7]**, and **[6.42]** and **[6.43]** *supra*. But signatures by both parties may also be a condition precedent to the coming into force of the contract, see para **[7.06]** *post*. In the *Embourg* case (fn 446 *supra*) the Supreme Court held that the parties in that case had made an "exchange" a condition precedent to the contract coming into force. See also *Smith v Mansi* [1963] 1 WLR 26.

solicitor to the effect that his client will not regard himself as bound by the contract until the vendor has signed the contract and returned one copy so signed. He may enclose also the deposit stipulated in the contract, or else indicate that this will be forwarded when the vendor "accepts" the contract. At this stage, the contract may be enforceable against the purchaser, in that there is in existence written evidence of it signed by him,[448] but not against the vendor until he signs. Thus, the purchaser often finds himself in a state of limbo; he cannot be absolutely certain, even at this late stage, whether the vendor will sign and, if he is willing, when he will sign. If the purchaser's solicitor has not enclosed the deposit with the signed copy of the contract, the vendor's solicitor will often notify him, by post or telephone, of the vendor's willingness to sign the contract provided the deposit is forwarded forthwith. When this is forwarded the vendor then signs the contract,[449] thereby rendering it enforceable against him as well, and his solicitor sends a copy to the purchaser or his solicitor, together with a receipt for the deposit.

[6.63] The question of whether the English system of exchange of contracts should be adopted in Ireland has been raised from time to time, and, indeed, the Conveyancing and Law of Property Committee of the Incorporated Law Society of Northern Ireland did recommend as long ago as 1969 that it should be adopted in that part of Ireland.[450] The Committee felt that it did have a number of advantages. First, they considered that it disposes of the unsatisfactory (from the purchaser's point of view) waiting period between the purchaser signing the contract and the vendor's "acceptance," which was mentioned in the previous paragraph. It is, however, fair to point out that the exchange system is not entirely free from uncertainty, eg, there remains the doubt as to when exchange takes place where it is conducted, as is usually the case, by post.[451] Secondly, they considered that it avoided the uncertainty

---

448. See para **[6.32]** *supra*. But note that there may be a condition precedent of signature by the vendor also, **[6.62]** *supra*, or this may be specified by a letter such as the one referred to above in the text.

449. In practice the vendor may have signed already and his solicitor simply delays sending a copy to the purchaser or his solicitor until the deposit is received. The danger in this practice is, of course, that once the vendor signs the contract it is technically enforceable against him, whether or not the deposit has been received, but in reality little hangs on this, in that the purchaser still does not have in his possession the evidence he needs to produce in court and, so long as he delays in paying the deposit, he is in breach of the contract and unlikely to receive a sympathetic hearing from the court, see para **[10.18]** *post*. In the *Embourg* case (fns 437 and 446 *supra*) both parties had signed the contract but it never came into operation because the Supreme Court held that they had stipulated for a further requirement, viz, an exchange

450. See *Memorandum on Proposed New Conditions of Sale and Enquiries Before Contract* (13 November 1969).

451. See para **[6.61]** *supra*.

as to payment of the deposit that often arises under the present system[452] Yet it is questionable whether the exchange system necessarily resolves the uncertainty if, again as is usual, it is conducted by post.[453] In that case exactly the same problem arises: the purchaser's solicitor should enclose the deposit with his client's signed copy of the contract, but, if he does not do so, the vendor's solicitor still has to clarify the matter before putting his client's signed copy in the post.[454] Thirdly, it was considered that the new system would avoid uncertainties which often arise from the purchaser or his solicitor making various amendments to the contract, without telling the vendor or his solicitor, who becomes aware of these only when the signed contract is returned for signature by the vendor. It may be true that the exchange system encourages better communication, eg, having the draft contract passing back and forth until a final agreed draft is approved before each party signs his copy,[455] but there have been some problems in England. For example, sometimes there the purchaser's signed copy is sent to the vendor's solicitor leaving the date for completion blank,[456] and this runs the risk that the vendor's solicitor may insert a date not acceptable to the purchaser.[457] Finally, it was thought that the exchange system would encourage laymen to consult their solicitors more and, in particular, guard against the dangers involved in a purchaser signing a contract before consulting his solicitor,[458] eg, a contract supplied by the vendor's estate agent.[459] It may be true that the extra formality involved might have this result and there is some evidence, albeit largely impressionistic, that such informal signing of contracts is rarer in England and Wales. But it is difficult to draw a firm causal connection, especially when it is remembered that there is no obligation in England and Wales to have an exchange - this

---

[452.] See para **[6.62]** *supra*. See also para **[10.22]** *post*.

[453.] If it is conducted by a formal exchange, eg, in the vendor's solicitor's office, then it will resolve the doubts in that presumably the deposit will have to be handed over with the purchaser's signed copy of the contract in return for the vendor's signed copy and receipt for the deposit.

[454.] *Cf* para **[6.62]** *supra*. See further, para **[10.22]** *post*.

[455.] By analogy with the process relating to the draft conveyance before engrossment, see para **[17.07]** *post*.

[456.] Insertion of the contract date is normally left to the vendor's solicitor.

[457.] It is doubtful if such insertion binds the purchaser instead of the date otherwise specified by the Conditions of Sale, see para **[9.05]** *post*; it depends upon whether the vendor's solicitor has authority from the purchaser to insert the date, which is unlikely, in that leaving the date blank could be construed as an indication of intention to be governed by the Conditions of Sale. See (1968) 65 L Soc Gaz 160.

[458.] See generally, Chs 2-5 *ante*.

[459.] See the remarks of Meredith J in *Donnelly v O'Connell* (1924) 58 ILTR 164 at 164, see para **[7.13]** *post*.

remains a matter of intention on the part of the two sides to the transaction, though its existence is now generally assumed.[460] The more recent adoption in England of telephonic exchanges has by no means solved the problems of exchanges by post; notwithstanding the Law Society's attempts to regulate the practice,[461] a number of further problems have come to light, partly due to practitioner's failure to follow the Society's formulae strictly.[462]

IV. REGISTRATION

[6.64] There is no statutory requirement that a contract for the sale of land should be registered and it is rare for it to be done in Ireland.[463] The reason for non-registration is the inconvience of creating a "flaw" on the title when there is usually a small risk of some other dealing being made with the land during the relatively short interval between the contract and completion, when registration of the conveyance will take place.[464] Any searches are usually made prior to completion[465] which will reveal whether any such dealing has been registered so as to gain priority over the purchaser buying under the unregistered contract, and these are brought up to date with registration of the purchaser's deed, in the case of unregistered land. If the searches do reveal any other dealing with the land purported to be conveyed to the purchaser, he should insist upon the person having rights under that dealing joining in the conveyance to him to release those rights and, if he refuses, the purchaser will be entitled to call the sale off, though, of course, that may not be much comfort if he had his heart set on that particular property. The rare occasions when the purchaser's solicitor might take the precaution of registering the contract are where there is likely to be a long delay between the date of the contract and completion, and so there is a

---

[460] See *Eccles v Bryant* [1948] Ch 93 at 102 (*per* Lord Greene MR). Note that there is no requirement in s 2 of the Law of Property (Miscellaneous Provisions) Act 1989 (see fn 16 *supra*), but it does expressly recognise that the parties may still want to exchange copies of the written contract which is required: see subs (1) and (3).

[461] See **[6.61]** *supra*.

[462] See Barnsley, *Conveyancing Law and Practice* (3rd ed, 1988), pp 210-212.

[463] It is also fairly rare in England, though such a contract is an "estate contract" registerable in the Land Charges Registry, see Barnsley, *Conveyancing Law and Practice* (3rd ed, 1988), pp 213-214. See also Adams, 'A Fly in the Ointment: Estate Contracts and the Land Charges Computer' (1971) 35 Conv 155. If, however, a dispute occurs leading one of the parties to institute proceedings, his rights will usually be protected by registration of a *lis pendens*: see Farrell, *Irish Law of Specific Performance* (1994), para [10.10] *et seq*. And if a judgment is obtained, this may be registered as a judgment mortgage: see *ibid*, Ch 11 and para **[12.03]** *et seq, post*.

[464] See para **[20.42]** *et seq, post*.

[465] See para **[15.39]** *post*.

greater risk of some other dealing taking place which takes priority over the purchaser, or where this risk exists anyway by virtue of the nature of the transaction being entered into by the purchaser.[466] One example of the latter situation which is often quoted is where the purchaser is entering into a building contract with a builder and an agreement to acquire the land from the site owner.[467] The risk here is that the builder or developer usually has to borrow substantial sums of money to cover the initial capital outlay for the development, eg, in preparation of the site and in laying down drains and sewers, and the lender will usually demand security for the loan by way of a mortgage or charge on the site. If the purchaser registers his contract relating to the site before the mortgage or charge is registered then he will have priority over the lender[468] should the builder go into insolvency.[469]

[6.65] Where the land is unregistered land, the contract for sale may be registered in the Registry of Deeds. At first sight this may appear surprising, in that the Registry of Deeds, as it name suggests, was primarily designed for registration of deeds and other conveyances.[470] However, it has always been recognised in Ireland that the system here covers transactions involving use of unsealed instruments, such as the very common creation of an equitable mortgage by deposit of title deeds, accompanied by a written, but unsealed, memorandum of the mortgage.[471] The result is that the Registries in both parts of Ireland have been prepared to accept for registration a memorial[472] of any written instrument which involves the transfer of any kind of interest in land from one person to another. In relation to contracts for the sale of land, the view has been taken that the purchaser becomes the

---

[466.] Needless to say, another occasion is where the purchaser or his solicitor does not trust the vendor and suspects that some "double-dealing" may occur!

[467.] See also *Midland Bank Trust Co Ltd v Hett, Stubbs and Kemp* [1979] Ch 384, where the solicitors were held negligent for failure to register an option to purchase. See also *Armstrong & Holmes Ltd v Holmes* [1994] 1 All ER 826.

[468.] Assuming the mortgage or charge is not an equitable one which is unregistrable because no written document is involved in its creation, eg, where it is created by deposit of the title deeds or land certificate, see *Irish Land Law* (2nd ed, 1986), paras 12.29 and 12.43-6. In such a case priority will depend upon the respective times of creation, see *ibid*, paras 3.087 and 13.133.

[469.] See para **[11.17]** *post*.

[470.] Indeed, in England it was firmly established, at least in relation to the Yorkshire Registry of Deeds, that a contract for sale was not an assurance, or deed or conveyance, and so was no registerable. See the decision by the Court of Appeal in *Rodger v Harrison* [1893] 1 QB 161 (which involved a building contract). There is no equivalent in either part of Ireland of the Land Charges Registry and the concept of an "estate contract".

[471.] See *Irish Land Law* (2nd ed, 1986), para 22.03.

[472.] See *ibid*, paras 22.05-8.

owner of the property in equity under the contract[473] and that this equitable interest justifies his being entitled to register the contract in the Registry of Deeds. In view of the absence of a Land Charges Registry in Ireland, there is no doubt that the practice followed by the Registries of Deeds in both parts of Ireland of allowing contracts for sale to be registered is an extremely convenient one. It has now been given express judicial recognition.[474] And the standard contract form issued by the Law Society also seems to recognise the practice, for, on rescission of a contract for failure to comply with a completion notice,[475] the purchaser is to procure the cancellation of any entry relating to the contract in any register.[476]

[6.66] So far as registered land is concerned, the purchaser under a contract for sale can lodge a "caution" in the Land Registry.[477] It is provided by statute that this can be done by any person "entitled to any right in, to, or over registered land,"[478] and it is accepted that a purchaser under a contract for sale comes into this category.[479] The effect of lodging a caution is to prevent any further dealings by the registered owner (ie, the vendor) until notice is served on the cautioner (ie, the purchaser).[480] Such notice enables the purchaser to take action to prevent adverse dealings by the vendor becoming registered.

[473.] But see the discussion of the nature of the purchaser's interest under the contract by the Supreme Court in *Tempany v Hynes* [1976] IR 101, which suggests that the purchaser cannot register unless he has paid the deposit or some portion of the purchase money or other consideration. See paras **[12.02]** *et seq, post.*

[474.] *O'Connor v McCarthy* [1982] IR 161 at 171 (*per* Costello J) (citing the first edition of this book).

[475.] See paras **[13.19-24]** *post.* Of course, these provisions could also be referring to entries relating to registered land, see fn 476 *infra.*

[476.] *General Conditions of Sale* (1995 ed), cond 40(e). This could, of course, by a reference to an entry in the Land Registry, para **[6.66]** *infra.*

[477.] See Fitzgerald, *Land Registry Practice* (2nd ed, 1995), p 161 *et seq.*

[478.] Registration of Title Act 1964, s 97.

[479.] See para **[12.02]** *post.*

[480.] See Fitzgerald, *op cit*, p 161.

Chapter 7

CONDITIONAL CONTRACTS

[7.01] Perhaps one of the most difficult areas of the law concerns the enforceability of conditional contracts, ie, where the contract for sale is made subject to some condition relating to the property or the parties.[1] There are usually two principal reasons why contracts may be so qualified. The first arises from considerations the parties themselves may have where they conduct the preliminary negotiations without consulting their solicitors. They may make an informal agreement but, in doing so, they may have at least a vague idea that some formalities may be necessary. They may not be familiar with the precise requirements of the Statute of Frauds - thus, if aware of the need for writing, they are likely to make the common error of assuming this means the contract itself must be in writing[2] - but they may realise that matters should not be left on an informal basis and so agree that the matter should be referred to their respective solicitors for completion of the formalities.[3] Though how they express this desire may vary considerably from case to case.[4] Another consideration which may weigh heavily with the parties, especially the purchaser, is that he may doubt the wisdom of committing himself to the contract before seeking advice or before conducting further enquiries or checks with respect to the property. So again some qualification may be attached to the agreement designed to give one or other, or both, of the parties a "let out" if something adverse is discovered.[5] But it is not only the parties who may seek to qualify the agreement initially; their solicitors may also wish to impose conditions, even on the formal contract finally approved for signing by both parties. Here again the desire is to obtain the best of both worlds - on the one hand, it is intended to commit the other party to the extent of preventing him from changing his mind and backing out of the transaction[6]; on the other hand, it is intended that the

---

1. See the discussion in Farrell, *Irish Law of Specific Performance* (1994), para [3.19] *et seq.* Also Barnsley, *Conveyancing Law and Practice* (3rd ed, 1988), p 132 *et seq.*
2. See para **[6.06]** *ante.*
3. See the discussion by Gannon J in *Black v Kavanagh* (1974) 108 ILTR 91 at 95-6, see paras **[3.33]** and **[6.42]** *ante.* See also *Donnelly v O'Connell* (1924) 58 ILTR 164 at 164 (*per* Meredith J) para **[7.13]** *infra.*
4. See para **[7.05]** *et seq, infra.*
5. See *Donnelly v O'Connell* (1924) 58 ILTR 164 at 164 (*per* Meredith J).
6. This condition may have a role to play in preventing "gazumping", ie, by preventing the vendor from accepting a higher offer, see para **[6.04]** *infra.*

condition will enable the party imposing it to abandon the contract later without liability, if the matter covered by the condition is not resolved satisfactorily. There may be a variety of considerations prompting such "half-hearted" arrangements.[7] In his desire to commit the vendor, the purchaser may not want to be finally committed himself until he has completed certain matters, eg, in respect of surveying the property[8] or raising the purchase money,[9] or his solicitor has completed any preliminary conveyancing steps he considers necessary, eg, searches and enquiries.[10] The result is that the use of conditional contracts has become very common. Contracts subject to a mortgage loan being obtained are used frequently, as are contracts subject to the obtaining of planning permission. Contracts subject to a satisfactory survey are also used sometimes.

[7.02] Though it is fairly easy to identify the motives behind the imposition of conditions, it is far from easy to state with certainty the precise effect of many of the conditions which are often imposed in practice. The courts on both sides of the Irish Sea have been faced with a considerable variety of conditions and we consider some of them in a moment. But first an attempt will be made to clarify the basic principles which should be taken into account in considering the effect of any particular condition - though the caveat is entered that the judges have not always analysed the cases in this way nor have they always expressly recognised the principles discussed in the following paragraphs.

I. GENERAL PRINCIPLES

[7.03] It is crucial to recognise that there is one basic distinction to be drawn when considering so-called "conditional" contracts.[11] This is the distinction between a condition which must be satisfied *before* any contract at all becomes binding on either party, ie, a condition *precedent*[12] and a condition which results in a contract which is already binding on both parties ceasing *afterwards* to be binding, usually as regards one of the parties only and then

---

7. *Cf* the use of options, see para **[8.03]** *post.*
8. See para **[3.41]** *ante* and para **[7.19]** *infra.*
9. See para **[7.14]** *infra.*
10. See Ch 5 *ante* and para **[7.20]** *infra.*
11. Though note also that the expression "conditional contracts" is itself vague. Thus, it may cover all cases where a condition is attached to a contract and it is in this sense that it is used above. But some writers confine it to certain types of conditions only, eg, conditions subsequent, Barnsley, *Conveyancing Law and Practice* (3rd ed, 1988) p 132.
12. Alternatively, imposition of such a condition by a vendor may be construed as a qualified acceptance only, see *Brien v Swainson* (1877) 1 LR Ir 135 at 141 (*per* Chatterton V-C).

at his option, ie, a condition *subsequent*.[13] Though the courts have not often put the matter in quite these terms, there is no doubt that they recognise the distinction in substance in relation to conveyancing contracts.[14] Thus, in *Thompson v King*[15] Gibson J stated:

> "Where an offer and acceptance are made subject to a subsequent formal contract, if such contract is a condition or term which until performed keeps the agreement in suspense, the offer and acceptance have no contractual force. On the other hand, if all the terms are agreed on, and a formal contract only is contemplated as putting the terms in legal shape, the agreement is effectual before and irrespective of such formal contract."[16]

On the other hand, in *Brien v Swainson*,[17] where a vendor accepted an offer from a purchaser "subject to letter and agreement to be sent to your solicitor," Chatterton V-C remarked:

> "If there be a concluded agreement, it will be specifically enforced, though by its terms it contemplates some more formal contract being entered into."[18]

It follows that it is essential in every case to determine first the crucial issue whether the parties ever reached the stage of a concluded agreement. If they did not, ie, they remained in a stage of negotiation or an offer by one party had not been accepted by the other or acceptance had not been communicated to the other party, there is no contract to be evidenced as

---

13. This passage in the first edition was cited with approval by Costello J in *Dorene Ltd v Suedes (Ireland) Ltd* [1981] IR 312 at 324. *Cf* Gannon J in *Gaelcrann Teo v Payne* ILRM 109 at 114-116. It is considered that this formulation makes the distinction clearer than alternatives such as one which distinguishes between a condition precedent to *formation* of the contract and a condition precedent to *performance* of the contract.

14. For further analysis of the effect of different conditions see the Privy Council decision in *Aberfoyle Plantations Ltd v Cheng* [1960] AC 115 and Goff J in *Wood Preservation Ltd v Prior* [1968] 2 All ER 849 at 855 (affd [1969] 1 All ER 364). *Cf* eg, *Thompson v King* [1920] 2 IR 365 (affd [1921] 2 IR 438) and *Black v Kavanagh* (1974)108 ILTR 91. See also *Louis v Willson* [1949] IR 347 at 349-50 (*per* Dixon J). And see the discussion in Davies, 'Conditional Contracts for the Sale of Land in Canada' (1977) 55 CBR 289; Oakley, 'Conditional Contracts for the Sale of Land' [1982] CLP 151; Harpum, 'The Construction of Conditional Contracts and the Effect of Delay in Completion' (1992) Conv 318.

15. [1920] 2 IR 365 (KBD), affd. without argument [1921] 2 IR 438 (CA).

16. [1920] 2 IR 365 at 386. In *Embourg Ltd v Tyler Group Ltd* Supreme Court, unrep, 5 March 1996 (223/1995), it was held that the parties, through their agents, had made the conclusion of a binding contract dependent upon the "exchange" of contracts: see paras **[6.61]** *ante* and **[7.08]** *infra*. See also *Ridgway v Wharton* (1857) 6 HLC 238 at 268 (*per* Lord Cranworth LC); *Von Hatzfeldt-Wildenburg v Alexander* [1921] 1 Ch 284 at 288 (*per* Parker J).

17. (1877) 1 LR Ir 135.

18. *Ibid*, pp 139-40. In fact, his conclusion was that the vendor's acceptance was so qualified that no concluded agreement had been entered into in this case.

required by the Statute of Frauds. In such a case any written correspondence is relevant only to the issue of whether it reveals a concluded agreement and the court is not concerned with the issue of whether that correspondence constitutes a sufficient memorandum or note in writing for the purpose of the Statute. That issue arises only if the court first makes the determination that the parties reached the stage of a concluded agreement, so that the further issue then arises as to whether that agreement is enforceable, by being evidenced by a sufficient memorandum or note in writing as required by the Statute of Frauds.

[7.04] The other essential principle to be borne in mind is that it is a question of construction in each case what is the effect of the condition. As Pim J stated in *Thompson v King*[19]:

> "The gist of all the cases is that the Court should in each case, having considered the wording of the document containing the alleged contract, the correspondence before and after, and the nature of the transactions, say whether in fact the parties meant that the matter in negotiation should remain in a state of negotiation until a formal contract was signed, or whether they only meant that the contract which had been entered into should be embodied afterwards in a formal contract. It is in every case an issue of fact for the Court."[20]

In the appeal to the King's Bench Division, Gibson J stated:

> "The relevant principles of law are clear. The only difficulty in each case is as to their application."[21]

The case law illustrates that the courts may be willing to imply terms in order to give effect to the conditions, especially if it is a condition subsequent. For example, a party will not usually be allowed to withdraw from the contract on the basis of non-fulfilment of the conditions, if he has not used his best endeavours to achieve the fulfilment in question, eg, by applying for Land Act consent.[22] And, where necessary, the other party will be expected to co-operate by performing any incidental acts required on his part[23] and, of course, must not attempt to thwart the other party's efforts to

---

[19.] [1920] 2 IR 365, reversed on other grounds by the KBD and appeal dismissed (without argument) [1921] 2 IR 438.

[20.] *Ibid* p 373.

[21.] *Ibid* p 386. See also para **[7.01]** *supra*.

[22.] See *Costelloe v KN Maharaj Properties (Ireland) Ltd* High Court, unrep, 10 July 1975 (1974/1564P). See also as regards getting the landlord's consent to an assignment of a lease *Royal Avenue Hotel Ltd v Richard Shops Properties Ltd* [1985] 6 NIJB 52. *Cf Draisey v Fitzpatrick* [1981] ILRM 219, para **[7.14]** *infra*.

[23.] See *Neville v Slattery Estates Co Ltd* High Court, unrep, 15 February 1984 (1981/14038P).

secure fulfilment.[24] If no express time limit for fulfilment is specified,[25] the condition must be fulfilled within a reasonable time,[26] but no later than the date fixed for completion.[27] Of course, the parties or their solicitors should not leave such matters to chance and care should be taken to spell out in detail precisely what it is which must be achieved in order to satisfy the condition, within what time-scale and what the consequences are of non-fulfilment.[28] It must be remembered that if the condition is vague or imprecise the courts may hold that it is too uncertain to be enforceable.[29] Finally, the party for whose benefit the condition has been inserted may choose to waive it and insist upon performance of the contract without the need for fulfilment of the condition.[30] There can, however, be no unilateral waiver of this kind unless the condition is for the waiving party's sole benefit.[31] For example, in the case of a condition concerning the obtaining of planning permission,[32] the vendor will usually also have an interest in this matter for the availability of such permission clearly affects the value of his land, including any land retained by him after the sale.[33]

II. ILLUSTRATIONS

[7.05] In the next few paragraphs we consider some of the more common conditions attached to conveyancing contracts. Though some indication will be given of the various terminology that may be used in respect of each type of condition, it must be remembered that this is by no means exhaustive. Not surprisingly laymen tend to use a bewildering variety of forms of condition,

---

[24.] See *Massarella v Massarella* High Court, unrep, 10 July 1980 (1978/630 Sp).

[25.] Where such a limit is expressed, it must be adhered to strictly: see *Crean v Drinan* [1983] ILRM 82 at 85 (*per* Barrington J).

[26.] See *Re Longlands Farm* [1968] 3 All ER 552.

[27.] See *Moloney v Elf Investments Ltd* [1979] ILRM 253.

[28.] Note cond 10(d) of the Law Society's *General Conditions of Sale* (1995 ed) (dealing with the landlord's consent to alienation): see para **[14.75]** *post*.

[29.] See *O'Mullane v Riordan* [1978] ILRM 73. *Cf Lee-Parker v Izzet* [1971] 3 All ER 1099 at 1105; *Lee-Parker v Izzet (No 2)* [1972] 2 All ER 800; *Janmohamed v Hassam* (1976) 241 EG 609.

[30.] *Healy v Healy* High Court, unrep, 3 December 1973 (1973/244 Sp).

[31.] *Moloney v Elf Investments Ltd* [1979] ILRM 253; *Tiernan Homes Ltd v Sheridan* [1981] ILRM 191. For an express provision covering waiver, see *Draisey v Fitzpatrick* [1981] ILRM 219, para **[7.14]** *infra*.

[32.] See para **[7.16]** *infra*.

[33.] See *McKillop v McMullen* [1979] NI 85. See also *Heron Garage Properties Ltd v Moss* [1974] 1 All ER 421; *cf Sepia Ltd v O'Hanlon Ltd* [1979] ILRM 11; *Ee v Kakar* (1979) 40 P & CR 223.

and even solicitors can hardly be said to be consistent about or agreed on the forms that should be used.

A. Subject to Contract

[7.06] One of the most common conditions attached to contracts for sale is one specifying that the contract is still "subject to contract". This is frequently done by the parties themselves when they are in the preliminary stages of negotiation, but it is also often done by their solicitors while they are either negotiating the contract or settling the precise terms of the formal contract for sale prior to signature by the parties. In the case of the parties, the intention is usually to indicate that they envisage that, after their preliminary negotiations, the matter will be taken over by their respective solicitors for completion of the formalities at the very least. Whether it means that they intend that no binding contract should be regarded as coming into force until that later stage is, of course, a matter of construction.[34] So far as their solicitors are concerned, the intention is almost certainly to indicate that no contract is to come into force until they have completed their negotiations over the draft contract and the finally approved draft is signed by both parties. We also pointed out earlier that such a qualification ought to be inserted in all correspondence conducted by each solicitor to guard against the risk of inadvertently bringing into existence a sufficient memorandum for the purposes of the Statute of Frauds,[35] and thereby rendering the contract enforceable before they wish their clients to be bound by it.[36] Over the years the issue of the effect of the "subject to contract" formula has been a matter of considerable controversy, but recently the Supreme Court clarified the position to a large extent.[37]

[7.07] In *Thompson v King*,[38] the contract was marked "subject contract" and it was held that this was a condition or term which, until performed by execution of a subsequent formal contract, kept the "agreement" in suspense. Gibson J stated:

[34.] See especially the discussion by Gannon J in *Black v Kavanagh* (1974) 108 ILTR 91 at 95 and the Supreme Court in *Boyle v Lee* [1992] 1 IR 555 and *Embourg Ltd v Tyler Group Ltd* Supreme Court, unrep, 5 March 1996 (223/1995). See also para **[7.03]** *supra*.

[35.] See paras **[6.15]**, **[6.42]** and **[6.47]** *ante*.

[36.] Arguably this was the mistake the solicitors made in *Black v Kavanagh, supra*. See also para **[7.09]** *infra*.

[37.] In *Boyle v Lee* [1992] 1 IR 555. For a detailed discussion of the caselaw and the implications of the decision in *Boyle* see Farrell, *Irish Law of Specific Performance* (1994), Ch 4.

[38.] [1920] 2 IR 365 (KBD), [1921] 2 IR 438 (CA).

"Did this expression 'subject contract' defer contractual obligation until a formal contract was settled, accepted, and executed; or does it mean that the purchase terms having been fully and finally settled, a further contract was only contemplated for the purpose of putting the bargain into legal shape, without substantial additions or alterations? I adopt the former construction ... the expression conveys an essential condition without performance of which the proposed contract is incomplete."[39]

Gordon J also stated:

"... the provision 'subject contract' was a necessary and vital provision to ensure that before the parties were bound there should be such a document signed as would eliminate all questions of doubt as to what they were agreeing to, and that until the document was signed there was no final or concluded agreement between them."[40]

Similarly, in *Re Hibernian Transport Companies Ltd*,[41] where an offer was made "subject to contract" after an abortive auction in a sale under a court order, Walsh J stated:

"... in the ordinary course of events an agreement for the sale or purchase of land subject to contract means nothing more than an agreement to enter into a contract for the sale of land and, as such, it is not enforceable as if it were a contract."[42]

[7.08] A similar construction of the "subject to contract" formula has been given by several English judges.[43] However, it had also been held by the English Court of Appeal that a contract so qualified could become binding by the parties or their solicitors agreeing subsequently to remove the qualification and that this could be done orally.[44] It was even suggested by that Court in *Law v Jones*[45] that solicitors' correspondence so qualified could

---

[39.] [1920] 2 IR 365 at 391-2 (KBD).The decision of the KBD was affirmed without argument by the Court of Appeal.

[40.] *Ibid* p 396.

[41.] [1972] IR 190.

[42.] *Ibid* p 202. See also *Barry v Buckley* [1981] 1 IR 306; *Dorene Ltd v Suedes (Ireland) Ltd* [1982] ILRM 126. In the *Embourg* case (fn 34 *supra*) the Supreme Court held that a condition that "no binding contract shall be deemed to exist between the parties until contracts have been executed and exchanged" meant that no contract had come into existence prior to an "exchange": see para **[6.61]** *et seq, ante*.

[43.] See *Keppel v Wheeler* [1927] 1 KB 577 at 584 (*per* Bankes LJ); *Spottiswoode, Ballantyne & Co Ltd v Doreen Appliances Ltd* [1942] 2 KB 32 at 35 (*per* Lord Greene MR).

[44.] See *Griffiths v Young* [1970] Ch 675 and note the discussion of this case by the Court of Appeal in *Law v Jones* [1974] Ch 112 and *Tiverton Estates Ltd v Wearwell Ltd* [1974] 2 WLR 176. See also Pritchard, 'An Aspect of Contracts and Their Terms' (1974) 90 LQR 55.

[45.] [1974] Ch 12.

nevertheless constitute a sufficient memorandum of an oral agreement made by the parties themselves,[46] but any such suggestion was firmly rejected by the Court in *Tiverton Estates Ltd v Wearwell Ltd.*[47] In the latter case, the Court emphasised that any alleged memorandum which purports to deny the existence of a contract (which it held a qualification such as "subject to contract" did) could not constitute a sufficient memorandum or note for the purposes of the Statute of Frauds,[48] even though the parties themselves had actually reached a concluded agreement and parol evidence could be adduced to prove this.[49] The position in Ireland had also become somewhat confused because in two decisions reported in 1979 the Supreme Court seemed to hold that the formula did not necessarily prevent the written evidence in question from being a sufficient note or memorandum for the purposes of the Statute of Frauds,[50] if the evidence suggested that the parties had concluded an unqualified oral agreement.[51] However, shortly afterwards, in a comprehensive survey of both the Irish and English caselaw,[52] Keane J came to the conclusion[53] that generally the sounder position was that determined by the English Court of Appeal in the *Tiverton* case. In particular, he was of the view that, apart from exceptional cases,[54] the note or memorandum should acknowledge the existence of a contract. Then in *Boyle v Lee*[55] the Supreme Court seized the opportunity to restate its position. Finlay CJ was emphatic:

> "In modern times, probably the most important legal transaction a great number of people make in their lifetimes is the purchase or sale of their house. The avoidance of doubt and, therefore, the avoidance of litigation concerning such a transaction must be a well worthwhile social objective, as far as the law is concerned. To that end certainty in the question of what

---

[46.] But note that not all the correspondence relied upon in that case seems to have been so qualified and see especially the judgments of Buckley and Orr LJJ on this point. *Cf Thirkell v Cambi* [1919] 2 KB 590. See Wilkinson '*Law v Jones*: Problems for Conveyancers' (1973)123 New LJ 941.

[47.] [1974] 2 WLR 176.

[48.] Or, in that case, s 40 of the English Law of Property Act 1925.

[49.] In so far as the actual decision in *Griffths v Young* [1970] Ch 675 suggested to the contrary, the Court in Tiverton disapproved of it.

[50.] See *Kelly v Park Hall School* [1979] IR 340; *Casey v Irish Intercontinental Bank* [1979] IR 364. See also *Carthy v O'Neill* [1981] ILRM 443.

[51.] See *McInerney Properties v Roper* [1979] ILRM 119.

[52.] See also Clark, 'Subject to Contract - I English Problems' (1984) Conv 173 and 'Subject to Contract - II Irish Solutions' (1984) Conv 251.

[53.] In *Mulhall v Harem* [1981] IR 364. See also *Ballyowen Castle Homes Ltd v Collins* High Court, unrep, 26 June 1986 (1985/246P).

[54.] Keane J was clearly aware of the earlier Supreme Court decisions in *Kelly* and *Casey supra*.

[55.] [1992] 1 IR 555.

is or is not sufficient note or memorandum is a desirable aim. In my view, the very definite statement that a note or memorandum of a contract made orally is not sufficient to satisfy the Statute of Frauds unless it directly or by very necessary implication recognises, not only the terms to be enforced, but also the existence of a concluded contract between the parties, and the corresponding principle that no such note or memorandum which contains any term or expression such as 'subject to contract' can be sufficient, even if it can be established by oral evidence that such a term or expression did not form part of the originally orally concluded agreement, achieves that certainty."[56]

Finlay CJ then stated that in his view this statement of the law did not allow for the "exceptional cases" referred to by Keane J in *Mulhall v Haren*, so that the previous decisions of the Supreme Court in *Kelly* and *Casey* should not be followed. In this he was supported by Hederman J[57] and McCarthy J,[58] thereby forming the majority view.[59] Notwithstanding the apparent lack of unanimity on the point,[60] it is considered that solicitors and their clients should now feel satisfied that the incorporation of a formula such as "subject to contract" in all[61] written documentation will prevent it being regarded as a sufficient note or memorandum for the purposes of the Statute of Frauds.

[7.09] It cannot be emphasised too strongly that solicitors must bear in mind that there have been several cases where the parties or their solicitors failed to enter an express qualification such as the Supreme Court has now approved and the courts have held that a binding contract came into existence. Thus, in *Godley v Power*[62] the Supreme Court held that a

---

[56.] *Ibid* p 574.

[57.] Who simply concurred with the CJ's judgment, *ibid*, p 574.

[58.] *Ibid* p 578.

[59.] *Cf* O'Flaherty J at p 588 ("subject to contract" is *"prima facie* a strong declaration that a concluded agreement does not exist" - "there must be cogent evidence of a contrary intention before such a phrase is put to one side") and Egan J at p 596 (approving Keane J's judgment in *Mulhall v Haren*).

[60.] Note that another issue in *Boyle v Lee* was whether in fact a concluded agreement had ever been made by the parties and on this too the judges were split: Finlay CJ (Hederman J concurring) and O'Flaherty J held there was no such agreement (because, eg,they had not agreed everything they thought essential): see para **[6.18]** *ante.* Note also the the Court (in a unanimous judgment given by Blayney J) held in the *Embourg* case (fn 34 supra) that a contract stated in documentation (estate agent's and solicitor's letters) to be subject to contracts being "exchanged" meant that no binding contract came into existence because no exchange was made - despite the fact that both parties had signed copies of the formal contract drawn up by the vendor's solicitors. See also para **[7.03]** *supra.*

[61.] It is not clear how far the "umbrella" principle (initial qualification covering later documentation without the need for repetition) would be applied in Ireland: see *Tevanan v Norman Brett (Builders) Ltd* [1972] 223 EG 1945; *Sherbrooke v Dipple* (1980) 41 P & CR 173; *Cohen v Nessdale Ltd* [1982] 2 All ER 97.

[62.] (1961) 95 ILTR 135.

sufficient memorandum existed in the purchaser's solicitor's letter to the vendor's solicitor confirming a telephone conversation about an oral agreement made by the parties. Similarly, in *Black v Kavanagh*[63] Gannon J held the solicitors' correspondence constituted a sufficient memorandum of an oral agreement previously made by the parties.[64]

[7.10] It is clear from the decision in *Boyle v Lee* that any expression which purports to deny the existence of a concluded contract will protect the parties in negotiation. It is true that a number of qualifications similar to "subject to contract" have come before the courts on both sides of the Irish Sea and the conclusions on their effect have not always appeared to be consistent. But, then, perhaps this is only to be expected since in the end of the day the question of construction has to be decided by the court in each case according to what it thinks the parties or their solicitors intended by the qualification in question. It is doubtful whether anything is gained by adding to the "subject to contract" formula another like "contract denied" or one denying the solicitor's authority to act as agent for his client, but it does no harm and serves to reinforce the point. The following are some of the other expressions that have come before the courts in Ireland.

1. Subject to a Formal Agreement

[7.11] One very common qualification inserted by one or other, or both, of the parties in the preliminary stages of negotiation is one which specifies that any agreement made at that stage is "subject to a formal agreement," usually stated to be one drawn up by a solicitor. Thus, in *Brien v Swainson*[65] the vendor accepted an offer from the purchaser by telegraphing as follows: "Accept your offer of £1200, subject to letter and agreement to be sent to your solicitor." Chatterton V-C held that there was no binding contract between the parties and that the qualification attached to the vendor's acceptance did not mean simply that a more formal version of the parties' contract was to be sent later.[66] In *Lowis v Wilson*[67] the purchaser agreed to buy freehold land from the vendor "subject to the preparation of a formal contract to be prepared" by the vendor's solicitor. The purchaser subsequently refused to sign a formal contract drawn up by the vendor's solicitor and he was held not to be bound by the earlier agreement. Dixon J stated:

[63.] (1974) 108 ILTR 91. See also *Law v Roberts & Co* [1964] IR 292; *Stinson v Owens* (1973) 24 NILQ 218: *Barrett v Costelloe* (1973) 107 ILT SJ 239.

[64.] See para **[6.42]** *ante*.

[65.] (1877) 1 LR Ir 135.

[66.] *Ibid* p 141. *Cf Kelly v Irish Nursery & Landscape Co Ltd* [1981] ILRM 433 (until exchange of contracts): see para **[6.62]** *ante*; see also *Embourg Ltd v Tyler Group Ltd* Supreme Court, unrep, 5 March 1996 (223/1995) (fns 42 and 60 *supra*).

[67.] [1949] IR 347.

" ... the weight of all cases from *Winn v Bull*[68] onwards is that similar wording to that here was held to have had the effect of preventing an agreement, although it contained sufficient to satisfy the Statute of Frauds, from being a binding and enforceable agreement. The reasons given in those cases was that the agreement was intended to be subject to the parties entering into a further agreement, and it was only when such further agreement had been entered into that the parties would have arrived at a firm and enforceable contract."[69]

He then went on to consider the effect of the condition quoted above:

"It seems to me that the condition contemplates the completion between the parties of a contract and in that respect the use of the word, 'contract,' is of importance ... In my view, the word 'preparation,' is used in a different sense to the words, 'to be prepared,' unless the latter words are superfluous; and a literal interpretation would make the provision a futile and purposeless one ... I hold that the agreement comes into the category of the cases already cited, that is to say, that it is a contract to enter into a contract. It is a case where the parties had agreed up to a point, but were not fully agreed, and where the expression of their full agreement was to be embodied in a formal document. If my view is right, then it follows that the agreement is not enforceable and never was."[70]

[7.12] On the other hand, in *Law v Roberts & Co*,[71] where a director of the estate agents firm employed by the vendor wrote a letter to the purchaser's solicitor confirming the sale and stating "We have asked [the vendor's solicitors] to have a contract forwarded to you immediately," it was held by the Supreme Court that the reference to a contract in this letter was not intended to create a term or condition of the agreement between the parties. The Court affirmed the decision of Kenny J that the correspondence in that case constituted a sufficient memorandum or note for the purposes of the Statute of Frauds. In *Scott v McCombe*,[72] where agents of the landlord and

---

68. (1877) 7 Ch D 29. See also *Rossdale v Denny* [1921] 1 Ch 57; *Chillingsworth v Esche* [1924] 1 Ch 97; *Lockett v Norman-Wright* [1925] Ch 56; *Spottiswoode, Ballantyne & Co Ltd v Doreen Appliances Ltd* [1924] 2 All ER 65; *Riley v Troll* [1953] 1 All ER 966.
69. [1949] IR 347 at 349 And see para **[7.03]** *supra*.
70. *Ibid* p 350. *Cf Irish Mainport Holdings Ltd v Crosshaven Sailing Centre Ltd* High Court, unrep, 16 May 1980 (1978/11247P); *Devlin v Northern Ireland Housing Executive* [1982] NI 377; *Silver Wraith Ltd v Siuicre Éireann Cpt* High Court, unrep, 8 June 1989 (1987/6178P).
71. [1964] IR 292. See also *Rossiter v Miller* (1878) 3 App Cas 1124; *Bonnewell v Jenkin* (1878) 8 Ch D 70. And note the extent to which the English Court of Appeal went in *Branca v Cobarro* [1947] KB 854, where a binding agreement was found despite inclusion of this clause: "This is a provisional agreement until a fully legalised agreement drawn up by a solicitor and embodying all the conditions herewith stated is signed."
72. (1965) 16 NILQ 122.

tenant of a property were negotiating a renewal of the tenant's lease, the tenant's agent wrote to the landlord's agent indicating the terms their client agreed to and added: "Perhaps you would kindly arrange for the draft to be prepared and forwarded to us." Lord MacDermott LCJ[73] held that the preparation and completion of a formal document was not intended to be a prerequisite of the existence of a binding contract.[74] Though he did say that the position might have been different if the words used had been instead, "subject to the preparation and completion of a tenancy agreement."[75] This point arose again in *City of Glasgow Friendly Society Ltd v Gilpin Ltd*,[76] where a letter written in connection with negotiations for the grant of a new lease acknowledged that the parties' agreement was not in its final form as their respective solicitors had still to draft the precise terms of the new lease. Gibson J held that this drafting by the solicitors was contemplated by the parties as being only ancillary to their earlier agreement and as necessary to clothe the matter with legal formality.[77] The letter was, therefore, sufficient evidence of a concluded agreement. Similarly, in *Usitravel Ltd v Freyer*,[78] where the parties agreed on the various detailed terms of the sale of a leasehold flat, but subject to the purchaser's solicitors preparing a contract to embody the agreed terms, Finlay J held that the reference to preparation of a contract by the solicitors was not a condition nor intended to give the solicitors power to add to or vary the terms. It was included simply because the parties thought their agreement should be enshrined in a legal document.

2. Subject to Title/Conditions of Sale

[7.13]   Another variant on the same theme occurred in *Donnelly v O'Connell*,[79] where the parties signed a document arranging for a sale of premises, "the vendor's solicitors to prepare title and conditions of sale". Meredith J held that this was a condition which prevented that document operating as a firm contract. He stated:

[73.] His decision was varied on appeal, but on a different ground, see (1965) 16 NILQ 418.

[74.] *Ibid* p 123.

[75.] See *Wilcox v Redhead* (1880) 49 LJ Ch 539; *Raingold v Bromley* [1931] 2 Ch 307; *Berry Ltd v Brighton and Sussex BS* [1939] 3 All ER 217. *Cf* "subject to approval of the lease" (eg by the tenant's solicitor), see *Chipperfield v Carter* (1895) 72 LT 487; *Caney v Leith* [1937] 2 All ER 532.

[76.] (1971) 22 NILQ 196.

[77.] *Cf Black v Kavanagh* (1974) 108 ILTR 91, see para **[6.42]** *ante*.

[78.] High Court, unrep, 29 May 1973 (Cir App). See also *O'Flaherty v Arvan Properties Ltd* Supreme Court, unrep, 21 July 1977 (1976/211).

[79.] (1924) 58 ILTR 164. See also *Hussey v Horne-Payne* (1879) 4 App Cas 311("subject to the title being approved by our solicitors").

"I must construe the expression 'conditions of sale' in its ordinary meaning. I would like to say that, in my opinion, any document in which reference is made to a solicitor should be construed generously by the Court so that the parties may have all reasonable protection. This remains the proper rule to be enforced even though the parties may not realise the importance of obtaining legal advice. I shall always interpret such documents generously."[80]

Similarly, in *Lynch v O'Meara*,[81] a document drawn up by the auctioneer acting for both parties to the sale of a farm stated that certain terms, eg, as to the date for possession and the title, were to be fixed by special conditions to be drawn up by a solicitor. The Supreme Court held that there was no concluded contract[82] since it was clearly intended that several matters still had to be closed by the conditions drawn up by the solicitor. Until that was done there was no binding agreement but only one subject to a condition still unsatisfied.

B. Subject to Mortgage

[7.14] Because of the difficulties and delay that may be experienced by the purchaser in raising the necessary finance for the purchase, it is quite commonly found that his solicitor insists on making the contract conditional upon the purchaser obtaining a satisfactory mortgage or loan.[83] This sort of condition was considered in *Rooney v Byrne*,[84] where a written proposal form detailing the terms of the parties' agreement for the sale of a house contained a statement by the purchaser in the following form: "This proposal is subject to me getting an advance on the property from the Royal Liver Friendly Society." It was held that the purchaser was bound by this agreement and that the mere fact that the insurance company named had refused an advance, on the ground that the property was not suitable security, did not release him from it. Evidence was given that he could have obtained an advance on reasonable terms from other sources after being refused by the insurance company.[85] O'Byrne J stated:

[80.] *Ibid* p 164. *Cf Irish Mainport Holdings Ltd v Crosshaven Sailing Centre Ltd* High Court, unrep, 16 May 1980 (1978/1247P).

[81.] Supreme Court, unrep, 8 May 1975 (1974/12).

[82.] Not even an agreement as to an "open" contract, to be "closed" later by the special conditions. as to which concepts, see para **[14.05]** *post*.

[83.] See *Incorporated Law Society of Ireland v Browne* (1961) 95 ILTR 6 ("subject to purchase obtaining Building Society Loan within one month"). See also Wilkinson, 'Subject to a Satisfactory Mortgage' (1972) 132 New LJ 70. *Re* building agreements see para **[11.19]** *post*.

[84.] [1933] IR 609.

[85.] *Ibid*, p 615 (*per* Sullivan P).

"It is argued that this proposal must be taken at its face value and that it makes the contract conditional on an advance being in fact obtained. In my opinion the stipulation means something more than that. We have to consider what was in the minds of the parties at the time the contract was signed. It is fairly clear that, in the contemplation of the parties, the purchaser would require to get an advance for the purpose of providing the purchase money, and the object was to provide that, in the event of his failing to get such an advance, the contract also failed.[86] But in my opinion it was equally contemplated that the purchaser should make an effort to secure the advance. [Counsel] contends that it was competent for the purchaser to elect whether he would get an advance or not, and that, if he elected not to do so, the contract failed, even though he could get such an advance on reasonable terms. That, in my opinion, was not the intention of the parties. In my view the purchaser was bound to make reasonable efforts to secure the necessary advance, and, if he failed after such reasonable efforts to secure an advance on reasonable terms, the contract was then at an end."[87]

In *Draisey v Fitzpatrick*[88] the condition was in the following terms:

"The obligations of both parties under this contract are subject to the purchasers being approved for a loan by the Irish Permanent Building Society on the security of the premises in the amount of £25,000 on or before 2 January next. Should the said loan approval be not forthcoming on or before that date then this contract shall be at an end and all amounts furnished by the purchasers will be refunded without any interest or compensation. This clause is to be specifically for the benefit of the vendor who alone shall have the right of waiver."

Loan approval was given but subject to various conditions, including conversion of the property into a single dwelling, execution of repairs to the satisfaction of the building society's valuers and completion of the loan transaction within forty days. The purchaser purported to repudiate the contract on the basis that it was impossible to complete the purchase because of the "abnormal, unusual and unreasonable" conditions attached to the loan. Ellis J rejected this claim and, finding that the purchasers had effectively made no effort to fulfil the loan conditions, held that the vendor could forfeit the deposit. He stated that such a condition relating to a loan in a contract for sale is subject to:

[86.] Ie, it was a condition *subsequent* rather than a condition precedent, see, see para **[7.03]** *supra*.

[87.] [1933] IR 609 at 615-6. These principles were applied by Finlay P in *Costelloe v Maharaj Krishna Properties (Ir) Ltd* High Court, unrep, 10 July 1975 (1974/15641P), see para **[7.23]** *infra*.

[88.] [1981] ILRM 219.

"the implied terms that the conditions of the loan approval mentioned therein were and are subject to the implied terms that they should be reasonable; that they should reasonably have been in the contemplation of the parties when the contract was made, and that they should be to the satisfaction of the plaintiffs acting reasonably. I am of the opinion also that they should be subject to the further implied terms that the plaintiffs were under an obligation at all times to act reasonably and to take and make all reasonable steps and efforts to fulfil and carry out the conditions of the loan approval. In my view ... the onus of proving that they have complied with these implied terms to the satisfaction of the court on the balance of probabilities lies on the plaintiffs to discharge."[89]

Attention was drawn in the case to that fact that the condition under consideration did not contain the "purchaser's protection clause" recommended by the Law Society.[90] This is designed to protect a purchaser against the risk that the lending institution will approve a loan only on extremely onerous terms and a solicitor opens himself to the risk of a negligence claim if he does not advise his client of such a possibility. The obvious safe course is to use a clause in the form recommended. This reads:

"THIS CONTRACT shall be subject to the purchaser obtaining approval for a loan of £___ from _____ on the security of the premises PROVIDED ALWAYS that if this loan has not been approved in writing within ___ weeks from the date hereof either party shall be entitled to rescind this contract and in such event the purchaser shall be refunded his deposit without interest, costs or compensation.

(If the loan approval is conditional on a survey satisfactory to the lending institution or a mortgage protection or life assurance policy being taken out or some other condition compliance with which is not within the control of the purchaser the loan shall not be deemed to be approved until the purchaser is in a position to accept the loan on terms which are within his reasonable power or procurement),
(Delete as appropriate)."

It is not entirely clear what the brackets around the second paragraph of this provision are meant to indicate. Arguably its contents, adapted as appropriate to the circumstances of the particular case, should be incorporated expressly into the condition as a matter of substance, in order to give the purchaser necessary protection against conditions which may be attached to the loan offer. They should not be treated as guidelines only, which do not form part of the condition. The Society's Conveyancing Committee also strongly advised against a solicitor giving an undertaking to

---

89. *Ibid*, p 223.
90. See the *Gazette* December 1979, reproduced on p 11.5 of the *Conveyancing Handbook*.

a bank to obtain bridging finance unless and until he is certain that all the conditions of the loan can be complied with.[91]

[7.15] The English courts, however, have had more difficulty with a "subject to mortgage" condition, largely on the ground that it is too vague and uncertain.[92] In *Lee-Parker v Izzet (No 2)*[93] a contract for the sale of a house was made "subject to the purchaser obtaining a satisfactory mortgage". Goulding J held that the contract was void for uncertainty on the ground that far too many terms relating to the mortgage were omitted, eg, the rate of interest, the amount of the loan and the repayment period.[94] However, in *Graham v Pitkin*[95] the Privy Council doubted this finding on the ground that, if the purchaser's circumstances had been different (he had no money at all), he could have declared that a mortgage offer from his brother-in-law was "satisfactory".[96] Furthermore, in *Lee-Parker v Izzet*[97] Goff J had held that a condition in a contract for sale of several properties, relating to the vendor arranging for the purchasers "satisfactory mortgages" within twenty-eight days of the contract, was not uncertain and was to be construed as meaning mortgages to the satisfaction of each purchaser acting reasonably. This latter decision seems to be more in line with the Irish decision in *Rooney v Byrne*.[98]

C. Subject to Planning Permission

[7.16] In view of the importance of planning permission where the purchaser intends to develop the land, it is becoming increasingly common to make the contract conditional upon the purchaser obtaining planning permission for his proposed development.[99] In the vast majority of cases the courts seem to

---

[91.] See further on undertakings para **[20.14]** *post*.

[92.] See Wilkinson, 'Sale Subject to Satisfactory Mortgage' (1972) 122 New LJ 708. *Cf* the New Zealand courts, see *Barber v Cricket* [1958] NZLR 1057; *Scott v Rains* [1966] NZLR 527 and Australian courts, see *Meehan v Jones* (1982) 56 ALJR 813 (Wilkinson [1984] Conv 243). See generally the discussion of British Commonwealth case law in Coote, 'Subject to Finance' (1976) 40 Conv 37. See also Davies, 'Conditional Contracts for the Sale of Land in Canada' (1977) 55 CBR 289.

[93.] [1972] 1 WLR 775. See also *Re Rich's Wills Trusts* (1962) 106 Sol Jo 75 (instructions in contract that vendor's solicitors were "to obtain and fix a suitable mortgage advance on the premises" held to be too vague and contract void for uncertainty).

[94.] Yet if the condition is construed as a condition subsequent as appears was done in *Rooney v Byrne*, see para **[7.14]** *supra* arguably only the condition is void and the contract survives, but no longer subject to the condition, see *Irish Land Law* (2nd ed, 1986), para 4.053. See also *Healy v Healy* High Court, unrep, 3 December 1973 (1973/244 Sp) para **[7.16]** *infra*.

[95.] [1992] 2 All ER 235.

[96.] *Per* Lord Templeman, *ibid*, p 237.

[97.] [1971] 1 WLR 1688.

[98.] Para **[7.14]** *supra*.

[99.] See Wilkinson, 'Sale of Land Subject to Planning Permission' (1974) 38 Conv 77.

treat such a condition as a condition *subsequent*, ie, one which does not prevent a contract from coming into existence between the parties but which may enable one or other or both of them to rescind the agreement on the ground of non-fulfilment of the condition.[100] Thus, in *Healy v Healy*[101] a special condition in the contract for sale made it subject to full planning permission for a residential development of at least seven houses being obtained within seventeen months. If such permission was not obtained by then, the purchaser was to be entitled to return of his deposit, subject to certain deductions. Completion was to be within two months of planning permission being received for part of the land, and within six months for the rest of it. In fact permission was not so obtained and the purchaser sought to waive that condition and to have the contract treated as absolute and to be completed within two months, whereas the vendor sought a declaration that it was determined. Kenny J upheld the purchaser's claim, holding that a party to a contract could waive such a condition inserted solely for his benefit and which is severable from the rest of the contract.[102] Thus, the condition as to planning permission was at most treated as a condition subsequent, non-fulfilment of which would avoid a contract otherwise fully binding up to that point, and, indeed, it seems the condition was really regarded as being no different than many other conditions normally included in a contract and known as the "conditions of sale".[103] Similarly in *International Securities Ltd v Portmarnock Estates Ltd*,[104] Hamilton J did not consider as preventing a contract for the sale of a house coming into force a condition that the contract was subject to full detailed planning permission (which was already applied for) being granted on or before a

---

[100.] See *O'Mullane v Riordan* [1978] ILRM 73 at 77 (*per* McWilliam J). See also *Sepia Ltd v O'Hanlon Ltd* [1979] ILRM 11; *Moloney v Elf Investments Ltd* [1979] ILRM 253; *Tiernan Homes Ltd v Sheridan* [1981] ILRM 191. *Cf McKillop v McMullen* [1979] NI 85, where Murray J described the planning condition as a condition precedent "to the coming into existence of an effective and enforceable contract of sale". Arguably he meant a condition precedent to *performance* of the contract rather to its formation: see para **[7.03]** *supra*.

[101.] High Court, unrep, 3 December 1973 (1973/244 Sp).

[102.] See also *Sepia Ltd v O'Hanlon Ltd* [1979] ILRM 11; *Batten v White* (1960) 12 P & CR 66. But such a condition cannot be waived if it benefits both parties, see *Heron Garage Properties Ltd v Moss* [1974] 1 All ER 421, or the *other* party only, see *Tiernan Homes Ltd v Sheridan* [1981] ILRM 191, nor if the contract cannot stand on its own without the waived clause, see *Boobyer v Thorville Properties, Ltd* (1968) 19 P & CR 768. *Cf* a qualified waiver, see *McKillop v McMullen* [1979] NI 85, or purported waiver *after* the time limit on fulfilment: see *Moloney v Elf Investments Ltd* [1979] ILRM 253. See also Robinson 'Waiver of Benefit of Conditional Clauses' (1975) 39 Conv 251.

[103.] See generally Ch 10 *post*. See also re licences and consents, para **[7.22]** *infra*. There is also English authority for regarding a planning permission condition as just another term of the contract, see eg, *Batten v White* (1960) 12 p & CR 66 at 71 (*per* Russell J); *Property & Bloodstock Ltd v Emerton* [1968] Ch 94 at 121 (*per* Sachs LJ).

[104.] High Court, unrep, 9 April 1975 (1974/2257P), see also the Law Society's *Gazette* July/August 1975, p 176. *Cf Earl v Mawson* (1973) 228 Est Gaz 529.

specified date, closing date being fixed as twenty-one days after receipt of such permission. If the permission was not obtained by that date, the closing date was to be extended by six months, subject to interest charges. Permission was actually received after the specified date and the vendor claimed completion was to take place twenty-one days after the actual date of receipt, whereas the purchaser claimed he was entitled to the six months extension. Hamilton J held that the six months extension was to operate only to allow extra time for the obtaining of permission and not once it was obtained, so that the twenty-one day period applied.

[7.17] It would seem that some care should be exercised in the drafting of such conditions if they are to operate as the parties intend, or even to avoid the risk of being held void for uncertainty. In particular, the various rules and regulations of the planning system ought to be borne in mind. Thus, it ought to be made clear whether the condition will be satisfied by a grant of "outline" permission only[105] or whether full detailed permission is necessary (which will take much longer to obtain).[106] In *Tiernan Homes Ltd v Sheridan*[107] the Supreme Court interpreted the expression "full planning permission" as not meaning just the notification of the decision to the applicant and any other interested party.[108] It meant the actual grant of permission made either after expiration of the period allowed for appeals or after any appeal taken is withdrawn, ie when the permission became effective.[109] Similarly, there may be a doubt as to whether a grant of permission subject to conditions[110] fulfils a condition as to planning permission in a contract for sale. It would seem that it depends upon whether or not the conditions are so onerous that they prevent the permission being considered as consent to the purchaser's development in reality.[111] One way round this difficulty may be to qualify the reference to permission by adding the epithet "satisfactory" (eg, to the purchaser),[112] but the courts are reluctant to apply a subjective test to such a qualification, so as to prevent the person to be satisfied from being arbitrary in the view he takes.[113]

[105.] See *Hargreaves Transport Ltd v Lynch* [1969] 1 All ER 455. As to "outline" permission, see Scannell, *Environmental and Planning Law in Ireland* (1995), p 231 *et seq*.

[106.] As was specified in the two Irish cases discussed in para **[7.16]** *supra*.

[107.] [1981] ILRM 191.

[108.] See s 26 of the Local Government (Planning and Development) Act 1963.

[109.] Section 26(9).

[110.] See s 26(2); O'Sullivan and Shepherd *Irish Planning Law and Practice* Pt 3; *Scannell, op cit* p 200 *et seq*.

[111.] *Richard West and Partners (Inverness) Ltd v Dick* [1969] 2 Ch 424 at 433 (*per* Megarry J), affd at 433 (CA).

[112.] See *Tesco Stores Ltd v William Gibson & Son Ltd* (1970) 314 Est Gaz 835. See also *Re Longlands Farm* [1968] 3 All ER 552.

[113.] *Richard West and Partners (Inverness) Ltd v Dick* [1969] 2 Ch 424. *Cf Hargreaves Transport Ltd v Lynch* [1969] 1 All ER 455.

[7.18] Care should also be taken to impose some time limit for the receipt of permission,[114] otherwise the party to apply may delay in making his application and leave the other party in a state of uncertainty whether the transaction is going to be completed and, if it is, when. Though it seems that, if no time limit is imposed, the courts will imply a term that the permission must be obtained within what the court considers is a "reasonable" time of the contract.[115] Imposition of a specific time limit avoids the difficult question of construction as to what is "reasonable" in the particular case and, in this respect, is better than requiring the purchaser, or other person responsible for seeking the permission, to "use his best endeavours".[116] However, unless the purchase is a simple case, eg, a single site, the complexities of the planning position may make it impossible to draft a practical planning condition. With a major development, such as a building site with no services, which at present is not zoned for residential or other proposed development, there may be a host of conditions attached to any planning permission eventually granted and then there may be appeals against the grant. The result might be a delay of many months, even years, before the matter is finally resolved. In such a case it is often more practical for the purchaser to take an option to purchase which he is free to exercise or not when the question of planning permission is finally settled.[117] Though it should be pointed out that there are risks from the vendor's point of view in granting such an option. If the application for planning permission is eventually rejected or is granted subject to unacceptable conditions, it may reduce considerably the value of his land and, yet, by the very nature of an option to purchase, he has no redress against the purchaser for refusing to exercise it. But some protection may be afforded by requiring the purchaser to submit his application for permission and plans to the vendor for his approval before they are sent to the planning authority. This should at least ensure that the value of the vendor's land is not reduced by rejection of an application or plans submitted by the purchaser which are so unsuitable or frivolous as to have no possibility of acceptance.

[114.] As was done in the Irish cases discussed in para **[7.16]** *supra*. See also *Sepia Ltd v O'Hanlon Ltd* [1979] ILRM 11; *Moloney v Elf Investments Ltd* [1979] ILRM 253; *Tiernan Homes Ltd v Sheridan* [1981] ILRM 191.

[115.] *Re Longlands Farm* [1968] 3 All ER 552. See also *Sepia Ltd v O'Hanlon Ltd* [1979] ILRM 11; *Earl v Mawson* (1973) 228 Est Gaz 529.

[116.] See *NW Investments (Erdington) Ltd v Swani* (1970) 214 Est Gaz 1115.

[117.] See para **[8.03]** *post*.

D. Subject to Survey

[7.19] In an effort to speed matters along in a particular transaction, the purchaser may enter into a contract subject to a surveyor's report or subject to a satisfactory survey. There seems to be no authority in Ireland on the effect of such a qualification, but in England it was once held that it left the purchaser free to refuse to proceed,[118] perhaps whether or not the report or survey was favourable.[119] This seemed to suggest that the condition was being construed as a condition precedent[120] to any contract coming into force, yet on principle it is difficult to see the distinction between it and one relating to planning permission.[121] They both relate to matters of equal importance, the one relating to the existing physical state of the property and the other to its legal fitness for the use or development intended by the purchaser. Perhaps not surprisingly the English courts have been having second thoughts on the matter. In *Ee v Kaker*,[122] where the parties had agreed a sale "subject to survey of the property", Walton J concluded that there was a conditional contract in force. Under this the purchaser was under an obligation to obtain a survey within a reasonable time; if he failed to do so, he would be deemed to have waived his right to have one and could not then withdraw from the contract; he was also under an obligation to act *bona fide* when considering the results of the survey and in deciding whether to proceed. The "reasonableness" of the purchaser's conduct in this regard was to be assessed on an objective basis. This seems to be an eminently sensible approach which hopefully will commend itself to the Irish courts.

E. Subject to Enquiries and Searches

[7.20] In view of the increasing prevalence of pre-contract enquiries or requisitions,[123] and in particular in view of the considerable delay frequently experienced in receiving some replies, solicitors may be tempted to attach such a condition to contracts for sale. However, it is doubtful whether it will achieve what would presumably be the desired effect, namely, to bring into existence a contract binding the vendor to the sale, but allowing the purchaser a "let out" if any of the replies turn out to be unsatisfactory.

[118.] *Marks v Board* (1930) 46 TLR 424. See also *Graham and Scott (Southgate) Ltd v Oxlade* [1950] 2 KB 257.

[119.] *Cf Astra Trust Ltd v Adams* [1969] 1 Lloyd's Rep 81. See also *John Howard & Co (Northern) v Knight* [1969] 1 Lloyd's Rep 364.

[120.] See para **[7.03]** *supra*.

[121.] See para **[7.16]** *supra*.

[122.] (1980) 40 P & CR 223; see commentary by Adams [1980] Conv 446; Oakley (1981) 40 Cambr LJ 23; Wilkinson (1981) 131 New LJ 771.

[123.] See para Ch 5 *ante*.

Sometimes the English courts have taken the view that expressions such as "subject to preliminary enquiries" and "subject to searches" are void for uncertainty, so that no contract at all comes into existence.[124] On the other hand, the dangers inherent in such a conditional contract were illustrated by *Aquis Estates Ltd v Minton*,[125] where the purchaser entered into a contract to buy an old building subject to the condition that it would be "found free from adverse entry on the [purchaser's] local land charge, land charge and land registry searches". The purchaser planned to knock the building down, but the local land charge search revealed that this would be impossible because it was a "listed" building, ie, a Grade II historic building. The English Court of Appeal took the view that, viewed objectively, the condition was not satisfied, but went on to hold that the purchaser had, in effect, waived the right to withdraw from the contract because he had continued to negotiate with the vendor after becoming aware of the listing.

F. Subject to Approval

[7.21] In *Dyas v Stafford*,[126] the purchaser at an auction signed a memorandum appended to the particulars and conditions of sale, acknowledging the purchase from the vendor "subject to his approval". It was held that as a result of this qualification there was no binding contract in existence.[127] FitzGibbon LJ commented:

> "Unless and until that approval was given, [the vendor] had made no contract; there was nothing more than a proposal by [the purchaser] for the vendor's consideration ..."[128]

G. Subject to Consent or Licence

[7.22] Provisions relating to the obtaining of consent eg, of the landlord to the assignment of a lease or the grant of a sublease, or of the Land Commission to sub-division of land or to a conveyance to a non-national,[129]

[124.] *Smith and Olley v Townsend* (1949) 1 P & CR 28. Note also that the English Law Society found it difficult to draft a satisfactory condition, see (1972) 69 L Soc Gaz 1502.

[125.] [1975] 3 All ER 1043.

[126.] (1882) 9 LR Ir 520.

[127.] Law C stated that it was a "peculiar case," *ibid*, p 523, but agreed that "there was as yet no contract, but only a proposal which [the vendor] might or might not accept as he pleased," *ibid*, p 524.

[128.] *Ibid*, p 529. See also Deasy LJ at p 528: "... how can it be held that the name of the vendor was inserted for the purpose of authenticating this document as a binding agreement, when the right to withhold his approbation to it was expressly reserved to him? It would not have been binding when signed by the purchaser, and there is no subsequent signature by the vendor."

[129.] See para **[7.23]** *infra*.

are usually to be found in the conditions of sale and to that extent may be regarded as simply one of the many terms of the contract. In other words, they are not generally to be regarded as creating a condition precedent, satisfaction of which is a prerequisite to the coming into effect of a binding contract.[130] Failure to comply with that term simply results in the aggrieved party being able to pursue his various remedies for breach of contract, including rescission.[131] The same principle would seem to apply to provisions requiring the obtaining of a licence, eg, for the sale of intoxicating liquor.[132] However, this principle is subject to the overriding principle that the precise effect of any particular provision is a matter of construction in each case, and there is nothing to stop the parties making the obtaining of consent or of a licence a condition precedent to a binding contract.[133]

[7.23] In *Costelloe v Maharaj Krishna Properties (Ir) Ltd*,[134] the agreement in question was conditional upon the obtaining of Land Commission consent under s 45 of the Land Act 1965, but this did not prevent an agreement coming into force; it simply meant that, in the event of the Commission refusing consent, the purchaser was entitled to withdraw and to return of his deposit. It was argued by the vendor that the purchaser had not made a proper application for consent, but rather one designed to induce a refusal, and Finlay J held that, in such a case, the purchaser is obliged to make a *bona fide* application.[135] A similar view of the effect of a condition relating to consent was taken by the same judge in *Sibel v Kent*.[136] On the other hand, it may be argued that no contract can come into existence where the purchaser is not a "qualified person" within s 45, for this matter seems in effect to go to his capacity to contract and so vitiates the contract.[137] However, in practice this point will not arise very often, because the parties will use the Law Society's contract for sale form. Under condition 28 of the *General Conditions of Sale (1995 Edition)* the onus is put on the purchaser

---

[130.] See *Property and Bloodstock Ltd v Emerton* [1968] Ch 94 at 118 (*per* Danckwerts LJ).

[131.] See generally, paras **[14.75]** and **[16.93]** *post*.

[132.] See *County Estates Ltd v Aco Ltd* (1955) 89 ILTR 8. See para **[16.104]** *post*.

[133.] It might be argued that it would be prudent to make the obtaining of consent of a spouse under the Family Home Protection Act 1976 a condition precedent. However, of course, in a sense the Act does this automatically in that it renders void any contract entered into without the consent where required in the case of that contract see para **[16.62]** sub-paras (c) and (g) *post*.

[134.] High Court, unrep, 10 July 1975 (1974/1564P).

[135.] Applying *Rooney v Byrne* [1933] IR 609 see para **[7.14]** *supra*.

[136.] [1976-77] ILRM 127.

[137.] Note that the words used by s 45 are that no "interest ... shall become vested" in an unqualified person without the necessary consent. See para **[16.53]** *post*.

to obtain any necessary certificate or consent under s 45 and "the sale is not conditional upon such consent being obtained.[138] It is imperative, therefore, that solicitors acting for purchasers explain this point to their clients and, in particular, that there will be no right to withdraw from the contract if it transpires that consent is needed and it is not granted.

[138.] See para [16.53] *post.*

Chapter 8

OTHER SPECIAL CASES

[8.01] Before closing the discussion of the formalities for creation of a contract for the sale of land it may be useful to note some special cases. These are special in the sense that the usual conveyancing procedures of negotiation of the contract between the parties or their solicitors, as in the case of a sale by private treaty, are not adopted or are adopted in part only because of the type of transaction in question.

I. SALE BY PUBLIC AUCTION

[8.02] The differences between a sale by public auction and a sale by private treaty were discussed at some length in earlier chapters[1] and little further need be added here. The requirements of the Statute of Frauds apply equally to such sales and we saw in an earlier chapter that the auctioneer is regarded as having extensive authority to see that these are met.[2] An important difference from sales by private treaty is, of course, that the purchaser's solicitor usually has a much more limited role to play prior to the contract, eg, the terms of it, as determined by the conditions of sale, are largely fixed by the vendor's solicitor.[3] This is done frequently by using the same standard form applicable to sales by private treaty.[4] It is true that there used to be a separate standard form for auction sales issued by the Law Society, but the *General Conditions of Sale (1976 Edition)* amalgamated in one document both the old auction[5] and private treaty[6] conditions (with amendments). This has remained the position in successive editions.[7] Finally, the actual bringing into effect of a contract in the case of a sale by public auction is, of course, governed by the special rules of contract law applicable to auctions, eg, the purchaser's bid is the offer which is not accepted until he is declared the highest bidder and the property is knocked

---

1. Chs 2 and 3 *ante*.
2. Para **[6.38]** *ante*.
3. See para **[2.53]** *ante*.
4. See Ch 9 *post*.
5. *Public Auction Particulars and Conditions of Sale* (1968 ed).
6. *Private Contract Agreement for Sale* (1968 ed).
7. See now the *General Conditions of Sale* (1995 ed).

down to him, which creates the contract,[8] though it does not become enforceable until the written memorandum is signed as required by the Statute of Frauds[9]

II. Option to Purchase

[8.03] An option to purchase is an arrangement whereby the owner of property is committed to selling it to the person given the option, if that person chooses to exercise it.[10] Until the latter does exercise it, however, there is no contract for the sale of land, and, of course, he may choose never to exercise it; but the owner is bound by the contract creating the option to the extent that he may not dispose of the property so as to deprive the option-holder of his right to exercise it. Though it has been held that for this contract to bind the owner it must be created either by deed or be supported by consideration[11] and, if not created by deed, must be evidenced in writing as it creates an interest in land for the purpose of the Statute of Frauds.[12] Such an arrangement has obvious advantages for a prospective purchaser who does not wish to commit himself to a binding contract to purchase the property at this stage,[13] but at the same time wishes to prevent the vendor from selling to someone in the meantime. For this reason it has been suggested that from the purchaser's point of view it might be an admirable guard against the practice of "gazumping,"[14] *if* he could persuade the vendor to grant such an option. But therein lies the problem - in times when there is a property boom, which is when the risk of gazumping is at its greatest, a vendor is unlikely to be willing to commit himself in such a way and will prefer to preserve his freedom to contract with the highest offeror.

[8.04] An option to purchase is often granted by a landlord to his tenant as part of the tenancy agreement, but such an option - in effect to purchase the

---

8. See paras **[2.09]**, **[2.21]** and **[6.38]** *ante*.

9. See para **[6.38]** *ante*.

10. See the discussion in *Cassidy v Baker* (1969) 103 ILTR 40. See also *Griffith v Pelton* [1958] Ch 205 at 225 (*per* Jenkins LJ); *Mountford v Scott* [1975] 1 All ER 198. And see Bodkin, 'Options to Purchase' (1943) 7 Conv 137 and (1944) 8 Conv 139; Holland, 'The Incidence of Options to Purchase Land' (1949) 13 Conv 49; Barnsley *Land Options*, (2nd ed, 1992).

11. But nominal consideration may be sufficient, *Mountford v Scott* [1975] 1 All ER 198.

12. *Birmingham Canal Co v Cartwright* (1879) 11 Ch D 421. As to its registration, see Wylie, *Irish Landlord and Tenant Law*, para 20.11.

13. The device has been much favoured by property developers, whose success often depends upon obtaining an option to purchase at a low price a piece of land with development potential. This can then be exercised to secure maximum profit when that potential is realised, eg, by the local planning authority's adoption of favourable planning proposals or for the grant of planning permission.

14. See paras **[6.04-5]** *ante*.

freehold reversion, or leasehold reversion, in the case of a sublease - should be distinguished from an option to renew a lease.[15] This distinction is of importance, eg, in relation to the application of the rule against perpetuities, which does not apply to the latter, but does apply to the former.[16] An option to purchase should also be distinguished from a right of pre-emption,[17] which simply gives the holder a right of first refusal if the owner of the property in question decides to sell it.[18] But there is no way in which the holder of the right of pre-emption can force the owner to sell, so as to enable the holder of the right of pre-emption to exercise it,[19] whereas, of course, the holder of an option to purchase forces the owner to sell to him by exercising it. It is important to emphasise that the distinction between an option to purchase and a right of pre-emption (or first refusal) is a matter of substance and it makes no difference what name is ascribed to the right of the parties.[20] Furthermore, it seems to be settled now on both sides of the Irish Sea that, unlike an option to purchase, a right of pre-emption does not create an interest in land and so an agreement conferring such a right does not have to comply with the Statute of Frauds.[21] No such interest arises until the owner of the land in question, whether the freeholder or holder of a leasehold

---

[15.] See the discussion of this distinction in *Jameson v Squire* [1948] IR 153; *Sims-Clarke v Ilet Ltd* [1953] IR 39. This distinction is blurred in Ireland because of the frequently adopted practice of "selling" land (already subject to a fee farm grant or long lease) by way of sub-grant or sublease. This practice has been recognised and enforced by the courts in both parts of Ireland in several contexts, see *Re Clarke's Will Trusts* [1920] 1 IR 47; *Re Braithwaite's Settled Estate* [1922] 1 IR 71; *McGowan v Harrison* [1941] IR 331; *Re Murphy* [1957] NI 156. See also *Irish Land Law* (2nd ed, 1986), paras 8.050, 8.069 and 10.015.

[16.] See *Irish Landlord and Tenant Law*, para 20.10.

[17.] See *Du Sautoy v Symes* [1967] Ch 1146; *Brown v Gould* [1972] Ch 53 at 58 (*per* Megarry J). This distinction has relevance, eg, in connection with mortgages, ie, an option may be a clog on the equity of redemption whereas a right of pre-emption may not be a clog, see *Irish Land Law* (2nd ed, 1986) para 13.091. Also it seems that a right of pre-emption does not create an interest in land and so presumably does not need to be evidenced in writing, see *infra*. See also Albery, (1973) 89 LQR 462.

[18.] See *Homsey v Searle* [1996] EGCS 43. *Cf* a right of re-purchase, *Re South City Market Co* (1884) 13 LR Ir 245.

[19.] Though, if the owner does sell to someone else without first offering the property to the holder of the right of pre-emption, the latter can sue for damages, *Gardner v Coutts & Co* [1967] 3 All ER 1064.

[20.] *Massarella v Massarella* High Court, unrep, 10 July 1980 (1978/630 Sp) at p 16 of Transcript (*per* Keane J). See also *Lac Minerals Ltd v Chevron Mineral Corporations of Ireland* [1995] 1 ILRM 161 (distinguishing the substantive right from machinery relating to its exercise).

[21.] See the discussion by the English Court of Appeal in *Pritchard v Briggs* [1980] Ch 338. See also *Aga Khan v Firestone* [1992] ILRM 31 at 50 (*per* Morris J), following the earlier English decisions in *Manchester Ship Canal Co v Manchester Racecourse Co* [1901] 2 Ch 37; *Murray v Two Stokes Ltd* [1973] 3 All ER 357. Apparently the *Pritchard* case was not opened to Morris J. *Cf* a "lock-out" agreement: see *Pitt v PHH Asset Management Ltd* [1993] 4 All ER 961.

reversion, decides to sell, whereupon the right of pre-emption "crystallises" into what is, in effect, then an option to purchase entitling the holder to require the sale to be made to him.

[8.05] The contract creating the option to purchase may contain various terms as to its exercise and as to the conditions of sale applicable.[22] Exercise of the option creates automatically the relationship of vendor and purchaser between the owner of the land and the person exercising the option,[23] ie, it brings into effect a binding contract for the sale of the land.[24] If the contract does contain provisions as to its exercise these must be complied with strictly, as *Cassidy v Baker*[25] illustrates. In that case a three-year lease gave the lessee the option to purchase the reversion for £5,000 on giving the lessor three months' notice in writing of his desire to purchase. The lessee purported to exercise the option less than two months before expiration of the three year term by writing to the lessor as follows: "This is to inform you that I now wish to exercise the option in my lease which entitles me to purchase these premises for £5,000." Kenny J held that this was an invalid exercise of the option because, first, it was not a three months' notice as required by the terms of the contract and, secondly, service at that date was too late as any notice should have been given so as to expire during the currency of the lease. It seems that time is of the essence of the contract in such a case.[26]

---

22. See *Cassidy v Baker* (1969) 103 ILTR 40; *Vone Securities Ltd v Cooke* (1969) 103 ILTR 40. *Cf Sunnybank Inn Ltd v East Coast Inns Ltd*, High Court, unrep, 11 May 1979 (1978/ 3042P); *Croft Inns Ltd v Scott* [1982] NI 95.

23. Thus if the contract creating the option contains no terms as to the conditions of sale, the parties will be deemed to have entered into an "open" contract, *Weldman v Spinks* (1861) 5 LT 385. *Cf Re Crosby's Contract* [1949] 1 All ER 830. See also as regards options granted by will, *Re Fison's Will Trusts* [1950] Ch 394; *Talbot v Talbot* [1968] Ch 1. And see *Re Davidson and Torrens* (1865) 17 Ir Ch R 7 (donee of option held not to be entitled to an abstract of title).

24. Note the recent English decisions considering the effect of s 2 of the Law Reform (Miscellaneous Provisions) Act 1989: *Spiro v Glencrown Properties Ltd* [1991] 1 All ER 600; *Armstrong & Holmes Ltd v Holmes* [1994] 3 All ER 826. *Cf* the effect of a notice served by a lessee of his intention to acquire the freehold under the statutory provisions in force in Ireland, see para **[8.09]** *infra*.

25. (1969) 103 ILTR 40. See also *Rafferty v Schofield* [1897] 1 Ch 937; *Cockwell v Romford Sanitary Steam Laundry Ltd* [1939] 4 All ER 370.

26. See *Lord Ranelagh v Melton* (1864) 2 Drew & Sin 278 at 282-3 (*per* Kindersley V-C) See also *Dibbins v Dibbins* [1896] 2 Ch 348; *Re Avard* [1948] Ch 43. See also *Vone Securities Ltd v Cooke* [1979] IR 59, where the majority of the Supreme Court, upholding the decision of Costello J, held that the holder of the option had fallen foul of the common law rule that a "month" means a lunar month of twenty-eight days, rather than a calendar month. The Interpretation Act 1937 (s 12) changes this for statutes and the Law Reform Commission has recommended a similar rule for private documents: *Report on Land Law and Conveyancing Law: (1) General Proposals* (LRC 30-1989), paras 21-22.

[8.06] It follows from the proposition that an option to purchase creates an interest in land that the agreement granting it must be evidenced by a sufficient note or memorandum in writing as required by the Statute of Frauds.[27] This must contain a clear statement of the basic terms, such as the purchase price, or else it must prescribe machinery for ascertaining such terms in accordance with the maxim *id certum est quod certum reddi potest*.[28] That machinery must, however, be unambiguous[29] and must not attempt to confer jurisdiction which would be an extension of that conferred on an official by statute.[30]

III. Acquisition of the Freehold

[8.07] Under the Landlord and Tenant (Ground Rents) Acts 1967-84 certain tenants may acquire the freehold of their land by invoking the statutory procedures.[31] It is important to note that the Act governs cases only where the tenant decides to invoke its compulsory procedures. There is nothing to prevent the tenant and superior owners getting together and making a voluntary agreement, in which case the transaction will be carried out in accordance with normal conveyancing procedures. If that is done, the parties have no right to use the special procedures laid down by the Acts, as *Carr v Phelan*[32] illustrated. In that case a contract was entered into for the purchase of the freehold, but no specific price was fixed by the contract. Instead it contained a clause that the price was to be the number of years' "purchase" as would be fixed by the county registrar under the 1967 Act,[33] if the rent had been a ground rent within the meaning of that Act,[34] and the case had, therefore, come within its provisions. The county registrar refused to fix the price on the ground that his jurisdiction extended only to cases brought under the Act and he was under no obligation to perform functions purported to be imposed on him by act of parties to a private contract. In an action by the tenant for specific performance of the contract, Hamilton J refused to grant the decree because the contract failed to specify a price or to provide a

---

[27.] See Ch 6 *ante*.

[28.] See para **[6.22]** *ante*. See also *Homsey v Searle* [1996] EGCS 43 (right of pre-emption).

[29.] *Lonergan v McCarthy* [1983] NI 129, discussing the limited scope for the court to substitute its own machinery, as suggested by the House of Lords in *Sudbrook Trading Estate Ltd v Eggleton* [1983] 1 AC 444.

[30.] See *Carr v Phelan* [1976-7] ILRM 149: see para **[8.07]** *infra*.

[31.] See Wylie, *Irish Landlord and Tenant Law*, Ch 31.

[32.] [1976-7] ILRM 149.

[33.] By arbitration under s 17. See para **[8.10]** *infra*.

[34.] See s 3(2).

227

method of fixing it with certainty, and, in the absence of an effective agreement for arbitration made by the parties, the court had no power to appoint an arbitrator for them. Thus, in his opinion, the agreement lacked one of the essentials for a binding contract for the sale or purchase of land.[35]

[8.08] The procedure to be followed by a qualifying lessee or tenant[36] varies from case to case. The original "notice procedure" was introduced by the Landlord and Tenant (Ground Rents) Act 1967,[37] but a much more simplified procedure was introduced for dwellinghouses by the Landlord and Tenant (Ground Rents) (No 2) Act 1978, involving a "vesting" certificate issued by the Land Registry.[38] In the present context what is of interest is the "notice procedure" because it accords more with the traditional conveyancing procedure for the sale of land. Where a tenant, who qualifies, wishes to invoke that procedure, his first step is to serve a notice of intention to acquire the fee simple on all the owners of superior interests in the land and all owners of incumbrances, eg, mortgages of such interests.[39] The form of notice is prescribed by regulations[40] made under the Act[41] and this form[42] requires inclusion of sufficient particulars to identify the property, particulars of the applicant's lease or tenancy[43] and, where part only of land held under a lease is to be acquired, which part is excluded from the notice. However, in *Smiths (Harcourt Street) Ltd v Hardwicke Ltd*[44] it was held that this notice does not have to have the same precision as a deed of conveyance, so long as it identifies to the vendor the land sought to be acquired. In that case the notice did not mention a right of way over adjoining lands, but it was held that "land" was to be interpreted as specified in the Schedule to the Interpretation Act 1937, which includes incorporeal hereditaments.[45] The vendor was to be taken as having understood that the fee simple in the lands was to be acquired together with such appurtenant

---

35. See para **[6.24]** *ante*.
36. See Pt II of the Landlord and Tenant (Grounds Rents) (No 2) Act 1978.
37. See Wylie, *Irish Landlord and Tenant Law*, para 31.46 *et seq*.
38. See *ibid* para 31.52 *et seq*. Note also the transfer order procedure applicable to housing authority tenants under s 26 of the 1978 (No 2) Act and s 90 of the Housing Act 1966: see *ibid*, paras 31.58 and 31.76.
39. Section 4. Service by post is to be by registered post, s 23(1).
40. Landlord and Tenant (Ground Rents) Act 1967 (Forms) Regulations 1967 (SI 1967/43).
41. Made under powers conferred on the Minister for Justice by s 34.
42. 1967 Regulations, Form No 1 (and see especially notes A-D).
43. Ie, the amount of rent and whether the land is held under a yearly tenancy or under a lease. If held under a lease, it should state its date, length of term and the parties to it.
44. High Court, unrep, 30 July 1971 (1970/3225P).
45. Cl 14.

rights as the right of way.[46] Where, as is common in the urban areas of Ireland,[47] there are several superior owners, it may be necessary to trace them by serving notices requiring information,[48] so as to secure the joinder of all necessary parties in the conveyance of the fee simple to the applicant.[49] Furthermore, if the applicant is responsible for payment of rent also in respect of other land held under the same lease, he may have the rent apportioned between that land and the land of which he wants to acquire the freehold.[50] This he can achieve by invoking the general provisions for apportionment of rent in the Act,[51] which lay down similar procedures, ie, service of a notice of intention to have the rent apportioned.[52] However, probably because of the complexities involved, these provisions as to apportionment of rent have been rarely invoked in practice.

[8.09] The effect of service of a notice of intention to acquire the fee simple is specified in s 6 of the 1967 Act. It creates a statutory duty on the person serving it and on the person upon whom it is served to take "without unreasonable delay" all "necessary steps" to effect a conveyance free from incumbrances of the fee simple and any intermediate interests in the land to the person serving the notice. This statutory duty to effect a conveyance thus takes the place of the contractual duty which would arise where the parties entered into a private contract for sale apart from the Act,[53] as in the *Smiths* case referred to above.[54] The "necessary steps" under the Act include,

---

46. On reference of a dispute as to the tenant's right to acquire the fee simple, the county registrar had fixed the purchase price on the basis that the right of way was attached to the freehold. Note, however, the restrictive interpretation of "land" in this context applied by O'Flaherty J in *Metropolitan Properties Ltd v O'Brien* [1995] 1 IR 467 where he held that it does not apply where the demised premises are separated from the ground, as in the case of a flat or apartment. The other members of the Supreme Court (Hamilton CJ and Egan J) expressly left the point open, confining the decision to another ground disqualifying the lessee in that case, *viz* that the landlord's interest has passed to the Commissioners of Public Works who are not bound by the legislation under s 4 of the 1978 (No 2) Act.

47. On the subject of "pyramid" titles, see *Irish Land Law* (2nd ed, 1986) paras 4.180-2 and 18.40.

48. Section 7. See 1967 Regulations, Form Nos 2 (Notice requiring information from a lessor) and 3 (Notice requiring information from a person receiving rent).

49. As to persons, eg, under a disability or who cannot be traced, see the special provisions in s 8.

50. Section 5(3).

51. Sections 11-6. As regards persons under a disability, etc, see s 14.

52. Section 12. See 1967 Regulations, Form No 5.

53. *Cf* ss 5 and 8 of the English Leasehold Reform Act 1967 which provide expressly that service of the notice creates a contractual relationship, under which the parties' rights and obligations are enforceable to the like extent as under a contract for sale freely entered into between them.

54. Para **[8.08]** *supra*.

therefore, the execution of a deed by all the appropriate parties transferring the fee simple to the applicant.[55]

[8.10] The scope of the statutory duty to effect a conveyance is defined to a certain extent by the 1967 Act. First, we saw in the previous paragraph that it is a duty to convey the fee simple "free from incumbrances," but this does not include mortgages or charges on the applicant's interest and it is provided that, on conveyance of the fee simple to him, any such mortgage or charge is, unless extinguished, to be deemed to be a mortgage or charge on the fee simple.[56] Secondly, if the parties cannot agree on the purchase price for the fee simple, the question may be referred to the county registrar for the area,[57] for determination by his arbitration.[58] Though the registrar is under a general duty to make such award as justice requires,[59] the Landlord and Tenant (Amendment) Act 1984 now gives guidance in providing that the purchase price is to be the sum which, in his opinion, a willing purchaser would give and a willing vendor would accept, having regard to a number of factors,[60] eg, the current rent, the current interest yields on Government securities, the price in previous sales, mortgages or other charges on superior owners' interests and costs and expenses of investing the purchase money. In practice, of course, awards made in arbitration by the registrars over a passage of time tend to form a body of precedents which are applied in similar cases and, for this reason, it is important to note that all awards relating to prices of fees simple are noted on a special register maintained by each country registrar.[61] The register, which is kept at the relevant Circuit Court Office,[62] is available for public inspection and copies of entries in it are available on payment of the prescribed fee.[63] A copy purported to be

---

[55.] See further on various problems which can arise in respect of the drafting of such deeds, para **[8.11]** *infra*.

[56.] Section 6(2).

[57.] Where the land straddles two or more areas, it should be referred to the registrar for the area in which the larger or largest portion of the land is situate, see s 2(3).

[58.] Section 17(1). The registrar may enlist the assistance of the Commissioner of Valuation, eg, by requesting a valuation or estimate in respect of any matter relating to determination of the purchase price of the fee simple, s 20. An appeal lies from the registrar's award to the Circuit Court, s 22.

[59.] *Ibid.*

[60.] Section 7. This section also applies where a lessee invokes the Land Registry "vesting" procedure (see para **[8.08]** *supra*) and the Registrar of Titles has to conduct an arbitration.

[61.] The duty to maintain a register of purchase price awards is imposed by s 21(1)(a) of the 1967 Act. A separate register is kept of all other awards, eg, as to apportionment of the purchase price or as to costs or expenses, s 21(1)(b). As to the forms of the two registers, see Ground Rents Registers Regulations 1967 (SI 1967/152) 1st Schedule, Parts I and II.

[62.] 1967 Regulations, reg 4.

[63.] Section 21(2). See also 1967 Regulations, 2nd Schedule.

signed by the registrar[64] is evidence of the matters stated, unless the contrary is proved.[65]

[8.11] The draftsman of the 1967 Act did not deal expressly with the question whether there is a merger of the tenant's interest as lessee in the fee simple conveyed to him. Merger is a question of intention,[66] though it is usual conveyancing practice, when a lessee is acquiring the lessor's interest, to have an express declaration of merger. The provision in the Act that a mortgage or charge affecting the lessee's interest is "to be deemed to be a mortgage on the fee simple in the land"[67] suggests that the effect of the conveyance is otherwise to merge the lessee's term of years in the freehold without any express declaration in the deed and it is suggested that solicitors should proceed on this basis.

[8.12] If the applicant to purchase the freehold under the Act held under a lease which contained restrictive covenants and there was an estate scheme in operation,[68] there is also the question of whether the merger of the leasehold in the freehold abolishes the rights of other tenants to enforce the covenants under the scheme. It is true that what is now s 28 of the Landlord and Tenant (Ground Rents) (No 2) Act 1978 keeps alive any covenants in the lease which protect or enhance the amenities of any land occupied by the owner of the lessor's interest in the lease, but it says nothing about covenants protecting or enhancing the amenities of any adjoining owner or person who could invoke the estate scheme doctrine. It would seem that, as the lessee's interest merges in the freehold, the covenants in the lease are extinguished except to the extent that they are saved by s 28. The all-embracing effect of s 28 was confirmed by Murphy J in *Whelan v Cork Corporation*[69] and his decision was upheld by the Supreme Court.[70] The result is that adjoining owners may be deprived of any benefit of the estate scheme doctrine. It is also doubtful if an express declaration of non-merger will be effective to protect their rights, even assuming that the lessor and acquiring lessee are likely to put one in the conveyance through altruistic motives. Such a declaration would reduce or restrict the rights or interest which the acquiring

---

[64.] Ie, without proof of the signature or that the person signing was the county registrar.

[65.] Section 21(3).

[66.] See *Irish Land Law* (2nd ed, 1986) Ch 24.

[67.] Section 6(2). See para **[8.10]** *supra*.

[68.] See *Irish Land Law* (2nd ed, 1986) paras 19.34-7.

[69.] [1991] ILRM 19.

[70.] *Ex temporare* judgment given on 15 November 1990. As regards the unsatisfactory nature of this, see the Law Reform Commission's *Report Land Law and Conveyancing Law (1): General Proposals* (LRC 30-1989), paras 60-61. On the constitutional difficulties, see Wylie *Irish Landlord and Tenant Law* paras 31.75 and 31.77-78.

lessee would otherwise be entitled to under the Act, and to that extent it would seem that such a declaration is rendered void under s 33 of the 1967 Act.

IV. COURT SALES

[8.13] We saw in an earlier chapter that a sale of land under a court order, eg, one obtained by a mortgagee on default by the mortgagor,[71] is normally carried out by public auction, under the general control of the court.[72] The procedure is not really very different from an ordinary sale by auction, except that the sale is subject to the approval of the court and a lower scale of auctioneers' fees is enforced as the court, and not the auctioneer, determines the fees. However, there may be other cases involving the court where a special procedure may be adopted. Thus, where a purchaser under an ordinary contract for the sale of land obtains an order for specific performance against the vendor, but the latter refuses to comply and to execute the requisite conveyance, the court may order the purchaser to lodge the purchase money in court and appoint another person to carry out the sale by executing the requisite conveyance in the name and on behalf of the vendor.[73] This power is conferred on the courts by the Trustee Act[74] and is an alternative to, though it has the same effect as, a vesting order made by the court under the Act. The court is empowered to make orders vesting estates or interests in land in persons in a variety of cases, eg, consequential on a court order for the sale or mortgage of land[75] or on an order for specific performance of a contract for the sale of land.[76]

V. COMPULSORY PURCHASE

[8.14] Another example of special procedures for the purchase of land is where land is acquired compulsorily by a public authority under statutory powers.[77] Powers of compulsory acquisition of land were granted by legislatures with increasing rapidity from the early part of the nineteenth

---

[71.] See *Irish Land Law* (2nd ed, 1986) paras 13.040-1.

[72.] See para **[2.27]**, *ante*. See also para **[11.01]** *et seq, post*.

[73.] See *Irish Land Law* (2nd ed, 1986) para 3.144. See also Farrell, *Irish Law of Specific Performance* (1994), para [8.25] *et seq*.

[74.] Trustee Act 1893, s 33. See *Moorhead v Kirkwood* [1919] 1 IR 225.

[75.] 1893 Act, s 30.

[76.] 1893 Act, s 31. *Cf* re vesting orders in respect of trustees, *Re Ruthven's Trusts* [1906]1 IR 236; *Re Kenny's Trusts* [1906] 1 IR 531.

[77.] See generally McDermott and Woulfe, *Compulsory Purchase and Compensation in Ireland: Law and Practice* (1992).

century to facilitate the execution of public works, eg, the building of railways, canals, roads and bridges.[78] The statutory procedures for acquisition varied from statute to statute until the Westminster Parliament decided to provide some rationalisation by devising one basic system of procedures which could be incorporated in all future statutes conferring powers of compulsory acquisition, unless it was decided that some special procedure was required for the particular case. This was done by passing the Lands Clauses Consolidation Act 1845,[79] which applied to both Ireland and England. The 1845 Act provided for what is usually known as the "notice to treat" system of acquisition,[80] ie, the acquiring authority, after determination of the land it wished to acquire, was to serve a notice on all persons interested in that land, requiring them to specify their interests in or claims to it and to enter into negotiations with the authority for its transfer to the authority.[81] In other words, the notice to treat in effect created a contract for sale between the authority and each landowner[82] and the acquisition then followed normal conveyancing procedures, ie the contract was to be carried out by a conveyance of the land to the acquiring authority.[83] In *Eaton v Midland Great Western Railway Co*[84] Blackburne CJ stated:

> "It is clearly settled that the effect of that notice [to treat] was to create the relation of vendor and purchaser between the parties, and the plaintiff was bound thereby to give the land, and the defendants were bound to take it and pay for it. The estate being thus bound, nothing was to be done but to ascertain the purchase money."[85]

---

78. See *Irish Land Law* (2nd ed, 1986) para 1.62.
79. See also Railway Clauses Consolidation Act 1845 and the Companies Clauses Consolidation Act 1845.
80. To operate if there was no purchase "by agreement," see ss 6-15. See *R (Secretary of State for War) v County Cork JJ* [1900] 2 IR 105.
81. See ss 18-20.
82. This analogy should not be pushed too far. Thus, unlike in the case of an ordinary contract for sale, if specifically enforceable (see para **[12.02]** *post*), it was settled that the notice to treat did not create an equitable interest in the acquiring authority; at the date of service of the notice to treat no price has been fixed, so that one of the essentials for an enforceable contract is missing (see para **[6.24]** *ante*). Thus, in *Blount v GS & W Rly Co* Brady LC remarked: "Serving notice does to a certain extent establish between the parties the relationship of vendor and purchaser, but not so as of itself to attach upon the case the jurisdiction of this Court, because notice operates only to determine one branch of the contract, namely, the thing to be taken; price is also to be determined" (1851) 2 Ir Ch R 40 at 47. See also *Haynes v Haynes* (1861) 1 Drew & Sm 426 at 450 (*per* Kindersley V-C); *Harding v Metropolitan Rly Co* (1872) 7 Ch App 154.
83. See ss 81-3 and Schedules A and B. As to entry on the land and proceedings where an owner refused to give up possession, see ss 85-91.
84. (1847) 10 Ir LR 310.
85. *Ibid*, p 314.

The purchase price or, to be more accurate, the compensation payable to each landowner was to be fixed by agreement or, in default of agreement, by arbitration.[86] However, it appears that the procedures of the 1845 Act were found to be not entirely satisfactory in Ireland and substantial amendments were made, initially in respect of acquisition for railway purposes, by the Railways (Ireland) Act 1851.[87] But the amendments introduced by the 1851 Act were given much wider scope in Ireland by the Railways (Ireland) Acts 1860 and 1864.[88] The 1851 Act required the acquiring authority to prepare maps and schedules of the lands in question and to lodge these with the Board of Works in Dublin.[89] Notices were to be published in the *Dublin Gazette* and local newspapers.[90] The Board appointed an arbitrator to determine any claims for compensation[91] and, once he had made his award, the land was to be conveyed to the acquiring authority in the normal way.[92] The 1845 and 1851 procedures, as amended by the Housing of the Working Classes Act 1890,[93] continued to govern most compulsory acquisition of land in Ireland until after 1920. Since then there have been introduced various substantial amendments to the nineteenth century provisions,[94]

---

86. By a jury, if desired, see s 24.

87. See the preamble to the 1851 Act, and see also *Parl Debs* (3rd series), Vol 117 cols 1114-21. On the significance of the 1851 Act and later Acts in Ireland, see Suffern, *Law Relating to Compulsory Purchase and Sale of Lands in Ireland* (1882). See also Trimble, 'The Procedure Governing compulsory Acquisition of Land in Northern Ireland' (1973) NILQ 466; McDermott and Woulfe, *op cit*, Ch 1.

88. The 1864 Act extended the 1851 Act to any company undertakers, commissioners, drainage board, corporation or private person empowered to take or use lands compulsorily, see 1864 Act s 13.

89. Sections 3-4. *R (Moore) v Abbott* [1897] 2 IR 362; *R (Montgomery) v Belfast Corporation* [1915] 2 IR 36.

90. Section 8. *Re Connor* (1894) 28 ILTR 67; *Re Fishguard and Rosslare Rlys* [1908] 1 IR 321.

91. Sections 5-15. See *Cork and Youghal Rly Co v Harnett* (1871) LR 5 HL 111; *Re Dublin (South) City Markets Co* (1888) 21 LR Ir 245; *Callow v Flynn* (1890) 26 LR Ir 179. In *Re Doyne's Traverses* (1888) 24 LR Ir 287, it was held that publication of the notice of the arbitrator's appointment was equivalent to service of a notice to treat under the Lands Clauses Act. See also *Re Parkinson* [1898] 1 IR 390.

92. *Re Baltimore Extension Rly Co* [1895] 1 IR 169. If no claims were forthcoming, the compensation could be lodged in court and the receipt operated as a conveyance to the acquiring authority, s 17. A deposit in court could also be made where a landowner refused to accept the compensation awarded or to make out title for the conveyance, s 19. As to entry on the land by the acquiring authority see ss 16 and 25; *Lambert v Dublin, Wicklow and Wexford Rly Co* (1890) 25 LR Ir 163. See also Railways (Ir) Act 1860 s 2; *Re Belfast Water Commissioners* (1884) 12 LR Ir 13; *Re Dublin, Wicklow and Wexford Rly Co* (1891) 27 LR Ir 79.

93. See Schedule 2.

94. For criticism of the "thoroughly confusing patchworth" of statute law, see the *Report of the Committee on the Price of Building Land* (Prl 3632; 1973), para 147.

though there has not, as yet, been introduced a consolidation measure such as the English Compulsory Purchase Act 1965.[95] Before considering the amendments, it may also be noted that the rules for assessment of compensation in most cases of compulsory purchase were set out in s 2 of the Acquisition of Land (Assessment of Compensation) Act 1919, which provided for establishment of a panel of official arbitrators to assess compensation in particular cases.

[8.15] A substantially revised procedure for many cases of compulsory purchase is now contained in the Housing Act 1966, which relates not only to compulsory purchase by housing authorities[96] but may be used by local authorities wherever they consider that this would be convenient.[97] In view of the importance of the 1966 procedure, it may be useful to give an outline of its main features,[98] though it must be emphasised that there exist also numerous statutes conferring special powers of compulsory purchase on local and other authorities which do not require use of this procedure.[99]

A. Compulsory Purchase Order

[8.16] The first step is for the housing or local authority to make a compulsory purchase order,[100] in the prescribed form,[101] describing by reference to a map the land in question.[102] In *Moran v Dublin Corporation*,[103] the Supreme Court emphasised that such an order must not relate only to land to be acquired by another authority. The order has to be submitted to the Minister for the Environment for confirmation, but, before its submission, the authority must do two things.[104] One is to publish a notice, in the

---

95. This lays down the basic system of procedure whereby a compulsory purchase order is made first and the acquisition is carried out by a notice to treat, followed by a conveyance. *Cf* the system under the Housing Act 1966 (see para **[8.15]** *infra*). But note the special "general vesting declaration" system introduced by the English Town and Country Planning Act 1968, s 30 and Schedule 3.

96. Section 76.

97. Section 86, which substitutes a new s 10 in the Local Government (No 2) Act 1960.

98. See further McDermott and Woulfe, *op cit*, Ch 2; Keane, *The Law of Local Government in the Republic of Ireland* (1982) Ch 8.

99. See the discussion in McDermott and Woulfe, *op cit*, Chs 3-6.

100. 1966 Act, s 76 and 3rd Schedule.

101. Housing Act 1966 (Acquisition of Land) Regulations 1966 (SI 1966/278), Schedule, Form Nos 1 (housing authorities) and 7 (local authorities).

102. 1966 Act, 3rd Schedule, art 1.

103. (1975) 109 ILTR 57. Though note that s 77 enables a housing authority to acquire land for a future building programme (see also s 55), so that it may not be used immediately, see *Russell v Minister for Local Government* [1976] IR 185.

104. *Op cit*, art 4.

prescribed form,[105] in one or more newspapers circulating in the authority's functional area, stating the fact that the order has been made and indicating where a copy of the order and map may be seen at all reasonable hours.[106] The other is to serve a notice[107] on every owner, lessee and occupier[108] of any land within the order, stating the order's effect and that it is about to be submitted to the Minister for confirmation and specifying the time within which and the manner in which objections can be made to the order.[109] The Minister has a discretion either to annul the order[110] or to confirm it, with or without modification.[111] However, he cannot confirm the order so far as it relates to any land in respect of which an objection has been made by any person served with notice of the order,[112] until he has caused a local public inquiry to be held into the objection and he has considered the objection and report of the person holding the inquiry.[113] The courts have increasingly stressed that the inspector appointed to conduct such an inquiry must observe fair procedures and abide by the rules of natural justice.[114] Furthermore, they have held that the Minister is also fulfilling a quasi-judicial role as *persona designata* and not simply an executive function.[115]

[8.17] Once the Minister confirms the compulsory purchase order, the housing or local authority must publish in the newspaper circulating in their functional area a notice[116] stating that it has been confirmed and naming a place where a copy of the order as confirmed and the related map can be

---

[105.] 1966 Regulations, Schedule, Form Nos 2 (housing authorities) and 8 (local authorities).

[106.] 1966 Act, 3rd Schedule, art 4(a).

[107.] For the prescribed form, see 1966 Regulations, Schedule, Form Nos 3 (housing authorities) and 9 (local authorities).

[108.] Except tenants for a month or a lesser period: 1966 Act, 3rd Schedule, art 4(b).

[109.] *Ibid.*

[110.] By an annulment order, 1966 Act, 3rd Schedule, art 5(1)(a).

[111.] By an confirmation order, *ibid*, art 5(1)(b).

[112.] Unless the objection is withdrawn or the Minister is satisfied that it relates exclusively to matters which can be dealt with by the arbitrator who assesses the compensation, *ibid*, art 5(2) and see para **[8.18]** *infra*.

[113.] The *Report of the Committee on the Price of Building Land* (Prl 3632; 1973) stated that this provision "causes long delays" and ought to be dispensed with in certain cases of "urgency," when a different procedure, involving strict time limits, should be adopted, see para 147. See the discussion of the role of the Minister when such an inquiry is held in *Murphy v Corporation of Dublin* [1972] IR 215.

[114.] See *Killiney and Ballybrack Development Association v Minister for Local Government* (1978) 112 ILTR 69; *Kiely v Minister for Social Welfare* [1977] IR 267; *O'Brien v Bord na Mona* [1983] ILRM 314.

[115.] See *Murphy v Corporation of Dublin* [1972] IR 215; *Geraghty v Minister for Local Government* [1976] IR 153.

[116.] Again in the prescribed form, 1966 Regulations, Schedule, Form Nos 4 (housing authorities) and 10 (local authorities).

seen.[117] The authority must also serve a like notice on every person with an interest in the land who objected to the order and appeared at the public local inquiry.[118] Any person aggrieved by the confirmed order may challenge its validity by application, not later than three weeks from publication of the confirmation notice, to the High Court.[119] The court may suspend the order's operation by an interim order, until final determination of the proceedings,[120] and ultimately may quash it, generally or in part, if satisfied that it is not within the statutory powers or that the interests of the applicant have been substantially prejudiced by any of the statutory provisions not having been complied with.[121] If no application is made to the High Court, the order becomes operative twenty-eight days after publication of the confirmation notice or, if one is made but later withdrawn, twenty-eight days after its withdrawal[122]; otherwise it becomes operative on the date of determination of the application.[123] Once it becomes operative, the authority must serve a copy of the order on every person previously served with notice of intention to submit the order for confirmation by the Minister.[124]

B. Notice to Treat

[8.18] The next step is for the authority to serve a notice to treat on each of the landowners and occupiers[125] affected by the compulsory purchase order.[126] This should state that the authority is willing to treat for the purchase of the several interests in the land and should require each owner to state, within the specified period,[127] the exact nature of the interest in respect of which he wishes to claim compensation and details of the compensation claimed.[128] Where the purchase money or compensation does not exceed

---

[117.] 1966 Act, s 78(1).

[118.] *Ibid.*

[119.] *Ibid* s 78(2). See *Fuller v Dublin CC* [1976] IR 20. Subject to this, a person may not question a compulsory purchase order by prohibition or *certiorari* or in any legal proceedings whatsoever, s 78(4).

[120.] Section 78(2)(a).

[121.] Section 78(2)(b). As to judicial review proceedings generally see Order 84 of the Superior Court Rules 1986 and *State (Furey) v Minister for Defence* [1988] ILRM 89.

[122.] Section 78(3)(a)(i)

[123.] Section 78(3)(a)(ii) and (b).

[124.] Section 78(5).

[125.] Again this does not have to be served on tenants for a month or lesser period, see para **[8.16]** *supra*.

[126.] Section 79(1). See *Green Dale Building Co v Dublin CC* [1977] IR 256. Such a notice is deemed to be a notice to treat for the purposes of the Acquisition of Land (Assessment of Compensation) Act 1919, s 79(2). See also para **[8.14]** *supra*.

[127.] Not being less than one month from the date of service of the notice to treat.

[128.] Section 79(1).

£500, the authority may complete the purchase by paying it to the person who can be dealt with as absolute owner of each interest in the land,[129] or to the first (in priority) mortgagee or chargee of that interest,[130] and the receipt, if in the prescribed form,[131] is "effectual to vest absolutely in the authority, free from incumbrances and all estates, rights, titles and interests of whatsoever kind (other than a public right of way) the fee simple of the land."[132] If the authority considers that the claimant is not absolutely entitled to the land or his title is not satisfactorily shown, and the purchase money or compensation does not exceed £5,000, they may pay the money into the Circuit Court[133]; otherwise it must be paid into the High Court.[134] Once the money is deposited in court, the authority may execute a deed poll, which has the effect of vesting the fee simple in the authority absolutely.[135] This procedure may also be adopted where a landowner refuses to accept compensation or to make out title.[136] But the 1966 Act now provides an alternative procedure, as outlined in the next few paragraphs.

C. Entry on Land

[8.19] At any time after service of notices to treat,[137] the authority may, on giving not less than fourteen days notice in writing to each owner and occupier, enter on, take possession of and use the land, without previous consent or compliance with the provisions of the Lands Clauses Acts relating to entry on lands,[138] but the authority is liable to pay compensation in the ordinary way and interest on it from the date of entry.[139]

D. Vesting Order

[8.20] Once the authority has entered on and taken possession of the land, then, if, after six months from the date of entry, the several interests have still not been conveyed or transferred to them and they consider that it is

---

[129.] 1966 Act, 3rd Schedule, art 2(a) (as modified by s 6 of the Housing Act 1970). Art 2 provides modifications to the Lands Clauses Acts and Acquisition of Land (Assessment of Compensation) Act 1919.

[130.] Article 2(b).

[131.] See 1966 Regulations, Schedule, Form No 12. Other persons may lodge claims to the money by applying to the High Court within six years, art 2(1).

[132.] Article 2(c).

[133.] Article 2(g) (as modified by s 6 of the Housing Act 1970).

[134.] Lands Clauses Consolidation Act 1845, ss 69-75.

[135.] *Ibid*, ss 73-5. But a deed poll is only as good as the title of the vendor, see *Wells v Chelmsford Local Board of Health* (1880) 15 Ch D 108.

[136.] *Ibid* ss 76-9.

[137.] But not before the notice to treat, see *Fitzpatrick v Dublin Corporation* [1971] IR 169.

[138.] See 1845 Act, ss 85-91.

[139.] Section 80(1). On the subject of interest, see *Nestor v Galway Corporation* High Court, unrep, 17 April 1983.

urgently necessary to complete the acquisition of the land and they have made a proper offer in writing for every interest of which they have been furnished particulars, they may make a vesting order acquiring the land.[140] If they do, they must, within seven days, publish a notice in one or more newspaper circulating in their functional area stating that the order has been made, describing the land and indicating where a copy may be seen.[141] They must also serve a notice, stating that it has been made and its effect, on every person appearing to them to have an interest in the land in question.[142]

[8.21] The vesting order must be in the prescribed form[143] and have attached to it a map of the land in question.[144] It must be expressed and does operate to vest the land in the authority in fee simple "free from incumbrances and all estates, rights, titles and interests of whatsoever kind (other than any public right of way)" on the specified date (the "vesting" date), which is to be not earlier than twenty-one days after the making of the order.[145] If the land is registered land, they must send the order to the Land Registry for registration of the authority as owner of the land.[146]

E. Assessment of Compensation

[8.22] In default of agreement as to the amount of compensation payable by the authority acquiring the land, it is assessed by arbitration under the Acquisition of Land (Assessment of Compensation) Act 1919, as amended by later Acts,[147] and as modified by the 1966 Act.[148] Section 2 of the 1919 Act, as amended, lays down various rules to be applied in the assessment, the principal one of which is rule 2, which requires the assessment of the value of the land to be made on the basis of the amount the land, if sold on the open market by a willing seller at the date of the notice to treat,[149] might

---

[140.] Section 81(1). If they become aware that the land, or part of it, is subject to, eg, a land purchase annuity they must inform the Land Commission of the intention to make a vesting order, s 81(2). See also s 82(2).

[141.] Section 81(3)(a)

[142.] Section 81(3(b).

[143.] See 1966 Regulations, Schedule, Form Nos 5 (housing authorities) and 11 (local authorities).

[144.] 1966 Act, s 82(1).

[145.] *Ibid.*

[146.] Section 82(3).

[147.] See McDermott and Woulfe, *op cit* Pt 2.

[148.] Section 84, 3rd Schedule, art 2(k) and (l) and 4th Schedule.

[149.] In *Re Murphy* [1977] IR 243 the Supreme Court held that the assessment date should be taken as the date of a notice served after the decision on an application to the High Court to test the validity of the CPO, not a subsequent notice served after an appeal to the Supreme Court from that decision. *Cf Re Green Dale Building Co Ltd* [1977] IR 256 (first notice *ultra vires* since served before High Court decision).

be expected to realise. In *Re Deansrath Investments*,[150] which involved compulsory acquisition of agricultural land, the Supreme Court held that the compensation awarded by the arbitrator should include enhancement of value existing at the date of the notice to treat due to the possibility that the land might become subject to a scheme of development by someone other than the acquiring authority.[151]

[150.] [1974] IR 228.

[151.] Rule 13 in s 2 of the 1919 Act (inserted by s 69(1) of and 4th Schedule to the Local Government (Planning and Development) Act 1963) provides that no account is to be taken of the existence of proposals for development by or the possibility or probability of such a scheme being undertaken by a local authority. See *Re Murphy* [1977] IR 243. For full discussion of the operation of the assessment rules see McDermott and Woulfe *op cit*, Chs 9-12.

Chapter 9

CONTENTS OF THE CONTRACT

[9.01] In this chapter and the next two chapters we are concerned with the contents of a contract for the sale of land. The first point which should be emphasised about this subject is that, in theory, the contents are largely a matter for the parties to determine, as in the case of any contract. The one qualification to this rule is, of course, that the Statute of Frauds (Ir) 1695, requires a written memorandum or note as evidence of the contract,[1] but even that is subject to the exception that a contract may be enforced without the requisite written evidence if there are acts of part performance.[2] If the parties enter into an informal agreement they may agree only on the minimum contents required for a sufficient memorandum or note for the purposes of the Statute of Frauds. If, however, the parties' contract is the subject of a formal agreement drawn up by their solicitors, or one of them,[3] it usually consists of a standard form document containing three principal parts.[4] One part contains the written memorandum required by the Statute of Frauds, another the "Particulars of Sale" and another the "Conditions of Sale," which are usually sub-divided into "General" and "Special" conditions. We consider each of these parts in detail later in this and the next chapter, but first some further preliminary remarks should be made.

[9.02] The need for a formal contract containing much more than the basic requirements of the Statute of Frauds has been recognised in Ireland, as in England,[5] for well over a century.[6] The reason is that most conveyancing

---

1. See generally, Ch 6 *ante*.
2. See para **[6.48]** *et seq, ante*.
3. This is invariably the case in a sale by public auction, para **[2.51]** *ante*. Even in the case of a sale by private treaty, the contract is usually drawn up by the vendor's solicitor, though it may be sent to the purchaser's solicitor for approval, para **[3.35]** *ante*.
4. The Law Society's current standard form contract, which covers sales by both private treaty and public auctions, is one document containing all three parts: see *General Conditions of Sale (1995 ed)*. The Society's Conveyancing Committee has recently disapproved of the practice adopted by some vendor's solicitors of furnishing simply conditions of sale which cross-refer to the Society's *General Conditions*, without including a print of those *General Conditions* with the contract for sale. The Committee insists that it is in everyone's interest that the Society's full contract form is used, particularly to avoid doubts or uncertainties as to the full context of the agreement: see the *Gazette*, December 1994, p 367.
5. See Wilkinson, *Standard Conditions of Sale of Land* (1st ed, 1990), pp 1-2.
6. See *Willis v Latham* (1837) S & Sc 441; *Lahey v Bell* (1843) 6 Ir Eq R 122; *Irvine v Deane* (1849) 2 Ir Jur (os) 209; *Boyd v Dickson* (1876) IR 10 Eq 239. See also Stubbs and Baxter, *Irish Forms and Precedents* (1910), pp 353-64 and 576-653.

transactions involve so many matters of importance to the parties and create such substantial financial commitments that they ought not to leave their agreements in an informal state, but rather ought in their own interests to have a formal agreement drawn up dealing with each of the matters involved in their transaction in detail, and not just providing for the basic requirements of the memorandum under the Statute of Frauds.[7] One of the original reasons for the drafting of "Conditions of Sale" seems to have been the complexity of title to land,[8] but it is important to note that formal contracts usually cover a much wider range of matters than questions of title.[9] This point is relevant to a question which is often raised by conveyancers, namely, whether there is any need for a detailed formal contract of sale where the land is registered land. It has been mooted from time to time that, since the title registered in the Land Registry is guaranteed[10] and investigation of title is thereby simplified,[11] there is no need for a formal contract of sale.[12] Indeed, it has been suggested that the transaction may be conducted on a purely informal basis by the vendor handing over his land certificate[13] in return for the purchase money. But, apart from the practical difficulty that the vendor may not have the certificate,[14] the certificate may not be up-to-date and may not, therefore, be an accurate reflection of the state of the registered title at the date of purchase.[15] Thus, the land certificate need not be produced for registration of a judgment mortgage against the land. Furthermore, the registered title is not

---

[7.] See paras **[6.17]** *ante* and **[9.05]** *infra*.

[8.] See cases cited in fn 6 *supra*. Note that where a contract for sale of land is described as being "open," as opposed to "closed," ie, containing express provision on the matter in question, this is usually taken as referring to the lack of provisions determining the title to be deduced by the vendor, see para **[14.05]** *post*.

[9.] See Ch 10 *post*.

[10.] See Fitzgerald *Land Registry Practice* (2nd ed, 1995), Ch 1.

[11.] See para **[15.07]** *et seq, post*.

[12.] See Brickdale and Stewart-Wallace *The Land Registration Act 1925* (4th ed, 1939), pp 28-9. *Cf* Potter, *Principles and Practice of Conveyancing under the Land Registration Act 1925* (1934), pp 318-9; Farrand, *Contract and Conveyance* (4th ed, 1983), pp 147-8. And see *Re Stone and Saville's Contract* [1963] 1 WLR 163; *Faruqi v English Real Estates Ltd* [1979] 1 WLR 963.

[13.] See para **[14.31]** *post*.

[14.] Eg, if his property is subject to an outstanding mortgage, it may be lodged with his mortgagee (see para **[2.43]** *ante*), though it is questionable whether this is desirable. Indeed, under s 67 of the Registration of Title Act 1964, a mortgagee of registered land is not entitled, by reason only of being the owner of a registered charge, to possession of the mortgagor's land certificate. Instead, the mortgagee is usually entitled to a charge certificate endorsed on the deed of charge: Fitzgerald *op cit*, pp 154-5.

[15.] Hence the practice of furnishing copies of the folio as part of deduction of title, see para **[14.33-5]** *post*, and making searches prior to completion, see para **[15.40]** *post*.

a complete mirror of the state of the title, eg, there are many burdens which affect registered land without registration.[16] Quite apart from these matters, normally the transferee from the registered owner must produce a transfer in the appropriate form to get himself registered as the new owner.[17] However, perhaps the most telling point of all is that a formal contract is needed to cover many other matters equally relevant to both registered and unregistered land, eg, the deposit payable,[18] whether vacant possession is to be given to the purchaser,[19] the closing date and interest charges for non-completion by then.[20]

[9.03] Where a formal contract is drawn up, it is common practice for the standard form issued by the Law Society to be used. The Law Society has recently revised its contract form and there is now a new general contract form entitled *General Conditions of Sale (1995 Edition)*. This form is the successor to a single contract form first issued in 1976 which amalgamated into one document the old private contract[21] and public auction[22] forms and may also be used to cover the case of a private sale entered into after an abortive auction.[23] The form issued in 1976 was revised substantially in 1986 and, although the 1986 version was further revised in 1988 and 1991, the 1995 edition largely maintains the 1986 format.[24] The form incorporates into one document the three principal parts referred to above, ie, the memorandum, the particulars of sale and the conditions of sale.[25] The front cover or "title" page refers to the two alternative methods of sale, ie by private treaty or by auction, with instructions to delete one as appropriate. In the case of a sale by auction the page provides space for entry of such details as the venue, date and time and the particulars of the auctioneer, the vendor and his solicitor.

[9.04] In the rest of this and the next chapter, we consider the provisions of the standard form in use in Ireland, though in the case of some of the provisions covered by the form more detailed discussion will be found

---

16. See Fitzgerald *op cit* Ch 13 and para **[14.27]** *post.*
17. See Fitzgerald *op cit* Ch 2 and para **[20.44]** *post.*
18. See para **[10.16]** *post.*
19. See para **[10.44]** *post.*
20. See paras **[13.10]** *et seq, post.*
21. *Agreement for Sale* (1968 ed).
22. *Particulars and Conditions of Sale* (1968 ed).
23. See *Judd v Donegal Tweed Co* (1935) 69 ILTR 117; *Rooney v Thomas* (1947) 81 ILTR 64.
24. Its contents are examined in this and the next chapter. The form itself is reproduced in Appendix II *post.*
25. See para **[9.01]** *supra*. Note also the "documents" and "searches" schedules added in 1986 and continued in the 1995 edition: see para **[9.39]** *et seq, infra.*

elsewhere in the book, in which case the appropriate place will be indicated. For the most part the order of discussion follows the format of the contract form which is structured sequentially to follow closely the steps usually taken in a straightforward conveyancing transaction. However, as will quickly become clear, it is not always practicable to maintain this approach.

I. MEMORANDUM OF SALE

[9.05] We discussed in an earlier chapter the need for a written memorandum of the sale and its requisite contents, as interpreted by the courts.[26] The *General Conditions of Sale (1995 Edition)* form contains a section beginning with the words "MEMORANDUM OF AGREEMENT..." on its first page. The section lists the various entries to be completed, detailing the date of the agreement, the names and addresses[27] of the vendor and purchaser, the purchase price, the deposit paid,[28] the balance owing, the closing date and the interest rate for late completion.[29] It also contains spaces for the signature by the two parties or their agents, which is required by the Statute of Frauds,[30] and for the signature and address of a witness to each such signature, which is not required by the Statute of Frauds. But, though the latter is not strictly required by the Statute, inclusion of such witnesses' signatures may constitute an extra safeguard against a subsequent questioning of the authenticity of the contract by any party. The memorandum acknowledges that the parties have agreed for the sale and purchase, in accordance with the terms of the contract,[31] of the property described in the particulars, ie, cross-referring to the section on the second page.[32]

[9.06] It is crucial to note that the MEMORANDUM on page 1 of the contract form is preceded (at the top of the page) by the spouse's consent

---

26. See para **[6.17]** *et seq, ante.*
27. Care should be taken over these since it may be necessary at a later stage to serve notices (eg, a completion notice: see para **[13.19]** *post*) on a party or to issue proceedings against him: see Ch 12 *post.*
28. Plus space at the bottom of the page for signed acknowledgement by the vendor of receipt of the specified deposit, see para **[10.16]** *post.*
29. It is doubtful if all these details are strictly necessary under the Statute of Frauds, see para **[6.18]** *ante*, but a record of them is obviously desirable in each case.
30. See para **[6.32]** *ante.*
31. Ie, as contained in the following conditions of sale. On the importance of such an acknowledgement especially in sales by auction, see para **[2.15]** *ante.*
32. See para **[9.07]** *infra.* This reiterates that the memorandum may be constituted by linking together different sections of one document or, even, different documents altogether, see para **[6.28]** *ante.*

required under the Family Home Protection Act 1976, in the case of a sale of a family home.[33] The reason for its position here[34] is, of course, to emphasise that such consent must be given "prior" to the "conveyance", which is defined in the Act as including a contract.[35] The purchaser's solicitor must ensure that the vendor's spouse completes this part of the form where this is appropriate. Whether it is appropriate is, of course, a matter which should be elicited by appropriate enquiries or requisitions, a subject which is examined in a later chapter.[36]

II. PARTICULARS AND TENURE

[9.07] The essential distinction between the particulars of sale, which we consider here, and the conditions of sale, which we consider in the next chapter, is that the former describe the subject-matter of the contract, whereas the latter state the terms upon which it is sold.[37] This distinction was discussed by Palles CB in *Irish Land Commission v Maquay*[38] in these terms[39]:

> "It will be observed that the 'Particulars' are referred to in this contract for the purpose only of describing the subject-matter of the sale, and that the 'Conditions of Sale' are referred to as those upon which the sale is to be made, in other words as the terms of the contract. I do not wish to be understood as saying that there may not be statements in the 'Particulars,' as distinguished from the 'Conditions of Sale,' which may be such as the Court may construe as amounting to a contract. But *prima facie* the contract is: 'We refer to the "Particulars" for the purpose of making certain the thing sold; and that thing, so sold, one of us sells and the other purchases upon the terms and conditions contained in the "Conditions of Sale". The reason I make this distinction between these different portions of the printed matter is that if we find, as possibly we may, something not exactly similar in the 'Conditions of Sale' and in the 'Particulars,' some variances between them, it appears to me that in determining this question the contract and 'Conditions' must prevail ..."[40]

[33.] See para **[5.08]** *ante*.

[34.] This transposition (from the back of the form) was first made in the 1986 edition of the contract form.

[35.] Section 1(1).

[36.] Para **[16.61]** *post*. Note also re pre-contact enquiries para **[5.08]** *ante*.

[37.] *Peilow v O'Carroll* (1972) 106 ILTR 29 at 47 (*per* Budd J).

[38.] (1891) 28 LR Ir 342.

[39.] See also *Torrance v Bolton* (1872) LR 14 Eq 124 at 130 (*per* Malins V-C); *Blaibery v Keeves* [1906] 2 Ch 175 at 184 (*per* Warrington J).

[40.] *Op cit* p 352.

Thus, the distinction is one based largely on conveyancing tradition and should not be regarded as absolutely rigid.[41] As we shall see, it is usually the case that the two parts of the contract form are linked together, eg, by the conditions purporting to qualify or restrict the scope of, or the vendor's liability for, the particulars of sale.[42]

[9.08] It is settled that the particulars of sale should delimit the land sold by giving both a physical and legal description.[43] As to the former, the duty of the vendor is to ensure that the property is identified with certainty, so that, in the event of a dispute, the Court will be able to determine exactly what is included within the contract for sale.[44] Subject to that basic principle, the vendor is protected by the *caveat emptor* rule[45] and, as we shall see, may be further protected by the conditions of sale.[46] On the other hand, care must be taken not to misdescribe the property,[47] though here again some protection may be afforded by the conditions of sale.[48] As to the latter, the duty is to indicate what title to the property is to be transferred to the purchaser, or, as it is sometimes put, the tenure, plus all benefits and burdens attaching to it. If this is not done, the general law implies that the vendor is contracting to sell the fee simple in possession free from incumbrances,[49] so that the vendor is regarded as being under a general duty to disclose when this is not what he is undertaking.[50] But, as we shall see, this duty of disclosure is a limited one only[51] and may be further restricted by the conditions of sale.[52]

A. Physical Description

[9.09] There is no absolute rule as to how the physical description of the property should be framed in the particulars of sale, but there are a number

41. See *Re Courcier and Harold's Contract* [1923] 1 Ch 565; *Cook v Taylor* [1942] Ch 349.
42. Para **[9.28]** *infra*. We have also seen that the particulars may be linked with the memorandum, para **[9.05]** *supra*. As regards linking them with other materials, eg, an auctioneers or estate agent's advertisement, see para **[9.16]** *infra*.
43. See the discussion in *McGillicuddy v Joy* [1959] IR 189. See also paras **[4.03-4]** *ante*. Note that the Law Society's contract form has the dual title "Particulars and Tenure" on p 2.
44. *Ibid*, p 211 (*per* Budd J). *Cf* the parcels clause in the conveyance, see para **[18.50]** *post*.
45. See generally para **[4.07]** *et seq, ante*. See also para **[9.22]** *infra*.
46. Para **[9.28]** *post*.
47. See para **[9.29]** *et seq, infra*.
48. Para **[9.36]** *infra*.
49. See the discussion in *Molphy v Coyne* (1919) 53 ILTR 177; *Healy v Farragher*, Supreme Court, unrep, 21 December 1972. See also *Martin v Cotter* (1846) Ir Eq R 351; *Larkin v Lord Rosse* (1846) 10 Ir Eq R 70; *Perrin v Roe* (1889) 25 LR Ir 37; *Hamilton v Bates* [1894] 1 IR 1. *Cf Re Ossemsley Estate Ltd.* [1937] 3 All ER 774 at 778 (*per* Greene MR); *Timmins v Moreland Street Property Co Ltd* [1958] Ch 110 at 118 (*per* Jenkins LJ).
50. See para **[9.24]** *infra*.
51. Paras **[9.21-3]** *infra*.
52. Para **[9.28]** *infra*.

of guiding principles which should be borne in mind. Failure to abide by these may result in the purchaser being able to pursue various remedies, eg, for misdescription. These remedies we consider later.[53]

1. Title Documents

[9.10] It should always be borne in mind that the contract for sale is only one step in the conveyancing process, and leads eventually to the stage when the vendor will be obliged to show his title to the property,[54] by producing appropriate documentation.[55] This documentation will usually include title deeds, in the case of unregistered land, or the land certificate or a copy of the Land Registry folio and map, in the case of registered land. One common rule of practice which is often invoked by solicitors is to adopt in the contract the description of the land contained in the vendor's title deeds or, in the case of registered land, to use the Land Registry reference, ie, the folio number relating to the land.[56] The point is that considerable difficulties may be created if it turns out that there is a discrepancy, in relation to the description of the land, between the particulars of sale in the contract and in the vendor's title documents. At the very least, the purchaser's solicitor is likely to raise requisitions on title about the matter.[57] However, care must be taken not to push this practice too far.[58] For example, the present contract may relate to part only of the land dealt with in the vendor's title documents, in which case the description in the latter is obviously inappropriate. Apart from such a case, title deeds relating to unregistered land sometimes have inconsistencies, so that the vendor's solicitor should not adopt the description in the latest deed without checking earlier deeds. Measurements given in title deeds are not always reliable and, as we shall see, maps or plans annexed to deeds are notoriously unreliable.[59]

[53.] Para **[9.29]** *infra*.

[54.] Though note that the conditions of sale may restrict this duty, or even seek to exclude it altogether, see para **[14.05]** *post*. Note also that, particularly in substantial commercial transactions, the title of the property may be disclosed prior to the contract in response to a "due diligence" exercise carried out by the purchaser's solicitor: see para **[5.14]** *et seq, ante. Cf* where the purchase of a rack rent-lease is involved: see para **[5.12]** *ante*.

[55.] See generally Ch 14 *post*.

[56.] See Fitzgerald, *Land Registry Practice*, (2nd ed, 1995) p 14.

[57.] See para **[15.10]** *post*. See also *Doran v Delaney* [1996] 1 ILRM 490, paras **[5.28]** *ante* and **[15.37]** *post*.

[58.] See *Gordon-Cumming v Houldsworth* [1910] AC 537 at 547 (*per* Lord Kinnear); *Re Sharman and Mead's Contract* [1936] Ch 755 at 758 (*per* Farwell J).

[59.] See *Re Pryde and Metson's Contract* (1968) 19 NILQ 214. Also *Healy v Farragher*, Supreme Court, unrep, 21 December 1972 (1/1971); *O'Reilly v Gleeson* [1975] IR 258. And see para **[9.12]** *infra*.

[9.11] It is common for the conditions of sale to seek to confer some protection in this regard. Thus, condition 14 of the Law Society's *General Conditions of Sale (1995 Edition)* requires the purchaser to accept "such evidence of identity as may be gathered from the description in the documents of title".[60] However, it has been held in England that such a provision is to be regarded as being subject to the implied restriction that it is effective only if the title deeds, or copies, do in fact identify the property satisfactorily.[61] If they do not do so, the vendor cannot enforce the contract against the purchaser.[62] However, such a condition may be drafted more widely, eg, by specifying that the description in the title documents is to be treated as "conclusive,"[63] in which case presumably the purchaser is bound by it whether or not it is accurate, though it is doubtful if the vendor would get specific performance where it was hopelessly inaccurate or misleading, so that the subject-matter of the sale could hardly be said to be identified at all.[64] As a general rule the courts take the view that conditions in a contract for the sale of land should be subject to the implied terms that they should (1) be reasonable; (2) have been reasonably within the contemplation of the parties when the contract was made; (3) be to the satisfaction of each party acting reasonably.[65] Furthermore, the *General Conditions*[66] do allow the purchaser to require the vendor to furnish[67] further evidence by way of a statutory declaration[68] that the property has been held and enjoyed for at least twelve years"[69] in accordance with the title shown.[70] But it is important to note that the conditions specify the twelve-year period only as a minimum, so that, where the failure to identify occurs in a much earlier

---

[60] The documents of title made available to the purchaser prior to the entering into of the contract should be listed in the "documents schedule" on p 3 of the contract form: see para **[9.39]** *infra.*

[61] *Curling v Austin* (1862) 2 Dr & Sm 129 at 135 (*per* Kindersley V-C).

[62] *Flower v Hartopp* (1843) 6 Beav 476. See also *Re Bramwell's Contract* [1969] 1 WLR 1659.

[63] See *Nicholl v Chambers* (1852) 11 CB 996.

[64] See *Beyfus v Lodge* [1925] Ch 350.

[65] *Per* Ellis J in *Draisey v Fitzpatrick* [1981] ILRM 219 at 223. He also held that the onus of proving unreasonableness, on the balance of probabilities, lies on the party alleging it.

[66] Cond 14.

[67] At the purchaser's expense, *ibid.*

[68] See Statutory Declarations Act 1835, largely replaced by the Statutory Declarations Act 1938. See O'Connor, *The Irish Notary* (1987), Ch VII.

[69] This is, of course, the limitation period under the Statute of Limitations 1957 and is the crucial period so far as the vendor's "good holding" title is concerned. On the latter concept, see para **[14.12]** *post.*

[70] It seems that the purchaser can insist upon the declaration being made by a person independent of the vendor, see *Hobson v Bell* (1839) 2 Beav 17. Cond 14 of the *General Conditions* refers to it being made by a "competent person".

deed, the purchaser should, and may under the conditions,[71] require better evidence of the title.[72]

2. Plans

[9.12] It is not uncommon for the particulars of sale to describe the property by reference to a map or plan, eg, in the time-honoured form - "more particularly described on the map hereunto annexed."[73] This may be particularly useful where part only of land hitherto the subject of a single title is being sold, so that there is nothing in the existing title documents to explain where the boundary between the two parts[74] lies and this may not be obvious on inspection. Unfortunately, a map is only as good as its mapper and all too often the map is an ill-drafted piece of rough-work, totally lacking in accuracy as to scale and measurements. So far from being useful, it turns out to be positively misleading and gives rise to disputes later.[75] And this is something to be borne in mind if reference is going to be made to maps attached to old title deeds. Here there is a double risk: first, that the map was inaccurate from the beginning and, secondly, even if it was accurate when drawn up, it has ceased to be accurate due to changes in the property since then. Yet it cannot be emphasised too often that, if a map is going to be incorporated by reference into the particulars of sale, it must be drawn with accuracy, if necessary by a professional mapper. This is particularly the case where property is being divided into numerous parts, eg, a building estate, for then a plan or map covering the whole estate becomes extremely important, if not essential.[76] Each part or lot on the estate can then be sold by reference to the plan or map covering the whole area of the estate.

[71.] It is arguable that the vendor can be required to furnish a declaration as to possession earlier than twelve years ago, since his obligation under the condition is to furnish "at least" a twelve-year declaration. There is also the positive statement in cond 14 that the vendor "shall be obliged to furnish such information as is in his possession relative to the identity and extent of the subject property". He is not, however, required to define exact boundaries etc nor parts held under different titles: see para **[9.14]** *infra*.

[72.] See *Bird v Fox* (1853) 11 Hare 40.

[73.] See *Healy v Farragher* Supreme Court, unrep, 21 December 1972 (1/1971); *O'Reilly v Gleeson* [1975] IR 258. The alternative is to avoid such a formula and to refer the map or plan "for the purposes of identification only"; this avoids the risk of a misdescription, which is particularly prevalent with an old map now out-of-date. *Cf* in deeds, see para **[18.64]** *post*.

[74.] Ie, the part sold and the part retained. *A fortiori*, where a major subdivision into several parts is being made, eg, a building estate.

[75.] See *Re Pryde and Metson's Contract* (1968) 19 NILQ 214. And note the criticism in *Scarfe v Adams* [1981] 1 All ER 843 about use of an ordnance survey map of too small a scale. See also para **[18.63]** *post*.

[76.] See further, para **[19.09]** *post*. See also on development schemes and multi-storey buildings, Fitzgerald *Land Registry Practice* (2nd ed, 1995), p 73 *et seq*.

[9.13] Some of these problems can be avoided in relation to registered land, because one of the essential features of the Land Registry system is that registered land is defined by reference to a registry map, which is based on the Ordnance Survey map for the area.[77] Thus, normally the Land Registry map can be relied upon, but it should be noted that technically the map is not conclusive as to the boundaries or extent of the land in question.[78] However, adjoining owners may apply to have the boundaries between their lands entered on the register as conclusive as between them and their successors in title, though this does not confirm the title to their lands.[79] And it seems that little use is made of this procedure in practice.[80] The Registrar may also enter the boundaries as conclusive, where part of registered land only is transferred, between the part transferred and the part retained,[81] and may settle any question as to the boundaries or extent of registered land when it is being transferred.[82] In each of these cases a cross-reference in the particulars of sale to the registry map is obviously the best form of physical description of the land. Fortunately, the advantages to be gained from using a copy of the Land Registry map which used to be lost in practice because of considerable delays met in obtaining such a copy, which were caused largely by severe staffing problems in the Registry, have been improved in recent times with advances in Land Registry procedures.[83] There are some cases where a copy of the map must be obtained, eg, to obtain consent of the Land Commission to a sub-division, yet, although it is advisable to obtain a copy in all cases, all too often the sale is completed without waiting for the Registry to issue one. The dangers of this practice, however understandable its adoption, cannot be emphasised too strongly.

[77.] See Fitzgerald, *op cit*, pp 68-69.

[78.] See Registration of Title Act 1964, s 85. This was also the rule under the Local Registration of Title (Ir) Act 1891, s 55. See *Hickey v Broderick* [1931] LJ Ir 136; *McManus v Kiernan* [1939] IR 297; *Gillespie v Hogg* [1947] Ir Jur Rep 51 (where a distinction was drawn between minor and substantial errors); *Geraghty v Rohan Industrial Estates Ltd* [1988] IR 419; *Tomkin Estates Ltd v O'Callaghan* High Court, unrep, 16 March 1995 (1992/8152P). The register is conclusive as to boundaries in certain cases, eg, where they have been ascertained and defined in an Incumbered or Landed Estates Court conveyance or Land Commission vesting order, see 1964 Act, s 86; *cf* 1891 Act, s 57. See generally Fitzgerald, *op cit*, Ch 4.

[79.] 1964 Act, s 87.

[80.] Fitzgerald, *op cit*, p 69.

[81.] 1964 Act, s 88(1).

[82.] 1964 Act, s 88(2).

[83.] *Fitzgerald, op cit*, p 71 *et seq.*

3. Boundaries

[9.14] In view of the problems of exact definition of boundaries in the case of unregistered land,[84] it is not surprising that the conditions of sale usually seek to protect the vendor from having to give a precise definition. Thus, condition 14 of the Law Society's *General Conditions of Sale (1995 Edition)* specifies that the vendor "shall not be required to define exact boundaries, fences, ditches, hedges[85] or walls or to specify what walls (if any) are of a party nature,[86] or separately identify parts of the property held under different titles.[87] The reason for these provisions is that it is often very difficult to determine questions as to the ownership of boundaries and, of course, impossible to anticipate when such questions will arise.

4. Fixtures and Fittings

[9.15] We have mentioned in earlier chapters the importance of determining precisely what fixtures, fittings or chattels are to be included in the sale.[88] One way of doing this is to include in the particulars a list of the items in question, or to incorporate by reference an inventory attached to the contract. If this is done, it has the advantage that it will attract the warranty by the vendor contained in the Law Society's *General Conditions of Sale (1995 Edition)* that at the date of actual completion they "shall not be subject to any lease, rental hire, hire-purchase or credit sale agreement or chattel mortgage."[89] In this respect the standard form contract recognises the provisions contained in s 12 of the Sale of Goods Act 1893, whereby there is implied into a contract for the sale of goods on behalf of the seller a condition that he has a right to sell the goods, a warranty that the buyer will enjoy quiet possession and a warranty that the goods will be free from any charge or incumbrance not declared or known to the buyer before the contract was made.[90] Thus, if after the sale a hire purchase company repossesses what was in effect its property, the purchaser can sue the vendor

---

84. See para **[9.12]** *supra*.
85. See further para **[18.62]** *post*.
86. On this thorny question, see *Irish Land Law* (2nd ed, 1986), paras 7.53-62.
87. The provision as to identification of parts of property held under different titles reverses the common law rule requiring the vendor to identify them, see *Dawson v Brinckman* (1850) 3 M & G 53; *Munro v Taylor* (1852) 3 M & G 713.
88. See paras **[3.40]** and **[5.07]** *ante*.
89. Cond 46. Note that cond 2 of the *General Conditions* defines "purchase price" as extending to cover additional moneys to be paid for "purchased chattels", which are, in turn, defined as "such chattels, fittings, tenant's fixtures and other items as are included in the sale".
90. On s 12 see *Stock v Urey* [1955] NI 1. See also *O'Reilly v Fineman* [1942] Ir Jur Rep 36; *Anderson v Ryan* [1967] IR 34. These provisions cannot be contracted out of unless it can be shown that the buyer is not a consumer and that the exemption clause is fair and reasonable: see s 22 of the Sale of Goods and Supply of Services Act 1980 (inserting s 55(4) of the 1893 Act): see Clark, *Contract Law in Ireland* (3rd ed, 1992), p 164 *et seq*.

for breach of warranty.[91] It should, however, be noted that if such items are included in the contract in this way, thereby increasing the total consideration for the transaction, the risk may be that the purchaser will incur a higher amount of stamp duty, ie, the amount attributable to the extra items may be just sufficient to push the total purchase price for the entire transaction to a level which attracts a higher amount of duty.[92] Where items which are clearly chattels are included in the sale, the purchaser's solicitor should advise his client to consider making a separate contract with the vendor as to the items in question. Indeed, the most prudent course may be to advise the parties to deal with the sale of such personal chattels themselves and verbally, and to put no mention of the transaction in any of the documents relating to the transfer of the land. This may avoid any query as to whether the transfer of the land is part of a larger transaction or series of transactions relating to the land.[93] However, the parties must beware that, in doing so, they apportion realistic values to the items regarded as chattels. Under no circumstances should they or their solicitors[94] attempt to evade stamp duty payable on the property being sold by inflating the value of the chattels and thereby seeking to reduce the value attributed to the land. The penalties and sanctions which can be imposed by the Revenue Commissioners for this sort of action are severe indeed[95] and the Law Society's Conveyancing Committee was recently prompted to issue a warning to solicitors that they also run the risk of sanctions for unprofessional conduct.[96]

5. Other Documents

[9.16] The question sometimes arises as to whether other documents not specifically referred to or expressly incorporated in[97] the particulars of sale may nevertheless be read with the particulars so as to add to or vary or otherwise explain them. The classic example is a leaflet or advertisement

---

[91.] Note that the warranty is confined to items which are personalty as opposed to realty, ie fixtures in the technical sense, see *Irish Land Law* (2nd ed, 1986), para 4.155. Thus the warranty covers so-called tenants' "fixtures" as the definition of "purchased chattels" in cond 2 makes clear: see fn 89 *supra*. Fixtures in the technical sense, as part of the land conveyed, are covered by the covenants for title in the conveyance, see para **[21.05]** *et seq, post*.

[92.] See para **[20.40]** *post*.

[93.] As to "certificates for value" see para **[18.108]** *post*.

[94.] Note the warning to solicitors issued by the English Court of Appeal in *Saunders v Edwards* [1987] 2 All ER 651.

[95.] See the Revenue Commissioners' Statement of Practice *Collection and Enforcement of Stamp Duty* (SP-SD/1/91). See also Donegan and Friel, *Irish Stamp Duty Law* (1995), Ch 13; *Butterworths Tax Guide 1995-96*, Ch 66.

[96.] Drawing attention to a memo issued by the DSBA: see the *Gazette* May/June 1995, p 159.

[97.] *Cf* documents listed in the "Documents Schedule": see para **[9.39]** *infra*.

relating to the property prepared by an auctioneer or estate agent, which, indeed, is often expressly referred to as containing "particulars of sale". The general rule is that such external documentation may not be referred to unless the contract itself justifies such a reference to it. Thus, in *Thomson v Guy*[98] an auctioneer's advertisements were admitted in evidence to show that the contract itself misdescribed the premises sold. Crampton J explained:

> "It is said that the effect of admitting this advertisement will be to enlarge the contract; that would be against all principle, but it is not so; the advertisement is referred to for a full and particular description of the thing to be sold, and is as much part of the contract as if it were recited in terms in it. Where a document refers to another, it thereby makes that other evidence."[99]

On the other hand, in *Peilow v O'Carroll*[100] the Supreme Court held that an auctioneer's advertisement and leaflet could not be regarded as part of the contract for sale, even though the conditions of sale contained (as is often the case prior to an auction) an invitation to interested persons to apply to the auctioneer for further particulars. Budd J said:

> "It would seem to me that what was intended by the invitation to apply for further particulars was that further particulars of that which was offered for sale in the conditions of sale, such as the accommodation in the house and the like, would be furnished on request. To hold that every particular furnished by an auctioneer with regard to the nature of a premises for sale becomes incorporated into the contract on his furnishing such particulars seems to me prima facie a somewhat untenable proposition in that it would involve the inclusion in the contract of puffing descriptions by an auctioneer.[101]

---

98. (1844) 7 Ir LR 6.

99. *Ibid*, p 15. *Cf* Pennefather CJ at p 12.

100. (1972) 106 ILTR 29. In fact, the actual decision of the Court was that the statements made in the auctioneer's advertisement and leaflet were misrepresentations inducing the purchaser to enter into the contract, entitling him to repudiate the contract and to resist successfully a claim for specific performance by the vendor, see paras **[5.26]** *ante* and **[13.51]** *post*.

101. *Ibid*, p 47. *Cf Thomson v Guy* (1844) 7 Ir LR 6 at 15 (*per* Crampton J): "Exaggerated representations, as puffing advertisements, are not to be taken into consideration....."; *Smith v Lynn* [1951] NI 69 at 76-7 (*per* Curran J): "Such advertisements, however, must be looked at in their true perspective. They do not purport to be detailed reports by experts as to the condition of the property to be sold. It is common knowledge that the purpose of such advertisements is to draw attention to the good points of the property and that one usually finds in such advertisements rather flourishing statements ...." See also *National Bank v Beirne* (1901) 35 ILTR 9 (solicitor having carriage of sale by auction responsible for accuracy of the particulars of sale; not part of duty of auctioneer to add description particulars).

B. Legal Description

[9.17] Just as the vendor must give a physical description of the subject matter of the sale, so must he give an accurate legal description.¹⁰² Thus, he should indicate the tenure by which the vendor holds, eg, whether it is freehold or leasehold and, if the latter, whether he holds under a lease or underlease.¹⁰³ If nothing is said on the matter, the vendor is deemed to contract to sell the fee simple in possession free from incumbrances,¹⁰⁴ and, if he has less than that, he may be guilty of misdescription or, at least, in breach of his duty of disclosure.¹⁰⁵ The rule relating to tenure would seem to apply equally to registered land, ie, it should indicate what sort of registered title the vendor has, eg, whether freehold or leasehold and whether absolute, qualified or possessory.¹⁰⁶ Though, here again incorporation of the Land Registry description by cross-reference should ensure compliance with the rule.¹⁰⁷

[9.18] The particulars may also indicate rights the benefit of which attaches to the land sold, eg, easements or restrictive covenants enjoyed in respect of other land. However, this is not always strictly necessary as the conveyance will pass some such existing rights without express mention, eg, easements.¹⁰⁸ This point arose in *Peilow v O'Carroll*,¹⁰⁹ where one issue involved was whether a right of way appurtenant to the premises was included in the sale, though it was not mentioned in the particulars of sale. The Supreme Court held that the sale of land includes appurtenant rights. Budd J said:

> "It may be remarked apart from any citation of authority for the proposition
> that it seems well founded in common sense having regard to the ideas
> usually held by those having to deal with the sale of land either for vendor
> or purchaser. The usual view of such persons is I venture to think that when

---

¹⁰² See para **[9.08]** *supra*. See also *Re Mitchell and McElhinney's Contract* [1902] 1 IR 83; *Re McDermott and Kellett's Contract* (1904) 4 NIJR 89. And see *Re Robb and Spillane's Contract* (1901) 1 NIJR 206 at 207 (*per* Chatterton V-C).

¹⁰³ *Re Robb and Spillane's Contract* (1901) 1 NIJR 206; *Power v Coates* (1905) 39 ILTR 221. See also *Re Russ and Brown's Contract* [1934] Ch 34; *Re Thompson and Cottrell's Contract* [1943] Ch 97. *Cf Becker v Partridge* [1966] 2 QB 155.

¹⁰⁴ *Healy v Farragher* Supreme Court, unrep, 21 December 1972. See also para **[9.08]** *supra*.

¹⁰⁵ See para **[9.24]** *infra*.

¹⁰⁶ *Re Brine and Davies' Contract* [1935] Ch 388. See also Fitzgerald, *Land Registry Practice* (2nd ed, 1995).

¹⁰⁷ See para **[9.10]** *supra*.

¹⁰⁸ Under s 6 of the Conveyancing Act 1881; *cf* the rule in *Wheeldon v Burrows* (1879) 12 Ch D 31. See the discussion in *Irish Land Law* (2nd ed, 1986), paras 6.061-8. See also para **[9.43]** *infra*.

¹⁰⁹ (1972) 106 ILTR 29.

a house is sold there goes with it such rights in the way of easements as are appurtenant to it. There readily occur to the mind such easements as rights of ancient lights and the right to have one's water supply and drainage system under a neighbour's lands. It would surprise most people engaged in the sale of houses to find that such rights would not pass on the sale of a house unless expressly mentioned."[110]

The Court also emphasised the obvious corollary of this rule, namely, that, if the sale does not include such rights, the vendor must make this clear in the particulars of sale, or otherwise bring it to the notice of the purchaser by the time of the sale. Thus, Budd J said later:

"... where in a sale of land a vendor has inadvertently described the property for sale in such a fashion that the contract includes either expressly or by implication of law such rights of way as are appurtenant to the property it is the duty of the vendor to correct the conditions of sale so as to exclude that which he does not wish to sell or convey or which he cannot sell or convey. If he does not do this he must make it clear to any would-be purchaser either before or at the sale, that such a right is not in fact included in the sale."[111]

[9.19] Much more important, however, is the rule that the vendor should disclose certain burdens on the land being sold. This duty of disclosure arises only in some cases, for it must be remembered that the general principle governing contracts for the sale of land remains *caveat emptor*.[112] Furthermore, non-disclosure of burdens must be distinguished from a misdescription of them in the particulars.[113] Like a misrepresentation,[114] a misdescription involves a positive statement or act, whereas, of course, non-disclosure involves an omission.

1. Duty of Disclosure

[9.20] The general rule of contract law is, of course, that there is no general duty of disclosure by the vendor; this arises only in special cases, eg, contracts *uberrimae fidei*, such as insurance contracts.[115] Contracts for the

---

[110.] *Ibid*, p 47.

[111.] *Ibid*, p 49. See also Fitzgerald J at p 59: "It appears to me that when it is admitted that such a contract would carry the right of way, if it still subsisted, the onus of proving that in this case the effect of the contract should be limited, rested upon the vendor to establish such a limitation."

[112.] See *Re Flynn and Newman's Contract* [1948] IR 104 at 109-10 (*per* Kingsmill Moore J) See also para **[4.04]** *ante*.

[113.] See further, para **[9.31]** *infra*.

[114.] See para **[5.26]** *ante*. As distinct from a misdescription, a misrepresentation does not involve a breach of contract, see para **[9.29]** *infra*.

[115.] See Clark, *Contract Law in Ireland* (3rd ed, 1992), p 247 *et seq*.

sale of land are not such contracts, but they do occupy an intermediate position in that the vendor is bound to disclose certain defects in title.[116] It is necessary, therefore, to examine the precise scope of this duty and how it may be restricted by the conditions of sale.

(i) Physical Defects

[9.21] It is clear that the duty of disclosure relates only to defects in title and does not cover physical defects. In respect of the latter, the *caveat emptor* rule applies fully and the purchaser must protect himself by eg, inspecting the property.[117] However, it may sometimes be difficult to distinguish between defects in title and defects in the physical condition of the property, and, indeed, in a particular case the distinction may be blurred. Thus, in *Re Flynn and Newman's Contract*,[118] the vendor-lessee did not disclose that his lessor had served a notice on him requiring repairs to be made to the property. The lease contained the usual covenant to keep the property in good repair, but not a provision for forfeiture or re-entry on breach of that covenant. Kingsmill Moore J said:

> "A liability to ejectment for forfeiture, crystallised by service of a repairing notice by the landlord, is clearly a defect in title to which the vendor must call attention. Mere disrepair which may involve an action for breach of covenant, but which, in the absence of a proviso for re-entry, cannot be a ground of forfeiture, is not a defect of title, but a defect in subject-matter. Provided that the terms of the lease were known to the purchaser before signing the contract, and the inspection of the property was open to him if he so desired, it seems to me that no breach of any legal obligation would be involved in failure to disclose the state of repair or the letter from the landlord ..."[119]

On the other hand, in *McCann v Valentine*,[120] where a sanitary notice served by the local authority under the Public Health (Ireland) Act 1878, requiring the vendor to abate a nuisance, was not disclosed to the purchaser, Porter MR said:

[116.] *Re Flynn and Newman's Contract* [1948] IR 104 at 109 (*per* Kingsmill Moore J). See also *Thompson v Lambert* (1868) IR 2 Eq 433 at 438-9 (*per* Walsh MR). And see further on this duty in relation to deduction of title, Ch 14 *post*.

[117.] *Geryani v O'Callaghan* High Court, unrep, 25 January 1995 (1994/677 Sp). See generally, Ch 4, *ante*. Note the exception where there is an implied warranty as to fitness or quality, see para **[4.12]** *ante*.

[118.] [1948] IR 104.

[119.] *Ibid*, p 112. This was so even in the absence of a condition of sale whereby the purchaser was deemed to have full knowledge of the state of the property, *ibid*, p 113, and see para **[9.43]** *infra*.

[120.] (1901) 1 NIJR 28.

"... the receipt of the sanitary notice should have been disclosed at the auction, as it was most necessary that a purchaser should know what he was buying. The knowledge that such a notice had been received, and had not been complied with (whether it was enforceable by the sanitary authority or not) would undoubtedly prevent a purchaser from giving as large a sum as he otherwise would."[121]

(ii) Patent Defects

[9.22] It is clear that the *caveat emptor* rule applies to the extent that the vendor need not disclose patent defects in title, ie, those which would be reasonably discoverable by the purchaser from inspection of the land or which are otherwise obvious from facts or materials brought to his attention.[122] In *Re Flanagan and McGarvey and Thompson's Contract*,[123] Black J stated:

"It is well settled that a purchaser of property must take it subject to any defects which are patent on inspection and are not inconsistent with the description contained in the contract for sale ... In order that a defect may be a patent defect within the meaning of this rule it is not enough that there exists on the land an object of sense that might put a careful purchaser on inquiry. To be a patent defect the defect must either be visible to the eye, or arise by necessary implication from something visible to the eye."[124]

Thus, the existence of a right of way enjoyed by some other landowner, or the public at large, may be apparent on inspection.[125] Indeed, this question arose in the *Flanagan* case and Black J concluded:

"I think that the existence and the nature of the path, leading nowhere but to the back door of the house, showed that it served no purpose other than as a way from the road to this back door to which there was no other means of access, and necessarily indicated as a practical certainty to anyone who saw it that the occupier of the house would have a right of way over it to the back door of his house."[126]

[121.] *Ibid*, p 28. See also *Re Lewis* (1908) 42 ILTR 210. *Cf Re Leyland and Taylor's Contract* [1900] 2 Ch 625; *Carlish v Salt* [1906] 1 Ch 335; *Re Englefield Holdings Ltd and Sinclair's Contract* [1962] 1 WLR 1119. And see the contractual duty under the Law Society's *General Conditions of Sale* para **[9.28]** *infra*.

[122.] *Re Flynn and Newman's Contract* [1948] IR 104 at 110 (*per* Kingsmill Moore J), where it was emphasised that this rule applied only "where no question of actual misdescription is involved". See also *Dykes v Blake* (1838) 4 Bing NC 463; *Denny v Hancock* (1870) 23 LT 686.

[123.] [1945] NI 32.

[124.] *Ibid*, p 38.

[125.] *Cf Hibernian Bank v Cassidy* (1902) 36 ILTR 156. See also *Ashburner v Sewell* [1891] 3 Ch 405.

[126.] *Op cit*, p 39. *Cf O'Brien v Kearney* [1995] 2 ILRM 232.

Nevertheless, many solicitors take the view that in practice it is much safer for the vendor to disclose all rights of way which affect the property.

[9.23] A point of some controversy has been whether the existence of occupiers other than the vendor is a patent defect, in the sense that the vendor need not disclose to the purchaser the precise rights or interests of such persons. The general principle of law is that the fact of occupation is constructive notice to a purchaser of the rights or interests of the occupier.[127] In Ireland this principle was applied in *Carroll v Keayes*,[128] where it was held that notice of the existence of tenants was notice of the fact that they were yearly tenants. Christian LJ stated:

> "... the principle of it [ie, the doctrine of constructive notice] is that the vendee's duty of inquiry, springing from notice of possession, supersedes the vendor's duty to disclose, and if both remain silent the purchaser is held to take subject to all existing rights ..."[129]

Later he stated bluntly:

> "... constructive notice of right, springing from actual notice of possession, closes the mouth of a purchaser as against his own vendor, as it unquestionably does as against the tenant himself."[130]

Carroll v Keayes was followed by the Irish Court of Appeal in *Clements v Conroy*,[131] where it was held that, since the purchaser had been apprised by the particulars and conditions of sale of the existence of tenants occupying the property, it was his duty to enquire as to the particular tenure by which the tenants held.[132] Holmes LJ stated:

---

127. Often known as the rule in *Hunt v Luck* [1902] 1 Ch 428. See *Ulster Bank Ltd v Shanks* [1982] NI 143, but *cf* the approach of the Supreme Court in *Bank of Ireland v Smyth* [1996] 1 ILRM 241 (a case where a spouse's consent was required under the Family House Protection Act 1976): see para **[16.69]** sub-para (b) *post. Cf* rights of persons in actual occupation under s 72 (1)(j) of the Registration of Title Act 1964: see para **[16.23]** *post*.

128. (1873) IR 8 Eq 97, following the English decision in *James v Litchfield* (1869) LR 9 Eq 51. But the latter was not followed by the English Court of Appeal in *Caballero v Henty* (1874) LR 9 Ch 447. See also *Nelthorpe v Holgate* (1844) 1 Coll 203; *Penny v Watts* (1849) 1 Mac & G 150; *Phillips v Miller* (1875) LR 10 CP 420; *Yandle & Sons v Sutton* [1922] 2 Ch 199. *Cf Timmins v Moreland Street Property Co Ltd* [1958] Ch 110.

129. *Ibid*, p 136. See also Lord O'Hagan LC at pp 117-8.

130. *Ibid*, p 138.

131. [1911] 2 IR 500. The Court stated that, in the event of any conflict between the *Carroll* decision and the English decision in *Caballero v Henty* (see fn 128 *supra*) the former should be followed in Ireland. See *ibid*, p 525 (*per* Walker LC). See also *Healy v Farragher* Supreme Court, unrep, 21 December 1972 (1/1971).

132. *Ibid*, p 524 (*per* Walker LC). See also *Spunner v Walsh* (1847) 10 Ir Eq R 386 (*affd* 11 Ir Eq R 597); *Vignolles v Bowen* (1847) 12 Ir Eq R 194.

"In the absence of authority, I should hold that the true rule of law is that, when a purchaser is informed by the vendor that the premises are held by tenants at certain specified rents, it is for him to inquire what their tenure is; and that he cannot complain that he has been misled if he afterwards discovers that such tenure is greater than what he, without any reason, assumed it to have been."[133]

When the purchaser inspects the lands before signing the contract, he should take particular care, if he finds livestock grazing on them, to confirm with the vendor that he (the vendor) owns the animals. Sometimes they may be grazing there under an agistment contract,[134] which may not even be in writing and so no document exists which might be shown to the purchaser or his solicitor, and, if the purchaser enters into the contract without looking into the matter, he may find himself involved in a dispute with the owner of the livestock.

(iii) Latent Defects

[9.24] The duty of disclosure in relation to contracts for the sale of land arises essentially in respect of latent defects in title, ie, those which are not "patent to the eye," eg, from inspection of the property.[135] The purchaser cannot complain if the defects were obvious to him[136] or should have been so if he or his solicitor had taken the normal precautions reasonably to be expected in such a case. However that raises the interesting point as to whether the purchaser may be fixed with notice in cases where the vendor or his solicitor does not follow traditional conveyancing practice, eg, where he adopts what has become a fairly common practice of furnishing a photocopy of the root of title deed, or even all the relevant deeds, with a draft contract.[137] It may be argued that the purchaser should then be deemed to have notice of all the contents of that deed or those deeds, at the time of

---

[133.] *Ibid*, p 530. Earlier he stated: "Premises of this kind in a country town [ie, Omagh Co Tyrone] are as likely to be held for a term of years as from year to year." *Ibid*, p 529.

[134.] See Wylie, *Irish Landlord and Tenant Law*, para 3.29 *et seq.*

[135.] *Re Flynn and Newman's Contract* [1948] IR 104 at 110 (*per* Kingsmill Moore J). See also *Geryani v O'Callaghan* High Court, unrep, 25 January 1995 (1994/677 Sp).

[136.] Actual knowledge of the defect, whether patent or latent, on the part of the purchaser when he enters into the contract clearly excludes any breach of duty to disclose by the vendor, see *Hibernian Bank v Cassidy* (1902) 36 ILTR 156 at 157 (*per* Porter MR). See also *Timmins v Moreland Street Property Co Ltd* [1958] Ch 110 at 132 (*per* Romer LJ). But this rule as to knowledge in the purchaser applies only to "irremovable" defects. If they are "removable, ie, the vendor can get rid of them by the time of completion, eg, by discharging a mortgage, the purchaser may, subject to the terms of the contract, require this to be done, see *Re Gloag and Miller's Contract* (1883) 23 Ch D 320.

[137.] See para **[14.02]** *post*. But note the contractual provisions discussed later, see para **[9.39]** *infra*.

signing the contract, including all defects discoverable from investigation of the title so deduced.[138] On the other hand, it may be questioned whether the vendor can in this way reverse the traditional practice that title is not deduced by him and investigated by the purchaser until after the contract is entered into.[139] But if the purchaser's solicitor finds photocopies of some or all of the title documents included with the draft contract, he is rather put on the spot and, perhaps, ought to insist, before he allows his client to sign the contract, that it is made clear that the vendor is still expected to show a good title to the property, including disclosure of all latent defects.[140] In recent times the Law Society's Conveyancing Committee has reminded practitioners that its standard conditions of sale are drafted on the basis that the vendor should disclose sufficient details of his title prior to the contract to enable the purchaser to judge the adequacy of the title before committing himself to contract, but this is not meant to displace the traditional *post-contract* investigation of title.[141] In particular the Committee has disapproved of the practice of furnishing purchaser's solicitors with copies of all the title documents along with a draft contract containing a restrictive special condition along the following lines:

> "The title shall consist of the documents listed in the Documents Schedule and shall be accepted by the purchaser as full and adequate evidence of the Vendor's title to the subject property."

Such a condition in effect forces the purchaser's solicitor to make a full investigation of the title[142] prior to the contract, which is particularly unfair where the sale is by public auction, because in such cases the client is, at most, a *potential* purchaser only (like all other possible bidders) until the auction takes place and the property is knocked down to the highest bidder.[143] In the Conveyancing Committee's view the Documents Schedule should be limited to:

(a) the root of title[144];

[138.] See Barnsley, *Conveyancing Law and Practice* (3rd ed, 1988), pp 138 and 331. See also (1962) L Soc Gaz 480, 667 and 757; (1963) L Soc Gaz 42, 97 and 300.

[139.] See Chs 14-16 *post*.

[140.] But note that the conditions of sale may seek to restrict the duty of disclosure, see paras **[9.28]** and **[9.39]** *infra*.

[141.] See the *Gazette* January/February 1990, p 8 and March 1995, p 83.

[142.] Note that cond 6 of the *General Conditions of Sale (1995 ed)* puts the purchaser on notice of covenants etc in documents specified in the documents schedule: see para **[9.39]** *infra*.

[143.] See para **[2.54]** *ante*.

[144.] On this concept see para **[14.56]** *post*.

(b) any document to which title is stated to pass under the special conditions;

(c) any document specifically referred to in a special condition.

In the light of this the purchaser's solicitor should clearly resist the inclusion of the type of condition quoted above and, if the vendor's solicitor insists upon it, should not proceed without fully warning his client in writing of the risks involved.[145]

[9.25] It is also settled that the vendor is obliged to disclose only latent defects of which he is aware or of which he should have been aware.[146] Thus, as a general rule,[147] a vendor of leasehold property is under a duty to disclose onerous covenants in the lease,[148] and on this Chatterton V-C said in *Power v Barrett*[149]:

> "I take the law to be as there[150] laid down, and that there is now no question that it is so - that if the purchaser state the object which he has in purchasing, and the seller is silent as to a covenant in the lease prohibiting or interfering with that object, his silence would be equivalent to a representation that there was no such prohibitory covenant, *although he was not aware of the extent or operation of the covenant*. I am of opinion that a vendor in the position of the plaintiff here *is bound to know what covenants are in his lease*, and that he is bound, moreover, to communicate such knowledge to an intending purchaser - provided such covenant can be reasonably interpreted as affecting the object which he is aware the purchaser has in view of purchasing the premises, and I think that the plaintiff has not fulfilled that obligation."[151]

It should be noted, however, that the Law Society's standard form contract contains a provision whereby the vendor may relieve himself of this

---

[145.] It must, of course, be recognised that there may be cases where a full investigation of the title prior to the contract is justified and the client should be so advised. An obvious example would be where a highly valuable industrial or commercial property is being acquired and the investigation of the title should be part of a "due diligence" exercise carried out by the purchaser's solicitor: see para **[5.14]** *ante*.

[146.] *Molphy v Coyne* (1919) 53 ILTR 177 at 179 (*per* Powell J).

[147.] But the conditions of sale may restrict its application, see para **[9.39]** *infra*.

[148.] See further, para **[9.27]** *infra*. *Cf* as regards usual covenants, *Spunner v Walsh* (1847) 10 Ir Eq R 386 (*affd* 11 Ir Eq R 597); *Vignolles v Bowen* (1847) 12 Ir Eq R 194. See Wylie, *Irish Landlord and Tenant*, para 5.09.

[149.] (1887) 19 LR Ir 450. See also *Re Haedicke and Lipski's Contract* [1901] 2 Ch 666; *Molyneux v Hewtry* [1903] 2 KB 487; *Melzak v Lilienfield* [1926] Ch 480; *Flexman v Corbett* [1930] 1 Ch 672.

[150.] Eg, *Flight v Barton* (1832) 3 My & K 282, applied in *Spunner v Walsh, supra* and *Cullen v O'Meara* (1869) IR 4 CL 537.

[151.] *Op cit* pp 457-8 (italics added). *Cf Spunner v Walsh* (1847) 10 Ir Eq R 386 at 400 (*per* Smith MR) (*aff'd* 11 Ir Eq R 597).

obligation by providing the purchaser with the title documents in question and requiring him to discover the defects for himself.[152]

[9.26] A wide variety of matters have been held to be defects in title which ought to have been disclosed by the vendor (subject to conditions of sale restricting the duty). Thus, defects which will prevent the vendor from conveying the precise title or estate he is contracting to sell should be disclosed.[153] Similarly, onerous burdens, such as incumbrances on the land, must be disclosed. There was considerable case law in Ireland on the subject of whether tithe rentcharges should be disclosed.[154] Prior to the Irish Church Act 1869, which, *inter alia*, provided a scheme for their redemption,[155] the general rule seems to have been that so much land in Ireland was subject to these charges that a purchaser was bound to assume that the land was subject to such a charge and to make suitable enquiries.[156] The vendor was not, therefore, under a duty to disclose the existence of the charge.[157] After the 1869 Act, however, views differed on the matter. The Landed Estates Court[158] continued to take the view that the vendor was not under a duty of disclosure,[159] but other judges took a different view.[160] This particular point was resolved finally by the Land Act 1984, under s 7(3) of which such rent charges are deemed to have been extinguished on 28 September 1975 and to be no longer payable. Other burdens which should be disclosed are easements[161] and restrictive covenants,[162] and any other rights reserved or

---

[152.] See further, para **[9.39]** *infra*.

[153.] See *Re McVicker's Contract* (1890) 25 LR Ir 307; *Manifold v Johnston* [1902] 1 IR 7. See also *Re Brine and Davies' Contract* [1935] Ch 388 (non-disclosure that "freehold registered property" held by possessory title only).

[154.] On such charges, which are not as common as they once were, see *Irish Land Law* (2nd ed, 1986), paras 6.120-30.

[155.] *Ibid*, paras 6.124-7.

[156.] *Hamilton v Bates* [1894] 1 IR 1 at 3 (*per* Porter MR). *Cf re* lands known to be held under letters patent and part of the plantation of Ulster (see *Irish Land Law* (2nd ed, 1986), paras 1.30-3), *Stewart v Marquis of Conyngham* (1851) 1 Ir Ch R 534.

[157.] *Re Barnewall's Estate* (1867) IR 1 Eq 304.

[158.] See *Irish Land Law* (2nd ed, 1986), paras 1.42 and 1.51.

[159.] *Re Neligan's Estate* (1892) 29 LR Ir 300; *Re Bailie's Estate* (1893) 31 LR Ir 373.

[160.] *Perrin v Roe* (1889) 25 LR Ir 37; *Hamilton v Bates* [1894] 1 IR 1. *Cf Madill v Blakely* (1900) 34 ILTR 28. See also *Williams on Title* (4th ed, by Battersby 1975), p 111. And see *Mahony v Davoren* (1892) 30 LR Ir 664, in which an action against a solicitor for negligence in not disclosing the rentcharge failed.

[161.] *Martin v Cotter* (1846) 9 Ir Eq R 351 at 355 (*per* Sugden LC); *Molphy v Coyne* (1919) 53 ILTR 177 at 179 (*per* Powell J). See also *O'Brien v Kearney* [1995] 2 ILRM 232. Though rights of way may be apparent on inspection, see *Hibernian Bank v Cassidy* (1902) 36 ILTR 156; *Re Flanagan and McGarvey and Thompson's Contract* [1945] NI 32 (para **[9.22]** *supra*). See also *Yandle & Sons v Sutton* [1922] 2 Ch 199.

[162.] *Power v Barrett* (1887) 19 LR Ir 450 at 457 (*per* Chatterton V-C),see para **[9.25]** *supra*. See also *Reeve v Berridge* (1888) 20 QBD 523; *Re White and Smith's Contract* [1896] 1 Ch 637.

excepted by the title deeds.[163] But, as we shall see,[164] there may be special provisions in the conditions of sale dealing with such rights.

[9.27] So far as leases are concerned, if the contract is for the sale of freehold property with vacant possession, clearly the existence of a lease or other tenancy agreement affecting the land must be disclosed.[165] Care must be taken to see that the terms of the lease or tenancy agreement are not misdescribed, eg, as to the rent reserved,[166] though, as we have seen, it is sufficient to draw the purchaser's attention to the existence of the lessees or tenants and leave it to him to enquire as to the precise terms upon which they hold.[167] We also saw that there is a general duty to disclose onerous covenants in a lease where this is being sold by the vendor,[168] and it seems that he must also disclose whether any notices have been served on him which materially affect or are likely to affect the lessee's position, eg, a notice to quit[169] or a notice as to disrepair.[170] However, this position as to leases and tenancies may be considerably affected by conditions of sale relating to the vendor's duty of disclosure, a matter to which we will turn in a moment.[171]

2. Contractual Provisions

[9.28] Condition 35 of the Law Society's *General Condition of Sale (1995 Edition)* requires the vendor to see that the purchaser receives notice before the sale of a wide range of matters affecting the property which may have been notified[172] to the vendor before the sale.[173] This covers closing orders, demolition orders and clearance orders made under housing legislation and

---

[163.] *Barton v Lord Downes* (1842) Fl & K 505; *Martin v Cotter* (1846) Ir Eq R 351; *Larkin v Lord Rosse* (1846) 10 Ir Eq R 70.

[164.] See para **[9.43]** *infra*.

[165.] *Healy v Farragher* Supreme Court, unrep, 21 December 1972 (1/1971). See also *Edwards v Wickwar* (1865) LR 1 Eq 68.

[166.] *Martin v Cotter* (1846) 9 Ir Eq R 351 at 353-4 (*per* Sugden LC). See also *Jones v Rimmer* (1880) 14 Ch D 588.

[167.] Para **[9.23]** *supra*.

[168.] Para **[9.25]** *supra*.

[169.] *Dimmock v Hallett* (1866) 2 Ch App 21. *Cf Devenport v Charsley* (1886) 54 LT 372.

[170.] *Re Flynn and Newman's Contract* [1948] IR 104 at 112 (*per* Kingsmill Moore J), see para **[9.21]** *supra*. See also *Re Englefeld Holdings Ltd and Sinclaire's Contract* [1962] 1 WLR 1119. *Cf McCann v Valentine* (1901) 1 NIJR 28 (local authority sanitary notice).

[171.] Para **[9.42]** *infra*.

[172.] Whether personally or by advertisement or posting on the property. Note that there is no requirement that the vendor be notified in writing, so that, eg, a radio announcement may bring his duty into effect.

[173.] Note that there is no restriction of this duty to notices served on the vendor "subsequent to commencement of the negotiations".

dangerous building notices made by a "competent authority"[174] under public health legislation and other legislation like the planning legislation.[175] It also covers any award or grant which is or may be repayable by the vendor's successor in title, ie, the purchaser. Failure to show that the purchaser received notice or was aware of the matter in question entitles the purchaser to rescind the contract[176] before completion and claim the return of his deposit, under condition 37.[177] It should be noted, however, that the vendor will not be in breach of this duty if he can show either that the order, notice, award or grant is no longer applicable or material, or does not prejudicially affect the value of the property,[178] or that the subject in question can be fully dealt with in the Apportionment Account.[179]

C. Remedies for Misdescription

[9.29] We now turn to the remedies available to a purchaser for misdescription by the vendor in the particulars of sale, whether physical or legal misdescription.[180] These remedies for misdescription in the contract for sale should not be confused with the remedies available for a misrepresentation made apart from, and usually prior to, the contract.[181] The former constitutes a breach of contract whereas the latter does not, and as Palles CB said in *Irish Land Commission v Maquay*[182]:

> "We all know that, in dealing with a contract in writing it is the province of the Court to determine whether any particular statement in it is a matter of contract or representation; and that the rights of the parties are different, according to the statement being one of one class or the other."[183]

[174.] Note the wide definition in cond 2 which now includes building control authorities under the Building Control Act 1990: see para **[16.79]** *post*.

[175.] Not being part of the contents of the Development Plan other than actual or proposed designation for compulsory purchase.

[176.] By giving notice in writing (in accordance with cond 49: see para **[10.64]** *post*) to the vendor or his solicitor, but note that no period of notice is specified, so presumably it should be "reasonable" notice.

[177.] As to which, see para **[15.35]** *post*.

[178.] This provision was added to the 1995 edition of the *General Conditions*.

[179.] See para **[20.03]** *post*.

[180.] The same remedies are available generally for breach of the duty of disclosure, but note the special criminal sanction against fraudulent concealment of an instrument or incumbrance material to the title, see paras **[9.31]** *infra* and **[14.61]** *post*.

[181.] These were discussed at para **[5.20]** *et seq, ante*. Note that the expression "misrepresentation" may be used in a wide and narrow sense. In its wide sense, it can cover inaccurate statements made both before the contract and in the contract (ie, including misdescriptions); in the narrow sense, it is confined to statements not part of the contract. See *Bank of Ireland v Smith* [1966] IR 646 at 656 (*per* Kenny J).

[182.] (1891) 28 LR Ir 342.

[183.] *Ibid*, p 351. See also *Bank of Ireland v Smith* [1966] IR 646 at 659 (*per* Kenny J).

However, whether the alleged inaccurate statement be regarded as a misdescription or a misrepresentation, it must be a statement of fact, and not of law or mere opinion.[184] As Crampton J once said: "Exaggerated representations, as puffing advertisements, are not to be taken into consideration."[185]

[9.30] In considering remedies for misdescription, a distinction must be drawn between the position under the general law and under the contract. It is usual for the contract to contain express provisions dealing with the matter,[186] and, indeed, we see below that there are several provisions contained in the Law Society's *General Conditions of Sale (1995 Edition)*.[187]

1. General Law

(i) Fraud

[9.31] It is clear that the making of a misdescription of the property, knowing that it is false, is a fraud on the purchaser which entitles him to both contractual and tortious remedies.[188] He may rescind the contract, demand his deposit back and seek damages for breach of contract on the basis of loss of bargain.[189] He may also sue in tort for damages for deceit.[190] It is also clear that a breach of the duty to disclose latent defects in title[191] may amount to fraud, with like consequences[192] This is certainly the case where there is a representation by the vendor that his title is good, or at least an inference to this effect,[193] and then he fails to disclose a defect in title known to him.[194] What is not so clear is whether mere non-disclosure in itself, eg, without any positive representation at all as to title, can amount to fraud, though there are

---

[184.] See the discussion in *Smith v Lynn* [1951] NI 69. See also para **[5.26]** *ante*.

[185.] *Thomson v Guy* (1844) 7 Ir LR 6 at 15. *Cf Peilow v O'Carroll* (1972) 106 ILTR 29 at 47 (*per* Budd J) ("puffing descriptions by an auctioneer"), see para **[9.16]** *supra*. See also *Watson v Burton* [1957] 1 WLR 19 at 24 (*per* Wynn-Parry J) ("typical auctioneers' 'puff'").

[186.] We have already noted some provisions dealing with non-disclosure, see paras **[9.28]** *supra*. The provisions discussed below (para **[9.36]** *et seq*) also deal to some extent with non-disclosure.

[187.] See para **[9.36]** *infra*.

[188.] See also as regards fraudulent misrepresentation, paras **[5.23-5]** *ante*.

[189.] Fraud has always been recognised as an exception to the rule, limiting damages for breach of contract, known as the rule in *Bain v Fothergill*, see para **[13.80]** *post*.

[190.] See the discussion in *Delany v Keogh* [1905] 2 IR 267, and see para **[5.24]** *ante*.

[191.] See paras **[9.24-27]** *supra*.

[192.] See *Delany v Keogh* [1905] 2 IR 267.

[193.] *Ibid*, pp 286-7 (*per* Holmes LJ), see para **[5.24]** *ante*. See also *Cullen v O'Meara* (1869) IR 4 CL 537 at 558 (*per* Pigot CB).

[194.] *Edwards v McLeay* (1818) 2 Swan 287. See also *Legge v Croker* (1811) 1 Ba & B 506.

some *dicta* in English cases which seem to suggest that it may be fraud.[195] It should also be noted that it is both a criminal offence and actionable in damages for the vendor or his solicitor or other agent to conceal, with intent to defraud, an instrument or incumbrance material to the title or to falsify any pedigree upon which the title may depend in order to induce the purchaser to accept the title.[196]

(ii) Substantial Misdescription

[9.32] Apart from fraud, it is settled that where a misdescription is "substantial," the vendor cannot enforce the contract either at common law or in equity, even on the basis of an abatement of the purchase price. This is often referred to as the rule in *Flight v Booth*,[197] the leading English case on the subject, which has been expressly recognised by the Irish courts.[198] On the other hand, the purchaser has the option either to rescind the contract (or to resist specific performance, if the vendor seeks this first)[199] or to insist upon taking the property despite the misdescription, but subject to abatement of the purchase price.[200] The same rules apply in respect of a breach of duty to disclose a latent defect in title which is substantial.[201]

[9.33] The essence of the concept of a "substantial" misdescription is that it would result (if the contract were enforced against the purchaser) in the purchaser not getting what he bargained for or what he was entitled to under

---

[195.] See *Edwards v McLeay* (1815) G Coop 308 at 312 (*per* Grant MR) (*affd* (1818) 2 Swan 287); *Wilde v Gibson* (1848) 1 HLC 605 at 632-3 (*per* Lord Campbell). See also *Hart v Swaine* (1877) 7 Ch D 42. *Cf* as regards non-disclosure of onerous covenants in leases, *Power v Barrett* (1887) 19 LR Ir 450 at 457-8 (*per* Chatterton V-C), and see para **[9.25]** *supra*.

[196.] Law of Property Amendment Acts 1859, s 24. and 1860, s 8. See para **[14.61]** *post*.

[197.] (1834) 1 Bing NC 370. See also *Re Weston and Thomas's Contract* [1907] 1 Ch 244.

[198.] See *Molphy v Coyne* (1919) 53 ILTR 177 at 170 (*per* Powell J); *Re Flynn and Newman's Contract* [1948] IR 104 at 109 (*per* Kingsmill Moore J). See also *Spunner v Walsh* (1847) 10 Ir Eq R 386 (*affd* 11 Ir Eq R 597); *Cullen v O'Meara* (1869) IR 4 CL 537.

[199.] See further on such remedies, Ch 13 *post*.

[200.] *Molphy v Coyne* (1919) 53 ILTR 177 at 170 (*per* Powell J). See also *Rutherford v Acton-Adams* [1915] AC 866 at 870 (*per* Viscount Haldane). Note, however, that the purchaser cannot be forced to complete (whether as a result of specific performance proceedings or service of a completion notice) until the amount of compensation or abatement is quantified, eg, as a result of an arbitration award: see *Keating v Bank of Ireland* [1983] ILRM 295; *O'Brien v Kearney* [1995] 2 ILRM 232 and para **[9.34]** *infra*. But the right to compensation may be excluded by the conditions of sale, *Molphy case*, 180, and see para **[9.47]** *infra*; or the vendor may have a right of rescission conferred by the conditions, see again para **[9.47]** *infra*. And the purchaser may be deemed to have waived his right to object, see *Martin v Cotter* (1846) 9 Ir Eq R 351.

[201.] *Molphy v Coyne* (1919) 53 ILTR 177 at 179 (*per* Powell J). See also *Power v Barrett* (1887) 19 LR Ir 450.

the contract, either in terms of the physical state of the property or the title to the property.[202] The Irish judges have put the point in various formulations, eg:

> "Courts of Equity have held that the reservation of rights in themselves of even small value, but which would break in too much upon the enjoyment and ownership of a purchaser, would not be capable of compensation, and that the purchaser would not be held to the purchase."[203]

Or again:

> "The only question for me is ... whether under these circumstances the purchaser got what he was entitled to get under the conditions of sale."[204]

Or again:

> "It appears that the deed [stipulated as the root of title] is in a material particular inconsistent with the title which was stipulated for in the contract of sale ... I do not feel at liberty under these conditions to force this title upon the purchaser."[205]

Whether or not a particular misdescription is substantial is clearly a matter to be determined by the court in the light of the circumstances of the particular case.[206] It also seems that the test is an objective one, ie, not a subjective one dependent upon the views of the individual purchaser.[207] And it seems that the courts will take a serious view of a misdescription in a court sale, for as Sugden LC once said:

[202.] See *Flight v Booth* (1834) 1 Bing NC 370 at 377 (*per* Tindal CJ); *Lee v Rayson* [1917] 1 Ch 613 at 618 (*per* Eve J).

[203.] *Larkin v Lord Rosse* (1846) 10 Ir Eq R 70 at 74 (*per* Smith MR). *Cf Vignolles v Bowen* (1847) 12 Ir Eq R 194 at 196 (*per* Smith MR).

[204.] *Re Deighan* (1897) 31 ILTR 45 at 46 (*per* Palles CB). See also *Linehan v Cotter* (1844) 7 Ir Eq R 176 at 179 (*per* Blackburne MR) ("entirely different from that which was professed to be sold, and which he contracted to purchase"); *Re McVicker's Contract* (1890) 25 LR Ir 307 at 310 (*per* Chatterton V-C) ("sufficient title in accordance with the conditions"); *Manifold v Johnston* [1902] 1 IR 7 at 10 (*per* Porter MR) ("what he was entitled to under the contract"); *Re Flynn and Newman's Contract* [1948] IR 104 at 110 (*per* Kingsmill Moore J) ("misdescription in a vital matter of title"). And see *Re Pryde and Metson's Contract* (1968) 19 NILQ 214.

[205.] *Re McDermott and Kellett's Contract* (1904) 4 NIJR 89 at 90 (*per* Barton J). See also *Molphy v Coyne* (1919) 53 ILTR 177 at 179 (*per* Powell J)("such a defect as would materially affect the contract from the point of view of the purchaser"). Note in these two quotations the references to a "material" misdescription or defect as opposed to a "substantial" one, see further, para **[9.47]** *infra. Cf Stewart v Marquis of Conynyham* (1851) 1 Ir Ch R 534 at 573 (*per* Smith MR) para **[9.34]** *infra.* And see further on the general principle that the court will not force a bad title on a purchaser, para **[13.52]** *post.*

[206.] *Re Deighan* (1897) 31 ILTR 45 at 46 (*per* Palles CB and FitzGibbon LJ).

[207.] See *Ridley v Oster* [1939] 1 All ER 618 at 620 (*per* Oliver J); *Watson v Burton* [1957] 1 WLR 19.

"... it is particularly requisite that an officer of this Court should be accurate in the preparation of the statement of what is to be done at a sale under the Court."[208]

(iii) Insubstantial Misdescription

[9.34] If the misdescription, or the defect in title not disclosed, is insubstantial, so that the purchaser will still get substantially what he contracted for, the vendor may still enforce the contract against the purchaser.[209] The purchaser cannot resist this, though he will be entitled to an abatement of the purchase price by way of compensation for the insubstantial misdescription or defect.[210] As Sugden LC said in *Martin v Cotter*[211]:

"I should not allow a purchaser to take advantage of a mere slip by which he could not be damaged."[212]

And in *Stewart v Marquis of Conyngham*,[213] Smith MR said:

"The general rule on the subject is, that although the vendor cannot make a good title to a small portion of the estate, if compensation can be made for the deficiency in consequence of such a portion not being material to the possession and enjoyment of the estate, specific performance will be decreed."[214]

However, recently the Irish courts have emphasised that the purchaser is entitled to resist completing until he knows precisely what amount of compensation or abatement in the purchase price he is entitled to. In *Keating v Bank of Ireland*[215] the parties had referred the question of compensation to arbitration[216] and the vendors argued that they were entitled to enforce completion by way of an order for specific performance, on the basis that

---

[208.] *Martin v Cotter* (1846) 9 Ir Eq R 351 at 353. *Cf Re Collis's Estate* (1864) 14 Ir Ch R 511 at 514-5 (*per* Hargreave J). See also *National Bank v Beirne* (1901) 35 ILTR 9; *Manifold v Johnston* [1902] 1 IR 7; *Re Flynn and Newman's Contract* [1948] IR 104. *Cf Hibernian Bank v Cassidy* (1902) 36 ILTR 156 at 157 (*per* Porter MR).

[209.] Unless, of course, he was fraudulent, see para **[9.31]** *supra*. See also *Re Moorehead's Estate* (1861) 12 Ir Ch R 371 at 374 (Hargreave J); *Re Ward and Jordan's Contract* [1902] 1 IR 73.

[210.] *Hibernian Bank v Cassidy* (1902) 36 ILTR 156 at 157 (*per* Porter MR). See also *Re Irwin* (1856) 5 Ir Ch R 290; *Re Moorehead's Estate* (1861) 12 Ir Ch R 371; *McCann v Valentine* (1901) 1 NIJR 28; *Re Lewis* (1908) 42 ILTR 210.

[211.] (1846) 9 Ir Eq R 351.

[212.] *Ibid*, p 353.

[213.] (1851) 1 Ir Ch R 534. See also *Magennis v Fallon* (1830) 2 Mol 590.

[214.] *Ibid*, p 573. See also *Re Robb and Spillane's Contract* (1901) 1 NIJR 206 at 207 (*per* Chatterton V-C): "It seems to me that this misnomer of calling the deed an assignment was not such a misdescription as to entitle the purchaser to be discharged."

[215.] [1983] ILRM 295.

[216.] Under cond 21 of the 1978 edition of the Law Society's *General Conditions of Sale*. See now cond 33 of the 1995 edition, para **[9.44]** *et seq, infra*.

any disputed amounts claimed for compensation or interest[217] should be placed on joint deposits pending the outcome of the arbitration award. Barrington J rejected this argument and held that a purchaser cannot be forced to close a sale before the issue of compensation has been determined.[218] Similarly, in *O'Brien v Kearney*[219] where again the vendor sought to force a closing through service of a completion notice,[220] McCracken J held that the purchaser was not obliged to comply until the issues whether he was entitled to compensation and, if so, the amount were settled.[221] The following have been held to be insubstantial misdescriptions or defects in title: a reservation of manorial rights which have ceased to exist[222]; a statement that timber on an estate was included in the sale, to which title was not made out in relation to a very small part of the estate[223]; misdescribing a deed as an assignment[224]; non-disclosure of a sanitary notice served on the vendor prior to the sale[225]; non-disclosure on an endorsement on the licence of a public house[226]; omission of a portion of a lot sold by auction.[227] On the other hand, the following have been held to be substantial misdescriptions or defects in title: an obscure statement leaving it doubtful for which lives a tenancy was held[228]; misdescribing lands held for a long term of years as held in fee farm[229]; describing premises as "licensed

---

[217.] The vendor's had made a claim for this on the basis of late completion: see para **[20.09]** *post*.

[218.] He made it clear that both parties can, of course, together enter into a supplementary agreement to close on such a basis.

[219.] [1995] 2 ILRM 232.

[220.] See para **[13.19]** *post*.

[221.] He took the view that this was a principle applicable to all cases where a purchaser is entitled to an abatement of the purchase price and is not confined, as alleged, to cases of possible fraud, *op cit*, p 240.

[222.] *Martin v Cotter* (1846) 9 Ir Eq R 351. Sugden LC said: "... although there is a reservation, yet if the Court is satisfied that there is no subject on which it can be exercised, or if all the legal rights under it have ceased ie, if, notwithstanding the reservation, the title of the seller is perfectly good and the purchaser's title cannot be disturbed, this Court will not do so idle a thing as to give the purchaser liberty to reject the title merely because in words there is such a reservation." *Ibid*, p 355. *Cf Re Irwin* (1856) 5 Ir Ch R 290 at 303 (*per* Brady LC).

[223.] *Stewart v Marquis of Conyngham* (1851) 1 Ir Ch R 534. *Cf Geraghty v Rohan Industrial Estates Ltd* [1988] IR 419 (shortfall in total acreage of farm): see para **[9.45]** *infra*.

[224.] *Re Robb and Spillane's Contract* (1901) 1 NIJR 206. *Cf Re Kavanagh and Balfe's Contract* (1898) 32 ILTR 6 (underlease described as lease). See also *Palmer v Coates* (1905) 39 ILTR 221. See para **[9.17]** *supra*.

[225.] *McCann v Valentine* (1901) 1 NIJR 28; *Re Lewis* (1908) 42 ILTR 210.

[226.] *Re Ward and Jordan's Contract* [1902] 1 IR 73.

[227.] *National Bank v Beirne* (1901) 35 ILTR 9.

[228.] *Martin v Cotter* (1846) 9 Ir Eq R 351.

[229.] *Re McDermott and Kellett's Contract* (1904) 4 NIJR 89. *Cf Vignolles v Bowen* (1847) 12 Ir Eq R 194; *Tuohy v Courtney* [1994] 3 IR 1, appeal dismissed by the Supreme Court, unrep, 26 July 1994 (333/345/1992).

premises" when only a temporary transfer of licence had been granted to the owner's assignee in bankruptcy[230]; non-disclosure of a tithe rentcharge affecting the property[231]; non-disclosure of responsibility to maintain fences and keep drains and watercourses clear[232]; misdescribing a life estate as an interest held under a fee farm conversion grant[233]; a misleading statement as to an indemnity in respect of a leasehold rent[234]; non-disclosure of a right of way[235]; describing the vendors as trustees when the property has been assigned to them by a trustee in breach of trust.[236]

(iv) Misdescription Against the Vendor

[9.35] In passing it may be noted that there is no converse rule that the vendor is entitled to increase the price where the purchaser will get more from the contract than he bargained for.[237] Nor is the purchaser under any duty of disclosure,[238] though he must not make misrepresentations as to the property (eg, as to its value) or otherwise mislead the vendor.[239] If he does, at the very least the court may exercise its discretion to refuse him specific performance.[240]

2. Contractual Provisions

[9.36] We now turn to a consideration of how far the remedies available under the general law may be varied by the terms of the contract for sale, ie, by the conditions of sale. From the outset it should be emphasised that the

---

[230.] *Re Deighan* (1897) 31 ILTR 45. *Cf Irish Industrial Benefit BS v O'Brien* [1941] IR 1. See also *O'Neill v Ryan* [1944] Ir Jur Rep 9; *Geryani v O'Callaghan* High Court, unrep, 25 January 1995 (1994/677 Sp).

[231.] *Perrin v Roe* (1889) 25 LR Ir 37; *Hamilton v Bates* [1894] 1 IR 1. But see para **[9.26]** *supra*. And *cf Re Moorehead's Estate* (1861) 12 Ir Ch R 371 (incorrect names of rentchargees).

[232.] *Larkin v Lord Rosse* (1846) 10 Ir Eq R 70. *Cf Cullen v O'Meara* (1869) IR 4 CL 537.

[233.] *Re McVicker's Contract* (1890) 25 LR Ir 307.

[234.] *Manifold v Johnston* [1902] 1 IR 7.

[235.] *Molphy v Coyne* (1919) 53 ILTR 177. *Cf O'Brien v Kearney* [1995] 2 ILRM 232.

[236.] *Re O'Flanagan and Ryan's Contract* [1905] 1 IR 280.

[237.] See *Re Lindsay and Forder's Contract* (1895) 72 LT 832. But the court might refuse the purchaser specific performance in a case of substantial misdescription on the ground of hardship, see *Mauser v Back* (1848) 6 Hare 443; *Cato v Thompson* (1882) 9 QBD 616. *Cf Alvanley v Kinnaird* (1849) 2 Mac & G 1. See further on the concept of hardship, para **[13.48]** *post*.

[238.] If only because there can be no question of him concealing defects in the vendor's title, see *Fox v Mackreth* (1788) 2 Bro CC 400 (on appeal, (1791) 4 Bro PC 258). *Cf Phillips v Homfray* (1871) 6 Ch App 770.

[239.] *Thompson v Lambert* (1868) IR 2 Eq 433 at 439 (*per* Walsh MR); *Coates v Boswell* (1886) 11 App Cas 232 at 235 (*per* Lord Selborne). See also *McPherson v Watt* (1877) 3 App Cas 254.

[240.] *Turner v Harvey* (1821) Jac 169 at 173 (*per* Lord Eldon LC); *Walters v Morgan* (1861) 3 De GF & J 718 at 724 (*per* Lord Campbell LC).

provisions discussed in the next few paragraphs are simply illustrations of those which are commonly inserted in the conditions of sale - largely because they are contained in the standard form issued by the Law Society over the years.[241] There is nothing to prevent the parties, or one of them, inserting special conditions of sale in the contract, as the Law Society's standard form expressly recognises.[242] However, before considering the standard conditions of sale on the subject, some general principles may be mentioned.

[9.37] The first is that the vendor must take care in framing conditions purporting to restrict what would otherwise be his liability under the general law. The reason was stated by O'Connor MR in *Re White and Hague's Contract*[243]:

> "It is a well-recognised canon of construction that if conditions are ambiguous they are to be construed in favour of the purchaser."[244]

The second, which is not unconnected with the first, is that the vendor must not frame his conditions deliberately to mislead the purchaser[245]; for otherwise the court is likely to hold that the purchaser is not bound by the conditions in question and may, therefore, pursue his remedies under the general law unrestricted in any way.[246] Thus, again in *Re White and Hague's Contract*,[247] O'Connor MR had this to say about conditions of sale in that case which purported to relieve the vendor of the duty to disclose his title to the property and to require the purchaser to assume that the title was good[248]:

> "There is nothing unreasonable in cases like these, nor anything to suggest dishonesty, if the vendor offers to a purchaser only such title as he may have, and a contract on this basis may be enforced. But in a case like that with which I am dealing, which suggests no reason for not disclosing the vendor's title, except an effort to foist upon the purchaser a worthless title, or mere perversity on the part of the vendor, I entertain the gravest doubt that the contract would be enforceable. It seems to be against common right and common honesty that a purchaser should be obliged to pay his

---

[241.] See further, Ch 10 *post*.
[242.] See para **[10.67]** *post*.
[243.] [1921] 1 IR 138.
[244.] *Ibid*, p 146. See also *Geoghegan v Connolly* (1858) 8 Ir Ch R 598 at 607 (*per* Smith MR); *Peilow v O'Carroll* (1972) 106 ILTR 29 at 49 (*per* Budd J).
[245.] *Re Mitchell and McElhinney's Contract* [1902] 1 IR 83 at 87 (*per* Porter MR). See also *Clements v Conroy* [1911] 2 IR 500 at 523-4 (*per* Walker LC).
[246.] *Re O'Flanagan and Ryan's Contract* [1905] 1 IR 280 at 286 (*per* Porter MR).
[247.] [1921] 1 IR 138.
[248.] See paras **[14.38-9]** *post*.

purchase-money without any assurance of getting value when no fair reason is alleged for not giving at least some evidence of title."[249]

[9.38] This second principle is particularly relevant in relation to the vendor's duty to disclose latent defects in title known to him.[250] If he knows that there is a defect, he is in an obvious dilemma: if he says nothing about it, he may be in a breach of his duty of disclosure; if he does mention it every time he tries to sell his property, he may render it unsaleable. So his only solution is to draft appropriate conditions of sale to protect himself against objections or requisitions as to title on the ground of the defect.[251] But how far can he go? The Irish judges have laid down very firm guidance on the matter.[252] Thus, in *Re Turpin and Ahern's Contract*,[253] FitzGibbon LJ stated:

> "The general rule is that, where a title is in fact defective, and the defect is, or ought to be, within the knowledge of the vendor, a condition against investigation will not prevent a purchaser from declining to complete, unless the condition which precludes investigation gives him some fair intimation or warning of the existence of the defect. Here the vendor, being a party to the settlement, must be taken to have known its provisions; if it created a blot on the title, he cannot estop the purchaser by the condition, unless it indicates the blot."[254]

Similarly in *Re Flynn and Newman's Contract*,[255] Kingsmill Moore J stated:

> "In the absence of any express provision to the contrary, the vendor undertakes and is bound, in law, to show a good title to the property to be sold and to convey land corresponding, substantially in all respects, with the description contained in the contract. If he fails to do these things, the purchaser may rescind and recover his deposit. The vendor may, of course, limit his obligation to show good title by suitable special conditions but, if he does so, he must fairly indicate what is the defect in his title to which the

---

[249.] *Op cit*, p 144.

[250.] See para **[9.24]** *supra*.

[251.] Conditions purporting to protect the vendor against known defects should not be confused with conditions relating to unknown defects, see *Re Mitchell and McElhinney's Contract* [1902] 1 IR 83 at 86-7 (*per* Porter MR).

[252.] See the discussion in *McMahon v Gaffney* [1930] IR 576 at 586-7 (*per* Johnston J).See also *Musgrave v McCullagh* (1864) 14 Ir Ch R 496 at 499 (*per* Brady LC).

[253.] [1905] 1 IR 85.

[254.] *Ibid*, p 103. See also Walker LJ at p 107. And see *Re Davys and Verdon and Saurin's Contract* (1886) 17 LR Ir 334 at 337 (*per* Chatterton V-C); *Re O'Flanagan and Ryan's Contract* [1905] 1 IR 280 at 286 (*per* Porter MR); *Molphy v Coyne* (1919) 53 ILTR 177 at 184 (*per* Powell J).

[255.] [1948] IR 104.

purchaser must submit, and must take care that he is not guilty of misrepresentation."[256]

(i) Notice of Documents

[9.39] One of the rules of the common law which can give rise to difficulties from the vendor's point of view is that, in respect of leases,[257] the vendor's duty of disclosure of latent defects in title extends only to "onerous" covenants[258] as opposed to the "usual" covenants,[259] which, of course, begs the question in every case as to which covenants are to be regarded as onerous and which as usual.[260] It is common, therefore, to have a special provision in the contract dealing with this matter, whereby the vendor usually gives the purchaser an opportunity of discovering the covenants for himself. Thus, condition 6 of the Law Society's *General Conditions of Sale (1995 Edition)* states that the documents specified in the Documents Schedule to the contract form,[261] or copies of them, have been available for inspection by the purchaser or his solicitor prior to the sale. It then goes on to provide that, if all or any of the property is stated in the particulars or special conditions to be held under a lease[262] or to be subject to any covenants, conditions, rights, liabilities or restrictions and the lease or other document containing the same is specified in the Documents Schedule, the purchaser, whether availing of such opportunity of inspection or not, is deemed to have purchased with full notice of the contents of those documents.[263]

[9.40] This provision will operate so as to fix the purchaser with notice of covenants (onerous or otherwise) in fee farm grants or leases only, of course,

---

[256.] *Ibid*, p 112. *Cf* Sullivan MR in *Boyd v Dickson* (1876) IR 10 Eq 239 at 255: "... the 8th condition is a mere subterfuge, and it deliberately suppresses the true facts in relation to the gross defect which it seeks to cover."

[257.] This same principle applies in Ireland to fee farm grants which share many common features with leases, especially the inclusion of various covenants and conditions binding successors in title, see *Irish Land Law* (2nd ed, 1986), para 4.057 *et seq*, and para **[19.37]** *et seq, post*.

[258.] See para **[9.25]** *supra*.

[259.] *Spunner v Walsh* (1847) 10 Ir Eq R 386 (*affd* 11 Ir Eq R 597); *Vignolles v Bowen* (1847) 12 Ir Eq R 194. See also *Re Haedicke and Lipski's Contract* [1901] 2 Ch 666; *Melzak v Lillienfield* [1926] Ch 480.

[260.] The position may vary from case to case in respect of the same covenant, see *Flexman v Corbett* [1930] 1 Ch 672.

[261.] Since the 1986 edition of the form this Schedule and the "Searches Schedule" are to be found *before* the conditions of sale: see p 3 of the 1995 edition. On the subject of searches, see para **[15.39]** *post*.

[262.] Note the wide definition of "lease" in cond 2, which includes fee farm grants and licences and agreements for occupation and use of land.

[263.] The purchaser is fixed with notice "notwithstanding any partial statement of the contents": see para **[9.40]** *infra*.

if the grants or leases are actually made available for inspection;[264] merely mentioning their existence is not enough.[265] Furthermore, although under the general law the purchaser is not bound by it if the contents of the grant or lease have been misrepresented by the vendor or misdescribed in the contract,[266] Condition 6 of the *General Conditions* even provides protection against this for it states that the purchaser has full notice "notwithstanding any partial or incomplete statement of such contents in the Particulars or in the Conditions".

[9.41] It must be reiterated, as was pointed out earlier,[267] that the vendor's solicitor should not seek to use this provision to prevent the purchaser's solicitor from making the usual *post*-contract investigation of title. The Law Society's Conveyancing Committee has, on more than one occasion, specifically disapproved of this practice and has insisted that there should be a limit to the documents listed in the Schedule. In essence, the list should be confined to the root of title and other documents which are the subject of special mention elsewhere in the contract (eg, in the Special Conditions). For example, the sale may be subject to and with the benefit of specified leases; it may be subject to charges or other incumbrances created by specified deeds. In this respect condition 6 should not be confused with condition 7 of the *General Conditions*, which requires the vendor to deliver copies of the documents necessary to vouch the title. Needless to say, it is vital that the purchaser's solicitor closely examines the documents listed in the Document Schedule and advises his client of any potentially adverse matter found before the contract is entered into. It will be too late to do so afterwards because the purchaser will be deemed to have contracted subject to the rights and interests in question.[268]

(ii) Tenancies

[9.42] Where the property is sold subject to any lease or tenancy, we saw that under the general law the vendor is under a duty to disclose not only the existence of the lease or tenancy, but also any notices, eg, to quit or as to disrepair, which have been served, and that care must be taken not to misdescribe the terms of the lease or tenancy agreement.[269] Condition 22 of the Law Society's *General Conditions of Sale (1995 Edition)* recognises this

---

[264]. And, apparently, only if the particulars or special conditions state that the property is held subject to such a grant, lease or sub-lease, see fn 262, *supra*.

[265]. See *Reeve v Berridge* (1888) 20 QBD 523; *Re White and Smith's Contract* [1896] 1 Ch 637.

[266]. *Flight v Barton* (1832) 3 My & K 282, approved in *Spunner v Walsh* (1847) 10 Ir Eq R 386 at 400 (*per* Smith MR) (affd 11 Ir Eq R 597); *Power v Barrett* (1887)19 LR Ir 450 at 457 (*per* Chatterton V-C). See also *Charles Hunt Ltd v Palmer* [1931] 2 Ch 287; *Pagebar Properties Ltd v Derby Investments Ltd* [1972] 1 WLR 1500.

[267]. Para **[9.24]** *supra*.

[268]. See *Hill v Harris* [1965] 2 All ER 358, para **[5.12]** *ante*.

[269]. See para **[9.27]** *supra*.

duty by providing that the vendor provides for inspection a copy of the lease or tenancy agreement,[270] together with copies of any notices in the vendor's possession served by or on the tenant. Subject to any provision to the contrary in the Special Conditions, condition 23 then specifies that the purchaser is entitled to assume that the lessee named in any lease so provided is still the lessee, that there has been no variation in the terms of the lease (other than one evident from an inspection of the property or apparent from documentation furnished to the purchaser prior to the contract) and that the terms and conditions (save those pertaining to the actual state and condition of the property) have been complied with. This clearly imposes an onus on the vendor who, in effect, is warranting the matters in question and his solicitor should check them thoroughly before issuing the draft contract. They are, of course, all matters which should be within the first-hand knowledge of the vendor and upon which the purchaser of what will usually be a substantial commercial or investment property will rightly expect to be satisfied before committing itself to the contract.

(iii) Easements and Other Rights

[9.43] We saw earlier that, under the general law, the vendor's duty of disclosure of latent defects in title extended to easements and other similar rights not already known to the purchaser or apparent from inspection.[271] Condition 15 of the Law Society's *General Conditions of Sale (1995 Edition)* expressly recognises this by providing that the vendor is to disclose before the sale, in the particulars, special conditions or otherwise, all easements, rights, privileges, taxes and other liabilities,[272] which are known by the vendor to affect the property or to be likely to affect it.[273] Subject to this, condition 16 then states that the purchaser is deemed to buy with full notice of the actual state and condition of the property and subject to all leases[274] mentioned in the Particulars and Special conditions and to all easements, rights, reservations, privileges, liabilities, covenants, rents, outgoings and incidents of tenure.[275]

---

[270] Or, if there is no written tenancy agreement, such evidence of its nature and terms as the vendor may be able to supply.

[271] See para **[9.26]** *supra*.

[272] The reference to "taxes" was added in the 1995 edition.

[273] It seems that at common law the vendor was liable to disclose even defects that he did not know about and had no reason to suspect existed, see *Re Brewer and Hawkin's Contract* (1899) 80 LT 127 (underground sewer). See also *Re Puckett and Smith's Contract* [1902] 2 Ch 258 (underground culvert). *Cf* as regards an earlier edition of the condition, *Molphy v Coyne* (1919) 53 ILTR 177 at 179 (*per* Powell J); *Re Flynn and Newman's Contract* [1948] IR 104 at 113 (*per* Kingsmill Moore J).

[274] As regards tenancies see further para **[9.42]** *supra*.

[275] Note that the purchaser has no right to compensation under cond 33 in respect of matters of which he is deemed to have notice under cond 16: see para **[9.45]** *infra*.

(iv) Misdescription and Compensation

[9.44] The remedies available to a purchaser under the general law for misdescription have been modified by the contract form and the provision in question is to be found in condition 33 of the Law Society's *General Conditions of Sale (1995 Edition)*.[276] The effect of the new provision[277] may be summarised as follows[278]:

(a) No Compensation

[9.45] First, it is provided that there is to be no compensation for loss of "trifling materiality" unless attributable to recklessness or fraud on the part of the vendor.[279] It is arguable that this alters the general law to the extent that it deprives the purchaser of compensation in respect of insubstantial errors.[280] It is also reiterated that there can be no compensation in respect of matters of which the purchaser is deemed to have notice,[281] nor in relation to any error in a location or similar plan furnished for identification only.[282]

[276.] First introduced in cond 21 of the 1976 edition. Prior to that cond 19 of the *Private Contract General Conditions of Sale* (1968 ed) and cond. 21 of the *Public Auction General Conditions of Sale* (1968 ed) simply provided that no error, misstatement or misdescription in the particulars or conditions or in any poster, advertisement or map was to annul the sale, nor was any compensation to be allowed. Note that this provision related to misdescription in the contract for sale and did not apply to misrepresentations apart from the contract, see *Bank of Ireland v Smith* [1966] IR 646 at 656 (*per* Kenny J). *Cf* the current condition, see para **[9.46]** *infra*. But it was well-settled that such a condition could not prevent a purchaser from rescinding for" substantial" misdescription or non-disclosure, see *Molphy v Coyne* (1919) 53 ILTR 177 at 179-80 (*per* Powell J), applying *Flight v Booth* (1834) 1 Bing NC 370. See also *Peilow v O'Carroll* (1972) 106 ILTR 20 at 52 (*per* Budd J).

[277.] Cond 33 involves some re-casting of the previous version. Note, in particular, that the definition of "error" in 33(a) now drops the reference to "communicated" (*cf* cond 33(d) in the 1991 edition) and includes "non-disclosure", thereby meeting the point made by Costello J in *Geryani v O'Callaghan* High Court, unrep, 25 January 1995 (1994/677 Sp). He held that a purchaser could not claim his costs under cond 33 of the 1991 ed in that case because the loss had been caused by the vendor's non-disclosure that the cafe business the subject of the contract had a provisional registration only under the Food Hygiene Regulations 1950 (SI 205/1950) and that full registration was subject to compliance with 21 conditions required by the Health Board.

[278.] In this context we are concerned with misdescription etc in the contract itself, but note that cond 33 applies expressly also to misstatements or misrepresentations made "in the course of any representation, response or negotiations leading to the sale": cond 33(a). See para **[5.20]** *et seq, ante*.

[279.] Cond 33(b).

[280.] See para **[9.34]** *supra*.

[281.] Under cond 16: see para **[9.43]** *supra*.

[282.] Cond 33(b). *Cf* where the map or plan is for more than this: see *Geraghty v Rohan Industrial Estates Ltd* [1988] IR 419.

(b) Compensation

[9.46] Subject to the provisions outlined in the previous paragraph, condition 33 provides that the purchaser is entitled to be compensated by the vendor for any loss suffered by the purchaser in his bargain relative to the sale as a result of an error "made"[283] by or on behalf of the vendor[284] and, subject to exceptions outlined below, there is no right by either party to rescind the contract.[285] Any dispute as to the right to, or the amount of, compensation is to be settled by arbitration in accordance with the provisions of condition 51.[286] It has recently been made clear that a purchaser cannot be forced to close the sale until the arbitration has been completed.[287]

(c) Rescission

[9.47] The common law rule is recognised that a purchaser may always rescind where the property "differs substantially from the property agreed to be sold," whether in "quantity, quality, tenure or otherwise".[288] But the provision seems to go further than this. In *Geryani v O'Callaghan*[289] where the vendor had failed to disclose that a cafe business had a provisional licence only and would have to comply with numerous requirements under the Food Hygiene Regulations 1950,[290] Costello J emphasised that due weight should be given to the word "otherwise" in this context, so that a right of rescission arises in respect of errors relating to matters other than quantity, quality and tenure. He further reiterated that the difference must be "substantial" and the purchaser must be "prejudiced materially" by reason of it. This seems to require an element additional to the need at common law for the misdescription or non-disclosure to be substantial, for it goes on to add the qualification - if the purchaser or vendor would be "prejudiced". In so far as this additional requirement purports to restrict further the purchaser's right of rescission at common law for substantial misdescription, it is might be questioned whether it should be enforceable,[291] though it has been accepted by at least one English judge,[292] and, apparently, by Costello

---

[283.] See fn 277 *supra*.

[284.] Note again that this includes *pre*-contract misrepresentations, etc: see fn 278 *supra*.

[285.] Cond 33(d).

[286.] See *Geraghty v Rohan Industrial Estates Ltd* [1988] IR 419.

[287.] *Keating v Bank of Ireland* [1983] ILRM 295; *O'Brien v Kearney* [1995] 2 ILRM 232.

[288.] Cond 33(c)(i). See para **[9.32]** *et seq, supra*.

[289.] High Court, unrep, 25 January 1995 (1994/677 Sp).

[290.] SI 205/1950 (made under the Health Act 1947). The vendor's solicitor also gave incorrect information in replies to requisitions on title: see para **[15.37]** *post*.

[291.] See paras **[9.32]** and **[9.46]** *supra*.

[292.] Wynn-Parry J in *Watson v Burton* [1957] 1 WLR 19, criticised at (1957) 21 Conv 7.

J. In fact in the *Geryani* case he held that the purchaser had a right to rescind under condition 33 on two grounds:

(1) considerable work would have to be done to the premises if it was to achieve full registration[293];

(2) there was a risk that the cafe business, which had been sold as a going concern, could not be carried on the premises.[294]

As regards the position under the common law, the vendor argued that, since there is no duty to disclose defects in the physical condition of the property,[295] but only defects in title which are latent;[296] the purchaser had no cause for complaint because she could have ascertained the position *re* the provisional registration by making appropriate *pre*-contract enquiries. Costello J accepted the general principle that there was no duty to disclose notices served on the vendor by the Health Board or the facts concerning registration of the cafe. However, he considered that it was important that the right to rescission claimed in that case was the contractual one in condition 33 which was "independent of any obligations imposed by general legal principles." It had to be borne in mind that this was in a standard form developed by the Law Society over a period of years and, in his view, it imposed no new requirement of disclosure because such statutory notices are required to be disclosed under the Society's standard *Requisitions on Title*.[297] In his view this meant that "if a vendor has knowledge of facts where non-disclosure might confer contractual rescission rights under Clause 33 prudence would suggest either *pre*-contract disclosure or that they be made the subject of special contractual conditions."[298] It is suggested that practitioners should note these comments. In particular, they serve to

---

[293]. "The difference is substantial in that customer space will be reduced, which will have a substantial effect on the business carried on in the premises. This difference was materially prejudicial to the purchaser in that her financial position would be adversely affected, bearing in mind the very high rent of the premises and the considerable purchase price payable for them." Transcript, p 8.

[294]. "The risk was significant because the purchaser could not be certain that the vendor was financially capable of carrying out the requirements of the Health Board, or that she could be relied on to carry out the work to the satisfaction of the officials of the Board, particularly in the light of the untrue statements made in the course of the transaction. The purchase was materially prejudiced by this difference because she was asked to make a substantial payment for a property which might prove useless to her and involve her in very substantial financial loss." Transcript, p 9.

[295]. Para **[9.21]** *supra*

[296]. Para **[9.24]** *supra*.

[297]. See para **[16.89]** *post*. However, the duty to disclose by way of reply to requisitions must surely depend upon the terms of the contract - the requirement to reply stems from the contract: see para **[5.02]** *ante* and **[15.17]** *post*.

[298]. Transcript p 10. *Cf* the English Court of Appeal decision in *Sindall plc v Cambridgeshire County Council* [1994] 3 All ER 932.

emphasise the wisdom from the purchaser's solicitor's point of view of raising appropriate *pre*-contract enquiries or requisitions in a case involving valuable commercial property, as part of a "due diligence" exercise.[299] From the vendor's solicitor's point of view, while it may not be the law that he is to be regarded as owing a duty of care to the purchaser in answering *pre*-contract enquiries,[300] he clearly owes a duty to his client, the vendor, and as Costello J has indicated, this involves acting in such a way that he does not give the purchaser a right to rescind the contract made with his client.

[9.48] Finally, it should be noted that condition 33 also recognises the purchaser's right of rescission where compensation for a claim attributable to a material error made by or on behalf of the vendor "cannot be reasonably assessed".[301] Presumably, the use of the word "material" here requires something more than a "trifling" matter, ie, it must be something more "substantial" involving some prejudice to the purchaser.[302]

[299.] See para **[5.14]** *et seq, ante*.

[300.] See the English Court of Appeal decision in *Gran Geloto Ltd v Richcliff (Group) Ltd* [1992] 1 All ER 865 and para **[5.28]** *ante*.

[301.] Cond 33(c)(i).

[302.] By analogy with cond 33(c)(i); para **[9.47]** *supra*.

Chapter 10

CONDITIONS OF SALE

[10.01] We turn now to the core standard provisions of the Law Society's contract form. These are the "conditions of sale" which are essentially the terms upon which the property, the subject of the contract, is sold.[1] The latest version is the *General Conditions of Sale (1995 Edition)*, which follows the format introduced by the 1986 Edition. It must be reiterated that this document, despite its title, is designed to incorporate the entirety of the contract for sale and not just the "general conditions".[2] Thus, quite apart from containing the memorandum necessary for the Statute of Frauds,[3] it also contains the particulars and tenure of the property being sold.[4] Furthermore, again despite its title, the form recognises that "special" conditions may be necessary for the particular transaction and will have to be added to the printed form.[5]

[10.02] Of course, it should not be forgotten that the normal practice may not be followed and the parties may not have drawn up any formal conditions of sale, or may sign a document drawn up by a non-lawyer, eg, an estate agent. If the former has happened, the parties may have agreed on the bare essentials for a sufficient memorandum or note for the purposes of the Statute of Frauds[6] and nothing more.[7] The contract is then said to be "open" in that so many of the parties' rights and duties are left to be determined by the general law, ie, centuries of case-law and statute law. As we shall see, the distinction between an open and closed contract, ie, one subject to express conditions of sale, is particularly important in relation to questions of title, eg, as to what title has to be deduced by the vendor and as to how far the purchaser is restricted in his investigation of title and in making requisitions on title.[8] Though it may not be desirable for the parties to leave

---

1. See para **[9.07]** *ante.*
2. See para **[9.03]** *ante.*
3. See para **[9.05]** *ante.*
4. See para **[9.07]** *ante.* Note also the Documents and Searches Schedules: see para **[9.24]** *ante.*
5. See p 4 of the form and para **[10.67]** *infra.*
6. See para **[6.17]** *et seq ante.*
7. Nothing more is necessary for enforcement, see generally Ch 6, *ante.*
8. This whole subject is dealt with in detail later, see Chs 14-16, *post.*

their contract open in this way,[9] it is at least the case that their respective positions will be reasonably clear from the general law, particularly where there are statutory provisions governing the matter in question. If, on the other hand, the parties have signed a document drawn up by a non-lawyer, this may be far from being the case! Fortunately, the courts seem prepared to strive to protect the parties in such a case. Thus, in *Donnelly v O'Connell*[10] the parties signed a document, drawn up by a house agent, in the latter's office without consulting their solicitors. This document contained a clause which read - "the vendor's solicitors to prepare title and conditions of sale."[11] In holding that this clause was a condition precedent to a contract coming into existence, Meredith J remarked:

> "I would like to say that, in my opinion, any document in which reference is made to a solicitor should be construed generously by the Court so that the parties may have all reasonable protection. This remains the proper rule to be enforced even though the parties may not realise the importance of obtaining legal advice. I shall always interpret such documents generously."[12]

[10.03] Considerable care should be exercised in drawing up the conditions of sale, as is the case with any document purporting to fix the terms of the parties' agreement. The simplest, and arguably the most sensible, course for the vendor's solicitor to adopt is to use the relevant Law Society's standard form, especially since it covers sales by both public auction and private treaty.[13] The dangers of mixing different contract forms or sets of conditions was commented upon by Kingsmill Moore J in *Re Flynn and Newman's*

---

9. To some extent this depends upon from which party's point of view one considers the matter. As a general rule, the purchaser's position is stronger under an open contract, since conditions of sale are usually drafted or required by the vendor's solicitor, see para **[10.05]** *infra*. However, the new general conditions drawn up by the Law Society are designed to draw a fair balance between the vendor and purchaser. See further as to construction of conditions of sale, *ibid*.

10. (1924) 58 ILTR 164.

11. See further, para **[7.13]** *ante*. Note that the expression "conditions of sale" should not be confused with the expression "conditional contracts." The former is simply the traditional expression used to describe the express terms of a contract which has come into existence and is fully enforceable. The latter is the expression used to indicate that the alleged contract is subject to some condition which either prevents it becoming a binding contract in the first place, ie, a condition precedent, or restricts the full operation of the contract in that one or other, or both, of the parties may withdraw on its non-fulfilment, ie, a condition subsequent, see para **[7.03]** *ante*. See also *Property and Bloodstock Ltd v Emerton* [1968] Ch 94 at 118 (*per* Danckwerts LJ).

12. *Op cit*, p 164.

13. See paras **[9.03]** *ante* and **[10.10]** *infra*.

Contract,[14] where he referred to the contract involved in that case in these terms:

> "Indeed, the contract for sale was a most unfortunate and confusing document. It incorporated not one, but two sets of conditions of sale - those used at the Court sale and a printed set of conditions suitable for use in a sale by private contract - together with supplementary conditions in the body of the contract ...."[15]

It was also mentioned earlier that the Law Society's Conveyancing Committee has disapproved of the practice adopted by some vendor's solicitors of furnishing a short contract form which simply cross-refers to the Society's *General Conditions* but does not reproduce them. The Committee is of the view that the Society's full printed form should always be used to avoid any doubts or uncertainties as to the precise contents of the parties' contract.[16]

[10.04] Apart from that, the common vices of vagueness and ambiguity are to be avoided and, unfortunately, the law reports are replete with criticisms in this regard. Thus, in *Re White and Hague's Contract*,[17] O'Connor MR uttered these trenchant remarks:

> "With all due respect to the vendor's adviser, he laid claim to an excellence in his conditions which they certainly have not. He describes them as 'clear and unambiguous.' Whatever merit they may have, they do not warrant this description. I would rather call them confused, contradictory, and misleading."[18]

Even worse were the vices castigated by Sullivan MR in *Boyd v Dickson*[19] in these terms:

> "In the present case, whether there was deliberate intention or not, I think the framing of the conditions was highly calculated to throw a purchaser off his guard and to mislead him, and there is palpable suppression and management on the face of them."[20]

[10.05] The courts have also recognised that it is invariably the vendor or his solicitor who draws up the conditions of sale[21] and so, when a question of interpretation arises, they will be construed against the vendor and in favour

---

[14]. [1948] IR 104.

[15]. *Ibid*, p 107.

[16]. The *Gazette* December 1994, p 367: see para **[9.01]** *ante*.

[17]. [1921] 1 IR 138.

[18]. *Ibid*, p 145. See also *Allman v McDaniel* [1912] 1 IR 467 at 472 (*per* O'Connor MR).

[19]. (1876) IR 10 Eq 239.

[20]. *Ibid*, p 255.

[21]. See paras **[2.45-6]** and **[3.35]** *ante*.

of the purchaser.[22] In the case of a court sale, the court will be particularly meticulous in its scrutiny of the conditions to ensure that neither party,[23] but especially the purchaser, suffers from the way they were drafted.[24] It also seems that the courts will take into account the fact that, in the case of a sale by public auction, the purchaser or his solicitor may have little opportunity in practice to scrutinise the conditions of sale.[25] As Sullivan MR said in *Boyd v Dickson*,[26] often the purchaser or his solicitor is "only able to make a very hurried perusal of the conditions of sale on the morning of the day of sale".[27] So also, in *Re Mitchell and McElhinney's Contract*,[28] Porter MR said:

> "No doubt a purchaser is often placed at a disadvantage where the condition is one which he does not understand, and the effect of which he cannot foresee: and when he buys at an auction he often does so without legal advice."[29]

[10.06] Finally, it is provided in the Law Society's standard form that, in the event of any conflict between the general conditions and special conditions, the special conditions are to prevail.[30] Though some of the printed general conditions may not be applicable in a particular case,[31] it is not the practice for solicitors to delete them from the printed form, but rather to make any appropriate amendments through the special conditions.[32] The Law Society's form recognises this by a "Note" contained at the beginning of *General Conditions of Sale*[33] in the following terms:

---

22. See *Allman v McDaniel* [1912] 1 IR 467 at 472 (*per* O'Connor MR). See also para **[9.37]** *ante*.

23. As regards protection of the vendor, see the remarks of Porter MR in *Hibernian Bank v Cassidy* (1902) 36 ILTR I56 at 157. See also *Hopkins v Geoghegan* [1931] IR 135 at 139 (*per* Johnston J).

24. See *Martin v Cotter* (1846) 9 Ir Eq R 351 at 353 (*per* Sugden LC); *Manifold v Johnston* [1902] 1 IR 7 at 13 (*per* Porter MR); *Re Flynn and Newman's Contract* [1948] IR 104 at 107 (*per* Kingsmill Moore J). See also as to the need for "reasonableness" *Draisey v Fitzpatrick* [1981] ILRM 219: para **[7.14]** *ante*.

25. See para **[2.53]** *ante*.

26. (1876) IR 10 Eq 239.

27. *Ibid*, pp 241-2. Later he again referred to "the very slender opportunity afforded by the vendor's solicitor of considering the conditions before the sale." *Ibid*, p 255.

28. [1902] 1 IR 83.

29. *Ibid*, pp 86-7.

30. Special cond 2(a): see para **[10.67]** *infra*.

31. Eg, those relating to sales by public auction when it is a sale by private treaty and those relating to registered land when it is unregistered land.

32. One argument is that deletion of one condition may have unforeseen consequences for conditions left in. See the discussion in *Re Priestley's Contract* [1947] Ch 469 (and see (1948) 12 Conv 40).

33. On p 5 of the printed form.

"These General Conditions are not to be altered in any manner. Any required variation or addition should be dealt with by way of Special Condition."

Over the years the Law Society has received complaints from vendors' solicitors about purchasers' solicitors returning draft contracts with amendments made to the general conditions but not drawing attention to the amendments in question. Such a failure to alert vendors' solicitors to such amendments to the printed conditions is regarded by the Society's Professional Purposes Committee as a breach of professional etiquette. The purchaser's solicitor should, therefore, adhere to the long-established practice of leaving the printed general conditions unamended and dealing with any desired amendment or variation by way of special condition on page 4 of the form, supplemented by further annexed pages as necessary.

[10.07] In the next few paragraphs we consider the various matters covered by the special and general conditions in the Law Society's standard contract form. In the case of some of them the comments will be kept to the minimum because detailed discussion of the operation of the condition in question will be found elsewhere in the book. In such cases an appropriate cross-reference to that discussion will be made. However, before considering the various conditions there is one further matter to be considered and that is the statutory regulation of conditions of sale which must be borne in mind. This is particularly important for the vendor's solicitors when drawing up special conditions.

I. STATUTORY REGULATION

[10.08] The parties to a contract for sale of land are restricted to a certain extent by statute in respect of the conditions of sale which they may include. Though there are not as many restrictions in Ireland as there are in England, eg, there is no equivalent of s 48(1) of the Law of Property Act 1925, which renders void any stipulation restricting a purchaser in the selection of a solicitor or requiring, subject to a few exceptions, his conveyancing to be carried out by the vendor's solicitor at the purchaser's expense.[34] But it seems that such a stipulation is rarely, if ever, found in practice in the Republic, though it is not unknown for builders to suggest verbally that the purchase may be handled quicker and more cheaply by their solicitors. However, it must also be reiterated that the courts generally frown on the

---

[34.] Section 48(2) renders void stipulations requiring assignments of leases to be prepared by the assignor or his solicitor at the assignee's expense. See, as regards Ireland para **[10.11]** *infra*.

same solicitor acting for both parties in the same transaction and solicitors must endeavour to avoid putting themselves in a position where they are faced with a conflict of interest.[35]

A. Stamping on Deeds

[10.09] Under s 117 of the Stamp Act 1891, any condition framed with a view to precluding the purchaser from objecting to title on the ground of absence or insufficiency of stamps on any instrument executed after May 16 1888, is void.[36] We return to this matter in a later chapter.[37]

B. Auctioneer's or Agent's Fees

[10.10] We saw in an earlier chapter that any provision or stipulation in an agreement whereby the purchaser is required to pay the vendor's auctioneer's or estate agent's fees or commission is void.[38]

C. Solicitor's Costs

[10.11] Section 32 of the Landlord and Tenant (Ground Rents) Act 1967, renders void any contractual provision whereby payment of all or any of the solicitor's costs of the lease of any party is to be borne by any other party. Though it seems that "solicitor's costs" in this section are confined to the scale charges to which the solicitor is entitled and do not include items of outlay, eg, the cost of furnishing evidence of the lessor's title to make the lease.[39]

D. Requisitions

[10.12] There are some statutory provisions protecting a purchaser's right to raise requisitions on title. Thus, s 115 of the Registration of Title Act 1964, renders void any stipulation in a contract for the sale or charge of registered land, or for the transfer of a registered charge, whereby the purchaser or intending chargeant or transferee is precluded from making requisitions on title in relation to burdens which may affect the land without registration.[40] Section 12(7) of the Land Act 1965, renders "null and void" any stipulation

---

35. See para **[1.34]** *ante*.
36. Section 117 also renders void any arrangement for assuming the liability on account of such absence or insufficiency of stamps or for indemnifying against such liability, absence or insufficiency. *Cf Nixon v Albion Marine Insurance* (1867) LR 2 Exch 338. And see *IRC v Maple & Co (Paris) Ltd* (1907) 77 LJKB 55 at 59 (*per* Lord Macnaghten).
37. Para **[20.38]** *post*.
38. Auctioneers and House Agents Act 1973, s 2(1). See paras **[2.35]** and **[3.32]** *ante*.
39. See Wylie, *Irish Landlord and Tenant Law*, para 13.13.
40. See para **[16.58]** *post*.

in a contract for the sale of land whereby the purchaser is precluded from making requisitions in relation to the letting, sub-letting or sub-division of an agricultural or pastoral holding.[41]

II. GENERAL CONDITIONS

[10.13] In the following paragraphs we deal with the various general conditions set out in the Law Society's printed form.[42] It should be noted that in dealing first with the general conditions we are reversing the order in the Law Society's contract form. This puts the special conditions first which serves to draw the parties' and their solicitors' attention to amendments or variations being made in the general conditions.[43] However, it facilitates exposition in the text to deal first with the general conditions. It should also be noted that the Law Society's Conveyancing Committee has taken care over the order in which the general conditions are set out. The first batch[44] deal with matters which are fairly routine and unlikely to give rise to difficulty or contentious issues. For the most part they follow the various stages of progression in a typical conveyancing transaction.[45] The remaining general conditions[46] deal with matters which are more incidental or are more likely to give rise to difficulties or disputes in the particular transaction.

A. Definitions

[10.14] Conditions 1 and 2 provide a number of important definitions applicable to the rest of the general conditions. Condition 1 largely provides some shorthand expressions which are used frequently such as "the Purchaser" and "the Vendor". The subject of the contract for sale, ie, the property or interest being sold, is referred to as "the subject property". Condition 2 provides some important definitions which affect the operation of other particular provisions. For example, there is a detailed definition of "Apportionment Date" which is designed to cater for a number of possible situations concerning completion of the sale and interest charges which may arise on late completion.[47] Connected with the same subject are the definitions of "closing date"[48] and "stipulated interest rate".[49] In places the general conditions require steps to be taken within certain time limits.[50] Here

---

[41.] See para **[16.30]** *post.*
[42.] Note that the full text is reproduced in Appendix II *post.*
[43.] On the importance of this see para **[10.06]** *supra.*
[44.] Conds 1-27.
[45.] See para **[1.05]** *et seq ante.*
[46.] Conds 28-51.
[47.] See para **[20.09]** *post.*
[48.] See para **[13.12]** *post.*
[49.] See para **[12.18]** *post.*
[50.] Eg, raising of objections on the title and requisitions, and replies thereto: see cond 17.

the definition of "working day" is important, though it should be noted that it is extended by a later condition.[51] The definition not only excludes any Saturday or Sunday and any bank or public holiday but also, in recognition of what has become a traditional period where offices and businesses remain closed, the seven days immediately succeeding Christmas Day. The definition of "Competent Authority" is a wide one covering the whole range of public authorities which have statutory powers. We have already met this in the context of the vendor's duty of disclosure of notices.[52] The definition of "lease" is also very wide, for not only does it include a fee farm grant and other arrangement creating the relationship of landlord and tenant, it also includes licences and agreements for the occupation and use of land which may not create that relationship.[53] This definition is relevant not only to the title of the property being sold,[54] but also to interests subject to which the property is being sold.[55] Finally, it should be noted that the definition of "Requisitions" is a wide "inclusive" one which is designed to reflect a major change in Irish conveyancing practice which has occurred in recent times. This is that a wide variety of enquiries are made in the form of "requisitions" at both the *pre-* and *post*-contract stage of the transaction, many of which do not come within the technical meaning of a "requisition on title".[56] The definition should forestall the argument that a response is not required because the requisition in question is not a "proper" requisition.

B. Interpretation

[10.15] Condition 3 contains some important interpretation provisions which are necessary in Ireland in private documents because there is no equivalent here for such documents[57] of the useful provisions for statutes contained in the Interpretation Act 1937.[58] The condition includes the standard interpretation provisions to the effect that the masculine gender includes the feminine, neuter and common genders and the singular includes the plural

---

51. See cond 50 which covers matters like notice periods, including dates of expiry of such periods: para **[10.64]** *infra*. Note that cond 40 (completion notices) does not refer to "working" days: see para **[13.19]** *post*.

52. See also cond 35: paras **[9.28]** *ante* and **[10.54]** *infra*. The definition is also relevant to the risk of loss or damage to the property between contract and completion: see conds 43-45: paras **[10.60]** *infra* and **[12.36]** *post*.

53. See Wylie, *Irish Landlord and Tenant Law*, Chs 2 and 3.

54. See conds 9 and 10: paras **[10.35]** *infra* and **[14.74]** *post*.

55. See conds 22 and 23: paras **[9.42]** *ante* and **[10.45]** *infra*.

56. See paras **[5.02]** *ante* and **[16.01]** *post*.

57. See *Vone Securities Ltd v Cooke* [1979] IR 59; Wylie, *Irish Landlord and Tenant Law*, para 20.06.

58. Part III. The Law Reform Commission recommended some time ago the enactment of such definitions for documents relating to interests in land: see *Land Law and Conveyancing Law: (1) General Proposals* (LRC 30-1989) paras 21-22. This was done in England by s 61 of the Law of Property Act 1925: see para **[17.17]** *post*.

and *vice versa*. The expressions "vendor" and "purchaser" include their successors in title[59] and where there is more than one such party the conditions are enforceable on a joint and several basis. References to statutes[60] include any amendment, modification and so on, plus any rules and regulations made under them. Finally, it is provided that headings and marginal notes[61] do not affect the construction of the conditions nor do they have any contractual significance. All these interpretation provisions are subject to what the context otherwise requires or implies.

C. Auction

[10.16] Condition 4 deals with the case of sale by auction and is largely concerned with ensuring compliance with the provisions of the Sale of Land by Auction Act 1867.[62] This subject was discussed in an earlier chapter.[63] Apart from that the condition deals with the deposit to be paid by the successful bidder to the vendor's solicitor as stakeholder.[64] The question of the amount of the deposit has been an extremely controversial one over the years. For many years the conditions specified a figure of 25% of the purchase price, but this was clearly out-of-line with the 10% figure long accepted in England. Quite apart from the shock it tended to create in overseas buyers, it came to be recognised increasingly that having to find such a substantial sum created considerable burdens on many purchasers. Furthermore, the practice developed of vendors agreeing, often on the advice of auctioneers, to accept less than 25%.[65] Eventually the Law Society's Conveyancing Committee recommended that 10% would generally be more appropriate,[66] but emphasised later that this was not an absolute rule and that there might be cases where 25% was justified.[67] After further discussion, the Committee settled on 15% as the figure in the 1986 Edition of the standard contract form, but this was reduced to 10% in the 1991 Edition, which remains the figure in the 1995 Edition.[68]

[59.] See further on, eg, the death of parties to the contract paras **[12.26]** and **[12.46]** *post*.

[60.] See, eg, conds 8, 11, 13 and 20.

[61.] Note the marginal note to cond 36: see para **[10.55]** *infra*.

[62.] Especially cond 4(b) and (c).

[63.] See para **[2.14]** *et seq, ante*.

[64.] The method of payment is discussed later, see para **[10.24]** *infra*.

[65.] The Law Society's Conveyancing Committee recommended that such arrangements should be agreed in advance of the bidding: see the *Gazette* March 1984, p 41. However, there could be an element of unfairness to other bidders if such an arrangement was a private one with one or some only of the bidders.

[66.] The *Gazette* September 1981, p 162.

[67.] The *Gazette* March 1984, p 41.

[68.] It remains the case, of course, that this figure may be altered by a special condition; *cf* in the case of a sale by private treaty: para **[10.17]** *infra*.

D. Private Treaty Sale

[10.17] Condition 5 makes an equivalent provision for payment of a deposit in the case of a sale by private treaty, though it does not specify an amount. Rather it leaves it to the vendor or his solicitor to enter the amount in the Memorandum on page 1 of the contract form.[69] This will usually be 10% but it is, of course, open to the vendor to specify a larger or smaller amount.[70] It cannot be emphasised too strongly how important the deposit is from both the parties' point of view and so it is worth discussing the subject in some more detail.[71]

1. Part Payment and Security

[10.18] Payment of a deposit on entering into a contract for the sale of land[72] is usually regarded as an essential part of the transaction.[73] As McVeigh J said in *Morrow v Carty*[74]:

"There can be little doubt that the payment of a deposit is a most important matter in the sale of land and everybody knows this."[75]

The point is that not only is the deposit paid under the contract as part payment of the purchase price,[76] it is also generally regarded as "security" for the performance of the agreement by the purchaser, in the sense that, on default by the purchaser, the vendor may forfeit it.[77] Indeed, condition 41 of the Law Society's *General Conditions of Sale (1995 Edition)* specifically provides that, on failure of the purchaser to comply in any material respect

---

[69.] See para **[9.05]** *ante*.

[70.] In this instance there is no need to do so by way of a special condition; *cf* in the case of an auction sale: para **[10.16]** *supra*.

[71.] Its role in connection with enforcement of the contract is discussed in a later chapter: see para **[13.30]** *et seq, post*.

[72.] On pre-contract deposits, eg, paid to an estate agent, see para **[3.15]** *et seq, ante*.

[73.] But see para **[6.25]** *ante*. See also para **[10.22]** *infra*.

[74.] [1957] NI 174.

[75.] *Ibid*, p 177. See also *Soper v Arnold* (1889) 14 App Cas 429 at 435 (*per* Lord Macnaghten); *Myton Ltd v Schwab-Morris* [1974] 1 WLR 331.

[76.] So stated expressly in conds 4(d) and 5(b). See also *Rooney v Byrne* [1933] IR 609 at 615 (per Sullivan P) and 617 (*per* O'Byrne J); *White v Spendlove* [1942] IR 224 at 252 (*per* Geoghegan J); *Leemac Overseas Investments Ltd v Harvey* [1973] IR 160 at 167-8 (*per* Kenny J).

[77.] *Re Commins and Hanafy's Contract* (1905) 39 ILTR 85 at 86 (*per* Lord Ashbourne C); *Morrow v Carty* [1957] NI 174 at 178 (*per* McVeigh J). See also *McGuire v Conwell* (1932) 66 ILTR 213; *International Securities Ltd v Portmarnock Estates Ltd* High Court, unrep, 1975 (1974/2257P); *Doyle v Ryan* [1981] ILRM 374. And see *Howe v Smith* (1884) 27 Ch D 89 at 98 (*per* Bowen LJ) and 101 (*per* Fry LJ) and the review by the Privy Council in *Workers Trust and Merchant Bank Ltd v Dojap Investments Ltd* [1993] 2 All ER 370. This subject is discussed later, see para **[13.31]** *et seq, post*.

with the conditions of sale, the vendor "shall be entitled to forfeit the deposit" and is at liberty to re-sell the property.[78] Furthermore, condition 31 provides that failure by the purchaser to pay in full the deposit constitutes a breach of condition entitling the vendor to terminate the contract or to sue for damages or both. This covers the case which sometimes used to occur, particularly in auction sales, of the purchaser stopping the cheque for the deposit or paying a portion of the account due only and failing to pay the balance at a later date. Condition 32 deals with the case where the cheque taken for the deposit is not honoured.[79] The subject of forfeiture of the deposit is considered in detail in a later chapter in the general context of enforcement of the contract for sale.[80] However, it should be noted that payment of the deposit is so important only because it is expressly required by the contract made between the parties. In the absence of such an agreement, ie, on an "open" contract, there is no requirement to pay a deposit, for the rule then is that no part of the purchase money is due until completion.[81]

2. Amount

[10.19] This subject was discussed above and little more need be said. It should be noted that in fixing the actual amount of the deposit as a percentage of the "purchase price", account is to be taken of the fact that condition 2 defines the latter expression as *including* additional moneys which the parties agreed should be paid for "goodwill, crops, or purchased chattels.[82] It should also be emphasised that there are dangers in accepting a deposit less than that specified in the contract for it seems that, if the vendor later exercises his right to rescind the contract for breach of contract by the purchaser, he can forfeit only the deposit actually paid by the purchaser, not the deposit he should have paid according to the contract.[83] This greatly

---

[78.] See further on this condition, para **[13.73]** *post*.

[79.] See para **[10.50]** *infra*.

[80.] See para **[13.31]** *et seq, post*.

[81.] *Binks v Rokeby* (1818) 2 Swanst 222 at 225-6 (*per* Lord Eldon LC); *Cyril Andrade Ltd v Sotherby & Co* (1931) 47 TLR 244. See also *Chillingworth v Esche* [1924] 1 Ch 97. And see para **[6.25]** *ante*.

[82.] Note that cond 2 defines "purchased chattels" as "chattels, fittings, tenant's fixtures and other items" included in the sale: see para **[9.15]** *ante*.

[83.] See *Lowe v Hope* [1970] Ch 94 (decision based on the principle that, by electing to rescind the contract, the vendor cannot thereafter insist upon its performance in relation to the deposit). *Cf Dewar v Mintoft* [1912] 2 KB 373. Note that the principle in *Lowe v Hope* can no longer stand in the light of the House of Lords decision in *Johnson v Agnew* [1980] AC 367 as regards the effect of "rescission" in such cases (see para **[13.04]** *post*), but the decision that a vendor can forfeit only the deposit in his or his agent's hands or those of a stakeholder from whom the vendor is entitled to call for the money, remains good law. See para **[13.31]** *post*.

reduces the "security" value of the deposit[84] from the vendor's point of view and it seems clear that it would be negligence on the part of the vendor's solicitor to accept a reduced deposit without the vendor's express authority.[85] Having said that, it is clear now that under the general law, even though the vendor has exercised his right to "rescind" the contract for non-payment of part of the deposit, he can still sue the purchaser in damages to recover the unpaid amount.[86] This position is recognised by condition 31 of the *General Conditions*.[87]

3. Payment

[10.20] There are several matters to be considered with respect to payment of the deposit, eg, when it is to be paid, to whom it should be paid and how it should be paid? Only some of these questions are answered by the *General Conditions* and the rest must be determined according to the general law.

(i) When

[10.21] Condition 4(d) of the *General Conditions of Sale (1995 Edition)* provides that, in the case of a sale by public auction, the deposit must be paid "forthwith." A somewhat similar expression, *viz* "immediately after the sale" was considered by McVeigh J in the Northern Ireland case of *Morrow v Carty*, [88] where the purchaser of a bungalow at an auction held on a Saturday, after signing the agreement after the auction, stated his inability to pay the deposit then. He was given an hour to produce it and, on failure to return with it within that time limit, the bungalow was resold to another person. He then tendered on the following Monday a cheque drawn in favour of his stepfather, but which he claimed he had authority to endorse, but this was refused.[89] McVeigh J rejected his application for specific performance and commented:

> "My view is that the words 'immediately after the sale' in condition 4 meant 'without any delay' ... I think it means that the purchaser must place himself at the disposal of the vendor or his agent so that it may be ensured that payment of the deposit takes place as soon as it is convenient to bring that about after the sale ... the vendor is not obliged to wait until the next

---

[84.] See para **[10.18]** *supra*.

[85.] *Morris v Duke-Cohan & Co* (1975) 119 Sol Jo 826.

[86.] This follows from the decision in *Johnson v Agnew* [1980] AC 367 (fn 83 *supra*): see *Millichamp v Jones* [1983] 1 All ER 267; *Damon Cia Naviera SA v Hapag-Lloyd International SA* [1985] 1 All ER 475.

[87.] See para **[10.18]** *supra*.

[88.] [1957] NI 174. See also, in a different context (delivery of the abstract of title), *Re Todd and McFadden's Contract* [1908] 1 IR 213 at 220 (*per* Kenny J), see para **[14.45]** *post*.

[89.] McVeigh J held that the auctioneer or vendor was entitled, apart from the question of delay, to insist upon payment in cash, see para **[2.10]** *ante* and **[10.24]** *infra*.

day to enable the purchaser to produce cash even where the purchaser is a person of credit."[90]

It had been argued that there was a local practice relating to auctions, whereby "immediately after the sale" was interpreted widely to allow payment at any time on the day of the sale or, in the case of a sale on a Saturday, on the following Monday. McVeigh J rejected this argument with the following comment:

"... I do not think there is any such practice, and my view, on the evidence, is that the local practice is to pay the deposit 'then and there' at the conclusion of the sale."[91]

[10.22] In the case of a sale by private treaty, condition 5(a) of the *General Conditions of Sale (1995 Edition)* requires payment "on or before the date of the sale". This is defined in condition 2 as the "date upon which the contract for the sale shall have become binding on the Vendor and Purchaser".[92] This provision[93] seems to be intended to prevent what was previously the standard practice in Ireland, namely, that the vendor or his solicitor, upon receipt of the contract signed by the purchaser, insisted upon payment of the deposit before the vendor signed the contract, ie, payment of the deposit was regarded almost as a pre-condition of the vendor's signature and the purchaser was expected to send the deposit with the return of the signed contract.[94] Under condition 2 it is questionable whether the vendor can insist upon this, because the contract does not become binding on him until he signs it.[95] Furthermore, the principle that payment of the deposit is a

---

[90.] *Op cit*, p 177.

[91.] *Op cit*, p 176. *Quaere* whether delay due to an oversight will excuse the purchaser: see *Millichamp v Jones* [1983] 1 All ER 267 and para **[10.22]** *infra*.

[92.] Note the reference to *both* parties.

[93.] It was first introduced in the 1986 Edition of the *General Conditions*.

[94.] See *Myton Ltd v Schwab Morris* [1974] 1 WLR 331, where Goulding J held that a condition requiring payment of the deposit "on or before the signing" of the agreement was a condition precedent to the agreement taking effect. He stated:

"The vendor, in the normal case, never intends to be bound by the contract without having the deposit in his own or his stakeholder's possession as a protection against possible loss from default by the purchaser. No doubt, it may be thought that where building operations are in progress and still unfinished, the vendor is even more concerned to have such a protection than in other cases. In any ordinary case where a deposit on signing is demanded, if the purchaser says, 'I am sorry, I cannot find the deposit,' the vendor would naturally reply, 'I do not propose to hand over the contract signed by me until I am paid'."

Ibid, p 336. As to counsel's inability to find direct authority on the point, he commented: "Perhaps its absence is due to the point being a clear one on the ordinary everyday understanding of transactions of sale of land." *Ibid*, p 336.

[95.] See para **[6.32]** *et seq, ante*.

condition precedent to the formation of the contract has been rejected in recent times.[96] Rather non-payment is regarded as a fundamental breach of the contract which has come into force and so the vendor is entitled to invoke remedies for breach of contract.[97] This view is reinforced by the *General Conditions*. Thus, the deposit is specified as "part payment" of the purchase price,[98] which, of course, is payable only if there is a contract in existence. Furthermore, condition 31 specifies that non-payment of the deposit in full constitutes "a breach of condition entitling the Vendor to terminate the sale or to sue the Purchaser for damages or both."[99]

(ii) To Whom

[10.23] Conditions 4(d) and 5(a) of the *General Conditions of Sale (1995 Edition)* require that the deposit should be paid to the vendor's solicitor "as stakeholder" in the cases of sales by both public auction and private treaty. Condition 5(b) recognises that in the case of a sale by private treaty it is not uncommon for part of the deposit to be paid to someone else, eg, a *pre*-contract deposit paid to an estate agent.[100] It provides that where a part of the deposit payable under condition 5(a) "has been or is"[101] paid to "any other person appointed or nominated by the vendor that other person shall be deemed to receive or to have received said part as stakeholder". This provision does, of course, provide limited protection only to a purchaser who unadvisedly pays a *pre*-contract deposit.[102] The vendor is bound by condition 5(a) only if the contract containing it is entered into by him. All too often the parties never get to the stage of entering into the contract and the purchaser is left to his remedies, such as they are, under the general law in order to recover a deposit which has been paid to an estate agent or builder or developer.[103]

---

96. *Damon Cia Naviera SA v Hapag-Lloyd International SA* [1985] 1 All ER 475, where the English Court of Appeal rejected the views of Goulding J in *Myton Ltd v Schwab-Morris* quoted in fn 94 *supra*. See also *Millichamp v Jones* [1983] 1 All ER 267 at 274 (*per* Warner J). A similar view has been taken by the Australasian courts: see *Brien v Dwyer* (1979) 141 CLR 378; *cf Watson v Healy Lands Ltd* [1965] NZLR 511.

97. *Culhane v Hewson* [1979] IR 8. See para **[10.19]** *supra*.

98. See para **[10.18]** *supra*.

99. This is without prejudice to other rights available. The vendor might, eg, prefer to enforce payment by seeking specific performance: see para **[13.37]** *post*. Note also the right either to rescind (in the sense of treating himself as discharged from the contract) or to enforce payment where the cheque is dishonoured conferred on the vendor by cond 22: see para **[10.18]** *supra*.

100. *Cf* a "booking" deposit or "stage payment" paid to an agent of a builder or developer: see *Desmond v Brophy* [1985] IR 449, paras **[3.15]** *ante* and **[10.31]** *infra*.

101. Ie, it may have been paid *prior* to the contract being entered into.

102. On the dangers see para **[3.15]** *et seq ante*.

103. *Desmond v Brophy* [1985] IR 449: see para **[3.17]** *ante*.

(iii) How

[10.24] The method of payment is not specified in the *General Conditions* and is, therefore, left to be determined by the general law. We saw in an earlier chapter[104] that the general rule is that the vendor or his agent is entitled to insist upon payment in cash[105] and cannot be required to accept a bill of exchange,[106] IOU[107] or even, it seems, a cheque.[108] This last point is the traditional view and may be questioned nowadays in terms of convenience, in view of the almost universal acceptance of a cheque as a method of payment in general commercial practice. There is some authority in England to support the view that a cheque is now an acceptable method of payment,[109] but the traditional view was accepted as recently as 1957 by McVeigh J in *Morrow v Carty*,[110] where he said:

"... what is required is payment in cash (not cheque) ..."[111]

In fact, in that case what had been tendered by the purchaser was a cheque drawn in his stepfather's name, which the purchaser claimed he had authority to endorse, and McVeigh J had no hesitation in holding that this was not satisfactory payment.[112] On the other hand, it is arguable that the Law Society's *General Conditions* impliedly recognise that payment by cheque is acceptable under the standard contract because condition 32 makes specific provision to cover the case where "a cheque taken for the deposit" is not honoured.[113]

4. Capacity of Deposit-Holder

[10.25][114] If the deposit is not paid to the vendor personally, the question arises as to what is the capacity of the third party who receives it.[115] The general law recognises two basic capacities in such a case, namely, receipt

---

[104.] See para **[2.10]** *ante*.

[105.] *Hodgens v Keon* [1894] 2 IR 657; *Morrow v Carty* [1957] NI 174.

[106.] *Boothman v Bryne* (1923) 57 ILTR 36. See also *O'Connor v Faul* (1957) 91 ILTR 7. And see *Williams v Evans* (1866) LR 1 QB 352; *Pape v Westacott* [1894] 1 QB 272.

[107.] *Hodgens v Keon* [1894] 2 IR 657. *Cf Wilson v Wilson* (1854) 14 CB 616; *Hinton v Sparkes* (1868) LR 3 CP 161.

[108.] *Johnston v Boyes* [1899] 2 Ch 73, followed by McVeigh J in *Morrow v Carty* [1957] NI 174.

[109.] See *Farrer v Lacy, Hartland & Co* (1885) 31 Ch D 42 at 46 (*per* Baggalley LJ). and 48 (*per* Bowen LJ).

[110.] [1957] NI 174, and see fn 108 *supra*, and para **[10.21]** *supra*.

[111.] *Ibid*, p 177, where he did also accept that the vendor could waive this requirement.

[112.] *Ibid*, pp 177-8.

[113.] See para **[10.18]** *supra*.

[114.] This paragraph in the first edition was quoted with approval by Barrington J in *Desmond v Brophy* [1985] IR 449 at 454.

[115.] A deposit paid under the contract should not be confused with a pre-contract deposit, eg, one paid to a house or estate agent, see paras **[3.10]** and **[3.15]** *et seq, ante*.

as *agent* for the vendor and as *stakeholder*. The significance of the distinction is this. If the deposit is paid to the vendor's agent, eg, his auctioneer or solicitor acting in that capacity,[116] the agent is liable to pay it to the vendor on demand.[117] He must also account to the vendor for any interest earned or other profit made from the deposit.[118] If the sale falls through, the purchaser can sue the vendor only, not the agent, for recovery.[119] The advantage from the vendor's point of view is that he can demand the deposit immediately and use it, eg, in connection with some other transaction such as the purchase of a new house. It has been suggested that there are dangers in this from the purchaser's point of view in that, if the vendor suddenly goes bankrupt and the deposit has been spent by him, the purchaser may have difficulty in recovering it.[120] The same principle applies to, eg, a *pre*-contract deposit paid to an agent receiving it on behalf of a builder or developer, for then the builder or developer can use the money immediately in connection with the building or development.[121] On the other hand, it is settled that, if the deposit is paid under the contract to the vendor's agent, the purchaser has a lien on the vendor's land for its return,[122] and in this respect the purchaser is better off than he would be if the deposit were paid to a stakeholder.[123]

[10.26] If the deposit is paid to a stakeholder, it is settled that he is personally responsible for its safe-keeping[124] and must not hand it over to the vendor without the purchaser's permission.[125] In this respect he is agent for both parties, obliged to hold onto the deposit until the vendor becomes entitled to it[126], eg, on forfeiture due to default by the purchaser or on

---

[116.] See para **[10.30]** *infra*.

[117.] *Edgell v Day* (1865) LR 1 CP 80.

[118.] *Harrington v Hoggart* (1830) 1 B & Ald 577 at 586 (*per* Tenterden LCJ). As regards solicitors see the Solicitors (Interest on Client's Moneys) Regulations 1995 (SI 108/1995), made under s 73 of the Solicitors (Amendment) Act 1994.

[119.] *Ellis v Goulton* [1893] 1 QB 350 at 353 (*per* Bowen LJ).

[120.] See the controversy in England, (1968) 65 L Soc Gaz 160 and (1972) 69 L Soc Gaz 359, 422 and 469. See also Adams, (1970) 120 New LJ 1128 and 1139.

[121.] See *Desmond v Brophy* [1985] IR 449: paras **[3.15]** *ante* and **[10.31]** *infra*.

[122.] *Whitbread & Co Ltd v Watt* [1902] 1 Ch 835. See also *Lee-Parker v Izzet* [1971] 1 WLR 1688. See also para **[12.44]** *post*.

[123.] See *Combe v Swaythling* [1947] Ch 623. But *cf Skinner v Reed's Trustee* [1967] Ch 1194.

[124.] *Wiggins v Lord* (1841) 4 Beav 30; *Furtado v Lumley* (1890) 54 JP 407. See further, para **[3.17]** *ante*.

[125.] *Smith v Jackson* (1816) 1 Madd 618; *Yates v Farebrother* (1819) 4 Madd 239.

[126.] *Leemac Overseas Investments Ltd v Harvey* [1973] IR 160 at 164 (*per* Kenny J). Note, however, that in England it was recently held that a stakeholder is not an *agent* but rather a *principal* who can exercise his own judgment as to whether to pay the money to one or other of the parties, subject, however, to the risk that if his judgment is later held to be wrong he will be personally liable to the other party: see *Hastingswood Property Ltd v Saunders Bearman Anselm* [1990] 3 All ER 107. *Cf Rockeagle Ltd v Alsop Wilkinson* [1991] 4 All ER 659 (duties lying in contract or *quasi*-contract and so solicitor-stakeholder obliged to hand funds over to another stakeholder when *both* parties so instructed him).

completion of the transaction, or the purchaser becomes entitled to its return, eg, on rescission of the contract due to the vendor's default.[127] However, it seems that a stakeholder is not a "trustee" for both parties and so is not obliged under the general law to account for any interest or profit earned by him from the deposit - this, as one English judge said, is his "reward" for holding the stake.[128] But it is extremely doubtful whether this rule applies to a solicitor - stakeholder governed by Solicitors' Accounts Regulations.[129] Finally, although there has been considerable controversy on the point,[130] it seems that there is no reason why a vendor who is acting in a fiduciary capacity, eg, a trustee or personal representative, should not allow the deposit to be paid to a stakeholder rather than an agent under the vendor's sole control.[131]

[10.27] It seems to be accepted now on both sides of the Irish Sea that the vendor is responsible to the purchaser for the loss of the deposit under the contract,[132] whether it is paid to his agent or a stakeholder. So far as payment to his agent is concerned, the general law of principal and agent confirms the principal's liability.[133] Where the payment is to a stakeholder, the vendor is responsible partly for a reason stated by Kenny J in *Leemac Overseas Investments Ltd v Harvey*[134]:

> "Where the sale is by public auction, the stakeholder will be nominated by the vendor who drafts the conditions of sale and who is therefore liable for his default. Similarly if the sale is by private contract and if the stakeholder is nominated by the vendor, he is liable for his default ..."[135]

[127.] *Skinner v Reed's Trustee* [1967] Ch 1194 at 1200 (*per* Cross J). See also *Collins v Stinson* (1883) 11 QBD 142.

[128.] *Smith v Hamilton* [1951] Ch 174 at 184 (*per* Harman J). See also *Harrington v Hoggart* (1830) 1 B & Ald 577 at 586-7 (*per* Tenterden LCJ); *Potters v Loppert* [1973] 1 All ER 658 at 668 (*per* Pennycuick J). On another aspect of the *Smith* case, see para **[13.17]** *post*.

[129.] See *Burt v Claude Cousins & Co Ltd* [1971] 2 QB 426 at 449-50 (*per* Sach LJ), citing in support *Brown v IRC* [1965] AC 244. The Law Society has recommended that a solicitor holding client money in which having regard to all the circumstances (including the amount and length of time for which the money is likely to be held) interest ought in fairness to the client to be earned, should put that money on deposit and account for the interest or pay the equivalent sum: see the *Gazette* November 1980, p 209. See also para **[10.32]** *infra*. See also the Solicitors (Interest on Client's Moneys) Regulations 1995 (SI 108/1995).

[130.] Note the varying views of textbook writers. See Farrand, *Contract and Conveyance* (4th ed, 1983), p 208; Gibson's *Conveyancing* (20th ed by Kersley; 1970), p 126, *Williams on Title* (4th ed by Battersby; 1975), p 91.

[131.] *Edmonds v Peake* (1843) 7 Beav 239 at 242 (*per* Lord Langdale MR).

[132.] *Cf re* a pre-contract deposit, see paras **[2.10]** and **[3.15]** *et seq, ante*

[133.] *Ellis v Goulton* [1893] 1 QB 350.

[134.] [1973] IR 160.

[135.] *Ibid*, p 165. See also *Annesley v Muggridge* (1816) 1 Madd 593 at 596 (*per* Plummer V-C); *Rowe v May* (1854) 18 Beav 613 at 614 (*per* Page-Wood V-C).

The stakeholder will usually be nominated by the vendor in a sale by private treaty, but the question remains as to what the position is if the deposit is paid to a stakeholder not nominated by him. Kenny J considered this matter at length in the *Leemac* case[136] and, after a review of the judicial and academic authorities, concluded:

> "There is thus consistent authority from 1816[137] for the rule that the vendor must bear the loss when the stakeholder cannot pay the deposit. The reasons originally given for the rule were unsatisfactory but I think it is the law to-day because the deposit paid by a purchaser to a stakeholder is a payment in part of the purchase money ... and when a sale cannot be completed and the purchaser becomes entitled to recover the deposit from the stakeholder, the vendor should be held liable for his default."[138]

[10.28] There remains to be considered the question of what is the capacity in which each of the various parties who may be involved in a sale of land receives the deposit. The first principle is that this may be specified expressly in the contract and we saw earlier that the *Law Society's General Conditions of Sale (1995 Edition)* provide that the deposit is to be paid to the vendor's solicitor as "stakeholder,"[139] whether the sale is by public auction[140] or private treaty.[141] Otherwise, the matter must be determined according to the general law, a subject to which we now turn.[142]

(i) Auctioneer

[10.29] It is settled that, in the absence of an agreement to the contrary, an auctioneer receives a deposit as a stakeholder and not as agent of the vendor.[143] He is not liable to pay interest on it for the period he holds it as stakeholder,[144] unless there is some special arrangement for its investment.[145] The deposit does, however, carry interest after a demand for its handing over by a person entitled to call for its receipt.[146]

---

136. Note that the *Leemac* case actually involved a *pre*-contract deposit, see paras **[3.16-17]** *ante*.
137. See the English cases cited in fn 135 *supra*.
138. *Op cit*, pp 167-8. See also at p 165.
139. See para **[10.22]** *supra*.
140. Cond 4(d).
141. Cond 5(a).
142. See also paras **[2.10]**, **[2.26]** and **[3.15]** *et seq*
143. *Dickie v White* (1901) 1 NIJR 128 at 131 (*per* FitzGibbon LJ) (*cf* at p 131, *per* Lord Ashbourne C). See also *Leemac Overseas Investments Ltd v Harvey* [1973] IR 160. And see *Harrington v Hoggart* (1830) 1 B & Ald 577; *Skinner v Reed's Trustee* [1967] Ch 1194.
144. *Lee v Mann* (1817) 8 Taunt 45.
145. See para **[10.32]** *infra*.
146. *Gaby v Driver* (1828) 2 Y & J 549.

(ii) Solicitor

[10.30] Again in the absence of a contrary agreement,[147] a deposit paid to the vendor's solicitor is treated as paid to him as the vendor's agent rather than as a stakeholder.[148]

(iii) Estate Agent

[10.31] In the case of a sale by private treaty, it is usual that the "deposit" received by a house or estate agent will be a pre-contract deposit, and it would seem, in the light of recent authorities, that as a general principle this should not be regarded as being received as agent for the vendor, in the absence of express authority conferred by the latter.[149] At most, therefore, the "agent" should be regarded as receiving such a deposit as a stakeholder.[150] This position is now confirmed by the 1995 Edition of the Law Society's *General Conditions* which contains a new provision not to be found in the earlier Editions. Condition 5(b) now provides that where a "part"[151] of the deposit, which should, under condition 5(a) be paid to the vendor's solicitor as stakeholder, "has been or is paid to any other person appointed or nominated by the vendor that other person shall be deemed to receive or to have received said part as stakeholder." It is important to appreciate the limitations to this provision. It is predicated on the assumption that the "part" so paid is part of the deposit payable under condition 5(a). The implication may be that the parties are to be taken as agreeing that any *pre*-contract payment already made, say to an estate agent, is "converted" once the contract is signed into part-payment of the deposit and so the obligation on the purchaser under condition 5(a) is to pay only the *balance* of the deposit specified. If that is the true interpretation of the provision, then, of course, it would mean that the vendor assumes responsibility for the loss of the *pre*-contract payment as well as the balance paid on the signing of the contract, in accordance with the principle governing *contractual*, as opposed to *pre-contractual,* deposits paid to a stakeholder.[152] This suggests that the vendor should insist, once the contract is entered into, upon the money held by the estate agent or other person holding the *pre*-contract payment being handed over to his solicitor to be held with the balance paid

---

147. Which there is if the Law Society's *General Conditions* are used, see para **[10.28]** *supra*. See also *Hall v Burnell* [1911] 2 Ch 551.

148. *Edgell v Day* (1865) LR 1 CP 80; *Ellis v Goulton* [1893] 1 QB 350.

149. See the discussion at para **[3.15]** *et seq, ante*.

150. See *Leemac Overseas Investments Ltd v Harvey* [1973] IR 160. See also the English cases cited in paras **[3.16-17]** *ante*.

151. The provision clearly envisages the situation where a *pre*-contract deposit has been paid to an estate agent, which will usually be less than the 10% payable under the contract; *cf* a "booking" deposit paid or "stage payment" made before the contract: see *Desmond v Brophy* [1985] IR 449, para **[3.15]** *ante*.

152. See para **[10.27]** *supra*.

by the purchaser.[153] All this, of course, only becomes relevant if condition 5 comes into play which it will not do if the parties never get as far as entering into a contract in the Law Society's standard form or, at least, one incorporating the *General Conditions* contained therein.[154] In that case the parties' position remains governed by the law relating to *pre*-contractual dealings and the purchaser will usually be at severe risk of being unable to recover any loss of deposit from the vendor.[155]

(iv) Investment

[10.32] In the absence of an express agreement on the matter, it seems that neither the vendor nor his agent, nor indeed, a stakeholder, is obliged to invest the deposit.[156] But, of course, the deposit may be invested[157] and, if it is, the vendor's agent must account for interest to his principal,[158] whereas the stakeholder can keep it, unless, like a solicitor, he is governed by special rules.[159] However, if the deposit is a very substantial amount and if completion is likely to be delayed for some substantial time, eg, because the contract is subject to fulfilment of some condition such as obtaining planning permission, the contract may provide expressly for investment of the deposit. In that case, a common practice in Ireland, as was illustrated by the case of *International Securities Ltd v Portmarnock Estates Ltd*,[160] is to require that the money be placed on deposit receipt[161] with a bank in the joint names of the vendor's and purchaser's solicitors. Although the Law Society has in more recent times cast doubt on the appropriateness of the use of deposit receipts for holding client's money, because of the various disadvantages associated with them,[162] it acknowledged that their use was most justified where the money is placed on joint deposit in the names of two solicitors.[163]

[153.] The purchaser should not object to this for it provides the protection of the Solicitors' Professional Indemnity Insurance Scheme (see the Solicitor's Acts 1954 to 1994 (Professional Indemnity Insurance Scheme) Regulations 1995 (SI 312/1995).

[154.] Note that the Society's Conveyancing Committee disapproves of the practice of using part only of its standard from: see para **[10.03]** *supra*.

[155.] *Re Barrett Apartments Ltd* [1985] IR 350. See para **[3.15]** *et seq, ante*.

[156.] *Harrington v Hoggart* (1830) 1 B & Ald 577.

[157.] See *Leemac Overseas Investments Ltd v Harvey* [1973] IR 160 at 166 (*per* Kenny J).

[158.] See para **[10.25]** *supra*.

[159.] See para **[10.26]** *supra*.

[160.] High Court, unrep, 9 April 1975 (1974/225P). See also *Healy v Healy* High Court, unrep, 3 December 1973 (1973/244P).

[161.] As to which, see Wylie *Irish Land Law* (2nd ed, 1986), para 9.044.

[162.] Eg, interest is paid only when the deposit receipt is uplifted and then it is simple interest only, not compound. See the summary of benefits and disadvantages set out in the Law Society *Newsletter*, April/December 1986 and reproduced in the *Conveyancing Handbook*, paras 13.19-20.

[163.] "Clearly, this is the best and most convenient method of putting money in a joint account." *Ibid*, para 13.20.

E. Purchaser on Notice of Certain Documents

[10.33] This matter is dealt with by condition 6 and relates to the Documents Schedule on page 3 of the contract form. The operation of this provision was fully considered in the previous chapter.[164]

F. Delivery of Title

[10.34] Condition 7 sets out the vendor's duty to deliver copies of title documents in compliance with the requirements of deduction of title. It is important to reiterate that this condition relates to the full set of title documents and should not be confused with the documents made available under condition 6. This matter is considered in detail in a later chapter.[165]

G. Title

[10.35] Conditions 8-10 deal with the title to be deduced by the vendor and the investigation of that title by the purchaser. Traditionally this subject is one of the key features of the *post*-contract stage of the conveyancing process and, therefore, the subject of conditions of sale. The whole matter is discussed in later chapters where the significance of these conditions is fully considered.[166]

H. Prior Title

[10.36] Condition 11 deals with the question of how far the purchaser can insist upon investigating the "prior" title, ie, prior to the commencement of title which the vendor has agreed to in the Special Conditions. This too is considered in a later chapter.[167]

I. Intermediate Title

[10.37] Condition 12 is linked with the previous conditions relating to deduction and investigation of title and is discussed in a later chapter.[168]

J. Registered Land

[10.38] Condition 13 deals with deduction and investigation of title in cases involving registered land, ie, where the title to the land being sold is registered in the Land Registry. This too is considered in a later chapter.[169]

[164.] See paras **[9.39-41]** *ante*. See also para **[9.24]** *ante*.

[165.] See, in particular, para **[14.46]** *post*.

[166.] See Chs 14-16 *post*.

[167.] See para **[15.52]** *post*.

[168.] See para **[14.61]** *post*.

[169.] See para **[14.21]** *et seq, post*.

K. Identity

[10.39] Condition 14 deals with the "particulars" of the property being sold and was discussed in the previous chapter.[170]

L. Rights - Liabilities - Condition of Subject Property

[10.40] Conditions 15 and 16 deal with the difficult question of the vendor's duty of disclosure and its relationship with the *caveat emptor* principle. This subject was also discussed in the previous chapter.[171]

M. Requisitions

[10.41] Conditions 17 and 18 deal with requisitions on title, an integral part of the purchaser's investigation of title. This subject is discussed in detail in later chapters.[172]

N. Searches

[10.42] Condition 19 deals with searches which are also an integral part of the investigation of title. The condition recognises the Law Society's recommended practice whereby the vendor should not only furnish with the draft contract any searches in his possession, but also a draft requisition for a negative search against the vendor and other parties immediately on the title, covering the period of title which the vendor has agreed to deduce. It was pointed out by Conveyancing Committee that a failure to lodge a requisition for a negative search at the contract stage inevitably results in it not being ready at the closing.[173] The consequence of this is that the purchaser may incur the additional expense of having to make a hand search and delays in closing may occur. This need to follow the recommended practice is reiterated by the Searches Schedule at the bottom of page 3 of the Law Society's contract form, which specifically refers to a negative search. The subject of searches is discussed fully in a later chapter.[174]

O. Assurance

[10.43] Condition 20 deals with the deed of conveyance or transfer essential to put into effect the contract for sale, a subject dealt with in a later

---

[170.] See para **[9.11]** *ante*.
[171.] See para **[9.43]** *ante*.
[172.] See Ch 15-16, especially para **[15.27]** *post*.
[173.] The *Gazette* July/August 1978, p 125.
[174.] See para **[15.39]** *post*.

chapter.[175] It also deals with the vitally important subject of tax clearance certificates which have become a feature of modern tax legislation. This too is dealt with in a later chapter.[176]

P. Vacant Possession

[10.44] In the absence of any provision in the contract,[177] it is settled that there is an implied condition at common law that the purchaser will be given vacant possession on completion.[178] This means that the vendor must see not only that he and other occupiers, such as tenants[179] or squatters,[180] leave the premises, but also that the physical state of the property itself is left vacant, eg, it must not be left cluttered up with rubbish.[181] Condition 21 provides expressly that, subject to any contrary provision in the particulars or conditions or implied by the nature of the transaction, the purchaser is entitled to vacant possession on completion. It was common to find this specified expressly in the contract even if no such provision was contained in the general conditions.[182] The importance of such a condition, and of strict compliance with the closing date,[183] in the case of a sale of a farm was emphasised by O'Connor J in *Guerin v Heffernan*[184]:

> "A contract for the sale of a farm is one which ought to be expeditiously carried out. A farm is a property which requires immediate attention and treatment. The times for doing things on a farm wait not for the farmer. He must always be up and doing. When he buys his farm he ought to get immediate possession. If he is delayed he may miss a sowing, or a reaping,

---

175. See Ch 17, especially para **[17.04]** *post*.
176. See para **[16.25]** *post*.
177. Eg. that the property is sold subject to existing tenancies, see para **[10.45]** *infra*. See also *Hibernian Bank Ltd v Harrington* (1912) 46 ILTR 27.
178. *Bank of Ireland v Waldron* [1944] IR 303 at 305 (*per* Overend J). See also *Guerin v Heffernan* [1925] 1 IR 57 at 67-8 (*per* O'Connor J). And see *Cook v Taylor* [1942] Ch 349 at 352 (*per* Simonds J). As regards possession *before* completion, see para **[12.32]** *post*.
179. *Irish Land Commission v Maquay* (1891) 28 LR Ir 342; *Re Postmaster-General and Colgan's Contract* [1906] 1 IR 287 (*affd* 477).
180. *Dickie v White* (1901) 1 NIJR 128.
181. *Cumberland Consolidated Holdings Ltd v Ireland* [1946] KB 264. *Cf Viscount Securities Ltd v Kennedy* Supreme Court, unrep, 6 May 1986 (168/1985) para **[13.20]** *post*. See also *Norwich Union Life Insurance Society v Preston* [1957] 1 WLR 813 (furniture left on premises). As to assessment of damages for failure to give vacant possession, see *Beard v Porter* [1948] 1 KB 321.
182. See *Irish Land Commission v Maquay* (1891) 28 LR Ir 342 at 352-3 (*per* Palles CB); *Dickie v White* (1901) 1 NIJR 128 at 131 (*per* FitzGibbon J); *Re Postmaster-General and Colgan's Contract* [1906] 1 IR 287 at 292 (*per* Barton J) (*affd* 477).
183. See para **[13.15]** *post*.
184. [1925] 1 IR 57.

or a market. Consequently, if there is a dispute between a vendor and a purchaser of a farm, the purchaser should know at once whether he is to be on or off with his contract. He ought not to be kept in suspense."[185]

Q. Leases

[10.45] Conditions 22 and 23 deal with a converse case, ie, where no vacant possession is to be given on completion because the property is sold subject to existing leases whereunder it is occupied by the lessees currently holding under those leases. The significance of these provisions was discussed in the previous chapter.[186]

R. Completion and Interest

[10.46] Conditions 24-26 deal with various matters relating to completion, including the formalities for closing the sale.[187] It also deals with interest charges which will arise on delays the fault of the purchaser, a matter also dealt with in a later chapter.[188]

S. Apportionment and Possession

[10.47] Condition 27 deals with a different area of the law, *viz*, apportionment as between the vendor and purchaser of various rents, profits, rates, taxes and other charges or outgoings relating to the property. This subject is dealt with in a later chapter.[189]

T. Section 45, Land Act 1965

[10.48] Condition 28 deals with cases where consent to the vesting of the property in the purchaser or his nominee is required under s 45 of the Land Act 1965. Since the 1986 Edition of the *General Conditions* the obtaining of such consent has no longer been a condition of the sale, failure to meet which would justify the purchaser rescinding the contract. This subject is discussed in a later chapter.[190]

---

185. *Ibid*, pp 67-8.
186. See para **[9.42]** *ante*.
187. See para **[20.25]** *post*.
188. See para **[20.09]** *post*.
189. See para **[20.03]** *post*.
190. See para **[16.37]** *post*.

U. Compulsory Registration

[10.49] Condition 29 deals with the situation where the property is still unregistered land but has become, or will become as a consequence of the sale, subject to compulsory registration of the title in the Land Registry. This is dealt with in a later chapter.[191]

V. Signing "in Trust" or "as Agent"

[10.50] Condition 30 contains a special provision dealing with the case where a purchaser signs the memorandum of agreement "in Trust," "as Trustee," or "as Agent" or with any similar qualification or description, without specifying therein the identity of any principal. We saw earlier that there is a danger in such a case that under the general law the person signing will be held liable personally to complete the purchase.[192] Indeed, if the contract is signed by a person expressly "as Agent" and there is no indication as to his principal in the contract, it is arguable that there is no sufficient memorandum of the agreement for the purposes of the Statute of Frauds. The name of one of the parties to the contract is missing and the names of both parties should normally be specified.[193] Condition 30 may save the contract by providing that the person who signs is to be personally liable to complete the purchase unless and until he discloses to the vendor the name of his principal. This condition may also act as a deterrent to solicitors or other persons from signing contracts as agents or trustees without specifying (1) the agency or trusteeship and (2) even if the agency or trusteeship is specified, the name of the principal or beneficiary. In any case, care should be taken to ensure that the principal or beneficiary is able to complete and will, if necessary, indemnify the agent or trustee.

W. Failure to Pay Deposit

[10.51] Conditions 31 and 32 deal with the vendor's remedies where the purchaser fails to pay the deposit in full, as required by the contract, or where the cheque taken for it is not honoured. This subject was dealt with earlier in this chapter.[194]

[191.] See para **[16.55]** *post.*
[192.] See para **[6.35]** *ante.*
[193.] See para **[6.20]** *ante.*
[194.] See para **[10.16]** *et seq, supra.*

X. Differences - Errors

[10.52] Condition 33 deals with the difficult area of misdescription of the property in the contract itself, and misrepresentation in the negotiations leading up to the contract, and the purchaser's remedies. This subject was dealt with in the previous chapter.[195]

Y. Documents of Title relating to other Property

[10.53] Condition 34 recognises that in a case where the sale involves the disposal of part only of a larger property held under a single title, the vendor will retain the original title documents since they relate also to the land retained by him. The condition makes provisions for furnishing the purchaser with certified copies of the documents and the usual acknowledgment of the right of production and undertaking for safe custody of original documents retained by the vendor.[196] This subject is dealt with in a later chapter.[197]

Z. Disclosure of Notices

[10.54] Condition 35 also deals with the vendor's duty of disclosure[198] and was dealt with in the previous chapter.[199]

AA. Development

[10.55] Condition 36 deals with another very difficult area of the law for conveyancers, *viz*, the impact on property of the planning legislation and related legislation like the Building Control Act 1990. It imposes substantial duties on the vendor for the protection of the purchaser. There is also an important marginal note referring to the possibility that protection may exist under, eg, the Bye-Law Amnesty contained in s 22(7) of the Building Control Act and recommending that this be dealt with expressly by way of a special condition.[200] This whole subject is considered in detail in a later chapter.[201]

[195.] See para **[9.44]** *et seq, ante.*
[196.] It also deals with the sale of a property in lots to different purchasers: see para **[19.09]** *post.*
[197.] See para **[18.102]** *post.*
[198.] See also conds 15 and 16, para **[9.43]** *ante.*
[199.] See para **[9.28]** *ante.*
[200.] See para **[10.69]** *infra.*
[201.] See para **[16.74]** *post.*

BB. Rescission

[10.56] Condition 37-39 deal with the effect of exercise by either party of a right of rescission conferred by other conditions.[202] This is dealt with in a later chapter.[203]

CC. Completion Notices

[10.57] Condition 40 deals with completion notices, often the most effective remedy for bringing a procrastinating party "to heel"! This too is dealt with in a later chapter.[204]

DD. Forfeiture of Deposit and Resale

[10.58] Condition 41 deals with what is often the most effective remedy for the vendor against a defaulting purchaser, *viz*, forfeiture of the deposit and resale of the property to another buyer. This is discussed fully in a later chapter.[205]

EE. Damages for Default

[10.59] Condition 42 confirms what now appears to be accepted as the general law in cases where an order for specific performance is not complied with, ie, the purchaser can claim an award of damages.[206] This matter is dealt with in a later chapter.[207]

FF. Risk

[10.60] Conditions 43-45 deal with the controversial subject of the allocation of risk of loss or damage to the parties in the interim period between contract and completion.[208] They were first introduced in the 1986 Edition and have now become generally accepted. They are discussed in a later chapter.[209]

[202.] See cond 10(d) (failure to obtain landlord's consent: see para **[14.75]** *post*), 18 (purchaser persisting with objection or requisition: see para **[15.27]** *post*) 33(c)(ii) (compensation for material error not assessable: see para **[9.48]** *ante*), 35 (non-disclosure or failure to explain away notices affecting the property: see para **[9.28]** *ante*), 40 (non-compliance with completion notice: see para **[13.19]** *post*) and 45 (damage to property: see para **[12.36]** *post*).

[203.] See para **[13.68]** *post*.

[204.] See para **[13.19]** *post*.

[205.] See para **[13.30]** *post*.

[206.] See the House of Lords decision in *Johnson v Agnew* [1979] 1 All ER 883.

[207.] See para **[13.03]** *post*.

[208.] See the detailed survey of the current law and recommendation contained in the Law Reform Commission's report on *Interests of Vendor and Purchaser in Land during the period between Contract and Completion* (LRC 49-1995).

[209.] See para **[12.36]** *post*.

GG. Chattels

[10.61] It is not uncommon for the sale to include chattels and condition 46 contains a long-standing warranty by the vendor that these are unencumbered. This subject was discussed in the previous chapter.[210]

HH. Inspection

[10.62] Condition 47 requires the vendor to accede to inspections by the purchaser "on a number of reasonable occasions and at reasonable times". This was first introduced in the 1986 Edition of the *General Conditions* to deal with reports received by the Law Society that vendors were being unco-operative. It must be recognised that the purchaser will often wish to make such inspections after the contract has been entered into. These may be linked to a survey made of the property or to the state of repair which may be the subject of a special condition. The condition also refers to "purchased chattels"[211] and the purchaser may wish to check that fixtures and fittings and other items included in the sale have not been removed.

II. Non-Merger

[10.63] The general rule is that the contract merges in the conveyance on completion,[212] so that thereafter the parties can no longer invoke their rights under the contract and must rely on the provisions of the deed of conveyance or transfer, eg, the covenants for title.[213] This is often an inconvenient rule, which is, however, based upon the presumed intention of the parties. It is, therefore, possible to mitigate its effect by an express provision and this done by condition 48. This is discussed in a later chapter.[214]

JJ. Notices

[10.64] The conditions[215] in various places make provision for the service of notices[216] and condition 49 contains detailed provisions governing the making or serving of such notices. They have to be in writing delivered by hand to the recipient personally or to his address or registered office (in the

---

[210.] See par **[9.15]** *ante*.

[211.] Note the wide definition in cond 2: see para **[9.15]** *ante*.

[212.] See para **[21.02]** *post*.

[213.] See para **[21.05]** *post*.

[214.] See para **[21.03]** *post*.

[215.] The Special Conditions may also do so; note that cond 49 refers to "Conditions" which is defined in cond 1 as meaning both the Special and General Conditions.

[216.] See conds 18, 25(b), 40 and 50.

case of a company) or his solicitor's office, or posted to such address or office. In the case of posting, a notice deemed to be delivered at the expiration of three working days[217] after it is put in the post with the correct address on the envelope. This condition is confined to "notices" and does not apply to service of other documents required under the *General Conditions*, eg, requisitions on title.[218]

KK. Time Limits

[10.65] The conditions also require various steps to be taken within certain time limits[219] and condition 50 deals with the situation where the last day for taking steps is not a "working" day.[220] In such a case the last day is to be the next following working day.[221]

LL. Arbitration

[10.66] Condition 51 contains an arbitration provision for the settling of differences and disputes between the parties to the contract. It is important to note that this applies only to differences and disputes relating to the matters listed, such as interest payable for late completion,[222] compensation for misdescription or misrepresentation[223] and questions relating to loss or damage to the property in the interim period between contract and completion.[224] In the absence of agreement the sole arbitrator is to be appointed by the President of the Law Society, and the arbitration is to be conducted in accordance with the Arbitration Acts 1954 and 1980.[225] There

---

217. Note the definition in cond 2: see para **[10.14]** *ante*.

218. See cond 17, para **[15.20]** *post*.

219. See conds 7 (delivery of title), 12 (objections and requisitions on title), 20 (delivery of draft assurance), 38 (return of deposit following rescission by purchaser), 40 (completion notices) and 49 (notices generally).

220. Note that for this purpose the expression "working day" is given a wider meaning than that which operates under the *General Conditions* as a whole (see cond 2). In addition to Saturdays, Sundays, Bank and Public Holidays and the 7 days immediately succeeding Christmas Day, also excluded are days when registers or record offices are not open to enable searches to be made in them and any day "recognised by the solicitors' profession at large as being a day on which their offices are not open for business".

221. Apparently no such extension is implied under the general law: see *Mesure v Britten* (1796) 2 Hy Bl 717.

222. Para (b). Note that this covers now, not only the rate or amount etc, but also the issue whether interest is payable at all.

223. Para (d). See *Geraghty v Rohan Industrial Estates Ltd* [1988] IR 419.

224. Para (f), which now covers also the question of the amount of compensation payable: see para **[12.41]** *post*.

225. See Forde, *Commercial Law in Ireland* (1990), Ch 20.

is provision for the appointment of a substitute, if the original arbitrator resigns, dies, becomes unable, unfit or unsuited to complete his duties or is removed from office by the court under its powers in the Arbitration Acts. It must be borne in mind that arbitration is not necessarily either a speedy or cheap procedure and the parties should consider, where it is open to them, the possibility of settling a dispute in another way, eg, through a vendor or purchaser summons under s 9 of the Vendor and Purchaser Act 1874.[226] It would also appear that an arbitrator cannot order specific performance of a contract for the sale of land.[227]

III. SPECIAL CONDITIONS

[10.67] What Special Conditions should be included in the contract clearly must depend upon the circumstances of the particular transaction.[228] Subject to statutory restrictions[229] and those imposed by the general law,[230] the parties are free to add as many special conditions as they see fit. However, if they are using the Law Society's standard contract form they must bear in mind that, in the event of a conflict between the General and Special Conditions, it is the Special Conditions which prevail.[231]

A. Printed Conditions

[10.68] The Law Society's standard contract form contains three printed conditions on page 4. The first one is an interpretative one incorporating into the Special Conditions the definitions and interpretation provisions of the General Conditions.[232] The second one provides that the Special Conditions prevail over the General ones in a case of conflict,[233] and reiterate the view of the Law Society's Conveyancing Committee that any amendment of the General Conditions should be made by way of Special Condition rather than simply making an alteration to the text of the General Conditions.[234] The third printed condition is of more substance and requires the purchaser to

---

[226.] See Farrell, *Irish Law of Specific Performance* (1994) para [8.53] *et seq*. See para **[13.26]** *post*.

[227.] See Arbitration Act 1954, s 26.

[228.] See the discussion in *Allman v McDaniel* [1912] 1 IR 467. See also *Healy v Healy* High Court, unrep, 3 December 1973 (1973/2445P); *Neighbourhood Public House Ltd v McInerney & Co Ltd* High Court, unrep, 21 June 1983 (1979/7213P).

[229.] See para **[10.08]** *supra*.

[230.] In respect of the need for certainty and lack of ambiguity: see para **[10.04]** *supra*.

[231.] See para **[10.06]** *supra*.

[232.] See conds 1 and 2 of the latter: paras **[10.14-5]** *ante*.

[233.] See para **[10.67]** *supra*.

[234.] See para **[10.06]** *supra*.

pay *in addition to* the purchase price any VAT arising as a consequence of the transaction under the Value-Added Tax Act 1972. This is designed to protect the vendor who might otherwise find that his net proceeds from the sale are reduced by VAT liability. It follows also that the purchaser must be advised by his solicitor of this additional liability, especially if it is not recoverable by the client.[235] Of course, not all transactions will give rise to VAT liability and enquiries or requisitions must be made to determine this matter.[236] A marginal note on the contract form reminds solicitors to delete the third printed condition if it turns out that no VAT liability arises on the particular transaction.

B. Other Conditions

[10.69] It may be useful at this point to refer to some typical special conditions in common use in Ireland. One obvious category is where there are potential problems over unauthorised use or development of the property and the protection of, eg, the Bye-Law Amnesty introduced by s 22(7) of the Building Control Act 1990 or s 19 of the Local Government (Planning and Development) Act 1992 is being invoked.[237] The marginal note to condition 36 of the General Conditions contains a recommendation that this matter should be dealt with by way of special condition.[238] Mention of planning matters leads to another extremely common category of special condition, ie, where the contract is made subject to a condition "subsequent" which has to be fulfilled before an obligation to complete arises.[239] Examples are conditions subject to the purchaser obtaining a mortgage loan[240] or planning permission for specified development.[241] Other common examples are conditions subject to consent being obtained under the Land Act 1965[242] and consent of the landlord to the assignment of a lease.[243]

[10.70] Another common category of special condition relates to the title to be deduced by the vendor and often seeks to limit the purchaser's

---

[235.] See further para **[11.11]** *post.*

[236.] See, eg, para **[5.12]** *ante.*

[237.] See para **[16.77]** *post.*

[238.] See para **[10.55]** *supra.*

[239.] The operation of such "conditional" contracts was considered in Ch 7 *ante.*

[240.] See para **[7.14]** *et seq, ante.*

[241.] See para **[7.16]** *et seq, ante.*

[242.] Note that under cond 28 of the General Conditions s 45 consent is *not* a condition (see para **[10.47]** *supra*), so that this would involve an amendment to the General Conditions. Cond 28 does not deal with s 12 consent: see para **[16.30]** *post.*

[243.] Note, however, that this matter is covered by cond 10(d) of the General Conditions: see para **[14.75]** *post.*

investigation further than the General Conditions do. Condition 8(a) of the latter requires the vendor to set forth in the Special Conditions the title to be shown, such as the root of title.[244] If there are any technical flaws in the title,[245] or missing title documents,[246] or the title is a possessory one only,[247] or any other matter relating to the title which the vendor should disclose,[248] the Special Conditions is the place to deal with them.[249]

[10.71] Where the property being sold is subject to an existing mortgage and it is sought, as is common practice, to avoid the vendor having to raise a "bridging" loan to discharge it before completion, great care should be exercised over the arrangements for securing the discharge after completion out of purchase money paid by the purchaser.[250] The Law Society's Conveyancing Committee has recently reiterated that it is not enough to rely on a simple undertaking by the vendor's solicitor to discharge the mortgage from the proceeds of sale. Instead a special condition should be inserted in the contract requiring payment of the balance of the purchase money by way of "split" draft, ie, two bank drafts, one for the discharge money and the other for the balance of the purchase money after deducting the discharge amount.[251]

[10.72] We discuss in a later chapter other matters which should usually be the subject of special conditions. Thus, the Law Society's Conveyancing Committee has recommended that a sale of farm land should have a special condition dealing with the complex subject of any milk quota attaching to the land.[252] The same applies to any premises subject to some form of licensing regulation, such as pubs and restaurants.[253]

---

[244] See para **[14.56]** *post.* This is obviously also linked with conds 11 and 12: see paras **[10.36-7]** *supra* and **[14.61]** and **[15.25]** *post.*

[245] See para **[14.17]** *post.*

[246] See para **[14.51]** *post.*

[247] See para **[14.80]** *post.* Note also the provisions of cond 8(b) in the General Conditions: see para **[14.82]** *post.*

[248] On the duty of disclosure see para **[9.20]** *et seq, ante.*

[249] On the need to "come clean" on matters of this kind see para **[14.07]** *post.*

[250] This subject is discussed in a later chapter: see para **[20.32]** *post.*

[251] See the *Gazette* July 1995, p 212. See previous recommendations in the *Gazette* of June 1979, p 94, September 1983 (in a Supplement issued by the Joint Committee of the Building Societies/Law Society), both reproduced respectively on pp 11.4 and 11.13 of the *Conveyancing Handbook.*

[252] See para **[16.101]** *post.*

[253] See para **[16.103]** *et seq, post.*

Chapter 11

SPECIAL CONTRACTS

[11.01] In this chapter we consider two special cases concerning contracts relating to sales of land which merit some attention. One is where the sale takes place under the supervision of the court. The other is where the sale involves a plot of land upon which a new building, such as a house, is going to be erected and acquired by the purchaser of the land.

I. COURT SALES

[11.02] Where a sale takes place under an order of the court,[1] the court has a wide jurisdiction to exercise control over the method and conduct of the sale. It has often been said that the court will strive to see that all parties to the sale are treated fairly.[2] In particular, the court will see that purchasers are not prejudiced by the way the sale has been conducted. Thus, in *Re Lewis*,[3] Meredith MR said:

> "... while I must admit that there is no law rendering it obligatory for the parties having a sale in Court to be more superlatively honest that others with a purchase, it is at least desirable for a purchaser buying in Court to know that the Court will see that right and justice will be done."[4]

Similarly, in *Bank of Ireland v Waldron*,[5] Overend J said:

> "... the Court expects exemplary conduct on the part of vendors selling under its order and will see that purchasers are fairly dealt with in every respect."[6]

---

1. See further, paras **[2.25]**, **[2.27]** and **[8.13]** *ante*. See also Farrell, *Irish Law of Specific Performance* (1994), para [3.54] *et seq*.
2. See *Connolly v Keating (No 2)* [1903] 1 IR 356 at 361 (*per* Porter MR). See also the same judge in *Hibernian Bank v Cassidy* (1902) 36 ILTR 156 at 157 and in *Manifold v Johnston* [1902] 1 IR 7 at 13. And see the Supreme Court in *Van Hool McArdle v Rohan Industrial Estates Ltd* [1980] IR 237: see para **[11.06]** *infra*.
3. (1908) 42 ILTR 210.
4. *Ibid*, p 211.
5. [1944] IR 303.
6. *Ibid*, p 307. See also *Bank of Ireland v Smith* [1966] IR 646 at 659 (*per* Kenny J): "... it would be against conscience that the vendor in a Court sale should not be bound by a representation made by his agent in connection with that sale."

Notwithstanding these sentiments, it must be acknowledged that a court sale arises from the unfortunate circumstances of the owner of the property, ie, he is being pursued by his creditors and the sale is being carried out by the Official Assignee, or the liquidator in the case of a company, who wants to raise funds as quickly as possible. He frequently knows little about the property and is conscious that prospective purchasers will be aware that a "forced" sale is in process. These circumstances tend to be reflected in the conditions of sale and in the price ultimately achieved. Subject to this, the following general principles apply to court sales.

A. Conduct of Sale

[11.03] The conduct of the sale is usually committed by the court to the applicant for the order of sale, though he clearly acts under the general supervision of the court, as we saw in the previous paragraph. It is settled in Ireland that the vendor in a court sale is, therefore, not the court, but the person so having carriage of the sale. In *Bank of Ireland v Waldron*,[7] Overend J rejected the opposite view[8] and stated:

"In my opinion the plaintiffs are the vendors; they sought a sale under the order of the Court; they obtained carriage of that sale."[9]

Kenny J agreed with this view in *Bank of Ireland v Smith*.[10] Overend J also reiterated in the *Waldron* case that normally the purchaser in a court sale should be given vacant possession on completion. He stated:

"In my view it is the duty of the vendor having carriage to be in a position to give clear possession on the date fixed for completion, and, in any case of doubt, application can be made to the Court in good time for an order for possession with a view to sale. I recollect frequent applications for such orders, and I think this was the normal procedure in the past unless in cases in which it was clearly unnecessary. I am at a loss to understand why this practice was discontinued, for it seems to me that the certainty that a purchase would be promptly and punctiliously carried out, or adequate compensation awarded in case of default, should be an incentive to purchasers to give better prices which should benefit both mortgagees and mortgagors."[11]

Similar views were stated by Lowry J (as he then was) in *Re O'Neill*.[12]

---

7. [1944] IR 303.
8. Suggested, eg in Prideaux, *Forms and Precedents in Conveyancing* (22nd ed), vol 1, p 382, fn (f).
9. *Op cit*, p 306.
10. [1966] IR 646 at 656. See also *Popham v Exham* (1860) 10 Ir Ch R 440 at 451 (*per* Smith MR).
11. *Op cit*, p 307. See also *Kidd v O Neill* [1931] IR 664 at 669-70 (*per* Johnston J).
12. [1967] NI 129 at 132-5. See *Irish Land Law* (2nd ed, 1986), para 13.018.

B. Mode of Sale

[11.04] This question is a matter for the court, but it is usual to order the person having carriage of the sale to hold a public auction. The reserve price is usually fixed by the court,[13] whereas the particulars[14] and conditions of sale[15] are usually drawn up by the solicitor acting for the party having carriage of the sale, in accordance with the rules of court.[16] However, the court usually insists upon approving the conditions of sale and, if necessary, directs that they be settled by counsel appointed by the court.[17] In *Law v Roberts & Co (No 2)*,[18] Kenny J insisted upon fixing a rate of interest, payable for failure to complete on the closing date,[19] which was "realistic" and would act as a deterrent to the purchaser against delaying completion.[20] The court may also lay down the terms of appointment of the auctioneer, including details of his remuneration.[21]

[11.05] The general rule as to bidding at the auction is that the person having carriage of the sale may not do so without the leave of the court. The law on this matter was clearly stated by Smith MR in *Popham v Exham*,[22] in a judgment which contains an admirable survey of the duties of that person and his solicitor:

> "It is a well-settled principle of Courts of Equity, that neither the plaintiff nor his solicitor can bid without the leave of the Court ... The rule, however, is not a rule of practice or procedure; it is a rule of Equity, founded on the well-understood principle, that the same person is not to be permitted to fill the double character of vendor and purchaser. A party who has the carriage of proceedings in a cause stands in a fiduciary position to

---

13. *Bank of Ireland v Smith* [1966] IR 646 at 650 (*per* Kenny J). See para **[2.27]** *ante*.
14. See *National Bank v Beirne* (1901) 35 ILTR 9.
15. *Popham v Exham* (1860) 10 Ir Ch R 440 at 451 (*per* Smith MR).
16. See *Belfast Bank v Callan* [1910] 1 IR 38 at 43 (*per* Meredith MR); *Bank of Ireland v Waldron* [1944] IR 303 (*per* Overend J). See also Rules of the Superior Courts 1986, Order 51.
17. See *Bank of Ireland v Smith* [1966] IR 646 at 650 (*per* Kenny J). See also *Belfast Bank v Callan* [1910] 1 IR 38 at 42 (*per* Meredith MR); *Irish Industrial Benefit Building Society v O Brien* [1941] IR 1 at 6 (*per* Murnaghan J). And see *Lahey v Bell* (1843) 6 Ir Eq R 122. See also Rules of the Superior Courts 1986, Order 51, rules 4 and 9. *Cf* where a liquidator exercises his power of sale under s 231 of the Companies Act 1963: see paras **[11.06]**, fns 28 and 32 and **[11.07]**, fn 43 *infra*.
18. [1964] IR 306.
19. See para **[20.09]** *post*.
20. See further, para **[2.27]** *ante*.
21. *Provincial Bank of Ireland Ltd v Goulding* [1942] IR 108 at 109 (*per* Gavan Duffy J). See also para **[2.33]** *ante*.
22. (1860) 10 Ir Ch R 440. As regards the rules for private auctions. see paras **[2.14]** *et seq*.

all the parties and incumbrancers in the cause. The jurisdiction exercised
by the Court, of taking the carriage of the proceedings from a party who
does not conduct the suit with due diligence, establishes that. The
plaintiff's solicitor prepares the conditions of sale. He is bound to see that
these conditions are not of such a character as to deter parties from bidding.
It is the duty of the plaintiff, acting through his solicitor, to see that the
intended sale shall be duly advertised, and hand-bills posted and circulated,
so as to give publicity to the sale. The time when the sale should take place
is often important. The plaintiff and his solicitor, in their character of
vendors, have a duty imposed on them to sell for the best price that can be
obtained. If the plaintiff, or his solicitor, purchase, their interest is in direct
conflict with their duty, because in their character of purchasers they would
or might be anxious to purchase at an undervalue. The Court, therefore,
when giving a plaintiff or his solicitor liberty to bid, makes it part of the
order that the carriage of the proceedings should be given to some other
party or incumbrancer. If no other person will take the carriage of the
proceedings, the notice of motion has informed all persons interested of the
fact that the plaintiff or his solicitor have obtained liberty to bid, and the
proceedings connected with the sale can be narrowly watched. If a plaintiff
or his solicitor was to bid openly in his own name, without the leave of the
Court, the sale would, in my opinion, be impeachable; at all events, if it
appeared to have been at an undervalue, and if the proceedings to impeach
the sale are taken within a reasonable time. But the objection becomes
much more serious if, as in the present case, the purchase is made through a
trustee, and where the fact of the plaintiff or his solicitor being the real
purchaser is kept concealed from the Court, and the Master, and the parties
in the case. In such a case, the authorities would appear to establish that the
sale is not simply impeachable for undervalue, but is actually void."[23]

[11.06] It should also be noted that s 7 of the Sale of Land by Auction Act
1867, severely restricted the former practice of the Courts of Equity,
whereby biddings at an auction held under a court order for sale were always
liable to be re-opened until the report on the sale was confirmed finally by
the court.[24] Section 7 now confines re-opening of biddings to cases of fraud
or other improper conduct in the management of the sale.[25] It has since been
held in Ireland that this restriction on re-opening of biddings in court sales

---

[23.] *Ibid*, pp 450-2. See also *Drought v Jones* (1841) Fl & K 316; *Byrne v Lafferty* (1845) 8 Ir
Eq R 47; *Atkins v Delmege* (1847) 12 Ir Eq R 1. *Cf: Dean v Wilson* (1878) 10 Ch D 136.

[24.] See the discussion of this practice in *Vesey v Elwood* (1842) 3 Dr & War 74 at 79-81 (*per*
Sugden LC). Under Order 51, rule 8 of the Rules of the Superior Courts 1986, it is sufficient
for the auctioneer and solicitor of party having carriage of the sale to certify (in the form set
out (No 21) in Appendix G to the Rules) the particulars of the sale; there is no need to file
any affidavit verifying the particulars or the result of the sale.

[25.] *Woods v Brown* [1915] 1 IR 29 at 36-7 (*per* Palles CB); see also at p 35 (*per* O'Brien LC).
See para **[2.25]** *ante*.

applies also to tenders or offers in a sale by private treaty after an abortive auction.[26] Thus, in *Re Hibernian Transport Companies Ltd*,[27] after a public auction of property of a company being wound up[28] proved abortive, an offer was made subject to a condition that it be accepted in writing by a certain time on a set date. Kenny J informed the liquidator in chambers that the court would approve a sale at the price offered (£65,000), and the offeror was sent acceptance in writing on that same day. A few days later, the liquidator applied in court for formal approval of the sale at £65,000, but at the same time another offer of £101,000 was made to the court by a different body. Kenny J refused to accept the new offer and made an order confirming the sale at the price originally offered. The Supreme Court[29] held that there were reasonable grounds for the initial approval of the first offer and that Kenny J's subsequent confirmation of the sale at the price so offered should not be disturbed. Walsh J pointed out that, while, all things being equal, the higher offer should be accepted, they were not equal in this case because the original offer had been accepted informally and that acceptance had been communicated to the offeror, who had acted upon it to its disadvantage. In those circumstances, it was quite right for Kenny J "to regard himself as being bound, if not in law certainly in honour, to permit the liquidator to complete the contract."[30] It is vital to note that this was a case where the court had approved the sale *before* the other offer was received. In *Van Hool McArdle Ltd v Rohan Industrial Estates Ltd*,[31] the liquidator entered into a contract to sell the land for £730,000 "subject to and conditional upon the consent of the High Court thereto".[32] A few days later he received another offer for £850,000 which he reported when he applied for the Court's approval of the contract. McWilliam J took the view that he had to confirm the first contract on the basis that the liquidator had acted in good faith,[33] but the Supreme Court emphatically rejected this approach. Kenny J

[26.] *Munster and Leinster Bank v Munster Motor Co* [1922] 1 IR 15; *Provincial Bank of Ireland Ltd v Farris* [1944] IR 150.

[27.] [1972] IR 190.

[28.] Note that, in fact, the official liquidator did not need the sanction of the court for the sale in view of his powers under s 231(2) of the Companies Act 1963. See *ibid*, p 201 (*per* Walsh J).

[29.] O'Dálaigh CJ, Walsh, Budd, Fitzgerald and McLoughlin JJ.

[30.] *Op cit*, p 203.

[31.] [1980] IR 237.

[32.] Note again that he did not need to make the sale conditional (see fn 28 *supra*), but this is common practice, particularly where substantial sums are involved: see Keane, *Company Law in the Republic of Ireland* (2nd ed, 1991), para 38.57.

[33.] A mortgagee selling out of court must act reasonably and ensure that it gets a fair price: see *Holohan v Friends Provident and Century Life Office* [1966] IR 1; *Re Brook Cottage Ltd* [1976] NI 78.

distinguished cases relied upon by McWilliam J, such as *Re Hibernian Transport Companies Ltd*,[34] in the following terms:

> "Those cases deal with an entirely different matter and are not authorities for the proposition advanced. Each of them relates to an application to discharge a court order, which had approved a sale, because a higher bid was received *after* the court's sanction had been given. In all three of them the court, having approved the sale, had to keep faith with the purchaser. In the instant case the High Court had not given its consent to the sale when *Van Hool's* offer of £850,000 was received."[35]

In the *Van Hool* case the liquidator had made the contract conditional and O'Higgins CJ stated that this "required the court to consider whether its consent should be given to the sale, having regard to the circumstances obtaining not merely at the time when the sale was effected but also at the time of the application for such consent."[36] And as Kenny J stated, the "primary duty of the court and of the liquidator in a court winding-up is to get the maximum price of the assets. A system under which a bid of £730,000 is accepted when one of £850,000 has been made would bring the court into well-deserved ridicule."[37]

[11.07] Strictly speaking, a purchaser under a court sale, ie, the highest bidder at the auction, does not become the purchaser until the result of the auction is reported to the court and a certificate is filed confirming the court's approval of the sale.[38] Once the court makes an order confirming the sale, it is conclusive as regards the purchaser, whether or not the purchaser knows of any irregularity.[39] But it has been held in Ireland that the purchaser

---

34. Which, of course, he had himself decided at first instance: see *supra*. The other cases relied on by McWilliam J were *Re Bartlett* (1880) 16 Ch D 561; *Munster Bank v Munster Motor Co* [1922] 1 IR 15.

35. *Op cit*, p 242.

36. *Op cit*, pp 240-1.

37. *Op cit*, pp 242-3. See also as to the need to get the "best price" in a court sale, Rules of the Superior Courts 1986 Order 51 rule 5.

38. See *Vesey v Elwood* (1842) 3 Dr & War 74 at 79-80 (*per* Sugden LC). It may be argued that the Lord Chancellor's view was based on the court's power to re-open biddings which was severely restricted by s 7 of the Sale of Land by Auction Act 1867 (see para **[11.06]** *supra*), but it has been held in England that s 7 did not remove the necessity for certification of the sale to convert the highest bidder into the accepted purchaser, see *Re Joseph Clayton Ltd* [1920] 1 Ch 257. See also *Hodder v Ruffin* (1830) Taml 341; *Dewell v Tuffnell* (1855) 1 K & J 324. *Cf Gowan v Tighe* (1835) Ll & G *temp* Plunk 168 at 175 (*per* Plunkett LC); *Vincent v Going* (1841) 3 Dr & War 75 at 76 (*per* Lord Plunket LC).

39. Conveyancing Act 1881, s 70(1): "An order of the Court under any statutory or other jurisdiction shall not. as against a purchaser, be invalidated on the ground of want of jurisdiction, or of want of any concurrence, consent, notice, or service, whether the purchaser has notice of any such or not." See *Woods v Brown* [1915] 1 IR 29 at 34 (*per* O'Brien LC).

nevertheless acquires some interest before that final confirmation is given. Thus, in *Vesey v Elwood*,[40] Sugden LC stated:

> "Now I apprehend, that the contract does not date only from the confirmation of the Master's report, and that the purchaser has before that period an insurable interest; but as the Court has great power over these contracts, it might feel itself at liberty to throw a loss by fire, before the confirmation of the report, upon the sellers."[41]

In *Smyth v Smyth*,[42] a storm caused damage to the property two days after it was sold to the purchaser in an auction held under a court order for sale, but the certificate of the Chief Clerk certifying the sale was not filed until the day after the storm. Porter MR held that the purchaser was entitled to compensation for the damage suffered prior to the filing of the certificate, ie, the vendor had to bear the loss.[43]

II. BUILDING AGREEMENTS

[11.08] An area of considerable complexity is that which concerns building agreements, ie, where the purchaser is buying a piece of land upon which a new building is in the course of erection or, indeed, may not even be started yet. This is a common phenomenon in the field of house purchase, where the new house may be a "one-off" job or part of a large estate development. The complications arise from the fact that it is common for such transactions not to be executed in what would appear to be the most straightforward manner. This would be for the builder to purchase the site, build the house and then sell the house and ground to a purchaser; or, if the owner of the site (the developer) and the builder are separate persons or companies, for the developer to employ the builder to build the house and, when this is completed, for the developer to sell the completed house and the ground to the purchaser. The main reason why this apparently straightforward procedure is often not followed, is that most developers and builders do not have the funds readily available for development and building and so wish to get their hands on funds from prospective purchasers as early as possible.[44]

---

40. *Op cit.*

41. *Ibid*, p 81.

42. (1903) 37 ILTR 82.

43. Note the difference now on the subject of who is subject to the risk of loss or damage between the general law and the Law Society's standard contract form: see para **[12.36]** *et seq post*. A sale by a liquidator under his powers in s 231 of the Companies Act 1963, will usually be made under the Law Society's *General Conditions*: see para **[11.06]** *supra*.

44. A second reason was based on stamp duty law, but this has changed in recent times: see para **[11.10]** *infra*.

The way in which this is usually achieved in a typical housing development[45] is as follows.

[11.09] First, the builder enters into an agreement with the owner of the site, under which the latter undertakes to sell each plot to nominees of the builder, ie, to convey or transfer the freehold[46] to each purchaser, when each house is completed. Alternatively, of course, the builder may purchase the site, but this will, of course, involve him in raising the purchase price. In major commercial or industrial developments financing may be provided by investors or financial institutions through a joint venture scheme. The builder then enters into two agreements with each prospective purchaser, though there is no reason why they should not be combined in one document, provided care is taken in the drafting of it, as we discuss later.[47] One is usually an agreement for a sale[48] of the plot, under which the builder undertakes to nominate the purchaser as transferee[49] and the purchaser undertakes to employ the builder to build his house on the site. The second is a building agreement under which the purchaser employs the builder to erect his house and which usually provides for "stage" payments, ie, payment of the purchase price of the house by instalments. Both these agreements can be comprised in one document, and frequently the agreement for sale is conditional upon the purchaser entering into a building agreement with the builder.[50]

[11.10] Two matters of considerable importance in this context are stamp duty and VAT. Until recently care had to be taken as to creation of two separate agreements, because this could produce a considerable saving in stamp duty.[51] However, anti-avoidance provisions were introduced by the

---

45. Variations on this theme, often involving several other parties, such as those involved in financing the development, occur in the case of commercial developments.

46. It must be a freehold in the case of dwellings coming within the Landlord and Tenant (Ground Rents) Act 1978: see Wylie, *Irish Landlord and Tenant Law*, para 2.22. This prohibition on leasing does *not*, however, apply to separate and self-contained flat developments (provided the premises comprising the development are divided into two or more such flats), nor to commercial developments, where leasing is more common.

47. Para **[11.12]** *infra*.

48. Or in the case of flat developments or commercial developments an agreement for the grant of a lease. For the distinction between an agreement for lease and the lease itself, see *Wylie op cit*, para 5.04.

49. Or lessee in the case of flats or commercial premises.

50. Note that the Law Society's Conveyancing Committee has recently deemed unacceptable the practice of builders instructing the solicitors not to return the contracts executed by the builder until closing. This practice clearly poses difficulties for the purchaser's solicitor in preparing a certificate of title for the purchaser's lending institution: see the *Gazette* August/September 1995, p 233.

51. If the agreement for sale of the site was independent of the building agreement, duty would be payable on the value of the site only, ie not including the building.

Finance Act 1990 and by s 112 of that Act[52] stamp duty on residential developments[53] will often be payable on the combined cost of the site and building, irrespective of whether separate agreements are entered into.[54] In essence the position as regards such developments may be summarised as follows:[55]

1. no stamp duty is payable in case of "grant type"[56] houses and apartments, but in such case the purchaser's solicitor must make sure he obtains a copy of the requisite Floor Area Certificate[57] to be produced to the Stamp Office when the deed of conveyance or transfer is lodged for adjudication;

2. no stamp duty will be payable in the case of "non-grant type" houses and apartment where the purchaser either:

    (a) buys the site and employs a builder "unconnected" with the sale of the site, ie, there is no "connection or arrangement" with the vendor of the site for the building of the house or apartment, [58]

    (b) buys the site and builds the house or apartment by his own labour;

[52.] As amended by s 100 of the Finance Act 1993. See Donegan and Friel, *Irish Stamp Duty Law* (1995), paras 11.13-14 and p 306 *et seq.*

[53.] Ie "houses and apartments".

[54.] The charge is levied on the greater of the consideration for the site (or fine in the case of a lease of an apartment) or 25% of the total consideration including the building contract.

[55.] See the Revenue Commissioners' Statement of Practice (SP-SD/2/90).

[56.] Note that under the Housing (New House Grant) Regulations 1990 (SI 24/1990) the builder must hold a Tax Clearance Certificate or current Form C2 and the purchaser's solicitor must check this and, if necessary, should make the contract conditional on the builder getting the necessary documentation prior to closing to enable the purchase to secure the grant for completion: see the warning by the Law Society's Conveyancing Committee, the *Gazette*, December 1990, p 358.

[57.] From the builder who should have been obtained the Certificate from the Department of the Environment. This confirms that the floor area is within the limits (ie, at least 38 square metres and not more than 125 square metres) set for exemption by s 49 of the Finance Act 1969 and para 8 of the Housing (New House Grants etc) Regulations 1990 (SI 296/1990).. The minimum floor area was increased from 35 to 38 square metres where the foundations were completed on or after 1 April 1996 by the Housing (New House Grants etc) Regulations 1990 (Amendment) Regulations 1996 (SI 88/1996).

[58.] This depends on the facts of the particular case and the Revenue Commissioners have stated that they will have regard to whether a building has commenced prior to execution of the sale or lease agreement and whether any relationship or association exists between the builder and the owner of the site: SP-SD/2/90, para 2.1. The Commissioners may require statements and/or statutory declarations from people concerned with the development or their agents, *ibid*, para 2.2. *Cf Dunne v Revenue Commissioners* [1982] ILRM 438.

3. in all other "non-grant type" cases stamp duty will be payable on the combined cost of the site and building.

Under s 112(5) the deed of conveyance or transfer[59] must now contain the appropriate certificate confirming whether or not the provisions of s 112 apply. The Revenue Commissioners have stipulated the form of the alternative certificates[60] and if the deed does not contain one of them it will not be accepted for stamping.[61] In the case of commercial and industrial property, where the building is not "substantially completed"[62] at the date of the signing of the agreements and the agreement for sale of the site and the building agreement are not "interlocked", stamp duty will be assessed on the market value of the site together with the cost of works done at the date of the signing of the agreements.[63] An architect's certificate should be obtained by the purchaser's solicitor detailing the works performed and their cost to the date of the agreements.[64] If the building is substantially completed and/or the agreement for sale and building agreement are interlocked, stamp duty will be assessed on the entire consideration passing for both the site and the building.

[11.11] The sale of land for the purpose of building on it usually involves a development which attracts VAT under s 4 of the Value Added Tax Act 1972.[65] The charge usually extends to the whole of the property, ie, both the site and the new building on it, but it was recognised in the original Act that difficulties might arise where the purchaser acquires his interest in the site from one person and enters into a building agreement with another. An example is the one given earlier,[66] where the owner of the site enters into a licence agreement with a builder permitting him to build on the site and agrees to convey the building or buildings (eg, new houses) to the builder's nominees (the house purchasers). Section 4(5) of the 1972 Act provides that in such circumstances the site owner is to be regarded as the taxable person accountable for the VAT on both any site fines payable under the licence agreement with the builder and the value of the interest conveyed to the

---

59. If executed on or after 1 September 1990.
60. SP-SD/2/90 para 5.1. See also Laffoy *Irish Conveyancing Precedents*, Precedent F1.10; the *Gazette,* December 1990, pp 357-8.
61. *Ibid*, para 5.3. It may also constitute a revenue offence under s 94 of the Finance Act 1983; *ibid*, para 5.2.
62. See again the *Dunne* case (fn 58 *supra*).
63. SP-SD/2/90 para 8.1.
64. *Ibid*.
65. See generally Somers, *Irish Value Added Tax* (1994), Ch 14. Also the Revenue Leaflet *VAT on Property Transaction* (1990).
66. Para **[11.09]** *supra*.

purchaser.[67] The same applies where a person purchases an undeveloped site from a company and then enters into a building agreement with a related company.

[11.12] We return now to the two agreements usually entered into where a new building, such as a house, is being acquired. As we saw earlier,[68] these comprise, first, an agreement for the sale or, in the case of flats or commercial property, the leasing of the site upon which the building is going to be erected. This agreement will be entered into by the purchaser with the owner of the site, who may or may not be the builder.[69] The other agreement is a building agreement between the purchaser and the builder,[70] which is our primary concern here.

A. Agreement for Sale

[11.13] The agreement for a sale will obviously vary in form according to whether the builder is also the owner of the site, or the developer, or is merely undertaking to nominate the purchaser as transferee to the owner or developer. The standard contract form issued the Law Society, incorporating general conditions of sale, may be adapted for this agreement.[71] Where this is done, obviously a considerable number of special conditions will have to be added. In the case of a builder who is not the owner of the site, one is the undertaking by the builder to nominate the purchaser as transferee. In the case of a commercial developemnt, whereby the purchaser is to get a lease only, the special conditions will specify the length of lease to be granted and the site fine and ground rent payable. It may also specify that the lease is to contain a covenant by the purchaser that he is to erect a building according to plans and details approved by the lessor, including a completion date for this and an undertaking to employ the builder to carry out the building. In

---

[67.] See the 1990 Revenue Leaflet (fn 65 *supra*), paras 29-31. Doubts raised by an appeal in 1994 were laid to rest by a substituted s 4(5) enacted by s 122 of the Finance Act 1995, thereby preserving the long-standing Revenue practice: see the note by Law Society's Taxation Committee in the *Gazette,* October 1995, pp 283-4. See also *Butterworths Tax Guide 1995-96*, para 46.21A.

[68.] Para **[11.09]** *supra.*

[69.] See *ibid.*

[70.] Of course, there is nothing to stop the owner of the site entering into this agreement with a view to selling off or leasing the building when it is completed, or even before that, as is commonly done in commercial developments.

[71.] See Chs 9 and 10 *ante*. Often the full contents of the Law Society's form (in particular the General Conditions) are not set out but only cross-referred to, but this is contrary to the Conveyancing Committee's recommended practice: see para **[9.01]** *ante.*

view of the importance of these matters it is usual to incorporate a draft lease in the contract.

B. Building Agreement

[11.14] The Law Society and Construction Industry Federation (CIF) have jointly issued a standard form of *Building Agreement*, the latest edition being dated 1987, and this is often used. Otherwise the standard form of building agreement issued by The Royal Institute of the Architects of Ireland may be adopted.[72] However, to some extent the form of agreement used may depend upon the circumstances of the case.[73] When the house in question is part of a large development, the builder will probably insist upon using a standard form of agreement drawn up by his solicitor for that development and the purchaser's solicitor is given no choice in the matter. In that case, the most he can do is to warn his client of any risks involved in signing the builder's form and he should proceed with the transaction only if he has clear instructions from the client to do so. If, however, the transaction is a single development, the purchaser's solicitor is likely to be in a stronger position to negotiate the form and terms of the agreement to be entered into. If the builder is registered with the HomeBond Scheme,[74] it is imperative that the building agreement, or agreement for sale,[75] contains a clause requiring the builder to enter into a Guarantee Agreement (Form HB 10). It must be remembered that major lending institutions will not lend on the security of new houses unless they are covered by this Scheme, which applies only to builders registered under it.[76] The Scheme does not apply to commercial or industrial property and here the purchaser must rely heavily on the terms of the building agreement itself and collateral warranties from sub-contractors.[77] The following are the salient features usually found in a building agreement.[78]

[72.] See *Hegarty & Sons Ltd v Royal Liver Society* [1985] IR 524; *Rohan Construction Ltd v Antigen Ltd* [1989] ILRM 783.

[73.] As to the dangers of entering into a substantial building contract other than by means of a proper written agreement, see *O'Neill & Co Ltd v Roche* High Court, unrep, 19 January 1972 (1970/722P).

[74.] See para **[4.25]** *et seq, ante*.

[75.] Or else a collateral agreement to this effect should be entered into.

[76.] See para **[4.25]** *ante*.

[77.] See para **[11.22]** *infra*.

[78.] See generally the leading English textbooks: Emden and Gill, *Building Contracts and Practice* (7th ed, by Gill; 1969; 1972 Supp); *Hudson, Building and Engineering Contracts* (10th ed, by Wallace; 1970).

1. Agreement to Build

[11.15] The primary term of a building agreement is, of course, the undertaking by the builder[79] to build the house on the land in question, as may be specified in the site plan, drawings or other specifications, which are usually prepared by an architect. The Law Society/CIF standard form *Building Agreement* contains an undertaking by the builder to do so in a "good substantial and workmanlike" manner,[80] similar to the warranty implied at common law,[81] but the builder may seek to exclude any such warranty and liability on any other basis, eg, for negligence,[82] but, generally this should be resisted by the purchaser's solicitor.[83] It is wise to make provision for variation or deviation in any plans incorporated in the agreement, and for additional work which may be required by the purchaser (employer) at a later stage.[84] Care should also be taken to see that the builder is under an obligation to comply with local or public authority requirements and standards with respect to basic services, eg, supply of water, gas and electricity, sewerage services, roads and access points and lighting.[85]

2. Payment of the Price

[11.16] It is common for the price to be paid by instalments, sometimes referred to as "stage payments",[86] eg, the first payment on signing the agreement, the next when the house reaches eaves level, the next when it is roofed, the next when plastering is completed and the final one when the house is substantially completed. It may also be required that each stage payment is subject to a condition precedent of issue of an architect's certificate approving the work completed as satisfactory.[87] Provision is also usually made for payment of interest if any instalment is overdue[88] and the purchaser is usually not entitled to occupy the premises until all instalments

---

[79.] Referred to as the "contractor" in the Law Society/CIF Building Agreement (1976 ed). The purchaser is referred to as the "employer".

[80.] Cl 1. Cond 2 deals with materials and workmanship and cond 3 with local and other authorities' requirements.

[81.] Recognised in *Morris v Redmond* (1936) 70 ILTR 8; *Doyle v Youell* (1938) 72 ILTR 253; *Brown v Norton* [1954] IR 34; *McGeary v Campbell* [1975] NI 7. See the discussion in para **[4.12]** *et seq.*

[82.] See para **[4.14]** *et seq.*

[83.] See para **[11.21]** *infra.*

[84.] See cond 2(c) and (d) of the Law Society/CIF *Building Agreement.*

[85.] See *ibid*, conds 3 and 10.

[86.] See *ibid*, cl 3.

[87.] See *Richardson v Mahon* (1879) 4 LR Ir 486; *McKee v McMahon* (1935) 69 ILTR 180; *Sisk and Son Ltd v Lawter Products BV* High Court, unrep, 13 November 1976 (1976/1124); *Hegarty & Sons Ltd v Royal Liver Society* [1985] IR 525; *Rohan Construction Ltd v Antigen Ltd* [1989] ILRM 783.

[88.] Cond 4(a) of the Law Society/CIF *Building Agreement* specifies 4% above the single A Bank overdraft rate charged by the Irish Clearing Banks to borrowers.

have been paid.[89] Because of the effect of inflation on the cost of materials and goods in the building industry, and, of course, rises in wages and other costs and expenses, the builder may insist upon a clause allowing increases to be made in the price according to such rises.[90] Purchasers should be made aware of the risks involved in stage payments, especially where paid before any transfer of the site. If the builder becomes insolvent the purchaser is particularly exposed, a matter to which we now turn.

[11.17] It is not uncommon for builders to demand money from prospective purchasers at a very early stage in the development of a site; indeed, often before any building has commenced at all. Sometimes this takes the form of what is called a "booking deposit"[91] and may be paid before any contract is entered into. The dangers of paying such a pre-contract deposit or any other money before a contract is signed cannot be emphasised too much.[92] If, as is often the case, the money is paid to a builder which is a limited liability company, the prospective purchaser runs the risk that, in the event of the company becoming insolvent or going into liquidation, he will be treated as an unsecured creditor with little hope of recovery of his money.[93] Once he has entered into an agreement for sale and building agreement, his position is better to the extent that he has an equitable interest in,[94] and lien on,[95] the site to which the agreement for lease relates. However, even when this is done, he may find that someone else or some institution has a prior claim to the site. Most builders and developers have to borrow extensively in the early stages of development, to cover the cost of such items as preparation of the site and laying down sewers and drains. This initial capital outlay is usually borrowed from a lending institution, like a bank, which will insist upon being provided with security for its loan, normally by way of a mortgage or charge on the site and building in progress. If this mortgage or charge is created before the purchaser enters into his agreement for sale, it will normally have priority over the purchaser's interest[96] and, in the event of the builder's insolvency, the purchaser will suffer the shock of finding that the bank claims not only the site but also any partly- or wholly-built house on it.[97] There is not much that the purchaser or his solicitor can do

---

[89]. *Ibid*, cond 4(d).

[90]. *Ibid*, cond 6 (which also covers decreases to be made in the price if costs and expenses fall).

[91]. *Cf* a *pre*-contract deposit paid to a house or estate agent, see paras **[3.15]** *et seq*.

[92]. Note the warning issued by the Law Society's in the *Gazette*, January/February 1977, p 17.

[93]. This passage in the 1st ed was approved by McCarthy J in the Supreme Court decision in *Re Barrett Apartments Ltd* [1983] IR 350 at 361: see para **[3.15]** *ante*.

[94]. On this controversial subject, see para **[12.02]** *et seq, post*.

[95]. On this, see para **[12.44]** *post*.

[96]. For discussion of this subject, see *Irish Land Law* (2nd ed, 1986), para 13.127 *et seq*.

about this,[98] but it does emphasise the importance for solicitors to advise their clients fully as to the risks involved. In particular, a warning should be given that the mere fact that the deposit or other monies are paid through the medium of the purchaser's solicitor does *not* necessarily provide any protection to the purchaser, since the risk of insolvency of the builder remains. It was the existence of these risks which led various bodies to make representations for extension of the old National House Building Guarantee Scheme to provide cover for lost deposits, but this was not done until 1990.[99] Under the HomeBond Scheme there is now an indemnity in the form of the "stage payment bond" which not only cover deposits but also stage payments.[100] It must be emphasised that solicitors should advise clients that the cover is not unlimited. Furthermore, it must be reiterated that this cover applies only to property covered by the Scheme and does not apply to, eg, commercial property.

3. Insolvency

[11.18] Apart from those aspects of insolvency discussed in the previous paragraph, it is common to provide in the building agreement that it may be determined by the builder in the event of the purchaser's bankruptcy, subject to payment for all work completed to that date,[101] and by the purchaser in the event of the builder's insolvency, subject to an adjustment in the price for any extra costs incurred thereby.[102]

[97.] See again the *Barratt* case fn 93 *supra*. See also *Desmond v Brophy* [1985] IR 449: para **[3.15]** *ante*.

[98.] One precaution would be to make searches against the builder *before* the client pays any money or enters into any agreement, to see if any mortgage or charge has already been created. Such searches should be made in the Registry of Deeds or Land Registry (depending upon whether the title to land is registered or not) and in the Companies Register if the builder is a company; see generally, para **[15.39]** *et seq, post*. It was the failure to make such searches that led the Supreme Court to hold the purchaser's solicitor negligent in *Roche v Peilow* [1985] IR 232, despite the fact that he has followed what was accepted as the usual practice at that time amongst conveyances in Ireland of not making searches until *after* the contract and just before closing: see para **[15.43]** *post*. Note the subsequent recommendation for searches made by the Law Society's Conveyancing Committee: see the *Gazette*, October 1985, p 278. Of course, such searches will merely provide a more definite picture of the risk for the client. If they show up an existing mortgage or charge, the client must decide, after advice from his solicitor, whether to proceed. If they do not, the client's contract should be registered in the Registry of Deeds, or a caution registered in the Land Registry, at once, see para **[6.64]** *ante*.

[99.] See para **[4.25]** *ante*.

[100.] Note that the limits on the indemnity provided differs: see **[4.26]** *ante*.

[101.] The Law Society/CIF *Building Agreement* does not contain such a provision, but entitles the builder to rescind the agreement for non-payment of any amounts due: see cond 4.

[102.] *Ibid*, cond 5.

4. Subject to Loan

[11.19] It is common for the building agreement to be subject to the purchaser obtaining approval for a loan for a specified amount.[103] This is usually in the form of a condition "subsequent",[104] whereunder either party may rescind the contract if the loan has not been approved by the time limit set.[105] The Law Society/CIF *Building Agreement* provides for return of the purchaser's deposit and for return to the builder's solicitors of all documents furnished to the purchaser if the condition is not met.[106]

5. Insurance

[11.20] Under the Law Society's standard contract for sale form the risk of damage to the property remains with the vendor[107] and the Law Society/CIF *Building Agreement* follows this by providing that the builder is to indemnify the purchaser against all losses, claims, demands, actions or proceedings in respect of personal injury or death or damage to the property.[108] Furthermore, it also imposes on the builder an obligation to effect appropriate insurance cover for these matters, including employer's and public liability.

6. Defects

[11.21] It is clearly in the purchaser's interest to see that the building agreement includes a provision imposing an obligation upon the builder to put right any defects in the building, due to faulty or defective materials or workmanship and which come to light within a reasonable period after completion. Under the Law Society/CIF *Building Agreement*, where the builder is registered under the National House Building Guarantee Scheme (now the HomeBond Scheme[109]) the expectation is that a collateral agreement will be entered into for the furnishing of the guarantee under that Scheme.[110] As we saw earlier, the HomeBond Scheme provides a ten-year structural guarantee against "major defects", under which (as under the NHBGS) the builder is responsible for remedying such defects during the

---

[103.] *Ibid*, cl 5.
[104.] See para **[7.03]** *ante*.
[105.] The Law Society/CIF *Building Agreement* provides for specification of a precise date which avoids the uncertainties created by "reasonable time" provisions. On the operation of such conditional contracts see para **[7.14]** *et seq, ante*.
[106.] Cl 5.
[107.] See para **[12.36]** *post*.
[108.] Cond 7.
[109.] See para **[4.25]** *et seq, ante*.
[110.] Cond 8(a).

first two years. He also has the option to remedying defects during the remaining eight years, but if he declines to do so, HomeBond will have that responsibility. The *Building Agreement* also provides a guarantee in respect of "major defects" for the first six months after completion. If the builder is not registered,[111] the *Building Agreement* contemplates that the builder will give a similar guarantee[112] for the period specified.[113] The *Building Agreement* also recognises that the NHBGS/HomeBond Scheme excludes liability for a wide range of matters, such as hair cracks in plaster work, defects or damage in paint work or decoration, normal shrinkage or expansion of timber, items covered by separate guarantees issued to the purchaser by manufacturers of the items in question and consequential loss arising from such defects.[114] In view of the limitations of the HomeBond Scheme and such exclusions,[115] it is important from the purchaser's point of view to preserve his common law rights, such as suing under the implied warranty[116] or for negligence.[117] This should be done expressly as is done in the *Building Agreement*.[118]

[11.22] Where commercial property is concerned, which, of course, is not covered by the HomeBond scheme, the purchaser is likely to be concerned not only with the liability of the builder, but also the various sub-contractors employed by him.[119] Frequently, the purchaser is not a party to the building agreement, which is entered into between the developer and the builder. Because of the limitations of the doctrine of privity of contract, and the uncertainties of the scope of the law of negligence in respect of pure economic loss,[120] it is usual for the purchaser, or lessee, to seek collateral warranties from the builder and others involved, such as sub-contractors. The developer should ensure that the building agreement entered into with the builder contains an obligation to enter into such warranties and to procure a similar obligation in any agreements entered into with sub-

---

[111.] Note the difficulties this will create if the purchaser intends seeking a loan from one of the major lending institutions: see para **[11.14]** *supra*.

[112.] Cond 8(b).

[113.] Cl 4. See *Brohan v Crosspan Developments Ltd* (noted [1985] ILRM 702).

[114.] Cond 8(d). *Cf* the list of items not covered by the NHBGS/HomeBond Scheme.

[115.] See para **[4.28]** *ante*.

[116.] See para **[4.12]** *et seq, ante*.

[117.] See para **[4.14]** *et seq, ante*.

[118.] Cond 8(e).

[119.] For discussion as to the liability of the builder for a sub-contractor's work see *Norta Wallpapers (Ir) Ltd v Sisk & Sons (Dublin) Ltd* [1978] IR 114. As to the relationship between the builder and sub-contractors see *Lift Manufacturers Ltd v Irish Life Assurance Co Ltd* [1979] ILRM 277; *Glow Heating Ltd v Eastern Health Board* [1988] IR 110.

[120.] See para **[4.14]** *et seq, ante*.

contractors. A purchaser or lessee is unlikely to be covered adequately[121] by an assignment of the benefit of the building agreement by the developer, because any such assignment cannot increase the liability of the builder to the developer under the building agreement.[122] It is true that the English courts in recent times have been prepared to allow a third party for whose benefit a building contract is entered into to sue for substantial damages relating to defects which it was foreseeable to the builder would cause loss to that third party (like a purchaser from the developer or a lessee),[123] but it is by no means certain that the Irish courts will follow this trend. For this reason it is prudent to continue to seek collateral warranties and, furthermore, to insist that the terms of these do not exclude common law rights.[124]

7. Completion

[11.23] One of the most difficult points to settle in a building agreement is the completion date.[125] The Law Society/CIF *Building Agreement* enables the builder to fix the completion date by giving notice in writing to the purchaser of completion of the works, unless the purchaser has previously agreed in writing that they have been completed.[126] The purchaser naturally wants to take possession of his new house as quickly as possible, yet, while it may be in the builder's financial interest to complete as early as possible, his experience of the trade will warn him of the need to have a sufficiently flexible completion clause to cover hold-ups caused by strikes, shortage of materials, bad weather and so on. The purchaser must bear in mind that the

---

[121.] It would appear, however, that the purchaser or lessee has a sufficient interest in the performance of the building agreement that such an assignment does not fall foul of the rule against maintenance or champerty: see *Trendex Trading Corporation v Credit Suisse* [1981] 3 All ER 520.

[122.] Ie, the builder is liable for loss suffered by the *other party* only, the developer, whereas the purchaser or lessee of a defective building may suffer more extensive loss, especially consequential loss.

[123.] See the House of Lords decision in *Linden Gardens Trust Ltd v Lenesta Sludge Disposals Ltd* [1993] 3 All ER 417, applied by the Court of Appeal in *Darlington Borough Council v Wiltshire Northern Ltd* [1995] 3 All ER 895.

[124.] This point is reinforced by the Privy Council's recent recognition that negligence liability for economic loss is still enforceable in New Zealand despite recent retrenchment by the English courts: see *Invercargill City Council v Hamlin* [1996] 1 All ER 756, para **[4.14]** *ante*. As regards rights of set off, see *Hegarty & Sons Ltd v Royal Liver Friendly Society* [1985] IR 524; *Rohan Construction Ltd v Antigen Ltd* [1989] ILRM 783.

[125.] See *O'Donoghue & Co Ltd v Collins* High Court, unrep, 10 March 1972 (1970/2771P); *Treacy v Dwyer Nolan Developments Ltd* [1979] ILRM 163.

[126.] Cond 8(a). Note also cl 2 which contains an obligation to complete the works within a stated number of calendar months of the date of the agreement. And note the provision for determination of disputes over minor defects: see para **[11.24]** *infra*.

more delays there are, the more his house is likely to cost in the end and so any clause protecting the builder against delays should be carefully scrutinised. In particular, it should be made clear who is to bear any increases in costs due to delays. However, in practice little attention is paid in many cases to the completion date and all too often an agreement drawn up on behalf of the builder contains some general provision such as: "The builder will do his best to finish the house as soon as possible." And that raises another matter upon which disputes often arise, ie, as to when a house is actually "finished", which in the end may have to be settled by arbitration.

8. Disputes

[11.24] In view of the complexity of a building agreement, and particularly in view of the considerable risk of something going wrong and disputes arising during its currency, it has become almost axiomatic now that it should contain an arbitration clause.[127] Arbitration is often the only practical way of resolving a dispute on such matters as when payments are due, whether work is progressing satisfactorily, delays in completion and so on. Though it should be noted that formal arbitration can be a very expensive process and many solicitors prefer determination of a dispute rather more informally by a single expert acceptable to both sides. The Law Society/CIF *Building Agreement* adopts both systems. In the case of a dispute as to whether there are defects resulting in the works not being properly completed, or whether they are minor, so that the purchaser should complete on the basis of an undertaking by the builder to rectify them within a reasonable time, this is to determined by an expert appointed, in the absence of agreement, by either the President of the Law Society or the President of the CIF from the list of approved experts.[128] Otherwise any dispute is to be referred to an arbitrator similarly appointed from the approved list.[129]

[127.] For early forms of such clauses, see *Mansfield v Doolin* (1869) IR 4 CL 17; *Richardson v Mahon* (1879) 4 LR Ir 486. See also *McKee v McMahon* (1935) 69 ILTR 180.

[128.] Cond 12(b)-(e).

[129.] Cond 11. See the discussion as to the duties of such an arbitrator by the Supreme Court in *Grangeford Structures Ltd v SH Ltd* [1990] 2 IR 351. See also *Wilson (Builders) Ltd v NIHE* [1989] NI 208.

Chapter 12

POSITION OF PARTIES PENDING COMPLETION

[12.01] In this chapter we consider the position of the parties in the intermediate stage in the conveyancing process between contract and completion. As we shall see, this is a subject which has given rise to considerable controversy in Ireland.[1] We also examine in the next chapter the various remedies for enforcement of the contract open to the parties, should one or other of them refuse to complete.[2]

I. VENDOR AS TRUSTEE

[12.02] According to traditional theory, the effect in equity of a contract for the sale of land is to make the vendor a trustee for the purchaser of the estate in the land agreed to be sold.[3] However, the precise application of the trust concept in this context has been the subject of considerable dispute amongst the courts on both sides of the Irish Sea. Particularly at issue is the question of when the beneficial interest in the land is to be regarded as passing to the purchaser and from the vendor. In England there appears to be a conflict between two lines of authorities.[4] The predominant view seems to be that the vendor becomes a trustee of the legal estate and the purchaser becomes the owner of the beneficial interest as soon as the contract for sale is entered into[5] - subject to the qualification that the contract must be one of which a court would grant a decree of specific performance.[6] In other words, the

---

1. See para **[11.03]** *et seq, infra*.
2. *Post* - completion remedies are considered in Ch 21 *post*.
3. See Waters, 'Constructive Trust: Vendor and Purchaser' (1961) 14 CLP 76; Wellings, 'Vendor as Trustee' (1959) 23 Conv 173.
4. See the discussion by Kenny J in *Tempany v Hynes* [1976] IR 101 at 114-6. See also the discussion by the English Court of Appeal in *Rayner v Preston* (1881) 18 Ch D 1. For detailed analysis of the issues involved, and discussion of both the English and Irish authorities see the Law Reform Commission's Report on *Interests of Vendor and Purchaser in Land during the Period between Contract and Completion* (LRC 49-1995). See also Farrell, *Irish Law of Specific Performance* (1994), Ch 11; Lyall, *Land Law in Ireland* (1994), Appendix A.
5. *Shaw v Foster* (1872) LR 5 HL 321 at 338 (*per* Lord Cairns); *Lysaght v Edwards* (1876) 2 Ch D 449 at 506 (*per* Jessel MR).
6. *Holroyd v Marshall* (1862) 10 HLC 191 at 209-10 (*per* Westbury LC). See further on specific performance, para **[13.37]** *post*.

relationship of trustee and beneficiary arises from the making of the contract and from that date the purchaser is to be regarded as having the entire beneficial interest in the land. Yet there is also authority for the view that the crucial factor is not signing of the contract, but rather the payment of the purchase money by the purchaser.[7] Under this theory, the purchaser does not acquire the entire beneficial interest in the land until he has paid the whole of the purchase money and, if he has paid part only, eg, by way of deposit, the vendor is a trustee for him only to the extent to which he has paid that part. And, of course, in the normal course of events the purchaser will have paid only a part of the purchase money prior to completion.[8] As we shall see,[9] as a result of the majority decision of the Supreme Court in *Tempany v Hynes*[10] the position in Irish law currently is that the purchaser obtains only a beneficial interest commensurate with the proportion of the purchase price paid.[11] In other words, if he pays the usual 10% deposit on signing the contract, he has only a 10% beneficial interest.[12] Notwithstanding the apparent logic of this position, it is not without its difficulties, as commentators have since pointed out.[13] For example, it suggests that in assessing the carrying of the risk of damage to the property between contract and completion, the general law would require an apportionment as between the two parties.[14] If the purchaser agrees to a sub-sale before completion, the sub-purchaser presumably acquires only a fraction of the purchaser's beneficial interest, commensurate with the proportion of the sub-purchase price paid, eg 10% of 10%, ie, 1% only.[15] If the purchaser does not pay any deposit or other part of the purchase price,[16] it would appear that he cannot protect himself against further dealings by the vendor and so may lose priority to third parties.[17]

---

[7] *Rose v Watson* (1864) 10 HLC 672 at 383-4 (*per* Lord Cranworth). *Cf* at p 678 (*per* Lord Westbury). But *cf* the doctrine of conversion, para **[12.11]** *infra*. See also *Bridges v Mees* [1957] Ch 475.

[8] Para **[13.30]** *post*.

[9] Para **[12.04]** *infra*.

[10] [1976] IR 101 (Kenny J, O'Higgins CJ concurring). Henchy J dissented on this point, adhering to the view that the beneficial interest arises on the signing of the contract regardless of any payment.

[11] *Ibid*, pp 114-6.

[12] Henchy J subsequently accepted that this was the effect of the majority holding in *Tempany v Hynes*: see *Hamilton v Hamilton* [1982] IR 466 at 484. See also *Re Grange Developments Ltd* [1987] ILRM 733; *Murnaghan Bros v O'Maoldomhnaigh* [1991] 1 IR 455.

[13] See fn 4 *supra*.

[14] Fortunately, this will usually be avoided in practice by an express provision: see para **[12.40]** *infra*.

[15] See the Law Reform Commission Report (fn 4 *supra*), para 2.105.

[16] A *pre*-contract payment (eg, a booking deposit paid to a builder) may not count: see *Re Barrett Apartments Ltd* [1985] IR 350, paras **[3.15]** and **[10.31]** *ante* and **[13.31]** *post*.

[17] See Lyall (fn 4 *supra*) pp 1028-30.

[12.03] This issue has arisen in Ireland in a number of cases where the question involved the validity of a judgment mortgage[18] registered between the date of the contract and completion. The point is that such a mortgage can be registered only against an interest in land[19] and so the question arose as to whether after the contract for sale the vendor retained such an interest against which the judgment mortgage could be validly registered. In *Re Kissock and Currie's Contract*,[20] the majority of the Irish Court of Appeal[21] held that the vendor did still retain an interest in the land.[22] O'Brien LC stated:

> "I think that, from the point of view of the judgment creditor, as regulated by the statute, his debtor had an interest in land after the date of the contract for sale and until completion, capable of being affected by the judgment ... If the contract of sale should not be carried out the estate of the vendor will be the same as before the contract; no doubt if the purchase money is paid and the sale is completed he loses that estate, but meanwhile it is to my mind clearly an interest in land, and as such capable of being affected by a registered judgment."[23]

[12.04] It was this same issue which was considered by the Supreme Court in *Tempany v Hynes*,[24] wherein all the judges[25] agreed that between contract and completion the vendor retained an interest in the land capable of being charged by a judgment mortgage. On the more general point, however, Kenny J[26] rejected the predominant view of English judges referred to above[27]:

[18.] See on this subject, *Irish Land Law* (2nd ed, 1986), para 13.163 *et seq.*

[19.] *Ibid*, para 13.166.

[20.] [1916] 1 IR 376.

[21.] O'Brien LC and Moriarty LJ, though note that the latter died before revising his judgment and the report was taken from the Registrar's note, *ibid*, p 391.

[22.] Cherry LCJ dissented on this point. He stated: "It is well-settled law that the effect of such an agreement is to make the purchaser the owner in equity of the property, and the vendor, if he remains in possession, merely a trustee for him ... It is a principle applied every day in the case of sales under the Land Purchase Acts, where, after the agreement has been signed and approved of by the Land Commission, the purchasing tenant is treated as owner in fee simple long before the legal estate is vested in him or the purchase money is paid ... The most that the vendor could retain would be a lien for unpaid purchase-money, and that has never, so far as I am aware, been held to be an estate or interest in the lands which can be captured by a judgment mortgage." *Ibid*, p 391.

[23.] *Ibid*, p 388.

[24.] [1976] IR 101.

[25.] O'Higgins CJ, Henchy and Kenny JJ.

[26.] O'Higgins CJ concurred with his judgment, [1976] IR 101 at 107.

[27.] Para **[12.02]** *supra.*

"A vendor who signs a contract with a purchaser for the sale of land becomes a trustee in the sense that he is bound to take reasonable care of the property until the sale is completed but he becomes a trustee of the beneficial interest to the extent only to which the purchase price is paid. He is not a trustee of the beneficial interest merely because he signs a contract."[28]

On the other hand, Henchy J accepted the more traditional view:

"When a binding contract for sale of land has been made, the law (at least in cases where the parties proceed to the stage of conveyance) treats the beneficial ownership as having passed to the purchaser from the time the contract was made ... From then until the time of completion, regardless of whether the purchase money has been paid or not, the vendor, in whom the legal estate is still vested, is treated for certain purposes (such as the preservation of the property from damage by trespassers[29] as a trustee for the purchaser. But, coupled with this trusteeship, there is vested in the vendor, pending completion, a substantial interest in the property. Save where the contract provides otherwise, he is entitled to remain in possession until the purchase money is paid[30] and, as such possessor, he has a common law lien on the property for the purchase money; even if he parts with possession of the property, he has an equitable lien on it for the unpaid purchase money[31]; and he is entitled to take and keep for his own use the rents and profits up to the date fixed for completion.[32] It is clear, therefore, that between contract and completion the vendor has a beneficial interest in the property which is capable of being charged by a judgment mortgage."[33]

It must be emphasised that Henchy J's views were in the minority and it is Kenny J's view (with which O'Higgins CJ concurred) which states current Irish law on the matter of principle. However, though there was a divergence of views on the basic principle involved, as a matter of substance the conclusion as to the position of the respective parties was the same and, indeed, it is fair to say that the judges on both sides of the Irish Sea are generally agreed on the various aspects of this subject. However, before we examine these aspects in further detail, it may be useful to note the actual

---

[28]. *Op cit*, p 114. Thus, he preferred the views of Lord Cranworth to those of Lord Cairns and Jessel MR, see fns 5 and 7, para **[12.02]** *supra*, *Cf Connolly v Keating (No 2)* [1903] 1 IR 356 at 361 (*per* Porter MR); *Re Murphy and McCormack* [1939] 1 IR 322 at 327 (*per* Kennedy CJ); *Re Strong* [1940] IR 382 at 394-4 (*per* Murnaghan J), 399 (*per* Meredith J) and 402 (*per* O'Byrne J).

[29]. Para **[12.21]** *infra*.

[30]. Para **[12.13]** *infra*.

[31]. Para **[12.15]** *infra*.

[32]. Para **[12.14]** *infra*.

[33]. *Op cit*, p 109.

decision in the *Tempany* case, for it has considerable importance for conveyancers in Ireland.

[12.05] The contract for sale and judgment mortgages in the *Tempany* case involved registered land[34] and raised the question of whether the mortgages registered between contract and completion would bind the purchaser when he was registered as owner after completion. This point had arisen in a number of earlier cases. In *Pim v Coyle*[35] Barton J held a judgment mortgage registered after a voluntary transfer by the registered owner, but before the transferee was registered, ranked in priority to the transfer even when registered. However, subsequent cases have not followed this principle in relation to transfers for valuable consideration.[36] In *Re Murphy and McCormack*,[37] the Supreme Court[38] held that, where a judgment mortgage was registered after execution of a transfer for value and payment of the purchase price, but before registration of the transferee as the new registered owner, the latter took free of the judgment mortgage. Kennedy CJ pointed out that by statute[39] a registered owner of land can create rights over the registered land without their being registered and that "the right or estate which a purchaser acquires by virtue of a contract for sale to him is such a right."[40] This unregistered right of the purchaser was liable to be defeated by subsequent registered charges or transfers for valuable consideration, but the point was that it had long been settled that a judgment mortgage was not a charge in this sense, at most it was a "process of execution."[41] This view was followed by the majority of the Supreme Court in *Re Strong*,[42] where it was held that the purchaser of registered land was entitled to have the registration of the judgment mortgage cancelled, where this registration had been made

---

[34.] See further on registered land para **[12.49]** *infra*.

[35.] [1907] 1 IR 330 approved by Cherry LJ in *Mooney v McMahon* [1911] I IR 125.

[36.] See the criticisms of *dicta* in *Pim v Coyle* by Kennedy CJ in *Devoy v Hanlon* [1929] IR 246 at 256 and *Re Murphy and McCormack* [1930] IR 322 at 322-7 and by Johnston J in *Quinn v McCool* [1929] IR 620 at 622.

[37.] [1930] IR 322.

[38.] Affirming the decision of Wylie J [1928] IR 479, which was followed by Johnston J in *Quinn v McCool* [1929] IR 620.

[39.] Ie, s 44(2) of the Local Registration of Title (Ir) Act 1891, now replaced by s 68(2) of the Registration of Title Act 1964. See para **[12.50]** *infra*.

[40.] [1930] IR 322 at 328. See also his judgment in *Devoy v Hanlon* [1929] IR 246 at 256, para **[12.50]** *infra*.

[41.] *Ibid*, p 327, approved by O'Byrne J in *Re Strong* [1940] IR 382 at 403. See also *Reid v Miller* [1928] NI 151; *Tempany v Hynes* [1976] IR 101 at 117 (*per* Kenny J).

[42.] [1940] IR 382 (Sullivan CJ, Geoghegan and O'Byrne JJ; Murnaghan and Meredith JJ dissenting).

after the purchase money had been paid and execution of the transfer, but before registration of the purchaser as transferee.[43]

[12.06] There still remained the question of what the position was where the judgment mortgage was registered after the contract but before any transfer was executed or the full purchase money was paid by the transferee. This issue arose in *Tempany v Hynes*,[44] where the point was not dealt with as clearly as it might have been. This was due in part, no doubt, because of the facts of the case. There the land owned by a company, which was registered land, was subject to a floating charge, which crystallised when the debenture holder appointed a receiver. The effect of this was to create an equitable assignment to the debenture holder of all property subject to the charge[45] and Kenny J, speaking for the majority, held that this ranked in priority to the judgment mortgages. The receiver who had contracted to sell the land had, therefore, in his view a good title to pass to the purchaser, who would, deriving title from the debenture holder through the receiver, take free of the judgment mortgages.[46] Henchy J took a different approach and argued that the vendor's interest affected by the judgment mortgage was a "transient" one which passed out of existence once completion of the purchase took place and the purchaser was registered as the new owner.[47] Furthermore, in his view s 71(4) of the Registration of Title Act 1964,[48] paragraph (c) of which states that a registered judgment mortgage is subject, *inter alia*, to "all unregistered rights subject to which the judgment debtor held that interest at the time of registration of the affidavit", supported this view. He pointed out that s 3(1) of the 1964 Act defines "right" as including "estate, interest, equity and powers", thus covering the purchaser's interest in this case. He then went on to say:

> "It follows, therefore, that if the defendant completes the purchase and becomes registered as full owner, the *post*-contract judgment mortgages[49]

---

43. Note that Murnaghan J stated that, in the case of unregistered land, a judgment mortgage would not affect the land after it had been agreed to be sold and after the purchase money had been paid, 'as the vendor no longer had a beneficial interest in the land after he had received the purchase money.' *Ibid*, p 395.
44. [1976] IR 101.
45. See *Re Interview Ltd* [1975] IR 382; *Re Keenan Bros* [1985] IR 401.
46. *Ibid*, p 117. Note that Kenny J stated that this applied to both *pre*- and *post*-contract judgment mortgages, all of which should be cancelled from the folios by the Registrar of Titles.
47. *Ibid*, p 109.
48. No equivalent provision existed in the Local Registration of Title (Ir) Act 1891.
49. Note that, unlike Kenny J (fn 46 *supra*), Henchy J refers only to the *post*-contract judgment mortgages.

will no longer affect the lands and he will be entitled to have them cancelled from the folios."[50]

The result, at least as regards the *post*-contract[51] judgment mortgages, was the same, but the issue remains as to the law governing such charges in cases where there are no complicating factors like the debenture in the *Tempany* case. On this point, it seems clear that the majority view in *Tempany* leads to the conclusion that such charges attach on registration to any beneficial interest retained by the vendor, ie, where the purchaser has still not paid the full purchase price, but only, say, a 10% deposit, they attach to the vendor's 90% beneficial interest. On completion the purchaser apparently takes subject to those charges.[52]

[12.07] There is no doubt that the decision in the *Tempany* case is unsatisfactory, not least because the difficulties created by the majority view of the respective interests of the vendor and the purchaser were not faced up to. In particular, by insisting that the purchaser acquires no beneficial interest until some part of the purchase money is paid, the majority view exposes the purchaser to considerable risks which it may not be possible to avoid. If the purchaser makes no payment towards the purchase price,[53] the vendor is, apparently, free to create all sorts of rights in favour of third parties, or they may acquire such rights through their own actions, which will take priority over the purchaser because, according to the majority, he has no estate or interest, whether legal or equitable, in the land. It would appear, therefore, that he cannot protect his interest against such dealings by registering the contract in the Registry of Deeds, in the case of unregistered land, or lodging a caution in the Land Registry, in the case of registered land.[54] Quite apart from the risk that charges like judgment mortgages may be registered, as occurred in the *Tempany* case itself, the vendor may contract to sell to a third party who does pay a deposit and, thereby, acquires an equitable interest which, being first in time, takes priority over the first purchaser.[55] It is true, of course, that this will be a very rare case because

---

50. Kenny J referred to the argument based on s 71(4) (*ibid*, p 116), but did not pursue it, going on instead to decide the appeal on the equitable assignment effected by the appointment of the receiver under the debenture.

51. See fn 49 *supra*.

52. See Keane, *Equity and the Law of Trusts in the Republic of Ireland* (1988), para 5.16; Law Reform Commission *op cit*, para 2.79. *Cf* Lyall, *Land Law in Ireland* (1935), p 1011.

53. Note again that the Supreme Court has held that *pre*-contract payments (such as booking deposits paid to a builder) do not count: see para **[3.15]** *ante*. *Quaere* whether they become converted later, if a contract is entered into: see paras **[10.31]** *ante* and **[13.31]** *post*.

54. See paras **[6.65]** and **[6.66]** *ante*. See also the Law Reform Commission *op cit*, para 2.80.

55. See the Law Reform Commission *op cit*, para 2.82.

usually the purchaser will pay a deposit on signing the contract,[56] but even where he does make some such payment, if it is not the full purchase price, he remains at risk to the extent that the vendor is free to deal with the proportion of the beneficial interest retained by him. In *Tempany v Hynes* it was judgment mortgages registered against that interest which apparently would survive completion. It is not clear that registration of the contract will protect the purchaser against such rights, for the argument might be that this protects the purchaser's interest only (commensurate with the proportion of the price paid), and does not affect vendor's interest.

[12.08] There is much to be said for the view that the majority in *Tempany*, by putting such emphasis on the need for a payment by the purchaser, were confusing two quite distinct doctrines, *viz*, the notion that the vendor becomes a trustee for the purchaser and the principle that the purchaser acquires a lien over the land.[57] In respect of the latter, clearly a payment must have been paid to justify the court holding that the purchaser has an equitable lien to secure its recovery, but it seems settled now that, although the purchaser must establish the existence of a contract, it is not necessary to show that specific performance would be available.[58] It is arguable that the minority view of Henchy J, that the vendor becomes a trustee and purchaser acquires the full beneficial interest on the signing of the contract, regardless of any payment made, is much to be preferred. It recognises the purchaser's interest from the date of the contract, which is surely what the parties intend in most, if not all, cases. It avoids the absurdities created by trying to split the beneficial interest between the vendor and purchaser. For example, when a purchaser who had paid only the deposit seeks specific performance of the contract, he expects an order affecting the entire land, not just a proportion commensurate with his beneficial interest. It may be that a full court sitting in the Supreme Court will some day take the opportunity to reverse the majority view[59] and the Law Reform Commission has recently come down firmly in favour of a statutory provision to the effect that when a binding contract is entered into, the beneficial ownership should be treated as

---

56. Another reason for advising a purchaser to do so: see para **[10.19]** *ante*.

57. To some extent even Kenny J recognised in *Tempany v Hynes* that there may be two levels of trusteeship: "A vendor who signs a contract with a purchaser for the sale of land becomes a trustee in the sense that he is bound to take reasonable care of the property until the sale is completed, but he becomes a trustee of the beneficial interest to the extent only to which the purchase price is made." [1976] IR 101 at 114.

58. See the Supreme Court decision in *Re Barratt Apartments Ltd* [1985] IR 350, especially at 360 (*per* McCarthy J). See Lyall, *op cit*, pp 1014, 1025 and 1029; *cf* Coughlan 'Equitable Liens for the Recovery of Booking Deposits' (1988) 10 DULJ 90.

59. This was suggested as a possibility by Henchy J in *Hamilton v Hamilton* [1982] IR 466 at 484. See also *Doyle v Hearne* [1987] IR 601 at 617 (*per* McCarthy J).

passing to the purchaser from the time of the contract, subject to the condition subsequent that the purchaser completes.[60]

[12.09] It follows from what has been said above that a purchaser in the vast majority of cases, where part only of the purchase price is paid prior to completion, must beware of judgment mortgages registered prior to completion. These must be registered in the Registry of Deeds in the case of unregistered land,[61] or in the Land Registry in the case of registered land.[62] Thus, their existence will be disclosed by the usual pre-completion searches.[63] If they are disclosed in this or any other way,[64] the purchaser's solicitor should advise his client to insist upon them being discharged by the vendor, either prior to completion or out of the proceeds of sale as in the case of ordinary mortgages to which the vendor is subject.[65] The client must be warned that if this is not done, he will take the property subject to the judgment mortgages in question. Quite apart from the risk of the creditor seeking a court order to enforce the mortgage,[66] the purchaser's title will be subject to incumbrances which may hinder further dealings with it. It should be noted, however, that if the creditor does not take action to enforce the judgment mortgage, it will become statute-barred after twelve years from the date of the judgment.[67] Judgment mortgages are included within the definition of a "mortgage" for the purposes of the Statute of Limitations 1957.[68] Thus, as is so often the case,[69] a flaw on the title may be cured in time by the doctrine of adverse possession.[70]

[12.10] It must also be said that, despite the theoretical dispute in the Supreme Court decision in *Tempany v Hynes* and the practical difficulties it

---

60. *Op cit*, para 4.19.
61. Judgment Mortgage (Ir) Act 1850, s 6. See *Irish Bank of Commerce Ltd v O'Hara* High Court, unrep 10 May 1989 (1988/578 Sp); *Allied Irish Banks plc v Griffin* [1992] 2 IR 70. See also Wylie, *Irish Land Law* (2nd ed, 1986), para 13.167.
62. Registration of Title Act 1986, s 69(1)(i). See also Fitzgerald *Land Registry Practice*, (2nd ed, 1995) Ch 8.
63. See para **[15.39]** *et seq, post*.
64. Eg, through the requisitions on title: see para **[16.22]** *post*.
65. See para **[20.37]** *post*.
66. The usual method of enforcement is to obtain a court order declaring that the sum for which the judgment was obtained is well charged and an order for sale of the land if it is not paid within a specified period (eg, three months). See *First National Building Society v Ring* [1992] 1 IR 375.
67. Statute of Limitations 1957, s 11(5).
68. See s 2(1) of the 1957 Act and Brady and Kerr *The Limitations of Actions* (2nd ed, 1994), pp 130-31.
69. See para **[14.80]** *post*.
70. See *Brady and Kerr op cit*, p 94 *et seq*; *Wylie op cit*, Ch 23.

may create in particular instances, as outlined above, for the most part the position of the vendor and purchaser between contract and completion is relatively clear. It is time, therefore, to consider this matter in some more detail.

A. Doctrine of Conversion

[12.11] The entering into of a contract for the sale of land has long been held to attract the application of the controversial equitable doctrine of conversion.[71] Equity treats the purchaser as owner of the land and the vendor as owner of the purchase money from the date of the contract,[72] so that, eg, on death of one or other of the parties before completion succession to property may be governed by the application of the doctrine.[73] This doctrine has been recognised and applied many times by the Irish courts,[74] which have also recognised its extension to options to purchase.[75] But the Irish courts have been very reluctant to further the latter extension in cases involving a vendor and purchaser,[76] and have been always ready to find evidence of an intention that the doctrine should not apply.[77]

[12.12] The traditional view is that the doctrine of conversion operates only in respect of a contract which is binding in the sense that specific performance would be available to enforce it.[78] To some extent this is bound up with the notion that the vendor becomes a constructive trustee of the legal title for the purchaser.[79] However, it must be questioned whether the availability of specific performance should be a prerequisite to operation of conversion,[80] and there are some English authorities suggesting that it is not.[81] That remedy is essentially a discretionary one which may not be available to the purchaser due to circumstances not linked to any default on

---

71. Pettit, 'Conversion under a Contract for the Sale of Land' (1960) 24 Conv 47. See also on the doctrine generally, *Irish Land Law* (2nd ed, 1986), paras 3.094-111.
72. *McDonnell v Stenson* [1921] 1 IR 80.
73. See *Irish Land Law* (2nd ed, 1986), para 3.095.
74. *Ibid*, paras 3.097-111.
75. Under the rule in *Lawes v Bennett* (1785) 1 Cox CC 167. See also *Re Isaac* [1894] 3 Ch 506. See Brady *Succession Law in Ireland* (2nd ed, 1995), para [6.94] *et seq*.
76. *Re Sherlock's Estate* [1899] 2 IR 561 at 608 (*per* Holmes LJ). *Cf Belshaw v Rollins* [1904] 1 IR 284.
77. *Steele v Steele* [1913] 1 IR 292 at 305 (*per* Palles CB). See also *Duffield v McMaster* [1896] 1 IR 370; *Miley v Carty* [1927] IR 541.
78. *Holroyd v Marshall* (1862) 10 HLC 191 at 209-10 (*per* Lord Westbury LC). *Cf Lysaght v Edwards* (1876) 2 Ch D 449.
79. See Oakley, *Construction Trusts* (2nd ed, 1987), Ch 6.
80. See *Pettit*, fn 61 *supra*.
81. *Rose v Watson* (1864) 10 HLC 672; *Gordon Hill Trust Ltd v Segall* [1942] 1 All ER 379. See also *Tailby v Official Receiver* (1888) 13 App Cas 523, especially at 546 (*per* Lord Macnaghten).

his part, eg, hardship to the vendor.[82] Arguably, therefore, all that the purchaser need establish is a "valid contract"[83] or "binding contract *simpliciter*".[84]

B. Possession

[12.13] It is settled that the vendor may retain possession of the land until completion or until the full purchase money is paid,[85] unless some special contractual variation is made by the parties.[86] Where he does retain possession of the land, he has a common law lien on it for the unpaid purchase money.[87] If he parts with possession, he has an equitable lien on the land for the unpaid purchase money.[88]

C. Rents and Profits

[12.14] The vendor is entitled to the rents and profits from the land until the time fixed for completion.[89] If completion does not take place on that date, the vendor is regarded as a trustee of the rents and profits from completion date[90] and is liable to account to the purchaser for them.[91] Indeed, this is a strict liability, for the vendor must account for any rents and profits he would have received if, eg, he had not allowed the property to go to waste.[92] Rents and profits include the proceeds from sale of crops harvested from the land

---

82. See Farrell, *Irish Law of Specific Performance* (1994), Ch 9.
83. See Keane, *Equity and Law of Trusts in the Republic of Ireland* (1988), para 24.03. See also his judgment at first instance in *Re Barratt Apartments Ltd* [1985] IR 350, especially at p 354.
84. Law Reform Commission, *op cit*, para 2.27.
85. *Re Kissock and Currie's Contract* [1916] 1 IR 376 at 392 (*per* Moriarty LJ); *Tempany v Hynes* [1976] IR 101 at 109 (*per* Henchy J). See also *Phillips v Silvester* (1872) LR 8 Ch 173.
86. Para **[12.32]** *infra*.
87. *Tempany v Hynes* [1976] IR 101 at 109 (*per* Henchy J). See *Irish Land Law* (2nd ed, 1986), para 12.15.
88. See *Irish Land Law* (2nd ed, 1986), para 12.16. See further, para **[12.15]** *infra*.
89. *Gowan v Tighe* (1835) L1 & G *temp* Plunk 168 at 175 (*per* Plunkett LC); *Tempany v Hynes* [1976] IR 101 at 109 (*per* Henchy J). See also *Johnston v Johnston* (1869) IR 3 Eq 328; *Neville v Slattery Estates Co Ltd* High Court, unrep, 15 February 1984 (1981/14036P). *Cf O'Brien v White-Spunner* [1979] ILRM 240. If no date for completion is fixed by the parties, then the date is when the vendor first makes out a good title to the property, *Monro v Taylor* (1848) 8 Hare 51. See also *Cuddon v Tite* (1858) 1 Giff 395.
90. Or the date he makes out good title, see fn 89 *supra*.
91. *Johnston v Johnston* (1869) IR 3 Eq 328. See also *Wilson v Clapham* (1819) 1 Jac & W 36; *Plews v Samuel* [1904] 1 Ch 464. See para **[12.18]** *infra*. See further on apportionment of rents and other outgoings, para **[20.03]** *post*.
92. *Phillips v Silvester* (1872) 8 Ch App 173.

in the normal course of husbandry[93] and from sale of minerals produced from working mines,[94] but do not include anything which forms part of the land itself, ie, part of its capital value as opposed to its income. If the vendor takes the latter the purchaser may seek an injunction against him.[95]

D. Lien

[12.15] As mentioned above,[96] the vendor has a lien on the land for unpaid purchase money. Where he has retained possession, he has a common law lien, ie, the right to retain possession until the debt is paid, but not the right to sell or otherwise deal with the property in discharge of the debt.[97] If he has parted with possession he still has an equitable lien on the land, ie, an equitable charge which entitles him to apply to the court for an order of sale of the land and discharge of his debt out of the proceeds of sale.[98] As Meredith J put it in *Munster and Leinster Bank Ltd v McGlashan*:[99]

> "... equity recognises a lien on the lands in favour of the vendor to secure the unfulfilled obligation of the purchaser, which in equity is of course binding on a third party with notice. This lien is bestowed by equity for the protection of vendors - as in the converse case for the protection of purchasers, who have paid the purchase money but not obtained the conveyance[100] - quite independently, as is well settled, of any contract between the parties. That is only reasonable, because the typical cases are those where the obligations on one side or the other are prematurely performed ... and consequently where what gives rise to the lien was from the nature of the case not in contemplation."[101]

[12.16] The lien arises on the signing of the contract,[102] but relates only to the land which forms the subject-matter of the contract.[103] It also arises even

---

93. *Webster v Donaldson* (1865) 34 Beav 451.
94. *Leppington v Freeman* (1891) 66 LT 357.
95. See the discussion in *Hadley v London Bank of Scotland Ltd* (1865) 3 De GJ & Sm 63.
96. Para **[12.13]** *supra*.
97. See *Irish Land Law* (2nd ed, 1986), para 12.15. See also *Tempany v Hynes* [1976] IR 101 at 109 (*per* Henchy J).
98. *Ibid*, para 12.16.
99. [1937] IR 525 (*aff'd* by the Sup Ct). See also *Stuart v Ferguson* (1832) Hayes 452; *Eyre v Sadlier* (1863) 15 Ir Ch R. 1; *Re Durrow Brick and Tile Works Co* [1904] 1 IR 530.
100. See para **[12.44]** *infra*.
101. *Op cit*, pp 528-9. See also *Bank of Ireland Finance Ltd v Daly Ltd* [1987] IR 79; *Highland Finance Ireland Ltd v Sacred Heart College of Agriculture Ltd* [1992] 1 IR 472.
102. And must be discharged by the purchaser's successors in title if he dies before it is discharged. *Dowdall v McCartan* (1880) 5 LR Ir 642. See also *Re Birmingham* [1959] Ch 523.
103. *Stuart v Ferguson* (1832) Hayes 452 at 468 (*per* Joy CB).

though the purchase money is payable by instalments or is not payable until some future date.[104] Indeed, as Meredith J again pointed out[105]:

"As authority for the proposition that the lien exists in the case of an annuity or of a sum of money to be paid at a date subsequent to the conveyance as well as in the case of purchase money to be paid at the time of transfer, it is sufficient to refer to the Irish case of *Richardson v McCausland*.[106]"

The lien subsists so long as any part of the purchase money remains owing.[107] It may still be invoked even though a conveyance of the land has been executed which contains the usual receipt clause purporting to suggest that the full consideration has been paid,[108] if in fact it has not been paid.[109] Thus, in *Saunders v Leslie*,[110] Lord Manners LC stated:

"It is established by many Decisions, that the Vendor's lien on the Estate is not gone by accepting either a Bond or a Note from the Purchaser; nor will a Receipt for the Purchase-Money discharge the Lien until the Money be paid."[111]

Similarly, in *Croly v O'Callaghan*,[112] Lefroy B stated:

"... though the recital or receipt in a deed is *prima facie* evidence of the payment of the consideration, yet if the court comes to the conclusion that the consideration has not been paid, and directs an inquiry upon the subject, the onus of proving the payment lies upon the party insisting that it has been paid."[113]

It should also be noted that the purchaser's lender may be entitled to claim a similar lien by way of subrogation. The Irish courts have held that *prima facie* where the lender advances money for the express purpose of it being applied in payment of the purchase price of property, the lender is entitled to the lien on the property which the vendor would have been entitled if the

---

[104.] *Nives v Nives* (1880) 15 Ch D 649; *Langen and Wind Ltd v Bell* [1972] Ch 685.

[105.] *Munster and Leinster Bank Ltd v McGlashan* [1937] IR 525 at 529 (*aff'd* by Sup Ct).

[106.] (1817) Beat 457.

[107.] *Re Kissock and Currie's Contract* [1916] 1 IR 376 at 391: "... in order to support a lien of any kind, there must be a debt due by the purchaser to the vendor." (*per* Cherry LCJ). See also *Lysaght v Edwards* (1876) 2 Ch D 449 at 506 (*per* Jessel MR).

[108.] See para **[18.43]** *post*.

[109.] *Winter v Lord Anson* (1827) 3 Russ 488. Note that this remains so despite s 55(1) of the Conveyancing Act 1881: see para **[18.45]** *post*.

[110.] (1814) 2 Ba & B 509.

[111.] *Ibid*, p 514.

[112.] (1842) 5 Ir Eq R 25.

[113.] *Ibid*, p 32. See also *Munster and Leinster Bank Ltd v McGlashan* [1937] IR 525 at 529 (*per* Meredith J) para **[12.17]** *infra*.

purchase price had not been paid by the purchaser.[114] This principle is, however, subject to the terms of the agreement between the purchaser and the lender and will not apply if those are inconsistent with retention by the lender of a right of subrogation.[115]

[12.17] A question that often arises is whether the vendor is to be regarded as having relinquished his lien,[116] particularly where the parties have arranged some additional security for payment of the outstanding purchase money.[117] The effect of taking such security is a matter of the intention of the vendor,[118] and the onus lies on the purchaser to show that the vendor agreed to rely upon this security and to abandon his lien.[119] As Meredith J explained in *Munster and Leinster Bank Ltd v McGlashan*[120]:

> "Where some particular and special security for the payment of money is given, then, according to the fundamental agreement for the sale and purchase, the giving of this security may be a full and complete performance of the purchaser's obligation. In that case the occasion on which equity confers a lien does not arise. Then the question is simply one of what the consideration really was. But even where the consideration was the payment of money there may be a question of whether the security given was agreed to be taken in substitution for the security conferred by the usual vendor's equitable lien. Of course if there is any such agreement between the parties for the substitution of the particular security given in place of that which equity would give in the absence of agreement then equity will give effect to such an arrangement. But it is well settled that the mere insertion into the conveyance of a covenant for the payment of the purchase price is not a circumstance from which an agreement for the substitution of the security of the covenant for the usual vendor's lien can be inferred."[121]

In *Re Aluminium Shop Fronts Ltd*,[122] a company which had an agreement for the grant of a lease of factory premises built by it resolved to sell its interest

---

[114.] *Bank of Ireland Finance Ltd v Daly Ltd* [1978] IR 79. *Cf Re Farm Fresh Frozen Foods Ltd* [1980] IR 131.

[115.] *Highland Finance Ireland Ltd v Sacred Heart College of Agriculture Ltd* [1992] 1 IR 472.

[116.] See *Stuart v Ferguson* (1832) Hayes 452 at 466 (*per* Joy CB).

[117.] See *Saunders v Leslie* (1814) 2 Ba & B 509; *Doyne v Harvey* (1816) 1 Hog 2. *Cf* Murphy J in *Re Aluminium Shop Fronts Ltd* [1987] IR 419 at 423.

[118.] *Re Stewart* [1925] 2 IR 51 at 60: "... the vendors took another security for the amount or the unpaid purchase-money, and the question whether by doing so they abandoned their lien is one of their intention to be inferred from their acts." (per FitzGibbon J). *Cf* the English Court of Appeal in *Barclays Bank plc v Estates and Commercial Ltd* London Times, 13 March 1996, where it held that the test is an objective, rather than a subjective, one.

[119.] *Hughes v Kearney* (1803) 1 Sch & Lef 132 at 135 (*per* Lord Redesdale).

[120.] [1937] IR 525 (*aff'd* by Sup Ct).

[121.] *Ibid*, p 529.

[122.] [1987] IR 419.

to an associated company. The landlord was informed and subsequently granted the lease to the associated company. The company was a party to this lease which recited that it had resolved to waive its rights under the earlier agreement in favour of the associated company. It also requested its bank to transfer loan facilities created in connection with the building works to the associated company. The associated company never paid the full purchase price to the company and. upon liquidation of both companies, the liquidator sought directions as to whether the company was entitled to an unpaid vendor's lien over the premises for the unpaid balance of the purchase money. Murphy J held that the restructuring of the financial facilities was "ample evidence" of waiver or abandonment of the lien.[123]

E. Interest

[12.18] As a corollary of the rule that the vendor ceases to be entitled to the rents and profits after the date fixed for completion,[124] he becomes thereafter entitled to interest on the balance of the purchase money outstanding until it is actually paid by the purchaser.[125] It is usual for the contract for sale to provide for payment of interest in such circumstances and, indeed, the Law Society's standard contract form so provides.[126] However, it is a well recognised qualification to this rule that the vendor is not entitled to claim interest where the delay in completion results from his "wilful default."[127] It is also the general law that the vendor is entitled to interest if the purchaser is allowed into possession of the land prior to completion.[128]

[12.19] To some extent the general law is modified by the Law Society's *General Conditions of Sale (1995 Edition)*. The matter is dealt with by condition 25 whereunder the purchaser is liable to pay interest where, by reason of any default on his part,[129] the purchase is not completed on or

---

[123.] *Ibid*, p 425.

[124.] Para **[12.14]** *supra*. If the contract fixes no date for completion, interest is payable from the date the vendor makes title to the property, *Enraght v Fitzgerald* (1842) 2 Dr & War 43 at 48 (*per* Sugden LC). See also *Barsht v Tagg* [1900] 1 Ch 231.

[125.] *Blount v GS & W Rly Co* (1851) 2 Ir Ch R 40; *Johnston v Johnston* (1869) IR 3 Eq 328.

[126.] See paras **[10.46]** *ante* and **[12.19]** *infra*. See further on delay over completion, para **[13.10]** *et seq, post*.

[127.] *Re Postmaster-General and Colgan's Contract* [1906] 1 IR 287 and 477; *Manton v Mannion* [1958] IR 324: *Sheridan v Higgins* [1971] IR 291; *Northern Bank Ltd v Duffy* [1981] ILRM 308. In such cases, if he retains possession, the vendor may be required to take the rents and profits in lieu of interest, see para **[20.09]** *post*.

[128.] *Blount v GS & W Rly Co* (1851) 2 Ir Ch R 40; *Greene v Quinn* (1941) 75 ILTR 107. See further para **[12.34]** *infra*.

[129.] The purchaser is deemed not to be in default where the vendor cannot complete due to his own default and is entitled to at least five working days' notice of when the vendor will be able ready and willing: cond 25(b). The vendor is not obliged to give such notice where his apparent default is occasioned by the purchaser: see para **[20.09]** *post*.

before the later of (a) the closing date or (b) such subsequent date whereafter the delay is "not attributable to default on the part of the vendor". This complies with the common law rule that the vendor cannot claim interest if he is the cause of the delay,[130] but avoids the niceties as to what constitutes "wilful" default.[131] Interestingly, this latest version of the "interest" provision in the Law Society's contract also provides now that the vendor has the right to take, in addition to interest,[132] the rents and profits less the outgoings of the property. This change was made to deal, in particular, with "investment" property, eg, where the property being sold is the reversion on a lease such as the landlord's interest in an office block or shopping centre. In the case of a sale which involves giving possession of the property which the vendor enjoys, the vendor is entitled to retain possession if completion is delayed, whereas in the case of investment property there is no such right. It was felt that the lack of this sanction justified a vendor being able to claim both the rents from the property and interest on the purchase money. This does involve a substantial change in the general law according to which the vendor is a trustee of the rents and profits from the *contractual* date for completion and liable to account strictly to the purchaser.[133] Condition 25 reverses this rule and allows the vendor to keep the rents which would otherwise be owing to the purchaser and, in addition, can charge the purchaser interest, thereby imposing what might be regarded as a "double" penalty. It remains to be seen whether the courts will accept that the different nature of investment property justifies this sanction against a defaulting purchaser.[134]

[12.20] In the absence of an express provision in the contract,[135] the court will fix the rate of interest. It seems that what has amounted to the "court" rate has fluctuated over the years in Ireland,[136] though in England the rate seems to have been fixed for many decades at 4 per cent.[137] In Ireland, the court rate seems to have been 6 per cent in the early part of the nineteenth

---

130. Eg, by failing to furnish title documents: see *Cellulose Processors Ltd v Flynn & O'Flaherty Ltd* High Court, unrep, 28 April 1986 (1982/2508P); or failing to answer proper requisitions on title: see *Meagher v Mount* [1984] ILRM 671.

131. See *Northern Bank Ltd v Duffy* [1981] ILRM 308 at 314 (*per* Costello J).

132. Previously (see, eg, cond 25 in the 1991 Edition) the vendor could opt only for interest *or* the rents and profits.

133. See para **[12.14]** *supra*. See also para **[20.09]** *post*.

134. In the case of non-investment property the vendor's retention of possession is some thing he is entitled to under the general law and, there being no rents and profits, the contractual penalty is simply the interest.

135. See para **[10.46]** *ante*.

136. See the discussion by Kenny J in *Law v Roberts & Co (No 2)* [1964] IR 306 at 306-7. See also para **[2.27]** *ante*.

137. *Calcraft v Roebuck* (1790) 1 Ves 221; *Carling v GN Rlys Co* (1869) 21 LT 17; *Re Davy* [1908] 1 Ch 61.

century,[138] but later in that century 5 per cent seems to have been the rate adopted.[139] But during this century 4 per cent came to be regarded as the appropriate court rate,[140] until recently. In *Law v Roberts & Co (No 2)*,[141] Kenny J refused to adopt the "so-called" court rate of 4 per cent in the absence of any Rules of Court or authorities compelling him to do so. He pointed out that in 1964 the rate specified in most private contracts for sale for failure by the purchaser to complete on the closing date was 6 per cent,[142] and commented:

> "I think it undesirable that an unrealistic rate of interest should be adopted in Court sales or in proceedings for specific performance ... If a purchaser has to borrow the purchase money from a bank, he will probably have to pay interest at 6¼ per cent to the bank: if, however, he is liable to the vendor for interest at 4 per cent it will be in his interest to delay completion of the sale for the longest possible period."[143]

So he fixed the rate in that case at 6 per cent. Since then, of course, there has been a considerable fluctuation in the level of interest rates generally, so that, if the approach of Kenny J is to be followed, a rate much higher than 6 per cent might be fixed by the courts from time to time. Court sales involving the Official Assignee certainly involve the fixing of higher rates. Under the Law Society's standard contract form the stipulated rate, if one is not entered in the Memorandum of Agreement,[144] is 4 per cent above the interest rate on tax chargeable under the Capital Acquisitions Tax Act 1976.[145]

F. Duty to Maintain

[12.21] The general rule is that the vendor is under a duty to maintain the property during the intermediate period between contract and completion, in the interests of himself, since the sale may fall through and leave him with

---

[138.] *Croly v O'Callaghan* (1842) 5 Ir Eq R 25 at 29 (*per* Richards B).

[139.] *Law v Roberts & Co (No 2)* [1964] IR 306 at 307 (*per* Kenny J). *Cf Re Day's Estate* (1876) 10 ILTR 18 (4% for "merely equitable claims") (criticised by Kenny J *ibid*).

[140.] *Manton v Mannion* [1958] IR 324 at 325 (*per* Budd J). See also *Greene v Quinn* (1941) 75 ILTR 107. 4% was the rate fixed for debts proved in an administrative action and on legacies by the Rules of the Supreme Court 1905, Order 55, rules 66-8. See *Law v Roberts & Co (No 2)* [1964] IR 306 at 307 (*per* Kenny J).

[141.] *Ibid.*

[142.] See also *Manton v Mannion* [1958] IR 324 at 324-5 (*per* Budd J).

[143.] [1964] IR 306 at 307. *Cf Vandeleur v Dargan* [1981] ILRM 75; *Taylor v Smyth* [1990] ILRM 377.

[144.] See paras **[9.05]** and **[10.14]** *ante*.

[145.] See cond 2 of the *General Conditions of Sale* (1995 Ed). See also s 41 of the 1976 Act, as amended by the Finance Act 1978, s 43 (1.25% per month or part of a month).

the property,[146] and of the purchaser, for whom he holds the property as trustee.[147] This duty lasts so long as the vendor retains possession and so may continue if completion is delayed, unless the delay is due entirely to the purchaser's refusal to take possession.[148] As Overend J stated in *Bank of Ireland v Waldron*[149]:

> "... a vendor is bound, until possession is given to the purchaser, to manage and preserve the property with the same care as a trustee would exercise in regard to the property subject to his trust ..."[150]

Thus, under the general law, the vendor is not only liable for damage which he actively causes to the property,[151] but also if he passively allows the property to deteriorate,[152] ie, he is under a duty to carry out repairs to the property without entitlement to an indemnity for the expenditure.[153] However, his duty as to repairs seems to extend only to matters which can be regarded as day-to-day expenditure, to be met out of the rents and profits to which the vendor is entitled so long as he remains in possession or until the time fixed for completion.[154] Thus, he ceases to be liable for repairs if the purchaser takes over possession,[155] and, if the vendor remains in possession after completion date has passed, and so is liable to account to the purchaser for the rents and profits,[156] he is entitled to a credit for expenditure on repairs as against those rents and profits.[157] But the duty as to repairs does not extend to making improvements and, unless, perhaps, they are necessary for

---

146. In this sense he is *entitled* to preserve the property. *Ecclesiastical Commrs v Pinney* [1899] 2 Ch 729 at 735-6 (*per* Byrne J); *Re Watford Corporation's and Ware's Contract* [1943] Ch 82 at 85 (*per* Simonds J).

147. *Tempany v Hynes* [1976] IR 101 at 114 (*per* Kenny J) and 109 (*per* Henchy J). Note that all members of the Supreme Court were agreed on this point. See also *Re Dwyer* [1901] 1 IR 165 at 167 (*per* Ross J); *Lyons v Thomas* [1986] IR 66 at 673-6 (*per* Murphy J). See Adams, 'Property Damage Between Contract and Completion' (1971) 68 L Soc Gaz 224.

148. *Phillips v Silvester* (1872) 8 Ch. App 173 at 178 (*per* Lord Selborne LC); *Clarke v Ramuz* [1891] 2 QB 456 at 463 (*per* Kay LJ).

149. [1944] IR 303. See also *Harris v Swordy (No 2)* High Court, unrep, 16 June 1975 (1960/71 Sp).

150. *Ibid* p 306. *Cf Clarke v Ramuz* [1891] 2 QB 456 at 459-60 (*per* Lord Coleridge CJ) and 462 (*per* Kay LJ).

151. Ie, acts which would constitute voluntary waste, see *Irish Land Law* (2nd ed, 1986), para 4.152. See also *Cumberland Consolidated Holdings Ltd v Ireland* [1946] KB 264; *Phillips v Lambin* [1949] 2 KB 33.

152. Ie, acts which would constitute permissive waste, see *ibid*, para 4.151. See also *Royal Bristol Permanent BS v Bomash* (1887) 35 Ch D 390.

153. *Re Watford Corporation's and Ware's Contract* [1943] Ch 82 at 85 (*per* Simonds J).

154. See para **[12.14]** *supra*.

155. See para **[12.32]** *infra*.

156. See para **[12.14]** *supra*.

157. *Phillips v Silvester* (1872) 8 Ch App 173 at 176 (*per* Lord Selborne LC).

preservation of the property,[158] the vendor cannot recover expenditure on them.[159]

[12.22] The vendor's duty to maintain extends to protecting the property against trespassers.[160] In the case of agricultural land, he must keep it in a proper state of cultivation.[161] It has even been suggested that the garden of a private residence should be kept in good order.[162] In the case of leasehold property, the vendor should continue to perform the covenants in the lease, otherwise there is the risk of forfeiture of the lease and a resultant defect in title.[163] Where the property being sold is subject to existing tenancies, it seems that the vendor should relet them if the tenants are given notice before completion.[164] Thus, in *Malone v Henshaw*,[165] Porter MR stated:

> "In considering the position of the parties from that time on the date of the contract for sale, it is vital to remember that the property dealt with consisted of houses let in rooms to weekly tenants, and could only be enjoyed or turned to account as matters then stood by letting and receiving the rents. It is not a residential property or *pleasaunce*. Its value was, as an investment of money, to yield a weekly return. If empty the houses would be a mere burden to the purchaser ... Of course, if the house became uninhabited by reason of pestilence, or a migration of the people who usually occupied them, or a strike against the rents, or any other unavoidable cause, the vendors would not be to blame. But I think they were bound to treat them in a fair and reasonable manner; not to have them derelict, or suffer them to become a source, not of profit, but of loss to the purchaser, who bought them relying on the vendors' own statements."[166]

---

158. *Ibid*, p 177.

159. *Munro v Taylor* (1850) 8 Hare 51 at 60 (*per* Wigram V-C). See also *Lyons v Thomas* [1986] IR 66. *Cf* as regards improvements by a prospective landlord or tenant, *Jennings and Chapman Ltd v Woodman, Matthews & Co* [1952] 2 TLR 409; *Brewer Street Investment Ltd v Barclay's Woollen Co Ltd* [1953] 1 All ER 1330. See also *Lloyd v Stanbury* [1971] 1 WLR 535.

160. *Clarke v Ramuz* [1891] 2 QB 456, applied in *Lyons v Thomas* [1986] IR 666.

161. *Foster v Deacon* (1818) 3 Madd 394; *Lord v Stephens* (1835) 1 Y & C Ex 222. *Cf re* business premises, *Golden Bread Co Ltd v Hemmings* [1922] 1 Ch 162.

162. *Foster v Deacon ibid*, p 395 (*per* Leach V-C).

163. *Palmer v Greene* (1856) 25 LJ Ch 841; *Newman v Maxwell* (1899) 80 LT 681; *Re Highett and Bird's Contract* [1903]1 Ch 287. Though it seems there is no defect if, as under the standard conditions of sale (see para **[9.43]** *ante*), the purchaser is deemed to buy with full notice of the actual state and condition of the property and is to take it as it stands, see *Lockharts v Bernard Rosen & Co Ltd* [1922] 1 Ch 433; *Butler v Mountview Estates Ltd* [1951] 2 QB 563. See also *Harris v Swordy (No 2)* High Court, unrep, 16 June 1975 (1966/71 Sp).

164. *Rafferty v Schofield* [1897] 1 Ch 937 at 944 (*per* Romer J).

165. (1891) 29 LR Ir 352.

166. *Ibid*, pp 359-60.

There is, however, authority in England for the proposition that where the tenant surrenders his tenancy, the vendor ought not to re-let the property, especially if it is subject to the rent restriction legislation, without first consulting the purchaser.[167] Indeed, it is arguable that prior consultation with the purchaser is a wise precaution to take in any case, though it should be remembered that the vendor has his own position to consider, especially the consequences if the sale falls through.[168]

[12.23] The Irish courts have emphasised that the performance by the vendor of his duty to maintain the property will come under particular scrutiny in the case of a court sale.[169] Indeed, it seems that the court will require that the property be preserved in the condition in which it stood at the time the order for sale was made and not just as it stood when the auction was held and it was knocked down to the purchaser, thereby creating a contract for the first time. Thus, in *Connolly v Keating (No 2)*,[170] Porter MR stated:

> "In the case of a private sale out of Court, in the absence of warranty or fraud, I think he [the purchaser] should be held to his bargain - obtaining the estate as it stood when the hammer fell. But in the case of a sale under the Court, particularly where there is a receiver, I think that the purchaser is entitled to expect that he will get that which the Court ordered to be sold; that is, that the fabric at least will be preserved as it stood, allowing for wear and tear and inevitable accident. I believe that he bought in that expectation and belief; and that, apart from his having taken his conveyance and its operation as a waiver of claim, that good faith which always attends sales by the Court would entitle him to be compensated ..."[171]

Indeed, it seems that the onus is shifted to the vendor in the case of court sales, as Overend J explained in *Bank of Ireland v Waldron*[172]:

> "When it is proved to the satisfaction of the Court that the property sold has been damaged between the date of sale and the time when the purchaser gets possession, the onus is shifted to the vendor, whose duty it was to preserve the property, and it is for him to establish, if he can, what portion of the damage pre-existed the sale and what portion could not have been prevented by the exercise of due care and forethought on his part."[173]

[167.] *Abdulla v Shah* [1959] AC 125. But *cf Earl of Egmont v Smith* (1877) 6 Ch D 469.
[168.] See *Golden Bread Co Ltd v Hemmings* [1922] 1 Ch 162 at 174 (*per* Sargant J).
[169.] See para **[11.02]** *et seq.*
[170.] [1903] 1 IR 356.
[171.] *Ibid*, p 361.
[172.] [1944] IR 303.
[173.] *Ibid* p 30.

[12.24] The *Connolly* case[174] also emphasised that any claim the purchaser has against the vendor for breach of his duty to maintain the property may be waived by him, even by implication from his acts. In that case the purchaser complained about damage in his requisitions on title and, though he later accepted a conveyance of the property and took possession, he did not withdraw his claim to compensation. In upholding his claim to compensation, Porter MR stated:

> "The acceptance of a conveyance does not of itself bar a claim for compensation if the damage was not known to the purchaser at the time... But where the damage ... had existed and was known, or ought to have been known, to the purchaser, the acceptance of a conveyance is very good evidence of a waiver by him of any right to damages in the nature of compensation. But while this is the general rule, the inference of waiver will not arise if the other facts show that the claim is not meant to be waived; for instance, if it is mentioned and insisted on before the deed is executed under such circumstances as to exclude the idea of an intention not to persist in the claim."[175]

[12.25] Finally, it should be noted that the Law Society's standard contract form now[176] reinforces the vendor's duty of maintenance by providing that the risk of damage to the property between contract and completion remains with the vendor.[177] This matter is discussed later in this chapter.[178]

G. Death or Insolvency

[12.26] The general rule is that the death of the vendor or purchaser before completion does not avoid the contract for sale. In the case of the vendor, his estate remains bound by the contract[179] and nowadays his personal representatives may enforce or have enforced against them the contract for sale.[180] Where the vendor has exercised his statutory powers as tenant for life

---

[174.] Para **[12.23]** *supra*.

[175.] [1903] 1 IR 356 at 359-60.

[176.] Prior to the 1986 Edition the contract form conformed to the common law rule that risk passes to the purchaser from the date of the contract, but this did not apply to damage occasioned by the vendor's wilful neglect or default: see cond 26 of the *General Conditions of Sale* (1978 Edition) and *Bradley v Donegal County Council* High Court, unrep, 14 November 1989 (1988/510 Cir App).

[177.] Cond 43.

[178.] Para **[12.36]** *et seq, infra*.

[179.] See *Heard v Cuthbert* (1851) 1 Ir Ch R 369; *Cumming v Reid* (1874) IR 8 CL 166. See also *White v Beck* (1871) IR 6 Eq 63.

[180.] See generally *Irish Land Law* (2nd ed, 1986), Ch 16; Brady *Succession Law in Ireland*, (2nd ed, 1995), Ch 10.

under the Settled Land Acts,[181] his successors in title are similarly bound by any contract for sale, lease or mortgage of the settled land.[182]

[12.27] The bankruptcy of the vendor or purchaser before completion also does not avoid the contract for sale.[183] However, upon adjudication of the bankrupt, his property vests in the Official Assignee and the purchaser thereafter will have to deal with that person.[184] If necessary the purchaser can seek specific performance against the Official Assignee[185] or claim it in the bankruptcy.[186] The Official Assignee may disclaim the contract as unprofitable,[187] but not so to deprive the purchaser of his interest in the land under the contract.[188] It seems that the purchaser can still call upon him to convey the property or can apply to the court for a vesting order.[189] If the Official Assignee, following a written application from the purchaser requiring him to decide whether to disclaim or not, fails within twenty-eight days[190] to disclaim the contract, he can no longer do so and is deemed to have adopted it.[191] The most the disclaimer will do is to free the vendor's estate from the obligation to perform the unprofitable acts in relation to the land, eg, where the contract binds him to spend money on it before conveying it, but another consequence of disclaimer is loss of the right to enforce it against the purchaser. Alternatively, of course, the Assignee may elect to perform the contract, in which case he becomes entitled to receive the purchase money.

[12.28] Until recently a purchaser had to exercise caution in the intermediate period between the vendor's act of bankruptcy[192] and his adjudication as a bankrupt following a creditor's petition.[193] A petition could be presented at

---

181. *Ibid*, para 8.091.

182. See the discussion in *Gilmore v The O'Connor Don* [1947] IR 462.

183. See generally on this subject Sanfey and Holohan, *Bankruptcy Law and Practice in Ireland* (1991), Ch 6.

184. See *Re Pooley* (1878) 8 Ch D 367.

185. *Re Bastable* [1901] 2 KB 518. See the discussion of this case in *Re Abbeyford Estates Ltd* High Court, unrep, 29 October 1993 (1993/4985P): para **[12.28]** *infra*.

186. *Re Taylor* [1901] 1 KB 562. Note that, if the whole of the purchase money has been paid before the act of bankruptcy, the vendor is treated as a mere trustee of the land for the purchaser and it does not become part of the assets in his bankruptcy, *ibid*. See also *Re Pooley* (1878) 8 Ch D 367; *Governors of St Thomas's Hospital v Richardson* [1910] 1 KB 271.

187. Bankruptcy Act 1988, s 56.

188. *Re Bastable* [1901] 2 KB 518.

189. As to inherent jurisdiction, see *Re O'Neill* [1967] NI 129. Note also the power to make an order rescinding the contract: 1988 Act, s 56(6).

190. Or such further period as the court may allow.

191. 1988 Act, s 56(5).

192. See 1988 Act, s 57.

193. 1988 Act, s 14.

any time within six months of the act of bankruptcy[194] and, if this was done and the vendor was adjudicated bankrupt, the Official Assignee's title related back to the first act of bankruptcy within that period.[195] Thus, even if the purchaser obtained a conveyance from the vendor prior to the petition and paid the purchase money to him, the conveyance could be rendered void subsequently, and the purchase money would be liable to be paid a second time to the Assignee,[196] *unless* the purchaser could establish that he was a *bona fide* purchaser without notice of any act of bankruptcy.[197] Commission of an act of bankruptcy constituted a defect in title and prevented the vendor from obtaining specific performance,[198] until the six months period elapsed and no petition was filed against the vendor.[199] However, a major difficulty in practice was that the purchaser might have no effective means of discovering the existence of an act of bankruptcy. Until the petition was presented, there was nothing which would be revealed by a bankruptcy search.[200] So in practice, if the search was clear, the purchaser's solicitor usually proceeded on the basis that all was in order. The Bankruptcy Law Committee recommended the removal of such uncertainties by abolition of the doctrine of relation back[201] and this was put into effect by s 44 of the Bankruptcy Act 1988. Under s 44(2) the title to any property vesting in the Official Assignee does not commence at any date earlier than the date of adjudication. This provision is followed up by another new provision contained in s 58. This provides, in this present context, that a contract for sale at a price which, in the opinion of the Court, is substantially below the market value of the property, or substantially reduces the sum available for distribution to creditors, is void as against the Official Assignee if the vendor is adjudicated bankrupt within three months of the vendor committing an act of bankruptcy. But the contract is not void if it was *bona fide* entered into by the vendor and the purchaser at the time of the contract had no notice of any prior act of bankruptcy.[202] It seems clear, then, that a purchaser must still

---

[194.] Irish Bankrupt and Insolvent Act 1857, s 115.

[195.] *Re Domville* (1879) 3 LR Ir 282.

[196.] *Powell v Marshall, Parkes & Co* [1899] 1 QB 710.

[197.] 1857 Act, ss 328 and 332.

[198.] *Lowes v Lush* (1808) 14 Ves 547.

[199.] *Hipwell v Knight* (1835) 1 Y & C Ex 401; *Powell v Marshall, Parkes & Co* [1899] 1 QB 710.

[200.] As to such a search, see para **[15.47]** *post*.

[201.] 1972 Report (Prl 2714), para 59.8.1. See *Sanfey and Holohan op cit*, para 6.

[202.] Note that this protection of purchasers does not extend to fraudulent preferences caught by s 57 nor to settlements caught by s 59. See *Sanfey and Holohan, op cit*, para 8.20, for the difficulties in interpreting these provisions. *Cf re* the English equivalent provisions *Barclays Bank plc v Eustice* [1995] 4 All ER 511.

raise appropriate requisitions[203] and ensure that a bankruptcy search is made.[204]

[12.29] Where the vendor is a company which goes into liquidation between contract and completion, the liquidator has power to carry the contract into effect, whether a winding-up order is made or a resolution for voluntary winding-up is passed.[205] As in the case of the Official Assignee[206] in whom a bankrupt individual's property vests, the liquidator has a power to disclaim onerous property,[207] but again this cannot be exercised so as to deprive the purchaser of his interest under the contract.[208] If the liquidator refuses to complete the sale, the purchaser can seek specific performance,[209] or else can prove in the winding-up.[210] Since the company's property does not vest in the liquidator on his appointment, unless a court order is made under the Companies Act,[211] the conveyance should still be made by the company[212] and it is doubtful if it is necessary for the liquidator to be joined in as a conveying party or to give a receipt for the purchase money.[213] Nevertheless, joining in the liquidator demonstrates the exercise of his power to sell.

II. PURCHASER AS BENEFICIARY

[12.30] It is a corollary of the principle that the vendor is to a certain extent regarded as trustee of the land in the post-contract stage pending completion that the purchaser is regarded as a beneficiary.[214] The application of this principle and its practical significance from the point of view of the purchaser may be illustrated by a consideration of the following topics.

[203.] See para **[16.24]** *post.*

[204.] See para **[15.47]** *post.*

[205.] Companies Act, 1963, ss 231(2)(b) and 276(1)(b). See also *Thames Plate Glass Co v Land and Sea Telegraph Co* (1870) LR 11 Eq 248.

[206.] See para **[12.27]** *supra.*

[207.] 1963 Act, s 290.

[208.] *Re Abbeyford Estates Ltd* High Court, unrep, 29 October 1993 (1993/4985P). See para **[12.26]** *supra.*

[209.] See *O'Connor v McCarthy* [1982] IR 161; *Ferguson v Merchant Banking Ltd* [1993] 3 IR 382.

[210.] See *Currie v Consolidated Kent Collieries Corp Ltd* [1906] 1 KB 134.

[211.] 1963 Act, s 230.

[212.] See 1963 Act, s 231(2)(b). See Laffoy, *Irish Conveyancing Precedents*, Precedents E.6.6, E.6.7 and E.6.9. *Cf* as regards a receiver *Industrial Development Authority v Moran* [1978] IR 159. See para **[18.131]** *post.*

[213.] This is a controversial point: see Barnsley, *Conveyancing Law and Practice* (3rd ed, 1988), p 239; *Emmet on Title* (19th ed), para 10.189; Marcus, 'Conveyances of Liquidators' (1970) 67 L Soc Gaz 329 (and see pp 459, 536, 626 and 714).

[214.] *Malone v Henshaw* (1891) 29 LR Ir 352 at 358 (*per* Porter MR); *Re Strong* [1940] IR 382 at 402 (*per* O'Byrne J); *Tempany v Hynes* [1976] IR 101 at 114 (*per* Kenny J) and 109 (*per* Henchy J).

A. Doctrine of Conversion

[12.31] This doctrine affects the position of the purchaser just as it affects the position of the vendor and was considered earlier in the chapter.[215]

B. Possession

[12.32] We also saw earlier that normally the vendor is entitled to retain possession of the land pending completion.[216] However, there is nothing to prevent the parties agreeing that the purchaser should be allowed into possession prior to completion, eg, to enable him to carry out repairs or improvement works. The dangers of this from the parties' point of view, especially the vendor's, cannot be emphasised too strongly and, if it is to be allowed, the greatest care should be exercised in seeing that the parties' legal position is defined clearly in the contract. It is generally unwise to leave the matter open, to be determined by the general law, for, apart from the fact that the general law may not be what the parties want to apply, it may not always be clear what the general law is or it may not be easy to apply it to the circumstances of the particular case. This point is particularly important in Ireland because the Law Society's standard contract form does not contain any printed condition dealing with the matter.[217] It may, however, be dealt with by way of a special condition set out in the contract.[218]

[12.33] From the vendor's point of view, the dangers in allowing the purchaser into possession before completion, especially before the balance of the purchase money is handed over, are obvious. First, there is the danger that the purchaser will be construed as having sufficient possessory rights to the property to be able to invoke the security of tenure conferred on tenants by legislation.[219] It seems that, at common law, the purchaser will usually be regarded as being in possession as a tenant at will, rather than a licensee,[220] and, therefore, may be within the protection of the legislation.[221] Though this may not be the case if payments he makes are in discharge of the purchase

---

[215] Para **[12.11]** *supra.*

[216] Para **[12.13]** *supra.*

[217] See the *General Conditions of Sale* (1995 Edition): Ch 10 *ante.*

[218] See para **[10.67]** *et seq, ante.*

[219] See Wylie, *Irish Landlord and Tenant Law,* Chs 29-32.

[220] *Ball v Cullimore* (1835) 2 Cr M & R 120. See also *Markey v Coote* (1876) IR 10 CL 149.

[221] *Chamberlain v Farr* [1942] 2 All ER 567. Note, however, that it has been held in Ireland that a tenant at will did not come within the protection of the rent restriction legislation and the same probably applies to the Housing (Private Rented Dwellings) Act 1982: *Delany (Blanchardstown Mill Ltd) v Jones* [1938] IR 826; *Irish Sailors' and Soldiers' Land Trust v Donnelly* [1944] IR 464; de Blacam *The Control of Private Rented Dwellings* (1984), p 9. See generally on tenancies at will, *Wylie op cit* para 4.21 *et seq.*

price and outgoings.[222] It is also the case that the courts tend nowadays to construe arrangements that might in earlier times have been regarded as creating a tenancy at will as creating, instead, a licence only.[223] Furthermore, arguably merely allowing the purchaser to enter the property to make repairs or alterations does not confer possession on him - this remains in the vendor.[224] Secondly, once he has obtained possession, the purchaser may be less concerned about completing on the agreed date. By giving up possession, the vendor relinquishes one of his strongest sanctions against a recalcitrant purchaser. If he seeks specific performance, the court is likely to give the purchaser the option of staying in possession and paying the balance of the purchase money with interest into court,[225] apparently even if substantial alterations have been made by the purchaser to the property.[226] In Ireland, the usual procedure adopted is for the purchaser to enter into a caretaker's agreement, so that the vendor may, if necessary, use the special summary procedure for ejectment available in the District Court to recover possession.[227]

[12.34] On the other hand, it has long been settled that, by taking possession, the purchaser impliedly undertakes to pay interest on the outstanding balance of the purchase money,[228] whether or not he derives any profit from his possession.[229] He is entitled to the rents and profits of the property,[230] but is responsible for repairs and payment of outgoings while he is in possession.[231] If the purchaser makes improvements to the property, he cannot recover his expenditure from the vendor, even though the sale falls through because of the vendor's default.[232] The purchaser also runs the risk that his taking of possession may be treated as a waiver of a breach of contract by the vendor. Generally, mere taking of possession is not sufficient

---

[222.] *Dunthorne and Shore v Wiggins* [1943] 2 All ER 678. *Cf* payments for use and occupation *Francis Jackson Developments Ltd v Stemp* [1943] 2 All ER 601.

[223.] See the views expressed by members of the Supreme Court in *Bellew v Bellew* [1982] IR 447; *Irish Shell & BP Ltd v Costello* [1984] IR 511. See also Wylie *op cit*, para 3.17 *et seq.*

[224.] *Cf* a lodger or guest or hirer of rooms for a special occasion: see also Wylie *op cit*, para 4.25.

[225.] *Greenwood v Turner* [1891] 2 Ch 144.

[226.] *Maskell v Ivory* [1970] Ch 502.

[227.] See *Corrigan v Woods* (1867) IR 1 CL 73; *Musgrave v McAvey* (1907) 41 ILTR 230; *Davies v Hilliard* (1965) 101 ILTR 50. See also *Wylie op cit* paras 3.14-15.

[228.] *Blount v GS & W Rly Co* (1851) 2 Ir Ch R 40 at 53 (*per* Blackburne LC); *Corrigan v Woods* (1867) IR 1 CL 73 at 75-6 (*per* Pigot CB). See also *Markey v Coote* (1876) IR 10 CL 149; *Greene v Quinn* (1941) 75 ILTR 107.

[229.] See *Ballard v Shutt* (1880) 15 Ch D 122.

[230.] See *Piers v Piers* (1847) 11 Ir Eq R 358 at 358 (*per* Smith MR). See also para **[12.14]** *supra*.

[231.] See para **[12.21]** *supra*.

[232.] *Lloyd v Stanbury* [1971] 1 WLR 535 at 546 (*per* Brightman J). See also *Warrington v Warrington* (1849) 8 CB 134; *Lee-Parker v Izzet* [1971] 3 All ER 1099.

to constitute a waiver or acceptance of title,[233] but it may be if accompanied by acts of ownership towards the property[234] or the making of structural alterations.[235] In Ireland, a purchaser entering into possession before completion is usually stipulated as doing so without prejudice to his rights under the contract and the balance of the purchase money is usually to be held on joint deposit by the vendor's and purchaser's solicitor.

C. Gains

[12.35] The general rule is that the purchaser is entitled to any gains which accrue in relation to the property between contract and completion. As Sugden LC explained in *Vesey v Elwood*:[236]

> "It is settled, but not without much previous conflict of opinion, that a purchaser in common cases is the owner of the estate from the time of the contract, and from that period must bear any loss, and is entitled to any benefit; and this applies as well to damage to the property, eg, by fire, as to the interest in the property, for example, the death of the life for which it was holden. So as to profit, for an accidental improvement of the property would belong to the purchaser as well as an additional interest by the dropping of a life, where the reversion was the subject of the sale."[237]

That case involved a sale under the court and the Lord Chancellor held that the same principle applied.[238] In *Re Grange Developments Ltd*[239] Murphy J applied the principle to a purchaser who was claiming compensation arising from a refusal of planning permission.

D. Losses

[12.36] As Sugden LC pointed out in *Vesey v Elwood*,[240] under the general law the corollary of the rule that the purchaser takes the gains between

---

[233.] *Boyd v Dickson* (1876) IR 10 Eq 239 at 253 (*per* Sullivan MR). See also *Johnston v Johnston* (1869) IR 3 Eq 328. The English cases draw a distinction between taking possession before and after delivery of an abstract of title revealing defects in title, see *Simpson v Sadd* (1854) 4 De GM 665 and *Bown v Stenson* (1857) 24 Beav 631.

[234.] *Re Barrington* (1834) 3 LJ Bey 122 (granting a lease); *Haydon v Bell* (1838) 1 Beav 337 (a mortgage).

[235.] *Cf Boyd v Dickson* (1876) IR 10 Eq 239. See also *Re Gloag and Miller's Contract* (1883) 23 ChD 320. See further para **[15.49]** *et seq, post*.

[236.] (1843) 3 Dr & War 74.

[237.] *Ibid*, p 79. See also *Enraght v Fitzgerald* (1842) 2 Dr & War 43. And see *Ex parte Manning* (1727) 2 P Wms 410.

[238.] *Ibid*, pp 79-82. See also para **[11.07]** *ante*.

[239.] [1987] ILRM 733.

[240.] Para **[12.35]** *supra*.

contract and completion is the rule that he also suffers the losses,[241] subject, of course, to the vendor's duty to maintain the property so long as he retains possession.[242] The standard form contract of the Law Society used to recognise this basic principle. Thus, condition 26 of the Law Society's *General Conditions of Sale (1978 Edition)* provided that the property was, as to any damage from whatever cause arising after the date of the sale, to be at the sole risk of the purchaser and no claim was to be made against the vendor for any deterioration or damage unless occasioned by the vendor's wilful neglect or default.[243] This position was reversed in the 1986 Edition and the condition 43 of the *General Conditions of Sale (1995 Edition)*[244] provides that the vendor is liable for any loss or damage "howsoever occasioned (other than by the Purchaser or his Agent)" to the subject property[245] between the date of sale and the actual completion of the sale.[246] However, it must be recognised that, if the Law Society's form is not used, the general law will apply[247] and so something must be said about this before returning to condition 43.

[12.37] It is clear that under the general law the purchaser bears the loss or damage caused to the property from the date of the contract by such things as fire, flood, storm and tempest. Furthermore, if the premises damage adjoining property or third parties, eg, by collapsing into a public highway, the purchaser will have to indemnify the vendor against third party claims, unless the vendor was at fault.[248] Until recently it was unclear to what extent the purchaser could invoke, in an appropriate case, the doctrine of frustration

---

[241.] See also *Vincent v Going* (1841) 3 Dr & War 75.

[242.] See para **[12.21]** *supra*.

[243.] See *Lyons v Thomas* [1986] IR 66. See also *Bradley v Donegal County Council* High Court, unrep, 14 November 1989 (1988/510 Cir App).

[244.] See para **[10.60]** *ante*.

[245.] Eg, fixtures and fittings: see the definition in cond 2, paras **[9.15]** and **[10.14]** *ante*.

[246.] This provision was endorsed by the Law Reform Commission, but it recommended that it should be put on a statutory basis rather than being dependent on the contractual position: see *Report on Land Law and Conveyancing Law: (5) The Passing of Risk from Vendor to Purchaser* (LRC 39-1991). The Commission has since reiterated its view in dealing with *Tempany v Hynes*, in respect of which it has recommended a statutory provision to the effect that the beneficial interest passes to the purchaser on the entering into of the contract, subject to the condition subsequent that he completes: see *Interest of Vendor and Purchaser in Land during the period between Contract and Completion* (LRC 49-1995) para **[12.08]** *supra*.

[247.] It was in recognition of this that the Law Reform Commission recommended a statutory provision to apply in all cases: fn 246 *supra*.

[248.] *Robertson v Skelton* (1849) 12 Beav 260. As regards the special case of a court sale, see para **[11.07]** *ante*.

of contract.[249] However, more recent cases suggest that there is no reason in principle why the doctrine should not apply to a contract for the sale of land, but, as the Supreme Court has made clear, it would have to be a case where the supervening event occurs without the default of either party and so significantly changes the nature of their outstanding rights and obligations from what they could reasonably have contemplated at the time they entered into the contract that it would be unjust to hold them to the contract.[250]

[12.38] All this makes it imperative, in a case where the Law Society's contract form is not used or there is no equivalent of condition 43 in the contract, that the purchaser should be advised to ensure that he takes out suitable insurance to cover the property from the date of the contract.[251] It is clear from the authorities that he must not rely upon any existing insurance held by the vendor. First, it is settled that the vendor is under no duty to keep up his insurance[252] and so he may allow it to lapse once the contract for sale is entered into.[253] Though it is unwise of the vendor to allow his insurance to lapse before completion since the sale may fall through and the risk of damage may thus be passed back to him.[254] Secondly, even if the vendor keeps up his insurance, it is settled that his "trusteeship" for the purchaser[255] is confined to the land itself and does not extend to anything which may be substituted for it, such as the proceeds of an insurance policy.[256] Thus, in the event of a fire, the vendor may claim the insurance money, but the purchaser

---

[249.] See *Hillingdon Estates Co v Stonefield Estates Ltd* [1952] Ch 267 at 631 (*per* Vaisey J).As regards leases, see the discussion in *Cricklewood Property and Investment Trust Ltd v Leighton's Investment Trust Ltd* [1945] AC 221. And see Wylie, *Irish Landlord and Tenant Law*, para 26.14 *et seq*. Of course, the event in question may have such serious consequences that a court would refuse to decree specific performance and the purchaser would cease to incur the risk of damage in this way, see *Hasham v Zenab* [1960] AC 316 and Farrell, *Irish Law Specific Performance* (1994), para [9.59] *et seq*.

[250.] *Neville & Sons Ltd v Guardian Builders Ltd* [1995] 1 ILRM 1, approving the views of the House of Lords in *National Carriers Ltd v Panalpina (Northern) Ltd* [1981] 1 All ER 161. See also *Browne v Mulligan* [1976-7] ILRM 327; *McGuill v Aer Lingus Teo* High Court, unrep, 3 October 1983 (1981/2238P). And see Thompson, 'Must a Purchaser Buy a Charred Ruin?' [1984] Conv 43.

[251.] Aldridge, 'Insurance of Buildings under a Contract for Sale' (1974) 124 New LJ 966; Peverett, 'Shifting the Insurance Burden: Another View' (1975) 125 New LJ 217.

[252.] *Paine v Meller* (1801) 6 Ves 349 .

[253.] If, however, the vendor's interest in the property is still subject to an outstanding mortgage there is little likelihood of the policy being allowed to lapse because his mortgagee, eg, a building society, will insist upon it being kept alive to protect its security.

[254.] *Simmons v Pennington & Son* [1955] 1 WLR 183. So long as the vendor is unpaid he has an insurable interest, *Collingridge v Royal Exchange Assurance Corp* (1877) 3 QBD 173.

[255.] See para **[12.02]** *supra*.

[256.] See the discussion in *Rayner v Preston* (1881) 18 Ch D 1.

may not and will still have to pay the full purchase price for the "charred remains."[257] Of course, since an insurance policy is a contract of indemnity only,[258] and in these circumstances the vendor receiving the full purchase price will suffer no loss, the insurance company can reclaim the insurance money from the vendor if he has been paid by the purchaser,[259] or can claim to be subrogated to the vendor on completion and recover the purchase money. Thirdly, there is no equivalent in either part of Ireland of the English legislation on the subject, though the general view in England is that this legislation[260] is not entirely satisfactory and the purchaser ought still to arrange his own insurance there.[261]

[12.39] In such cases, and it must be reiterated that we are still talking about comparatively rare situations where the parties are not using the Law Society's standard contract form or a contract incorporating condition 43 or an equivalent provision, the simplest procedure for the purchaser's solicitor to adopt is to make sure that his client takes out his own insurance cover from the date of the contract, regardless of what existing insurance cover the vendor has. If the purchaser's solicitor does not arrange the insurance for his client in such cases, he ought to advise his client about the matter in writing. The question of insurance is so important that failure to advise the client as to its necessity would doubtless constitute negligence on his solicitor's part, so, if the matter is left to the client to arrange for himself, the existence of written advice may be crucial in the event of his ignoring it and the property being damaged or destroyed by fire before completion. Arranging for the vendor's policy to be endorsed in favour of the purchaser is not so satisfactory for the practical reason that there may be delays while it is discovered whether he has an existing policy and with which company, whether the company is agreeable to the endorsement and, if so, what contribution towards the premium is payable by the purchaser. Indeed, insurance companies are extremely reluctant to allow such an endorsement and in some cases it might even render the policy void. Furthermore, generally a purchaser can succeed in obtaining fire cover only for the premises. While all this is being sorted out, the purchaser may be at risk. It is true that some insurance policies nowadays may have a clause in them to the

---

257. But *cf* Thompson fn 250 *supra*.

258. See *Gaggin v Upton* (1859) Dru *temp* Nap 427.

259. As happened after *Rayner v Preston supra*. See *Castellain v Preston* (1883) 11 QBD 380.

260. Two provisions are relevant. First, the Fires Prevention (Metropolis) Act 1774, s 83: see Foote, 'Liability for fire before 1800' (1969) 20 NILQ 141 and *Irish Land Law* (2nd ed, 1986), para 17.059. Secondly, the Law of Property Act 1925, s 47.

261. See Adams, 'Property Damage between Contract and Completion' (1971) 68 L Soc Gaz 224.

effect that the cover enures to the benefit of purchasers, but that still leaves the purchaser with the risk that the vendor may have allowed his policy to lapse[262] and, even if he has kept it up, with the trouble of discovering this and whether his policy contains such a clause. Finally, there is a problem for both parties to which attention has been drawn by the English Law Society, namely, that most household insurance policies, even if comprehensive, do not provide cover against burglary, theft, malicious damage or damage due to bursting or overflowing water tanks or pipes or sanitary fittings, if the property is left unoccupied for a certain period or unfurnished.[263] This creates a problem particularly for the purchaser if, as often happens, the vendor vacates the property some days, if not weeks, before the purchaser is due to take possession. In such a case the purchaser ought to arrange special cover, yet frequently he is unaware that the vendor has left the premises and may thereby have invalidated the purchaser's own insurance cover. In practice it is rare for this extra cover for unoccupied property to be arranged.[264] Finally, care should be taken over the insurance cover provided; in particular the purchaser really needs cover for the full cost of reinstatement of the property, rather than the value of the buildings,[265] but it is not always easy to obtain this in the insurance market.

[12.40] The problems outlined in the previous paragraphs induced the Law Society's Conveyancing Committee to examine the matter in the 1980s. Quite apart from the difficulties of securing adequate insurance for the purchaser and the inefficiency and expense of the resultant "double" insurance (ie, with both parties insuring the same property[266]), the Committee was concerned about the exposure of the purchaser where the vendor vacated the property before completion and left it prey to, eg, squatters or vandalism,[267] or left it unoccupied during the winter time without taking precautions to guard against damage caused by burst water pipes and the like. The committee came to the conclusion that the best solution to these problems, and one which was fair to both parties, was for

---

[262.] But see para **[12.38]** fn 253 *supra*.

[263.] (1965) 62 L Soc Gaz 478.

[264.] See the discussion in Adams, 'Property Damage between Contract and Completion' (1971) 68 L Soc Gaz 224.

[265.] See *St Albans Investment Co v Sun Alliance & London Insurance Ltd* [1983] IR 362. See also *Lonsdale & Thompson Ltd v Black Arrow Group plc* [1993] 3 All ER 648.

[266.] The difficulties of trying to apportion the insurance according to the respective proportionate interests of the parties which the majority in *Tempany v Hynes* held existed in most cases (see the remarks of Henchy J in *Hamilton v Hamilton* [1982] IR 466 at 484) were likely to be insurperable: see para **[12.08]** *supra*.

[267.] See *Evans v Glasgow District Council* 1978 SLT 17; *Lamb v Camden London Borough Council* [1983] 3 All ER 161.

the risk of damage to be carried by the party who generally remained in possession or control the property, and, therefore, in a better position to guard against the risk, *viz*, the vendor. As mentioned above,[268] this is now the position under condition 43 of the *General Conditions of Sale (1995 Edition)*.

[12.41] There are several matters to be noted about condition 43. First, the vendor is liable for "any loss or damage howsoever occasioned", but not where it is caused by the purchaser or his agent.[269] Secondly, the vendor's liability covers not only the "subject property",[270] but also the "purchased chattels", ie, any other items like fixtures and fittings included in the sale.[271] Personal property, and its transfer, is, of course, subject to different rules,[272] but it was felt appropriate to make it clear in the contract that the vendor is liable for their safe-keeping pending completion and delivery to the purchaser. Thirdly, the vendor's liability lasts from the date of sale[273] to the actual completion of the sale, not, eg, the contractual date for completion[274] nor, indeed, the "Apportionment Date".[275] It was felt that the actual date of completion is one which is easily recognised by the parties themselves. Fourthly, the vendor's liability extends to "consequential or resulting loss" but is not to exceed the purchase price. Fifthly, condition 44 excludes any liability for inconsequential damage or insubstantial deterioration from reasonable wear and tear in the course of normal occupation and use, and which does not materially affect value.[276] This is designed to discourage purchasers from seeking to use condition 43 to hold up completion because of some trifling matter. It also excludes liability for damage occasioned by the vendor's removal from and vacation of the property, provided he acts with reasonable care,[277] and for any loss or damage resulting from a requirement, restriction or obligation imposed by a "competent authority",[278] ie, matters outside the control of the vendor.[279]

[268.] Para **[12.36]** *supra*.

[269.] In the original version of cond 43 in the 1986 Edition this limitation did not exist, which raised concerns about the scope of the vendor's liability and the element of fairness.

[270.] Ie, the property or interest which is the subject of the contract: see the definition in cond 1.

[271.] See the definition in cond 2.

[272.] See Bell, *Modern Law of Personal Property in England and Ireland* (1989), Pt 3.

[273.] Ie, the date of the auction or the date the contract becomes binding in the case of a sale by private treaty: see cond 2 and Chs 2, 3, and 6 *ante*.

[274.] See para **[13.10]** *post*.

[275.] See para **[20.05]** *post*.

[276.] Cond 44(a). *Cf* exclusion of compensation for loss of "trifling materiality" in cond 33(b): see para **[9.45]** *ante*.

[277.] Cond 44(b).

[278.] Ie, the State or other public or statutory bodies or authorities: see cond 2.

[279.] Cond 44(c).

[12.42] In devising a provision which reverses the general law in what is an area of conveyancing law which is extremely uncertain,[280] the Conveyancing Committee was concerned to ensure that the provision did not have effects beyond the strictly limited purpose of dealing with the issue of which party carries the risk of loss or damage to the property, and items being sold with it, in the interim period between contract and completion. To this end condition 45 lists a number of matters which are not affected by the provision. The first one confirms the purchaser's right to specific performance in an appropriate case. Notwithstanding the transfer of the risk to the vendor, the purchaser should still be regarded as obtaining a beneficial interest in the property under the contract, at least to the extent that he pays part of the purchase price (such as the usual deposit).[281] Conditions 43 and 44 do not, therefore, affect the "normal rule" that specific performance is available to both parties to the contract.[282] The second matter is that condition 45 confirms the purchaser's right to rescind or repudiate[283] the sale where the vendor fails to deliver the property substantially in its condition at the date of sale, unless this failure has been occasioned by the purchaser or his agent. This was not in the original version in the 1986 Edition of the *General Conditions* and was added to allay doubts which had been expressed by some practitioners. Such a right of rescission exists under the general law, and is recognised by other parts of the contract form,[284] and it was certainly never intended that allocating the risk to the vendor should relieve him in any way from his contractual obligation to hand over on completion the property in substantially the same condition as it was when the contract was entered into. The third matter covered is confirmation that the doctrine of conversion still operates. This may follow from the continued availability of the remedy of specific performance, although the modern view is that the doctrine should operate wherever a valid or binding contract *simpliciter* is established.[285] The fourth matter is to confirm the purchaser's right to gains accruing to the property[286] and the fifth his right to effect his own insurance on or after the date of sale. It cannot be emphasised too strongly that condition 43 does not remove the need for both the vendor and purchaser to give careful thought to the question of insurance cover and for their respective solicitors to give appropriate advice on the matter.[287] From the vendor's point of view, of course, it is, as a result of condition 43, not

---

[280.] See **[12.02]** *et seq, supra.*

[281.] Ie, in accordance with the majority decision of the Supreme Court in *Tempany v Hynes*: see para **[12.02]** *supra.*

[282.] See Farrell, *Irish Law of Specific Performance* (1994), para [1.15-16].

[283.] See on this concept para **[13.09]** *post.*

[284.] Eg cond 33(c): see para **[9.47]** *ante.*

[285.] Para **[12.12]** *supra.*

[286.] See para **[12.35]** *supra.*

[287.] See paras **[12.38-9]** *supra.*

just a question of keeping up his insurance to protect his continuing interest in the property,[288] he must ensure that he has sufficient cover to enable him to discharge his obligations under the condition, which, it should be reiterated, would seem not only to require insurance to cover the cost of reinstatement of the property,[289] but also consequential loss.[290] From the purchaser's point of view, he clearly must make sure that he has insurance cover at the latest from the date of actual completion. It may be argued that he does not need cover any earlier than this because of the effect of condition 43. Indeed, it was one of the primary purposes of the condition to do away with such "double" insurance.[291] If the vendor maintains, or puts in place, the appropriate insurance, the purchaser will have the protection he needs if he wishes to take the property and not exercise his right of rescission. However, the purchaser will wish to be assured that the vendor has, indeed, done so and so it is incumbent upon his solicitor to check this matter, by making appropriate *pre*-contract enquiries.[292]

[12.43] Finally, condition 45 deals with three other matters. It provides that conditions 43 and 44 do not affect the rights and liabilities of parties other than the vendor and purchaser. As we have seen earlier,[293] the position of the vendor and purchaser during the interim period between contract and completion is an extremely complex one and all sorts of third parties may engage in dealing with them[294] or acquire rights over the property.[295] Conditions 43 and 44 effect a limited change, confined to the risk of loss or damage, and are not intended to affect other aspects of the relationship between vendor and purchaser. Condition 45 confirms also that this principle applies to any lease subsisting at the date of sale, the point being that, in the case of an investment property, involving the purchase of the landlord's interest in commercial or industrial property held under a long lease, responsibility for loss or damage to the property will be the responsibility of the tenant under the repairing and maintenance covenants, rather than that of the vendor-landlord.[296] Finally condition 45 confirms that conditions 43 and 44 do not affect any arrangement whereby the purchaser is allowed into occupation (or to take possession of chattels being sold with the

---

[288.] See para **[12.38]** *supra*.

[289.] See para **[12.39]** *supra*.

[290.] See para **[12.41]** *supra*.

[291.] See para **[12.40]** *supra*.

[292.] Note the *Pre-Contract* Check List issued by the Law Society's Conveyancing Committee for private dwellinghouses: see para **[5.06]** *ante*.

[293.] See para **[12.02]** *et seq, ante*.

[294.] Eg, the purchaser may arrange a sub-sale of the property he is buying: see para **[12.02]** *supra*.

[295.] Eg, by registering a judgment mortgage as occurred in *Tempany v Hynes*: see para **[12.03]** *et seq, supra*.

[296.] See Wylie, *Irish Landlord and Tenant Law*, Ch 15.

land) *prior* to completion. The parties are, therefore, free to enter into the usual caretaker's agreement,[297] which in the present context should contain a provision requiring the purchaser to maintain the property while in occupation.[298]

E. Lien

[12.44] Just as the vendor has a lien on the land for unpaid purchase money,[299] so also does the purchaser have a lien for purchase money paid to the vendor,[300] including the deposit,[301] and other costs incurred in what turns out to be an abortive sale.[302] Such a lien can also be invoked by a sub-purchaser.[303]

F. Interest

[12.45] We saw earlier that the purchaser is liable to pay interest on the unpaid purchase money where he takes possession before completion.[304] He is also usually under a contractual obligation to pay interest where a delay in completion is attributable to default on his part.[305]

G. Death or Insolvency

[12.46] On the death of the purchaser, his equitable interest in the land vests in his personal representatives and they can enforce or have the contract enforced against them.[306] If the purchaser made a specific devise of his interest in the land, his devisee takes it subject to any lien the vendor has on it for the purchase price[307] and cannot require the price to be paid out of any other part of the purchaser's estate, unless the purchaser signified a contrary

---

[297.] See para **[12.33]** *supra.*

[298.] See *Wylie, op cit*, para 3.15.

[299.] See para **[12.15]** *supra.*

[300.] *Woods v Martin* (1860) 11 Ir Ch R 148. See also *Munster and Leinster Bank Ltd v McGlashan* [1937] IR 525 at 528 (*per* Meredith J) (*aff'd* by Sup Ct), para **[12.15]** *supra.* And see *Rose v Watson* (1864) 10 HLC 672.

[301.] But only if paid to the vendor or his agent, not, apparently, if paid to a stakeholder, see *Combe v Swaythling* [1947] Ch. 625. See also *Re Barrett Apartments Ltd* [1985] IR 350: paras **[3.15]** *ante* and **[13.31]** *post.*

[302.] Eg, costs of investigating a title which proves to be bad, *Re Yeilding and Westbrook* (1886) 31 Ch D 344, and of a specific performance action, *Turner v Marriott* (1867) LR 3 Eq 744, but not for damages awarded in lieu of specific performance, *Cornwall v Henson* [1900] 2 Ch 298.

[303.] *Aberaman Ironworks v Wickens* (1868) 4 Ch App 101.

[304.] Para **[12.34]** *supra.*

[305.] This subject was mentioned earlier, para **[12.18]** *et seq, supra.*

[306.] *Dowdall v McCartan* (1880) 5 LR Ir 642. See also para **[12.26]** *supra.*

[307.] Succession Act 1965, s 47. See *Irish Land Law* (2nd ed, 1986), para 16.40; Brady, *Succession Law in Ireland* (2nd ed, 1995), para [10.17] *et seq.* See also *Re Birmingham* [1959] Ch 523.

intention.[308] But this is without prejudice to the right of the vendor to insist upon payment out of other assets of the deceased.[309]

[12.47] Where the purchaser goes bankrupt, the Official Assignee must complete the contract or disclaim it as unprofitable.[310] If the Official Assignee disclaims it, the vendor can forfeit the deposit and prove in the bankruptcy for any loss he has suffered thereby.[311] If the Official Assignee does not disclaim the purchaser's contract,[312] it would seem to be accepted now that the vendor can seek specific performance against him, though probably only if he has taken steps to force the Official Assignee to make a decision on disclaimer.[313] If he does not respond to this, the Official Assignee is deemed to have adopted the contract after twenty-eight days, or such extended period as may be allowed by the court.[314] There is no such deeming period where the parties do nothing.[315] We saw earlier that the Bankruptcy Act 1988 abolished the doctrine of "relation back", so, like the purchaser in relation to the vendor, the vendor is no longer subject to the risks created by that doctrine in respect of an act of bankruptcy committed by the purchaser.[316] The position now would seem to be that, provided the vendor acts *bona fide* and the sale price is not substantially below market value,[317] the vendor is safe in completing with the purchaser unless he has notice of an act of bankruptcy committed by the purchaser.[318] If he does have notice of such an act or of the presentation of a petition for adjudication of the purchaser as a bankrupt, it appears that the vendor cannot treat this as justifying him rescinding the contract, unless time is of the essence.[319] There would seem, however, no reason why the vendor should not be able to exercise contractual rights, such as service of a completion notice.[320]

[12.48] Where the purchaser is a company which goes into liquidation, the liquidator can elect to complete the contract or to disclaim it.[321] If the

---

[308.] *Re Cockcroft* (1883) 24 Ch D 94.

[309.] 1965 Act, s 47(3).

[310.] Bankruptcy Act 1988, s 56.

[311.] *Re Parnell* (1875) 10 Ch App 512; *Collins v Stinson* (1883) 11 QBD 142.

[312.] See on this para **[12.27]** *supra*.

[313.] Ie, by using the written application procedure laid down in s 56(5): see para **[12.27]** *supra*. Note also that the vendor could instead seek a court order rescinding the contract: s 56(6).

[314.] See Sanfey and Holohan, *Bankruptcy Law and Practice in Ireland* (1991) para 7.14.

[315.] See Farrell, *Irish Law of Specific Performance* (1994), para [8.17].

[316.] See para **[12.28]** *supra*.

[317.] On "good faith" see *Re O'Neill* [1989] 544 at 551-3 (*per* Hamilton P).

[318.] See para **[12.28]** *supra*.

[319.] *Jennings' Trustee v King* [1952] Ch 899, explaining *Collins v Stinson* (1883) 11 QBD 142.

[320.] See para **[13.19]** *post*.

[321.] Companies Act 1963, s 290.

liquidator adopts the latter course, the vendor can sue for specific performance, and this becomes in effect a money claim in the winding-up for any deficiency in the proceeds of a resale of the land.[322] Alternatively, the vendor can prove directly in the winding-up for any loss he has sustained.[323]

III. REGISTERED LAND

[12.49] It is a general principle of the Land Registry system that the registered owner can generally deal with the land by means of a registered disposition only,[324] which raises the question of what the position of the parties to a contract for the sale of registered land is in the intermediate period between the contract and registration of the purchaser as the new owner. This has been a very controversial point in Ireland,[325] but it is considered that the courts have now settled the following propositions.

[12.50] Once the transaction reaches the stage of the vendor executing and delivering to the purchaser the instrument of transfer and the purchaser paying over the balance of the purchase money, the purchaser has an "equity" to be registered as owner and has an unregistered right to the land valid against the registered owner (his vendor) and all other persons except a registered transferee for value. After doubts were expressed on the point at the turn of the century,[326] this point was settled by the Supreme Court in *Devoy v Hanlon*,[327] where Kennedy CJ stated with respect to the provisions of the legislation[328] then governing registration of title:

> "It is, therefore, clear that the statute was framed in contemplation of rights, estates, interests, equities, and powers in or over the land being created, and having valid existence and force outside the registered title."[329]

---

322. There is no point in ordering a conveyance of land to a company about to be dissolved, see *Thames Plate Glass Co v Land and Sea Telegraph Co* (1870) LR 11 Eq 248.
323. See *Currie v Consolidated Kent Collieries Corp Ltd* [1906] 1 KB 134.
324. Registration of Title Act 1964, s 68(1). See generally Fitzgerald, *Land Registry Practice*, (2nd ed, 1995).
325. See further, para **[12.05]** *et seq, supra*.
326. See especially *Pim v Coyle* [1903] 2 IR 457. See also *Mooney v McMahon* [1911] 1 IR 125. But *cf Re Furlong and Bogan's Contract* (1893) 31 LR Ir 191 at 195 (*per* Chatterton V-C): "It is true that the [purchaser] had not yet acquired any estate in the lands, but she had an inchoate right incapable of being defeated, and only waiting for an official duty to be performed to become an absolute estate."
327. [1929] IR 246.
328. Ie, Local Registration of Title (Ir) Act 1891, especially ss 44(2) and (3), 69 and 70. See now Registration of Title Act 1964, s 68(2) and (3) and 96-8.
329. *Op cit,* p 255.

As to the effect of execution and delivery to a purchaser of an unregistered instrument of transfer, he concluded:

"... it is competent for a registered owner by an unregistered instrument - for example, by an unregistered deed of transfer - to confer a beneficial right or estate or interest on another by way of gift or otherwise, valid against other persons claiming as volunteers under the registered owner.[330]

This view has since been accepted as correct both at first instance[331] and by the Supreme Court,[332] and a similar view was taken in a different context by the Court of Appeal of Northern Ireland.[333]

[12.51] That still leaves the question of what the position is earlier in the transaction, ie, immediately after the contract for sale is entered into and before the registered owner executes the instrument of transfer or the purchaser pays the balance of the purchase money. The generally accepted view amongst the Irish judges now seems to be that the purchaser has an unregistered right to the land equivalent to the right he would have under the contract in the case of unregistered land, but that right is, of course, liable to be defeated by registration of a transfer for value. Thus, Kennedy CJ stated in *Re Murphy and McCormack*[334]:

"In my opinion, the right or estate which a purchaser acquires by virtue of a contract for sale to him of land is such a right (which includes estate[335] ...) as an owner of registered land may as vendor create over the registered land within the meaning of section 44(2) of the 1891 Act,[336] a right or

---

[330.] *Ibid*, p 256. See also Murnaghan J at pp 262-3. The only question was whether the instrument had been sufficiently delivered to constitute a perfect gift, see *ibid*, pp 257 and 258 (*per* FitzGibbon J).

[331.] See, eg, *Quinn v McCool* [1929] IR 620 (Johnston J).

[332.] See, eg, *Re Murphy and McCormack* [1930] IR 322: *McManus v Kiernan* [1939] IR 297; *Re Strong* [1940] IR 382; *Coffey v Brunel Construction Co Ltd* [1983] IR 36.

[333.] See *Re Scarlett* [1958] NI 28. See also *McGirr v Devine* [1925] NI 94; *McParland v Conlon* [1930] NI 138; *McLean v McErlean* [1983] NI 258.

[334.] [1930] IR 322.

[335.] See the definition in s 95 of the Local Registration of Title (Ir) Act 1891. See now the Registration of Title Act 1964, s 3(1).

[336.] Which read: "Nothing in this Act shall prevent a person from creating any right in or over any registered land or, registered charge, but any right created or arising in relation to registered land after the first registration of the land shall not affect a registered transferee of the land or chargee for valuable consideration, or the registered owner of a charge created on the land for valuable consideration, unless that right is either - (a) Registered as a burden affecting the land; or (b) One of the burdens to which, though not registered, all registered land is by this Act declared to be subject." *Cf* now Registration of Title Act 1964, s 68(2) and (3).

estate outside the register, which is liable to be defeated by a registered transfer of, or charge on, the land for valuable consideration."[337]

The only dispute which seems to have existed amongst later judges was whether the interest of the purchaser under the contract could be called an "estate" in the land as Kennedy CJ seems to have thought,[338] or should be referred to as a "right" only, on the basis that no estate vested in the purchaser until he was actually registered as the new owner.[339] In the more recent case of *Tempany v Hynes*,[340] the members of the Supreme Court seem to have adopted Kennedy CJ's views, in relation to the provisions of the Registration of Title Act 1964.[341]

[12.52] It is accepted by all the authorities that the purchaser's right or estate in registered land under the contract for sale is, pending registration of his title as owner, vulnerable, in that it will be defeated if the vendor transfers the land to a third party *for value* and that party registers his title first.[342] The purchaser's unregistered right or estate is *not* a burden which affects registered land without registration[343] and so the question arises as to whether there is anything he can do to protect himself. The answer is that he can because, although he probably cannot register his right as a burden,[344] he can register a caution,[345] which prevents the registered owner from dealing

---

[337.] *Op cit*, p 328. *Cf* Murnaghan J at p 329.

[338.] Because of the wide definition in s 95 of the 1891 Act of "right" as including "estate, interest, equity and power". See also *Re Strong* [1940] IR 382 at 404 (*per* O'Byrne J). And see *McParland v Conlon* [1930] NI 138; *Re Scarlett* [1958] NI 28.

[339.] See *McManus v Kiernan* [1939] IR 297 at 305 (*per* Meredith J).

[340.] [1976] IR 101. See the discussion of this case, particularly its holding that the purchaser acquires a beneficial interest to the extent only that he pays some or all of the purchase money, at para **[12.02]** *et seq, supra*.

[341.] The equivalent of s 44(2) of the 1891 Act is s 68(2) and (3). which refers only to an unregistered "right", but, as Henchy J pointed out, right is defined by s 3(1) as including "estate, interest, equity and power," thus "covering the estate or interest of the purchaser". *Ibid* p 109. See also Kenny J at pp 116-7. See also Glover, *Registration of Ownership of Land in Ireland* (1934), pp 14-15, 34-9, 46 and 212.

[342.] *Devoy v Hanlon* [1929] IR 246 at 256 (*per* Kennedy CJ) and 363 (*per* Murnaghan J); *Re Murphy and McCormack* [1930] IR 322 at 328 (*per* Kennedy CJ); *Re Strong* [1940] IR 382 at 397 (*per* Murnaghan J) and 405 (*per* O'Byrne J); *Tempany v Hynes* [1976] IR 101 at 117 (*per* Kenny J) and 110 (*per* Henchy J).

[343.] Ie, it was not included in the list in s 47 of the 1891 Act, nor is it in the list contained now in s 72 of the 1964 Act. See *Re Strong* [1940] IR 382 at 406 (*per* O'Byrne J).

[344.] Ie, it was not included in the list in s 45 of the 1891 Act, nor is it in the list contained in s 69 of the 1964 Act. See *Re Strong* [1940] IR 382 at 406 (*per* O'Byrne J); *cf* at p 397 (*per* Murnaghan J) and the same judge in *Re Murphy and McCormack* [1930] IR 322 at 331.

[345.] 1964 Act, s 97. This provision replaces s 69 of the 1891 Act.

with the land without notice to the cautioner.[346] Thus, the purchaser will be warned if the vendor has executed a transfer in favour of another party and the latter has applied for registration as a transferee for value, having priority over the purchaser. He may then elect his remedy under the contract,[347] eg, rescind for breach of contract by the vendor[348] or specific performance. Or, of course, if he already has an executed transfer from the vendor, he can insist upon registering it before the other transfer in favour of the third party.[349]

[346.] A "caution" is more suitable for contracts of sale than an "inhibition" for the latter is more a restriction on dealings for a specified time or without consent of a specified person, eg, to protect a person during his disability. See McAllister, *Registration of Title in Ireland* (1973), pp 237-9; *Irish Land Law*, para 21.51. *Cf Re Strong* [1940] IR 382 at 397 (*per* Murnaghan J). See also para **[6.66]** *ante*.

[347.] See further, para **[13.03]** *et seq, post*.

[348.] Or treat the vendor as having repudiated the contract, see para **[13.09]** *post*.

[349.] See *Northern Banking Co v Devlin* [1924] 1 IR 90.

Chapter 13

REMEDIES FOR ENFORCEMENT OF THE CONTRACT

[13.01] We now turn to a consideration of the various remedies available to both parties to the contract for the sale of land in the event of the contract not being carried out. From the outset, it should be emphasised that in this chapter we are concerned with pre-completion remedies, ie, those available to the parties during the period between entering into the contract and completion of the transaction to which the contract relates. During this intermediate period the parties' remedies are largely concerned with taking action for breach of contract, but, as we shall see in a later chapter,[1] once completion takes place the contract generally ceases to have significance[2] and the parties' remedies are largely based upon other considerations, eg, the covenants for title in the conveyance.[3]

I. General Principles

[13.02] Before examining in some detail the various pre-completion remedies available to the parties, it may be useful to outline some general principles. First, though the remedies are established by the general law, the parties may have varied the detail of their application, by restricting or adding to them, in the contract for sale. Indeed, we have already noted that the Law Society's standard contract form in common use in Ireland does this.[4] Secondly, the injured party may have a number of remedies available in any particular case, but they are not all necessarily consistent with each other and so there will come a point when that party must elect which remedy or remedies he is going to pursue.[5] Thirdly, not all of the remedies discussed in the following paragraphs are available to each party. Thus, one of the vendor's most effective remedies, ie, forfeiture of the deposit,[6] is not

---

1. See Ch 21 *post*.
2. See the doctrine of "merger," para **[21.02]** *post*.
3. See para **[21.05]** *post*.
4. See paras **[9.44]** *et seq, ante*, in relation to remedies for misdescription. See also paras **[13.19]** and **[13.70]** *infra*.
5. See further on election, para **[13.03]** *infra*.
6. See further, para **[13.30]** *infra*.

available to the purchaser.[7] And, of course, some remedies may not be available to either party in every instance of a breach of contract, eg, rescission where the breach is trivial.[8] Fourthly, when the various remedies can be invoked in a particular case will depend upon its circumstances, eg, one crucial factor may be whether time is of the essence of the contract.[9] Finally, instead of invoking substantive remedies as soon as a dispute arises, the parties may find it useful to "test the temperature of the water" first, by issuing a vendor and purchaser summons. This is a special summary procedure for determining certain matters relating to contracts for the sale of land which was introduced by the Vendor and Purchaser Act 1874.[10]

A. Election

[13.03] Though a party may seek more than one remedy in the same action, eg, he may claim specific performance or damages or rescission,[11] it is essential to note that these remedies are alternatives and that he will not be awarded all three. At the very latest he must elect at the hearing of his action which he wants, but he may be held to have made his election at a much earlier stage.[12] It is, however, also important to note that the mere fact that a party has secured one remedy from the court does not necessarily prevent him from coming back to the court for another remedy if the first one proves to be ineffective. The classic illustration of this is where a party has obtained an order for specific performance but the other party still refuses to carry out part of the contract. It is settled law that it is open to the party who obtained the order for specific performance[13] to return to the court to ask for that order to be dissolved and for, eg, an order of rescission of the contract instead, plus an award of damages to cover losses incurred as a result of the other party's breach of contract.[14] Having said that, a party who is aggrieved at the actions of the other party ought to be aware of the different remedies available and

---

7. *Cf* recovery of the deposit, see para **[13.34]** *infra*.
8. See further, para **[13.67]** *infra*.
9. See further, para **[13.10]** *infra*.
10. Section 9. See further, para **[13.26]** *infra*.
11. See, eg, *Peilow v O'Carroll* (1972) 106 ILTR 29 (plaintiff sued for specific performance or damages in lieu thereof, plus forfeiture of the deposit); (defendant counter-claimed for specific performance with rectification or rescission, plus return of his deposit and auctioneers' fees paid by him).
12. See *Maconchy v Clayton* [1898] 1 IR 291 at 309 (*per* Walker LJ).
13. See the House of Lords decision in *Johnson v Agnew* [1980] AC 367.
14. See *Solomon v Estates Management and Development Agency* High Court, unrep 14 July 1980 (1975/1703P); *Vandeleur v Dargan* [1981] ILRM 75; *Croft Inns Ltd v Scott* [1982] NI 95. See also Farrell, *Irish Law of Specific Performance* (1994), para [10.28] and **[13.04]** *infra*. It is, of course, also open to the party who has secured the order for specific performance to ask the court to insist upon that order being enforced: see para **[13.55]** *infra*.

the consequences of electing to pursue one rather than another. The need for an election and its consequences may be best illustrated by considering the following example: V contracts to sell his house to P for £100,000 and P pays a deposit of £10,000; during the next few weeks, the parties' solicitors carry out the usual conveyancing steps, ie, V's solicitor deduces the title and P's solicitor prepares the draft conveyance; then, before the conveyance is executed and completion takes place, one or other of the parties decides to call the sale off and informs the other party of his refusal to proceed. The position of the innocent party in these two alternative situations may be summarised in the following way.[15]

1. Vendor

[13.04] If the purchaser refuses to proceed with the contract for sale, the vendor may elect between two alternative courses of action, which are quite inconsistent and the remedies available vary according to his election.[16] One course of action is to refuse to accept the repudiation of the contract by the purchaser and to insist upon its being carried out as agreed. If the vendor elects this course of action, then his remedies relate to enforcement of the contract as still existing. Thus, if the purchaser persists in refusing to complete by the closing date, he may seek a decree of specific performance against the purchaser, which may or may not be granted, and the court has jurisdiction to grant damages in lieu of specific performance.[17] If the vendor succeeds in obtaining a decree, but the purchaser refuses to comply with it, then the vendor can apply instead for an order of rescission and forfeiture of the deposit,[18] or for an order for forfeiture of the deposit and liberty to resell the property and, after the resale, to recover the damage which he has suffered if the price on the resale, plus the deposit forfeited, together are less than the original contract price.[19] However, in such a case, it is important to note that rescission in this context does not mean returning to the *status quo* before the contract. That is rescission in the strict sense, such as may be invoked by a party who claims that the contract is vitiated by some factor like fraud or undue influence.[20] Here, indeed, because the court's order seeks

---

[15.] Note that the discussion in the following paragraphs proceeds on the assumption that such a repudiation by one party is a sufficient breach of contract to justify the other party treating himself as discharged, see para **[13.04]** *infra*.

[16.] *Mills v Healy* [1937] IR 437 at 440 (*per* Sullivan P),442 (*per* O'Byrne J) and 447 (*per* Meredith J). See also *Murphy v Harrington* [1927] IR 339; *Bourke v Grimes* (1929) ILTR 53; *McGuire v Conwell* (1932) 66 ILTR 213.

[17.] See para **[13.54]** *infra*.

[18.] See *Bourke v Grimes* (1929) 63 ILTR 53.

[19.] *Cf* cond 41 in the Law Society's *General Condition of Sale* (1995 ed): see para **[13.31]** *infra*.

[20.] See para **[13.58]** *infra*.

to restore the parties to their position before the contract was entered into, ie, a *restitutio in integrum*,[21] a party seeking this remedy cannot expect to be able to claim damages for breach of contract, for, *ex hypothesi*, the court is proceeding on the basis that no contract exists or ever has existed. In other words, the apparent agreement made by the parties is treated as void *ab initio*.[22] In the example given above, on the other hand, the vendor is not making such a claim. Rather he is reiterating that a contract does exist but, because of the repudiation by the purchaser,[23] he is now entitled to treat himself as discharged from any *further* performance of the contract on his own part. Since the contract has existed up to this point, he is clearly entitled to demand damages for breach of that contract by the other party.[24] This vital distinction between rescission on the basis of a vitiating factor, treating the contract as void *ab initio* and seeking *restitutio in integrum* for the parties, on the one hand, and rescission on the basis of a repudiatory breach of contract by one party, justifying the other in treating himself as discharged from further performance of the contract and seeking damages for the breach, on the other hand, has been recognised by the Law Society's standard contract form. Thus, condition 41 of the *General Conditions of Sale (1995 Edition)* provides that, where the purchaser fails "in any material respect"[25] to comply with the "conditions",[26] the vendor is entitled[27] to forfeit the deposit, re-sell the property and recover from the purchaser any deficiency to cover his losses, costs and expenses (allowing credit for the deposit forfeited).[28] Condition 42 confirms the right of either party who has secured an order for specific performance to claim an award of damages in the event of the order not being complied with.[29]

[21.] See *Northern Bank Finance Corporation Ltd v Charlton* [1979] IR 149.

[22.] In the case of fraud, the innocent party may have an action for damages in *tort*, ie, for deceit: see *Delany v Keogh* [1905] 2 IR 267; McMahon and Binchy, *Irish Law of Torts* (2nd ed, 1990), Ch 35. Dishonesty must be established: see *Witter Ltd v TBP Industries Ltd* [1996] 2 All ER 573.

[23.] Which may be reinforced by his refusal to abide by an order for specific performance.

[24.] This point was settled finally in England by the House of Lords in *Johnson v Agnew* [1980] AC 367, the authority of which was accepted by McWilliam J in *Vandeleur v Dargan* [1981] ILRM 75. See further paras **[13.07-8]** *infra*. See also *Sepia Ltd v O'Hanlon Ltd* [1979] ILRM 11; *Taylor v Smyth* [1990] ILRM 377.

[25.] *Cf* cond 31 (failure to pay the deposit): see para **[13.31]** *infra*. Note also conds 37-39: see para **[13.70]** *infra*.

[26.] Ie, both the special and general conditions: see cond 1.

[27.] This is without prejudice to any rights or remedies he has at law or in equity, as to which see the rest of this chapter.

[28.] See para **[13.31]** *infra*.

[29.] *Cf* para **[13.56]** *infra*

[13.05] The main alternative to specific performance, as a remedy based on the continued existence of the contract despite the purchaser's refusal to complete, is for the vendor to sue the purchaser for damages for breach of contract. Here the vendor claims to be put in the position he would have been in had the purchaser performed the contract as agreed. Thus, whether the vendor recovers any substantial damages depends on the value of the land at the date of the breach, usually taken as its resale value within a reasonable time.[30] In practice, he will rarely be entitled to any such damages because, even if the land has fallen in value, so that its resale value is now below the contract price, that fall is more than off-set by the deposit paid, which must be taken into account.[31] So usually a vendor prefers to rescind the contract, forfeit the deposit and resell the property, whereby, in fact, he will often make a substantial profit as compared with the result if the purchaser had carried out the contract.[32]

[13.06] There may be one other alternative open to the vendor, especially where he wants to be rid of the land and yet be sure of recovery of the full contract price. It has been suggested in England that he may ignore the repudiation by the purchaser altogether, insist upon completion, if necessary by executing the conveyance unconditionally in the purchaser's favour, and then sue for the contract price.[33] Thus, the vendor may avoid the need to resort to the equitable remedy of specific performance, is not limited to damages for loss of profit and yet, if necessary, can presumably fall back on his equitable lien for unpaid purchase money.[34] But this alternative has been criticised, eg, on the ground that it is inconsistent with the principle of mitigation of loss,[35] and it is doubtful if it can be adopted if the vendor cannot complete without further action by the purchaser, eg, forwarding the draft conveyance to the vendor for approval and execution.[36] It has also been suggested that the courts may have a general equitable jurisdiction in exceptional cases to prevent the innocent party's otherwise unfettered right to insist on completing his own part of the contract.[37] It remains to be seen

[30] See para **[13.78]** *infra*.
[31] See *ibid*. Note also cond 41 of the *General Conditions*: para **[13.04]** *supra*.
[32] See para **[13.32]** *infra*.
[33] See the majority HL decision in *White and Carter (Councils) Ltd v McGregor* [1962] AC 413 (an appeal from Scotland and not involving a contract for the sale of land).
[34] See para **[12.15]** *ante*.
[35] See Goodhart (1962) 78 LQR 203 See also Megarry J's comments in *Hounslow London Borough v Twickenham Gardens Developments Ltd* [1971] Ch 233.
[36] See Lord Reid in the *White and Carter* case [1962] AC 413 at 428-9.
[37] See *Clea Shipping Corporation v Bulk Oil International Ltd* [1984] 1 All ER 129 at 137 (*per* Lloyd J) (again not a case involving a contract for the sale of land).

whether the Irish courts will accept the suggestion that an innocent party to a contract for the sale of land can act in this way.

[13.07] The alternative course which can be elected by the vendor, as was mentioned above,[38] is to accept the repudiation by the purchaser and to treat it as terminating the contract, thereby discharging the vendor from further liability to perform his obligations under the contract. Adoption of this course of action is often referred to as "rescission" of the contract, but it is crucial to note that it does not involve rescission in the technical sense, ie, restoration of the parties to their pre-contract position as if the contract had never existed. What it does is to put the vendor into the position of being able to pursue alternative remedies, one of which may be rescission in the technical sense. If he seeks rescission in the technical sense the parties must be restored to their original position[39] and he cannot also claim damages for breach of contract, for *ex hypothesi* the effect of rescission in this sense is to treat the parties as being in the position where there never was a contract to be breached.[40] On the other hand, if the vendor "rescinds" for a repudiatory breach of contract by the purchaser, he can forfeit the deposit, resell the property and recoup any losses, plus costs and expenses, through an action for damages.[41] In most cases damages will not concern the vendor because he will often be able to resell the land at a profit, as it has probably increased in value since the contract price was fixed, and, even if it has not increased in value, or has dropped in value, the deposit will usually more than off-set the difference. For this reason rescission in the sense of accepting the repudiation by the purchaser and treating oneself as discharged from further performance of the contract, plus forfeiture of the deposit, is, perhaps, the most popular course of action for vendors faced with defaulting purchasers. It has one further advantage and that is that there is no need for any application to the court,[42] whereas specific performance and an action for damages do require such an application.

[13.08] There is a further advantage for a vendor who elects to accept the repudiation by the purchaser. He may "rescind" immediately, and take such further action as he deems appropriate, eg, forfeit the deposit and put the

---

38. See para **[13.04]** *supra*. For early recognition of the confusion over the usage of the word rescission see *Mersey Steel and Iron Co v Naylor Benzon & Co* (1882) 9 QBD 648 at 671 (*per* Bowen LJ). See also *Clibborn v Horan* [1921] 1 IR 93 at 100 (*per* O'Connor MR).

39. See para **[13.59]** *infra*.

40. See para **[13.60]** *infra*.

41. See *Sepia Ltd v O'Hanlon Ltd* [1979] ILRM 11. See also paras **[13.04]** *supra* and **[13.57]** *infra*.

42. Unless, of course, there are complicating factors, eg, the purchaser has been allowed into possession before completion (see para **[12.32]** *ante*) and refuses to leave.

property up for sale again. On the other hand, if he does not accept the repudiation, he must wait until the purchaser breaks the contract by not completing on the closing date before taking action, such as seeking damages. We saw above that this may ensure that the damages amount to the full contract price.[43] It is important to note, therefore, that acceptance of the purchaser's repudiation (or his "rescission" as it is sometimes confusingly referred to) does not necessarily involve the vendor in disaffirmation of the contract. Only rescission by him in the technical sense involves that. By electing to sue for damages for breach of contract the vendor necessarily affirms the existence of the contract. Thus, the effect of accepting the purchaser's repudiation is to enable him to exercise his remedy immediately, instead of postponing that exercise by refusing to accept the repudiation. Also a refusal to accept the repudiation and thereby keeping the contract alive may ultimately cost the right of election, as Meredith J explained in *Mills v Healy*[44]:

> "But that is only so in the sense that if the right to elect is not promptly exercised subsequent events and occurrences may readily cause a loss of the right. The vendor may be enabled to mend his hand and restore and revert to his original position. But so long as the vendor maintains the position that gives the right of election so long he preserves and keeps alive the purchaser's right."[45]

2. Purchaser

[13.09] Where the vendor refuses to proceed with the contract, the purchaser may also elect between two alternative courses of action. If he refuses to accept the vendor's repudiation, and thus affirms the contract, he may seek either specific performance if the vendor persists in his refusal[46] or damages for breach of contract.[47] If he accepts the repudiation, he may rescind the contract, in the sense of treating himself as discharged from further performance of it,[48] and seek damages for breach of contract.[49] He may also seek the return of his deposit.[50]

---

43. Para **[13.06]** *supra*.
44. [1937] IR 437.
45. *Ibid*, p 447. See also *O'Mullane v Riordan* [1978] ILRM 73; *Horgan v Deasy* [1979] ILRM 71.
46. But again he may ask for rescission as an alternative, see para **[13.04]** *supra*.
47. Or the court may award damages in lieu of specific performance. See *ibid*.
48. See paras **[13.04]** and **[13.07]** *supra*.
49. Note that his claim for damages may be limited by the rule in *Bain v Fothergill*: see para **[13.79]** *infra*.
50. See para **[13.34]** *infra*.

B. Time

[13.10] A factor which most frequently induces one party to a contract for the sale of land to invoke remedies for enforcement of the contract against the other party is the failure or refusal of the latter to complete on time. We have already mentioned in earlier chapters[51] that the fixing of the closing date is usually regarded as a crucial matter in land transactions, if only because of the number of other matters, especially of major financial significance, which depend upon completion on time. The closing date is usually fixed by the contract, either as a specific date or by reference to some period linked to an event or other date.[52] The question then arises as to what the position of the innocent party is if the other party is guilty of delay and refuses or fails to close on that date. The answer is that it depends upon which remedy he wishes to pursue and the terms of the contract. If the innocent party wants to seek specific performance against the delaying party, it seems that he can apply for this as soon as the delay occurs,[53] because this remedy does not depend so much on a breach of contract as on the equitable duty to perform it.[54] Indeed, specific performance may be sought before any delay in completion occurs, eg, where one party repudiates the contract before completion.[55] On the other hand, where the innocent party wishes to rescind the contract for delay by the other party or to claim damages for breach of contract, the question of time becomes more significant.

1. Time Clauses

[13.11] The common law and equity adopted different attitudes to clauses in contracts requiring completion or performance within a set time.[56] The common law regarded time as being a crucial factor and, if a party failed to complete by the fixed date, he was immediately regarded as being in breach of the contract, ie, time was regarded as being of the essence of the contract. On the other hand, equity took the view that this was too harsh a rule and adopted the opposite presumption that time was not of the essence, so that mere delay did not necessarily involve a breach of contract and the defaulting party would be allowed to complete within a reasonable time after

---

[51.] See, eg, paras **[1.09]**, **[2.50]**, **[3.48]** and **[9.05]** *ante*.

[52.] See Ch 7 *ante*.

[53.] Unless he has waived his right to completion by the day specified in the contract, see para **[13.25]** *infra*.

[54.] See *Marks v Lilley* [1959] 1 WLR 749 at 753 (*per* Vaisey J).

[55.] *Hasham v Zenab* [1960] AC 316. See also (1969) 116 New LJ 1657.

[56.] See *Irish Land Law* (2nd ed, 1986), para 3.060. See also Graham, 'Stipulations as to Time' (1954) 18 Conv 452.

the contractual dale for completion.[57] This equitable approach was given statutory confirmation by the Judicature (Ireland) Act 1877,[58] and operates now as the general rule for all contracts.[59]

2. Time of the Essence

[13.12] As explained in the previous paragraph, the general rule in contracts for the sale of land is that time is not of the essence of the contract.[60] At most the closing date is to be regarded as a "target" date, for which the parties are aiming but, which, it is understood by both of them, neither of them may, as things turn out, quite hit. The result is, therefore, that in most cases either party is entitled to complete the contract after the closing date has passed and will not be regarded as being in breach of contract so long as he completes within a "reasonable time" thereafter.[61] Thus, the innocent party may not be able to exercise certain of his remedies, eg, rescission, until that further period has elapsed and, as we shall see, even then may have to give notice to the defaulting party.[62] This clearly puts the innocent party in a difficult position because what amounts to a "reasonable time" in this context must depend upon the circumstances of each case and there is always the risk that he will be regarded by a court as having acted too hastily in, eg, rescinding the contract.[63] As we shall see, one way of avoiding these difficulties is to ensure that there are contractual provisions regulating the matter, and we discuss this subject later.[64] They may also be avoided if time is of the essence of the contract from the outset.[65] There are two ways in which this can arise.

[57.] See *Stickney v Keeble* [1915] AC 386 at 415-6 (*per* Lord Parker). See also the discussion by the Supreme Court in *Hynes Ltd v Independent Newspapers Ltd* [1980] IR 204.

[58.] Section 28(7). See *Irish Land Law* (2nd ed, 1986), para 3.060.

[59.] The whole subject of time should he considered now in the light of the Supreme Court decision in the *Hynes* case, fn 57 *supra*. See also the House of Lords decision in *United Scientific Holdings Ltd v Burnley Borough Council* [1977] 2 All ER 62. And see Wylie, *Irish Landlord and Tenant Law,* para 11.09 *et seq*; Farrell, *Irish Law of Specific Performance* (1994), para [8.29] *et seq*.

[60.] See *Clegg v Wright* (1920) 54 ILTR 69; *Sheridan v Higgins* [1971] IR 291.

[61.] This concept is considered further later, see para **[13.17]** *infra*. There may, nevertheless, be liability in damages for the delay, see the House of Lords decision in *Raineri v Miles* [1980] 2 All ER 145.

[62.] See *ibid*. *Cf* the English Court of Appeal decision in *Behzadi v Shaftesbury Hotels Ltd* [1991] 2 All ER 477: see para **[13.17]** *infra*.

[63.] *Clegg v Wright* (1920) 54 ILTR 69 at 72 (*per* Powell J). See also *Healy Ballsbridge v Alliance Property Corp Ltd* [1974] IR 441.

[64.] Para **[13.19]** *infra*.

[65.] See Graham, 'Stipulations as to Time' (1954) 18 Conv 452.

(i) Expressly

[13.13] There is nothing to prevent the parties making time of the essence of their contract expressly,[66] but extreme caution should be exercised before adopting this course. Making time of the essence from the outset can prove to be a "two-edged sword" upon which either party is as likely to cut himself as his opponent. This point was illustrated by the case of *United Yeast Co Ltd v Cameo Investments Ltd*,[67] where there was a special condition of sale making time of the essence. During the course of the transaction the purchasers had difficulty in securing financial arrangements for proposed development of the property and explained their problems to the vendors, who were not sympathetic. Instead, the vendors continuously reminded the purchasers that time was of the essence of the contract. Part of the premises being sold were occupied by a third party and, though the vendors secured his agreement to vacate them by the closing date, he did not comply. By the time of the closing date the purchasers had managed to solve their financial problems and were ready to complete, but refused to do so because of the continued occupation by the third party. The next day they wrote to the vendors rescinding the contract and demanding return of the deposit. The vendors claimed that they were entitled to an equitable extension of time to enable them to eject the third party whom they claimed was a trespasser, and brought an action for specific performance. Butler J rejected their claim and upheld the purchasers' claim to rescission and return of the deposit.[68] Thus, the vendors, who had insisted on the time clause in the contract with the intention of being able to take prompt action against a defaulting purchaser, ended up being caught by it themselves. In the case of house purchases, where the parties are so often involved in a "chain" of transactions, the dangers of making time of the essence are particularly acute, since neither party is an entirely "free agent" with respect to any one particular sale or purchase. It is, therefore, perhaps not surprising that the contract form issued by the Law Society in Ireland assumes that time is *not* of the essence of the contract, unless there is a special condition to this effect.[69]

[66.] See *Dyas v Rooney* (1890) 27 LR Ir 4.

[67.] (1977) 111 ILTR 13.

[68.] Citing in support *Finkielkraut v Monohan* [1949] 2 All ER 234; *Quadrangle Development and Construction Co Ltd v Jenner* [1974] 1 WLR 68.

[69.] Cond 40 and para **[13.19]** *infra*. Note, however, that time is of the essence under cond 17 (requisitions): See *Coyle v Central Trust Investment Society Ltd* [1978] ILRM 211 and para **[15.22]** *post*.

(ii) By Implication

[13.14] Even if the parties do not say so expressly in so many words in their contract, time may be regarded as being of the essence by implication.[70] As a matter of construction of the terms of the contract, the court may take this to be the intention of the parties.[71] On the other hand, it is clear that the terms of the contract may negative this either expressly[72] or by implication. Thus, it seems to be settled that inclusion of a provision for payment of interest in the event of delay raises a presumption that time is not of the essence, since it indicates that the parties anticipate a possible postponement of completion.[73]

[13.15] The courts are more inclined to regard time as being intended to be of the essence where there are special circumstances relating to the subject-matter of the contract, eg, a grazing farm being let for the season[74] or, indeed, any farm property sold as a going concern,[75] or business property, such as licensed premises,[76] sold as a going concern.[77] The same principle has been applied where the property is of a hazardous or wasting nature, eg, a lease shortly to expire[78] or a life interest.[79] However, it seems that as a general rule it does not apply to residential property,[80] though there are suggestions by some English judges that time may be of the essence where, eg, the purchaser needs the property on completion day for occupation by himself and his family as their only home (their old one probably having been sold in anticipation of completion on that day) and the vendor is well aware of this.[81] Yet this is such a common occurrence nowadays that it may

---

[70.] See *Parkin v Thorold* (1852) 16 Beav 59 at (*per* Lord Romilly MR).

[71.] *Dyas v Rooney* (1890) 27 LR Ir 4 at 5 (*per* Lord Ashbourne C). See also *Barclay v Messenger* (1874) 43 LJ Ch 449 at 455 (*per* Jessel MR).

[72.] See para **[13.13]** *supra*.

[73.] So held by Finlay P in *O'Brien v Seaview Enterprises Ltd* High Court, unrep, 31 May 1976 Cir App). (Note, however, that the *O'Brien* case involved licensed premises where there is usually a presumption that time is of the essence, see para **[13.15]** *infra*). See also *Patrick v Milner* (1877) 2 CPD 342; *James Macara, Ltd v Barclay* [1945] 1 KB 148. *Cf Harold Wood Brick Co Ltd v Ferris* [1935] 2 KB 198 and see (1956) 20 Conv 347.

[74.] *Dyas v Rooney* (1890) 27 LR Ir 4 at 9.

[75.] *Guerin v Heffernan* [1925] 1 IR 57 at 67-8 (*per* O'Conner J), see para **[10.44]** *ante*. See also *Stickney v Keeble* [1915] AC 386 at 401 (*per* Lord Atkinson).

[76.] *Cf O'Brien v Seaview Enterprises Ltd* High Court, unrep, 31 May 1976. See also *Lock v Bell* [1931] 1 Ch 35.

[77.] *MacBryde v Weekes* (1856) 22 Beav 533 (mines).

[78.] *Hudson v Temple* (1860) 30 LJ Ch 251.

[79.] *Withy v Cottle* (1823) Turn & R 78.

[80.] *Smith v Hamilton* [1951] Ch 174 at 179 (*per* Harman J).

[81.] See *Tilley v Thomas* (1867) LR 3 Ch App 61 at 70 (*per* Rolt LJ) apparently approved by Lord Atkinson in *Stickney v Keeble* [1915] AC 386 at 402-3. *Cf Khodaram Irani v Burjorji Dhunjibai* (1915) 32 TLR 156 at 157 (*per* Lord Haldane). And see *Raineri v Miles* [1980] 2 All ER 145 at 155 (*per* Lord Edmund-Davies).

be questioned whether the Irish courts would regard time as being of the essence in the absence of an express stipulation one way or the other.

3 . Making Time of the Essence

[13.16] If time is not of the essence of the contract, or if it was originally but has ceased to be, eg, due to waiver,[82] the question arises as to whether the aggrieved party can subsequently make or remake time of the essence so as to bring the defaulting party to heel. The orthodox answer to this seems to be in the negative, as Kenny J explained in *Healy Ballsbridge Ltd v Alliance Property Corp Ltd*[83]:

> "I protest against the commonly held view that one party to a contract in which time is not of the essence can make it of the essence by serving a notice ... [84] The true position is that when time is not of the essence and the vendor or the purchaser has been guilty of unreasonable delay, the other party may by notice limit a reasonable time within which the contract must be completed if the party on whom the notice is served is not to lose the remedy of specific performance and have the contract terminated against him."[85]

It is important, therefore, to examine what exactly the aggrieved party can do at common law and how this may be modified by the terms of the contract for sale.

(i) At Common Law

[13.17] The position at common law of a party faced with delay in completion by the other party is far from satisfactory. Unless he chooses to seek specific performance, which he can do at once,[86] his position is bedevilled by uncertainty. First, it is settled that he cannot take action, such as to rescind the contract for delay, unless the "reasonable time" for completion allowed by the common law after the contract closing date has elapsed.[87] Secondly, it has long been held that he cannot serve notice on the delaying party as soon as the completion date fixed by the contract is passed,

---

[82.] See para **[13.25]** *infra*.

[83.] [1974] IR 441 (*aff'd* by Sup Ct).

[84.] Quoting FitzGibbon J in *Mills v Healy* [1937] IR 437 at 445-6 in support.

[85.] This passage was in fact a quotation from an earlier judgment of his in an unreported case, *Holohan v Ardmoyle Estates* High Court, unrep, 5 March 1966 (1964/449P) (also *aff'd* Supreme Court, unrep 1 May 1967). Similar views were expressed by Fry J in *Green v Sevin* (1879) 13 Ch D 589 at 599. See also *Cumberland Court (Brighton) Ltd v Taylor* [1964] Ch 29 at 37 (*per* Ungoed-Thomas J). *Cf Charles Rickards Ltd v Oppenheim* [1950] 1 KB 616 at 624 (*per* Denning LJ).

[86.] See para **[13.10]** *supra*.

[87.] See para **[13.12]** *supra*. See also *Taylor v Smyth* [1990] ILRM 377.

for the aggrieved party must wait until there is what has been called variously an "unnecessary,"[88] an "undue",[89] a "great and improper"[90] or a "gross, vexatious and unreasonable"[91] delay by the other party.[92] It is clearly very difficult, if not impossible, for a party to decide in a particular case what is the appropriate waiting period. Thirdly, once this waiting period has passed, any notice served on the delaying party must limit a "reasonable" time within which that party must complete.[93] This raises the further difficulty for the aggrieved party of deciding what is "reasonable" in the particular case. And this must clearly depend upon the circumstances of the particular case.[94] It seems that the question of reasonableness should be considered at the time of the giving of the notice and one factor to be taken into account is what remains to be done at that date.[95] It has been suggested that the ability of the purchaser to raise the purchase money is relevant,[96] though on principle it is difficult to see why the vendor should be concerned with the purchaser's financial arrangements, unless, of course, these formed part of the parties' agreement or, at least, the vendor induced the purchaser to believe that he would be sympathetic on this point.[97] It is also clear that the effect of the delay on the aggrieved party's position should be considered. *In Sepia Ltd v O'Hanlon Ltd*,[98] property developers had entered into two contracts for the purchase of blocks of houses, the first of which

---

88. *Hopkins v Geoghegan* [1931] IR 135 at 140 (*per* Johnston J). See also *Taylor v Brown* (1939) 2 Beav 180 at 183 (*per* Longdale MR).
89. *Healy Ballsbridge Ltd v Alliance Property Corp Ltd* [1974] IR 441 at 448 (per Kenny J). See also *Mills v Healy* [1937] IR 437.
90. *King v Wilson* (1843) 6 Beav 124 at 126 (*per* Langdale MR).
91. See *Wells v Maxwell* (1863) 331 1 Ch 44.
92. *Smith v Hamilton* [1951] Ch 174 at 181 (*per* Harman J). *Cf Phillips v Lamdin* [1949] 2 KB 33 at 42 (*per* Croom-Johnson J). See also *International Securities Ltd v Portmarnock Estates Ltd* High Court, unrep, 9 April 1975 (1975/2257P). Note, however, that the English Court of Appeal recently disapproved of the *Smith* case in *Behzadi v Shaftesbury Hotels Ltd* [1991] 2 All ER 477 and held that, as soon as a party fails to meet an agreed deadline, the other party can serve a notice making time of the essence without having to wait for some "unreasonable" delay. See also para **[13.18]** *infra*.
93. *Hopkins v Geoghegan* [1931] IR 135 at 140 (*per* Johnston J); *Mills v Healy* [1937] IR 437 at 445-6 (per FitzGibbon J). See also *Healy Ballsbridge Ltd v Alliance Property Corp Ltd* [1974] IR 441 at 447 (*per* Kenny J), para **[13.16]** *supra*, *International Securities Ltd v Portmarnock Estates Ltd supra*; *Sepia Ltd v Hanlon Ltd* [1979] ILRM 11.
94. *MacBryde v Weekes* (1856) 22 Beav 533 at 543 (per Romilly MR).
95. *Crawford v Toogood* (1879) 13 Ch D 153 at 158 (*per* Fry J); *Stickney v Keeble* [1915] AC 386 at 419 (*per* Lord Parker), approved by Costello J in *Sepia Ltd v Hanlon Ltd* [1979] ILRM 11 at 32. See also *Green v Sevin* (1879) 13 Ch D 589 (three weeks' notice insufficient); *Ajit v Sammy* [1967] AC 255 (six days' notice sufficient).
96. *Re Barr's Contract* [1956] Ch 551 at 558 (*per* Danckwerts J).
97. See *Stickney v Keeble* [1915] AC 386 at 398 (*per* Earl Loreburn) See also *Re Roger Malcolm Developments Ltd Contract* (1960) 176 Est Gaz 1237, (1961) 25 Conv 260.
98. [1979] ILRM 11.

was subject to the developers obtaining planning permission. Owing to difficulties over the furnishing of title, the closing dates were not met, but after the title issue was resolved the vendors gave the developers three months' notice to complete, declaring time to be of the essence. When the developers failed to complete within this time the vendors purported to rescind the contract on the basis of the developers' repudiation, forfeiting the deposit,[99] but the developers then brought proceedings for specific performance and a declaration that the vendors were not entitled to retain the deposits. In refusing the relief sought, Costello J considered the vendors' position *vis à vis* the notice they had given to the developers:

> "They were, in my opinion, entitled to have the uncertainty concerning the future of their property brought to an end within a reasonable time. The property was a very valuable one and delay in closing meant that the defendants' freedom in dealing with it was constrained by their obligations to the plaintiffs Their future trading plans were also affected by the delay and attendant uncertainties. Their business was carried on in most of the premises the subject of the contracts and in anticipation of closing they had made some alternative arrangements elsewhere. They were entitled to know, within a reasonable time, whether or not these alternative arrangements should be extended or terminated. Furthermore, delay in completion not only deferred the payment to them of a very substantial capital sum but they were contractually entitled to interest only on the purchase of Block A: the second contract did not contain any interest clause. Consideration of these factors would suggest that a three months notice given in April 1977 was a reasonable time."[100]

Costello J also pointed out that, since the condition relating to planning permission was for the developers' sole benefit,[101] they could have waived this. He remarked:

> "The length of time to consider this option was a reasonable one in my opinion having regard to the very lengthy periods which had already elapsed prior to this service for the preparation and presentation of the planning application."[102]

Finally, it is settled that a notice is invalid if the party serving it is not himself, at the date of service, ready, able and willing to complete.[103] Thus, in *Healy Ballsbridge Ltd v Alliance Property Corp Ltd*,[104] a notice served by

---

[99.] See para **[13.07]** *supra*.

[100.] *Op cit*, p 34.

[101.] See para **[7.04]** *ante*.

[102.] *Op cit*, p 34.

[103.] See *United Yeast Co Ltd v Cameo Investments Ltd* (1977) 111 ILTR 13: see para **[13.13]** *supra*.

[104.] [1974] IR 441.

the vendors was held to be invalid because they had not shown title when it was received by the purchasers.

[13.18] Apart from the uncertainties over the "waiting period" prior to service of the notice and the length of notice required, there are more fundamental doubts about the position at common law.[105] One is that it is not clear why, as seems to be the rule, the notice cannot be served as soon as the contractual closing date has passed, provided it limits a reasonable time for completion thereafter. It is arguable that the courts should be concerned solely to see that the purchaser is allowed the requisite reasonable time after the closing date and, if the notice provides for this, it is difficult to see why it matters how quickly it is given after the closing date has passed, when the other party is technically in breach of contract.[106] Most practitioners take the view that the closing date is fixed as being the date when it is hoped that the sale will be concluded. On the same reasoning, logically if a reasonable time has already elapsed since the contractual closing date, it is difficult to see why, as the authorities seem to suggest is the rule, some further period of notice must be given, or, indeed, why any notice at all must be given - the purchaser has had his reasonable time after the closing date and should be entitled to nothing more. Of course, in practice the aggrieved party has no way of knowing whether a court will agree with his view as to what is reasonable and so must be advised to take the precaution of delaying before serving a notice and of limiting a further period for completion in the notice. But, even then, there is some doubt as to whether the reasonable time may be calculated as being made up from two periods, ie, the period between the closing date and the date of the notice and the period limited in the notice. The authorities are not entirely clear on this point, but again on principle the aggrieved party's duty should be simply to ensure that the other party has a reasonable time in which to complete after the closing date. Thus, the longer the delay in service of the notice, the shorter the time which need be limited in the notice and *vice versa*. In view of these doubts at common law, it is not surprising that attempts have been made to clarify the position by special provisions in contracts for sale, a subject to which we now turn.

(ii) Contractual Completion Notices

[13.19] Condition 40 of the Law Society's *General Conditions of Sale (1995 Edition)* empowers *either* party to serve a completion notice on the other in any case except where the special conditions provide that time is of the essence of the contract.[107] This provision is designed to avoid the difficulties

---

[105.] See Graham. 'Stipulations as to Time' (1954) 18 Conv 452.
[106.] This was the view of the English Court of Appeal in *Behzadi v Shaftesbury Hotels Ltd* [1991] 2 All ER 477. See para **[13.17]** fn 92 *supra*.
[107.] See para **[13.13]** *supra*.

at common law which were discussed in the previous paragraphs. First, it provides that a completion notice may be served, where the sale is not completed on the contractual date, on that date or at any time thereafter.[108] Secondly, service of a notice makes it a term of the contract that the party served must complete the transaction within twenty-eight days[109] after the date of service (excluding the day of service) and time is to be of the essence of the contract in respect of that period of time.[110] It is now recognised that the effect of this provision is that the aggrieved party does not have to wait before service of the notice nor does he have to guess at what amounts to a reasonable time to be limited in his notice when he does serve it. Service of the notice makes time of the essence of the contract and so no question of "reasonableness" arises.[111]

[13.20] Condition 40 recognises the position at common law[112] in providing that a notice is effective only if the party giving it is either "able, ready and willing" to complete the sale or is not so ready by reason of the default or misconduct of the other party."[113] Indeed, if the party giving the notice is not in this position, not only is the notice invalid but the other party can rescind against him when the notice expires,[114] for it is settled that such a notice binds the giver as well as the receiver.[115] This emphasises once again the warning that making time of the essence of the contract is very much a two-edged sword.[116] Thus, it has been held by the Irish courts that a purchaser is not obliged to comply with a completion notice where the question of compensation for misdescription[117] has not been settled.[118] Rather more disconcerting from the point of view of Irish practitioners was the holding

---

[108.] Para (a). Such a notice cannot be served if the contract has already been rescinded or become void: para **[13.03]** *et seq, ante.*

[109.] Not, be it noted, "working" days: see **[10.14]** *ante.*

[110.] But without prejudice to any intermediate right of rescission of either party: para (b). As regard the "date of service" see cond 49: para **[10.64]** *ante.* Specific performance may still he sought, even if the notice is invalid, *Woods v MacKenzie Hill Ltd* [1975] 2 All ER 170.

[111.] *Cumberland Court (Brighton) Ltd v Taylor* [1964] Ch 29 at 38 (*per* Ungood-Thomas J). See *also Innisfail Laundry Ltd v Dawe* (1963) 107 Sol Jo 437; *Hooker v Wyle* [1973] 3 All ER 707.

[112.] *Healy Ballsbridge Ltd v Alliance Property Corp Ltd* [1974] IR 441; *United Yeast Co Ltd v Cameo Investments Ltd* (1977) 111 ILTR 13. See also *Horton v Kurzke* [1971] 1 WLR 769; *Pagebar Properties Ltd v Derby Investment Holdings Ltd* [1972] 1 WLR 1500; *Bechal v Kitsford Holdings Ltd* [1988] 3 All ER 985.

[113.] Para (a).

[114.] *United Yeast Co Ltd v Cameo Investments Ltd* (1977) 111 ILTR 13. See also *Finkielkraut v Monohan* [1949] 2 All ER 234; *Lutchmunsing v Rapp* (1967) 204 Est Gaz 1119.

[115.] *Quadrangle Development and Construction Co Ltd v Jenner* [1974] 1 WLR 68.

[116.] See para **[13.13]** *supra.*

[117.] Under, eg, cond 33 of the *General Conditions*, see para **[9.44]** *et seq, ante.*

[118.] *Keating v Bank of Ireland* [1983] ILRM 295; *O'Brien v Kearney* [1995] 2 ILRM 232. *Cf Bechal v Kitsford Holdings Ltd* [1988] 3 All ER 985.

by the Supreme Court in *Viscount Securities Ltd v Kennedy*[119] that the vendors in that case were not "able, ready and willing" to complete[120] because, *at the time they served the completion notice*,[121] they were not in a position to give vacant possession owing to large amounts of spoil on the land in question.[122] On this basis, the court held that the completion notice was invalid, notwithstanding that the spoil was removed ten days after service of the notice and within twenty-four hours of the vendor's solicitor becoming aware of it, ie, well within the period of notice. In *Dublin Laundry Co Ltd v Clarke*[123] Costello J refused to apply the *Viscount Securities* decision in a case where the property was subject to incumbrances[124] at the time the vendor served his completion notice. He commented:

> "I do not think that the Supreme Court's decision is to be construed as meaning that if a vendor has not got releases of incumbrances available on the date of service of the completion notice but could have had them on the date of its expiration that the notice is invalid."[125]

The uncertainty over the validity of completion notices created by the Supreme Court's decision led the Law Reform Commission to propose a statutory provision to the effect that a vendor would not be deemed to be other than able, ready, and willing to complete at the date of service of a completion notice by reason of (a) being unable to deliver vacant possession at that date or (b) not having discharged any mortgage affecting the property.[126] This has not been acted upon by the Oireachtas but meanwhile the Law Society has dealt with the matter[127] in condition 40 of the *General*

---

119. High Court, unrep, 6 May 1986.

120. Under cond 28 of the 1978 Ed of the *General Conditions of Sale*.

121. Emphasis was put on the word "then" which preceded "able, ready and willing" in cond 28 and still does in cond 40(a) of the 1995 Ed.

122. See the detailed discussion of the decision and its implications by the Law Reform Commission in *Report on Land Law and Conveyancing Law: (4) Service of Completion Notices* (LRC 40-1991).

123. [1989] ILRM 29.

124. Judgment mortgages registered against the land: see para **[12.03]** *et seq, ante.*

125. *Op cit*, p 35. The English courts have tended to draw a distinction between matters of title, and other substantive matters, and largely administrative matters to be discharged by the vendor: see *Re Stone v Saville's contract* [1963] 1 All ER 353; *Cole v Rose* [1978] 3 All ER 1121; *Bechal v Kitsford Holdings Ltd* [1988] 3 All ER 985; see the Law Reform Commission's Report, fn 122 *supra*, p 19 *et seq.*

126. Once a notice has been served, the vendor would, under the Commission's proposals, be required to give vacant possession and discharge an "encumbrance" within ten days of being requested to do so by the purchaser; *op cit*, p 27. It is not clear that the Commission intended to draw a distinction in these proposals between "mortgages" and other "encumbrances"; probably not.

127. Originally in cond 40 of the 1986 Ed.

Conditions of Sale (1995 Edition). Paragraph (g) provides that the vendor is not to be deemed other than able, ready and willing to complete:

(i) by reason of the fact that the subject property has been mortgaged or charged, provided that the funds (including the deposit) receivable on completion shall (after allowing for all prior claims thereon) be sufficient to discharge[128] the aggregate of all amounts payable in satisfaction of such mortgages and charges to the extent that they relate to the subject property; or

(ii) by reason of being unable, not ready or unwilling at the date of service of such notice to deliver vacant possession of the subject property provided that (where it is a term of the sale that vacant possession thereof by given[129]) the Vendor is, upon being given reasonable advice of the other party's intention to close the sale on a date within the said period of twenty-eight days or any extension thereof pursuant to condition 40(f),[130] able, ready and willing to deliver vacant possession of the subject property on that date.

[13.21] Though it is probably the case that the notice need not refer expressly to the condition in the contract under which it is served, it must make it clear that the party is invoking its special provisions.[131] Clearly the safest course is to refer explicitly to the condition in question in the contract, thereby incorporating its provisions, eg, the twenty-eight days period.[132]

[13.22] If the purchaser fails to comply with a notice to complete served by the vendor, the latter may forfeit the deposit and resell the property by public auction or private treaty.[133] If, on a resale within one year from the closing date,[134] the vendor incurs a loss, the purchaser is obliged to make up the deficiency and all costs and expenses incurred in the resale, subject to a credit allowed for the deposit forfeited.[135] Any surplus or profit made from the resale may be kept by the vendor.[136] Presumably the vendor is under a

---

[128.] See further on discharge of mortgages and charges on completion para **[20.18]** *post.*

[129.] See cond 21 of the 1995 Ed, para **[10.44]** *ante.*

[130.] See para **[13.24]** *infra.*

[131.] *Babacomp Ltd v Rightside Properties Ltd* [1974] 1 All ER 142; *Delta Vale Properties Ltd v Mills* [1990] 2 All ER 176. See also *Commane v Walsh* High Court, unrep, 2 May 1983 (1982/66 Sp) (noted [1985 ILRM 66]).

[132.] *Cf* (1973) 70 L Soc Gaz 1502.

[133.] Cond 40(d) and 41. See *Stud Managers Ltd v Marshall* [1985] IR 83.

[134.] Presumably the purchaser can still be sued outside this period at common law subject to rules as to remoteness of damage, see para **[13.77]** *infra.*

[135.] These provisions conform with the rules at common law, see para **[13.78]** *infra.*

[136.] *Ibid.* See *Doyle v Ryan* [1981] ILRM 374, para **[13.32]** *infra.*

duty to get the proper market value for the property before he can claim for any deficiency against the purchaser.[137]

[13.23] If the vendor fails to comply with a notice served by the purchaser, the purchaser may elect either to exercise his legal or equitable remedies without further notice or, without prejudice to any right to damages, to give notice in writing to the vendor forthwith to repay the deposit and any money paid on account of the purchase price.[138] If he adopts the latter course and the vendor does repay, the purchaser is no longer entitled to specific performance and must return all documents in his possession belonging to the vendor and, at the vendor's expense, must procure cancellation of any entry relating to the contract in any register.[139]

[13.24] If the party serving the notice extends its term for one or more specified periods of time, at the request or with the consent of the other party, the term of the notice is deemed to expire on the last day of the extended period. The notice is to operate as though the extended period has been specified in the conditions of sale instead of the twenty-eight days period and time is of the essence for the extended period.[140] This provision resolves any doubt that might exist as to whether the terms of the original condition, eg, as to time, apply to an extended period agreed by the parties.[141]

4. Waiver

[13.25] Where time is made of the essence of the contract originally the parties may waive it either expressly[142] or by implication, eg, by continuing negotiations after the date fixed for completion,[143] so that time thereafter ceases to be of the essence.[144] However, it has been held that, where the parties agree on a delay for a *definite* period, ie, in extension of a period in respect of which time was of the essence, time may become of the essence in respect of the extension instead.[145]

[137.] By way of analogy with a mortgagee exercising his power of sale. see *Holohan v Friends Provident and Century Life Office* [1966] IR 1; *Irish Land Law* (2nd ed, 1986), para 13.036.

[138.] Cond 40(e).

[139.] *Ibid.*

[140.] Cond 40(f).

[141.] See *Charles Rickards Ltd v Oppenheim* [1950] 1 KB 616. See also *Delta Vale Properties Ltd v Mills* [1990] 2 All ER 176.

[142.] *Lock v Bell* [1931] 1 Ch 35. See also *Charles Rickards Ltd v Oppenheim* [1950] 1 KB *op cit.*

[143.] *Dyas v Rooney* (1890) 27 LR Ir 4 at 7 (*per* FitzGibbon J); *Rooney v Byrne* [1933] IR 609 at 616 (*per* O'Bryne J). See also *Webb v Hughes* (1870) IR 10 Eq 281 at 286 (*per* Malins V-C).

[144.] *Mills v Healy* [1937] IR 437 at 445-6 (*per* FitzGibbon J).

[145.] See *Lock v Bell* [1931] 1 Ch 35.

II. Vendor and Purchaser Summons

[13.26] As mentioned earlier,[146] the Vendor and Purchaser Act 1874, introduced a special summary procedure to enable vendors and purchasers of land to settle disputes which may arise during the course of transactions relating to land without having to commence a full scale action or to invoke remedies for breach of contract.[147] Section 9 of the 1874 Act[148] as it applies in Ireland[149] reads:

> "[A vendor or purchaser of real or leasehold estate ... may at any time or times and from time to time apply in a summary way to a judge ... in chambers, in respect of any requisitions or objections, or any claim for compensation, or any other question arising out of or connected with the contract, (not being a question affecting the existence or validity of the contract) and the judge shall make such order upon the application as to him shall appear just, and shall order how and by whom all or any of the costs of and incident to the application shall be borne and paid.]

> A vendor or purchaser of real or leasehold estate in Ireland ... may in like manner[150] and for the same purpose apply to the [High Court] and the [judge] shall make such order upon the application as to him shall appear just, and shall order how and by whom all or any of the costs of and incident to the application shall be borne and paid."

[13.27] As s 9 itself indicates, it is clear that a vendor and purchaser summons cannot be used to determine a dispute over the validity of a

---

146. Para **[13.02]** *supra*.

147. See *Martin v Irish Permanent Building Society* High Court, unrep, 30 July 1980 (1980/608 Sp); *Mulligan v Dillon*, High Court, unrep, 7 November 1980 (1980/906 Sp) (wherein McWilliam J emphasised that it is not the function of the court "to take over the duties of Conveyancing Counsel or Solicitors on an investigation of title": see the Law Society Practice Note published in the *Gazette* December 1981, reproduced in the *Conveyancing Handbook*, p 13.5). For detailed discussion of the Irish caselaw on the remedy, see Farrell, *Irish Law of Specific Performance* (1994), para [8.53] *et seq*.

148. Now replaced in England by s 49(1) and (3) of the Law of Property Act 1925. See *Wilson v Thomas* [1958] 1 WLR 422. Note also the criticisms of the procedure in (1961) 25 Conv 90. The remedy is little used now in England because of the spread of registration of title: see *Practice Directions* [1967] 1 All ER 656 and [1970] 1 All ER 671.

149. The first part of the section (indicated by the brackets in the quotation) applied to England only: see Wylie, *Irish Conveyancing Statutes* (1994), p 145.

150. Ie, summary manner, but note the lack of reference to "in chambers", though this would appear to have been the procedure at one time in Ireland. Nowadays, the applications may be by special summons in the High Court, where the case is heard in open court in the usual way: Rules of the Superior Courts 1986 Order 3(12); see also Order 20, rule 1 and Order 38. For earlier times see *Re Vian and Gaffney* (1877) IR 11 Eq 521; *Drapers' Co v McCann* (1878) 1 LR Ir 13.

contract for the sale of land,[151] nor a question of fraud.[152] Rather its use should, in general, be confined to determination of disputes as between the vendor and purchaser (including the parties to a contract for the grant or assignment of a lease[153]) on matters of interpretation of their contract and related conveyancing matters, eg: whether the vendor has made out a good title in accordance with the contract[154]; whether the purchaser has raised a proper requisition on title or the vendor has sufficiently answered a requisition[155]; whether certain clauses need to be included in the conveyance[156]; whether a party has a right to rescind under the contract.[157] It has been used frequently in recent times to resolve disputes over the effect of modern legislation like the Family Home Protection Act 1976.[158] Other matters which have been held to be the proper subject of a summons include: the scope of the power of sale of executors and trustees[159] or of a personal representative[160] the necessity for an assent by a personal representative[161]; the proper execution of a power of appointment[162]; the duty to disclose notices[163]; the duty to deliver an abstract of title[164]; the appropriate form of a covenant for title[165]; the appropriate method of apportioning rent.[166]

[151.] *Re Scott* (1879) 13 ICLR 139 at 140 (*per* Chatterton V-C).

[152.] *Re Delany and Deegan's Contract* [1905] 1 IR 602 at 606 (*per* Porter MR). *Re* innocent misrepresentation see *Re Flynn and Newman's Contract* [1948] IR 104; *cf McCambridge v Winters* High Court, unrep, 28 May 1984 (1983/486 Sp).

[153.] *Re Lecky and Aiken's Contract* (1906) 40 ILTR 65 .See also *Sims-Clarke v Ilet Ltd* [1953] IR 39.

[154.] *Re Ashe and Hogan's Contract* [1920] 1 IR 159; *Kearns v Manresa Estates Ltd* High Court, unrep 25 July 1975 (1974/193). See also *Re Priestley and Davidson's Contract* (1892) 31 LR Ir 122; *Re Mitchell and McElhinney's Contract* [1902] 1 IR 83; *Re Murphy and Griffin's Contract* [1919] 1 IR 187.

[155.] *Kearns v Manresa Estates Ltd supra.*

[156.] *Re Doherty's Contract* (1884) 15 LR Ir 247; *Re Lecky and Aiken's Contract* (1906) 40 ILTR 65; *Colhoun v Trustees of Foyle College* [1898] 1 IR 233. See also *Re Cooper and Crondace's Contract* [1904] 90 LT 258. But it cannot be invoked to rectify a deed already executed. See *Re Ford and Ferguson's Contract* [1906] 1 IR 607 at 609 (*per* Meredith MR).

[157.] *Coyle v Central Trust Investment Society Ltd* [1978] ILRM 211; *Maloney v Elf Investments Ltd* [1979] ILRM 253; *Kennedy v Wrenne* [1981] ILRM 81; *Lyons v Thomas* [1986] IR 66. See also *Re Jackson and Woodburn's Contract* (1887) 37 Ch D 44; *Re Wallis and Barnard's Contract* [1899] 2 Ch 515.

[158.] See *Hickey v Keating* High Court unrep, 25 January 1980 (1979/3196P); *Mulligan v Dillon* High Court, unrep, 7 November 1980 (1980/966 Sp); *Guckian v Brennan* [1981] IR 478; *Reynolds v Waters* [1982] ILRM 335.

[159.] *Re McDonnell and Branigan's Contract* (1922) 56 ILTR 143.

[160.] *Shiels v Flynn* [1975] IR 296; *Crowley v Flynn* [1983] ILRM 513.

[161.] *Mohan v Roche* [1991] 1 IR 560.

[162.] *Re Walker and Elgee's Contract* (1919) 53 ILTR 22.

[163.] *Re Flynn and Newman's Contract* [1948] IR 104; *cf McCann v Valentine* (1990) 1 NIJR 28.

[164.] *Re Priestley and Davidson's Contract* (1892) 31 LR Ir 22.

[165.] *Re Geraghty and Lyon's Contract* (1919) 53 ITR 57.

[166.] *Re Doherty's Contract* (1884) 15 LR Ir 247.

[13.28] On the other hand, where the question referred to the court involves some particularly difficult question of construction of, eg, a deed or will upon which the vendor's title depends, the court may refuse to deal with the matter on such a summons. Thus, in *Re Antrim County Land, Building and Investment Co Ltd*[167] Meredith MR stated:

> "In ordinary circumstances, on a vendor and purchaser summons, an obligation lies on the Court as between vendor and purchaser to determine in one way or another matters that are capable of determination, without waiting for the presence of other persons who may be interested. Where the question involved is the construction of a will or deed, a judge cannot evade the obligation of making up his mind as to the true construction of the document, save in the case of ill-expressed or in artificial instruments where the meaning is so obscure that the Court or judge will not force the title on the purchaser."[168]

In *Re Brown and Mitchell's Contract*,[169] Chatterton V-C refused to decide a question of construction of a will as between the vendor and purchaser, because his decision might affect the rights of third parties under the will who were not represented in the proceedings.[170] Yet as Powell J said in *Re Hogan and Marnell's Contract*[171]:

> "There is a class of case in which, where a whole current of authority has settled what the legal effect of a certain construction of a written document is to be, and when there can be only one reasonable construction of such a document, and when that construction clearly shows that the vendor has a good title, the Court will not hesitate so to decide on a vendor and purchaser summons."[172]

[13.29] It seems that the court may not only answer the questions referred to it on a summons, but may also direct that the natural consequences should follow from its decision, eg, by ordering rescission of the contract, or that the vendor should return the deposit or pay the purchaser's costs of investigating the title or of the summons.[173] It is not appropriate, however, to

---

[167.] (1909) 43 ILTR 120. *Cf Re Nichols and Van Joel's Contract* [1910] 1 Ch 43. And see *Re Hogan and Marnell's Contract* [1914] 1 IR 422 at 429 (*per* Powell J).

[168.] *Ibid*, p 121. See also *Re Kissock and Currie's Contract* [1916] 1 IR 376 at 385 (*per* O'Brien LC); *Re Walker and Elgee's Contract* (1919) 53 ILTR 22 at 24 (*per* Powell J).

[169.] (1902) 2 NIJR 106. See also *Re Carolan and Scott's Contract* [1899] 1 IR 1.

[170.] See also *Re McDermott and Kellett's Contract* (1904) 4 NIJR 8 at 90 (*per* Barton J).

[171.] [1919] 1 IR 422.

[172.] *Ibid*, p 428.

[173.] *Re McDermott and Kellett's Contract* (1904) 4 NIJR 89; *cf Re Priestley and Davidson's Contract* (1892) 31 LR Ir 122. See also *Re Hargreaves and Thompson's Contract* (1886) 32 Ch D 454; *Re Walker and Oakhott's Contract* [1901] 2 Ch 383.

use such a summons to seek specific performance[174] nor rectification.[175] Finally, where s 9 of the 1874 Act refers to a "claim for compensation" it would appear that this must be connected with a dispute over the contract, eg, seeking an abatement of the purchase price[176] or compensation for misdescription.[177] The English courts have distinguished from such claims an action for damages, where the validity of the contract will often be put in issue.[178]

III. FORFEITURE AND RECOVERY OF DEPOSIT

[13.30] We saw earlier that the payment by the purchaser of a deposit on entering into the contract for sale is normally required by the conditions of sale and that this deposit is usually regarded both as part payment of the purchase price and as security for or a guarantee of performance of the contract by the purchaser.[179] The result is, therefore, that it is well-settled that as a general rule the vendor may forfeit the deposit if the purchaser defaults on the contract[180] and the purchaser may recover it if the vendor defaults.[181] However, both these aspects of the general rule have been the subject of considerable controversy over the years.

A. Forfeiture by Vendor

[13.31] It is settled that the vendor may forfeit the deposit as soon as the purchaser is in default on his contract,[182] and when this occurs, as we have seen,[183] may depend upon whether or not time is of the essence of the

---

174. See *Re Ford and Ferguson's Contract* [1906] 1 IR 607.
175. *Re McDermott and Kellett's Contract* (1904) 4 NIJR 89. *Cf Lyons v Murphy* [1986] IR 666. Nor may it be used to amend a contract the parties have agreed: *March Properties Ltd v Commissioners of Public Works in Ireland* Supreme Court, unrep 11 November 1993 (1992/384).
176. *Molphy v Coyne* (1919) 53 ILTR 177; *cf Re Terry and White's Contract* (1886) 32 Ch D 14.
177. *Cf Keating v Bank of Ireland* [1983] ILRM 295 and *O'Brien v Kearney* [1995] 2 ILRM 232, in both of which a claim for damages and specific performance with an abatement of the purchase price was made.
178. See *Re Hargreaves and Thompson's Contract* (1886) 32 Ch D 454; *Re Wilson and Steven's Contract* [1894] 3 Ch 546; *Barber v Wolfe* [1945] Ch 187.
179. See paras **[10.18]** and **[10.22]** *ante. Cf* a *pre*-contract deposit, as to which see para **[3.15]** *ante.*
180. *International Securities Ltd v Portmarnock Estates* Ltd High Court, unrep, 9 April 1975 (1974/2257P); *Doyle v Ryan* [1981] ILRM 375; *Draisey v Fitzpatrick* [1981] ILRM 219. See also *Morrow v Carty* [1957] NI 174.
181. *Dickie v White* (1901) 1 NIJR 128; *United Yeast Co Ltd v Cameo Investments Ltd* (1977) 111 ILTR 13.
182. *Levy v Stogdon* [1898] 1 Ch 478; *Sprague v Booth* [1909] AC 576.
183. See para **[13.10]** *et seq, supra.*

contract. This right of forfeiture does not depend upon the terms of the contract, but is implied from the purpose of paying the deposit as security for performance of the contract.[184] However, it is interesting to note that the Society's *General Conditions of Sale (1995 Edition)* contains express provisions to this effect. Condition 31 provides that a failure by the purchaser to pay in full the deposit constitutes a "breach of condition" which entitles the vendor to terminate the sale or to sue the purchaser for damages, or both. Condition 41[185] provides:

> "If the Purchaser shall fail in any material respect to comply with any of these Conditions, the Vendor (without prejudice to any rights or remedies available to him at law or in equity[186]) shall be entitled to forfeit the deposit and shall be at liberty (without being obliged to tender an Assurance) to re-sell the subject property, with or without notice to the Purchaser, either by public auction or private treaty ..."

It is, however, important to note that it seems that the vendor can forfeit only the sum of money actually paid over to him, rather than the sum of money which should have been paid to him as the deposit under the terms of the contract.[187] However, care should be taken over this proposition for in practice what it means is that the vendor initially can clearly only forfeit the amount which has actually been paid by the purchaser. Recent authorities in England have made it clear that it is also open to the vendor to sue the purchaser for the balance of the deposit payable under the contract, ie, in effect a claim for damages for breach of contract.[188] Of course, the vendor may take the view that it is not worth the trouble and expense of pursuing the defaulting purchaser in this way and that there are more effective remedies.[189] Normally the vendor will rescind the contract, provided the

---

[184.] *Hall v Burnell* [1911] 2 Ch 551. See also *Morrow v Carty* [1957] NI 174 at 177 (*per* McVeigh J.).

[185.] This has long been a feature of the Society's contract form: a similar provision was contained in cond 29 of the 1976 Ed.

[186.] Eg, an action for damages (see para **[13.75]** *infra*) or rescission (see para **[13.57]** *infra*).

[187.] *Lowe v Hope* [1970] Ch 94. *Cf Dewar v Mintoft* [1912] 2 KB 373.

[188.] See *Millichamp v Jones* [1983] 1 All ER 267; *Damon Cia Naviera SA v Hapag-Lloyd International SA* [1985] 1 All ER 475. This accords with the earlier case of *Dewar v Mintoft*, fn 187 *supra*; *Lowe v Hope* (also fn 187 *supra*) insofar as it may suggest otherwise is probably based on the false notion that a vendor who rescinds because of a repudiatory breach of contract by the purchaser cannot sue for damages: that notion was exploded by the House of Lords in *Johnson v Agnew* see para **[13.03]** *supra*. Cond 31 of the *General Conditions* confirms the vendor's right to sue: see para **[10.18]** *ante*.

[189.] Nevertheless, if the purchaser is allowed to pay less than the full deposit it reduces the "security" of the vendor and makes the threat of its forfeiture less effective: see para **[10.19]** *ante*.

purchaser's default is sufficiently serious to justify this,[190] thus enabling him to retain the land and resell it, probably in most cases for a profit which he is entitled to keep.[191] If, instead of rescinding the contract, he elected to affirm it and to sue for damages only, he would have to account for the deposit he received and thereby reduce his claim.[192]

[13.32] This, however, raises a controversial question, namely, whether the vendor is entitled to retain what is usually a substantial deposit, eg, at least 10 per cent. of the purchase price,[193] even in a case where he has rescinded and resold the property for at least the full contract price, if not more than that. To take a not uncommon example, at least when the property market is rising in step with inflation, a particular property might be contracted to be sold for £100,000 and a deposit of £20,000 might be paid. After a few months the sale might fall through due to circumstances particular to that purchaser, ie, not relating to general circumstances likely to affect the value of the property, eg, a refusal of planning permission. The vendor might then forfeit the £20,000 deposit and resell the property for £130,000 a few months later. Thus, instead of recovering the £100,000 under his original contract, he recovers £150,000 in total, ie, he makes a profit of £50,000 or 50 per cent. Under the general law of contract he almost certainly would not be allowed to do this, because equity would regard the forfeiture of the deposit in such circumstances as a "penalty" against which the court ought to grant relief.[194] The question remains, however, as to whether the penalty rules apply to contracts for the sale of land.

[13.33] From the outset it must be stated that there is very little firm authority on this point on either side of the Irish Sea. There seems to be no case where a deposit in a case of a sale of land has been struck down as a penalty.[195] On the other hand, there are cases where the courts seem to have accepted the generally held view amongst practitioners, and several

---

[190.] Hence the expression "in any material respect". See further, paras **[13.67-8]** *infra*.

[191.] *Doyle v Ryan* [1981] ILRM 375, para **[13.33]** *infra*. Cond 41 goes on to deal with the right of resale. see para **[13.22]** *supra*.

[192.] See para **[13.78]** *infra*.

[193.] See para **[10.17]** *ante*.

[194.] *Husband v Grattan* (1833) Alc & Nap 389; *Lombank Ltd v Kennedy* [1961] NI 192; *Irish Telephone Rentals Ltd v Irish Civil Service Building Society Ltd* [1991] ILRM 880. See also *Stockloser v Johnson* [1954] 1 QB 476; *Bridge v Campbell Discount Co Ltd* [1962] AC 600; Clarke, *Contract Law in Ireland* (3rd ed, 1992), p 468 *et seq*.

[195.] In *Windsor Securities v Loreldal* London Times 10 September 1975, in a sale of properties in London for over £2m the purchasers claimed relief on the ground that forfeiture of the deposit was a penalty as the property had increased in value by the date of failure to complete. Oliver J held that there was no reason for granting equitable relief in the circumstances and directed an inquiry as to the vendor's loss.

writers,[196] that the vendor is entitled to keep the deposit even though it exceeds any loss he may have suffered.[197] This traditional view was applied in the Circuit Court in *Doyle v Ryan*,[198] where the vendors rescinded a contract for the sale of premises for £20,000, forfeited the deposit of £2,000 and re-sold the premises at a profit.[199] The purchasers sued for return of the deposit[200] and argued that the vendors should not be entitled to forfeit the deposit *in toto* where the premises had appreciated in value on a re-sale. They claimed that this would constitute a penalty. Judge Sheridan held, after full arguments by counsel, that "the court cannot be concerned as to what transpires upon a re-sale except where there is deficiency". This decision involved an application of the *General Conditions of Sale*, under which the question of giving credit for the deposit arose only in a claim against the purchaser to make up a deficiency on a re-sale.[201] That remains the position under condition 41 of the *General Conditions of Sale (1995 Edition)*.[202] Furthermore, the condition provides[203] that any "increase in price obtained by the vendor on any re-sale, whenever effected, shall belong to the vendor". However, the penalty rules are based upon equitable jurisdiction to strike down an express provision in the contract. The whole matter was reviewed recently by the Privy Council[204] in an appeal from the Court of Appeal of Jamaica, *Workers Trust and Merchant Bank Ltd v Dojap Investments Ltd*.[205] That case involved a sale by the mortgagee bank of premises by public auction and, in accordance with the terms of the contract, a deposit of 25% was paid by the purchaser. The balance of the purchase money was to be paid within fourteen days and, when it was not paid, the bank rescinded the contract and forfeited the deposit. The Jamaican Court of Appeal had held

---

[196.] See Barnsley, *Conveyancing Law and Practice* (3rd ed, 1988), p 224; *Gibson's Conveyancing* (20th ed, by Kersley 1970), pp 128-9; Walford, *Sale of Land* (2nd ed, 1957), p 253; *Williams on Title* (4th ed, by Battersby 1975), p 744. *Cf* Farrand, *Contract and Conveyance* (4th ed, 1983), pp 203-5.

[197.] *Hinton v Sparkes* (1868) LR 3 CP 161; *Wallis v Smith* (1883) 21 Ch D 243.

[198.] [1981] ILRM 374.

[199.] They had invoked cond 29 of the 1976 Ed of the *General Condition of Sale*, the forerunner of cond 41 of the 1995 Ed; see para **[13.31]** *supra*. The size of the profit is not revealed by the report.

[200.] See para **[13.34]** *infra*.

[201.] See fn 199 *supra*.

[202.] Note that cond 29 referred to the deposit being forfeited "absolutely", but this epithet does not appear in cond 41. If is doubtful whether anything hangs on this and Judge Sheridan made no reference to the point in his judgment.

[203.] As did cond 29 of the 1976 Ed, though Judge Sheridan did not advert expressly to this point.

[204.] Note that a five-member Board heard the appeal (Lord Keith of Kinkel, Lord Jauncey of Tullichettle, Lord Donaldson of Lymington, Lord Browne-Wilkinson and Sir Christopher Slade) ie, including 3 law lords and a former Master of the Rolls.

[205.] [1993] 2 All ER 370.

that the purchaser was entitled to relief from the forfeiture to the extent that the deposit exceeded 10% of the price. The Privy Council[206] accepted the proposition that a deposit paid under a contract for the sale of land is an exception to the general penalty rules, ie, it can be forfeited even though it "bears no reference to the anticipated loss to the vendor flowing from the breach of contract"[207] However, it accepted that this exception is "anomalous" and recognised that the special treatment accorded to such deposits "is plainly capable of being abused". To receive the special treatment the sum paid must be a "deposit", ie, earnest money,[208] and in the Privy Council's view: "It is not possible for the parties to attach the incidents of a deposit to the payment of a sum of money unless such sum is reasonable as earnest money".[209] They then applied the test of "reasonableness" to the particular case, taking the position that by long continued usage in both the United Kingdom and Jamaica the customary deposit on a sale of land was 10%. It followed that: "A vendor who seeks to obtain a larger amount by way of forfeitable deposit must show special circumstances which justify such a deposit".[210] After reviewing the evidence, they concluded that special circumstances had not been shown by the bank. They also confirmed that, where the court concludes that the deposit is unreasonable and, therefore, a penalty, the court has jurisdiction to order its return to the purchaser.[211] However, unlike the Jamaican Court of Appeal, the Privy Council took the view that there was no question of splitting the deposit, so as to leave the bank with a reasonable amount (the normal 10%). The bank had contracted for "one globular sum" which, being unreasonable, was not a deposit at all, and so it could not keep any of it.[212] However, it was recognised that the bank had suffered some, as yet unquantified, losses as a result of the breach of contract and so it was held that the bank could keep back a proportion of the sum to cover what were anticipated to be a small amount of damages. It remains to be seen whether the Irish courts will follow the approach of the

---

206. The judgment was given by Lord Browne-Wilkinson.

207. *Op cit*, p 373.

208. See para **[10.08]** *ante*.

209. *Op cit*, p 374. Statements by Denning LJ in *Stockloser v Johnson* [1954] 1 All ER 630 at 638 and Lord Hailsham LC in *Linggi Plantations Ltd v Jagatheesan* [1972] 1 MLJ 89 at 94 were approved, *op cit*, p 373.

210. *Ibid*.

211. *Cf* where the purchase price is payable by instalments. The Privy Council refused to decide between the conflicting views on this subject expressed by members of the Court of Appeal in *Stockloser v Johnson* [1954] 1 All ER 630; *op cit*, p 276. See also *Kilmer v British Columbia Orchard Land Ltd* [1913] AC 319; *Steadman v Drinkle* [1916] 1 AC 275; *Starside Properties Ltd v Mustapha* [1974] 2 All ER 567.

212. It was also held that the purchaser was entitled to claim interest from the date the bank rescinded until it made the repayment.

Privy Council. It is suggested that vendors should be advised that, unless there are special circumstances applicable, the deposit specified in the contract[213] should not exceed what is customary in sales of that kind. In particular, they should be advised that an excessive deposit, such as 25% or more, may be regarded as a penalty, the whole of which may have to be returned unless losses deriving from the purchaser's breach of contract can be established. From the point of view of practical convenience, of course, it is preferable not to have litigation arising in every case as to whether or not the deposit forfeited is reasonable. The way to avoid this would seem to be to stick to the customary amount for sales of the type in question. Notwithstanding the absence so far of any indication by the Irish courts of a willingness to intervene, the niggling doubt must remain whether a court would refuse to exercise the equitable jurisdiction in a case where the vendor, so far from making a loss from the purchaser's default, is bound to make a substantial profit at the expense of a purchaser forced into defaulting by fortuitous and unforeseen circumstances.

B. Recovery by Purchaser

[13.34] It is settled that, if the vendor is in default, the purchaser may recover his deposit,[214] with interest, plus the costs of investigating title.[215] Though it has been held in Ireland that interest is not allowed where the vendor rescinds the contract under a condition allowing him to do so because the purchaser raises a requisition on title with which the vendor is not bound or willing to comply, provided there is no fraud on the vendor's part.[216] This was held to be so even though the vendor had not such a title as the court would force on an unwilling purchaser; it was, however, in accordance with the contract and a good "holding" title.[217] This, however, raises a controversial point. Normally the right to return of the deposit is based upon a breach of contract by the vendor. In most cases the purchaser

---

[213.] Note that the *General Conditions of Sale* (1995 Ed) now specifies 10% for auction sales: see cond 4(d), whereas the amount has to be specified in the Memorandum in sales by private treaty: see cond 5(a). See paras **[10.16]** and **[10.17]** *ante*

[214.] *Dickie v White* (1901) 1 NIJR 128; *White v Spendlove* [1942] IR 224; *Re Flynn and Newman's Contract* [1948] IR 104; *United Yeast Co Ltd v Cameo Investments Ltd* (1977) 111 ILTR 13.

[215.] *Peilow v O'Carroll* (1972) 106 ILTR 29 (interest at 6%); *cf Day v Singleton* [1899] 2 Ch 320 (4%). See also *Soper v Arnold* (1889) 14 App Cas 429; *Jacobs v Revell* [1900] 2 Ch 858.

[216.] *Re Commins and Hanafy's Contract* (1905) 39 ILTR 85. On such a condition (see cond 18 of the 1995 Ed of the *General Conditions*), see para **[15.27]** *post* and note the Supreme Court's recent review of its operation in *Williams v Kennedy* High Court, unrep 19 July 1993.

[217.] *Ibid*, p 86 (*per* FitzGibbon LJ).

can rescind the contract and sue for its recovery.[218] Indeed, as we have seen,[219] he also has a lien on the land for its recovery,[220] unless it was paid to a stakeholder rather than the vendor or his agent.[221] The question arises, however, as to what the position is where the vendor has not committed such a breach of contract as to allow the purchaser to rescind the contract[222] and sue for recovery of the deposit, yet the sale falls through because the vendor is refused specific performance. The classic case is that mentioned above, ie., where the vendor fails to establish a sufficiently good title to justify the court granting him equitable relief to force it on the purchaser,[223] but where the vendor is protected from breach of contract by conditions of sale which, eg, prevent the purchaser raising requisitions on or objections to title or even investigating it at all.[224]

[13.35] In England, it was finally established in the leading case of *Re Scott and Alvarez's Contract*[225] that in such a case the court had no power to order the return of the deposit to the purchaser. This rule was reversed for England by s 49(2) of the Law of Property Act 1925, which provided:

> "Where the court refuses to grant specific performance of a contract, or in any action for the return of a deposit, the court may, if it thinks fit, order the repayment of any deposit."[226]

Notwithstanding the absence of such a provision here,[227] it is questionable whether the Irish courts will adopt the principle of *Re Scott and Alvarez's Contract*, for it has been subject to a steady current of criticism by the Irish judges.

---

[218] *Dickie v White* (1901) 1 NIJR 128; *Peilow v O'Carroll* (1972) 106 ILTR 29; *United Yeast Co Ltd v Cameo Investments Ltd* (1977) 111 ILTR 13.

[219] Para **[12.44]** *ante*.

[220] *Combe v Swaythling* [1947] Ch 625.

[221] See para **[10.25]** *ante*.

[222] See paras **[13.67-8]** *infra*.

[223] See para **[13.38]** *infra*.

[224] See para **[15.25]** *post*.

[225] [1895] 2 Ch 603. See also *Re National Provincial Bank of England and Marsh* [1895] 1 Ch 90; *Beyfus v Lodge* [1925] Ch 350.

[226] It has been suggested that the jurisdiction is to return the whole deposit or nothing at all, ie, not a portion of it, see *James Macara Ltd v Barclay* [1944] 2 All ER 31 at 32 (*per* Vaisey J) (*aff'd* on other grounds [1945] KB 148). See also *Charles Hunt Ltd v Palmer* [1931] 2 Ch 287; *Finkielkraut v Monohan* [1949] 2 All ER 234. *Cf Dimsdale Developments (South East) Ltd v De Haan* (1983) 47 P & CR 1.

[227] The English Courts have now resolved that the jurisdiction under s 49(2) involves an unfettered discretion and does not require the purchaser to establish misconduct by the vendor or other special circumstances: see *Universal Corporation v Five Ways Properties Ltd* [1979] 1 All ER 552 (disapproving *Cole v Rose* [1978] 3 All ER 1121). See also *Schindler v Pigault* (1975) 30 p & CR 328; *Faruqi v English Real Estates Ltd* [1979] 1 WLR 963.

[13.36] The first salvo was fired by the Irish Court of Appeal the year after the English case was decided, in *Re Lyons and Carroll's Contract*.[228] Lord Ashbourne C stated that he could not accede to the argument that in such a case there was no jurisdiction to order return of the deposit. He felt that there was "ample" jurisdiction to do so under the wording of s 9 of the Vendor and Purchaser Act 1874, which recognised the jurisdiction of the court to make such order as it thought "just."[229] Barry LJ commented on the *Scott* case:

"That is a very complicated case, and I am bound to say not very creditable to our system of judicature."[230]

On the other hand, the other two members of the Court, FitzGibbon and Walker LJJ, felt it was unnecessary to express an opinion on the jurisdiction to order a return of the deposit.[231] Nevertheless, in *Re Turpin and Ahern's Contract*,[232] Porter MR commented at first instance,[233] but, as he recognised, *obiter*, that the *Scott* decision had not "satisfied" the Court of Appeal in Ireland on the question of return of the deposit nor, as he put it, "apparently anybody else."[234] More recently, Kingsmill Moore J, in *Re Flynn and Newman's Contract*,[235] commented that the *Scott* case had been "frowned on" in the *Lyons* case in Ireland. On the other hand, in *White v Spendlove*,[236] Geoghegan J stated, again *obiter*,[237]:

"It has also been suggested that even in a vendor's action for specific performance the Court has jurisdiction to order return of part payments of purchase money if the action fails. I have not been referred to any case where that was done in the absence of an appropriate counterclaim by the purchaser indicating precisely the case he was making for repayment. It is well established that even though a vendor has failed in his claim for

---

[228] [1896] 1 IR 383.

[229] *Ibid*, p 395. But note that s 9 of the 1874 Act is strictly confined to orders made on a vendor and purchaser summons, see para **[13.26]** *supra*.

[230] *Ibid*, p 396. But he went on to point out that the vendor and purchaser in the *Scott* case were innocent, whereas in the present case he felt there was an element of fraud on the part of the vendor. Fraud would, of course, normally entitle the purchaser to rescind (see para **[13.64]** *infra*) and it is settled that in such a case he can always sue to recover the deposit, para **[13.34]** *supra*.

[231] *Ibid*, pp 395 and 400.

[232] [1905] 1 IR 85.

[233] The point was not mentioned in the CA, the majority of which comprised FitzGibbon and Walker LJJ, who refused to deal with it in the *Lyons* case.

[234] *Ibid*, p 93.

[235] [1948] IR 104.

[236] [1942] IR 224.

[237] The actual decision of the majority of the Supreme Court was that the purchaser was estopped from suing in the circumstances, and Geoghegan J actually dissented from that decision.

specific performance the purchaser may not be entitled to enforce the return of his part payments. In the present case he conceived he had an answer on the ground that there was not total failure of consideration. In my opinion even if the Court had discretionary jurisdiction to order return of the moneys because the specific performance proceedings failed it was not a case for the exercise of that discretion, having regard to the state of the pleadings and the course of the trial."[238]

IV. SPECIFIC PERFORMANCE

[13.37] Where a party to a contract for the sale of land wishes to force the other party to go through with the contract, he may apply to the court for a decree of specific performance, ie, an order of the court requiring the other party to carry out the contract strictly according to its terms.[239] This is a remedy which was developed especially for contracts for the sale of land and so has particular significance for conveyancers. In the next few paragraphs we discuss the various principles applicable to the remedy and emphasise those matters which relate to conveyancing in particular. First, however, it may be worth emphasising some practical considerations which suggest that this remedy may prove inconvenient from either party's point of view. So far as the vendor is concerned, the disadvantage about seeking specific performance is that the property cannot be dealt with until the proceedings are finally determined. Thus, if he requires the purchase money in order to buy another property, he may find that the delay causes him considerable financial embarrassment and results in default on that other purchase. So it may prove more convenient to cut his losses by rescinding the first contract instead and reselling the property or using it as security for bridging finance. So far as the purchaser is concerned, the disadvantage is that he must usually show the court that he is able and willing to complete by not only tendering a conveyance but also proving that he has the necessary finance to pay the balance of the purchase money. At the very least the court will usually require clear evidence of the availability of finance from a lending institution, if not from his own resources, and in practice it is often difficult to furnish such evidence.

[238.] *Ibid*, p 252.

[239.] Or, in certain cases, subject to a variation, eg, an abatement in the purchaser price or compensation, see para **[12.51]** *infra*. See generally on the remedy as it is used in Ireland Farrell, *Irish Law of Specific Performance* (1994); see also Delany, *Equity and the Law of Trusts in Ireland* (1996), Ch 14.

A. General Principles

1. Equitable Remedy

[13.38] Specific performance is an equitable remedy, and, like all equitable remedies, lies in the discretion of the court.[240] However, as has long been emphasised by the courts, this is not an arbitrary discretion. Thus, at the beginning of the last century. Lord Manners LC stated:

" ... it is in the Discretion of the Court to decree or refuse the specific Execution of the Contract. It is so; but that Discretion is regulated and restrained by Principles as well known and established, as any other Branch of the Law of this Court ..."[241]

Similar views were expressed more recently by Black LJ in *Conlon v Murray*.[242] This question of discretion becomes very relevant in connection with the various so-called "defences" to an action for specific performance which we discuss below.[243]

2. Damages Inadequate

[13.39] The underlying rationale of the remedy of specific performance was enunciated a long time ago in *Harnett v Yielding*[244] by Lord Redesdale:

"Unquestionably the original foundation of these decrees was simply this, that damages at law would not give the party the compensation to which he was entitled; that is, would not put him in a situation as beneficial to him if the agreement were specifically performed. On this ground, the Court in a variety of cases, has refused to interfere, where from the nature of the case, the damages must necessarily be commensurate to the injury sustained."[245]

It was the inadequacy of damages at common law in the case of contracts for the sale of land, and certain other special cases,[246] that gave rise to the special significance of specific performance as a remedy for conveyancing transactions.

[240.] See Farrell, *op cit*, para [1.06] *et seq*.

[241.] *Revell v Hussey* (1813) 2 Ba & B 280 at 288.

[242.] [1958] NI 17 at 25. See also *Smelter Corporation of Ireland Ltd v O'Driscoll* [1977] IR 305 at 311 (*per* O'Higgins CJ); *O'Neill v Ryan (No 3)* [1992] 1 IR 166 at 191 (*per* Costello J) and 196 (*per* Finlay CJ).

[243.] Para **[13.43]** *infra*.

[244.] (1805) 2 Sch & Lef 549. He expressed similar views in *Davis v Hone* (1805) 2 Sch & Lef 341 at 347; on rehearing (1807) 2 Sch & Lef 741 (Ponsonby LC).

[245.] *Ibid*, p 553. See also *Bagnell v Edwards* (1876) IR 10 Eq 215; *Hennessy v Kiernan* (1904) 38 ILTR 250; *Rushbrooke v O'Sullivan* [1908] 1 IR 232.

[246.] See *Farrell, op cit*, para [1.14] *et seq*.

3. Conveyancing Contracts

[13.40] It has long been settled that a contract for the sale[247] or lease[248] of land may be the subject of a decree of specific performance. From the purchaser's point of view, the land in question usually has some special character and so damages will rarely be an adequate remedy.[249] It is true that the vendor's claim is essentially a monetary one, and so one which ought to be satisfied with damages, but it is settled that the vendor may also obtain a decree of specific performance.[250] It is also settled that the remedy may be invoked to enforce a contract for the exchange of lands[251] and the various kinds of options which may be granted in land transactions, such as an option to purchase.[252] However, as a general rule it does not apply to a contract to lend money, whether or not on the security of land.[253] Thus, in *Gorringe v Land Improvement Society,*[254] Porter MR stated:

> "As a general proposition it is correct to say that a mere agreement to lend money, even upon security, will not be specifically performed. If money is lent, the lender may call it in again, and therefore specific performance would be futile. Money compensation in such a case affords an adequate, and, indeed, the best remedy, and goes nearer to a complete restitution in integrum than the enforcement of a loan which the lender might straightway proceed to require back, leaving the borrower in no better position after the interference of the court."[255]

[247.] See, eg, *Corless v Sparling* (1874) IR 8 Eq 335; *Abbott v Ryan* (1901) 1 NIJR 75; *Heneghan v Davitt* [1933] IR 375; *Smith v Lynn* [1951] NI 69; *Barclay's Bank v Breen* (1962) 96 ILTR 179; *Sheridan v Higgins* [1971] IR 291; *Roberts v O'Neill* [1983] IR 47; *McCrystal v O'Kane* [1986] NI 123; *O'Brien v Kearney* [1995] 2 ILRM 232.

[248.] See, eg, *Lindsay v Lynch* (1804) 2 Sch & Lef 1; *Clarke v Moore* (1844) 7 Ir Eq R 515; *Moore v Crofton* (1946) 9 Ir Eq R 344; *McLoughlin v Alexander* (1910) 44 ILTR 253; *Hughes, Dickson & Co Ltd v Hughes Ltd* [1924] 1 IR 113.

[249.] See *Crowley v O'Sullivan* [1900] 2 IR 478.

[250.] *Jessop v Smith* [1895] 1 IR 508; *Abbott v Ryan* (1901) 1 NIJR 75. See also *Molphy v Coyne* (1919) 53 ILTR 177 at 179 (*per* Powell J). This is often said to be based on the principle of mutuality, see para **[13.47]** *infra*.

[251.] *Lowry v Reid* [1927] NI 142 at 157 (*per* Andrews LJ). See para **[6.51]** *ante*.

[252.] See *O'Hara v Flint* [1979] ILRM 156; *Croft Inns Ltd v Scott* [1982] NI 95. *Cf Jameson v Squire* [1948] IR 153: Wylie, *Irish Landlord and Tenant Law*, Ch 20.

[253.] *Duggan v Allied Irish BS* High Court, unrep, 4 March 1976 (1974/230P) (contract to lend in return for a mortgage). See also *Rogers v Challis* (1859) 27 Beav 175. *Cf Shannonside Holdings (US) v Associated Mortgage Investors* High Court, unrep, 12 March 1980 (1974/298P).

[254.] [1899] 1 IR 142.

[255.] *Ibid*, p 151.

However, in that case the Society agreed to lend money to the owner of an estate for improvements in return for an assignment of the Provisional Order from the Board of Works[256] sanctioning the proposed expenditure and creating a rentcharge on the estate. This assignment was duly made, but, after an initial loan, the Society refused to make further advances. Porter MR held that the estate owner was entitled to specific performance on the ground that the transaction was in substance a purchase by the Society of the rentcharge. He stated:

> "The defendants were to become owners of the rentcharge ... If there is anything plain it is that there was no loan in the ordinary sense ... It is an abuse of language to call that a loan. The rentcharge was not to be security to the defendants for an advance. It was to be their sole and absolute property. This is in substance a purchase of a rentcharge to be created in part by means of the purchase money to be paid for it."[257]

It also seems clear that where a lender has already advanced the loan money to the borrower it can obtain specific performance to make the borrower grant the agreed security.[258]

[13.41] As a general rule, a decree of specific performance will not be granted in respect of a contract where its performance would require constant supervision by the court.[259] Such supervision is impracticable and equity does nothing in vain.[260] This rule inhibited the courts in granting specific performance of contracts to build or repair, though they have not always been consistent on the subject.[261] However, since at least the turn of the century it has been recognised on both sides of the Irish Sea that specific performance of a building contract will be granted in exceptional circumstances, ie, where the particulars of the work to be done are defined sufficiently clearly that the court can see exactly what is to be performed, the plaintiff's interest could not be adequately compensated by damages and the

---

[256.] Made under the Improvement of Land (Ir) Act 1864. See *Irish Land Law* (2nd ed, 1986), para 8.009.

[257.] *Op cit*, p 155. Cf *Hermann v Hodges* (1873) LR 16 EG 18; *Starkey v Barton* [1909] 1 Ch 284.

[258.] *The Regina Coeli* [1976] 5 NIJB 40; cf *Re Lynch Monahan & O'Brien Ltd* High Court, unrep, 14 October 1986 (1984/2936P).

[259.] *Ryan v Mutual Tontine Westminster Chambers Association* [1893] 1 Ch 116; *Joseph v National Magazine Co* [1959] Ch 14. Cf *Beswick v Beswick* [1968] AC 58.

[260.] See *Irish Land Law* (2nd ed, 1986), para 3.067. Hence, the rule that specific performance of a contract for the provision of services will not be granted: see *Gillis v McGhee* (1862) 13 Ir Ch R 48.

[261.] *Rushbrooke v O'Sullivan* [1908] 1 IR 232 at 234 (*per* Meredith MR). See also *Bernard v Meara* (1861) 12 Ir Ch R 389; *Armstrong v Courtney* (1863) 15 Ir Ch R 138; cf *Todd & Co v M & GW Rly* (1881) 9 LR Ir 85.

defendant has by the contract obtained possession of the land on which the work is to be done[262] or, at least, is entitled to possession so that he will be in a position to carry out the work.[263] In *Rushbrooke v O'Sullivan*,[264] the defendant agreed to take a lease of premises from the plaintiff and within twelve months to expend £600 in such repairs and improvements as were mentioned in the schedule to the agreement, viz, to take down, rebuild and repair such portion of the premises as the plaintiff's architect should direct, under his directions and to his satisfaction. In refusing to grant specific performance to the plaintiff, Meredith MR stated:

> "The present case does not fall within the class of exceptional cases. It fails because there are no plans, particulars, or specifications."[265]

But, later, after commenting that he personally was not disposed to extend the class of exceptions further than it had already been extended, he conceded:

> "I agree that the question is a most difficult one; it must often be a matter of the utmost delicacy for the Court to determine how far it will go in granting specific performance of a covenant to build or repair, but in the present case I am clear that the exact nature of the work to be done has not been so specifically defined or ascertained as to justify a decree for specific performance."[266]

As to what is required, his criticisms of the schedule to the agreement in that case are instructive:

> "Where is there anything definite in that? Where is there any plan showing the particulars of the work to be done ... Could anything be less definite than this schedule? If the plaintiff's architect had before the action was brought made out his plans and specifications, and had said: 'There is what you must do: you must take down here; you must rebuild and repair there,' then the contract would have been specifically enforceable]." [267]

---

262. See the leading English case, *Wolverhampton Corp v Emmons* [1901] 1 KB 515 at 525 (*per* Romer LJ). See also *Carpenters Estates v Davies* [1940] Ch 160; *Hounslow LBC v Twickenham Developments Ltd* [1971] Ch 233. See also on building contracts, paras **[11.08]** *et seq*.

263. The *Carpenters Estates* case settled that the plaintiff does not necessarily have to have possession under the contract: see Keane, *Equity and the Law of Trusts in Ireland* (1988), para 16.04; Farrell, *Irish Law of Specific Performance* (1994), para [1.21]; Delany, *Equity and Law of Trusts in Ireland* (1996), p 446.

264. [1908] 1 IR 232.

265. *Ibid*, p 236.

266. *Ibid*, p 237.

267. *Ibid*, p 236.

In *Lift Manufacturers Ltd v Irish Life Assurance Co Ltd*[268] McWilliam J stated that the rule against granting specific performance where oversight of works is required clearly does not apply where there is no need for such oversight.[269] The principle that specific performance may in such exceptional circumstances be granted in respect of leasehold repairing covenants has recently been given statutory recognition in England,[270] in relation to a landlord's covenant.[271] In recent times, the English courts have been prepared to grant specific performance of other covenants commonly found in leases even against the tenant, eg, a "keep open" clause in a shopping centre lease held by the supermarket which was the "anchor" tenant.[272]

4. Breach of Contract

[13.42] Unlike the case of an action at common law for damages, a breach of contract is not a pre-condition to the right to sue for specific performance. Though a breach must probably be anticipated, eg, an indication by the other party that he is not going to complete on the closing date, for the court to be induced to grant the decree, and even then performance will not be required before the contractual date for completion.[273]

B. Defences

[13.43] Over the years the Irish courts have come to recognise a large number of defences to an action for specific performance,[274] and the following are those which have been most frequently raised in respect of

---

[268] [1979] ILRM 277 (injunction granted restraining new nomination of a sub-contractor under a building contract, pending hearing of an action for specific performance of a contract for supply and installation of lifts). See also *Treacy v Dwyer Nolan Developments Ltd* [1979] ILRM 163 (specific performance of building contract granted by consent).

[269] *Ibid*, p 280.

[270] Housing Act 1974, s 125, which contained the sweeping provision (now in s 17 of the Landlord and Tenant Act 1985) that the court may order specific performance "notwithstanding any equitable rule restricting the scope of that remedy, whether on the basis of mutuality or otherwise." See *Joyce v Liverpool Corporation* and *Wynne v Liverpool Corporation* [1995] EGCS 77. See further on the "defences" to specific performance, para **[13.43]** *et seq, infra.*

[271] Thus confirming *Jeune v Queen's Cross Properties Ltd* [1974] Ch 97. *Cf Todd & Co v M & GW Rly* (1881) 9 LR Ir 85. See also *Francis v Cowliffe Ltd* (1976) 33 P & CR 368; *Hammond v Allen* [1993] 08 EG 122.

[272] *Co-operative Insurance Society Ltd v Argyll Stores (Holdings) Ltd* [1996] 09 EG 128. *Cf Retail Parks Investments Ltd v Royal Bank of Scotland plc* London Times 18 July 1995 (injunction to stop bank closing its branch office in shopping centre).

[273] See the discussion in the leading English case on this subject, *Marks v Lilley* [1959] 1 WLR 749. See also *Hasham v Zenab* [1960] AC 316; *Manchester Diocesan Council for Education v Commercial and General Investments Ltd* [1970] 1 WLR 241.

[274] See Farrell, *Irish Law of Specific Performance* (1994), Ch 9.

actions concerning contracts for the sale or lease of land. But first it should be emphasised that many of these defences are but illustrations of more general principles that govern equity's approach to all its special remedies, eg, the maxim - "he who comes into equity, must come with clean hands."[275] Thus, in *O'Rourke v Percival*,[276] Lord Manners LC summarised equity's approach in this way:

> "I take it to be an established Principle of this Court, not to decree specific Execution of an Agreement, unless it appears that the Party, who calls for this peculiar Aid of the Court, has acted, not only fairly, but in a Manner clear of all Suspicion. If there be a reasonable Doubt upon the Transaction, the Court will leave the Party to his legal Remedy, for the Non-Performance of the Contract."[277]

Secondly, one should take heed of the warning issued by Black LJ in *Conlon v Murray*[278]:

> "It was argued on behalf of the plaintiff that cases in which equity refuses the remedy of specific performance fall within one or other of certain defined categories. I cannot accept this view. Certainly equity acts on certain broad and ascertained principles but it has always refused to be forced into rigid categories."[279]

Thirdly, since it is the "normal" rule to grant specific performance of a contract for the sale of land, the onus is on the defendant to establish the ground or grounds upon which that relief should be refused.[280]

1. Lack of Formalities

[13.44] It is clear that as a general rule specific performance will not be decreed of a contract for the sale or lease of land which is not fully binding on the parties because it lacks some formality,[281] eg, evidence in writing as required by s 2 of the Statute of Frauds (Ireland) 1695.[282] However, it is important to remember that equity may still grant specific performance of

---

[275.] See Wylie, *Irish Land Law* (2nd ed, 1986), para 3.058. See also *Harnett v Yielding* (1805) 2 Sch & Lef 549 at 554 (*per* Lord Redesdale).

[276.] (1811) 2 Ba & B 58.

[277.] *Ibid*, p 62. And see *O'Neill v Ryan (No 3)* [1992] 1 IR 166 at 196 (*per* Finlay CJ).

[278.] [1958] NI 17.

[279.] *Ibid*, p 26.

[280.] *McCrystal v O'Kane* [1986] NI 123 at 132 (*per* Murray J).

[281.] *A fortiori* if there is no contract because, eg, it is still "subject to contract" (see *Boyle v Lee* [1992] 1 IR 555; see also *Dorene Ltd v Suedes (Ireland) Ltd* [1981] IR 312; *Sun Fat Chan v Osseous Ltd* [1992] 1 IR 425) or unsupported by consideration (see *McCoubray v Thompson* (1868) IR 2 CL 226; *Clitheroe v Simpson* (1879) 4 LR Ir 59). *Cf* an incomplete gift: see *Jopling-Pursar v Jackman* Supreme Court, unrep, 31 March 1995 (49/95).

[282.] See Ch 6, *ante*.

such a contract, provided there has been sufficient part performance of the contract by the plaintiff.[283]

2. Uncertainty or Incompleteness

[13.45] Quite apart from a lack of formalities, the court may refuse specific performance because the alleged contract lacks certainty, whether as to the intention of the parties to be bound by it[284] or as to the precise terms of what the parties have agreed.[285] Thus, in *Lord Ormond v Anderson*,[286] Lord Manners LC stated:

> "The jurisdiction of this court is to compel specific performance of a contract between parties, but the contract must be complete; the court cannot supply any term that had not been agreed upon; for that would be to make, and not to execute an agreement, a jurisdiction which this court can never assume ... when a party comes into this court for the specific execution of an agreement, he must accurately state the terms of the agreement he seeks to have executed, and prove the case he has stated on the record, otherwise the court will not assist him."[287]

An obvious example is where the parties have failed to state clearly enough the price for which the property is to be bought[288] or have specified an ineffective method of ascertaining it.[289]

[13.46] Sometimes the defence of uncertainty is linked with the defence of incompleteness, ie, the evidence of the contract does not contain all the essential terms of the parties' agreement.[290] We discussed this subject in an earlier chapter in connection with the requirements of the memorandum or note under s 2 of the Statute of Frauds (Ireland) 1695.[291]

3. Lack of Mutuality

[13.47] This is a more controversial defence.[292] The traditional view is that if a party to the contract cannot enforce it for some reason, eg lack of capacity,

---

[283.] See the discussion of this doctrine at para **[6.48]** *et seq, ante*.

[284.] *Harnett v Yielding* (1805) 2 Sch & Lef 549 at 554 (*per* Lord Redesdale).

[285.] *McLoughlin v Alexander* (1910) 44 ILTR 253; *Williams v Kenneally* (1912) 46 ILTR 292.

[286.] (1813) 2 Ba & B 363. See also *Clinan v Cooke* (1802) 1 Sch & Lef 22 at 33 and *Lindsay v Lynch* (1804) 2 Sch & Lef 1 at 8 (*per* Lord Redesdale).

[287.] *Ibid*, p 369. See also the same judge in *Pentland v Stokes* (1812) 2 Ba & B 68 at 73; *Lowe v Swift* (1814) 2 Ba & B 529 at 535; *Savage v Carroll* (1815) 2 Ba & B 444 at 451.

[288.] *Lonergan v McCartney* [1983] NI 129.

[289.] *Carr v Phelan* [1976-7] ILRM 149.

[290.] See the discussion by the Supreme Court in *Boyle v Lee* [1992] 1 IR 555.

[291.] See para **[6.17]** *et seq, ante*.

[292.] See Ames, 'Mutuality in Specific Performance' (1903) 3 Col L Rev 1. See also Farrell, *Irish Law of Specific Performance* (1994) paras [9.70-3].

the other party cannot enforce it against him.[293] Yet the courts have recognised so many exceptions to the rule that it is doubtful whether much of it survives.[294] Thus, it is well settled that a memorandum of a contract for the sale of land can be enforced against the party who has signed it, though it could not be enforced by him against the plaintiff because he has not signed it[295] - the Statute of Frauds requires signing by the defendant or his agent only.[296] In *Fennelly v Anderson*,[297] Brady LC said:

> "That the objection of want of mutuality of remedy to enforce the contract does not in all cases prevail, is manifested by cases decided under the Statute of Frauds, where it has been held that the plaintiff may obtain a decree of specific performance of a contract signed by the defendant but not signed by the plaintiff. The reason of this doctrine is, that the plaintiff by filing his bill submits to perform his part of the contract; and of the plaintiff's non-signature the other party is not allowed to avail himself, because although he could not have compelled the plaintiff to complete the contract, yet he (the defendant) has by signing, thought proper to run the chance of the plaintiff performing his part, which, if he do not rely upon the Statute of Frauds, the Court will decree him to perform. True it may be, however, that these decisions rest upon the particular language of that Statute ..."[298]

Normally the question of mutuality must be considered at the time when the contract was made, so that, if at that stage the vendor could not show a good title, he should not be granted specific performance, nor should it be granted against him,[299] yet it has been held that the vendor may still obtain specific performance if he is in a position to show good title by the time of the hearing of the action.[300] Similarly, normally an infant cannot obtain specific performance because a contract cannot be enforced against him so long as he

---

[293.] See *Lawrenson v Butler* (1802) 1 Sch & Lef 13 at 18 (*per* Lord Redesdale). See also *Murphy v Harrington* [1927] IR 339 at 344 (*per* Meredith J).

[294.] See also the attitude of the English legislature as exhibited by s 125 of the Housing Act 1974 (now s 17 of the Landlord and Tenant Act 1985), see fn 270 para **[13.41]** *supra*. See also *O'Regan v White* [1919] 2 IR 339 at 395 (*per* O'Connor LJ).

[295.] *Lord Ormond v Anderson* (1813) 2 Ba & B 363 at 370 (*per* Lord Manners LC). *Cf Doherty v Waterford and Limerick Rly Co* (1850) 13 Ir Eq R 538 at 543 (*per* Brady LC). See also the leading English case, *Flight v Bolland* (1828) 4 Russ 298 at 301 (*per* Leach MR): "by [the] act of filing the bill, [the plaintiff] has made the remedy mutual."

[296.] See para **[6.32]** *ante*.

[297.] (1851) 1 Ir Ch R 706.

[298.] *Ibid*, p 711.

[299.] *Murphy v Harrington* [1927] IR 339 at 344 (*per* Meredith J).

[300.] *Hoggart v Scott* (1830) 1 Russ & M 293; *Eastern Counties Rly v Hawkes* (1855) 5 HLC 331; *Price v Strange* [1977] 3 All ER 371.

is under age,[301] yet it has been held that an infant may obtain specific performance provided he commences his action after attaining his majority,[302] even though presumably he is entitled to the defence for a "reasonable time" thereafter.[303]

4. Hardship or Lack of Fairness

[13.48] This category, which may be said to consist of a number of sub-categories, covers a wide range of conduct or circumstances which may justify the court in refusing specific performance. When the courts speak of a want of fairness they tend to have in view the plaintiff's conduct, whereas hardship is something which, looking at the effect of an order against the defendant, justifies refusal to make it.[304] Frequently the acts or circumstances in question are so serious that not only do they form a defence to an action for specific performance, but they would found a successful counterclaim by the defendant for rescission of the contract.[305] This is the case where the acts involve fraud,[306] duress,[307] undue influence[308] or mistake,[309] However, it is also settled that there may be acts or circumstances which, though not sufficient to found a claim for rescission, may nevertheless be a sufficient defence to an action for specific performance. As Black LJ said in *Conlon v Murray*[310]:

> "And it is well established that there is a class of cases in which a contract may be such and entered into in such conditions that the court will not order it to be rescinded but, at the same time, looking to the substantial justice of the case, will not order it to be specifically performed."[311]

[301.] Wylie, *Irish Land Law* (2nd ed, 1986), paras 25.06. See also *Flight v Bolland* (1828) 4 Russ 298.

[302.] *Clayton v Ashdown* (1714) 2 Eq Ca Abr 516.

[303.] See *Irish Land Law* (2nd ed, 1986), para 25.06.

[304.] See the discussion by McCarthy J in *Roberts v O'Neill* [1983] IR 47 at 55-57. See also *McCrystal v O'Kane* [1986] NI 123.

[305.] See further, paras **[13.67-8]** *infra*.

[306.] *Carbin v Somerville* [1933] IR 276; *Maguire v Conway* [1950] IR 44. See para **[13.64]** *infra*.

[307.] *Blackwood v Gregg* (1831) Hayes 277.

[308.] *Conlon v Murray* [1958] NI 17 at 20 (*per* Black LJ); *Buckley v Irwin* [1960] NI 98; *McCrystal v O'Kane* [1986] NI 123. See also *Doherty v Gallagher* High Court, unrep, 9 June 1975 (1973/2830P). And see para **[13.64]** *infra*.

[309.] *Gun v McCarthy* (1883) 13 LR Ir 304; *Monaghan CC v Vaughan* [1948] IR 306; *JL Smallman Ltd v O'Moore* [1959] IR 220; *National Bank Ltd v O'Connor* (1969) 103 ILTR 73. See also *Sibel v Kent* [1976-7] ILRM 127. And see para **[13.66]** *infra*.

[310.] [1958] NI 17.

[311.] *Ibid*, p 25. See also *Buckley v Irwin* [1960] NI 98 at 104 (*per* McVeigh J).

Thus, while inadequacy of consideration is not usually sufficient hardship to justify a refusal of specific performance,[312] in *Buckley v Irwin*[313] McVeigh J felt it was, as he was faced with an "unethical bargain" which infringed "the principles of fairness," where it was a "snap bargain at a considerable undervalue, even if it was not a gross undervalue."[314] Similarly, in an appropriate case, the court may refuse to grant specific performance against a party who was drunk when he entered into it, though this would seem to go also to the question of intention to create legal relations.[315]

[13.49] The courts are careful, in recognising the defence of hardship, that they do not allow a party to escape from a contract which has not turned out as favourable as he originally expected.[316] Thus, in *Lavan v Walsh*,[317] Budd J explained:

> "The Court, it is well established, will not enforce the specific performance of a contract the result of which would be to impose great hardship on either of the parties to it. It is conceded, however, that the question of hardship of a contract is generally to be judged at the time it is entered into. Changes of circumstances taking place later, making the contract less beneficial to one party, are immaterial as a rule unless brought about by the action of the other party."[318]

In *Roberts v O'Neill*,[319] McCarthy J, giving the judgment of the Supreme Court, stated:

> "Hardship is permitted to defeat specific performance where an existing hardship was not known at the relevant time, being the date of the contract. While recognising that there may be cases in which hardship arising after the date of the contract is such that to decree specific performance would result in great injury, there must be few such cases and, in my view, they should not include ordinarily cases of hardship resulting from inflation alone. To permit, as an ordinary rule, a defence of subsequent hardship, would be to add a further hazard to the already trouble-strewn area of the law of contracts for the sale of land."[320]

---

[312] See *Moore v Crofton* (1946) 9 Ir Eq R 344 at 348 (*per* Sugden LC) *Cf* "improvident" settlements see para **[21.35]** *post*.

[313] [1960] NI 98.

[314] *Ibid*, p 104. In the end he also concluded that there was sufficient fraud to justify rescission *ibid*, p 105.

[315] See *White v McCooey* [1976-7] ILRM 72; *McCrystal v O'Kane* [1986] NI 123 (plea of drunkenness not sustained) See also *Nagle v Baylor* (1842) 3 Dr &War 60.

[316] See *Smyth v Lynn* [1951] NI 69 at 78 (*per* Curran J).

[317] [1964] IR 87.

[318] *Ibid*, p 101. See also at p 105.

[319] [1983] IR 47.

[320] *Ibid*, p 56.

In England, hardship arising after the contract has succeeded as a defence to specific performance in a case where the defendant vendor had one child only and appeared to be in good health at the date of the contract, but when the purchaser sought specific performance she had two more children and, as a result of a diagnosis of bone cancer, had had her leg amputated.[321] Goulding J heard evidence that if she were forced to go through with the sale, she would have to move from the neighbourhood and would lose the daily assistance of friends and relations. In his view the purchaser should be left to his remedy in damages for breach of contract. In this sort of case the court must balance the hardship to the defendant against the hardship to the plaintiff in not getting specific performance.[322] One common example of the hardship defence succeeding is where the court refuses specific performance on the principle that it is unwilling to force a bad title on the purchaser or to force the purchaser[323] "to buy a law suit."[324] It is also settled that specific performance will be refused where to order it would involve hardship on third parties.[325]

5. Laches

[13.50] The doctrine of laches applies to specific performance as it applies to other equitable remedies - "delay defeats equity."[326] Thus, in *Moore v Blake*[327] Manners LC stated:

> "A Bill of this Description (that is, for the specific Performance of an Agreement) is an Application to the Discretion, or rather to the extraordinary Jurisdiction of this Court, which I apprehend cannot be exercised in Favour of Persons, who have so long slept on their rights, and acquiesced in a Title and Possession adverse to their claim. Due Diligence is necessary to call this Court into Activity, and where it does not exist, a Court of Equity will not lend its Assistance, it always discountenances Laches and Neglect."[328]

[321.] *Patel v Ali* [1984] 1 All ER 978. The delay in completion was the fault of neither party.

[322.] *O'Neill v Ryan (No 3)* [1992] 1 IR 166 at 192 (*per* Finlay CJ).

[323.] See further, para **[13.52]** *infra*.

[324.] *Re Nichols and Van Joel's Contract* [1910] 1 Ch 43 at 46 (*per* Cozens-Hardy MR). See also *Wroth v Tyler* [1974] Ch 30.

[325.] *Meara v Meara* (1858) 8 Ir Ch R 37 at 40 (*per* Brady LC). And see *Conlon v Murray* [1958] NI 17 at 25-6 (*per* Black LJ); *Lavan v Walsh* [1964] IR 87 at 102-5 (*per* Budd J). See also *Thomas v Dering* (1837) 1 Keen 729; *Willmott v Barber* (1880) 15 Ch D 96.

[326.] See *Irish Land Law* (2nd ed, 1986), para 3.066, wherein the related concept of "acquiescence' is discussed.

[327.] (1808) 1 Ba & B 62. See also *Murphy v A-G* [1982] IR 241; *Van Nierop v Commissioners of Public Works* [1980] 2 IR 189.

[328.] *Ibid*, p 69. See also *Clarke v Moore* (1844) 7 Ir Eq R 515 at 517 (*per* Sugden LC).

Clearly it is a matter for the court in each case as to whether the plaintiff has "slept too long" on his right to apply for specific performance. Thus, in *Haire-Foster v McIntee*,[329] Monroe J stated:

> "I know of no cases in which a plaintiff has ever succeeded in getting a decree for specific performance of an agreement six years and a-half after it is alleged to have been entered into, four years after it has been repudiated in open Court, and nearly two years after the defendant had himself instituted proceedings entirely inconsistent with the existence of such a contract."[330]

In *Lydon v Lydon*,[331] a delay in filing a bill for specific performance of seven months after being given notice disputing the validity of the agreement was held to disentitle the plaintiff to relief. It must also be emphasised that for laches to succeed as a defence the circumstances must be such as to render it inequitable to grant specific performance.[332]

6. Misdescription

[13.51] We discussed the remedies for misdescription under the general law, and as likely to be varied by the conditions of sale, in an earlier chapter[333] and what was said there need not be repeated here.[334] Suffice it to say that the effect of misdescription varies according to whether it is substantial or not, and, of course, according to the terms of the contract for sale.[335] Thus, depending on these factors, the purchaser may be able in certain cases to elect to accede to specific performance in favour of the vendor, but subject to compensation or an abatement of the purchase price to take account of the misdescription, as an alternative to claiming rescission.[336] Whereas, in other cases, there may be no alternative and he will be forced to accede to specific performance, but may still claim compensation or an abatement of the purchase price.[337]

---

[329] (1889) 23 LR Ir 529. See also *Guardian Builders v Kelly* [1981] ILRM 127.

[330] *Ibid*, p 535. See also *Moore v Blake* (1808) 1 Ba & B 62 (nineteen years); *Re Browne's Estate* [1913] 1 IR 165 (over thirty years).

[331] (1874) 8 ILTR 85. *Cf Martin v Cotter* (1846) 9 Ir Eq R 351 (also seven months). *Cf Giffard v Hort* (1804) 1 Sch & Lef 386; *Murphy v Harrington* [1927] IR 339.

[332] *Burke v Lynch* (1814) 2 Ba & B 426; *JH v WJH* High Court, unrep, 20 December 1979 (1977/5831P); *Horgan v Deasy* [1979] ILRM 71.

[333] Para **[9.29]** *et seq, ante*.

[334] See also Farrell, *Irish Law of Specific Performance* (1994), para [9.85] *et seq*.

[335] See para **[9.44]** *et seq*.

[336] See para **[9.32]** *ante*.

[337] See para **[9.34]** *ante*. See also paras **[9.44]** *et seq, ante*.

7. Lack of Title

[13.52] One of the primary objects of a decree of specific performance of a contract for the sale of land is that the purchaser should become the owner of the land to the extent agreed in the contract. Clearly this will not be the result if the vendor has a bad title and so is unable to transfer the title he undertook to transfer by his agreement with the purchaser.[338] So it is an oft-quoted principle that the court will not force a bad title on the purchaser by granting a decree of specific performance to the vendor.[339] However, there are bad titles and bad titles and, where the title is merely doubtful, and the court can easily resolve the doubt, eg, by determining a question of law dependent upon the construction of title documents, the court may do so and then decree specific performance if the result favours the purchaser.[340] Otherwise, the court will not force the purchaser, in effect, "to buy a law suit."[341]

[13.53] However, as in the case of a misdescription,[342] the purchaser may elect to take whatever title the vendor has to give,[343] subject, if he wishes, to compensation or an abatement of the purchase price.[344] Thus, in *Leslie v Crommelin*,[345] where it turned out that the intended lessor could not grant as substantial a lease as he had contracted to grant, Chatterton V-C stated:

> "It is now settled that if the landlord, from the limited extent of his estate or power, is unable to give in point of duration a lease for the whole interest which he agreed to give, then, if the intended lessee is willing to take - for it cannot be forced upon him - the interest which the landlord can give, the latter must grant a lease to the full extent which his estate or power

---

338. See further on deduction of title, Ch 14 *post*.

339. *Larkin v Lord Rosse* (1846) 10 Ir Eq R 70 at 74 (*per* Smith MR); *Boyd v Dickson* (1876) IR 10 Eq 239 at 255-6 (*per* Sullivan MR); *Re McDermott and Kellett's Contract* (1904) 4 NIJR 89 at 90 (*per* Barton J); *Molphy v Coyne* (1919) 53 ILTR 177 at 179 (*per* Powell J). Nor will the court decree specific performance against the vendor, unless the purchaser is willing to take such title as the vendor can give, see *Harnett v Yielding* (1805) 1 Sch & Lef 559 at 554 (*per* Lord Redesdale). See also *Leslie v Crommelin* (1867) IR 2 Eq 134 at 140 (*per* Chatterton V-C), para **[13.53]** *infra*.

340. *Wilson v Thomas* [1958] 1 WLR 422. *Cf* where the doubt involves third party interests, see *Poole v Coates* (1842) 2 Dr & War 493 at 496-7 (*per* Sugden LC), or questions of fact or mixed law and fact, see *Re Handman and Wilcox's Contract* [1902] 1 Ch 599; *Selkirk v Romar Investments Ltd* [1963] 1 WLR 1415. See also para **[13.28]** *supra*.

341. *Re Nichols and Van Joel's Contract* [1910] 1 Ch 43 at 46 (*per* Cozens-Hardy MR). See also *Re Hogan and Marnell's Contract* [1919] 1 IR 422.

342. See para **[13.51]** *supra*.

343. *Harnett v Yielding* (1805) 1 Sch & Lef 549 at 554 (*per* Lord Redesdale); *Leitch v Simpson* (1871) IR 5 Eq 613 at 615 (*per* Chatterton V-C). See also *Hughes, Dickson & Co Ltd v Hughes Ltd* [1924] 1 IR 113.

344. *Molphy v Coyne* (1919) 53 ILTR 177 at 179 (*per* Powell J). See also *O'Brien v Kearney* [1995] 2 ILRM 232.

345. (1867) IR 2 Eq 134.

authorises, and compensation will be made by the Court to the lessee for any loss that he may have sustained by reason of the agreement not being carried to its full extent."³⁴⁶

Furthermore, the purchaser may, by his words or actions, be taken to have waived all objection to the vendor's title and so cannot raise any defence to an action for specific performance based on lack of title.³⁴⁷ He may also be prohibited by the conditions of sale from raising any requisitions or objections to the vendor's title, but it is well recognised that the courts will scrutinise such conditions carefully.³⁴⁸ Generally speaking they will not allow vendors to use them in a deliberate attempt to conceal defects in title and to force a bad title on the purchaser.³⁴⁹ To grant equitable relief to the vendor in such circumstances would be contrary to the basic principles of equity³⁵⁰ and so the parties will be left to their remedies at law.³⁵¹

C. Damages

[13.54] Prior to the Judicature (Ireland) Act 1877, damages could be awarded generally only in the common law courts, but this rule was amended by s 2 of the Chancery Amendment Act 1858³⁵² (usually known as Lord Cairns' Act³⁵³) which gave the Court of Chancery a discretionary power to award damages *either* in addition to *or* in substitution for specific performance, to be assessed in such a manner as the court directs. It is important to realise that this jurisdiction, which has been, of course, generally available to all the superior courts since the Judicature (Ireland) Act 1877,³⁵⁴ may be invoked only in cases where the court would have jurisdiction to award specific performance, so that it does not apply where the contract in question is of such a type that it is not specifically enforceable.³⁵⁵ But it may still be invoked even though in the particular case

---

³⁴⁶· *Ibid*, p 140.

³⁴⁷· See *Boyd v Dickson* (1876) IR 10 Eq 239 at 253 (*per* Sullivan MR). See also *Healy v Healy* High Court, unrep, 3 December 1973 (1973/2445P).

³⁴⁸· See further on this subject, para **[15.25]** *post*.

³⁴⁹· *Boyd v Dickson* (1876) IR 10 Eq 239 at 255-6 (*per* Sullivan MR); *Molphy v Coyne* (1919) 53 ILTR 177 at 184 (*per* Powell J). See also paras **[15.25-6]** *post*.

³⁵⁰· See para **[13.43]** *supra*.

³⁵¹· The purchaser may recover his deposit, but damages may be restricted, see para **[13.79]** *infra*.

³⁵²· See Jolowicz (1975) CLJ 224. Section 2 of the 1858 Act remains in force in Ireland.

³⁵³· See Heuston, "Hugh McCalmont Cairns" (1975) 26 NILQ 269 espec at 272-4.

³⁵⁴· See *Duggan v Allied Irish BS* High Court, unrep, 4 March 1976 (1974/230P). See also *Irish Land Law* (2nd ed, 1986), paras 3.034-7.

³⁵⁵· *Lavery v Purcell* (1888) 39 Ch D 508. See also *Leeds Industrial Co-operative Society Ltd v Stack* [1924] AC 851. And see paras **[6.51]** *ante* and **[13.40-41]** *supra*. Of course, all the courts may now award damages at *common law*, but this is an entirely separate jurisdiction and the measure of damages may not he the same, see *infra* and para **[13.75]** *infra*.

specific performance is refused on some discretionary ground.[356] Furthermore, this jurisdiction may be invoked in cases where damages could not be awarded at common law, eg, where the contract lacks some legal formality but is nevertheless enforceable in equity.[357] It has also been held in recent English cases that the measure of damages under Lord Cairns' Act is different from the traditional view.[358] At common law, damages are assessed as at the date of the breach of contract,[359] but in *Wroth v Tyler*,[360] where Megarry J decided to refuse specific performance but to grant damages in lieu, the learned Judge held that, in order to be a true substitute for specific performance, the damages ought to put the plaintiffs in as good a position as if the contract had been performed. In that case the contract price for the house in question was £6,000 and at the date of breach of contract (by the vendor's non-completion) it was worth £7,500, but by the date of the judgment this had risen to £11,500. So, instead of fixing damages at £1,500 (the common law measure), Megarry J fixed damages at £5,500, ie, measured at the date of judgment.[361] This same principle was adopted by Goff J in fixing damages in addition to specific performance under Lord Cairns' Act.[362] The Irish courts have similarly been quite prepared to assess damages by taking the value of the property at the date of judgment.[363] This may be a convenient way round the restrictions on damages at common law.[364]

---

[356] See *Murphy v Harrington* [1927] IR 339 at 344 (*per* Meredith J). See also *Wroth v Tyler* [1974] Ch 30.

[357] Eg, under the doctrine of part performance, see para **[13.44]** *supra*. It also seems that damages may be claimed under Lord Cairns' Act where a party refuses to comply with the specific performance order: see *Johnson v Agnew* [1980] AC 367, approved by Hutton J in *Croft Inns Ltd v Scott* [1982] NI 95 and McWilliam J in *Vandeleur v Dargan* [1981] ILRM 75. See also para **[13.04]** *supra*.

[358] See *Fry on Specific Performance* (6th ed), p 602.

[359] See para **[13.78]** *infra*. Note, however, that the House of Lords held in *Johnson v Agnew* [1980] AC 367 that the common law rule in not inflexible, so that the court has a discretion to chose the most appropriate date for assessment to ensure that justice is done to the party seeking damages.

[360] [1974] Ch 30. See also *Brownlee v Duggan* [1976] 5 NIJB 11; *O'Connor v McCarthy* [1982] IR 161. See Lawson, 'Damages - An Appraisal of *Wroth v Tyler*' (1975) 125 New LJ 300.

[361] The logical corollary is, of course, that the damages under Lord Cairns' Act would be less than at common law if the property falls in value by the date of judgment! Damages under the Act may also cover future loss: see *Jaggard v Sawyer* [1995] 13 EG 132.

[362] *Grant v Dawkins* [1973] 1 WLR 1406.

[363] See *Roberts v O'Neill* [1983] IR 47 at 50 (*per* McWilliam J) (on appeal, the Supreme Court held specific performance should be granted: *ibid*, p 57, *per* McCarthy J); *O'Connor v McCarthy* [1982] ILRM 201 T 202-3 (*per* Costello J). See also *Murphy v Quality Homes* High Court, unrep, 22 June 1976 (1975/4344P).

[364] Ie, the rule in *Bain v Fothergill*, see para **[13.79]** *infra*.

D. Enforcement of the Order

[13.55] Enforcement of an order for specific performance varies according to whether it is obtained by the vendor or purchaser,[365] apart from the question of contempt of court which applies in either case. Where the vendor has obtained an order against a purchaser who refuses to comply, he may apply to the court to dissolve the order for specific performance and for an order of rescission,[366] seeking to forfeit the deposit and, on a resale of the property, recover damages to meet any loss.[367]

[13.56] Where the purchaser obtains an order against a vendor who refuses to comply with it, he may apply to the court for an order permitting him to lodge the purchase money in court and authorising a third person to execute the necessary conveyance in the name and on behalf of the vendor.[368] Alternatively he may apply for a vesting order from the court.[369]

V. RESCISSION

[13.57] The second main remedy available to the parties is rescission, but the greatest care must be exercised over this concept, for it is commonly used in a bewildering variety of meanings by judges and commentators alike.[370] In its strict sense, rescission involves restoring the parties to their original pre-contractual position, so that their rights are largely based on the assumption that they never made a contract. Thus, as we shall see, there can in general be no question of an action for damages for breach of contract, because after such rescission there is *ex hypothesi* no contract to sue on. This may be described as rescission *ab initio*, and it is vital to note that a party seeking this remedy must apply to the court for an appropriate order of rescission.[371] We examine the nature of this remedy in more detail in a

---

[365.] See Farrell, *Irish Law of Specific Performance* (1994), para [8.25] *et seq.*

[366.] *Abbott v Ryan* (1901) 1 NIJR 75. See also *Hall v Burnell* [1911] 2 Ch 551. Note that he must establish a good reason for replacing the order for specific performance, see the strictures issued in *Bourke v Grimes* (1929) 63 ILTR 53 at 55 (*per* Kennedy CJ) and 56 (*per* FitzGibbon J).

[367.] See *Solomon v Estates Management and Development Agency Ltd* High Court, unrep 14 July 1980 (1975/1703P); *Vandeleur v Dargan* [1981] ILRM 75; See also **[13.03]** *supra*. *Taylor v Smyth* [1990] ILRM 377.

[368.] Under the Trustee Act 1893, s 33. See *Moorhead v Kirkwood* [1919] 1 IR 225.

[369.] 1893 Act, s 31. See *Re Ruthven's Trusts* [1906] 1 IR 236.

[370.] See the discussion in *Maconchy v Clayton* [1898] 1 IR 291, espec at 310 (*per* Holmes LJ). See also *Mersey Steel and Iron Co v Naylor Benzon & Co* (1882) 9 QBD 648 at 671 (*per* Bowen LJ). Albery, 'Mr Cyprian Williams 'Great Heresy' (1975) 91 LQR 337. And see para **[13.04]** *supra*.

[371.] See *Northern Bank Finance Corporation Ltd v Charlton* [1979] IR 149.

moment. It must be distinguished from what is often confusingly referred to as "rescission for breach"[372] which really means that the innocent party elects to treat himself as discharged from the contract because of the breach of contract by the other party. But, having done that, the innocent party still has a further election to make, namely, as to what precise remedies he seeks. One may be rescission in the strict sense,[373] but he may instead prefer to treat himself as discharged from further performance and to sue for damages for breach of contract on the basis that the contract has substituted up to that point.[374] In the following paragraphs we are confining our attention to rescission in the strict sense.

A. General principles

1. Common Law and Equity

[13.58] Even at common law it was accepted that a contract could be rescinded by the innocent party on certain grounds, eg, fraud or for a breach of contract going to the root of the transaction.[375] The remedy could be exercised unilaterally without recourse to the court,[376] but the restriction existed that the common law courts insisted that rescission could only apply provided the parties could revert strictly to the *status quo* which existed before the contract.[377] One of the major contributions of the courts of equity was that they were not so strict in their requirement of restoration to the *status quo*.[378] Another was that, while recognising the same grounds for

---

[372.] Or "repudiation," but even this word can be used in different senses. Thus, to take the example given in para **[13.03]** *supra*, the party who decides to call the sale off may he said to "repudiate" the contract (ie, break it by refusing to carry out his obligations) and the other party may be said to "repudiate" (or "rescind") the contract (ie, treat himself as discharged from it) because of the first party's breach of contract (or "repudiation"). See also *Clibborn v Horan* [1921] 1 IR 93 at 100 (*per* O'Connor MR); Bate, 'Rescission' (1955) 19 Conv 116.

[373.] But only if grounds exist justifying the court ordering rescission in the strict sense: see *infra*. See also *Dickie v White* (1901) 1 NIJR 128; *McGuire v Conwell* (1932) 66 ILTR 213.

[374.] See *Mills v Healy* [1937] IR 437; *Industrial Yarns Ltd v Greene* [1984] ILRM 15; *House of Spring Gardens Ltd v Point Blank Ltd* [1984] IR 611; *Taylor v Smith* [1991] 1 IR 142. The remedy of damages is discussed in detail later, see para **[13.75]** *et seq, infra*.

[375.] *Simmons v Heseltine* (1858) 5 CBNS 554; *Phillips v Caldcleugh* (1868) LR 4 QB 159.

[376.] See the discussion by Buckley J in *Re Stone and Saville's Contract* [1962] 2 All ER 114 at 121 (*aff'd* [1963] 1 WLR 163).

[377.] *Hogan v Healy* (1876) IR 11 CL 119. See also *Hunt v Silk* (1804) 5 East 447; *Blackburn v Smith* (1848) 2 Exch 783.

[378.] See *Carbin v Somerville* [1933] IR 276 at 289 (*per* FitzGibbon J), quoted at para **[5.23]** *ante*. See also *Erlanger v New Sombrero Phosphate Co* (1878) 3 App Cas 1218 at 1278 (*per* Lord Blackburn) followed by the Supreme Court in *Northern Bank Finance Corporation Ltd v Charlton* [1979] IR 149; *cf* the discussion by the English Court of Appeal in *Cheese v Thomas* [1994] 1 All ER 35. And see para **[13.59]** *infra*.

rescission as the common law courts,[379] equity allowed rescission on grounds not recognised at common law, eg, innocent misrepresentation.[380] However, such equitable relief could, of course, only be obtained on application to the court and this remains the case today.

2. Restitutio in Integrum

[13.59] It is of the essence of the remedy of rescission that the innocent party is entitled to *restitutio in integrum*, ie, to be restored to his position before the contract was entered into, subject to the corollary that he must return to the other party any property already received under the contract. The consequences of the principle for the two parties may be summarised as follows.

(i) Vendor

[13.60] Where the vendor rescinds, he is entitled to recover possession of the land, if the purchaser has been in possession,[381] and to an account from the purchaser for any rents and profits actually received by him.[382] The vendor must account for any payments received from the purchaser,[383] but not the deposit, which he is still entitled to forfeit, because it is security or a guarantee for the purchaser's performance of the contract as well as part payment of the purchase price under the contract.[384] But he can only forfeit the actual deposit paid; since rescission in the strict sense destroys the contract *ab initio*, he cannot sue on the contract to recover the balance of the deposit which should have been paid.[385]

[13.61] Since rescission restores the vendor to his pre-contractual position as owner of the property, he may resell it regardless of any contractual provision to this effect.[386] But if he makes a loss on such a resale he cannot, in the absence of some special contractual provision, sue to recover this as

---

[379.] Eg, a breach going to the root of the contract, see *Linehan v Cotter* (1844) 7 Ir Eq R 176 at 179 (*per* Blackburne MR). See also *Boothman v Brown* (1900) 1 NIJR 41 at 41-2 (*per* Porter MR).

[380.] See *Re Otway's Estate* (1862) 13 Ir Ch R 222 at 235 (*per* Brady LC). See also para **[5.26]** *ante*.

[381.] See para **[12.32]** *ante*.

[382.] *Clarke v Wallis* (1966) 35 Beav 460. But the vendor cannot charge an occupation rent, *Barber v Wolfe* [1945] Ch 187.

[383.] *Mayson v Clonet* [1924] AC 980.

[384.] *Hall v Burnell* [1911] 2 Ch 551, followed in *McGuire v Conwell* (1932) 66 ILTR 213. See also paras **[13.31-32]** *ante*.

[385.] *Lowe v Hope* [1970] Ch 94. Note that in so far as this case suggest that this rule applies also to rescission in the sense of treating oneself discharged from further performance of the contract, it is not good law: see paras **[13.31]** and **[13.57]** *supra*.

[386.] *Howe v Smith* (1884) 27 Ch D 89.

damages for breach of contract, because once again the effect of rescission in the strict sense is to destroy the contract and removes the basis for such a claim.[387] The most he is entitled to under the general law is an indemnity for his costs in deducing title.[388] However, as we saw earlier, the contract for sale may contain a special provision conferring a right of resale which includes the right to recover any deficiency, plus the costs and expenses of the resale, from the purchaser.[389] Under condition 41 of the Law Society's *General Conditions of Sale (1995 Edition)* the vendor has this right in any case where the purchaser fails "in any material respect" to comply with the conditions. This will sometimes enable the vendor to pursue a more satisfactory remedy than seeking a court order for rescission in the strict sense.

(ii) Purchaser

[13.62] Where the purchaser rescinds the contract, he is entitled to recover his deposit, plus any legal expenses incurred in investigating the title to the property.[390] But he will have to account for any rents and profits he may have received from the land.[391] Like the vendor, he cannot sue for damages for breach of contract if he seeks rescission in the strict sense,[392] though he also may elect to sue for damages as an alternative to rescission in the strict legal sense.[393] If he does, as we shall see,[394] he will be no better off than if he rescinded where the ground for his action is the failure of the vendor to show good title to the property.[395]

B. Grounds

[13.63] In the next few paragraphs we list the main grounds for exercising the right of rescission at common law and for applying to the court for equitable relief by way of an order for rescission. The discussion will be kept to a minimum as several of these grounds have been dealt with elsewhere in the book.[396]

[387.] *Barber v Wolfe* [1945] Ch 187. Again this case is not good law in so far as it suggests the same rule applies to rescission for repudiatory breach.

[388.] *Newbigging v Adam* (1886) 34 Ch D 582 at 594 (*per* Bowen LJ). See also *Whittington v Seale-Hayne* (1900) 82 LT 49.

[389.] See para **[13.22]** *supra*.

[390.] *McMahon v Gaffney* [1930] IR 576 at 587 (*per* Johnston J). See also *Dickie v White* (1901) 1 NIJR 128; *Re Flynn and Newman's Contract* [1948] IR 104. See also para **[13.34]** *supra*.

[391.] *Whitbread & Co v Watt* [1902] 1 Ch 835.

[392.] See para **[13.61]** *supra*.

[393.] See *Mills v Healy* [1937] IR 437.

[394.] See para **[13.79]** *infra*.

[395.] Ie, the rule in *Bain v Fothergill*, see *ibid*.

[396.] See also Farrell, *Irish Law of Specific Performance* (1994), para [10.32] *et seq*; Delany, *Equity and the Law of Trusts in Ireland* (1996), Ch 16.

1. Misrepresentation

[13.64] At common law a misrepresentation was a ground for rescission only if it was made fraudulently.[397] And as Pigot CB put it in *Cullen v O'Meara*[398]:

> "To nullify a contract on the ground of fraud, in a Court of Common Law, the fraud must be shown to have been connected with the transaction of the contract, and, so connected, to have induced the making of the contract."[399]

Equity followed the law and would also grant relief for fraud,[400] as it would for other improper conduct such as undue influence.[401] However, there was no right of rescission at common law for an innocent misrepresentation, unless it became a term of the contract amounting to a condition, ie, in effect a misdescription.[402] On the other hand, equity would grant rescission for an innocent misrepresentation inducing the contract and we considered this jurisdiction in an earlier chapter.[403]

2. Misdescription and Non-Disclosure

[13.65] We considered this subject in detail in an earlier chapter,[404] in connection with the content of a contract for sale, for it is usual for the contract to contain provisions dealing with misdescription and non-disclosure. It is unnecessary to repeat here what was said earlier.

3. Mistake

[13.66] Mistake is another well recognised ground for rescission,[405] though it is sometimes difficult from the decisions to define precisely the scope of the remedy. At common law it seems that mistake was regarded as rendering the contract void *ab initio*, so that it had to be something so fundamental to the

---

[397] *Legge v Croker* (1811) Ba & B 506 at 514 (*per* Manners LC).

[398] (1869) IR 4 CL 537.

[399] *Ibid*, p 558. See also para **[5.23]** *ante*.

[400] *Re Moorhead's Estate* (1861) 12 Ir Ch R 371 at 374 (*per* Hargreave J); *Thompson v Lambert* (1868) IR 2 Eq 433 at 438-9 (*per* Walsh MR). See also *Re Commins and Hanafy's Contract* (1905) 39 ILTR 85 at 86 (*per* Lord Ashbourne C); *Carbin v Somerville* [1933] IR 276 at 288-9 (*per* FitzGibbon J) (quoted in para **[5.23]** *ante*).

[401] *Provincial Bank of Ireland v McKeever* [1941] IR 471; *R (Proctor) v Hutton* [1978] NI 139. And see *Cheese v Thomas* [1994] 1 All ER 35. See *Irish Land Law* (2nd ed, 1986), para 9.075.

[402] See paras **[9.29]** *et seq, ante* and **[13.65]** *infra*.

[403] See paras **[5.26]** *et seq, ante*.

[404] See paras **[9.17]** *et seq, ante*.

[405] It is also a ground for rectification, see the discussion in *Gun v McCarthy* (1884) 13 LR Ir 304 and para **[21.37]** *post*. See also *Monaghan CC v Vaughan* [1948] IR 306; *Nolan v Nolan* (1958) 92 ILTR 94.

contract, or going to the root of the transaction, that it destroyed the element of consent between the parties - their minds were never *ad idem*.[406] In effect no contract ever came into existence and in this respect it is somewhat misleading to talk of rescission of a contract at common law.[407] Indeed, this is a point of distinction from rescission on other grounds, eg, fraud or misrepresentation, or in equity where the contract is voidable only and thus remains valid until avoided.[408] The courts are more reluctant to grant rescission on the basis of a unilateral mistake made by one of the parties to the contract.[409]

[13.67] A mistake which renders the contract void at common law may relate, provided that in each case it is fundamental, to such things as the existence of the subject-matter of the contract,[410] the identity of the parties to the contract,[411] the title to be transferred[412] and, perhaps, even in a rare case the quality of the subject-matter.[413] Equity generally follows the law with regard to the grounds for granting rescission on the basis of mistake, but, as one would expect, is not quite so strict in its requirements.[414] As Flanagan J said in *Gun v McCarthy*,[415] the more important question in the eyes of equity is "whether the facts of the case raise a sufficient equity to justify the Court in making a decree for the rescission of the contract."[416] Thus, the courts are more likely to grant equitable relief for a mistake as to the quality of the subject-matter of the contract.[417]

[406.] See the leading English case, *Bell v Lever Bros Ltd* [1932] AC 161, espec at 217 (*per* Lord Atkin).

[407.] See *Cundy v Lindsay* (1878) 3 App Cas 459.

[408.] See *Irish Land Law* (2nd ed, 1986), para 3.159.

[409.] See *Riverplate Properties Ltd v Paul* [1979] 2 All ER 656 at 661 (*per* Russell LJ), quoted with approval by Keane J in *Irish Life assurance Co Ltd v Dublin Land Securities Ltd* [1986] IR 332 at 352 (his decision was upheld by the Supreme Court, [1989] IR 253); *Ferguson v Merchant Banking Ltd* [1993] ILRM 136.

[410.] Eg, sale of life interest when the *cestui que vie* is already dead, see *Strickland v Turner* (1852) 7 Exch 208; *Scott v Coulson* [1903] 2 Ch 249. See also *Cooper v Phibbs* (1867) LR 2 HL 149. *Cf Sindall plc v Cambridgeshire County Council* [1994] 3 All ER 932.

[411.] See *JL Smallman Ltd v O'Moore* [1959] IR 220. *Cf Smith v Wheatcroft* (1878) 9 Ch D 223; *Dyster v Randall & Sons* [1926] Ch 932.

[412.] See *Coleman v Fry* (1873) IR 7 CL 247; *Dickie v White* (1901) 1 NIJR 128; *National Bank Ltd v O'Connor* (1969) 103 ILTR 73.

[413.] See *Bell v Lever Bros Ltd* [1932] AC 161 at 218 (*per* Lord Atkin). *Cf Solle v Butcher* [1950] 1 KB 671.

[414.] See *Cooper v Phibbs* (1867) LR 2 HL 149. *Cf Sindall v Cambridgeshire County Council* [1994] 3 All ER 932.

[415.] (1883) 13 LR Ir 304.

[416.] *Ibid*, p 310.

[417.] See *Solle v Butcher* [1950] 1 KB 671 (contract upheld at law but relief in equity), approved by Costello J in *O'Neill v Ryan* [1992] 1 IR 166. *Cf Coleman v Fry* (1873) IR 7 CL 247. See also *Grist v Bailey* [1367] Ch 532.

4. Defect in Title

[13.68] It is clear that where the purchaser discovers a fundamental defect in the vendor's title, he may immediately repudiate the contract in the sense that he treats himself as discharged from it.[418] He may then elect whether to sue for damages or to rescind the contract in the strict sense.[419] However, if he decides to rescind there has been considerable controversy[420]as to whether this is a right at common law, which, when exercised, puts an end to the contract, or it is merely an equitable right, which, when exercised, enables the purchaser to resist specific performance but leaves the contract standing, so that the vendor may redeem himself by subsequently acquiring title.[421] The Irish cases seem to support the view that the purchaser can rescind the contract at common law as soon as he discovers the vendor's defect, ie, without having to wait for completion.[422] However, it is clear that he must exercise his right without delay, otherwise he may be treated as having elected to keep the contract in existence.[423] He then runs the risk that the vendor may subsequently cure the defect and ultimately succeed in obtaining specific performance.[424] If the title is defective, the purchaser should, when raising requisitions, specifically object to the title before raising the requisitions. It should also be noted that both parties have some protection if the contract incorporates the Law Society's *General Conditions of Sale (1995 Edition)*. Under condition 39 it is provided that the right to rescind "shall not be lost by reason only of any intermediate negotiations or attempts to comply with or to remove the issue giving rise to the exercise of

---

[418.] *Clibborn v Horan* [1921] 1 IR 93 at 96 (*per* O'Connor MR); *Cf Forrer v Nash* (1865) 35 Beav 167 at 170 (*per* Romilly MR). See also *Maconchy v Clayton* [1898] 1 IR 291; *Dickie v White* (1901) 1 NIJR 128; *Re Flynn and Newman's Contract* [1948] IR 104.

[419.] See para **[13.57]** *supra*.

[420.] *Cf Halkett v Dudley* [1907] 1 Ch 590 at 596 (*per* Lord Parker of Waddington) (followed in *Proctor v Pugh* [1921] 2 Ch 256; *Elliot and H Elliot (Builders) Ltd v Pierson* [1948] Ch 452; *Price v Strange* 1977] 3 All ER 371) and Williams *Law of Vendor and Purchaser* (4th ed, 1936) Vol 1 p 203 supported by *Phillips v Caldcleugh* (1886) IR 4 QB 159; *Re Atkinson and Horsell's Contract* [1912] 2 Ch 1; *Pips (Leisure Production) Ltd v Walton* (1980) 43 P & CR 415. See also *Re Stone and Saville's Contract* [1963] 1 WLR 163.

[421.] See Emery 'A Purchaser's Right of Repudiation: Mr Cyprian Williams versus Lord Parker of Waddington' (1977) 41 Conv 18. See also Albery 'Mr Cyprian Williams' Great Heresy' (1975) 91 LQR 337.

[422.] *Maconchy v Clayton* [1898] 1 IR 291; *Dickie v White* (1901) 1 NIJR 128; *Clibborn v Horan* [1921] 1 IR 93. See also *Re Flynn and Newman's Contract* [1948] IR 104.

[423.] *Mills v Healy* [1937] IR 437 at 447 (*per* Meredith J). See also *Maconchy v Clayton* [1898] 1 IR 291 at 309 (*per* Walker LJ) *Eyston v Simonds* (1842) 1 Y & C Ch Cas 608; *Re Deighton and Harris's Contract* [1898] 1 Ch 458 and 310 (*per* Holmes LJ).

[424.] *Ibid*. See also *Eyston v Simonds* (1842) 1 Y & C Ch Cas 608; *Re Deighton and Harris's Contract* [1898] 1 Ch 458.

such right". This provision applies, as condition 37 makes clear, not only where rescission is being exercised under the provisions of the Society's contract form, but "otherwise", ie, under the general law.

5. Failure to Complete

[13.69] We considered this subject earlier in .this chapter in connection with the significance of time in relation to completion of the sale.[425]

6. Contractual Rights

[13.70] It is usual for the contract for sale to contain several provisions conferring a contractual right of rescission. One common one which we have already discussed is the right of either party to rescind for failure to comply with a completion notice.[426] There are, however, other common contractual rights.

(i) Requisitions

[13.71] The Law Society's *General Conditions of Sale (1995 Edition)* contains a provision enabling the vendor to rescind the contract in certain circumstances if the purchaser insists on certain objections or requisitions as to title.[427] We examine this important provision later in connection with the subject of investigation of title.[428]

(ii) Non-Disclosure of Notices

[13.72] Condition 35 of the Law Society's *General Conditions of Sale* gives the purchaser a right of rescission where the vendor fails to show that before the sale the purchaser received notice or was aware of various orders and notices that may have been served on the vendor. We considered these provisions in an earlier chapter.[429]

(iii) Deposits

[13.73] Condition 31 of the Law Society's *General Conditions of Sale* now provides that failure by the purchaser to pay in full the deposit specified as payable constitutes a breach of condition entitling the vendor to terminate the sale. We considered the operation of this provision in an earlier chapter.[430]

[425.] See para **[13.10]** *et seq, supra.*
[426.] See para **[13.19]** *et seq, supra.*
[427.] Cond 18.
[428.] Para **[15.27]** *post.*
[429.] Para **[9.28]** *ante.*
[430.] See para **[10.18]** *ante.*

(iv) Conditions of Sale

[13.74] Apart from the above provisions condition 41 of the Law Society's *General Conditions of Sale* contains a more general provision to the effect that failure by the purchaser to comply in "any material respect" with the conditions of sale entitles the vendor to forfeit the deposit and re-sell the property. This too was considered earlier.[431]

VI. DAMAGES

[13.75] The third main remedy available to both parties is an action for damages for breach of contract. We have already seen that the effect of a breach varies according to its seriousness.[432] If the breach is sufficiently serious the offended party may have alternative remedies open to him, ie, he may apply to the court for an order of specific performance,[433] or an order rescinding the contract in the strict sense,[434] or may, without application to the court, "rescind" in the sense of treating himself as discharged from any further performances of the contract.[435] In the case of specific performance and rescission in the sense of treating oneself discharged from performance, it is clear that damages[436] may also be sought to cover losses suffered as a result of the breach of contract by the other party. Damages may not be claimed where a party seeks a court order for rescission in the strict sense because this proceeds on the basis that the contract is treated as void *ab initio* and the parties should be restored to their *pre*-contractual position, ie, *restitutio in integrum*.[437] Of course, in a particular case it is always open to a party to claim alternative remedies, but there will come a point when the court will require him to elect as between them which one he wishes to enforce.[438] If the breach is a minor one, generally the offended party will succeed only in an action for damages.[439]

[13.76] There is, however, even a limitation to the recovery of damages and that is the general principle that on completion the contract merges in the

---

[431.] See para **[13.31]** *supra*.

[432.] See, eg, the distinction between substantial and insubstantial misdescription, para **[9.32]** *et seq*.

[433.] See para **[13.37]** *et seq, supra*.

[434.] If a vitiating factor like fraud or misrepresentation by other party exists: see para **[13.57]** *et seq, supra*.

[435.] See paras **[13.04]** and **[13.57]** *supra*. Note also the contractual right of rescission which may be available: see par **[13.70]** *et seq, supra*.

[436.] See paras **[13.04]** and **[13.54]** *supra*.

[437.] See paras **[13.57]** and **[13.59]** *supra*.

[438.] See para **[13.03]** *et seq, ante*.

[439.] Or in securing an abatement in the purchase price: see para **[9.34]** *ante*.

conveyance and therefore all remedies based on the contract are lost.[440] Thereafter an action for damages must be founded on the covenants for title in the conveyance rather than on the contract for sale.[441] Though this is the general rule, there are several well-recognised exceptions to it. Thus, an action may still be brought for fraudulent misrepresentation inducing the contract,[442] or for breach of a collateral warranty.[443] It is also, of course, important to remember that the doctrine of merger is largely based upon the parties' intention nowadays and the particular term broken may not have merged in that particular case.[444]

A. Vendor

[13.77] So far as the vendor is concerned, his right to damages for breach of contract is governed by the normal rules of contract law. He is entitled to be put in the position he would have been in had the contract been performed according to its terms. This is, of course, subject to the rules as to remoteness of damage, ie, he is entitled only to damages which may fairly and reasonably be considered as arising naturally from the breach or may reasonably be supposed to have been within the contemplation of the parties, when they contracted, as the probable result of it.[445]

[13.78] The amount of damages recoverable must obviously vary according to the circumstances of the case, and in each case the assessment to be made is of the actual loss the vendor has suffered. Thus, he cannot sue for the contractual purchase price unless the land has already been conveyed to the purchaser and the title has been vested in him.[446] Apart from this exceptional case, the vendor, on breach of contract by the purchaser, is left with the land in his hands and obviously cannot have both the land and the full contract

---

[440] The doctrine of merger is considered later see para **[21.02]** *et seq, post.*

[441] *Re Otway's Estate* (1862) 13 Ir Ch R 222 at 235 (*per* Brady LC). See also *Irish Leisure Industries Ltd v Gaeity Theatre Enterprises Ltd* High Court, unrep 12 February 1975 (1972./253P). On the covenants for title see para **[21.05]** *post.*

[442] See para **[5.23]** *ante.*

[443] See para **[5.26]** *ante.* Note also the possibility of an action for negligence, such as negligent misstatement: see para **[5.27]** *ante.*

[444] See also *Connolly v Keating (No 2)* [1903] 1 IR 356 at 359-60 (*per* Porter MR).

[445] Ie, the rule in *Hadley v Baxendale* (1854) 9 Exch 341. See *Murphy v Quality Homes* High Court, unrep, 22 June 1976 (1975/4344P); *Malone v Malone* High Court, unrep, 9 June 1982 (1978/66847P). See also *Seven Seas Properties Ltd v Al-Essa* [1993] 3 All ER 577. See further Clark, *Contract Law in Ireland* (3rd 1992), p 453 *et seq.*

[446] *East London Union v Metropolitan Rly Co* (1869) LR 4 Exch 309; *Leader v Tod-Heatly* [1891] WN 38. For the suggestion that the vendor may try to secure the full purchase price by unilaterally executing the conveyance see *White and Carter (Councils) Ltd v McGregor Ltd* [1962] AC 413 and para **[13.06]** *supra.*

price which was intended to represent its value.[447] Instead, his damages must be limited to any loss he suffers by reason of the land having fallen in value since the contract price was determined. Thus, the general rule is that the damages are to be assessed as the difference in value between the contract price and the value of the land at the date of the breach of contract.[448] However, in more recent times the courts on both sides of the Irish Sea have come to recognise that strict application of this rule may cause hardship, especially in times of inflation in property prices. It is now accepted that the common law rule is not inflexible and that the court has a discretion to choose the most appropriate date at which to value the land for the purposes of calculating the damages to be awarded.[449] This might be the date of the plaintiff's application to the court,[450] the date of hearing of the plaintiff's action,[451] the date of the judgment in his favour[452] or some other date which the court chooses because of the circumstances of the particular case.[453] Apart from this, in the absence of a resale by the vendor, the latter value is to be estimated as that realisable on the sale within a reasonable time of the breach.[454] But the vendor will not be allowed to inflate this resale price by "nursing" the property.[455] He may, however, claim the expenses of the resale,[456] but not those incurred in respect of the abortive sale, eg, his legal fees.[457] He must also bring into account to be credited against the damages any deposit forfeited by him,[458] and it is largely for this reason that most vendors prefer to elect to pursue alternative remedies to suing for damages,

---

[447] See paras **[13.04-8]** *supra*.

[448] *Laird v Pym* (1841) 7 M & W 474; *Watkins v Watkins* (1849) 12 LT (os) 353; *Suleman v Shahsavari* [1989] 2 All ER 460. *Cf Surrey County Council v Bredero Homes Ltd* [1993] 3 All ER 705.

[449] See the House of Lords decision in *Johnson v Agnew* [1980] AC 367, applied by McWilliam J in *Vandeleur v Dargan* [1981] ILRM 75.

[450] *Vandeleur v Dargan supra*.

[451] *Forster v Silvermere Golf and Equestrian Centre Ltd* (1981) 42 P & CR 255; *Radford v De Froberville* [1978] 1 All ER 33.

[452] *Wroth v Tyler* [1973] 1 All ER 897: see para **[13.54]** *supra*. See also *Suleman v Shahsavari* [1989] 2 All ER 460.

[453] *Malhotra v Choudhury* [1979] 1 All ER 186 (one year before judgment because of the plaintiff's delay in bringing proceedings).

[454] *Ockenden v Henly* (1888) 1 B & E 485.

[455] *Keck v Faber* (1915) 60 Sol Jo 253.

[456] *Laird v Pym* (1841) 7 M & W 474 at 478 (*per* Parke B) *Noble v Edwardes* (1877) 5 Ch D 378 at 385 (*per* Bacon LC). See also para **[13.22]** *ante*.

[457] Alternatively, it seems that, instead of claiming for loss of profit, he may claim for wasted expenditure in respect of both the abortive sale and resale see *Anglia Television Ltd v Reed* [1972] 1 QB 60. But presumably he cannot both forfeit the deposit and claim his expenses unless there is a contractual provision to this effect: see *Essex v Daniel* (1875) LR 10 CP 538.

[458] *Ockenden v Henly* (1858) 1 B & E 485; *Shuttleworth v Clews* [1907] 1 Ch 176.

ie, rescission and forfeiture of the deposit, which he can keep notwithstanding that he resells at a profit.[459] In *Vandeleur v Dargan*,[460] McWilliam J allowed the vendor's claim for interest at the rate fixed in the contract for late completion,[461] for the period between the closing date in the contract and the date fixed for completion in an order for specific performance obtained by the vendor.[462] In *Taylor v Smyth*,[463] where an earlier action by the vendor had been settled on the basis of a compromise agreement which provided for interest at the rate of 22% if the sale was delayed, Lardner J awarded interest at this rate for a period of five and a half years which had elapsed since the closing date specified in the compromise agreement. In his view the rate specified, though "almost penal" at the date of trial, was not so when it was fixed.[464] Finally, the vendor cannot sue the purchaser for breach of contract if the purchaser's obligation to perform the contract is nullified by reason of the vendor being unable to show good title, or being otherwise not ready and willing to perform his side of the agreement.[465]

B. Purchaser

[13.79] The recovery of damages by the purchaser for breach of contract by the vendor is also governed by the general law of contract, but this is subject to one major restriction, usually known as the rule in *Bain v Fothergill*.[466] This rule states that, where the breach of contract relied upon by the purchaser is the vendor's failure to show good title to the property in question, then, provided the vendor was not fraudulent and did not act otherwise in bad faith, the purchaser is not entitled to recover damages for loss of bargain but is limited to recovery of his deposit with interest and any expenses incurred in investigation of the title. This is a most controversial rule,[467] but it has not been reversed in Ireland.[468] However, the Law Reform

---

[459] See paras **[13.04]** and **[13.31-3]** *supra*.

[460] [1981] ILRM 75.

[461] 18%: see para **[12.18]** *et seq, ante*.

[462] The vendor subsequently applied for this to be dissolved because of non-compliance and for rescission and damages instead: see para **[13.03]** *supra*.

[463] [1990] ILRM 377.

[464] *Ibid*, p 390-1.

[465] *Noble v Edwardes* (1877) 5 Ch D 378 at 392 (*per* James LJ). See also *Bellamy v Debenham* [1891] 1 Ch 412.

[466] (1874) LR 7 HL 158.

[467] See Emery 'In Defence of the Rule in *Bain v Fothergill*' (1978) Conv 338; Lewis '*Bain v Fothergill* and the Maggots' (1985) New LJ 1129; Sydenham 'The Anomalous Rule in *Bain v Fothergill*' (1977) 41 Conv 341.

[468] It was abolished in England by s 3 of the Law of Property (Miscellaneous Provisions) Act 1989, following the recommendation of the Law Commission: see Report No 166, *Transfer of Land - The Rule in Bain v Fothergill*.

Commission has recommended that it should be abolished,[469] but this has not yet been acted upon.

1. The Rule in Bain v Fothergill

[13.80] Though universally called after a House of Lords decision of 1874, the rule is of much greater antiquity and probably dates back to the earlier decision in *Flureau v Thornhill*.[470] After considerable discussion in subsequent cases,[471] the rule was eventually settled in England in the form given above. The rationale which has come to be accepted for its existence is the principle that the vendor ought not to suffer, provided he acts in good faith, where his default results from the complexity of titles to land.[472] But the rule has frequently been castigated by the English judges as anomalous[473] and, therefore, not to be extended,[474] and in recent times, until it was abolished in 1989,[475] they have refused to apply it in actions for damages based on defects in title relating to modern statutes which, they have held, could not, *ex hypothesi*, have been within the contemplation of the judges who decided *Flureau v Thornhill* and *Bain v Fothergill*.[476]

2. In Ireland

[13.81] The decision in *Flureau v Thornhill* was recognised and applied in Ireland at least as early as 1854,[477] ie, some twenty years before it was confirmed by the House of Lords in *Bain v Fothergill*. Since then what has

---

[469] *Land Law and Conveyancing Law: (1) General Proposals* (LRC 30-1989), paras 30-32. See also O'Driscoll 'A Note on the Rule in *Bain v Fothergill*' (1975) 9 IR Jur (ns) 203.

[470] (1776) 2 Wm Bl 1078. See the survey of this history of the rule by O'Connor MR in *Kelly v Duffy* [1922] 1 IR 62. See also the discussion by the Supreme Court in *McDonnell v McGuinness* [1939] IR 223.

[471] See, eg, *Sikes v Wild* (1863) 4 B & S 421, *Engell v Fitch* (1869) LR 4 QB 659, *Bain v Fothergill* (1874) LR 7 HL 158; *Day v Singleton* [1899] 2 Ch 320; *Keen v Mear* [1920] 2 Ch 574.

[472] See eg, *Silkes v Wild* (1861) 1 B & S 587 at 596 (*per* Cockburn CJ) (on appeal (1863) 4 B & S 421); *Engell v Fitch* (1869) LR 4 QB 659 at 666 (*per* Kelly CB); *Bain v Fothergill* (1874) LR 7 HL 158 at 210-1 (*per* Lord Hatherley).

[473] *Ibid*.

[474] Especially as it is of questionable relevance when all land in England and Wales is now subject to compulsory registration of title.

[475] See fn 468 *supra*.

[476] See eg, *Wroth v Tyler* [1974] Ch 30 espec at 56 (*per* Megarry J); *Watts v Spence* [1975] 2 WLR 1039 espec at 1049 (*per* Graham J). A similar view was adopted by O Higgins J *in Irish Leisure Industries Ltd v Gaiety Theatre Enterprises Ltd* High Court, unrep 12 February 1975 (1972/253P). *Cf Malhotra v Choudhury* [1979] 1 All ER 186; *Sharneyford Supplies Ltd v Edge* [1987] 1 All ER 588.

[477] *Buckley v Dawson* (1854) 4 ICLR 211. *Cf Fitzgerald v Browne* (1854) 4 ICLR 178, where the Irish Court of Exchequer refused to apply the principle where the contract had been partly executed: see at pp 184-5 (*per* Richards B).

become known as the rule in *Bain v Fothergill* has been followed consistently by the Irish judges,[478] but not without criticism. Thus, in *Kelly v Duffy*,[479] O'Conner MR, in giving an admirable survey of the history of the rule, commented with respect to *Flureau v Thornhill*:

> "As has been more than once remarked, the report of the case is meagre. Indeed, so meagre is it, having regard to the importance of the decision, it justifies Dr. Johnson's remark that the English reports in general were very poor, only the half of what was said having been taken down, and of that half much was mistaken."[480]

However, he later concluded:

> "Unsatisfactory, however, as the decision may be, it is now too late to question it. It is settled law."[481]

And as regards the ascription of the epithet "anomalous," he had this to say:

> "I do not know what is meant by an anomalous rule of law. A rule is either good or bad. If it is good, as founded on some principles, it cannot be called anomalous. If it is bad, it ought not to be followed. The rule in *Flureau v Thornhill* is as well established as any rule of law can be. It would only become anomalous if so interpreted as to make it applicable to cases which it was not designed to cover. It was only intended to rule transactions in which the vendor deals unfairly with his purchaser."[482]

O'Conner MR's view that the rule was settled law in Ireland has been accepted without question ever since,[483] though some later judges have, like their English counterparts, questioned whether it has not lost most of its justification in twentieth century conditions.[484] It is not surprising, therefore, that the Law Reform Commission has recommended its abolition, as has been done in England.[485]

---

[478] *Re Kavanagh and Balfe's Contract* (1898) 32 ILTR 6; *Nolan v Feely* (1899) 33 ILTR 132; *Re McDermott and Kellett's Contract* (1904) 4 NIJR 89; *Kelly v Duffy* [1922] 1 IR 62; *McMahon v Gaffney* [1930] IR 576; *McDonnell v McGuinness* [1939] IR 223; *McQuaid v Lynam* [1965] IR 564. See O'Driscoll, 'A Note on the Rule in *Bain v Fothergill*' (1975) 9 Ir Jur (ns) 203.

[479] [1922] 1 IR 62.

[480] *Ibid*, p 65.

[481] *Ibid*, p 66.

[482] *Ibid*, p 69.

[483] See, eg, *McDonnell v McGuinness* [1939] IR 223 (HC and Sup Ct; *McQuaid v Lynam* [1965] IR 564 at 574 (*per* Kenny J).

[484] See, eg, *McDonnell v McGuinness, op cit*, p 232 (*per* Gavan Duffy J) (*affd* by Sup Ct). See also *Irish Leisure Industries Ltd v Gaiety Theatre Enterprises Ltd* High Court, unrep, 12 February 1975 (1972/253P).

[485] See para **[13.79]** *supra*.

3. Its Application

[13.82] Where the rule applies, it limits the purchaser to recovery of his deposit with interest[486] and of his expenses, if any, in investigation of the title to the property, eg, his solicitor's conveyancing costs.[487] It has been held in England that such expenses can include the amount of an insurance premium paid as a result of entering into the contract,[488] but not in Ireland auctioneers' fees paid by the purchaser under the contract.[489] The purchaser cannot recover damages for loss of bargain.[490]

[13.83] The rule has been applied in Ireland in respect of the following instances of defects in title: the vendor had previously demised the leasehold premises to a third party, who was also the lessee of a reversionary lease, and the purchaser was evicted by the assignee of the reversionary lease[491]; the root of title deed did not convey the fee farm grant interest contracted to be sold[492]; the vendor had no title in the premises at the date of the contract and died before completion, the action being founded solely on breach of contract and not fraud or deceit[493]; the vendor was unable to make title because of an outstanding right of dower[494]; the vendor had entered into an undertaking with the local authority not to sell the house for fifteen years and to let it only subject to certain conditions.[495] On the other hand, the rule was not applied in *Fitzgerald v Browne*[496] where the vendor agreed to let three parcels of land at fourteen shillings per acre and, while he was able to put the purchaser in possession of one parcel, he failed with respect to the other two. In a suit for breach of contract the purchaser claimed that the true value of the parcel he had occupied was only twelve shillings per acre and argued that the measure of damages should be the difference between twelve shillings. and the fourteen shillings per acre he had been obliged to pay. The Irish Court of Exchequer accepted this argument. Richards B said:

[486.] *McMahon v Gaffney* [1930] IR 576 at 586 (*per* Johnston J). See also *Nolan v Feely* (1899) 33 ILTR 132; *Re McDermott and Kellett's Contract* (1904) 4 NIJR 89.

[487.] *Re McDermott and Kellett's Contract* (1904) 4 NIJR 89; *McQuaid v Lynam* [1965] IR 564.

[488.] *Keen v Mear* [1920] 2 Ch 574. See para **[12.36]** *ante*.

[489.] *Re Priestley and Davidson's Contract* (1892) 31 LR Ir 122; *McNulty v Hanratty* (1918) 52 ILTR 43; *McMahon v Gaffney* [1930] IR 576. But see now para **[10.10]** *ante*. *Cf* a surveyor's fee, *McQuaid v Lynam* [1965] IR 564 at 574 (*per* Kenny J).

[490.] *Buckley v Dawson* (1854) 4 ICLR 211; *Nolan v Feely* (899) 33 ILTR 132; *McDonnell v McGuinness* [1939] IR 223.

[491.] *Buckley v Dawson* (1854) 4 ICLR 211.

[492.] *Re McDermott and Kellett's Contract* (1904) 4 NIJR 89.

[493.] *Kelly v Duffy* [1922] 1 IR 62.

[494.] *McDonnell v McGuinness* [1939] IR 223.

[495.] See *McQuaid v Lynam* [1965] IR 564.

[496.] (1854) 4 ICLR 178.

"I agree that when the contract is concerning the sale of land, damages cannot be recovered by the vendor, for the fancied loss of his bargain. For the mere case of such a contract unfulfilled, no damages can be recovered; but this case is clear of that principle, because it is not the case of a contract wholly unfulfilled, where both parties are left in their original position. This contract has been partially executed, and the defendant seeks to hold the plaintiff bound as to part of it."[497]

And more recently, in *Irish Leisure Industries Ltd v Gaiety Theatre Enterprises Ltd*,[498] where the lease executed by the vendor was rendered ineffective by the existing tenants obtaining a new one under the Landlord and Tenant Act 1931, O'Higgins J (as he then was) refused to apply the rule since the lease was already executed and the action was more akin to an action on the covenants for title than for breach of contract.[499] Apart from that, he took the view that the rule was anomalous and ought not to be extended, and, adopting an approach similar to that adopted in England,[500] he held that there was no "defect in title" within the meaning of the rule, since the problem arose over the special modern statutory form of protection afforded to existing tenants which they did not enjoy at common law.[501]

[13.84] Finally, it must be reiterated that the rule itself admits of the important qualification that it does not prevent a purchaser from recovering full damages for loss of bargain if he can establish that the vendor was fraudulent[502] or otherwise acted in bad faith.[503] However, it seems that the test may be a subjective one, so that even though the vendor knew of a defect when he contracted, he may still invoke the rule successfully if he *bona fide* believed he would be able to remove it by completion, but failed to do so.[504] Furthermore, it seems that the courts will apply the rule in cases where the vendor could with reasonable diligence have discovered the existence of the defect and then made provision for it in the contract.[505]

---

[497] *Ibid*, pp 184-5.

[498] High Court, unrep, 12 February 1975 (1972/253P).

[499] See para **[13.76]** *supra*.

[500] Ie in *Wroth v Tyler* [1974] Ch 30: see para **[13.80]** *supra*.

[501] On this see Wylie, *Irish Landlord and Tenant Law*, Ch 30.

[502] Of course, in a case of fraud the purchaser can instead seek damage in tort for deceit *Kelly v Duffy* [1922] 1 IR 62 at 67 (*per* O'Connor MR); *McMahon v Gaffney* [1930] IR 576 at 586 (*per* Johnston J); *McDonnell v McGuinness* [1939] IR 223 at 231-2 (*per* Gavan Duffy J) (affd by Sup Ct). See para **[5.24]** *ante*.

[503] See *Malhotra v Choudhury* [1979] 1 All ER 186; *Sharneyford Supplies Ltd v Edge* [1987] 1 All ER 588.

[504] See *Sikes v Wild* (1863) 4 B & S 421.

[505] See *Re McDermott and Kellett's Contract* (1904) 4 NIJR 89.

4. Substantial Damages

[13.85] Where the rule in *Bain v Fothergill* does not apply and the purchaser is entitled to substantial damages, then, subject to the usual rules as to remoteness,[506] he is entitled to the return of the deposit, with interest for loss of its use,[507] and to damages for "loss of bargain."[508] In this context, loss of bargain means the difference between the contract purchase price and the property market value at the date of the breach.[509] Moreover, it seems that, in appropriate cases, a loss of prospective profits from development of the property, which may reasonably be taken to have been within the contemplation of the parties and, therefore, not too remote,[510] may be included.[511] These are matters which go towards placing the purchaser in the same position he would have been in had the contract been performed. However, since, even if it had been performed, he would still have incurred his conveyancing expenses, he is not in general entitled to claim these in addition to damages for loss of bargain.[512]

[13.86] On the other hand, where the purchaser cannot establish a loss of profit and so cannot claim on the basis of loss of bargain, the court may instead seek to restore him to his position prior to the contract, ie, as if it had never been made. In that case he is entitled to those out of-pocket expenses which he would not have incurred had he never entered into the contract,[513] eg: (1) pre-contract expenditure reasonably within the contemplation of the parties as wasted if the contract was broken,[514] such as survey fees[515]; (2) conveyancing costs, such as preparation and execution of the contract,[516] investigation of title[517] (including searches[518] and examination of deeds[519])

[506.] See para **[13.77]** *supra*.

[507.] *McMahon v Gaffney* [1930] IR 576 at 586-7 (*per* Johnston J). See also *Lloyd v Stanbury* [1971] 1 WLR 535.

[508.] *Engell v Fitch* (1869) LR 4 QB 659.

[509.] See para **[13.78]** *supra*. See also *Suleman v Shahsavari* [1989] 2 All ER 460.

[510.] See para **[13.77]** *supra*.

[511.] See *Cottrill v Steyning and Littlehampton BS* [1966] 1 WLR 753. *Cf Diamond v Campbell-Jones* [1961] Ch 22.

[512.] *Re Daniel* [1917] 2 Ch 405, *Anglia Television Ltd v Reed* [1972] 1 QB 60. *Cf Engell v Fitch* (1869) LR 4 QB 659; *Godwin v Francis* (1870) LR 5 CP 295.

[513.] See the discussion in *Lloyd v Sanbury* [1971] 1 WLR 535; *Anglia Television Ltd v Reed* [1972] 1 QB 60.

[514.] *Ibid.*

[515.] See *McQuaid v Lynam* [1965] IR 564. *Cf Hodges v Earl of Litchfield* (1835) 1 Bing NC 492.

[516.] *Hanslip v Padwick* (1850) 5 Exch 615. *Cf* cost of negotiating the contract, *Wright v Chatteris* (1846) 7 LT (os) 111.

[517.] *Day v Singleton* [1899] 2 Ch 320; *Keen v Mear* [1920] 2 Ch 574. *Cf* expenses of raising finance, *Hanslip v Padwick* (1850) 5 Exch 615, or expenditure on repairs or improvements, *Worthington v Warrington* (1849) 8 CB 134.

[518.] *Hanslip v Padwick* (1850) 5 Exch 615.

[519.] *Hodges v Earl of Litchfield* (1835) 1 Bing NC 492.

and preparation of the conveyance after acceptance of title.[520] It seems that these expenses may be claimed whether or not the purchaser's solicitor has actually been paid.[521]

[13.87] Apart from these general rules, some special ones may apply depending upon the nature of the breach of contract in question. Thus, where the vendor fails to give vacant possession, the purchaser may recover the cost of alternative temporary accommodation and conveyancing costs incurred in the purchase of a second house.[522] There may also be special contractual provisions, eg, those governing delay in completion.[523] Finally, there is a distinction between damages for breach of contract and damages in tort for deceit.[524] In the case of breach of contract, the award is essentially compensatory and is designed to put the aggrieved party in the position he would have been if the contract had been performed.[525] In the case of a tort, the award is designed instead to restore the aggrieved party to his position before the tort occurred.[526]

---

[520] *Cf* if the title is shown to be had, *Hodges v Earl of Litchfield* (1835) 1 Bing NC 492, or preparation before acceptance, *Jarmain v Egelstone* (1813) 5 C & P 172.

[521] *Richardson v Chasen* (1847) 10 QB 756.

[522] *Beard v Porter* [1948] 1 KB 321. See also *Cumberland Consolidated Holding Ltd v Ireland* [1946] KB 264.

[523] See paras **[13.22-3]** *supra*.

[524] See para **[5.24]** *ante*.

[525] See para **[13.77]** *supra*.

[526] See Clark, *Contract Law in Ireland* (3rd ed, 1992), p 442 *et seq*.

Chapter 14

DEDUCTION OF TITLE

[**14.01**] We now turn to the next major stage of the conveyancing process, the post-contractual stage which is usually referred to as the investigation of title stage.[1] As soon as the contract for sale is entered into the vendor becomes obliged to deduce title, ie, to establish that he is in a position to transfer the property he has contracted to convey to the purchaser for the estate he has agreed to sell. We examine the nature of this duty, and its extent in practice as it varies according to the circumstances of different cases, in this chapter. In the next chapter we will examine the extent to which the purchaser ought to investigate the title so deduced by the vendor.

I. INTRODUCTION

[**14.02**] As we mentioned in an earlier chapter,[2] the traditional conveyancing theory is that the vendor's duty of deduction of title does not arise until the contract for sale is entered into.[3] In practice, however, it is not uncommon for the vendor's solicitor to send the purchaser's solicitor some documentary evidence of title, eg, a copy of what is proposed as the root of title,[4] or to provide the opportunity for examination of some title documents prior to the sale.[5] There is, however, the danger in this practice from the purchaser's point of view that he may be fixed with constructive notice of any defects in title revealed by such documents and may be taken subsequently to contract subject to them, even though his solicitor did not in fact spot them. This is a particular risk if the full title is made available. In other words, by sending photocopies of the documents along with the draft contract for sale, the vendor's solicitor may reduce considerably, if not destroy altogether, the protection otherwise afforded the purchaser by the general duty to disclose latent defects in title.[6] Furthermore, it must be remembered that the Law

---

1. See para [**5.02**] *ante*.
2. See para [**1.29**] *ante*.
3. See *Reeve v Berridge* (1888) 20 QBD 523 at 528 (*per* Fry LJ). See also para [**14.08**] *infra*.
4. See para [**14.56**] *infra*. Note the standard conditions of sale dealing with this, see para [**9.39**] *ante*.
5. Note the standard conditions of sale dealing with this, see para [**9.39**] *ante*.
6. See para [**9.24**] *ante*.

Society's standard contract form also provides that the purchaser is deemed to have purchased with "full knowledge" of the contents of documents specified in the Documents Schedule.[7] This covers matters like "covenants, conditions, rights, liabilities or restrictions" and it is important to note that it applies to copies of documents available for inspection by the purchaser or his solicitor "whether availing of such opportunity of inspection or not."[8] Notwithstanding the dangers of making available full title documentation *prior* to the entering into the contract for sale, it has become an increasingly common practice in recent years. It cannot be emphasised too strongly that this puts the purchaser's solicitor in a difficult position. In order to protect his client's interests he will have to carry out a full *pre*-contract investigation of the title or else must make it clear, if necessary by insisting upon insertion of a special condition in the contract to this effect, that the purchaser reserves the right to raise objections to defects in the title upon investigation of the title after the contract is entered into.

[14.03] It would appear that the Law Society's Conveyancing Committee has also become concerned at such developments. It recently pointed out that the Society's standard contract form[9] is drafted on the basis that the vendor will disclose at the contract stage only sufficient title to enable the purchaser's solicitor to consider properly the "adequacy" of such title "before completion of contracts in accordance with long standing conveyancing practice", ie, where the full investigation takes place *after* the contract is entered into.[10] The Committee disapproved, in particular, of the practice of furnishing copies of all documents of title and inserting a special condition in the contract along the following lines:

> "The title shall consist of the documents listed in the Documents Schedule and shall be accepted by the purchaser as full and adequate evidence of the vendor's title to the subject property."

The Committee castigated, rightly, this practice as "highly undesirable and unfair" to purchasers, since it is a clear attempt to restrict the raising of proper requisitions on title.[11] It also pointed out that it poses particular problems in the case of a sale by auction, where the purchaser does not become identified until he is successful in the bidding, but that also creates

---

[7.] *General Conditions of Sale* (1995 ed), cond 6: see para **[9.39]** *et seq, ante*.
[8.] *Ibid*.
[9.] This applies equally to the latest version - the 1995 ed.
[10.] The *Gazette*, March 1995, p 83.
[11.] Arguably a court would regard such a special condition as unenforceable if there is any suspicion or suggestion of fraud or sharp practice by the vendor, such as deliberate concealment of a flaw in the title: see para **[9.37]** *et seq, ante* and **[14.07]** *infra*.

the contract and leaves no time for a *pre*-contract investigation. It is one thing to expect a prospective purchaser at an auction to ask his solicitor to do a preliminary check on the title, but it is quite another to ask him to carry out a full investigation in respect of a property which may be knocked down to another bidder. The Committee recommended that the documents listed in the Documents Schedule to the contract should be limited to: (a) the root of title being shown;[12] (b) any document to which title is stated to pass under the special conditions; (c) any document which is specifically referred to in a special condition. Items (b) and (c) are partly a recognition of the fundamental principle that the vendor is under a duty to disclose latent defects in title[13] and must not seek to perpetrate a fraud or engage in "sharp practice" by means of special conditions.[14] Instead, he must disclose the difficulties by giving due warning in the special conditions and leaving it to the purchaser and his solicitor to decide whether to accept those conditions.[15] Of course, it must be recognised that there will be circumstances justifying the furnishing of full documentation of title and investigation by the purchaser's solicitor prior to the contract. The obvious example is where the property comprises a substantial commercial investment by the purchaser. Here the likelihood is that the transaction will involve lengthy negotiations and include a number of parties, such as investment institutions providing much of the financing, in addition to the vendor and purchaser. The expectation in such cases will often be that a thorough "due diligence" exercise will be carried out before the contract to buy is entered into. This will include comprehensive *pre*-contract enquiries and searches, such as planning and environmental "requisitions".[16] Some other investors are likely to insist upon a full investigation of, and report[17] on, title before they commit themselves to contractual obligations. Here it is a case of the purchaser and other parties interested in the acquisition of the property seeking to protect their substantial investment and to minimise the risk by eschewing traditional procedures which were developed for much less complicated conveyancing transactions, eg, the typical house purchase. In the case of such commercial transactions the duty of the purchaser's solicitor will clearly be different.[18]

[12.] See para **[14.46]** *infra*.

[13.] See para **[9.24]** *ante*.

[14.] *Re Turpin and Ahern's Contract* [1905] 1 IR 85; *Re Flynn and Newman's Contract* [1948] IR 104: para **[9.38]** *ante*.

[15.] See para **[9.47]** *ante*.

[16.] See para **[5.14]** *ante*.

[17.] See para **[15.05]** *post*.

[18.] See Spence 'Contaminated Sites - Clean up or Be Cleaned Out?' (1994) IPELJ 57; Fanagan, 'Environmental Due Diligence' [1995] IPELJ 3.

A. Registered and Unregistered Land

[14.04] The primary purpose of a system of registration of title is the simplification of conveyancing by reducing considerably the complications of deduction and investigation of title.[19] It is at this stage in the conveyancing process that the system has most impact and we consider this subject further in this[20] and the next chapter.[21]

B. Open and Closed Contracts

[14.05] The extent of the vendor's duty will vary according to whether the contract for sale is left "open" as to title (an "open contract") or is "closed" by the conditions of sale. As we shall see,[22] if the contract is "open", the general law, including statute law, defines the extent of the vendor's duty as to the length of title to be shown for different types of case and, of course, in this way indicates the limits to investigation of title by the purchaser. However, it is rare for the contract to be left open, for it is usually in the interests of the parties to vary the general law - frequently the vendor will want to restrict further his duty of deduction,[23] perhaps even to exclude it altogether,[24] and the purchaser will sometimes want to be shown and to investigate more title than is allowed under the general law.[25] This may be done by inserting special conditions in the contract for sale, but even that may not be necessary because the general conditions included in the standard form contract issued by the Law Society contains provisions relating to title.[26]

C. Obligation to show Good Title

[14.06] As a general rule the vendor is under an obligation to show good title to the property he has contracted to sell.[27] As Walker LJ said in *Clarke v Taylor*[28]:

[19.] See McAllister, *Registration of Title in Ireland* (1973), Ch 1; Fitzgerald, *Land Registry Practice* (2nd ed, 1995), Ch 1.

[20.] Para **[14.21]** *infra*.

[21.] Para **[15.07]** *post*.

[22.] Para **[14.54]** *et seq, infra*.

[23.] See para **[14.07]** *infra*.

[24.] See para **[9.37]** *ante*.

[25.] See para **[14.73]** *infra*.

[26.] See paras **[10.35]** *ante* and **[14.74]** *et seq, infra*.

[27.] *Wright v Griffith* (1851) 1 Ir Ch R 695 at 702 (*per* Brady LC); *Re Flynn and Newman's Contract* [1948] IR 104 at 112 (*per* Kingsmill Moore J). See also *Re Lyons and Carroll's Contract* [1896] 1 IR 383; *Re Geraghty and Lyon's Contract* (1919) 53 ILTR 57; *Re White and Hague's Contract* [1921] 1 IR 138.

[28.] [1899] 1 IR 449.

"The law of the land applicable to vendors and purchasers always has been that where a man proposes to sell land he must make out his title."[29]

This, as Lord Ashbourne C said in the same case, stems from "the ordinary right of a purchaser to see that he is getting what he desires to buy."[30] In fact, this duty is often said to have two aspects, ie, to show good title, in the sense of stating all matters essential to the title contracted to be sold, and to make good title, in the sense of proving by proper evidence those matters.[31]

[14.07] It is important to note that this duty operates with full force only in respect of an open contract.[32] There is no reason why the vendor should not restrict this duty, or possibly even exclude it,[33] by the terms of the conditions of sale,[34] and this is often done.[35] But the greatest caution must be exercised in framing such conditions, as we saw in an earlier chapter.[36] The vendor must take care not to be fraudulent, nor ambiguous, for the courts will construe the conditions in favour of the purchaser.[37] Thus, in *Re O'Flanagan and Ryan's Contract*,[38] where the vendors contracted to sell property as trustees, a condition of sale stated that the property had been conveyed to them by a testator's widow who had herself been appointed by his will a trustee for sale of the property, and that they would not be bound to procure the concurrence of any other parties to the sale. The purchaser refused to complete on the ground that a good title had not been shown, as the testator's will contained no power by the widow to delegate her trust. Porter MR upheld the purchaser's objection to title and had this to say about the vendor's argument that the conditions of sale informed the purchaser of what he was buying, that, if the title proved bad, it was all the vendors were prepared to give and the purchaser was precluded from objecting.

"In my opinion this argument is founded on a fallacy. A purchaser under such a condition is entitled to assume that he is getting a good title if it be possible consistently with what is stated that the title may be a good one; and it is plain that, consistently with what is stated, the title here might be a perfectly good one ... Anyone reading that condition could be entitled to

---

[29.] *Ibid*, p 460. See also at p 458 (*per* FitzGibbon LJ).

[30.] *Ibid*, p 457. See also *Re O'Flanagan and Ryan's Contract* [1905] 1 IR 280 at 286 (*per* Porter MR).

[31.] On this distinction, see *Higgins v ILC* [1960] IR 277 at 279 (*per* Teevan J). See also *Parr v Lovegrove* (1858) 4 Drew 170.

[32.] See *Re Geraghty and Lyon's Contract* (1919) 53 ILTR 57 at 58 (*per* Powell J); *Re White and Hague's Contract* [1921] 1 IR 138 at 143 (*per* O'Connor MR).

[33.] See para **[14.08]** *infra*.

[34.] *Re Flynn and Newman's Contract* [1948] IR 104 at 112 (*per* Kingsmill Moore J), see para **[14.08]** *infra*.

[35.] See para **[9.37]** *ante*.

[36.] See para **[9.37]** *et seq, ante*.

[37.] See *ibid* and para **[15.04]** *post*.

[38.] [1905] 1 IR 280. See also *Pryde v Pryde* (1968) 19 NILQ 214.

assume, and would assume, that there was some provision in the will, or in some other instrument of title, enabling [the widow] to delegate her trust... If then, on the condition of sale, he is entitled to assume that a power to do what was done would be shown, the meaning of that is that he was entitled to have this by the contract, and as he has not got it, a good title has not been shown pursuant to the conditions of sale."[39]

Similarly, in *Re White and Hague's Contract*,[40] O'Connor MR commented:

"And there is also authority for the further proposition, that a contract by a purchaser to take such title as a vendor has does not relieve the vendor from the necessity of showing a *bona fide* title, and producing the best title he can from the materials in his power ... a proposition which has special application to a case in which no explanation can be offered for refusal to make title, except dishonesty or perversity."[41]

1. Implied Term or Rule of Law

[14.08] There has been a divergence of views amongst judges on both sides of the Irish Sea as to whether the vendor's obligation to show good title rests upon an implied term of the contract for sale or exists as a general rule of law.[42] The more traditional view seems to have been that the duty arises from an implied term of the contract,[43] but in *Re White and Hague's Contract*,[44] O'Connor MR was firmly of the view it was not a right arising from the parties' agreement, but rather one given by law.[45] This also seems to have been the view of Kingsmill Moore J in *Re Flynn and Newman's Contract*,[46] when he said:

"In the absence of any express provision to the contrary, the vendor undertakes and is bound, *in law*, to show a good title to the property to be sold and to convey land corresponding substantially, in all respects, with the description contained in the contract."[47]

However, nothing of substance seems to turn on the distinction for it is clear that, even if the duty is accorded the status of a rule of law, it does give way

---

[39] *Ibid*, p 286.
[40] [1921] 1 IR 138.
[41] *Ibid*, p 145. See also para **[9.37]** *ante*.
[42] *Re Geraghty and Lyons Contract* (1919) 53 ILTR 57 at 58 (*per* Powell J). See also *Ellis v Rogers* (1885) 29 Ch D 661 at 670-1 (*per* Cotton LJ).
[43] See, eg *Souter v Drake* (1834) 5 B & Ald 992. See also *Parvis v Rayer* (1821) 9 Price 488; *Hall v Betty* (1842) 4 Man & G 410.
[44] [1921] 1 IR 138.
[45] *Ibid*, p 145, quoting *Ogilvie v Foljambe* (1817) 3 Mer 53 at 64 (*per* Grant MR).
[46] [1948] IR 104.
[47] *Ibid*, p 112 (italics added). *Cf McGrory v Alderdale Estate Co Ltd* [1918] AC 503 at 508 (*per* Finlay LC); *Timmins v Moreland Street Property Co Ltd* [1958] Ch 110 at 118-9 (*per* Jenkins LJ) and 132 (*per* Romer LJ).

to an express provision to the contrary in the contract,[48] as Kingsmill Moore J accepted. Rather the distinction seems to be one of emphasis in that judges, who want to emphasise the courts' vigilance to prevent vendors from escaping from their obligations by fraudulently or ambiguously drafted conditions of sale, tend to speak of those obligations being imposed by the general law rather than as being dependent on the vagaries of the parties' agreement. This seems to have been the attitude of O'Connor MR in *Re White and Hague's Contract*.

2. Good Title

[14.09] The word "title" is used in a variety of senses by lawyers.[49] In the context of conveyancing there are at least two meanings. One is the equivalent of ownership of land, ie., the person who has "title" to it is the person who enjoys such attributes of ownership that he has the right to maintain and recover possession of the land as against all other persons. The other is the proof of ownership, ie., the evidence, such as documents like "title" deeds, which establishes the claim to ownership, or title in the first sense. In the context of the vendor's duty to show good title, the word is usually taken as being used in the first sense, ie., the vendor is to show that he enjoys such ownership of the property that, when he conveys it to the purchaser, the latter will be able to resist any claims or challenge made by any third parties.[50]

[14.10] The vital test is usually whether the vendor would succeed, in an application for specific performance, in securing a court order forcing the title he had deduced on the purchaser.[51] If the answer to this question is in the affirmative, then, the title is "good" or, as it is sometimes described, at least "marketable."[52] On the other hand, if the court would not decree specific performance, the title must be either "bad," in the sense that there is a clear defect in title,[53] or so "doubtful" that the court is not prepared to force it on an unwilling purchaser,[54] unless, perhaps, the contract has been fairly

---

48. *Cf* other so-called "rules of law", eg, the Rule in *Shelley's* Case, see *Irish Land Law* (2nd ed, 1986), para 4.036.

49. See Rudden, 'The Terminology of Title' (1964) 80 LQR 63. See also *Irish Land Law* (2nd ed, 1986) paras 23.07-8.

50. See *Jeakes v White* (1851) 6 Exch 873 at 881 (*per* Pollock CB).

51. See *Re McDermott and Kellett's Contract* (1904) 4 NIJR 89 at 90 (*per* Barton J). See also *Re Murphy and Griffin's Contract* [1919] 1 IR 187; *Re Hogan and Marnell's Contract* [1919] IR 422.

52. See *Maconchy v Clayton* [1898] 1 IR 291 at 308 (*per* FitzGibbon LJ). See also the same judge in *Clarke v Taylor* [1899] 1 IR 449 at 460 and Costello J in *Dublin Laundry Co Ltd v Clarke* [1989] ILRM 29 at 36. *Cf Re Spollen and Long's Contract* [1936] Ch 713 at 713 (*per* Luxmoore J); *MEPC Ltd v Christian-Edwards* [1979] 3 All ER 752.

53. See *Re McLoughlin and McGrath's Contract* (1914) 48 ILTR See also *Wiles v Latham* (1837) S & Sc 441 at 442 (*per* O'Loghlen MR).

54. See *Re Walker and Elgee's Contract* (1919) 53 ILTR 22. See also para **[13.52]** *ante*.

"closed" and the purchaser has committed himself to accepting that title.[55] Finally, there may be what is called a "good holding" title[56] which is one which may have had some technical defect but which is no longer open to any serious doubt,[57] probably because of the operation of the Statute of Limitations.[58] Such a title may be forced on a purchaser despite the technical flaw.[59] It may be useful to examine these gradations of title in a little more detail.

(i) Marketable

[14.11] It is settled that a title need not be absolutely perfect to be forced on a purchaser; it is sufficient if, when transferred to the purchaser, it will enable the purchaser to sell it in turn without having to insert special conditions in the contract for sale to cover any defects.[60] Thus, in *Maconchy v Clayton*,[61] the Irish Court of Appeal held that a title based upon a renewable leasehold fee farm conversion grant[62] was not a "marketable" one, unless the title to the lease that existed before the conversion grant was proved. The reason was, of course, that under the Renewable Leasehold Conversion Act 1849, such grants took effect subject to all covenants, conditions, exceptions and reservations,[63] and to all uses, trusts, charges, liens, incumbrances and equities,[64] which previously affected the lease which had been converted into a fee farm grant.[65] Though it is arguable that,

---

55. *Re White and Hague's Contract* [1921] 1 IR 138 at 144 (*per* O'Connor MR).
56. See *Re Mitchell and McElhinney's Contract* [1902]1 IR 83 at 88 (*per* Porter MR). See also Lindley LJ's oft-quoted dictum in *Re Scott and Alvarez's Contract* [1895] 2 Ch 603 at 613: "... there are bad titles and bad titles; bad titles which are good holding titles, although they may be open to objections which are not serious, are bad titles in a conveyancer's point of view, but good in a business man's point of view ..."
57. *Re Murphy and Griffin's Contract* [1919] I IR 187.
58. See *Re McClure and Garrett's Contract* [1899] 1 IR 225.
59. *Re Mitchell and McElhinney's Contract* [1902] 1 IR 83. See also *Re Atkinson and Horsell's Contract* [1912] 2 Ch 1, but see the comments on this case of O'Connor MR in *Clibborn v Horan* [1921] 1 IR 93 at 100, para **[14.82]** *infra*.
60. *Re Spollen and Long's Contract* [1936] Ch 713 at 718 (*per* Luxmoore J). *Cf Barclays Bank plc v Weeks Legg and Dean* [1996] EGCS 29.
61. [1898] 1 IR 291.
62. On such grants, see *Irish Land Law* (2nd ed, 1986) para 4.081 *et seq*.
63. Section 1.
64. Section 7. See *Irish Land Law* (2nd ed, 1986) para 4.086.
65. Section 74 of the Landlord and Tenant (Amendment) Act 1980, which purports to vest the fee simple in the holder of any unconverted lease for lives renewable for ever does not necessarily improve the marketability of the title in this respect because the estate so vested is deemed to be a "graft" on the previous leasehold interest and subject to "any rights or equities arising from its being such a graft." This would seem to cover not only covenants and conditions in the lease but also, arguably, the rent: see Lyall, *Land Law in Ireland* (1994), pp 202-3 and 250-2; Wylie *Irish Landlord and Tenant Law*, pp 1181-2. See further, para **[14.56]** *infra*.

since many of these grants are now over 100 years old, they ought to be accepted as a good root of title. To require production of the antecedent lease for lives may be regarded as unreasonable and it is now common practice to accept the conversion grant as the root of title. In *Clarke v Taylor*,[66] the Court of Appeal refused to accept as marketable vendors' title based on the fact that they were the executors of a person who had remained in occupation after expiration of a lease, paying the same rent as reserved by the lease. On the other hand, in *Dublin Laundry Co Ltd v Clarke*[67] Costello J rejected various arguments put forward by the purchaser from a company in support of the propositions that it did not have a good marketable title and so a completion notice served by the vendor was invalid. For example, although at the date of service of the notice the liquidator of the company had not got releases of charges on the company's land, arrangements for releases had been made and they could have been obtained by the date of expiration of the notice.[68] Similarly, although a statutory declaration and certificate for the purpose of the Family Home Protection Act 1976,[69] had not been executed at the date of service of the completion notice, the form of both had been agreed and it was simply a matter of signature which could again be done without difficulty before the expiry of the notice.

(ii) Good Holding

[14.12] The classic case of a good holding title is one which, though not supported by the usual documentary evidence of title, is supported by long and undisturbed possession of the land by the vendor. Indeed, by virtue of the doctrine of adverse possession,[70] once the statutory period of limitation has run the title of the previous owner is "extinguished" and so arguably the vendor's title thereupon becomes "good" in the fullest sense,[71] provided, of course, sufficient proof of the requisite adverse possession is forthcoming.[72] Indeed, in England the general proposition has been laid down that in such a case the vendor may force a possessory title on the purchaser, even though the contract specified a documentary title.[73] However, this has been doubted in Ireland in relation to leasehold land, because of the consequences of the

---

66. [1899] 1 IR 449.
67. [1989] ILRM 29.
68. See para **[13.20]** *ante*.
69. See para **[16.64]** *post*.
70. See *Irish Land Law* (2nd ed, 1986), Ch 23.
71. See para **[14.10]** *ante*. See also *Re McClure and Garrett's Contract* [1899] 1 IR 225 at 228 (*per* Chatterton V-C).
72. Eg, supported by statutory declarations.
73. *Re Atkinson and Horsell's Contract* [1912] 2 Ch 1. *Cf George Wimpey & Co Ltd v Sohn* [1967] Ch 487.

"no parliamentary conveyance" doctrine.[74] As O'Connor MR pointed out in *Re Ashe and Hogan's Contract*,[75] unless there are special circumstances creating a tenancy by estoppel,[76] the vendor relying upon such a title in relation to leasehold land does not have the leasehold estate vested in him.[77] He went on:

> "He cannot then convey it. The most he can convey is the right to hold possession of the lands during the residue of the term. From one point of view that may be a more beneficial estate, because it does not carry with it the personal obligations which the assignee of a leasehold estate assumes: but on the other hand, not being in privity with the lessor, he does not get the benefits which pass to an assignee of a leasehold estate. For instance, he cannot sue on the lessor's convenants for title and quiet enjoyment which, when not expressed, are implied in leases by the Landlord and Tenant Act 1860."[78]

[14.13] Another point which has arisen several times in Ireland relates to registered land. It has been questioned whether a vendor shows good title to registered land when he has not yet himself become the registered owner because the formalities for registration following a previous transfer to him have not yet been completed, or, perhaps, he has never applied to have himself registered as owner. The same point arises when, on the transfer to the vendor of unregistered land, the land becomes subject to compulsory registration, as it did, eg, when land was vested in the tenant-purchaser under the Land Purchase Acts.[79] In respect of the latter situation, s 25 of the Local Registration of Title (Ireland) Act 1891, provided that no estate was to vest in the tenant-purchaser until he was registered as owner, but, on being so registered, his title was to relate back to the date of the execution of the conveyance in his favour.[80] The question then arose as to what the position was if the tenant-purchaser contracted to resell the land before he became so registered. In *Re Furlong and Bogan's Contract*,[81] Chatterton V-C held that

---

74. This is discussed in detail in *Irish Land Law* (2nd ed, 1986), paras 23.09-19. See also Brady and Kerr, *the Limitation of Actions* (2nd ed, 1994), p 135 *et seq.*

75. [1920] 1 IR 159.

76. See *Irish Land Law* (2nd ed, 1986), paras 23.124.

77. On this at least both the House of Lords (see *Fairweather v St. Marylebone Property Co Ltd* [1963] AC 510) and the Irish Supreme Court (see *Perry v Woodfarm Homes Ltd* [1975] IR 104) are agreed. See *Irish Land Law* (2nd ed, 1986), paras 23.11-9.

78. [1920] 1 IR 159 at 169. See also the same judge in *Clibborn v Horan* [1921] 1 IR 93 at 100-1. *Cf Mohan v Roche* [1991] 1 IR 560. As to the 1860 Act, see . Wylie, *Irish Landlord and Tenant Law*, Ch 14.

79. See *Irish Land Law* (2nd ed, 1986), paras 1.60 and 21.05. See also para 21.21. See also Fitzgerald, *Land Registry Practice* (2nd ed, 1995), p 380 *et seq.*

80. A similar provision (but including time limits for registration) is now contained in the Registration of Title Act 1964, s 25.

81. (1893) 31 LR Ir 191.

such a vendor had sufficient title to the land to be forced on a purchaser. He said:

> "It is true that the vendor had not yet acquired any estate in the lands, but she had an inchoate right incapable of being defeated, and only waiting for an official duty to be performed to become an absolute estate."[82]

Similarly, in *Re Mitchell and McElhinney's Contract*,[83] where the tenant-purchaser died before registration of his ownership and left the land to the vendor, one of the conditions of sale stated that the vendor's title was not registered and that the purchaser was not to raise any objection on this ground nor to require the vendor to register before completion. The purchaser nevertheless objected that the vendor had failed to show good title and was bound to register prior to completion. Porter MR rejected this argument and insisted that the vendor had a "perfectly good holding title."[84]

[14.14] In *McGirr v Devine*,[85] a contract for the sale of registered land was entered into on 29 May 1924. However, at that date the vendor had not yet become the registered owner, though he had lodged his application for registration on 8 January 1924. The contract fixed completion for June 1924, but the vendor did not in fact become registered until 18 August 1924. However, under the Land Registry Rules[86] the registration of the vendor dated back to the date of lodgment and acceptance of his application for registration, ie, 8 January 1924. Wilson J held that the vendor had shown good title to the property, and that the purchaser was not entitled to rescind. The vendor was absolutely entitled to be registered as from 8 January 1924, and became registered and was, therefore, in a position to convey as registered owner on 18 August 1924, before time had been made of the essence of the contract. Presumably, however, this rule does not hold good in a case of land already registered where the vendor has not even lodged his application for registration by the date of the contract for sale, when his duty to show good title arises.[87] Prior to his application for registration, the vendor's rights under the unregistered transfer[88] are subject to the risk that

---

82. *Ibid*, p 195. See further on the nature of the vendor's title prior to registration, para **[12.49]** *et seq, ante*.
83. [1902] 1 IR 83.
84. *Ibid*, p 88.
85. [1925] NI 94. *Cf Dublin Laundry Co Ltd v Clarke* [1989] ILRM 29.
86. 1910 Rules, Order IV, rules 30 and 31. See now in NI Land Registration Rules (NI) 1977, rule 50. *Cf* the Republic's Land Registration Rules 1972, rule 63.
87. *Cf* a case of unregistered land which becomes subject to compulsory registration on execution of the conveyance to the vendor, where title relates back to the date of the conveyance, not just the date of the application to the Registry, see para **[14.13]** *supra*.
88. See further, para **[12.05]** *ante*.

the registered owner may execute a transfer or a charge in favour of a third party who, by lodging his application for registration first, may gain priority over the vendor.[89] Thus, until he lodges his application for registration, or otherwise protects himself, eg, by entering a caution,[90] such a vendor patently does not have a good holding title and the purchaser ought to be able to call the sale off on that ground.

(iii) Doubtful

[14.15] In *Re Hogan and Marnell's Contract*,[91] Powell J decided that there was a difficult question of construction of the will under which the vendor claimed title, so that the title was sufficiently doubtful that he ought not to force it on the purchaser in a vendor and purchaser summons,[92] but rather ought to adjourn the summons so that the question could be determined on an originating summons the decision on which would bind all parties. On the other hand, in *Re Walker and Elgee's Contract*,[93] which involved a question of the effect of a purported exercise of a power of appointment by a testatrix in favour of the vendors, the same judge took the view that there was no "real difficulty or doubt" on the question of title and decided, on a vendor and purchaser summons, that the vendors had shown a good title.

[14.16] In *Re McDermott and Kellett's Contract*,[94] Barton J had this to say about the vendor's title:

> "The vendors have agreed to sell the whole legal and equitable estate in premises held for ever in fee-farm, and have agreed that the deed of January 4th 1881, shall be the commencement of title. It appears that the deed of January 4th 1881, is in a material particular inconsistent with the title which was stipulated for in the contract of sale which is deduced by the subsequent fee-farm grant. I do not feel at liberty under these circumstances to force this title upon the purchaser."[95]

(iv) Bad

[14.17] There have been numerous cases where the Irish courts have held that a vendor's title had so clear a defect that it had to be held that it was bad.

[89.] See Fitzgerald, *Land Registry Practice* (2nd ed, 1995), p 31.

[90.] See *ibid*, Ch 10. See also para **[6.66]** *ante*.

[91.] [1919] 1 IR 422, applying *Re Nichol and Van Joel's Contract* [1910] 1 Ch 43. See also *Nottingham Patent Brick and Tile Co v Butler* (1886) 16 QBD 778; *Re Hollis' Hospital and Hague's Contract* [1899] 2 Ch 540.

[92.] See para **[13.26]** *ante*.

[93.] (1919) 53 ILTR 22.

[94.] (1904) 4 NIJR 89.

[95.] *Ibid*, p 90.

Thus, in *Mulholland v Corporation of Belfast*,[96] Blackburne LJ said with respect to the title being purchased in that case:

> "... it is a valid and insuperable objection to the title to an underlease, that the premises in it are comprised with others in an original lease, under which the lessor has a right to re-enter for breach of covenant, so that the under-lessee or his assignee might be evicted without any breach of covenant on his part ..."[97]

In *Boyd v Dickson*,[98] where the vendor had bought the property on behalf of one of the trustees of the property,[99] Sullivan MR referred to the title as "a radically bad title, or rather, as it was described at the Bar, no title at all."[100] In *Clegg v Wright*,[101] the vendor failed to show good title because the vendor had only a life interest in one-third of the property as dower.[102] In *Re Geraghty and Lyon's Contract*,[103] it was admitted by the vendor that he could not give a good title since it was clearly defeasible.

3. Matters of Conveyance

[14.18] A distinction must be drawn between a defect in title, in respect of which the purchaser can raise objections immediately and resist specific performance, and a flaw which is a "matter of conveyance" only, which the vendor has until completion to put right. Such a matter is something which the vendor can deal with immediately and independently, ie, without having to get some third party's consent. Examples are discharging a mortgage[104] or securing appointment of trustees to receive the purchase money.[105] In *Re Conlon and Faulkener's Contract*,[106] O'Connor MR held that the furnishing of a statutory declaration to verify a fact stated on the face of the abstract of

---

96. (1859) Dru *temp* Nap 539.
97. *Ibid*, p 554-5.
98. (1876) IR 10 Eq 239.
99. Which was, therefore, a breach of trust, see *Irish Land Law* (2nd ed, 1986), para 10.075. See also *Re O'Flanagan and Ryan's Contract* [1905] 1 IR 280 (improper delegation of trust), para **[14.07]** *supra*.
100. *Op cit*, p 256. *Cf Re Stone and Saville's Contract* [1963] 1 WLR 163 at 169 (*per* Lord Denning MR) ("a thoroughly bad title").
101. (1920) 54 ILTR 69.
102. *Ibid*, p 70 (*per* Powell J). See *Irish Land Law* (2nd ed, 1986), para 4.158.
103. (1919) 53 ILTR 57. *Cf Molphy v Coyne* (1919) 53 ILTR 177.
104. *Re Daniel* [1917] 2 Ch 405. See also *Dublin Laundry Co Ltd v Clarke* [1989] ILRM 29: para **[14.11]** *supra*.
105. *Hatten v Russell* (1888) 38 Ch D 334. See *Irish Land Law* (2nd ed, 1986), para 8.094. As to planning matters, see Mellows, 'The Use and Title' (1962) 26 Conv 269; Potter, 'Caveat Emptor' (1949) 13 Conv 36.
106. [1916] 1 IR 241.

title was a matter of conveyance, the expense of which ought to be borne by the purchaser.[107] As he put it:

> "The declaration asked for is not required for the purpose of adding to the abstract of title, or completing it ... a declaration verifying it would not be part of the abstract. His title would not depend on the declaration; he would still have a good title even though he refused to make the declaration, or was unable to do so, if the fact of the heirship existed."[108]

On the other hand, he held that the abstract was defective in not showing whether or not succession and estate duty, to which the property became liable on the death of a previous owner through whom the vendor's title was traced, had been paid.[109] In *Hopkins v Geoghegan*,[110] Johnston J held that production of a certificate from the Revenue Commissioners that no arrears of income tax were outstanding was not a defect in title, but a matter of conveyance,[111] the expense of which should again be borne by the purchaser.[112] However, he did also hold that the lack of a "PD" stamp[113] on a deed of assignment was a matter of title for which the vendor was responsible.[114]

4. Waiver

[14.19] Once the purchaser discovers that the vendor cannot show good title to the property, the purchaser has a choice of remedies[115] and must, as FitzGibbon LJ said in *Clarke v Taylor*,[116] "elect whether he will insist on strict proof of a marketable title, or will accept such evidence of title as the vendor can reasonably give, rather than break off the purchase."[117] Thus, in *Clegg v Wright*,[118] where Powell J held that the purchaser's solicitor had treated the contract as subsisting after discovery of the defect in title,[119] the vendor was held to be entitled to a reasonable opportunity to cure the defect.[120] In such cases the purchaser is often said to waive the right to be

---

[107.] Under the Conveyancing Act 1881, s 3(6). See para **[14.48]** *infra*.

[108.] *Op cit*, pp 245-6.

[109.] *Op cit*, p 247.

[110.] [1931] IR 135.

[111.] *Ibid*, p 141.

[112.] Conveyancing Act 1881 s 3(6).

[113.] See para **[20.41]** *post*.

[114.] *Op cit*, p 142.

[115.] See *Re Geraghty and Lyon's Contract* (1919) 53 ILTR 57 at 58 (*per* Powell J).

[116.] [1899] 1 IR 449.

[117.] *Ibid*, p 460. Or he can sue for damages, *per* Powell J fn 115 *supra*.

[118.] (1920) 54 ILTR 69.

[119.] *Ibid*, p 73.

[120.] *Ibid*, p 72.

shown good title, or at least, the right of objection to title and whether or not there is such a waiver must obviously depend upon the circumstances of the particular case.[121] The courts seem to be very reluctant to accept that there has been a waiver, no doubt because of the serious consequences for a purchaser. Thus, in *Wright v Griffith*,[122] where the purchaser had taken possession of the property, Brady LC stated:

> "... it seems manifest to me, that the parties did not intend or consider that the taking of possession was to operate as a waiver of title; their acts prove this, because they continued the negotiations with respect to the title."[123]

In *Boyd v Dickson*,[124] not only had the purchaser taken possession of the property, he had also made some alterations to it.[125] Nevertheless, Sullivan MR said:

> "I feel bound to say that I see nothing in the supposed case of waiver on either side. The vendor did nothing in my opinion, to give up his right to insist on the strictest construction of the conditions; and neither the possession taken by Mr. Dickson nor his subsequent acts have, under the circumstances surrounding them, sufficient force to prevent him from rejecting the title, if he can show that he is not bound to accept it."[126]

II. DEDUCTION OF TITLE

[14.20] We now turn to the question of how in a particular case the vendor must actually deduce title, or, to put it another way, discharge his obligation to show good title to the property contracted to be sold. As we mentioned earlier, a crucial distinction must be drawn between registered and unregistered land.

A. Registered Land

[14.21] As has been said many times, the primary object of the registration of title system is to simplify conveyancing by abolishing the need for repetitive investigations of title every time a parcel of land is sold or otherwise disposed of.[127] Instead, once the title is registered in the Land

---

[121.] See *Corless v Sparling* (1874) IR 8 Eq 335. See also *Re Priestley and Davidson's Contract* (1892) 31 LR Ir 122. And see para **[12.34]** ante.

[122.] (1851) 1 Ir Ch R 695.

[123.] *Ibid*, p 703.

[124.] (1876) IR 10 Eq 239.

[125.] For the significance or such acts in another context, see paras **[6.56-8]** *ante*.

[126.] *Op cit*, p 253.

[127.] See McAllister, *Registration of Title in Ireland* (1973) Ch 1; Fitzgerald, *Land Registry Practice* (2nd ed, 1995) Ch 1.

Registry, a prospective purchaser should be concerned solely with the existing state of the register, which is supposed to be a "mirror" of the title, backed by a state guarantee.[128] He should not, so the theory goes, be concerned with the previous history of the title, as he would be in a case of unregistered land.[129] He should no longer be concerned with title deeds, for on registration of the title the owner should have been issued with a land certificate, or in the case of a charge, a charge certificate.[130] These certificates fulfil largely the same role as title deeds; thus they can even be used to create equitable mortgages by way of deposit.[131]

[14.22] 1t is essential to realise, however, that, admirable though the Land Registry system is, it is by no means perfect. It may be useful, therefore, to examine the limitations of the system before considering deduction of registered titles.[132] There are limitations which exist quite apart from the fact that most urban land is not yet subject to compulsory registration of title,[133] so that unregistered conveyancing is still the norm in urban areas.[134]

1. Limitations of Registration of Title System

(i) Title Registered

[14.23] It is crucial to note that the benefits of the Land Registry system accrue in respect only of the actual registered estates or interests in any particular parcel of land. Thus, while the freehold title in a parcel of land may be registered, the leasehold title may not[135] and clearly, if the transaction in question concerns only the leasehold title, the conveyancing will still be unregistered conveyancing and the title in the Land Registry will often be ignored.[136] Though, where the lease is registered as a burden on the

---

128. See *McAllister, op cit*, pp 298-302; Fitzgerald *op cit*, pp 6 and 23-4.

129. See para **[14.54]** *infra*.

130. See *McAllister, op cit*, Ch VIII; Fitzgerald *op cit*, Ch 20. But note that the land certificate has often not been issued in the past, see para **[14.31]** *infra*.

131. *Irish Land Law* (2nd ed, 1986), paras 12.13 and 12.29.

132. See the critique of the English system in Hayton, *Registered Land* (3rd ed, 1981). See also Dworkin, 'Registered Land Reform' (1961) 24 MLR 135; Jackson, 'Registration of Land Interests - The English Version' (1972) 88 LQR 93.

133. *Irish Land Law* (2nd ed, 1986), paras 4.182 and 21.20; Fitzgerald, *Land Registry Practice* (2nd ed, 1995) pp 7-8.

134. But the registration of deeds system, not to be confused with registration of title system (*ibid*, para 21.01), is relevant, *ibid*, Ch 22.

135. Indeed, if the original lease is for a term not exceeding twenty-one years, it cannot be registered, see *Irish Land Law* (2nd ed, 1986), para 21.38.

136. It depends largely on whether the purchaser of the lease wishes to insist on investigation of the freehold title as well as the leasehold title, as, eg, a developer might wish to do, see para **[14.73]** *infra*. In that case, the purchaser should insist on a special contractual provision for this, see para **[14.74]** *infra*.

freehold title, a copy or copy extract of the folio may be furnished showing this registration.

(ii) Class of Title

[14.24] Even where the transaction involves an estate in the land which is registered, the extent to which the register "mirrors" that title varies according to the class of title registered. This has become a particularly important point since additional classes were introduced by the Registration of Title Act 1964.[137] Thus, there is a considerable difference between an absolute title,[138] on the one hand, and a qualified, possessory, and good leasehold title on the other. Thus, while a qualified title has the same general effect as an absolute title, it is subject to the estates or rights included in the qualification or exception noted on the register.[139] A possessory title may be even less of a mirror because the registration does not affect or prejudice enforcement of any rights adverse to or in derogation of the registered holder's title at the time of registration and which, of course, are not disclosed by the register.[140] A good leasehold title does not affect or prejudice any estates or rights arising from superior leases or grants and there may be many of these hidden, ie, not disclosed by the register, in the sort of "pyramid" titles so common in major urban areas of both parts of Ireland.[141] Of course, these titles may be converted or reclassified into a better class, and ultimately into absolute titles,[142] but that is small comfort for a prospective purchaser who has to deal with the titles as currently classified. Though it should be noted that, until the benefits of the ground rents purchase scheme have come through in recent years, few pyramid titles had been registered, since they largely relate to land in towns and cities which are not yet subject to compulsory registration.

(iii) Equities Note

[14.25] One of the significant features of Irish conveyancing practice is that most agricultural land in both parts of Ireland is registered freehold land. This is because it was made a part of the land purchase scheme that the titles vested in the tenant-purchasers should be compulsorily registered under the Local Registration of Title (Ireland) Act 1891,[143] and this remains the case

---

[137.] See *McAllister op cit* Chs 11 and 111. *Irish Land Law* (2nd ed, 1986), paras 21.24-31.

[138.] Though even this is not a complete mirror, see para **[14.27]** *infra*.

[139.] *Irish Land Law* (2nd ed, 1986), para 21.25.

[140.] *Ibid*, para 21.26.

[141.] *Ibid*, paras 4.179-82 and 21.27-8.

[142.] *Ibid*, paras 21.29-31. See also McAllister *op cit*, Ch 111; Fitzgerald, *Land Registry Practice* (2nd ed, 1995), Ch 23.

[143.] *Irish Land Law* (2nd ed, 1986), paras 1.60 and 21.07.

under the Registration of Title Act 1964.[144] However, there is one major drawback about such titles and that is that most of them were registered "subject to equities".[145] The fee simple was vested under the Land Purchase Acts in the person who was ostensibly the tenant of the farm in question and so was only a "graft" on his existing tenancy.[146] In other words, the note as to equities entered on the register in such a case protects, but does not disclose, any third party rights which attached to the pre-vesting tenancy and continue to attach to the registered freehold title. These may be commercial interests such as mortgages or charges, or family interests such as those existing under a settlement or on an intestacy. Whatever their nature, or, indeed, whether or not any survive at the date of a subsequent purchase of the land, the note as to equities on the register constitutes a serious blot on the owner's title which the purchaser must take account of.[147] As O'Connor MR said in *Re White and Hague's Contract*[148]:

> "... the graft which springs from a Land Commission sale is not dependent on a constructive trust. It is expressly declared by statute, and the trust is as clearly established as if the purchaser by deed under his hand declared that he held the lands purchased upon the same trusts and to and for the same purposes as the previous tenancy had been held for. A purchaser from him is therefore in the strongest way coerced to make an inquiry into the title of his vendor previous to the Land Commission sale."[149]

We return to this subject later.[150]

[14.26] It is true that the note as to equities could be cancelled provided sufficient proof as to the prior title can be produced, but until recently this was rarely done. This is now governed by the provisions for conversion of titles contained in the Registration of Title Act 1964.[151]

---

[144] Section 23(1)(a).

[145] *Ibid*, para 21.07. See also *McAllister op cit* Ch 111.

[146] See *Re Smith* [1917] 1 IR 170 at 175 (*per* Madden J) (*affd* [1918] 1 IR 45). On the doctrine of graft, see further, *Irish Land Law* (2nd ed, 1986), paras 9.063-7.

[147] Note that owners holding under titles already registered subject to equities are deemed to be registered with possessory titles, and all titles vested by the Land Commission since 1967 have been registered as possessory, *Irish Land Law* (2nd ed, 1986), paras 21.30-1. But such possessory titles are subject to special conversion or reclassification procedures, see Fitzgerald, *Land Registry Practice* (2nd ed, 1995), Ch 23.

[148] [1921] 1 IR 138.

[149] *Ibid*, p 143. O'Connor MR suggested that on an "open" contract the purchaser would be entitled to investigate the equities, see para **[14.38]** *infra*.

[150] Para **[14.38]** *infra*.

[151] Section 50. For detailed discussion of their operation see Fitzgerald, *op cit*, Ch 23.

(iv) Unregistered Burdens

[14.27] Even where a title is registered as absolute, it is still not a complete mirror of the title because it has always been the case that not all interests which may attach to a parcel of land need be registered. These are referred to as "burdens" and they fall into two categories.[152] The first consists of burdens which may be registered and should be in order to preserve priority as against a transferee for value of the registered land to which they relate, eg, leases for lives or for a term exceeding twenty-one years, easements, profits and restrictive covenants, certain rights of residence and judgment mortgages. From the conveyancing point of view, these do not create many problems, provided, of course, the transaction involves a transfer for value[153]: the burdens will be either registered, in which case the transferee will discover them easily, or not registered, in which case he will take priority over them. The problems really arise in respect of the second class of burdens which affect registered land. As is the position under the English Land Registry system,[154] there is a long statutory list of burdens ("s 72" burdens) which may not be registered, but nevertheless affect the registered land without registration, eg, death duties, land purchase annuities, tenancies for terms not exceeding twenty-one years, rights acquired or in the course of being acquired under the Statute of Limitations and the rights of every person in actual occupation of the land or in receipt of the rents and profits (unless not revealed on inquiry to such persons).[155] In respect of these the Land Registry system is of no help at all,[156] and a prospective purchaser must rely upon the ordinary precautionary steps taken in a case of unregistered land in order to discover the existence of many of such rights, eg, by making appropriate requisitions on title.[157] The existence of persons who may have, rights to the property other than the registered owner, such as tenants, squatters or other persons in "actual occupation," may be revealed by an inspection of the property,[158] though in England this category of unregistered rights has given rise to particular difficulties and has resulted in some very controversial decisions.[159] It is also clear from the Supreme Court's decision

---

[152] See McAllister, *op cit*, Ch VI; Fitzgerald, *op cit*, Chs 12 and 13.

[153] *Cf* if it is a voluntary transfer, including acquisition of the land by succession or adverse possession. See **[12.05]** *et seq, ante*.

[154] The notorious "overriding interests" protected by s 70 of the Land Registration Act 1925. See Hayton, *Registered Land* (3rd ed, 1981), Ch 6.

[155] See *Fitzgerald, op cit*, Ch 13.

[156] Unless in respect of some of the burdens the Registrar has complied with a request or court order to enter a notice on the register as to their existence or non-existence, see *Fitzgerald, op cit*, p 229.

[157] See para **[16.58]** *post*.

[158] See para **[4.21]** *ante*.

[159] See Barnsley *Conveyancing Law and Practice* (3rd ed, 1988), p 50 *et seq*.

in *Northern Bank Ltd v Henry*[160] that mortgagees and chargees are particularly at risk that someone other than the mortgagor or chargor will have a right, such as a beneficial or equitable interest, which is a s 72 burden because that person is still in "actual occupation" of the property mortgaged or charged.[161] It should be noted, however, that in *Guckian v Brennan*[162] Gannnon J held that the power of a spouse to refuse consent under the Family Home Protection Act 1976, is *not* a s 72 burden. Thus, registration of a transfer without the requisite consent is valid and the transferee can assert that his title is inviolable on the basis of the conclusiveness of the register,[163] unless fraud is involved.[164]

2. Deduction of Title

[14.28] Deduction of title in the case of registered land must obviously depend upon the nature of the Land Registry system, including the limitations of that system which we have just outlined. Thus, if the transaction involves an estate or interest in the land which is not itself registered, then the rules relating to unregistered land[165] apply, even though some other estate or interest in that same land is registered. For example, the transaction may involve the assignment of a ten-year lease, which is not registered,[166] though the landlord's freehold title is. In such a case the vendor's immediate root of title[167] is the lease, which is not registered, and whether the purchaser can insist upon being shown evidence of the landlord's registered title depends upon the usual rules governing open contracts for the sale of unregistered land, or upon the terms of the contract for sale.[168]

[14.29] So far as purchase of an estate or interest the title to which is registered is concerned, it is important to note that there is no statutory provision specifying what documents must be furnished to the purchaser by way of deduction of title by the vendor.[169] Nor does there seem to be any judicial authority on the matter. However, it is usual to cover the point by the

---

[160.] [1981] IR 1. See also *McC v McC* [1982] ILRM 277.

[161.] See the discussion by Conlon, 'Beneficial Interests, Conveyances and the Occupational Hazards', the *Gazette*, March 1985, p 59. See also para **[16.23]** *post*.

[162.] [1981] IR 478. *Cf Barclays Bank Ltd v Carroll* High Court, unrep, 10 September 1986.

[163.] Under s 31 of the 1964 Act: see Fitzgerald *op cit*, pp 227 and 389-91.

[164.] See s 30 of the 1964 Act. As to the courts' jurisdiction to direct rectification of the register for fraud see *Re Walsh* [1916] 1 IR 40.

[165.] See para **[14.42]** *infra*.

[166.] Para **[14.27]** *supra*.

[167.] On this concept, see para **[14.56]** *infra*.

[168.] Para **[14.68]** *et seq, infra*.

[169.] Ie, there is no equivalent of s 110 of the English Land Registration Act 1925.

terms of the contract for sale and, indeed, the conditions of sale in the contract form issued by the Law Society do contain provisions dealing with it.

(i) Inspection of Registers

[14.30] Unlike in England where the vendor's register of title was until recently[170] private and the purchaser needed his authority to inspect it,[171] in Ireland the practice since 1891 has been to treat the registers in the Land Registry as open to public inspection,[172] and this has now been confirmed by statute.[173] It is true that the rules may seek to impose limits on the categories of persons able to inspect documents filed in the Registry,[174] in an attempt to exclude "curiosity mongers" and "mischief makers,"[175] but it seems clear that a person who has entered into a contract for sale with the registered owner does not come into this category.[176] So there is no need for the vendor to furnish authority to the purchaser to inspect the registers; the purchaser is entitled to do this without such authority, and, indeed, ought to make his own searches prior to completion, unless it is provided by the contract that the vendor is going to supply these.[177]

(ii) Land Certificate

[14.31] As mentioned earlier,[178] on registration of a title in the Land Registry the title deeds are replaced by the land certificate[179] which may be issued by the Registry to the registered owner.[180] This certificate is a copy of the folio[181] relating to the title in question and is *prima facie* evidence of the

---

[170.] The English register became open to public inspection as a result of the Land Registration Act 1988, s 1: see also Land Registration (Open Register) Rules 1991 (SI 122/1991); Pryer 'Land Register goes Public' (1990) L Soc Gaz 19

[171.] Land Registration Act 1925, s 112; see also s 110(1).

[172.] See *Re Fitzgerald* [1925] 1 IR 39; *Re Fairbairn* (1940) 74 ILTR 4; *Re Nolan* (1941) 75 ILTR 56.

[173.] Registration of Title Act 1964, s 107(1).

[174.] See, eg, the Land Registration Rules 1972, rule 188 (authority of registered owner or court order needed to inspect filed documents); *cf* rule 198 (any person, on payment of the prescribed fee, may search in the registry maps, folios and indexes and obtain copies of them or of extracts from them).

[175.] See McAllister, *Registration of Title* (1973), p 315.

[176.] 1972 Rules, rules 188(1) and (2).

[177.] See para **[15.41]** *post*.

[178.] Para **[14.21]** *supra*.

[179.] Or charge certificate in the case of a registered charge (which is a mortgage of registered land), *ibid*. And see Fitzgerald, *Land Registry Practice* (2nd ed, 1995), pp 154 and Ch 20.

[180.] Despite the duty imposed by s 28 of the Registration of Title Act 1964, land certificates are frequently not issued and where they were, were often lodged with the Land Commission.

[181.] *Fitzgerald op cit*, Ch 20.

registered title,[182] though not of burdens mentioned in it.[183] Thus, at first sight the primary method of deduction of title would be for the vendor to furnish the purchaser with a copy of the land certificate. However, there is one point which a purchaser must remember and that is that the land certificate is evidence only of the matters referred to in it as at *the date of its issue*.[184] If the certificate has not been lodged by the vendor in the Registry to be made conformable with the register and then reissued, it may be out-of-date and the purchaser cannot safely rely upon any copy furnished by the vendor. Thus, at the very least, the purchaser will have to protect himself by making appropriate searches in the Registry prior to completion.[185] Not surprisingly, given that a land certificate may not have been issued or the one issued has not been kept up-to-date, the Law Society's standard contract form provides[186] that the purchaser is not entitled to require production or issue of a land certificate, if none has previously been issued or the one which has been was issued to the Land Commission.[187] Instead the vendor is required to furnish a copy of the folio or folios relating to the land in question, written up-to-date, and a copy of the relevant Land Registry map or file plan.[188] Another point is that a high proportion of registered land cases involve a leasehold folio where the original lease is not retained by the Land Registry, but is returned to the registered owner. The Registry keeps a certified copy only. In all cases, a copy of the original lease must be furnished by the vendor as in a case of unregistered land.

[14.32] However, it should be noted that it is usual for a requisition on title to be made requiring the land certificate to be handed over on completion.[189] Apart from this, the certificate will have to be produced to the Registry for registration of the new ownership resulting from the current transaction.[190] Once the purchaser is registered as the new owner, he is, by statute, entitled to delivery of a certificate,[191] and this will usually be the existing certificate previously held by the vendor, but written up-to-date. If, however, the sale relates to part only of the land registered, the Registrar may either allow the vendor to retain his certificate subject to an entry in it as to the part of the

---

[182.] Registration of Title Act 1964, s 105(4).
[183.] See 1972 Rules, rule 159.
[184.] 1972 Rules, rule 161.
[185.] See para **[15.41]** *post*.
[186.] Cond 13(e).
[187.] See fn 180 *supra*.
[188.] Cond 13(c). See para **[14.33]** *et seq, infra*
[189.] See para **[16.59]** *post*.
[190.] 1964 Act, s 105(1). See also 1972 Rules, rule 162.
[191.] 1964 Act, s 51(3). See para **[14.33]** *infra*.

land transferred to the purchaser, or issue a new certificate to the vendor as to the land retained by him.[192]

(iii) Copy of Folio

[14.33] Instead of furnishing a copy of the land certificate, as we have seen[193] the vendor provides the purchaser with a copy of the folio or folios relating to the land in question. This is certainly necessary where a land certificate has never been issued in respect of the land (which is often the case) or where it has been issued to the Land Commission.[194] Since 1922 a copy of the folio has invariably been furnished by the vendor to vouch his title, because so few land certificates have been issued to registered owners.[195] There are some advantages in producing a copy of the folio. A sealed copy of the folio is conclusive evidence of the title shown thereon and of the original, though not the subsequent, title to burdens registered thereon[196]; the land certificate is *prima facie* evidence only of the title, as it reflects the state of the title only at the date of its issue or re-issue, and it is not evidence of the ownership of the burdens on the folio.[197] The register is divided into folios relating to each title, which with the passage of time consist of pages of entries detailing various successive changes of ownership and other dealings with the land. However, since 1973 each folio has been divided into three parts, which makes it easier to decipher the current state of the title.[198] Furthermore, computerisation of the system was launched in a major way during the 1980s, beginning with the Dublin folios.[199] Though financial and staffing restrictions imposed by successive Governments has hampered the programme, considerable progress has been made and the hope is that the benefits of computerisation will soon apply comprehensively to other parts of the system, such as the maps.[200]

[14.34] A copy of the folio, or of extracts from it, may be obtained from the Registry on payment of the prescribed fee.[201] Since it is usual for the vendor's solicitor to obtain this close to the date of the contract it should be fairly up-to-date, though again it must be remembered that the copy shows the state of the title only as at the date of its issue. There will still be a gap

---

[192.] 1964 Act, s 51(4).

[193.] See para **[14.31]** *supra*.

[194.] Cond 13(c) of the Law Society's *General Conditions of Sale* (1995 ed).

[195.] See the discussion in Glover, *Registration of Ownership of Land in Ireland* (1933), pp 254-8.

[196.] 1964 Act, s 31.

[197.] See McAllister, *Registration of Title in Ireland* (1973), p 252; Fitzgerald, *Land Registry Practice* (2nd ed, 1995) p 347.

[198.] See *McAllister, op cit* pp 26-7; *Fitzgerald, op cit*, p 14.

[199.] This is now completed.

[200.] Computer-generated digital maps are now accepted: see *Fitzgerald op cit*, Ch 4 and generally on new developments, Ch 29.

[201.] 1972 Rules, rule 198(1).

between that date and the date of completion, when the purchaser is still subject to the risk of some third party rights being registered and getting priority over him.[202] Once again the only sure method of protection is to make a search in the Registry prior to completion.[203]

[14.35] Condition 13(c) of the Law Society's *General Conditions of Sale (1995 Edition)* imposes a duty on the vendor to furnish to the purchaser a copy of the folio or folios relating to the property written up-to-date, or as nearly as practicable written up-to-date. In the case of a leasehold folio, where the original lease is usually returned to the registered owner, a copy of the original must also be furnished in all cases and the original handed over on closing, as in the case of unregistered land.[204]

(iv) Copy of Map

[14.36] One of the advantages of the Land Registry system is that titles are registered by reference to a registry map,[205] which, being based on Ordnance Survey maps, is usually considerably more accurate than any map or plan attached to title deeds of unregistered land.[206] Though the map is not conclusive, except in special cases,[207] it can usually be relied upon.[208] Thus, the conditions of sale issued by the Law Society require the vendor to furnish to the purchaser a copy of the Land Registry map or file plan of the land comprised in the folio relating to the registered title the subject-matter of the sale.[209] A copy of the map may be obtained on payment of the prescribed fee.[210]

(v) Special Cases

(a) Non-Absolute Title

[14.37] We saw earlier that, if the registered title in question is not absolute, the purchaser cannot rely entirely upon evidence of title produced by the vendor which relates solely to Land Registry documentation.[211] For the most part the purchaser will have to insert special conditions into the contract for

---

[202.] Unless he has taken the precaution (which is unusual) of registering a caution based on the contract for sale, see para **[6.66]** *ante*.

[203.] Paras **[14.31]** *ante* and **[15.41]** *post*.

[204.] See Cond 22. See para **[14.31]** *supra*.

[205.] See McAllister, *op cit* pp 57-9; Fitzgerald, *op cit*, Ch 4.

[206.] See para **[18.63]** *post*.

[207.] Fitzgerald, *op cit*, p 69.

[208.] *Gillespie v Hogg* [1947] Ir Jur Rep 51. See also *McManus v Kiernan* [1939] IR 297; *Tomkin Estates Ltd v O'Callaghan* High Court, unrep, 16 March 1996 (1992/8152 P).

[209.] Cond 13(c) of the 1995 ed.

[210.] 1972 Rules, rule 198(1).

[211.] Para **[14.24]** *supra*.

sale if he is concerned about the class of title with which the vendor is registered.[212] However, the Law Society's *General Conditions of Sale (1995 Edition)* contains two provisions on this subject. Condition 13(b) provides that, where the vendor is registered with a possessory title, the purchaser is not to require him to be registered with an absolute title, but he must furnish sufficient evidence of title prior to registration to enable the purchaser to be registered with an absolute title.[213] It is important to note that now all titles registered subject to equities are deemed to be as possessory titles.[214] Thus, technically the process formerly known as discharge or cancellation of the equities is now called conversion of the possessory title.[215] Although all new folios opened since 1964 "subject to equities" will have the title classified as possessory, folios opened prior to that will have the old "Equities Note" and so Condition 13(a) of the Law Society's *General Conditions of Sale* requires the vendor to furnish sufficient evidence of the *pre*-registration title to enable the purchaser to procure discharge of the equities, a subject to which we now turn.

(b) Equities Note

[14.38] Where the title is registered subject to equities, we also saw earlier that there may be various major third party interests not disclosed by the register. The dangers of such a title for a purchaser were admirably portrayed by O'Connor MR in *Re White and Hague's Contract*[216]:

> "I must now point out the possible result of taking such a title without investigation. The purchaser might get absolutely no beneficial interest, because his vendor might have had no interest in the tenancy of the purchased holding, for he might have been a mere occupier without any title: or the purchaser might get only a limited interest-such as for the life of his vendor if the latter had been only tenant for life of the holding before it was sold in the Land Commission Court; or the purchaser might get only an individual share if his vendor's share in the holding had been that of one of numerous next-of-kin. It is, therefore, obvious that under an open contract the purchaser would be entitled to a full investigation of title. It is, however, no less obvious that the right to a full investigation may be cut down by conditions of sale."[217]

[212.] See further, para **[14.40]** *infra*.

[213.] See McAllister, *op cit* Ch 111; Fitzgerald, *op cit*, Ch 23.

[214.] Registration of Title Act 1964, s 35.

[215.] See *Fitzgerald, op cit*, p 398.

[216.] [1921] 1 IR 138. See also para **[14.25]** *supra*.

[217.] *Ibid*, p 143.

In fact, in that case the conditions of sale contained a large number of provisions to "cut down" the purchaser's right to full investigation and, as a corollary, the vendor's duty of deduction of title. In summary, they provided, *inter alia*, that: (1) the vendor was not to be required to furnish an abstract of title, but was to be deemed to have a good and sufficient title; (2) the purchaser was to be furnished with a plain copy of the folio, but no other document of title; (3) the purchaser was not to require the note as to equities to be discharged, nor was the title to the previous interest of the purchaser under the Land Purchase Acts to be called for nor investigated, nor was the purchaser to be entitled to serve any objections or requisitions; (4) the title of the vendor prior to registration was not to be called for or investigated, nor again were any objections or requisitions to be made; (5) no evidence was to be furnished as to the existence or non-existence of unregistered burdens and it was to be assumed that the property was free from all such burdens except as appeared in the particulars of sale or the registered folio; (6) the purchaser was not to call upon the vendor to discharge any equities, including any appearing on the register, and the purchaser was presumed to buy subject to them; (7) if any proper objection were made with which the vendor was unable or unwilling to comply, the vendor was at liberty to rescind the contract by repaying the deposit, without interest, costs or other charges.

[14.39] These provisions were a classic case of "overkill," and the vendor's solicitor fell into the trap of failing to ensure that the conditions were clear and unambiguous and consistent with each other.[218] The result was that they were construed against the vendor.[219] As regards the argument that the vendor was entitled to say to the purchaser that he had to be satisfied with his title so registered subject to equities and could make no enquiries about the equities, O'Connor MR had this to say:

> "If that is the law, it leaves the gate wide open to many frauds in this country, because it has become a common practice to limit the investigation of title in land purchase cases in the same way as here. Any day a purchaser may find that he has paid his money for land from which he is liable to immediate eviction - a situation which will be all the more distressing if he finds that the vendor (as in the present case) had bade adieu to his native country, and has gone to America. There is no doubt that a purchaser may preclude himself by agreement from making any inquiry as to title, and specific performance may be enforced against him. There are many precedents of agreement to take only such title as the vendor has.

[218.] Thus O'Connor MR held, eg, that item (7) was inconsistent with item (1): "This[(7)]is absolutely inconsistent with a contract to take only such title as the vendor has. It implies a right to make objections to the title, with a corresponding obligation on the vendor's part to give a reasonable answer to them. What objections could this condition have referred to, except objections arising out of the equities mentioned in the register? None; because the register is absolutely conclusive on all other points." *Ibid*.

[219.] See paras **[9.37]** and **[10.03-4]** *ante*.

There are many cases in which vendors with good holding titles cannot prove them by documentary evidence, and in which it is quite reasonable that they should provide that no evidence of title should be asked for. For instance, the assignee in bankruptcy of an absconding bankrupt may know nothing and may not be able to get any information, about the bankrupt's title to business premises. He may in such cases set up for sale such interest as the bankrupt had, and the purchaser may be bound not to make any inquiry. Or an heir-at-law may be anxious to sell lands into which he has entered as heir-at-law, and may know nothing of his ancestor's title. It would be quite allowable for him to provide that the purchaser should accept his title without investigation, without deeds, without evidence of tenure, etc. There is nothing unreasonable in cases like these, nor anything to suggest dishonesty, if the vendor offers to a purchaser only such title as he may have, and a contract on this basis may be enforced. But in a case like that with which I am dealing, which suggests no reason for not disclosing the vendor's title, except an effort to foist upon the purchaser a worthless title, or mere perversity on the part of the vendor, I entertain the gravest doubt that the contract would be enforceable."[220]

[14.40] As we saw above,[221] the Law Society's *General Conditions of Sale (1995 Edition)* now provide that, where the registration is subject to equities under the pre-1964 legislation,[222] the purchaser is not to require the equities to be discharged, but the vendor must furnish sufficient evidence of title prior to first registration to enable the purchaser to procure their discharge.[223] This clearly meets O'Connor MR's objections to restrictive conditions of sale.

(c) Unregistered Burdens

[14.41] Condition 13(d) of the Law Society's *General Conditions of Sale (1995 Edition)* provides that the vendor must furnish a statutory declaration, by some person competent to make it, confirming that there are not in existence any burdens which affect registered land without registration,[224] except as regards any which are specifically mentioned in the particulars or special conditions of sale. In fact, by s 115 of the Registration of Title Act 1964, any stipulation in a contract for the sale or charge of registered land, or for the transfer of a registered charge, whereby the purchaser or intending chargeant or transferee is precluded from making requisitions on title in relation to burdens generally, or to any particular burden which may affect the land without registration, is void.[225]

[220.] *Op cit*, p 144. See also para **[9.37]** *ante*.
[221.] Para **[14.37]** *supra*.
[222.] See para **[14.25]** *supra*.
[223.] Cond 13(a).
[224.] See para **[14.27]** *supra*.
[225.] See para **[10.12]** *ante*.

B. Unregistered Land

1. Abstracts or Copies of Deeds

[14.42] The traditional method of deducing title was for the vendor to deliver to the purchaser an "abstract of title."[226] As Lord Ashbourne C once said, it was "the ordinary right of a purchaser to have an abstract furnished and title shown before he pays his purchase-money."[227] An abstract of title is a summary of the title documents by which dispositions of the property in question have been made during the period for which title has to be shown,[228] together with a statement of all facts which may have affected that title, eg, births, deaths and marriages.[229] There is no doubt that abstracts were at one time commonly used in Ireland, for there are many reported cases in which references to them will be found,[230] though in *Re Furlong and Sheehan*[231] it was held that in Irish practice it was not enough simply to furnish a full abstract of the deeds and to offer the purchaser an inspection of the deeds themselves - the vendor had to furnish copies of the deeds abstracted as well.[232] However, in recent decades abstracts have become so rare that many solicitors in Ireland will have never met an abstract in day-to-day practice, and for this reason we do not propose to examine the nature of an abstract in detail.[233] Instead, the practice has become for the vendor's solicitor to furnish the purchaser's solicitor with copies of the relevant title deeds and in this regard the development of modern photocopying machines has been a boon to solicitors. This practice is now recognised by the standard

---

[226.] Many believe that the vendor's duty to furnish an abstract was a rule of practice first evolved by Sir Edward Sugden (later Lord St Leonards), successively Lord Chancellor of Ireland and of Great Britain; see his famous treatise on conveyancing, *Law of Vendors and Purchasers* (14th ed, 1862), p 406.

[227.] *Clarke v Taylor* [1899] 1 IR 449 at 458. See also *Re Priestley and Davidson's Contract* (1892) 31 LR Ir 122 at 126 (*per* Porter MR).

[228.] See further on this, para **[14.54]** *infra*.

[229.] See *Oakden v Pike* (1865) 34 LJ Ch 620 at 622 (*per* Kindersley V-C).

[230.] See, eg, *Corless v Sparling* (1874) IR 8 Eq 335; *Boyd v Dickson* (1876) IR 10 Eq 239; *Phelps v White* (1881) 7 LR Ir 160: *Clarke v Taylor* [1899] 1 IR 449; *Re Todd and McFadden's Contract* [1908] 1 IR 213; *Re Conlon and Faulkener's Contract* [1916] 1 IR 241; *Re Ashe and Hogan's Contract* [1920] 1 IR 159; *Bourke v Grimes* (1929) 63 ILTR 53; *Hopkins v Geoghegan* [1931] IR 135. See para **[1.33]** *ante*. See also the precedent in Stubbs and Baxter, *Irish Forms and Precedents* (1910), pp 5-13.

[231.] (1889) 23 LR Ir 407.

[232.] The right to an abstract could he waived, see *Re Priestley and Davidson's Contract* (1892) 31 LR Ir 122. See also as to waiver or acceptance of title generally, para **[15.49]** *post*.

[233.] Reference may he made to the discussion in English Textbooks, see, eg, Barnsley, *Conveyancing Law and Practice* (3rd ed, 1988) pp 257-65; *Emmet on Title* (19th ed by Farrand) Ch 5; *Williams on Title* (4th ed by Battersby; 1975), pp 573-86. But the practice of sending photocopies of the deeds instead of an abstract is a fast growing one in England and Wales and has now been sanctioned by the Law Society, subject to certain restrictions, see (1969) 66 L Soc Gaz 492; also Emmet *op cit*, para 5.052.

contract form issued by the Law Society. Condition 7 of the *General Conditions of Sale (1995 Edition)* provides that the vendor is to deliver or send by post to the purchaser or his solicitor "copies of the documents necessary to vouch the title to be shown". Earlier versions of this condition used to add that he may also, but is not bound to, deliver an abstract of title.[234]

[14.43] Few solicitors will regret the disappearance of abstracts, for their preparation was usually an extremely tedious and cumbersome task for vendors' solicitors.[235] Good abstracting was a very skilled job and, if it was not done well, it could give rise to a host of difficulties, not the least of which was a flood of requisitions on title from the purchaser's solicitor. On the other hand, the practice, which was once very common in Ireland, of sending to the purchaser's solicitor the original title deeds was most dangerous. One danger was the not inconsiderable risk of loss of some or all of the deeds, whether in transit or otherwise, with embarrassment for all concerned, solicitors and clients alike. Another was the risk of the vendor's solicitor being in breach of an undertaking,[236] eg, where he obtained the deeds from the vendor's mortgagee on accountable receipt.[237] It is much wiser in the pre-completion stage of the transaction to send copies of the deeds only and to hand the originals over on completion.[238] In this respect the advent of modern photocopying machines has proved extremely useful to solicitors.

[14.44] It should, however, be pointed out that, however convenient the modern practice is from the vendor's solicitor's point of view, it does, of course, throw a greater burden of investigation of the title onto the purchaser's solicitor. So long as the vendor's solicitor ensures that he sends copies of all the relevant deeds to the purchaser's solicitor, he can sit back and let the purchaser's solicitor work out for himself whether or not a good title has been shown. He will generally avoid the difficulties with which the vendor's solicitor was faced in *Mahony v Davoren*.[239] In that case the vendor's solicitor was sued by his own client for negligence in preparation of the abstract of title furnished to the purchaser.[240] The solicitor had failed to disclose the existence of a tithe rentcharge affecting the land and, because

---

[234.] See, eg, Cond 8 of the 1976 ed.

[235.] See the views of the English Law Society on the furnishing of an "epitome" of title plus photocopies of the deeds: *Law Society's Digest*, Opinion No 94 in Fourth (Cumulative) Supplement: Emmet, *op cit* para 5.052.

[236.] See para **[20.17]** *post*.

[237.] See para **[2.43]** *ante*.

[238.] See para **[20.34]** *post*.

[239.] (1892) 30 LR Ir 664.

[240.] Negligence was also claimed in respect of the drafting of the particulars and conditions of sale. which, of course, remains a problem for vendor's solicitors: see on the duty of disclosure, para **[9.20]** *et seq, ante*.

it had recently been held in Ireland that a purchaser was no longer obliged to assume the existence of such charges,[241] the purchaser was able to insist that the charge be redeemed out of the purchase money, thereby reducing the amount ultimately received by the vendor. In fact, the majority of the Irish Queen's Bench Division[242] held that there was no negligence, for the solicitor had asked his client for all the relevant documents and papers relating to the land and the client, though he had paid one instalment of the rentcharge and had a receipt, forgot about this and did not hand over the receipt. However, even if he had known about the rentcharge, the majority took the view that the point of law involved was not sufficiently clear,[243] so that the vendor's solicitor would still have not been negligent. As Holmes J put it:

> "There is a wide distinction between professional negligence and an error of judgment or failure to apprehend legal subtleties: to make solicitors responsible for the latter would be to impose upon them an intolerable burden."[244]

However, on the more general point of the solicitor's duty, O'Brien CJ said:

> "... the solicitor to be rendered liable must have been guilty of a want of ordinary care, or must have exhibited a want of ordinary skill ..."[245]

And Johnson J commented:

> "There is no hard-and-fast line defining what amounts to actionable negligence in a solicitor under all circumstances. He is bound to bring reasonable skill, knowledge, and diligence to the discharge of the professional duty which he undertakes to perform: that is his duty; whether he has discharged it or not depends on the facts of the particular case."[246]

(i) Time for Delivery

[14.45] In the absence of a special provision in the contract for sale, the rule is as stated by Kennedy CJ in *Bourke v Grimes*[247]:

> "It is, in my opinion, an implied term of the contract that the vendor shall deliver an abstract of title within a reasonable time."[248]

[241.] Due to the redemption scheme introduced by the Irish Church Act 1869, see para **[9.26]** *ante*.

[242.] O'Brien CJ and Holmes J. The jury had found for the plaintiff and Johnson J thought there should be a new trial.

[243.] See para **[9.26]** *ante*. Note that such rentcharges were deemed to be extinguished on 28 September 1975 and no longer payable by s 7(3) of the Land Act 1984.

[244.] *Op cit*, pp 676-7.

[245.] *Op cit*, p 668.

[246.] *Op cit*, p 671.

[247.] (1929) 63 ILTR 53.

[248.] *Ibid*. See also *Compton v Bagley* [1892] 1 Ch 313 at 321 (*per* Romer J).

However, it is usual for the contract for sale to specify a time for delivery, though not usually one so short as in *Re Todd and McFadden's Contract*,[249] where the conditions of sale required delivery of the abstract "immediately" after the sale. The sale took place on 30 December 1907, but the abstract was not delivered until 4 January 1908. The purchaser argued that this was too late and was upheld by the court. Kenny J said:

> "I accede to the purchaser's argument that 'immediately' means 'forthwith', 'instanter,' and that the purchaser's solicitor might with reason say that he expected the abstract at the latest on the 1st January. His letter of that date shows that he did. In my opinion, a delivery five days after the sale did not, in the circumstances of the case, satisfy the condition."[250]

Modern decisions, however, cast doubt upon the correctness of this view.[251]

[14.46] Condition 7 of the Law Society's *General Conditions of Sale (1995 Edition)* requires delivery, or sending by post, of copies of the title documents within "seven working days from the date of sale". The "date of sale" is either the date of the auction or, in the case of a sale by private treaty, the date on which the contract becomes binding on the Vendor and the Purchaser.[252] Presumably, the crucial signing is that of the vendor, since until he signs he is not bound by the contract and so is under no duty to deliver the title.[253]

[14.47] In accordance with the general rule, in the absence of a special provision in the contract, time is not of the essence in relation to such time limits.[254] However, if the vendor fails to comply with the time limit for delivery of the title, there may be two immediate consequences. First, if the contract requires the purchaser to send his requisitions on title within a period fixed by reference to the date of delivery of the title, late delivery of the latter clearly affects the purchaser's duty in respect of the former.[255] Secondly, by failing to keep to the time limit governing himself, the vendor

---

[249.] [1908] 1 IR 213.

[250.] *Ibid*, p 220. See also, in a different context (payment of the deposit). *Morrow v Carty* [1957] NI 174 at 177 (*per* McVeigh J), para **[10.21]** *ante*.

[251.] See, eg, the views expressed by Supreme Court in *Hynes Ltd v Independent Newspapers Ltd* [1980] IR 204 (see Wylie *Irish Landlord and Tenant Law*, para 11.05). *Cf* those of the House of Lords on the subject of time clauses, in *United Scientific Holdings Ltd v Burnley BC* [1977] 2 All ER 62. See also para **[13.10]** *et seq, ante*.

[252.] See the definition of Cond 2: para **[10.14]** *ante*.

[253.] See paras **[6.32]** *et seq, ante*. *Cf* where the parties require an "exchange" to take place: see para **[6.61]** *et seq, ante*.

[254.] See para **[13.12]** *ante*. See also *Roberts v Berry* (1853) 3 De GM & G 284.

[255.] *Cf* the provisions on requisitions in the contract form issued by the Law Society, see para **[15.20]** *post*.

may be held to have waived his right to insist on strict performance of the terms of the contract by the purchaser.[256] In particular, as Kenny J said in *Re Todd and McFadden's Contract*:[257]

> "I think it is settled ... that if the abstract be not delivered within the time named in the conditions, the purchaser cannot be held bound to send in his objections within the time limited in the conditions for that purpose."[258]

Apart from this, of course, if the vendor fails to deliver the appropriate documents within the time limit, the purchaser may serve a notice on him requiring him to deliver them within a reasonable time, after which he may call the sale off.[259]

(ii) Verification

[14.48] Where under the traditional method of deducing title the vendor furnished an abstract of title, the general rule was that it was the purchaser's duty to see that the abstract was verified and the vendor's duty to produce the necessary evidence for examination by the purchaser. However, while the vendor had to bear the expense of obtaining the documentation necessary for preparation of the abstract[260] and the title deeds for handing over on completion,[261] it was usual to include a special condition in the contract requiring the purchaser to meet the cost of production of title documents or other materials not in the vendor's possession, which were necessary for verification of the abstract. This practice was given statutory recognition by s 3(6) of the Conveyancing Act 1881, which provides:

> On a sale of any property, the expenses of the production and inspection of all ... deeds, wills, probates, letters of administration, and other documents, not in the vendor's possession, and the expenses of all journeys incidental to such production or inspection, and the expenses of searching for, procuring, making, verifying, and producing all certificates, declarations, evidences, and information not in the vendor's possession, and all attested, stamped, office or other copies or abstracts of ... documents aforesaid, not in the vendor's possession, if any such production, inspection, journey, search, procuring, making, or verifying is required by a purchaser, either for verification of the abstract, or for any other purpose, shall be borne by the purchaser who requires the same; and where the vendor retains

---

[256.] *Cf Fitzgerald v McCullagh* (1858) 7 ICLR 457 (waiver by purchaser of right to insist upon delivery by vendor strictly according to the contract). See also *Hipwell v Knight* (1835) 1 Y & C Ex 401.

[257.] [1908] 1 IR 213.

[258.] *Ibid*, p 220.

[259.] See paras **[13.17-8]** *ante*. See also *Compton v Bagley* [1892] 1 Ch 313.

[260.] *Re Johnson and Tustin* (1885) 30 Ch D 42.

[261.] *Re Duthy and Jesson's Contract* [1898] 1 Ch 419.

possession of any document, the expenses of making any copy thereof attested or unattested, which a purchaser requires to be delivered to him, shall be borne by that purchaser.

In *Re Conlon and Faulkener's Contract*,[262] O'Connor MR applied this provision in a case where the purchaser required the vendor to furnish a statutory declaration to prove that he was the heir-at-law of a deceased owner of the property, as was stated in the abstract of title. As O'Connor MR put it:

> "... it is required merely for the purposes of verifying a fact which is stated on the face of the abstract ... The declaration asked for is not required for the purpose of adding to the abstract of title, or completing it ..."[263]

On the other hand, he held that failure to disclose in the abstract whether or not succession and estate duty had been paid on the death of the previous owner through whom the title was traced, or that no duty was payable, rendered the abstract incomplete. The expense of proving this would have to be borne by the vendor.[264] However, in *Hopkins v Geoghegan*,[265] as we saw earlier,[266] Johnston J held that production of a certificate from the Revenue Commissioners[267] that no arrears of income tax were outstanding was a matter of conveyance rather than of title, and so the expense should be borne by the purchaser under s 3(6) of the 1881 Act.[268]

[14.49] There are several points which should be noted about s 3(6). First, it was clearly dealing with the subject of verification of the abstract and, since an abstract is never furnished in modern Irish practice, it would seem to have little, if any, practical significance now. It did not alter the common law rule that the vendor must bear the expense of production of documents necessary for preparation of the abstract[269] and this would seem to cover the modern practice of furnishing copies of the title documents. Nor did it alter the common law rule that the vendor must meet the cost of production of documents of title to be handed over on completion,[270] which also applies to

---

[262] [1916] 1 IR 241. See also para **[14.18]** *ante*.

[263] *Ibid*, pp 245-6, and thereby he distinguished *Re Moody and Yates' Contract* (1885) 30 Ch D 344. See also *Re Wright and Thompson's Contract* [1920] 1 Ch 191.

[264] *Ibid*, p 247.

[265] [1931] IR 135.

[266] Para **[14.18]** *supra*.

[267] Under s 6 of the Finance Act 1928, since repealed by the Income Tax Act 1967, Sched, 19, Pt II.

[268] *Op cit*, p 141. *Cf* as regards the "PD" stamp on an assignment, p 142. And see also para **[14.49]** *infra* and **[20.41]** *post*.

[269] See para **[14.48]** *supra*.

[270] See *ibid*.

modern practice.[271] Secondly, it relates only to the documents of title not in the vendor's possession, eg, in the possession of his mortgagee[272] or trustee.[273] In fact, in England it was felt that the provision imposed too great a burden on purchasers in this respect, and in 1925 it was amended to exclude not only documents in the vendor's possession but also those in the possession of his mortgagee or trustee.[274] Thirdly, it operates only if and as far as a contrary intention is not expressed in the contract for sale.[275] It should be noted, for example, that under condition 8(b) of the Law Society's *General Conditions of Sale (1995 ed)*, the vendor is obliged, in cases where the title is based on possession,[276] to furnish to the purchaser a Certificate of Discharge from Capital Acquisitions Tax pursuant to s 146 of the Finance Act 1994.[277] Indeed, in modern conveyancing practice it is usual for the vendor to have furnish a variety of certificates relating to tax matters[278] and other matters like planning, building control and multi-storey buildings.[279]

[14.50] Apart from the requirements of s 3(6) of the 1881 Act, production of the original deeds is regarded in conveyancing practice as sufficient proof of title. In the absence of suspicious circumstances, a deed is presumed to have been duly executed and, generally speaking, no questions are asked in practice as to how the vendor acquired possession of it, though strictly the presumption is supposed to operate only if the deed comes from a source that might reasonably be expected, eg, the vendor's mortgagee.[280] Indeed, the rule at common law was that a deed thirty years old coming from proper custody proved itself,[281] Furthermore, recitals, statements and descriptions in deeds twenty years old at the date of the contract for sale are, by s 2(2) of the Vendor and Purchaser Act 1874, to be taken, unless proved to be inaccurate, to be sufficient evidence of the truth.[282]

[271.] See para **[20.34]** *post*.

[272.] *Re Willett and Argenti* (1889) 60 LT 735.

[273.] *Re Ebworth and Tidy's Contract* (1889) 42 Ch D 23 at 24 (*per* North J).

[274.] Law of Property Act 1925, s 45(4)(a).

[275.] Section 3(9). See *Hopkins v Geoghegan* [1931] IR 135 at 141 (*per* Johnston J).

[276.] See para **[14.80]** *infra*.

[277.] This subject is discussed at para **[14.82]** *post*.

[278.] See Requisition No 16 in the Law Society's *Objections and Requisitions on Title* (1996) (Rev ed): see para **[16.25]** *post*.

[279.] *Ibid*, Nos 27, 28 and 35: see paras **[16.74]**, **[16.79]** and **[16.95]** *post*.

[280.] *Crongliton v Blake* (1843) 12 M & W 205 at 208 (*per* Parke B). See also *Meath v Winchester* (1836) 4 Cl & Fin 445 at 640 (*per* Tindal CJ).

[281.] *Donegall v Templemore* (1858) 9 ICLR 374. See also *Marsh v Collnett* (1798) 2 Esp 665; *Doe d Oldham v Walley* (1828) 8 B & C 22. And see *Re Acrey* [1897] 1 Ch 164.

[282.] See para **[18.28]** *post*.

(iii) Lost or Destroyed Deeds

[14.51] It is settled that, if the title documents are lost or destroyed, the purchaser cannot repudiate the contract provided the vendor can produce adequate secondary evidence of the contents and execution of the missing deeds.[283] However, the vendor cannot force the purchaser to accept secondary evidence, such as a completed copy or draft of the original deed, unless he can establish clearly that the original deed is destroyed or, after a proper search, is still lost.[284] An affidavit or statutory declaration may be provided as to the result of the search.[285] It seems that execution of the missing deed must be proved,[286] though it may be presumed in the case of a very old deed.[287] In addition, it is common practice in Ireland to require evidence that the missing documents have not been pledged or otherwise adversely dealt with, plus the furnishing by the vendor of an insurance company bond to protect the purchaser against any claims made by any person claiming under or through those documents. However, it seems that due stamping will be presumed.[288]

[14.52] In respect of unregistered land, a form of secondary evidence of a lost deed commonly tendered in Ireland is the memorial registered in the Registry of Deeds.[289] This has long been accepted as suitable secondary evidence.[290] As is the general rule with respect to secondary evidence, the memorial can be used instead of the deed only if the latter is not found after a proper search,[291] and, apparently, only if the possession of the land has since been in accordance with what the memorial would lead one to

---

[283.] *Re Halifax Commercial Banking Co Ltd and Wood* (1898) 79 LT 536; *Halkett v Dudley* [1907] 1 Ch 590. See Walford, 'Missing Title Deeds' (1949) 13 Conv 349.

[284.] *Re JPR* (1970) 74 ILTR 11 at 14 (*per* Sullivan CJ). See also *Breslin v Hodgens (No 2)* (1874) IR 8 Eq 397. *Cf Staples v Young* [1908] 1 IR 135.

[285.] *Stewart v Marquis of Conyngham* (1851) 1 Ir Ch R 534 at 568 (*per* Smith MR). See also *Sadlier v Higgs* (1853) 4 HLC 435 at 460 (*per* Lord St. Leonards). *Cf Breslin v Hodgens (No 2)* (1874) IR 8 Eq 397 (oral evidence in court).

[286.] *Bryant v Busk* (1872) 4 Russ 1.

[287.] *Moulton v Edmonds* (1859) 1 De GF & J 246. See also *Donegal v Templemore* (1858) 9 ICLR 374.

[288.] *Hart v Hart* (1841) 1 Hare 1; *Marine Investment Co v Haviside* (1872) LR 5 HL 624.

[289.] See *Irish Land Law*, (2nd ed, 1986), paras 22.02 and 22.05-6.

[290.] See *Hobhouse v Hamilton* (1803) 1 Sch & Lef 207; *Re Harding's Estate* (1860) 11 Ir Ch R 29; *Brown v Armstrong* (1873) IR 7 CL 130; *Earl of Antrim v Gray* (1875) IR 9 Eq 513; *Chism v Lipsett* 11905) 1 IR 60; *Re Turpin and Ahern's Contract* [1905] 1 IR 85; *Re Ward's Estate* (1909) 43 ILTR 113.

[291.] See the discussion by Lord St Leonards in *Sadlier v Higgs* (1853) 4 HLC 435 at 460-1. Also *Stewart v Marquis of Conyngham* (1851) 1 Ir Ch R 534 at 568 (*per* Smith MR); *McKay v McNally* (1878) 4 LR Ir 438 at 449 (*per* Palles CB); *Miller v Wheatley* (1891) 28 LR Ir 144 at 156 (*per* O'Brien J); *Re JPR* (1940) 74 ILTR 11 at 14 (*per* Sullivan CJ). *Cf Staples v Young* [1908] 1 IR 135.

expect.[292] At one time it was thought that the original memorial had to be produced, and not just a copy,[293] but by statute now an office copy may be received and taken as evidence of the contents of the memorial in any court proceedings, unless, on giving notice to the other party, the latter demands by counternotice the production of the original.[294] So far as matters stated in the memorial are concerned, it is *prima facie* evidence against the party who executed it, and anyone claiming through him,[295] but not against a party who did not execute it.[296]

[14.53] Generally the issue of lost documents does not pose such problems in the case of registered land, because the vendor meets his deduction of title obligations by furnishing a copy of the folio and map in the Land Registry.[297] However, problems can arise where a land certificate has been issued and is required to be handed over on completion to enable the purchaser to register his new ownership.[298] In such cases an application may have to be made for issue of a duplicate certificate,[299] or for an order dispensing with its production.[300]

2. Length of Title

[14.54] It has long been accepted that the vendor must do more than simply produce as evidence of his title to the property the document by which he acquired the title, unless he has held the property under that document for a long time. The point is that there may have been some defect in the last transfer document - it may even be a forgery - which the vendor did not observe; if so, he may never have received a good title and so is in no position to transfer one to the purchaser. Such a defect may, of course, be cured, in the sense that third party claims may become barred, through the operation of the doctrine of adverse possession,[301] but, though the limitation

---

[292.] *McKay v McNally* (1878) 4 LR Ir 438 at 449 (*per* Palles CB); *Miller v Wheatley* (1891) 28 LR Ir 144 at 156-7 (*per* O'Brien J). See also *Re Harding's Estate* (1860) 11 Ir Ch R 29.

[293.] *Hobhouse v Hamilton* (1803) 1 Sch & Lef 207 at 207 (*per* Lord Redesdale).

[294.] Registry of Deeds (Ir) Act 1832, s 32. See *Reidy v Pierce* (1861) 11 ICLR 361 espec at 368-9 (*per* Pigot CB). See also *Earl of Antrim v Gray* (1875) IR 9 Eq 513; *McKay v McNally* (1878) 4 LR Ir 438; *Miller v Wheatley* (1891) 28 LR Ir 144.

[295.] *Miller v Wheatley* (1891) 28 LR Ir 144 at 161 (*per* Johnson J). See also *Peyton v McDermott* (1838) 1 Dr & Wal 198; *Sadlier v Higgs* (1853) 4 HLC 435.

[296.] *McKay v McNally* (1878) 4 LR Ir 438 at 449 (*per* Palles CB).

[297.] See para **[14.33]** *et seq, supra.*

[298.] See para **[14.32]** *supra.*

[299.] See Land Registration Rules 1972, rule 170. See Fitzgerald, *Land Registry Practice* (2nd ed, 1995), p 351.

[300.] *Ibid*, rule 165. See Fitzgerald, *op cit*, p 349.

[301.] See para **[14.80]** *infra.*

period is now only twelve years, most purchasers are reluctant to accept a possessory title based on such a short period.[302] At common law, the rule evolved by conveyancers for freehold land[303] was that the vendor should trace his title back for sixty years,[304] but the Vendor and Purchaser Act 1874, reduced this to forty years for open contracts, ie, subject to any stipulation to the contrary in the contract for sale.[305] This remains the position in Ireland, but it may be noted that in England the period was reduced in 1925 to thirty years[306] and in 1969 to fifteen years.[307] In Ireland it has become increasingly common in modern times for purchasers' solicitors to accept twenty years' title in the case of freehold land and, in the case of leasehold land, commencement with the original lease and then passing to an assignment some fifteen years old. Not surprisingly, then, the Law Reform Commission recommended that the statutory period should be reduced to twenty years.[308] It considered a reduction to fifteen years as in England but regarded this as "uncomfortably close" to the twelve-year limitation period under the Statute of Limitations 1957.[309] The point here is that the twelve-year period may be extended in certain cases, eg, where the landowner with the right to recover possession is under a disability.[310] The Commission was concerned about such persons losing their rights without redress, though it would appear that no such problems have come to light since the fifteen-year period was

---

302. Especially in view of the judicial controversy over the operation of the doctrine and, in Ireland, its application to leasehold property, see *Irish Land Law* (2nd ed, 1986), Ch 23.

303. Leasehold land is subject to special rules, see para **[14.68]** *infra*.

304. *Barnwell v Harris* (1809) 1 Taunt 430 at 432 (*per* Heath J); *Bryant v Taylor* (1867) IR 2 QB 161 at 178-81 (*per* Cockburn LJ). It has been suggested that sixty years was chosen as the duration of a lifetime, after which no one was likely to upset the title, see *Cooper v Emery* (1844) 1 Ph 388 at 389 (*per* Lyndhurst LC).

305. Section 1. Note that the suggestion (see *Bolton v London School Board* (1878) 7 Ch D 766) that s 2 of 1874 Act (which provided, *inter alia*, that recitals in deeds twenty years old at the date of the contract are sufficient evidence of their own truth, unless proved inaccurate, see para **[18.28]** *post*) meant in effect that a purchaser could not call for title earlier that such a recital was disapproved of in *Re Wallis and Grout's Contract* [1906] 2 Ch 206.

306. Law of Property Act 1925, s 44(1).

307. Law of Property Act 1969, s 23. This resulted from the Law Commission's Interim Report on Root of Title to Freehold Land (1966) (Law Com No 9), espec paras 34-6. For criticisms, see Cretney, 'Land Law and Conveyancing Reforms' (1969) 32 MLR 477; Hallett and Nugee, 'Root of Title' (1966) 110 Sol Jo 179 at 201. See also (1966) 30 Conv 158.

308. *Land Law and Conveyancing Law (1) General Proposals* (LRC 30-1989), paras 8-9. The Commission pointed out that the adequacy of twenty years had already been recognised in certain cases for the purposes of an application for first registration of the title: see Land Registration Rules 1972 rule 19; Fitzgerald, *Land Registry Practice* (2nd ed, 1995), pp 365-68.

309. See Brady and Kerr, *The Limitation of Actions* (2nd ed, 1994), Ch 4.

310. *Ibid*, pp 31-334.

introduced in England.[311] Regrettably the Law Reform Commission's proposal has not been acted upon.

[14.55] It has also been settled that the statutory period of title is a minimum period in the sense that, if tracing the title back to a date exactly 365 days multiplied by forty years earlier, does not bring one to a "good root of title," one must go back further until one does reach a good root. As an English judge once put it, the title "cannot commence in *nubibus*".[312]

(i) Root of Title

[14.56] There is no statutory definition as to what constitutes a good root of title,[313] but certain characteristics have come to be accepted by conveyancers over the years. First, it should be a document dealing with the whole legal and equitable estate contracted to be sold. Thus, on a sale of the fee simple, a lease would not be a good root; on the sale of the legal estate, a transfer of the equity of redemption would not be a good root, since the legal title outstanding in the mortgagee[314] is not dealt with. On the other hand, the mortgage deed itself is a good root, as, of course, is a conveyance on sale. In both these cases, one can expect that the title was investigated and found satisfactory. This is not the case with a voluntary conveyance, but the general view is that on an open contract such a conveyance is a good root.[315] Secondly, the document must contain a description by which the property can be identified. Thus, a general devise was not a good root because it did not indicate that the testator owned the property the subject of the contract for sale.[316] Moreover, since wills now operate in equity only,[317] a will is not a good root and the vital title document is the assent by the personal

---

[311.] Barnsley, *Conveyancing Law and Practice* (3rd ed, 1988), p 251. Also arguably the Statute of Limitations protects such persons by extending the limitation period, so that it is purchasers who are at risk.

[312.] North J in *Re Cox and Neve's Contract* [1891] 2 Ch 109 at 118

[313.] The English Law Commission refused to draft one on the ground that it might do more harm than good. Law Com No 9 (1966), paras 40-1. The definition in *Williams on Vendor and Purchaser* (4th ed), p 124, is often quoted as acceptable: "an instrument of disposition dealing with or proving on the face of it, without the aid of extrinsic evidence, the ownership of the whole legal and equitable estate in the property sold, containing a description by which the property can be identified and showing nothing to cast any doubt on the title of the disposing parties." See Pritchard, 'Roots of Title today' (1975) 28 CLP 125.

[314.] See *Irish Land Law* (2nd ed, 1986), para 12.32.

[315.] *Re Marsh and Earl Granville* (1882) 24 Ch D 11 at 24 (*per* Cotton LJ).

[316.] *Parr v Lovegrove* (1858) 4 Drew 170. *Cf* a specific devise: see *Clarke v Taylor* [1899] 1 IR 449 at 459 (*per* FitzGibbon LJ).

[317.] See *Irish Land Law* (2nd ed, 1986), para 5.30; Brady, *Succession Law in Ireland* (2nd ed, 1995), Ch 9.

representatives, supported by the grant of probate or letters of administration.[318] Thirdly, the document must not depend for its validity on some other instrument, eg, a document exercising a power of appointment is not a good root of title, since it depends for its validity on the instrument creating the power.[319] As it is sometimes put, the root must not cast doubt upon its own validity.[320] It has long been held in Ireland that a fee farm conversion grant is not a good root of title because by the terms of the Renewable Leasehold Conversion Act 1849,[321] the grant is subject to the same covenants, conditions, exceptions and reservations,[322] and the same uses, trusts, charges, liens, incumbrances and equities,[323] as affected the lease before conversion.[324] But, as we mentioned earlier, it may be questioned whether this holds good today.[325] On the other hand, a conveyance from the Landed Estates Court[326] is a good root of title, for, by virtue of the legislative provisions under which the Court operated in the nineteenth century, it had power to vest an indefeasible title in the purchaser of the land being sold. As Chatterton V-C explained in *Earl of Antrim v Gray*[327]:

"There can be no question now that a conveyance from those [Incumbered Estates Court] Commissioners, or from the judges of the Landed Estates Court, effectively conveys the estate of every one, whether a party to the proceedings before them or not, whether with full notice of those proceedings or in entire ignorance of them. The legislature, on grounds of public policy, thought it expedient to grant these somewhat arbitrary powers to these tribunals; and it is not for the ordinary Courts of the realm

[318.] *Ibid*, Ch 16 especially paras 16.44-7. See also *Re Miller and Pickergill's Contract* [1931] 1 Ch 511. And see *Mohan v Roche* [1991] IR 560, paras **[14.79]** *infra* and **[16.54]** *post*.

[319.] *Re Copelin's Contract* [1937] 4 All ER 447; *Re Holmes and Cosmopolitan Press Ltd Contract* [1944] Ch 53.

[320.] See *Re Duce and Boots Cash Chemists (Southern) Ltd Contract* [1937] Ch 642.

[321.] See *Irish Land Law* (2nd ed, 1986), para 4.081 *et seq*.

[322.] Section 1.

[323.] Section 7.

[324.] See the leading authority *Maconchy v Clayton* [1898] 1 IR 291. Also *Dawson v Baxter* (1886) 19 LR Ir 103; *Re Carew's Estate* (1887) 19 LR Ir 483; *Smyth v Shaftesbury* (1901) 1 NIJR 34; *Re Garde Browne* [1911] 1 IR 205. *Cf McClenaghan v Bankhead* (1874) IR 8 CL 195.

[325.] See para **[14.11]** *supra*.

[326.] Or the Incumbered Estates Court see *Irish Land Law* (2nd ed, 1986), paras 1.42 and 8.008. See also on the effect of conveyances from this Court *Rutledge v Hood* (1853) 3 ICLR 447; *Scott v Anderson* (1857) 2 Ir Jur (ns) 422; *Rorke v Errington* (1859) 7 HLC 617; *De Vesci v O'Kelly* (1869) IR 4 CL 269; *Corless v Sparling* (1874) IR 8 Eq 335. The judges were not always unanimous in their views, as to the effect of the statutory provisions see the discussion in *O'Donnell v Ryan* (1854) 4 ICLR 44.

[327.] (1875) IR 9 Eq 513.

to attempt, even for the redress of manifest wrong in particular cases, to cut down or limit them.''[328]

In *Re Tottenham's Estate*,[329] Christian LJ described the effect of such a conveyance in these terms:

> "... by a sort of conveyancing magnetism, it would draw out, not merely from the owner whose estate was under sale, or from whatever persons might intervene as parties in the proceedings, but from the absent, the helpless, the infant, the married woman, the mentally imbecile, nay, even the unborn, every particle of estate and interest, legal or equitable, present and future, known or unknown, patent or latent, in the land expressed to be conveyed, and would concentrate the whole in the purchaser, freed from everything that the conveyance itself did not save."[330]

[14.57] It is usual for the contract to specify the root of title and the Law Society's standard form contract provides for specification of the title to be shown by the vendor in the special conditions.[331] Presumably, the root specified need not be a good root, provided the purchaser is prepared to accept it. However, the vendor must take care not to mislead the purchaser as to the nature of the document in question, especially where he is seeking to restrict the amount of title to be shown, ie, to reduce the length of title to which the purchaser would otherwise be entitled to under an open contract.[332]

[14.58] Finally, it is clear that the title may commence without a good root of title in the traditional sense, ie, a document of title.[333] The obvious case is where the vendor proposes to show a possessory title to the property.[334] However, though the limitation period is now twelve years only, it seems that on an open contract[335] the vendor must still show forty years' title,[336] ie., possession by himself for that period[337] or at least twelve years' possession by himself preceded by the title of the barred owner for the balance of the

---

[328.] *Ibid*, p 518.

[329.] (1869) IR 3 Eq 528.

[330.] *Ibid*, p 547. It was, however, common for the conveyance to "save", eg existing tenancies on the estate, see *Lauder v Alley* (1867) IR 1 CL 82; *Hamilton v Musgrove* (1871) IR 6 CL 129; *Cussack v Hudson* (1880) 6 LR Ir 309; *Oliver v Rooney* [1895] 2 IR 660.

[331.] *General Conditions of Sale* (1995 ed) Cond 8(a).

[332.] *Re Marsh and Earl Granville* (1883) 24 Ch D 11 at 22 (*per* Baggallay LJ).

[333.] See *Cottrell v Watkins* (1839) 1 Beav 361 at 365 (*per* Lord Langdale MR).

[334.] See further, para **[14.80]** *infra*.

[335.] *Cf George Wimpey & Co Ltd v Sohn* [1967] Ch 487.

[336.] The point is that he may not have barred third party rights created during the forty-year period, but before his twelve years of adverse possession, see *Re Nisbet and Port's Contract* [1906] 1 Ch 386. See para **[14.81]** *infra*.

[337.] *Jacobs v Revell* [1900] 2 Ch 858 at 869 (*per* Buckley LJ).

forty years.[338] But a possessory title cannot be used as a substitute for a lost deed, for here proper secondary evidence must be produced.[339]

(ii) Pre-Root Title

[14.59] By statute a purchaser is precluded from requiring production of any title documents dated or made before the time prescribed by law or stipulated in the contract for commencement of the title and from making requisitions, objections or enquiries as to the prior title, whether or not such prior documents are recited or noted in the documents of title furnished.[340] This provision applies subject to any contrary stipulation in the contract for sale,[341] but in fact the Law Society's standard contract for sale contains a similar provision.[342] However, it does not bind a purchaser to complete his purchase in any case where specific performance would not be enforced against him by the court, ie, where the title is clearly shown to be bad or so doubtful that the court will not force it on him.[343] Indeed, there is a line of authority that such a statutory or contractual provision does not prevent the purchaser from showing *aliunde*, eg, by enquiries of third parties, that the pre-root title is defective.[344] However, the terms of the contract may be so widely drafted as to exclude even this, as the Law Society's contract appears to be. Thus, condition 11(a) of the Law Society's *General Conditions of Sale (1995 Edition)* provides that title prior to the date of the instrument specified as the commencement of title (ie, the root of title) "whether or not appearing by recital, inference or otherwise, shall not be required, objected to or

---

[338.] *Re Atkinson and Horsell's Contract* [1912] 2 Ch 1 at 11 (*per* Cozens-Hardy MR).

[339.] *Re Halifax Commercial Banking Co Ltd and Wood* (1898) 79 LT 536. See para **[14.52]** *infra*.

[340.] Conveyancing Act 1881, s 3(3). See *Nottingham Patent Brick and Tile Co v Butler* (1885) 15 QBD 261. Note the exceptions added in England by s 45(1) of the Law of Property Act 1925. See *Re Copelin's Contract* [1937] 4 All ER 447.

[341.] *Ibid*, s 3(9).

[342.] *General Conditions of Sale* (1995 ed) Cond 11(a): see *infra* Note that this provision does not prevent a purchaser of registered land raising requisitions relating to burdens affecting the land without registration: see cond 11(b) which thereby expressly recognises the force of ss 52 and 115 of the Registration of Title Act 1964 (para **[10.12]** *ante*). Cond 11(b) also preserves the right to raise *pre*-root requisitions in respect of voluntary dispositions aimed at disinheriting the deceased's spouse or children, which may be set aside by the court under s 121 of the Succession Act 1965: see *MPD v MD* [1981] ILRM 179; Brady, *Succession Law in Ireland* (2nd ed, 1995) para **[7.89]** *et seq*.

[343.] See paras **[13.52]** *ante* and **[14.15-7]** *supra*. Though the purchaser may be unable to recover damages at law and may even be unable to recover his deposit, see paras **[13.34-5]** and **[13.79]** *et seq, ante*.

[344.] *Leathem v Allen* (1850) 1 Ir Ch R 683 at 691 (*per* Brady LC). See also *Willes v Latham* (1837) S & Sc 441 at 442 (*per* O'Loghlen MR); *Re Cox and Neve's Contract* [1891] 2 Ch 109. *Cf Smith v Robinson* (1879) 13 Ch D 148 (vendor accidentally produced pre-root documents).

investigated."[345] But it must be emphasised that a distinction has to be drawn between the basic overriding rule that the vendor must show good title and subordinate rules defining the manner of proof. Thus, the purchaser will still be able to object if incumbrances, such as restrictive covenants, come to light which the vendor knew or ought to have known about,[346] ie, the vendor cannot so disregard his duty to disclose latent defects in title.[347]

(iii) Shortened Length

[14.60] There is nothing to prevent the parties contracting for less than the statutory forty years' title to be shown by the vendor, but it is important to realise that the purchaser runs a risk if he accedes to this. The risk is that he will nevertheless be fixed with constructive notice of all interests which he would have discovered had he insisted upon deduction for the full period.[348] This is something which a purchaser and his solicitor must bear in mind when faced with a draft contract proposing a shortened length of title. In many cases there may be little risk in practice of third party rights affecting the purchaser, but in others the risk may be too great, eg, where the purchaser intends to develop the land and may be restricted by covenants created by earlier deeds and still binding the land.[349]

(iv) Chain of Title

[14.61] The general rule is that the vendor must show an unbroken chain of title running from the root of title to some document of title or event whereby he acquired the estate in the property contracted to be sold.[350] The links in the chain will usually consist of various conveyances of the land and events, such as deaths, which caused the title to be transferred from one person to another. If there is a missing link, then the title is bad and the

---

[345.] See *Hume v Bentley* (1852) 5 De G & s 520: *Re National Provincial Bank of England v Marsh* [1895] 1 Ch 190.

[346.] See *Nottingham Patent Brick and Tile Co v Butler* (1886) 16 QBD 776; *Re Cox and Neve's Contract* [1891] 2 Ch 109. It is also a criminal offence to conceal an incumbrance with intent to defraud the purchaser, see para **[14.61]** *infra*.

[347.] See para **[9.24]** *et seq, ante*.

[348.] *Re Nisbet and Pott's Contract* [1906] 1 Ch 386 at 408 (*per* Romer LJ). *Cf* the rule in *Patman v Harland* in the case of leasehold land. see para **[14.71]** *infra*.

[349.] Freehold restrictive covenants have given rise to particular difficulties in England despite their registration in the Land Charges Registry since 1925, see Law Commission *Report on Land Charges Affecting Unregistered Land* (Law Com No 18) and Law of Property Act 1969, s 25. Mercifully Irish conveyancers have been spared this particular twist, since there is no such Registry in either part of Ireland, para **[1.27]** *ante*.

[350.] Or, at least, whereby the estate vested in some person whom the vendor can compel to convey to the purchaser. see *Re Bryant and Barningham's Contract* (1890) 44 Ch D 218; *Re Butler and Selmon's Contract* [1907] 1 Ch 238; *Elliott v Pierson* [1948] Ch 452: *Jones v Lipman* [1962] 1 WLR 832.

purchaser can rescind the contract for failure to show good title.[351] However, the vendor may seek to cover this by a special condition relating to the intermediate title between a particular instrument and a later one. Thus, condition 12 of the Law Society's *General Conditions of Sale (1995 Edition)* provides that, where the special conditions specify that the title is to commence with a particular instrument and then pass to a second instrument or specified event, "the title intervening between the first instrument and the second instrument or specified event, whether or not appearing by recital, inference or otherwise, shall not be required, objected to or investigated". Once again, though this is a widely drafted restriction,[352] it does not relieve the vendor of his basic duty to disclose latent defects in title of which he is aware, or ought to have been aware.[353] Furthermore, it must also be remembered that it is both a criminal offence and a civil wrong actionable in damages by the purchaser or persons deriving title under him for the vendor or his solicitor or other agent to conceal, with intent to defraud,[354] from the purchaser any instrument or incumbrance material to the title or to falsify any pedigree upon which the title may depend in order to induce the purchaser to accept the title offered or produced.[355] Subject to these general principles, it may be useful to consider the various links in a chain of title which are usually appropriate and those which are not.

(a) Conveyances on Sale

[14.62] Clearly any conveyance on sale of the estate in the land contracted to be sold is one of the strongest links in any chain of title and a copy of all such conveyances should be furnished by the vendor. Normally, the original will have to be handed over on completion, unless special circumstances apply, eg, the current sale is of part only of the land the subject-matter of the earlier transaction and the vendor wishes to keep the deed which still forms a vital link in the chain of title to the land he retains after the current sale.[356]

[351.] Though the defect caused by the missing link may be cured by adverse possession; see the dispute on this amongst the members of the English Court of Appeal in *Re Atkinson and Horsell's Contract* [1912] 2 Ch 1, especially at 19-20 (*per* Buckley LJ) and at 16 (*per* Fletcher Moulton LJ, *dissentiente*). See further, para **[14.81]** *post.*

[352.] Thus, it excludes objections as to the intermediate title discovered *aliunde*, see para **[14.59]** *supra.*

[353.] *Ibid*, and see para **[9.24]** *ante.*

[354.] This must be established see *District Bank Ltd v Luigi Grill Ltd* [1943] Ch 78 (on s 183 of the Law of Property Act 1925). See also para **[9.31]** *ante.*

[355.] Law of Property Amendment Acts 1859, s 24 and 1860, s 8 (still in force in both parts of Ireland, but replaced in England by s 183 of the 1925 Act fn 154 *supra*). In *Smith v Robinson* (1879) 13 Ch D 148 at 151, Fry J doubted whether s 24 of the 1859 Act covered concealment of a *pre*-root incumbrance; *sed quaere.*

[356.] See para **[20.35]** *post.*

Also, if the current sale is made subject to an outstanding mortgage on the land which is not to be discharged on completion,[357] the mortgagee will usually insist upon retention of the deed.[358]

(b) Leases

[14.63] Where the current transaction involves an assignment of an existing lease, the lease and previous assignments of it form the major links in the chain of title and, as we shall see, are subject to the 40-year deduction of title rule.[359] Where, however, it involves a conveyance of the freehold, the general rule is that copies of expired leases, ie, those which have come to their natural determination,[360] in the chain of title need not be produced, since there is no possibility of their affecting the purchaser. On the other hand, a copy of a surrendered lease probably should be produced, so that the purchaser can satisfy himself that the surrender was effective[361] and that the lease no longer survives.[362] Subsisting leases, subject to which the property is sold, must, of course, be disclosed as incumbrances affecting the title.[363]

(c) Mortgages

[14.64] As regards previous mortgages on the land which have been discharged, it seems that, as with surrendered leases, the purchaser is entitled to see that they have been properly discharged.[364] An existing mortgage is clearly an incumbrance which ought to be disclosed and a copy of the relevant deed ought to be furnished, even though, as is usually the case, it is going to be redeemed out of the purchase money raised on the current sale.[365] On principle copies of equitable mortgages created by written document should not be furnished, unless they have been registered in the Registry of Deeds, since a purchaser of the legal estate without notice of them takes free of them - the general rule is that trusts and equities should be kept off the

---

[357.] Which will usually be the case and is provided for by cond 8(c) of the Law Society's *General Conditions of Sale* (1995 ed): see para **[20.18]** *post*.

[358.] See para **[20.17]** *post*.

[359.] There are, however, special rules as to the landlord's title (eg, the freehold reversion) and where the current transaction involves the grant of a sub- or sub-sub-lease. see para **[14.68]** *et seq, infra*.

[360.] See Wylie *Irish Landlord and Tenant Law*, para 26.01 *et seq*.

[361.] *Ibid*, Ch 25.

[362.] See *Re Heaseman and Tweeedie's Contract* (1897) 69 LT 89; *Knight v Williams* [1901] 1 Ch 256; *Barclay's Bank Ltd v Stasek* [1957] Ch 28.

[363.] See para **[9.42]** *ante*.

[364.] See *Irish Land Law* (2nd ed, 1986), para 13 088 *et seq*. See also *Heath v Crealock* (1874) IR 10 Ch 22. *Cf Cumberland Court (Brighton) Ltd v Taylor* [1964] Ch 29.

[365.] See para **[20.29]** *post*.

title.[366] But there is authority to the contrary in England[367] and, if the mortgage has been registered in the Registry of Deeds, it will have priority over the purchaser[368] and will be disclosed by the usual search in the Registry.[369] Thus, the purchaser is likely to want to see a copy of the mortgage document. However, in practice in Ireland most equitable mortgages are created by deposit without any written document to avoid the need for registration, so it might be thought that such mortgages need not be disclosed and the purchaser should not raise any requisition in respect of them; being equitable only, a *bona fide* purchaser for value without notice of them takes free of them. However, that begs the question as to whether the purchaser is fixed with constructive notice and the point is that the absence of the deeds in the vendor's hands gives rise to such notice. Thus, in practice, a requisition is usually made and the equitable mortgage is disclosed in the vendor's reply, with a letter of release from the mortgagee being furnished in due course.[370]

(d) Equitable Interests

[14.65] The general rule is that equitable interests should be kept off the title,[371] ie, those interests which will not affect a *bona fide* purchaser for value of the legal estate without notice of the equities or equitable interests.[372] Thus, where property is held by trustees on trust for beneficiaries, it is the former who may have the legal title and with whom a purchaser is primarily concerned on a sale of the trust property. If the trustees sell under an express or statutory trust for sale,[373] the beneficiaries' interests are generally "overreached" and the purchaser takes free of them. This applies, of course, only if the trustees hold on a trust *for sale*.[374] If the trust is in any other form, eg, a mere power or discretion whether to sell, the land will be settled if there is a "succession" of beneficial interests for the

---

366. Para **[14.65]** *infra*.

367. See *Drummond v Tracey* (1860) John 608 at 612 (*per* Wood V-C), accepted as correct in Sugden, *Law of Vendors and Purchasers* (14th ed, 1862), p 411. For criticisms, see (1962) 26 Conv 445.

368. *Irish Land Law* (2nd ed, 1986), para 13.141 *et seq*.

369. Para **[15.42]** *post*.

370. No 14 in the Law Society's *Objections and Requisitions on Title* (1996 Rev Ed) asks whether the property is subject to "any" mortgage or charge: see para **[16.22]** *post*.

371. See *Carritt v Real and Personal Advance Co* (1889) 42 Ch D 263 at 272-3 (*per* Chitty J). See also *Re Harman and Uxbridge and Rickmansworth Rly Co* (1883) 24 Ch D 720; *Jared v Clements* [1903] 1 Ch 428.

372. See *Irish Land Law* (2nd ed, 1986), para 3.069 *et seq*.

373. *Ibid*, paras 10.015-7.

374. See *ibid*, paras 8.011 *et seq* and 8.083 *et seq*; also para **[14.77]** *infra*.

purposes of the Settled Land Acts 1882-90. In that situation it is the beneficiary who is the tenant for life who has the power to sell the land and with whom the purchaser must deal.[375]

(e) Wills

[14.66] Since wills now operate in equity only in Ireland,[376] theoretically they should be kept off the title. Until recently, a will was a vital title document and still is in respect of persons who died some years ago. Thus, where a person died before 1 June 1959, his real property passed directly under his will to his devisee, and, on intestacy, to his heir-at-law, and so when examining the title the will had to be read.[377] If he died testate, his executors could make title if he left his realty to them; otherwise they could sell only under Lord St Leonard's Act 1859.[378] In the case of intestacy, only the heir-at-law had power to sell. Thus, when dealing with a title which involves a death of an owner prior to 1959, the will must be examined. So far as deaths after that date are concerned, the vital links where property has been transferred by succession on death are the grant of probate or letters of administration to the deceased's personal representatives and the assent by the latter to the vesting of the property in the appropriate successor, ie, the beneficiaries named in the will or, in the case of intestacy, the next-of-kin.[379] The same applies where the personal representatives exercise a power to sell the property.[380] However, as a copy of the will still forms part of the grant of probate or letters of administration with the will annexed, and, indeed, is physically attached by the Probate Office to the grant form, the will always appears amongst the documents of title furnished. However, it has been made clear by statute that the will is *not* a document of title in the case of registered land and the Registrar of Title is required to act on the basis of the personal representatives' assent or transfer in favour of the deceased's successor.[381]

---

375. *Ibid*, para 8.014, 8.020 and 8.028 *et seq*.
376. See *ibid*, para 5.030.
377. Administration of Estates Act 1959. See generally, *Irish Land Law* (2nd ed, 1986), Ch 15; Brady, *Succession Law in Ireland* (2nd ed, 1995), Ch 9.
378. Ie, Law of Property Amendment Act 1859. See *Irish Land Law* (2nd ed, 1986), para 16.50.
379. See *Irish Land Law* (2nd ed, 1986), paras 16.44-6. *Cf Mohan v Roche* [1991] 1 IR 560, paras **[14.79]** *infra* and **[16.54]** *post*.
380. *Ibid*, paras 16.48-51.
381. Registration of Title Act 1964, s 61(3), substituted by s 54(2) of the Succession Act 1965 to clarify the position: see Fitzgerald, *Land Registry Practice* (2nd ed, 1995), pp 90-91. If the application to register the transmission on death quotes the provisions of the will, it will be rejected by the Registry: see Note (1) to Form 48 in the Land Registration Rules 1972.

(f) Voluntary Conveyances

[14.67] At first sight it might appear that voluntary conveyances are weak links in a chain of title because of their statutory liability to be set aside, eg, where made to defraud purchasers[382] or by way of settlement to defraud creditors[383] or otherwise void as against the Official Assignee under the provisions of the Bankruptcy Act 1988.[384] However, the crucial point to note in respect of all these situations is that a *bona fide* purchaser for value without notice of the fraud or bankruptcy, as the case may be, is protected and obtains a good title to the property.[385]

3. Special Cases

(i) Fee Farm Grants and Leases

[14.68] Under an open contract for sale of land there are special statutory provisions relating to leasehold transactions and it is also usual to have special provisions in the contract for sale dealing with leases. Furthermore, since in Ireland fee farm grants. though involving transfer of freehold estates, share many of the features of leasehold estates, eg, payment of rent and easy enforceability of covenants and conditions, and. indeed, have much leasehold law directly applicable to them,[386] it is usual for similar contractual provisions to apply in Ireland to fee farm grants.[387]

(a) Open contract

[14.69] So far as a transaction involving a lease is concerned, there are in fact four statutory provisions governing an open contract. First, the requirement of deduction of title for forty years contained in s 1 of the Vendor and Purchaser Act 1874,[388] applies except to the extent it is restricted by the other statutory provisions. Secondly, where the contract relates to a grant or assignment of a term of years, whether to be derived out of a freehold or leasehold estate, the intended lessee or assignee is not entitled to call for the title to the freehold. This is provided by s 2 of the Vendor and

---

[382.] Conveyancing Act (Ir) 1634, ss 1 and 3 and Voluntary Conveyances Act 1893. See *Irish Land Law* (2nd ed, 1986), para 9.078.

[383.] Conveyancing Act (Ir) 1634, ss 10 and 14. See *Re O'Neill* [1989] IR 544 and *McQuillan v Maguire* [1996] 1 ILRM 394; *Ibid*, paras 9.076-7.

[384.] See ss 57 and 59; Sanfey and Holohan, *Bankruptcy Law and Practice in Ireland* (1991), Ch 8.

[385.] See *ibid*.

[386.] See *ibid*, para 4.057 *et seq*.

[387.] Under cond 2 of the Law Society's *General Conditions of Sale* (1995 ed) "lease" includes a "fee farm grant and every contract (whether or not in writing or howsoever effected, derived or evidenced) whereby the relationship of Landlord and Tenant is or is intended to be created and whether for any freehold or leasehold estate or interest ..."

[388.] Para **[14.54]** *supra*.

Purchaser Act 1874, and deals with four situations: the grant of a lease by the freeholder; the assignment of such a lease; the grant of a sub-lease out of such a lease; the assignment of such a sub-lease. Thirdly, s 3(1) of the Conveyancing Act 1881, provides that on a contract to sell and assign a term of years derived out of a lease of land, the intended assignee does not have the right to call for the title to the leasehold reversion. This also deals with the case of an assignment of a sub-lease. Fourthly, s 13(1) of the 1881 Act provides that, on a contract to grant a term of years to be derived out of a leasehold interest with a leasehold reversion, the intended lessee does not have the right to call for the title to the reversion. This deals with the case of a grant of a sub-sub-lease.

[14.70] The operation of these rules in the case of an open contract are best explained by examples illustrated diagramatically:

Example I

In 1890 L granted a 999-year lease to T, who assigned the lease in 1930 to A, who in turn assigned it in 1940 to B, who assigned it in 1950 to C, who assigned it in 1970 to V, who contracted in 1996 to assign it to P.
This chain of title may be illustrated thus -

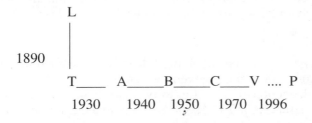

Under an open contract P can in 1996 call for deduction of the following title: (1) forty years' title back, or more if the first good root[389] is not forty years back,[390] so that the title must begin with the 1950 assignment and cannot begin with the 1970 assignment; (2) the 1890 lease the residue of which he is buying.[391] He cannot call for: (1) the title to L's freehold estate[392] (no doubt now held by some successor in title); (2) the 1930 and 1940 assignments, since these are more than forty years old[393] and pre-date the

---

389. 1874 Act, s 1.
390. Para **[14.55]** *supra.*
391. Ie, none of the statutory provisions prohibit this and all of the subsequent assignments are only as good as the original lease.
392. 1874 Act, s 2.
393. 1874 Act, s 1

first assignment after forty years back from 1996 (the 1950 assignment). The risk of some defect existing in either of those earlier assignments and surviving to affect P is fairly remote, but of much greater danger to him is the fact that he cannot see L's title and, therefore, cannot check whether L had sufficient title to the land to enable him to grant a valid lease in 1890. Admittedly, since all concerned seemed to have acted on this basis since then, it is unlikely that some successor of L is going to be able to upset the title so much later, but there is the further problem that L's freehold title may be subject to incumbrances which may affect P indirectly if he buys the lease, eg, restrictive covenants.[394] This may be a particular problem if P proposes to develop the property.[395] Furthermore, if L's freehold interest is held under a fee farm or sub-fee farm grant, it may be subject to all sorts of exceptions and reservations, covenants and conditions, which may again affect any person, such as P, who acquires an interest derived out of the grant.[396] It is true that, if, as is likely, the property includes a permanent building on the land the title will in recent times have ceased to be a leasehold title because the tenant will have exercised his statutory right to acquire the fee simple.[397] However, that will not necessarily resolve title problems caused by covenants because some may continue to affect the land.[398]

Example 2

In 1960 L granted a 999-year lease to T, who assigned the lease in 1970 to A, who assigned it in 1980 to V, who contracted in 1996 to assign it to P. This chain of title may be illustrated thus -

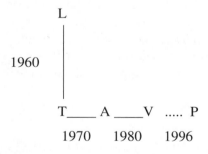

[394.] See *Irish Land Law* (2nd ed, 1986), Ch 19.

[395.] *Ibid*, para 19.46.

[396.] *Ibid*, paras 4.179-82.

[397.] Under the Landlord and Tenant (Ground Rents) Acts 1967-87: see Wylie, *Irish Landlord and Tenant Law* Ch 31.

[398.] Under s 28 of the 1978 (No 2) (Ground Rents) Act: see *ibid*, paras [31.74-7].

In 1996, P can call for: (1) the 1980 and 1970 assignments; (2) the 1960 lease. The 1970 assignment is less than forty years back from 1996, as indeed is the 1960 lease, but P cannot call for any earlier title because this would involve L's freehold title, which he cannot call for.

Example 3

In 1960 L granted a 999-year lease to T, who in 1970 assigned the lease to A, who in 1980 granted a sub-lease to V, who in 1996 contracted to assign the sub-lease to P. This may be illustrated thus -

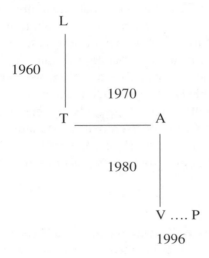

In 1996, P can call for the 1980 sub-lease, but nothing more, ie, he cannot call for: (I) the 1970 assignment since this relates to the head-lease, ie, the "leasehold reversion" on the sub-lease,[399] even though it is less than forty years back from 1996; (2) the 1960 lease, the leasehold reversion[400]; (3) L's freehold title.[401] This is strictly in accordance with the statutory provisions,[402] though it is particularly risky from P's point of view in that the

---

[399.] 1881 Act, s 3(1).

[400.] *Ibid.*

[401.] 1874 Act, s 2.

[402.] The dictum of Romer LJ in *Drive Yourself Hire Co (London) Ltd v Strutt* [1954] 1 QB 250 at 278 to the effect that P could see also the 1960 head-lease is usually discounted. Romer LJ cited *Gosling v Woolf* [1893] 1 QB 39, but that case involved a grant of a sub-lease, ie, someone in V's position in 1980. It is clear that in 1980 V could call for the title to the head-lease of 1960 and the 1970 assignment, since s 3(1) of the 1881 Act prohibits calling for the leasehold reversion only on a contract to *sell and assign* a term of years already derived out of leasehold land (ie, an existing sub-lease), not on a contract for the grant of the sub-lease in the first place

sub-lease is only as good as the head-lease out of which it is derived, and the sub-lessee is clearly subject indirectly to the covenants and conditions contained in the head-lease.[403]

Example 4

In 1960 L granted a 999-year lease to T, who in 1970 assigned the lease to A, who in 1980 granted a sub-lease to B, who in 1990 assigned the sub-lease to V, who in 1996 contracted to grant a sub-sub-lease to P. This may be illustrated thus -

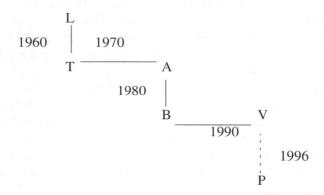

In 1996, P can call for: (1) the 1990 assignment since this is less than forty years old[404]; (2) the 1980 sub-lease, since this is the title held by his vendor and none of the statutory provisions prohibit him from calling for this. He can not call for: (1) the 1970 assignment, since this relates to the leasehold reversion on the leasehold interest out of which his sub-sub-lease is to be derived[405]; (2) the 1960 lease, the said leasehold reversion[406]; (3) L's freehold title.[407]

(b) Rule in Patman v Harland

[14.71] Prior to the statutory provisions just discussed, the position at common law seems to have been that the purchaser of leasehold property was entitled to call for his lessor's title.[408] However, it was recognised that

---

[403.] See Wylie, *Irish Landlord and Tenant Law* para 24.23 *et seq.* See also *Becker v Partridge* [1966] 2 QB 155.

[404.] 1874 Act, s 1.

[405.] 1874 Act, s 13(1).

[406.] *Ibid.*

[407.] 1881 Act, s 2.

[408.] *Mulholland v Corporation of Belfast* (1859) Dru *temp* Nap 539 at 554 (*per* Blackburne J). See also *Lahey v Bell* (1843) 6 Ir Eq R 122; *Leathem v Allen* (1850) 1 Ir Ch R 683; *Wright v Griffith* (1851) 1 Ir Ch R 695.

the vendor[409] could seek to preclude this by an express stipulation in the contract.[410] As Brady LC put it in *Leathem v Allen*[411]:

"The common rule is, that the vendor of a leasehold is, if required, bound to produce the title of his lessor; but he may stipulate against that necessity, and, if he do so, the Court will give him the benefit of it. And there is no doubt that this stipulation may be made either by express words or inferred from the mode of description."[412]

The question arose, however, as to what the position of a purchaser was under an open contract after the passing of the legislation precluding investigation of the freehold or leasehold reversion. It was soon decided, according to what is now known, after the leading English case, as the rule in *Patman v Harland*,[413] that a purchaser is fixed with constructive notice of not only all matters he would have discovered by investigating the title he is allowed to see under the statutory provisions, but also all matters he would have discovered by investigating the superior title which the statutory provisions precluded him from investigating on an open contract.[414] In other words, the purchaser runs the risk of being affected by hidden defects or incumbrances in the superior title both if he contracts for *less* than the legislation allows him and if he fails to contract for more than the legislation allows him. The only absolutely safe course for a purchaser of leasehold property to adopt is, therefore, to contract for *more* than the legislation allows, ie., not to leave the contract open, but to close it by stipulating that the vendor should deduce the relevant superior title.

[14.72] At first sight this may appear to be hard on purchasers, but it is important also to look at the matter from the point of view of third parties whose interests in the land were created as part of transactions affecting the superior title. The rule in *Patman v Harland* does at least ensure that the owners of interests such as restrictive covenants are protected in that purchasers of the land under transactions to which those owners are not parties and of whom they may know nothing will continue to be bound by

---

[409.] Or the Court in a sale under its jurisdiction, see *Willes v Latham* (1837) S & Sc 441 at 441 (*per* O'Loghlen MR). See also *Lahey v Bell* (1843) 6 Ir Eq R 122 at 122 (*per* Brady CB).

[410.] *Wright v Griffiths* (1851) 1 Ir Ch R 695 at 702-3 (*per* Brady CB) *Mulholland v Corporation of Belfast* (1859) Dru *temp* Nap 539 at 554 (*per* Blackburne LJ).

[411.] (1850) 1 Ir Ch R 683.

[412.] *Ibid*, p 690.

[413.] (1881) 17 Ch D 353 (decided in relation to s 2 of the Vendor and Purchaser Act 1874). This rule as to notice also operated prior to the statutory provisions, see *Wilson v Hart* (1866) IR 1 Ch 463 at 467 (*per* Turner LJ).

[414.] See *Imray v Oakshette* [1897] 2 QB 218. See also *Re Cox and Neve's Contract* [1891] 2 Ch 109; *Oliver v Hinton* [1899] 2 Ch 264; *Re Nisbet and Pott's Contract* [1906] 1 Ch 386.

their interests. Thus, the criticism has been levelled at the draftsman of the English Law of Property Act 1925, that, in seeking to abrogate the rule to the extent that a purchaser is not to be fixed with notice of any matters he would have discovered if he had contracted to see the superior title,[415] he may have provided a cure that was worse than the disease.[416] So far no similar provision has been enacted in Ireland, where the rule survives in full force.

[14.73] In view of the continued operation of the rule in *Patman v Harland* in Ireland, it may be questioned whether a purchaser's solicitor should be content to allow his client to enter into an open contract for the grant or assignment of a leasehold interest, or, as is not uncommon, to allow him to accede to a contractual stipulation seeking to restrict the vendor's duty even further than the statutory provisions applicable to an open contract. At first sight a negative answer suggests itself and, indeed, it has been suggested from time to time that a solicitor who does not ensure[417] that the purchaser contracts for the fullest deduction of title may be negligent.[418] Yet s 66(1) of the Conveyancing Act 1881,[419] provides:

> "... a solicitor shall not be deemed guilty of neglect or breach of duty, or become in any way liable, by reason of his omitting, in good faith, in any ... instrument, or in connection with any ... contract or transaction, to negative the giving, inclusion, or application of the ... provisions, stipulations, or words, or to insist or apply any others in place thereof, in any case where the provisions of this Act would allow of his doing so."

Admittedly, this covers only the provisions for open contracts contained in the 1881 Act and not those in the Vendor and Purchaser Act 1874,[420] but a court would be likely to adopt a similar approach to the latter, where, eg, a

---

[415.] Section 44(5). However, note that this provision has to be read with s 198(1) of the same Act, under which the purchaser is deemed to have notice of all registered land charges. and since 1925 all freehold restrictive covenants must be so registered. See *White v Bijou Mansions Ltd* [1937] Ch 610 at 621 (*per* Simonds J) (*affd* on other grounds [1958] Ch 351). See also now the Law of Property Act 1969, s 25(9); Law Commission *Report on Land Charges Affecting Unregistered Land* (Law Com No 18).

[416.] Barnsley, *Conveyancing Law and Practice* (3rd ed, 1988), pp 268-70; *Emmet on Title* (19th ed by Farrand) para 5.152; Cretney, 'Land Law and Conveyancing Reforms' (1869) 32 MLR 477, especially at 485.

[417.] Or at least advise his client of the dangers of not demanding a full deduction of title. *Cf* where the right to investigate the superior title exists, but the solicitor fails to exercise it, see *Hill v Harris* [1965] 2 QB 601 at 618 (*per* Russell LJ). and see (1965) 29 Conv 162. See also para **[5.12]** *ante*.

[418.] See, eg, *Imray v Oakshette* [1897] 2 QB 218 at 225 (*per* Lopes LJ) and 229 (*per* Rigby LJ), approved in Walford, *Sale of Land* (2nd ed, 1957), p 113; *cf* Barnsley, *Conveyancing Law and Practice* (3rd ed, 1988) pp 267-8; (1963) 60 L Soc Gaz 479; (1971) 68 L Soc Gaz 476.

[419.] Replaced in England by s 182(1) of the Law of Property Act 1925.

[420.] Para **[14.69]** *supra*.

solicitor did not stipulate in the contract for deduction of the freehold title contrary to s 2 of the 1874 Act. On the other hand, s 66(2) of the 1881 Act impliedly warns of the need to consider insertion of special stipulations by providing that nothing in the Act is to be taken "to imply that the insertion in any such instrument, or the adoption in connection with, or the application to, any contract or transaction, of any further or other powers, covenants, provisions, stipulations, or words is improper." The fact is that it is probably dangerous to generalise and each case must be considered on its own merits. There is all the world of difference between a contract for the grant of a short lease at a rack rent, where the lessee intends to continue the existing use of the property for the duration of the lease,[421] and a contract for the grant or assignment of a long lease at a substantial premium, where the purchaser may decide to develop the property in the future, if he does not intend to do it immediately upon purchase.[422] In most cases of sales of leasehold or sub-leasehold titles for long terms, the contract for sale provides that the title is to begin with the lease or sub-lease creating the term sold. In the case of residential property or property used for the same business for many years, there is little risk of the purchaser being concerned with restrictive covenants affecting the freehold interest or included in the head-lease. The real risk arises when it is intended to develop open land by building upon it. In such cases the purchaser's solicitor should insist upon production of the title to the freehold and, in cases of sales of sub-leases, the intermediate lease as well, for it may have been granted for residential purposes seventy years ago when the land to be developed was in the country and nobody contemplated development of the property leased. Many leases of a house surrounded by extensive lands contained a covenant by the lessee that the lands leased would be used as a single private residence. Such a covenant would prevent the lands being developed and could be enforced by the owner of the freehold interest. Relief against the covenant could probably be obtained by invoking the provisions relating to covenants restricting user or against improvements in the Landlord and Tenant (Amendment) Act 1980, but the purchaser should insist that the vendor brings the proceedings.[423]

(c) Contractual Provisions

[14.74] The statutory provisions governing open contracts operate only so far as an express stipulation to the contrary is not contained in the contract for sale.[424] Condition 9 of the Law Society's *General Conditions of Sale*

[421.] See *Clayton v Leech* (1889) 41 Ch D 103 at 105.

[422.] *Cf Becker v Partridge* [1966] 2 QB 155.

[423.] Or joins with the purchaser in bringing proceedings: see Wylie, *Irish Landlord and Tenant Law*, para 18.16. See also *McMullen v Farrell* [1993] 1 IR 123.

[424.] Vendor and Purchaser Act 1874, s 2; Conveyancing Act 1881, ss 3(9) and 13(2).

(1995 Edition) reiterates the open contract rule as to leases, and applies the same rule to fee farm grants,[425] namely, that the purchaser of any property held under a fee farm grant, lease or sub-lease, is not to call for or investigate the title of the grantor or lessor to make the same, but is to assume conclusively that it was well and validly made and is a valid and subsisting grant or lease.[426]

[14.75] Apart from these matters, the Law Society's contract contains other provisions relating to fee farm grants and leases. First, where the sale involves a sub-grant or sub-lease of part of a larger portion of land held under a superior grant or lease, reserving a larger rent, in respect of which there may or may not be an apportionment or exclusive charge of rent, and various other covenants, conditions, and agreements, the purchaser is not to object because of these facts or to require any further indemnity.[427] Secondly, no objection or requisition can be made where there is a discrepancy between covenants, conditions and provisions in any sub-lease and those in any superior lease, unless this is such as could give rise to forfeiture or a right of re-entry.[428] Thirdly, production of the receipt for the last rent payable under the grant or lease is to be conclusive evidence, without proof of the title of the person giving it, that all rent accrued due has been paid and all covenants, conditions and agreements have been complied with or that any breaches (including breaches of a continuing nature) have been effectively waived or sanctioned up to the date of actual completion.[429] This provision extends the protection afforded the vendor by s 3(4) and (5) of the Conveyancing Act 1881, which states that such a receipt in respect of a lease or sub-lease raises a rebuttable presumption only, so that a purchaser could still object on discovery of the non-payment or breach.[430] The contractual provision as to conclusive evidence precludes such objection,[431] except presumably in relation to breaches committed after the contract for sale,[432] but it purports to preclude objection even where it appears that the vendor knew of the breaches and should have disclosed them to the

---

[425.] They are included in the definition of "lease": see para **[14.68]** *supra*.

[426.] This deals with the sale of an existing grant or lease. There is no provision dealing with the original granting of a fee farm grant or lease.

[427.] Cond 10(a). See *Re Doherty's Contract* (1884) 15 LR Ir 247. See also *Irish Land Law* (2nd ed, 1986), paras 4.107 and 6.136.

[428.] Cond 10(b).

[429.] Cond 10(c). We saw earlier that, where the fee farm grant or lease or copies are made available for inspection, the purchaser is deemed to have bought with full notice of their contents, see para **[9.39]** *ante*.

[430.] *Becker v Partridge* [1966] 2 QB 153 at 169 (*per* Danckwerts LJ). See also the controversial decision in *Re Highett and Bird's Contract* [1903] 1 Ch 287; *cf Re Allen and Driscoll's Contract* [1904] 2 Ch 226 at 231 (*per* Romer LJ).

[431.] *Lawrie v Lees* (1881) 7 App Cas 19.

[432.] *Howell v Kightley* (1856) 21 Beav 331 at 336 (*per* Romilly MR).

purchaser.[433] This provision also deals with the situation where such a receipt is not available. This often occurs where the rent is not a rack rent, but some nominal sum only.[434] Instead a statutory declaration[435] that no notices or rent demands have been served on or received by the vendor, that he has complied with the all covenants (other than in respect of payment of rent) and conditions and that he is not aware of any breaches by himself or his predecessors in title is to be accepted again as conclusive evidence.[436] Fourthly, where consent is required for assignment by the vendor,[437] the vendor is to apply for and endeavour to obtain it and the purchaser is to satisfy all reasonable requirements of the landlord in relation to the application, but the vendor is not to be required to institute legal proceedings[438] for a declaration that such consent has been unreasonably withheld.[439] This seems to accord with the common law position.[440]

(ii) Leases for Lives Renewable For Ever

[14.76] Where the purchaser was buying a lease for lives renewable for ever,[441] it was held in *Anderson v Higgins*[442] that the vendor was obliged to show which lives were in existence, and where they lived, but, if some were dead, he was not obliged to apply for their renewal. If all were dead without being renewed, the vendor would fail to show a good title.[443] Sugden LC said:

> "Evidence to show which of the *cestui qui vies* were then *in esse* must be part of such a title ... I should be of opinion that a good title can now be made out under the contract, by the seller showing which of the lives were in existence at the time of the contract, and by a conveyance of the interest

---

[433.] See para **[9.27]** *ante*. And see *Beyfus v Lodge* [1925] Ch 350.

[434.] Many such rents were created during the period immediately preceding enactment of the Landlord and Tenant (Ground Rents) Act 1978, which prohibited the creation of further ground rents in respect of dwellinghouses: see Wylie, *Irish Landlord and Tenant Law*, para 2.22.

[435.] As recommended in 1982 in a Practice Note issued by the Joint Committee of the Building Societies and Law Society, reproduced in the Society's *Conveyancing Handbook* p 4.3.

[436.] Cond 10(c). The Practice Note (fn 435 *supra*) was based on s 3(4) and (5) of the 1881 Act and so stated that the declaration was *prima facie* evidence only.

[437.] Eg under an express provision in a lease.

[438.] See Wylie, *Irish Landlord and Tenant Law*, para 21.11-12.

[439.] Cond 10(d).

[440.] *Lehmann v McArthur* (1868) 3 Ch App 496. See also *Lipmans Wallpaper Ltd v Mason and Hodgron Ltd* [1969] 1 Ch 20 at 25 (*per* Goff J).

[441.] These were not very common in modern times as all those created since 1849 operated automatically as fee farm grants under s 37 of the Renewable Leasehold Conversion Act 1849. See generally *Irish Land Law* (2nd ed, 1986), paras 8.167-76.

[442.] (1844) 1 Jo & Lat 718.

[443.] But note that the vendor might have been able to have the lives renewed despite lapse of time under the Tenantry (Ir) Act 1779. See *Irish Land Law* (2nd ed, 1986), paras 4.171-5.

under the lease for the then existing lives and that the seller would not be bound to obtain a renewal of the lease, in case any of the *cestui qui vies* were then dead. The seller of a lease for lives must be prepared to show what lives in the lease are in existence: his title depends on the fact of the lives or some of them being in existence; and the purchaser has a right to know where the *cestui qui vies* are living."[444]

This continued to be a problem down to modern times because, although all lessees holding under *pre*-1849 leases for lives renewable for ever were given the right to convert them into fee farm grants,[445] all too often this right was not exercised. It was resolved by s 74 of the Landlord and Tenant (Amendment) Act 1980, under which the interest of any person entitled to an interest the title to which originated under such an unconverted lease is converted into an estate in fee simple. This estate is, however, deemed to be a graft upon the previous leasehold interest and so is subject to the same "rights and equities".This clearly covers covenants and conditions in the leases and, arguably, also the rent.[446] If so, s 74 would seem to create another category of fee farm grant, analogous to conversion grants created under the Renewable Leasehold Conversion Act 1849.[447]

(iii) Settlements and Trusts for Sale

[14.77] Conveyancers in Ireland have so far been spared the complexities that have resulted in England from the provisions introduced there in relation to settlements[448] and statutory trusts for sale.[449] Thus, there is no statutory requirement of use of two conveyancing documents for creation of a settlement, ie, a principal vesting deed, which is the sole concern of the purchaser, and a trust instrument (or will, in the case of a settlement by a testator) dealing with the beneficial interests, which is generally none of his concern.[450] In Ireland, the settlement is usually contained in one document, and a copy of this will have to be furnished by a vendor purporting to sell as entitled under the settlement or as tenant for life exercising the powers conferred by the Settled Land Acts 1882-90. This whole subject is dealt with in detail elsewhere.[451]

[444.] *Op cit*, p 722.

[445.] Renewable Leasehold Conversion Act 1849, s 37: see Wylie, *Irish Landlord and Tenant Law* para 4.45.

[446.] See *ibid*, p 1181; cf Lyall, *Land Law in Ireland* (1994), pp 202-3 and 250-1.

[447.] Note the effect of ss 1 and 7. See *Irish Land Law* (2nd ed, 1986), para 4.086.

[448.] Settled Land Act 1925.

[449.] Law of Property Act 1925, ss 23-33.

[450.] See Albery, 'The Settled Land Act Curtain' (1939) 4 Conv 203.

[451.] *Irish Land Law* (2nd ed, 1986), Ch 8. See Lyall, *Land Law in Ireland* (1994), Ch 14

[14.78] So far as trusts for sale are concerned, the provisions of the Settled Land Acts 1882-90, are not well drafted and do cause some conveyancing difficulties. These too have been discussed elsewhere.[452]

(iv) Succession

[14.79] We mentioned earlier[453] that, where a link in the chain of title consists of a succession by one person on the death of the owner, the vital documents of title to be produced by the vendor are the grant of probate or letters of administration to the deceased's personal representatives upon whom his property will devolve on death and the assent by them vesting the property in his successors in title, ie, the beneficiaries named in his will or his next-of-kin (on intestacy). But as we also mentioned earlier, the practice remains that the will is attached physically to the grant of probate or letters of administration with the will annexed. This subject is also discussed elsewhere.[454]

(v) Possessory Titles

[14.80] The general nature of possessory titles, and, in particular, the controversy over the application of the doctrine of adverse possession to leasehold land, which most urban land is in Ireland, has been considered elsewhere.[455] Where the vendor's title is entirely possessory, it is clear that, on an open contract, merely showing the statutory twelve years' adverse possession dating back from the contract for sale is not enough. Indeed, it is arguable that the traditional forty years' title is not enough in many cases. The point is that the possession by the vendor bars only the rights of those to whom his possession is "adverse" in the modern sense, ie, possession giving rise to a right of action which, after twelve years from the date of its accrual, will be barred.[456] But the vendor may have dispossessed only one of the persons with an interest in the land, eg, the tenant for life under a settlement. So long as the tenant for life remains alive, the remainderman has no right to possession and time does not run against him until the tenant for life dies.[457] This may not occur until several years, even decades, after the vendor completes his twelve years' possession against the tenant for life. So that a sale by the vendor in the meantime based solely on his adverse possession

---

[452.] *Irish Land Law* (2nd ed, 1986), paras 8.043-50.

[453.] See para **[14.66]** *supra*.

[454.] *Ibid* and para [16.54] *post*, which discusses the position where the personal representative is also the deceased's successor in title.

[455.] *Irish Land Law* (2nd ed, 1986), Ch 23. See also Brady and Kerr, *The Limitations of Actions* (2nd ed, 1995), Ch 4.

[456.] *Ibid*, para 23.04-5.

[457.] *Ibid*, para 23.32.

would, in effect, pass an estate *pur autre vie* to the purchaser, ie, for the life of the tenant for life, and not the freehold. The result is, therefore, that, on an open contract, it is often necessary for the vendor to trace the title back to a good root of title preceding the adverse possession, then forward to the point of dispossession and then at least twelve years' possession thereafter.[458] This may be particularly onerous for a vendor who may know nothing of the previous owners (they may have long since disappeared) and so it is necessary then to stipulate in the contract that a possessory title for the specified period of years only will be shown.[459] But care must be exercised to ensure that the vendor will be able to prove uninterrupted possession for the stipulated period, for it seems that the court will not substitute twelve years for any longer period stipulated in the contract.[460] And it is usual for the purchaser to require that proper proof of the alleged possession be furnished, eg, supported by appropriate statutory declarations.[461]

[14.81] We mentioned earlier that a controversial point on both sides of the Irish Sea has been whether a vendor, who has contracted to deduce title by documentary evidence in the normal way, but who later discovers that he cannot furnish an unbroken chain of title in this way, can supply the missing link by furnishing a possessory title. This was held in England to be the case on an open contract, ie, where it did not specify the title to be shown,[462] and the same view was taken by the majority of the Court of Appeal in *Re Atkinson and Horsell's Contract*[463] in relation to a case where the vendor contracted expressly to commence title with a specified instrument. It was held that in such a case the court would force the possessory title on the purchaser as a substitute for the documentary title contracted for. But that case was questioned in Ireland by O'Connor MR in two cases he decided some eight or nine years later dealing with the sale of leasehold property. In *Re Ashe and Hogan's Contract*[464] he had this to say about the principle enunciated in the English case:

[458.] See *Jacobs v Revell* [1900] 2 Ch 858.

[459.] See *Re McClure and Garrett's Contract* [1899] 1 IR 225.

[460.] This was the trap the vendors fell into in *George Wimpey & Co Ltd v Sohn* [1967] Ch 487 (20 years stipulated). See also *Re Spence and Hauser's Contract* [1928] Ch 598.

[461.] See Statutory Declarations Act 1835 and Statutory Declarations Act 1938.

[462.] *Games v Bonner* (1884) 54 LJ Ch 517.

[463.] [1912] 2 Ch 1 (Buckley LJ and Cozens-Hardy MR) Fletcher-Moulton LJ dissented vehemently, *ibid*, p 16. Some of his views seem to have been echoed in *George Wimpey & Co Ltd v Sohn* [1967] Ch 487, though the Court of Appeal expressly distinguished between the two cases.

[464.] [1920] 1 IR 159.

"There is, no doubt, authority for this, but I do not think that it has gone so far as to establish as a universal proposition that when a vendor has contracted to make title in the usual way by conveyances, devises, or descent he can force on a purchaser a title depending entirely on possession. This might place a purchaser in a singularly disadvantageous position. Very frequently a purchaser has to get an advance from his banker or a private lender on the security of the property purchased to enable him to complete the purchase. A banker or private lender might be very ready to lend on the security of a title deduced in the ordinary way, but might absolutely refuse to lend on the security of a mere possessory title."[465]

He then went on to point out that, on the basis of the "no parliamentary conveyance" doctrine,[466] the leasehold estate is not transferred to the adverse possessor, so that the possessor does not enjoy the benefits resulting from privity of estate with the landlord that an assignee enjoys.[467] O'Connor MR returned to this theme in *Clibborn v Horan*,[468] where he stated that, though he felt bound to accept the general proposition laid down in *Re Atkinson and Horsell's Contract*, he thought that -

"... the question is still open whether - although it must be accepted as a general rule that a possessory title can be substituted for a documentary title - this is a proposition of universal application, no matter what the nature of the estate the subject of the contract."[469]

And again he pointed out "the difficulty in applying it to leasehold estates, having regard to the quality of the title acquired by possession."[470] It is doubtful if developments in the law since then have suggested sufficient improvements in the quality of such titles in Ireland to warrant disagreement with O'Connor MR's views. The Supreme Court approved the "no parliamentary conveyance" doctrine, which O'Connor MR had in mind, in *Perry v Woodfarm Homes Ltd*[471] and, though the majority took the view that the squatter's title was not as vulnerable (eg, to surrender by the

---

[465.] *Ibid*, p 166. He distinguished *Scott v Nixon* (1843) 3 Dr & War 388 on the ground that there the title had been investigated by the court and proved by evidence contained in affidavits. Apart from that, the *Scott* case is tainted with Sugden's "parliamentary conveyance" heresy, see *Irish Land Law* (2nd ed, 1986), para 23.09.

[466.] Since upheld by the Supreme Court, see *ibid*, paras 23.10-19.

[467.] Nor, on the other hand, the burdens, but see *ibid*, para 23.16. But note that it has often been held in Ireland that the possessor may become a tenant by estoppel, as O'Connor MR held in fact in the *Ashe* case, see *op cit*, p 169. See also *Irish Land Law* (2nd ed, 1986), para 23.13.

[468.] [1921] 1 IR 93.

[469.] *Ibid*, p 100.

[470.] *Ibid*.

[471.] [1975] IR 104. See *Irish Land Law* (2nd ed, 1986), paras 23.15-18.

dispossessed lessee or merger of title brought about by him) as the majority of the House of Lords decided in *Fairweather v St Marylebone Property Co Ltd*,[472] they did accept that there was a difference in quality between his title and that of an assignee of the lease.[473] The doubts expressed by O'Connor MR were echoed by Keane J in *Mohan v Roche*,[474] where he expressed the view that "there are clearly serious difficulties in holding that a vendor is entitled to insist upon a purchaser accepting such a title where he has contracted for a documentary title".[475]

[14.82] There is one further problem which has arisen recently in cases where the title is a possessory one only. Under s 146 of the Finance Act 1994, such a title may not be registered in the Land Registry unless a certificate has been issued by the Revenue Commissioners to the effect that they are satisfied that the property did not become chargeable to gift tax, probate tax or inheritance tax or else that any charge to tax has been discharged or will be discharged within a time considered reasonable by the Commissioners.[476] This is a matter which purchasers' solicitors must beware of in all cases where an application will have to be made to the Land Registry, eg, where the title[477] is already registered or the land is in an area of compulsory registration. The latest version of the Law Society's contract form now puts the onus on the vendor's solicitor to furnish the appropriate certificate.[478] This matter is considered further in a later chapter.[479]

[472.] [1963] AC 510. See *ibid*, paras 23.11-2.

[473.] At least in respect of unregistered land, see *ibid*, para 21.16.

[474.] [1991] 1 IR 560.

[475.] *Ibid*, p 568.

[476.] For a discussion of the difficulties this raised for conveyancers, see Grogan 'A Conveyancing Disaster - Waiting to Happen' The *Gazette* April 1995, p 125.

[477.] Or part of it, eg, where the land borders agricultural land bought out under the Land Purchase Acts and an encroachment has been made on the latter, giving rise to a claim to title by adverse possession.

[478.] *General Conditions of Sale* (1995 ed), cond 8(b).

[479.] Para **[16.25]** *post*.

Chapter 15

INVESTIGATION OF TITLE

[15.01] The purchaser ought to investigate the title deduced by the vendor.[1] The reason for this is that, even if the purchaser fails to investigate title, he will nevertheless be fixed with constructive notice of those defects in title which he would have discovered had he carried out an investigation.[2] This doctrine of notice has been discussed in detail elsewhere.[3] Its effect is to impose on the purchaser the duties to peruse the title deduced by the vendor, to raise with the vendor any queries which are suggested by that perusal, to ensure that a satisfactory explanation is given and to make searches in public registers relating to the title. We examine each of these matters in this chapter. Added force to the doctrine has been given by the Family Home Protection Act 1976 because that Act makes it imperative that a purchaser, or other person or body wishing to acquire an interest in the land in question, such as a mortgagee, ensures that consent to the transaction is obtained from any "non-owning" spouse if any part of the land comprises a "family home".[4] The Supreme Court has recently emphasised that the burden of proving that the appropriate consent was obtained rests with the purchaser or mortgagee and the duty to engage in an appropriate investigation of the title is not one owed to the non-owning spouse. Rather it is a duty which the purchaser or mortgagee owes to himself, which must be carried out if he is to get good title to the property.[5] It must be reiterated that in this instance the penalty for failing to carry out the appropriate steps is that the purchaser or mortgagee gets no title at all.[6]

[1.] Deduction of title was dealt with in the previous chapter.

[2.] *Gilmore v The O'Connor Don* [1947] IR 463 at 484 (*per* Murnaghan J). See also para **[4.02]** *ante*.

[3.] *Irish Land Law* (2nd ed, 1986), paras 3.069-93; Lyall, *Land Law in Ireland* (1995), p 116 *et seq* and 467 *et seq*.

[4.] If such consent is not obtained in a case where it is needed, a purchaser will obtain good title only if he pays full value and acts in good faith: see s 3(3)(a) and (b) of the 1976 Act; *Somers v Weir* [1979] IR 94. For further discussion of the need for such consent see para **[16.61]** *post*.

[5.] *Bank of Ireland v Smyth* [1996] 1 ILRM 241; *Allied Irish Banks plc v Finnegan* [1996] 1 ILRM 401.

[6.] Generally under the doctrine of notice the purchaser gets the legal title conveyed but subject to the equitable interest of which he has actual or constructive notice, or such notice in his agent which is imputed to him: see *Northern Bank v Henry* [1981] IR 1.

[15.02] Investigation of title, especially in respect of unregistered land, can be a complex process and so is usually left to the purchaser's solicitor. It is clear, as was laid down by the Supreme Court in *Somers v Erskine (No 2)*,[7] that it is negligence on the part of the purchaser's solicitor not to investigate the title at all or to do so in an incompetent manner. In that case the solicitor was retained to act for the purchaser of a 500-year building lease. The proposed landlord's[8] solicitor informed the purchaser's solicitor that doubts had been expressed as to the landlord's power to grant leases and, indeed, he expressed the view that the landlord could not grant a lease for more than 150 years.[9] Nevertheless, without investigating the title or making enquiries as to the true legal position, the purchaser's solicitor permitted his client to enter into the 500-year lease, which was subsequently held by the Supreme Court to be wholly invalid.[10] In a subsequent action by the purchaser against his solicitor's estate,[11] the Supreme Court held that he had been negligent and his estate was liable in damages. As O'Byrne J said, if the solicitor "had investigated the matter and advised his client after a full and careful consideration," then he would have had a good defence, even though his advice later turned out to be unsound.[12] More recently, in *Doran v Delaney*,[13] where there was a doubt as to the boundaries of a parcel of land which the purchaser was acquiring with the benefit of planning permission for development, Hamilton J held the purchaser's solicitor negligent for failing to ensure that the boundaries were staked out and in agreeing to deletion of a special condition in the draft contract for sale which would have provided for the furnishing of an Ordnance Survey map showing the site and all boundaries clearly marked.[14]

[15.03] Normally, of course, investigation of title requires the expertise of a lawyer, but in a straight-forward case the purchaser may employ a non-lawyer. If he does, the person employed must conduct a full investigation and enquiry to the best of his ability, or he too may find himself liable in

---

7. [1944] IR 368.
8. Who was a receiver appointed at the instance of a mortgagee.
9. Ie the statutory limit for leases granted by a tenant for life, as extended by the Landlord and Tenant Act 1931 s 62. see *Irish Land Law* (2nd ed, 1986), para 8.071.
10. *Levingston v Somers* [1941] IR 183.
11. He died pending the hearing of the action and it was continued against his personal representative.
12. [1944] IR 368 at 384. *Kehoe v Louth & Son* [1992] ILRM 282; *cf McMullen v Farrell* [1993] 1 IR 123.
13. [1996] 1 ILRM 490. *Cf Glendinning v Orr* [1989] NI 171.
14. Expert evidence was given by experienced conveyancing solicitors that these actions were not in accordance with "standard and good practice": transcript p 39. Note that a claim for negligence against the vendor's solicitors failed: see para **[15.37]** *infra*.

negligence. This is what happened in *Crawford v Boyd & Co*,[15] where the Northern Ireland Court of Appeal held a property broker liable for negligence in failing to ascertain what kind of tenancy existed in the premises and whether there were any restrictions on the kind of business that could be conducted on them.[16] As to the argument that it was not the duty of a property broker to investigate the title, Andrews LJ commented:

> "This investigation of title is in name only as there was really no title to be examined, there was no mortgage or other documents requiring examination by a solicitor: the defendant only had to make enquiries as to the nature of the tenancy, and if a man is instructed to value a business one of the first things he should do is to ascertain what kind of business can be carried on and what is the nature of the tenancy."[17]

And Best LJ stated:

> "The most elementary enquiries on the defendant's part would have brought to light the necessary information, but he has failed in his duty and not only advised his client to buy a business which is prohibited under the agreement but drew up an agreement under which the vendor sold a business she had no right to carry on."[18]

The courts have increasingly recognised that a professional person may step outside his usual role by, eg, tendering advice to a prospective purchaser and doing so in such a way that he should anticipate that the prospective purchaser is likely to rely on that advice.[19] In such circumstances the professional person may be taken to have assumed responsibility for the advice given and, therefore, be liable in negligence if the purchaser suffers loss as a result of relying upon the advice.[20]

[15.04] It is important to note that the purchaser's investigation of the title may be circumscribed by the terms of the contract for sale. Thus, it is common for the conditions of sale to restrict the requisitions on title that may be raised, or even any objections as to title, and we discuss this later.[21] However, the conditions may purport to go even further and seek to preclude all investigation of title, eg, because the vendor is aware of some defect, or

---

[15.] (1935) 69 ILTR 65.

[16.] See para **[5.28]** *ante*.

[17.] *Op cit*, p 66.

[18.] *Op cit*, p 67.

[19.] Note the views of Hamilton J in *Doran v Delaney* ie, the possibility that a *vendor's* solicitor may in special circumstances be liable to the *purchaser*: see para **[15.37]** *infra*.

[20.] See *McAnarney v Hanrahan* [1993] 3 IR 492. See also *Irish Permanent Building Society v O'Sullivan* [1990] ILRM 598.

[21.] Para **[15.25]** *infra*.

suspects that it exists. But, as we saw in an earlier chapter, there is a limit to how far the vendor can by this means "foist upon the purchaser a worthless title".[22] Such a condition of sale is generally construed against the vendor and, if it is drafted with the intention of misleading the purchaser, it will not be enforced by the courts,[23] and the purchaser will have a good defence to an action for specific performance by the vendor.[24] Furthermore, if the vendor wishes to exclude the purchaser's investigation of title because of a defect of which he is aware, it is settled that he must give the purchaser fair warning of the existence of the defect.[25] This point must be borne in mind in relation to the provisions in the Law Society's standard form contract precluding investigation of the title prior to the root of title.[26] It was held in *Re Turpin and Ahern's Contract*[27] that such a condition does not debar the purchaser from making his own enquiries, independently of the vendor, or from raising objections to title based on those. As FitzGibbon LJ said:

> "The general rule is that, where a title is in fact defective, and the defect is, or ought to be, within the knowledge of the vendor, a condition against investigation will not prevent a purchaser from declining to complete, unless the condition which precludes investigation gives him some fair intimations or warning of the existence of the defect."[28]

However, there is a matter of construction which is relevant in this context. Thus, the condition of sale in question may be interpreted as relieving the purchaser from investigation independently of the vendor[29]; or, where it purports to preclude requisitions on title, it may be interpreted as relating only to requisitions based on the title deduced by the vendor and as not precluding objections or any requisitions based on information coming from third parties.[30] Yet the condition may purport to preclude investigation of any kind and all requisitions and objections based on information coming from any source whatever. However, presumably even this provision is

---

22. *Re White and Hague's Contract* [1921] 1 Ch 138 at 144 (*per* O'Connor MR), see para **[9.37]** *ante*.

23. *Ibid*.

24. See para **[13.52]** *ante*.

25. See para **[9.38]** *ante*.

26. See para **[14.59]** *ante*. Note also the provision in the contract precluding investigation into the "intermediate" title, see para **[14.61]** *ante*.

27. [1905] 1 IR 85.

28. *Ibid* p 103. See also *Musgrave v McCullagh* (1864) 14 Ir Ch R 496 at 499 (*per* Brady LC); *Re Davys and Verdon and Saurin's Contract* (1886)17 LR Ir 334 at 337 (*per* Chatterton V-C).

29. See *Musgrave v McCullagh* (1864) 14 Ir Ch R 496.

30. See *Re Davys and Verdon and Saurin's Contract* (1886) 17 LR Ir 334. See further, para **[15.25]** *post*.

subject to the courts' overriding jurisdiction to refuse to enforce a provision deliberately designed to cheat the purchaser[31] or one which is grossly misleading[32] and, where the court suspects misconduct or lack of fairness[33] or is doubtful as to whether the purchaser will obtain a good title,[34] it may refuse to grant the vendor specific performance.

[15.05] Although investigation of the title is regarded as primarily of concern to the purchaser, it is important to note that there may be other parties involved in the transaction who may be interested in it. The obvious example is the purchaser's mortgagee in the common case where the purchaser is borrowing a substantial proportion of the purchase price from a lending institution, such as a building society or bank. Since the property to be conveyed to the purchaser is also to be the security for the mortgagee's loan, it is crucial for the mortgagee to be certain that the title is good so that, in the event of the security having to be realised, eg, by exercising the power of sale,[35] there will be no difficulties. One way of ensuring that this is so is for the mortgagee to insist upon its own investigation of the title, parallel to that conducted by the purchaser. Alternatively, the mortgagee may be willing to authorise the purchaser's solicitor to act as its agent in the matter, in which case the purchaser's solicitor will have to issue a report on title based upon his investigation. Until recent times it was rare for a lending institution such as a building society to permit the purchaser's solicitor to act as its agent in the transaction, but a consequence of this was that the purchaser's costs were increased substantially by having to pay the costs of both his own solicitor's and the mortgagee's solicitor's investigation. In more recent times the main lending institutions like the building societies and banks have moved to a system whereby they rely upon the investigation of title carried out by the purchaser's (borrower's) solicitor, in respect of which the solicitor will issue to the lender a "certificate of title". This was designed to reduce the overall costs of the transaction for the borrowers, by removing the need for an investigation of title by the lender's own solicitor. Some years ago the Law Society's Conveyancing Committee and the Joint Law Society/Building Societies Committee issued guidelines to be followed by solicitors when completing such certificates for building societies[36] and clearly there is a risk that a *prima facie* case of negligence will arise if this is

---

[31.] *Re White and Hague's Contract* [1921] 1 IR 138 at 144 (*per* O'Connor MR). See para **[10.04]** *ante*.

[32.] *Re Flynn and Newman's Contract* [1948] IR 104 at 112 (*per* Kingsmill Moore J).

[33.] See paras **[13.48-9]** *ante*.

[34.] See paras **[13.52-3]** *ante*.

[35.] See *Irish Land Law* (2nd ed, 1986), para 13.013 *et seq*.

[36.] They are set out on pp 11.23-4 of the *Conveyancing Handbook*.

not done. They also issued standard forms of certificates which may be used,[37] but some words of caution must be issued. The Law Society standard forms incorporate the usual formula whereby the purchaser's solicitor certifies that the borrower has a "good marketable title". This is defined as a "title of a quality commensurate with prudent standards of current conveyancing practice in the Republic of Ireland".[38] A number of points should be emphasised. First, it is imperative that the purchaser's solicitor does, indeed, carry out a full investigation of the title before issuing a certificate of title. Failure to do so clearly opens the solicitor issuing the certificate to an action for negligence by the lender to whom the certificate is issued, if it subsequently suffers loss as a result of its security turning out not to be in accordance with the title certified.[39] Secondly, the solicitor must have regard to the form of certificate being given and to any special requirements of the lender in question. In so far as the "good marketable title" concept is incorporated a full disclosure must be made, or a suitable qualification must be entered, relating to any incumbrance or other flaw on the title which might render it less than marketable. We discussed this concept in the previous chapter.[40] Thirdly, the solicitor must make sure that he raises the full pre-contract enquiries[41] and requisitions on title[42] which are appropriate to the property in question and follows up any matter disclosed by these which suggests that further enquiries should be made. This is particularly important where commercial or industrial property is being bought, for here there may be all sorts of planning and environmental problems.[43] In this exercise the purchaser's solicitor will often rely upon information provided by various third parties, eg, the vendor and his solicitor's replies to pre-contract enquiries and requisitions on title. Much information may be supplied by experts, such as architects and engineers, which may be qualified.[44] In all cases the purchaser's solicitor must exercise professional judgment as to whether full reliance should be put on such

---

[37.] They are reproduced on pp 11.25-8 of the *Handbook*.

[38.] The forms also provide that any dispute with regard to the quality of title may be referred to the Society's Conveyancing Committee, but this is without prejudice to the right to seek a determination by the court, eg, through a vendor and purchaser summons: see para **[13.26]** *ante*.

[39.] See *Barclays Bank plc v Weeks Legg & Dean* [1996] EGCS 29, London Times 28 February 1996. See also as to the duty to disclose relevant information to the lender *Mortgage Express Ltd v Bowerman & Partners* [1996] 04 EG 126.

[40.] See para **[14.11]** *et seq, ante*.

[41.] See Ch 5 *ante*.

[42.] See Ch 16 *post*.

[43.] See para **[5.14]** *et seq, ante* and **[16.74]** *et seq, post*.

[44.] See further on such certificates issued by such professional experts paras **[16.76]** and **[16.82]** *post*.

information, for if he thinks that there is cause for concern or doubt, he must consider whether he should qualify the certificate he issues to warn the lender or its solicitor and to protect himself against a claim for negligence. Further, to the extent that the solicitor issuing the certificate is relying upon such information, it may serve to reiterate the true nature of such a certificate if the fact of such reliance, in accordance with standard conveyancing practice, is expressly stated in the certificate in relation to the information in question. In this respect it is important to stress that the whole process of investigating title, and issuing a certificate on the basis of it, is an exercise of professional judgment. It would be surprising if the courts took the view that anything more was required than that the purchaser's solicitor adopted good conveyancing practice to ensure that he elicited the information necessary to enable him to make a sensible judgment as to the quality of the title. Despite the use of the word "certificate" its substance usually indicates, and this is certainly true of the Law Society's standard forms, that it is *not* a guarantee as to the title.[45] There is, therefore, usually no question of the solicitor being under a strict liability or being taken as providing the lender or other recipient with an indemnity in respect of it. His liability will usually be dependent upon proof that he was negligent in issuing the particular form of certificate of title. That proof will, in turn, usually depend upon the plaintiff establishing that the conduct of the purchaser's solicitor, especially in carrying out the investigation of title, fell below the standard of good conveyancing practice. That is why the courts tend to rely heavily on expert evidence as to such practice,[46] though universal practice is not necessarily to be equated with good practice.[47] Fourthly, the solicitor issuing the certificate ought to be clear as to the use to be made of it; in particular, he should beware of it being passed on to and relied upon by unknown third parties. The Law Society's standard forms state expressly that the certificate is for the benefit of the specified building society in connection with the loan sought for the particular property. The solicitor should understand that if the certificate is not limited in any way, it may be relied upon by other parties involved in the transaction, eg, investors in a complicated commercial development, or in later transactions. This greatly increases the solicitor's exposure to the risk of a suit for negligence, especially since under the law of

---

[45.] It has been argued that the point would be reiterated if the document signed by the solicitor was called a "report" or "opinion" rather than a "certificate", but this would seem to be a change in name only.

[46.] See, eg, *Doran v Delaney* [1996] 1 ILRM 490, para **[15.02]** *supra*. *Cf* relying upon counsel's opinion: *Park Hall School Ltd v Overend* [1987] ILRM 345.

[47.] *Roche v Peilow* [1985] IR 232; *Desmond v Brophy* [1985] IR 449: see paras **[3.15]** and **[11.17]** *ante* and **[15.48]** *infra*.

joint and several liability a plaintiff is liable to sue the most convenient "deep pocket" defendant for the entire loss.[48] Finally, the Law Society's Conveyancing Committee has recently reiterated that responsibility for certificates of title rests with the solicitor issuing it and so a lender's solicitor should accept them at face value.[49] He should not seek to go behind them unless a particular certificate is qualified in such a way as to justify rejection of the certificate or the raising of queries relating to the matter referred to in the qualification. If the lender's solicitor seeks to go behind an unqualified certificate, he defeats the whole purpose of the certificate of title system and runs the risk of fixing his client with notice of matters which would not otherwise affect its title.

I. PERUSAL OF TITLE

[15.06] The first step in the investigation of title is perusal of the title documents furnished by the vendor.[50] We saw in the previous chapter that in practice in Ireland it is rarely, if ever, that an abstract of title will be supplied,[51] so that the documentation usually consists of copies of the title deeds or of the Land Registry folio and map, depending upon whether the title is unregistered or registered. In each case the purchaser, or more usually his solicitor, must examine this documentation in order to check whether or not it confirms that the vendor is in a position to convey the estate or interest in the land which he has contracted to sell. This is also a vital step for the purchaser's solicitor if he is expected to issue a certificate of title, eg, to the purchaser's lending institution.[52]

A. Registered Land

[15.07] Perusal of the title documentation in the case of registered land is generally straightforward in the sense that the purchaser is usually furnished with copies of Land Registry material which can be relied upon as being accurate, eg, copies of the folio and map relating to the land in question.[53]

[48.] The recent spectacular claims made in England against accountancy firms acting as auditors of company accounts illustrate the risks, but note that the English Law Commission is against reform: see its Common Law Team's *Feasibility Investigation of Joint and Several Liability* (1996 Consultation Paper for the Department of Trade and Industry, HMSO). In particular the Team rejected the notion of "proportionate" liability as introduced in some jurisdictions, like the USA. See also Byrne, 'Joint and Several Liability: A Need for Reform?' (1996) 14 ILT 46.

[49.] See the *Gazette*, March 1995, p 83.

[50.] As to these, see Ch 14 *ante*.

[51.] Para **[14.42]** *ante*.

[52.] See para **[15.05]** *supra*.

However, there may be complications in a particular case, which will necessitate an investigation more akin to that which prevails where the land is unregistered. Thus, the purchaser may be concerned with the pre-registration title where the land has been registered "subject to equities,"[54] and, if he proposes to secure cancellation of these,[55] he will need to be furnished with appropriate evidence of the title to them.[56] The same applies to unregistered burdens affecting the land.[57] For these reasons the view which is sometimes expressed, that requisitions on title are unnecessary in the case of registered land, is not accurate.[58]

B. Unregistered Land

1. The Chain of Title

[15.08] In the case of unregistered land, the purchaser's solicitor should check the vendor's chain of title, making sure that it runs in an unbroken series of links from the root of title to the vendor.[59] This should result in the vendor being able to convey the estate in the land contracted to be sold, free from all incumbrances other than those subject to which the property is being sold. If the original title deeds have not been furnished, in strict theory any abstract or copies should be checked against the originals, but in practice this may be deemed unnecessary provided good quality photocopies are furnished.[60] The originals will usually be handed over on completion anyway.[61]

[15.09] Clearly each case must depend upon its own circumstances, but there are several generally recognised principles to be observed in checking the title. If on application of any of these the purchaser's solicitor is doubtful

---

53. Paras **[14.31-6]** *ante*.
54. Para **[14.25]** *ante*.
55. Or, to be more accurate, conversion of what are now "possessory" titles, see para **[14.26]** *ante*.
56. Note the provision in Cond 13(a) of the Law Society's standard contract form, para **[14.40]** *ante*.
57. Para **[14.27]** *ante*.
58. Para **[16.57]** *post*.
59. Though some links in the intermediate title may be missing and are covered by a condition of sale governing the intermediate title, see para **[14.61]** *ante*.
60. See the English Law Society's ruling on the use of photocopies, quoted in *Emmet on Title* (19th ed by Farrand), para [5.052].
61. See para **[20.34]** *post*. In England, where abstracts are still sometimes used, there has been considerable controversy over the practice of leaving the checking of the title against the original deeds to the completion day. See Emmet, *op cit* para [5.087].

or puzzled about a matter, he should make a note of it and raise it by way of special requisition on title.[62]

2. Points to Check

(i) Description of the Property

[15.10] It is important to check that the description of the property in the title deeds conforms with that in the contract for sale,[63] and, indeed, that the descriptions in the various deeds are consistent *inter se*. If the title deeds refer to maps or plans, a check should be made to see that these have also been furnished[64] and, if they have been, they should be checked against the verbal descriptions of the property in the deeds, eg, in the parcels clauses.[65] Photocopies of maps or plans should be checked to see that they are coloured in accordance with what is stated in the deeds. The map or plan may help to explain the description in the parcels clause, but it should always be remembered that such maps or plans attached to title deeds are notoriously inaccurate[66] and, in the case of an inconsistency, the description in the deed usually prevails.[67] If there are any discrepancies of this kind, the purchaser's solicitor should raise them with the vendor's solicitor for explanation.

(ii) Execution of Deeds

[15.11] A check should be made to see that each deed has been properly executed by all necessary parties.[68] It is true that every party to a deed need not necessarily execute it, eg, the grantee is bound by it in equity without execution because he takes the benefit of it.[69] But it is usual for the purchaser to execute the deed, especially where he is entering into covenants,[70] or interests such as easements and profits are being reserved for the vendor,[71] or he is giving any kind of certificate, eg, for stamp duty purposes.[72] Where a company has purported to execute the deed, it is imperative to check that the

---

[62.] See para **[15.17]** *infra*.

[63.] See para **[9.07]** *et seq, ante*.

[64.] If they have not been furnished, they should be requisitioned from the vendor's solicitor.

[65.] See para **[18.50]** *post*.

[66.] See paras **[9.12-3]** *ante*.

[67.] *Wyse v Leahy* (1875) IR 9 CL 384. See para **[18.66]** *post*.

[68.] This subject is discussed later, see para **[18.119]** *post*. As regards pre-root documents referred to in recitals, see Conveyancing Act 1881, s 3(3); also para **[14.59]** *ante*.

[69.] *Burnett v Lynch* (1826) 5 B & C 589: *May v Belleville* [1905] 2 Ch 605.

[70.] See para **[18.95]** *post*.

[71.] See para **[18.77]** *post*.

[72.] See para **[18.108]** *post*.

requirements of its Memorandum and Articles of Association have been followed.[73]

(iii) Technical Words

[15.12] The purchaser's solicitor should keep in mind his knowledge of basic land law when reading the deeds. Thus, the need for technical words of limitation in an *inter vivos* conveyance should be checked.[74] If one of the deeds is a voluntary conveyance, it should be remembered that a conveyance to the "use" of the grantee is still necessary in both parts of Ireland to avoid a resulting use in favour of the grantor being executed by the Statute of Uses (Ireland) 1634, and rendering the conveyance a nullity.[75]

(iv) Stamping of Deeds

[15.13] A check should be made to see that, where necessary, the deeds have been properly stamped.[76] As Kennedy CJ said in *Tyrell v Imperial Tobacco Co Ltd*[77]:

> "It is well settled that a purchaser is entitled to have all instruments and documents which constitute the muniments of title to the property sold, and which are liable to stamp duty, properly stamped at the vendor's expense ... This rule springs from the statutory prohibition[78] against the admission in evidence of instruments which are insufficiently stamped."[79]

Any condition of sale which purports to preclude the purchaser from objecting as to the absence or insufficiency of a stamp on any instrument executed after 16 May 1888 is void.[80] In practice, however, the purchaser's solicitor assumes that the deeds have been properly stamped, unless it is glaringly obvious that this is not so - if only because there have been so many changes in the details of stamping requirements over the years.

(v) Registration of Deeds

[15.14] Each deed should have been registered in the Registry of Deeds immediately after completion of the transaction to which it relates and of its stamping. Failure to do this may have caused a loss of priority for that

---

73. This whole subject is considered in later chapters: see paras **[16.27]** and **[18.128]** *post.*
74. *Re Courtney* [1981] NI 58. See *Irish Land Law*, (2nd ed, 1986) para 4.024 *et seq.* Also para **[18.86]** *post.*
75. See Laffoy, *Irish Conveyancing Precedents* pp J5-6. See also para **[18.86]** *post.*
76. See para **[20.38]** *post.*
77. [1926] IR 285. See also *Whiting to Loomes* (1881) 17 Ch D 10.
78. Stamp Act 1891, s 14. See Donegan and Friel, *Irish Stamp Duty Law* (1995), para 3.10 *et seq.*
79. *Op cit*, p 291.
80. Stamp Act 1891, s 117. See para **[10.09]** *ante.*

transaction in relation to subsequent transactions affecting the same land.[81] The question whether a deed is registered or not will be answered by examining the deed to see if the Registrar's certificate stating the date of registration is stamped on it.[82] If a defective copy (eg, photocopy) of the deed has been furnished by the vendor, so that the certificate does not appear on it, a requisition on the matter should be raised.

(vi) Capacity of Parties

[15.15] It is important to check the capacity of the parties to each deed, especially the grantor, to do what they purported to do by virtue of that deed. For example, if the grantor was a tenant for life under a settlement, exercising his statutory power of sale, the grantee would not have obtained a clear title to the land unless the purchase money was paid to the trustees of the settlement and a receipt was issued by them.[83] This receipt should be included in the "premises" part of the deed,[84] or else endorsed on the deed. In the case of a company it is imperative to check that it has power to make the conveyance in question.[85]

(vii) Incumbrances

[15.16] A note should be made of all incumbrances on the land created by various deeds, eg, mortgages, charges and restrictive covenants and all rights excepted and reserved, eg, easements and profits. If these have not been discharged or released, the purchaser will take subject to them.[86]

II. Requisitions on Title

[15.17] If, on perusing the title, the purchaser or his solicitor has any queries, he may raise these with the vendor by furnishing "requisitions on title"- so-called because the purchaser "requires" the vendor to remove the doubt or difficulty specified. However, as we shall see, "requisitions" often not only deal with matters of doubt or difficulty, but also cover a wide range of matters, many of which simply remind the vendor to do various things before or by completion or ask for confirmation that the usual steps in the conveyancing process will be followed. Furthermore, though strictly requisitions should be confined to matters relating to the "title", they also

---

[81.] See *Irish Land Law* (2nd ed, 1986), para 3.084 *et seq*; Lyall, *Land Law in Ireland* (1995), p 139 *et seq*.

[82.] See para **[20.43]** *post*.

[83.] See *Irish Land Law* (2nd ed, 1986), para 8.094. Alternatively, the money may have been paid into court, *ibid*.

[84.] See para **[18.43]** *post*.

[85.] See para **[16.27]** *post*.

[86.] See para **[10.18]** *et seq, ante*.

tend in practice to cover various matters relating more to the property itself.[87] This is particularly so now in Ireland because it is envisaged that often parts of the Law Society's standard form of *Objections and Requisitions on Title*[88] will be extracted and used to make pre-contract enquiries.[89] It should also be noted that requisitions on title are sometimes distinguished from objections to title.[90] A requisition usually relates to some particular matter of title which the purchaser expects the vendor to explain or put right, whereas an objection is usually made on the ground that the title shown is bad and, therefore, the purchaser will not get a good title.[91] But it is not always easy to make this distinction in practice.[92] Detailed discussion of the Law Society's standard form is to be found in the next chapter, but it may be useful to discuss here some general principles before going on to consider some other matters relating to investigation of title.

A. General Principles

[15.18] The general rule is that requisitions on title should be specific and should not be used by the purchaser or his solicitor to embark upon a general "fishing" expedition for information. As we shall see, technically the vendor or his solicitor may refuse to answer a requisition which is too vague or general.[93] On occasion, especially where the Law Society's standard form of requisitions may not be used, a requisition is made along the following lines: "Have all material facts in connection with the title been disclosed?" The vendor should always decline to answer such a wide-ranging requisition. Nor should the purchaser or his solicitor indulge in raising all sorts of trivial items, if only because the contract will usually have a clause in it enabling the vendor to rescind the contract if he is unable or unwilling to comply with a particular requisition.[94]

[15.19] Care should be taken to avoid raising two particular types of requisition. First, a requisition should not be raised in respect of a matter of no concern to the purchaser. The classic example of this is where a statutory provision makes it none of the purchaser's concern. Thus, where the vendor

---

87. See the standard form discussed in Ch 16 *post*. See also the comments in *Goody v Baring* [1956] 2 All ER 11 at 16-7 (*per* Danckwerts J); *cf* (1959) 23 Conv 153.

88. 1996 Edition.

89. See para **[5.02]** *ante*.

90. As its title indicates, the Law Society's standard form recognises the distinction. This distinction may be important in relation to contractual restrictions, see para **[15.25]** *infra*.

91. See *Martin v Cotter* (1846) 9 Ir Eq R 351.

92. Thus, the Law Society's standard contract for sale refers to the purchaser sending a written statement of all "objections and requisitions," see para **[15.20]** *infra*.

93. *Re Ford and Hill* (1878) 10 Ch D 365. See also Wilkinson, 'Requisitions on Title or Request for Information' (1967) 111 Sol Jo 591; and see (1966) 110 Sol Jo 930 and 960. And see para **[15.25]** *infra*.

94. Para **[15.27]** *infra*.

is a mortgagee exercising his power of sale, the purchaser does not have to, and should not, enquire as to whether or not the circumstances of the case justify the exercise of that power or whether or not due notice has been given.[95] Similarly, where the vendor is a tenant for life exercising his statutory power of sale under the Settled Land Acts 1882-90, the purchaser does not need to enquire whether or not he has given notice to the trustees of the settlement,[96] provided he acts in good faith.[97] Under s 53 of the Succession Act 1965, an assent by a personal representative relating to unregistered land is, in favour of a purchaser, *conclusive* evidence that the person in whose favour it is given is entitled to have the land vested in him.[98] Notwithstanding that the Act defines "purchaser" as a person acquiring property "in good faith", it is considered that a purchaser should not seek to go behind an assent, but should take it at face value and accept it as conclusive, even though he may be aware of circumstances which *suggest* that other parties *may* be interested in the property. Thus, the mere fact that an assent is made in favour of the personal representative himself, who is one only of the deceased's intestate successors as part of a family arrangement,[99] does not mean necessarily that something improper has taken place. The personal representative might, eg, have bought out the other successors as part of a family arrangement. Similarly, again in the case of an intestacy, the mere fact that the assent is in favour of someone with a different surname from the deceased could be capable of explanation; eg, the assent is in favour of a woman using her married name or some relative who has changed his name by deed poll. It is suggested that the better view is that it would defeat what must surely have been the intention of the Oireachtas in using the word "conclusive"[100] to expect a purchaser to pursue such speculation. So long as there is a possible explanation which would not involve something improper, the purchaser or his solicitor should accept the

---

95. Conveyancing Acts 1881, s 21(2) and 1911, s 5(1). See *Re Irish Civil Service Building Society and O'Keeffe* (1880) 7 LR Ir 136. See also *Irish Land Law*, (2nd ed, 1986) paras 13.028-30. It would appear that a purchaser can invoke this protection once he has entered into a contract to buy from the mortgagee (s 2 of the 1881 Act defines "purchaser" as including "intending" purchaser: *National Provincial Building Society v Ahmed* [1995] 38 EG 138).

96. Settled Land Act 1882, s 45(3). See *Irish Land Law* (2nd ed, 1986), paras 8.098-9.

97. See *Hughes v Fanagan* (1891) 30 LR Ir 111; *Gilmore v The O'Connor Don* [1947] IR 462.

98. See McGuire, *The Succession Act 1965* (2nd ed by Pearce) p 124.

99. And so ordinarily would be entitled to a share of his estate: see Brady, *Succession Law in Ireland* (2nd ed, 1995), Ch 8.

100. The obvious contrast to be made is with the equivalent English provision, s 36(7) of the Administration of Estates Act 1925, which provides that an assent is "sufficient" evidence only: see *Re Duce and Boots Cash Chemists Ltd's Contract* [1937] 3 All ER 788. *Cf* s 35(3) of the Administration of Estates Act (NI) 1955; Leitch, *A Handbook on the Administration of Estates Act (NI) 1955* pp 103-4.

conclusiveness of the assent.[101] Of course, some meaning must be given to the reference in the Succession Act to "good faith", but it is suggested that this will cover cases of fraud, where, eg, the purchaser is a party to some improper scheme being carried out by the personal representative, ie, he has full knowledge of the impropriety.[102] Secondly, the purchaser should try to avoid making requisitions which may result in his being fixed with notice of something which would not otherwise have affected him. The classic example is where the property is subject to an undisclosed trust and the vendors are in fact trustees. Normally trusts are "kept off the title" and the purchaser is safe in dealing solely with the trustees and will take free of the beneficiaries' interests.[103] Thus, though the purchaser or his solicitor may have a remote suspicion that the vendors are trustees, generally the temptation should be resisted to pursue the matter by raising requisitions.[104] The fact that what seems to be a conveyance is stamped with a nominal amount only is not notice that it is a conveyance to a new trustee.[105] However, there is a narrow dividing line to be observed in this context, which it is not always easy to see in practice. If the purchaser has notice, actual or constructive, of the existence of the trust, he must satisfy himself that the trustees have full power to sell so as to overreach the beneficiaries' interests.[106] If they do not have such full power, the beneficiaries may have to be joined in the conveyance. In view of the difficulty in deciding whether or not the purchaser is fixed with constructive notice, many solicitors adopt the rule in practice that, if they are in doubt as to whether or not there is a trust in existence, they make enquiries. This is an understandable reaction, especially since the general doctrine of notice is pervasive and a purchaser in such a case does not have protection such as that provided by statute in respect of assents. Nevertheless, every effort should be made to avoid upsetting careful conveyancing. If conveyances have clearly been drafted to keep trusts off the title, requisitions should not be raised which will have the

---

[101.] The Law Reform Commission has apparently taken the same view: see *Brady, op cit*, para [10.54-58].

[102.] If the vendor's solicitor furnishes a copy of the will, which has been attached to the grant of probate, arguably the purchaser's solicitor should reject this by analogy with Land Registry practice where an application to register a transmission quotes the will: see para **[14.66]**, fn 381 *ante*. The Law Reform Commission apparently considers that the "good faith" reference should be replaced by a requirement of proof of fraud in order to deprive the purchaser of the protection of s 53: see *Brady, op cit*, para [10.55].

[103.] See Bailey, 'Trusts and Titles' (1942) 8 CLJ 36.

[104.] See *Re Harman and Uxbridge and Rickmansworth Rly Co* (1883) 24 Ch D 720 at 725 (*per* Pearson J). See also *Re Chafer and Randall's Contract* [1916] 2 Ch 8; *Re Soden and Alexander's Contract* [1918] 2 Ch 258.

[105.] See *Hadgett v IRC* (1877) 3 Ex D 46.

[106.] *Re Blaiberg and Abrahams* [1899] 2 Ch 340. See also *Coyle v Central Trust Investment Society Ltd* [1978] ILRM 211.

effect of bringing them on to the title. Thus, the mere fact that the purchaser knows that the conveying parties are persons unlikely to own property beneficially, eg, members of a religious order, does not justify going behind the wording of the deed. Arguably the same applies where other documentation furnished with the title makes reference to a charitable organisation, eg, a planning permission. Furthermore, the mere fact that the grantors are expressed to convey "as trustees" does not put a purchaser on enquiry as to the nature of the trust, since these words are simply the formula used to imply the appropriate covenant for title under s 7 of the Conveyancing Act 1881.[107]

B. Time for Making

[15.20] In the absence of a special provision in the contract for sale, the requisitions on title must be made within a reasonable time.[108] However, it is usual for the contract for sale to cover the matter. Thus, condition 17 of the Law Society's *General Conditions of Sale (1995 Edition)* requires the purchaser to send to the vendor's solicitor a "written statement of all his Objections (if any) on the title and his Requisitions " within fourteen days[109] after the delivery of the copy documents of title.

[15.21] At common law, the rule is that the vendor cannot rely upon such a time limit if he himself is in default in not furnishing the abstract of title or title documents within the time limit for that. Thus, in *Re Todd and McFadden's Contract*,[110] Kenny J stated:

> "I think it is well settled ... that if the abstract be not delivered within the time named in the conditions, the purchaser cannot be held bound to send in his objections within the time limited in the conditions for that purpose."[111]

This would seem to remain the rule under the Law Society's condition 17. Furthermore, it is also the rule at common law that the time limit on the purchaser does not operate in favour of the vendor if the abstract of title or other evidence of title furnished by him is not "perfect" ie, as good as he can

---

[107] See Laffoy, *Irish Conveyancing Precedents*, pp D7-D9, D13 and D17. *Cf Coyle v Central Trust Investment Society Ltd* [1978] ILRM 211 (freehold interest purchased by trustee of leasehold interest and both interests being sold together as one transaction and documents of title read together clearly revealing the trust). See also para **[21.18]** *post*.

[108] *Spurrier v Hancock* (1799) 4 Ves 667. See also *Re Todd and McFadden's Contract* [1908] 1 IR 213.

[109] Note the definition of "working day" in Cond 2: see para **[10.14]** *ante*.

[110] [1908] 1 IR 213.

[111] *Ibid* p 220. See also *Southby v Hunt* (1837) 2 My & Cr 207; *Upperton v Nickolson* (1871) 6 Ch App 436.

furnish having regard to the documents and evidence within his control,[112] though the onus of establishing imperfection rests with the purchaser.[113]

[15.22] The Law Society's contract form provides in condition 17, contrary to the general rule for the standard form conditions,[114] that time is to be of the essence for the condition relating to requisitions and objections.[115] If the purchaser does not meet the time limit he is deemed to have waived all objections and requisitions[116] and to have accepted the title.[117] However, Condition 17 expressly recognises to a certain extent common law restrictions on a "time of the essence" provision in the contract. Thus, it states that it does not apply where the objection or requisition goes "to the root of the title," for the courts have always held that the purchaser can object that the vendor has no title at any time before completion.[118] It is also the rule at common law, which, in the absence of an express exclusion in the conditions, presumably still applies, that the purchaser can still raise, despite the time clause in the contract, requisitions relating to matters discovered apart from perusal of the abstract or title documents furnished by the vendor, eg, from his own enquiries or searches.[119] Indeed, it is common for the purchaser to reserve expressly in his original requisitions sent to the vendor the right to make further objections or requisitions arising out of the vendor's replies or on the result of searches.[120] Finally, as is generally the case, even though the purchaser is out of time with his objections or requisitions, the court may refuse to grant specific performance against him where it is clear that the title is bad or, at least, so doubtful as to make the court reluctant to force it on the purchaser.[121]

C. Restrictions

[15.23] The extent to which the purchaser may raise objections or requisitions is restricted by statute and, usually, the contract for sale. So far as contractual restrictions are concerned, these are subject to the normal

---

[112.] See *Want v Stallibrass* (1873) LR 8 Exch 175, espec at 184 (*per* Pollock B).

[113.] *Ward v Grimes* (1863) 8 LT 782.

[114.] See para **[13.12]** *ante*.

[115.] *Cf* replies by the vendor, see para **[15.36]** *infra*.

[116.] Cond 17.

[117.] *Ibid*. See para **[15.51]** *infra*.

[118.] *Re Carrige and McDonnell's Contract* [1895] 1 IR 288 at 296 (*per* Chatterton V-C); *Coyle v Central Trust Investment Society Ltd* [1978] ILRM 211. See also *Want v Stallibrass* (1873) LR 8 Exch 175 at 181 (*per* Kelly CB).

[119.] *Warde v Dixon* (1858) 28 LJ Ch 315. See also para **[15.25]** *infra*.

[120.] See para **[15.37]** *infra*.

[121.] See para **[13.52]** *ante*.

close scrutiny of the courts and, being in derogation of the purchaser's right
to have a good title proved, will be construed against the vendor.[122]

1. Statutory

[15.24] By s 3(3) of the Conveyancing Act 1881, a purchaser is prohibited
from requiring "any information" or making "any requisition, objection. or
inquiry" with respect to the title prior to that which must be deduced under
an open contract or which is stipulated for by the contract for sale. However,
this provision has been interpreted as not precluding the purchaser from
showing *aliunde* that the pre-root title is defective or that incumbrances
created in the pre-root title were not disclosed by the vendor.[123] Once again
this is an illustration of the basic principle that the courts are reluctant to
allow the vendor to disregard his fundamental obligation to show good title
to the property[124] by sheltering behind provisions designed to reduce the
amount of proof of title he has to furnish or to restrict the purchaser's
investigation of title.[125] Thus, it has been held that the purchaser may still
object in respect of a pre-root defect in title which he has discovered as a
result of enquiries made of a third party,[126] or because the vendor by mistake
produced the pre-root title documents for inspection.[127] Apart from this, it
must be remembered that s 3(11) of the 1881 Act states that nothing in the
section is to be construed as binding the purchaser to complete the purchase
where, on a contract containing similar provisions as to the title, the court
would not enforce specific performance against him. So, even if the
purchaser is precluded in law from raising objections or requisitions in
respect of a defect in title, he may still be able to convince the court that the
title is so doubtful that it ought not to be forced on him.[128]

2. Contractual

(i) Pre-Root Title

[15.25] The Law Society's standard form contract contains restrictions as to
objections and requisitions relating to the pre-root title similar to the 1881
provisions.[129] Condition 11(a) of the Law Society's *General Conditions of
Sale (1995 Edition)* simply provides that the prior title, "whether or not

---

[122] See para **[15.04]** *supra*.
[123] See *Nottingham Patent Brick and Tile Co v Butler* (1885) 15 QBD 261 at 272 (*per* North J), on appeal (1886) 16 QBD 778.
[124] See para **[14.06]** *et seq, ante*.
[125] See para **[14.07]** *ante*.
[126] *Re Cox & Neve's Contract* [1891] 2 Ch 109.
[127] *Smith v Robinson* (1879) 13 Ch D 148.
[128] See para **[13.52]** *ante*.
[129] See para **[14.59]** *ante*.

appearing by recital, inference or otherwise, shall not be required, objected to or investigated".[130] But the Irish courts, like their English counterparts,[131] have been reluctant to allow vendors to enforce such a provision so as to prevent the purchaser from showing that the title is in fact bad. Thus, in respect of the analogous case of a provision in the conditions of sale purporting to prevent the purchaser from requiring evidence of the lessor's title,[132] or from objecting in respect of incumbrances contained in that title,[133] O'Loghlen MR had this to say in *Willes v Latham*[134]:

> "The purchaser has always been at liberty, by his own research, to show that the title is bad, and where he has done so, I have known cases where he has been let off."[135]

And more directly in point, in *Re Davys and Verdon and Saurin's Contract*,[136] Chatterton V-C had to consider a condition of sale prohibiting requisitions in respect of the prior title and stated:

> "I consider that this condition only precludes the purchaser from making requisitions upon the vendor as to his title, but does not preclude the purchaser from showing that upon searches or inquiries made by himself *aliunde*, the title is defective ..."[137]

However, Chatterton V-C did go on to say:

> "... it is well settled that there is nothing invalid in conditions even precluding all objections to title; but it is necessary that all restrictions interfering with the legal rights of purchasers must be clear and explicit."[138]

Thus, it may be argued that condition 11(a)[139] of the Law Society's *General Conditions of Sale (1995 Edition)* satisfies this test in that it not only precludes requisitions but also objections, which may cover objections

---

[130.] Cond 12 contains a similar provision in respect of the "intermediate" title where the special conditions provide for the title to be shown to pass from one instrument to another or to a specified event: see para **[14.61]** *ante*.

[131.] See *Waddell v Wolfe* (1874) LR 9 QB 515. See also *Darlington v Hamilton* (1854) Kay 550.

[132.] See para **[14.69]** *ante*.

[133.] See *Musgrave v McCullagh* (1864) 14 Ir Ch R 496.

[134.] (1837) S & Sc 441.

[135.] *Ibid* p 441-2. See also *Leathem v Allen* (1850) 1 Ir Ch R 683 at 691 (*per* Brady LC): "... the vendee having *aliunde* discovered defects in the lessor's title, it was held that notwithstanding that condition, he was entitled to insist upon the defects." And see the remarks of Brady LC in *Musgrave v McCullagh* (1864) 14 Ir Ch R 496 at 499.

[136.] (1886) 17 LR Ir 334.

[137.] *Ibid* p 337. *Cf Re Turpin and Ahern's Contract* [1905] 1 IR 85 at 103 (*per* FitzGibbon LJ),and see para **[15.04]** *supra*.

[138.] *Ibid*. See also his remarks in *Re McClure and Garrett's Contract* [1899] 1 IR 225 at 229.

[139.] And cond 12 see fn 130 *supra*.

arising from information gained otherwise than by perusing the title documents furnished by the vendor.

[15.26] However, as Chatterton V-C pointed out, the vendor may be prevented by the courts from relying upon even so widely drafted a restriction in certain circumstances. Thus, he will not be able to rely upon it if it is ambiguous[140] or misleading.[141] Still less will he be able to rely upon it if it involves fraud or deception,[142] such as an intention to "foist a thoroughly bad title on the purchaser".[143]

(ii) Vendor Unable or Unwilling to Comply

[15.27] Condition 18 of the   Law Society's *General Conditions of Sale (1995 Edition)* provides that if the purchaser makes and insists on any objection or requisition as to title, the assurance or any other matter relating to or incidental to the sale which the vendor is unable or, unwilling to remove or comply with, the vendor may rescind the contract by giving notice to the purchaser.[144] Under condition 18 the vendor is to give the purchaser or his solicitor not less than five working days notice in writing to rescind. Several points should be noted about these provisions.[145]

[15.28] First, it covers objections or requisitions not only as to title but also as to matters of conveyance,[146] and, indeed, any other matter relating to the sale, eg, objections as to the description of quantity.[147] Secondly, the vendor's right of rescission does not arise until the purchaser is given the opportunity of reconsidering his position; as it is usually put, he is entitled to a *locus poenitentiae*. Condition 18 makes this clear by requiring the purchaser to make "and insist" on the objection or requisition.[148] Thus, in substance several steps must take place under Condition 18, ie, (1) the

---

140. *Geoghegan v Connolly* (1858)8 Ir Ch R 598 at 607 (*per* Smith MR). See also *Re White and Hague's Contract* [1921] 1 IR 138 at 145-6 (*per* O'Connor MR).

141. *Clements v Conroy* [1911] 2 IR 500 at 523 (*per* Walker LC).

142. *Re Cummins and Hanafy's Contract* (1905) 39 ILTR 85 at 86 (*per* Lord Ashbourne C and FitzGibbon LJ).

143. *Clegg v Wright* (1920) 54 ILTR 69 at 71 (*per* Powell J).

144. Such a condition is inconsistent with a condition that the purchaser is to take only such title as the vendor has without question, since it clearly implies a right to make objections, see *Re White and Hague's Contract* [1921] 1 IR 138 at 146 (*per* O'Connor MR), para **[14.39]** *ante*. See also Harpum, 'Recission for Insistence on a Requisition' [1990] Conv 150.

145. As to the consequences of the vendor exercising this right of rescission, see para **[15.35]** *infra*.

146. See para **[14.18]** *ante*. See also *Kitchen v Palmer* (1877) 46 LJ Ch 611; *Re Jackson and Oakshott* (1880) 14 Ch D 851; *Re Deighton and Harris's Contract* [1898] 1 Ch 458. *Cf Hardman v Child* (1885) 28 Ch D 712 at 718 (*per* Pearson J).

147. See *Re Terry and White's Contract* (1886) 32 Ch D 14 at 24-5 (*per* Lord Esher MR).

148. *Lyons v Thomas* [1986] IR 666 at 679 (*per* Murphy J). See also *Re Starr-Bowkett Building Society and Siburn's Contract* (1889) 42 Ch D 386. See also *Re Dames and Wood* (1885) 29 Ch D 626.

purchaser makes the objection or requisition; (2) the vendor decides he is unable or unwilling to remove it or comply with it; (3) he communicates this unwillingness to the purchaser; (4) the purchaser refuses to withdraw it.[149]

[15.29] At common law, if the vendor continued to perform acts under the contract or attempted to comply with the requisition, he might be regarded as having waived his right of rescission.[150] However, condition 18 protects the vendor against this by preserving his right "notwithstanding any intermediate negotiation or litigation".[151] However, this protection is not absolute, for it is settled that the right of rescission cannot be exercised after judgment has been given in litigation,[152] or while the vendor's own action for specific performance is proceeding.[153] Furthermore, it has also been held that "negotiation" is not the same as "dispute," so that the vendor is not protected by the provision if he instead denies that any defect exists to justify the objection or requisition.[154]

[15.30] This right of rescission constitutes a considerable restriction on the purchaser's rights[155] and so it is not surprising that the courts have been alert to see that it is not abused.[156] In fact, the courts have laid down a number of qualifications to the vendor's right of rescission.[157] First, it is settled that the vendor must exercise it in a reasonable manner or, as it is more usually put, he must not invoke it without reasonable cause.[158] He must not act capriciously or arbitrarily and, if necessary, will have to convince the court

---

[149.] *Duddell v Simpson* (1866) 2 Ch App 102 at 109 (*per* Cairns LJ). Sec also *Mawson v Fletcher* (1870) 6 Ch App 91.

[150.] *Shoreditch Vestry v Hughes* (1864) 17 CBNS 137.

[151.] It also adds, it would appear *ex abundanti cautela*. "or attempts to remove or comply with the same". See *Isaacs v Towell* [1898] 2 Ch 285; *cf Gray v Fowler* (1873) LR 8 Ex 249.

[152.] *Re Quigley and McClay's Contract* [1918] 1 IR 347, following *Re Arbib and Class's Contract* [1891] 1 Ch 601.

[153.] *Public Trustee v Pearlberg* [1940] 2 KB 1. See also *Re Spindler and Mear's Contract* [1901] 1 Ch 908.

[154.] *Gardom v Lee* (1865) 6 H & C 651.

[155.] See the adverse criticisms of its reservation in Williams, *The Contract of Sale of Land*, p xi. It is no longer included in the English contract form now usually adopted: see the *Standard Conditions of Sale* (3rd ed); Silverman, *The Law Society's Conveyancing Handbook* (1995) p 683.

[156.] See the discussion by Johnston J in *McMahon v Gaffney* [1930] IR 576 at 586-7. See also *Selkirk v Romer Investments Ltd* [1963] 1 WLR 1415 at 1422 (*per* Viscount Radcliffe). And see *Re Dames and Wood* (1885) 29 Ch D 626 at 634 (*per* Lindley LJ).

[157.] The following formulation was approved by the Supreme Court in *Williams v Kennedy* unrep, 19 July 1993 (*ex tempore* judgment given by Finlay CJ). See also *Kennedy v Wrenne* [1981] ILRM 81; *Lyons v Thomas* [1986] IR 66.

[158.] *Kennedy v Wrenne ibid* p 83 (*per* Costello J). See also the Supreme Court in *Williams v Kennedy ibid; Quinion v Horne* [1906] 1 Ch 596 at 604 (*per* Farwell J).

that the objection or requisition which has caused him to invoke his right of rescission is one which will cause him substantial expense or involve him in litigation if he is to comply with it or remove it.[159] Thus, he cannot use the right as a convenient method of getting out of his contract with the purchaser, eg, in order to be able to accept a higher offer for the property from a third party.[160] Condition 18 recognises this principle for it provides that the vendor must be unable or unwilling "on the grounds of unreasonable delay or expense or other reasonable ground".

[15.31] Secondly, the courts have refused to allow the vendor to invoke the right where he was guilty of "recklessness" in entering into the contract.[161] In this context, recklessness is to be distinguished from fraud or dishonesty, and generally consists of an indifference towards the purchaser as regards whether he will obtain the title contracted to be sold.[162] Thus, the vendor must not induce the purchaser to enter into the contract by making some misrepresentation which he had little or no grounds for believing was true and then purport to exercise his right of rescission when the purchaser raises an objection or requisition about that same matter.[163] Similarly, where the vendor has entered into a collateral agreement, or pre-condition to the contract for sale, which he has failed to meet.[164]

[15.32] Thirdly, it is clear that the vendor cannot invoke his right of rescission where he has no title at all to the property,[165] or, to put it another way, where the objection or requisition goes to the root of the contract.[166] Similarly, where damage has resulted to the property as a consequence of the vendor's default.[167]

[159.] *McMahon v Gaffney* [1930] IR 576 at 581 (*per* Meredith J), and 586-7 (*per* Johnston J). See also *Re Weston and Thomas's Contract* [1907] 1 Ch 244.

[160.] *Smith v Wallace* [1895] 1 Ch 385.

[161.] *Molphy v Coyne* (1919) 53 ILTR 177 at 184 (*per* Powell J), following *Re Jackson and Haden's Contract* [1906] 1 Ch 412.

[162.] *Selkirk v Romar Investments Ltd* [1963] 1 WLR 1415 at 1422-5 (*per* Viscount Radcliffe). See also *Williams v Kennedy* fn 157 *supra*.

[163.] *Molphy v Coyne* (1919) 53 ILTR 177 at 184 (*per* Powell J). See also *Baines v Tweddle* [1959] Ch 679, wherein the point was mooted, but not decided, whether the recklessness must be the vendor's own personally or whether it also extends to that of his solicitor or other agent, see at pp 689-90 (*per* Lord Evershed MR) See also *Re Milner and Organ's Contract* (1920) 89 LJ Ch 31. *Cf Re Des Reaux and Setchfield's Contract* [1926] Ch 178.

[164.] Eg, for release of a mortgage: see *Kennedy v Wrenne* [1981] ILRM 81.

[165.] *Cf* where he can show title to part of the property and wishes to rescind on the ground of an objection that he has no title to the remainder, see *Heppenstall v Hose* (1884) 51 LT 589.

[166.] *Baines v Tweddle* [1959] Ch 679 at 687-8 (*per* Lord Evershed MR) and 698 (*per* Pearce LJ). See also *Bowman v Hyland* (1878) 8 Ch D 588.

[167.] *Lyons v Thomas* [1986] IR 66 (flooding due to burst pipe and damage by squatters getting into vacant premises).

[15.33] Fourthly, the vendor can exercise his contractual right of rescission only so long as the contract survives, so that if the purchaser has already rescinded the contract,[168] eg, for misrepresentation, the right is lost.[169]

[15.34] Finally, it should be noted that there may be another sanction operating against the vendor and that is that, by entering into the contract which he is now rescinding, he may have become liable to pay his house or estate agent's commission and will remain so even though he has to reemploy him to resell the property after the rescission. As we saw in an earlier chapter, this depends very much upon the construction of the contract between the vendor and the agent in question.[170]

[15.35] Upon valid exercise of the right of rescission by the vendor, the purchaser becomes entitled to the return of his deposit, but without interest thereon.[171] This shows the advantage to the vendor of himself exercising this contractual right of rescission rather than allowing the purchaser to exercise his common law right of rescission for failure to show a good title or for misrepresentation, under which the purchaser could recover both interest on his deposit and the costs of investigating the title.[172] However, it seems that the courts will not construe the making of a good objection to title as rescission by the purchaser, ie, on the argument that the purchaser has really brought the contract to an end by making a requisition with which the vendor is unable to comply and thus forcing the vendor to rely upon the condition of sale giving him the right of rescission. As Johnston J said in *McMahon v Gaffney*:

> "I may say at this stage that a purchaser cannot defeat the object of such a condition by taking a good objection to the title disclosed and then cutting in himself with a rescission of the contract."[173]

E. Replies and Rejoinders

[15.36] The general rule is that the vendor must answer satisfactorily all proper[174] requisitions, otherwise he may be held not to have shown a good

---

[168.] See para **[13.57]** *et seq, ante.*

[169.] *Holliwell v Seacombe* [1906] 1 Ch 426. *Cf Proctor v Pugh* [1921] 2 Ch 256 at 268 (*per* Sargant J).

[170.] See para **[3.19]** *et seq, ante.*

[171.] Cond 37(a).

[172.] *McMahon v Gaffney* [1930] IR 576 at 587 (*per* Johnston J). See also *Re Priestley and Davidson's Contract* (1892) 31 LR Ir 122. See para **[13.62]** *ante.*

[173.] *Ibid.*

[174.] Ie, those which are not too vague or general. see *Re Ford and Hill* (1878) 10 Ch D 365 and para **[15.18]** *supra.*

title to the property.[175] Technically this rule probably applies only to requisitions relating to the "title",[176] so that the vendor may be entitled strictly not to reply to other requisitions, such as those seeking general information about the property,[177] on the ground that these are not concerned with the title deduced by the vendor.[178] However, if only as a matter of courtesy, it is usual for the vendor's solicitor to reply to each requisition. In the absence of any contractual time limit, presumably the vendor must reply within a reasonable time, though there appears to be no authority for this directly in point. However, should he delay, it seems that the purchaser may serve a notice on him requiring an answer within a specific time and, if he fails to reply within that time limit, the purchaser can rescind the contract.[179] The Law Society's standard contract form does not impose a time limit on the vendor's replies to any objections or requisitions[180] raised by the purchaser.[181]

[15.37] The vendor's solicitor should clearly endeavour to give accurate replies to proper requisitions, otherwise he runs the risk of being sued for negligence[182] or fraud,[183] though it has been held in England that a reply given in accordance with conveyancing practice does not give rise to any action by the vendor against his own solicitor, even though it resulted in the purchaser being able to rescind the contract.[184] On the other hand, if the vendor's solicitor gives a reply to a requisition without taking any reasonable steps to check its accuracy (by, eg, seeking information from his client which the client most likely has) he will find it difficult to defend an action for negligence brought by his client to recover any loss flowing from

---

175. *Re Delany and Deegan's Contract* [1905] 1 IR 602. See also *Embankment Properties Ltd v Calaroga Ltd* High Court, unrep, 28 January and 24 October 1975; *Dublin Laundry Co Ltd v Clarke* [1989] ILRM 29.
176. See para **[15.17]** *supra*.
177. See para **[16.06]** *post*.
178. See *Re Ford and Hill* (1879) 10 Ch D 365 at 370 (*per* James LJ); *Wilkes v Spooner* [1911] 2 Ch 473 at 484 (*per* Vaughan-Williams LJ) and 486 (*per* Farwell J). See also Wilkinson, 'Requisition on Title or Request for Information' (1967) 111 Sol Jo 591; and see (1966) 110 Sol Jo 930 and 960.
179. See *Re Stone and Saville's Contract* [1963] 1 WLR 163.
180. *General Conditions of Sale* (1995 ed), cond 17.
181. It does, however, impose a time limit on the purchaser's rejoinders or answers to the vendor's replies, see para **[15.38]** *infra*.
182. See paras **[5.27-8]** *ante*.
183. See para **[5.23]** *ante*. Misrepresentation is not a ground for an action since the reply could not be regarded as inducing the purchaser to enter into a contract already made, see paras **[5.21]** and **[5.26]** *ante*.
184. *Simmons v Pennington and Son* [1955] 1 WLR 183. See also *Geryni v O'Callaghan* High Court, unrep, 25 January 1995 (1994/677 Sp), para **[16.89]** *post*.

the inaccurate reply. Ordinarily the vendor's solicitor's duty of care is owed to his own client (the vendor) and, as Hamilton J stated in *Doran v Delaney*,[185] no duty of care is owed to the purchaser who "can reasonably be expected to rely upon his own solicitor to investigate title and similar matters".[186] However, he went on to state that "it is clearly established that situations can arise in which a solicitor owes a duty not only to his own client but to a third party who relies upon what the solicitor tells them".[187] Solicitors must be aware that the courts are increasingly prepared to hold that the circumstances of a particular case created a "special relationship" between the solicitor or other professional person and a third party who was not his client.[188] If that is so, the solicitor or other professional person may be taken to have assumed personal responsibility for statements made to that party (eg, the purchaser) and thereby be open to a claim for negligent misstatement for any inaccuracies resulting in loss.[189] In fact, in the *Doran* case, it was held that the vendor's solicitor was not liable to the purchaser because the replies given to requisitions were based entirely upon information acquired from the vendor and related to matters within the special knowledge of the vendor.[190] It would seem that it is not appropriate for the vendor's solicitor to be ultra cautious in his replies, eg, by entering non-committal answers such as "not so far as we are aware," especially where the vendor is asked specifically to confirm something.[191] On the other hand, where the purchaser has furnished his requisitions out of time,[192] any replies should be marked "without prejudice," otherwise the vendor may be deemed to have waived the time clause.[193]

---

[185] [1996] 1 ILRM 490.

[186] *Ibid*, p 10.

[187] *Ibid*. He cited in support the Scottish case *Midland Bank plc v Peterkin and Duncan* (1988) SLT 611 and 627 (*per* Lord Jauncey).

[188] Ie the principle enunciated by the House of Lords in *Hedley Byrne & Co Ltd v Heller & Partners Ltd* [1964] AC 464: see para **[5.27]** *ante*.

[189] See *McAnarney v Hanrahan* [1993] 3 IR 492 (auctioneer); *Greyhill Property Co Ltd v Whitechap Inn Ltd* High Court, unrep, 5 October 1993 (1990/2384P) (receiver replying to purchaser solicitor's queries); *Donnellan v Dungoyne* [1995] ILRM 388: see para **[5.28]** *ante*

[190] Ie, whether there were any boundary disputes with adjoining owners or litigation pending or threatened or adverse claims; the reply was: "Vendor says none". Note that the purchaser's solicitor was held negligent for not ensuring that the boundaries of a property his client was purchasing for development purposes were staked out: see again para **[5.28]** *ante* and **[16.07]** *post*.

[191] *Cf* in respect of pre-contract enquiries, see para **[5.02]** *ante*.

[192] See para **[15.26]** *supra*.

[193] *Cutts v Thodey* (1842) 13 Sim 206; *Oakden v Pike* (1865) 34 LJ Ch 620.

[15.38] The purchaser or his solicitor may not be satisfied with the replies given by the vendor or his solicitor and so may feel it necessary to send rejoinders or answers[194] and this process may be repeated several times before a satisfactory conclusion is reached.[195] Condition 17 of the Law Society's *General Conditions of Sale (1995 Edition)* requires the purchaser's answers to the vendor's replies to be sent in writing within ten days after delivery of the replies and so on toties quoties.[196] If they are not so answered, the replies are deemed to have been accepted as satisfactory.[197]

III. SEARCHES

[15.39] The investigation of title by the purchaser should be completed by making or having made searches in one or more registries for entries relating to the land being purchased. This is essential because of the risk that some other interest in the land may be registered prior to completion which will enjoy priority over the purchaser.[198] What searches should be made will vary from case to case and we consider the various alternatives in the next few paragraphs.

A. Land Registry

[15.40] Where the title to the land is registered, the purchaser should make a search in the Land Registry immediately prior to completion to cover the interval between the date of issue of the copy document of title, eg, the folio,[199] and the lodgment of his application to be registered as the new owner. It is up to the purchaser to protect himself by seeing that such a search is made on his behalf. In theory there is no reason why he should not seek to include a provision in the contract requiring the vendor to furnish him with the result of such a search on completion, but this is rarely done in practice.[200]

[194.] Though before he does so he should consider whether it would not be wiser to rescind the contract forthwith, if he feels that he has discovered a matter justifying this. The point is that, by continuing correspondence with the vendor, he may be deemed to have waived his right to rescind, see *Elliott v Pietson* [1948] Ch 452 at 456 (*per* Harman J) and para **[15.49]** *et seq, infra*.

[195.] See *Dublin Laundry Co Ltd v Clarke* [1989] ILRM 29.

[196.] Again this is of the essence, see para **[15.22]** *supra*.

[197.] See further. Para **[15.49]** *infra*.

[198.] As to the protection against registration in the intermediate period between the contract and completion which may be gained by registering the purchaser's contract, see para **[6.64]** *et seq, ante*.

[199.] See para **[14.31]** *et seq, ante*.

[200.] *Cf* Registry of Deeds searches in the case of unregistered land, para **[15.42]** *infra*.

[15.41] Recent legislation in both parts of Ireland has introduced the concept of official searches made by the Land Registry[201] as opposed to "hand" searches made by the parties themselves, or a firm of private searchers on their behalf.[202] However, notwithstanding that this system has existed for many years it is surprisingly underutilised, perhaps because some practitioners have not appreciated the protection it can afford a purchaser. Under the system the Registrar issues a certificate of the result of an official search[203] and the advantage of applying for such a search is the period of priority which it may obtain for the applicant.[204] In such a case, where the Registrar is satisfied that the certificate is issued to a person who is a prospective purchaser, lessee or chargee of the land in question, he may, at that person's request, make a priority entry on the register.[205] The effect of this is to secure priority for registration of the document completing the transaction in question (eg, the purchase) provided the application is in order and is delivered to the Land Registry within fourteen days of issue of the certificate.[206] So clearly the purchaser ought to apply for a priority search less than two weeks immediately prior to completion, because lodgment of his application for registration of his new ownership will usually take place some days after the closing date.[207] Furthermore, where such a priority search has been obtained in anticipation of closing the transaction on the date fixed by the contract, but there is a last minute hitch which causes completion to be delayed, it is essential to beware that the fourteen-day priority period does not expire before the date when completion finally takes place. If it does, a fresh application should be made so as secure the priority for a further period. Alternatively, a last minute search may be made by the purchaser's solicitor by telephone[208] or, telegram,[209] in which case the search is made forthwith and the result sent by telephone,[210] or telegram, as the case

---

[201.] Registration of Title Act 1964, s 107(2). See *Irish Land Law* (2nd ed, 1986), para 21.17.

[202.] 1964 Act, s 107(1). See also Land Registration Rules 1972, r 198.

[203.] 1964 Act, s 107(2).

[204.] Another advantage from the purchaser's solicitor's point of view is that a solicitor or other person who obtains an official search certificate is not answerable for loss that may arise from any error therein, see Land Registration Rules 1972, r 195. A person who conducts a "hand" search is clearly liable if he is negligent in making it. eg, by missing some vital entry on the register.

[205.] An inhibition is engrossed on the folio in Form 106 in the 1972 rules, inhibiting "all dealings with the property" for a period of fourteen days: 1964 Act, s 108(1). See Fitzgerald, *Land Registry Practice* (2nd ed, 1995) p 168.

[206.] 1964 Act, s108(2). See the Land Registration Rules 1972, rr 190-4.

[207.] See para **[20.44]** *et seq, post.*

[208.] Only a solicitor may do this in 1972 Rules, r 196(1) The fee is to be sent by letter, 1972 Rules, r 196(3).

[209.] Any person may do this, r 196(1), but the fee is to be sent by money order with the telegram and the reply is to be pre-paid, r 196(4).

[210.] But in this case it is also confirmed in writing sent on the same day from the Registry 1972 Rules, r 197(2).

may be.[211] It is, however, important to note that such a fresh application, however made, does not confer priority retrospectively. It protects the purchaser only against dealings lodged for registration *after* the *fresh* application is made and during the fourteen-day priority period running from the date of the original application. Once that original fourteen-day priority period running from the date of the *fresh* application. It does *not* carry forward the protection conferred by the *original* application; that covered dealings lodged for registration *after* the *original* application was made and during the fourteen-day priority period running from the date of the *original* application. Once that original fourteen-day priority period expires without the purchaser lodging his documents for registration, the priority is lost and any dealings lodged during the priority period must then be registered by the Land Registry and have priority as of the date of their lodgement.[212] Any fresh application for priority by the purchaser made after expiry of the original fourteen-day priority period operates only as to the future and does not revive or continue that priority. Indeed, the official search certificate will include a notice of the dealings pending and lodged during the original priority period.[213]

B. Registry of Deeds

[15.42] Where the title to the land is unregistered, a search should be made in the Registry of Deeds, again to ensure that no document relating to some other transaction with respect to the land has been registered so as to gain priority over the purchaser.[214] Such a search may be made by the purchaser himself, or by a firm of law searchers on his behalf, ie, a "hand" search, or by the Registry in the form of either a "common" search, which is not warranted, or a "negative" search, which is.[215] Though it was held at one time in Ireland that a purchaser was entitled, in the absence of a contractual provision to the contrary, to be furnished by the vendor with a negative search in both the Index of Names and the Index of Lands,[216] later practice was to confine this requirement to such a search in the Index of Names.[217] In

---

211. 1972 Rules, r 197(1).

212. Fitzgerald, *Land Registry Practice* (2nd ed, 1995), pp 168-9.

213. *Ibid*, p 169.

214. As to protection of the purchaser by registration of the contract for sale, see para **[6.65]** *ante*.

215. See on this subject, *Irish Land Law* (2nd ed, 1986), paras 22.12-4. Note that progress in computerisation of the Registry of Deeds has been rapid in recent years and records for the past 25 years have now been computerised so as to facilitate "on-line" searches: *Irish Times* 1 November 1995.

216. See *Langford v Mahoney* (1843) 3 Jo & Lat 109.

217. See *Re Kissock and Currie's Contract* [1916] 1 IR 376 at 383 (*per* O'Brien LC). In fact the Lands Index was not kept up to date until recently in Dublin, see *Irish Land Law* (2nd ed, 1986), para 22.11.

the leading case on the subject, *Re Murray and Hegarty's Contract*,[218] Chatterton V-C stated:

> "There was nothing better settled than that, on a sale of land in this country, searches were always furnished by the vendor at his expense ... In this country, where registration is universal, it is absolutely necessary for a purchaser to obtain searches in the Registry of Deeds for his protection: and it is provided that the registrar is responsible in damages for their accuracy."[219]

In that case the issue was whether the provisions of s 3(6) of the Conveyancing Act 1881, enabled the vendor to push the expense of procuring searches onto the purchaser, as documentary evidence of title not in his possession.[220] Chatterton V-C held that it did not[221] and said:

> "A Registry search is not an existing document forming part of the evidence of title. It is a process to obtain a statement that no other deeds or instruments are registered than those stated in the abstract of title. The name of the search is a 'negative search'; and the form of it is negative. It is outside the abstract altogether, and independent of it; and it is not for the purposes of verifying the abstract that such searches are required, but in order to ascertain the fact whether any other instrument than those disclosed in the abstract appears on the Registry, which might affect the title . . . Therefore, in the absence of words clearly applying to Registry searches, or the certificates of the result of such searches, I do not feel compelled to overturn the practice so long established in this country on the subject. I therefore hold that the expense of procuring these searches is not to be thrown on the purchaser."[222]

[15.43] Condition 19 of the Law Society's *General Conditions of Sale (1995 Edition)* provides that the purchaser is to be furnished with searches, if any, specified in the Searches Schedule to the contract form and that any searches already in the vendor's possession are to be furnished with the copy documents of title. Any other searches required by the purchaser are to be obtained by him at his own expense. In fact some years ago there was a variation in practice between Dublin and elsewhere in the State. Outside Dublin the practice was for the purchaser to make his own Registry of Deeds searches, but the Conveyancing Committee of the Law Society recommended adoption of this practice in Dublin as well, as from 1 January

---

[218.] (1885) 15 LR Ir 510.

[219.] *Ibid*, p 512.

[220.] See para **[14.48]** *ante*.

[221.] He commented: "I should be slow to change the established practice, and I shall not do so unless I am coerced by the 3rd section of the Conveyancing Act." *Op cit*, p 512.

[222.] *Op cit*, p 513.

1977.[223] Expressly excluded from this recommendation were building estates, where the usual and convenient practice was for the vendor or builder to obtain a "master" search and to distribute certified copies to purchasers in each case.[224] However, the Conveyancing Committee reviewed the matter shortly thereafter and recommended in 1978 that the previous practice of the vendor furnishing searches should be resumed.[225] The problem which came to light was that the purchaser's solicitors usually did not arrange to lodge negative searches at the contract stage and so had to commission hand searches at closing and, since these cannot be kept open to cover the subsequent registration of the purchase deed,[226] further hand searches would have to be commissioned.[227] In changing its recommendation the Committee drew attention to the protection afforded by negative searches, but emphasised that the system operates smoothly only if the vendor's solicitor remembers to furnish his draft requisition for a negative search along with the draft contract for sale and existing searches already in the vendor's possession. Failure to do this usually results in the negative search not being available by closing date and so the expense of last minute hand searches is incurred. Despite this warning, the advice is frequently, and regrettably, ignored. Condition 19 goes on to provide that the vendor is to explain and discharge any acts appearing on searches made for the period running from the commencement of title to the date of actual completion, but where the special conditions specify that title is to commence with a particular instrument and then pass to a second instrument or specified event, he is not obliged to explain and discharge any act appearing on a search covering the intermediate period, unless it goes to the root of the title.[228]

[15.44] Subject to what the contract for sale specifies, the search should be made against every person[229] appearing on the title from the date of his accrual of title to the date of registration of a conveyance by him which

---

[223.] See the *Gazette*, November 1976, p 184.

[224.] See reiteration of this point in the *Gazette*, August/September 1977, p 138.

[225.] See the *Gazette*, July/August 1978, p 125.

[226.] See para **[20.43]** *post*.

[227.] Such hand searches might also have to be commissioned to cover the closing of subsequent mortgage transactions. The Joint Committee of the Building Societies and Law Society has stated that lenders' solicitors can reasonably refuse to accept searches carried out by solicitors rather than professional Law Searchers (even though the solicitor may have professional indemnity insurance covering searching): see the *Gazette* June 1983, p 125.

[228.] See also cond 12. See para **[14.61]** *ante*.

[229.] But not against persons such as the owner of an expired lease or a mere grantee to uses. See Madden, *Registration of Deeds, Conveyances and Judgment Mortgages* (2nd ed, 1901), p. 246; Stubbs and Baxter, *Irish Forms and Precedents* (1910), p 555.

renders all subsequent documents executed by him ineffectual. It is important to search against common variations of forenames (including the Irish version) and to be aware of hyphenated names. Examples illustrating what should be included in a requisition for a search have been given elsewhere.[230] It is crucial that the requisition includes all descriptions by which the land is or was known at any time.[231]

C. Judgments Office

[15.45] A search should be made on behalf of the purchaser in the Judgments Office for any *lis pendens*,[232] or judgment, affecting the land.[233] Generally, a search is not necessary for ordinary judgments because any of these entered up or made after 15 July 1850, do not affect land[234] and so a purchaser is not concerned with them. A purchaser is concerned about such judgments only if they are registered as a judgment mortgage in the Registry of Deeds or Land Registry, according to whether the land is unregistered or registered land.[235] This will be disclosed by the search in the appropriate Registry.[236] As regards a *lis pendens* the search in the Judgments Office needs cover a five-year period prior to completion only, as entries expire if they are not re-docketed or reregistered every five years.[237] Furthermore, to affect to purchaser the *lis pendens* must be registered within five years before execution of the conveyance or transfer to the purchaser.[238]

D. Sheriff's Office

[15.46] Chattel real, ie, leasehold, property may be seized by the sheriff under a writ of *fieri facias*, but, though the lodgment of the writ with the

---

[230.] See *Irish Land Law* (2nd ed, 1986), para 22.16. See also Madden, *op cit* p 251 *et seq*; *Stubbs and Baxter, op cit*, p 557 *et seq*.

[231.] *Dardis and Dunns Seeds Ltd v Hickey* High Court, unrep, 11 July 1974. See *Irish Land Law* (2nd ed, 1986), para 22.18 .

[232.] See on this topic, *Irish Land Law* (2nd ed, 1986), para 13.165.

[233.] See Stubbs and Baxter, *Irish Forms and Precedents* (1910) pp 559-60.

[234.] See Judgment Mortgage (Ir) Act 1850. As to pre-1850 judgments, see *Guardians of Limerick Union v Heffernan* (1877) IR 11 Eq 302; *O'Rourke v Copeland* (1892) 26 ILTR 126.

[235.] See *Irish Land Law* (2nd ed, 1986), para 13.163 *et seq*. See also *Tempany v Hynes* [1976] IR 101 and para **[12.03]** *et seq, ante*.

[236.] See paras **[15.40]** and **[15.42]** *supra*.

[237.] See Judgments Registry (Ir) Act 1871, s 12.

[238.] Judgment Mortgage (Ir) Act 1850, s 5. See *Giles v Brady* [1974] IR 462. Note that it is settled now that the court has jurisdiction to order vacation of a *lis pendens* without the consent of the person who registered it, if the suit or proceedings are not being *bona fide* prosecuted: see *Flynn v Buckley* [1980] IR 423 and Farrell, *Irish Law of Specific Performance* (1994), para [10.10] *et seq*.

sheriff binds. the judgment debtor's leasehold interest,[239] the creditor acquires no title to the land as against a *bona fide* purchaser for value without notice of the lodgment until the sheriff "actually seizes" the property under the writ. However, it is settled that this does not require the sheriff to take actual possession of the land; it is sufficient for him to do any act which indicates to the debtor an intention on his part to execute the writ.[240] Seizure by the sheriff effectively prevents any subsequent disposition of the property by the debtor, and therefore an assignment by the sheriff to a purchaser takes priority over any purported assignment by the debtor after seizure, even though the debtor's deed may be registered before the sheriff's.[241] The result is that a purchaser of a legal leasehold interest may consider it to be a wise precaution to make a search in the Sheriff's Office for the lodgment of writs against the property, especially if he has any doubts about the solvency of the vendor.

E. Bankruptcy

[15.47] Where a landowner is adjudged bankrupt, the certificate of the vesting of his estate in the Official Assignee must be registered in the Land Registry or Registry of Deeds, depending on whether the land is registered or unregistered, within two months, otherwise a *bona fide* purchaser for value without notice of the bankruptcy has priority and obtains a good title to the land.[242] So once again the Land Registry or Registry of Deeds search should reveal the bankruptcy and protect the purchaser as regards certificates issued more than two months previously.[243] However, because of the risk of one issued during the two months prior to completion of the sale, it is also

---

[239.] Only if it is a legal interest, for a mere equitable interest cannot be taken in execution. Although under the common law property could not be seized by the sheriff unless it was descendible to the debtor's executor, it must be doubted whether the assimilation of the law of devolution for both freehold and leasehold property by modern statutes (the Administration of Estates Act 1959 and Succession Act 1965) was intended to render freehold property liable to seizure: see the Law Reform Commission Report, fn 241 *infra*, paras 54-57; *cf* Macauley and MacCann 'Methods of Enforcement of Revenue Debts' *Irish Tax Review* July 1991 at p 448. The point is that the writ of *fieri facias* authorised the seizing of chattels, with which personal property leaseholds came to be categorised: see *Gilbert on Executions* (2nd ed, 1763), pp 18-19.

[240.] *O'Brien v Murray* (1864) 17 ICLR 46; *White v Bateman* (1891) 29 LR Ir 281.

[241.] See Law Reform Commission's *Report on Debt Collection: (1) The Law Relating to Sheriffs* (LRC 27-1988).

[242.] Bankruptcy Act 1988, s 46. See Sanfey and Holohan, *Bankruptcy Law and Practice in Ireland* (1991) Ch 17.

[243.] See paras **[15.40]** and **[15.42]** *supra*.

standard practice for purchaser's solicitors to search the Bankruptcy Office against the vendor's name.

F. Companies Office

[15.48] Charges created by companies[244] or existing on property acquired by companies[245] must be registered with the Registrar of Companies within 21 days of their creation or the acquisition of the property. The Registrar keeps a register of these in relation to each company, which is open to public inspection,[246] and a purchaser from a company vendor ought always to take the precaution of searching that company's file. We saw in earlier chapters that the Supreme Court emphasised the need to make such a search against a building company *before* a building agreement or contract to purchase is entered into with that company.[247]

IV. ACCEPTANCE OF TITLE

[15.49] The final act in the process of investigation of title is the acceptance of it by the purchaser. In practice this often does not take place in full until completion because up to the closing date there may still be certain matters outstanding, eg, requisitions still not complied with[248] or the result of final searches still to be forthcoming.[249] Furthermore, a distinction must be drawn between acceptance of the title in the strict sense of the title deduced by the vendor, which precludes only further requisitions or objections relating to it, and such acceptance which precludes further objection to any matter, ie, including matters relating to the contract and matters of conveyance. Usually the last kind of acceptance occurs only on completion when the conveyance takes effect[250] and the contract merges into it.[251]

[15.50] So far as acceptance of the title deduced by the vendor is concerned, the question often arises as to when the purchaser is to be taken to have accepted the title or, as it is sometimes put, to have waived all further objections to it. This is a matter of intention to be considered in the light of the purchaser's acts or words[252] and, for this reason, his solicitor ought

---

[244.] Companies Act, 1963, s 99.

[245.] 1963 Act, s 101.

[246.] 1963 Act, s 103.

[247.] See *Roche v Peilow* [1985] IR 232 (also *Re Barrett Apartments Ltd* [1985] IR 350): paras **[3.15]**, **[4.25]** and **[11.17]** *ante*. See also para **[16.27]** *post*.

[248.] See para **[20.23]** *post*.

[249.] See para **[20.22]** *post*.

[250.] See para **[20.42]** *post*.

[251.] See para **[21.02]** *post*.

[252.] *Flexman v Corbett* [1930] 1 Ch 672 at 682-3 (*per* Maughan J).

always to make it clear that his client has not yet accepted the title by, eg, marking all correspondence "without prejudice," until he is ready finally to accept it without further question.[253] In the absence of an express indication of intent to accept the title, the following acts may be relevant.

A. Failure to send Requisitions

[15.51] Under the general law, a failure to raise any requisitions at all or, even more significant, to call for an abstract of title or documents of title, may be held to constitute a waiver of the right to investigate the title.[254] So far as failure to send the requisitions or objections within the time limit is concerned, the Law Society's contract form provides that this operates as a waiver unless the requisition or objection goes to the root of title.[255] Furthermore, it provides that, if the purchaser's answers or rejoinders to the vendor's replies to requisitions or objections are not made within the time limit, the replies are to he considered satisfactory.[256]

B. Delivery of Draft Conveyance

[15.52] It seems that even under the general law delivery of the draft conveyance by the purchaser does not of itself constitute a waiver.[257] Indeed, it is common practice to send the draft conveyance to the vendor with the requisitions on title,[258] though it may be wise to state expressly that this is "subject to the vendor's replies to requisitions being satisfactory". However, if the Law Society's standard form contract has been used, this is probably not strictly necessary since it provides that "delivery of the draft or engrossment shall not prejudice any outstanding Objection or Requisition validly made".[259]

[253.] See *Maconchy v Clayton* [1898] 1 IR 291. Note the usual reservation included with requisitions on title, see para **[16.04]** *post.*

[254.] *Fleetwood v Green* (1809) 15 Ves 594; *Sibbald v Lowrie* (1853) 23 LJ Ch 593. See also the discussion in *Corless v Sparling* (1874) IR 8 Eq 335.

[255.] *General Conditions of Sale* (1995 ed) Cond 17. See para **[15.22]** *supra.* As to delays generally, see *Martin v Cotter* (1846) 9 Ir Eq R 351. As to continuing correspondence, see *Maconchy v Clayton* [1898] 1 IR 291.

[256.] *Ibid.* See para **[15.38]** *supra.*

[257.] See the discussion in *Connolly v Keating (No 2)* [1903] 1 IR 356 at 359-60 (*per* Porter MR). See also *Burroughs v Oakley* (1819) 3 Swanst 159 at 171 (*per* Plummer MR).

[258.] See para **[1.08]** *ante* and para **[17.01]** *post.* See also *Re Spollen and Long's Contract* [1936] Ch 713.

[259.] Cond 20.

C. Taking Possession

[15.53] Under the general law, the purchaser's taking possession may raise a presumption of a waiver,[260] unless the contract for sale contained a special provision for possession before completion.[261] But, as we saw in an earlier chapter, Law Society's *General Conditions of Sale (1995 Edition)* contains no provision dealing with this matter and so the need to exercise caution is clear.[262] Any arrangement entered into should be put strictly on a "without prejudice" basis.[263]

[260.] *Bown v Stenson* (1857) 24 Beav 631 at 637 (*per* Romilly MR). Cf *Re Gloag and Miller's Contract* (1883) 23 Ch D 320 at 327-8 (*per* Fry J). See also para **[12.34]** *ante*.

[261.] *Stevens v Guppy* (1828) 3 Russ 171; *Bolton v London School Board* (1878) 7 Ch D 766.

[262.] See para **[12.32]** *ante*.

[263.] Note also the dangers from the vendor's point of view: see para **[12.33]** *ante*.

Chapter 16

REQUISITIONS ON TITLE

I. INTRODUCTION

[16.01] In this chapter we consider an important aspect of investigation of title. As was mentioned in the previous chapter, it is standard practice for the purchaser's solicitor to raise with the vendor's solicitor "requisitions" on title.[1] These are usually a combination of queries relating to the property and its title, which require an answer,[2] and instructions to the vendor's solicitor as to matters which must be attended to before the transaction is completed.[3] We also discussed in an earlier chapter[4] that it has become increasingly the practice for a purchaser's solicitor to raise such matters *before* the contract is entered into, by way of *pre*-contract enquiries rather than *post*-contract requisitions in accordance with the traditional system of investigation of title. This development has been recognised by the Law Society, even to the extent of furnishing practitioners with standard forms to be used *pre*-contract.[5] These forms[6] are, however, of limited scope and the Society's Conveyancing Committee has continued to revise and recommend use of a comprehensive *Objections and Requisitions on Title* form.[7] The latest version of this is the 1996 Edition. It is important to emphasise that, although this form remains one essentially for use by purchaser's solicitors as part of a traditional *post*-contract investigation of title, it is envisaged that parts of it can be extracted and used as *pre*-contract enquiries or requisitions in appropriate cases.[8]

[16.02] In this chapter we go through the Law Society's form item by item, drawing attention to the purpose of each. There are, however, some further

---

[1.] See para **[15.17]** *et seq, ante*.

[2.] See para **[5.02]** *ante*.

[3.] Eg, documentation to be handed over on closing: see para **[16.108]** *infra*.

[4.] See para **[5.01]** *et seq, ante*.

[5.] Eg, the *Check List* for private dwellinghouses (see para **[5.06]** *ante*) and *Guidelines* on rack rent leases (see para **[5.12]** *ante*).

[6.] See fn 5 *supra*.

[7.] The form is reproduced in Appendix III *post*. Note, as its title indicates, that it can also be used to raise an "objection" to title. As to this distinction, see para **[15.17]** *ante*.

[8.] See para **[5.02]** *ante*.

points to mention. First, it is clear that some of the items on the standard form will not be applicable to a particular transaction, eg, No 10, which concerns the Housing (Private Rented Dwellings) Acts 1982-1983,[9] clearly does not apply to commercial property. The ensuing discussion of the individual items on the form will reinforce this point. It is also one recognised by the Conveyancing Committee for the form itself contains the instruction under its main heading on the first page: "Please strike out and/or detach (where appropriate) Requisitions not Applicable". Regrettably this instruction tends to be ignored in practice. Secondly, at the end of the form is the following statement: "The right is reserved by the Purchaser to make any further objections or requisitions arising out of the above and the answers thereto and on the result of searches." This is an important provision designed to protect the purchaser against, eg, the operation of the doctrine of waiver.[10]

II. THE STANDARD FORM

[16.03] We turn now to the form itself. This is set out in the traditional manner with double columns. However, as mentioned above,[11] the form caters for the raising of both "objections" and "requisitions".

A. Objections

[16.04] The first page of the form provides space for the raising of objections notwithstanding the use of the heading "Requisitions on Title" This is reinforced by the wording at the top of page 2 of the form, *viz*: "without prejudice to the foregoing objections (if any) the following Requisitions on Title are made: "Any objections will, of course, be specific to the title in question and so both columns on page 1 of the form are left blank. The purchaser's solicitor can enter the objection or objections in the left-hand column and leave the right-hand column blank for the vendor's solicitor's response. Of course, it will often be the case in practice that a summary only of the objection and response will be entered, or a cross-reference to documentation where more details are set out. An objection to title is an extremely serious matter and the purchaser's solicitor will be expected to spell out precisely the nature of the objection and the basis for making it. Conversely, if the vendor's solicitor does not accept the purchaser's solicitor's arguments, he will be expected to give a properly

---

9. See para **[16.18]** *infra*.
10. See paras **[15.22]**, **[15.37]** and **[15.50]** *ante*.
11. See para **[16.01]** *supra*.

reasoned rebuttal which deals with all the points raised by the purchaser's solicitor. The limited space on the form will often not be suitable for this.

B. Requisitions

[16.05] Page 2 and the subsequent pages of the form set out numerous requisitions under 44 headings. These are all printed on the left-hand column in each page and the vendor's solicitor is expected to enter his replies or answers in the blank left on the right-hand column.[12]

1. Premises

[16.06] The requisitions under this heading relate to the property which is the subject-matter of the sale or other transaction. They cover a number of matters. One concerns the situation where the sale includes fixtures, fittings or chattels[13] and if any of these are subject to any lease, rental, hire purchase agreement or chattel mortgage, it requests the vendor's solicitor to furnish a copy of the agreement. It also requires him to prove on closing that payments under any such agreement are up-to-date or else that the agreement in question has been discharged. It should be remembered that under the *General Conditions of Sale (1995 Edition)*, unless otherwise disclosed to the purchaser *prior* to the sale, the vendor warrants that, at the *actual completion*, all "purchased chattels"[14] will be his "unencumbered property" and "shall not be subject to any lease, rental hire, hire-purchase or credit sale agreement or chattel mortgage".[15]

[16.07] Another requisition addresses the important subject of the boundaries of the property, requiring identity of "boundaries" belonging to the property and those which are "party". This must be taken to refer to the situation where walls, fences, hedges, ditches and the like are on the boundary line and it is desired to determine the ownership of these.[16] Care should be taken over this particular requisition for the matter of boundaries is also dealt with by Condition 14 of the *General Conditions of Sale (1995 Edition)*. As we saw in an earlier chapter,[17] under Condition 14 the vendor is *not* required to "define exact boundaries, fences, ditches, hedges or walls or to specify which (if any) of the same are of a party nature". If that condition

---

12. If the purchaser's solicitor has ignored the instruction to strike out inapplicable requisitions (see para **[16.02]** *supra*), this may involve the vendor's solicitor doing so and/or entering "not applicable" or the abbreviation "N/A" in the right-hand column.
13. See paras **[3.40]** and **[5.07]** *ante*.
14. See the definition in Cond 2.
15. Cond 46: see para **[9.15]** *ante*.
16. See Wylie, *Irish Land Law* (2nd ed, 1986), para [7.53] *et seq*; see also para **[18.61]** *post*.
17. See para **[9.14]** *ante*.

is not struck out or qualified by a special condition, the vendor's solicitor may regard the requisition as an improper one. However, it should be noted that Condition 14 does oblige the vendor to furnish such information as is in his possession relative to the identity "and extent" of the property, and in this respect the other parts of the requisition are important. These require the vendor to furnish with the replies to the requisitions[18] any agreements as to repair, maintenance or otherwise and to state whether there are disputes with any adjoining owner. The need to determine whether such disputes exist is particularly important where the vendor plans to develop the property. This was illustrated by the recent case of *Doran v Delaney*,[19] where Hamilton J held the purchaser's solicitor negligent for failing to ensure that the boundaries were staked out in relation to land being bought with the benefit of planning permission. The land was registered land and not only did the solicitor disregard the suggestion for such staking out made by the builder, he also agreed to deletion of a special condition in the draft contract which would have provided for the furnishing of an Ordnance Survey map showing the site and its boundaries clearly marked. Instead he acceded to the vendor's solicitor's suggestion that the latter was unnecessary as the sale involved the whole of the land comprised in the Land Registry folios and shown on the File plan. In fact there was a discrepancy between the Land Registry documentation and the documentation submitted to the local authority as part of the planning application. There was also a long-standing dispute over the boundary and it transpired after the sale that the purchaser had no effective access to the site and so could not develop it as planned. It is important to note that, although his claim for negligence against his own solicitor succeeded the claim against the vendor's solicitor failed notwithstanding the replies he made to requisitions concerning disputes with adjoining owners in relation to party walls and fences (reply: "Vendor says no") and pending or threatened litigation (reply: "Vendor says none"). Hamilton J held that these replies were made after taking express instructions from the vendor and, in making them, the solicitor did not step outside the role of agent for the client and so did not assume responsibility as a principal to the purchaser. This point was considered in the previous chapter.[20]

[16.08] The final matter covered is raising the question whether the property is registered under the National House Building Guarantee Scheme or, its recent replacement, the HomeBond scheme. If it is, and this, of course,

---

18. Hence the word "now" in Rq No 1.3.a.
19. [1996] 1 ILRM 490. See further paras **[5.28]**, **[15.02]** and **[15.37]** *ante*. *Cf* the recent English case *Darville v Lamb*, para **[5.23]** fn 95 *ante*.
20. Paras **[15.02-3]** and **[15.37]** *ante*.

relates only to residential property,[21] the vendor's solicitor is required to furnish with the replies the Guarantee Certificate/Final Notice (depending upon which Scheme apples) in respect of the property if it is still covered by the Scheme in question.[22] The significance of this subject was discussed in an earlier chapter.[23]

2. Services

[16.09] Here the requisitions seek to determine what services (drainage, water, electricity, telephone[24] and gas) are supplied to the property and to what extent services such as roads, lanes, footpaths, sewers and drains have been taken in charge by the local authority. If they have not been taken in charge, an indemnity under seal is to be furnished by the vendor or if one was provided to him or his predecessor, this is to be assigned to the purchaser. Frequently these are matters which will be checked prior to the contract being entered into.[25]

3. Easements and Rights

[16.10] This is a related matter and concerns easements and similar rights like wayleaves relating to pipes, drains, sewers, wires, cables or septic tanks serving the property. The vendor is required to furnish details of such rights and other rights like rights of way and rights of light benefiting the property or to which the property is subject. This includes obligations relating to such matters, such as any liability to repair. We saw in an earlier chapter,[26] that under the Law Society's *General Condition of Sale (1995 Edition)* the vendor is obliged to disclose *before* the sale, in the particulars or special conditions, all easements, rights, reservations and such like which are known to him to affect the property "or which are likely to affect it".[27] Subject to that the purchaser is deemed to buy subject to all such rights.[28] The reply to

---

21. See para **[4.25]** *ante.*
22. Under the NHBG scheme cover was provided for 6 years but the Homebond scheme covers property for 10 years: see para **[4.25-6]** *ante*. Where the purchase involves a newly-erected property, see Rq No 23, para **[16.60]** *infra.*
23. See para **[4.25]** *et seq, ante*. Note also the point about lodging claims relating to existing defects: see para **[5.10]** *ante.*
24. A letter consenting to transfer of any telephone line, instrument and number is to be furnished (if applicable): Rq No 2.2
25. Note the reference to them in the Law Society's *Pre-contract Check List*: see para **[5.07]** *ante*. See also para **[16.10]** fn 28 *infra.*
26. See para **[9.43]** *ante.*
27. Cond 15. A point which frequently gives rise to problems and of which purchaser's solicitors should be aware is that the percolation area of a septic tank may extend beyond the property in which the tank is located.
28. Cond 16. A point which frequently gives rise to problems and of which purchaser's solicitors should be aware is that the percolation area of a septic tank may extend beyond the property is which the tank is located.

these requisitions will, therefore, frequently refer the purchaser's solicitor to the matters disclosed in the contract and copy documentation of title supplied as part of the deduction of title.

4. Obligations/Privileges

[16.11] This is also a related matter and seeks to determine in the case where a service or facility is not in charge of the local authority whether it is used in common with a neighbouring owner or occupier. The vendor is required to disclose his rights and obligations in such cases and to furnish any agreements relating to the user in question.

5. Forestry

[16.12] The form then turns to more specialised matters relating to country rather than urban property. This requisition requires the vendor to furnish details of timber felling licences and forestry grants still in existence or payable, plus any unfulfilled conditions requiring the planting or replanting of timber.[29]

6. Fishing

[16.13] This requisition requires the vendor to furnish details of any fishing licence[30] or right appurtenant to the property or to which the property is subject and a copy of any deed granting such a right.[31] If the vendor claims that such a licence or right not granted by deed has not been exercised for 20 years, an affidavit to this effect is to be furnished on closing.[32]

7. Sporting

[16.14] This requisition contains a similar provision relating to sporting licences or rights. However, reference in this case is made also to the special provision in s 18 of the Land Act 1965, whereby sporting rights[33] reserved to a person other than the owner of registered land cease to exist if they have not been exercised for 12 years. The vendor is required to furnish an affidavit to this effect which may be used by the purchaser to procure cancellation of the entry relating to such rights.[34]

---

29. See the Forestry Acts 1948-88: Scannell, *Environmental and Planning in Law in Ireland* (1995), p 273 *et seq.*
30. See the Fisheries Acts 1959-90: *Scannell op cit* p 313 *et seq.*
31. This may, of course, have already been furnished as part of the documentation of title.
32. Non-user for 20 years may raise a presumption that an easement or profit has been released by implication: see Wylie, *Irish Land Law* (2nd ed, 1986), para 6.105.
33. Other than fishing rights. Nor does s 18 apply to sporting rights reserved to the Land Commission.
34. See Fitzgerald, *Land Registry Practice* (2nd ed, 1995), p 250.

8. Possession

[16.15] This requisition requires the vendor to confirm that "clear vacant possession of the entire property" will be handed over at closing. This is the duty of the vendor both at common law[35] and under *General Conditions of Sale* (1995 ed), unless the parties have agreed otherwise.[36] This matter was discussed in an earlier chapter.[37]

9. Tenancies

[16.16] This requisition requires the vendor to furnish details of tenancies in any part of the property.[38] Apart from supplying names of tenants, the rents payable and gale days, other important information must be supplied which is relevant to statutory rights which the tenants may have acquired under the Landlord and Tenants Acts. Thus the vendor must state the date when the tenant commenced occupation, which is a vital element in determining whether the right to a new tenancy has been or will be acquired under the Landlord and Tenant (Amendment) Act 1980.[39] Related questions concern tenant's claims or future claims for compensation[40] and improvements carried out by tenants.[41]

[16.17] The vendor is also required to furnish the lease or tenancy agreement in each case, or prove the terms of any tenancy not in writing, and furnish with the replies to the requisitions a copy[42] of any renunciation of the right to a new tenancy executed by the tenant of an "office".[43] He must also hand over on closing letters addressed to the tenants to notify them of the sale and authorising payment of rents to the purchaser, who becomes the new landlord. Finally, he must furnish copies of notices served in respect of private residential lettings coming within the Housing (Miscellaneous

---

[35.] *Bank of Ireland v Waldron* [1994] IR 303 at 305 (*per* Overend J).

[36.] Cond 21.

[37.] See para **[10.44]** *ante*. See also para **[13.20]** *ante* and **[20.13]** *post*.

[38.] Note also Rq No 10 which deals with dwellings coming within the Housing (Private Rented Dwellings) Acts 1982-83: see para **[16.18]** *infra*.

[39.] See Wylie *Irish Landlord and Tenant Law* paras 30.06 and 30.10 *et seq*. Note the amendments introduced by the Landlord and Tenant (Amendment) Act 1994.

[40.] Eg, for disturbance, if a new tenancy is successfully opposed: see Wylie, *op cit* para 32.26 *et seq*.

[41.] Which may also give rise to claims for compensation: *ibid*, para 32.04 *et seq*. There may also be implications on future rent reviews: *ibid*, para 11.38.

[42.] The original of the renunciation must be furnished on closing. Note the form of renunciation recommended by the Law Society's Conveyancing Committee which was set out in the *Gazette*, May/June 1995, p 160.

[43.] Executed under s 4 of the Landlord and Tenant (Amendment) Act 1994.

Provisions) Act 1992,[44] and confirm that the tenant in each case has been furnished with the requisite rent book.[45]

10. Housing (Private Rented Dwellings) Acts 1982-1983

[16.18] These requisitions relate to dwellings coming within these Acts and seek information which will enable an assessment of the effect of the Acts to be made.[46] They also require the vendor to furnish relevant documentation in each case, such as the tenancy agreement, the certificate of registration with the local authority and certificates of registration of changes in the terms of the tenancy and certified copies of any court order, Rent Tribunal or rent officer decision on the rent.[47] Where an increase in the rent has been agreed or fixed, the vendor must furnish a statutory declaration to vouch compliance with the statutory requirements for registration of the new rent and a certification of registration.[48] He must also confirm that a rent book has been furnished to each tenant in compliance with the relevant regulations.[49] Finally, the requisition requires information about any improvements made by tenants which may have been taken into account in fixing the rent, ie, the "gross" rent may have been reduced by an allowance for such improvements.[50]

11. Outgoings

[16.19] These requisitions cover outgoings like rates and other periodic or annual charges affecting the property. They require the vendor to furnish information as to the rateable valuation of both lands and buildings, notices of changes in the valuation, any work on the property likely to result in a revision and particulars of any remission of rates in force. They also enquire whether there is a separate water or refuse charge payable and, if so, particulars of these and the furnishing of the agreement or contract regulating the payments. The vendor must furnish receipts to the last accountable date for all such outgoings and furnish an Apportionment

---

44. Note the requirements as to registration contained in the Housing (Registration of Rented Houses) Regulations 1996 (SI 30/1996). A certified copy of the entry on the Register must be furnished.
45. See Housing (Rent Books) Regulations 1993 (SI 146/1993).
46. See de Blacam, *The Control of Private Rented Dwellings* (1984); Wylie, *Irish Landlord and Tenant Law* Ch 29.
47. See the Housing (Private Rented Dwellings) Regulations, 1982 (SI 217/1982) and 1983 (SI 286/1983). See also the Housing (Rent Tribunal) Regulations 1983 (SI 222/1983) and 1988 (SI 140/1988).
48. See s 11(2) of the Housing (Private Rented Dwellings) Act 1982; *Wylie, op cit*, para 29.34
49. Housing (Private Rented Dwellings) Regulations 1982 (SI 217/1982); *Wylie, op cit*, para 5.50
50. See *Wylie, op cit*, para 29.31.

Account for completion purposes.[51] Also to be furnished on closing is a letter to the rating authority notifying them of the change of ownership.

12. Notices

[16.20] These requisitions reflect the huge range of statutory provisions which now affect land and which any purchaser must beware of. They first require the vendor to state whether any notice, certificate or order has been served upon or received by him, or whether he has notice of any intention to serve any notices, under a long list of Acts "or under any other Act or any Statutory Rule Order or Statutory Instrument". The list ranges from the more traditional property legislation like the Conveyancing Acts, Land Acts, Landlord and Tenant Acts, Registration of Title Act and Succession Act to legislation governing planning and the environment. It is important to note that the requisitions under this heading are primarily concerned with determining whether any such notices have been served upon or received by, or, indeed, whether notices have been served by, the vendor and, if so, requiring him to furnish them and confirm whether they have been complied with.[52] The vendor is also required to state whether any notice of intention to acquire the property compulsorily[53] or to resume possession[54] has been served by a statutory body and, if so, he must furnish a copy with his reply.

13. Searches

[16.21] This requisition requires the vendor to give information necessary to enable the purchaser's solicitor to make the various searches he will expect to make before completion as part of the investigation of title.[55] Thus it requires confirmation of the vendor's full name and address and a statement of whether he has executed any document in relation to the property in Irish or any other variant of his name.[56] The requisition also makes it clear that the vendor must explain, and discharge where applicable, not only any acts

---

[51.] With supporting vouchers: see para **[20.03]** *post*. It must be remembered that rates are levied on the occupier and the incoming purchaser or tenant is exposed to the risk of liability for arrears already accumulated.

[52.] Much of the legislation in question is also the subject of more specific requisitions under later headings: see *infra*.

[53.] See generally McDermott and Woulfe, *Compulsory Purchase and Compensation in Ireland: Law and Practice* (1992); also para **[8.14]** *et seq, ante*.

[54.] Note the power of the Land Commission to "resume" tenancies as part of a scheme to amalgamate uneconomic holding: see Land Acts 1923 (s 29), 1939 (s 39) and 1965 (s 42); Wylie *Irish Land Law* (2nd ed, 1986), para 1.66; Fitzgerald, *Land Registry Practice* (2nd ed, 1995), Ch 24. The Commission's functions in this respect have, of course, been transferred to the Minister for Agriculture, Food and Forestry: see the Irish Land Commission (Dissolution) Act 1992.

[55.] See para **[15.39]** *et seq, ante*.

[56.] Eg, the Index of Names is a valid element in a Registry of Deeds search: see para **[15.44]** *ante*.

appearing on searches in the vendor's possession which the Law Society's contract for sale form requires him to furnish,[57] but also any acts appearing on any searches carried out by the purchaser.

14. Incumbrances/Proceedings

[16.22] This requisition requires the vendor to disclose incumbrances which may affect property, including mortgages or charges and charges created under the Public Health Acts. Mortgages or charges are expected to be discharged before completion and evidence of release must be furnished on closing.[58] The vendor must disclose whether any grant[59] has been received in respect of the property and, if so, must give details and indicate whether any part is repayable. Also to be disclosed is any judgment obtained against the vendor which is capable of being registered as a judgment mortgage and which, according to the Supreme Court in *Tempany v Hynes*[60] will, if registered prior to closing, affect the purchaser's interest even after completion.[61] The vendor must further disclose whether any litigation is pending or threatened, or a court order has been obtained or any adverse claim has been made to the property by any person.[62] It must be remembered that a court will not force a purchaser to "buy a law suit".[63]

[16.23] The other matter covered by the requisition is a subject of increasing concern in recent times. Purchasers must beware of the fact that nowadays the courts recognise that various persons other than the legal owner of property may acquire an equitable interest in it by virtue of a direct or indirect financial contribution or as a result of some agreement or arrangement with the legal owner.[64] Given the numerous decisions in recent

---

57. *General Conditions of Sale* (1995 ed), cond 19: see para **[10.42]** *ante*. The requisition requires such searches to be furnished with the replies, if not already furnished with the other title documents.

58. This is provided by cond 8(c) of the *General Conditions* (see para **[14.62]** *ante*), but in practice the discharge is invariably arranged after completion on the basis of an undertaking given by the vendor's solicitor: see paras **[20.18]** and **[20.32]** *post*.

59. Eg, a new house grant: see **[11.10]** *ante*.

60. [1976] IR 101.

61. See on this subject para **[12.03]** *et seq, ante*.

62. See *Doran v Delaney* [1996] 1 ILRM 490; para **[16.07]** *supra*.

63. See para **[13.52]** *ante*.

64. The Irish courts have shown a willingness to go further than their English counterparts: see the Supreme Court decision in *McC v McC* [1986] ILRM 1 (*cf* the House of Lords in *Gissing v Gissing* [1971] AC 886, the Court of Appeal in *Midland Bank plc v Cooke* [1995] 4 All ER 562 and the NI Court of Appeal in *McFarlene v McFarlene* [1972] NI 59). But see *C v C* [1976] IR 254; *BL v ML* [1992] 2 IR 77; *Murray v Murray* High Court, unrep, 15 December 1995. For detailed discussion of this area of the law see Lyall, *Land Law in Ireland* (1994), Ch 17.

decades, the doctrine of constructive notice impels the purchaser to make appropriate enquiries to determine if any such rights exist, hence this requisition.[65] It is important to note, also, that this applies equally to registered land, at least to the extent that the claimant is in "actual occupation" of the land.[66] This is because s 72 of the Registration of Title Act 1964 lists amongst the burdens which affect registered land *without* registration the "rights of every person in actual occupation of the land or in receipt of the rents and profits thereof, save where, upon enquiry made of such person, the rights are not disclosed".[67] A purchaser must, therefore, make enquiries in respect of such interests if he is to avoid taking subject to them. It must also be remembered that this rule applies to anyone acquiring an interest in the land and it is something which lending institutions must bear in mind, since at risk is the priority of the mortgage or charge over the property in question. What follows from this is that, if any such interests or potential interests come to light as a result of the enquiries or requisition, the claimant should be required to join in the transaction or to release or agree to postpone the claim. It is also suggested that the purchaser's or mortgagee's solicitor should consider whether to advise any such claimant to obtain independent legal advice. The Supreme Court has recently insisted upon this requirement in cases where a "non-owning" spouse's consent is required under the Family Home Protection Act 1976.[68] In doing so it has applied the doctrine of constructive notice and emphasised that the burden of establishing "informed" consent rests on the lender where the transaction involves a mortgage or charge.[69] The English courts have taken the view, at least in cases where the equitable claimant, or even a joint owner, is being asked to join in a transaction as surety for the other owner, that the lending institution must be alert to the risk that the claimant or joint owner has been

---

[65.] *Northern Bank Ltd v Henry* [1981] IR 1: see para **[4.02]** *ante*.

[66.] If not in actual occupation, it would appear that the equitable claimant must protect his interest by lodging a caution, otherwise the purchaser who registers his legal title subsequently will take free of the unprotected equitable interest: see Fitzgerald, *Land Registry Practice* (2nd ed, 1995) Ch 10.

[67.] Section 72(1)(j). See on the English equivalent (s 70(1)(g) of the Land Registration Act 1925) *Williams and Glyn's Bank Ltd v Boland* [1981] AC 487; *Lloyds Bank v Rossett* [1991] 1 AC 107. See also Conlon 'Beneficial Interests - Conveyances and the Occupational Hazard' The *Gazette*, March 1985; Pearce 'Joint Occupation and the Doctrine of Notice' (1980) 15 Ir Jur (ns) 211; Sparkes 'The Discoverability of Occupiers of Registered Land' [1989] Conv 341; Fitzgerald, *op cit* p 223 *et seq*.

[68.] *Bank of Ireland v Smyth* [1996] 1 ILRM 241; *Allied Irish Bank plc v Finnegan* [1996] 1 ILRM 401.

[69.] It may be argued that this firm line is justified because it is the validity of the mortgage or charge which is at stake - lack of consent under the 1976 Act renders the "conveyance" void: see para **[16.62]** sub-para (g) *infra*.

subject to undue influence or a misrepresentation or other vitiating conduct.[70] This is particularly so where the claimant is, eg, an elderly relative or has some other relationship with the other owner which gives rise to a presumption of undue influence.[71] In such cases the Supreme Court may, when faced with the issue, adopt the approach of the House of Lords in England[72] and hold that a lender loses priority if it cannot establish that it took steps to explain to the claimant the nature and implications of the transaction and advised the claimant of the desirability of obtaining independent legal advice.[73] It should instruct its solicitor, who may, of course, be the purchaser's solicitor,[74] to ensure that this is done and, so that appropriate evidentiary documentation becomes available, that any release, waiver or consent includes an acknowledgment by the claimant that the explanation and advice was given.[75] Indeed, given the uncertainty of the position under Irish law on this question, it is recommended that a solicitor acting for a purchaser or lender who becomes aware, as a result of enquiries or replies to requisitions, of a claim or potential claim to an interest in the land in question by a person other than the vendor should take the precautionary steps indicated above.[76] On the other hand, it is important to view this part of the requisition in the context in which it was introduced some years ago, viz, as its wording indicates, to reflect the fact that the courts recognise in modern times that certain persons (usually relatives or friends of the legal owner of property) can acquire an equitable interest in

---

70. *Barclays Bank plc v O'Brien* [1993] 4 All ER 417; *CIBC Mortgages plc v Pitt* [1993] 4 All ER 433.

71. See the survey of the law by Lowry LCJ in *R (Proctor) v Hutton* [1978] NI 139. See also *Gregg v Kidd* [1956] IR 183; Delany, *Equity and the Law of trusts in Ireland* (1996), p 479 *et seq.*

72. See fn 70 *supra.*

73. Note that Geoghegan J at first instance in *Bank of Ireland v Smyth* (fn 68 *supra*) (see [1993] 2 IR 102) went even further than the House of Lords, relying on the Court of Appeal decision in the *O'Brien* case. He did not draw a distinction between cases where, eg, a spouse obtained a direct benefit from the transaction in question and cases where the spouse acted as a surety for the other spouse. On appeal, the Supreme Court studiously ignored this approach and decided the case strictly according to the application of the doctrine of constructive notice to the Family House Protection Act 1976 (see [1996] 1 ILRM 241). *Cf* Keane J in *Bank of Nova Scotia v Hogan* High Court, unrep, 21 December 1992 (1991/97 Sp).

74. See para **[1.35]** *ante.*

75. It is unlikely that the Court would expect the lender's solicitor to check whether the party so advised actually obtained independent advice, still less to check on the competence of any such advice: see *Massey v Midland Bank plc* [1995] 1 All ER 929; *Banco Exterior International v Mann* [1995] 1 All ER 936; *cf TSB Bank plc v Camfield* [1995] 1 All ER 951.

76. As regard family home consents see para **[16.63]** *infra.*

the land and so, as required by the doctrine of constructive notice, "reasonable" enquiries or requisitions must be made by the purchaser. It is questionable whether the courts would expect a purchaser to pursue similar enquiries or requisitions in a purely commercial context, eg, where property has been put in the name of a nominee company which holds it as a "bare" trustee for another company. If the title documents have been carefully drafted to keep this bare trust off the title, the purchaser should not pursue the matter and, it is suggested, the vendor could, quite properly, reply "not applicable" to this part of the requisition.

15. *Voluntary dispositions/bankruptcy*

[16.24] This requisition is designed to protect the purchaser against the risk that certain dispositions on the title may be void as against Official Assignee.[77] For example, under s 59 of the Bankruptcy Act 1988, a "settlement"[78] is void if the settlor is adjudicated bankrupt within two years after the date of the settlement and at any subsequent time within five years, unless the parties claiming under it can prove that, at the date of the settlement, the settlor was able to pay all his debts without the aid of the property comprised in the settlement. This does not apply, however, to a settlement made before and in consideration of marriage or in favour of a purchaser or incumbrancer "in good faith and for valuable consideration". Similarly, under ss 10 and 14 of the Conveyancing Act 1634, a conveyance "with intent to delay, hinder or defraud creditors and others of their just and lawful debts, rights and remedies"[79] is "clearly and utterly void", but not where conveyed "upon good consideration and *bona fide*" to any person not having "any manner of notice or knowledge of the intended fraud".[80] The requisition requires the vendor to furnish with the replies a statutory declaration that the disposition in question was made *bona fide* and without fraudulent intent or, if this is not within the reasonable procurement of the vendor,[81] confirmation that he is not aware of any such fraudulent intent. In the case of a disposition within five years, a declaration as to the solvency of the disponer is required, but in the case of one within two years, an insurance bond equal to the value of the property must be furnished. Also to be furnished is a bankruptcy search against the disponer.[82]

[77.] See generally Sanfey and Holohan, *Bankruptcy Law and Practice in Ireland* (1991) Ch 8.

[78.] This includes "any conveyance or transfer of property": see s 59(4).

[79.] See *Re Moroney* (1887) 21 LR Ir 27.

[80.] See *Re O'Neill* [1989] IR 544. See also *Bryce v Fleming* [1930] IR 376.

[81.] Eg, it relates to some earlier transaction to which he was not a party.

[82.] See para **[15.47]** *ante*.

16. Taxation

[16.25] There are now numerous taxes affecting interests in land and it is crucial from the purchaser's point of view that he does not become subject to unexpected liabilities once he becomes the owner. This requisition requires the vendor to furnish various certificates relating to potential liabilities, viz:

1. **Estate duty**: Where a person on the title died before 1 April 1975,[83] payment of estate duty arising on the passing of a reversionary interest on the death may have been deferred; if so the vendor must furnish a certificate of subsequent discharge of duty in any case where the reversionary interest fell into possession within six years of the present sale to the purchaser.

2. **Capital Acquisitions Tax**: A number of certificates may have to be furnished by the vendor. One is a certificate of absolute discharge in respect of any gift or inheritance within the last twelve years, since unpaid tax is a charge on property which transfers to subsequent owners until it lapses in favour of a *bona fide* purchaser for full consideration after twelve years from the date of gift or inheritance.[84] If a taxable gift has been made within the previous two years, additional tax may arise if the donor dies within that two-year period,[85] so the vendor is required to furnish a statutory declaration that the disponer is still alive and a security, such as term assurance or a cash deposit to cover potential liability arising from death within two years. Another is a certificate of discharge in relation to tax arising by virtue of the property or any part of it being the subject of a discretionary trust as defined by the Finance Act 1984.[86] As from 25 January 1984 a discretionary trust becomes subject to an inheritance tax charge on the later of various specified events.[87] Where any part of the title to registered land[88] depends on a claim of adverse possession, the vendor must furnish a certificate of discharge to enable the purchaser to be registered in the Land Registry as the new owner of the land.[89]

[83.] The date when inheritance tax replaced estate duty: Capital Acquisitions Tax Act 1976, s 10.

[84.] 1976 Act, s 47. The certificate should also cover discharge of any liability arising from "connected dispositions" within s 8 of the 1976 Act.

[85.] 1976 Act, s 3(1)(c).

[86.] Section 105.

[87.] Section 106, as amended by the Finance Acts 1984, s 109 and 1985, s 64. See O'Callaghan, *Taxation of Trusts: the Law in Ireland* (1994), Chs 17 and 18.

[88.] Or the purchaser expects to make a first application for registration of the title because, eg, the land is in a compulsory registration area: see Fitzgerald, *Land Registry Practice* (2nd ed, 1995), Ch 22.

[89.] Finance Act 1994, s 146: see para **[14.82]** *ante*. See also *Fitzgerald, op cit*, p 201 *et seq*; Grogan, 'A Conveyancing Disaster - Waiting to Happen' The *Gazette*, April 1995, p 125.

3. **Probate Tax**: Where there is a death on the title after 17 June 1993, probate tax may be payable[90] and in such cases the vendor is required to furnish a certificate of discharge.

4. **Capital Gains Tax**: Where the consideration in the purchase, or in the aggregate of the purchase and previous sales of the land between the same parties, exceeds £100,000 the purchaser must deduct from the consideration paid 15% tax unless the vendor furnishes a tax clearance certificate.[91] If the consideration is such that a monetary deduction could not be made and the vendor cannot furnish a tax clearance certificate, the purchaser must notify the Revenue Commissioners of the purchase and the vendor must provide 15% of the estimated market value of the property on closing, which the purchaser has to pay to the Collector-General.[92]

5. **Residential Property Tax**: As from 1 August 1993 the vendor is required on a sale of residential property[93] to furnish the purchaser on or before closing with a certificate of clearance, where the consideration exceeds the RPT threshold.[94] Otherwise, the purchaser is obliged to deduct from the purchase price the "specified amount" and to pay it to the Revenue Commissioners. In the case of a transfer between spouses from 17 June 1993, any RPT plus accrued interest is a charge on the property for twelve years.[95] The requisition requires the vendor to furnish a certificate of discharge in respect of any previous transfer.[96]

6. **Stamp duty**: It has long been the duty of a vendor or lessor for a term exceeding 14 years to present the instrument of transfer or lease to the Revenue Commissioners, so that it could be stamped with a stamp denoting that all the particulars have been delivered (the "PD" stamp) to the Commissioners.[97] Failure to comply with this rendered the deed not duly stamped and so not receivable in evidence.[98] The PD requirements have been changed with respect to instruments

---

90. Finance Act 1993, ss 109-119: see *Butterworths Tax Guide 1995-96*, Ch 45.
91. Capital Gains Tax Act 1975, Sch 4 para 11 (substituted by s 34(1) of the Finance Act 1982).
92. *Ibid*, para 11(7) (as amended by s 76 of the Finance Act 1995).
93. Note the definition in s 95 of the Finance Act 1983.
94. Finance Act 1993, s 107 (inserting s 110A in the 1983 Act).
95. But not as against a subsequent *bona fide* purchaser or mortgage unless the purchase price or mortgage amount exceeds the relevant market value exemption limit: s 110A(9).
96. See s 110A(10).
97. Finance (1909-10) Act 1910, s 4: see Donegan and Friel, *Irish Stamp Duty Law* (1995), para 6.18 and Appendices 2 and 3.
98. Stamp Act 1891, s 14.

executed[99] after 31 August 1995,[100] and the vendor is required to comply with the new regulations.[101]

17. Non-Resident Vendor

[16.26] Under the Finance (Miscellaneous Provisions) Act 1968, there are anti-avoidance charges to income tax or corporation tax in respect of certain capital gains arising from the disposal of land in the State or other property (eg shares) deriving its value from such land.[102] In particular, the Revenue Commissioners are empowered to direct the purchaser to deduct income tax or corporation tax at the standard rate before paying the purchase price to the non-resident vendor.[103] The requisition requires the vendor to confirm that no such direction has been served by the Commissioners and to reconfirm this on closing.

18. Body Corporate Vendor

[16.27] Great care must be taken by the purchaser's solicitor where the vendor is a company, for a number of reasons. First, it is important to determine whether it is incorporated in the State,[104] which the requisition requires the vendor's solicitor to confirm, and that it has power to enter into the sale.[105] It is also important to determine the company's rules as to the sealing of documents.[106] Thus, the vendor's solicitor is required to furnish with the replies a certified copy of the Certificate of Incorporation, together with the Memorandum and Articles of Association or other constitution evidencing such matters.[107] Secondly, the purchaser's solicitor must beware of various mortgages and charges which may have been created over the company's assets, including the land being sold, and of steps being taken for the winding-up of the company. The requisition, therefore, also requires the vendor to furnish with the replies copies of all existing mortgages, charges, debentures, receiverships and winding-up notices. Furthermore, he is to

---

[99.] They apply to conveyances (including voluntary dispositions) of the fee simple and leases exceeding 30 years.

[100.] Finance Act 1994, s 107, as amended by Finance Act 1995, s 149; Stamp Duty (Particulars to be Delivered) Regulations 1995 (SI 144/1995).

[101.] See *Donegan and Friel, op cit*, para 13.03. See also para **[20.41]** *post*.

[102.] Section 20, as amended by the Finance Act 1981, s 29. See Judge, *Irish Income Tax* (1995-96), para 12.410 *et seq*.

[103.] 1981 Act, s 21(2). See *Judge, op cit*, para 12.414.

[104.] Note the provisions governing non-resident vendors referred to in para **[16.26]** *supra*.

[105.] For the difficulties caused by *ultra vires* acts, see Keane, *Company Law in Ireland* (2nd ed, 1991), Ch 12. See also Courtney, *The Law of Private Companies* (1994), Ch 6.

[106.] See further para **[18.128]** *post*.

[107.] In the case of a foreign company, confirmation of the validity of due execution of documents by that company in the jurisdiction in question should be obtained from a lawyer qualified to practice in that jurisdiction: see again para **[18.128]** *post*.

furnish on closing a certificate of the company secretary that no charges have been executed other than those registered in the Companies Registration Office[108] and that no resolution to wind-up the company has been passed or notice issued or published of a meeting to propose winding-up, or petition presented or pending to wind-up, or steps taken to place the company in receivership or to have a receiver or examiner appointed.[109] If a debenture has been issued containing a floating charge, the vendor is required to prove, on closing, that it has not crystallised so as to attach to the property being sold.[110]

[16.28] The Companies Act 1990 introduced provisions designed to ensure that directors of companies do not abuse their position of trust, by, eg, causing the company to enter into transactions with themselves on more favourable terms than would be offered to an outsider. Under s 29 of the Act any arrangement, and any transaction entered into in pursuance of it, may be voidable by the company where there is a connection between the parties, such as the director and his own company, or a subsidiary company and its holding company.[111] To avoid this the transaction should be affirmed by a general meeting and so the requisition requires the company secretary to certify whether the present transaction is an arrangement caught by s 29 and to furnish the appropriate resolution of a general meeting to cover it and any other previous transaction on the title entered into since 1 February 1991.[112] The other provision in the 1990 Act which must concern the purchaser's solicitor is s 31 which prohibits various loans, quasi-loans, credit transactions and guarantees in favour of directors, including "shadow" directors and persons connected with directors like members of his family. These are very wide-ranging provisions[113] and again the requisition requires a certificate of the company's secretary or auditors identifying which particular exception in the Act[114] protects any transaction apparently coming within s 31.[115]

[108.] See para **[15.48]** *ante*.

[109.] On these various matter, see *Keane op cit* Chs 38-40; *Courtney, op cit*, Chs 17-19.

[110.] See *Keane, op cit*, Ch 22; *Courtney, op cit*, para [14.040] *et seq*.

[111.] See *Keane, op cit*, Chs 29-19; *Courtney, op cit*, para [7.102] *et seq*.

[112.] Note the Law Society's recommended certificates for inclusion in deeds, as appropriate: see the *Gazette*, December 1991, p 419; para **[18.113]** *post*.

[113.] See *Keane, op cit*, para 29.16 *et seq*; *Courtney, op cit*, para [7.106] *et seq*.

[114.] Set out in ss 32-37.

[115.] Note the warning issued to solicitors by the Law Society's Company Law Committee about giving unqualified certificates to financial institutions on behalf of clients. Unless the solicitor is fully satisfied that he has all the relevant information about the company, its directors and shareholders, he runs considerable risks in issuing an unqualified certificate in respect of s 31: see the *Gazette,* December 1991, p 420. See also Courtney, 'The Latest Hazard Guarantees: The Effects of s 31, Companies Act 1990 on Inter-Company Guarantees', the *Gazette,* September 1991, p 261.

19. Land Act 1965

[16.29] This requisition is concerned with compliance with the provisions of the Land Act 1965, in particular the need to obtain consent to the transaction from the Land Commission.[116] This is a matter which has caused conveyancers difficulties ever since the foundation of the State and, although becoming part of the EEC and subject to the provisions of the Treaty of Rome, such as the right of establishment, has reduced the effect of the 1965 Act,[117] it is still a matter which conveyancers must have regard to.[118] There are three forms of consent which may be needed.

(i) Section 12

[16.30] Section 12 of the Land Act 1965, contains provisions which have been part of the land purchase scheme in Ireland for decades.[119] That scheme involved the removal of leasehold tenure from the Irish agricultural scene and the vesting of freehold titles in the tenant-farmers. It is not surprising, therefore, that the legislators wished to impose restrictions on the further subletting or sub-division of the land and the possibility of the problem which they had striven for so long to solve growing up again. Another factor motivating the imposition of the restrictions was that the freehold titles vested in the tenant-farmers were subject to land purchase annuities in repayment of the sums advanced to buy out the landlords' interests. These annuities were charged on the land, like mortgages, and the legislators were concerned about the effect sub-division of holdings would have on the value of the security, ie, the dangers of having the liability for payment of the annuity in respect of any one holding fragmented amongst several owners on sub-division of the holding. A third factor, which has assumed considerable importance in the Republic, has been that many of the holdings occupied by tenant-farmers have been too small to be economic. Rather than encourage further sub-division of holdings, one of the main functions of the Land Commission has been to promote amalgamation and consolidation schemes

---

[116.] The Irish Land Commission (Dissolution) Act 1992 provided for the Commission's dissolution and the consequent devolution of its powers to the Minister for Agriculture, but the Minister has yet to make the statutory instrument bringing this part of the Act into operation.

[117.] See Laffoy, 'Section 45 of the Land Act 1965 and the Right of Establishment in European Communities' (1982-83) 6 Journal of Irish Society for European Lawyers 26; *cf* Murphy, *op cit*, p 32. See also O'Farrell and Cawley, 'Section 45 Consents and the Treaty of Rome', the *Gazette,* September 1993, p 191.

[118.] Note the Law Society's pamphlet 'The Land Act 1965: Notes on Certain Provisions Affecting Conveyancing and Title', published in September 1965.

[119.] See *Irish Land Law* (2nd ed, 1986), para 1.66 *et seq.*

to produce more economic holdings and relieve congestion.[120] Under the early legislation of the land purchase scheme, the restrictions on subletting or sub-division were effective only so long as the land purchase annuity was payable in respect of the holding in question.[121] Once the annuity was paid off, the holding became free of the restrictions.[122] Under the scheme as it operated in the Republic after 1923, however, the restrictions remained in force even after the annuity was paid off.[123] These post-1923 provisions have now been largely replaced by those contained in s 12 of the Land Act 1965.[124]

[16.31] Section 12 relates only to "agricultural holdings," ie, holdings which are substantially agricultural and/or pastoral in character, held under freehold or leasehold tenure, whether or not subject to statutory conditions, held jointly or in common or alone or in severalty, and whether or not purchased under the Land Purchase Acts or registered in the Land Registry.[125] Section 12(1) states the general restriction that such a holding cannot be let, sublet or sub-divided[126] without the consent in writing of the Land Commission.[127] It goes on to say that such consent may be either general or particular and may be subject to such conditions (if any) as the Land Commission think fit. However, s 12(2) qualifies this by providing that the power to withhold consent can be exercised solely to prevent the creation or continuance of holdings which, in the opinion of the Land Commission, are not economic holdings. Thus the Commission may seek to attach

---

[120.] *Cf* partition of holdings held on commonage: see *Re Commonage at Glennamaddoo* [1992] IR 297.

[121.] See, eg, Irish Land Act 1903, s 54(1). On this provision, see *Foley's* case [1957] NI 130. See also *O'Leary v Buckley* (1922) 56 ILTR 14; *Re Geoghegan* [1918] 1 IR 188.

[122.] See Leitch, 'Present-Day Agricultural Tenancies in Northern Ireland' (1965) 16 NILQ 491.

[123.] See Land Acts 1923, s 65; 1927, ss 3 and 4;1936, s 44;1939, s 23;1946, ss 3 and 6. See also *Re Morris* (1940) 74 ILTR 235.

[124.] See 1965 Act, s 47 and 1st Sched.

[125.] Section 12(8).

[126.] This includes the case of any claim whatsoever to title to part or parts of a holding, whether by disposition to one or more than one person, see s 12(8). *Cf Re Cleary* [1922]1 IR 94; *Re Lennon* [1928] NI 195. See also *Allied Irish Banks plc v O'Neill* [1996] ICLC 36. Consent is also required for acquisition of title to part or parts of a holding by adverse possession (except where acquired by possession wholly antecedent to the passing of the 1965 Act), see s 12(6). *Cf re Smith* [1939] IR 244; *Murphy v Forde* (1943) 77 ILTR 130. As to adverse possession, see *Irish Land Law* (2nd ed, 1986), Ch 23.

[127.] With respect to holdings which may still come under the land purchase scheme, whether by vesting the land in the Land Commission for the first time or "resumption" of land previously bought out under the scheme, s 13 of the 1965 Act contains a similar restriction applicable to the land until the termination of the proceedings under the Land Purchase Acts, see para **[16.36]** *infra*.

conditions requiring consolidation of more than one holding, though it is important to note that the power of consolidation is subject to the consent of the tenant or proprietor of the holdings in question.[128] The owner should consider in such a case whether the condition is reasonable before he gives his consent to its imposition, because, if he does give it, subsequent sub-division of the consolidated holdings, such as a sale of the one the subject of the current application for consent, will again require consent. Any attempted or purported letting, subletting or subdivision without consent is "null and void" as against all persons.[129] However, if the Commission grant consent subsequently, they may direct that it operates retrospectively so as to validate the attempted or purported letting, subletting or sub-division.[130] It was held in *Carew v Jackman*[131] that a letting rendered void under the legislation in force prior to the 1965 Act could not be validated retrospectively by a consent purported to be given under the 1965 Act, even though the earlier legislation was repealed and replaced by the 1965 Act.

[16.32] It is important to note that s 12(4) excludes the need for consent in cases where the holding is no longer subject to a land purchase annuity or other payment payable to the Land Commission[132] and either the whole of the holding in question is situated in an urban area[133] or the Commission certify that in their opinion the holding, by reason of its proximity to an urban area, is required for urban development.[134]

[16.33] As any letting, subletting or sub-division without the consent of the Land Commission "shall be null and void as against all persons," the owner who has made the letting may repudiate it at any time by relying on the section and may bring proceedings for recovery of possession immediately after the transaction is completed. The owner is not bound by the transaction in any way and he is not estopped by his action in making the letting, subletting or sub-division, even though he has accepted rent or the purchase price of part of the holding has been paid to him. There cannot be an estoppel which would have the result that the effect of a statute would be nullified as this would give the courts power, in effect, to repeal the

---

128. See 1965 Act, s 25, which amends s 66 of the Land Act 1923, so as to extend the power of consolidation to any two or more holdings, whether or not subject to a purchase annuity. See *Re Stevenson* [1928] NI 135.

129. Section 12(3).

130. *Ibid.*

131. [1966] IR 177.

132. As under the pre-1923 legislation applicable to both parts of Ireland, see para **[16.30]** *supra*.

133. Ie, within the boundary of any county borough, borough, urban district or town, s 12(4)(a) A list of these is given later, see para **[16.44]** *infra* and Appendix IV *post*.

134. Section 12(4)(b).

provisions of the statute. The question whether any purchase money paid to the owner in respect of a void sub-division could be recovered from the owner is one of great difficulty: we believe that it could be under the rapidly developing concept of unjust enrichment[135] or, possibly, as money paid under a mistake in law,[136] but the matter has not been considered in any reported case in Ireland.[137]

[16.34] In respect of *registered* land, an important change was made in 1977 because the Land Commission then issued a general consent to sub-division of such land, provided the severed plots do not exceed one hectare[138] in size and various other conditions are met.[139] In such cases there is no need to apply for consent.[140]

[16.35] Requisition 19 takes the above into account and requires the vendor's solicitor to indicate whether the present transaction[141] gives rise to a letting, sub-letting or sub-division which requires consent under s12. If it does, the original letter of consent, together with the appropriate map, and a letter from the Land Commission[142] confirming that all relevant conditions have been met must be furnished. Otherwise the vendor's solicitor must confirm that the general consent procedure[143] applies or, if the land is subject to a land purchase or reclamation annuity, that sub-divisions in excess of two hectares have not been effected under that scheme.

(ii) Section 13

[16.36] Where a provisional list of holdings which will vest in the Land Commission has been published, the lands or any part thereof mentioned in the provisional list cannot be sold, transferred, let, sublet, or sub-divided without the written consent of the Land Commission, until the proceedings

---

[135.] See, generally, Goff and Jones, *The Law of Restitution* (4th ed, 1993). See also Birks, *Introduction to the Law of Restitution* (1985); Burrows, *The Law of Restitution* (1993).Note also the House of Lords decision in *Lipkin Gornan v Karpanale Ltd* [1991] 2 AC 548.

[136.] But see *O'Loghlan v O'Callaghan* (1874) IR 8 CL 116. And generally Clark, *Contract Law in Ireland* (3rd ed, 1992), p 202 *et seq.*

[137.] But see *Dolan v Nelligan* [1967] IR 247; *Dublin Corporation v Trinity College, Dublin* [1986] ILRM 283. And note the English Law Commission's Report, *Restitution of Payments made under a Mistake of Law* (Law Com No 120; 1991).

[138.] One hectare = 2.471 acres.

[139.] Eg the severed plot will be discharged from the land purchase annuity, which will remain charged on the rest of the holding, and the purchaser is a 'qualified person' for the purposes of s 45 of the 1965 Act: see para **[16.50]** *infra.*

[140.] See the Direction SR 13/77, dated 8 December 1977. The procedure agreed with the Land Registry is set out in Fitzgerald, *Land Registry Practice* (2nd ed, 1985), p 53 *et seq.*

[141.] Or any previous transaction in the case of *unregistered* land.

[142.] Or its successor, see fn 116 *supra.*

[143.] See para **[16.34]** *supra.*

under the Land Purchase Acts for the acquisition of the lands have terminated. Under s 40(6) of the Land Act 1923, any inspector or other person appointed by the Land Commission may, after notice sent to the owner or occupier of any lands, enter upon them to inspect them. Service of such a notice is usually an indication that the Land Commission are considering the compulsory acquisition of the lands.[144] Section 13(2) of the Land Act 1965, provides that, where such a notice has been served after the passing of that Act, the lands or any part of them mentioned in the notice shall not be sold, transferred, let, sublet or sub-divided without the written consent of the Land Commission within three months from the date of the service of the notice. The period of three months may be enlarged to six months by an order of the Land Commissioners. It is accordingly essential for a purchaser who is buying agricultural lands of any kind to find out whether a notice of intention to enter has been served by the Land Commission. However, a copy of any provisional list or notice affecting registered land (as it usually will do) is furnished to the Registrar of Titles, so that an appropriate entry can be made in the register. This will be disclosed by the usual search,[145] so that a special requisition on the matter is rarely necessary.[146]

(iii) Section 45

[16.37] This section has over the years profoundly affected the transfer and mortgaging of all land in the State which was not wholly situate within a county borough, a borough, an urban district or a town. It had the extraordinary result that, if a company incorporated in the State recovered judgment against a farmer, it could not convert that judgment into a judgment mortgage without the consent of the Land Commission: it had the bizarre effect that a company which was incorporated in the State and all of whose shareholders were Irish citizens could not purchase agricultural land in the State without that consent. It was, however, only the second step in the legislative effort to prevent persons who were not Irish citizens from buying agricultural land in the State. An understanding of the first stage and its complete failure explains many of the strange features in s 45 which have been removed only in recent times.

[16.38] Shortly after the end of the Second World War, a Labour Government was elected in Britain. Many of the wealthy in Britain feared

---

[144.] See *Horgan v Deasy* [1979] ILRM 71; *Keane v Irish Land Commission* [1979] IR 429; *State (Callaghan) v Irish Land Commission* [1978] ILRM 201.

[145.] See para **[15.40]** *ante*.

[146.] Note, however, that Rq 19 does require the vendor's solicitor to furnish with the replies a copy of any vesting order made for consolidation with the land being sold.

penal taxation and the possible confiscation of their property, and some of them moved to the State and bought land with the intention of farming it. The Irish Government decided to counter this by the imposition of a penal 25 per cent. stamp duty on all purchases of land in any part of the State when the conveyance did not contain the appropriate certificate.[147] Originally this 25 per cent. stamp duty applied to purchasers of all land in the State, including that in cities, boroughs, urban districts and towns. The Revenue Commissioners took the opportunity to increase the stamp duty in all cases, even when the necessary certificate was given, from 1 per cent. to 5 per cent.

[16.39] By s 13 of the Finance (No. 2) Act 1947, the stamp duty payable on a conveyance was increased to £2.50 for each £50 of the consideration, except in cases where the purchase money was under £1,000. The rate of 5 per cent. was, however, to apply only when the conveyance contained a statement by the party to whom the property was being conveyed that the person becoming entitled to the entire beneficial interest in the property was, *inter alia*, (a) an Irish citizen, or (b) a person ordinarily resident in the area now know as the Republic and who had been so resident continuously during the three years preceding 15 October 1947, or (c) a body corporate incorporated in the area now known as the Republic before that date, or (d) a body corporate incorporated in the area now know as the Republic after that date where the issued shares of each class were, to an extent exceeding one half in nominal value thereof, in the beneficial ownership of Irish citizens or a body corporate incorporated in the Republic before that date. If the conveyance did not contain this certificate, stamp duty of 25 per cent. of the purchase price was payable.[148]

[16.40] Avoidance of this penal tax was, to a company lawyer, very easy. The proposed non-Irish purchaser formed a company with a nominal capital of £500 or some other amount. The company allotted 51 shares to an Irish citizen whom the foreigner trusted and 49 shares to the foreigner who then lent the purchase price to the company. The company then completed the sale and certified, with complete accuracy, that it was a body corporate incorporated in the State after the 15 October 1947, where the issued shares of each class were, to an extent exceeding one half in nominal value thereof, in the beneficial ownership of Irish citizens. Some months later the Irish citizen transferred all but one of his shares to the foreigner for the price he had paid for them and so the foreigner became the virtual owner of the company which owned the lands or the house. The Government dealt with

---

[147.] See Finance (No 2) Act 1947, s 13.
[148.] See *New Forest Estate Co Ltd v Revenue Commissioners* [1965] IR 172; *Parkes v Parkes* [1980] ILRM 137.

this method of avoiding payment of the 25 per cent. stamp duty by provisions of great obscurity in the Finance Act 1949.[149] The effect of these was that, when the shares in a company incorporated after 15 October 1947, which had acquired land after that date, ceased to be, to an extent exceeding one half, in the beneficial ownership of Irish citizens, the penal duty of 25 per cent. became payable on any conveyance executed after 15 October 1947.

[16.41] The device of forming a new company was no longer effective, but again company lawyers had little difficulty in finding another method of avoiding the penal duty. There are always dormant companies on the Register of Companies: they have usually been formed to carry out one transaction or have ceased to trade. If a foreigner bought all the shares in a company incorporated in the Republic before 15 October 1947, he could lend the purchase price of whatever land he wanted to buy to it and the conveyance could be made to it. The company could then with complete accuracy certify that the person who became entitled to the entire beneficial interest in the property was a body corporate incorporated in the State before 15 October 1947, and so the ordinary rate of stamp duty was payable. An active market developed in these companies and the price, which was originally about £250, went up to £1,000. This method of carrying out a sale to a person who was not an Irish citizen continued until 1965.

[16.42] The penal duty continued to apply to all sales of every kind of landed property when the purchaser could not give the necessary certificate until its application was restricted by s 30 of the Finance Act 1956. This section provided that the ordinary rate of stamp duty was to apply when there was a certificate in the conveyance that the property being conveyed was being acquired for private residential purposes and did not include land exceeding five acres in extent. Therefore the purchase of residential properties was liable to the ordinary rate of stamp duty, although the conveyance did not contain any certificate as to nationality or incorporation.

[16.43] We have dealt with the penal duty at some length because an understanding of it and of the way in which payment of it was avoided is essential to an understanding of s 45 of the Land Act 1965. The company had been such a flexible legal instrument that those who drafted the 1965 Act were determined that the sorry story of the penal stamp duty would not be repeated. It is not a coincidence that the 25 per cent stamp duty was removed in the same year as that in which s 45 of the 1965 Act became law. So all companies, whether incorporated in the Republic or not, were

---

[149.] Sections 26 and 27. See Plunkett, *The Stamp Duty Legislation 1890-1962* (1962), pp 14-5.

prohibited from buying land or acquiring any interest of any kind in it without the consent of the Land Commission, unless it was wholly situate within a county borough, a borough, an urban district or a town.

(a) Urban area

[16.44] It is important, therefore, in each transaction to determine whether any part of the property in question lies outside a county borough, borough, urban district or town. From time to time the Law Society's Conveyancing Committee has issued lists identifying such urban areas and these should be checked,[150] for this is a subject of some complexity. "Town" is defined by the Interpretation Act 1937, as meaning "the areas comprised in a town (not being an urban district) in which the Towns Improvement (Ireland) Act 1854 is in force."[151] The fact that a collection of houses and shops has the word "town" as part of its name does not mean that it is a town for the purposes of s 45 of the Land Act 1965 or the Act of 1854. The Anglo-Normans seem to have called every place where there is a castle a town. There are many Castletowns in the Republic but not one of them is a town for the purposes of the Land Act 1965. As Palles CB said in *Archer v The Earl of Calidon*[152]:

> "Town according to my view, like every other word in the English language, will bear a different signification according to the object with which it finds a place in any particular piece of legislation."[153]

That great authority on the English language, Dr. Johnson, defined a town as: "a collection of houses larger than a village," but as he defined a village as "an assemblage of houses smaller than a town," his dictionary does not assist. In *Dardis and Dunn's Seeds Ltd v Hickey*,[154] Kenny J had to consider whether Robinstown, in Co Kildare, was a town for the purposes of the Judgment Mortgage (Ireland) Act 1850, and, after an examination of the authorities, held it was not. There was, however, no Interpretation Act in force in 1850.

[16.45] The Towns Improvement (Ireland) Act 1854, is a very long statute dealing with such diverse topics as the adoption of the Act by the rated occupiers of cities and towns, the sale of gunpowder and the regulation of public bathing. In it "town" is defined as meaning and including "a city, town corporate, borough, market town in Ireland containing a population of

---

150. See the *Gazette*, December 1993, p 395. The list is reproduced in Appendix IV *post*. For earlier lists see the *Gazette*, May 1986, p 116.
151. Section 12 and Sched.
152. [1894] 2 IR 473.
153. *Ibid*, p 476.
154. High Court, unrep, 11 July 1974 (1972/1165 Sp). See *Irish Land Law* (2nd ed, 1986), paras 13.174-5.

1,500 inhabitants or upwards."[155] It provided that a meeting of occupiers of premises with a rateable valuation of £8 or over might be called by two local justices of the peace to consider a resolution for the adoption of the Act so that it applied to the city, borough or town. The resolution had to specify the boundaries but did not have to have a map attached showing these. If the resolution was passed and was approved by the Lord Lieutenant, he had to notify his approval by advertisement in the *Dublin Gazette*. When he did this, the Act was in force in the area as verbally defined. The function of approval of the resolution of the ratepayers was exercised by the Lord Lieutenant from 1854 to 1872, by the Local Government Board from 1872 to 1922 and by the Minister for Local Government (now for the Environment) from 1922 to date.

[16.46] The First Schedule to the Local Government (Planning and Development) Act 1963 contains a list of "scheduled towns", but it should be noted that the definition of "scheduled town"[156] for the purposes of that Act includes "non-municipal" towns.[157] Those towns were, however, removed in 1970 from the ambit of s 45 of the Land Act 1965, by the somewhat tortuous route of declaring that any person becoming entitled to an interest in land situate in any such town is a "qualified person".[158]

[16.47] The boundaries of county boroughs and boroughs do not present a very difficult problem, because the Acts establishing them always provided for the preparation of a map by the Commissioner of Valuation which is to show the boundaries, which may be inspected at the City or Town Hall and which is conclusive. Section 18 of the Local Government (Dublin) Act 1930, is an example of this. The boundaries of all urban districts are shown on the latest edition of the Ordnance Survey. While this is not evidence in a court of law (for it is impossible to have as a witness the person who made the Survey), a purchaser is safe in assuming that the boundaries of urban districts shown on it are correct unless there has been a statutory instrument made since the last revision of the Ordnance Survey. The Town Clerk will be able to say whether this has happened. It should also be noted that land in

---

[155.] See Vanston, *Law Relating to Municipal Towns under the Towns Improvement (Ireland) Act 1854* (1907), p 6.

[156.] See the definition in s 2(1) of the 1963 Act.

[157.] A "non-municipal" town is defined as a place (not being a county borough, borough, urban district or town in which the Towns Improvement (Ir) Act 1854, is in operation) which is designated a town in the report of the census of population taken in 1956.

[158.] See the Land Act 1965 (Additional Category of Qualified Person) Regulations 1970 (SI 40/1970). In such cases, the conveyance should contain an appropriate s 45 certificate: see para **[16.50]** *infra* and **[18.114]** *post*.

certain counties was removed from the ambit of s 45 in 1994, *viz*, Dublin South, Fingal, Dun Laoghaire-Rathdown.[159]

[16.48] The boundaries of towns present a more complex problem. In many cases they can be ascertained by reference only to the order of the Lord Lieutenant or of the Local Government Board where they are verbally described, usually, by reference to townlands. There are 62,000 townlands in Ireland,[160] and in many cases, but not in all, these boundaries are shown on the Ordnance Survey. The real difficulty lies in finding out the townlands by reference to which the town adopted the 1854 Act. The problem is made more difficult by the fact that the administration of some towns was transferred by the Local Government Act 1925, to the council of the county in which the town is situate. When purchasing land near what is popularly known as the boundary of a town on behalf of anyone who is not an Irish citizen, the greatest care should be exercised to ensure that all the land being purchased is within the boundaries of the town.

[16.49] It is important to emphasise that once it is determined that all the land the subject of the conveyance is within an "urban" area, s 45 does not apply and so there is no need for any consent.[161] Furthermore, there is no requirement under s 45 that any certificate should be included in the conveyance to the effect that the land is within such an area.[162] It is not like a case of the purchaser claiming to come within one of the "qualified person" categories, where a certificate is necessary.[163] In the case of urban land, s 45 does not apply at all and so, notwithstanding the common practice of including a certificate specifying that the land is situated in a particular urban area, any certificate is unnecessary.

[159.] See the Land Act 1965 (Additional Category of Qualified Person) Regulations 1994 (SI 67/1994). The boundaries of these countries were fixed by the Local Government (Dublin) Act 1993. Again in such cases an appropriate s 45 certificate should be inserted in the conveyance: see para **[16.50]** *infra* and **[18.114]** *post.*

[160.] See MacDermott, 'The Townlands of Ireland' (1972) 3 Cambrian L Rev 80; O'Dálaigh, 'Linguistically, in the Footsteps of Lord MacDermott' (1972) 3 Cambrian L Rev 89.

[161.] Hence the importance of para 5 in Rq 19, which asks whether any part of the holding is situate within the boundary of a County Borough, a Dublin County, a Borough, Urban District or Town. It also asks for confirmation that the land is not subject to a land purchase annuity, for if it is, consent of the Land Commission under s 12 of the 1965 Act will be needed: see para **[16.31]** *supra.*

[162.] A certificate should, however, be included in the two cases referred to in fns 158 and 159 *supra.*

[163.] See para **[16.50]** *infra.*

(b) Qualified person

[16.50] Section 45 provides that, if the land in question is situated outside an urban area, no interest will vest in the purchaser unless consent to the vesting has been given by the Land Commission or the purchaser is a "qualified person" as defined by the 1965 Act.[164] The section provides a wide definition of "qualified person",[165] including an Irish citizen, various statutory bodies and any category declared by statutory instrument to be an additional category. Over the years this ministerial power has been exercised with increasing rapidity. Apart from its use to exclude land from the scope of the section in the case of certain towns and counties,[166] it has become necessary to comply with various EEC Directives furthering the right of establishment and enabling nationals, companies and other organisations of one Member State to pursue activities in other Member States.[167] In all such cases, ie, whether it is claimed that consent has been given or, instead, the purchaser is such a "qualified person", s 45 requires that the instrument purporting to vest the land to contain a certificate by the person in whom the interest is purported to be vested. That certificate will usually certify that consent has been given and any conditions attached to it have been complied with[168] or else that the person becoming entitled to the land is a qualified person within the meaning of s 45 or one of the various statutory instruments adding to that category.[169]

[16.51] Care must be taken over such certificates, if only because it is a criminal offence knowingly to make any statement in connection with an application for consent or in a certificate which is knowingly false or misleading.[170] It is also an offence to do so in a reply to a requisition[171] or,

---

[164.] Section 45(3)(a)(i) and (ii). There is a third category, viz where the interest becomes vested, on the distribution of a deceased person's estate, in his 'heir' or other members of his family: see s 45(2)(b)(iii) and (3)(a)(iv). The use of 'heir' in this context seems to suggest that this category is confined to cases of intestacy, and that its applies to cases of testacy only where the vesting is in another member of the family. In either case the requisite s 45 certificate should be put in the personal representatives' vesting assent: see Laffoy, *Irish Conveyancing Precedents,* Precedent F.1.9, certificate (i).

[165.] Section 45(i). If must be remembered that 'person' includes a body corporate and incorporated bodies of persons : Interpretation Act 1937, s 11(c).

[166.] See paras **[16.46]** and **[16.47]** *supra.*

[167.] See the Land Act 1965 (Additional Category of Qualified Persons) Regulations 1972 (SI 332/1972), 1983 (SI 144/1983), and 1995 (SI 56/1995). Note the articles referred to in fn 117 *supra.*

[168.] See *Laffoy, op cit*, Precedent F.1.9, certificate (b).

[169.] *Ibid*, certificates (c)-(h). As regards certificate (i) see fn 164 *supra.*

[170.] Section 45(6)(a)(i)-(iii).

[171.] Section 45(6)(a)(iv).

indeed, to fail to comply with a requisition under the section[172] or to make a disclosure under it.[173] It should be noted that Requisition 19 requires the furnishing of evidence of compliance with s 45.[174] The section also provides that where an interest vested in a body corporate is transferred to a person who is not a qualified person, this must be disclosed to the Land Commission within one month, which may institute proceedings for the acquisition or resumption of the land.[175] Requisition 19 requires the vendor's solicitor to state whether such a transfer has taken place and, if so, whether the Commission was notified and whether any action has been taken on foot of this.[176]

[16.52] It seems clear that once an instrument has been executed containing the appropriate certificate, it can be relied upon. The section is couched in positive terms. In particular, s 45(3) states that an instrument by which an interest in land coming within the section "purports" to become vested "shall effect such vesting" provided it contains the appropriate certificate by the person in whom the interested is "purported" to be vested, "notwithstanding any objection to the accuracy of such certificate". Any person subsequently dealing with that person is, therefore, entitled to take the certificate at face value and should not seek to go behind it by requiring evidence to support it or raising any requisitions or objections in respect of it.[177]

(c) Consent

[16.53] In the case of land coming within s 45 which is being acquired by a person or body *not* a "qualified person", it is, of course, essential to acquire the requisite consent from the Land Commission. Under condition 28 of the Law Society's standard contract form[178] the duty to obtain such consent lies with the purchaser. It is imperative, therefore, that the purchaser applies as soon as practicable. It is true that the contract form no longer provides that failure to obtain such consent justifies the vendor in forfeiting the deposit and reselling,[179] but condition 28 does provide that the sale is not conditional upon such consent being obtained. Thus, unless this is countermanded by a special condition rendering the contract subject to obtaining consent, the purchaser will not be able to refuse to complete on the basis that he has not

---

[172.] Section 45(6)(b).

[173.] Section 45(6)(c).

[174.] Para 1.

[175.] Section 45(5).

[176.] Para 2.

[177.] *Cf Parkes v Parkes* [1980] ILRM 137 (Court will not aid a party who seeks to avoid s 45 as part of a scheme to evade stamp duty).

[178.] *General Conditions of Sale (1995 Ed)*: see para **[10.48]** *ante*.

[179.] As did Cond 25 of the 1976 Ed.

received consent.[180] The vendor may, instead, invoke other remedies under the contract, such as service of a completion notice and, if consent is not obtained on expiry of the notice, he may then forfeit the deposit and resell.[181] It would not seem likely, however, that the vendor would succeed in obtaining specific performance, because lack of consent required under s 45 prevents the interest in the land vesting in the purchaser[182] and a court will not force a bad title on a purchaser.[183] The vendor may, however, claim damages for any loss suffered as a consequence of the purchaser failing to obtain consent.[184] Conversely, it seems unlikely that a purchaser who fails to obtain consent would succeed in seeking to defend claims against him by the vendor on the basis that the contract has been rendered a nullity.[185] It is difficult to see upon what ground the purchaser could advance, eg, a case for rescission, since the need for consent in such cases is something which both parties and their solicitors must be taken to be fully aware of. There would appear to be no case for rescission on any of the usual grounds like fraud, misrepresentation and mistake.[186] Nor would the doctrine of frustration apply, since this operates only where the supervening event is one which was unforeseen by the parties when they entered into the contract.[187] It might be argued that, since any conveyance executed by the vendor without the requisite consent in favour of the purchaser will fail to vest any title in the purchaser,[188] there is a fundamental defect in title which justifies the purchaser rescinding the contract.[189] However, again it is difficult to see how this could succeed since the right of rescission in such cases is based upon discovery of such a defect *after* the contract has been entered into.[190] The need for s 45 consent is, or should be, known to the purchaser prior to entering into the contract and, as we saw above, the Law Society's standard form reinforces the point that the purchaser contracts on the basis that it is his duty to obtain it. Furthermore, in such cases, there is nothing wrong with vendor's title in the strict sense, if he could execute a fully effective

---

[180.] See *Costelloe v Maharaj Krishna Properties (Ir) Ltd* High Court, unrep, 10 July 1975 (1974/1564 P) ; *Sibel v Kent* [1976-7] ILRM 127; para **[7.23]** *ante. Cf Aga Khan v Firestone* [1992] ILRM 31.

[181.] Under Cond 40: see para **[13.19]** *et seq, ante.*

[182.] See para **[16.50]** *supra.*

[183.] See para **[13.52]** *ante.*

[184.] See para **[13.04]** *ante.* Damages may be claimed in lieu of specific performance : see para **[13.54]** *ante.*

[185.] Unless, of course, the obtaining of such consent has been made a special condition - precedent or subsequent : see Ch 7 *ante.*

[186.] See para **[13.63]** *et seq, ante.*

[187.] *Neville & Sons Ltd v Guardian Builders Ltd* [1990] ILRM 601: see para **[12.37]** *ante.*

[188.] See para **[16.50]** *supra.*

[189.] See para **[13.68]** *ante.* See also as to a defence to an action by the vendor for specific performance para **[13.52]** *ante.*

[190.] See *ibid.*

conveyance to a qualified person. The defect lies rather in the capacity of the purchaser to take the conveyance and it is difficult to see why the vendor should be deprived of his common law or contractual remedies in a case where the purchaser has freely entered into the contract.[191]

20. Unregistered Property

[16.54] This requisition deals with a number of matters which may concern unregistered land. Thus where any person on the title died after 31 May 1959,[192] a written assent by the personal representative must be furnished with the replies.[193] Such an assent is the vital document of title, whereby the deceased's land becomes vested in his successor in title. The one exception to this seems to be where the personal representative is also the successor in title. In *Mohan v Roche*[194] Keane J took the view that, since the legal title to the land is already vested in the personal representative,[195] there is no need for that person to execute an assent in his own favour. In so holding, Keane J departed from the English authorities,[196] which had been the subject of criticism.[197] In strict theory Keane J's holding is perfectly logical; since the personal representative already has the legal title vested in him, there is no need for any "vesting" in or "transfer" to him of that title once the administration of the estate is completed and the time for distribution to the deceased's successors has arrived.[198] Nevertheless, as Keane J himself conceded, it may be desirable for the personal representative to execute an assent in his own favour. This will make it clear that there has been a change in his capacity, ie, he has ceased to be a personal representative still charged with administration of the estate and has become the new beneficial owner of the estate.[199] Furthermore, it has been pointed out that difficulties may arise where the personal representative is not the sole successor in title.[200] An

---

[191.] Ie, where there is no question of the contract being vitiated by wrongful actions on the part of the vendor, such as undue influence or misrepresentation.

[192.] The date when the Administration of Estates Act 1959, came into force: see Brady, *Succession Law in Ireland* (2nd ed, 1995), Ch 9.

[193.] See *Brady, op cit*, para [10.34] *et seq*. Also paras **[14.66]** and **[14.79]** *ante*.

[194.] [1991] 1 IR 560. As to the conclusiveness of an assent see para **[15.19]** *ante*.

[195.] Under s 10 of the Succession Act 1965.

[196.] In particular *Re King's Will Trusts* [1964] Ch 542. See also *Re Hodge* [1940] Ch 260; *Re Edwards' Will Trusts* [1982] Ch 30.

[197.] See, eg, Garner, 'Assents Today' (1964) 28 Conv 298; Farrand, 'Dissent on Assents' 108 Sol Jo 698 and 719. See also *Emmet on Title* (19th ed by Farrand), para 11.121.

[198.] Note the wording of ss 52(2) and 53(1) of the Succession Act 1965.

[199.] In a subsequent sale of the property this change of capacity would govern what covenants for title would be appropriate, *ie*, whether the vendor is expressed to convey as personal representative or as beneficial owner : see para **[21.18]** *post*.

[200.] This was initially the position in *Mohan v Roche* but the other members of the family entitled on intestacy had entered into a deed of family arrangement releasing their interests to their mother, the personal representative of her deceased husband. See Brady, *Succession Law in Ireland* (2nd ed, 1995), para [10.37] *et seq*.

assent in favour of the personal representative who claims to be entitled to the land in question is *conclusive*[201] and forestalls any query as to claims by other members of the family. It completes the documentary chain of title.[202] Notwithstanding the decision in *Mohan v Roche* it is suggested that it remains good practice for a personal representative who is also the successor in title to the deceased to execute an assent in his own favour.

[16.55] The second matter covered by the requisitions concerns the possible need for compulsory registration of the title to the land in question.[203] The need for such registration may have already arisen as a result of some previous transaction, in which case the vendor's solicitor is required to procure registration prior to completion of the present sale. The need may, however, arise as a consequence of the present sale, because, eg, it is the first conveyance on sale or assignment of a leasehold interest to occur in respect of the land since the area in which it is situated was declared a compulsory registration area.[204] In such a case the vendor's solicitor is required to furnish with his replies a map which complies with the Land Registry requirements[205] and an undertaking to supply,[206] if requested, within two years of completion,[207] such further information and documents as may be necessary to effect registration.

[16.56] The third matter covered by the requisition relates to the title documents. As we saw in a previous chapter, in the case of unregistered land, the original deeds will be retained by the vendor's solicitor until completion.[208] The requisition requires the vendor's solicitor to indicate where the originals may be inspected and to identify which will be delivered on completion.[209] Of course, it may be that the vendor will retain the title deeds after completion. This arises where the land being sold is part only of a larger holding, in which case the vendor needs to retain the deeds as they evidence his title to the part of the holding retained by him after the sale. In such cases the requisition requires the vendor to give the purchaser the usual

---

201. See para [15.19] *ante*.

202. See Parry and Clark, *The Law of Succession* (9th ed, 1988), p 375.

203. See generally Fitzgerald, *Land Registry Practice* (2nd ed, 1995), pp 7-8 and 380 *et seq*.

204. This applies, eg, to the three counties of Carlow, Laois and Meath: see the Compulsory Registration of Ownership (Carlow, Laoighis and Meath) Order 1969 (SI 87/1969).

205. For full discussion of these see Fitzgerald, *op cit,* Ch 4.

206. At the purchaser's expense.

207. Where a conveyance gives rise to compulsory registration, that registration must take place within 6 months of execution of the conveyance, but the Registrar or, on appeal against his refusal, the Court may extend this Registration of Title Act 1964, s 25.

208. Ie the purchaser's solicitor is furnished with photocopies only by way of deduction of title: see para [14.42] *et seq, ante*.

209. See para [20.34] *post*.

statutory acknowledgment for production and undertaking as to safe custody.[210]

21. Identity

[16.57] This short requisition simply requires the vendor's solicitor to prove the identity of the property sold with that to which the vendor's title is purported to be shown. The Law Society's standard contract form provides that the purchaser should accept the descriptions in the documents of title, but he may, if the circumstances require it, require a statutory declaration of at least 12 years' enjoyment in accordance with the title shown.[211]

22. Registered Property

[16.58] This requisition deals with the case where the land being sold is registered land. Apart from requiring the vendor's solicitor to confirm that this is, indeed, the case and to state whether any dealings have been registered on the folio or are pending, which are not shown on the copy folio furnished to the purchaser's solicitor,[212] the vendor's solicitor is required to furnish two sets of documents, one with the replies to the requisitions and the other on closing. To be furnished with the replies, if not already furnished, are a certified copy of the folio written up-to- date and the Land Registry map or filed plan.[213] Since most registered land is agricultural land bought out under the Land Purchase Acts,[214] the land in question may be subject to a land purchase annuity, in which case the vendor's solicitor is to furnish a certificate of redemption value unless the annuity will be automatically removed on the sale of the land. Also to be furnished with the replies are a *draft* (for the purchaser's solicitor's approval) s 72 declaration and affidavit in cases where the title is not yet registered as absolute. The former applies where the land is subject to any burdens affecting registered land without registration and to which the purchaser will take subject.[215] The latter applies where the title has been registered as qualified or possessory only, but due to the passage of time, it may now be possible to have it converted to an absolute title.[216] If the transaction involves the transfer of part only of the land in a folio, it will be necessary to open a new folio for the transferred part.[217] In such cases the vendor's solicitor is required to furnish

---

[210.] This matter is discussed at para **[18.102]** *et seq, post.*

[211.] See para **[9.11]** *ante.*

[212.] The copy folio is, of course only up-to-date as of the date of its issue; see paras **[14.34]** and **[15.40]** *ante.*

[213.] See para **[14.33]** *et seq, ante.*

[214.] See Fitzgerald, *Land Registry Practice* (2nd ed, 1995), Ch 24. See also *Irish Land Law* (2nd ed, 1986), para 1.38 *et seq.*

[215.] See paras **[14.27]** and **[14.41]** *ante.*

[216.] See paras **[14.24]** and **[14.37]** *ante.*

[217.] See *Fitzgerald, op cit,* Ch 3.

with the replies a site map of the transferred part complying with the Land Registry's requirements[218] or an Approved Scheme Map.[219]

[16.59] On closing the vendor's solicitor is required to furnish the original land certificate[220] or, in the case of a transfer of part only of the land in the folio, an undertaking to lodge it in the Land Registry immediately on completion, together with a letter consenting to its use in connection with registration of the purchaser's transfer.[221] In addition, if not furnished previously,[222] the vendor's solicitor must furnish, as appropriate, the Land Registry map or file plan, the site map or Approved Scheme Map, the certificate of redemption value of any land purchase annuity payable, the s 72 declaration and the affidavit or other sufficient evidence to enable the purchaser to convert the title to an absolute one.

23. Newly Erected Property

[16.60] This requisition relates to the case where the purchaser is buying a newly erected property, such as a new house on a housing estate.[223] The vendor's solicitor is required to furnish with the replies to the requisition drafts of documentation to be handed over at closing: the deed of assurance[224]; site map and statutory declaration by the vendor's architect or other competent person of identity and confirming that rights of way, easements and services relating to it form part of the land to which the vendor has shown title; an indemnity in relation to roads, footpaths, sewers and all services;[225] an indemnity in respect of defects. Also to be furnished with the replies is the floor area certificate,[226] the Particulars Delivered form for completion by the purchaser for stamp duty purposes[227] and the HomeBond Scheme Guarantee Agreement.[228] At closing the vendor's solicitor is required to hand over the original deed of assurance duly executed by the vendor and assessed for stamp duty or adjudged exempt from duty, with the PD stamp impressed,[229] and a certificate of compliance with the building or other covenants endorsed on it. A memorial of the deed

---

218. *Ibid*, Ch 4.

219. Governing development subleases and multi-storied buildings: see *ibid* p 73 *et seq*.

220. Or where it has not been issued, confirmation that an application has not been made for its issue: see para **[14.31]** *ante*.

221. See *Fitzgerald, op cit*, pp 61 and 348.

222. See **[16.57]** *supra*.

223. Flats and other "managed" properties are covered by Rq 36: see para **[16.97]** *infra*.

224. See Ch 18 *post*.

225. Which may not yet have been taken in charge by the local authority.

226. Which is necessary to show that the house is within the statutory limits for grant purposes and to obtain stamp duty reliefs in certain cases: see para **[11.10]** *ante*.

227. See para **[20.41]** *post*.

228. Form HB 10: see para **[4.27]** *ante*.

229. See para **[20.41]** *post*.

must also be furnished for registration in the Registry of Deeds,[230] and, where applicable, the HomeBond Final Notice determining the date from which the 10-year structural guarantee runs.[231]

24. Family Home Protection Act 1976 and Family Law Act 1995

[16.61] No piece of legislation enacted since the foundation of the State has caused conveyancers more difficulties than the Family Home Protection Act 1976. The fears expressed in the first edition of this book,[232] published shortly after its enactment, have, sadly, proved to be something of an underestimate of the problems, as the flood of litigation over the past 20 years has shown. The result has also been that the Law Society's Conveyancing Committee has had to work overtime to issue guidelines to practitioners from time to time.[233] The Act has been the subject of detailed analysis and discussion by various other authors[234] since the first edition of this book and there is little point in going over the same ground again. We are concerned primarily with the conveyancing implications and so confine the ensuing paragraphs to summarising these and then considering how to deal with them in practice.

(i) Conveyancing Implications

[16.62] The following is a summary of the more significant aspects of the Act from the conveyancing point of view:

(a) *Remedial social statute*: The Act is primarily a remedial social statute, rather than one concerned with conveyancing, and the courts have emphasised time and again that it will be interpreted widely and liberally to this end.[235] In particular it is designed to protect "non-owning"[236] spouses[237] and dependent children in their house, in furtherance of the State's

---

[230.] See para **[20.43]** *post*. In the case of registered land, a certified copy of the deed must be furnished.

[231.] See para **[4.26]** *post*.

[232.] See para **[6.31]** *et seq*.

[233.] See the Society's *Conveyancing Handbook* (1990) Ch 1 of which collects most of those issued up to 1990, but others have had to be issued since then: eg, the revised Family Home Declarations prepared by the Dublin Solicitors Bar Association and approved by both the Law Society's Conveyancing Committee and the Joint Committee of Building Society Solicitors and the Law Society, see para **[16.64]** *infra*.

[234.] See, eg, Duncan and Scully, *Marriage Breakdown in Ireland: Law and Practice* (1990), Ch 11; Farrell, *Irish Law of Specific Performance* (1994) Ch 7; Shatter, *Family Law in the Republic in Ireland* (3rd ed), Ch 16. Note also the annotations to the Act itself in Wylie, *Irish Conveyancing Statutes* (1994), p 356 *et seq*.

[235.] *Bank of Ireland v Purcell* [1989] IR 327.

[236.] It does not apply where both spouses are owners of the home: see sub-para (f) *infra*.

[237.] Usually the wife, but it is important to reiterate that the Act provides equal protection for a non-owning husband: see *Allied Irish Banks plc v O'Neill* [1996] ICLC 36: see para **[16.69]** sub-para (d) *infra*.

constitutional duty to protect the family.[238] This has led the Supreme Court to emphasise that the burden of proving that the Act's requirement, in terms, eg, of the non-owning spouse giving consent to the transaction in question, lies squarely on the purchaser, mortgagee or other person or body claiming to have acquired an interest in the land which includes a family home.[239]

(b) *Family home*: This is defined as meaning "primarily"[240] a "dwelling"[241] in which a "married couple ordinarily reside".[242] It would seem that the couple must have a valid marriage[243] and be in actual occupation.[244] However, the Act is designed to protect the interest of the non-owning spouse and so it still applies where that spouse was in occupation but has since left.[245] It is clear that the Act applies to cases where the couple reside in accommodation which forms part of a larger property, which may have a largely commercial use, eg, the farmhouse on a farm.[246] It also protects "any garden" or other land usually occupied with the dwelling. Clarification of this concept has recently been made,[247] so that it now means "land that is subsidiary and ancillary[248] to it [the dwelling], is required for amenity or convenience and is not being used or developed primarily[249] for commercial purposes". As originally enacted the 1976 Act referred to a "portion of ground attached to and usually occupied with the dwelling", which suggested that the family home might include an area rather larger than the

---

238. See *Somers v W* [1979] IR 94; *Nestor v Murphy* [1979] IR 326; *Hamilton v Hamilton* [1982] IR 466; *W v Somers* [1983] IR 122.

239. *Bank of Ireland v Smyth* [1996] IR 241; *Allied Irish Banks plc v Finnegan* [1996] 1 ILRM 401: see para **[16.69]** sub-para (b) *infra*.

240. See *National Irish Bank Ltd v Graham* [1994] 2 ILRM 109 at 113 (*per* Finlay CJ): see fn 249 *infra*.

241. This must be occupied as a separate dwelling, but it includes a part of a building, like a flat or apartment : s 2(2).

242. Section 2(1).

243. Under the law for the time being in force in the State : see *The State (Nicolaou) v An Bord Uchtála* [1966] IR 567, See para **[16.64]** *infra*.

244. An intention to occupy, however imminent, is probably not enough: *National Irish Bank Ltd v Graham* [1994] 2 ILRM 109 at 113-114 (*per* Finlay CJ).

245. See the second sentence of s 2(1): 'The expression ['family home'] comprises, in addition, a dwelling in which a spouse whose protection is in issue ordinarily resides or, if that spouse has left the other spouse, ordinarily resided before leaving.' See *Hegarty v Morgan* High Court, unrep, 15 March 1979 (1977/6037 P); *H & L v S* [1979] ILRM 105. Residence *before* leaving seems to essential : *Somers v W* [1979] IR 94 at 114 (*per* Griffin J).

246. *Bank of Ireland v Smyth* [1996] 1 ILRM 241; *Allied Irish Banks plc v O'Neill* [1996] ICLC 36.

247. Family Law Act 1995, s 54 (1)(*a*) of which substitutes a new s 2(2) in the 1976 Act. This comes into force on 1 August 1996 : see para **[16.70]** *infra*.

248. This is a concept used in the Landlord and Tenant Acts : see Wylie, *Irish Landlord and Tenant Law*, para 30.05.

249. Some commercial use is, therefore, permissible.

usual concept of a garden.[250] The new definition would seem designed to narrow down the amount of land around the dwelling which can be regarded as part of the family home.[251] Finally, it should be noted that the Act applies to dwellings which do not comprise land and so do not involve conveyancing, ie, "a vehicle or vessel, whether mobile or not, occupied as a separate dwelling".[252]

(c) *Alienation of an interest*: The Act affects an extremely wide range of *inter vivos*[253] transactions relating to property comprising a family home.[254] It covers the "conveyance" of an "interest". For these purposes "conveyance" includes a "mortgage, lease, assent, transfer, disclaimer, release and any other disposition of property otherwise than by a will or a *donatio mortis causa*" and "interest" means "any estate, right, title or other interest, legal or equitable".[255] And, as if that were not clear enough, "mortgage" is defined as including an equitable mortgage, a charge on registered land and a chattel mortgage.[256] Thus the Act applies to practically every *inter vivos* transaction likely to take place with respect to the family home, including the common equitable mortgage created by deposit of title documents.[257] It also applies to the common situation where a mortgage or charge on land covers not only loans already made but also further advances in the future.[258] However, the Act is aimed at dispositions by the owning

---

[250.] Note, however, that the original version of s 2(2) referred to "ground" in contradistinction to building and land. Thus it presumably excluded, eg the various outbuildings usually existing near the farmhouse on a farm. Under the new version they would appear to remain excluded as primarily used for commercial purposes, ie the farm business.

[251.] This is an important point in view of the possible scope for "severance": see para **[16.69]**, sub-para (d) *infra*. Care should also be taken where, eg part of the garden of an existing house is sold off as a building site. Although that site may have, as yet, no dwelling on it, it was part of the family home which comprises the existing house and so consent to the sale of the site may be needed; see the warning given by the Law Society's Conveyancing Committee in the *Gazette,* January/February 1984, p 15.

[252.] Section 2(2). This includes caravans, mobile homes, canal barges and boats.

[253.] It does not apply to dispositions by will or a *donatio mortis causa* (see the definition of "conveyance" in s 1(1)) presumably on the basis that the surviving spouse and children are protected by the provisions of Part IX of the Succession Act 1965: see Brady, *Succession Law in Ireland* (2nd ed, 1995), Ch 7. Note that s 121 of the 1965 Act covers an *inter vivos* disposition designed to disinherit the spouse or children: see *MPD v MD* [1981] ILRM 179. As regards an assent by a personal representative, see sub-para (d) *infra*.

[254.] *Somers v W* [1979] IR 94 at 113 (*per* Griffin J.).

[255.] See the definitions in s 1(1).

[256.] *Ibid.*

[257.] See *Bank of Ireland v Hanrahan* High Court, unrep, 10 February, 1987 (1985/100 Sp); *Bank of Ireland v Purcell* [1989] IR 327; *Allied Irish Banks plc v O'Neill* [1996] ICLC 36 (deposit of land certificate relating to farm).

[258.] *Bank of Ireland v Purcell* [1989] IR 327 at 330-331 (*per* Barron J), *aff'd* by Supreme Court (*per* Walsh J at p 333). Note, however, the provision for "general" consents contained in the Family Law Act 1995: see para **[16.69]** sub-para (h) *infra*.

spouse and so does not apply to the unilateral actions of a third party, such as a creditor on foot of a judgment mortgage registered against the home.[259] A judgment mortgage is a process of execution[260] over which the owning spouse has no control, but it is arguable that if that spouse has colluded with the creditor in enabling him to obtain the judgment which is registered,[261] this may amount to a disposition by that spouse coming within the Act.[262] The Act does, on the other hand, apply not only to a "conveyance" in the technical sense of the disposition which creates or transfers the interest in question but also to a contract - "an enforceable agreement (whether conditional or unconditional)".[263] In the case of a typical sale of land, where the parties initially enter into a contract for sale and later a deed of conveyance or transfer is executed,[264] this would suggest that the requisite consent is needed at both stages. However, the courts have taken the view that it is unlikely that the Oireachtas intended this and, if consent is given to the contract for sale, there is no need for a further consent to the conveyance giving effect to that contract.[265] Nevertheless, the obtaining of consent at both stages is standard practice because the danger about relying upon consent to the contract only[266] is that the consent may not be kept with the title deeds for reference in future dealings with the property. It is the better practice to have the requisite consent endorsed on the deed of a conveyance or transfer.[267]

(d) *Assents.* The inclusion of "assents" by personal representatives within the dispositions of property caught by the Act[268] is somewhat puzzling,

---

[259.] *Containercare (Ir) Ltd v Wycherley* [1982] IR 143; *Murray v Diamond* [1982] ILRM 113.

[260.] See *Irish Land Law* (2nd ed, 1986), para 13.163 *et seq.*

[261.] It is probable that the courts would require something more than merely getting into debt or acting irresponsibly in ignoring threats to take proceedings; it has been suggested that a failure to enter a defence to a claim which should have been defended might be enough: see Farrell, *Irish law of Specific Performance* (1994), para [7.15].

[262.] See *Murray v Diamond* [1982] ILRM 113 at 115 (*per* Barrington J). See also *Bank of Ireland v Purcell* [1989] IR 327 at 334 (*per* Walsh J).

[263.] See again the definition of "conveyance" in s 1(1). In view of the fact that the agreement must be "enforceable", presumably that Act does not apply when the condition is "precedent" to an agreement coming into force: see para **[7.03]** *ante.*

[264.] See para **[1.05]** *et seq, ante.*

[265.] *Kyne v Tiernan* High Court, unrep, 15 July 1980 (1978/6857 P), Transcript p 9 (*per* McWilliam J).

[266.] Conversely relying on consent to the conveyance only is impracticable since the absence of prior consent to the contract for sale renders the contract void. Either party could, therefore, refuse to execute the conveyance on the basis that there is no agreement to be put into affect by it and this is a risk which neither party would ordinarily wish to take. *Cf* where they decide to move quickly and to dispense with a prior contract and, instead, move immediately to execution of a conveyance or transfer.

[267.] See para **[16.69]**, sub-para (a) *infra.* This is the view of the Law Society's Conveyancing Committee, see the *Gazette,* May 1981, p 79.

[268.] Ie within the definition of "conveyance" in s 1(1).

especially since the Act otherwise excludes dispositions taking effect on a spouse's death.[269] Originally the Law Society's Conveyancing Committee advised that it was unnecessary to enquire into the position in relation to the Act where the purchaser was buying from a personal representative selling in that capacity.[270] In particular it was considered that the Act could bear no relevance to occupation of the premises by non-conveying beneficiaries. However, it came to be recognised that this advice was too simplistic and that particular danger existed where the personal representative is selling several years after the death. The point is that the personal representative may have been,[271] or be,[272] in occupation of the property and during this period it may have been his or her family home. After taking senior counsel's advice, the Committee issued new guidelines which, in essence, suggested that purchasers' solicitors should view the facts of each case carefully and seek appropriate declarations confirming the personal representative's position and consent of his or her spouse where appropriate.[273]

(e) *Company property.* On the face of it the Act should not apply where the property is being disposed of by a company, since a corporate body cannot have a family home.[274] However, the danger is that, although the company may own the property, it may have allowed an individual to occupy the property as his home under a tenancy, licence or other arrangement. Clearly the Act would apply to a disposition of that individual's interest but there is also the danger that the court would hold that the company is holding its interest in the property on trust for the individual, so that it applies also to the disposition of the company's interest.[275] This is a particular danger where the company is a small family company and the occupant is the controlling shareholder, or where the company provides the accommodation to a director or employee.[276] There is also the danger that the property has been put in the company's name as a device to get around the 1976 Act.[277] It is important, therefore, to determine in a particular case whether the property

---

[269] See sub-para (c) *supra.*

[270] Ie as part of the administration of the deceased's estate: see Brady, *Succession Law in Ireland* (2nd ed, 1995), para [10.61] *et seq.*

[271] Eg, while looking after the deceased in his or her latter days or nursing the deceased through an illness.

[272] Eg, the personal representative may be a relative who has always lived in the property or who moved in after the deceased's death.

[273] See the *Gazette,* April 1988, p 71. See also para **[16.64]** *infra.*

[274] See *Walpoles (Ir) Ltd v Jay* High Court, unrep, 20 November, 1980 (1980/996 Sp). See also *Carrigan v Carrigan* High Court, unrep, 2 May 1983 (1979/413 Sp).

[275] See *LB v HB* High Court, unrep, 31 July 1980 (1979/449 Sp).

[276] See the Law Society's Conveyancing Committee's Practice Note - "An Unmarried Company?", the *Gazette,* October 1983, p 217.

[277] See *Carrigan v Carrigan* High Court, unrep, 3 May, 1983 (1979/413 Sp), *per* O'Hanlon J (Transcript, p 8).

being disposed of by a company is occupied by any individual as a family home.

(f) *Joint disposition.* The primary purpose of the Act is to protect the "non-owning" spouse and the children against a disposition affecting the family home made by the "owning" spouse.[278] It has, therefore, been held by the Supreme Court that the Act does not apply where both spouses join in the disposition, by, eg both signing the contract for sale.[279]

(g) *Voidness.* The essential reason why conveyancers must beware of the Act is that it declares any disposition of an interest in the family home by the "owning" spouse "void" unless it had the "prior consent in writing of the other spouse" (ie the "non-owning" spouse).[280] Although the courts have over the years been somewhat ambiguous in their statements of the effect of this, it seems clear that "void" in this context should be given its technical meaning, ie, the disposition is "of no effect"[281] and not just voidable.[282] In recent cases involving mortgages and charges, the Supreme Court has emphasised that the effect of a failure to obtain the requisite prior consent is that the lender obtains no mortgage or charge over the family home, ie, no title to the property.[283]

(h) *Exceptions.* It is clear from the Act that there are several exceptions where the Act does not apply to a conveyance made by a spouse of the family home. One is where the conveyance is in favour of the other spouse.[284] Another is where the contract for sale is entered into before the marriage of the spouses in question; their subsequent marriage does not

---

[278.] See sub-para (a) *supra.*

[279.] *Nestor v Murphy* [1979] IR 326. See also *Barclays Bank Ireland v Carroll* High Court, unrep, 10 September 1986 (Bankruptcy). *Cf* a deed severing a joint tenancy: see the Circuit Court decision in *McCarthy v McCarthy* High Court, unrep, 1 May 1984; 30 ILT 216, discussed in Duncan and Scully, *Marriage Breakdown in Ireland: Law and Practice* (1990), pp 296-7.

[280.] Section 3(1). See *Bank of Ireland v Hanrahan*, High Court, unrep, 10 February, 1987 (1985 No 1000 Sp); *Somers v W* [1979] IR 326 at 328 (*per* McCarthy J).

[281.] See *Hamilton v Hamilton* [1982] IR 466 at 485-6 (*per* Henchy J); *Bank of Ireland v Purcell* [1989] 327 at 334 (*per* Walsh J). See the discussion in Farrell, *Irish Law of Specific Performance* (1994), para 7.18. Note, however, the effect of the Family Law Act 1995: para **[16.70]** *infra.*

[282.] In the sense that the disposition is valid until the non-owning spouse takes action to have it set aside ("avoided"). If such were the case, third parties could, in the meantime, acquire rights which took priority over the non-owning spouse's equitable right to apply for rescission. On this distinction, see Keane, *Equity and the Law of Trusts in the Republic of Ireland* (1988), Ch 14; Delany, *Equity and the Law of Trusts in Ireland* (1996), Ch 11.

[283.] *Bank of Ireland v Smyth* [1996] 1 ILRM 241. See also *Allied Irish Banks plc v Finnegan* [1996] ICLC 36.

[284.] Section 3(1) ("except the other spouse"). Note the exemption from stamp duty and other fees of any transaction creating a joint tenancy between the spouses: s 14 and para **[20.39]** *post.*

mean that prior consent is needed to a later conveyance giving effect to that contract.[285] However, far and away the most important exemption is where the conveyance is made to a "purchaser for full value".[286] To come within this exception the purchaser[287] must have given "such value as amounts or approximates to the value of that for which it is given".[288] Furthermore, the purchaser must have acted "in good faith".[289] The effect of these provisions is to incorporate the doctrine of constructive notice as enshrined in s 3 of the Conveyancing Act 1882,[290] ie, the purchaser must make appropriate "inquiries and inspections" in relation to the possible effect of the 1976 Act, in particular the need for consent from a non-owning spouse.[291] Indeed, the Act expressly extends the doctrine in this context, because a purchaser may be fixed with notice of information acquired by his solicitor in any capacity and not just, as provided by s 3 of the 1882 Act, while acting as solicitor for the purchaser.[292]

(i) *Burden of proof.* The Act reiterates the incorporation of the doctrine of constructive notice by providing that, if any question arises in any proceedings as to whether a conveyance is valid, the burden of proving validity is on the person alleging it.[293] This point cannot be emphasised too strongly. As the Supreme Court has recently stressed, if, for example, a non-owning spouse challenges the enforceability of a mortgage or charge against the family home, on the basis that his or her consent was not obtained as required under the Act, it is for the lender to prove that such consent was, indeed, obtained.[294]

---

[285] Section 3(2). See also *Hamilton v Hamilton* [1982] IR 466, especially at 477 (*per* O'Higgins CJ).

[286] Section 3(3)(*a*). Sub-para (*b*) excepts conveyances to purchasers "for value" by a person other than a spouse, but it is not clear why this was needed since s 3(1) renders void only a conveyance by "a spouse". Note, however, the explanation for this somewhat ambiguous provision given by the Law Reform Commission: see para **[16.70]**, fn 378 *infra*. Sub-para (*c*) excepts any conveyance which depends for its validity on the validity of a conveyance which itself comes within the other exemptions. Note also the provisions of the Family Law Act 1995, para **[16.70]** *infra*.

[287] Note, of course, that "purchaser" in this context means any person acquiring an estate or interest in the family home, including, eg, a lessee, assignee, mortgagee or chargee: s 3(6).

[288] Section 3(5).

[289] Section 3(6).

[290] See para **[4.02]** *ante*.

[291] See *Hamilton v Hamilton* [1982] IR 466.

[292] Section 3(7). See para **[4.02]** *ante*. It must, however, still be information gained in the "same transaction", eg, where the solicitor was also acting for the vendor: see *H & L v S* [1979] ILRM 105 at 108 (*per* McWilliam J).

[293] Section 3(4).

[294] *Bank of Ireland v Smyth* [1996] 1 IR 241; *AIB plc v Finnegan* [1996] 1 ILRM 401: see para **[16.69]** sub-para (b) *infra*.

(ii) Requisitions

[16.63] It follows from what has been said above that it has become essential for purchasers' solicitors to ensure that appropriate requisitions[295] are raised in respect of the Family Home Protection Act 1976. As Henchy J said in *Somers v W*:[296]

> "He must ascertain if the property, because of its present and past use, is a family home within the meaning of the Act of 1976. If it is, he must find out if it is a sale by a spouse and if so whether the conveyance should be preceded by the consent in writing of the other spouse so as to prevent its being rendered void under Section 3. If that other spouse omits or refuses to consent the purchaser should require the vendor to apply to the court for an order under Section 4 of the Act dispensing with the consent."[297]

It is compliance with these requirements that Requisition 24 in the Law Society's standard form is designed to achieve. In essence it requires the vendor's solicitor to confirm whether or not the property the subject of the sale or other disposition, or any part of it, is a family home within the 1976 Act - either the vendor's or any other person's.[298] It then requires the vendor's solicitor to furnish statutory declarations verifying the responses to these questions, exhibiting, as necessary, a copy of the civil marriage certificate covering the vendor and previous vendors in conveyances of the property made on or after 12 July 1976.[299]

(iii) Statutory Declarations

[16.64] Over the years considerable thought has been given as to the form and content of the declarations and in 1993 the Law Society's Conveyancing Committee and the Joint Committee of the Building Society Solicitors and the Law Society approved revised forms prepared by the Conveyancing Committee of the Dublin Solicitors Bar Association. There are eleven forms

---

[295.] Given that the Act also voids the contract for sale if the prior consent is not obtained, this is a classic case where the requisitions should be raised as *pre*-contract enquiries: see paras **[5.01]** *et seq* and **[5.08]** *ante*.

[296.] [1979] IR 94.

[297.] *Ibid*, p 111. See also *H & L v s* [1979] ILRM 105 at 108 (*per* McWilliam J).

[298.] The reference to "other person" covers, eg the case of an individual occupying property owned by a company: see para **[16.62]**, sub-para (e) *supra*.

[299.] The 1976 Act had no retrospective operation: see *Hamilton v Hamilton* [1982] IR 466. Note that in the case of registered land, a purchaser is not concerned with previous transfers because, in the absence of fraud, he is entitled to rely upon the conclusiveness of the register: see *Guckian v Brennan* [1981] IR 478 and para **[16.70]** fn 374 *infra*. In the case of unregistered land, a purchaser may, of course, after 12 years acquire a good possessory title as a result of the doctrine of adverse possession: see para **[14.80]** *ante* and **[16.70]** fn 376 *infra*.

covering the following situations: (1) where the family home is owned by one of the spouses; (2) where the family home is owned by both spouses; (3) where the spouses declare that the property is not a family home; (4) where a widow or widower declares that it is not a family home; (5) where a single person who has never been married is selling; (6) where a previously married person is selling after a decree of nullity; (7) where the spouses have separated; (8) where a company owns and has full commercial use of the property;[300] (9) where an executor[301] is selling; (10) where the vendor is conveying in accordance with a deed of separation; (11) where vendor is selling subsequent to the property being vested in him or her alone under a deed of separation. A number of points should be noted about these declaration forms.

[16.65] First, given the "official" approval of the forms, it would be unwise practice to depart from them.[302] In each case the form specifies the facts or grounds verifying the declaration in question and the courts seem to accept that the purchaser's solicitor should not seek to go behind the declaration unless there is a good reason to do so.[303] In essence the purchaser's solicitor is entitled to assume that what is stated is true unless he has information suggesting the contrary and such an assumption will not call into question the purchaser's "good faith".[304] On the other hand, it will clearly not be "good faith" to collude with the vendor making an obviously false statement or "a wild and inaccurate leap in the dark".[305]

[16.66] Secondly, each of the declarations also covers the possible effect of the Family Law Act 1981 and Judicial Separation and Family Law Reform Act 1989.[306] These Acts are the subject of separate requisitions on the Law Society's form and are considered later in this chapter.[307]

[300.] See para **[16.62]**, sub-para (e) *supra*.

[301.] Despite its title, the form itself deals with a personal representative (see para 3 thereof): see para **[16.62]**, sub-para (d) *supra*.

[302.] See, however, para **[16.67]** *infra*.

[303.] *Reynolds v Waters* [1982] ILRM 335. See also *Martin v Irish Permanent Building Society* High Court, unrep, 30 July 1980 (1980/608 Sp). The facts must, of course, be set out: *Hegarty v Morgan* High Court, unrep, 15 March 1979 (1977/6077 P).

[304.] See para **[16.62]**, sub-para (h) *supra*. The Law Society's Conveyancing Committee has stated that a purchaser's or mortgagee's solicitor should not require a separation agreement to be exhibited, as this is likely to contain highly confidential and private information: see the *Gazette*, January/February 1995, p 11.

[305.] *Somers v W* [1979] IR 94 at 107 (*per* Henchy J); *cf* McCarthy J at p 127.

[306.] Note that Part II (other than s 35) of the 1989 Act has been repealed by the Family Law Act 1995 (which comes into force on 1 August 1996 - Family Law Act 1995 (Commencement) Order, 1996, (SI 46/1996) and replaced by Part II of the 1995 Act.

[307.] See paras **[16.72]** and **[16.73]** *infra*.

[16.67] Thirdly, each of the forms include a declaration that the party or parties making it understand the effect and import of the declaration "which have been fully explained to me (us) by my (our) solicitor". This raises what has become an increasingly important point so far as the courts are concerned. As we shall see,[308] in cases where consent of a non-owning spouse is needed, the Supreme Court has recently emphasised that the party relying on the validity of that consent must prove[309] that it is "informed" consent.[310] This burden will not be discharged unless it is established that the non-owning spouse had the nature and import of the consent fully explained to him, or her, and, furthermore, that it was suggested that he or she should obtain independent legal advice.[311] Form 1 of the 1993 revised declarations arguably covers this since paragraph 2 contains the following statement:

> "I (other spouse) fully understand the nature and import of this consent. I have been advised that I have the right to be independently advised in connection therewith and I have waived this right."

In the case of a straightforward sale of the family home, it would seem that the purchaser's solicitor can rely on this statement and need not seek corroboration from the vendor's solicitor that what is stated is true.[312] Where, however, a mortgage or charge over the family home is being created, either as part of the purchase (where a portion of the purchase money is being loaned by a bank or building society, or other lending institution) or subsequently by the spouse in whose name the property is held, the solicitor acting for the lender,[313] who is often also the purchaser's solicitor, must see that such an explanation of the nature and effect of the transaction is given to the non-owning spouse giving consent and that the suggestion as to obtaining independent legal advice is made to that spouse.[314]

[16.68] Fourthly, the requisite statutory declaration from the vendor must be furnished in draft form with the replies to the requisitions, so that it can be approved by the purchaser's solicitor. The completed declaration should, of course, be handed over on closing, though, if the form has been agreed, failure to do so may not invalidate a notice to complete served by the vendor.[315] A dispute as to whether or not the particular declaration should be

---

[308.] See para **[16.69]**, sub-para (b) *infra*.

[309.] See para **[16.62]**, sub-para (i) *supra*.

[310.] *Bank of Ireland v Smyth* [1996] 1 ILRM 241; *Allied Irish Banks plc v Finnegan* [1996] 1 ILRM 401.

[311.] See para **[16.69]**, sub-para (c) *infra*.

[312.] See para **[16.65]** *supra*.

[313.] Or other agent of the lender, eg, the bank manager: see *Bank of Ireland v Smyth, op cit*.

[314.] See further para **[16.69]**, sub-para (c) *infra*.

[315.] See *Dublin Laundry Co v Clarke* [1989] ILRM 29.

relied upon, or whether the vendor should be required to furnish corroboration, or better evidence of title, may be dealt with by a vendor and purchaser summons.[316]

(iv) Consent

[16.69] It is the essential requirement of the 1976 Act that consent is obtained from the non-owning spouse prior to any disposition by the other spouse relating to the family home. There are several crucial aspects to this.

(a) *Form*: No particular form of such consent is prescribed except that it must be "in writing" and "prior" to the "conveyance" in question.[317] Although, as we have seen, there is strictly no necessity to have a consent to both the contract and conveyance,[318] it is usual to have it endorsed on both the contract and the deed of conveyance. The forms recommended by the Law Society[319] are as follows:

For the contract:

> "I, _____ being the spouse of the within-named Vendor hereby consent to the proposed sale of the property described in the within Contract (Conditions) at the price of £__ and hereby irrevocably agree to endorse a Consent in writing on any Assurance of the said property by the Vendor in furtherance of the within Contract (Conditions) for the purposes of Section 3 of the Family Home Protection Act 1976."

For the conveyance:

> "I, _____ being the spouse of the within-named Vendor hereby consent for the purposes of Section 3 of the Family Home Protection Act 1976, to the sale by the Vendor of the within premises for the sum of £__."

The wording should obviously be adapted for dispositions not involving a sale and purchase, so that, eg, "Mortgagor" may be substituted for "Vendor". An alternative to endorsing the consent on the deed is to include it as one of the certificates in the deed itself, but care must be taken to ensure that the non-owning spouse executes the deed before any of the other parties and the certificate should confirm this. The advantage of including the consent in the deed in the case of unregistered land is that it can be recorded

---

[316.] *Martin v Irish Permanent Building Society* High Court, unrep, 30 July 1980 (1980/608 Sp); *Mulligan v Dillon* High Court, unrep, 7 November 1980 (1980/966 Sp); *Guckian v Brennan* [1982] IR 478; *Reynolds v Waters* [1982] ILRM 335. See para **[13.26]** *et seq, ante*.

[317.] Section 3(1).

[318.] See para **[16.62]**, sub-para (c) *supra*.

[319.] In a letter sent by the President to members dated 23 July 1976. Note, however, that a shortened version of the form for the contract is now printed on p1 of the Law Society's *General Conditions of Sale (1995 ed)*: see Appendix II *post*.

in the memorial registered in the Registry of Deeds. This would be good secondary evidence of the consent if the deed itself were subsequently lost.

(b) *Informed:* We saw earlier that the courts insist now that the purchaser, mortgagee or other party relying upon the consent has the burden of proving that the consent is an "informed" one.[320] In *Bank of Ireland v Smyth*[321] the Court[322] laid down two requirements in this regard: (1) the non-owning spouse giving the consent must have full knowledge of what he or she is doing; (2) he or she should be given the opportunity to obtain independent legal advice on the matter. This decision arose in the context where the non-owning spouse had signed a consent to a charge over a farm to secure existing and future borrowings by her husband. The Court held that the bank's charge was unenforceable because the wife mistakenly believed that it applied only to the farm land and not to the farmhouse.[323] It was not suggested that the bank contributed to this belief, nor, indeed, that the bank owed the wife any duty of care.[324] Rather the Court took the view that the doctrine of constructive notice, as incorporated into the 1976 Act,[325] imposed a duty on the bank to itself, *viz,* to take steps to ensure that it got a valid charge.[326] This involved ensuring that the wife's consent was an informed one and seeing that the two steps stated above were carried out. In that case, the charge had been arranged by its branch manager and he had failed to carry out those steps when he called the farmer and his wife into the branch to sign the charge and consent documents. In *Allied Irish Banks plc v Finnegan*[327] the Court[328] reiterated its view in a case of a typical house purchase mortgage loan, where the wife alleged that her consent was vitiated by her mistaken belief that the documents she had signed related to a joint purchase and mortgage of the couple's new home, rather than consent to a purchase of the house in her husband's sole name and his mortgage of it to the bank to secure a substantial portion of the purchase price. In this case, as is commonly the situation,[329] the couple's solicitor was also acting for the

---

[320.] See paras **[16.62]**, sub-para (i) and **[16.67]** *supra.*

[321.] [1996] 1 ILRM 241.

[322.] The judgment of the Court was given by Blayney J.

[323.] The Court refused to decide the question of "severance" because the point had not been argued in the court below: see [1993] 2 IR 102.

[324.] This had been the approach of Geoghegan J in the court below, relying on recent English authorities: see para **[1.35]** *ante.*

[325.] See para **[16.62]**, sub para (h) *supra.*

[326.] This is the significance of the conveyance being "void": see para **[16.62]** sub-para (g) *supra.*

[327.] [1996] 1 ILRM 401.

[328.] Again the judgment of the Court was given by Blayney J.

[329.] See para **[1.35]** *ante.*

bank and the Court held that the burden lay on the bank to establish that the solicitor had taken the steps to ensure that the wife's consent was "informed".[330]

(c) *Independent advice*: The *Smyth* and *Finnegan* decisions established at the very least that in any case where a mortgage or charge is involved, it is essential to the validity of the lender's title[331] that not only should the consenting spouse have the implications of the transaction fully explained but also the suggestion of obtaining independent advice should be made. In this context "independent" must mean independent of the lender's agent, so that if the solicitor for the other spouse (the borrower) is also acting as solicitor for the lender, the advice would have to be obtained from someone else. In *Smyth* Blayney J. used the expression "independent advice", so that arguably it does not have to be "legal" advice in the sense of being given by another solicitor. However, for the suggestion to be effective in discharging the lender's duty to see that the consent is "informed", it must be a suggestion of advice to be obtained from someone competent to explain the full implications of the transaction and to answer queries about what has already been said by way of explanation, so that arguably, the safest course is to suggest independent legal advice. Blayney J also used the expression "suggestion" which seems to indicate that the Supreme Court took the view that, once the suggestion is made, it is for the non-owning spouse to decide whether to act on it. It is difficult to believe that the Court expects the bank's agent to pressure that spouse into acting on the advice,[332] still less that the agent should check that any advice sought is competent or appropriate.[333] The lender should insist upon the borrower's solicitor, who is also acting for

---

[330.] The actual decision on the appeal was that the court below had been wrong to deal with this issue on the basis of affidavit evidence only and so directed that the matter be remitted to be determined at a plenary hearing on oral evidence. It is important to note that the solicitors firm had filed an affidavit disputing the wife's account of what happened in its office.

[331.] Or, to put it another way, to prevent the mortgage or charge being held void under the 1976 Act.

[332.] Except, perhaps, in a case where the agent has doubts as to whether the non-owning spouse had the capacity to understand the explanation of the implications of the transaction. The court may set aside an "improvident" transaction even though full value was given: *Grealish v Murphy* [1946] IR 35 at 49-50 (*per* Gavan Duffy J). Increasingly the courts look to receipt of independent legal advice to counter a claim for rescission of a transaction entered into by a person suffering from a disadvantage like weakness of mind or old age: see *McQuirk v Branigan* High Court, unrep, 9 November 1992 (Cir App); Delany, *Equity and the Law of Trusts in Ireland* (1996), p 490 *et seq.*

[333.] This has certainly been approach of the English courts in the analogous context where it is alleged that a transaction is vitiated by some factor such as duress or undue influence: see *Massey v Midland Bank plc* [1995] 1 All ER 929; *Banco Exterior Internacional v Mann* [1995] 1 All ER 936; *cf TSB Bank plc v Camfield* [1995] 1 All ER 951; Sanfey, 'Consenting Adults: The Implications of *Bank of Ireland v Smyth*' (1996) 3 CLP 31.

it, confirming in writing that the explanation has been given and the suggestion has been made. Where the lender has not instructed the borrower's solicitor to act for it, it is probably sufficient to require the borrower's solicitor to confirm in writing that he has explained the transaction fully to the non-owning spouse giving consent.[334] It must surely be appropriate to rely upon the professional skill and expertise of the borrower's solicitor in this regard and to leave it to his judgment whether, eg, to interview the non-owning spouse separately from the borrower.[335] *A fortiori,* in a case where the non-owning spouse is consenting to the sale of the family home, it would seem sufficient for the purchaser's solicitor to rely upon advice given by the vendor's solicitor and the declaration contained in the standard form.[336]

(d) *Severance*: It will be recalled that the issue of validity of the bank's charge over the farm in *Bank of Ireland v Smyth*[337] stemmed from the non-owning spouse's mistaken belief that the charge related to the farm land only and did not include the farmhouse. The point was raised before the Supreme Court whether this belief could be acted upon, so as to "sever" the charge by regarding it as valid at least against the farm land. The Supreme Court refused to decide this issue because the point had not been argued in the court below,[338] but Blayney J., in giving the Court's judgment, cast great doubt upon whether it was appropriate to sever a charge in such circumstances. He relied upon the view expressed by Costello J, sitting as a member of the Supreme Court in *Hamilton v Hamilton*,[339] that the argument for severance was "not sustainable".[340] This view seems to have been based on the principle that s 3(1) of the 1976 Act rendered void "the purported conveyance" which relates to "any interest in the family home"[341] and the whole conveyance either stands or falls according to whether or not either the requisite consent was obtained or it is covered by one of the exceptions.[342] This was despite the fact that at least one previous case was

---

[334.] See the English cases cited in fn 333 *supra*.

[335.] This might be appropriate where the solicitor suspects that the borrower may be exercising undue influence over the non-owning spouse or that some other potentially vitiating factor is at play: see fn 332 *supra*.

[336.] See para **[16.67]** *supra*.

[337.] See sub-para (b) *supra*.

[338.] [1993] 2 IR 102.

[339.] [1982] IR 466. His views were strictly *obiter* and Costello J was dissenting from the majority decision that the 1976 Act had no retrospective operation.

[340.] *Ibid* p 490. *Cf* the view of the English Court of Appeal in *TSB Bank plc v Camfield* [1995] 1 All ER 951, where it refused to hold a charge partially valid, ie, for the fixed amount the husband had misrepresented to his wife.

[341.] See Farrell, *Irish Law of Specific Performance* (1994), para [7.12].

[342.] See para **[16.62]**, sub-para (h) *supra*.

cited to the Court in which the judge had, indeed, agreed to sever a charge.[343] The issue arose directly in *Allied Irish Banks plc v O'Neill*,[344] a case where the owning farmer had deposited the land certificate with the bank to secure, by way of equitable mortgage,[345] various loans. The non-owning spouse (her husband) had never given any consent and the bank accepted that its mortgage was not enforceable against the "family home". However, it argued that it was enforceable against the remainder of the farm land and Laffoy J. accepted this argument. In her view, notwithstanding the views expressed by the Supreme Court in *Bank of Ireland v Smyth*:

> "... whether a literal or a purposive approach is adopted to the construction of subsection (1) of section 3 to ascertain the intention of the legislature as to the effect of non-compliance with the prior consent requirement in relation to a conveyance of the family home, as defined, and other property included in the same instrument or transaction the result is the same. The purpose of the Act of 1976 is to protect the family home defined therein. A construction of subsection (1) which limits the invalidating effect to the family home, as defined, is entirely consistent with the legislative scheme as expressed in the Act of 1976 as a whole and fulfills its purpose."[346]

The key point is that the Oireachtas went to great pains in the 1976 Act to define what amounts to a "family home"[347] and, thereby, to limit the Act's protection to that property. It clearly contemplated that such property would often form part of a larger property and so there seems to be no reason in principle why the court should not apply the definition to the transaction in question. As the Supreme Court recognised in the *Smyth* case this will involve a finding of fact, ie, what part of the property may be said to constitute the dwelling and "any garden or portion of ground attached to and usually occupied with the dwelling or otherwise required for the amenity or convenience of the dwelling".[348] Laffoy J took the view that making such a finding "does not present any insuperable difficulty"[349] and so she adjourned the proceedings to enable the parties to consider the position and to make submissions on a resumed hearing. It remains to be seen how the Supreme Court will react to this holding, but it is to be hoped that the Court will revise

---

[343.] *Bank of Ireland v Slevin* High Court, unrep, 16 February 1989 (Cir App).

[344.] [1996] ICLC 36.

[345.] See *Irish Land Law* (2nd ed, 1986), para [12.29].

[346.] *Op cit* p 43.

[347.] And note the revised definition introduced by s 54(1) of the Family Law Act 1995: see para **[16.62]**, sub-para (b) *supra* and fn 340 *infra*.

[348.] 1976 Act, s 2, or as from 1 August 1996, "any garden or other land usually occupied with the dwelling, being land that is subsidiary and ancillary to it, is required for amenity or convenience and is not being used or developed primarily for commercial purposes".

[349.] *Op cit* p 43.

the view expressed earlier. It must be remembered that the consequences of refusing to allow a severance in appropriate cases can be very serious. In *Bank of Ireland v Smyth*, the bank was owed some £180,000 (in the *O'Neill* case it was some £50,000) and the refusal to sever the charge meant that it lost its entire security. It is difficult to see how the interests of justice are served by such a refusal, when a different interpretation of the 1976 Act would still achieve the protection of the non-owning spouse and children in the family home which the Court was so anxious to achieve.

(e) *Disability*: Where a spouse is incapable of giving consent by reason of "unsoundness of mind or other mental disability" or cannot be found after reasonable inquiries, the court may give consent on his or her behalf, if it appears to the court to be reasonable to do so.[350] It was pointed out in the first edition of this book[351] that this did not seem to cover a spouse who was still a minor and who could, under the general law[352] repudiate on attaining majority any consent given previously.[353] This omission was corrected by s 10 of the Family Law Act 1981, which validates consents given by minor spouses.[354]

(f) *Omission or refusal*: Where a non-owning spouse omits or refuses to consent, the court may, if it considers it, in all the circumstances, unreasonable to withhold consent, dispense with it.[355] If there are difficulties of this kind the purchaser's solicitor must insist upon the vendor applying for a court order before the contract is entered into, for a consent cannot be dispensed with retrospectively.[356]

(g) *Desertion*: The court has a similar power to dispense with consent where the non-owning spouse has deserted and continues to desert the other spouse.[357] Again the purchaser's solicitor should insist upon such an order being obtained, where necessary, before the contract is entered into.

[350.] 1976 Act, s 4(4).

[351.] Para 6.45. Note that in 1978 the age of majority was still 21 and was not reduced to 18 until the Age of Majority Act 1985 came into force.

[352.] See *Slator v Trimble* (1861) 14 ICLR 342; *Irish Land Law* (2nd ed, 1986), para 25.06.

[353.] See *Lloyd v Sullivan* High Court, unrep, 6 March 1981 (1982/39 Sp).

[354.] Including consents given before the 1981 Act and those given by guardians. Prior to the Act applications were often made for a court order under s 11 of the Guardianship of Infants Act 1964: See Duncan and Scully, *Marriage Breakdown in Ireland: Law and Practice* (1990), para 11.031.

[355.] 1976 Act, s 4(1) and (2). See the discussion by Costello J in *Hamilton v Hamilton* [1982] IR 466 at 498-9 and by Duncan and Scully, *op cit*, para 11.024 *et seq*.

[356.] *Somers v W* [1979] IR 94. See also *Hamilton v Hamilton* [1982] IR 466.

[357.] Note that "desertion" includes conduct by the non-owning spouse which leads the owning spouse, with just cause, to leave the family home and live separately: s 4(3).

(h) *General*: One of the great concerns about the operation of the 1976 Act has always been that its provisions seem to apply every time a new disposition takes place with respect to the family home. To take a common case, frequently a bank will arrange a loan secured on the property which involves an initial advance at the time the loan is first secured and an arrangement whereby the borrower may draw down further amounts, usually up to a set limit. Each such further advance, or borrowing, alters the amount secured by the mortgage or charge and involves a "conveyance" within s 3(1) of the Act to which fresh consent of the non-owning spouse is required. This was the view of Barron J. in *Bank of Ireland v Purcell*[358] and it was upheld by the Supreme Court.[359] The question arises as to whether a "general" or "blanket" consent given at the beginning would cover such subsequent transactions. Doubts have been expressed as to whether a court would accept this as sufficient, given the purpose of the Act to protect the non-owning spouse and children and the likelihood that the family circumstances might change substantially since the general consent was given.[360] This matter will, however, be resolved, at least to some extent, as from 1 August 1996 when the Family Law Act 1995 comes into force.[361] Section 54(1)(b) of that Act inserts a new sub-s (9) in s 3 of the 1976 Act, which reads:

(9) If, whether before or after the passing of the *Family Law Act 1995*, a spouse gives a general consent in writing to any future conveyance of any interest in a dwelling that is or was the family home of that spouse and the deed for any such conveyance is executed after the date of that consent, the consent shall be deemed, for the purposes of subsection (1), to be a prior consent in writing of the spouse to that conveyance.

A number of points should be noted about this provision. First, when it comes into force, it will operate retrospectively, so that a general consent already given may be effective. Secondly, such a consent operates to validate only "conveyances"[362] executed after it is given. Thirdly, as in the case of consents under the Act generally, no particular form is prescribed,

---

[358.] [1989] IR 327.

[359.] *Ibid* p 333 (*per* Walsh J).

[360.] Arguably there was nothing in principle in the 1976 Act to rule out a general consent: see Laffoy, *Irish Conveyancing Precedents*, p J9 and Precedent **J.1.5.** The existence of such a prior general consent might also be a factor taken into account where an application is made for a court order dispensing with consent on the ground that it is being unreasonably withheld in a later transaction: see Farrell, *Irish Law of Specific Performance* (1994), para [7.17] and sub-para (f) *supra*.

[361.] Family Law Act 1995 (Commencement) Order 1996 (SI 46/1996).

[362.] Ie, this has the wide meaning given by the 1976 Act and so includes contracts as well as various dispositions other than a sale involving the family home: see para **[16.62]**, sub-para (c) *supra*. Presumably the subsequent reference to "the deed" is not meant to cut down the earlier reference to "any future conveyance of any interest".

but a general consent must also be in writing.[363] The forms previously recommended by the Law Society are not suitable[364] because they are designed for inclusion in the contract, and endorsement on the deed giving effect to it, relating to one particular transaction. The whole point of a general consent is to avoid the need for this in subsequent transactions. Thus something along the following lines would seem to be appropriate:

> "I, _____ being the spouse of _____ hereby give my general consent for the purposes of section 3(9) of the Family Home Protection Act 1976, to any future conveyance of any interest in the property described below: _____"

Such a consent would cover any form of future transaction and the wording of the new subsection seems to contemplate this type of consent. It is not clear whether a more limited "general" consent comes within it, eg, a consent, in the case of a mortgage or charge securing a loan, which is designed to cover only further advances to be secured by that same mortgage or charge.[365] Notwithstanding the language of subs (9), it is difficult to believe that the Oireachtas did not intend to validate also such limited general consent. It is also arguable that, at least, an unlimited consent, in the sense that it covers any transaction, still comes within the subsection if it is restricted as to the period of its operation. Fourthly, the previous point illustrates the potentially extremely wide-ranging consequences for a non-owning spouse giving a general consent. Although the subsection makes no reference to the need for independent advice, it should be assumed that the courts will be even more vigilant in insisting that any general consent is truly "informed" consent.[366] This will be especially the case where the general consent is unlimited, so that the non-owning spouse is giving up the right to veto any type of *inter vivos* transaction which the other spouse may decide to engage in. Lastly, solicitors will have to take precautions in the future if general consents come to be widely used in practice. Quite apart from the point about the need for "informed" consent, it would seem essential that any conveyance executed in reliance on a general consent should at least contain a recital to this effect.[367] Furthermore, a purchaser's solicitor should insist upon production of the original general consent in the chain of title, or a certified copy, before closing the sale, by analogy with the case where a deed is executed under a power of attorney.[368] *A fortiori*, the purchaser's

---

[363.] See para **[16.69]**, sub-para (a) *supra*.

[364.] See *ibid*.

[365.] Ie, the *Bank of Ireland v Purcell* situation, see *supra*.

[366.] See sub-paras (b) and (c) *supra*.

[367.] There is, of course, nothing to prevent endorsing on or attaching to each such conveyance a certified copy of the general consent and this may be considered "good practice".

solicitor needs to see the general consent where the sale to his client is covered by it. In this respect the general consent becomes a vital title document which should be kept with the title deeds for future reference.

(i) *Power of attorney*: In principle there is no reason why a consent required under the 1976 Act, whether one given to a particular transaction or a general consent, should not be given by a properly authorised agent. One way of arranging this is for the non-owning spouse to give someone else a power of attorney, which may be a general power or one specific to a particular transaction.[369] The Law Society's Conveyancing Committee has rightly warned practitioners of the need to advise spouses as to the wisdom of giving such a power to someone else.[370] If a non-owning spouse should not give consent without being made fully aware of the implications, there is even more reason for him or her to be made aware of the implications of giving someone else the power to give consent. The Committee pointed out[371] that a power of attorney cannot confer on the agent any power to make the usual statutory declarations verifying facts relating to marriage and so on.[372] These must be made by the parties themselves and any declaration by an agent would be hearsay and inadmissible in evidence.[373]

(v) Family Law Act 1995

[16.70] The particular dangers from the conveyancing point of view created by the Family Home Protection Act 1976, stem from the fact that any conveyance of the family home without the requisite spouse's consent is void[374] in the case of unregistered land. The result is that a purchaser of property is at risk if the consent was not obtained in any transaction in the chain of title since 1976. It must be remembered that the consent had to be given in each case prior to the transaction in question;[375] there is no question

---

[368.] See *Re Copeliu's Contract* [1937] 4 All ER 447, but note that s 3(3) of the Conveyancing Act 1881 (still in force in Ireland) does not have the exceptions attached to s 45(1) of the English Law of Property Act 1925, in respect of pre-root title documents: para **[14.59]** *ante*.

[369.] See *Irish Land Law* (2nd ed, 1986), para 11.29 *et seq* and para **[18.129]** *post*.

[370.] The *Gazette*, April 1992, p 97.

[371.] *Ibid*.

[372.] See para **[16.64]** *supra*.

[373.] See Fennell, *The Law of Evidence in Ireland* (1992), Ch 9.

[374.] See para **[16.62]**, sub-para (g) *supra*. In the case of registered land, once the transfer is registered the transfer is protected by the rule that the register is conclusive: see s 31 of the Registration of Title Act 1964. Thus a subsequent purchaser need not be concerned with previous transfers and enquiries or requisitions are required only in respect of the immediate vendor and his or her spouse; *Guckian v Brennan* (1981) IR 478 at 488-9 (*per* Gannon J). See also *Barclays Bank Ireland v Carroll* High Court, unrep, 10 September 1986 (Bankruptcy).

[375.] Para **[16.69]**, sub-para (a) *supra*.

of the position being retrieved by getting a subsequent consent and the courts have no power to dispense with consent retrospectively.[376] With the passage of time the danger that the validity of a whole series of transactions might be called into question increased. The Law Reform Commission also pointed out that a particular problem arose from the fact that the practice of seeking appropriate statutory declarations to evidence facts relevant to the application of the 1976 Act began only gradually after its enactment and many subsequent transactions would stand on somewhat shaky evidentiary ground.[377] The Commission recommended that where a conveyance had been implemented without objection by the non-owning spouse for over six years, it should be deemed always to have been valid.[378] This recommendation has, at long last, made its way into legislation through s 54(1)(b)(ii) of the Family Law Act 1995, which comes into force on 1 August 1996.[379] This adds a new sub-s (8) to s 3 of the 1976 Act, whereunder proceedings cannot be instituted to have a conveyance declared void "after the expiration of 6 years from the date of the conveyance".[380] It is, then, provided that a conveyance shall be deemed not to be and never to have been void for failure to get the requisite prior consent unless *either* it was declared void in proceedings before the *passing*[381] of the 1995 Act or on or after that date and brought within 6 years of the date of the conveyance[382] *or* the parties to the conveyance, or their successors in title, state in writing that it is void for lack of consent within 6 years from the date of the conveyance[383]

[376.] *Ibid*, sub-para (f) *supra,* of course, once a purchaser or his predecessors in title have been in undisputed possession for at least 12 years after the void conveyance, a good possessory title may be acquired under the doctrine of adverse possession: see para **[14.80]** *ante.*

[377.] See its Report on *Land Law and Conveyancing Law: (1) General Proposals* (LRC 30 - 1989), para 39 *et seq.* The Law Society's Conveyancing Committee was also aware of this problem and recommended that solicitors should rely on consents endorsed on the deeds without seeking supporting evidence of the identity of the spouses where this was not available: see the *Gazette*, June 1981, p 115.

[378.] The Commission reported that apparently the draftsman of the Act thought that he had covered subsequent conveyances to purchasers for value in the exception in s 3(3)(*b*) relating to a conveyance by "a person other than the spouse making the purported conveyance" void under s 3(1). This, however, is difficult to square with meaning of "void" as interpreted by the courts (see para **[16.62]**, sub-para (g) *supra*). The notion of a void conveyance becoming valid later as a result of a subsequent conveyance is, as the Commission commented, "completely foreign to the basic doctrines of the law of property": *ibid*, para 41.

[379.] Family Law Act 1995 (Commencement) Order 1996 (SI 46/1996).

[380.] Subsection (8)(a)(i). Rules of court are to require the registration of such proceedings as a *lis pendens*: subs (8)(d).

[381.] Ie, 30 September 1995, *not* its date of commencement (see fn 379 *supra*).

[382.] Subsection (8)(b)(i).

[383.] Subsection (8)(b)(ii). Note that the non-consenting spouse cannot apparently do this on her own: see para **[16.71]** *infra.*

and a certified copy of this statement is registered, as appropriate, in the Land Registry[384] or Registry of Deeds.[385]

[16.71] A number of points should be noted about these provisions. First, the 6-year limitation period on proceedings does *not* apply to a spouse "who has been in actual occupation of the land concerned from immediately before the expiration of 6 years from the date of the conveyance concerned until the institution of the proceedings".[386] This somewhat convoluted provision seems designed to protect a spouse who has remained in occupation but whose consent was not obtained to an earlier transaction. The classic example would be where the family home has been mortgaged by the other spouse, perhaps several times over.[387] The result is that the new provision does not protect lenders, unless the non-consenting spouse ceases to be in actual occupation before proceedings are brought. Rather it is designed to cover cases where the family home has been sold, with the spouses vacating possession in the usual way. After 6 years a purchaser or other person can accept the conveyance on sale as valid under the 1976 Act unless either proceedings have been instituted or the parties to that conveyance, or their successors in title, have registered a statement declaring it void. These matters will be disclosed by the usual searches.[388] Secondly, by requiring the initiation of such proceedings or the registration of a statement the 1995 Act has altered the whole approach of the 1976 Act. The non-owning spouse must take action to have the conveyance without consent avoided, so that, in cases where the spouse does not remain in occupation, the conveyance is, in effect, voidable rather than void.[389] That, however, raises a third point. The registration of a statement,[390] which is the alternative to proceedings to declare a conveyance void for non-compliance with the 1976 Act, must be

---

[384.] As is prescribed under s 69(1)(s) of the Registration of Title Act 1964, ie as a burden which may be registered as affecting registered land.

[385.] Subsection (8)(c).

[386.] Subsection (8)(a)(ii).

[387.] See para **[16.69]**, sub-para (b) *supra.*

[388.] Ie in the Judgments Office (see para **[15.45]** *ante*), Land Registry (see para **[15.40]** *ante*) and Registry of Deeds (see para **[15.42]** *ante*).

[389.] See para **[16.62]**, sub-para (g) *supra.* Note that curiously a statement that a conveyance is void cannot be made and registered by the non-owning spouse on his or her own: see para **[16.70]** *supra.*

[390.] It is not entirely clear what is to be stated. Subs (8)(b)(ii) requires that the relevant parties "so" state, which must cross-refer to the wording at the beginning of para (b): "A conveyance shall be deemed not to be void and never to have been void by reason of subs (1) unless -". This suggests a statement along the following lines:

"We _____, being the parties (or the successors in title to the parties) to a purported conveyance dated _____ day of _____ and relating to the property described therein hereby declare, for the purposes of section 3(8)(*b*)(ii) of the Family Home Protection Act 1976, that the said purported conveyance is void by reason of s 3(1) of the said Act of 1976."

made by the "parties to the conveyance or their successors in title". It cannot be made by the non-owning spouse who should have given consent and who will usually not have been a party to the conveyance.[391] The explanation for this may be that the draftsman was concerned to have the statement registered in the names of the same parties to facilitate searches by a subsequent prospective purchaser.[392] In any event, it is likely to be a rare case where a non-owning spouse will succeed in persuading the other spouse and the other party, or parties, to whom the property was conveyed to make the requisite statement, still less their successors in title. The institution of proceedings will, therefore, be the only option for most spouses. Finally, the 6-year limitation period for proceedings is without prejudice to the right of the non-owning spouse "to seek redress" for contravention of the 1976 Act in any other way. Thus, the non-owning spouse might still seek a compensation order under s 5(2) of the 1976 Act.[393]

25. Family Law Act 1981 and Family Law Act 1995

[16.72] This requisition is designed to deal with the possible effect of the 1981 Act, which contains a number of provisions concerning the property of engaged couples.[394] The vendor's solicitor is required to state whether any disposition of the property has been made to which ss 3 and 4 of the Act apply. Those sections concern gifts to engaged couples made by other persons and gifts as between engaged couples and raise various presumptions as to, eg, return of the gift if the marriage does not take place. The Family Home Protection Act 1976 Declarations recommended by the Law Society's Conveyancing Committee and approved by the Joint Committee of Building Society Solicitors and the Law Society,[395] contain a clause which deals with the matter, in the sense that they contain a declaration by the vendor or vendors, that none of the provisions of the 1981 Act apply because they have not been parties to an agreement to marry

---

[391.] There may be rare cases where the consenting spouse is joined as a party, but later claims that her consent was not "informed" or was vitiated by some factor such as duress or undue influence: see para **[16.69]** sub-para (b) *supra*.

[392.] This would not apply, however, in the case of registered land since the s 69 burden would be registered on the folio in the usual way and the Act could have required the Registrar to accept for registration a statement by the non-owning spouse. In the case of unregistered land, if the non-owning spouse could register the statement in her name only, the purchaser would have to search in the Index of Names against her name, unless there was a requirement for registration in the Index of Lands.

[393.] Though the delay would obviously count against the non-owning spouse, as the court has a discretion in the matter: see Duncan and Scully, *Marriage Breakdown in Ireland: Law and Practice* (1990), para 11.032 *et seq.*

[394.] See Duncan and Scully, *Marriage Breakdown in Ireland: Law and Practice* (1990), para 12.014 *et seq.*

[395.] See para **[16.64]** *supra*.

which has terminated. If, on the other hand, there has been such a disposition then the other party to the agreement and the donor of any gift must join in the deed of conveyance to release their respective interests in the property. The requisition also asks the vendor's solicitor to confirm that s 5 of the 1981 Act does not affect the property. That section applies to an engaged couple, whose agreement to marry is terminated, "the rules of law relating to the rights of spouses in relation to property in which either or both of them has or have a beneficial interest".[396] The section also enables a formerly engaged couple to have a dispute over ownership of property deteermined by the court under s 12 of the Married Women's Status Act 1957.[397] These matters are also covered by the Family Home Protection Act declarations. As previously noted, the vendor's solicitor is to furnish the appropriate draft declaration for approval by the purchaser's solicitor with the replies to the requisitions and the approved declaration itself duly completed on closing.[398]

26. *Judicial Separation and Family Law Reform Act 1989 and Family Law Act 1995*

[16.73] This requisition deals with the possible application of the 1989 Act, under Part II of which the court has jurisdiction, in cases of judicial separation, to make various orders affecting the spouse's property, eg, property adjustment orders, ancillary orders, orders extinguishing succession rights and orders for the sale of property.[399] The requisition requires the vendor's solicitor to confirm that no application or order has been made under these Acts. This matter is covered by a clause in the Family Home Protection Act 1976 declarations approved by the Law Society's Conveyancing Committee and the Joint Committee of the Building Societies Solicitors and the Law Society.[400] The vendor's solicitor is also required to confirm that the current sale is not a disposition for the purposes of defeating

---

[396.] It was far from clear what precisely this wording covers: see Power, 'The Family Law Act 1981 - Yet Another Pandora's Box', the *Gazette,* June 1985, p 169; *cf* O'Donnell, "Conveyancing and the Family Home", SYS Lectures, No 146. See also Duncan and Scully, *op cit,* para 12.015. However, s 48 of the Family Law Act 1995 makes it clear that it is referring only to rules for determination of disputes between spouses (eg, presumptions of advancement or resulting trusts) and relating to claims in relation to beneficial ownership (see para **[16.23]** *supra*). It does not relate, and is to be deemed never to have related, to rules governing persons' rights under legislation like the Succession Act 1965, the Family Home Protection Act 1976, the Judicial Separation and Family Law Reform Act 1989 or the 1995 Act itself. There is, therefore, no question of consent under the 1976 Act being needed in the case of engaged or formerly engaged couples.

[397.] See *Duncan and Scully, op cit,* ch 10 and para 12.016 *et seq.* Note that, as from 1 August 1996, s 12 is replaced by s 36 of the Family Law Act 1995.

[398.] See para **[16.68]** *supra.*

[399.] See *Duncan and Scully, op cit,* Ch 13.

[400.] See para **[16.64]** *supra.* See also the Law Society's Conveyancing Committee's Practice Note, the *Gazette,* March 1990, p 66.

a claim for financial relief[401] and that, if the vendor acquired the property after 19 September 1989,[402] to confirm that he was a *bona fide* purchaser for value (other than marriage) without notice of any intention to defeat such a claim.[403] This too is covered by the standard 1976 Act declarations. It should be noted, however, that as from 1 August 1996 these provisions in Part II of the 1989 Act will be replaced by the provisions of Part II of the Family Law Act 1995,[404] and orders made already under the 1989 Act will continue in force and be treated as if made under the corresponding provision in the 1995 Act.

27. *Local Government (Planning and Development) Act 1963*

[16.74] This requisition is a lengthy one which raises a wide range of matters which arise under the planning legislation.[405] This is a complex subject beyond the scope of this book.[406] In essence what the purchaser's solicitor must be concerned about is that there has been compliance with the planning legislation up to the present time, because of the draconian sanctions which the planning authority may invoke against the property for non-compliance.[407] Special concerns obviously arise where the property is a newly constructed one, in respect of which appropriate planning permission should have been obtained, which may have been made subject to various conditions, and compliance with building bye-laws or regulations may have been required. If the purchaser is buying the property with a view to development, whether building or a change of use which requires such permission, his solicitor must ensure that this is available and, if not, should consider whether the contract for sale should be made conditional upon it being obtained.[408]

[401.] Which the court may set aside under s 29 of the 1989 Act. Note also relief under s 35 of the 1995 Act.

[402.] This probably should be 19 October 1989, which is the date the Act came into force, see s 46(2).

[403.] If this is so, the disposition is not reviewable by the court: s 29(4). See also s 35 of the 1995 Act.

[404.] 1995 Act, s 3(2)(a). The same applies to proceedings instituted under the 1989 Act before 1 August 1996: *ibid*, s 3(2)(c). The corresponding provision to s 29 of the 1989 Act (transactions intended to prevent or reduce relief) is s 35 of the 1995 Act.

[405.] Despite its title, the requisition also covers matters arising under other principal Acts like the Local Government (Planning and Development) Acts 1976, 1982, 1983, 1990, 1991, 1992 and 1993. Note also the immediately following requisition which deals with related legislation like the Building Control Act 1990 and Fire Services Act 1981. See Sweetman, 'Recent Developments in Conveyancing Practice' (1995) IPELJ 95.

[406.] For detailed treatment see O'Sullivan and Shepherd, *Irish Planning Law and Practice*; Scannell, *Environmental and Planning Law in Ireland* (1995).

[407.] See *O'Sullivan and Shepherd, op cit*, Part 5; *Scannell, op cit*, p 252 *et seq*.

[408.] See para **[7.16]** *et seq, ante*.

[16.75] The requisition must be viewed in the light of condition 36 in the Law Society's standard contract form.[409] Subject to a provision to the contrary in the Special Conditions, under condition 36 the vendor initially gives a two-part warranty:

(1) either no development has taken place on the property requiring planning permission or building bye-law approval or, if it has, that the appropriate permission and approvals were obtained and all conditions attached or notified were complied with substantially;

(2) no claim for compensation has ever been made under Part III of the Local Government (Planning and Development) Act 1990.[410]

This warranty does not, however, extend to cover development or works executed prior to 1 October 1964, when the modern planning system came into operation. It would clearly be unreasonable to expect a vendor to give a warranty in respect of matters which took place over 30 years ago and, in any event, the likelihood of any action being taken against the property or its owners or occupiers at the present time must be remote in the extreme.[411] The effect of this warranty, if it is not removed or reduced by a special condition, is to reverse the *caveat emptor* principle, under which the purchaser would be expected to check out the planning situation.[412] A breach of the warranty would entitle the purchaser to sue for damages[413] and, where the matter is a serious one going to the root of the contract or one which would seriously prevent the purchaser enjoying the property as expected, it is likely that he can rescind[414] or resist a claim for specific performance.[415] Condition 36 then goes on to require the vendor to furnish with the documents of title[416] copies of all relevant permissions and approvals.[417] He must also furnish on or prior to completion written confirmation from the

---

[409] *General Conditions of Sale (1995 ed)*: see para **[10.55]** *ante*.

[410] Such compensation relates to cases involving "adverse" planning decisions, ie where permission to develop land is refused or granted subject to conditions which reduce the value of the land: see *Scannell, op cit*, p 240 *et seq*.

[411] See the Law Society's Conveyancing Committee's views given in a Practice Note published in the *Gazette*, June 1988, p 141.

[412] *Edler v Auerbach* [1950] 1 KB 359 at 374 (*per* Devlin J), approved by the English Court of Appeal in *Hill v Harris* (1965) 2 QB 601: see paras **[4.08]** and **[5.12]** *ante*.

[413] See para **[13.75]** *et seq, ante*. *Quaere* whether planning matters would be regarded as a defect in title to bring the case within the rule in *Bain v Fothergill*: see para **[13.80]** *et seq, ante*.

[414] See paras **[13.58]** and **[13.74]** *ante*.

[415] See paras **[13.48]**, **[13.51]** and **[13.52]** *ante*.

[416] Under Cond 7: see paras **[10.34]** and **[14.42]** *ante*.

[417] Including, where relevant, fire safety certificates (see para **[16.83]** *infra*) and commencement notices issued under building control regulations which are referable to the property (see para **[16.79]** *infra*): Cond 36(b).

local authority of compliance with all conditions involving financial contributions or the furnishing of bonds in the permissions or approvals also formal confirmation from the local authority that the roads and other services abutting the property have been taken in charge by it without requirement for payment of money.[418] He must also furnish on or prior to completion a certificate or opinion by an architect or engineer, or other professionally qualified person competent to certify "substantial compliance" with the relevant permissions or approvals and any conditions relating to them.[419] Given the importance of these matters it is usually wise to insist upon the vendor furnishing the draft certificates or opinions for approval by the purchaser's solicitor *prior* to entering into the contract. This avoids delays at a later stage if the purchaser's solicitor is not happy with the form being offered or has doubts about the qualification of the person issuing it.

[16.76] Over the years much discussion has taken place over certificates or opinions[420] of compliance and both the Law Society and the Royal Institute of the Architects of Ireland have published standard forms. Both bodies have recently agreed to co-operate in developing a common set and, in the meantime, have agreed to encourage their respective members to accept the other body's forms.[421] For solicitors a continuing matter of concern are the qualifications of the person issuing such certificates. The Law Society's position remains that purchasers' and mortgagees' solicitors should adhere to the practice of accepting only certificates issued by professionally qualified architects (holding a degree in architecture),[422] chartered or civil engineers, building surveyors or other persons calling themselves architects or engineers who have been in independent (or similar) practice for at least 10 years.[423] Problems often arise in the remoter parts of the State because such professional experts are not readily available, but in such cases purchasers' and mortgagees' solicitors must be mindful of their duties to their respective clients and the dangers of opening themselves to a negligence claim by accepting a certificate from an inadequately qualified

---

418. Cond 36(c)(i).

419. Cond 36(c)(ii).

420. The Law Society's Conveyancing Committee has obtained Senior Counsel's advice that the nomenclature is not materially significant - it is the substance of what is issued and by whom which matters: see guidelines , "Who should Certify Compliance?" in a Law Society Newsletter issued on 26 October 1994.

421. See the *Gazette*, March 1995, p82. See also Sweetman, 'Recent Developments in Conveyancing Practice' (1994) IPELJ 133 and 179.

422. Or architects from elsewhere in the EU whose qualification is entitled to recognition under the Architect's Directive - EC Directive 85/384/EEC (10 June 1985).

423. See the guidelines referred to in fn 420 *supra*.

person.[424] The Law Society's Conveyancing Committee has endorsed a three-fold test to be applied in such situations:

1. In the solicitor's own opinion, is the particular matter in order and in accordance with good conveyancing practice?

2. Will it be acceptable under the rules or guidelines of the Bank or Building Society from whom the client is borrowing? and

3. Will it be acceptable to most other solicitors if the property were to be put up for sale again in the near future?[425]

If the answer to any of these questions is in the negative, or if the solicitor has doubts over the qualifications of the person issuing the certificate or opinion of compliance, the solicitor must discuss the matter with the client and leave it to the client to make an informed decision whether to proceed. Where the client does decide to proceed, taking a commercial view of the matter, despite the solicitor's reservations, it is wise and good practice for the solicitor to confirm his reservations in writing.

[16.77] A marginal note to Condition 36 in the Law Society's standard contract form recommends that consideration be given to dealing separately, by way of special condition, with the case where the property is affected by an unauthorised development or breach of condition or conditions in planning permission, or bye-law approval, amounting to a "non-conforming development".[426] The point here is that, although the non-conforming development may be no longer subject to enforcement action, it remains unauthorised and this fact may cause difficulties in the future, eg, if planning permission is sought for future works.[427] Similarly special consideration should be given where the property is covered by the amnesty in s 22(7) of the Building Control Act 1990.[428]

[16.78] Requisition 27 in a sense provides the vendor's solicitor with a checklist of information to be given and documentation (such as certificates

---

[424.] *Cf Glendinning v Orr* [1989] NI 171. See also *Lake v Bushby* [1949] 3 All ER 964.

[425.] See guidelines referred to in fn 420 *supra*.

[426.] See s 19 of the Local Government (Planning and Development) Act 1992, under which such developments may be immune from enforcement procedures.

[427.] Reliance could not be placed on the "exempted development" provision under Art 10(1)(*a*)(viii) of the Local Government (Planning and Development) Regulations 1994 (SI 86/1994), since these do not cover extensions, alterations, repair or renewal of "non-authorised" structures or structures the use of which is an "unauthorised use". The planning authority is also unlikely to be enthusiastic about granting permission for new works where previous ones have been unauthorised. See Sweetman, 'Recent Developments in Conveyancing Practice' (1995) IPELJ 20.

[428.] See para **[16.81]** *infra*.

of compliance) to be furnished if the vendor is to comply with the warranty in Condition 36. As we saw in an earlier chapter, the importance of these matters is such that the purchaser's solicitor will often wish to raise them as pre-contract enquiries or requisitions.[429] It will also often be necessary for the purchaser's solicitor to supplement such enquiries or requisitions with a search in the planning register.[430]

28. Building Control Act 1990 and any Regulation, Order or Instrument thereunder

[16.79] This requisition deals with the possible effect of the 1990 Act and regulations made under it. This Act introduced a system of building regulations to replace the old building bye-law system which had operated haphazardly since the last century.[431] The Act designates "building control authorities"[432] which are responsible for overseeing the operation of building regulations[433] and building control regulations.[434] In essence the building control system introduced is a somewhat controversial one of "self-certification" by designers and builders of individual projects of compliance with the relevant building regulations, and submission of fire safety certificates and applications for certificates of approval.[435] As a result it has become necessary to incorporate into letters of engagement and building contracts a requirement that certificates of compliance with the building regulations will be supplied at the appropriate time, usually on "practical completion of the works".[436] These are usually required from the architects, civil and structural engineers or mechanical and electrical engineers and the

---

[429.] See para **[5.09]** *ante*.

[430.] Maintained under s 8 of the Local Government (Planning and Development) Act 1963.

[431.] Such bye-laws could be made by "sanitary authorities" under s 41 of the Public Health (Ir) Act 1878. The Local Government (Planning and Development) Act 1963, made provision for building regulations (see ss 386-88), but, although draft regulations were circulated to local authorities, they were never brought into force. This highly unsatisfactory position was highlighted by the Stardust Tribunal: *Report of the Tribunal of Inquiry on the Fire at the Stardust, Artane, Dublin, on February 16, 1981*. Note also Requisition 35 dealing with multi-storey buildings: see para **[16.95]** *infra*.

[432.] Local authorities which are fire authorities under the Fire Services Act 1981: see para **[16.83]** *infra*.

[433.] Section 3. See the Building Regulations 1991 (SI 306/1991) and 1994 (SI 154/1994). The 1991 Regulations came into on 1 June 1992: see Reg 2.

[434.] Section 6. See the Building Control Regulations 1991 (SI 305/1991) and 1994 (SI 153/1994).

[435.] See s 6(2).

[436.] See further para **[16.82]** *infra*. Note also the need to appoint project supervisors for works at the design and construction stage, and to maintain a "safety file" in respect of projects started on site after 6 March 1996, under the Safety, Health and Welfare at Work (Construction) Regulations, 1995 (SI 138/1995), made under the Safety, Health and Welfare at Work Act 1989, in order to comply with the EU directive aimed at reducing accidents in the construction industry (Directive 92/57/EEC): see para **[16.84]** *infra*.

respective professional bodies have recommended appropriate forms to their members.

[16.80] This requisition must, like the previous one relating to planning,[437] be viewed in the light of condition 36 in the Law Society's standard contract form.[438] Under that condition[439] the vendor warrants[440] that there has been "substantial compliance" with the 1990 Act and regulations made under it. He is required to furnish, on or prior to completion, a certificate or opinion by an architect or engineer or other professionally qualified person[441] confirming such compliance. The requisition requires the vendor's solicitor to state whether the property is affected by the building control regulations. If it is claimed that it is not so affected, this must be verified by a statutory declaration by a "competent person", such as an architect or engineer, containing an appropriate explanation. If the property is affected, then draft certificates or opinions of compliance must be furnished with the replies,[442] together with a copy of any "commencement notice" given to the building control authority.[443] Where a fire safety certificate is required a copy of this must be attached to and referred to in the certificate or opinions of compliance, which should also confirm compliance with the fire safety certificate and that no appeal has been made against conditions imposed by the building control authority. Other documentation which must be furnished, if relevant, is a copy of any enforcement notice[444] (plus a certificate of compliance with it), details of any application to the District Court to annul, modify or alter the notice[445] and a copy of any High Court order made in respect of health and safety matters[446] (plus again a certificate of compliance with it).

[16.81] The marginal note to condition 36 of the Law Society's standard contract form[447] cautions practitioners to consider dealing with the bye-law

---

[437.] See para **[16.75]** *supra*.

[438.] *General Conditions of Sale (1995 Ed)*.

[439.] Cond 36(d). Note also Cond 36(b) requiring the furnishing of all fire safety certificates and commencement notices under the regulations.

[440.] Subject to stipulation to the contrary in the special conditions.

[441.] See para **[16.76]** *supra*.

[442.] Again the better practice is to raise these matters *pre*-contract and to seek the draft certificates or opinions for approval *before* the contract is entered into: see para **[16.75]** *supra*.

[443.] Such a notice must be submitted in respect of works to which the regulations apply and a copy furnished under Cond 36(b) of the Law Society's contract form.

[444.] See s 8 of the 1990 Act.

[445.] See s 9 of the 1990 Act.

[446.] See s 12 of the 1990 Act.

[447.] See para **[16.77]** *supra*.

amnesty given by s 22(7) of the 1990 Act by way of a special condition. That section provided transitional arrangements to cover cases where plans had been submitted under the old building bye-law system.[448] However, under subs (7) where work carried out before 13 December 1989[449] did not comply with the bye-laws, no proceedings for non-compliance can be taken unless the building control authority has served, within six months of the operative day,[450] a notice stating that the works constitute a danger to public health or safety. If no such notice has been served, approval to the carrying out of the works is deemed to have been granted.[451] This amnesty was designed to cover the common situation where relatively minor works, like small extensions to houses, were erected without obtaining the requisite bye-law approval.

[16.82] There is one further point to stress about this subject. Solicitors acting for developers and for prospective purchasers of, or investors in, new developments should bear in mind that, such is the complexity of the various regulations governing building works and of building techniques, it is often very difficult to secure certificates of compliance "after the event". If an architect or engineer has not been involved in the project from the beginning he is likely to be extremely reluctant to furnish a certificate of compliance and, if persuaded, is likely to enter substantial qualifications. Every effort should, therefore, be made to secure certificates of compliance whenever various stages of the project are completed from the professional people involved, and these should be kept with the title documents for future reference. Where this "good practice" has not been followed purchasers, investors and lending institutions must recognise that the certificates of compliance which can be made available at a later stage may not be entirely satisfactory and solicitors must adopt a cautionary approach. As was said earlier, the earlier such difficulties are brought to light and confronted the better, so that it is wise to deal with the matter at the pre-contract stage.[452] Again, as was said earlier,[453] it is vital that any such difficulty is thoroughly discussed with the client and that it is explained to the client that it is for him, having been informed of the difficulties, to make the decision whether to proceed. A failure to take such cautionary steps exposes the solicitor to a potential negligence claim.[454] It follows that the vendor's solicitor must also

---

[448.] See para **[16.79]** *supra*.

[449.] The date the Building Control Bill was passed by the Dáil.

[450.] The day the building regulations first came into operation in the area: s 22(4).

[451.] *Cf* the position in respect of "non-conforming" developments under s 19 of the Local Government (Planning and Development) Act 1992: see para **[16.77]** *supra*.

[452.] See paras **[16.75]** and **[16.80]** *supra*.

[453.] See para **[16.76]** *supra*.

[454.] See *ibid*.

take care. In many cases it will be clear that the vendor will not be in a position to honour the warranty in condition 36 of the Law Society's standard contract form and so this should be either deleted or modified by special condition.[455] The documentation immediately to hand must be checked carefully at the earliest stage against the requirements of condition 36 and the standard requisitions. The warning given above about the difficulties of securing certificates of compliance after the event must be heeded. In particular the vendor's solicitor should under no circumstances give an undertaking to produce certificates which are not already to hand. It is a golden rule that a solicitor should never undertake to do something which is dependent upon the performance of someone else. It must be remembered that the sanctions for breach of a solicitor's undertaking are extremely severe.[456]

29. Fire Services Act 1981

[16.83] This requisition requires the vendor to furnish with the replies copies of any notices served under this Act and to state whether any proceedings are pending and whether the property has been inspected by the fire authority. A certificate of substantial compliance must be furnished in respect of any such notices or requirements resulting from an inspection. These are matters of particular importance in respect of premises to be used by the general public, such as hotels, restaurants, pubs and entertainment venues.[457] We also saw earlier, that fire safety certificates are now part of the building control regime and the vendor is required under the Law Society's standard contract form to furnish all such certificates issued in respect of the property being sold.[458]

30. Safety Health and Welfare at Work (Construction) Regulations 1995

[16.84] The Regulations,[459] which give effect to an EEC Council Directive,[460] are designed to promote safety, health and welfare at construction sites. They require the developers to ensure that competent project supervisors are appointed at both the design and construction stages of the project, to develop and monitor health and safety plans and activities.

[455.] See para **[16.80]** *supra*.

[456.] See para **[20.15]** *post*.

[457.] See *Greyhill Property Co Ltd v Whitechap Inn Ltd* High Court, unrep, 5 October 1993 (1990/2384). See also Requisitions 40 and 41, paras **[16.103]** and **[16.105]** *infra*.

[458.] *General Conditions of Sale (1995 Ed)*, Cond 36(b): see para **[16.80]** *supra*. See also *Greaney Ltd v Dublin Corporation* High Court, unrep, 7 March 1994 (1993/117).

[459.] SI 138/1995. They came partly into force on 6 June 1995 but became wholly operational in respect of construction projects on 6 March 1996.

[460.] 92/57/EEC.

In particular, the project supervisor for the construction stage is to maintain a "Safety File" containing details of design specifications, construction methods and materials and a record of health and safety information, including risks to be considered in any subsequent maintenance, repair or construction work on the building or buildings.[461] This File is to be handed over to the owner of the property on completion of the project and kept for future reference.

[16.85] The Regulations are of obvious relevance in a number of situations. Apart from the developer who must see that there is appropriate compliance during construction,[462] clearly the first purchaser of a new building to which the Regulations apply must ensure that he obtains the Safety File and keeps it for future reference.[463] Although it would appear that most compliance obligations under the Regulations apply only during the construction period, the File may be required later for evidentiary purposes if claims are made within the usual statutory limitation periods. Furthermore, as mentioned in the previous paragraph, the File will be needed when subsequent work is done on the building. It is for this reason that there is a duty to keep the File available for inspection by any person who may need the information it contains for the purpose of compliance with the Regulations. With this in mind, requisition 30 asks whether there has been construction work at or in the premises coming within the Regulations and, if so, requires the furnishing of a copy of the Safety File with the replies. The original is to be handed over on completion.

31. Environmental

[16.86] This requisition raises a matter of increasing importance, *viz* the impact on property transactions in Ireland of implementation of the various European Directives for control and prevention of pollution and for preservation and improvement of the environment. This is a complex subject which is beyond the scope of this book and has been dealt with elsewhere.[464] Suffice it to say that anyone purchasing, or lending on the security of, or investing in, land must be concerned about compliance with the wide range

---

[461.] Reg 6.

[462.] The developer must obtain appropriate certificates of compliance, if not at each stage of the construction, certainly on completion of the project.

[463.] As with planning, building control, etc the first purchaser should also insist upon the furnishing by the vendor of appropriate certificates of compliance: see paras [16.76] and [16.80] *ante*.

[464.] See especially the comprehensive treatment in Scannell, *Environmental and Planning Law in Ireland* (1995). See also O'Sullivan and Shepherd, *Irish Planning Law and Practice*, Parts 7 and 8.

of legislation dealing with these matters, for the civil and criminal sanctions for non-compliance can be severe indeed.[465]

[16.87] Requisition 31 adopts a very broad approach, by referring to the environmental protection legislation in very general terms and requiring the vendor's solicitor to furnish with the replies copies of any "notice, certificate, order, requirement or recommendation"[466] served upon or received by the vendor and confirmation of compliance. The vendor is also asked whether he is aware of any breach of relevant environmental controls and is required to give particulars if he is. This matter should be viewed from the point of view of both the vendor's solicitor and the purchaser's or other interested party's solicitor.

[16.88] The vendor's solicitor is faced with obvious problems when confronted with such an open-ended requisition, given the large range of environmental controls now in existence. He will clearly have to rely on his client for the information and documentation needed for the response and appropriate certificates of compliance from professional experts will have to be obtained, if they are obtainable. Much will obviously depend upon the nature of the property in question and the transaction being negotiated. The likelihood of the legislation being relevant and of action having been taken, or the risk of it being taken in the future, will obviously vary from case to case. There is all the world of a difference between purchasing a good quality private residential home in a well-established area of one of the major cities and acquiring a commercial or industrial property like a chemical factory. However, although there is a clear difference, it should never be assumed in any transaction that environmental legislation is irrelevant. The vendor's solicitor must be particularly careful about undertaking to provide documentation, especially certificates from other professional people, which it may be impossible to obtain.[467]

[16.89] The need to take into account the nature of the property and the transaction in relation to it being negotiated applies equally to the purchaser's solicitor. Where there is a serious risk that there may be environmental problems, it is imperative that the matter is addressed as early as possible and certainly *before* the contract is entered into. The need to carry out a full "due diligence" exercise, ie an investigation of the current or potential environmental liabilities of the activity being carried on in the

---

[465] These were dealt with by Dr Scannell in a recent Law Society CLE seminar on 'Environmental Law and its Implications in Conveyancing Transactions' (26 September 1995).

[466] Including any notice of intention to serve any such notice.

[467] See para **[16.82]** *supra*.

property being acquired, has been increasingly recognised in recent years where commercial or industrial properties are concerned.[468] In such cases it may be appropriate to raise much more specific *pre*-contract enquiries or requisitions relating to environmental matters.[469] The purchaser's solicitor must consider each case on its own merits and go into specifics as seems appropriate. It should not be assumed that the need for detailed enquiries or requisitions is confined to commercial or industrial property. It is not unheard of for it to be discovered that a housing estate has been build on a "contaminated" site.[470]

[16.90] In matters of this kind the solicitors will need to draw a balance between the interests of their respective clients. The underlying principle remains *caveat emptor*[471] and so the vendor should resist attempts completely to overturn it, eg, where the purchaser seeks a warranty similar to the planning and building control one contained in condition 36 of the Law Society's standard contract form.[472] He must, however, appreciate that in cases where the risk of environmental problems is substantial, the prospective purchaser is likely to require a due diligence exercise to be carried out[473] and, if this brings to light potential problems, the purchaser is likely to seek appropriate warranties or indemnities. In the end, the parties and their advisers will probably have to engage in tough negotiations and make a commercial judgment as to whether to proceed.

32. Food Hygiene Regulations

[16.91] This requisition relates to premises, such as a restaurant or café, which are required to be registered as "food premises" with the relevant health authority.[474] Non-compliance with the authority's requirements can result in non-registration and a prohibition on carrying on the business. In *Geryani v O'Callaghan*[475] Costello J emphasised the need for the vendor to disclose the fact that premises were subject to provisional registration only and that full registration was dependent on satisfactory compliance with

---

[468] See Fanagan, 'Environmental Due Diligence' (1995) IPELJ 3.

[469] See, eg, the set of pre-contract enquiries furnished by Garrett Gill (of Matheson, Ormsby Prentice, Solicitors) at the Law Society's CLE Seminar referred to in fn 465 *supra*.

[470] Indeed, at the CLE seminar (fn 465 *supra*) reference was made to the report in the *Irish Times* (15 August 1995) that an asbestos dump had been found at a housing site in Kildare. See also Spence, 'Contaminated Sites - Clean Up or be Cleaned Out?' (1994) IPELJ 57.

[471] See Ch 4 *ante*.

[472] See paras **[16.75]** and **[16.80]** *supra*.

[473] See para **[16.89]** *supra*.

[474] See Food Hygiene Regulations 1950 (SI 205/1950), made under the Health Act 1947. See McDonald, *Hotel, Restaurant and Public House Law* (1992), Ch 2.

[475] High Court, unrep, 25 January 1995 (1994/677 Sp).

over 20 conditions required by the health authority. A failure to disclose this in the replies to the requisitions raised by the purchaser[476] was held to justify the purchaser rescinding the contract.[477]

[16.92] The requisition requires the vendor's solicitor to state whether the premises come within the Food Hygiene Regulations 1950, as amended,[478] and, if they do, to furnish evidence of registration and of compliance with any conditions or undertakings. It also requires the vendor's solicitor to state whether any notice has been served by the health authority, or whether the vendor or his agents have information of an intention to serve any notice. If any notice has been served full copies are to be furnished, plus details of any undertakings, with a statement of whether they have been complied with. Given the importance of these matters to the operation of the business in question, in most cases it will be prudent to raise them as *pre*-contract enquiries rather than leaving them to *post*-contract requisitions.[479]

33. Leasehold/Fee Farm Grant Property

[16.93] This requisition deals with the situation where the property being sold is held under a lease or fee farm grant. As such it should be read in the light of the provisions in the Law Society's standard contract form.[480] The first part of the requisition requires the vendor's solicitor to furnish evidence of the title to make the lease or grant and to prove performance and observance of covenants and conditions. This is dealing with the case where the transaction involves the original making of the lease or grant, where, especially in commercial transactions, it is wise to insist on seeing the vendor's title.[481] Conversely, where the transaction involves the transfer of an existing lease or grant, often the superior owner's title is not investigated. Thus under the Law Society's contract the purchaser is *not* entitled to call for or to investigate lessor's or grantor's title and is to assume conclusively that the lease or grant was "well and validly made" and is "valid and subsisting".[482] This is, of course, subject to a special condition to the contrary.[483] The requisition then goes on to ask questions about notices

---

[476.] The replies to the equivalent requisition (No 30) in the 1990 Ed of the Law Society's form stated that the premises were registered pursuant to the 1950 Regulations and that no notice had been served on the vendor, both incorrect.

[477.] Under the "errors" condition in the contract: see para **[9.47]** *ante*.

[478.] See, eg, the Food Hygiene Regulations 1961 (SI 24/1961) and 1971 (SI 322/1971).

[479.] See para **[9.47]** *ante*.

[480.] See para **[14.74]** *et seq, ante*.

[481.] Under an "open" contract the intended lessee or grantee is not so entitled: see para **[14.69]** *ante*.

[482.] *General Conditions of Sale (1995 Ed)*, Cond 9. See para **[14.74]** *ante*.

[483.] See para **[14.05]** *ante*.

served by the lessor or grantor[484] and observance and performance of covenants, conditions and stipulations. The last receipt for rent is to be produced for inspection[485] and handed over at closing. Where the rent is nominal, as is often the case with long leases or grants of residential property, and has not been demanded for 6 years (12 years in the case of a fee farm grant),[486] the vendor is to furnish the draft of a declaration to be handed over on closing confirming the non-demand and that no notices have been served and that there have been no breaches of covenants and conditions.[487] Finally, the landlord's consent to the assignment, where necessary, is to be furnished by way of endorsement on the deed.[488]

34. Acquisition of Fee Simple under the Landlord and Tenant (Ground Rents) Act 1967

[16.94] This requisition relates to cases where the property is subject to a ground rent and the lessee[489] is entitled to acquire the fee simple under the ground rents legislation. It requires the vendor's solicitor to indicate whether any steps have been taken in this matter, in particular whether the vesting certificate procedure operated by the Land Registry is being used and, if so, whether by the "consent" or "arbitration" procedure.[490] If the former, the vendor must furnish the consent of the original applicant to issue of the vesting certificate in the purchaser's name and, if the latter, consent to continuation of the arbitration on behalf of the purchaser. If the vesting certificate has already been issued, but has not yet been registered, the vendor is to arrange for registration prior to completion.[491] If steps have been taken to acquire this fee simple in any other way, details are to be furnished.[492]

---

484. Eg a notice of breach of covenant under s 14 of the Conveyancing Act 1881: see Wylie, *Irish Landlord and Tenant Law* para 24.10 *et seq.*

485. Note that under the Law Society's contract this is *conclusive* evidence of payments up-to-date and compliance with covenants, etc: see Cond 10(c) and para **[14.75]** *ante.*

486. The limitation periods: see *Wylie, op cit,* para [28.02]. See also Wylie, 'The Effect of Non-payment of a Fee Farm Grant' Western Law Gazette (Dli), Winter 1992, p 50.

487. The vendor's solicitor is also asked to confirm that an allowance will be made in the apportionment account for any unpaid rent for the past 6 years, ie rent still recoverable within the limitation period: see para **[20.06]** *post.*

488. See para **[14.75]** *ante.*

489. And, possibly, also a fee farm grantee (in the sense of getting rid of the rent and covenants): see Wylie, *Irish Landlord and Tenant Law*, para 4.44.

490. This procedure was introduced by Part III of the Landlord and Tenant (Ground Rents) (No 2) Act 1978. See *Wylie, op cit,* para 31.52 *et seq.* See also Fitzgerald, *Land Registry Practice* (2nd ed, 1995), Ch 17.

491. See *Fitzgerald, op cit,* p 314 *et seq.*

492. Eg under the 1967 Act's "notice" procedure: see *Wylie, op cit,* para 31.46 *et seq.*

35. Local Government (Multi-Storey Buildings) Act 1988

[16.95] This requisition deals with cases where the property is a multi-story building or part of such a building within the meaning of the 1988 Act, or part of a development in which there is such a building with which it shares a common management company.[493] The 1988 Act makes provision for structural approval of such buildings[494] by requiring owners to submit certificates of compliance with specified codes of practice and standards.[495] It does not apply, however, to buildings constructed before 1 January 1950,[496] but covers all kinds of multi-storey buildings, such as residential apartment blocks, office blocks and substantial buildings like hotels constructed before, or whose construction was begun before but not completed by, 14 November 1988.[497] Owners of such buildings must furnish, where necessary, a certificate signed by a "competent person"[498] to the effect that all reasonable actions[499] have been taken to minimise as far as is practicable the risk of accidental damage to the building.[500] Since this could involve substantial expenditure on the part of the owner it is essential that a purchaser of such a building checks out the position before buying it. The Law Society's Conveyancing Committee takes the view that this should be done by way of *pre*-contract enquiries or requisitions.[501]

[16.96] Requisition 35, which, of course, can be extracted and used for the purposes of pre-contract enquiries,[502] requires the vendor to state what the position is with respect to his property, ie, whether it comes within the 1988 Act and its regulations,[503] or building regulations.[504] If the local authority has

---

[493.] See further on "managed" properties, Requisitions 36 and 37: para **[16.97]** *et seq, infra.*

[494.] It must be 5 storeys or more (a basement counts as a storey): 1988 Act s 1(1). The Act was passed following the *Report of the Task Force on Multi-Storey Buildings* (1987), which had been commissioned after a gas explosion in a Dublin apartment house in January 1987.

[495.] 1988 Act, s 3 and 1st Schedule. See also the Local Government (Multi-Storey Buildings) Regulations 1988 (SI 286/1988) and 1990 (SI 95/1990).

[496.] See definition of "multi-storey building" in s 1(1) of the 1988 Act.

[497.] The date the 1988 Act came into operation: see the Local Government (Multi-Storey Buildings) Act 1988 (Commencement) Order 1988 (SI 285/1988). Section 4 of the Act deals with buildings whose construction was not completed in 1988. Buildings constructed since the Building Control Act 1990 came into operation must, of course, comply with its regulatory scheme: see s 23(i) of the 1990 Act and para **[16.79]** *supra.*

[498.] A chartered engineer with experience in the design or appraisal of the matter in question, eg gas installation or systems: see s 1(1) of the 1988 Act.

[499.] See the 3rd Schedule.

[500.] Section 3(2)(c). Note also the definition of "robustness" in s 1(1).

[501.] Published as a supplement to the *Gazette,* May 1990: See *Conveyancing Handbook,* para 13.32.

[502.] See para **[5.01]** *ante.*

[503.] A statutory declaration must be furnished to prove construction before 1 January 1950: see para **[16.94]** *supra.*

[504.] See fn 492 *supra.*

served a notice requiring the furnishing of a certificate under the Act,[505] a copy of this must be furnished with the replies to the requisition and, in any event, where it is necessary to comply with the Act and its regulations, a copy of any certificate submitted, with a statement as to whether or not it complies with the regulations, must be furnished. If no certificate has been furnished, one must be furnished with the replies. The Law Society's Conveyancing Committee warned purchaser's solicitors that sometimes the local authority has not accepted certificates[506] and so where it is claimed that one has been submitted, evidence should be sought that it has been accepted.[507] Requisition 35 now covers this point. If any work has been carried out which might have nullified an existing certificate and required submission of a further certificate, a certified copy of the further certificate must be furnished, as must a certified copy of any certificate submitted in respect of a building whose construction was not completed prior to 14 November 1988.[508]

36. New Flats/New Managed Properties

[16.97] This requisition[509] deals with a highly complex matter, viz where the property comprises part of a development such as a block of flats or apartments, or similar properties which are subject to a management scheme.[510] Because of the need to ensure that covenants and other rights are mutually enforceable in respect of each unit, such developments are usually leasehold developments,[511] though, with some very careful drafting, a freehold scheme may be effective.[512] A key feature of such schemes is usually that ownership of common areas like corridors, stairways, lifts and the exterior and structure of the building, plus areas outside the building like gardens and carparks, are reserved initially to the landlord. They are then vested in a management company which is responsible for the repair and

---

[505.] See s 2 of the Act.

[506.] And so they will not be recorded in the local authority's register of multi-storey buildings in its area: see s 2(1) of the Act.

[507.] The *Gazette,* October 1991, p 323.

[508.] See fn 492 *supra.*

[509.] Note also Requisition 37, which deals with the purchase of second-hand flats and managed properties: para **[16.99]** *infra.*

[510.] See Aldridge, *Law of Flats* (3rd ed, 1993); Cawthorn and Barraclough, *Sale and Management of Flats - Practice and Precedents* (2nd ed, 1996).

[511.] The prohibition on the creation of new ground rents in respect of dwellings in the Landlord and Tenant (Ground Rents) Act 1978, does not apply to a separate and self-contained flat in premises divided into two or more such flats: see the definition of "dwelling" in s 1 and Wylie, *Irish Landlord and Tenant Law,* p 976. See also para **[19.11]** *et seq, post.*

[512.] Incorporating the so-called "estate scheme" rules which can also be used for similar schemes like housing estates: see Laffoy, *Irish Conveyancing Precedents,* pp E20-22 and Precedents E.8.1 and E.8.2.

maintenance of these areas, plus, their insurance (usually through a "block" policy), and for the provision of various other services for the entire development. Each unit owner is expected to pay, in addition to any rent, a service charge designed to cover a proportionate part of the cost of provision of the various services.[513] It is also common for the management company to comprise the unit owners, who may be the members and shareholders, though sometimes the actual management will be delegated to managing agents.[514]

[16.98] Requisition 36 lists a long series of items relating to the development scheme governing the new flat or other property being bought. It requires the vendor's solicitor to produce a substantial amount of documentation relating to the property, the management company and its operation, any managing agents to be employed, the block insurance policy and the service charge payments. All of this must be closely scrutinised by the purchaser's solicitor. The other very important matter it covers is the question whether the property is a "qualifying" premises for tax concessions under the urban renewal schemes for "designated areas" like the Temple Bar area of Dublin.[515]

37. Second Hand Flats/Second Hand Managed Properties

[16.99] This requisition deals with the situation where the owner of the flat or apartment sells it on. A second or subsequent owner should be just as concerned as the first purchaser about precisely how the development scheme operates and the requisition here is equally detailed. Indeed, it is even more comprehensive than the previous requisition because it is also designed to elicit information about how the scheme has worked in practice and requires the furnishing of appropriate documentation.[516] Here it covers the issue of whether there are any claims against the management company's funds or outstanding repairs or other expenditure which may affect the level of service charges payable. It is also important again to determine whether the flat or apartment qualifies for tax relief.

---

[513] Similar provisions are, of course, common in office and other commercial developments which are multi-let; see *Laffoy, op cit,* pp L7-12 and Precedent L.2.4. See also para **[19.14]** *et seq, post.*

[514] In larger developments it is more usual for the company to be one limited by guarantee: see para **[19.16]** *post.* See also Cox, *Running a Flat Management Company* (2nd ed, 1993).

[515] For detailed discussion of these see Judge, *Irish Income Tax* (1995-96 Ed), Part 18.5. See also Requisition 38, para **[16.100]** *infra.*

[516] It also deals with the situation of a sale before the development is completed and the management company has yet to be established.

38. Tax Based Incentives/Designated Areas

[16.100] To some extent this matter is covered by the previous two requisitions, but it is important to have a separate requisition because the tax incentive schemes and designated area scheme also cover property which is not within those two requisitions. There is a wide range of allowances covering industrial buildings or structures, multi-storey car parks, toll roads and bridges, farm buildings, holiday cottages and even some houses qualify.[517] The vendor is required to hand over on closing all documentation required to transfer allowances to the purchaser.

39. Milk Quotas

[16.101] Where the property being bought is farm land used for milk production, a matter of vital concern to the purchaser will be the "milk quota" allocated to it. This is part of the regime introduced by the EC in 1984 to tackle the widely-criticised surpluses which were a consequence of the Common Agricultural Policy.[518] Under the scheme a milk producer is obliged to pay a levy on any quantity of milk or milk products which are in excess of his quota for any particular year.[519] Hence the quota allocated to a particular farm is a very valuable asset and, in the Law Society's Conveyancing Committee's view, ought to be checked by a prospective purchaser as a *pre*-contract matter. Requisition 39 is a detailed one which has been drafted in a format so that it can be so used.[520] The Committee also recommends that, in view of the complexity of the Milk Quota Regulations, the purchaser should include in the contract for sale a special condition whereby the vendor warrants that no circumstances exist by virtue of which the quota, or the apportioned part thereof in the case of the sale of part of a farm, will not pass in full to the purchaser.[521]

[16.102] The requisition seeks to elicit detailed information with respect to the milk quota attaching to the property being bought, plus appropriate

---

[517.] See *Butterworths Tax Guide 1995-6*, especially Chs 5, 16 and 58.

[518.] Regulation 857/84. See *Dowling v Ireland* [1991] 2 IR 379; *O'Brien v Ireland* (1991) 2 IR 387. See also Ryan-Purcell 'Law Relating to Milk Quota Transactions in Ireland' (1994) CLP 179.

[519.] The European Communities (Milk Quota) Regulations 1994 (SI 70/1994) made the important change that the quota attaches to the land used for milk production in the quota year (April to March) prior to the year of transfer. Thus a purchaser must enquire as to the vendor's farming practice in the previous year. See also the 1995 Regulations (SI 266/1995).

[520.] An earlier version was issued with covering notes in February 1995. For earlier guidance, see the *Conveyancing Handbook*, Ch 6. See also *O'Brien v Kearney* [1995] 2 ILRM 232.

[521.] See the covering notes *ibid*.

documentation to evidence the various matters covered. This includes details of any apportionment of the quota where part only of the farm is being sold. It also requires the vendor's solicitor furnish various documents on closing, in particular the requisite transfer form duly completed by the vendor.

40. Licensing

[16.103] This and the next three requisitions deal with premises which require a license in order to carry out the activity conducted therein.[522] Clearly the existence of this licence is of vital concern to a purchaser if he intends to continue the activity after he has completed the purchase. As in the case of a milk quota attaching to a dairy farm,[523] the matter is of su:h crucial importance and such a vital factor in the value of the property that it is something which should be thoroughly checked out by the purchaser prior to entering into the contract.[524] The requisition under consideration and the next three requisitions are also drafted in such a way that they can be used for the purposes of pre-contract enquiries.

[16.104] Requisition 40 deals with the sale of a public house and seeks to elicit detailed information relating to its intoxicating liquor license, the hours it covers, the property it covers, alterations which may have affected the licence and any convictions under the Intoxicating Liquor Act 1927, or summonses pending. The vendor is required to endorse the licence and hand it over to the purchaser on closing and to take all steps necessary to facilitate its transfer to him. He is also required to confirm compliance with any requirement of the fire authority.[525]

41. Restaurant/Hotel

[16.105] This requisition deals with various licences applicable to restaurants[526] and hotels. Thus, it covers a full or limited restaurant licence granted under the Intoxicating Liquor Act 1927. So far as hotels are concerned, it covers a hotel licence issued under the Licensing (Ireland) Act

---

[522] See generally Cassidy, *The Licensing Acts 1933-1994* (1996); McDonald, *Hotel, Restaurant and Public House Law* (1992).

[523] See para **[16.101]** *supra.*

[524] And again, the question of inserting a vendor's warranty by way of special condition should be considered: *ibid.*

[525] See also para **[16.83]** *supra.* Note also the need for the vendor to discharge any tax liabilities - the vendor's solicitor may obtain a tax clearance certificate on the basis of an undertaking to discharge the liabilities out of the proceeds of sale (after payment of prior mortgage and costs of sale): see the *Gazette,* March 1996, p 78 and para **[20.18]** *post.*

[526] See also Requisition 42, dealing with special restaurant licenses: see para **[16.106]** *infra.* Note also the requirement to comply with the Food Hygiene Regulations: Requisition 32 and para **[16.91]** *supra.*

1902 and an order authorising the sale of intoxicating liquor under the Intoxicating Liquor Act 1960. It also covers certification and registration with Bord Fáilte.

42. Special Restaurant Licence

[16.106] This is a licence granted under the Intoxicating Liquor Act 1988 which permits a restaurant to sell the full range of intoxicating liquor in the context of a substantial meal.[527] It also covers the Bord Fáilte certificate of compliance with the Special Restaurant Licence (Standards) Regulation 1988,[528] which is issued under s 8 of the 1988 Act.

43. Dancing, Music and Singing

[16.107] This requisition covers premises where a licence is needed for public dancing[529] or music and singing.[530]

44. Completion

[16.108] This requisition reminds the vendor's solicitor to hand over on closing all documents specified in the preceding requisitions and provides space for the purchaser's solicitor to list any other documents he considers necessary. In such a case the purchaser's solicitor is concerned that not all the documents necessary to prove the title have been furnished rather than raising a defect in title.

[527.] See McDonald, *op cit*, ch 12.

[528.] SI 147/1988.

[529.] Under the Public Dance Halls Act 1935: see *McDonald, op cit,* Ch 16.

[530.] Under s 51 of the Public Health Acts (Amendment) Act 1890, which covers a wide variety of public "places", including hotels, restaurants and pubs. See *McDonald, op cit,* Ch 17.

Chapter 17

DRAFTING AND CONSTRUCTION OF DEEDS

[17.01] We now turn to the next major stage in the conveyancing process, the preparation of the conveyance for the transaction in question. By tradition the conveyance is not prepared until the purchaser has completed his investigation of title, but, as we saw in an earlier chapter,[1] the conveyance may in practice be prepared in draft and sent to the other party at an earlier stage, eg, it may be sent by the purchaser's solicitor to the vendor's solicitor together with the requisitions on title.[2] Furthermore, as we shall see later,[3] in certain cases the conveyance may be drafted by the vendor's solicitor instead of the purchaser's solicitor and may be furnished to the purchaser's solicitor at an even earlier stage, eg, it may be annexed to the contract for sale in accordance with a special condition designed to avoid the purchaser's solicitor drafting it.

I. DRAFTING THE CONVEYANCE

[17.02] The history of the forms of conveyance of land in Ireland is a long and tangled one, which has been discussed in detail elsewhere.[4] Suffice it to say that the ancient forms, eg, feoffment with livery of seisin, the bargain and sale and the lease and release, will rarely trouble the conveyancer today.[5] Since the passing of the Real Property Act 1845,[6] the "deed of grant" has become the standard mode of conveyance for unregistered land in Ireland, as in England. However, unlike England,[7] the older forms have not been abolished in either part of Ireland and in theory may still be used, though this is rarely done in practice.[8] Furthermore, though a deed, ie, a

---

1. See para **[1.08]** *ante*.
2. See also para **[15.52]** *ante*.
3. See para **[17.04]** *infra*.
4. See *Irish Land Law* (2nd ed, 1986), paras 3.023-30.
5. Note, however, the case of *Re Sergie* [1954] NI 1, which is discussed fully at *ibid* paras 3.026-30.
6. Section 2 of the Act introduced the deed as an alternative to livery of seisin. Section 3 required most feoffments with livery of seisin made after the Act to be evidenced by a deed.
7. See Law of Property Act 1925, s 51.
8. But see *Re Sergie* fn 5, *supra*.

document under seal,[9] is used in most cases, it is important to note that there are several conveyancing transactions where a deed is not required and where a written, unsealed document is sufficient or even no writing of any kind is required. Thus an assent by personal representatives to the vesting of a deceased person's land in his successors need be in writing only.[10] The same applies to certain disclaimers made under bankruptcy legislation,[11] as it does to leases for freehold estates[12] or terms of years.[13] A grant of a periodic tenancy, eg, from year to year, or for a period of less than a year, but not, it appears, for one year,[14] may be made orally without any writing at all.[15] Other transactions may also be effected without any writing, eg, a surrender of an interest in land by operation of law.[16]

[17.03] Where the land is registered land, generally the document of transfer must be one of the forms prescribed by statutory regulations.[17] Execution of such a transfer does not, of course, in itself vest the legal title to the registered land in the transferee. He must complete the conveyance of the land by applying to the Land Registry for registration of himself as the new owner of the land.[18]

A. Responsibility

[17.04] As a general rule it is the responsibility of the purchaser to prepare at his own expense the conveyance for execution by the vendor and all other necessary parties.[19] This rule is recognised expressly by the standard form contract issued by the Law Society.[20] However, in certain cases it is common practice for the conveyance to be drafted by someone else. Thus, in the case

---

9. See further, para **[18.122]** *post*.
10. Succession Act 1965, s 52(5). See *Irish Land Law* (2nd ed, 1986), paras 16.44-6. See also Brady, *Succession Law in Ireland* (2nd ed, 1995), para [10.34] *et seq*. *Cf* an endorsed receipt put on the mortgage deed by a building society, see Building Societies Act 1989, s 27 (*Stamers v Preston* (1859) 9 ICLR 351) or other mortgage, see Housing Act 1988, s 18. Note also satisfaction of a judgment mortgage: see *Irish Land Law* (2nd ed, 1986), para 13.163 *et seq*.
11. See Bankruptcy Act 1988, s 56. See Sanfey and Holohan, *Bankruptcy Law and Practice in Ireland* (1991) para 7.6 *et seq*.
12. Ie, fee farm grants or leases for lives, see Wylie, *Irish Landlord and Tenant Law* para 5.26.
13. Deasy's Act, 1860, s 4. See *ibid*, para **[5.25]** *et seq*.
14. See *Wright v Tracy* (1874) IR 8 CL 478.
15. See *Wylie, op cit*, para 5.28 *et seq*.
16. See *ibid*, para 25.10 *et seq*.
17. See Land Registration Rules 1972, r 69 and Sched of Forms: Fitzgerald, *Land Registry Practice* (2nd ed, 1995) pp 24 and 27 *et seq*. See para **[18.04]** *post*.
18. See para **[20.44]** *post*.
19. See *Tennent v Robinson* (1852) 2 ICLR 142. See also *Poole v Hill* (1840) 6 M & W 835.
20. *General Conditions of Sale* (1995 ed), cond 20: see para **[10.43]** *ante*.

of a grant of a lease, it is usual for the lessor's solicitor to draft this, rather than the lessee's.[21] Similarly, it is usual for the grantor's solicitor to draft the fee farm grant. However, it is provided by statute that the grantee or lessee does not have to pay the grantor's or lessor's solicitor's costs and any stipulation to the contrary, eg, in the contract for sale, is void.[22] In the case of a mortgage, the mortgage deed is usually drafted and engrossed by the mortgagee's solicitor, at the mortgagor's expense.

[17.05] Even though the purchaser may be responsible for drafting and engrossing the conveyance, he may be required by the contract for sale to use the form furnished by the vendor, often by annexation to the contract. Use of the vendor's draft is frequently stipulated where the property forms part of a larger development, eg, a new house on a housing estate. This practice has obvious advantages from the building developer's point of view, in that it standardises the documentation relating to that estate and helps to ensure the applicability of the "estate scheme" rules.[23] However, it should be noted that there may be considerable disadvantages, even serious dangers, in the practice from the purchaser's point of view. All too often the documents are drafted in a rather "one-sided" fashion, favouring the developer rather than individual purchasers, and the purchaser's solicitor must consider whether it is wise to allow his client to enter into a contract which commits him to a particular form of conveyance before the title to the property has been fully investigated. He will usually find that there is very little, if any, scope for having the draft conveyance amended at a later stage. There is also the risk, which is inherent in attempts at standardisation of documents for several transactions, that the standard document has not been drafted in a sufficiently flexible form to cover each particular case.

B. Delivery of Draft and Engrossment

[17.06] It is usual for these matters to be regulated by the contract for sale. Thus condition 20 of the Law Society's *General Conditions of Sale (1995 Edition)* requires that the draft assurance be submitted to the vendor's solicitor not less than seven days and the engrossment not less than *four* working days before the closing date. The draft conveyance is frequently sent with the requisitions on title,[24] "without prejudice".[25] The Law Society's

---

21. See Wylie, *Irish Landlord and Tenant Law* para 5.04.
22. Landlord and Tenant (Ground Rents) Act 1967, s 32. See para **[10.11]** *ante*.
23. Laffoy, *Irish Conveyancing Precedents* pp E20-22 and Precedent E.8.1.
24. See paras **[17.01]** *supra*.
25. Though in strict theory delivery of the draft conveyance or an engrossment is not usually a waiver of defects in the title see para **[15.52]** *ante*.

standard contract form expressly provides that the "delivery of the said draft or engrossment shall not prejudice any outstanding Objection or Requisition validly made".[26]

[17.07] The purchaser's solicitor sends the draft conveyance to the vendor's solicitor for his approval.[27] To the extent that the responsibility for determining the form of the conveyance rests with the purchaser, the vendor's solicitor's duty in considering the draft is strictly limited.[28] He must, of course, see that the proposed form is sufficient to carry out the objects of the contract for sale. In particular, he must ensure that, when executed, it will not give the purchaser more than he is entitled to under the contract, and that it does not impose restrictions on the vendor which are not authorised by the contract. He should also check for technical errors which might render the conveyance ineffective or give rise to disputes later. And he should correct any typing errors. However, it is not the function of the vendor's solicitor to redraft the conveyance in another form, even though he would prefer that form to the purchaser's solicitor's draft and may regard it as superior, whether in terms of style, conciseness, neatness or whatever. Arguably, it is not even his function to point out omissions which affect the purchaser only, even though the contract for sale makes it clear that there is an omission in the draft conveyance. But there is the risk that a failure to point out the omission at this stage may result in a claim for rectification of the conveyance being made by the purchaser after completion.[29]

C. Forms and Precedents

1. Unregistered Land

[17.08] In preparing the draft conveyance it is usual for the purchaser's solicitor, or the vendor's solicitor in cases where he supplies the draft, to use, or adapt as necessary, an appropriate form or precedent to be found in one of the recognised practitioners' books containing such forms and precedents. Alternatively, the solicitor's firm may have devised its own set of precedents which have been built up over the years in the light of experience, though many of these may be adaptations of ones appearing in precedent books. In this respect Irish solicitors, until recently, were not as well-served as their English counterparts. The only major precedent book containing forms and precedents specifically designed for Irish conveyancers was Stubbs[30] and

---

[26.] Cond 20: see *ibid*.

[27.] See para **[1.08]** *ante*.

[28.] See *Cooper v Cartwright* (1860) John 679 at 685 (*per* Page-Wood V-C).

[29.] See para **[21.39]** *post*.

[30.] William Cotter Stubbs was sometime Examiner of Titles for the Irish Land Commission.

Baxter's[31] *Irish Forms and Precedents*,[32] which was published in 1910 as a supplementary volume to the English *Encyclopaedia of Forms and Precedents*.[33] Though still of considerable value to Irish conveyancers, the 1910 volume contained much material which has been rendered obsolete with the passage of time and does not, of course, provide precedents to deal with developments since then. This is especially so with modern legislation, such as that relating to landlord and tenant law,[34] enacted since the establishment of the State. The result was that often solicitors in Ireland had to devise their own precedents or use those to be found in the editions of English books, such as the *Encyclopaedia*.[35] The position has now changed dramatically with the publication of Laffoy's *Irish Conveyancing Precedents*, the first issue of which appeared in 1992. This contains introductory notes and annotations to individual precedents which should be closely studied by conveyancers. The project is a long-term one but, when it is completed, it will provide practitioners in Ireland with a comprehensive set of modern precedents.

[17.09] It should also be noted that in certain cases a form or precedent may be provided by statute. Thus, the Conveyancing Act 1881,[36] provides precedents relating to a statutory form of mortgage, but these are rarely used in Ireland.[37] In an earlier chapter we saw that statutory regulations prescribe various forms to be used in the case of compulsory purchase of land by a public authority.[38]

2. Registered Land

[17.10] Where the transaction involves registered land, in general the appropriate form prescribed by statutory regulation must be used. These

---

[31.] James Sinclair Baxter managed to combine, *inter alia*, a busy practice at the Bar on the North-East Circuit of Ireland with the post of Regius Professor of Feudal and English Law in the University of Dublin (Trinity College).

[32.] The Consulting Editor was John H Edge, KC, sometimes Legal Assistant Commissioner to the Irish Land Commission, and much of his earlier work, *Forms of Leases and Other Forms Relating to Land in Ireland* (1884), was incorporated into the 1910 volume.

[33.] This work is now in its 5th edition and runs to 42 volumes!

[34.] In the field of succession many useful forms were included in Leitch's *Handbook on the Administration of Estates Act (NI) 1955* (1956), and many of these were adapted for the Republic and incorporated in McGuire's *Succession Act 1965* (2nd ed by Pearce).

[35.] Other established works are: *Kelly's Draftsman* (16th ed, 1993); Hallett, *Conveyancing Precedents* (1965); Key and Elphinstone, *Precedents in Conveyancing* (11th ed, 1922; 15th ed, 1953-4), 3 vols; Prideaux, *Forms and Precedents in Conveyancing* (25th ed, 1958-9), 3 vols.

[36.] See Pt V and 3rd Sched. See also the short forms of deeds contained in the 4th Sched.

[37.] See *Irish Land Law* (2nd ed, 1986), para 12.31.

[38.] See paras **[8.14]** *et seq*.

forms are contained in the Land Registration Rules 1972.[39] These must be used in all transactions to which they refer or to which they are capable of being applied or adapted, with such alterations and additions as are necessary and the Registrar allows.[40] Instruments or documents for which no form is prescribed are to be in such form as the Registrar directs or allows, the scheduled forms being followed as closely as circumstances permit.[41] Where any instrument appears to the Registrar to be improper or not clearly expressed, he may refuse registration absolutely or require modifications subject to his approval before registration.[42]

D. Wording

[17.11] As we shall examine in more detail in the next chapter,[43] the wording of conveyances of unregistered land has had a long and hallowed ancestry. Though the days are long gone when conveyancers were paid by the number of words inserted in the conveyance,[44] the verbosity and somewhat archaic language of the conveyancers of the past has tended to survive down to modern times, as a perusal of most of the modern precedent books will indicate. It is true that various suggestions for simplification have been made from time to time, but they have often been met with a marked lack of enthusiasm on the part of conveyancers.[45] Conveyancers, perhaps understandably, given the amount of money at stake in most conveyancing transactions, are always concerned that omission of a time-honoured phrase will deprive the conveyance of its effectiveness. And they remain sharply divided on such matters as the use of punctuation[46] and figures instead of words for dates. It is, perhaps, one of the advantages of the registration of title system that the forms prescribed by the Land Registry Rules[47] are much more concise than the equivalent conveyances for unregistered land.[48]

[39.] See r 52 and Sched of Forms.

[40.] Rule 52(1).

[41.] *Ibid.*

[42.] Rule 53. See Fitzgerald, *Land Registry Practice* (2nd ed, 1995), pp 24-5 and 27 *et seq.*

[43.] Ch 18, *post.*

[44.] See paras **[20.48]** *post.*

[45.] Note the radical attempt at simplification by Parker in his *Modern Conveyancing Precedents* (1964). *Cf* Ross *Drafting and Negotiating Commercial Leases* (4th ed, 1994).

[46.] Note that as regards the English precedent books mentioned in para **[17.08]** fn 35 *supra*, punctuation is fully used in *Prideaux*, but rarely in *Hallett* or the *Encyclopaedia* (or Stubbs and Baxter's Irish Supplement of 1910). It is also used sparingly in *Laffoy*.

[47.] See para **[17.10]** *supra.*

[48.] See the comparison discussed later, paras **[18.02]** *et seq, post.*

[17.12] The drafting of conveyances for unregistered land must remain very much a matter of personal taste and style. It would be pointless to try and lay down rigid rules on the subject, but a few general remarks may be made.[49] First, it is suggested that those conveyancers who insist upon strict adherence to the traditional forms and phraseology should consider whether that approach remains appropriate at a time when conveyancers are frequently being required by the public at large to justify the practices and, indeed, the very existence of their profession. In particular, they should consider whether the perpetuation of the use of terminology which is often quite meaningless to their clients is always necessary. On the other hand, it would be foolish to believe that conveyances can be drafted completely in terminology with which a layman can be expected to be familiar, for it must be remembered that conveyancing is based upon the concepts of land law which even most law students find extremely difficult to master.[50]

II. CONSTRUCTION OF CONVEYANCES

[17.13] Before examining the form and contents of conveyances in greater detail, it may be useful to discuss briefly the construction of conveyances, especially the general rules of interpretation which have been applied by the courts over the years. These rules must be borne in mind by conveyancers for at least two reasons. First, they are guidelines to be followed when drafting a conveyance for a particular transaction, which may be particularly useful in cases of doubt, eg, where the draftsman cannot find a precedent which covers his case exactly. Secondly, conveyancers are frequently called upon to interpret conveyances drafted by someone else, in which case a knowledge of the rules which would be applied by the court, if the matter were referred to it, is vital. The obvious example is where the purchaser's solicitor has to peruse the title documents furnished by the vendor's solicitor as part of his investigation of title.[51] What follows is necessarily a summary only of the main rules of construction applicable to conveyances. For a more detailed discussion readers are referred to the standard texts on the subject.[52]

[49.] Further reference may be made, eg, to Piesse and Gilchrist Smith, *The Elements of Drafting* (3rd ed, 1965) and to other works dealing with the drafting of legal documents or instruments generally, including legislation, eg Bennion, *Statutory Interpretation* (2nd ed, 1992); Thornton, *Legislative Drafting* (4th ed, 1996).

[50.] See *Irish Land Law* (2nd ed, 1986), paras 1.01-4.

[51.] See para **[15.06]** *et seq, ante*.

[52.] Eg *Norton on Deeds* (2nd ed, 1928); Odgers, *The Construction of Deeds and Statutes* (5th ed, by Dworkin; 1967).

A. General Principles

[17.14] We begin our summary with a statement of the general principles which govern construction of conveyances[53] and then go on to mention some specific rules which are invoked by the courts from time to time.

1. Intention of the Parties

[17.15] The overriding rule of construction of a deed is to give effect to the intention of the parties as expressed in the deed.[54] It is important to note that this does not justify the ignoring of the express words in pursuance of what is otherwise conceived to be the intention of the parties. The essential question is what is the meaning of the words actually used by the parties, not what did the parties mean to say and, perhaps, fail to make clear by the words they used.[55] As Ball J put it in *O'Donnell v Ryan*[56]:

> "The very plain and well-established principle is, that in construing legal instruments, we are not at liberty either to transpose language or to reject words out of the instrument, or to import them into it, unless it becomes necessary to do so in order to carry out the manifest intention of the parties, appearing by the language they have used. I say the manifest intention apparent on the instrument; for it would be obviously a vicious construction to transpose, or reject, or supply words, in order to give effect to an intention not manifested by the parties, but only conjectured by the court, that is, an intention which, in the mind of the court, the parties may have entertained, but which the language of the instrument did not clearly import that they did. To reject words having a definite signification, and treat them as insensible, or to import into the instrument words which the parties themselves have not thought fit to use, or to transpose words so as to alter the meaning of a legal instrument, would be manifestly to take such a liberty with it as neither law nor reason could justify, unless it be absolutely necessary to do so for the purpose of preventing the defeat of the object which the parties have clearly shown they had in view."[57]

---

53. For discussion of these principles as they apply to wills, see *Irish Land Law* (2nd ed, 1986), paras 14.36-50; Brady, *Succession Law in Ireland* (2nd ed, 1995), Ch 5.
54. See the discussion in *Wharton v Kelly* (1861) 14 ICLR 293. See also *Mansfield v Doolin* (1869) IR 4 CL 17; *Quinn v Shields* (1877) IR 11 CL 254; *Di Munro v Childs* High Court, unrep, 14 December 1979 (1978/5526 P).
55. For illustration of this distinction, see *Re Hopkin's Lease* [1972] 1 WLR 372.
56. (1854) 4 ICLR 44. See also *Drummond v Attorney-General* (1849) 2 HLC 837. In the context of a will, see *Fitzpatrick v Collins* [1978] ILRM 244.
57. *Ibid* pp 56-7.

The meaning of a deed must be gained from reading it as a whole,[58] and where the transaction is effected by two or more documents these should be construed together.[59]

2. Ordinary Meaning of Words

[17.16] In determining the meaning of the words used in the conveyance, the general rule is that the "grammatical and ordinary" sense of the words is to be taken, unless this would lead to some absurdity, repugnance or inconsistency with the rest of the deed.[60] This principle is also frequently applied to wills.[61]

3. Technical Words

[17.17] On the other hand, where technical words or terms, whether legal, scientific or otherwise, are used, the assumption to be made is that they are used in their technical sense, unless the contrary appears from the conveyance.[62] It should be noted, however, that there is no equivalent in Ireland of the English statutory provision[63] defining for the purposes of deeds, contracts, wills and other instruments, eg, "month" as meaning calendar month,[64] "person" as including a corporation, the singular as including the plural and *vice versa*, and the masculine as including the feminine and *vice versa*.[65]

[58.] *Wharton v Kelly* (1861) 14 ICLR 293 at 297 (*per* O'Brien J); *Delmer v McCabe* (1863) 14 ICLR 377 at 383-4 (*per* Monahan CJ).

[59.] *Atkinson v Pillsworth* (1787) 1 Ridgw PC 449 at 461-2 *per* Yelverton LCB). See also *Massy v O'Dell* (1859) 9 Ir Ch R 441.

[60.] *Clements v Henry* (1859) 10 Ir Ch R 79 at 87-8 (*per* Smith MR), applying the principle enunciated by Lord Wensleydale in *Grey v Pearson* (1857) 6 HLC 61 at 106; *cf Thompson v Thompson* (1871) IR 6 Eq 113 at 118 (*per* Chatterton V-C). See also *Caulfield v Maguire* (1856) 5 Ir Ch R 78; *McNeill v Crommelin* (1858) 8 ICLR 61; *Listowel v Gibbings* (1858) 9 ICLR 223.

[61.] See *Heron v Ulster Bank Ltd* [1974] NI 44 at 53 (per Lowry LCJ), applied by Carroll J in *Howell v Howell* [1992] 1 IR 290. See *Brady, op cit*, para [5.07] *et seq*.

[62.] *Meyler v Meyler* (1883) 11 LR Ir 522. See *Irish Land Law* (2nd ed, 1986), para 4.033. Again this applies to wills: *Brady, op cit*, para [5.13] *et seq*.

[63.] Law of Property Act 1925, s 61. The Law Reform Commission has recommended enactment of a similar provision here: see *Land Law and Conveyancing Law: (1) General Proposals* (LRC 30-1989), paras 20-21.

[64.] It seems that at common law "month" means lunar month, see *Phipps & Co Ltd v Rogers* [1925] 1 KB 14; *Vone Securities Ltd v Cooke* [1979] IR 59 (discussed in *Irish Landlord and Tenant Law* para 20.06).

[65.] Though the similar definitions for statutes contained in, eg, the Interpretation Act 1937 (see ss 11 and 12) may be incorporated into a conveyance by reference.

4. Recitals

[17.18] That part of a deed which is known as the "recitals," which is the part near the beginning which usually begins with the word "WHEREAS,"[66] may help to explain the effect of the deed by, eg, setting out its purpose and stating the vendor's title to the property. However, it is important to remember that recitals are not essential to a deed and, even where they are included, they do not form an "operative" part of it and must, in the event of an inconsistency, give way to an operative part,[67] eg, the words of grant[68] or *habendum.*[69] We examine the role of recitals in greater detail in the next chapter.[70]

5. Extrinsic Evidence

[17.19] The general rule is that extrinsic evidence is not admissible to add to, vary or contradict the terms of a deed.[71] The construction of a deed cannot be controlled by the antecedent or subsequent acts of the parties,[72] nor, indeed, by the terms of the contract[73] or the draft conveyance.[74] However, there are several well-known exceptions to this rule.[75] Thus it is clear that extrinsic evidence is admissible to explain the meaning of words used, eg, to resolve a latent ambiguity.[76] However, where there is a clear contradiction between two parts of a deed, generally extrinsic evidence is not admissible and instead the rule is that the first statement or description prevails over the

---

66. See para **[18.25]** *post.*
67. See *Butler v Gilbert* (1890) 25 LR Ir 230 at 241-2 (*per* Porter MR); See also *Macnamara v Carey* (1867) IR 1 Eq 9 at 22 (*per* Blackburne C); *Re Carter's Trusts* (1869) IR 3 Eq 495 at 501 (*per* Chatterton V-C).
68. See para **[18.48]** *post.*
69. See para **[18.84]** *post.*
70. See para **[18.25]** *et seq, post.* See also *Renwick v Daly* (1877) IR 11 CL 126; *O'Sullivan v Weekes* (1903) 4 NIJR 153.
71. *Blake v Marnell* (1811) 2 Ba & B 35 at 47 (*per* Lord Manners LC); *Davis v Fitton* (1842) 4 Ir Eq R 612 at 615-6 (*per* Sugden LC). See also *O'Donnell v Ryan* (1854) 4 ICLR 44 at 56-7 (*per* Ball J) (see para **[17.15]** *supra*); *Hollier v Eyre* (1842) 2 Dr & War 590. Garner, 'Admission of Extrinsic Evidence and Deeds Conferring Rights in Land' (1965) 29 Conv 175.
72. *Burrowes v Hayes* (1834) Hay & Jon 597. See also *Douglas v Allen* (1842) 2 Dr & War 213.
73. But note that if a mistake has been made, parol evidence may be admissible to prove this and to found a claim for rectification, see *infra* and para **[21.39]** *post.*
74. *Re Carter's Trusts* (1869) IR 3 Eq 495 at 501 (*per* Chatterton V-C). See also *City and Westminster Properties (1934) Ltd v Mudd* [1959] Ch 129. *Cf White v Taylor (No 2)* [1969] 1 Ch 160.
75. *Lord Waterpark v Fennell* (1855) 5 ICLR 120 at 129-30 (*per* Moore J).
76. *Bradford v Dublin and Kingstown Rly Co* (1858) 7 ICLR 624 at 630 (*per* Lefroy CJ). See also *Drummond v Attorney-General* (1849) 2 HLC 837; *Donegall v Templemore* (1858) 9 ICLR 374. *Cf* the introduction of secondary evidence where the original deed is lost or destroyed: see *Savage v Nolan* [1978] ILRM 151. See para **[14.51]** *ante.*

second.[77] However, it is admissible to show that the deed is not binding, eg, on account of fraud, or to establish a claim for rectification on the ground of mistake.[78] In *Revenue Commissioners v Moroney*[79] an assignment of leasehold premises by a father to himself and his sons for a stated consideration of £16,000 contained a receipt clause whereby the father purported to acknowledge receipt of this sum. In fact, the sum was never intended to be paid, nor was it ever paid, and when later the Revenue Commissioners argued that two-thirds of the sum constituted a debt owed to the father upon which estate duty was payable on his death, the sons challenged this. Kenny J, whose decision was affirmed by the Supreme Court, held that extrinsic evidence was admissible to refute the receipt clause. As he put it:

> "It is not necessary to give authority for the proposition that evidence may be given to show that, despite the receipt, the consideration was not paid. Similarly, evidence is admissible when it is relevant to explain to circumstances in which the deed was executed and to establish that the parties did not intend that the purchase price mentioned in the deed should ever be paid".[80]

The object of the receipt clause was to expedite processing of the deed in the stamp office,[81] but if the purpose is to evade duty or otherwise to pursue a fraud or illegality the courts will not render assistance.[82]

[17.20] In passing it may be noted that the extrinsic evidence rule was given statutory recognition in s 90 of the Succession Act 1965, which reads:

> Extrinsic evidence shall be admissible to show the intention of the testator, and to assist in the construction of, or explain any contradiction in, a will.

Unfortunately, the courts have had some difficulty in interpreting the precise scope of the provision[83] and, in particular, have had doubts as to how far it extends the traditional scope of the extrinsic evidence rule as it applied to

---

[77.] *Bradford v Dublin and Kingstown Rly Co* (1858) 7 ICLR 624; *Roe v Lidwell* (1860) 11 Ir Ch R 320, *Kenny v La Barte* [1902] 2 IR 63. See also *Boyle v Mulholland* (1860) 10 Ir Ch R 150. In the case of wills the rule is that the second description prevails over the first, see *Irish Land Law* (2nd ed, 1986), para 14.40.

[78.] *Flood v Finlay* (1811) 2 Ba & B 9 at 15 (*per* Lord Manners LC); *Macnamara v Carey* (1867) IR 1 Eq 9 at 22 (*per* Blackbourne C). See also *Davis v Fitton* (1842) 4 Ir Eq R 612. See also para **[21.39]** *post*.

[79.] [1972] IR 372.

[80.] *Ibid*, p 377.

[81.] If the transfer has been for natural love and affection, the amount of duty would have required adjudication: see Keane, *Equity and the Law of Trusts in Ireland* (1988), para 28.06.

[82.] See *Parkes v Parkes* [1980] ILRM 137.

[83.] See the full discussion in *Brady, op cit* para [5.25] *et seq*.

wills.[84] The Supreme Court has appreciated the difficulties and recently reserved its position on the subject.[85]

B. Some Specific Rules

[17.21] The following are some specific rules frequently invoked by the courts when faced by a problem of construction. From the outset it must be mentioned that this summary is by no means exhaustive.

1. Contra Proferentem

[17.22] In a case of doubt or ambiguity, a deed is construed against the grantor in favour of the grantee. This rule has particular significance in relation to exceptions or reservations, eg, of easements or profits.[86] It is also a rule which landlords must bear in mind, for a consequence is that ambiguities in the terms of the lease will generally be construed in the tenant's favour.[87]

2. Id Certum Est Quod Certum Reddi Potest

[17.23] We met this rule, that what is capable of being rendered certain is to be treated as certain, in an earlier chapter in connection with the requirements of a memorandum or note of a contract for sale for the purposes of the Statute of Frauds.[88]

3. Falsa Demonstratio Non Nocet

[17.24] Under this rule a false description in the deed may not prejudice its intended effect, eg, where more than one description appears in the deed, and one is clearly accurate, the other or others may be disregarded.[89] This

---

[84.] The so-called "armchair principle" seemed to confine the admissibility of such evidence to explain what the testator had written rather than what he intended to write: see *Re Julian* [1950] IR 57.

[85.] *Curtin v O'Mahoney* [1991] 2 IR 562. *Cf* its earlier decision in *Rowe v Law* [1978] IR 55. See also *Bennett v Bennett* High Court, unrep, 24 January 1977 (1974/109 Sp); *Re Clinton* [1988] ILRM 80; *Re Egan* High Court, unrep, 16 June 1989 (1988/399 Sp).

[86.] *Connell v O'Malley* High Court, unrep, 28 July 1983 (1979/8260 P). *Cf re* a restrictive covenant, *St Luke's and St Anne's Hospital Board v Mahon* High Court, unrep, 18 June 1993 (1992/895 P). See the discussion of this in *Irish Land Law* (2nd ed, 1986), paras 6.058-72.

[87.] See *Sepes Establishment Ltd v KSK Enterprises Ltd* [1993] 2 IR 225 at 235 (*per* O'Hanlon J). See also *CIF Holdings Ltd v Barclays Bank (Ir) Ltd* High Court, unrep, 25 July 1986 (see *Irish Landlord and Tenant Law* para 11.31).

[88.] See paras **[6.20]** and **[6.22]** *ante*.

[89.] *Roe v Lidwell* (1860) 11 Ir Ch R 320. See also *Boyle v Mulholland* (1860) 10 Ir Ch R 150; *Rochfort v Ennis* (1861) 13 ICLR 324; *Re McDermott and Kellett's Contract* (1904) 4 NIJR 89.

rule is frequently invoked where there is an inconsistency between the parcels clause in the body of the deed and a map annexed or attached to it.[90] We return to this subject later.[91]

4. Omnia Praesumunter Rite Esse Acta

[17.25] This rule, that everything should be presumed to have been done properly, is frequently invoked in cases of doubt as to whether, eg, a deed has been properly executed.[92] It is a rule also invoked frequently where the issue is whether a will has been properly executed, so that, eg, it may be presumed that alterations have been made before execution of the will itself.[93]

5. Expressum Facit Cessare Tacitum

[17.26] It is clear that inclusion of an express provision on a matter in a deed excludes the implication of any other provision on the same matter. This principle has particular significance, eg, where statutory provisions, such as covenants for title, would otherwise be implied in a conveyance.[94] We discuss this subject later.[95]

6. Ut Res Magis Valeat, Quam Pereat

[17.27] The courts may invoke the principle that, in cases of doubt or ambiguity, it is better to adopt a construction of a deed or other document which will permit it to have force than one which will render it inoperative.[96]

---

90. See the discussion in *Bradford v Dublin and Kingstown Rly Co* (1858) 7 ICLR 624.
91. Para **[18.58]** *et seq, post.*
92. See the discussion of the rule by Davitt J in *In b McLean* [1950] IR 180 at 185. See also *Reid v Miller* [1928] NI 151. As to execution, see para **[18.119]** *et seq, post.*
93. See *Clarke v Early* [1980] IR 229. See the discussion in *Brady, op cit*, para [2.46] *et seq.*
94. *Thompson v Thompson* (1871) IR 6 Eq 113 at 125 (*per* Chatterton V-C).
95. See para **[21.05]** *et seq, post.*
96. See *Blakeney v Hardie* (1874) IR 8 Eq 381 at 389 (*per* Brooke CS).

Chapter 18

FORM AND CONTENTS OF DEEDS

[18.01] In this chapter we examine in general the form and contents of deeds relating to both registered and unregistered land. In the next chapter we consider some of the more important aspects of deeds used for particular transactions. We begin with a comparison between the documents used for registered and unregistered land.

I. Documents for Registered and Unregistered Land

[18.02] As we discussed in the previous chapter,[1] the documents to be used in dealings with registered land are largely prescribed by statutory regulation, whereas documents for unregistered land are usually based upon well-recognised precedents. A comparison between the form and contents of the two types of deed is best shown by giving a simple illustration. This illustration also serves to point out the main parts of such documents which are examined in greater detail later in the chapter.[2] Let us suppose that V is the owner of the fee simple in Blackacre and has agreed to convey it to P for £50,000.

[18.03] If Blackacre were unregistered land, the conveyance from V to P would take a form such as that which follows[3]:

THIS INDENTURE made the 1st day of January 1996 BETWEEN   of (hereinafter called "the Vendor") of the one part and   of (hereinafter called "the Purchaser") of the other part

WHEREAS:

A.   The Vendor is seised of the premises described in the Schedule hereto (hereinafter called "the Premises") for an estate in fee simple in possession free from incumbrances.

[1.]   See paras **[17.02-3]** and **[17.08-10]** *ante*.

[2.]   See para **[18.02]** *et seq, infra*.

[3.]   It must be emphasised that this is something of a "skeleton" used solely for the purposes of illustration. In practice such a conveyance. even for such a straightforward transaction, would be likely to contain rather more provisions. eg exceptions. reservations, covenants and restrictions. See, generally, Laffoy, *Irish Conveyancing Precedents*, Division E. The precedent reproduced follows Precedent E.1.1.

B. The Vendor has agreed with the Purchaser for the sale to the Purchaser of the Premises for an estate in fee simple in possession free from incumbrances at the price of IR£50,000.

NOW THIS INDENTURE WITNESSETH as follows:

1. In pursuance of the said agreement and in consideration of the sum of IR£50,000 now paid by the Purchaser to the Vendor (the receipt whereof the Vendor hereby acknowledges) the Vendor as beneficial owner hereby conveys unto the Purchaser ALL THAT AND THOSE the Premises TO HOLD the same unto and to the use of the Purchaser in fee simple.

2. It is hereby certified by the purchaser being the person becoming entitled to the entire beneficial interest in the Premises hereby conveyed that he is an Irish citizen and as such a qualified person within the meaning of Section 45 of the Land Act, 1965.

3. It is hereby further certified that the transaction hereby effected does not form part of a larger transaction or series of transactions in respect of which the amount or value or the aggregate amount or value of the consideration exceeds IR£50,000.

4. It is hereby further certified for the purposes of the stamping of this Conveyance that this is an instrument to which the provisions of Section 112 of the Finance Act, 1990 do not apply for the reason that the Premises constitute an existing house.

IN WITNESS whereof the parties hereto have hereunto set their respective hands and seals the day and year first above WRITTEN

SCHEDULE

(The Premises)

ALL THAT AND THOSE

SIGNED SEALED and DELIVERED
by the VENDOR
in the presence of:

SIGNED SEALED and DELIVERED
by the PURCHASER
in the presence of:

[18.04] If instead Blackacre were registered land and V were the registered owner, the transfer document, as prescribed by the Land Registry rules,[4] would be in the following form:

LAND REGISTRY

County   Folio [5]

Transfer dated, 1st day of January 1996. [V] the registered owner, in consideration of £50,000 (the receipt of which is hereby acknowledged) as beneficial owner[6] hereby transfers all the property described in folio [the Registry number for Blackacre] of the register County [where Blackacre is situated] to [P]

The address of [P] in the State for service of notices and his description are:

It is hereby certified [certificate of value for stamp duty purposes and other revenue certificates, Land Act consents and Family Home Protection Act 1976, consent]

Signed, sealed and delivered [signature of V]
by [V] in the presence of:-

[18.05] It is clear then that Land Registry forms tend to be rather shorter and simpler documents than conveyances of unregistered land and also have the merit that they usually omit much of the archaic terminology still so prevalent in conveyances. It is also to be noted that the Registry form quoted above omits altogether some of the parts of the conveyance quoted, eg, the recitals clause,[7] including parts which are essential in a conveyance of unregistered land, eg, the words of limitation.[8]

II. CONTENTS OF DEEDS

[18.06] We now examine in some detail the various parts of typical conveyances of unregistered land, comparing in each case the equivalent (if any) parts of Land Registry documents. At each stage we shall refer to the examples given above[9] for illustration purposes.

---

4. The form given here is that prescribed by the Land Registration Rules 1972, Sched of Forms, No 19 (transfer of freehold property by a registered full owner).
5. Inserted here will be the Land Registry reference number relating to Blackacre, see para **[9.10]** *ante.* and see later in the transfer form.
6. Form 19 specifies that these words may be inserted if desired. See further para **[21.06]** *post.*
7. Ie, the clause beginning with the word "WHEREAS." See para **[18.25]** *infra.*
8. Ie, the words "in fee simple" But, in practice words of limitation are commonly inserted. See para **[18.88]** *infra.* Note also the omission of the reference to holding unto "and to the use of" the purchaser, see para **[18.86]** *infra.*
9. Paras **[18.03-4]** *supra.*

A. Commencement

[18.07] A conveyance of unregistered land usually begins with a statement or description indicating the nature of the document. The traditional practice was to begin with the words "THIS INDENTURE," to distinguish a deed made between two or more parties, ie, a deed *inter partes*, from one made by one party only, ie, a deed "poll," so-called because the top of it was usually "polled" or shaved. In earlier times, a deed *inter partes* was written out in duplicate on the same piece of parchment and was then cut into two parts by an irregular or "indented" line.[10] Each party then retained one part which fitted the other and so proved its genuineness as the counterpart of the same deed. A conveyance may still be called an indenture, and it is still common to do so in Ireland,[11] but it may instead be called by a name appropriate to the transaction in question, eg, "THIS CONVEYANCE" in the case of a sale of freehold land,[12] "THIS LEASE" in the case of a grant of a lease, "THIS ASSIGNMENT" in the case of an assignment of an existing lease, "THIS MORTGAGE" in the case of a mortgage and "THIS ASSENT" in the case of an assent by personal representatives. Though it is to be noted that there is as yet no equivalent in Ireland[13] of s 57 of the Law of Property Act 1925, whereby it is confirmed by statute that any deed, whether or not an indenture, may be described as a deed simple, or as a conveyance, settlement, mortgage, charge or whatever, according to the nature of the transaction. However, by s 5 of the Real Property Act 1845,[14] a deed in Ireland, purporting to be an indenture,[15] has the effect of an indenture, although not actually indented.

[18.08] As we saw earlier,[16] generally the forms prescribed for registered land do not contain a description of the form in question like a conveyance,

---

[10.] Later only one copy would be written out which would be "indented" by, eg, cutting the top of the first page or sheet of the document in a wavy line.

[11.] Note that most of the precedents in *Stubbs and Baxter* (see para **[17.08]** *ante*) used the expression "THIS INDENTURE", see, eg, pp 117-26 (fee farm grants), 239-336 (leases), 418-26 (mortgages) and 702 (settlement). *Laffoy* continues this practice, see especially Division E (Conveyances an Sale).

[12.] See Division L in *Laffoy*.

[13.] See, however, the recommendations in para 177 of the *Survey of the Land Law of Northern Ireland* (1971).

[14.] Replaced in England by s 56(2) of the Law of Property Act 1925.

[15.] It is not entirely clear whether this requires the deed to be expressed to be an indenture. Presumably not; ie, it need not begin with the words "THIS INDENTURE," so long as the rest of the deed makes it clear that it is made *inter partes*. Section 56(2) of the English 1925 Act (fn 14, *supra*) does make this point clear by providing that a deed operates as an indenture "though not indented *or expressed to be an indenture*". (Italics added).

[16.] Para **[18.04]** *supra*.

but rather a heading containing the appropriate Land Registry reference, eg, the folio number. However, as we saw before,[17] transfer forms then go on to begin with the word "Transfer".[18] In passing, it may be noted that it has been held in England[19] that a Land Registry transfer is more in the nature of a deed poll than a deed *inter partes*, so that it is not governed by rules applicable to the latter, eg, the restriction that a party to such a deed can take a benefit under it or sue on it only if named a party to it.[20] However, that restriction, which never applied to deeds poll, was substantially modified also by s 5 of the Real Property Act 1845, which reads:

> "Under an indenture executed after the first day of October one thousand eight hundred and forty-five an immediate estate or interest in any tenements or hereditaments, and the benefit of a condition or covenant respecting any tenements or hereditaments, may be taken, although the taker thereof be not named a party to the same indenture."[21]

B. Date

[18.09] It is usual to date a conveyance of unregistered land with the date of actual completion, though it has long been established that insertion of a date is not strictly a necessary part of the deed.[22] Furthermore, it is also clear that the date from which a deed operates, ie, transfers the estate to be conveyed to the purchaser, is the date of delivery of the deed, which is not necessarily the closing date or date of completion.[23] However, the courts have recognised a presumption that any date actually appearing on a deed is the correct one, though they have been careful to emphasise that this is a presumption only, which may be rebutted by evidence to the contrary.[24] If

---

17. *Ibid.*
18. See the Schedule of Forms of the Land Registration Rules 1972.
19. *Chelsea and Walham Green BS v Armstrong* [1951] Ch 853, espec at 857-8 (*per* Vaisey J).
20. See *McArdle v Irish Iodine Co* (1864) 15 ICLR 146 at 153 (*per* Pigot CB).
21. This was replaced in England by s 56(1) of the Law of Property Act 1925. The views of Denning LJ (as he then was) on the effect of s 5 of the 1845 Act, and s 56(1) of the 1925 Act (expressed in cases such as *Drive Yourself Hire Co (London) Ltd v Strutt* [1954] 1 QB 250 at 273), especially as regards the general doctrine of privity of contract, must be reconsidered now in the light of the view of the House of Lords expressed in *Beswick v Beswick* [1968] AC 58. See Wylie, 'Contracts and Third Parties' (1966) 17 NILQ 351 at 402-12.
22. *Goddard's Case* (1584) 2 Co Rep 46, which also supports the proposition that parol evidence is admissible to establish the correct date of a deed. Note, however, that it is essential that a contract for a lease shows the commencement of the term granted by it, see para **[6.26]** *ante*. See also *Landlord and Tenant Law*, para 6.03.
23. *Clayton's Case* (1585) 5 Co Rep 1a; *Halter v Ashe* (1696) 3 Lev 438.
24. *Browne v Burton* (1847) 17 LJQB 49 at 50 (*per* Patterson J); *Re Slater* (1897) 76 LT 529 at 530 (*per* Wright J). Cf *Roberts v Church Commrs for England* [1972] 1 QB 278 at 283 (*per* Russell LJ).

two documents bear the same date, eg, a conveyance and mortgage, there is a presumption that they have been executed in the order which gives effect to the parties' manifest intention.[25]

[18.10] Though the date is not essential for the validity of the deed, the determination of the date from which it operates may be important for a variety of reasons and, in view of the presumptions mentioned in the previous paragraph, it is not surprising that when solicitors ask clients to execute deeds they usually request them to leave the date blank, so that it can be inserted later. First, much legislation, eg, Finance Acts and other legislation concerning taxation,[26] applies to instruments operating before or after certain dates. Secondly, under the Stamp Act 1891,[27] many conveyancing documents, eg, conveyances on sale, leases, mortgages and settlements, may be stamped after, instead of before, execution, but must be stamped or presented for adjudication within thirty days of execution, if a penalty is to be avoided.[28] Thirdly, there are other time limits which are linked to the date of operation of a conveyance. Thus, the grantee of a conveyance of land in a compulsory registration of title area, which is subject for the first time to compulsory registration, must become the registered owner within six months after the conveyance.[29] A failure to register his title means that the grantee does register the estate or interest purportedly granted to him,[30] though, once he does register it, his title relates back to the date of execution of the conveyance.[31] Fourthly, rights in the nature of quasi-easements which may arise by implication on a conveyance of land under s 6(1) of the Conveyancing Act 1881, include those enjoyed with the land "at the time of the conveyance".[32] Fifthly, subject to the rules governing priorities in relation to unregistered land,[33] an unregistered conveyance may take priority from the date it was made.[34] Sixthly, if a date

---

[25.] *Gartside v Silkstone and Dodsworth Iron and Coal Co* (1882) 21 Ch D 762 at 767-8 (*per* Fry J).

[26.] See para **[1.24]** *ante*.

[27.] Sections 1(3) and 15(2). Sections 1 and 15 were substituted respectively by ss 94 and 100 of the Finance Act 1991.

[28.] See further on this subject. Para **[20.38]** *post*. For these purposes, "execution" is governed by the general law (see para **[18.119]** *et seq, infra*) and cannot be altered by the date inserted on the deed by the solicitor: see para **[9.15]** *ante*.

[29.] Registration of Title Act 1964, s 25. See para **[20.42]** *post*.

[30.] See Fitzgerald, *Land Registry Practice* (2nd ed, 1995), p 387.

[31.] Apparently the Registrar as a matter of practice frequently allows registration "out-of-time": See *Fitzgerald, op cit*, p 387.

[32.] See *Irish Land Law* (2nd ed, 1986), paras 6.066-8.

[33.] See *ibid* para 3.069 *et seq*.

[34.] Of course, in Ireland this is qualified substantially by the existence of the Registry of Deeds system, under which the crucial date is the date of registration of the conveyance, see *ibid* para 3 084 *et seq*.

is going to be inserted in a conveyance, care should be taken to see that it is the correct one, if only because under the Forgery Act 1913, it is a criminal offence to forge a document "with intent to defraud or deceive"[35] and making a false document includes falsely stating in it "the time or place of making, where either is material."[36] It is true that in many cases where the wrong date is inserted there may be no requisite "intent"[37] or the date may not be "material,"[38] but where, eg, a deed is deliberately antedated or post-dated in order to avoid the effect of legislation, a court may well regard this as technically a forgery under the 1913 Act.[39] Furthermore, apart from the criminal sanction, it must be remembered that a forged deed is null and void and, therefore, passes no estate to the purchaser.[40]

[18.11] So far as registered land transfers are concerned, the forms prescribed in Ireland do in fact require insertion of a date.[41] However, the date of the transfer is not the crucial date in such cases; the crucial date is the date of registration of the purchaser as the new owner of the registered land.[42]

C. Parties

[18.12] There are two matters to be considered: who are the necessary parties to a deed (ie, who should be joined in it), and how should they be described? The answer to the first question will obviously vary from case to case.

1. Necessary Parties

[18.13] In a straightforward transaction, it is usually clear who are the parties to be joined in the conveyance, eg, the vendor and purchaser, lessor and lessee, mortgagor and mortgagee, as the case may be. In certain cases there may be only one party, eg, where a personal representative assents to the vesting of land in himself as sole beneficiary. Apart from that, the general rule is that persons should be joined as parties to the deed only where this is necessary because otherwise the deed would fail to achieve all its objects.[43] Thus any person intended to take the benefit of or to become

---

35. Section 1(1).
36. Section 1(2).
37. See *R v Kitson* (1869) LR 1 CCR 200.
38. See *R v Wells* [1939] 2 All ER 169.
39. See *ibid*.
40. *Re Cooper* (1882) 20 Ch D 611; *Kreditbank Cassel v Schenkers Ltd* [1927] 1 KB 826, *cf Kwei Tek Chao v British Traders and Shippers Ltd* [1954] 2 QB 459 at 476 (*per* Devlin J).
41. Land Registration Rules 1972, Sched of Forms. See para **[18.04]** *supra*.
42. See para **[12.50]** *ante*.
43. See *Corder v Morgan* (1811) 18 Ves 344.

subject to an obligation created by the deed should be joined,[44] though, as we saw earlier,[45] under s 5 of the Real Property Act 1845, a person may take the benefit, but not the burden, of a deed without being named a party to it. However, the considerable controversy surrounding the scope of that section, and its replacement in England,[46] suggests that the wisest course is still to join all parties intended to take a benefit or to become subject to a burden under the deed, eg, under covenants contained in it.[47] Apart from these cases, there are some special ones to be considered.

(i) Persons Giving Receipts

[18.14] The classic illustration of this case is where the purchase price, or capital money raised on the sale, has to be paid to third parties, who must issue a receipt to effect a good discharge and thereby render the conveyance fully effective. Thus on a sale by the tenant for life of land under the Settled Land Acts 1882-90, the capital money must be paid to the trustees of the settlement[48] and they should be joined in the conveyance to give a receipt for the purchase money.[49]

(ii) Persons Giving Consent

[18.15] Where some third party's or parties' consent is required for the conveyance, he or they may give the consent by endorsement on it or by being joined in it, eg, where a lessor's consent is required for an assignment of a lease. In practice, the consent of a landlord to an assignment or subletting is usually given by a separate document, eg, by letter, but this may be dangerous if the assignor wishes to be relieved of continuing liability on the covenants in accordance with s 16 of Deasy's Act.[50]

---

44. This is the result of the *inter partes* rule, see the discussion by Lord Upjohn in *Beswick v Beswick* [1968] AC 58 at 102-3. See also *McArdle v Irish Iodine Co* (1864) 15 ICLR 146 at 153 (*per* Pigot CB).

45. See para **[18.08]** *supra*.

46. Ie, s 56(1) of the Law of Property Act 1925. See the survey of the authorities by Lord Upjohn in the *Beswick* case, *op cit* pp 106-7. See also Wylie, 'Contracts and Third Parties' (1966) 17 NILQ 351.

47. Unless, of course. this is impracticable, eg, where the purchaser enters into a restrictive covenant with the vendor "and the owners for the time being of land adjacent to that conveyed", see *Re Ecclesiastical Commrs for England's Conveyance* [1936] Ch 430.

48. See *Irish Land Law* (2nd ed, 1986), para 8.094. See also **[15.15]** *ante*.

49. See para **[18.47]** *infra*.

50. See *Irish Landlord and Tenant Law*, para 21.30. Note that the consent of the trustees of the settlement is required for certain transactions by a tenant for life, eg a sale of the "principal mansion house." See *Irish Land Law* (2nd ed, 1986), para 8.101.

(iii) Mortgagees

[18.16] Unless an existing mortgage is to be discharged before completion, the mortgagee should be joined in a conveyance by the mortgagor to release the mortgage, if the purchaser is to take free of it. This is, however, unusual nowadays. Instead, the mortgagee and purchaser may be satisfied with an appropriate undertaking from the vendor's solicitor to discharge the outstanding debt from the proceeds of sale and a receipt will be endorsed on the mortgage deed when this is done.[51]

(iv) Owners of Overreachable Interests

[18.17] Clearly there is no need to join the owners of interests which are "overreached" on a sale of land, eg, the holders of other interests in settled land on a sale by the tenant for life.[52]

(v) Nominees

[18.18] Subject to any agreement to the contrary, the purchaser can require the vendor to convey the land to a nominee or nominees as directed, eg, where he has effected a sub-sale. If, however, this would prejudice the vendor, eg, where the purchaser has entered into personal obligations and his personality is fundamental to the transaction, the vendor may compel the purchaser to join in the conveyance to guarantee performance of those obligations.[53]

2. Description

(i) Name

[18.19] It is usual to describe each party by his full name, ie, Christian or forename or names in full and the surname. Care should be taken over this, as a mistake can cause considerable difficulties in later transactions. If the name now differs from that given in an earlier deed, or a mistake was made in the latter, it may be useful to draw attention to the discrepancy expressly, eg, by stating that the party (probably the vendor) was called by such and such a name when reciting the deed in question. It is, however, settled that, if a mistake does occur, the court will correct it on being shown sufficient evidence of the error.[54] The need for accuracy in respect of names is vital for

---

[51.] See para **[20.37]** *post*.

[52.] See *Irish Land Law* (2nd ed, 1986), paras 8,041-2. *Cf* where the land is held under a trust for sale, see *ibid*, para 8.043 *et seq*. See also *Martin v Lysaght* (1850) 2 Ir Jur (os) 184; *Re Davison's Estate* (1893) 31 LR Ir 249 at 256 (*per* Monroe J), affd [1894] 1 IR 56.

[53.] See *Curtis Moffat Ltd v Wheeler* [1929] 2 Ch 224.

[54.] *Alexander Mountain & Co v Rumere* [1948] 2 KB 436; *Establissement Bandelot v RS Graham & Co* [1953] 2 QB 271. See also *Simmons v Woodward* [1892] AC 100 at 105 (*per* Lord Halsbury); *cf Fung Ping Shan v Tong Skun* [1918] AC 403 at 406.

registration purposes, for the key to the Registry of Deeds system is the Index of Names.[55]

(ii) Address

[18.20] It is also usual to give each party's address or, in the case of a company, its registered office. This helps to identify the parties more clearly and may resolve any doubt created by the name given.

(iii) Occupation

[18.21] It was also the traditional practice to give each party's occupation, though in the case of a women it was more usual to give her status, eg, "spinster," "widow" or "married woman." But most solicitors regard this as superfluous nowadays, since the full name and address are usually quite sufficient to identify the party in question.

(iv) Registered Land

[18.22] The prescribed forms for registered land in Ireland require insertion of the names of the parties and, in the case of the transferee, his address for service of notices and his description (ie, occupation).[56] As regards the transferor, the entry on the folio relating to him as owner of the property is required to give his name and description and his address for service of notices.[57]

3. Format

[18.23] In a deed *inter partes*, it is usual to express the persons joined as parties as being of a separate part of the deed, thus emphasising that it is not a deed poll. Where there are two only, they are usually designated as being "of the one part" and "of the other part," the grantor (vendor) coming first.[58] If there are more than two, they are usually designated as being "of the first part," "of the second part", "of the third part" and so on.[59] In order to save needless repetition in the rest of the deed, it is usual to put in brackets a

---

[55.] See *Irish Land Law*, (2nd ed, 1986) para 22.11. See also para **[15.44]** *ante*. For the possible disastrous consequences of even a slight discrepancy in relation to land charges searches in England, see *Oak Co-operative BS v Blackburn* [1968] Ch 730. See also *Diligant Finance Co Ltd v Alleyne* (1972) 23 P & CR 346.

[56.] Land Registration Rules 1972, Sched of Form See also para **[18.04]** *supra*.

[57.] 1972 Rules, r 3(3)(a).

[58.] See para **[18.03]** *supra*.

[59.] Persons regarded as one owner eg joint tenants, are designated together as being of one part. See *Irish Land Law* (2nd ed, 1986), para 7.07. On the other hand, a person who executes a deed in more than one capacity, eg, a vendor-tenant for life who is also one of the trustees of the settlement (see para **[18.14]** *supra*) may be designated in more than one part.

short-form reference description by which each party will be called elsewhere in the deed, eg, hereinafter called "the Vendor."[60]

[18.24] Generally the prescribed forms for registered land, being much shorter and simpler documents,[61] do not adopt the format of *inter partes* deeds of unregistered land.[62]

D. Recitals

[18.25] It is common for deeds relating to unregistered land to contain as the next part what are known as "recitals," which can usually be identified as the part beginning with the word "WHEREAS." As we shall discuss in a moment,[63] recitals are designed primarily to make the deed more intelligible. However, from the outset it must be emphasised that they are not an essential part of the deed[64] and may be omitted altogether without damaging its efficacy. And, while they may help to explain other parts of a deed,[65] in the event of an inconsistency between the recitals and an operative part of the deed, it is clear that the latter must prevail.[66]

[18.26] The general view is that recitals are not necessary nor, indeed, appropriate[67] for documents dealing with registered land and there is no mention of them in the prescribed forms.[68] In so far as recitals explain the history of the title,[69] this should be clear from the register, at least since the property was first registered. On the other hand, where recitals explain the purpose of the deed in which they are included,[70] there may be occasions where their inclusion may be useful in relation to registered land, eg, where a disposition is made by a personal representative of a deceased owner and the representative has never been registered as owner.[71] Furthermore, if recitals are included, they will attract the incidental advantages which accrue in respect of recitals under the general law, whether the land is registered or

---

[60.] See para **[18.03]** *supra*.

[61.] See para **[18.04]** *supra*.

[62.] Hence the view that such documents are more akin to deeds poll, see para **[18.08]** *supra*.

[63.] See para **[18.35]** *infra*.

[64.] *Blake v Marnell* (1811) 2 Ba & B 35 at 44 (*per* Lord Manners LC). See also *Borrowes v Borrowes* (1871) IR 6 Eq 368 at 379 (*per* Sullivan MR).

[65.] See para **[18.40]** *infra*.

[66.] *Butler v Gilbert* (1890) 25 LR Ir 230 at 241-2 (*per* Porter MR). See para **[17.18]** *ante*.

[67.] See eg, *Emmet of Title* (19th ed by Farrand), para 12.013.

[68.] Land Registration Rules 1972, Sched of Forms.

[69.] Ie narrative recitals. see para **[18.38]** *infra*.

[70.] Ie introductory recitals, see para **[18.40]** *infra*.

[71.] See Registration of Title Act 1964, s 61(2). Also *Irish Land Law* (2nd ed, 1986), para 21.48.

unregistered. And it is to the effect of recitals under the general law that we turn first.

1. Effect

(i) Evidence

[18.27] There are several statutory provisions which establish that recitals may be treated as evidence of the facts stated in them in certain circumstances.

(a) Twenty Years' Old

[18.28] Section 2(2) of the Vendor and Purchaser Act 1874, provides that recitals, statements and descriptions of facts, matters and parties in deeds, instruments, Acts of Parliament or statutory declarations 20 years' old at the date of the contract (for sale) are to be taken as "sufficient" evidence of the truth of such facts, matters and descriptions, unless and except so far as they are proved to be inaccurate.[72] Thus the existence of recitals in a title document may be of advantage from the point of view of deduction and investigation of title.[73]

(b) Pre-Root Title

[18.29] Section 3(3) of the Conveyancing Act 1881, precludes the purchaser from requiring production of pre-root title documents or making requisitions, objections or enquiries as to the pre-root title, notwithstanding that such documents of title are recited.[74] It then goes on to require the purchaser to assume, unless the contrary appears, that such recitals of any documents forming part of the pre-root title are correct, give all the material contents of the documents and that every recited document was duly executed by all necessary parties.

(c) Trustee Appointments

[18.30] In some jurisdictions there is a special provision governing such appointments. In Northern Ireland, s 37(1) of the Trustee Act (NI) 1958, now provides that a statement in an instrument appointing a new trustee of land as to the ground for his appointment[75] is conclusive[76] evidence of the

---

72. Replaced in England by s 45(6) of the Law of Property Act 1925.
73. See *Re Marsh and Earl Granville* (1882) 24 Ch D 11. See also para **[14.50]** *ante*.
74. See para **[14.59]** *ante*.
75. Ie a cross-reference to one of the grounds for appointment of new or additional trustees specified in s 35 of the 1958 Act, see *Irish Land Law* (2nd ed, 1986), para 10.008. *Cf* s 38 of the English Trustee Act 1925.
76. Note that in the previous two statutory provisions mentioned above recitals are subject to contrary proof.

matter stated as regards a *bona fide* purchaser. There is no equivalent provision in the Republic of Ireland so that purchasers have to rely on the 20-year rule referred to earlier.[77]

(d) Civil Proceedings

[18.31] Under legislation governing admissibility of evidence in civil proceedings, statements, such as recitals, made in documents by persons may be admissible in certain circumstances and this may be useful where, eg, the maker of the statement cannot reasonably be called as a witness.[78]

(ii) Estoppel

[18.32] Quite apart from any statutory provisions, it is settled that a recital in a deed may operate by way of estoppel against the party making it in any action relating to that deed.[79] It is, however, crucial to recognise the limitations to this doctrine, whereby, in effect, what is untrue may nevertheless be held to have the effect of the truth.[80] First, an estoppel will arise only in respect of a party who, on a proper construction of the deed, can be regarded as making the statement in the recital[81] and those claiming through him.[82] It will not bind parties who do not claim through him[83]; nor, of course, will it operate in his favour. Secondly, an estoppel will not operate in favour of all the world, but only in favour of those persons who are intended to and do act on the faith of the statement in question, eg, successors in title of one of the original parties to the deed containing the recital.[84] Thirdly, an estoppel can be raised only in an action on the deed in question and not in relation to some matter collateral to the deed.[85] Fourthly, for a recital to raise an estoppel, it must contain a clear and definite statement of fact,[86] or, as Chatterton V-C once put it, it must be a "clear and

---

[77.] Where the Trustee Act 1893, still governs the subject. See *Irish Land Law*, (2nd ed, 1986) para 10.008.

[78.] See Documentary Evidence Acts 1868, 1882 and 1895 and generally, Fennell, *The Law of Evidence in Ireland* (1992), Ch 13. And see *Nagle v Shea* (1875) IR 9 CL 389.

[79.] *Murphy d Wray v Morrisson* (1831) 2 Hud & Br 406; *Hungerford v Bechier* (1855) 5 Ir Ch R 417.

[80.] It is clear that no estoppel will operate if the falsity of the recital was known to the party invoking the estoppel, see *McCormick v Duke* [1907] 1 IR 339, *Cf Duggan v O'Connor* (1828) 1 Hud & Br 459.

[81.] *Re Davison's Estate* (1893) 31 LR Ir 249 (affd [1894] 1 IR 56.) See also *Nagle v Shea* (1875) IR 9 CL 389 at 401 (*per* Palles CB).

[82.] *Clarke v Hall* (1888) 24 LR Ir 316.

[83.] *Blackhall v Gibson* (1878) 2 LR Ir 49 at 57 (*per* May CJ).

[84.] See *Re King's Settlement* [1931] 2 Ch 294.

[85.] *Donegall v Templemore* (1858) 9 ICLR 374 at 408 (*per* Christian J).

[86.] *Munster and Leinster Bank Ltd v McGlashan* [1937] IR 525 at 527-8 (*per* Meredith J) (*aff'd* by Sup Ct).

unequivocal representation."[87] A "general" recital or one which is vague or uncertain is not enough to justify a court in holding a party or his successors bound by the statement.[88] The courts will exercise caution in this regard.[89]

[18.33] Where a deed includes the common recital as to the grantor's title,[90] a considerable breach of the *nemo dat quod non habet* principle may occur. If the grantor in fact has no title at the date of the deed's operation, he may nevertheless be estopped from denying that he has the title recited.[91] Furthermore, if the grantor subsequently acquires that title, it passes automatically to the grantee without any further conveyance, or, as it is often put, the estoppel is "fed."[92] A recital of the grantor's title is particularly useful because it is settled that, without it, no estoppel as to the title can be raised from other parts of the deed.[93] It is common for such a recital to state that the grantor is seised "free from incumbrances,"[94] even though in fact the grantor may hold subject to rights coming within the definition of an "incumbrance" in the broad sense, eg, easements and restrictive covenants.[95] It is, perhaps, more important for the grantor's solicitor to check that such a reference to freedom from incumbrances does not appear in the operative part of the deed. since this may amount to an express covenant imposing wider obligations that the usual covenant implied by statute.[96]

---

87. *Guardian Assurance Co v Viscount Avonmore* (1872) IR 6 Eq 391 at 400. And see the same judge in *Thompson v Thompson* (1871) IR 6 Eq 113 at 124: "...the Court requires that the assertion should be definite and clear and one on which a reasonable man would be warranted in acting without inquiry." (Affd at p 322.).

88. *Kelly v Power* (1812) 2 Ba & B 236 at 251 (*per* Lord Manners LC). See also *Thompson v Thompson* (1871) IR 6 Eq 113 at 125 (*per* Chatterton V-C). *Cf Delmer v McCabe* (1863) 14 ICLR 377 at 382 (*per* Monahan CJ).

89. *Borrowes v Borrowes* (1871) IR 6 Eq 368 at 378-9 (*per* Sullivan MR).

90. See para **[18.38]** *infra*.

91. *Thompson v Thompson* (1871) IR 6 Eq 113 at 125 (*per* Chatterton V-C) (affd at p 322).

92. *Re Bridgwater's Settlement* [1910] 2 Ch 342. See also *Cumberland Court (Brighton) Ltd v Taylor* [1964] Ch 29. Note that the English Court of Appeal held recently that the doctrine of "feeding the estoppel" is not dependent upon there being a recital; furthermore it applied the doctrine to registered land: see *First National Bank plc v Thompson* [1996] 1 All ER 140.

93. *General Finance, Mortgage and Discount Co v Liberator Permanent Benefit BS* (1878) 10 Ch D 15.

94. *Cf* para **[18.03]** *supra*.

95. *Cf* the definition in s 2(vii) of the Conveyancing Act 1881, as including " mortgage in fee, or for less estate. and a trust for securing money, and a lien, and a charge of a portion, annulty, or other capital or annual sum." As regards a lease, see *District Bank Ltd v Webb* [1958] 1 WLR 148. See also paras **[9.26-7]** *ante*.

96. See the discussion of this subject by Chatterton V-C in *Thompson v Thompson* (1871) IR 6 Eq 113 at 117-25 (affd at p 322). It might also be regarded as an "express" provision which casts doubts on the force of the "all estate" provision in s 63 of the Conveyancing Act 1881: see para **[18.82]** *infra*. As to implied covenants for title, see para **[21.05]** *post*.

(iii) Creation of Covenants

[18.34] It is settled that the wording of a recital may, in effect, create a covenant by a party to the deed, eg, where it shows an intention by him to do or not do something and there is nothing elsewhere in the deed to contradict this.[97] However, as Sullivan MR explained:

> "On the other hand, it is plain that the Court ought to be cautious in spelling a covenant out of a recital of a deed; because that is not the part of a deed in which covenants are usually expressed."[98]

Furthermore, any statement in the recital may be explained or cut down by express covenants later in the deed.[99]

(iv) Construction

[18.35] As mentioned in an earlier chapter,[100] the recitals may help to explain the purpose of the deed and so facilitate resolution of a question of construction.[101] But their role is strictly limited in this regard, because in the event of a conflict the recitals must give way to the operative parts of the deed.[102]

(v) Trusts

[18.36] Recitals in a deed forming part of the title to a property may contain a reference to trustees or a trust of the land and so fix the purchaser with notice of the trust. However, by statute in both parts of Ireland a purchaser from trustees is exonerated from seeing to the destination or application of the purchase money, provided he obtains a receipt from at least two trustees.[103] Furthermore, a purchaser is not affected with notice of matters which he would not have discovered except by questioning the truth of recitals or other contents of the document of title.[104] Thus as a general rule the purchaser should not enquire further, eg, as to whether the trustees mentioned were duly constituted.[105] In particular, the purchaser should not

---

[97.] *Borrowes v Borrowes* (1871) IR 6 Eq 368 at 378 (*per* Sullivan MR).

[98.] *Ibid*, p 379.

[99.] *Thompson v Thompson* (1871) IR 6 Eq 113 at 125 (*per* Chatterton V-C) (*aff'd* at p 322). See also *Delmer v McCabe* (1863) 14 ICLR 377.

[100.] Para **[17.18]** *ante*.

[101.] *Re Carter's Trusts* (1869) IR 3 Eq 495 at 501 (*per* Chatterton V-C). See also *Delmer v McCabe* (1863) 14 ICLR 377 at 382 (*per* Monahan CJ).

[102.] *Macnamara v Carey* (1867) IR 1 Eq 9 at 22 (*per* Blackburne C); *Butler v Gilbert* (1890) 25 LR Ir 230 at 241-2 (*per* Porter MR).

[103.] Trustee Act 1893, s 20. See *Irish Land Law* (2nd ed, 1986), para 10.018.

[104.] *Earl of Gainsborough v Watcombe Terra Cotta Clay Co Ltd* (1885) 54 LJ Ch 991.

[105.] See *Re Chafer and Randall's Contract* [1916] 2 Ch 8 at 18 (*per* Cozens-Hardy MR).

seek to go behind recitals clearly drafted to keep the trusts "off the title," eg, by enquiring into the beneficial interests created by the trust document.[106]

2. Categories

[18.37] There are two main categories of recitals, narrative and introductory. If a deed does contain recitals, it is usual to have both, first a narrative recital followed by an introductory one.[107]

(i) Narrative

[18.38] A narrative recital explains the entitlement of the grantor to make the conveyance in question.[108] It used to be common for such a recital to give a fairly detailed statement in chronological order[109] of the relevant documents and events showing how the vendor became the owner of the land being conveyed. However, nowadays it is usual not to give a complete history of the title and, instead, it is common practice in a straightforward sale simply to recite that the vendor is seised of the property for the estate in question.[110] Alternatively, a good rule of thumb is to recite the seisin of a vendor who bought the land, but if he inherited it to recite the seisin of the first predecessor in title who bought the land. In the case of a sale of leasehold property, the original lease and the last assignment should be recited. Also clearly there are cases where rather more detailed recitals are necessary to explain the operative parts of the deed, eg, a sale following the death of the owner, probably made by his personal representatives. And if the conveyance involves several parties with different interests in the land, or several parcels of land, the inclusion of full narrative recitals may be the only practical way of indicating exactly what is being done. It must always be remembered that, in the case of unregistered land, the current conveyance will form part of the title deeds relating to the property which will be examined by solicitors acting for parties involved in subsequent dealings

---

106. Conversely; the drafter of recitals should beware of revealing too much, otherwise he may deprive the purchaser of statutory protection, see *Re Duce and Boots Cash Chemists (Southern) Ltd's Contract* [1937] Ch 642. But note, as regards the issue in the *Duce* case, s 53(3) of the Succession Act 1965, and see *Irish Land Law* (2nd ed, 1986), para 16.46; Brady, *Succession Law in Ireland* (2nd ed, 1995), para [10.53] *et seq*; para **[15.19]** *ante*. See also Laffoy, *Irish Conveyancing Precedents* Division D (charities and clubs).

107. See *Delmer v McCabe* (1863) 14 ICLR 377. See also para **[18.03]** *supra*.

108. See *Blackhall v Gibson* (1878) 2 LR Ir 49; *Clarke v Hall* (1888) 24 LR Ir 316; *Re Davison's Estate* (1893) 31 LR Ir 249 (affd [1894] 1 IR 56).

109. Though in a complicated conveyance, where several parties' estates or interests are being dealt with, it is usual to deal with each separately.

110. See the example given in para **[18.03]** *supra*. See also *Duggan v O'Connor* (1828) 1 Hud & Br 459; *Delmer v McCabe* (1863) 14 ICLR 377; *Guardian Assurance Co v Viscount Avonmore* (1872) IR 6 Eq 391.

with the property, and such examinations may occur several decades later. The solicitors will derive considerable benefit if full recitals were contained in earlier deeds.[111]

[18.39] In drafting narrative recitals, advantage may be taken of s 53(1) of the Conveyancing Act 1881, which provides:

> "A deed expressed to be supplemental to a previous deed, or directed to be read as an annex thereto, shall, so far as may be, be read and have effect as if the deed so expressed or directed were made by way of indorsement on the previous deed, or contained a full recital thereof."[112]

It seems to be accepted that, if this course is adopted, it does not confer on the purchaser any right to production of the previous deed and he may accept the same evidence that the previous deed does not affect the title as if it had been merely mentioned in the supplemental deed.[113]

(ii) Introductory

[18.40] An introductory recital links the narrative recital or recitals with the rest of the deed.[114] It does this by explaining the intended operation of the current deed, eg, that it is to give effect to a contract for sale entered into by the parties.[115] However, in referring to the agreement for sale, it is usual to state the barest essentials only and not to go into the details of its terms. The danger is that, if the details of its terms are referred to, subsequent purchasers may be obliged, when investigating the title, to make enquiries as to whether the contract's terms have been carried out.[116]

E. Testatum

[18.41] We now come to the operative part of the deed,[117] which begins with the *testatum*, ie, a declaration that what follows contains the details of the

---

[111.] And, of course, they can also invoke the statutory provisions mentioned earlier, see, eg, paras **[18.28-9]** *supra*.

[112.] This applies to deeds executed before or after 1881, s 53(2).

[113.] This is stated expressly in s 58 of the English Law of Property Act 1925, which replaced s 53 of the 1881 Act.

[114.] And so, if there is no narrative recital, there should be no introductory recital.

[115.] See the example given in para **[18.03]** *supra*. See also *Delmer v McCabe* (1863) 14 ICLR 377; *Re Davison's Estate* (1893) 31 LR Ir 249 (affd [1894] 1 IR 56).

[116.] *Cf* the operation of the doctrine of merger in this context, see para **[21.02]** *post*. See also *Munster and Leinster Bank Ltd v McGlashan* [1937] IR 525 at 527-8 (*per* Meredith J).

[117.] In fact, strictly all the operative parts from the *testatum* to, but not including, the *habendum* (see para **[18.84]** *infra*) constitute the "premises". See *Kerr v Kerr* (1854) 4 Ir Ch R 493 at 497 (*per* Brady LC). However, in modern parlance "premises" has come to mean the same as "parcels" (see para **[18.50]** *infra*), see *Gardiner v Sevenoaks RDC* [1950] 2 All ER 84 at 85 (*per* Lord Goddard).

operation of the deed. The usual formula in the case of unregistered land is: "NOW THIS INDENTURE WITNESSETH ...."[118] The general view seems to be that the word deed, or indenture, should be used here, on the ground that the *testatum* should indicate the nature of the current document, ie, a sealed instrument, whereas the commencement[119] may indicate what particular kind of instrument or its operation, ie, a lease, mortgage or whatever, in this particular case. The *testatum* may also run on so as to include further words before the next part of the deed, the statement of the consideration. Thus it is common to insert after the word "WITNESSETH" a phrase such as "in pursuance of the said agreement,"[120] thereby providing a link with the introductory recital.[121] The forms prescribed for registered land do not contain any *testatum*.[122]

F. Consideration

[18.42] Unless the transaction is a voluntary one, it is usual for the deed to contain a statement of the consideration paid for the property,[123] though it seems that at common law such a statement is not essential to a deed and parol evidence may be adduced to prove what the consideration was.[124] However, there are several reasons why the consideration should be stated. First, it shows that the deed is not a voluntary one and thus avoids the weaknesses inherent in such deeds, eg, their liability to be set aside.[125] Secondly, it rebuts the presumption of a resulting trust in favour of the grantor,[126] though this should also be rebutted by the words of the *habendum*.[127] Thirdly, it ensures compliance with several statutory provisions. Thus under s 5 of the Stamp Act 1891 (as substituted by s 5 of the Finance Act 1991), it is an offence to execute or prepare a document which does not set out all the facts and circumstances affecting liability to stamp duty with intent to defraud the revenue authorities. The vendor may

---

118. See para **[18.03]** *supra*.
119. See para **[18.07]** *supra*.
120. See para **[18.03]** *supra*.
121. See para **[18.40]** *supra*.
122. Land Registration Rules 1972, Sched of Forms. See also para **[18.04]** *supra*.
123. Whether the document relates to unregistered or registered land, see paras **[18.03]** *supra*.
124. See the discussion in *Doe d Kearns v Sherlock* (1824) 1 Fox & Sm 79, espec at 89 (*per* Bushe CJ). See also *Pratt v Barker* (1828) 1 Sim 1.
125. See *Irish Land Law* (2nd ed, 1986), paras 9.076-8. See also Sanfey and Holohan, *Bankruptcy Law and Practice in Ireland* (1991), Ch 8. As to a voluntary conveyance's status as a root of title, see para **[14.56]** *ante*. See also the interesting aspect of this rule raised in *Revenue Commissioners v Moroney* [1972] IR 372, espec at 376 (*per* Kenny J) para **[18.44]** *infra*.
126. See *ibid*, paras 3.018-9 and 9.057-8.
127. Ie, a conveyance "unto and to the use of" the grantee, see para **[18.86]** *infra*.

be obliged by statute to sell for the "best" consideration, eg, a tenant for life exercising his power of sale under the Settled Lands Acts,[128] and so a clear statement of just what it was may be useful. Fourthly, a statement of the consideration facilitates insertion of a receipt clause and, as we shall see, a receipt may be vitally important.[129]

G. Receipt Clause

[18.43] It is usual now in both conveyances of unregistered land[130] and registered land transfers[131] for the receipt clause to be inserted in brackets immediately after the statement of the amount of the consideration. Prior to 1882, a formal receipt was endorsed usually on the back of the deed,[132] but that is no longer necessary because of the provisions of s 54(1) of the Conveyancing Act 1881, which reads:

> A receipt for consideration money or securities in the body of a deed shall be a sufficient discharge for the same to the person paying or delivering the same, without any further receipt for the same being endorsed on the deed.

There are several reasons why it is important for the deed to contain or have attached to it a receipt for the consideration paid.

1. Sufficient Discharge

[18.44] As between the vendor and purchaser, a receipt in the body of the deed is a "sufficient" discharge, as s 54(1) of the Conveyancing Act 1881, quoted in the previous paragraph, provides. It is, however, important to note that this protection is limited, for s 54(1) does not say that it is a "conclusive" discharge. It is true that at common law the courts treated a receipt clause as generally conclusive evidence of payment, in the sense that it was said to estop the person giving it from asserting non-payment.[133] But the Courts of Equity adopted a different rule and held that evidence may

---

[128.] Settled Land Act 1882 s 4(1). See *Irish Land Law* (2nd ed, 1986), para 8.066. The same applies to building societies exercising their power of sale as mortgagees. Building Societies Act 1989, s 26. Sec *ibid* para 13.036 and Lyall, *Land Law in Ireland* (1994), p 754.

[129.] Para **[18.43]** *infra*.

[130.] See para **[18.03]** *supra*.

[131.] See para **[18.04]** *supra*.

[132.] Note, however, that a statutory form of receipt by a building society endorsed on the mortgage deed operates as a discharge and a reconveyance of the property, see Building Societies Act 1989, s 27(2). As regards other mortgages, see the Housing Act 1988, s 18(2) and registered land, see the Registration of Title Act 1964, s 65. See also the discussion in *Stamers v Preston* (1859) 9 ICLR 351 and *Irish Land Law*, (2nd ed, 1986) paras 13.125-6; Lyall *Land Law in Ireland* (1994), pp 788-9; Fitzgerald, *Land Registry Practice* (2nd ed, 1995) Ch 15.

[133.] See *Potts v Nixon* (1870) IR 5 CL 45. See also *Baker v Dewey* (1823) 1 B & C 704.

always be adduced to prove the non-payment of consideration despite the receipt. As Lefroy B. put it in *Croly O'Callaghan*[134]:

" ... though the recital or receipt in a deed is *prima facie* evidence of the payment of the consideration, yet if the Court comes to the conclusion that the consideration has not been paid, and directs an inquiry upon the subject, the onus of proving the payment lies upon the party insisting that it has been paid."[135]

And, of course, under s 28(11) of the Judicature (Ireland) Act 1877, the equitable rule now prevails,[136] as was illustrated by *Revenue Commissioners v Moroney*.[137] In that case, a father assigned leasehold premises to himself and his sons "in consideration of" £16,000 and the deed contained a receipt clause by which the father acknowledged payment of that amount to him. In fact no purchase money was ever paid or intended to be paid,[138] but on the father's death the Revenue Commissioners claimed that a sum equal to two-thirds of the £16,000 was to be treated as a debt due to the father's estate and part of the property passing on his death. At first instance, Kenny J held, *inter alia*,[139] that extrinsic evidence was admissible to refute the receipt clause and this established that the deceased had not expected to receive, and his sons had not agreed to pay, any purchase money.[140] He stated:

"It is not necessary to give authority for the proposition that evidence may be given to show that, despite the receipt, the consideration was not paid. Similarly, evidence is admissible when it is relevant to explain the circumstances in which the deed was executed and to establish that the parties did not intend that the purchase price mentioned in the deed should ever be paid."[141]

2. Subsequent Purchaser

[18.45] If a purchaser has not, in fact, paid the full purchase price, the vendor has a lien on the property for the unpaid money,[142] which will bind any subsequent purchaser of the property unless he can prove that he is a

---

[134.] (1842) 5 Ir Eq R 25. See also *Wilson v Keating* (1859) 27 Beav 121.

[135.] *Ibid* p 32.

[136.] See *Irish Land Law* (2nd ed, 1986), paras 3.036-7.

[137.] [1972] IR 372.

[138.] The "consideration" was entered to prevent the deed being treated as a voluntary conveyance so as to avoid delays in the Stamp Office relating to such conveyances, *ibid* p 376 (*per* Kenny J). See also para **[17.19]** *ante*.

[139.] Another issue involved representations made by the father prior to execution of the deed and raised some interesting questions concerning the doctrine of "promissory estoppel," see Brady, 'An English and Irish View of Proprietary Estoppel' (1970) 5 Ir Jur (ns) 239.

[140.] The appeal to the Supreme Court was disallowed, [1972] IR 372.

[141.] *Ibid*, p 377.

[142.] See para **[12.15]** *ante*.

bona fide purchaser for value without notice. And it is established that this lien remains so long as the purchase money or any part of it is owing and despite execution of a deed containing the usual receipt clause.[143] This rule is not abrogated by what might appear to be a contradictory provision in s 55(1) of the Conveyancing Act 1881, which reads:

> A receipt for consideration money or other consideration in the body of a deed or indorsed thereon shall, in favour of a subsequent purchaser, not having notice that the money or other consideration thereby acknowledged to be received was not in fact paid or given wholly or in part, be sufficient evidence of the payment or giving of the whole amount thereof.

There are two points to be noted about this provision. First, it does not provide that the receipt is "conclusive" evidence, but only "sufficient" evidence, so that proof to the contrary remains admissible. Secondly, it provides expressly that a subsequent purchaser's protection remains dependent upon him establishing that he is a *bona fide* purchaser without notice. It must be remembered that "notice" in this context has a wide meaning, eg, it includes "constructive" notice,[144] so that a subsequent purchaser may be fixed with notice of a previous vendor's lien from the fact that the latter has retained the title deeds pending payment of the balance of the purchase money.[145] His protection depends therefore, more on the doctrine of notice than on the receipt. However, s 55(1) may be invoked by a subsequent purchaser in other contexts, eg, where the validity of the previous conveyance is dependent upon the existence of a receipt for capital money, such as is the case where settled land was sold.[146]

3. Payments to Solicitors

[18.46] As we shall see later, when the balance of the purchase money is paid over on completion, it is often not handed over to the vendor or other person named in the deed as acknowledging receipt of it.[147] It is in this respect that the provisions of s 56(1) of the Conveyancing Act 1881, are most relevant. It reads:

---

[143] *Saunders v Leslie* (1814) 2 Ba & B 509 at 514 (*per* Lord Manners LC). See para **[12.16]** *ante*.

[144] See generally, *Irish Land Law*, (2nd ed, 1986) para 3.069 *et seq*; Lyall *Land Law in Ireland* (1994) p 117 *et seq*.

[145] See *Spencer v Clarke* (1878) 47 LJ Ch 692. For discussion of the applicability of the statutory provision (in England now s 68 of the Law of Property Act 1925) to a registered land transfer, see *London and Cheshire Insurance Co Ltd v Laplagrene Property Co Ltd* [1971] Ch 499; (1971) 35 Conv 188.

[146] See para **[18.47]** *infra*.

[147] See para **[20.27]** *post*.

Where a solicitor produces a deed, having in the body thereof or indorsed thereon a receipt for consideration money or other consideration, the deed being executed, or the indorsed receipt being signed, by the person entitled to give a receipt for that consideration, the deed shall be sufficient authority to the person liable to pay or give the same for his paying or giving the same to the solicitor, without the solicitor producing any separate or other direction or authority in that behalf from the person who executed or signed the deed or receipt.

Though, no doubt, this provision is much relied upon in practice, albeit probably often without realising the fact, it is important to note its limitations. First, again the statutory protection is not "conclusive"; it provides for "sufficient" authority only, so that proof to the contrary may be produced. Secondly, the authority in question is confined to a "solicitor" and so presumably does not apply to unqualified employees who may deal with the completion, eg, a solicitor's apprentice or clerk.[148] Thirdly, it seems that it is confined further to the solicitor acting for the person giving the receipt and so it may not cover another solicitor acting as his agent in the completion.[149] Though, in fact, it is common, at least in Ireland, for one solicitor to close the transaction for another. Fourthly, it is confined to deeds and so does not apply to an unsealed document handed over on completion in return for money, eg, a receipt endorsed on a mortgage deed in discharge of the mortgage[150] or a written assignment of an equitable interest in land.[151] In all these cases not coming within the section technically special authority to receive the money in question should have been obtained and the purchaser or his solicitor would be entitled to require it to be produced. Indeed, to take the matter to extremes, proof of the fact that the payee is a solicitor could be demanded, but, of course, in practice this is not done.

4. Capital Money

[18.47] In certain cases it is essential from a purchaser's point of view that a receipt for capital money raised on a sale is issued, eg, where the land is sold by a tenant for life under the Settled Land Acts, a receipt must be issued by the trustees of the settlement or the court.[152] Furthermore, trustees may authorise a solicitor to receive and give a discharge for the money by

---

148. *Cf Day v Woolwich Equitable BS* (1889) 40 Ch D 491.

149. *Re Hetling and Merton's Contract* [1893] 3 Ch 269 (CA). See also the *Day* case, cited in fn 148 *supra*. This is the view of the English Law Society, see Digest, Opinions Nos 163 and 164. *Cf* Williams, *Law of Vendor and Purchaser* (4th ed, 1936), p 743.

150. See *Irish Land Law* (2nd ed, 1986), para 13.125.

151. *Ibid*, para 9.025. As to other transfers of an interest in land which do not require a deed. See para [17.02] *ante*.

152. See *Irish Land Law* (2nd ed, 1986), para 8.094.

permitting him to have custody of, and to produce, a deed containing a receipt or having one endorsed on it, signed by them.[153] This is a special provision for trustees similar to the general one discussed in the previous paragraph.

H. Words of Grant

[18.48] The next part of the deed contains the operative part usually known as the words of grant. This states what the grantor does by virtue of the deed, eg, conveys the property to the purchaser.[154] It is no longer necessary to use any particular operative word such as "grant",[155] because s 49(1) of the Conveyancing Act 1881, provides:

> "It is hereby declared that the use of the word grant is not necessary in order to convey tenements or hereditaments, corporeal or incorporeal."

The most appropriate word or words for the conveyance in question may be selected, eg, "conveys" or "grants"[156] in the case of a sale; "demises" for a grant of a lease; "assigns" for an assignment of a lease; "surrenders" for surrender of an interest such as where a lessee gives up a lease; "releases" where a reversioner transfers his interest to the person in possession[157]; "confirms" where some third party joins in the conveyance, such as where a beneficiary joins in a conveyance by the trustees; "appoints" where the conveyance involves the exercise of a power of appointment. In the case of registered land, the prescribed forms use the words "transfer" or "charge" as the case requires.[158]

[18.49] It is also usual for the words of grant to include a statement, using the appropriate statutory formula, of the capacity in which the party in question, eg, the vendor, conveys, eg, "as beneficial owner."[159] The reason for this is that there are then implied in the conveyance the appropriate covenants for title laid down in s 7 of the Conveyancing Act 1881.[160] Under

---

[153.] Trustee Act 1893, s 17. See *ibid* para 10.033.

[154.] See para **[18.03]** *supra*.

[155.] Previously it was thought that the word "grant" had to be used because of the reference in s 2 of the Real Property Act 1845, to corporeal hereditaments lying "in grant", see para **[17.02]** *ante*. Hence the common practice of using combined words of grant, one of which is always the word "grants," eg, "grants and conveys". See also fn 160, *infra*.

[156.] This is clearly the appropriate word for a fee farm grant, see para **[0.00]** *post*.

[157.] Or an incumbrancer gives up his incumbrance, eg, a release by the owner of his rentcharge on land. *Cf* the release of an option to purchase land: see *Cherry Court v Revenue Commissioners* [1995] 2 ILRM 228.

[158.] Land Registration Rules 1972, Sched of Forms. See para **[18.04]** *supra*.

[159.] See para **[18.03]** *supra*.

[160.] Note that s 4 of the Real Property Act 1845, provided that use of the word "give" or "grant" in a conveyance after 1845 does not imply any covenant in respect of the land other than any otherwise implied by statute.

this section different covenants for title are implied according to whether the person in question conveys and is expressed to convey,[161] eg, "as beneficial owner,"[162] "as settlor," or "as trustee." This complex subject is dealt with in detail in a later chapter.[163] Finally, it should be noted with respect to conveyances of unregistered land, that words of limitation are not inserted in the words of grant. Rather they appear in the *habendum*, which we discuss below.[164]

I. Parcels

[18.50] The next part of a deed is the parcels clause, which contains a physical description of the land conveyed in the case of unregistered land and usually begins with the words "ALL THAT...."[165] This should not be confused with the description of the estate or interest in the land which it is, in strict theory, the primary function of the deed to convey. The delimitation of the estate or interest to be passed to the grantee is performed by a later part of the deed, the *habendum*.[166] In addition to providing a physical description of the land, the parcels clause may include a statement of any new rights created in respect of the land in favour of the grantee, eg, easements to be enjoyed over land retained by the grantor.[167] It may also include a statement of any exceptions or reservations in favour of the grantor.[168]

1. Description of the Land

(i) Unregistered Land

[18.51] The greatest care should be exercised in the case of unregistered land to see that the description of the land contained in the parcels clause is accurate.[169] The law reports are littered with illustrations of how this principle is so often ignored in practice, and we examine later some of the problems of construction which can arise.[170] Many of these could be avoided

---

161. On the difficulties caused by this requirement, see para **[21.08]** *post.*

162. And in this case the covenants vary according to the nature of the conveyance eg, a sale of freehold property, assignment of a lease or a mortgage of freehold or leasehold property.

163. See para **[21.05]** *et seq, post.* As to the applicability of implied covenants to registered land transfers, see para **[21.06]** *post.*

164. See para **[18.86]** *infra.*

165. As regards registered land, see para **[18.55]** *post.*

166. See para **[18.84]** *infra.*

167. See para **[18.71]** *infra.*

168. See para **[18.73]** *infra.*

169. We have already emphasised the need for accuracy in relation to the description of the land in the contract for sale, see para **[9.10]** *et seq, ante.*

170. See para **[18.58]** *infra.*

if certain elementary precautions are taken by the draftsman of the clause, eg the purchaser's solicitor. First, he should check his draft against the description of the land in previous title deeds. But caution must be exercised, because there is no guarantee that the previous deeds were accurate or, if they were at the date of their execution, are still so in the light of changed circumstances. Furthermore, the descriptions in the various deeds may not be entirely consistent with each other. In such cases, once the solicitor drafting the current deed is satisfied that his clause is accurate, it may be wise to include a cross-reference to the description in earlier deeds so as to indicate to conveyancers involved in subsequent dealings that it is the same land which is dealt with in all the deeds. Secondly, the description may be checked against any map or plan attached to earlier deeds, but here even greater caution should be exercised, for such maps or plans are notoriously inaccurate.[171] If it is intended to attach a map or plan to the current deed, again extreme care should be exercised to see that it is accurate and properly drawn to scale. It is useless, indeed it is positively dangerous, to incorporate[172] a map or plan which is not strictly accurate and it may be questioned whether it should be done at all unless it is drawn by an expert, eg, a surveyor. However, in practice there may not be the time for, or the client may not be prepared to meet the expense of, a proper survey of the property by an expert. Though there are cases where it is almost essential to provide a map or plan, eg, where part only of a larger estate is being conveyed and it is necessary to identify which part of the larger area previously dealt with in the title deeds is being conveyed by the current deed. Thirdly, the client should be asked to check particularly the description of the land to see that it accords with his view of what he is selling or buying, and of course, the description in the deed should accord with the description in the contract for sale.[173]

[18.52] The purchaser is entitled to ensure that the description of the land is accurate and identifies the land he has contracted to buy.[174] Conversely, the vendor is entitled to ensure that the description in the deed so accords with the description in the contract for sale (provided it is accurate) that he will be

---

171. We discuss this subject later, see para **[18.63]** *infra*. See also para **[9.12]** *ante*.

172. As to problems of construction which may arise over the degree of "incorporation", see para **[18.64]** *infra*.

173. See para **[9.09]** *et seq, ante*.

174. And, perhaps, so accords with the description in previous title deeds as to connect the current deed with them, see *Re Sansom and Narbeth's Contract* [1910] 1 Ch 741 at 749 (*per* Swinfen Eady J). But this is on the assumption that the previous description is accurate, see para **[18.51]** *supra*.

conveying, and entering into covenants for title[175] relating to, the land he contracted to sell and nothing more.

[18.53] There are several alternative methods of description, eg, a purely verbal one in the parcels clause in the body of the deed[176] or by cross-reference to a map or plan annexed or attached to the deed or a combination of both.[177] We consider the use of maps or plans later.[178] Where a verbal description is given, especially on its own, the amount of detail necessary varies from case to case. In the case of residential property, it may be sufficient description to refer to its usual address, eg, "ALL THAT AND THOSE the premises known as 22 Park Road situate in the parish of _____ barony of _____ and City of Dublin." On the other hand, in the case of agricultural property, it is usual to give the measurements of the land, eg, so many hectares, acres,[179] roods and perches.

[18.54] It is no longer necessary to incorporate into the description of the property a long list of the various items included in it, because these are covered by the "general words" implied in conveyances by s 6 of the Conveyancing Act 1881.[180] This section was included in the Act in furtherance of its policy of shortening conveyances.[181]

Thus s 6(1) provides:

> A conveyance of land shall be deemed to include, and shall by virtue of this Act operate to convey, with the land, all buildings, erections, fixtures, commons. hedges, ditches, fences, ways, waters, watercourses, liberties, privileges, easements, rights, and advantages whatsoever, appertaining or reputed to appertain to the land, or any part thereof, or at the time of

---

[175.] See para **[18.49]** *supra* and **[21.05]** *et seq, post.*

[176.] Where the description is a very lengthy one, it may be inserted instead in a schedule at the end of the deed, with a cross-reference to this schedule in the parcels clause. See Division E (conveyances on sale) in Laffoy, *Irish Conveyancing Precedents.*

[177.] Where the third approach is adopted, considerable problems may arise where there is an inconsistency between the verbal description in the parcels clause and the map or plan, see para **[18.66]** *infra.*

[178.] Para **[18.63]** *infra.*

[179.] Usually statute measure. See *Myers v Burke* (1892) 26 ILT 306. Note also that this is the definition in s 1 of Deasy's Act 1860 (Landlord and Tenant Law Amendment Act Ireland).

[180.] As regards the significance of this section in relation to implied rights in the nature of *quasi-*easements and profits. See *Irish Land Law* (2nd ed, 1986), paras 60.066-8; Lyall, *Land Law in Ireland* (1994) p 695 *et seq.* As to the practice prior to the Act, see *Geoghegan v Fegan* (1872) IR 6 CL 139.

[181.] Just as, of course, the Solicitors' Remuneration Act 1881, provided for remuneration according to a statutory scale of charges instead of according to the number of words in the conveyance, see para **[20.49]** *et seq, post.*

conveyance demised, occupied or enjoyed with, or reputed or known as part or parcel of or appurtenant to the land or any part thereof.

Section 6(2)[182] provides:

> A conveyance of land, having houses or other buildings thereon, shall be deemed to include and shall by virtue of this Act operate to convey, with the land, houses, or other buildings, all outhouses, erections, fixtures, cellars, areas, courts, courtyards, cisterns, sewers, gutters, drains, ways, passages, lights, watercourses, liberties, privileges, easements, rights, and advantages, whatsoever, appertaining or reputed to appertain to the land, houses or other buildings conveyed, or any of them, or any part thereof, or at the time of conveyance demised, occupied, or enjoyed with, or reputed or known as part or parcel of or appurtenant to, the land, houses, or other buildings, conveyed, or any of them, or any part thereof.

These provisions apply only if and as far as a contrary intention is not expressed in the conveyance, and have effect subject to the terms of the conveyance and its provisions.[183] Furthermore, it is important to note that it is provided expressly that they are not to be construed as giving to any person a better title to any property than the title which the conveyance gives to him, nor are they to be construed as conveying to him any property further or otherwise than what could have been conveyed by the conveying parties.[184]

(ii) Registered Land

[18.55] In the case of a transfer of the whole of the land contained in a particular folio, the prescribed form simply requires a cross-reference to that folio, eg, "all the property described in folio _____ of the register County _____".[185] For some time now folios have been divided into three parts and the first part contains a description of the property registered with a cross-reference to the plan of the land on the Registry map.[186] The map is an essential part of the Registry system.[187] By statute the Registry description is to be by the names of the denominations on the

---

[182.] Section 6(3) deals with the conveyance of a manor and is probably obsolete now, see *Irish Land Law* (2nd ed, 1986), paras 2.29-33 and 6.066. However, to the extent that the word "manor" may still he used merely as a term of reference or description in a conveyance (ie whether or not manorial or copyhold tenure in the strict sense exists in respect of the land, see *ibid*, para 2.33), s 6(3) may still be of use since it incorporates many items still relevant. eg pastures, mines, minerals, quarries, trees, woods, fisheries, etc.

[183.] Section 6(4). See *Steele v Morrow* (1923) 57 ILTR 89.

[184.] Section 6(5). See further *Irish Land Law* (2nd ed, 1986), para 6.067.

[185.] Land Registration Rules 1972, Form 19.

[186.] 1972 Rules, r 3. See *Irish Land Law* (2nd ed, 1986), para 21.16; McAllister, *Registration of Title in Ireland* (1973), pp 26-7.

[187.] See para **[9.13]** *ante*.

Ordnance Survey map or maps in which the land is included or in such manner as the Registrar considers best calculated to secure accuracy.[188] However, though this description can usually be taken as accurate, it is important to note that it is provided expressly in Ireland that the Registry description is not conclusive as to the boundaries of the land or its extent.[189] As we shall discuss later, this limitation applies also to the Registry maps.[190] Though there is provision made for the Registrar to enter boundaries as conclusive in certain cases, eg, on application by adjoining owners or on transfer of part of registered land,[191] but it seems that this is rarely invoked.

[18.56] Where the transfer involves part only of the land contained in a particular folio, it is necessary to include in the transfer form a description of the part sold, ie, a reference to the land in the folio in question with a description of the part transferred in a schedule to the form.[192] Furthermore, unless that part is clearly defined on the Registry map and may be identified thereon from the description, the transfer form must be accompanied by a plan drawn on the current largest scale Ordnance Survey map and referred to in the form, or drawn on such Ordnance Survey map signed by the grantor and grantee, or his solicitor, showing the part transferred.[193] Where agricultural land is concerned it should be noted that a transfer which involves a sub-division of land may require the consent of the Land Commission under s 12 of the Land Act 1965.[194] We discussed this subject in an earlier chapter.[195]

[18.57] It is provided that a transfer of registered land operates. on registration of the transferee as full owner, as a conveyance by deed within the meaning of the Conveyancing Acts[196] and so the "general words" provision in s 6 of the 1881 Act[197] applies, subject to certain limitations.[198]

---

188. Registration of Title Act 1964, s 85. See *Irish Land Law* (2nd ed, 1986), para 21.15; Fitzgerald, *Land Registry Practice* (2nd ed, 1995), p 20. See also *Geraghty v Rohan Industrial Estates Ltd* [1988] IR 419.

189. 1964 Act, s 85. See *Irish Land Law* (2nd ed, 1986), para 21.15; *McAllister, op cit* pp 58-9.

190. See para **[18.69]** *infra*.

191. See *Irish Land Law* (2nd ed, 1986), para 21.15; *Fitzgerald op cit* pp 69-70.

192. See 1972 Rules, Form 22.

193. 1972 Rules, r 56. For details of Land Registry mapping procedures see *Fitzgerald op cit* Ch 4. See also the discussion by Hamilton J in *Walsh v McGauran* High Court, unrep 14 June 1977 (1975/444 P); para **[18.62]** *infra*.

194. *Fitzgerald, op cit*, p 53. But note the "general consent" issued in 1977: see para **[16.34]** *ante*.

195. See para **[16.30]** *et seq, ante*.

196. Registration of Title Act 1964, ss 52(1) and 55(l).

197. See para **[18.54]** *supra*.

198. Eg, such registration is obviously subject to registered burdens and unregistered burdens affecting land without registration.

(iii) Construction

[18.58] We have already outlined the general rules of construction applying to deeds as a whole,[199] and these apply equally to construction of the parcels clause itself and for resolution of conflicts between the parcels clause and other parts of the deed.[200] Thus the parcels clause may be explained by the recitals,[201] and the maxim *falsa demonstratio non nocet* is frequently invoked.[202] And extrinsic evidence may be resorted to in a cause of doubt or ambiguity.[203] More particularly in relation to the parcels clause, the description may be filled-out by certain presumptions of law which may be applicable.

(a) Roads

[18.59] The presumption is that the person owning the land adjoining a public or private road or street is presumed to own the soil[204] of one-half of the road,[205] so that a conveyance of the land is presumed to include this soil.[206] Like all presumptions it may be rebutted by evidence to the contrary. eg, by a description clearly excluding half of an adjoining road or a map drawn or coloured so as to exclude the road.[207] Thus the developer of a building estate usually retains ownership of the soil for construction of roads and subsequent dedication to the public.[208] Indeed, the need for this has led

---

[199.] See Ch 17 *ante*.

[200.] See discussion of the dangers of conflict within the parcels clause itself, due to use of a multiple description or incorporation of a map, by the House of Lords in *Eastwood v Ashton* [1915] AC 900, espec at 914-6 (*per* Lord Sumner). See further as to incorporation of maps, para **[18.64]** *infra*.

[201.] See the discussion in *Butler v Gilbert* (1890) 25 LR Ir 230 at 241-2 (*per* Porter MR). See also paras **[17.18]** *ante* and **[18.35]** *supra*.

[202.] See para **[17.24]** *ante* and **[18.66]** *infra*.

[203.] See para **[17.19]** *ante*.

[204.] *Cf* the surface of a public road or street, see Local Government Acts 1925, s 25 and 1953, s 2. See *Irish Land Law*, (2nd ed, 1986) para 6.041; Keane, *The Law of Local Government in the Republic of Ireland* (1982) p 66 *et seq*. See also *Tithe Redemption Commission v Runcorn UDC* [1954] Ch 383.

[205.] See the discussion in *Central London Rly Co v City of London Land Tax Commrs* [1911] 1 Ch 467 at 474 (*per* Cozens-Hardy MR) (affd *sub nom City of London Land Tax Commrs v Central London Rly Co* [1913] AC 364). See also *Tottenham v Byrne* (1861) 12 ICLR 376. This presumption does not apply to a railway line, *Thompson v Hickman* [1907] 1 Ch 550.

[206.] *LNW Rly v Mayor of Westminister* [1902] 1 Ch 269. See also *Re White's Charities* [1898] 1 Ch 659.

[207.] *Dwyer v Rich* (1871) IR 6 CL 144 at 149 (*per* Fitzgerald J). See also *Mappin Bros v Liberty & Co Ltd* [1903] 1 Ch 118. *Cf* the position *re* registered land: *Geraghty v Rohan Industrial Estates Ltd* [1988] IR 419.

[208.] *Leigh v Jack* (1879) 5 Ex D 264.

to the suggestion that no presumption arises in the case of a building estate.[209]

(b) Rivers

[18.60] A similar presumption arises in relation to the soil of a river[210] adjoining land. The position of the parties owning the land on the opposite banks of the river was described by Lefroy CJ in *Beauman v Kinsella*[211] in this way:

> "... each party is entitled to the soil of the river up to the middle of the stream, *usque ad medium filum aquae*; and is, therefore, entitled also, as a matter of right, to the fishing therein - not as an easement *in alieno solo*, but as a right of fishery in the party's own land; and inasmuch as the river is not divided by any abutments marking the respective rights of the parties, and as the fish run freely from one side to the other, this right of fishery is, in its very nature, a species of tenancy in common."[212]

As was explained in *Tennant v Clancy*,[213] it is common for fishing rights to be granted over a river or lake, as an incorporeal hereditament held by someone other than the owner of the soil on the bank and the bed of the river or lake (the riparian owner).[214] As Costello J held in that case, the riparian owner cannot act so as to interfere substantially with the exercise of the fishing rights.

(c) Walls and Fences

[18.61] Clearly a wall or fence built exclusively on one side of a boundary line belongs to the owner of the land on whose side it is built[215] The difficulties arise where the structure straddles the boundary and this subject has been considered elsewhere.[216] The general presumption at common law is that such a "party wall" is owned by the adjoining landowners as tenants

---

[209.] *Ibid*, p 274 (*per* Cotton LJ).

[210.] *Cf* a tidal river, see *Irish Land Law* (2nd ed, 1986), para 6.116.

[211.] (1858) 8 ICLR 291 (reversed on other grounds (1859) 11 ICLR 249). See also *Donegall v Templemore* (1858) 9 ICLR 374.

[212.] *Ibid* p 298. Islands in the river are not presumed to pass, the half-way line being drawn between the island and the bank, see *Great Torrington Commons Conservators v Moore Stevans* [1903] 1 Ch 347.

[213.] [1987] IR 15.

[214.] See *Irish Land Law* (2nd ed, 1986), para 6.117.

[215.] *Hutchinson v Mains* (1812) Alc & Nap 155. Though the adjoining owner may have an easement of support, see *Hanly v Shannon* (1834) Hay & Jon 645; *Toole v Macken* (1855) 7 Ir Jur (os) 385.

[216.] See *Irish Land Law* (2nd ed, 1986), paras 7.53-62.

in common, with mutual rights of support.[217] But this presumption too may be rebutted.[218] It is by no means necessarily the case that the parties' legal position accords with the commonly held layman's view that a fence belongs to the landowner on whose side the posts are placed. In view of the difficulties of this area of law, it is wise to insert in conveyances express provisions on the matter in certain cases, eg, where a building estate is being sub-divided into numerous plots.[219]

(d) Hedges and Ditches

[18.62] In this context a "hedge" is usually taken to mean the bank of earth separating two parcels of land rather than the bushes or "hedgerows" which may be growing on it. The common law also assumed that such a bank of earth would be created by digging up the soil and throwing it onto the bank, thus making a ditch along the edge of the bank. From this stems the common law "hedge and ditch" rule or presumption that the boundary between the adjoining lands runs along the edge of the ditch away from the bank or hedge.[220] It seems, therefore, that the presumption arises only where such a ditch has been made and not where, eg, there is a natural hedge or ditch.[221] It may also be rebutted by clear evidence to the contrary,[222] eg, where the parcels describe the boundary by reference to a map which clearly draws the boundary down the centre of hedges.[223] However, considerable caution must be exercised in the use and construction of the word "ditch" as it is used in different senses in various parts of Ireland. In some it means an excavation in the ground; in others it means a bank extending from the ground upwards. Having said that, in *Walsh v McGauran*,[224] Hamilton J applied the general rule in a case involving a dispute which had arisen in respect of an eight-foot high whitethorn hedge. The plaintiffs had argued that the hedge straddled the boundary between their property and the defendants, so that the boundary

---

[217.] See the discussion in *Kempston v Butler* (1861) 12 ICLR 516 and *Jones v Read* (1876) IR 10 CL 315. As regards projections overhanging adjoining property, *cf Truckell v Stock* [1957] 1 WLR 161 with *Layburn v Grindley* [1892] 2 Ch 13. See also *Corbett v Hill* (1870) IR 9 Eq 671; *Fox v Clarke* (1874) IR 9 QB 565; (1957) 21 Conv 164.

[218.] *Kempton v Butler, op cit* p 526 (*per* Christian J); *Jones v Read op cit* p 320 (*per* Palles CB).

[219.] See Adams 'Ownership of Fences The Conveyancer's Choice' (1971) 68 L Soc Gaz 275 and 375. See also generally, Powell-Smith, *Law of Boundaries and Fences* (2nd ed, 1975).

[220.] *Vowles v Miller* (1810) 3 Taunt 137 at 138 (*per* Lawrence J). See also *Weston v Lawrence Weaver Ltd* [1961] 1 QB 402; *Hall v Dorling* [1996] EGCS 58.

[221.] *Marshall v Taylor* [1895] 1 Ch 641.

[222.] See *Henniker v Howard* (1904) 90 LT 157.

[223.] See *Fischer v Winch* [1939] 1 KB 666: *Davey v Harrow Corp* [1958] 1 QB 60.

[224.] High Court, unrep, 14 June 1977 (1975/444). It was pointed out that the Land Registry map is not conclusive to boundaries, unless an application for this has been made in the particular case: see para **[18.55]** *supra*.

lay down the centre of the hedge. Hamilton J was not convinced by this argument and considered the physical evidence in these terms:

"It is quite clear and indeed uncontested that there is in the vicinity of the hedge a slight depression on the plaintiffs' side of the hedge, which said depression has been grassed in. There is then on the side of the depression furthest from the plaintiffs' premises a slight bank upon which the hedge is growing. The slight depression is referred to as a ditch or gripe; the bank upon which the hedge is erected is on the defendant's side of the ditch or gripe. It is well settled that when two estates are separated by a hedge and a single ditch the presumption is, in default of evidence, that both ditch and hedge belonged to the owner of the land on which the hedge is planted. The presumption is that both the ditch and hedge are owned by one person. The evidence does not establish to my satisfaction by whom the hedge was planted and I must have regard to the probabilities of the matter. It would appear to me that a person erecting a bank on which a hedge was to be planted for the purpose of establishing a boundary between the two properties would dig the ditch or gripe at the extremity of his land and shovel the earth therefrom on to his land. Consequently, it appears to me that the ditch and hedge are situate on the defendants' lands and in this view I am fortified by photograph A produced on behalf of the defendant which shows an old post, which appears to be on a line on the plaintiffs' side of the said hedge. This would appear to me to constitute the boundary between the two properties and be in accordance with the presumption of law to which I have already referred."[225]

2. Maps or Plans

(i) Unregistered Land

[18.63] As we mentioned earlier,[226] it is common practice to describe the land in the parcels clause by reference to a map or plan. In this context we are concerned with express incorporation of a map or plan into the deed and the problems of construction which may arise from this. But, in passing, it may be mentioned that a map or plan, eg, the relevant Ordnance Survey map, may be referred to to explain the terms of a deed, though it is not incorporated expressly into the deed. However, under the rules governing use of extrinsic evidence,[227] this can be done only where the deed itself is uncertain or ambiguous, for otherwise such a map cannot be used to explain or control the deed.[228]

[225.] Transcript, pp 3-5.

[226.] Para **[18.53]** *supra*.

[227.] See para **[17.19]** *ante*.

[228.] *Wise v Leahy* (1875) IR 9 CL 384. *Cf Leachman v L & K Richardson Ltd* [1969] 1 WLR 1129.

(a) Incorporation

[18.64] The usual method of incorporation of a map or plan is to refer to it in the parcels clause and then to attach it at the end of the deed. Thus a common formula adopted is: "all the land and premises more particularly described in the schedule hereto and delineated and coloured red on the map hereon annexed." If the premises are described in a schedule, the reference to the map or plan will, of course, appear here rather than in the parcels clause. As we shall discuss in a moment, a wide range of words of incorporation may be used with varying effects, so that it is often a difficult question of construction whether the map or plan is to govern any verbal description in the parcels or *vice versa*. If there are no words of incorporation in the parcels clause or elsewhere in the body of the deed, but nevertheless a map or plan has been attached to it, it seems that the map or plan may not be referred to, except as a piece of extrinsic evidence to explain an ambiguity or doubt.[229]

[18.65] The question is sometimes raised as to whether the purchaser is entitled to insist upon incorporation of a map or plan in the deed. The case law on this question is far from clear and the cases are not easily reconciled.[230] It seems clear that the vendor cannot object to a plan in the deed if the contract for sale described the property by reference to one. Apart from that, the general rule is that, where the purchaser is to draw up the conveyance, he is entitled to decide on its form and the vendor is entitled only to object to this if it is inaccurate or fails to carry out the contract.[231] As against that, it is arguable that, where the verbal description in the parcels clause is clear and sufficient to describe the property, the purchaser's insistence upon incorporation of a map or plan as well would put the vendor to the needless expense of having this checked for accuracy.[232] Conversely, if the verbal description is not sufficient, it would seem proper for the purchaser to insist upon incorporation of a map or plan and the vendor cannot object to this or seek to minimise its effectiveness to describe the property being conveyed.[233]

---

[229] *Ibid.* See also the discussion in *Dennehy v Corrigan* [1902] 2 IR 63. And note *Wigginton & Milner Ltd v Winster Engineering Ltd* [1978] 3 All ER 436.

[230] See *Re Sansom and Narbett's Contract* [1910] 1 Ch 741; *Re Sparrow and James' Contract* [1910] 2 Ch 60; *Re Sharman and Meade's Contract* [1936] Ch 755.

[231] *Re Sansom and Narbett's Contract, op cit,* pp 749-50 (*per* Swinfen Eady J). See also para **[15.06]** *ante.*

[232] *Re Sharman and Meade Contract, op cit,* p 760 (*per* Farwell J).

[233] *Re Sparrow and James' Contract, op cit,* p 62 (*per* Farwell J).

(b) Construction

[18.66] There are several different constructions as to the effect of incorporation of a map or plan in a deed and, of course, each case must depend upon its own facts and, in particular, the precise words of incorporation used.[234] Most problems arise where the deed combines a verbal description in the parcels clause (with, perhaps, a fuller verbal description in a schedule) and a map or plan.[235] If there is any inconsistency or conflict between the verbal description or descriptions and the map or plan the question arises as to which prevails. The Irish courts have drawn a distinction between two formulae in particular, *viz*, where the words in the parcels clause incorporating the map or plan begin with the conjunction "and" or "as."[236] If the verbal description in the parcels clause is followed by a formula such as "and described in the annexed map," the courts seem to take the view that the deed contains two descriptions of equal force, which must both be looked at. Thus if the verbal description is unclear it may be rendered certain by the map.[237] As Walker LJ put it in *Dennehy v Corrigan*[238]:

"... a grant referring to a map may be so worded that the map is an essential part of the grant, and that there can be no certainty without it."[239]

If, however, the verbal description is clear and sufficient in itself to describe the property, and the map conflicts with it, then a different rule applies, as Andrews J explained in *Kenny v La Barte*.[240]

"The common law principle upon which, in my opinion, the map must be rejected is, that where two adequate descriptions occur in a deed, each purporting to describe what the deed conveys, and these descriptions are in fact at variance and inconsistent with each other, the earlier description must prevail."[241]

And there have been several such cases where the Irish courts have rejected the map in favour of the parcels clause[242] and have applied, in effect, the principle of *falsa demonstratio non nocet*.[243]

[234.] See the discussion in *Dennehy v Corrigan* [1902] 2 IR 63n.

[235.] See the formula quoted in para **[18.64]** *ante*.

[236.] *Kenny v La Barte* [1902] 2 IR 63 at 77 (*per* Andrews J); *Dennehy v Corrigan* [1902] 2 IR 63n at 67n (*per* FitzGibbon LJ).

[237.] *Errington v Rorke* (1859) 7 HLC 618; *Boyle v Mulholland* (1860) 10 ICLR 150.

[238.] [1902] 2 IR 63n.

[239.] *Ibid*, p 71n.

[240.] [1902] 2 IR 63.

[241.] *Ibid*, p 76.

[242.] See *Bradford v Dublin and Kingstown Rly Co* (1858) 7 ICLR 624 at 630 (*per* Lefroy CJ); *Dennehy v Corrigan* [1902] 2 IR 63n at 66n (*per* Lord Ashbourne C).

[243.] *Boyle v Mulholland* (1860) 10 ICLR 150 at 157 (*per* Fitzgerald B); *Roe v Lidwell* (1860) 11 ICLR 320. See para **[17.24]** *ante*.

[18.67] On the other hand, if the parcels clause uses the formula "as described in the annexed map," then there may be a presumption that the map is intended to be the governing description.[244] However, this is not an absolute rule as the case of *Dennehy v Corrigan*[245] illustrates. In that case the description in the parcels clause, which was held to be sufficient in detail,[246] was followed by the formula "as more particularly described" in the map. Lord Ashbourne LC stated:

> "I can see no reason for imputing in this case any prerogative significance to the word 'as.' That word is followed by the words 'more particularly,' which convey that there had been another antecedent description. There may, of course, be cases where 'as' is so used as to make the map it refers to the governing part of the description, but this is not such a case."[247]

Nevertheless, it has often been held that the formula "and more particularly described" suggests that the map or plan is enlarging upon the verbal description and so governs it, particularly if that description is uncertain or ambiguous.[248] But again it was emphasised in *Dennehy v Corrigan* that this must not be taken to be a universal rule, especially where the verbal description is in fact complete on its own. Thus Walker LJ stated:

> "I cannot attach any special force to the words 'more particularly' where the words 'and described' follow a complete description. They import *per se* a further and more particular description, and the words 'more particularly' are only an expansion of that."[249]

[18.68] Sometimes an attempt may be made by the draftsman of the deed to reduce or qualify the effect of any map or plan annexed to it, eg, by adding such words as "for the purpose of identification only." The English courts seem to have taken the view that such a qualification does, indeed, reduce the effect of the map or plan, so that usually the parcels will prevail over it.[250] However, even this is not a rigid rule, because if the parcels clause in such a case is not entirely clear as to the identity of or the boundaries of the

---

[244.] *Kenny v La Barte* [1902] 2 IR 63 at 77 (*per* Andrews J); *Dennehy v Corrigan* (1902) 2 IR 63n at 67n (*per* Lord Ashbourne C) and 67n (*per* FitzGibbon LJ).

[245.] [1902] 2 IR 63n.

[246.] "I cannot see anything in the words of the deed referring to the map to cut down or regulate or control the already sufficient and adequate description". *Ibid*, p 66n (*per* Lord Ashbourne C).

[247.] *Ibid*, p 67n. See also Walker LJ at p 75n.

[248.] See *Wallington v Townsend* [1939] Ch 588; also *Neilson v Poole* (1969) 20 P & CR 909 at 916 (*per* Megarry J).

[249.] *Op cit*, p 74n.

[250.] *Hopwood v Brown* [1955] 1 WLR 213 at 228 (*per* Jenkins LJ). See also *Willson v Greene* [1971] 1 WLR 635.

property being conveyed, the map or plan may still be referred if it elucidates the matter.[251] However, care should be taken to see that such a qualification is not used in conjunction with a formula which suggests that the map or plan is to have a more substantial effect, eg, in conjunction with the "more particularly described" formula.[252] Furthermore, if the contract for sale described the land by reference to a map and the purchaser insists upon incorporating this in the deed, the vendor cannot require insertion of such a qualification.[253]

(ii) Registered Land

[18.69] As we saw earlier,[254] the Land Registry description of land, which is incorporated by reference in the prescribed transfer forms,[255] includes a cross-reference to the plan of the land on the Registry map. These maps are based upon the Ordnance Survey maps. Many of them, of course, date back to 1891, when the Local Registration of Title (Ireland) Act of that year provided for compulsory registration of all land bought under the Land Purchase Acts, and are drawn to a scale of 6 inches to the mile. However, rule 174(3) of the Land Registration Rules 1972, required adoption, as far as possible, of 25 inch or larger scale maps, subject to the Registrar's directions.[256] Under rule 3 of the Land Registration Rules 1986, registry maps for property in urban areas are, as far as possible, to be on the 1/1000 scale and all plans of such property are to be on such scale as conforms, with necessary or obvious adjustments, to ordnance map detail. It is imperative, therefore, that solicitors lodging documents for registration of a transfer of a property ensure that the architect, surveyor or engineer who has drawn up the plan has fully met the Registry's requirements.[257]

[18.70] Though the Registry maps may generally be relied upon as accurate,[258] they are not conclusive as to the boundaries or extent of the

---

[251.] See the discussion in *Wigginton & Milner Ltd v Winster engineering Ltd* [1978] 3 All ER 436.

[252.] See the warning on this given by Megarry J in *Neilson v Poole* (1969) 20 P & CR 909 at 916.

[253.] *Re Sparrow and James' Contract* [1910] 2 Ch 60.

[254.] Para **[18.55]** *supra*.

[255.] *Ibid*.

[256.] Metric maps with the National Grid values printed on them have increasingly come into use see Griffith 'Land Registry Practice' (1977) 71 Gaz ISLI 99 at 104.

[257.] See the full discussion of the Registry requirements in Fitzgerald, *Land Registry Practice* (2nd ed, 1986), Ch 4.

[258.] The Registrar has of course power to rectify errors see Registration of Title Act 1964 s 32(1). However, this power arises only if all interested parties consent to the rectification: see *Crumlish v Registrar of Deeds and Titles* [1990] 2 IR 471. See also *Geraghty v Rohan Industrial Estates Ltd* [1988] IR 419. See also *Re Trainor* [1936] NI 197.

land.[259] However, it is a general principle of the system that the register is otherwise conclusive evidence of the title of the registered owner. This question arose in the controversial Northern Ireland case of *Miscampbell v McAlister*,[260] which involved a grant by a registered owner of land of a right to take water from, and to divert, a stream at certain points. These were marked on a map annexed to the deed but, on registration of the right as a burden on the grantor's land,[261] with a cross-reference to the stream shown on the Registry map, an error was made on the map so that it showed the stream as including waters not delineated on the map annexed to the deed of grant. In an action later by a purchaser from the grantee to prevent the grantor from diverting water to which he was not entitled according to the deed map, but which was included in the parts of the stream still belonging to him according to the Registry map, the Northern Ireland Court of Appeal held that the principle of the register being conclusive was confined by s 34 of the Local Registration of Title (Ireland) Act 1891, to the title to "land," which covered "corporeal" hereditaments only[262] and not "incorporeal" hereditaments[263] such as the burden or easement in this case.[264] However, this would no longer appear to be the law in either part of Ireland, because it is now provided[265] that the register is conclusive evidence not only of the title[266] but also of "any right, privilege, appurtenance or burden" appearing or shown thereon.

3. Grantee's Rights

[18.71] The parcels clause may go on to specify additional rights passing to the grantee, eg, easements and profits *à prendre*.[267] Of course, so far as existing easements and profits are concerned, these will pass automatically

---

[259.] See *Gillespie v Hogg* [1947] Ir Jur Rep 51. The provisions for entry of boundaries as conclusive are rarely used see para **[18.55]** *supra*. As to such entries see 1972 Rules rr 148-50.

[260.] [1930] NI 74. The decision resulted in a lengthy argument between the Republic's then Registrar of Titles, WE Glover and the then Dean of the Faculty of Law QUB Professor JL Montrose, see (1938) 2 NILQ 38, 63 and 142: (1939) 3 NILQ 34 and 68.

[261.] It was also entered in the grantee's folio as an appurtenance to his land.

[262.] See the definition in s 59(1).

[263.] *Cf* ss 19 and 21 of the 1891 Act and see Andrews LJ at [1930] NI 74 at 96.

[264.] See *ibid* pp 96 (*per* Andrews LJ) and 102-3 (*per* Best LJ).

[265.] Registration of Title Act 1964, s 31(1), *re* NI see Land Registration Act (NI) 1970, s 11(1). See also *Geraghty v Rohan Industrial Estates Ltd* [1988] IR 419.

[266.] Section 31(1) of the 1964 Act also refers to the owner's title "to the land" and "land" is now defined in s 3(*e*) of the Act as including "incorporeal hereditaments." Section 11(1) of the 1970 Act does not mention the word "land." though note the wide definition in s 45(1)(a) of the Interpretation Act (NI) 1954. See *Irish Land Law* (2nd ed, 1986), para 1.01 fn 3.

[267.] See generally on this subject *Irish Land Law* (2nd ed, 1986), Ch 6; Lyall, *Land Law in Ireland* (1994), Ch 22.

on a conveyance of the dominant land and there is no need to refer to them expressly in the parcels clause or elsewhere in the deed of conveyance.[268] However, most conveyancers prefer to insert some reference to them, if only a statement that the land is conveyed to the purchaser together with all easements, profits, and other rights and incidents created by earlier deeds. Where, however, the easements or profits are being created for the first time by the current conveyance in favour of the grantee,[269] it is, of course, necessary to deal with them in the deed. They may be set out in the parcels clause, usually introduced by the words "TOGETHER WITH,"[270] but if, as is often the case, the description is rather lengthy, the details may be set out in a schedule to which cross-reference is made.[271]

[18.72] Care should be taken in drafting the details of rights such as easements and profits. First, the requirements of the general law on this subject, especially relating to the nature and scope of such rights, must be taken into account. This is a subject which has been considered in detail elsewhere,[272] Secondly, it is important to define precisely the person ors persons entitled to enjoy the rights, particularly since subsequent dealings with the dominant land may increase the user of the servient land or the exercise of the rights in question.[273] Thirdly, the dominant and servient land to which the rights relate should be defined.[274] Fourthly, it should be remembered that the grant of an easement or profit to arise in the future is subject to the rule against perpetuities,[275] so that care should be exercised in granting, eg, a right to use sewers and drains passing "or hereafter to pass" under land.[276]

[268.] *Peilow v O'Carroll* (1972) 106 ILTR 29 at 47 (*per* Budd J), see para **[9.18]** *ante*.

[269.] As regards reservation of such rights in favour of the grantor see para **[18.73]** *infra*.

[270.] See *Tisdall v Parnell* (1863) 14 ICLR 1; *Poole v Griffith* (1865) 15 ICLR 239.

[271.] Of course, rights in the nature of easements and profits may pass to the grantee by implied grant under eg the rule in *Wheeldon v Burrows* or s 6 of the Conveyancing Act 1881. This whole subject is considered in *Irish Land Law* (2nd ed, 1986), paras 6.060-8. See also paras **[9.43]** *ante* and **[18.54]** *supra*.

[272.] See *ibid* paras 6.023-38 and 6.052-5. See also *Lyall, op cit, et seq*.

[273.] See *White v Grand Hotel, Eastbourne Ltd* [1913] 1 Ch 113; *Jelbert v Davis* [1968] 1 All ER 1182.

[274.] See *Shannon Ltd v Venner Ltd* [1965] Ch 682.

[275.] The Law Reform Commission has recommended that easements, profits and other interests like options should be removed from the scope of the rule and that it be declared that the rule never applied to them. See *Land Law and Conveyancing Law: (1) General Proposals* (LRC 30-1969), para 18-20. The exclusions in s 9(1) of the Perpetuities Act (NI) 1966, are confined to existing rights or to ancillary rights (eg for executing repairs or alterations) exercisable in respect of these see *Irish Land Law*, (2nd ed, 1986) para 5.149.

[276.] See *Dunn v Blackdown Properties Ltd* [1961] Ch 433 and see (1962) 106 Sol Jo l46; (1964) 61 L Soc Gaz 59.

4. Exceptions and Reservations

[18.73] Exceptions and reservations in favour of the grantor, which necessarily delimit what is not to pass to the grantee, are usually introduced in the parcels clause by the words "EXCEPTING AND RESERVING"[277] However, as we shall discuss in a moment,[278] exceptions and reservations are quite different things and technically should not be lumped together in the parcels clause as if they were the same. Reservations do not relate to part of the land as it exists immediately before the conveyance and so should not strictly be included in the parcels clause. Rather they relate to new rights over the land being granted to the grantor and, as such, ought really to be mentioned later in the deed, after the *habendum*.[279] However, the modern tendency is to lump them together in the parcels clause, though if the draftsman of the deed is incorporating rights created by earlier deeds it is usual to refer to these after the *habendum*, introducing them with the words "SUBJECT TO ...." The courts seem prepared to interpret such clauses so as to give effect to the parties' substantive intention,[280] and thus will give effect to the deed despite the lack of strict adherence to the correct form or terminology.[281]

(i) The Distinction

[18.74] There are two main points of distinction between an exception and a reservation. First, as mentioned in the previous paragraph, an exception relates to the land as it exists immediately before the conveyance; it refers to something *in esse*, a part of the land being conveyed. A reservation, on the other hand, relates to some newly created right which, *ex hypothesi*, was not *in esse* prior to the current conveyance. Thus Chatterton V-C explained in *Earl of Antrim v Gray*[282]:

[277.] See *Brown v Chadwick* (1857) 7 ICLR 101; *Listowel v Gibbings* (1858) 9 ICLR 223; *Quinn v Shields* (1877) IR 11 CL 254. Another common formula is "SAVING AND RESERVING" " see *Tottenham v Byrne* (1861) 12 ICLR 376.

[278.] Para **[18.74]** *infra*.

[279.] See para **[18.84]** *infra*.

[280.] See *Earl of Inchiquin v Burnell* (1795) 3 Ridgw P C 376 at 420-4 (*per* Yelverton CB). See also *Re Dances Way* [1962] Ch 490 at 502 (*per* Lord Evelshed MR) and 506 (*per* Upjohn J).

[281.] Thus what is really an exception may, in fact, be referred to in the deed as a reservation see eg *Fishbourne v Hamilton* (1890) 25 LR Ir 483 and *Staples v Young* [1908] 1 IR 135 (mines and minerals). See also *Attorney-General for NSW v Dickson* [1904] AC 273. Cf *British Railways Board v Glass* [1965] Ch 538 (right of way which should have been "reserved". introduced by the words "SAVE AND EXCEPT"). And see *Waterpark v Fennell* (1855) 5 ICLR 120 ("exception" of fishing, fowling, hunting and hawking rights).

[282.] (1875) IR 9 Eq 513.

> "It is plain that mines and minerals, being an integral part of the land, form properly the subject of an exception and not of a reservation. The right to enter and dig for them is the subject of a reservation, and a reservation is in law a re-grant to the grantor by the grantee."[283]

Secondly, as Chatterton V-C pointed out, a reservation, unlike an exception, operated at common law as a re-grant of a right by the grantee and so, as we shall discuss later,[284] care had to be taken to see that the grantee executed the deed so as to ensure that the re-grant took effect.[285] Indeed, in early law the term "reservation" had a more restricted meaning, being confined to services rendered to the grantor or feudal lord, such as provision of a beast[286] or payment of rent.[287] Its modern meaning of a re-grant of rights in the nature of easements and profits in favour of the grantor was a later development.

[18.75] At this point it may be useful to give examples of exceptions and reservations to illustrate the distinction. The most obvious category of an exception is where the grantor keeps back part of an estate granted to someone else,[288] eg, a road running through it[289] or the land traversed by a railway line.[290] Another common exception is mines and minerals,[291] though as Chatterton V-C pointed out in the quotation given in the previous paragraph, the usual accompanying rights to enter the land and work the mines or dig for the minerals involve the creation of new rights and, therefore, properly form the subject of a reservation.[292] Another is quarries, which may be distinguished from mines as Monohan CJ stated in *Brown v Chadwick*[293]:

---

283. *Ibid*, p 520.
284. Para **[18.77]** *infra*.
285. This does not apply in Ireland. of course. where the rights in question operate by way of demise under Deasy's Act 1860, see *Radcliff v Hayes* [1907] 1 IR 101 (reservation of sporting and shooting rights in lease). *Cf Bayley v Conyngham* (1863) I5 ICLR 406 (oral letting of fishing rights). See also *Irish Landlord and Tenant Law* paras 2.18 and 2.25.
286. Ie, a heriot, see *Irish Land Law* (2nd ed, 1986), paras 2.30 and 2.49.
287. See the discussion of *Earl of Inchiquin v Burnell* (1795) 3 Ridgw PC 376. See also *Mason v Clarke* [1954] 1 QB 460 at 467 (*per* Denning LJ) (rev'd on another point [1955] AC 778).
288. See *Ellis v The Lord Primate* (1864) 16 Ir Ch R 184.
289. *Tottenham v Byrne* (1861) 12 ICLR 376. *Cf* reservation of a right of way over the road, see *Bradford v Dublin and Kingstown Rly Co* (1858) 7 ICLR 624.
290. *Bradford v Dublin and Kingstown Rly Co, op cit.*
291. See *McDonnell v Kenneth* (1850) 1 ICLR 113; *Brown v Chadwick* (1857) 7 ICLR 101; *Listowel v Gibbings* (1858) 9 ICLR 2223; *Earl of Antrim v Gray* (1875) IR 9 Eq 513; *Fishbourne v Hamilton* (1890) 25 LR Ir 483; *Staples v Young* [1908] 1 IR 135.
292. Note, of course, that there are few private rights in mines and minerals as a result of their statutory acquisitions by the State, see *Irish Land Law* (2nd ed, 1986), para 6.115.
293. (1857) 7 ICLR 101.

"The distinction between a mine and a quarry appears to me to be this - a mine is a place where the substratum is excavated, but the surface is unbroken; whereas in a quarry the surface is opened, and the material in the present case, limestone, is exposed and raised."[294]

In that case, the Court of Common Pleas held that an exception of mines and mineral did not include open limestone quarries and this was followed in *Listowel v Gibbings*,[295] where the Court of Queen's Bench held that a "mine" usually imports a cavern or subterraneous place containing metals or minerals and not a quarry and "minerals" ordinarily means metallic fossil bodies and not limestones. However, these decisions were not followed by the Court of Appeal in *Fishhourne v Hamilton*,[296] where it was held that beds of limestone were included within an exception of "mines and minerals," whether they were got at by quarrying or surface working. And the *Fishbourne* case was approved by the Court of Appeal in *Staples v Young*,[297] though it was held in that case that pure sand of several feet in depth which constituted most of the grantee's holding some six feet below the surface was not included within a "reservation"[298] of mines and minerals. Walker LC stated:

"Though a reservation uses only the words 'mines and minerals,' and there may be in the district covered by it a subject-matter such as coal and iron which would in the popular sense furnish a subject for the reservation, any substance which is a mineral in the view of the law may, notwithstanding, be covered by the reservation."[299]

Finally, in *Quinn v Shields*[300] it was held that an exception of "all mosses" meant all the places in which turf, or matter in the course of becoming turf, was found, including the soil of such places. The exception also referred to "turbaries" and on this Palles CB stated:

"No doubt, turbary in the singular would prima facie mean 'a right of cutting turf,' but I doubt whether the word 'turbaries' in the plural, in a context like the present, does not more properly mean 'places in which turf may be cut.'"[301]

[294.] *Ibid*, p 106.

[295.] (1858) 9 ICLR 223.

[296.] (1890) 25 LR Ir 483, following *Hext v Gill* (1872) IR 7 Ch 699.

[297.] [1908] 1 IR 135.

[298.] See para **[18.73]**, fn 281 *supra*.

[299.] *Op cit* p 143. *Cf McDonnell v McKinty* (1847) 10 Ir LR 514 (exception of mines, minerals and quarries held to include quarries of limestones).

[300.] (1877) IR 11 CL 254. See also *Irons v Douglas* (1841) 3 Ir Eq R 601; *Boyle v Olpherts* (1841) 4 Ir Eq R 241.

[301.] *Ibid*, p 266.

[18.76] The most common type of reservation, apart from payment of rent and other charges, is rights in the nature of easements and profits *à prendre*, eg, rights of way, turbary (the right to cut turf), fishing rights, shooting and hunting rights and timber rights. These have all been considered in detail elsewhere.[302]

(ii) Execution by Grantee

[18.77] Since a reservation operates as a re-grant,[303] it was the rule at common law that. unlike in the case of an exception, the grant had to be executed by the grantee for the reservation to be fully effective in favour of the grantor. If the grantee did not execute the grant, it operated at most to confer equitable rights on the grantor, in the sense that the grantee was bound in equity to give effect to the intended easements or profits.[304] This remains the position in Ireland,[305] unless the special mechanism introduced by s 62(1) of the Conveyancing Act 1881, is adopted. Under this the reservation will be effective in law without execution by the grantee if the grantor conveys the land to X and his heirs "to the use" that the grantor should have the easements and profits in question and, subject thereto, to the use of the grantee and his heirs. The Statute of Uses (Ireland) 1634, then "executes"[306] the use and the legal title to the easements and profits vests automatically in the grantor. This mechanism was also considered elsewhere.[307]

(iii) Construction

[18.78] The general rule is that a grantor may not derogate from his grant and so express exceptions are clearly construed against the grantor of a conveyance.[308] However, to the extent that an express reservation still operates in Ireland[309] as a re-grant by the grantee of the conveyance (ie, the purchaser or lessee of the land rather than the vendor or lessor), strict adherence to this rule of construction results in the reservation being construed in favour of the grantor of the conveyance (who is the grantee of

---

[302] *Irish Land Law* (2nd ed, 1986), paras 6.107-19; Lyall, *Land Law in Ireland* (1994), Ch 22.

[303] See para **[18.74]** *supra*.

[304] See *May v Belleville* [1905] 2 Ch 605.

[305] *Cf* England where, under s 65 of the Law of Property Act 1925, a reservation is effective in law without execution by the grantee.

[306] Note the special meaning of this word in relation to the Statute see *Irish Land Law* (2nd ed, 1986), para 3.016.

[307] See *ibid*, para 6.057, wherein it is explained why this mechanism was not effective prior to the 1881 Act.

[308] See the discussion in *Irish Land Law* (2nd ed, 1986), para 6.058 *et seq*.

[309] Para **[18.77]** *supra*.

the reservation).³¹⁰ It would seem that the non-derogation principle is applied against the grantor of the conveyance as a whole only when the question of implied reservation arises, as we shall see in a moment.

(iv) Rule Against Perpetuities

[18.79] Since a reservation, unlike an exception, relates to the creation of new rights,³¹¹ it is subject to the rule against perpetuities and so care must be exercised in drafting a reservation purporting to bring easements or profits into existence at some indefinite time in the future.³¹²

(v) Implied

[18.80] The question of implied exceptions or reservations is governed largely by the principle that the grantor of a conveyance may not derogate from his grant. This subject is considered in detail elsewhere³¹³ and need not be dealt with further here.

(vi) Registered Land

[18.81] On a transfer of registered land, exceptions and reservations may be made by express reference in the transfer form, as in the case of unregistered land. This may be done by listing the exceptions or reservations in the body of the form or in a schedule to it.³¹⁴ Where they involve creation of rights like easements and profits *à prendre*, they constitute burdens affecting the servient land and should be entered in the folio relating to the land.³¹⁵ The registered owner of the dominant land may require an entry in the folio³¹⁶ relating to that land showing the existence of the easement or profit.³¹⁷ Every

---

³¹⁰· See *South Eastern Rly v Associated Portland Cement Co* [1910] 1 Ch 12; *Foster v Lyons* [1927] 1 Ch 219. Note, however, that in England, since s 65 of the Law of Property Act 1925 (see fn 305, *supra*) has largely abolished the concept of a re-grant by the grantee of the conveyance, judges have taken the view that express reservations should be construed like exceptions, ie against the grantor of the conveyance, see *Cordell v Second Clanfleld Properties Ltd* [1969] 2 Ch 9; *St Edmondsbury and Ipswich Diocesan Board of Finance v Clarke (No 2)* [1973] 1 WLR 1572. *Cf Johnstone v Holdway* [1963] 1 QB 601.

³¹¹· Para **[18.74]** *supra*.

³¹²· See para **[18.72]** *supra*. See also (1962) 106 Sol Jo 123 and 147.

³¹³· *Irish Land Law* (2nd ed, 1986), para 6.058 *et seq*. Note that there may be a distinction in this context between construction of the wording of a deed already completed and executed and determination of the wording or form of a deed still to be executed. In the case of the latter, it is still a matter of contract and the court should strive to give effect to the parties' intention as exhibited by it. See the discussion in *Re Flanagan and McGarvey and Thompson Contract* [1945] NI 32 at 40-1 (*per* Black J).

³¹⁴· See the Land Registration Rules 1972, Form 29.

³¹⁵· Registration of Title Act 1964, s 69(1)(j); see Fitzgerald, *Land Registry Practice* (2nd ed, 1995), Ch 14.

³¹⁶· 1964 Act, s 82; 1972 Rules, r 25(b).

³¹⁷· Ie as an "appurtenance".

application for registration of an easement or profit *à prendre* must be accompanied by a map[318] or plan[319] identifying the servient land, unless this can be clearly identified from the description in the transfer instrument. Any plan not endorsed on and referred to[320] in that instrument must be signed by the registered owner of the servient land and the grantee, or his solicitor.[321]

5. All Estate Clause

[18.82] Prior to 1882 it was the practice of conveyancers to insert at the end of the parcels clause a clause designed to ensure that there passed to the grantee any outstanding estate in the land vested in the vendor that might not be mentioned expressly.[322] This was known as the "all estate" clause and ran something like this: "and all the estate right title interest use trust benefit property claim and demand whatsoever at law and in equity of the grantor therein." It is, however, no longer necessary to include this clause, because s 63(1) of the Conveyancing Act 1881, provides:

> "Every conveyance shall, by virtue of this Act, be effectual to pass all the estate, right, title, interest, claim, and demand which the conveying parties respectively have, in, to, or on the property conveyed, or expressed or intended so to be, or which they respectively have power to convey in, to, or on the same."

This provision applies, however, only if and as far as a contrary intention is not expressed in the conveyance and has effect subject to its terms and provisions.[323] Thus a demise of a term of years does not pass the lessor's freehold reversion as the *habendum* should clearly indicate.[324] It is also considered not to be good practice to have the *habendum* or any other operative part[325] of the deed refer to the grantor as conveying "free from incumbrances" as this might be construed as an "express" provision which casts doubts on the operation of s 63.[326] On the other hand, a conveyance of

---

318. Sufficient to enable the servient land to be identified on the Registry maps, see *Fitzgerald op cit* p 236.

319. Drawn on the current largest scale Ordnance Survey Map, 1972 Rules r 130(1). Rule 130(2) relates to the appurtenant land.

320. 1972 Rules, r 130(3).

321. *Ibid.*

322. See *Drew v Earl of Norbury* (1846) 3 Jo & Lat 267 at 284 (*per* Sugden LC). See also *Taylor v London and County Banking Co* [1901] 2 Ch 231 at 255 (*per* Stirling LJ). However, many solicitors still insert an all estate clause in a conveyance of a possessory estate.

323. Section 63(2).

324. Para **[18.84]** *post.* See also *Buckler's* Case (1597) 2 Co Rep 55.

325. *Cf* the recitals: see para **[18.33]** *supra.*

326. Another reason is that it may be regarded as imposing on the grantor wider obligations than would be implied under the usual covenants for title implied under s 7 of the 1881 Act: see *Thompson v Thompson* (1871) IR 6 Eq 113 at 117-25 (*per* Chatterton V-C); *Borrowes v Borrowes* (1871) IR 6 Eq 368 at 378 (*per* Chatterton V-C).

the fee simple will pass to the grantee any outstanding terms of years vested in the grantor and not merged with the freehold.[327] Furthermore, all estates or interests actually vested in the conveying party will pass and not just those vested in him in the capacity in which he may be expressed to convey in the deed, eg, as trustee.[328] It should, however, be noted that s 63 of the 1881 Act is confined in operation to a "conveyance", which, though defined widely in s 2(v) of the Act, is not as widely defined as in the equivalent legislation in England.[329] And it has been held that s 63 should be construed strictly, so that the various instruments included within the definition of "conveyance" are not to be read into it *mutatis mutandis*, eg, an instrument expressed to be a conveyance is not effectual to appoint all the estate, etc, although the definition includes an appointment.[330] But the section would apply if the instrument were also expressed to be an appointment instead of a conveyance.[331] However, this principle has not been followed in England since 1925,[332] for in *Re Stirrup's Contract*[333] Wilberforce J held that an assent executed under seal by personal representatives passed the legal estate vested in them, even though technically they had no power to execute the assent,[334] ie, the assent could operate as a conveyance.[335]

[18.83] It is not entirely clear whether s 63 of the 1881 Act has any relevance to transfers of registered land. There is no reference to the matter in the legislation, except that it is provided that a transfer operates as a conveyance by deed within the Conveyancing Acts,[336] which technically

---

327. *Burton v Barclay* (1831) 7 Bing 745; *Thellhuson v Liddard* [1900] 2 Ch 635. *Cf Re Hume's Estate* (1905) 5 NIJR 196 (charge on land conveyed).

328. *Drew v Earl of Norbury* (1846) 3 Jo & Lat 267 at 284 (*per* Sugden LC). See also *Parker v Judkin* [1931] 1 Ch 475; *Re Stirrup's Contract* [1961] 1 WLR 449 (conveyances by personal representatives as beneficial owners without first making formal assents in their own favour), but note the wide definition of conveyance in the English Law of Property Act 1925, see *infra*.

329. Ie ss 205(1)(ii) and 63 of the Law of Property Act 1925 which correspond respectively to ss 2(v) and 63 of the 1881 Act. Thus s 205(1)(ii) includes within the definition (which is not included in s 2(v) of the 1881 Act), eg, an assent. See *Re Stirrup's Contract* [1961] 1 WLR 449 fn 328 *supra*. It has recently been held in England to apply to a claim for rectification of an earlier deed of transfer of the land in question: see *Berkeley Leisure Group Ltd v Williamson* [1996] EGCS 18.

330. See *Hanbury v Bateman* [1920] 1 Ch 313.

331. *Ibid*, p 320 (*per* Sargant J).

332. And, therefore, under the Law of Property Act 1925 see fn 329, *supra*.

333. [1961] 1 WLR 449.

334. Because it did not "devolve" on them within s 36(1) of the Administration of Estates Act 1925 but rather was vested in them by the personal representatives of a deceased testator as the representatives of a beneficiary who died after the testator but before it could be vested in him. See Elphinstone, 'Assent to the Vesting of a Legal Estate' (1961) 25 Conv 491.

335. Note, however, that *Hanbury v Batemam*, fn 231 *supra*, was not cited in *Re Stirrup's Contract*.

336. Ie, Registration of Title Act 1964 s 52(1).

includes s 63. However, the general principle of the registered land system is that the transferee on registration gets the estate or interest with which the transferor was registered and neither more nor less.[337] If s 63 does apply, it is not clear as to how it could operate,[338] except, possibly, in respect of unregistered rights in the registered land.[339]

J. Habendum

1. Unregistered Land

[18.84] The next part of a deed of unregistered land, coming after all those parts which make up the "premises,"[340] is what is usually called the *habendum*, from the Latin *habeo* (to have). In fact, this is something of a misnomer nowadays since the clause usually begins with the words "TO HOLD,"[341] ie, a *tenendum*, from the Latin *teneo* (to hold), instead of the earlier form of "TO HAVE AND TO HOLD." At common law, the *habendum* was not regarded as an essential part of a deed,[342] for its primary function of determining the quantum of the estate granted could be performed by the premises and, if not, the law had rules which applied automatically anyway to determine this. Nevertheless, an *habendum* is invariably included in a deed of unregistered land for a number of reasons.

(i) Grantee

[18.85] The first obvious function of the *habendum* is to specify the grantee of the conveyance, though, of course, this may have been made clear by other parts of the deed, eg, the introductory recitals[343] or the premises.[344] There may, of course, be more than one grantee and we consider the question of co-owners and the capacity in which they may take the property later.[345] It should also be noted that at common law a person could not

---

[337.] See 1964 Act, ss 52-8.

[338.] See Potter, *Principles and Practice of Conveyancing under the Land Registration Act 1925* (1934), pp 91-2.

[339.] As to which, see further paras [12.05-6] and [12.49] *et seq*. Note, however, the *Berkeley Leisure Group* case (fn 329 *supra*), where it was held to apply to a purchaser of land who claimed that an earlier transfeer of the land, which was registered land, should be rectified.

[340.] Ie the operative parts coming after the recitals, see para [18.41] *supra*. The "premises" part or a deed is, strictly speaking. "that which went before", ie, the parcels. Then, in popular speech. it came to mean the lands conveyed. When reading law books or legal documents it is essential to hear this double meaning in mind.

[341.] See para [18.03] *supra*.

[342.] See *Kennedy v Hayes* (1840) 2 Ir LR 186 at 189 (*per* Burton J *in arguendo*). As to the significance of this on a question of construction, see para [18.87] *infra*.

[343.] See para [18.40] *supra*.

[344.] Eg, the words of grant, see para [18.48] *supra*.

[345.] Under the general heading of "Declaration of Trusts", see para [18.89] *infra*.

convey land to himself alone except by a conveyance to uses.[346] However, s 50(1) of the Conveyancing Act 1881,[347] now provides that freehold land may be conveyed by a person to himself *jointly* with another person by the like means by which it might be conveyed by him to another person.[348] Since then it has also been provided that a personal representative may make an assent in favour of himself.[349]

(ii) Words of Limitation

[18.86] The second major purpose of the *habendum* is to specify the *quantum* of the estate conveyed to the grantee. This involves, of course, the insertion of words of limitation where they are necessary. This is still an extremely complex subject in Ireland, but one which has been discussed at length elsewhere[350] and so little further need be added here.[351] It is also common for the *habendum* still to contain a conveyance to uses,[352] ie, the time-honoured formula "unto and to the use of"[353] the grantee. This is necessary in the case of a voluntary conveyance to prevent a resulting use in favour of the grantor coming into effect.[354] These words are, however, not strictly necessary in the case of a conveyance for consideration,[355] but obviously their presence may be useful in the event of a dispute as to whether or not consideration was involved.[356]

[346.] See *Irish Land Law* (2nd ed, 1986), paras 3.009 and 3.020.

[347.] A similar provision for leaseholds was made by s 21 of the Law of Property Amendment Act 1859. However, it remains the case that a person cannot grant land to himself alone, and so a nominee cannot grant an effective lease to his principal of land which he is holding for that principal: see *Ingram v IRC* [1995] 4 All ER 334.

[348.] It also provided that a husband could convey to his wife *alone* or *jointly* and *vice versa*. As regards covenants with himself and another, or with two or more persons, see para **[18.96]** *infra*.

[349.] Succession Act 1965, s 52(1)(b)(i) and (2).

[350.] See *Irish Land Law* (2nd ed, 1986), paras 4.024-42 (fees simple), 4.062, 4.082, 4.095-6 (fee farm grants), 4.127-34 (fees tail), 4.145-7 (life estates) and 4.167 (leases for lives renewable for ever). See also the discussion in *Re Courtney* [1981] NI 58 (assignment of land under a fee farm grant). Note that the Law Reform Commission has recommended the abolition of the need for words of limitation in conveyances of unregistered land (thus conforming with the position as regards registered land: see para **[18.88]** *infra*): see *Land Law and Conveyancing Law: (5) Further General Proposals* (LRC 44-1992), pp 6-8.

[351.] As to registered land. see para **[18.88]** *infra*.

[352.] The Statute of Uses (Ir) 1634. being still in force, see *Irish Land Law* (2nd ed, 1986), para 3.015-30.

[353.] *Ibid*, para 3.022. See *Re Luby's Estate* (1909) 43 ILTR 141.

[354.] Which would, of course, be "executed" by the Statute of Uses so as to render the conveyance a nullity. see *ibid* para 3.018.

[355.] See para **[18.42]** *supra*. Note that they are *not* contained in the conveyances on sale precedents in Laffoy *Irish Conveyancing Precedents*, Division E.

[356.] See *Revenue Commissioners v Moroney* [1972] IR 372, para **[18.44]** *supra*.

(iii) Construction

[18.87] The question sometimes arises as to how the *habendum* should be interpreted *vis-à-vis* the rest of the deed, especially where there appears to be a conflict between its terms and the terms of other parts of the deed, eg, the premises. The courts now seem to be agreed on the rules of interpretation for such cases.[357] First, where the conflict relates as to who is the grantee of the conveyance, the general rule seems to be that the premises prevail over the *habendum*, ie, if X is named as grantee in the former and Y is named in the latter, X takes and not Y.[358] Secondly, where the conflict relates to the estate being conveyed, the *habendum* may be read so as to explain or modify the premises.[359] However, it seems clear now that it cannot be used to cut down the estate specified in the premises. Thus, in *Kerr v Kerr*,[360] Brady LC stated:

> "No doubt there is authority in the text-books, that if an absolute interest be conferred in the premises, it cannot be narrowed to a more limited estate by the *habendum*."[361]

Thirdly, where the conflict related to the *property* itself,[362] the *habendum* should generally be ignored as exceeding its function.[363]

2. Registered Land

[18.88] No *habendum* clause is included in the prescribed forms of transfer of registered land,[364] nor is one necessary. First, each transfer form simply names the grantee. Secondly, the form cross-refers to the registered title of the transferor and the nature of this will obviously be indicated by the register. Apart from that the need for words of limitation has been removed now by statute.[365] It is provided that the transfer of registered land without the appropriate words of limitation is to be construed as passing the fee simple or other the whole interest which the transferor had power to convey,

---

[357.] The *habendum* may, of course, be used to explain other parts of the deed, *Kennedy v Hayes* (1840) 2 Ir LR 186 at 189 (*per* Burton J, in *arguendo*).

[358.] *Reynold v Kingman* (1587) Cro Eliz 115.

[359.] See *Hagarty v Nully* (1862) 13 ICLR 532. See also *Kendal v Micfield* (1740) Barn Ch 46 at 47 (*per* Verney MR); *Spencer v Registrar of Titles* [1906] AC 503 at 507 (*per* Lord Davey).

[360.] (1854) 4 Ir Ch R 493.

[361.] *Ibid* p 497. See also *Throckmerton v Tracy* (1555) 1 Plow 145. *Cf Altham's* Case (1610) 8 Co Rep 150b.

[362.] Which should be rare since the *habendum* should not be concerned with describing the property; this is the function of the parcels clause, see para **[18.50]** *et seq, ante*.

[363.] *Carew's Case* (1585) Moore 222 at 223 (*per* Markwood CB). *Cf Gregg v Richards* [1926] 1 Ch 521 at 533 (*per* Warrington LJ).

[364.] Land Registration Rules 1972, Sched of Forms. See para **[18.04]** *supra*.

[365.] Registration of Title Act 1964, s 123. Note that the Law Reform Commission has recommended a similar provision for unregistered land: see para **[18.86]** fn 350 *supra*.

unless a contrary intention appears from the transfer.[366] However, especially in view of the qualification relating to a contrary intention, many conveyancers continue to insert words of limitation in transfer forms.[367] It is also provided that a resulting use or trust for the transferor is not to be implied merely because the property is not expressed to be transferred to the use or benefit of the transferee.[368] Once again no reference to uses is contained in the prescribed forms, though some conveyancers may insert one *ex abundanti cautela*.

K. Declaration of Trusts

[18.89] This part of the deed which, if included, usually follows on from the *habendum* may cover a variety of matters. In particular, where the conveyance is to trustees, it may declare the details of the trust and, where it is to co-owners, it should indicate the form of co-ownership.[369]

1. Trusts

[18.90] The traditional method of conveying property to trustees to be held for specified beneficiaries, which developed after the passing of the Statute of Uses (Ireland) 1634, is to use the formula "unto and to the use of X and Y and their heirs in trust for A, B and C ...."[370] The deed may then go on to spell out the details of the beneficiaries' interests and the trustees' powers,[371] either immediately or in a schedule.[372] Care must be taken to see that the beneficial interests comply with the rule against perpetuities[373] and arguably, the trustees' powers should also be limited as to their exercise within the perpetuity period.[374]

2. Co-Owners

[18.91] Where the conveyance is made to more than one grantee, it ought to be specified exactly how they are to take the property, ie, as joint tenants or

---

[366.] 1964 Act s 123(1) and (2).

[367.] See McAllister, *Registration of Title in Ireland* (1973), pp 100-2. See also as regards covenants for title, para **[21.06]** *post*.

[368.] 1964 Act, s 123(3).

[369.] Note that there is no general provision of a statutory trust for sale in cases of co-ownership in Ireland, see *Irish Land Law* (2nd ed, 1986), Ch 7.

[370.] See *Gorman v Byrne* (1857) 8 ICLR 394. See also *Irish Land Law* (2nd ed, 1986), para 3.022.

[371.] See generally on this, *Irish Land Law* (2nd ed, 1986), Ch 10.

[372.] Or by a separate instrument.

[373.] See generally, *Irish Land Law* (2nd ed, 1986), Ch 5; Lyall, *Land Law in Ireland* (1994), Chs 11 and 12.

[374.] See *ibid*, paras 5.116-32. See also *Re Allot* [1924] 2 Ch 498.

tenants in common.[375] Clearly this matter must be discussed with the parties themselves and they should be advised as to the distinction between the two types of co-ownership and, in particular, as to the advantages (if any) of one form over another. Thus in the case of trustees it is usual to convey to them as joint tenants, because the right of survivorship ensures continuance of the full operation of the trust by the survivors until a replacement is appointed.[376] Similarly, in the case of a conveyance to a husband and wife, a joint tenancy ensures that the surviving spouse succeeds automatically to the other spouse's interest in the property. There may be other considerations, eg, fiscal ones.[377] Thus under s 14 of the Family Home Protection Act 1976,[378] a conveyance of a family home to the spouses as joint tenants is exempt from stamp duty, land registration fees, Registry of Deeds fees or Court fees, where the home was immediately prior to this transaction owned by either spouse or by both of them otherwise than as joint tenants. In the case of a conveyance to co-owners as tenants in common, their precise shares in the property should be specified.

3. Registered Land

[18.92] Where a transfer of registered land involves the creation of a trust, it is arguable that this should be done by two documents instead of one. One should consist of a transfer to the trustees in the usual form to be lodged in the Registry for registration of the trustees as owners of the land. The other should consist of a declaration of the beneficiaries' interests which should not be sent to the Registry, because trusts should be kept off the title and are not entered in the register.[379] Furthermore, even if one document is used or both are lodged in the Registry, neither the Registrar nor transferees, chargees and persons claiming an interest in burdens created for valuable consideration are affected by notice of any trust contained in, or arising out of matters contained in, that document.[380] In special cases, however, it may

---

[375.] See generally *Irish Land Law*, (2nd ed, 1986) Ch 7; Lyal,l *Land Law in Ireland* (1994), Ch 16.

[376.] See *ibid*, para 10.004.

[377.] As to other fiscal considerations which were once important, e.g., in relation to estate duty, see Bevan and Taylor, 'Spouses as Co-owners' (1966) 30 Conv 354 and 438; Pritchard, 'Co-ownership, Estate Duty and Additional Powers' (1972) 36 Conv 182. Note that under the Capital Acquisitions Tax Act 1976, liability to gift and inheritance tax in respect of gifts taken by joint tenants is the same in all respects as if they took as tenants in common in equal shares, see ss 7 and 14. See Bohan, *Capital Acquisitions Tax* (1995) Ch 14.

[378.] See further on the implications of this Act para **[16.61]** *et seq, ante*. See also para **[18.115]** *infra*.

[379.] Registration of Title Act 1964, s 92(1); see Fitzgerald, *Land Registry Practice* (2nd ed, 1995) pp 116-7.

[380.] 1964 Act, s 92(2).

be wise to insist upon entry of an "inhibition" in the register to prevent dealings by the trustees to the prejudice to the beneficiaries' interests,[381] eg, to prevent dealings except by way of sale in the case of a simple transfer to trustees for sale.[382]

L. Covenants

[18.93] The next part of the deed usually contains the various covenants which may be entered into by the grantor and grantee of the conveyance. This is a complex subject, many of the aspects of which, eg, as to the enforceability of covenants as between the original parties and as between their respective successors in title, have been considered elsewhere.[383] Some further points may be mentioned here.

1. Words of Creation

[18.94] A covenant is simply a promise under seal and so no technical words need be used in a deed so long as it makes it clear that the party in question agrees to do or refrain from doing something.[384] It is, however, common to specify that the party "covenants," but this may be made clear by other words suggesting that an obligation has been entered into, eg, "provided that" or "on condition that".[385] Thus a recital may be construed as creating a covenant.[386]

2. Execution of Deed

[18.95] Though liability may arise in equity, there is no legal liability on the covenantor to abide by a covenant unless he executes the deed containing it.[387] For this reason, it is usual to have the deed executed by the grantee as well as the grantor.[388]

3. Joint and Several Covenants

[18.96] Although a person may convey to himself jointly with another,[389] covenants contained in such a conveyance may be unenforceable because of

---

381. See *Fitzgerald, op cit*, pp 163-4.

382. See McAllister, *Registration of Title in Ireland* (1973) p 105.

383. See *Irish Land Law* (2nd ed, 1986), Ch 19; Lyall, *Land Law in Ireland* (1994), Ch 21.

384. *Luttrell v McCreery* (1850) 1 ICLR 7 at 15 (*per* Moore J).

385. *Brookes v Drysdale* (1877) 3 CPD 52.

386. *Duckett v Gordon* (1860) 11 Ir Ch R 181. See also para **[18.34]** *supra*.

387. *Re Rutherford's Conveyance* [1938] Ch 396 at 404 (*per* Simonds J).

388. See para **[18.77]** *supra*.

389. See para **[18.85]** *supra*.

the rule that a man may not covenant with himself and liability under such covenants is joint.[390]

[18.97] Where a covenant is entered into with two or more covenantees, the rule at common law was that it had to be made as either one covenant with them all jointly or separate covenants with each of them severally; it could not be made as one covenant with the covenantees jointly and severally at one and the same time. However, s 60(1) of the Conveyancing Act 1881, provided that where a covenant is made with two or more persons jointly, then, unless the contrary intention is expressed,[391] it is to be construed as in effect being made with each of them. However, in the case a covenant entered into by two or more covenantors, it remains necessary to draft the covenant in the form of covenants by each of them if they are to be liable severally.

4. Indemnity Covenants

[18.98] As a general rule the covenantor remains liable personally for the performance of covenants he has entered into, even though he has sold the land in respect of which he entered into the covenants in the first place.[392] The point is that he usually covenants expressly on behalf of himself and his successors in title and, even if he does not do so expressly, he is deemed to do so by s 59 of the Conveyancing Act 1881.[393] Though it is arguable that such personal liability for the actions of his successors should not survive his parting with the land, despite the doctrine of privity of contract, unless the wording of the covenant itself is drafted widely, eg, by enjoining the covenantor not only to refrain from doing the prohibited acts but also not to "permit or suffer"[394] or "cause or permit"[395] those acts to be done (ie, by other persons such as his successors). And, in Ireland, s 16 of Deasy's Act 1860, provides that the assignment of a lease with the lessor's consent (given as prescribed therein) releases and discharges the lessee from all future liability under the lease.[396]

[390.] See *Napier v Williams* [1911] 1 Ch 361. See also the general discussion in *Rye v Rye* [1962] AC 496. Thus, a nominee cannot grant an effective lease to his principal for whom he is holding the land: see *Ingram v IRC* [1995] 4 All ER 334, fn 347 *supra*.

[391.] Section 60(3).

[392.] See *Irish Land Law* (2nd ed, 1986), para 19.22.

[393.] See *ibid*, para 19.20.

[394.] See *Powell v Hemsley* [1909] 1 Ch 680 at 689 (*per* Eve J) (affd [1909] 2 Ch 252).

[395.] See *Earl of Sefton v Tophams Ltd* [1967] AC 50 at 81 (*per* Lord Wilberforce).

[396.] See *Irish Land Law* (2nd ed, 1986), para 17.030; *Irish Landlord and Tenant Law,* para 21.29 *et seq. Cf* the English Law of Property Act 1925, s 77 and note now the Landlord and Tenant (Covenants) Act 1995.

[18.99] The standard mechanism for protecting a covenantor against continuing liability on his covenants after parting with the land in question is an "indemnity" covenant entered into by the purchaser or other person to whom he conveys the land.[397] The need for such an indemnity covenant will also arise, of course, in each successive conveyance of the land, because each grantor might otherwise remain liable on the indemnity covenant entered into by him. The vendor's right to insertion of an indemnity covenant in the conveyance may be stated expressly in the contract for sale, but there is no such provision in the Law Society's *General Conditions of Sale (1995 Edition)*. Nevertheless, it seems that at common law the vendor is entitled to such an indemnity covenant and may, if necessary, ask the court to require the purchaser to enter into one.[398] Thus in *Adair v Carden*[399] it was held that on a conveyance for value of land subject to a mortgage there is, in the absence of express agreement, an undertaking implied by law on the part of the purchaser to indemnify the vendor against personal liability on foot of the mortgage.[400] As Porter MR put it:

> "It is, no doubt, reasonable to suppose that one who sells a property charged with a debt, and who therefore presumably receives for it just so much less money than he would otherwise have received, would regard himself as having got rid of the whole thing, liability as well as security."[401]

5. Covenants for Title

[18.100] Express covenants for title on the part of the vendor may be inserted in the conveyance and, even if they are not, there are several which may he implied by statute.[402] These may be extremely important to the purchaser once the conveyance takes effect, since, after that, the general rule is that he loses all remedies he had previously under the contract for sale. The whole question of post-completion remedies is considered in a later chapter,[403] and therein we discuss the covenants for title.[404]

[397.] See *ibid*, para 19.22.

[398.] *Moxhay v Inderwick* (1847) 1 De G & Sm 708; *Re Poole and Clarke's Contract* [1904] 2 Ch 173.

[399.] (1892) 29 LR Ir 469.

[400.] *Cf* the purchaser's right to an indemnity, eg, in respect of rents, on a sale of part of the vendor's land *vis-à vis* the other parts, see *Hatton v Waddy* (1837) 2 Jon 541; *Massy v O'Dell* (1859) 9 Ir Ch R 441; *Re Doherty's Contract* (1884) 15 LR Ir 247. See also *Irish Land Law*, (2nd ed, 1986) para 5.136.

[401.] *Op cit* p 482.

[402.] Ie, s 7 of the Conveyancing Act 1881.

[403.] Ch 21 *post*.

[404.] Para **[21.05]** *post*.

6. Registered Land

[18.101] There are no special rules relating to covenants in transfers of registered land. The usual covenants may be inserted in the prescribed forms.[405] and covenants for title may be implied by use of the appropriate formula after the name of the transferor.[406]

M. Acknowledgment and Undertaking

[18.102] As a general rule, on a conveyance of land the vendor must hand over the documents of title to the purchaser.[407] If, however, the vendor is conveying part only of his land, it is usual for him to retain possession of the title deeds.[408] Indeed, condition 34(a) of the Law Society's *General Conditions of Sale (1995 Edition)* contains an express reservation of such a right of retention.[409] Condition 34(c) provides, however, that the vendor is to give the purchaser certified copies of all documents so retained.[410] By statute, it is provided that the expenses of making any copy (attested or unattested) of retained title deeds required by the purchaser must be borne by him.[411] Condition 34(d) of the *General Conditions* then goes on to state that, subject to the provisions mentioned above, the vendor is to give the usual statutory acknowledgment of the right of production and undertaking, which is to be prepared by and at the purchaser's expense. This is a reference to the provisions of s 9 of the Conveyancing Act 1881, which spell out the obligations which arise when such an acknowledgment and undertaking are given.

[18.103] Before examining the details of the acknowledgment and undertaking, there are several points to be noted about the provisions of s 9 of the 1881 Act. First, they apply only if an acknowledgment or undertaking "in writing" is given. There is no obligation to put this in the deed of conveyance, but it is usual now for it to be inserted after the covenants in a form such as: "The vendor hereby acknowledges the right of the purchaser to production of the documents referred to in the schedule hereto (the

---

[405.] See, eg, Land Registration Rules 1972, Form 31.

[406.] 1972 Rules, Form 19. See para **[21.06]** *post.*

[407.] *Re Duthy and Jesson's Contract* [1898] 1 Ch 419.

[408.] In England. it is now provided that, subject to any contractual stipulation, a vendor may retain the title documents only where (a) he retains part of the land to which they relate and (b) they consist of a trust instrument or other instrument creating a subsisting trust, see Law of Property Act 1925, s 45(9) and (10).

[409.] Cond 34(b) reserves a right of intention in the case of a sale of property in lots, until all the lots are sold.

[410.] Plain copies only of documents of record.

[411.] Conveyancing Act 1881 s 3(6). This is subject to a contrary intention expressed in the contract for sale. s 3(9). See para **[14.48]** *ante.*

possession of which is retained by the vendor) and to delivery of copies thereof and hereby undertakes for the safe custody of the same." Secondly, s 9 operates only where the acknowledgment or undertaking is given "to another," so that any given by a personal representative in an assent to himself is worthless.[412] This means that any subsequent purchaser from him should not rely upon the assent[413] and should insist upon inclusion of a fresh acknowledgment in the conveyance to him. Also, where the property is mortgaged, the deeds are usually retained by the mortgagee[414] rather than the vendor-mortgagor and so the acknowledgment should be made by the mortgagee,[415] probably with an undertaking by the vendor as to their safe custody when they come into his possession, eg, on discharge of the mortgage. In practice, trustees, mortgagees and personal representatives should give the acknowledgment only (if anything) and should not commit themselves to a covenant for safe custody.

1. The Acknowledgment

[18.104] The acknowledgment as to the right of production of deeds binds the person in possession or control of the documents in question so long as he retains such possession or control.[416] The benefit of it accrues to the successors in title (other than a lessee at a rent) of the original purchaser.[417] The obligations imposed by the acknowledgment are: (i) production of the documents "at all reasonable times" for inspection and comparison with copies or abstracts by the person entitled to request production or by any person authorised by him in writing; (ii) production in court or elsewhere to prove or support the title or claim of the person requesting production; (iii) delivery of copies or abstracts, attested or unattested, as requested to the person entitled to them.[418] The person under these obligations is obliged to perform them specifically, unless prevented from doing so by fire or other inevitable accident,[419] but all costs and expenses of or incidental to specific

---

412. See *Re Skeat's Settlement* (1889) 42 Ch D 522.

413. As to the position of successors, see para **[18.104]** *infra*.

414. *Quaere* whether such a purchaser has an equitable right to production of all the title deeds. see *Fain v Ayers* (1826) 2 Sim & St 533; *Re Jenkins and Commercial Electric Theatre Co's Contract* (1917) 61 Sol Jo 283. See para **[2.43]** *ante*.

415. It seems that a mortgagee cannot be compelled to give an acknowledgment, *Re Pursell and Deakin's Contract* [1893] WN 152; Rowley (1962) 26 Conv 453.

416. 1881 Act, s 9(2). Such an acknowledgment satisfies any liability to give a covenant for production and delivery of copies of or extracts from documents, s 9(8). Such a liability arose at common law in respect of documents of title subsequent to the commencement of title, see *Cooper v Emery* (1844) 1 Ph 388.

417. Section 9(3).

418. Section 9(4). Note that this does not give the purchaser or his successors the right to make his or their own copies.

419. Section 9(2).

performance must be paid by the person requesting it.[420] However, the statutory acknowledgment does not confer any right to damages for loss or destruction of, or injury to, the documents arising from any cause whatever.[421] For this reason it is usual to accompany the statutory acknowledgment with a statutory undertaking for safe custody.[422]

2. The Undertaking

[18.105] The undertaking under the Act, like the acknowledgment, binds the person in possession or control of the documents so long only as he retains such possession or control.[423] It creates an obligation to keep the documents "safe, whole, uncancelled, and undefaced, unless prevented from so doing by fire or other inevitable accident."[424] The person claiming the benefit of the undertaking may apply to the court for assessment of damages for any loss, destruction of, or injury to the documents and the court may, if it thinks fit, direct an enquiry as to the amount of damages, order payment by the person liable, and make such order as to costs as it thinks fit.[425] It seems, however, that, since destruction of title documents merely affects proof of title, and not its validity, damages normally will be restricted to the cost of furnishing equivalent proof,[426] eg, statutory declarations.[427]

3. Registered Land

[18.106] No acknowledgment or undertaking is contained in the prescribed forms for transfers of registered land[428] and the general view seems to be that normally the transferee will have no need of one. Where a land certificate exists in respect of the land,[429] this must be produced in later dealings with the land, whether it was retained by the transferor on a previous transfer of part of the land or a new one was issued to the transferor in respect of the

---

[420.] Section 9(5). As to the powers of the court on an application for specific performance, see s 9(7).

[421.] Section 9(6).

[422.] See para **[18.102]** *supra*.

[423.] Section 9(9). Curiously there is no express provision as to the running of the benefit of the undertaking with the land. *cf* s 9(3) as to the acknowledgment, para **[18.104]** *supra*. Perhaps the draftsman look the view that s 58 of the 1881 Act (dealing generally with the benefit of covenants attaching to the covenantee's land) covered the point, see *Irish Land Law* (2nd ed, 1986), para 19.20.

[424.] Such an undertaking satisfies any liability to give a covenant for safe custody of documents, s 9(1). See fn 416 *supra*.

[425.] Section 9(10).

[426.] *Cf Barrett v Brahms* (1967) 111 Sol Jo 35.

[427.] See para **[14.80]** *ante*.

[428.] See Land Registration Rules 1972, Sched of Forms.

[429.] Note that frequently no certificate is ever issued, see para **[14.31]** *ante*.

part retained by him.[430] And the Registrar may by order require production by the person who has custody of it.[431] There may, however, be cases where an acknowledgment and undertaking may be useful, eg, on a transfer of part of land in respect of which the transferor is registered with a possessory title only. In such a case the original registration is made without prejudice to any rights adverse to or in derogation of the registered owner's title and subsisting or capable of arising at the time of registration,[432] and so any pre-registration documentation of title remains relevant. On a transfer of part of land comprised in a registered leasehold title, an acknowledgment for production of the lease itself should be required.

N. Certificates

[18.107] It is usual to insert after the acknowledgment and undertaking any certificates which are necessary for the conveyance in question. There are several which may be relevant.

1. Revenue Certificates

(i) Certificates for Value

[18.108] As we shall see later,[433] stamp duty is payable in respect of conveyances on sale or leases on an *ad valorem* basis, ie, according to rates varying according to the amount of the consideration. However, there are special rates which apply only if a "certificate for value" is contained in the conveyance in question.[434] This is designed to ensure that advantage is not taken of the special rates in one large transaction by splitting it up into several smaller ones, each involving a part only of the total consideration. Thus the usual certificate is in a form certifying that "the transaction does not form part of a larger transaction or series of transactions in respect of which the amount or value, or the aggregate amount or value, of the consideration exceeds IR£___"[435]

(ii) Relationship Certificate

[18.109] Again the purpose of this is to take advantage of the stamp duty relief (consanguity relief) available on transactions between persons with a

---

[430.] See Fitzgerald, *Land Registry Practice* (2nd ed, 1995) p 61.

[431.] Registration of Title Act 1964, s 105(2); *Fitzgerald, op cit*, p 439.

[432.] 1964 Act, s 38(1).

[433.] See para **[20.38]** *post*.

[434.] See Donegan and Friel, *Irish Stamp Duty Law* (1995), para 4.11.

[435.] See Laffoy, *Irish Conveyancing Precedents* Precedent F.1.10(a). In the case of a voluntary transaction the word "property" should be substituted for "consideration": Precedent F.1.10(b).

certain degree of family relationship, whereby reduced rates of *ad valorem* duty are payable.[436] The certificate is usually in a form by the purchaser, as the person becoming entitled to the actual beneficial interest in the premises, that "he is related to the vendor being the person immediately heretobefore so entitled as lineal descendant".[437]

[18.110] There is another type of relationship certificate which is commonly included in certain conveyances involving a "family home" within the meaning of the Family Home Protection Act 1976.[438] Under s 14 of that Act, conveyance of the family to the spouses as joint tenants is exempt from stamp duty, where immediately prior to the transaction it was owned by either of them or both or them otherwise than as joint tenants. This exemption applies automatically where the circumstances come within s 14, so that strictly there is no need to include a certificate confirming this. Nevertheless it is often done.[439]

(iii) Finance Act 1990, s 112

[18.111] The purpose of s 112[440] is to prevent evasion of stamp duty payable where a new house or apartment is being constructed under a building agreement.[441] Section 112(5) requires conveyances of such property to contain a certificate as to the applicability or non-applicability of the section, in one of the forms stipulated by the Revenue Commissioners.[442]

(iv) Finance Act 1990, s 120

[18.112] Stamp duty is not payable in respect of commercial woodlands, ie, the consideration attributable to the value of the trees growing on land managed for commercial profits.[443] This exemption does not apply unless the conveyance contains a certificate in relation to the trees.[444]

2. Companies Act 1990, s 29

[18.113] The implications of s 29 for transactions between a company and one of its own directors, or a director of one its holding companies, or with a

---

[436] See *Donegan and Friel, op cit*, para 12.08.

[437] See *Laffoy, op cit*, Precedent F.1.10(c).

[438] See para **[16.61]** *et seq, ante*.

[439] For an example see *Laffoy, op cit*, Precedents J.1.1 to J.1.4. As regards consent under the Act see para **[18.115]** *infra*.

[440] As amended by s 100 of the Finance Act 1993.

[441] See para **[11.10]** *ante*.

[442] See the Commissioners' Statement of Practice (SP-SD/2/90); also *Laffoy, op cit*, Precedent F.1.10(d).

[443] See *Donegan and Friel, op cit*, para 12.18.

[444] See *Laffoy, op cit*, Precedent F.1.10(e).

person connected with him, were considered in an earlier chapter.[445] The Law Society's Conveyancing Committee has recommended appropriate forms of certificates which may be included in conveyances involving companies to cover the section. [446] It must be emphasised that there is no need for any such certificate in a transaction between two natural persons - a company must be involved for the section to apply. Furthermore, unlike in the case of certificates mentioned above, there is no statutory requirement for such a certificate. The object of including one is to deal with an important matter which would otherwise give rise to queries in later transactions involving the property in question.

3. Land Act Certificates

[18.114] The question of consents needed under the Land Act 1965, especially ss 12 and 45, was considered in an earlier chapter.[447] We saw that a general consent procedure for sub-divisions coming within s 12 was introduced in 1977 for registered land, but if this is to be relied upon the transfer must contain a certificate in the appropriate form.[448] So far as s 45 is concerned, the numerous additions to the categories of "qualified person" made in recent times to comply with European Directives has resulted in a range of certificates which must be used, as appropriate, to ensure that non-urban land vests in the purchaser.[449] It must be reiterated that no certificate is needed where the entirety of the land conveyed or transferred in situated within an "urban" area.[450]

3. Spouse's Consent

[18.115] We also saw in an earlier chapter[451] that, as a result of the Family Home Protection Act 1976, it is necessary that the vendor's spouse should give consent to any conveyance of the home.[452] It might be thought that the obvious place for incorporation of this consent is to insert it along with the certificates mentioned in the previous paragraphs. Alternatively. the consent may be endorsed on the conveyance and this, in fact, is the recommended practice. The problem about incorporating the consent as a certificate in the conveyance is that the consent must be "prior" consent and, therefore, given

---

[445.] See para **[16.28]** *ante.*

[446.] See the *Gazette* December 1991, pp 419-20.

[447.] See para **[16.29]** *et seq, ante.*

[448.] See *Laffoy, op cit*, Precedent F.1.9(a).

[449.] *Ibid*, (b)-(i).

[450.] See para **[16.49]** *ante.*

[451.] Para **[16.61]** *et seq, ante.*

[452.] See para **[16.69]** *ante.* As to the content required for the contract for sale, see para **[16.62]**, sub-para (c) *ante.*

before the conveyance is executed.[453] Therefore if it is proposed to include it as a certificate in the body of the deed the wording should confirm that the spouse subscribed his or her name to the deed prior to execution of it by the vendor. We gave earlier the form recommended by the Law Society.[454]

4. Registered Land

[18.116] The various certificates mentioned above must also be inserted in a transfer of registered land and the prescribed forms in Ireland provide for this expressly.[455]

O. Testimonium and Execution

[18.117] The *testimonium* of a deed of unregistered land links the contents of the deed with the last part, the attestation clause, which contains the parties' seals and signatures for its execution and attestation by witnesses.[456] If the deed contains any schedules,[457] they are usually sandwiched between the *testimonium* and the attestation clause. The reason for this is to make it clear that these are part of the deed which has been executed by the parties, a point reiterated in the next paragraph.

1. Testimonium

[18.118] The *testimonium* is usually in the form. "IN WITNESS whereof the parties hereto have hereunto set their hands and seals the day and year first written above",[458] or in the case of a company: "IN WITNESS whereof the company has caused its common seal to be hereunto affixed." The prescribed forms for registered land, however, contain no *testimonium*.[459] The attestation clause containing the parties' seals and signatures appears immediately after the certificates (if any). However, any schedule should probably be inserted before the attestation clause[460] and certainly should be inserted before the signatures. The practice of inserting schedules after the signatures is very dangerous, since it may be claimed that they were added after the deed was executed and so are not part of the deed.

---

[453] See para **[16.69]** *ante*.
[454] See *ibid*, sub-para (a).
[455] Land Registration Rules 1972, Sched of Forms. See also para **[18.04]** *supra*.
[456] As to registered land transfers, see para **[18.132]** *infra*.
[457] See paras **[18.53]**, **[18.71]**, **[18.81]** and **[18.90]** *supra*.
[458] See para **[18.03]** *supra*.
[459] Land Registration Rules 1972, Sched of Forms. See also para **[18.04]** *supra*.
[460] *Cf* 1972 Rules, Form 22.

2. Execution

[18.119] We saw earlier that it is usual to have the conveyance "executed" not only by the grantor but also by the grantee,[461] indeed all persons who are parties to it. If a party is joined more than once in the conveyance in different capacities, it seems that he need execute it once only, ie it is not necessary, eg, to sign and seal it twice.[462] Furthermore, where a party purports to transfer more than one interest in the land by the same conveyance, he need again execute it once only,[463] since the "all-estate" clause, express or implied,[464] has the effect of passing all his interests unless a contrary intention appears.

[18.120] At common law execution involved two things, not three, in order to make a written document operate as a deed, namely, sealing and delivery.[465] Technically that remains the case in Ireland, but it has long been the practice that the parties in question also sign the deed.[466] Though not strictly necessary, a signature by each executing party further proves that the document is authentic.

(i) Signature

[18.121] Presumably "signing" should be given a wide interpretation, as it is usually given in other contexts, eg, in respect of the memorandum or note of the contract for sale required by the Statute of Frauds.[467]

(ii) Sealing

[18.122] In the days before hand-writing became common, the usual, indeed the only, way of effectively authenticating a document was to "seal" it by putting molten wax on it and impressing upon the hot wax one's own crest or coat-of-arms, eg, by using a signet ring. One does not have this formality occurring very often in practice now and, instead, a small red wafer is usually attached to the deed, without the signing party paying any attention

---

[461.] See para **[18.77]** *supra*.

[462.] *Young v Schuler* (1883) 11 QBD 651.

[463.] *Drew v Lord Norbury* (1846) 9 Ir Eq R 524.

[464.] See para **[18.82]** *supra*.

[465.] *Blennerhassett v Day* (1813) Beat 468 at 470 (*per* Lord Manners LC). See also *Goddard's Case* (1584) 4 Co Rep 46 at 5a. Note the comprehensive discussion of execution of documents including deeds of land in Kearney, 'Execution of Commercial Documents' (1994) 16 DULJ 1.

[466.] Signature, or placing one's mark, was required in England by s 73 of the Law of Property Act 1925 but note that sealing by an individual was abolished by s 1 of the Law Property (Miscellaneous Provisions) Act 1989, which replaces s 73 of the 1925 Act.

[467.] See para **[6.32]** *ante*. In England placing one's mark is a statutory alternative, see s 1(4) of the 1989 Act: *cf Goodman v Eban Ltd* [1954] 1 QB 550 at 561 (*per* Denning LJ).

to it.[468] However, despite some *dicta* suggesting the contrary,[469] it seems clear that some mark or impression must be put on the deed, even if only one caused by the end of a ruler, to act as the seal.[470] A circle enclosing the letters "LS" (for *locus sigilli*, the place of the seal) may be enough,[471] and this may be done on a copy made of a deed to indicate that the original has a seal on it.[472] Furthermore, as regards deeds relating to registered land, it is provided by rule 58 of the Land Registration Rules 1972, that, except in the case of the seal of a corporation, the Registrar is entitled to assume that every deed expressed to be sealed by any party executing it has, in fact, been so sealed, notwithstanding the fact that the deed bears no trace of such sealing.

(iii) Delivery

[18.123] The final[473] formality to make the deed operative is "delivery" of it. As Sullivan MR put it in *Evans v Grey*[474]:

> "In law a deed binds property from its delivery which is necessary to make it a perfect conveyance of the property comprised in it."[475]

However, it is crucial to realise that delivery in this context has a special meaning.

(a) Manner

[18.124] The essential purpose of delivery is to indicate an intention that the deed should become operative,[476] and it is clear that such an intention may be shown in a number of ways. One obvious way is to deliver the deed in the popular sense of the word, ie, to hand it over physically to the appropriate

---

[468.] See the remarks of Danckwerts J in *Stromdale and Ball Ltd v Burden* [1952] Ch 223 at 230.

[469.] Eg, in *Re Sandilands* (1871) IR 6 CP 411 at 413 (*per* Bovill CJ). See the comments on this dictum in *National Provincial Bank v Jackson* (1886) 33 Ch D 1 at 11 (*per* Cotton LJ) and 14 (*per* Lindley LJ). See also the more recent comments by the English Court of Appeal in *First National Securities Ltd v Jones* [1978] 2 All ER 221, but note the views of Browne-Wilkinson V-C in *TCB Ltd v Gray* [1986] 1 All ER 58 (affd on other grounds [1988] 1 All ER 108).

[470.] *Re Smith* (1892) 67 LT 64 *Cf Linton v Royal Bank of Canada* (1967) 60 DLR (2d)398.

[471.] *First National Securities v Jones* (fn 469, *supra*), not following *Re Balkis Consolidated Co Ltd* (1888) 58 LT 300.

[472.] *Quaere* whether merely using the time-honoured formula in the *testimonium* "set their hands and *seals*" (italics added) creates any estoppel so as to prevent the party in question denying that he sealed it, *cf Re Smith* (1892) 67 LT 64 and *Stromdale and Ball Ltd v Burden* [1952] Ch 223.

[473.] Thus, if the signing or sealing is performed later, the deed must he redelivered *Tupper v Foulkes* (1861) 9 CBNS 797.

[474.] (1882) 9 LR Ir 539.

[475.] *Ibid* p 544.

[476.] See *Devoy v Hanlon* [1929] IR 246 at 358 (*per* FitzGibbon J).

person, eg, the other party to the transaction.[477] But this is not necessary, for as Sullivan MR said again in *Evans v Grey*:

"It is clear ... that the mere fact of the grantor retaining a deed in his possession does not contradict the idea that the grantor intended the deed to be operative."[478]

Thus a statement made in reference to the deed, eg, by pointing to it or holding it, so that it is delivered as the speaker's deed is sufficient, even if made unilaterally with no one else present.[479] Furthermore, delivery may be presumed from the actions of the parties, eg, their acts of signing and sealing the deed. Thus, Sullivan MR said in *Evans v Grey*:

"When a man signs and seals a deed, and the attestation clause states that it was signed, sealed and delivered, the attestation clause is *prima facie* evidence that he delivered the deed. If there is nothing in the attestation clause about delivery, something must be proved to have been done; leaving the deed on the table for a few seconds of time would be a sufficient delivery."[480]

(b) Escrows

[18.125] The requirement of delivery to render the deed effective has significance in respect of one particular point of practice and that is the concept of an "escrow," ie, delivery subject to a condition precedent[481] which must be performed before the deed becomes operative.[482] The classic example is where the vendor executes the deed some days before the closing date and gives it to his solicitor for handing over on completion in return for the balance of the purchase money.[483] The condition of the escrow is, of course, that the balance of the purchase money must be so handed over[484]

[477.] See *ibid* p 264 (*per* Murnaghan J).

[478.] (1882) 9 LR Ir 539 at 546. See also *Xenox v Wickham* (1866) LR 2 HL 296 at 312 (*per* Blackburn J) and 326 (*per* Lord Cranworth).

[479.] Though this gives rise to obvious difficulties of proof.

[480.] *Op cit* p 546. See also at p 544. *Cf Powell v London and Provincial Bank* [1893] 2 Ch 555 at 556 (*per* Kay J).

[481.] See further para **[7.03]** *ante*.

[482.] See Farrand 'Escrows' (1961) 25 Conv 126. And see the comments of Cross LJ in *Vincent v Premo Enterprises Ltd* [1969] 2 QB 609 at 623; (1969) 33 Conv 227; (1970) 34 Conv 145.

[483.] It seems that the Courts may infer an escrow in such a situation, without an express declaration of the condition by the vendor see *Thompson v McCullough* [1947] KB 447. *Cf,* however, *Blennerhassett v Day* (1813) Beat 468 at 470: "... when an escrow is intended the grantor must at the time declare it to be delivered as such" (*per* Lord Manners LC).

[484.] See *Jessop v Smith* [1895] 1 IR 508 (court order for delivery as an escrow).

and the deed will not operate, even though in fact handed over, so long as any of this remains outstanding.[485]

[18.126] Whether or not a deed is an escrow is largely a matter of intention.[486] As Blackburne LC put it in *Wood v Knox*[487]:

> "It is now clearly settled that if the real intention of the parties be that the instrument shall not operate at all except and until a specified condition be performed, there is no form of words in which that intention need be expressed."[488]

Thus, though the courts in general presume that delivery of a deed is absolute,[489] in certain circumstances the usual conveyancing practice suggests an inference of an escrow. One is the common situation outlined in the previous paragraph.[490] Another is where a lessor executes a lease on condition that the lessee executes a counterpart.[491] However, if the deed was delivered unconditionally, it cannot be converted subsequently into an escrow. Thus in *Blennerhassett v Day*[492] Lord Manners LC. stated:

> "It cannot be denied that the character of the instrument, whether it is to be considered as a deed or an escrow, must depend upon what passed at the time of the execution, and then, if it were duly executed as a deed, any subsequent act or declaration of the grantor could not vary the nature of it, or suspend its legal operation."[493]

[18.127] If an escrow has been created, and the condition in question is subsequently fulfilled. the deed becomes operative from the date of its original delivery without any redelivery, ie, it relates back so as to pass the title from that date retrospectively.[494] This principle operates, however, only

---

[485.] See the English cases of *Vincent v Premo Enterprises Ltd* [1969] 2 QB 609; *Kingston v Ambrian Investment Co Ltd* [1975] 1 All ER 120; *Alan Estates Ltd v WG Stores Ltd* [1981] 3 All ER 481; *Bentray Investments Ltd v Vennar Time Switches Ltd* (1985) 274 EG 43. An escrow may, however, be stamped, *Byrne v Revenue Commissioners* [1935] IR 664 at 671 (*per* Johnston J).

[486.] *Blennerhassett v Day* (1813) Beat 468 at 470 (*per* Lord Manners LC).

[487.] (1852) 3 Ir Ch R 109.

[488.] *Ibid*, p 116.

[489.] See *Silva v Lister House Development Ltd* [1971] Ch 17.

[490.] See fn 483, *supra*.

[491.] See *Beesly v Hallwood Estates Ltd* [1961] Ch 105.

[492.] (1813) Beat 468.

[493.] *Ibid* p 469.

[494.] *Foundling Hospital v Crane* [1911] 2 KB 367 at 376 (*per* Farwell J). This doctrine of relation back does not apply to registered land, for it is provided that a transfer is not completed until registration of the transferee as owner and, until registration. the document does not operate to transfer the land, see Registration of Title Act 1964, s 51(2). See also *Irish Land Law* (2nd ed, 1986), para 21.44.

in respect of the transfer of title and does not, eg, create any right to intermediate rents and profits or validate any acts otherwise invalid.[495] However, once a lease ceases to be an escrow, the tenant may be liable for rent as from the date the lease was delivered in escrow.[496] If the condition is never fulfilled, the deed never comes into operation and, in the event of unreasonable delay in fulfilment, the court may release the grantor.[497] On the other hand, having delivered the deed in escrow, the grantor cannot revoke it and the escrow survives his death.[498] If an express power of revocation or right of recall was reserved on delivery, then in effect no delivery at all, conditional or otherwise, has been made.[499]

(iv) Corporations

[18.128] So far as execution of a deed by a corporation is concerned, the general rule in Ireland remains that it must be done as required by its articles of association.[500] In practice, this usually means the affixing of the company's seal by authority of the directors in the presence of a director and the secretary or other director.[501] It is, therefore, important to make appropriate enquiries as to the sealing requirements of the company in question and to ensure that these have been met.[502] Where a foreign company is concerned, enquiries must be made as to the requirements for proper execution of a conveyance by such a company in that jurisdiction and the prudent step is to requisition a statement from a lawyer practising in that jurisdiction confirming the execution requirements. At common law there is a presumption, albeit a rebuttable one, that the affixing of the common seal

---

[495.] See *Hooper v Ramsbottom* (1815) 6 Taunt 12.

[496.] *Alan Estates v WG Stores Ltd* [1981] 3 All ER 481.

[497.] *Beesly v Hallwood Estates Ltd* [1961] Ch 105 at 118 (*per* Harman LJ) and 120 (*per* Lord Evershed MR). See also *Kingston v Ambrian Investments Co Ltd* [1975] 1 All ER 120. An escrow may, however, be stamped, *Byrne v Revenue Commissioners* [1935] IR 664 at 671 (*per* Johnston J).

[498.] *Perryman's* Case (1599) 5 Co Rep 84a; *Graham v Graham* (1791) 1 Ves 272.

[499.] *Foundling Hospital v Crane* [1911] 2 KB 367 at 375 (*per* Vaughan Williams LJ).

[500.] Ie there is as yet no equivalent of s 74 of the English Law of Property Act 1925, which is intended to remove the need for a purchaser to enquire whether the appropriate formalities have been adopted. See *O'Shea v Lister House Development Ltd* [1971] Ch 17. The lack of an equivalent of s 74 was regarded as important by Morris J in the *Safeera* case, fn 502 *infra*.

[501.] Ie, where the articles of association incorporate Table A of the Companies Act 1963.

[502.] *Safeera Ltd v Wallis* High Court, unrep 12 July 1994 (1994/518 Sp) (company incorporated under the Companies Act 1908 and so Table A of the 1963 Act not applicable). See para **[16.27]** *ante*. The Law Reform Commission has recommended that the Land Registry should accept execution by a foreign company in accordance with the legal requirements of the foregn jurisdiction, eg, there is no requirement of use of a company seal in the Netherlands: see *Report on Land Law and Conveyancing Law: (5) Further General Proposals* (LRC 44-1992), pp 3-4.

of a company imports delivery and, therefore, due execution.[503] On this basis, it is arguable that no further delivery is necessary and this has led to the suggestion that a corporation cannot deliver a deed as an escrow.[504] Yet to the extent that the common law's view of the effect of affixing a seal is based on the intention of the corporation,[505] which is also the basis of the concept of an escrow,[506] there seems to be no reason in principle why a corporation should not deliver a deed in escrow if it wishes to, so long as the intention is made clear.[507]

(v) Agents

[18.129] As a general rule no part of execution of a deed, including delivery, can be performed by an agent of a party to it unless he has been authorised under seal,[508] eg, by a power of attorney.[509] In practice, of course, this is rarely obtained and solicitors frequently deliver the conveyance on completion on behalf of their clients without it. So far as signing or sealing by an agent is concerned, Pigot CB had this to say in *McArdle v Irish Iodine Co*[510]:

> "... where a deed is executed by one person on behalf of another, either he must, in order to bind that other person, execute it, either using the name of his principal, or he must employ such words as show that he executed it, not as himself a party to the deed, but as the agent, in the act of executing it, of his principal. The form of words is immaterial, if in substance this is done."[511]

[503.] See *McArdle v Irish Iodine Co* (1864) 15 ICLR 146 at 153 (*per* Pigot CB). See also *Willis v Jermin* (1590) Cro Eliz 167. *Cf Mowall v Castle Steel & Iron Works Co* (1886) 34 Ch D 58 at 62 (*per* Cotton LJ): *Beesly v Hallwood Estates Ltd* [1960] 1 WLR 549 at 562 (*per* Buckley LJ) (*cf* CA at [1961] Ch 105); *Windsor Refrigeration Co Ltd v Branch Nominees Ltd* [1961] Ch 88 at 98 (*per* Cross J).

[504.] See *Gartside v Silkstone* (1882) 21 Ch D 762 at 768 (*per* Fry J).

[505.] See *Staple of England v Bank of England* (1887) 21 QB 160 at 165-6 (*per* Wills J).

[506.] Para **[18.126]** *supra*.

[507.] See *Lloyd's Bank v Bullock* [1896] 2 Ch 192; *Beesly v Hallwood Estates Ltd* [1961] Ch 105.

[508.] *Powell v London and Provincial Bank* [1893] 2 Ch 555 at 563 (*per* Bowen LJ); *Re Seymour* [1913] 1 Ch 475 at 481 (*per* Joyce J).

[509.] The law on this complex subject is considered elsewhere. See *Irish Land Law* (2nd ed, 1986) para 11.29 *et seq*. See also *Gosford v Robb* (1845) Ir LR 217. Note that major changes to the law governing powers of attorney will be effected if and when the Power of Attorney Bill before the Oireachtas at the time of writing is enacted and comes into operation. It will replace the much criticised provisions in Part IX of the Conveyancing Act 1881 and introduce the concept of an "enduring" power of attorney which comes into effect when the donor becomes mentally incapable. *Cf* the English Powers of Attorney Act 1971. See also para **[18.131]** *infra*.

[510.] (1864) 15 ICLR 146.

[511.] *Ibid*, p 153.

(vi) Liquidators

[18.130] The liquidator has a statutory power to execute deeds and other documents on behalf of the company in liquidation and, for that purpose, may affix the company's seal to the deed of conveyance or transfer.[512] It is also usual for the liquidator to execute the deed on his own behalf.[513]

(vii) Receivers

[18.131] Unlike a liquidator, a receiver, such as one appointed by a mortgagee under the Conveyancing Act 1881[514] or by a chargee under a company debenture,[515] does not, generally, have power to affix the company's seal. In *Industrial Development Authority v Moran*,[516] the debenture stated that a duly appointed receiver had power to sell the company's assets and to act as attorney of the company "to execute, seal and deliver" any deed required for such a sale. The debenture also stated that the receiver could effect a sale "by deed in the name of and on behalf of" the company. The receiver had purported to effect execution of a deed of transfer of registered land by the company, by affixing its seal opposite the attestation. The Supreme Court held that this was ineffective since it had no authority given by the company's directors, as required by the company's articles of association. Kenny J gave the following advice to receivers operating under such debenture provisions:

> "When a receiver is selling under such a clause, the more usual and better practice is for him to execute the deed of transfer by writing the name of the company and underneath this to write words that indicate that the name of the company has been written by the receiver as attorney of the company under the power of attorney given by the debenture. In addition, he should execute the deed in his own name. In that way he has the best of both worlds. The writing of the name of the company by the authority of the company given when it executed the debenture brings the case within the words of the debenture itself and execution by the attorney personally gives the advantage of s 46 of the Conveyancing Act 1881."[517]

Section 46 of the 1881 Act provides that execution of any instrument by the donee of a power of attorney is "as effectual in law" as if the instrument had been executed by the donee in the name and with the signature and seal of

---

[512.] Companies Act 1963, s 231(2)(b). this applies equally to voluntary liquidators, *ibid*, s 276.

[513.] See Laffoy *Irish Conveyancing Precedents* Precedents E.6.7-E.6.9. See also para **[18.131]** *infra*.

[514.] See s 24. And *Irish Land Law* (2nd ed, 1986), para 13.048 *et seq*.

[515.] See Courtney, *The Law of Private Companies* (1994), para [16.011] *et seq*.

[516.] [1978] IR 159.

[517.] *Ibid*, p 166.

the donor.[518] Thus the Supreme Court held that what the receiver had done in that case was rendered effective by s 46, so as to vest the company's land in the purchaser. The better practice now is to follow Kenny J's advice.[519]

(vi) Registered Land

[18.132] The prescribed forms for transfers of registered land in both parts of Ireland provide for execution as in the case of conveyances of unregistered land, ie, signing, sealing and delivery.[520] So presumably the rules discussed above apply in the same way.[521] There is, however, the additional requirement that, where part only of the land comprised in a folio is being transferred, the transfer must be accompanied by a plan signed by the grantor and the grantee, or his solicitor.[522] Furthermore, as we mentioned earlier, the Registrar is entitled to assume that every deed expressed to be sealed by the parties, other than a corporation, executing it is in fact so sealed although the deed bears no trace of such sealing at the time of lodgment in the Registry.[523]

3. Attestation

(i) Unregistered Land

[18.133] At common law attestation of execution of a deed was not necessary to its effectiveness, but it has become the invariable practice to have each party sign, seal and deliver "in the presence of" a third party, a witness, who signs the attestation clause, giving his name, address and occupation.[524] Such attestation has obvious evidentiary value, even if it is not strictly necessary, and, as we saw earlier,[525] it provides *prima facie* evidence that the deed was duly executed.[526] Of course, in the end of the day the court may require production of the witness, as Pennefather CJ pointed out in *Gosford v Robb*[527]:

---

518. Cl 17 of the Powers of Attorney Bill (see fn 509 *supra*), which would replace s 46 of the 1881 Act, provides for the alternative of the donee either executing in his own name or in the name of the donor, but in both cases by making it clear that this is done by the authority of the donor of the power of attorney.

519. See Laffoy, *Irish Conveyancing Precedents* Precedents E.6.5.

520. Land Registration Rules 1972, Sched of Forms. See para **[18.04]** *ante*.

521. See *Devoy v Hanlon* [1929] IR 246 at 257 (*per* Kennedy CJ). 258 (*per* FitzGibbon J) and 264 (*per* Murnaghan J).

522. 1972 Rules, r 56. See para **[18.56]** *ante*.

523. 1972 Rules, r 58. See para **[18.122]** *supra*.

524. See para **[18.03]** *supra*. Note also the requirements as to witnessing for the purposes of registration of deeds, see para **[18.136]** *infra*.

525. Para **[18.124]** *supra*.

526. *Evans v Grey* (1882) 9 LR Ir 539 at 546 (*per* Sullivan MR). See also *Hope v Harman* (1847) 16 QB 751n.

527. (1845) 8 Ir LR 217.

"No rule is better settled than this, that to prove execution of a deed, you must produce the subscribing witnesses; and the only exception to that is, when the witnesses have died, or gone out of the jurisdiction; in such case, proof of their hand-writing is sufficient. So great strictness may not be required when the deed is above thirty years old; then actual proof is dispensed with, if possession be proved."[528]

Of course, the chances are that the witnesses will prove to be of little help, especially if the execution occurred several years ago.[529]

[18.134] A party to the deed cannot be a competent witness,[530] nor, apparently by tradition, should a party's spouse act as a witness, though there is no rule against this.[531] At common law the purchaser could not require the vendor to execute the conveyance in his or his solicitor's presence, unless special circumstances justified this.[532] Because of doubts as to what amounted to such circumstances, s 8(1) of the Conveyancing Act 1881, provided instead:

> On a sale, the purchaser shall not be entitled to require that the conveyance to him be executed in his presence, or in that of his solicitor, as such; but shall be entitled to have, at his own cost, the execution of the conveyance attested by some person appointed by him, who may if he thinks fit, be his solicitor.

This right is rarely invoked in practice and arguably should not be unless fraud or forgery is suspected. The maxim adopted by practitioners and the courts alike tends rather to be *omnia praesumuntur rite esse acta*.[533]

(ii) Registered Land

[18.135] The prescribed forms for registered land transfers also provide for attestation.[534] Execution by a blind or illiterate person must be verified by affidavit of an attesting witness to the effect that it was read over and explained to such person and that he appeared to understand it.[535] Execution

---

[528] *Ibid*, p 219.

[529] See *National Provincial Bank v Jackson* (1886) 33 Ch D 1 and *Stromdale and Ball Ltd v Burden* [1952] Ch 223, in both of which the witness was a solicitor's managing clerk.

[530] *Seal v Claridge* (1881) 7 QBD 516.

[531] *Cf* witnessing a will, see *Irish Land Law* (2nd ed, 1986), paras 14.13 and 14.34 and Brady, *Succession Law of Ireland* (2nd ed, 1995), para [2.32] *et seq* or sealing by a corporation in the presence of directors, **[18.128]** *supra*. *Quaere* whether the Land Registry will accept a spouse as a witness.

[532] *Ex parte Swinbanks* (1879) 11 Ch D 525.

[533] See para **[17.25]** *ante*. See also *Re Airey* [1897] 1 Ch 164 at 169 (*per* Kekewich J).

[534] Land Registration Rules 1972, Sched of Forms.

[535] 1972 Rules, r 54.

by a person by his mark, due solely to physical disability, must be verified by affidavit of an attesting witness giving reasons for such execution.[536] Where execution is by attorney, the power of attorney, or a copy,[537] must be produced to the Registrar, together with evidence that the principal was alive at the time of execution.[538] and that the power was then unrevoked.[539]

(iii) Registration of Deeds

[18.136] It is important to note that there are special requirements in respect of registration of deeds.[540] If the deed is to be registered in the Registry of Deeds, one witness at least appears to be essential to the execution of the *deed* by the grantor. However, it is particularly important to note that s 6 of the Registration of Deeds (Ireland) Act 1707, makes two witnesses to the execution of the *memorial* of the deed by the grantor or grantee necessary for registration.[541] By implication the section makes it essential that there should be one witness at least to the execution of the *deed* by the grantor. One of the witnesses to the execution of the *deed* must be one of the two witnesses to the execution of the *memorial*. There has been much debate as to whether execution of the deed by the *grantor* is essential or whether proof of execution by the *grantee* is sufficient.[542] It is wiser to assume that execution of the deed by the grantor is required. The safest course is to have the same two witnesses to the execution of the deed and the memorial by the grantor. If a company is the grantor, there must usually be two witnesses to the execution of the deed and memorial by the company, *in addition* to the director and secretary or two directors or other persons who under the articles of association must sign the deed when the seal has been affixed.[543] The theory is that the officers of the company who are "authorising" the execution by *signing* the deed cannot also attest as witnesses to that execution.[544]

[536.] *Ibid.*
[537.] Office copy 1972 Rules, r 55(1).
[538.] 1972 Rules, r 55(1).
[539.] *Ibid.*
[540.] See further *Irish Land Law* (2nd ed, 1986), paras 22.05-8.
[541.] See *ibid.* para 22.05.
[542.] See *ibid* para 22.05.
[543.] See para **[18.128]** *supra.*
[544.] *Cf* Land Registration Rules 1972, r 77(4): Register entitled to assume company deed duly executed where seal appears to have been affixed in the presence of and attested by the secretary, deputy secretary or a member of the board of directors of the company.

Chapter 19

DOCUMENTS FOR PARTICULAR TRANSACTIONS

[19.01] In this chapter we consider the deeds or other documents used for the more common conveyancing transactions relating to unregistered land. The forms to be used for dealings with registered land are, of course, largely prescribed by statutory regulation.[1] Space does not, of course, permit anything other than a highlighting of the main variations from the outline of a typical deed of conveyance given in the previous chapter. We do. however, attempt to draw attention to the main points to be borne in mind when drafting any of the documents mentioned in this chapter.[2]

I. SALES

[19.02] The deed used by way of illustration in the previous chapter[3] was a very simple one suitable for the conveyance by the owner of the fee simple of land of his entire interest in the property. It is, however, the case that "sales" of land involve a considerable variety of conveyances, depending upon both the nature of the property itself and the nature of the title of the person selling.[4] Thus it may involve the sale of part only of a larger property, eg., a sale of a new house on a housing estate or a flat in a large purpose-built block of flats or in a larger property which was once a single dwelling, but is now converted into several dwellings.[5] Similarly, the sale may involve the assignment of a lease held by the vendor[6] or the conveyance of property held by the vendor under a fee farm grant.[7] Indeed, it is quite common for the original grant of the lease or fee farm grant to be a "sale" in the sense that

---

[1.] See Land Registration Rules 1972, Sched of Forms.
[2.] Further reference should be made to Laffoy *Irish Conveyancing Precedents*, which also contains introductory notes to the various Divisions, as well as annotations to each precedent. The only other major precedent book dealing with Irish law is of course Stubbs and Baxter, *Irish Forms and Precedents* (1910) which is somewhat out of date now. See para **[17.08]** *ante.*
[3.] See para **[18.03]** *ante.*
[4.] See *Laffoy, op cit*, Division E (Conveyances on Sale).
[5.] These matters are considered later, see para **[19.08]** *et seq, infra.*
[6.] See para **[19.31]** *infra.*
[7.] See para **[19.46]** *infra.*

it is made partly in return for a "fine," ie, a capital sum paid in addition to the rent reserved.[8] A sale transaction may be complicated by the existence of incumbrances on the property, eg, mortgages or charges, and the conveyance will obviously vary according to whether or not the incumbrance is to be discharged on the sale, so as to transfer the property to the purchaser free of it. Other variations may occur where the vendor is selling under special statutory powers, eg, a tenant for life selling under the Settled Land Acts 1882-90,[9] or a mortgagee selling under s 19 of the Conveyancing Act 1881,[10] or under a power of sale conferred by the mortgage deed.

A. Land Subject to a Mortgage or Charge[11]

1. Unregistered Land

[19.03] In the case of unregistered land, the form of the deed will vary according to whether or not the land is to be sold to the purchaser subject to the mortgage. If it is, then the mortgagor is, in effect, conveying his equity of redemption only.[12] If, as is more usual, it is not, because the mortgage debt is to be discharged out of the proceeds of sale, the mortgagee must join in the deed or give a separate release, so as to ensure that the discharge occurs and the purchaser gets an unincumbered title. Thus in the case of a building society mortgage, the society will insist upon the vendor's mortgage being discharged, whether out of the proceeds of sale or otherwise, and the purchaser taking out a new mortgage on the property.

(i) Conveyance of Equity of Redemption[13]

[19.04] It is usual for the deed to contain narrative recitals[14] relating in chronological order: (a) that before the mortgage deed the vendor was seised in unincumbered fee simple (or other estate); (b) the creation of the mortgage by a deed of a certain date to secure a stated capital sum, plus interest; (c) the current state of the debt, ie, how much of the principal sum remains owing. Then the introductory recital[15] relates that the vendor has agreed to sell the property subject to the said mortgage for the price stated. Then the *habendum*[16] usually states that the property is held unto and to the use of the purchaser in fee simple subject to the mortgage and to payment of

---

8. See para **[19.25]** *infra*.
9. See further *Irish Land Law* (2nd ed, 1986), paras 8.066-70.
10. See *ibid*, paras 13.022-39.
11. See *Laffoy, op cit*, Division E.7.
12. See *Irish Land Law* (2nd ed, 1986), para 12.05.
13. See *Laffoy, op cit*, Precedent E.7.6.
14. Para **[18.38]** *ante*.
15. Para **[18.40]** *ante*.
16. Para **[18.84]** *ante*.

the mortgage debt and all interest henceforth to accrue due in respect thereof. And the purchaser enters into a covenant to pay the mortgage debt and interest henceforth to become due under the mortgage and to indemnify the vendor and his successors in title from all actions, proceedings, costs, charges, claims and demands on account thereof.[17]

(ii) Conveyance Free of Mortgage

[19.05] If the mortgage is to be discharged out of the proceeds of sale, this will usually be arranged separately from the conveyance and the mortgagee will not be joined in the deed. Indeed, the mortgage may not even be recited in the deed. There may, however, be cases where the mortgagee will be joined in, eg, where a building estate is subject to a first charge in favour of a bank which gave the developer or builder a loan to cover the initial outlay for laying sewers, drains and roads. Here the bank may be joined in to release particular sites sold while work is still progressing on the estate. In such a case the mortgagor is usually joined as the party of the first part (to be called the "vendor"), the mortgagee as the party of the second part and the purchaser as the party of the third part.[18] Then again there are usually narrative recitals relating to the creation of the mortgage and specifying the state of the debt[19] and an introductory recital recording the agreement to sell the property to the purchaser free from incumbrances, that it was part of the agreement that a stated amount out of the purchase money should be paid to the mortgagee in satisfaction of all monies owing on foot of the mortgage and that the mortgagee should join in the conveyance in the manner appearing thereafter. Following on from this, the consideration and receipt clauses[20] will state that part of the purchase money is paid to the mortgagee by the direction of the vendor and the balance to the vendor, the mortgagee and vendor each acknowledging receipt of these sums. In the words of grant,[21] the mortgagee confirms or grants and releases "by direction of the vendor" (often "without warranty of title") and the vendor conveys or grants unto the purchaser. Then the *habendum* states that the property is held unto and to the use of the purchaser freed and discharged from the mortgage and all monies and interest thereby secured and all claims and demands thereunto. If the mortgage was by subdemise, there will then be a declaration that the term of years created by the mortgage merges in the superior interest.[22]

[17.] Para **[18.99]** *ante.*

[18.] Para **[18.23]** *ante. Cf Laffoy, op cit*, Precedents E.7.1 and E.7.2.

[19.] Para **[19.04]** *supra.*

[20.] Paras **[18.42-3]** *ante.*

[21.] Para **[18.48]** *ante.*

[22.] *Cf Laffoy, op cit*, Precedents E.7.4 and E.7.5.

2. Registered Land

[19.06] No specific form is prescribed for a transfer of registered land subject to an existing charge, where this is to remain charged on the land, eg, where there is a local authority mortgage. The purchaser will simply take subject to this registered burden in the normal way and an ordinary transfer form may be used.[23] There is, however, a prescribed form of transfer where the registered owner of a charge joins to release the charge[24] This is a very simple form compared with a deed for unregistered land. As is usual with registered land forms, there are no recitals[25] The form simply states that the registered owner transfers all the land in the folio in question to the transferee and then that the registered owner of the charge for the amount stated registered in that folio releases the said lands from the charge.

B. Under Statutory Powers

[19.07] Where a sale is being made under statutory powers it is usual for that fact to be recited. For example, in the case of a sale by the tenant for life under a settlement, it is usual to recite that the vendor is such a person and to state who are the trustees of the settlement for the purposes of the Settled Land Acts.[26] The trustees are also parties to the conveyance and the consideration and receipt clauses state that the purchase money is paid to them by direction of the vendor (tenant for life) and they acknowledge receipt of it.[27] Similar consideration and receipt clauses are contained in the prescribed form for a transfer of registered land by a limited owner in exercise of his powers under the Settled Land Acts.[28]

C. New House on Housing Estate

[19.08] As we mentioned in an earlier chapter,[29] this is a case where the conveyance is usually in a form provided by the vendor, ie, the builder or developer of the estate as a whole, rather than the purchaser.[30] This form is usually designed to be a standard form for use in sales of all the houses on the estate. This makes it all the more imperative that the purchaser's solicitor

---

[23.] Ie the form of transfer of the freehold by a registered full owner, see Land Registration Rules 1972, Form 19. See para **[18.04]** *ante*.

[24.] 1972 Rules, Form 21.

[25.] Para **[18.26]** *ante*.

[26.] See *Laffoy, op cit*, Division E.4.

[27.] See para **[18.47]** *ante*.

[28.] Land Registration Rules 1972, Form 24.

[29.] Para **[17.05]** *ante*.

[30.] See *Laffoy, op cit*, Division E.8.

scrutinises the deed to see that it contains provisions sufficient to protect his client in respect of the special circumstances necessarily involved in buying such property. The following are some of the points to which attention should be paid.

[19.09] Since the property forms part of a larger area, it is essential, as in any conveyance involving a sub-division of land, to see that the description of the property in the parcels clause,[31] and any map intended to be enclosed in the deed,[32] is accurate. Because of the property's location on an estate, where it shares common facilities, eg, sewers, drains and roads. with other properties, it is usually essential for each conveyance of a property on that estate to contain various easements relating to these facilities. Thus the purchaser should be granted[33] a right of way for all purposes connected with the land conveyed to him over all the estate roads, whether existing or still to be built (where the site is still being developed), but subject to the rule against perpetuities. This right may be expressed to be enjoyed in common with the vendor and all other owners on the estate. Similarly the purchaser should be granted the right to connect with and use all sewers, drains, watercourses, pipes, cables, wires and other services laid or to be laid (again subject to the rule against perpetuities) in, under or over adjacent land. Conversely. there should be a reservation of such rights in respect of the purchaser's land in favour of the vendor and his successors in title for the benefit of the rest of the estate.[34] Unfortunately, in practice difficulties often arise. Thus, in Dublin, it is commonly discovered that the builder has not built strictly according to his map or plan of the estate, and so it is sometimes provided in the deeds that rights of way are granted or reserved over roads on the estate which are actually built, rather than by reference to the estate map or plan. Though sometimes there is no mention at all of rights of way, probably on the assumption that the roads and footpaths are likely to be taken in charge by the local authority fairly quickly. Apart from that, it is likely that residents of estates will have rights of way of necessity. In certain cases, it may be necessary to grant the purchaser a right of entry on adjacent land for the purposes of maintenance and repair of such things as drains or waterpipes running under that land or eaves or gutters overhanging it. There may also be imposed obligations to erect dividing fences or walls between adjacent plots, with associated obligations in respect of maintenance and repair or, alternatively, a declaration that they are to be party walls or

---

[31.] See para **[18.51]** *et seq, ante.*

[32.] Especially if it is intended to control the description in the parcels clause, see para **[18.63]** *et seq, ante.*

[33.] See paras **[18.71-2]** *ante.*

[34.] See para **[18.73]** *et seq, ante.*

fences.[35] Though again in practice there is sometimes no mention of these matters.

[19.10] It is the invariable practice of estate developers to insist upon imposition, by way of covenant,[36] of numerous restrictions on each of the purchasers of a plot on the estate for the purpose of enhancing and preserving the amenities of the estate.[37] The enforceability of such restrictions by or against the original covenantor and covenantee and their respective successors in title, and how this varies according to whether the purchaser buys the freehold or a lease or whether an estate scheme exists, is considered in detail elsewhere.[38] In this respect, it is crucial to note the change in the law which was effected when the Landlord and Tenant (Ground Rents) Act 1978.[39] The consequence of this Act was that housing developments since 1978 have had to be executed by way of freehold conveyancing, so that conveyancers have been faced with the difficulties of the law relating to freehold covenants. In order to maximise the likelihood of covenants being enforceable by and against successors in title, it is important to use wording likely to attract the "building" or "estate" scheme rules[40] and the reciprocity principle of mutual benefit and burden usually known as the rule in *Halsall v Brizell*.[41]

D. Flats

[19.11] The sale of flats,[42] which is a comparatively new development in Ireland, gives rise to some particularly acute conveyancing problems.[43]

[35.] See *Irish Land Law* (2nd ed, 1986), para 7.53 *et seq*.

[36.] Para **[18.93]** *et seq, ante*.

[37.] See *Irish Land Law* (2nd ed, 1986), paras 19.34-7.

[38.] *Ibid*, Ch 19. See also Lyall *Landlaw in Ireland* (1994), Ch 21.

[39.] See *Irish Landlord and Tenant Law* para 2.22 and Ch 35.

[40.] Sometimes known as the rule in *Elliston v Reacher* [1908] 2 Ch 655; see *Irish Land Law* (2nd ed, 1986), para 19.34 *et seq*; *Lyall, op cit*, p 674 *et seq*.

[41.] [1957] 1 All ER 371. See *ibid*, para 19.23; *Lyall, op cit*, p 659 *et seq*. But see the House of Lords discussion in *Rhone v Stephens* [1994] 2 All ER 65. See also *Laffoy, op cit*, Precedent E.8.1.

[42.] And related properties such as apartments and townhouses, In England maisonettes are common. The distinction between a flat and a maisonette is usually taken to be this: a flat is an independent dwelling forming part of a larger structure and sharing common facilities with other parts, including the entrance or entrances to the structure: a maisonette is such a dwelling which has its own separate entrance from ground floor level. which is not shared with other parts of the structure. As to maisonettes, see George, *The Sale of Flats* (5th ed, 1984).

[43.] The leading English texts on the subject apart from *George, supra* are: Aldridge *Law of Flats* (2nd ed, 1989); Cawthorn and Barraclough, *Sale and Management of Flats* (2nd ed, 1996); Cox, *Running a Flat Management Company* (2nd ed, 1993). See para **[16.97]** *ante*. See also Leyser, 'Ownership of Flats: Comparative Study' (1958) 7 ICLQ; Scamell, 'Legal Aspects of Flat Schemes' (1961) 14 CLP 161.

These arise from the physical state of such property. Looked at from the point of view of the owner of a flat, there are several things of particular concern to him. First, as it is part of a larger structure, eg, one flat in a large block of flats, it is dependent for support on other flats or parts of the structure. Secondly, the owner will have to share various parts of the structure in common with other occupiers or flat owners, eg, entrances, stairways, lifts, passages, gardens, paths and access roads. Thirdly, he will have to share various services and facilities in common with other occupiers or flat owners, eg, electricity, gas, water, sewers, drains and heating. It is essential, therefore, that each flat owner should have the benefit of some scheme whereby the continuance, maintenance and repair of each of these matters is assured. As we shall see, there are several ways in which this may be achieved, but each of them involves imposing obligations in respect of maintenance and repair on someone or some body and, of course, reciprocal rights to use and enjoy the common parts, services and facilities. Thus, from the conveyancing point of view, it is essential for any solicitor acting for a prospective purchaser of a flat to check that the scheme applicable to that flat provides, and will continue to do so in the future, adequate protection for his client on all these matters.

1. Freehold and Leasehold Flats

[19.12] As we shall discuss later,[44] one of the crucial aspects of conveying flats is the question of how far obligations, usually imposed by means of covenant, can be made to bind and to be enforceable by successors in title. As a general rule, the enforceability of covenants is achieved more easily where the relationship of landlord and tenant is created, for leasehold covenants run with the land to a greater extent than freehold covenants.[45] This point has particular significance in respect of flats because so many of the covenants required for flat schemes are positive in nature, eg, to repair facilities. For this reason, it is arguably better practice for developers of flat schemes to adopt leasehold conveyancing rather than freehold conveyancing.[46] However, it should be noted that in Ireland the best of both worlds may be achieved by using fee farm grants made under Deasy's Act.[47]

[44.] Para **[19.15]** *infra*.

[45.] See generally, *Irish Land Law* (2nd ed, 1986), Ch 19; Lyall, *Land Law in Ireland* Ch 21.

[46.] See the English *Report of the Committee on Positive Convenants Affecting Land* (Cmnd 2719; 1965) Law Com No 11; *Restrictive Covenants* (1967); Law Com No 127, *Report on Positive and Restrictive Covenants* (1984). See also the Lord Chancellor's Working Group Report: *Commonhold: Freehold Flats and Freehold Ownership of other Interdependent Buildings* (1987), which proposed a new "commonhold" system similar to the Australian strata title schemes.

[47.] See para **[19.15]** *infra*. Commonly a leasehold scheme is used involving rent reviews, thereby aimed at excluding the right to acquire the fee simple in accordance with s 16(2)(a) of the Landlord and Tenant (Ground Rents) (No 2) Act 1978: see *Irish Landlord and Tenant Law* para 31.37.

It is important to note that the Landlord and Tenant (Ground Rents) Act 1978, which we mentioned earlier, prevented the future creation of leases in respect of "dwellings" only, and s 1 of the Act defines "dwelling" as not including "a separate and self-contained flat in premises divided into two or more such flats."

[19.13] There is one further preliminary point which should be mentioned. It has been alleged from time to time that the whole notion of flats, particularly where a building is divided horizontally, so that all flats, other than those at ground level, exist "in the air" offends against the basic principles of our land law. The maxim *cuius est solum, eius est usque ad coelum et ad inferos*[48] is often cited in this context, in particular to support the view that it is conceptually impossible to create freehold flats which are not at ground level, so-called "flying freeholds." However, this view now seems to be discredited,[49] for it seems clear that, while this maxim states the general rule that a person owning land also owns the vertical column of air space above it,[50] there is no reason at common law why the owner of the land cannot convey horizontal slices of the air space above it to others, whether by way of lease or by conveying the freehold interest in it.[51] In other words, there can be separate ownership of the air space above the surface of the land just as much as there can be such ownership of the subterranean area below the surface, which is also mentioned in the maxim and which may contain valuable assets such as minerals. And the fact is that the English courts seem to have recognised the validity of such a division of the air space as occurs through flat developments for many decades. Thus in *Dalton v Angus*,[52] a

---

[48.] See *Irish Land Law* (2nd ed, 1986), para 4.022. But see the warnings about too literal an interpretation of this maxim given in *Lord Bernstein of Leigh v Skyviews and General Ltd* [1977] 3 All ER 136.

[49.] See Tolson, 'Land without Earth: Freehold Flats in English Law' (1950) 14 Conv 350.

[50.] So that any interference by a third party may involve a trespass, see Richardson, 'Private Property Rights in Air Space' (1953) 31 CBR 117. See also the *Bernstein* case cited in fn 48 *supra*.

[51.] See *Humphries v Broglan* (1850) 12 QB 739 at 747 and 755-7 (*per* Lord Campbell CJ). See also *Bonomi v Backhouse* (1858) El Bl & El 622 at 654-5 (*per* Willes J).

[52.] (1881) 6 App Cas 740. Note that this case and the ones cited in the previous footnote were decided well before 1925. The concept of freehold flats was recognised well before 1925 in England and is not dependent on the definition of "land" in s 205(1)(ix) of the Law of Property Act 1925, which includes "parts of buildings (whether the division is horizontal, vertical or made in any other way)," *Cf* the definition in s 2(ii) of the Conveyancing Act 1881. As regards the "flying" freeholds which have existed for centuries in Lincoln's Inn, London, see Vitoria, 'New Square, Lincoln's Inn and its Flying Freeholds' (1977) 41 Conv 11. And see *Grigsby v Melville* [1973] 3 All ER 455 at 458 (*per* Russell LJ).

leading case on the subject of rights of support,[53] Lord Selborne LC commented:

> "If a building is divided into floors or 'flats' separately owned (an illustration which occurs in many of the authorities) the owner of each upper floor or 'flat' is entitled, upon the same principle, to vertical support from the lower part of the building, and to the benefit of such lateral support as may be of right enjoyed by the building itself."[54]

This view of the law was recently accepted by O'Flaherty J in the Supreme Court in *Metropolitan Properties Ltd v O'Brien*,[55] which involved a bookshop on the ground floor of a building which was nevertheless separated from the ground underneath by a "void" of some feet in depth. It should also be noted that the Oireachtas has recognised it so far as registered land is concerned. Thus the Land Registry Rules provide for registration of land which is a "flat or floor, or part of a flat or floor, of a house" and require, *inter alia*, the Registry to be furnished with a plan of the surface "over which" the land to be registered lies, together with such other plans and descriptions as the Registrar deems necessary and with particulars "of any appurtenant rights of access, whether held in common with others or not, or obligations affecting other land" for the benefit of the land the title to which is being registered.[56] And it is further provided that, before such registration is completed, notice may be given to the reputed owners or occupiers of other property or properties "above or below" the land to be registered.[57]

2. Flat Schemes

[19.14] The fact is that, as in the case of a building estate,[58] the purchaser of a flat, especially one which is part of a large block of flats, has little opportunity to correct the main features of the conveyancing scheme applicable. These will have already been determined by the vendor's legal advisers and almost certainly will be applied to all purchasers of flats

---

53. See *Irish Land Law* (2nd ed, 1986), paras 6.039 and 6.111.
54. *Op cit* p 793.
55. [1995] 2 ILRM 383. His views were strictly *obiter* as the issue whether the tenant could acquire the fee simple under the Landlord and Tenant (Ground Rents) (No 2) Act 1978, was determined by the Court on the ground that the landlords were the Commissioners of Public Works and s 4 of the Act provides that it does not bind them. The other two members of the Court (Hamilton CJ and Egan J) refused to go into the issue of whether the tenant held "land" within the Act.
56. Land Registration Rules 1972, r 30(1)(a).
57. 1972 Rules, r 30(i)(b). See Fitzgerald, *Land Registry Practice* (2nd ed, 1995), pp 75-7 and 379.
58. See para **[19.08]** *supra*.

belonging to the scheme. It may, therefore, be useful to examine at this point the likely features of such schemes and, in so doing, to highlight the advantages and disadvantages involved in each of them.

(i) Conveyance to Purchaser

[19.15] It is invariably a part of a flat scheme that the purchaser is to receive the benefit of various covenants and rights relating to common parts of the building and other flats and to become subject to various obligations, again usually imposed by covenant. Such a scheme is effective so far as all are concerned only if such covenants remain fully enforceable in the future, in particular by or against successors in title of all concerned. Because of the difficulties of enforcement of positive covenants, eg, in respect of maintenance and repair, which are so essential to flat schemes, it is the generally accepted view that the developer ought to grant leases only to purchasers of flats rather than convey the freehold.[59] In this way the common lessor can enforce the covenants contained in each lease against any successor in title of an original lessee and his co-operation in this regard may be achieved, if he or his solicitor will allow it, by inserting in each lease an undertaking to enforce, on request and at the expense of the lessee, covenants against any other lessees.[60] However, if it is desired to convey the freehold to flat purchasers, it should be noted that it is much easier to do so and still preserve enforceability of covenants in Ireland than in England.[61] The reason for this is, of course, that a fee farm grant made under Deasy's Act 1860,[62] achieves the best of both worlds by passing the fee simple to the grantee and, yet, creating the relationship of landlord and tenant between the grantor and grantee, so that the enforceability of covenants is the same as in the case of a lease.[63] The alternative is to try and ensure that the estate scheme rules apply to the block of flats,[64] and to link the benefit and burden of covenants in such a way that the principle of reciprocity may require their

---

[59.] See the discussion in *Irish Land Law* (2nd ed, 1986), Ch 19; Lyall, *Land Law in Ireland* (1994) Ch 21. Often rent review provisions are included to make sure that there is no risk of the scheme being upset by flatowners seeking to acquire the freehold of individual flats: see s 16(2)(a) of the Landlord and Tenant (Ground Rents) (No 2) Act 1978: fn 47 *supra*.

[60.] On the need for such a covenant by the common lessor, see *Malzy v Eichholz* [1916] 2 KB 308.

[61.] In England, if it is desired to convey the freehold to flat purchasers, some of the problems may he avoided by doing so subject to a rentcharge and attempting to annex the obligations to this by reserving a right of re-entry for breach of covenant.

[62.] Ie the Landlord and Tenant Law Amendment Act Ireland 1860, especially s 3. See *Irish Land Law*, (2nd ed, 1986) para 4.091 *et seq*.

[63.] See *ibid*, paras 4.099-101.

[64.] For a discussion of these rules, see *Irish Land Law* (2nd ed, 1986), para 19.34-7; *Lyall, op cit*, Ch 7. See also para **[19.10]** *supra*.

full enforcement.[65] But it is difficult to see why conveyancers in Ireland should adopt such mechanisms, where conveyances of the freehold are required, when the concept of a fee farm grant is a tailor-made device to achieve all that is desired or necessary. Once again it is important to note that the Landlord and Tenant (Ground Rents) Act 1978, in preventing future creation of ground rents in respect of dwellings does not apply to separate and self-contained flats.[66]

(ii) Developer's Responsibilities

[19.16] It must be emphasised that the use of a lease or fee farm grant, while it solves the problem of the theoretical unenforceability of certain covenants, does not necessarily guarantee in practice the continued performance of the developer's obligations, eg, in respect of maintenance and repair of the structure of the building as a whole or the management of its common services and facilities. There is always the danger that the developer will lose interest in the property as time goes by, or may sell his interest to some other person or body that turns out to be even more unsatisfactory. For this reason it is often recommended that the flat owners themselves ought to be given a greater say in the management of the building and everything connected with it, eg, gardens, garages, car parks and so on. The device most commonly suggested is the formation of a management company, whose members comprise the flat owners and which should take over all the responsibilities of the developer, including ownership of all parts of the building and environs retained by him.[67] To ensure that the company has the fullest powers to do this properly, it seems desirable that each flat owner should be a member and that any successor automatically becomes a member. If, however, a large scheme is involved, it is preferable for the management company to be one limited by guarantee rather than having numerous shareholders. Under one type of scheme the developer leases the common areas to the management company, so that, even if individual flat owners later buy out the developer's freehold interest, the company's interest survives. In essence what happens is that the developer forms a management company and leases to it all the common areas. The lease is made between the developer of the first part, the company of the second part and the lessee of the third part. The developer then demises the flat to the lessee and the management company demises a right to use the common areas in common with other flat owners. The lessee enters into detailed

---

[65.] See *Halsall v Birizell* [1957] Ch 169. See again *Irish Land Law* (2nd ed, 1986), para 19.23, and also para 19.22 for the possible use of a chain of indemnity agreements.

[66.] See para **[19.12]** *supra*.

[67.] See Cox, *Running a Flat Management Company* (2nd ed, 1993).

covenants with the developer and the management company. When the last flat in the development is sold, control of the management company is transferred to the flat owners, so that between them they control the common areas and can enforce the covenants against any individual owner. It may also be convenient for the management company to take out one insurance policy on the entire property. The service charges or other annual sums paid by members of the company must be sufficient to cover the cost of maintenance and repairs and. in these days of inflation, ought to be subject to regular revision. And therein lies what has been alleged is a practical drawback of a management company so constituted. In many cases it will have as members a large collection of people who may be inexperienced in the operation of a company or in the management of a large property like a block of flats. Furthermore, from the very nature of the situation, the members may frequently face a conflict of interest, each as a member of the company concerned with management of the building as a whole and as an individual flat owner occupying a small part of the same building. For this reason, it has been suggested from time to time that the management company should be independent of the flat owners and preferably an established company expert in managing such property. This could be achieved by the developer granting a "concurrent" lease to the company, ie, a lease of the same building granted by the developer as reversioner of the prior leases granted to flat owners, usually at a rent somewhat less than the receivable rents under the flat owners' leases.[68] All service or maintenance charges payable by the flat owners also go to the company to meet the cost of carrying out the management responsibilities imposed by the concurrent lease. However, the drawback of this scheme seems to be that if, in fact, the company turns out to be inefficient, the owners are stuck with it. It is, therefore, common now for the developer to retain ownership of the common parts until that last flat is sold and then for him to transfer his entire interest (eg, the freehold) in the development to an independent management company. Indeed, even where the flatowners are members of the management company there is no reason why that management company should not employ another management company to carry out its functions on a contract basis. In this way the ultimate control remains in the hands of the members of the first company, ie the flat owners, and if they are not satisfied with the experts they have called in, they can always sack them.

[68.] See Andrae-Jones, 'A Concurrent Lease to Secure Flat Maintenance (1962) Conv 348, and see the precedent for such lease given on p 723.

(iii) Contents of Conveyance

[19.17] At this point it may be useful to summarise the most important contents of a conveyance, whether by lease, fee farm grant or otherwise, to any particular purchaser of a flat in a larger building. It must be emphasised, of course, that any particular scheme may be subject to numerous variations and what follows is at most a very general outline.[69]

(a) Parcels Clause

[19.18] It is vital to define the precise boundaries of the flat in question, whether by reference to a map or plan or otherwise. We saw earlier the strict requirements where registered land is concerned.[70] It is also important to make clear exactly what is included in the grant, eg, in respect of walls, floors and ceilings, and which, if any, are "party" walls. However, it is wise to exclude altogether from the grant the exterior of all walls of the whole building; indeed, arguably the basic fabric of the entire structure should be left in the ownership of the management company, so that there is no question as to the right to carry out maintenance and repairs.

(b) Grantee's Rights

[19.19] It is clear from the nature of the property granted that the grantee must be given various rights in respect of the rest of the building, whether as a whole or as regards parts of it, usually in the form of easements.[71] These will include rights of support, access to the building, use of common areas shared with other flat owners, both internal (halls, stairways. passages, landings and so on) and external (gardens, paths, car parks and so on) and use of shared facilities (lifts, central heating system, gas and electricity services, water and sewerage services and so on).

(c) Grantor's Exceptions and Reservations

[19.20] There will usually be exceptions and reservations[72] in favour of the grantor, and for the benefit of the other flat owners, eg, exceptions of those areas which will not be occupied by any of the flat owners and reservation of rights in respect of the grantee's flat necessary to enable the grantor to carry out maintenance and repairs to services and facilities in it and in respect of such things as wires, pipes and cables running through it and serving other flats as well.

[69.] *Cf* the precedent lease with service charge provisions for letting of part of a multi-tenanted building in Laffoy, *Irish Conveyancing Precedents* Precedent L.2.4.

[70.] Para **[19.13]** *supra.*

[71.] See para **[18.71]** *ante.*

[72.] See para **[18.73]** *ante.*

(d) Covenants

[19.21] So far as the grantee is concerned, no doubt he will be required to enter into a variety of covenants, both negative and positive.[73] Thus he will almost certainly enter into restrictive covenants as to the use of his flat, so as to protect the enjoyment of other flat owners living in the same building, eg, restricting use of the flat otherwise than as a private residence for one family, prohibiting the causing of nuisances, the obstructing the common access ways, the interference with shared facilities, the support or protection afforded by the flat to other flats and parts of the building, and the making of any structural alterations to the flat. He will also be expected to enter into positive covenants relating to repairs, insurance and contributions by way of annual service charges to meet the cost of maintaining common areas of the building and provision of services. These covenants will, of course, be in addition to the usual covenants in leases or fee farm grants in respect of, eg, payment of rent, rates and other outgoings.

[19.22] The grantor will also enter into various covenants relating to the responsibilities in respect of management of the building which he is to assume, though these may, as we saw earlier,[74] be assigned to some other body such as a management company. The grantor should covenant not only on behalf of his successors, including the other flat owners, but also undertake to enforce covenants entered into by them when requested to do so by the grantee.[75] Though in practice this is rarely, if ever, done and the developer's responsibilities in this regard are often left unspecified.

II. LEASES

[19.23] The first point to be emphasised is that leases are used in a variety of quite different transactions.[76] Their contents will obviously vary according to the nature of the subject-matter, eg, a private residence, business premises or a farm.[77] They will also vary according to the length of the term granted by the lease. The balance between the respective rights and duties of the lessor and lessee usually shifts according to the length of this term because the longer it is, the larger is the lessee's interest and, conversely, the smaller the lessor's interest in the property and *vice versa*. Secondly, it must be remembered that in many cases there is no need to use a deed for the grant of

---

[73.] See para **[18.93]** *ante*.
[74.] See para **[19.16]** *supra*.
[75.] See para **[19.15]** *supra*.
[76.] See *Irish Landlord and Tenant Law*.
[77.] See Laffoy, *Irish Conveyancing Precedents* Division L.

the lease in question; indeed in some cases there is no need for a written document of any kind.[78] It is proposed to say something in the next few paragraphs about the form of a lease in general and then to discuss some aspects of particular types of lease.

A. Forms of Lease

The form of a lease usually differs in several respects from the typical form of a deed given by way of illustration earlier.[79]

1. Recitals

[19.24] It is not usual now to insert recitals in a grant of a lease for the first time,[80] unless there are some special circumstances in the particular case justifying this.[81] The form of lease is usually prescribed by the lessor's solicitor[82] and the lessee is generally not entitled to question the lessor's title to grant the lease.[83]

2. Consideration

[19.25] The consideration for the grant of a lease is usually the rent to be paid and the covenants entered into by the lessee. But it may also involve payment of a capital sum, usually called a "fine,"[84] or "premium",[85] in which case the normal receipt clause will be included.[86]

3. Words of Grant

[19.26] The operative word of grant in the case of a lease is usually "demises,"[87] but the lessor does not do so in any stated capacity since the

---

78. See *Irish Landlord and Tenant Law*, Ch 5.
79. See para **[18.03]** *ante*. As to various precedents for leases, see Stubbs and Baxter, *Irish Forms and Precedents* (1910) pp 176-339 (which incorporates many of the precedents originally contained in Edge, *Forms of Leases and Other Forms Relating to Land in Ireland* (2nd ed, 1884). (Edge was consulting editor for *Stubbs and Baxter*). For modern precedents see *Laffoy, op cit*. Note also that the contents of a lease may be prescribed partly by statute, eg where granted by a tenant for life or a mortgagee, see para **[19.33]** *infra*.
80. *Cf* as assignment of an existing lease, para **[19.31]** *infra*.
81. Note, however, that several of the precedents in *Stubbs and Baxter* (fn 79 *supra*) contain recitals. *Cf Laffoy*.
82. See para **[17.04]** *ante*.
83. See para **[14.69]** and **[14.74]** *ante*.
84. See *Landlord and Tenant Law* paras 7.03 and 7.05.
85. *Ibid* paras 7.04, 7.06 and 13.11A.
86. See para **[18.43]** *ante*.
87. See para **[18.48]** *ante*. See *Irish Landlord and Tenant Law* paras 1.04 and 7.08.

covenants for title implied by s 7 of the Conveyancing Act 1881,[88] do not apply to "a demise by way of lease at a rent.[89]

4. Habendum

[19.27] No words of limitation are required, of course, for a grant of a term of years, since this is not an estate of freehold, but the precise length of the term,[90] including the date of its commencement, should be stated.[91] Special rules applied to the once common "freehold" leases in Ireland, eg, the lease for lives renewable for ever and the lease for lives combined with a term of years. These have been considered in detail elsewhere.[92]

5. Reddendum

[19.28] This is a special clause usually inserted in a lease after the *habendum* and beginning with the words "YIELDING AND PAYING." It specifies the amount of rent payable, when it is payable and how, eg, by two half-yearly instalments on the first day of May and the first day of November in every year.

6. Covenants

[19.29] It is usual for a lease to contain a large number of covenants, especially ones entered into by the lessee, though some may be entered into by the lessor. Because of their length it is sometimes the practice to set them out in detail in a schedule or schedules attached to the lease.[93] Clearly these covenants will vary considerably according to the nature of the subject-matter of the property, eg, there is a considerable difference in the interests of the lessor and lessee as between a single residential house and a flat in a large block of flats,[94] or an office in a town or city and a farm.[95] Subject to these variations, however, there are some covenants which are to be found in most leases, in some form or other.[96] Thus, the lessee usually covenants to

---

[88.] See para **[21.05]** *post.*

[89.] 1881 Act, s 7(5). *Cf* the covenants implied under s 41 of Deasy's Act 1860. See *Irish Landlord and Tenant Law* paras 14.04-5.

[90.] Commencement "from" a certain date usually means that the term begins on the following day, see *Dempsey v Tracy* [1924] 2 IR 171. *Cf Brakspear & Sons Ltd v Barton* [1924] 2 KB 88. See also *Irish Landlord and Tenant Law* para 6.04.

[91.] See *McNally v Donnelly* (1894) 28 ILTR 85. And see also *Simms v Sinclair* (1884) 18 ILTR 60. As regards the need for certainty in relation to a *contract* for a lease, see para **[9.26]** *ante.*

[92.] *Irish Land Law* para 4.167 *et seq.*

[93.] *Cf* Laffoy, *Irish Conveyancing Precedents* Division L.2.

[94.] See para **[19.21]** *supra.*

[95.] See paras **[19.34]** and **[19.35]** *infra.*

[96.] *Cf* the implied covenants contained in ss 41 and 42 of Deasy's Act 1860, see *Irish Landlord and Tenant Law* paras 14.04-7 and 15.24.

pay the rent and, perhaps, other outgoings such as rates and taxes, to do certain repairs, to meet the cost of insurance taken out by the lessor (perhaps in the joint names of the lessor and lessee), not to make alterations without the lessor's consent, not to assign, sublet or otherwise part with possession without consent, to permit the lessor to enter and inspect the premises and to execute repairs, where necessary, to use the property subject to specified restrictions and to give it up on determination of the term granted. The lessor usually covenants for the "quiet enjoyment" of the lessee, to do certain repairs and, perhaps, to undertake responsibility for certain outgoings. All these matters have been considered in detail elsewhere.[97]

7. Proviso for Re-Entry

[19.30] Most leases contain in relation to the covenants entered into by the lessee a "proviso for re-entry", ie, a clause conferring on the lessor a right (with or without demand) to re-enter the property for non-payment of rent by the lessee or other breach of covenant on his part. This clause is usually inserted in the body of the deed, often beginning with the words "PROVIDED THAT". The need for such a clause, and its effect, was also considered elsewhere.[98]

B. Assignments

[19.31] An assignment of an existing lease or sub-lease accords more with an ordinary conveyance of the freehold.[99] Thus it should contain recitals,[100] eg, a narrative recital of the vendor's (ie, assignor's) title as derived from a lease of a certain date and, depending upon what is the root of title,[101] the subsequent history of that lease (eg, later assignments of it)[102] down to themethod by which it became vested in the vendor. Then there follows an introductory recital of the agreement for the assignment of the lease for a stated price. This price is then stated to be the consideration in the *testatum* clause and the vendor acknowledges receipt in the usual way. However, the

---

[97.] *Ibid*, Chs 11-20. See also Deale, *The Law of Landlord and Tenant in the Republic of Ireland* (1968), Chs 4 and 5.

[98.] *Ibid*, para 24.07. See also *Deale, op cit*, p 259 *et seq*; Laffoy, *Irish Conveyancing Precedents* pp L.7-12.

[99.] See para **[18.03]** *ante*. See also *Laffoy, op cit*, Division E.2

[100.] *Cf* a grant of a lease. Para **[19.24]** *supra*.

[101.] See paras **[14.56]** *et seq* and **[14.63]** *ante*.

[102.] Details of intermediate transfers may he omitted and may, instead, be covered by a general formula such as "by virtue of divers *mesne* assurances acts in the law and events and ultimately by an Indenture of Assignment dated ..." the premises were assigned to the vendor for the residue then unexpired of the term of years granted by the lease. See *Laffoy op cit* Precedent E.2.2.

operative word of grant is usually "assigns" and there are no words of limitation. The vendor usually assigns to the purchaser for the residue now unexpired of the term of years created by the lease, subject to payment of the rent thereby reserved and to the performance and observance of the covenants on the lessee's part and the conditions contained therein. He also assigns "as beneficial owner" so as to attract the covenants for title implied by s 7 of the Conveyancing Act 1881. Then the purchaser usually covenants to pay the rent and perform and observe the covenants and conditions in the lease and to indemnify the vendor against all claims in respect of them.[103] If the assignment consists of part only of the land comprised in the original lease, it may be necessary to insert a clause dealing with apportionment of the rent, covenants and conditions as between the part assigned to the purchaser and the part retained by the vendor, with mutual indemnity covenants.[104] It is usual for the apportioned rents to be "charged" on that part of the land to which they relate, thereby in effect creating rentcharges in addition to the leasehold rents.[105] It is important to note that such apportionment and indemnity schemes do not bind the lessor, unless, of course, he joins in the assignment, and he is free to enforce all the covenants and conditions of the lease fully against all or any part of the premises comprised in the lease. It may also be necessary to include an acknowledgment and undertaking for safe custody in respect of title documents not to be handed over on completion.

C. Sub-leases

[19.32] A grant of a sub-lease is generally in the same form as a grant of a lease.[106] It is important to remember, however, that a grant of a sublease creates the relationship of landlord and tenant between the grantor and grantee which is quite independent of the continuing relationship between the grantor (sub-lessor) and the head-lessor.[107] Thus it is essential for the sub-lease to protect the sub-lessee against failure by the sub-lessor to perform and observe the covenants and conditions of the head-lease.[108] Conversely, the sub-lessor should obtain a covenant of indemnity from the

---

[103.] See para **[18.98]** *ante*. Note, however, the provision in s 16 of Deasy's Act 1860, see *Irish Landlord and Tenant Law* para 21.29 *et seq*.

[104.] Note that there is no equivalent in Ireland of s 77 of the English Law of Property Act 1925. which deals with this matter, see *Whitham v Bullock* [1939] 2 KB 81.

[105.] See *Irish Land Law* (2nd ed, 1986), para 6.136, see also *Laffoy, op cit*, Precedents E.2.7, E.2.8 and E.2.9.

[106.] Para **[19.25]** *et seq, ante*.

[107.] See *Irish Landlord and Tenant Law*, para 17.028.

[108.] Note, however, the provisions in ss 19-21 of Deasy's Act, see *ibid*, paras 22.09-10.

sub-lessee against action by the latter which may involve a breach of covenants or conditions in the head-lease.[109]

D. Particular Cases

1. Leases Granted under Statutory Powers

[19.33] It is important to note that, where a lease is being granted under statutory powers, the statute may require the insertion of certain provisions in the lease or may otherwise control its contents. Thus a lease granted by a tenant for life under his statutory powers conferred by the Settled Land Acts 1882-90, is subject to the statutory limits on duration and various provisions as to its terms.[110] Similar provisions apply to leases granted by mortgagors or mortgagees under the Conveyancing Act 1881.[111] On the other hand, the statutory power to grant leases conferred on personal representatives is rather less restricted.[112] Furthermore, where there is a statutory right to obtain a lease, eg, as an extension of an existing one or to replace or renew an existing one, it is again usual for the statute or statutes in question to limit the term of that lease to some extent. This subject was considered elsewhere.[113]

2. Business Leases

[19.34] As is to be expected, a lease of business premises may contain special clauses which relate to the particular nature of the property and the fact that the tenant is running his business there, ie, he intends to occupy the premises for profit.[114] Thus a clause which in recent years has become almost invariably a part of a lease of business or industrial premises is a rent review clause, ie, one requiring the rent to be revised periodically during the course of the term of years granted, rather than leaving it fixed at the original amount for the whole term. The increase in the rate of inflation in recent years has resulted in revision periods becoming shorter and shorter, so that where a few years ago the revision would have been required every seven years, nowadays it may be required every five years. However, the voluminous case law on this subject in England clearly points to the need for the exercise of the greatest care in the drafting of such a clause.[115] First, it

---

[109.] See *Clare v Dobson* [1911] 1 KB 35. See also *Hornby v Cardwell* (1881) 8 QBD 329.

[110.] See *Irish Land Law* (2nd ed, 1986), paras 8.071-7; *Irish Landlord and Tenant Law* para 5.41.

[111.] *Ibid*, paras 13.1 14-7; *ibid* para 5.42.

[112.] *Ibid*, paras 16.57-8. *Cf* trustees, see *ibid*, paras 10.015 and 10.028.

[113.] See *Irish Landlord and Tenant Law* Chs 30 and 31.

[114.] See Ross *Drafting and Negotiating Commercial Leases* (4th ed, 1994). See also Laffoy, *Irish Conveyancing Precedents* pp L5-15 and Division L.2.

[115.] See *Irish Landlord and Tenant Law* Ch 11. See also Clarke and Adams, *Rent Reviews and Variable Rents* (3rd ed, 1990).

must make it clear exactly when the revision is to be made and is to take effect. Secondly, it must lay down a clear procedure for making the revision and indicate who has to do what and when. Thirdly, some clear, and preferably simple, mechanism by which the new rent is to be worked out must be laid down, eg, by arbitration or by an expert. Fourthly, and this has perhaps given rise in England to more disputes than anything else, it ought to be made clear to what extent time is of the essence with regard to any steps to be taken to operate the procedures for revision or to any purported time limits expressed in the lease.[116] Many of the problems are avoided by relying upon the clauses recommended by the Law Society and IAVI.[117]

3. Agricultural Leases

[19.35] Agricultural leases are comparatively rare in Ireland because of the statutory restrictions on the letting, sub-letting or sub-division of land bought under the Land Purchase Acts.[118] The consent of the Land Commission is required for such a lease, unless it is covered by the "general consent" provision made in 1977.[119] Where such consent is sought, it is frequently given subject to conditions which may affect materially the terms of the lease or tenancy agreement in question. Apart from that, as is to be expected from the nature of the subject-matter, such a lease will usually contain special provisions, eg, as to the running of the farm, which areas are to be used for grazing and which for growing crops, which particular crops are to be sown and their rotation, use of manure and fertilisers, maintenance and repair of fences and ditches and so on.

[19.36] Largely as a result of the statutory restrictions mentioned in the previous paragraph, it has become the practice to use special forms of "letting" which do not create the relationship of landlord and tenant between the parties and so are not subject to the restrictions. These are "conacre" and "agistment" lettings, which were considered elsewhere.[120] These, however, are often created informally with little regard for the niceties of drawing up a detailed formal document like a lease.[121] Note should also be taken of the

---

116. This whole subject must be read now in the light of the House of Lords decisions in *United Scientific Holdings Ltd v Burnley Corp* and *Cheapside Land Development Co Ltd v Messels Service Co*, both reported at [1977] 2 All ER 62 and *cf* the Supreme Court decision in *Hynes Ltd v Irish Independent Newspapers Ltd* [1980] IR 204; *Irish Landlord and Tenant Law* para 11.10 *et seq.*

117. See Laffoy, *Irish Conveyancing Precedents* p L7; *cf* the earlier Law Society/RICS clauses: see *Irish Landlord and Tenant Law* para 11.14 *et seq.*

118. See *Irish Land Law* (2nd ed, 1986), para 18.03; *Irish Landlord and Tenant Law* para 1.11.

119. See para **[16.30]** *et seq, ante.*

120. See *Irish Land Law* (2nd ed, 1986), para 20.25 *et seq*; *Irish Landlord and Tenant Law* para 3.20 *et seq.*

121. See *ibid*, para 20.27 Note, however, the precedents for agistment contracts in Stubbs and Baxter, *Irish Forms and Precedents* (1910), pp 25-30.

"Master Lease" for agricultural property launched in 1983 by Allied Irish Banks and the Irish Farmers' Association, in co-operation with the Law Society and Royal Institution of Chartered Surveyors. This was facilitated by the repeal of old nineteenth century legislation by the Land Act 1984, but does not seem to have been taken up to any great extent.[122]

III. FEE FARM GRANTS

[19.37] Over the centuries in Ireland fee farm grants have taken several forms,[123] but since the second half of the nineteenth century the most common form has been a grant made under s 3 of Deasy's Act so as to create the full relationship of landlord and tenant between the grantor and grantee, despite the passing of the fee simple to the latter.[124] The result is that the form of grant has more in common with a lease[125] than a conveyance of the fee simple,[126] though, as we shall see, account must be taken of the fact that a fee simple, ie, freehold, estate passes to the grantee.[127]

A. Grants

1. Parties

[19.38] The parties to a fee farm grant are, as might be expected, usually referred to as the grantor and grantee. Though, in the case of a conveyance of land held under an existing grant, the parties are usually called the vendor and purchaser in the usual way.

2. Recitals

[19.39] Unlike in the case of the grant of a lease,[128] a fee farm grant does usually contain a recital to indicate what type of grant it is.[129] Thus a grant

---

[122.] See *Irish Landlord and Tenant Law* para 1.12.

[123.] See generally, *Irish Land Law* (2nd ed, 1986), para 4.057 *et seq.*

[124.] See *ibid*, para. 4.091 *et seq.*

[125.] See para **[19.24]** *et seq, supra.*

[126.] See para **[18.03]** *ante.*

[127.] For various precedents, see Stubbs and Baxter, *Irish Forms and Precedents* (1910) pp 87-131.

[128.] See para **[19.24]** *supra.*

[129.] A conversion grant made under the Renewable Leasehold Conversion Act 1849 (see *Irish Land Law*, (2nd ed, 1986) para 4.081 *et seq*), usually recited the lease for lives renewable for ever and various renewals, etc, see *Stubbs and Baxter, op cit* p 117. *Cf* a conveyance of either the grantee's or grantor's interest in such a grant: Laffoy, *Irish Conveyancing Precedents* Precedents E.1.10 and E.1.11. And note a conveyance of a freehold estate created by virtue of s 74 of the Landlord and Tenant (Amendment) Act 1980: see *ibid*, Precedent E.1.12.

under Deasy's Act usually contains a recital in this form: "WHEREAS the parties hereto have agreed that a contract of tenancy and the relation of landlord and tenant shall be created between them in respect of the land hereinafter described upon the terms hereafter appearing".[130]

3. Consideration

[19.40] As in the case of a lease,[131] the consideration for a grant is the rent reserved, though, of course, a capital sum may also be payable receipt of which the grantor will acknowledge in the usual way.

4. Words of Grant

[19.41] The words of grant, where the grant is made under Deasy's Act, are usually "grants and demises," thus emphasising the fact that in substance the grant shares many of the features of a lease and creates the relationship of landlord and tenant.[132] It is also usual to state that the grantor grants and demises unto the grantee "his heirs and assigns," though this hardly seems necessary in view of the usual *habendum* in such a grant.

5. Habendum

[19.42] Despite the doubts that have been expressed from time to time, the better view seems to be that, since a fee farm grant passes the fee simple to the grantee, words of limitation must be used,[133] at least in a grant under Deasy's Act.[134] This view of the necessity for words of limitation was accepted by Murray J in *Re Courtney*.[135] The standard formula is: "TO HOLD the said premises unto the grantee his heirs and assigns for ever."[136] However, nowadays the usual formula for a conveyance of the fee simple is more commonly used, ie, "in fee simple".[137]

6. Reddendum

[19.43] A fee farm grant contains a *reddendum* clause just like a lease,[138] though relating to payment of the fee farm rent "during the grant" rather than during the term.

[130.] See *Stubbs and Baxter, op cit*, p 122.

[131.] See para **[19.25]** *supra*.

[132.] See para **[19.26]** *supra*.

[133.] See *Irish Land Law* (2nd ed, 1986), paras 4.095-96.

[134.] Special considerations apply in other cases, eg a conversion grant, see *ibid* para 4.082. *Cf Stubbs and Baxter, op cit*, p 120.

[135.] [1981] NI 58, a case involving a conveyance of the fee farm grantee's interest. See *Irish Landlord and Tenant Law* para 2.16.

[136.] *Cf* the "gilding of the lily" which occurred in *Twaddle v Murphy* (1881) 8 LR Ir 123. See *Irish Land Law* (2nd ed, 1986) para. 4.095.

[137.] See Laffoy, *Irish Conveyancing Precedents* Precedent E.1.10; *cf* E.1.11 and E.1.12.

[138.] See para **[19.28]** *supra*.

7. Covenants

[19.44] It also usually contains a series of covenants very similar to those to be found in a lease,[139] though again these are entered into for the period of the grant rather than for that of the term.

8. Proviso for Re-Entry

[19.45] A proviso for re-entry for non-payment of rent or breach of any other covenant or condition is also included as in the case of a lease.[140] Contrary to what is often said to be the case, there is no doubt that, in theory, a forfeiture or re-entry clause can be invoked in respect of a fee farm grantee's freehold interest.[141] A court would, of course, be sympathetic to giving the grantee relief against the forfeiture, because of the very substantial nature of his interest, as compared with the minor interest of the grantor in the rent and covenants.[142]

B. Conveyances

[19.46] A conveyance of land held under a fee farm grant is very similar in form to an assignment of a lease, subject to different terminology (references to "grant" instead of "lease" and so on) and special provisions to take account again of the fact that a fee simple is being conveyed to the purchaser.[143] Thus the recitals should refer to the original grant, but it is to be more usual for the word of grant to be "grants" (or "grants and conveys") rather than "assigns."[144] The vendor also usually conveys "as beneficial owner," thereby attracting the covenants for title implied by s 7 of the Conveyancing Act 1881.[145] Then, because the conveyance involves the fee simple, the *habendum* states that the vendor holds the premises "unto and to the use"[146] of the purchaser "his heirs and assigns for ever,"[147] but subject to

---

[139.] See para **[19.29]** *supra*.

[140.] See para **[19.30]** *supra*. The precedents in *Stubbs and Baxter, op cit*, also contain an express power of distress. see pp 121 and 123, but this would not be done nowadays in view of constitutional doubts about the remedy, see *Irish Landlord and Tenant Law*.

[141.] See *Walsh v Wightman* [1927] NI 1. Note that s 14 of the Conveyancing Act 1881 specifically applies to a "grant a fee farm rent": see s 14(3). This applies, of course, largely to commercial property only; a right of re-entry is no longer enforceable in respect of non-payment of rent relating to a dwelonghouse whose lessee has the statutory right to acquire the fee simple: see Landlord and Tenant (Ground Rents) (No 2) Act 1978, s 27(1).

[142.] See *Irish Landlord and Tenant Law* para 24.19 *et seq*.

[143.] See para **[19.31]** *supra*.

[144.] See *Stubbs and Baxter, op cit*, p 125. *Cf Laffoy, op cit*, Precedent E.1.10.

[145.] See para **[21.05]** *post*.

[146.] See para **[18.86]** *ante*.

[147.] See para **[19.42]** *supra*. But note fn 137 *supra*.

the fee farm rent, covenants and conditions. Finally, the purchaser should enter into covenants to pay the fee farm rent, observe and perform the covenants and conditions in the grant and indemnify the vendor in respect of these.[148]

IV. MORTGAGES

[19.47] The various methods of creating a mortgage over both registered and unregistered land were considered in detail elsewhere.[149] So far as registered land is concerned, the relevant forms are prescribed by statutory regulation and these include a charge for payment of a principal sum,[150] for future advances[151] and by way of annuity.[152] So far as unregistered land is concerned, subject to the fact that many lending institutions have their own standard forms of mortgages to be used in the case of all borrowers from them, the form of mortgage used will vary according to the interest held or to be purchased by the mortgagor. From the mortgagee's point of view it may appear preferable to take a mortgage by conveyance, or assignment in the case of a leasehold interest, since this passes the whole legal interest to the mortgagee, though subject to the proviso for redemption.[153] The mortgagee may feel that this facilitates a sale of the property by way of realisation of its security on subsequent default by the mortgagor.[154] And, in the case of a lease, an assignment enables the mortgagee to reduce the risk of forfeiture of the lease as a result of a breach of covenant by the mortgagor. If, however, the interest being mortgaged is a leasehold interest, held under a lease containing onerous covenants binding the lessee and his successors in title, it may be preferable to create the mortgage by sub-demise, so that the mortgagor remains liable on the covenants.[155] The same applies where the land being mortgaged is held under a fee farm grant.[156] Apart from these general points, the following remarks may be made about the forms of a mortgage of unregistered land.[157]

[148.] See para **[19.31]** *supra.*

[149.] *Irish Land Law* (2nd ed, 1986), Ch 12. See also Lyall, *Land Law in Ireland* (1994), Ch 23.

[150.] Land Registration Rules 1972, Form 67.

[151.] 1972 Rules, Form 68.

[152.] 1972 Rules, Form 72.

[153.] See *Irish Land Law* (2nd ed, 1986), paras 12.32-3 and 12.36.

[154.] But in most cases a full power of sale will exist whatever the form of mortgage, see *ibid* para 13.022 *et seq.*

[155.] See *ibid*, para 12.37.

[156.] See *Re Sergie* [1954] NI 1. See also *ibid*, paras 3.026-30 and 12.34.

[157.] Note, of course, the types of informal mortgage so common in both parts of Ireland, eg, by deposit of title documents, see *Irish Land Law* (2nd ed, 1986), paras 12.13. 12.29 and 12.43-6.

A. Freehold

1. Recitals

[19.48] In a mortgage of freehold land by way of conveyance, it is usual to recite the mortgagor's title and the agreement of the mortgagee to lend the mortgagor the stated capital sum upon having its repayment secured with interest.

2. Testatum

[19.49] The traditional form of mortgage of freehold land contains more than one *testatum*.[158] The first states the consideration in the usual way (ie, the loan made by the mortgagee), contains the usual receipt clause and then a covenant by the mortgagor to repay the loan plus interest at the rate stated by a certain date (ie, a legal date for redemption usually three or six months later), followed by a covenant to pay interest at the same rate by equal half-yearly instalments so long as any principal money remains due under the mortgage.[159] The second *testatum* states that in pursuance of the agreement and for the consideration mentioned the mortgagor conveys the land, ie, leading into the words of grant and ultimately the habendum.

3. Habendum

[19.50] The *habendum* states in the usual way that the mortgagor holds the property unto and to the use of the mortgagee in fee simple, but then the deed runs on to say that this is subject to the proviso for redemption[160] which follows.

4. Proviso for Redemption

[19.51] This usually begins with the words "PROVIDED ALWAYS" and states that, if the mortgagor repays the loan plus interest on a date usually three or six months later, which is the legal date for redemption,[161] then the mortgagee will at any time thereafter, upon the request and at the cost of the mortgagor, reconvey the property to the mortgagor or as he shall direct.

[158.] See Stubbs and Baxter, *Irish Forms and Precedents* (1910), pp 418-21.

[159.] And. perhaps. a proviso for reduction of interest for prompt payment, payment by instalments over a period of time and a period of notice before early redemption, see *ibid* pp 419-20. Note that, under the Consumer Credit Act 1995, early redemption fees will not be chargeable in respect of home loans except in the case of fixed-rate interst loans: see para **[2.40]** fn 215 *ante*.

[160.] See *Irish Land Law* (2nd ed, 1986), paras 12.32 and 12.40.

[161.] As to the significance of this, see *ibid*, paras 12.32, 13.026, 13.072 and 13.093.

5. Other Provisions

[19.52] It is then usual for the mortgage to contain a number of other provisions which relate specifically to the law of mortgages or the nature of a mortgage transaction, eg, express incorporation by reference to the mortgagee's statutory powers of sale and other powers conferred by the Conveyancing Act 1881,[162] exclusion or variation of the mortgagor's power of leasing,[163] and exclusion of statutory restrictions on consolidation.[164] If the mortgagee wishes to secure some "collateral advantage," eg, where he is in the same line of business or trade as the mortgagor, care must be taken to see that the provision does not amount to a "clog" on the equity of redemption.[165] Finally, the mortgage may contain an "attornment" clause, whereby the mortgagor "attorns" or acknowledges himself to be the tenant of the mortgagee, so as to enable the latter to recover possession of the land on that basis.[166]

6. Covenants

[19.53] The mortgagor usually enters into various covenants, eg, to insure the property with a specified insurance company,[167] to keep it in repair and to pay any outgoings in respect of it.

B. Leasehold

[19.54] A mortgage of a leasehold interest by way of assignment follows very closely the form of a conveyance of a freehold interest, as outlined in the previous paragraphs, subject, of course, to modifications to take account of the fact that a leasehold and not a freehold interest is passing. Where, however, there is a mortgage by demise or sub-demise, some special clauses are required to take account of the fact that the head-interest, ie, the fee simple in the case of a fee farm grant or the head-leasehold interest, is retained by the mortgagor. Thus it may contain a clause conferring a power of attorney on the mortgagee which enables him to convey the reversion to himself or to a purchaser from him on exercise of his power of sale. It may also contain, as an additional or alternative clause, one whereby the

---

162. See *ibid*, para 13.022 *et seq*.
163. See *ibid*, para 13.111 *et seq*.
164. See *ibid*, para 13.069 *et seq*.
165. See *ibid*, para 13.089 *et seq*.
166. See *ibid*, paras 13.020 and 17.020.
167. Note, however, the mortgagor's statutory power to arrange his won "equivalent" insurance: see Building Societies Act 1989, ss 35 and 36. *Cf* the mortgagee's statutory powers, see *ibid* paras 13.007-9.

mortgagor declares that he holds the reversion on trust for the mortgagee and any person to whom he may have sold the property.[168]

C. Discharges

[19.55] A discharge, or release, as it is commonly called, of a mortgage of unregistered land is effected by a reconveyance by the mortgagee to the mortgagor or, in the case of a mortgage by sub-demise,[169] by a surrender of the sub-lease.[170] In the case of a building society mortgage, a special form of statutory receipt endorsed on the mortgage deed operates both as a discharge of the mortgage and a reconveyance or surrender to the person entitled to the equity of redemption.[171] A similar provision for non-building society mortgages was introduced by the Housing Act 1988.[172] In the case of a charge on registered land, the same effect is achieved by the Registrar cancelling the charge on the register, eg, at the request of the owner of the charge or on production to the Registrar of a receipt[173] of the owner of the charge or a release[174] in the deed signed by him or under seal of a body corporate.[175] It is necessary in cases of unregistered land outside urban districts or towns to include a Land Act vesting certificate in the release and to have the deed of release signed by the mortgagee so to certify.

[19.56] There is one important point to note in the common case where the vendor's existing mortgage is being discharged out of the proceeds of sale and the property is being conveyed to the purchaser freed and discharged from that mortgage.[176] The reconveyance or surrender from, or receipt endorsed by, or receipt or release given by, the vendor's mortgagee or chargee ought to take effect before the conveyance by the mortgagor-vendor to the purchaser from him. Thus the usual practice is to date this a day or so before the date of the conveyance to the purchaser, though it must be remembered that a deed takes effect from the date of its "delivery" in the

---

[168.] See *ibid*, para 13.024.

[169.] As regards a mortgage by demise. redemption produces a "satisfied term." See *Irish Land Law* (2nd ed, 1986), para 13. 125.

[170.] *Ibid*.

[171.] Building Societies Act 1989, s 27. See also fn 180 *infra*.

[172.] Section 18.

[173.] No form is prescribed and instead the owner of the charge makes a requisition for discharge in the prescribed form. see Land Registration Rules 1972, Form 71A, or else some other person, such as the registered owner (chargor), makes a requisition in the Form 71B.

[174.] A requisition in Form 71A or 71B is again made, see fn 173 *supra*.

[175.] See *Irish Land Law* (2nd ed, 1986), para 13 126.

[176.] Though, of course, it may in turn become subject to a mortgage in favour of the lending institution from whom the purchaser is borrowing a proportion of the purchase price.

technical sense[177] rather than the date entered in it. If the discharge does not take effect before the conveyance, then the latter in effect operates initially as a transfer to the purchaser still subject to the vendor's mortgage.[178] It is true that, in practice, the purchaser may be protected by an undertaking[179] by the vendor's solicitor to see that this mortgage is discharged out of the proceeds of sale, but theoretically if the conveyance pre-dates the reconveyance or other form of discharge it may be strictly inaccurate, eg, by stating that the vendor is conveying free from incumbrances, and, therefore, may be technically open to an action for rectification.[180] Though it seems that if the conveyance contains such a recital on behalf of the vendor, he may be estopped from denying it and the estoppel is "fed" by the subsequent reconveyance or other form of discharge.[181] The problem is, of course, that the vendor's lending institution is usually not prepared to issue the reconveyance or receipt until it actually receives the discharge money from the vendor's solicitor and he may not be in a position to give this money until after the closing date for the sale to the purchaser and delivery of the conveyance to his solicitor. Thus the discharge may be arranged by the vendor's solicitor some time after that date, on the basis of an undertaking given by him on the matter.[182] And in practice the purchaser's solicitor does not delay while this is being done and lodges the conveyance to his client for stamping immediately.[183] Yet, arguably, the purchaser's solicitor should not simply accept the vendor's undertaking as to discharge of the mortgage and close without production of a prior reconveyance or other form of discharge of the vendor's mortgage, without his client's express authority to do so. If in fact the vendor's solicitor fails in his undertaking and the mortgage is not

---

[177.] See paras **[18.09]** and **[18.123]** *et seq, ante*.

[178.] In England, where under s 115 of the Law of Property Act 1925, mortgages generally may be discharged by endorsed receipt, a receipt issued in respect of money appearing to have been paid by a person who is not entitled to the immediate equity of redemption operates not to discharge the mortgage but rather as a transfer of it to the mortgagor, see s 115(2). See, however, on this *Cumberland Court (Brighton) Ltd v Taylor* [1964] Ch 29 (original mortgagor-vendor held to be estopped by recital in conveyance to purchaser that he was seised in fee simple "free from incumbrances"). See also on estoppel, paras **[18.32-3]** *ante*. And see Adams, (1971) 68 L Soc Gaz 175 and (1973) 70 L Soc Gaz 1360.

[179.] See para **[20.14]** *et seq, post*.

[180.] See para **[21.39]** post. A building society receipt cannot operate as a transfer of the mortgage to the vendor-mortgagor because normally it does not name the payer, and under s 84 of the Building Societies Act 1989, the receipt operates to vacate the mortgage and vest the property in the person for the time being entitled to the equity of redemption. As regards other mortgages, see s 18 of the Housing Act 1988: para **[19.55]** *supra*.

[181.] See *Cumberland Court (Brighton) Ltd v Taylor* [1964] Ch 29, fn 178, *supra*.

[182.] See para **[20.17]** *post*. See also the English Law Society's opinions on the subject, (1949) 46 L Soc Gaz 230 and (1970) 67 L Soc Gaz 753.

[183.] See para **[20.38** *post*.

subsequently discharged, it may be argued that the purchaser's solicitor was negligent in closing the sale on that basis.[184] Indeed, for this reason many solicitors refuse to accept such an undertaking and insist upon the vendor's mortgage being discharged prior to completion, evidence of the discharge being produced at completion and an undertaking to furnish the mortgage deed in due course. The view is taken that the vendor ought to obtain a bridging loan to effect the discharge and the purchaser should not be obliged to help the vendor to escape the cost of this. Where purchasers' solicitors are prepared to accept an undertaking from the vendor's solicitor to redeem the mortgage out of the proceeds of sale and to furnish the vacated mortgage on redemption, it is usually only in a case where they know that there is unlikely to be much delay, eg, building societies tend to be speedy about such matters, whereas some local authorities are notoriously tardy! If the vendor's mortgage is to be redeemed out of the proceeds of sale, it is wiser not to have the purchaser's banker's draft made out entirely in favour of the vendor's solicitor but rather a "split" draft, ie, two cheques, one in favour of the vendor's mortgagee for the discharge money and the other in favour of the vendor's solicitor for the balance of the purchase money.[185] If, on the other hand, the vendor's mortgage is to be redeemed prior to completion, the proper course for the vendor's solicitor is to arrange bridging finance and not. as is sometimes done, to pay it off by a draft drawn on the client's account on the morning of completion in anticipation of obtaining the proceeds of sale from the purchaser that afternoon. Quite apart from infringement of the Solicitors' Accounts Rules, there is always the risk of a last minute hitch which results in closing being postponed.

V. WILLS AND ASSENTS

[19.57] Wills and assents are the two important types of document relating to the transfer of property on death. The will, where the deceased dies testate, specifies the beneficiaries entitled to succeed to his property[186] and the assent is the method usually adopted now[187] by the deceased's personal representatives to vest the property in those beneficiaries or, in the case of intestacy, in the persons decreed by statute to be his successors.[188]

[184.] See *Edward Wong Finance Co Ltd v Johnston, Stokes & Master* [1984] AC 296: see para **[20.32]** *post.*

[185.] The Law Society's Conveyancing Committee has recently reiterated this point: see *ibid.*

[186.] See *Irish Land Law* (2nd ed, 1986), Ch 14.

[187.] See *ibid*, paras 16.44-6.

[188.] See *ibid*, para 15.16 *et seq.*

A. Wills

1. Formalities

[19.58] It is axiomatic that a solicitor must, when drawing up a will, have regard to the formalities of the law for the making of a valid will. The various matters which are relevant to this subject have been dealt with elsewhere[189] and so we shall confine our discussion here to a summary of the main points to be considered. First, it should be noted that there are certain statutory restrictions as to the capacity to make a will.[190] Secondly, there are strict requirements as to the form of a will, relating particularly to its execution, ie, signing and witnessing.[191] Though it should be noted that there is no need for a deed; writing only is required.[192] Thirdly, care should be taken to see that nothing appears in the written document likely to create difficulties when the will is submitted for proving,[193] eg, pin or clip marks suggesting something was once attached to it.[194] Furthermore, obliterations, interlineations and other alterations should be avoided if at all possible.[195] Fourthly, special rules relating to the effect or construction of wills must be borne in mind, eg, the effect of the testator's subsequent marriage,[196] rules relating to lapsed gifts[197] and gifts to witnesses,[198] the doctrines of satisfaction and ademption[199] and, of course, the rules against remoteness of gifts and accumulations.[200]

2. Contents

[19.59] The precise contents of any particular will must depend upon a variety of factors, such as the personal circumstances of the testator and his family and the size and nature of his estate. It is very difficult to generalise about what provisions should be included in a will, but it may be useful to mention some matters which, because of their general significance, are at

---

[189.] *Ibid*, Ch 14. See also Brady, *Succession Law in Ireland* (2nd ed, 1995), Chs 2-4.

[190.] *Ibid*, paras 14.04-5.

[191.] *Ibid*, paras 14.09-13; *Brady, op cit*, Ch 2.

[192.] *Ibid*, para 14.08; *Brady, op cit*, para [2.04] *et seq*.

[193.] *Ibid*, para 16.04 *et seq*.

[194.] Eg, another will or codicil. see *ibid* paras 14.17 and 14.22-3. See also the list of "don'ts" in (1977) 71 Gaz ILSI 86; *Brady, op cit*, Ch 3.

[195.] *Ibid*, paras 14.14-6. *Brady, op cit*, Ch 5.

[196.] *Ibid*, paras 14.19-20.

[197.] *Ibid*, paras 14.28-31.

[198.] *Ibid*, para 14.34.

[199.] *Ibid*, para 3.115 *et seq*.

[200.] *Ibid*, Ch 5. As regards rules of construction of wills, see *ibid*, para 11.36 *et seq*.

least worthy of consideration in most, if not all, cases and ought, therefore, to be drawn to the testator's attention.

(i) Freedom of Disposition

[19.60] It must be remembered that a testator does not have an entirely free hand in making dispositions of his property by will so far as his immediate family is concerned. He is restricted by the provisions in the Succession Act 1965, relating to the legal right of the spouse and the making of proper provision for his children.[201] And it is important to note that the matrimonial home and household chattels may be appropriated by the personal representatives in satisfaction of the surviving spouse's share, regardless of the terms of the will.[202]

(ii) Tax Considerations

[19.61] It is essential nowadays that a testator should be advised as to the tax implications of the dispositions made by his will. He must be warned particularly of the incidence of inheritance tax[203] and probate tax.[204] The testator should also be advised to take into account the future liabilities to tax of his beneficiaries after his will comes into operation. This is a highly complex subject which is outside the scope of this book.

(iii) Commorientes

[19.62] It is usual to insert a *commorientes* clause in a will of a married person leaving property to his or her spouse absolutely, to ensure that children of the family are not deprived of property in favour of one of the spouse's next-of-kin.[205] This clause should provide that, in the event of the spouse dying within, say, 30 days of the testator,[206] the testator's estate should be held on trust for his children or other beneficiaries he wishes to benefit.

(iv) Apportionment and Related Rules

[19.63] As a general rule, some thought should be given to making the executors' duties as straightforward as possible. For this reason it is usual to insert special clauses negativing the application to the will of the complex

---

[201] *Ibid*, paras 14.56-64. See also *Brady, op cit*, Ch 7.

[202] *Ibid*, para 14.60; *Brady, op cit*, para [7.26] *et seq*.

[203] Introduced by the Capital Acquisitions Tax Act 1976. See generally Bohan, *Capital Acquisitions Tax* (1995). See also O'Callaghan, *Taxation of Estates: The Law in Ireland* (1993).

[204] Introduced by the Finance Act 1992, ss 109-119. See *Bohan, op cit*, Ch 19.

[205] See *Irish Land Law* (2nd ed, 1986), para 14.32-3.

[206] The period should not be too long. since probate cannot be issued during this period and so administration of the estate will be held up.

rules relating to apportionment as between capital and income,[207] in particular the rules in *Howe v Lord Dartmouth*,[208] *Re Earl of Chesterfield's Trusts*[209] and *Allhusen v Whittell*.[210]

(v) Property Subject to Charges

[19.64] If property left by will is still subject to a charge on the testator's death, the donee takes it subject to the charge and is primarily liable for its payment, unless a contrary intention is signified.[211] Thus, if the testator wants to avoid saddling his beneficiary with such a charge, which can relate to both realty and personalty, he should be advised to make this clear in the will.

(vi) Advancements

[19.65] Advancements made to children must be taken into account in reckoning each child's share in the estate.[212] Since this may give rise to considerable complications in the distribution of the testator's assets, it is arguable that his will ought to contain a clause excluding the application of this rule.

(vii) Executors

[19.66] The executors ought to be named in the will and care ought to be taken to see that they are suitable persons or bodies. There is little point in selecting relatives of the testator who have no knowledge of legal or business affairs, except as a last resort. Most banks have departments specialising in executor and trustee work (though their fees tend to be high) and, of course, the client's solicitor may be willing to undertake the work.[213]

(viii) Trustees

[19.67] Many wills involve the creation of trusts and frequently the persons appointed as executors are also to act as trustees.[214] In such cases it is vital to pay particular attention to the express powers to be conferred on the trustees by the will, a matter we mention later.[215]

---

207. See *Irish Land Law* (2nd ed, 1986), para 10.077 *et seq.*
208. (1802) 7 Ves 137. *Ibid*, para 10.079 *et seq.*
209. (1883) 24 Ch D 643. *Ibid*, para 10.082.
210. (1867) LR 4 Eq 295. *Ibid*, para 10.083.
211. *Ibid*, para 16.40; *Brady, op cit*, para [10.17] *et seq.*
212. *Ibid*, para 15.29; *Brady, op cit*, para [8.26] *et seq.*
213. See *ibid*, paras 16.04-5.
214. *Ibid*, para 10.004.
215. Para **[19.70]** *infra.*

B. Assents

[19.68] Like wills, assents by personal representatives, even when dealing with the vesting of land, do not have to be by deed and need, in the case of land, be in writing only.[216] The law relating to assents has been discussed elsewhere,[217] and various precedents for use in both parts of Ireland in connection with unregistered land have also been given in other works.[218] Forms for registered land are prescribed by statutory regulation.[219]

VI. SETTLEMENTS AND TRUSTS

[19.69] Several of the matters considered in connection with wills are equally relevant in respect of an *inter vivos* settlement or trust. Attention is drawn specifically to the following matters. First, so far as tax considerations are concerned,[220] particular account must be taken of capital acquisition tax.[221] Furthermore, a settlement is to be regarded as a "disposal" of the entire settled property by the settlor for the purposes of capital gains tax,[222] notwithstanding any power of revocation or interest retained by the settlor.[223] In this connection, it should be noted that a deed of family arrangement or similar deed varying dispositions made by a testator to his beneficiaries or their interests acquired on intestacy will not, if executed not more than two years after the death, involve a disposal for the purposes of capital gains tax[224]

[19.70] The remarks made earlier with respect to avoidance of apportionment rules apply to some extent to trustees[225] and it is particularly important to have regard to the question of conferring various express powers on the trustees, ie, by way of variation of or addition to their statutory powers.[226] Thus, it is usually considered wise to confer express

---

[216.] Succession Act 1965, s 52(5).

[217.] *Irish Land Law* (2nd ed, 1986), paras 16.44-7. See also Brady, *Succession Law in Ireland* (2nd ed, 1986), para [10.34] *et seq*; para **[15.19]** *ante*.

[218.] See Leitch, *A Handbook on the Administration of Estates Act (NI) 1955* (1956), App IV; Maguire, *The Succession Act, 1965* (2nd ed by Pearce), App C.

[219.] Land Registration Rules 1972, Forms 37, 48 49 and 58. See Fitzgerald, *Land Registry Practice* (2nd ed, 1995), p 107 *et seq*.

[220.] See para **[19.61]** *supra*.

[221.] See Bohan *Capital Acquisitions Tax* (1995) Chs 16 and 17. See also O'Callaghan, *Taxation of Trusts: The Law in Ireland* (1994).

[222.] See *O'Callaghan, op cit*, Chs 15 and 16.

[223.] *Ibid,* paras 15.07 and 16.03.

[224.] 1975 Act, s 14(6); *O'Callaghan, op cit*, para 16.09.

[225.] Para **[19.63]** *supra*.

[226.] As to which see *Irish Land Law* (2nd ed, 1986), Ch 10.

powers of investment on trustees, generally giving them a wide or absolute discretion in the matter.[227] Other matters worth particular consideration for inclusion in the trust instrument are an express power to raise money,[228] an extended power of maintenance and express power of advancement,[229] and reservation to the trustees of the right to charge fees.[230]

[227.] See *ibid* para 10.054 *et seq*. There has been in more recent years a welcome extension of the range of trustee securities. Personal representatives and trustees are not tied now to so-called gilt-edged securities. Thus Bank of Ireland stock and shares in other banks like Allied Irish Banks are now trustee securities. See Trustee (Authorised Investments) Orders 1967 (SI/285), 1969 (SI/241), 1974 (SI/41), 1979 (SI/407), 1983 (SI/58). 1985 (SI/224), 1986 (SI/372).

[228.] *Ibid*, paras 10.023-4.

[229.] *Ibid*, paras 10.042-9.

[230.] *Ibid*, para 10.069 *et seq*.

Chapter 20

COMPLETING THE TRANSACTION

[20.01] We come now to the final stage in the conveyancing process, the completion of the transaction.[1] There are three main matters to be considered. First, there are the various steps to be taken by the vendor's and purchaser's solicitors in preparation for the day of completion, the closing date for the transaction. Secondly, there is the procedure for completion on that date, ie, the date agreed or such later date when actual completion takes places. Thirdly, there are various steps to be taken by the solicitors subsequent to that date before the transaction can be said to be finally completed.

I. PREPARATION FOR COMPLETION

[20.02] This subject is best considered from the point of view of the two parties' solicitors. The steps they have to take are clearly governed by the terms of the contract for sale and by what is to take place on the closing day itself.

A. Vendor's Solicitor

1. Apportionment Account

[20.03] The first thing which the vendor's solicitor must do is to furnish the purchaser's solicitor with an "apportionment account." The object of this is to apportion as between the vendor and purchaser income and outgoings relating to the property and to indicate the balance of purchase money owing and to be paid by the purchaser on the closing date. The point is that such income and outgoings may have been received or paid partly in respect of a period of time *after* the closing date, when the purchaser becomes the owner and the vendor ceases to be the owner. If no apportionment were made, one or other of them may secure a financial advantage, eg, if the vendor has paid the rates for the current year or half-year and completion occurs two months later, the purchaser would obtain the advantage of ten months', or four

---

[1.] See para **[1.09]** *ante*.

months', payment of rates. This may be adjusted on the apportionment account by crediting the vendor with the ten months' payment.

[20.04] The Law Society's standard contract form recognises the vendor's solicitor's responsibility in this regard. Condition 27[2] contains a comprehensive set of provisions whereby "All rents, profits, rates, taxes, outgoings and moneys (including rent, outgoings and money payable in advance[3] but not including impositions derived from hypothecation[4]) referable to the subject property" are to be apportioned (whether apportionable by law or not[5]) on a day-to-day basis as at the Apportionment Date.[6] There are several aspects of this matter which should be considered.

(i) Apportionment Date

[20.05] Practitioners must note the definition in condition 2 of the *General Conditions*. The date is usually the later of either the closing date specified in the Memorandum section of the standard contract[7] or the date subsequent to that when delay in completion ceases to be attributable to default by the vendor. It is important to note, therefore, that ordinarily the apportionment date is *not* the date of *actual* completion. This protects the vendor in the situation where he might face severe practical difficulties arising from delaying tactics adopted by the purchaser. For example, where a vendor is trying to get rid of a property subject to a rack rent and has agreed to sell the lease for a nominal amount, or, perhaps, a "reverse" premium is involved, the danger is that, if the purchaser delays completion, the vendor is stuck with the rent. The interest penalty is no help to the vendor because, of course, it is payable on the price payable by the purchaser, which in this instance is really a nominal sum only. Under the *General Conditions*, however, the "cut-off" date in such a case is the closing date specified in the contract, unless the vendor is also in default, in which it is the date on which he ceases to be in default. If, however, the vendor, as in the sale of an investment property, elects to take the rents and profits in addition to claiming interest from the purchaser for delay,[8] the apportionment date is the date of actual completion. Subject to this, it is always open to the parties to agree some other date, as the definition recognises expressly. Furthermore,

---

2. *General Conditions of Sale* (1995 ed).
3. See para **[20.06]** *infra*.
4. This is the process of giving security to a creditor over property which does not involve either the passing of legal ownership or possession. It is more commonly used in civil-law countries, including Scotland: see Sheridan, *Rights in Security* (1974), p 7 and Ch 12.
5. See para **[20.06]** *infra*.
6. Cond 27(b).
7. See para **[9.05]** *ante*.
8. This applies only where the purchaser is in default: see paras **[12.19]** *ante* and **[20.09]** *infra*.

condition 27(b) provides that, where delay in completion is through default by the vendor, the purchaser may opt for apportionment as at the specified closing date or the date at which the purchaser ceased to be in default (if he was also in default). The position in each case is that the vendor is liable for or entitled to the apportioned amount up to the apportioned date and is regarded as owner of the property until midnight on that date.[9] The purchaser is liable or entitled thereafter.

(ii) Items Apportionable

[20.06] Under the general law, the vendor must account to the purchaser for all income in the nature of rents and other profits from the property which accrues after the contractual date for completion.[10] And, under s 2 of the Apportionment Act 1870,[11] all rents, annuities, dividends and other periodical payments in the nature of income are to be considered as accruing "from day to day" and apportionable in respect of time accordingly. Conversely, again under the general law, the purchaser must repay to the vendor all outgoings in the nature of rent and rates paid by the vendor in respect of the period after completion.[12] It has long been accepted that rents are apportionable,[13] though not, apparently, where rent is payable in advance and is already due before completion.[14] It should be noted, however, that condition 27 of the Law Society's contract, as quoted above,[15] expressly covers rent and other sums payable in advance. It is not clear, how far apportionment applies to payments similar to rent, but which do not constitute rent in the strict sense of the word, eg, conacre or agistment monies in Ireland, where there is strictly no relationship of landlord and tenant between the parties.[16] It is true that, in *Foster v Cunningham*[17] Curran J held that such monies were apportionable as between a tenant for life and

---

9. Cond 27(c).
10. *Paine v Meller* (1816) 6 Ves 349 at 352 (*per* Lord Eldon): *Plews v Samuel* [1904] 1 Ch 464. As regards renewal fines see *De Voeux v Mara* (1963) 15 Ir Ch R 16, quit rents and tithe rentcharges: *Re Biggs-Atkinson and Ryan's Contract* [1913] 1 IR 125.
11. The Act does not apply where it is expressly stipulated that no apportionment is to take place, see s 7.
12. *Carrolus v Sharp* (1855) 20 Beav 56 at 58 (*per* Romilly MR); *Barsht v Tagg* [1900] 1 Ch 231.
13. See Apportionment Act 1814, and 1870 s 3; Deasy's Act 1860, s 50. See also *Re Leeks* [1902] IR 339; *Glass v Patterson* [1902] 7 IR 660: *Irish Land Law* (2nd ed, 1986), para 10.083 and 17.031; *Irish Landlord and Tenant Law* para 10.15 *et seq.*
14. See *Dublin Corp v Barry* [1897] 1 IR 65. *Cf Ellis v Rowbotham* [1900] 1 QB 740.
15. See para **[20.04]** *supra.*
16. See *Irish Land Law* (2nd ed, 1986), paras 20.25-27; *Irish Landlord and Tenant Law* para 3.20 *et seq.*
17. [1956] NI 29.

remainderman[18] "as if they had accrued from day to day",[19] but two caveats must be entered about this decision. First, throughout his judgment Curran J referred to the monies paid as "rent",[20] which clearly they were not if he was dealing with true conacre or agistment "lettings".[21] Secondly, Curran J did not make clear in respect of what period the day-to-day apportionment should be calculated, ie, whether over a calendar year or some other period. The point is that such lettings are commonly taken on a seasonal basis or for part only of a year[22] and it is arguable that the apportionment should be calculated accordingly, ie, by treating the monies payable as referable not to the whole calendar year in which they are paid but just for the part of it for which the "letting" is taken. On the other hand. since the farming activities, especially in the case of conacre,[23] engaged in under such an arrangement may be said in most cases to exhaust the profits of the land for the year in question, it may be fairer to calculate the apportionment with reference to the calendar year.

[20.07] Apart from rent,[24] it is clearly established that other outgoings in respect of property are apportionable. One obvious category is the rates payable in respect of the property.[25] This remains the case despite the fact that rates are not a charge on the property and are payable by the occupier under a personal obligation,[26] and despite the fact that they may be payable by instalments.[27] Nevertheless, if instalments are being paid it may be more convenient for the vendor to stop the instalments in the month of completion and for the purchaser to take them on in the following months.

---

18. See *Irish Land Law*, (2nd ed 1986) para 10.83.

19. *Op cit* p 30 citing in support a decision by Wilson J in an unreported case heard in 1931, *Swan v Kane op cit* p 29.

20. As, apparently, did Wilson J in *Swan v Kane* fn 19 *supra*.

21. *Allingham v Atkinson* [1898] 1 IR 239; see also *Carson v Jeffers* [1961] IR 44 at 57 (*per* Budd J). *Cf Dease v O'Reilly* (1845) 8 Ir LR 52.

22. See *Irish Land Law*, (2nd ed 1986) para 20.25.

23. *Cf* agistment, see *ibid*.

24. It is, of course, common to reserve as "rent" other sums payable by the tenant, such as service charges: see *Irish Landlord and Tenant Law*, para 17.07 and Laffoy, *Irish Conveyancing Precedents* p L6.

25. See *O'Connor v Harvey* (1910) 44 ILTR 242. See *Irish Landlord and Tenant Law* para 13.04; Keane, *The Law of Local Government in the Republic of Ireland* (1982), Ch 10. Full relief in respect of rates was, of course, introduced for dwellings by the Local Government (Financial Provisions) Act 1978, ss 3 and 5.

26. See *Lally v Concannon* (1853) 3 ILR 557; *Leathley v Dublin Corp* [1942] Ir Jur Rep 20. On the other hand, residential property tax is not apportionable as it is based upon the assessable person's income and the net market value of that person's residential property owned and occupied on the valuation date: see *Butterworths Tax Guide 1995-96* Pt 7.

27. *Belfast v Callen* (1910) 1 IR 38.

[20.08] Apart from the general law, the parties usually provide expressly for apportionment in the contract for sale. Thus, as we saw earlier,[28] condition 27 of the Law Society's *General Conditions of Sale (1995 Edition)* provides that all rents, profits, rates, taxes and outgoings and moneys are to be apportioned and then adds, to remove any doubt on the matter, that these are all to be apportioned "whether apportionable by law or not." This is a very wide category of payments relating to the property, Furthermore, it is expressly provided that excise and "kindred" duties payable in respect of the property, or any licence attaching to it, are to be apportioned on a day-to-day basis.

(iii) Interest

[20.09] Condition 25 of the Law Society's *General Conditions of Sale (1995 Edition)* requires the purchaser to pay interest at the stipulated rate[29] on the balance of the purchase money from the closing date up to the date of actual completion, but only if the delay is caused by reason of "any default" on the part of the purchaser.[30] This qualification confirms, if not simplifies, the rule at common law.[31] It has been held in several Irish cases that any express condition as to payment of interest by the purchaser for delay in completion should be read as subject to the qualification that he is not liable where the delay is caused by the vendor's "wilful default."[32] But this concept of "wilful default" is notoriously difficult to define[33] and it is to be noted that condition 25 does not use the adjective. We saw in an earlier chapter that condition 25 also allows the vendor to take the rents and profits less the outgoings of the property for the period between the closing date and the date of actual completion.[34] This right may, of course, be valuable where the subject-matter of the sale is a business or other property producing substantial income, though, as condition 25(a) makes clear, no such claim can be made where interest could not be claimed because of the vendor's own default, ie,

---

[28.] Para **[20.04]** *supra*. And see *Allman v McDaniel* [1912] 1 IR 467 (apportionment of expenses of sale of distillery as a going concern).

[29.] See para **[12.18]** *et seq.*

[30.] Cond 25(a). See the discussion at para **[12.19]** *ante*.

[31.] Note that, in *Beresford v Clarke* [1908] 2 IR 317, it was held that the purchaser must still pay interest even though he has also taken possession of the property and is paying rent.

[32.] *Re Kissock and Taylor* [1916] 1 IR 393 at 399 (*per* Barton J); *Manton v Mannion* [1958] IR 324 at 325 (*per* Budd J); *Sheridan v Higgins* [1971] IR 291 at 302-4 (*per* Ó Dálaigh CJ). See also *Northern Bank Ltd v Duffy* [1981] ILRM 308.

[33.] See the remarks of Barton J in *Re Postmaster-General and Colgan's contract* [1906] 1 IR 287 at 294 (*aff'd* at p 477). See also *Re Young and Harston's Contract* (1885) 31 Ch D 168 at 174 (*per* Bowen LJ); *Re London Corp and Tubb's Contract* [1894] 2 Ch 524 at 530 (*per* Lopes LJ); *Re Hewitt's Contract* [1963] 1 WLR 1298 at 1303 (*per* Wilberforce J).

[34.] Para **[12.19]** *ante*.

the right to rents and profits is dependent upon the right to interest.[35] Under an open contract, ie, where there are no provisions as to interest on delay in completion and the vendor is responsible for the delay, the purchaser can require the vendor to take the rents and profits in lieu of interest.[36]

(iv) Estimated Payments

[20.10] It is the case sometimes that at the apportionment date the payments in respect of the property are calculated on an "estimated" basis only. A typical example is service charges payable in respect of units in a shopping centre or flats in a block of flats, where the leases usually provide for the precise amounts to be determined following an audit of accounts at the year end.[37] Conditions 27(e) of the Law Society's *General Conditions of Sale (1995 Edition)* recognises this by providing for provisional apportionment "on a fair estimate" of such amounts and a final apportionment when the actual figures are ascertained. The difference between the provisional and actual figures is to be refunded within 10 working days of the liable party becoming aware of the difference.

(v) Balance of Purchase Price

[20.11] Condition 27(d) of the Law Society's *General Conditions* provides that the balance of the purchase price[38] is to be adjusted upwards or downwards to accommodate the apportionments calculated in accordance with the condition's provisions. As we saw in the previous paragraph, there may have to be refunds made after completion, where apportionments are made in respect of items like service charges which had to be calculated on an estimated basis.

2. Execution of Deed

[20.12] The vendor's solicitor must see that his client executes the engrossed deed or transfer for handing over on completion to the purchaser's solicitor. This is usually done some days before the closing date, either by getting the client to come into the office to execute the deed, which is preferable, or sending it to him with strict instructions on the matter. The requirements of execution, including the delivery of the executed deed to the vendor's

---

[35.] See in the context of a right to elect for rents and profits *in lieu of* interest. *Re Hewitt's Contract* [1963] 3 All ER 419 at 423 (*per* Wilberforce J).

[36.] *Ibid* p 422. See also *Esdaile v Stephenson* (1823) 1 Sim & St 122 at 123 (*per* Leach V-C).

[37.] See *Irish Landlord and Tenant Law* para 17.05.

[38.] Ie, owing after deduction of the deposit already paid (see paras **[10.18]** *et seq* and **[13.30]** *et seq, ante*) and payable on completion: see para **[20.31]** *et seq, post*. If the vendor's mortgage is to be discharged out of the proceeds of sale, the Apportionment Account should "split" the balance so as to show the redemption figure and the balance to which the vendor is entitled. This enables the purchaser's solicitor to furnish two bank drafts at closing, thereby complying with what is now clearly "best practice" in this matter: see para **[20.32]** *infra*.

solicitor as an "escrow" pending completion, were discussed in detail in an earlier chapter.[39]

3. Keys and Vacant Possession

[20.13] The vendor's solicitor must discuss with his client the final arrangements for the client vacating the premises on or before the closing date, where the property has been sold with vacant possession,[40] and the handing over of the keys to the purchaser. The keys are usually handed over at completion itself and so the client must be told to deliver them at his solicitor's office in time, if he is not going to attend at completion himself.

4. Undertakings

[20.14] As we have mentioned before,[41] one important aspect of modern conveyancing practice is the extent to which its processes depend upon solicitors' "undertakings" and their acceptance by fellow solicitors and other persons or bodies involved in conveyancing, eg, banks and building societies. In view of their importance, it may, therefore, be useful to draw attention to the nature of such undertakings and the types of undertaking frequently entered into in connection with conveyancing transactions. It is a subject which has come under review by the Law Society from time to time, as a result of which the Conveyancing Committee issued guidelines to practitioners[42] and agreed standard forms of undertakings with the Irish Bankers' Federation.[43]

(i) Nature of Undertaking

[20.15] An undertaking given by a solicitor is a promise or guarantee by him in his professional capacity and, as such, must be honoured by him. Failure to honour it involves professional misconduct and renders him liable to disciplinary proceedings.[44] Furthermore, as an officer of the court,[45] he is

---

[39.] See para **[18.119]** *et seq, ante*. Note the importance of having two witnesses to facilitate registration in the Registry of Deeds, see para **[18.136]** *ante*.

[40.] See para **[10.44]** *ante*.

[41.] See, eg, para **[2.43]** *ante*.

[42.] See the *Conveyancing Handbook* (1990), Ch 2.

[43.] To cover, eg, the lending of title documents for inspection only and return to the bank (Form No 1) and for a sale or mortgage and accounting to the bank for the net proceeds (Form No 2). See the *Gazette* June 1989 and December 1990.

[44.] Note the numerous pronouncements in recent times by the English courts on this subject: see, eg, *Fox v Bannister King and Rigbeys* [1987] 1 All ER 737; *Udall v Capri Lighting Ltd* [1987] 3 All ER 262; *United Bank of Kuwait Ltd v Hammoud* [1988] 3 All ER 418; *Hastingwood Property Ltd v Saunders Bearman Anselm* [1990] 3 All ER 107; *Rooks Rider v Steel* [1993] 4 All ER 716.

[45.] This has been the case for over a century: see Judicature (Ir) Act 1877, s 78 and the Solicitors (Ir) Act 1898, s 4.

subject to the jurisdiction of the court and may, therefore, be compelled by the court to implement his undertaking.[46] Depending upon the facts of the case, and, in particular, the wording of the undertaking, it may be enforced against him personally.[47] If the undertaking is given by the solicitor in the normal course of carrying out his duties within the firm of solicitors of which he is a partner or which employs him, in other words, if he acted within his ostensible authority given by the firm, the firm, ie, the partners, may be held liable.[48] If the court takes the view that it is inappropriate to order specific performance of the undertaking, because, eg, it is impossible of such performance or no help to the aggrieved party, it may instead order the solicitor or his firm to pay compensation to the aggrieved party.[49] It is essential, therefore, that a solicitor should exercise the greatest care when the question of giving an undertaking is concerned. It is suggested that there are several rules or guides to be observed.[50] First, no undertaking should be given unless the solicitor has clear and irrevocable authority from his client, preferably in writing, to give it. Secondly, the additional precaution should be taken of obtaining a written undertaking by the client that he will not withdraw his retainer in connection with the matter in respect of which the solicitor has given his undertaking.[51] Thirdly, no personal undertaking should be given unless the solicitor is and will remain in the position to carry it out. If he is not in that position, may never be in it or may not remain in it, he must not give a personal undertaking as to performance and should, instead, see that the terms of any undertaking (if any at all is necessary) are suitably qualified by its express terms to ensure that the solicitor is protected against all eventualities. Thus, if an undertaking is given to hold title deeds on trust. eg, for a lending institution,[52] they should be in the solicitor's hands at the time and remain so until, eg, the institution's mortgage is discharged.

---

46. *Re A Solicitor* (1919) 53 ILTR 51. See also *Re A Solicitor* [1966] 1 WLR 1604; *Geoffrey Silver & Drake v Baines* [1971] 1 QB 396. And see the Solicitor's Act 1960, s 8 (substituted by s 18 of the Solicitors (Amendment) Act 1994) and the 1994 Act, s 38.

47. *Marsh v Joseph* [1897] 1 Ch 213.

48. *United Bank of Kuwait Ltd v Hammoud* [1988] 3 All ER 418.

49. *Udall v Capri Lighting Ltd* [1987] 3 All ER 262.

50. *Cf* "dos" and "don'ts" recommended by the Law Society's Professional Purposes Committee in the *Gazette* November 1978 and the Society's Practice Note published in a Newsletter issued in September 1987, both reproduced in the *Conveyancing Handbook* pp 2.1-2.7. Note also the Practice Notes in the *Gazette* June 1989 and October 1989, *ibid*, pp 2.11-2.13; and the *Gazette* December 1990, June 1993 and November 1993.

51. Eg if the vendor solicitor obtains the title deeds from the vendor's mortgagee on accountable receipt and then, before the sale is completed and the proceeds of sale come to hand to discharge the mortgage, the vendor changes his solicitor, the first solicitor will remain liable on this undertaking, though he will no longer have any lien on the deeds, see para **[20.50]** *infra*.

52. See *ibid*.

Similarly, if an undertaking is to be given to account for money or to pay over the proceeds from a sale still to be completed, it must be so qualified that, rather than being an undertaking to pay a precise amount, it is confined to paying over whatever *net* proceeds, *if any*, result from the sale, *if and when* it is ever completed. The point is that an anticipated sale may never in fact be completed and, if it is, it may be uncertain exactly what net proceeds will result from it, ie, after all taxes, duties, costs, fees and expenses have been met. Furthermore, no such undertaking as to money should be given unless it is going to come into the solicitor's hands at some stage. Fourthly, no undertaking should be given to pay money where the amount is not stipulated at the time of giving it, for otherwise the solicitor may find that he has incurred an unlimited liability. The obvious example is an undertaking to pay taxes arising from the transaction, for the precise extent of the liability and the amount payable may not become clear until much later in the transaction. Finally, the greatest care should be taken to keep a clear and accurate record of all undertakings given. So far as conveyancing transactions are concerned, we mentioned in an earlier chapter the advantage of using a "progress" sheet pinned to each client's file upon which can be entered a note on this sort of thing, which also serves as a reminder to discharge the undertaking in due course.[53]

(ii) Examples

[20.16] There are several undertakings which may be entered into as part of a typical conveyancing transaction. For the moment we are concerned primarily with undertakings given by the vendor's solicitor, but it should be noted that the purchaser's solicitor may also be involved in giving undertakings, eg, to the purchaser's mortgagee.[54]

(a) To Vendor's Mortgagee

[20.17] We pointed out in an earlier chapter that one common form of undertaking given by a vendor's solicitor occurs where the property to be sold is subject to an existing mortgage and the deeds or other documents of title are held by the mortgagee.[55] Even where this mortgage is to be discharged out of the proceeds of sale, these will not become available until completion, yet the vendor's solicitor needs the title documents well before that, eg, in order to draw up the contract for sale[56] and to deduce title to the purchaser.[57] The mortgagee normally will release the deeds only on the

---

[53.] See para **[20.16]** *infra*.
[54.] See para **[20.24]** *infra*.
[55.] See para **[2.43]** *ante*.
[56.] See Ch 9 *ante*.
[57.] See Ch 14 *ante*.

vendor's solicitor's accountable receipt, which usually involves him in giving a written undertaking to hold the deeds on trust for or on behalf of and to the order of the mortgagee and to account to the mortgagee for the amount outstanding to ensure discharge of the mortgage on completion of the sale. The Law Society has recommended a form for use in such cases.[58] It is important to note, however, as the Supreme Court pointed out in *Re Galdan Properties Ltd*,[59] the solicitor in such a case holds the title documents for the mortgagee, not for his client, and so he cannot claim a lien over them for unpaid client fees.[60]

(b) To Purchaser's Solicitor

[20.18] There is one type of undertaking which may be given by the vendor's solicitor to the purchaser or his solicitor. Again where the property being sold is subject to a mortgage to be discharged out of the proceeds of sale, he may, depending upon what takes place at completion,[61] be required to give an undertaking that this mortgage will he discharged out of the purchase money and to furnish the purchaser or his solicitor with the mortgagee's receipt endorsed on the mortgage deed, in the case of unregistered land, or release, in the case of registered land, in due course.[62] Though we pointed out earlier that some solicitors are reluctant to accept such an undertaking and insist upon the vendor's mortgage being discharged prior to completion,[63] through bridging finance, if necessary.[64] The Law Society's Conveyancing Committee has also warned solicitors to take special care in giving undertakings to provide a release of a mortgage.[65] In particular, if it is intended to use the endorsed receipt procedure authorised by s 18 of the Housing Act 1988,[66] it is important to note that this can be used only where all monies secured by the mortgage or charge have been

---

[58.] Form No 2 of those agreed with the Irish Bankers' Federation: see para **[20.14]** *supra*.

[59.] [1988] IR 213.

[60.] See para **[20.50]** *infra*.

[61.] See para **[20.32]** *infra*.

[62.] See also para **[19.56]** *infra*. See also *Re A Solicitor* (1919) 53 ILTR 51. Note that, in so far as that case holds that a document relating to the same estate in registered land may also be registered in the Registry of Deeds (ie as if the land were unregistered), its authority must be doubted now, see Registration of Title Act 1964, s 117. See also McAllister, *Registration of Title in Ireland* pp 6405; *Irish Land Law* (2nd ed 1986), para 21.56.

[63.] See **[19.56]** *ante*. See also **[16.22]** *ante*.

[64.] Form No 4 in the Law Society's forms deals with bridging finance.

[65.] See the *Gazette* November 1990, p 318. Note also the warning to use the "split draft" procedure in such cases: see the *Gazette* March 1995, p 83 and July 1995 p 212 and para **[20.32]** *infra*.

[66.] See para **[19.55]** *ante*.

fully repaid. It is essential, therefore, to obtain full details of all such monies and up-to-date redemption figures before entering into any undertaking.[67]

[20.19] Another type of undertaking which used to be common arose where the vendor was, by the terms of the contract for sale, to furnish the purchaser with Registry of Deeds searches. In such cases the vendor's solicitor would requisition a negative search, as approved by the purchaser's solicitor, and, upon the search becoming available, would furnish the purchaser's solicitor with authority to inspect, close and take-up the search. This was presented by the purchaser's solicitor to the Registry of Deeds prior to closing, so as to enable him to inspect the search and to call upon the vendor's solicitor to explain any entries on it. Hand searches would also be made to continue the search from the date up to which the negative search had been initially written to the date of closing the transaction. After completion the purchaser's solicitor would register the deed executed in favour of his client[68] and close the negative search so as to show the registration of that deed. As we saw earlier,[69] the Law Society still encourages vendor's solicitors to requisition the appropriate negative search and, on receipt of this, to transmit it to the purchaser's solicitor with explanation of any entries.[70] The purchaser's solicitor is still expected to make continuation hand searches, to bring the negative search up-to-date to closing, he should also relodge the negative search following registration of the purchaser's deed, so that particulars of such registration will be entered on the search.

B. Purchaser's Solicitor

[20.20] There are several matters to be attended to by the purchaser's solicitor during the period immediately preceding the closing day. One obvious one is to check the apportionment account with the supporting vouchers or receipts, sent by the vendor's solicitor.[71] Apart from that, the following matters will usually require his attention.

1. Purchaser's Finance

[20.21] Perhaps the most important matter is to see that the requisite financial matters are sorted out in time. The purchaser is going to have to hand over on completion the balance of the purchase money shown as owing on the apportionment account. So his solicitor must ensure that he is put in

---

[67.] See the Committee's recommendation set out in the *Gazette* fn 65 *supra*.
[68.] See para **[20.43]** *infra*.
[69.] See para **[15.42]** *ante*.
[70.] Note the standard requisitions on title: see para **[16.21]** *ante*.
[71.] See para **[20.03]** *et seq, supra*.

funds by his client, usually a few days before the day of actual completion. The reason for this is that the normal method of payment now is by banker's draft and sufficient time must be allowed to arrange this.[72] For this to be obtained, technically the purchaser's cheque in favour of his solicitor should be cleared through his solicitor's client account before his solicitor asks his bank for the draft, which may be debited against the client account or issued against a cheque drawn on that account.[73] Of course, in most cases the purchaser is not supplying the bulk of the funds himself and is dependent on an advance or loan from a lending institution, in which case his solicitor must do his best to see that this is ready in good time. Unfortunately, this is where problems arise all too often in practice and the solicitor may find himself involved in a last minute rush, because the lending institution's cheque is not ready. In Ireland, until recent times,[74] it was not as common as it is in England for a lending institution to appoint the purchaser's solicitor as its agent to complete the mortgage. Indeed, this was rarely done and, provided the mortgagee's cheque was ready, completion took place at the mortgagee's solicitor's office. The mortgagee's cheque or draft was then usually endorsed over in favour of the vendor's solicitor and a draft for the balance of the purchase money was given to him by the purchaser's solicitor. In any event, whether or not the purchaser's solicitor is also acting for the lending institution, if the lending institution's cheque is not ready, the purchaser's solicitor may be forced to arrange "bridging" finance[75] for his client, which will, of course, involve more expense for the client.[76]

2. Searches

[20.22] The whole question of searches which should be made by the purchaser's solicitor prior to completion was discussed in an earlier chapter.[77]

3. Outstanding Requisitions

[20.23] It is a wise precaution for the purchaser's solicitor to check[78] whether he has received satisfactory replies to all the requisitions on title sent to the vendor's solicitor.[79] If he has not, he ought to contact the vendor's

---

[72.] See para **[20.31]** *infra*.

[73.] Depending upon the practice of the bank on these matters.

[74.] See paras **[1.35]** and **[16.67]** *ante*.

[75.] See paras **[20.18]** *supra*.

[76.] But it will not usually be more expensive than incurring interest charges for late completion see para **[12.20]** *ante*.

[77.] Para **[15.39]** *ante*.

[78.] Bearing in mind the time limits which may exist for rejoinders by the purchaser see para **[15.38]** *ante*.

[79.] See para **[15.36]** *et seq, ante*.

solicitor immediately and insist upon receipt of such replies by the closing date at the latest.[80]

4. Undertakings

[20.24] Just as the vendor's solicitor may have to give undertakings in connection with the transaction,[81] so may the purchaser's solicitor. Thus we mentioned above that bridging finance may have to be arranged for the purchaser to enable him to complete on time.[82] In such a case it is usual for the bank lending the finance to require the purchaser's solicitor to give an undertaking to hold the documents of title on trust for the bank, to lodge them with the bank on demand after stamping and registration, and to lodge the advance from the lending institution for the purchaser's long-term mortgage loan as soon as it comes to hand.[83] It is likely that the bank will require documentary evidence of the future availability of the advance, eg, a copy of the offer of the advance made by the lending institution or, if that has not yet been made, at least a letter of intention to make an advance to the purchaser.

II. COMPLETION

[20.25] We now turn to the day of actual completion itself. From the parties' point of view this is usually the most important day, in that usually the vendor gets the balance of the purchase money and the purchaser the title documents, the keys to the property and the possession that goes along with them.[84] However, it must be noted that from the strictly legal point of view the significant date is the day that the estate or interest contracted to be sold passes to the purchaser. This may not necessarily coincide with completion day for at least two main reasons. First, so far as unregistered land is concerned, the vital date is the "delivery" of the deed and, as we saw earlier,[85] this is a technical concept which may in a particular case be complicated by the law relating to escrows.[86] Secondly, in the case of registered land, the legal ownership does not pass to the transferee until he is

---

80. See para **[20.29]** *infra.*
81. See para **[20.14]** *et seq, supra.*
82. Para **[20.21]** *supra.*
83. See Form No 4 of the Law Society/Irish Bankers' Federation agreed forms of undertakings
84. See the discussion in *Palmer v Lark* [1945] Ch 182 at 194-5 (*per* Vaisey J); *Killner v France* [1946] 2 All ER 83 at 86 (*per* Stable J).
85. See para **[18.123]** *et seq, ante.*
86. Para **[18.125]** *et seq, ante.*

registered in the Land Registry as the new owner of the land,[87] which will not be completed until some time after completion.[88]

A. Place

[20.26] The place for completion varies according to the circumstances of the case, though it is usual for the contract for sale to contain a provision on this.[89] Thus condition 24(b) of the Law Society's *General Conditions of Sale (1995 Edition)* requires completion to take place at the vendor's solicitor's office. If, however, a mortgage on the property is to be discharged out of the proceeds of sale, the mortgagee's solicitor may require that completion takes place at his office. Furthermore, if the purchaser's solicitor is not acting as agent for the purchaser's mortgagee, who have had their own solicitor acting for them, eg, in investigating the title,[90] they usually insist upon completion at their solicitor's office.

[20.27] It is usual for the purchaser's solicitor to attend at completion in person or to send someone from his office, though, if his office is a long distance from the vendor's solicitor's office or other place of completion, he may arrange for another solicitor to represent him at completion. It is not usual for completion to take place by post. It is more common for completion by post to occur in England where the offices of the respective solicitors are some distance apart. In such a case the purchaser's solicitor sends the balance of the purchase money and receives in return the title documents. There are, of course, dangers inherent in this practice, in that it reduces, indeed in most cases excludes, the opportunity of the purchaser's solicitor to examine the original title documents before handing over the purchase money, which, at least from the technical point of view, is a vital part of the process of completion.[91] As a result of such concerns the English Law Society some years ago devised a "Code for Completion by Post", setting out the procedure to be followed.[92] A similar step was taken by the Law Society here with the issue of the 1986 Code of Practice.[93] This provides as follows:

[87.] As to the position pending this, see para **[12.05]** *ante*.

[88.] Para **[20.44]** *infra*. See also *Lever Finance Ltd v Needleman and Krentzer's Trustee* [1956] Ch 375.

[89.] It has been suggested that. in the contract is silent, the vendor can insist upon anywhere in the country, see Walford, *Contracts and Conditions of Sale of Land* (2nd ed, 1957), p 24. See also *Reading Trust Ltd v Spero* [1930] 1 KB 492 at 513-4 (*per* Slesser LJ).

[90.] See para **[15.05]** *ante*.

[91.] See para **[20.29]** *infra*.

[92.] See Silverman, *The Law Society Conveyancing Handbook* (1995) Appendix VII 2.

[93.] Published in the *Gazette* January/February 1986.

The sale shall be closed in the following manner:

(a) The Purchaser's Solicitor shall not later than four days prior to the closing date send to the Vendor's Solicitor a list of closing requirements (in accordance with the replies to Requisitions on Title and subsequent correspondence).

(b) When the Vendor's Solicitor is immediately able to satisfy or meet these closing requirements, notice shall be given (and where applicable mortgage redemption figures shall be furnished) to the Purchaser's Solicitor who shall then (save in the circumstances in paragraph (c)) send to the Vendor's Solicitor a Bank Draft for the balance of the purchase money or the balance due on the Apportionment Account (if any).

(c) If the Vendor's and the Purchaser's solicitors agree that the Vendor's mortgage is not to be redeemed prior to closing, the Purchaser's Solicitor should furnish to the Vendor's Solicitor two separate Bank Drafts, firstly for the amount required to redeem the Mortgage and secondly for the balance of the purchase monies. This shall imply an undertaking by the Vendor's Solicitor to forthwith discharge the Mortgage debt to the Vendor's Mortgagee and to furnish as soon as possible to the Purchaser's Solicitor proper evidence of such discharge and such release of Mortgage stamped and if registerable in the Registry of Deeds, duly registered, as may be appropriate.

(d) The Vendor's Solicitor will agree (without charge) to act as agent for the Purchaser's Solicitor with a view to receiving the Deed of Assurance containing the Receipt clause. This is with a view to the Purchaser's Solicitor getting a good receipt for payment of the purchase monies pursuant to the provisions of Section 56 of the Conveyancing and Law of Property Act 1881.

(e) Completion will be deemed to have taken place when the Vendor's Solicitor has received the balance purchase money outstanding and is at the same time in a position to furnish to the Purchaser's Solicitor the deeds and other items outstanding to close in accordance with the Vendor's Solicitor's replies to the Requisitions on Title and subsequent correspondence, in a position to satisfactorily explain all acts appearing on the Searches (if any) submitted by the Purchaser's Solicitor to the Vendor's Solicitor for explanation, and in a position to hand over or otherwise make available the keys of the property. The Vendor's Solicitor should confirm by telephone or telex to the Purchaser's Solicitor that completion has taken place and thereupon the Vendor's Solicitor shall be entitled to release to the Vendor the purchase monies.

(f) After completion and until posting or other dispatch, the Vendor's Solicitor holds the documents of title and other items to close as Agent for the Purchaser's Solicitor.

(g) As soon as possible after completion, the Vendor's Solicitor shall send to the Purchaser's Solicitor by registered post or as agreed the documents and other items and the keys (or an authority to the Auctioneers to release these) if they have not been made available on a telephone or telex instruction after completion is deemed to have taken place. The documents and items are sent by registered post or as agreed at the sole risk of the Purchaser's Solicitor.

It cannot be emphasised too strongly that solicitors should ensure that they follow these procedures strictly, for a failure to do so may lead to a claim that "good practice" has not has not been followed and so open the solicitor to a negligence claim. Furthermore, since the Code seems to require, in effect, such solicitor to give undertakings to the other solicitor, it would appear that a failure to carry out the requisite steps involves a breach of undertaking, with all the sanctions which arise thereby.[94] The Law Society's Conveyancing Committee has reiterated that its Code applies only where both solicitors have previously agreed to its operation. Indeed, the Committee expressly disclaimed responsibility for any adverse consequences of adopting completion by post[95] and, drawing attention to the risk of the loan cheque or the title documents being lost in the post, urged extreme caution in adopting the practice.[96] In view of the reliance each solicitor is putting on the other, it is suggested that, if completion by post is contemplated, the solicitors should each obtain written authority from their respective clients to complete in this way and should make adoption of the 1986 Code a special condition of the contract. In view of the point made above, it might also be wise to make it clear that each solicitor is proceeding on the basis of an "undertaking" from the other to follow the Code.

B. Date

[20.28] The matter of the precise date for completion, and the related question as to whether or not time is of the essence, were considered in earlier chapters to which reference should be made.[97]

---

94. The 1986 Code is not quite as explicit on this point as the English equivalent, which uses the word "undertakes", but arguably the substance is the same. As regards the sanctions for breach of undertakings see para **[20.15]** *supra*.

95. Fn 93 *supra*.

96. See *Newsletter* July 1987, reproduced in the *Conveyancing Handbook* p 13.23.

97. See para **[13.10]** *et seq, ante*.

C. Procedure

[20.29] The actual procedure to be followed at completion obviously varies according to the circumstances of the case and the number of interested parties present or represented at it.[98] In a simple case, the purchaser's solicitor hands over the cheque for the balance of the purchase money, which should always be in the form of a banker's draft, and the vendor's solicitor hands over the deed executed by the vendor,[99] the approved draft of this deed,[100] the original title documents,[101] the keys to the property and any undertakings necessary for that case.[102] The vendor's solicitor should never accept a personal cheque from the purchaser or his solicitor no matter how eminent he may be. Such a cheque may not be honoured and this is a risk which the vendor's solicitor must avoid at all costs.[103] If he has accepted such a cheque and it is not honoured, he will be liable in negligence for the amount of the cheque. The purchaser's solicitor should check that the current deed has been properly executed and check it against the approved draft. He should also check that all the original title documents have been handed over and compare them against the copies he has been using up to that point. It cannot be emphasised too strongly that this may be the first and last opportunity he has to "verify" the title[104] and he must seize the opportunity in his client's interest.[105] Failure to do so will almost certainly constitute negligence for which the solicitor may be sued if a defect is discovered later. It must be remembered that, if he discovers on examination a defect which goes to the root of the title, he can still raise a requisition on or make objection to the title at this late stage, ie, even though the usual time limit for this has long passed.[106] This raises another matter which he should check, namely, that there are no outstanding requisitions still awaiting a satisfactory reply from the vendor's solicitor.[107] If the vendor does not furnish such a reply at completion, the purchaser's solicitor ought not to

---

98. See *Palmer v Lark* [1945] Ch 182 at 194-5 (*per* Vaisey J).
99. See para **[20.12]** *supra.*
100. See paras **[17.06-7]** *ante.*
101. Up to this point the purchaser's solicitor will usually have seen copies only, see para **[14.42]** *et seq, supra.*
102. See para **[20.14]** *et seq, supra.*
103. See **[20.32]** *infra.*
104. See para **[14.48]** *et seq, ante.* The English Law Society officially does not approve of the common practice in England of examination of the deeds being left to completion, see Digest (Third Cumulative Supplement), Opinion No 95(a).
105. After closing the purchase on completion day, the purchaser will normally be deemed to have accepted the title. see para **[15.49]** *et seq, ante.*
106. See paras **[15.22]** and **[15.51]** *ante.*
107. See para **[20.23]** *supra.*

close the purchase unless, at the very least, the vendor's solicitor gives him an undertaking to provide a satisfactory reply, preferably by a certain time.

[20.30] The procedure may, of course, be rather more complicated in certain cases. For example, where there is an existing mortgage on the property to be discharged out of the purchase money, the solicitors may, on occasion, all meet at the vendor's mortgagee's solicitor's office.[108] In such a case the purchaser's solicitor often hands over a banker's draft[109] for the full balance of the purchase money to the vendor's solicitor who in turn hands over a cheque for the discharge money to the vendor's mortgagee's solicitor.[110] The mortgagee's solicitor then hands over to the vendor's solicitor the reconveyance or mortgage deed with endorsed receipt or release of the charge and other title deeds[111] held by the mortgagee. The vendor's solicitor then hands the deeds and keys to the purchaser's solicitor and gives an undertaking to stamp and register the reconveyance or release and send it on in due course. Otherwise, it too may be handed over to the purchaser's solicitor for stamping and registration.

(i) Purchase Price

[20.31] In strict theory the vendor is entitled to require payment in cash,[112] in legal currency.[113] He is not bound to accept a cheque, or any other form of negotiable instrument, if only because a personal cheque may not be honoured,[114] though there is nothing to stop him agreeing to accept such a cheque, however unwise that might be.[115] Needless to say the vendor's solicitor must not agree to accept a personal cheque without his client's authority and, if he does so, he will be liable if it is dishonoured and his client thereby suffers loss.[116] It used to be the practice for payment to be made by "certified" cheque, ie, a cheque drawn on the purchaser's solicitor's client account and certified by his bank as good for payment.[117] However,

---

108. See para **[20.26]** *supra.*

109. See para **[20.29]** *infra.*

110. Alternatively. the purchaser's solicitor may hand over a "split" draft, ie, two cheques, one for the vendor's mortgagee and the other for the vendor's solicitor and this is certainly the "better" practice in most, if not all, cases. See para **[20.32]** *infra.*

111. See para **[19.55]** *ante.*

112. *Cf* the deposit paid under the contract for sale see para **[10.24]** *ante.*

113. As to which see Coinage Acts 1927, 1950 and 1966; Currency (Amendment) Act 1930, Central Bank Acts 1942 and 1970, and Decimal Currency Acts 1969 and 1971.

114. *Blumberg v Life Interests and Reversionary Securities Corp* [1898] 1 Ch 27. See also *Johnston v Boyes* [1899] 2 Ch 73, followed in *Morrow v Carty* [1957] NI 174, para **[10.24]** *ante.*

115. See *Cubitt v Gamble* (1919) 35 TLR 223. See also para **[20.29]** *supra.*

116. *Pape v Westacott* [1894] 1 QB 272.

117. As to the protection afforded by such a cheque, see *Bank of Baroda Ltd v Punjab National Bank Ltd* [1944] AC 176.

this can no longer be done because some years ago the Irish banks discontinued the practice of marking, certifying and guaranteeing cheques in this way. Instead, the usual method used now in practice of effecting a guaranteed payment instead of cash is to pay by banker's draft, which is technically an order for payment of money drawn by one banker on another, but otherwise resembles a cheque.[118] A draft will not be issued unless the purchaser's solicitor lodges money to cover the amount in question, hence the importance of being put in funds before completion.

[20.32] If the property being sold is not subject to a mortgage to be discharged out of the purchase money, or if the vendor's solicitor is acting as agent for such a mortgagee, the draft may be a single one for the total balance of the purchase money owing. It has long been the view of many solicitors that the vendor ought to discharge any mortgages or charges on the property *before* closing - they are his problem and the purchaser should not be concerned with them.[119] This does, of course, put the onus on the vendor to raise any "bridging finance" necessary to secure such a discharge, thereby incurring additional expense, and so it is increasingly the practice to get the purchaser's solicitor to agree to the vendor's mortgage or charge being discharged out of the proceeds of sale received on closing. Purchaser's solicitors must be alert to the dangers of this and the Law Society's Conveyancing Committee have issued several warnings on the subject over the years,[120] which it has recently reiterated.[121] In particular the purchaser's solicitor must be mindful of his duty to his client to ensure that he obtains an unincumbered title to the property, in accordance with the contract for sale,[122] and of the requirement that the purchaser's lending institution obtains the title to the mortgage or charge it has specified.[123] This is particularly so where the purchaser's solicitor has also acted for lending institution and has issued a certificate of title to it.[124] A failure to safeguard his client's or his client's lender's interests in this regard opens the solicitor to a claim for negligence.[125] It is not sufficient to rely upon an undertaking given by the

---

[118.] *Capital and Counties Bank Ltd v Gordon* [1903] AC 240.

[119.] See paras **[2.40]** and **[16.22]** *ante*.

[120.] See the *Gazette* June 1979 and a supplement to the *Gazette* September 1983, both reproduced in the *Conveyancing Handbook* pp 11.4 and 11.13.

[121.] See the *Gazette* March 1995, p 83 and July 1995 p 212.

[122.] See fn 119 *supra*. Note also that if the vendor conveys "as beneficial owner" there is an implied covenant for "freedom from incumbrances": see para **[21.15]** *post*. Note, however, the doctrine of "feeding the estoppel": see paras **[18.33]** and **[19.56]** *ante*.

[123.] Note that under s 22 of the Building Societies Act 1989, it remains the case that a society may, in general, make housing loans by way of a first mortgage only, unless the prior mortgage is also in its favour.

[124.] See para **[15.05]** *ante*.

[125.] See *Edward Wong Finance Co Ltd v Johnson Stokes and Master* [1984] AC 296.

vendor's solicitor (which might be dishonoured), when there is a safer way of protecting his client's or his lender's interests.[126] Thus the Law Society's Conveyancing Committee has reiterated on more than one occasion that the practice of purchasers' solicitors agreeing to a special condition to the effect that "on closing the purchaser will accept the vendor's solicitor's undertaking to discharge out of the proceeds of sale the mortgage in favour of the [vendor's lending institution]" should not be adopted.[127] Instead the Committee recommends that the solicitors should agree that the purchaser's solicitor should furnish on closing *two* bank drafts: one for the redemption figure relating to the vendor's mortgage[128] and made out in favour of his mortgagee and one for the balance of the purchase money owing to the vendor and made out in favour of the vendor's solicitor.[129] The Committee has recommended a provision to cover this matter which may be put in the contract for sale, eg, by way of special condition[130]:

> When furnishing an Apportionment Account for the closing of the sale, the Vendor's Solicitors will furnish to the Purchaser's Solicitors a statement from the Vendor's Mortgagees setting out the amount required to redeem the mortgage as at the closing date together with the accruing daily rate of interest thereafter and, on closing, the Purchaser will furnish to the Vendor separate Bank Drafts for the amount required to redeem the mortgage and for the balance of the purchase monies respectively and the Vendor will forthwith discharge the mortgage debt to the Vendor's Mortgagees and will furnish to the Purchaser proper evidence of such discharge and will furnish to the Purchaser such release of the mortgage as may be appropriate.[131]

The Committee has recognised that sometimes a "three-way" closing is arranged, eg, where the vendor's mortgagee is also the purchaser's mortgagee. In such cases the lending institution may be prepared to split the purchaser's loan cheque, so that it can also be used to discharge the vendor's

---

[126.] This was the essential point of the Privy Council's decision in the *Edward Wong* case, where, it should be noted, the solicitors had acted in accordance with standard practice on completions in Hong Kong.

[127.] The *Gazette* June 1979 (*Conveyancing Handbook* p 11.4).

[128.] The Apportionment Account should, therefore, specify this: see para **[20.11]**, fn 38 *supra*.

[129.] See the *Gazette* July 1995 p 212.

[130.] See para **[10.71]** *ante*.

[131.] *Conveyancing Handbook*, p 11.4. The alternative recommended by the English Law Society to counter the dangers expressed by the *Edward Wong* case (fn 125 *supra*) is for the vendor's solicitor to secure authority from the vendor's mortgagee to receive the part of the purchase money needed to discharge its mortgage, ie, to act as its agent: see the Code for Completion by Post para 3(2) (para **[20.27]** *supra*). The problem is that lending institutions may be reluctant to give such authority and so the vendor's solicitor cannot provide the purchaser's solicitor with the written confirmation which he would need to be able to rely on this alternative.

mortgage at closing.[132] If it is proposed to adopt this procedure it is imperative that the lending institution's agreement is obtained in sufficient time (adequate notice must clearly be given to it) and the Conveyancing Committee has issued the warning that, since it departs from the recommended "two drafts" procedure, the agreement of the clients should be obtained by way of express written instructions.[133]

[20.33] In practice the receipt of the purchase money by the vendor's solicitor is treated as sufficient so far as the purchaser is concerned, because of the provisions of s 56 of the Conveyancing Act 1881. No doubt in most cases this view is justified, but it may be noted that there are limits to the protection afforded by s 56, as we discussed in an earlier chapter.[134] In certain cases, it may be the technical position that the vendor's solicitor or the other person receiving the money should have special authority to do so and the purchaser's solicitor would be entitled to require evidence of this to be produced before handing over the money Finally, it would seem that a transferee of registered land is safe in handing over the purchase money on completion in return for the transfer form and land certificate (if there is one issued), despite the fact that this does not transfer the legal ownership of the land to the purchaser, but only puts him in the position of being able to effect this transfer by lodging the form and certificate in the Land Registry and applying to be registered as the new owner.[135] But this safety should be secured by the purchaser's solicitor making a priority search before completion, but this is rarely done.[136]

(ii) Title Documents

[20.34] As mentioned earlier,[137] on completion all the title documents relating to the property are normally handed over to the purchaser's solicitor, who may be asked to sign a "schedule" listing all the documents received by him. In the case of registered land, the appropriate document of title is, of course, the land certificate, but this has frequently not been issued or has been issued to the Land Commission,[138] and so in such cases the purchaser is not entitled to require it to be handed over under the Law Society's *General Conditions of Sale (1995 Edition)*.[139]

[132.] See *Conveyancing Handbook* para 11.13 and the *Gazette* March 1995, pp 83 and 85.
[133.] The *Gazette* March 1995, p 85.
[134.] See para **[18.46]** *ante*.
[135.] See para **[12.49]** *et seq, ante*.
[136.] See para **[15.41]** *ante*.
[137.] See para **[20.29]** *supra*.
[138.] See paras **[14.31]** and **[14.33]** *ante*.
[139.] Cond 13(e): see para **[14.31]** *ante*.

[20.35] There may, of course, be certain cases where the vendor will retain the title documents and will be required to hand over, at most, certified copies of them only. We saw in an earlier chapter that this usually occurs where part only of a larger parcel of land is sold by the vendor and we discussed various contractual and statutory provisions which cover this case.[140] Indeed, it is usual in such a case for the purchaser to be required to hand over some documentary evidence of title relating to the part transferred to him. Thus, condition 34(e) of the Law Society's *General Conditions of Sale (1995 Edition)* requires, in the case of unregistered land, the purchase deed relating to the part sold to be engrossed in duplicate by the purchaser at his expense and he must then deliver to the vendor the counterpart when it is duly stamped and registered. In the case of registered land, on a sale of part only of land comprised in a folio, the Registrar may allow the transferor to retain his land certificate with an entry in it as to the part transferred, or may deliver to him a new certificate as to the part retained by him.[141]

III. AFTER COMPLETION

[20.36] Though the parties may consider that the completion day marks the end of their transaction, it will rarely, if ever, mean this, for both solicitors, especially the purchaser's, will usually have further tasks to perform before the transaction can be regarded as finally completed and their respective clients' files as closed. Once again this subject is best looked at from the point of each solicitor.

A. Vendor's Solicitor

[20.37] One matter which the vendor's solicitor will have to attend to is to discharge any undertakings he may have given, eg, in respect of discharge of a mortgage on the property[142] or, possibly, as to searches.[143] His client should be advised to cancel any insurance he has relating to the property sold and to notify the rating authority as to the change of ownership, if this has not been done already. If the property sold was leasehold, it is likely that one of the terms of the lease is that the landlord should be notified of all assignments or that they should be "registered" with him. Though, since this may involve production of a copy of the assignment, it may be arranged that the purchaser should do this. Apart from that, he must account to his client for the balance of the purchase money[144] and furnish his bill of costs. showing

---

[140.] See para **[18.102]** *et seq, ante.*

[141.] Registration of Title Act 1964, s 51(4).

[142.] See para **[20.17-8]** *supra.*

[143.] See para **[20.19]** *supra.*

[144.] Which may, of course, be needed urgently for another transaction, eg, the purchase of another property by the vendor.

the various expenses he has incurred in respect of the transaction, fees paid and, of course, his fees for doing the work. We consider the question of fees and costs later.[145]

B. Purchaser's Solicitor

There are several extremely important matters to be attended to by the purchaser's solicitor after completion.

1. Stamping

[20.38] One of the most important things to be done by the purchaser's solicitor is to see that the deed is taken to the Stamp Office for stamping.[146] There are two main reasons why this must be done. First, a deed which is not stamped or is stamped improperly is not admissible in evidence and this may cause the purchaser difficulties in future dealings with the property.[147] Secondly, the whole basis of stamp duty was changed dramatically by the Finance Act 1991.[148] It ceased to be a "voluntary" tax, in the sense that no one had a direct obligation to pay the duty and it was enforced through indirect sanctions like the admissibility point just mentioned, and became a mandatory one, whereby duty must be paid by the accountable person[149] within the specified time on any instrument liable to duty.[150] Unless written on stamped material, or lodged for adjudication,[151] the duty is payable within 30 days of the instrument's execution.[152] The 1991 Act also introduced new penalties to enforce the regime, covering both fraud and negligence.[153] These provisions are couched in very wide terms and solicitors should note that they may apply to them as well as their clients.[154] The detailed operation of the stamp duty law is outside the scope of this book,[155] but a few further words may be added.

---

[145] Paras **[20.49]** *infra*.

[146] See *New Forest Co Ltd v Revenue Commissioners* [1965] IR 172 at 176 (*per* Kenny J). See generally Donegan and Friel, *Irish Stamp Duty Law* (1995).

[147] We dealt with this matter earlier, see para **[15.13]** *ante*. See also para **[10.09]** *ante*.

[148] See Part IV thereof and *Donegan and Friel, op cit*, Ch 3.

[149] Eg, the purchaser or lessee: 1991 Act, s 96.

[150] 1991 Act, s 94, substituting a new s 1 in the Stamp Act 1891. See *Donegan and Friel, op cit*, para 3.18 *et seq*.

[151] In which case duty is payable within 14 days of notice of assessment: new s 1(3)(b) of the 1891 Act.

[152] Now s 1(3)(a): *Donegan and Friel op cit* para 3.19.

[153] 1991 Act, s 97 (substituting a new s 5 in the 1891 Act).

[154] See *Donegan and Friel, op cit*, para 3.20 *et seq* and Ch 13; *Irish Landlord and Tenant Law* para 5.51C, which considers, in particular, the exposure of solicitors under the new regime.

[155] For detailed treatment apart from *Donegan and Friel*, see also *Butterworths Tax Guide 1995-96* Part 6; and see Butterworths *Capital Tax Acts 1995-96*.

(i) Conveyances to be Stamped

[20.39] Most conveyances on sale, including sub-sales and exchanges of land, voluntary dispositions *inter vivos* and certain leases must be stamped. There are, however, several types of conveyance or transfer of land which are exempt from stamp duty.[156] For example, no stamp duty is payable on any transaction creating a joint tenancy between spouses in respect of a family home within the meaning of the Family Home Protection Act 1976,[157] where the home was immediately prior to such transaction owned by either spouse or by both spouses otherwise than as joint tenants.[158]

(ii) Rates of Duty

[20.40] Stamp duty rates are of two kinds. First, there are fixed rates which apply to certain instruments regardless of the consideration involved in the transactions to which they relate. Thus there used to be a 6d.[159] duty on contracts for sale, but this was abolished some years ago.[160] Other documents are still subject to a £10 duty eg, a conveyance or transfer made to effectuate the appointment of a new trustee.[161] Secondly, there are *ad valorem* duties which vary according to the amount of the consideration involved in the transaction in question and it is these which are of particular relevance to conveyances. The actual rates of duty charged vary according to the type of conveyance and the rates themselves have been altered several times over the years since the original rates were specified in Schedule 1 to the Stamp Act 1891.[162] Furthermore, it is crucial to note with respect to *ad valorem* rates that there are two rates, one which is the normal rate which will apply unless the instrument in question contains an appropriate certificate and a special lower rate which will apply if it does contain that certificate.[163]

(iii) Production of Conveyances

[20.41] It is crucial to remember that, whether or not stamp duty is payable, certain conveyances must be produced to the Stamp Office to be stamped with a special "Particulars Delivered" stamp denoting that it has been so produced. Failure to do this again involves a penalty[164] and absence of the

---

156. See *Donegan and Friel, op cit*, para 12.11 *et seq.*

157. See generally, para **[16.61]** *et seq, ante.*

158. 1976 Act, s 14. See para **[18.91]** *ante.*

159. Ie, pre-decimilisation currency.

160. See Finance Act 1970, s 40 and 1st Sched.

161. Stamp Act 1891, s 62; see also Finance Act 1902. s 9 and Finance (1909-10) Act 1910, s 74(6); Finance Act 1990, s 204(b). And see *Hadgett v IRC* (1877) 37 LT 612; *Re Kennaway* [1889] WN 70. *Cf Viscount Massereene v CIR* [1900] 2 IR 138.

162. See Butterworths *Capital Tax Acts 1995-96* p 41 *et seq.*

163. See para **[18.108]** *ante*. Note also the lower rates applicable to sales between relatives, see para **[18.109]** *ante.*

164. Finance Act 1994, s 107.

"PD" stamp means that the deed is not deemed to have been duly
and is not, therefore, admissible in evidence.[165] This is not the place
into the history of this requirement.[166] Suffice it to say that the pre
requirement was recently restated by s 107 of the Finance Act 1994,
amended by s 149 of the Finance Act 1995. In essence a PD stamp is now
required for transfers of the fee simple or any other interest in land and the
grant of a lease exceeding 30 years or any assignment of a lease where the
unexpired terms exceeds 30 years. The duty of complying with the
regulations, which provide for use of new forms,[167] rests on the transferee or
lessee.[168] It should be noted, however, that a PD stamp is not needed in the
case of a transaction creating a joint tenancy between the spouses pursuant
to s 14 of the Family Home Protection Act 1976, or to transfers or leases by
or to a housing authority pursuant to s 8 of the Housing (Miscellaneous
Provisions) Act 1992.

2. Registration

[20.42] Having seen to the stamping of the conveyance, the next most
important matter to be attended to by the purchaser's solicitor is registration.
In the case of unregistered land, he must see that the deed is registered in the
Registry of Deeds to secure the purchaser's priority. Furthermore, if the land
is in a compulsory registration area, ie, currently Counties Carlow, Laois and
Meath,[169] and the current transaction is the first conveyance on sale[170] since
the date of designation of the area as a compulsory registration area, the
grantee's estate or interest must be registered within six months, otherwise
he will not acquire that estate or interest.[171] If the land is already registered
land, then the grantee does not obtain any legal interest in it until he is
registered in the Land Registry as the new owner.[172]

(i) Registry of Deeds

[20.43] The subject of registration of deeds in the Registry of Deeds has
been considered elsewhere[173] and little need be added here. Registration is

---

[165.] See paras **[14.18]** and **[15.13]** *ante*.

[166.] See the discussion of its "chequered history" by Johnston J in *Hopkins v Geoghegan* [1931]
IR 135 at 142.

[167.] Stamp Duty (Particulars to be Delivered) Regulations 1995 (SI 144/1995).

[168.] Finance Act 1995, s 149, reversing s 107 of the 1994 Act. See *Donegan and Friel, op cit*,
para 13.03 *et seq*.

[169.] Since 1 January 1970, see Compulsory Registration of Ownership (Carlow, Laois and
Meath) Order 1969 (SI 87/1969). See Fitzgerald, *Land Registry Practice* (2nd ed 1995) pp
7-8.

[170.] Ie, a sale of the freehold or a grant or assignment on sale of a leasehold interest exceeding
21 years, see Registration of Title Act 1964, s 24(2).

[171.] 1964 Act, s 25. See *Fitzgerald, op cit*, p 387.

[172.] See paras **[12.05]** and **[12.49]** *et seq*. See also **[16.55]** *et seq*.

[173.] *Irish Land Law* (2nd ed, 1986), Ch 22.

a "memorial" which sets out the essential features of ~red. The memorial must comply with the statutory ontents[174] and must be lodged with the stamped deed tration, together with the appropriate fee. In practice, tains rather more detail than is strictly required.[175] ~eds for Northern Ireland some years ago pointed out ... ~is experience why deeds lodged for registration are ~~~ accepted or are later rejected on examination are omission of or improper stamping, discrepancies between the deed and the memorial and inaccurate setting out of the witnesses in the memorial.[176] Here the Dublin Solicitors Bar Association has issued similar guidelines over the years[177] and recently published a "Registration Checklist" sheet,[178] which should be pinned to every conveyancer's office wall!

(ii) Land Registry

[20.44] Where the transaction involves a transfer of land already registered, an application must be made to register the transferee as the new owner. This must be made in accordance with the rules governing such applications.[179] The transfer deed, properly stamped,[180] must be lodged with the appropriate form of application,[181] and prescribed fee,[182] in the Central Office in Dublin, or relevant local office for transmission to the Central Office.[183] The land certificate, if one exists,[184] must also be produced to the Registrar.[185] As we saw earlier, on a transfer of part only of registered land, a plan of the land sufficient to identify it on the Registry map may have to be lodged.[186]

[174.] These are discussed *ibid*, paras 22.05-8.

[175.] See the examples given by the former Registrar of Deeds for NI in Irwin, 'The Registry of Deeds for Northern Ireland' (1972) 22 NILQ 140 at 115-6.

[176.] *Irwin op cit* pp 143-4.

[177.] See, eg, the *Gazette* April 1980, reproduced in the *Conveyancing Handbook* p 13.2.

[178.] Available from law searchers, Dooley & Co, 9A Sundrive Road, Kimmage, Dublin 12.

[179.] See generally, Land Registration Rules 1972. See also McAllister, *Registration of Title in Ireland* (1973), Ch 1V.

[180.] If the original transfer is lost, a copy duly stamped may be accepted, see *Re Foley* (1951) 85 ILTR 61; *Nally v Nally* [1953] IR 19; *Gardiner v Irish Land Commission* (1976) 110 ILTR 21; see also *Fitzgerald, op cit*, p 188.

[181.] 1972 Rules, Form 17.

[182.] Fees may now be paid in cash, banker's draft, money order, postal order or cheque instead of by Land Registry stamps (which used to be the only method of payment), see Land Registration Fees Order 1991 (SI 363/1991). Payment by stamps was abolished as from 1 January 1988.

[183.] See *Fitzgerald, op cit*, Ch 22.

[184.] See para **[14.31]** *ante*.

[185.] 1972 Rules r 162. As to the Registrar's powers to order or dispense with production, sec *ibid*, rr 164-5. *Fitzgerald, op cit*, p 349 *et seq*.

[186.] See para **[18.56]** *ante*. See on mapping requirements *Fitzgerald, op cit*, Ch 4.

[20.45] In the case of an application for first registration, again the various regulations dealing with this must be complied with. These lay down the form of application[187] and prescribe the documents which must accompany the application, eg, all original title deeds, abstracts of title, contracts for or conditions of sale, searches, requisitions and replies, affidavits and statutory declarations.[188]

[20.46] From time to time the Land Registry has issued a comprehensive list of common omissions and errors made by solicitors in lodging applications relating to both dealings with registered land and applications for first registration.[189] All solicitors should study this list carefully.

3. Notices

[20.47] The purchaser's solicitor may consider it advisable in his client's interests to notify certain persons or bodies as to the transfer of ownership, eg, the local rating authority. In the case of leasehold property, the lease may require notice or "registration" of assignments with the lessor and the purchaser's solicitor may undertake to do this instead of the vendor.[190]

4. Undertakings

[20.48] Like the vendor[191] the purchaser must also discharge any undertakings he may have given, eg, to a bank in respect of a bridging loan arranged for the purchaser.[192]

C. Bill of Costs

[20.49] The last major step for each solicitor is to send his client his bill of costs, indicating the various expenses and charges incurred on behalf of the client in connection with the transaction, eg, stamp duty paid and Land Registry or Registry of Deeds fees, and, of course, the solicitor's fees for doing the work. These fees are still statutory scale fees,[193] which are *ad valorem* fees, ie, charged as a percentage of the value of the property being

---

187. 1972 Rules, r 14 and Forms 1 and 2.
188. 1972 Rules, rr 15-6; *Fitzgerald, op cit*, Ch 22.
189. See the checklists in *Fitzgerald, op cit*, pp 65-66 and 70. Note also the DSBA 'Registration Checklist' para **[20.43]** *supra*.
190. See para **[20.37]** *supra*.
191. *Ibid*.
192. See para **[20.24]** *supra*.
193. Laid down by statutory instrument made under the Solicitor's Remuneration Act 1881 in the form of Solicitors Remuneration Orders. See also *Re Boggs* (1951) 85 ILTR 1. As to the taxing of a solicitor's bill of costs, see *Morris v Allan* (1957) 91 ILTR 52; *Whitney Moore and Keller v Shipping Finance Corporation Ltd* [1964] IR 216.

conveyed.[194] If the land is registered land, the fee is lower than it would be for unregistered land, on the assumption that deduction and investigation of title in such cases is more simple.[195]

[20.50] Finally, it should be noted that a solicitor has, at common law, a lien over his client's documents in respect of his unpaid costs.[196] Furthermore, under s 3 of the Legal Practitioners (Ireland) Act 1876, which is still in force,[197] he may apply to the court by special summons for a declaration charging property recovered or preserved through his instrumentality in litigation with his taxed costs in relation to the suit.[198] The court is given power to make orders for raising and paying the costs out of the property, and any conveyance or act to defeat such a charge is void, unless made to a *bona fide* purchaser for value without notice.[199] Such an action should always be registered as a *lis pendens* against the land.[200]

[194.] Note the need to comply with the Solicitors (Interest on Client's Moneys) Regulations 1995 (SI 108/1995), made under s 73 of the Solicitors (Amendment) Act 1994.

[195.] Sec Chs 14 and 15 *ante*.

[196.] See *Brownlow v Keatinge* (1840) 2 Ir Eq R 243; *Smith v Chichester* (1842) 4 Ir Eq R 580; *Blunden v Desart* (1842) 5 Ir Eq R 221; *Taylor v Gorman* (1844) 7 Ir Eq R 259; *Molesworth v McCreith* (1845) 8 Ir Eq R 1; *Molesworth v Robbins* (1845) 8 Ir Eq R 223; *Re Bayly's Estate* (1860) 12 Ir Ch R 315; *Re Kavanagh Ltd* [1952] Ir Jur Rep 38. Note that the lien is confined to client's documents and does not extend, eg, to title deeds held by the solicitor on accountable receipt for the client's lending institution: see the Supreme Court decision in *Re Galdan Properties Ltd* [1988] IR 213.

[197.] See also Arbitration Act 1954, s 32.

[198.] See *Re Legal Practitioners (Ir) Act 1876* [1951] Ir Jur Rep 1; *Temple Press Ltd v Blogh* [1955-56] Ir Jur Rep 53; *Fitzpatrick v DAF Sales Ltd* [1988] IR 464.

[199.] No order may be made where the right to recover the costs is barred by any statute of limitations: 1876 Act, s 3.

[200.] See para **[15.45]** *ante*.

Chapter 21

POST-COMPLETION REMEDIES

[21.01] We considered in an earlier chapter the remedies available to the parties for enforcement of the contract for sale, particularly in the interim period between the date of the contract and the date of completion.[1] In this chapter we are concerned with the parties' remedies after completion. The first point to be emphasised in this connection is the operation of the doctrine of merger.[2]

I. MERGER

[21.02] The general rule is that, on completion, the contract for sale merges in the conveyance and the parties thereby lose the remedies they had for enforcement of the contract and must thereafter rely upon remedies available under the conveyance. As Porter MR put it in *Adair v Carden*[3]:

> "... I reject from consideration the evidence of correspondence and negotiations anterior to the conveyance itself; because when the transaction has been once completed by a formal deed, the rights of the parties to it must depend upon its terms, and the inferences to be derived from it."[4]

Thus, if the purchaser discovers subsequent to completion that there is a defect in his title, he cannot usually sue for breach of the contract for sale but must rely upon the covenants for title[5] in the conveyance.[6] The same rule as to the effect of merger would seem to apply to registered land,[7] except that it is not clear whether the merger occurs upon completion in the normal sense, ie, handing over the transfer deed in return for the balance of the purchase money,[8] or only upon the subsequent registration of the transferee as the new

---

1. Ch 13 *ante*.
2. See generally on this doctrine, *Irish Land Law* (2nd ed, 1986), Ch 24; *Irish Landlord and Tenant Law* para 21.19 *et seq*.
3. (1892) 29 LR Ir 469.
4. *Ibid*, p 481.
5. These are considered later see para **[21.05]** *infra*.
6. *Re Otway's Estate* (1862) 13 Ir Ch R 222 at 235 (*per* Brady LC).
7. See *Knight Sugar Co Ltd v Alberta Rly and Irrigation Co* [1938] 1 All ER 266. See also Robinson, 'Merger and Systems of Title of Land by Registration' (1973) 37 Conv 342.
8. Para **[20.25]** *ante*.

owner of the land.[9] To the extent that the vendor's handing over of the transfer deed may be said to exhaust his contractual responsibilities as regards transfer of the title to the purchaser, and completion of the transfer by registration is entirely a matter for the purchaser,[10] which he is free to perform as he chooses, though at his own risk,[11] it may be said that merger should be regarded as taking place on completion rather than on registration of the purchaser as the new owner.[12]

[21.03] It is important to recognise the limits to the doctrine of merger in this context. First, the doctrine is based upon the presumed intention of the parties[13] and must, therefore, give way to an express or implied indication that no merger is to take place. Indeed, condition 48 of the Law Society's *General Conditions of Sale (1995 Edition)* puts this principle into effect by providing:

> "Notwithstanding delivery of the Assurance of the subject property to the Purchaser on foot of the sale, all obligations and provisions designed to survive completion of the sale and all warranties in the Conditions contained, which shall not have been implemented by the said Assurance, and which shall be capable of continuing or taking effect after such completion, shall enure and remain in full force and effect."[14]

This is a very wide provision which should forestall most, if not all, arguments that a party cannot invoke the contract after completion. It should be noted, for example, that it covers not only "all obligations" but also "provisions", so that a party may even be able to invoke the arbitration provision in condition 51. The only question which will have to be determined in each case is whether the particular obligation or provision was "designed to survive completion".[15] Thus, the question becomes in every case one of construing the contract for sale to see which provisions in it, if any, are to be taken as being intended by the parties to survive completion.[16]

---

9. Para **[20.44]** *ante*.
10. Para **[20.42]** *ante*.
11. Para **[12.05]** *ante*.
12. *Cf Montgomery and Rennie v Continental Bags (NZ) Ltd* [1972] NZLR 884.
13. As it is where it applies to merger or estates of interests in land, see *Irish Land Law*, (2nd ed 1986) para 24.12. See also *McIlvenny v McKeever* [1931] NI 161; *Cherry Court v Revenue Commissioners* [1995] 2 ILRM 228.
14. See on the effect of a similar provision, *Hissett v Reading Roofing Co Ltd* [1970] 1 All ER 122.
15. It is arguable that "designed" is not confined to those expressed in the contract, so that it may even include implied obligations, eg, implied warranty as to fitness for human habitation in respect of new houses, see para **[4.12]** *et seq, ante. Cf Adair v Carden* (1892) 29 LR Ir 469 at 481 (*per* Porter MR). See also para **[17.26]** *ante*.
16. See Bowen LJ in *Palmer v Johnson* (1884) 13 QBD 351 at 357 and *Clarke v Ramuz* (1891) 2 QB 456 at 461.

Thus the following contractual provisions have on occasion been held to survive completion: one relating to vacant possession on completion[17]; one relating to compensation for misdescription[18]; one relating to an indemnity against tenant's claims[19]; one relating to erection and completion of a house.[20]

[21.04] Quite apart from the question of intention of the parties, the courts have recognised other limitations or exceptions to the general rule of merger of the contract in the conveyance. Thus, if the purchaser can prove the existence of a *collateral* warranty, ie, one independent of the main contract for sale, he can sue on it, for merger of the contract does not affect it. Thus in *Carrigy v Brock*,[21] on a sale by auction of land held under a lease containing the usual covenant against alienation without the consent of the lessor, the auctioneer signed and delivered to the purchaser a memorandum containing a stipulation that the purchaser would not have to pay the sum demanded by the lessor for giving his consent.[22] The subsequent deed of assignment made no mention of this and the purchaser was later compelled, on default of the vendor, to pay the sum in order to validate his title. The Irish Court of Exchequer held that the auctioneer's memorandum was a collateral document which did not merge in the deed of assignment and so the purchaser was entitled to sue the vendor for recovery of the sum paid by him.[23] It is also settled that there are certain other remedies which survive completion. Where fraud is involved, the conveyance may be set aside on application by the party damaged by it, ie, rescission may be a post-completion remedy as well as a post-contractual remedy.[24] Rescission may also be available in certain circumstances on the ground of mistake.[25] Furthermore, mistake may be a ground for invoking a different remedy, namely, rectification of the conveyance.[26]

[17.] *Hissett v Reading Roofing Co Ltd* [1970] 1 All ER 122.
[18.] *Palmer v Johnson* (1884) 13 QBD 351.
[19.] *Eagon v Dent* [1965] 3 All ER 334. *Cf Adair v Carden* (1892) 29 LR Ir 469.
[20.] *Lawrence v Cassel* [1930] 2 KB 83; *Hancock v Brazier (Anerley) Ltd* [1966] 3 All ER 901. See generally, para **[4.12]** *et seq, ante*.
[21.] (1871) IR 5 CL 501.
[22.] He had announced at the auction that the vendor had agreed to pay it.
[23.] An alternative remedy might have been to sue for rectification of the deed of assignment, see para **[21.39]** *infra*.
[24.] See paras **[13.57]** *et seq, ante* and **[21.35]** *et seq, infra*.
[25.] Para **[21.37]** *infra*.
[26.] Para **[21.39]** *infra*.

II. REMEDIES

A. Covenants for Title

[21.05] The object of the covenants for title which may be expressed or implied in a conveyance[27] is to protect the purchaser against the operation of the doctrine of merger,[28] by trying to ensure that he will be able to sue the vendor for breach of covenant in the event of a defect in title first coming to light after completion.[29] The concept of covenants for title goes back to the earliest days of the feudal system, under which, on a grant of land, a lord was required to warrant his tenant's title.[30] Later, after *Quia Emptores* 1290, prohibited further *subinfeudation* of freehold land,[31] it became the practice to insert express warranties as to title in conveyances of such land. It was from this medieval law of warranties that the modern form of covenants for title developed.[32] By the nineteenth century various express covenants for title were inserted by conveyancers in conveyances of land,[33] eg, that the grantor had a good title or full power to make the conveyance,[34] for quiet enjoyment,[35] freedom from incumbrances[36] or for further assurance.[37] These express covenants were extremely verbose clauses, which is hardly surprising during a time when a conveyancer was paid according to the number of words in the conveyance.[38] This was not changed until the 1880s[39] and it is no coincidence that the Conveyancing Act 1881 contained several provisions designed to simplify or shorten conveyances. One of

---

27. See para **[18.100]** *ante.*
28. See para **[21.02]** *et seq, supra.*
29. See the discussion by Powell J in *Re Geraghty and Lyon's Contract* (1919) 53 ILTR 57. See also *Soper v Arnold* (1887) 37 Ch D 96 at 101-2 (*per* Cotton LJ) (affd (1889) 14 App Cas 429).
30. See Bailey, 'Warranties of Land in the Thirteenth Century' (1942-4) 8 CLJ .274 and (1945-7) 9 CLJ 82.
31. See *Irish Land Law* (2nd ed, 1986), para 2.42 *et seq.*
32. *Ibid,* para 4 072.
33. See *Wood v Jamieson* (1844) 6 Ir Eq R 420; *Re Gardiner* (186l) 11 Ir Ch R 519.
34. *Delmer v McCabe* (1863) 14 ICLR 377; *Doyle v Kinsley* (1864) 9 Ir Jur (ns) 26. See further para **[21.27]** *infra.*
35. *Doyle v Hort* (1880) 4 LR Ir 455. See further, para **[21.30]** *infra.*
36. *Williams v Williams* (1861) 12 Ir Ch R 507; *Re Barker's Estate* (1879) 3 LR Ir 395. See further para **[21.31]** *infra.*
37. *Maguire v Armstrong* (1814) 2 Ba & B 538; *Doyle v Kinsley* (1864) 9 Ir Jur (ns) 26; *Weldon v Bradshaw* (1873) IR 7 Eq 168; *Rorke v Sherlock* (1877) IR 11 Eq 510. See further para **[21.33]** *infra.*
38. Scale fees based on consideration etc were introduced by the Solicitors Remuneration Act 1881.
39. *Ibid.*

these is s 7 which implies various covenants for title, set out at length in the section,[40] in conveyances of land, provided each conveyance contains the vital formula or "magic phrase" specified in the section as necessary for incorporation of the covenant in the conveyance.[41] Section 7 does not, however, apply to the grant of a lease at a rent,[42] but covenants for title on the part of a landlord in such a case are implied by s 41 of Deasy's Act 1860, namely that the landlord has a good title to make the lease and that the tenant will have quiet and peaceable enjoyment without interruption by the landlord or "any person whomsoever"[43] during the term, so long as the tenant performs his obligations under the lease.[44] Since the provisions of Deasy's Act have been considered elsewhere,[45] it is proposed to concentrate in the following paragraphs on the provisions of s 7 of the 1881 Act.[46]

[21.06] First, however, two preliminary points may be made. One is that there is nothing to stop the parties or their conveyancers inserting express covenants for title in the conveyance[47] and this is still quite commonly done in certain cases, eg, on the grant of a new lease.[48] The other is that in theory there would seem to be no reason why the statutory implied covenants should not be incorporated in transfers of registered land by the use of the

---

[40.] In the form which had by then become common for express covenants.

[41.] See on this section, *Re Geraghty and Lyon's Contract* (1919) 53 ILTR 57. See also *Re Hume's Estate* (1905) 5 NIJR 196; *Cherry Court v Revenue Commissioners* [1995] 2 ILRM 228.

[42.] Section 7(5). *Cf* an assignment of an existing lease, para **[21.15]** *infra*.

[43.] An express covenant is usually confined to interruption by the landlord or persons lawfully claiming through him see *Bowes v Dublin Corporation* [1965] IR 476; *Lapedus v Glavey* (1965) 99 ILTR 1. See also *Irish Land Law*, (2nd ed 1986) paras 17.042 and 17.052; *Irish Landlord and Tenant Law* Ch 14; Laffoy, *Irish Conveyancing Precedents* Precedent L.2.2.

[44.] See *Carew v Jackman* [1966] IR 177. As to other implied covenants in leases, see *Irish Land Law* (2nd ed 1986), paras 17.052-4.

[45.] *Irish Landlord and Tenant Law*, Ch 14.

[46.] As regards the former English provisions, *viz* Law of Property Act 1925, s 76 and Sched 2, which are very similar to the 1881 provisions, see Bicknell, 'Implied Covenants for Title' (1943) 7 Conv 3; Martin, 'Acts of Omission as Breaches of Covenants for Title' (1907) 23 LQR 3351: Pritchard, 'Mortgages and Covenants for Title' (1964) 28 Conv 205; Russell, 'Covenants for Title: Omissions' (1967) 31 Conv 268 and 'Covenants for Title: Implication' (1968) 32 Conv 123. See also Barnsley, *Conveyancing Law and Practice* (3rd ed, 1988), Ch 23. Those provisions have recently been replaced by new implied covenants, depending upon whether the conveyance is made with "full" or "limited" title guarantee, under the Law of Property (Miscellaneous Provisions) Act 1994.

[47.] See the discussion by Powell J in *Re Geraghty and Lyon's Contract* (1919) 53 ILTR 57, wherein he suggests that under an "open" contract the purchaser is entitled to require the vendor to enter into the "usual" covenants for title. see pp 58-9.

[48.] See *Irish Landlord and Tenant Law*, Ch 14. See also *O'Connor v Foley* [1906] 1 IR 20 (covenant for further assurance in assignment of lease).

appropriate "magic phrase," and this is sometimes done. Indeed, a note attached to the standard transfer form contained in the Schedule to the Land Registration Rules 1972, suggests expressly that this may be done "if desired".[49] This ties in with the general provision that, on registration of a transferee as full owner of land, the transfer operates as a conveyance by deed within the meaning of the Conveyancing Acts.[50] However, it may be questioned whether such incorporation will achieve any practical benefit for the transferee. It is doubtful if it will except in special cases, eg, where the transferor is transferring a qualified or possessory title only, so that the transferee wants protection against interests or rights subsisting against the land but not noted on the register.[51] In the case of transfer of an absolute title, it is provided expressly that the transfer operates subject to all registered burdens and unregistered ones affecting land without registration,[52] so that it would seem that the implied covenants for title could not be invoked to protect the transferee against such unregistered burdens later coming to light.[53] This, however, is a matter of controversy and, until the matter is judicially determined, no final conclusion can be drawn.

1. Implied Covenants

[21.07] Before considering the various covenants implied in different cases under s 7 of the Conveyancing Act 1881, it may be useful to examine some general points which should be noted about the operation of the section. By and large these are relevant to all the covenants and to every case coming within the section.

(i) General Points

(a) Conveys and Is Expressed to Convey

[21.08] One of the most controversial aspects of s 7 is that it is stated expressly that it operates to imply covenants for title only if the person in question "conveys and is expressed to convey" in a certain capacity, eg, as beneficial owner.[54] It might have been expected that the intention was that the protection afforded by the covenants should be provided wherever a

---

49. Form 19 (transfer of freehold property by a registered full owner), note (4).
50. Registration of Title Act 1964, s 52(1). See *Irish Land Law* (2nd ed, 1986), para 21.45.
51. See *Irish Land Law* (2nd ed, 1986), paras 21.25-6. The same may apply to a transfer of a good leasehold title. see *ibid*, paras 21.27-8.
52. 1964 Act, s 2(1).
53. *Cf* the provisions concerning "overriding interests" in r 77 of the English Land Registration Rules 1925, which have given rise to considerable controversy, see Potter, 'Covenants for Title and Overriding Interests' (1942) 58 LQR 356; Megarry, (1941) 57 LQR 564. See also Barnsley, *Conveyancing Law and Practice* (3rd ed, 1988), p 608 *et seq*.
54. See para **[21.15]** *infra*.

person was expressed to convey in a stated capacity, ie, that the grantee of a conveyance should not be concerned with the question of whether or not the grantor actually had that capacity. But the insertion of the antecedent words "conveys and" obviously suggests that the draftsman[55] intended that the covenants should operate only where the grantor both actually had the capacity in question and also was expressed to convey in the same capacity. This interpretation obviously reduces the protection afforded by the covenants, but, though there appears to be no authority on the point in Ireland, English decisions suggest that it is nevertheless the correct one.[56] Though, in view of the absence of Irish authority, it is to be noted that earlier English decisions suggested that the grantor's actual capacity was irrelevant, ie, that what was required was simply that he *purported* to convey and was expressed to convey in a stated capacity[57] The result of these doubts about the application of s 7 is that, in practice, it may fail to achieve what was precisely its function, namely, to operate as a piece of statutory "shorthand" by saving conveyancers from having to insert express covenants for title. It would appear that the only safe course for conveyancers to adopt to ensure that the grantee obtains full protection is to insist upon insertion of express covenants for title and not to rely upon the statutory implied ones. That, however, is rarely, if ever, done and purchaser's solicitors rely instead on the preservation of contractual rights by the "non-merger" provision in the Law Society's standard contract form.[58]

(b) Stated Capacity

[21.09] Section 7 does not apply unless the grantor is expressed to convey in one of the capacities mentioned in the section, ie, the conveyance must contain one of the statutory formulae or "magic phrases".[59] We consider what these are below.[60]

---

55. It seems that they were added at the last moment to the draft Bill which became the 1881 Act, see Russell 'Covenants for Title: Implication' (1968) 32 Conv 123 at 124.

56. *Fay v Miller, Wilkins & Co* [1941] Ch 360 at 363 (*per* Greene MR) and 366 (*per* Clauson LJ); *Pilkington v Wood* [1953] Ch 770 at 777 (*per* Harman J); *Re Robertson's Application* [1969] 3 All ER 257 at 758 (*per* Megarry J). These were all decisions on s 76 of the Law of Property Act 1925, which replaced s 7 of the 1881 Act in England, but retained the wording under discussion.

57. See *David v Sabin* [1893] 1 Ch 523 (tenant for life conveying "as beneficial owner"); *Eastwood v Ashton* [1915] AC 900 (vendor had lost title to a squatter by adverse possession); *Wise v Whitburn* [1924] 1 Ch 460 (executors assigning "as personal representatives" to a purchaser after having assented to the vesting of the property in a life tenant); *Parker v Judkin* [1931] 1 Ch 475 (personal representatives conveying "as beneficial owners").

58. See para **[21.03]** *supra*.

59. Section 7(4). See *Cherry Court v Revenue Commissioners* [1995] 2 ILRM 228.

60. Para **[21.15]** *infra*

(c) Variations

[21.10] The implied covenants may be varied or extended by deed and, where so varied or extended, they operate, so far as may be, in the same manner and with all the same incidents, effects and consequences as if the variations or extensions were directed to be implied by the section.[61] Indeed, it may be advisable to restrict the scope of the implied covenants in certain cases, eg, on assignment of a lease, where, if the vendor assigns "as beneficial owner", there is an implied covenant that all rents reserved by the lease have been paid and all covenants, conditions and agreements have been observed and performed up to the time of conveyance.[62] It seems, however, that there is a limit to how far the courts will allow a variation to reduce the scope of the covenants for title, eg, it must not destroy their effect altogether because the vendor remains subject to the general rule that he must show good title to the property.[63] However, there is nothing to stop the purchaser agreeing to buy the property subject, eg, to an incumbrance which would otherwise be a defect in title, in which case he cannot invoke the covenants for title in respect of that incumbrance.[64] The reason for this lies in the provision mentioned in the next paragraph.

(d) Subject-Matter of the Grant

[21.11] Under s 7 the covenants for title are implied only "as regards the subject-matter or share of subject-matter expressed to be conveyed.[65] The result is that, if the grantor conveys only such title as he has, the purchaser must be satisfied with this and cannot invoke the covenants to complain about any defect in that title.[66] Furthermore, it seems to follow that, in the case of a registered land transfer omitting the words of limitation for a fee simple, the purchaser again cannot invoke the covenants for title. Such a transfer operates to pass to the transferee the fee simple or other interest which the transferor had power to convey,[67] so that the purchaser cannot

---

[61.] Section 7(6). See *Butler v Mountview Estates Ltd* [1951] 2 KB 563.

[62.] *Cf* cond 10(c) of Law Society's *General Conditions of Sale* (1995 ed). See para **[14.75]** *ante.*

[63.] See *Watling v Lewis* [1911] 1 Ch 414.

[64.] See the discussion in *Re Geraghty and Lyon's Contract* (1919) 53 ILTR 57 at 58-9 (*per* Powell J).

[65.] Section 7(1).

[66.] *May v Platt* [1900] 1 Ch 616; *George Wimpey & Co v Sohn* [1967] Ch 487 at 505 (*per* Harman LJ) and 509 (*per* Russell LJ); *Re Geraghty and Lyon's Contract* (1919) 53 ILTR 57 (personal representatives conveying "as beneficial owners").

[67.] See para **[18.88]** *ante.* This is one reason for continuing to include words of limitation in registered land transfers.

complain if it subsequently turns out that the transferor had no power to convey the fee simple.

(e) Grantee's Knowledge

[21.12] It seems to be settled, however, that the covenants for title do cover defects in title or incumbrances fully known to the grantee at the time of the conveyance; indeed, even ones recited in the conveyance.[68] The grantor escapes liability only if the conveyance is made expressly subject to the defect or incumbrance.[69]

(f) Joint and Several Covenants

[21.13] So far as the covenantors are concerned in a conveyance by more than one person, s 7(1) provides that the covenants are implied "by *each* person who conveys",[70] which suggests that their liability is several, ie, there is an independent cause of action against each of them.[71] On the other hand, in the case of a conveyance to more than one person, s 7(1) states that the covenants are implied "with the persons jointly if more than one, to whom the conveyance is made, or with the persons jointly, if more than one, to whom the conveyance is made as joint tenants, or with each of the persons, if more than one, to whom the conveyance is made as tenants in common." In other words, the covenantees' rights are joint and they must join together in suing for breach of covenant unless the conveyance is made to them as tenants in common, in which case their rights are several and each of them can sue separately.[72]

(ii) The Covenants

[21.14] As was mentioned earlier,[73] s 7 of the Conveyancing Act 1881, implies covenants according to the capacity in which the grantor conveys and is expressed to convey the property. The terms of these covenants are set out in detail in the section with an extreme verbosity which has been criticised many times.[74] In the following paragraphs we attempt to

---

[68.] *Page v Midland Rly* [1894] 1 Ch 11; *GW Rly Co v Fisher* [1905] 1 Ch 316. See also *Re Geraghty and Lyon's Contract* (1919) 53 ILTR 57 at 59 (*per* Powell J).

[69.] Para **[21.10]** *supra*.

[70.] Italics added.

[71.] Ie "each" is a word of severance, see *Collins v Prosser* (1823) 1 B & C 682. See also *Irish Land Law* (2nd ed, 1986), para 7.15.

[72.] As to joint tenants and tenants in common, see generally, *Irish Land Law* (2nd ed, 1986), Ch 7; Lyall, *Land Law in Ireland* (1994), Ch 16.

[73.] See paras **[21.05]** and **[21.08]** *supra*.

[74.] See Russell 'Brevity v Verbosity' (1962) 26 Conv 45. The English Law Property (Miscellaneous Provisions) Act 1994, while retaining to some extent the substance of the old covenants, reduces dramatically their wording: see para **[21.05]** fn 46 *supra*.

summarise the covenants only and readers should refer to the section itself for their full wording. We then go on to consider their effect in more detail and their enforceability.

(a) As Beneficial Owner

[21.15] In a conveyance for valuable consideration,[75] other than a mortgage,[76] by a person who conveys and is expressed to convey "as beneficial owner," a covenant is implied on the part of the grantor which has four parts[77]: (1) that he has full power to convey the property; (2) that the grantee will have quiet enjoyment without lawful interruption or disturbance; (3) that the grantee will receive the property freed from incumbrances; (4) that the grantor will do anything reasonably requested in order further to assure the property to the grantee.[78] In the case of an assignment of an existing lease,[79] a further covenant, ie, in addition to the four-part one just mentioned, is implied consisting of two parts: (1) that the lease is valid and subsisting; (2) that the rent has been paid and the covenants in the lease have been duly observed and performed.[80] It is important to note that these covenants are not absolute covenants for title, but are qualified in several respects, as we discuss later.[81]

[21.16] On a conveyance by way of mortgage, in which the mortgagor conveys and is expressed to convey as beneficial owner, the same four-part or, in the case of leasehold property, six-part covenant is implied,[82] but with one important difference.[83] That is that the covenant is an absolute one and is not qualified in the way we discuss later.[84] However, there are some variations in the terms of the covenant to take account of the nature of a

---

75. Which includes marriage, see *Irish Land Law* (2nd ed, 1986), paras 9.042 and 9.077. Note. however, that in the covenants themselves a "purchase for value" does not include a gift in consideration of marriage, see para **[21.23]** *infra*.
76. See para **[21.16]** *infra*.
77. Ie, rather than 4 separate covenants, see *David v Sabin* [1893] 1 Ch 523 at 531 (*per* Lindley LJ).
78. Section 7(1)(A). It is arguable that (2) and (3) are really the same, in the sense that they form part of one obligation, see para **[21.31]** *infra*. Cf Russell, 'The Principal Covenants for Title' (1970) 34 Conv 178 at 187.
79. *Cf* the grant of a new lease at a rent, see para **[21.05]** *supra*. But it would appear that s 7 of the 1881 Act could apply to a grant of a lease at a premium only, ie, without reservation of a rent.
80. Section 7(1)(B).
81. See para **[21.23]** *infra*.
82. Section 7(1)(C) and (D).
83. See Pritchard 'Mortgagees and Covenants for Title' (1964) 28 Conv 205. *Cf* a conveyance by a person "as mortgagee" para **[21.18]** *infra*.
84. Para **[21.23]** *infra*.

mortgage transaction. Thus the part of the covenant for quiet enjoyment arises only on the mortgagee taking possession on default by the mortgagor in paying principal or interest.[85] The part of the covenant for further assurance operates at the cost of the mortgagor, ie, covenantor, so long as his equity of redemption[86] subsists.[87] And, in the case of a mortgage of leasehold property, the part of the further covenant relating to rent and covenants specifies that the mortgagor will pay the rent and perform and observe the covenants in the future, so long as any money remains owing on the security of the mortgage.

(b) As Settlor

[21.17] On a conveyance by way of settlement, in which a person conveys and is expressed to convey "as settlor," the only covenant implied is one for further assurance.[88] But in this case the covenant is even more limited than in the case of a conveyance by a person as beneficial owner.[89]

(c) As Trustee or Similar Owner

[21.18] In any conveyance, in which any person conveys and is expressed to convey in one of the following capacities, ie, "as trustee", "as mortgagee," "as personal representative", "as committee of a lunatic",[90] or under an order of the court, there is again only one covenant implied, a covenant against incumbrances, which is also even more limited than in the case of a conveyance by a person as beneficial owner.[91] It would seem to be proper for a tenant for life conveying under the Settled Land Acts to do so "as trustee", since he is a trustee of the exercise of his statutory powers,[92] though there is some authority for saying that he may convey "as beneficial owner".[93] On a conveyance to give effect to a sub-sale, ie, a conveyance by the original vendor to the sub-purchaser, with the original purchaser joining in, the original vendor may convey "as trustee" instead of together with the original purchaser "as beneficial owner".[94] On a transfer of a mortgage by the

---

[85.] See *Irish Land Law*, (2nd ed 1986) para 13.042 *et seq*.

[86.] See *ibid* para 12.05.

[87.] Normally it operates "on the request and at the cost of any person to whom the conveyance is expressed to be made". see s 7(1)(A).

[88.] Section 7(1)(E). Note that there is, of course, no requirement that the conveyance should be for valuable consideration.

[89.] See para **[21.24]** *infra*.

[90.] See *Irish Land Law* (2nd ed, 1986), para 25.17.

[91.] See para **[21.24]** *infra*.

[92.] See *Irish Land Law* (2nd ed, 1986), paras 8.058-9.

[93.] *Re Ray* [1896] 1 Ch 468 at 472 (*per* Lindley LJ). See Laffoy, *Irish Conveyancing Precedents* Precedent E.4.1.

[94.] Hallett *Conveyancing Precedents* (1965) p 227; *Laffoy, op cit*, Precedent E.10.1; *cf* Parker *Modern Conveyancing Precedents* (1964) p 18. See also (1962) 106 Sol Jo 132. And see para **[21.19]** *infra*.

mortgagee,[95] it would seem proper for him to convey "as beneficial owner" rather than "as mortgagee", since he is the full owner of the mortgage.[96] It should also be noted that it is provided that the covenant for title is implied in any assent signed by a personal representative unless the assent provides otherwise.[97] Thus there is no necessity to use the incorporating formula "as personal representative" in the assent; all that is required is that it should be signed by the personal representative.

(d) By Direction of Another Person

[21.19] Where a person conveys by the direction of another person who is expressed to direct as beneficial owner, then the same covenants are implied on the part of that other person as if he had himself conveyed and been expressed to convey as beneficial owner.[98] This provision may be useful where there is a sub-sale and the original vendor conveys direct to the sub-purchaser,[99] at the direction of the original purchaser.[100]

(e) Husband and Wife

[21.20] Where a wife conveys and is expressed to convey as beneficial owner, and the husband also so conveys, the wife is deemed to convey and to be expressed to convey by direction of her husband, as beneficial owner.[101] Furthermore, in addition to the covenant implied on the part of the wife, there are also implied on the part of the husband covenants as if he directed the wife to convey and covenants in the same terms as the covenant implied on the part of the wife.[102] Thus a husband in such a case could find himself liable for a breach of covenant by his wife. This provision seems to be somewhat out of keeping with the modern concept of a married woman being treated as a *feme sole* with respect to her own property.[103] It should also be noted that care should be exercised in the wording of a conveyance by a wife of a "family home" within the meaning of the Family Home Protection Act 1976.[104] Her husband's consent should not be signified by his joining in the conveyance but by means of a certificate of consent contained

---

[95.] See *Irish Land Law* (2nd ed 1986), para 13.122 *et seq.*

[96.] Parker, *Modern Conveyancing Precedents* (1964) pp 159-60. *Cf* Hallett, *Conveyancing Precedents* (1965) p 692.

[97.] Succession Act 1965, s 52(6). See Brady, *Succession Law in Ireland* (2nd ed, 1995), para [10.47].

[98.] Section 7(2).

[99.] See para **[21.18]** *supra.*

[100.] See (1962) 106 Sol Jo 132.

[101.] Section 7(3), and see para **[21.19]** *supra.*

[102.] *Ibid.*

[103.] See *Irish Land Law* (2nd ed, 1986), para 25.09 *et seq.*

[104.] See para **[16.61]** *et seq, ante.*

in or endorsed on the conveyance,[105] otherwise he may find himself liable on the covenants for title.

2. *Their Enforceability*

[21.21] There are two matters to be considered. The first is the extent of the benefit of the covenants in any particular case and how far they may be enforced by persons other than the original covenantee. The other is the extent of the burden of the covenants and their enforceability against persons other than the original covenantor.

(i) Benefit

[21.22] It is provided expressly that the benefit of any implied covenant is "annexed and incident to" and goes with the estate or interest of the covenantee and may be enforced by every person in whom that estate or interest is, for whole or part, vested from time to time.[106] It is to be noted that a successor in title will be able to sue only if he succeeds to the same estate or interest conveyed by the original covenantor, eg, if the grantee of a conveyance of the freehold subsequently mortgages the property by demise, the mortgagee cannot sue on the grantor's covenants.[107] However, a successor in title of a covenantee who procured the original conveyance by fraud may still sue provided he can establish that he is a *bona fide* purchaser for value without notice of the fraud.[108] Though a person may succeed to the benefit of a covenant for title entered into by a vendor in a sale which was a link in a chain of title consisting of several transactions, several of which are ones intermediate between that person's purchase and the sale by the vendor-covenantor, he may have difficulties in practice in suing on the covenants. First, there may not be an unbroken scheme of protection, because each vendor in the chain of title may not have been expressed to convey in the requisite capacity.[109] Secondly, it is settled that the onus of proving who in the chain of title has been guilty of a breach of covenant rests on the plaintiff and it may not be always possible to discharge this onus.[110] And, of course, having done this, the plaintiff may find that that person is deceased and his estate has been distributed or he is a person who is not worth suing. Apart from these problems, in many cases the covenants are so

---

[105.] See paras **[16.69]** and **[18.115]** *ante*.

[106.] Section 7(6).

[107.] Note that s 7(6) of the 1881 Act conforms with the general provisions as to the benefit of covenants contained in s 58 of the same Act, see *Irish Land Law* (2nd ed, 1986), para 19.20. It is not clear that the position was any different in England as a result of the wider wording of s 78 of the Law of Property Act 1925; see Pritchard, 'Mortgagees and Covenants for Title' (1964) 28 Conv 205.

[108.] *David v Sabin* [1893] 1 Ch 523.

[109.] See *Wyld v Silver* [1963] 1 QB 169.

[110.] See *Howard v Maitland* (1883) 11 QBD 695; *Stoney v Eastbourne* [1927] Ch 367.

qualified in relation to their burden that the plaintiff may again find that he has no remedy at all.

(ii) Burden

[21.23] Where a person conveys as beneficial owner,[111] his liability as covenantor is personal to him and there is no question of his successors in title being liable on his covenant. They will be liable only on covenants entered into by them and this is why, as we mentioned in the previous paragraph, a subsequent purchaser's protection depends often on establishing an unbroken chain of covenants entered into at each link or transaction relating to the property. But, even as regards each covenantor himself, his liability is not usually absolute or unlimited. Except in the case of a mortgage,[112] on a conveyance as beneficial owner the covenantor's liability extends only to the acts or omissions of (1) himself; (2) anyone through whom he derives title otherwise than by purchase for value[113]; (3) any person claiming by, through or under him, or some person within (2); (4) any person claiming in trust for him.[114]

[21.24] Thus a person conveying as beneficial owner is not liable for the acts or omissions of his predecessors, unless he derives title from such a person otherwise than for value. Thus in a series of successive conveyances for value, each purchaser's protection depends more on the investigation of title by his solicitor than on the covenants for title in his conveyance, since these provide protection only for the period which extends from the last conveyance to the vendor.[115] Thus if A conveyed to B who in turn conveyed to C, C could not sue B on his covenants in respect of A's acts. On the other hand, C could sue B on his covenants in respect of A's acts if A had instead devised the land to B or had it settled on him by way of gift or in consideration of marriage. The only case where, on a conveyance for value as beneficial owner, the covenantor is liable for predecessor's acts, is in a conveyance by way of mortgage.[116]

[21.25] A person conveying as beneficial owner is, however, liable for the acts or omissions of persons deriving title under him,[117] but not, be it noted, his successors in title.[118] In other words, he is liable for the acts or omissions

---

[111.] See para **[21.15]** *et seq, supra.*
[112.] See para **[21.16]** *supra* and **[21.24]** *infra*
[113.] Which does not include a conveyance in consideration of marriage.
[114.] *David v Sabin* [1893] 1 Ch 523 at 532 (*per* Lindley LJ).
[115.] *Ibid,* p 534 (*per* Lindley LJ). See also *Re Geraghty and Lyon's Contract* (1919) 53 ILTR 57 at 58 (*per* Powell J).
[116.] See the wording of the covenants in s 7(1)(C) and (D) of 1881 Act.
[117.] Section 7(1)(A) refers to persons claiming "by, through or under" him. In respect of the covenantor's predecessors, it refers simply to persons "through" whom he derives title, para **[21.24]** *supra.*
[118.] *David v Sabin* [1893] 1 Ch 523 at 544 (*per* AL Smith LJ).

of a tenant to whom he lets the land or a mortgagee in whose favour he mortgages it, but not a purchaser to whom he conveys the property outright.

3. Their Effect

[21.26] Having considered the extent of the covenants' enforceability, it may be useful to examine the precise effect of the main implied covenants, or, rather, the four parts of the main implied covenant.[119] As we have already seen,[120] this effect may vary from case to case, ie, according to the capacity in which the grantor conveys the property.

(i) Full Power to Convey

[21.27] That part of the main implied covenant to the effect that the grantor has full power to convey the property relates only to the "subject-matter expressed to be conveyed".[121] For this reason the implied covenant may be of little value in a transfer of registered land without words of limitation, for in such a case the transfer operates to convey the fee simple or *other the whole interest which the transferor had power to convey.*[122] If in fact the grantor has none, the transfer operates to convey none and the grantee cannot claim that it purports to do otherwise, so that he cannot sue for breach of covenant. If, however, the transfer does contain words of limitation, it purports to convey the estate which they indicate and so the grantee may be able to sue if it turns out that the grantor did not have power to convey it. It is also the case that this part of the covenant is confined by reference to the subject-matter expressed to be conveyed "subject as, if so expressed, and in the manner in which, it is expressed to be conveyed".[123] In other words, the grantee cannot sue for breach of covenant in respect of a defect expressly subject to which the conveyance is made.[124] Though, as we saw earlier, if the conveyance is not made expressly subject to it, the grantee is not debarred from suing because he knew of the defect or, indeed, it was apparent on the fact of the conveyance by, eg, being referred to in the recitals.[125]

[21.28] The covenantor is liable under this part of the covenant if he himself, or some person for whom he is responsible,[126] has created a defect in title, or

---

[119.] See para **[21.15]** *supra*.

[120.] See para **[21.14]** *et seq, supra*.

[121.] 1881 Act, s 7(1)(A).

[122.] See para **[18.88]** *ante*. This point has even greater force in England, where such a rule applies to unregistered land as well as registered land, see *Irish Land Law*, (2nd ed 1986) para 4.030.

[123.] 1881 Act, s 7(1)(A).

[124.] *Re Geraghty and Lyon's Contract* (1919) 53 ILTR 57 at 59 (*per* Powell J).

[125.] Para **[21.12]** *supra*.

[126.] See para **[21.25]** *ante*.

allowed it to come into existence, which prevents the grantee obtaining the estate or interest purported to be conveyed. Thus he is liable if he has previously conveyed or leased part of the land to be conveyed to the grantee,[127] or created a right of way over it[128] or allowed a squatter to obtain title to it by adverse possession.[129] Though in the last case there may be difficulties if the grantee cannot establish when the adverse possession began, so that he may fail to prove to the satisfaction of the court that the omission in question was the vendor's.[130] It must be emphasised again that the vendor is not liable for the acts or omissions of his predecessors, so that the grantee cannot sue the grantor for breach of covenant on eviction by someone claiming by title paramount, ie, through the act or omission of some previous owner.[131] Whether the grantee can sue the previous owner depends upon the circumstances of the case. Thus, if what had happened was that A had conveyed the land to B and had then purported to convey it to C, who in turn had purported to convey it to D, on D's eviction by B, D cannot sue C on the implied covenant, but he may be able to sue A. This depends on whether the conveyance from A to C incorporated the implied covenant, for, if it did, the conveyance to B was clearly a breach of it and D can sue to enforce the benefit of it as a successor in title of C.[132]

[21.29] It would appear that a breach of this part of the covenant is a single one occurring at the date of execution of the conveyance, so that the limitation period begins to run then.[133] Damages should be assessed as at that date, on the basis of the difference between the value of the property as

---

127. *May v Platt* [1900] 1 Ch 616. See also *David v Sabin* [1893] 1 Ch 523 (mortgage); *Jackson v Bishop* (1979) 48 P & CR 57 (double conveyance); *AJ Dunning & Sons (Shopfitters) Ltd v Sykes & Son (Poole) Ltd* [1987] 1 All ER 700 (registered land transfer including plot not within title).

128. *Turner v Moon* [1901] 2 Ch 825.

129. *Eastwood v Ashton* [1915] AC 900. It has been suggested that a drafting slip or printer's error occurred in the 1881 Act and that the word "omitted" should have read "committed", see Russell, 'Covenants for Title: Omissions' (1967) 31 Conv 268. But "omitted" was repeated in s 76 of the Law of Property Act 1925.

130. The same difficulty arises where the defect is an easement or profit arising by prescription. See also *Stoney v Eastbourne RDC* [1927] 1 Ch 367.

131. *Browning v Wright* (1799) 2 Bos & P 13 at 22 (*per* Lord Eldon); *Thackeray v Wood* (1865) 6 B & S 766 at 773 (*per* Erle J). The grantee may have another cause of action against the grantor, eg, for fraud, where the grantor conveyed knowing he had no title, see para **[21.35]** *infra*.

132. See para **[21.22]** *supra*. See also Sweetman 'Good Right to Convey' (1954) 18 Conv 362. Note that D's title may also be cured if B subsequently sells the land to C, eg, by a recital of seisin in the conveyance to D creating an estoppel which is thereby "fed", see para **[18.33]** *ante*.

133. *Turner v Moon* [1901] 2 Ch 825.

purported to be conveyed and its value as the grantor had power to convey it.[134] The former is usually taken as being the price actually paid by the grantee.[135]

(ii) Quiet Enjoyment

[21.30] This part of the covenant is designed to protect the grantee from disturbance. Disturbance in this context means, of course, physical disturbance such as dispossession, not disturbance caused by noise.[136] The disturbance must be "lawful", for any unlawful disturbance is covered by the law of tort, eg. trespass or nuisance.[137] Though again no action lies against the grantor where the disturbance is not caused by his acts, or those of persons for whom he is responsible.[138] Nor, again does one lie where eviction is by title paramount.[139]

(iii) Freedom from Incumbrances

[21.31] The generally accepted view seems to be now that this part of the covenant is really an extension only of the second part,[140] in that, in essence, the grantor is undertaking to provide the grantee with an indemnity in the event of disturbance.[141] If the grantee is to succeed under this part of the covenant, he must prove that he has actually been disturbed in his possession or had his enjoyment interrupted by some adverse claim actually made against him.[142] The mere existence of an incumbrance is not enough,[143] though, of course, it may involve a breach of another part of the covenant, eg, the full power to convey.[144] Nor can the grantee complain generally in respect of acts by the grantor on adjoining land,[145] though liability may arise in another way, eg, on the principle of non-derogation from grant.[146]

[21.32] Breach of this and the second part of the covenant occurs when the disturbance or interference with quiet enjoyment occurs and, though time

---

[134.] *Ibid.*

[135.] See *Jenkins v Jones* (1882) 9 QBD 128; *GW Rly Co v Fisher* [1905] 1 Ch 316.

[136.] *Howard v Maitland* (1883) 11 QBD 695. See also *Jenkins v Jones* (1888) 40 Ch D 71.

[137.] *Malzy v Eichholz* [1916] 2 KB 308. See also *Williams v Gabriel* [1906] 1 QB 155.

[138.] *Chiverst and Sons Ltd v Air Ministry* [1955] Ch 585.

[139.] *Baynes & Co Ltd v Lloyd & Sons* [1895] 2 QB 610.

[140.] *Cf* the views of Joyce J in *Turner v Moon* [1901] 2 Ch 825 at 828; also Russell, 'The Principal Covenants for Title' (1970) 34 Conv 178 at 187.

[141.] See Barnsley, *Conveyancing Law and Practice* (3rd ed, 1988), pp 604-5.

[142.] *Stock v Meakin* [1900] Ch 683.

[143.] *Howard v Maitland* (1883) 11 QBD 695.

[144.] See para **[21.27]** *supra.*

[145.] See *Davis v Town Properties Investment Corp Ltd* [1903] 1 Ch 797.

[146.] See *Harmer v Jumbil (Nigeria) Tin Areas* [1921] 1 Ch 200. On this principle, see *Irish Land Law*, (2nd ed 1986) para 6.058-9.

begins to run then for the purpose of limitation of actions, the breach is a continuing one, with a fresh cause of action occurring with every disturbance. Damages should be measured at the date of the breach in question, so that the plaintiff takes the benefit of any increase in the value of the land since the date of the conveyance, including an increase attributable to improvements made to the land since that date.[147] Where the disturbance does not consist of eviction or total dispossession, it is not clear whether a claim can be based on the ground of permanent damage to the property as opposed to the actual damage at the time of the disturbance.[148] For example, the damage caused by way of diminution in the value of the land may far exceed the actual damage caused by the particular disturbance, eg, one exercise of a right of way may cause little damage but the existence of it and its potential future exercise may have disastrous effects on the value of the land for development purposes.

(iv) Further Assurance

[21.33] This part of the covenant[149] requires the grantor to execute such further assurance or to do such further things as are necessary to perfect the grantee's title, provided the outstanding estate or interest is vested in the grantor or some person for whom he is responsible.[150] The grantee can require the grantor to execute the necessary conveyance,[151] but the grantee must meet the costs of this.[152] It is doubtful if the covenant applies where the original conveyance is subsequently lost or destroyed, so as to enable the grantee to require the grantor to execute a duplicate conveyance.[153] In such a

---

147. See *Bunny v Hopkinson* (1859) 27 Beav 565. *Quaere*, whether this includes improvements not within the contemplation of the parties at the date of the conveyance, see *Lewis v Campbell* (1819) 8 Taunt 715. But *cf Rolph v Crouch* (1867) IR 3 Exch 44 on this point. The *Rolph* case also establishes that the grantee can claim for loss which is a natural consequence of the breach, eg, the cost of moving to other premises.

148. *Cf Child v Stenning* (1879) 11 Ch D 82 and *Sutton v Bailli* (1891) 65 LT 528.

149. Note that this is the only part which applies in the case of a conveyance by a person "as settlor," see para **[21.17]** *supra*. Furthermore, the covenant is given only by the settlor himself and persons subsequently deriving title under him, ie, not persons through whom he derives title, see para **[21.18]** *supra*.

150. See *Maguire v Armstrong* (1814) 2 Ba & B 538. Note that in the case of a person conveying "as trustee" or in a similar capacity this part of the covenant is limited to his own acts only, see para **[21.18]** *supra*.

151. Eg, to discharge an undisclosed mortgage, see *Re Jones* [1893] 2 Ch 461; or to bar an entail, see *Bankes v Small* [1887] 36 Ch D 716. Note again the possibility of the grantee's title being perfected through operation of the doctrine of "feeding" an estoppel, see para **[18.33]** *ante*.

152. But not in the case of a conveyance by way of mortgage, see para **[21.16]** *supra*.

153. But see *Bennett v Ingoldsby* (1676) Cas Temp Finch 262. See also *Napper v Lord Allington* [1700] 1 Eq Cas Arb 166.

case the original conveyance is effective and it is difficult to see how the grantor can be said to have broken the covenant, especially if the loss or destruction is the fault of the grantee.

B. Recission

[21.34] A conveyance may be rescinded or set aside on a variety of grounds, some recognised at common law, some in equity. Since this subject has been discussed elsewhere,[154] the following is a summary only.

1. Fraud

[21.35] Fraud was a ground of rescission at common law and completion of the transaction by execution of the conveyance was no bar to relief. Alternatively, the injured party could affirm the transaction and sue for damages in an action of deceit.[155] Equity exercised concurrent jurisdiction in respect of fraud to the extent of granting rescission[156] and also had exclusive jurisdiction to order delivery up and cancellation of documents procured by fraud.[157] The concept of what constitutes fraud in equity is a very wide one[158] and includes, eg, a conveyance procured by undue influence.[159] Equity has also intervened on many occasions to set aside improvident or ruinous transactions, especially where they are tainted by clear unfair dealing.[160]

2. Innocent Misrepresentation

[21.36] We saw in an earlier chapter that the bar to rescission for innocent misrepresentation after completion of a transaction by execution of the conveyance remains.[161]

3. Mistake

[21.37] At common law mistake could be a ground for relief after completion of a contract for the sale of land where a party could prove total failure of consideration, ie, a mistake so fundamental as to render the

---

154. See Keane, *Equity and the Law of Trusts in the Republic of Ireland* (1988) Ch 17; Delany, *Equity and the Law of Trusts in Ireland* (1996), Ch 16. See also para **[13.57]** *et seq, ante.*

155. See para **[5.23]** *et seq, ante.*

156. See *Murray v Palmer* (1805) 2 Sch & Lef 474; *Legge v Croker* (1811) 1 Ba & B 506.

157. *Gun v McCarthy* (1884) 13 LR Ir 304. See on this subject, *Keane, op cit*, para 4.03.

158. See generally, Sheridan, *Fraud in Equity* (1957).

159. See *Keane, op cit*, Ch 29; *Delany, op cit*, p 479 *et seq.*

160. See *Grealish v Murphy* [1946] IR 35; *Duffy v Duffy* [1947] Ir Jur Rep 39; *Buckley v Irwin* [1960] NI 98. See also as regards acquisition of reversions at an undervalue, Sales of Reversions Act 1867; *Rae v Jones* (1892) 29 LR Ir 500. And see *Keane, op cit*, para 29.10 *et seq*; *Delany, op cit*, p 490 *et seq.*

161. See para **[5.26]** *ante.*

contract void *ab initio* and, therefore, any conveyance on foot of it totally ineffective.[162] Whether this rule can be applied in respect of fundamental mistakes not resulting in total failure of consideration is not so clear. Equity will generally set aside contracts on this basis,[163] but it is doubtful if this jurisdiction extends to rescission *after* completion.[164] Though the decision of the English Court of Appeal in *Solle v Butcher*[165] suggests that it may do so.

[21.38] Alternatively, a party to a deed may raise the plea of *non est factum*, ie, that it is void as against him on the ground that he was induced into executing it because he thought it was something entirely different in character.[166] Though designed primarily to protect the blind and illiterate, it seems that this plea is not confined to such persons,[167] though a considerable onus of proof will rest upon a person not suffering from any such disability.[168] And clearly no relief is available if the plaintiff was negligent in reading the document in question.[169]

C. Rectification

[21.39] Apart from the question of rescission, mistake may be a ground for another remedy, namely, rectification of the conveyance to conform with the terms of the contract for sale. This matter has been considered elsewhere.[170]

[162.] *Bingham v Bingham* (1748) 1 Ves Sen 126; *.Strickland v Turner* (1882) 7 Exch 208.

[163.] See para **[13.66]** *et seq, ante.*

[164.] See *Re Tyrell* (1900) 82 LT 675; *Debenham v Sawbridge* [1901] 2 Ch. 98; *Bligh v Martin* [1968] 1 All ER 1157.

[165.] [1950] 1 KB 671. See also *Grist v Bailey* [1967] Ch 532; *Magee v Pennine Insurance Co Ltd* [1969] 2 QB 507; *Laurence v Lexourt Holdings Ltd* [1978] 2 All ER 810. *Cf Svanosio v McNamara* (1956) 96 CLR 186. See *Keane op cit* para 17.12 *et seq.*

[166.] The leading discussion on this subject is now to he found in the House of Lords decision in *Saunders v Anglia BS* [1971] AC 1004. See also *United Dominions Trust v Western* [1976] QB 513; *Avon Finance Co Ltd v Bridges* [1985] 2 All ER 281; *Norwich and Peterborough BS v Steed (No 2)* [1993] 1 All ER 331.

[167.] *Ibid*, p 1026 (*per* Lord Wilberforce). *Cf* in the CA *sub-nom Gallie v Lee* [1969] 2 Ch 17 at 31-2 (*per* Lord Denning MR).

[168.] *Ibid*, p 1027 (*per* Lord Wilberforce).

[169.] *Ibid*, pp 1019 (*per* Lord Hodson) 1023 (*per* Viscount Dilhorne) and 1027 (*per* Lord Wilberforce).

[170.] The leading authority in Ireland is *Irish Life Assurance Co Ltd v Dublin Land Securities Ltd* [1989] IR 253; *cf Rooney and McParland Ltd v Carlin* [1981] NI 138. See *Keane, op cit,* Ch 18; *Delany op cit* Ch 15; Farrell, *Irish Law of Specific Performance* (1994), para [10.15] *et seq.* See also Bromley, 'Rectification in Equity' (1971) 87 1 QR 532.

Appendix I

PRE-CONTRACT DOCUMENTATION

1. PURCHASER'S SOLICITORS *PRE-CONTRACT* CHECK LIST ON ACQUISITION OF PRIVATE DWELLINGHOUSE

2. GUIDELINES ON ENQUIRIES TO BE MADE WHEN TAKING A RACK RENT LEASE OR A RENEWAL THEREOF

PURCHASER'S SOLICITORS *PRE-CONTRACT* CHECK LIST ON ACQUISITION OF PRIVATE DWELLINGHOUSE[1]

CLIENT ....

PROPERTY ....

Requisitions on title are designed to ensure that Title is given in accordance with the contract and act as a Check List for both the vendor's and purchaser's solicitors to remind them to obtain certain documentation and make certain searches prior to closing. The purchaser's rights are determined by the contract for sale. The basic rule is that *Caveat Emptor* applies except in so far as the contract for sale otherwise provides, for instance the warranty contained in General Condition 36 in relation to development. Because of this there are many items which have to be clarified *prior* to the signing of the contract. To defer enquiry into such matters until the requisition stage could result in the purchaser being bound to complete the purchase regardless of whether the results of such enquiries are satisfactory or not.

With this in mind the following Check List has been prepared for the use of purchaser's solicitors prior to their client being contractually committed to acquire the property.

Queries should be directed in the first instance to the purchaser. While some of the information will have to be obtained from the vendor the Check List is not designed for use as pre-contract requisitions.

This Check List is designed for general residential conveyancing. For Commercial Properties, Licensed Premises, Agricultural lands with Milk Quotas, Flats, Multi-Storied Buildings (or part thereof) special pre-contract enquiries should be raised and in many cases the issue of complete extracts from the Standard Requisitions on Title may be justified.

[1.] Prepared by the Law Society's *Conveyancing Committee* and issued with the July/August 1990 *Gazette*.

CHECK LIST

1. Check that Insurance will be available for property. In the event of property being of a special category confirm purchaser has obtained Insurance of his beneficial interest to cover any loss in the event of non completion or delay in completion.

    ....

    ....

2. Check that survey effected which includes planning and new roads and road widening search, zoning as to amenities (eg commercial/industrial developments, halting sites) etc, and identity.

    ....

    ....

3. Which of the walls and fences belong to the property and which are party walls or fences? Confirm if there are any agreements.

    ....

    ....

4. Is the property registered under the National House Building Guarantee Scheme? If so provide in contract for obtaining HG.6 Guarantee Certificate.

    ....

    ....

5   (a) How is the property serviced as to drainage, water supply and otherwise?

         ....

    (b) If the property is serviced by a septic tank, is the tank and percolation area within the property boundaries?

         ....

    (c) Is water supply from Local Authority mains or from a well? If the latter, is this within the boundaries, or are there suitable easements of access?

         ....

6. Have the services (including roads, footpaths, sewers, drains) abutting or servicing the property been taken over by the Local Authority or if not are there appropriate easements and indemnities in existence?

    ....

    ....

7. Are there any rights of way, easements, privileges or liabilities affecting the property known to the purchaser or apparent from an inspection of the property?

    ....

    ....

8. Is there a television aerial or cable on or attached to the property? If so obtain details of ownership.

    ....

    ....

9. Is there a telephone line to be supplied with the property?

    ....

    ....

10. Check what contents and/or fixtures or fittings are included in the sale.

    ....

    ....

11. Is the property or any part of it let or subject to a Lease or Licence?

    ....

    ....

12. Is there a service charge for refuse collection, water supply or other public services?

    ....

    ....

13. Is the property situate in a County Borough, Borough, Urban District or Town and if not, does the purchaser require consent under Section 45 of the Land Act 1965?

    ....

    ....

14. Is the property or any part thereof the vendor's "Family Home" within the meaning of the Family Home Protection Act 1976?

    ....

    ....

15. Has there been in relation to the property any development (including change of use or extensions) within the meaning of the Local Government (Planning and Development) Acts on or after the 1st October 1964?

    ....

    ....

GUIDELINES ON ENQUIRIES TO BE MADE WHEN TAKING A RACK RENT LEASE OR A RENEWAL THEREOF [2]

The Conveyancing Committee has received a number of queries as to the enquiries into the landlord's title which ought to be made by a tenant's solicitor when taking a lease at rack rent or on the renewal of such lease under the Landlord and Tenant Acts.

While the tenant is not entitled under the Conveyancing or Vendor and Purchaser Acts to enquire into the landlord's title both the practice of the profession and certain judicial pronouncements have made considerable inroads on this strict statutory provision.

The decision in *Hill v Harris* [1965] 2 All ER held that a solicitor acting for a tenant should take 'the ordinary conveyancing precautions before allowing his client take a sub-lease, or finding out by inspection of the head lease what were the covenants restrictive of user or otherwise contained in the head lease'

Therefore, while it is **not** necessary to fully investigate the landlord's title and raise a full set of standard Requisitions on Title, it is necessary to obtain *prima facie* evidence of the landlord's title and to make certain enquiries.

For the guidance of the profession the Conveyancing Committee has prepared a short set of Pre-Lease enquiries or Check List which it hopes will be found to be useful when acting for a tenant taking a lease.

These Enquiries or Check-List are primarily designed for the taking of a new lease.

On a renewal of a lease, it should not be necessary to raise all these matters. For example, it will only be necessary to request evidence of the landlord's title if this was not obtained on the grant of the original lease or if the landlord has in the meantime changed. It will not be necessary to raise Requisitions 2, 3, 9, 10 or 13. It may also not be necessary to raise any enquiries on planning matters if the tenant has already been in occupation of the property prior to 1964 or if planning documentation was obtained when the original lease was granted. Generally it is regarded as necessary to obtain satisfactory evidence of compliance with planning permission for any development or change of use of commercial property since 1 October 1964. If there was a development and an architect's certificate of compliance was not obtained then and is not now readily obtainable, then the tenant should be entitled to have any covenant in the lease requiring compliance with the Planning Acts modified so that it is not bound to comply or remedy any breach of planning permission that occurred prior to it taking the lease

March 1990

[2.] Prepared by the Law Society's *Conveyancing Committee*, March 1990, and issued with the May 1990 *Gazette.*

PRE-LEASE ENQUIRIES OR CHECK LIST

Landlord_____ Tenant_____

Demised Premises_____

Your Ref:_____ Our Ref:_____

Enquiries	*Replies*

TITLE

1. Furnish *prima facie* evidence of Landlord's title to grant the lease as follows:

Unregistered:

1.1 Certified copy Deed of Conveyance/Assignment to Landlord.

1.2 If Landlord's title is leasehold/fee farm grant, certified copy Head Lease or Fee Farm Grant.

1.3 Up-to-date Receipt for Rent under Head Lease/Fee Farm Grant.

1.4 If required, head Landlord's Consent to grant of Sub-Lease.

Registered:

1.5 Certified copy Land Registry Folio showing Landlord as registered owner with file plan attached.

1.6 If leasehold folio, certified copy of Head Lease/Fee Farm Grant.

1.7 Up-to-date Receipt for Rent under Head Lease/Fee Farm Grant.

1.8 If required, head Landlord's Consent to grant of Sub-Lease.

1.9 Section 72 Declaration.

1.10 Consent to registration of Lease as burden on Folio (may be contained in Lease.)

1.11 Has Land Certificate issued? If so, please undertake to lodge in the Land Registry and give Letter consenting to use of Land Certificate for the purpose of registering Lease.

Enquiries	*Replies*

SERVICES

2.1 Is the property serviced with:
Drainage
Water
Electricity
Telephone
Gas?

2.2 If applicable, furnish letter consenting to the transfer of the telephone to the Tenant.

2.3 Have the services (including roads, footpaths, sewers, drains) abutting or servicing the demised premises been taken over by the Local Authority and have all charges on account thereof been paid?

2.4 Furnish letter from Local Authority or Solicitor's Certificate based on the Local Authority Records or personal knowledge confirming the position.

2.5 If the services are not in charge, furnish an Indemnity under seal unless Landlord covenants to maintain same in Lease.

EASEMENTS AND RIGHTS

3.1 Are there any pipes, drains, sewers, wires, cables or septic tanks on, passing through or over property not included in the demised premises which serve or are in any way connected to or belong to the demised premises? If there are any, rights over same must be granted in the Lease and evidence of the Landlord's title to grant such easements and rights must be furnished.

3.2 Is the demised premises or any part of it subject to any right-of-way, water, light, air or drainage or to any other easement, reservation, covenant or restriction or to any public right of way or other public right or covenant or agreement restrictive of its user or other right of any kind.

Enquiries	*Replies*

3.3 If any road, path, drain, wire, cable, pipe, party wall or other facility (which is not in charge of the Local Authority) is used by the occupier of the demised premises in common with the owner oroccupier of any other property, please confirm that all rights to do so are contained in the Lease and furnish evidence of the Landlord's title to grant such rights.

3.4 If so, please also state what (if any) are the obligations attaching to such rights.

NOTICES

4.1 Has any notice, certificate or order been served upon or received by the Landlord or a previous Tenant of the Landlord or has the Landlord notice of any intention to serve any notice relating to the demised premises or any part of it under any Act or any statutory rule, order or statutory instrument or any amendment or extension of same?

4.2 If so, furnish now a copy of any such notice, certificate or order so served or received.

4.3 Has the same been complied with?

LITIGATION

5.1 Is there any litigation pending or threatened in relation to the demised premises or any part of it or has any adverse claim thereto been made by any person?

5.2 If the Landlord is an individual, confirm that no orders affecting the demised premises have been made pursuant to the provisions of the Judicial Separation and Family Law Reform Act 1989?

MORTGAGE

6. Is the Landlord's interest in the demised premises or any part of it subject to any mortgage or charge? If so, please give full particulars and, if necessary, join the mortgagee in the Lease in order to grant and confirm same or if it is a floating floating charge furnish letter confirming non-crystallisation.

Enquiries	*Replies*

SEARCHES

7.   The Tenant shall search against the Landlord in:

7.1   If unregistered title, Registry of Deeds from date of Deed to Landlord.

7.2   If registered, in the Land Registry.

7.3   If Landlord's interest is leasehold, in the Sheriff's Office

7.4   If the Landlord is a Company, in the Companies Office

7.5   If the Landlord is an individual, in the Bankruptcy Office

7.6   In the Judgments Office.

7.7   The Landlord shall explain and discharge all adverse acts appearing on such Searches.

LOCAL GOVERNMENT (PLANNING AND DEVELOPMENT) ACTS 1963 TO 1983 ("THE ACTS")

8.1   Has there been in relation to the demised premises any development (including change of use of exempted development) within the meaning of the Acts on or after the 1st October 1964?

8.2   In respect of any such development furnish (where applicable):

     a) Grant of Planning Permission or

     b) Outline Planning Permission and Grant of Approval

     c) Building Bye-Law Approval (if applicable).

8.3   In respect of development completed after the 1st November 1976 furnish evidence by way of statutory declaration of competent person that each development was completed prior to expiration of the Permission/Approval.

8.4   Has the demised premises been used for the use proposed under the Lease without material change continuously since the 1st day of October 1964? If so, please furnish statutory declaration evidencing same.

Enquiries	*Replies*

8.5 If the demised premises has been developed since the 1st October 1964 please furnish Architect's Certificate of Compliance with Planning Permission and (if applicable) Building Bye-Law Approval. (**Note**: If such a Certificate is not available, then the covenant in the Lease to comply with Planning Acts should be modified).

FIRE SERVICES ACT 1981

9.1 Have any notices been served on the Landlord or any previous Tenant under the Fire Services Act 1981?

9.2 Are there any proceedings pending under the Fire Services Act 1981?

9.3 Has the demised premises ever been inspected by the Fire Authority for the functional area within which the demised premises is situate? If so, what were its requirements?

9.4 Have the requirements of the Fire Authority been fully complied with in relation to the demised premises and (if applicable) the building of which it forms part?

RATES

10.1 What is the rateable valuation of the demised premises?

10.2 Furnish evidence of payment of rates for current year.

10.3 Confirm that rates will be apportioned as of the date the Tenant commences to be liable.

INSURANCE

11.1 If the Landlord is insuring, furnish certified copy of Landlord's insurance policy and receipt for latest premiums.

11.2 Confirm that either Tenant's interest will be noted on the policy or a letter from the Landlord's insurers will be furnished waiving subrogation rights.

Enquiries	*Replies*

MULTI-STOREY BUILDING

12.1 Is the demised premises a 'multi-storey building' (or part of such building) within the meaning of the Local Government (Multi-Storey Buildings) Act 1988?
or

12.2 Does it form part of a development in which there is a multi-storey building and in respect of which the Tenant may be required to make a contribution by way of service charge or otherwise to the cost of repair or compliance with statutory requirements?

12.3 If so, the Tenant reserves the right to raise specific Requisitions in regard to the Local Government (Multi-Storey Buildings) Act 1988.

FAMILY HOME PROTECTION ACT 1976/FAMILY LAW ACT 1981

13. Furnish Certificate that the demised premises are not affected by the above Acts.

Appendix II

STANDARD CONTRACT FOR SALE

WARNING:IT IS RECOMMENDED THAT THE WITHIN SHOULD
NOT BE COMPLETED WITHOUT PRIOR LEGAL ADVICE

LAW SOCIETY OF IRELAND
GENERAL CONDITIONS OF SALE (1995 EDITION)

PARTICULARS
and
CONDITIONS

of
*SALE BY PRIVATE TREATY
*SALE BY AUCTION

to be held at

on   the   day of   , 199

at   · o'clock.

*Auctioneer:

Address:

Vendor:

Vendor's solicitor:

Address:

Reference:

_____

*Delete if inappropriate

I,   being the Spouse of the under-named Vendor hereby, for the purposes of Section 3, Family Home Protection Act, 1976, consent to the proposed sale of the property described in the within Particulars at the price mentioned below.

Signed by the said Spouse
in the presence of:

MEMORANDUM OF AGREEMENT made this   day of
199

between

of   ("VENDOR")

and

of   ("PURCHASER")

whereby it is agreed that the Vendor shall sell and the Purchaser shall purchase in accordance with the annexed Special and General Conditions of Sale the property described in the within Particulars at the purchase price mentioned below.

Purchase Price	£ _____	Closing Date:	
less deposit	£ _____	Interest Rate:	per cent per annum
Balance	£ _____		
SIGNED	_____	SIGNED	_____
	_____		_____
	(Vendor)		(Purchaser)
Witness	_____	Witness	_____
Occupation	_____	Occupation	_____
Address	_____	Address	_____

As stakeholder I/We acknowledge receipt of Bank Draft/Cheque for £   in respect of deposit.

                                        Signed _____

PARTICULARS AND TENURE

DOCUMENTS SCHEDULE

SEARCHES SCHEDULE

1. Negative Search in the Registry of Deeds on the Index of Names only for all acts affecting the subject property by the Vendor from the   day of

    and

SPECIAL CONDITIONS

1. Save where the context otherwise requires or implies or the text hereof expresses to the contrary, the definitions and provisions as to interpretation set forth in the within General Conditions shall be applied for the purposes of these Special Conditions

2. The said General Conditions shall:

    (a) apply to the sale in so far as the same are not hereby altered or varied, and these Special Conditions shall prevail in case of any conflict between them and the General Conditions.

    (b) be read and construed without regard to any amendment therein, unless such amendment shall be referred to specifically in these Special Conditions.

3. In addition to the purchase price, the Purchaser shall pay to the Vendor an amount equivalent to such Value-Added Tax as shall be exigible in relation to the sale or (as the case may be) the Assurance same to be calculated in accordance with the provisions of the Value-Added Tax Act 1972, and to be paid on completion of the sale or forthwith upon receipt by the Purchaser of an appropriate invoice (whichever shall be the later).

e if
opriate)

NOTE: These General Conditions are not to be altered in any manner. Any required variation or addition should be dealt with by way of Special Condition.

Special Conditions should be utilised in instances where it is required to adopt Recommendations or Advices of the Law Society or of any Committee associated with it, where such Recommendations or Advices are at variance with provisions expressed in the General Conditions.

GENERAL CONDITIONS OF SALE
DEFINITIONS

1. In these General Conditions:

    "*the Conditions*" means the attached Special Conditions and these General Conditions.

    "*the Documents Schedule*", "*the Searches Schedule*" and "*the Special Conditions*" mean respectively the attached Documents Schedule, Searches Schedule and Special Conditions.

    "*the Memorandum*" means the Memorandum of Agreement of Page 1 hereof.

    "*the Particulars*" means the Particulars and Tenure on Page 2 hereof and any extension of the same

    "*the Purchaser*" means the party identified as such in the Memorandum.

    "*the sale*" means the transaction evidenced by the Memorandum, the Particulars and the Conditions.

    "*the Vendor*" means the party identified as such in the Memorandum.

2. In the Conditions save where the context otherwise requires or implies:

    "*Apportionment Date*" means either (a) the later of (i) the closing date (as defined hereunder) and (ii) such subsequent date from which delay in completing the sale shall cease to be attributable to default on the part of the Vendor or (b) in the event of the Vendor exercising the right referred to in conditions 25(a)(ii) hereunder, the date of actual completion of the sale or (c) such other date as may be agreed by the Vendor and the Purchaser to be the Apportionment Date for the purpose of this definitions.

    "*Assurance*" means the document orf documents whereby the sale is to be carried into effect.

    "*closing date*" means the date specified as such in the Memorandum, or, if no date is specified, the first working day after the expiration of five weeks computed from the datle of sale.

    "*Competent Authority*" includes the State, any Minster thereof, Government Department, State Authority, Local Authority, Planning Authority, Sanitary Authority, Building Control Authority, Fire Authority, Statutory Undertaker or any Department, Body or person by statutory provision or order for the time being in force authorised directly or indirectly to control, regulate, modify or restrict the development, use or servicing of land or buildings, or empowered to acquire land by compulsory process.

"*date of sale*" means the date of the auction when the sale shall have been by auction, and otherwise means the date upon which the contract for the sale shall have become binding on the Vendor or the Purchaser.

"*development*" has the same meaning as that conferred by the Local Government (Planning and Development) Act, 1963.

"*lease*" includes (a) a fee farm grant and every contract (whether or not in writing or howsoever effected, derived or evidenced) whereby the relationship of Landlord and Tenant is or is intended to be created and whether for any freehold or leasehold estate or interest and (b) licences and agreements relating to the occupation and use of land, cognate words being construed accordingly.

"*purchased chattels*" means such chattels, fittings, tenant's fixtures and other items as are included in the sale.

"*purchase price*" means the purchase price specified in the Memorandum PROVIDED HOWEVER that, if the sale provides for additional moneys to be paid by the Purchaser for goodwill, crops or purchased chattels, the expression "*purchase price*" shall be extended to include such additional moneys.

"*Requisitions*" include Requisitions on the title or titles as such of the subject property and with regard to rents, outgoings, rights, covenants, conditions, liabilities (actual or potential), planning and kindred matters and taxation issues material to such property.

"*stipulated interest rate*" means the interest rate specified in the Memorandum, or if no rate is so specified, such rate as shall equate to 4 per centum per annum over the rate (as annualised) of interest payable upon tax chargeable under the Capital Acquisitions Tax Act, 1976 and ruling at the date from which interest hereunder is to run.

"*working day*" does not include any Saturday, Sunday or any Bank or Public Holiday nort any of the seven days immediately succeeding Christmas Day.

INTERPRETATION

3. In the Conditions save where the context otherwise requires or implies:

Words importing the masculine gender only include the feminine, neuter and common genders, and word importing the singular number only include the plural number and vice versa.

The words "Vendor" and "Purchaser" respectively include (where appropriate) parties deriving title under them or either of them and shall apply to any one or more of several Vendors and Purchasers as the case may be and so that the stipulations in the Conditions contained shall be capable of being enforced on a joint and several basis.

Unless the contrary appears, any reference hereunder:

(a)   to a particular Condition shall be to such of these General Conditions of Sale as is identified by said reference

(b)   to a Statute of Regulation or a combination of Statutes or Regulations shall include any extension, amendment, modification or re-enactment thereof, and any Rule, Regulation, Order or Instrument made thereunder, and for the time being in force

Headings and marginal notes inserted in the conditions shall not affect the construction thereof nort shall the same have any contractual significance.

AUCTION

4. Where the sale is by auction, the following provisions shall apply:

(a) The Vendor may divide the property set forth in the Particulars into lots and sub-divide, consolidate or alter the order of sale of any lots

(b) there shall be a reserve price for the subject property whether the same shall comprise the whole or any part of the property set forth in the Particulars and the Auctioneer may refuse to accept any bid. If any dispute shall arise as to any bidding, the Auctioneer shall (at his option) either determine the dispute or again put up the property in question at the last undisputed bid. No person shall advance at a bidding a sum less than that fixed by the Auctioneer, and no accepted bid shall be retracted. Subject to the foregoing, the highest accepted bidder shall be the Purchaser.

(c) the Vendor may:

(i) bid himself or by an agent up to the reserve price

(ii) withdraw the whole of the property set forth in the Particulars or, where such property has been divided into lots, withdraw any one or more of such lots at any time before the same has been sold without disclosing the reserve price.

(d) the Purchaser shall forth with pay to the Vendor's Solicitor as stakeholder a deposit of ten per centum (10%) of the purchase price in part payment thereof, and shall execute an agreement in the form of the Memorandum to complete the purchase of the subject property in accordance with the Conditions.

PRIVATE TREATY SALE

5. (a) where the sale is by private treaty, the Purchaser shall on or before the date of the sale pay to the Vendor's solicitor as stakeholder a deposit of the amount stated in the Memorandum in part payment of purchase price

(b) if notwithstanding condition 5(a), a part of such deposit has been or is paid to any other person appointed or nominated by the Vendor that other person shall be deemed to receive or to have received said part as stakeholder.

THE FOLLOWING CONDITIONS APPLY WHETHER THE SALE IS BY AUCTION OR BY PRIVATE TREATY

PURCHASER ON NOTICE OF CERTAIN DOCUMENTS

6.   The documents specified in the Documents Schedule or copies thereof have been available for inspection by the Purchaser or his Solicitor prior to the sale. If all or any of the subject property is stated in the Particulars or in the Special Conditions to be held under a lease or to be subject to any covenants, conditions, rights, liabilities or restrictions, and the lease or other document containing the same is specified in the Documents Schedule, the Purchaser, whether availing of such opportunity of inspection or not, shall be deemed to have purchased withll full knowledge of the contents thereof, notwithstanding any partial statement of such contents in the Particulars or in the Conditions.

DELIVERY OF TITLE

7.   Within seven working days from the date of sale, the Vendor shall deliver or send by post to the Purchaser or his Solicitor copies of the documents necessary to vouch the title to be shown in accordance with the Conditions.

TITLE

8.   (a)   The Title to be shown to the subject property shall be such as is set forth in the Special Conditions.

     (b)   Where the title to be shown to the whole or any part of the subject property is based on possession, the Vendor shall, in addition to vouching that title and dealing with such further matters as are required of him by the Conditions, furnish to the Purchaser on or before completion of the sale a certificate from the Revenue Commissioners to the effect (i) that the subject property or (as the case may be) such part of the same as aforesaid is not charged with any of the taxes covered by the provisions of Section 146, Finance Act, 1994 or (ii) that the Revenue Commissioners are satisfied that any such charge will be discharged within a time considered by them to be reasonable.

     (c)   Save as stipulated in the Special Conditions the Vendor shall, prior to or at the completion of the sale, discharge all mortgages and charges for the payment of money (other than items apportionable under Condition 27(b)) which affect the subject property.

9.   Where any of the subject property is held under a lease, the Purchaser shall not call for or investigate the title of the grantor or lessor to make the same, but shall conclusively assume that it was well and validly made, and is a valid and subsisting lease.

10. Where any of the subject property is stated to be held under a lease or an agreement therefor then:

     (a)   no Objection or Requisition shall be made or indemnity required on account of such lease or agreement being (if such is the case) a sub-lease or agreement therefor, or on account of any superior lease comprising other property apart from the subject property or reserving a larger rent, or on the ground of any superior owner not having concurred in any apportionment or exclusive charge of rent.

(b)   no Objection or Requisition shall be made by reason of any discrepancy between the covenants, conditions and provisions contained in any sub-lease and those in any superior lease, unless such as could give rise to forfeiture or a right of re-entry.

(c)   the production of the receipt for the last gale of rent reserved by the lease or agreement therefor, under which the whole or any part of the subject property is held, (without proof of the title or authority of the person giving such receipt) shall (unless the contrary appears) be accepted as conclusive evidence that all rent accrued due has been paid and all covenants and conditions in such lease or agreement and in every (if any) superior lease have been duly performed and observed or any breaches thereof (past or continuing) effectively waived or sanctioned up to the actual completion of the sale, whether or not it shall appear that the lessor or reversioner was aware of such breaches. If the said rent (not being a rack rent) shall not have been paid in circumstances where the party entitled to receive the same is not known to the Vendor, or if the subject property is indemnified against payment of rent, the production of a Statutory Declaration so stating shall (unless the contrary appears) be accepted as such conclusive evidence, provided that the Declaration further indicates that no notices or rent demands have been served on or received by the Vendor under the lease or agreement on foot of which the subject property is held; that the Vendor has complied with all the covenants (other than those in respect of payment of rent) on the part of the lessee and the conditions contained in such lease or agreement and that he is not aware of any breaches thereof either by himself or by any his predecessors in title.

(d)   if any of the subject property is held under a lease or agreement for lease requiring consent to alienation, the Vendor shall apply for and endeavour to obtain such consent, and the Purchaser shall deal expeditiously and constructively with and shall satisfy all reasonable requirements of the lessor in relation to the application therefor, but the Vendor shall not be required to institute legal proceedings to enforce the issue of any such consent or otherwise as to the withholding of the same. If such consent shall have been refused or shall not have been procured and written evidence of the same furnished to the Purchaser on or before the closing date, or ift any such consent is issued subject to a condition, which the Purchaser on reasonable grounds refuses to accept, either party may rescind the sale by seven days prior notice to the other.

PRIOR TITLE

11. (a)   The title to the subject property prior to the date of the instrument specified in the Special Conditions as the commencement of title, whether or not appearing by recital, inference or otherwise, shall not be required, objected to or investigated.

    (b)   In the case of registered freehold or leasehold land registered under the Registration of Title Acts, 1891 to 1942 or the Registration of Title Act, 1964 the provisions of subparagraph (a) of this Condition shall apply without prejudice to Sections 52 and 115 of the last mentioned Act and shall not disentitle the Purchaser from investigating the possibility of there having been a voluntary disposition on the title within the period of twelve years immediately preceding the date of sale or a disposition falling within Section 121, Succession Act, 1965 and the Vendor shall be required to deal with all points properly taken in or arising out of such investigation.

INTERMEDIATE TITLE

12.   Where in the Special Conditions it is provided that the title is to commence with a particular instrument and then to pass to a second instrument or to a specified event, the title intervening between the first instrument and the second instrument or the specified event, whether or not appearing by recital, inference or otherwise, shall not be required, objected to or investigated.

REGISTERED LAND

13.   Where all or any of the subject property consists of freehold or leasehold registered land registered under the Registration of Title Acts, 1891 to 1942 ("the Acts of 1891 to 1942") or the Registration of Title Act, 1964 ("the Act of 1964") then:

    (a)   if the registration is subject to equities under the Acts of 1891 to 1942, the Purchaser shall not require the equities to be discharged, but the Vendor shall, with the copy documents to be delivered or sent in accordance with Condition 7, furnish sufficient evidence of title prior to first registration or otherwise to enable the Purchaser to procure their discharge.

    (b)   if the registration is with a possessory title under the Act of 1964 the Purchaser shall not require the Vendor to be registered with an absolute title, but the Vendor shall, with the copy documents to be delivered or sent in accordance with Condition 7, furnish sufficient evidence of the title prior to such registration or otherwise to enable the Purchaser to be registered with an absolute title.

    (c)   the Vendor shall, with the copy documents to be delivered or sent in accordance with Condition 7, furnish to the Purchaser a copy of the Land Registry Folio or Folios relating to the subject property written up-to-date (or as nearly as practicable up-to-date), together with a copy of the relevant Land Registry map or file plan.

(d)   the Vendor shall furnish a Statutory Declaration, by some person competent to make it, confirming that there are not in existence any burdens which under the Act of 1964 affect registered land without registration, save such (if any) as are specifically mentioned in the Particulars or the Special Conditions.

(e)   if the Land Certificate has been issued to the Land Commission or if no such Certificate has been issued, the Purchaser shall not be entitled to require such Certificate to be produced, handed over on completion or issued.

(f)   the Purchaser shall procure himself to be registered as owner of the subject property at his own expense

(g)   In the event of the subject property being subject to a Land Purchase Annuity the Vendor shall, prior to completion, redeem the same or (as the case may be) such proportion thereof as may be allocated to the subject property.

IDENTITY

14.   The Purchaser shall accept such evidence of identity as may be gathered from the descriptions in the documents of title plus (if circumstances require) a Statutory Declaration to be made by a competent person, at the Purchaser's expense, that the subject property has been held and enjoyed for at least twelve years in accordance with the title shown. The Vendor shall be obliged to furnish such information as is in his possession relative to the identity and extent of the subject property, but shall not be required to define exact boundaries, fences, ditches, hedges or walls or to specify which (if any) of the same are of a party nature, nor shall the Vendor be required to identify parts of the subject property held under different titles.

RIGHTS - LIABILITIES - CONDITION OF SUBJECT PROPERTY

15.   The Vendor shall disclose before the sale, in the Particulars, the Special Conditions or otherwise, all easements, rights, reservations, privileges, taxes and other liabilities (not already known to the Purchaser or apparent from inspection) which are known by the Vendor to affect the subject property or which are likely to affect it.

16.   Subject to Condition 15, the Purchaser shall be deemed to buy:

(a)   with full notice of the actual state and condition of the subject property

and

(b)   subject to (i) all leases (if any) mentioned in the Particulars and in the Special Conditions and (ii) all easements, rights, reservations, privileges, liabilities, covenants, rents, outgoings and incidents of tenure.

REQUISITIONS

17. The Purchaser shall, within fourteen working days after the delivery of the copy documents of title in accordance with Condition 7, send to the Vendor's Solicitor a written statement of his Objections (if any) on the title and his Requisitions. Any Objection or Requisition not made within the time aforesaid and not going to the root of the title shall be deemed to have been waived. The Vendor's Replies to any Objections or Requisitions shall be answered by the Purchaser in writing within seven working days after the delivery thereof and so on toties quoties, and, if not answered, shall be considered to have been accepted as satisfactory. In all respects time shall be deemed to be of the essence of this Condition.

18. If the Purchaser shall make and insist on any Objections or Requisitions as to the title, the Assurance to him or any other matter or incidental to the sale, which the Vendor shall, on the grounds of unreasonable delay or expense or other reasonable ground, be unable or unwilling to remove or comply with, the Vendor shall be at liberty (notwithstanding any intermediate negotiation or litigation or attempts to remove or comply with the same) by giving to the Purchaser or his Solicitor not less than five working days to rescind the sale. In that case, unless the Objection or Requisition in question shall in the meantime have been withdrawn, the sale shall be rescinded at the expiration of such notice.

SEARCHES

19. The Purchaser shall be furnished with the searches (if any) specified in the Searches Schedule and any searches already in the Vendor's possession, which are relevant to the title or titles on offer. Any other searches required by the Purchaser must be obtained by him at his own expense. Where the Special Conditions provide that the title shall commence with a particular instrument and then pass to a second instrument or to a specified event, the Vendor shall not be obliged to explain and discharge any act which appears on a search covering the period between such particular instrument and the date of the second instrument or specified event, unless same goes to the root of the title. Subject as aforesaid the Vendor shall explain and discharge any acts appearing on Searches covering the period from the date stipulated or implied for the commencement of the title to the date of actual completion.

ASSURANCE

20. Subject to the provisions of Paragraph 11, Schedule 4, Capital Gains Tax Act, 1975 (as substituted), and (if relevant) to those contained in Section 107, Finance Act, 1993 (in relation to Residential Property Tax) on payment of all moneys payable by him in respect of the sale, the Purchaser shall be entitled to a proper Assurance of the subject property from the Vendor and all other (if any) necessary parties, such Assurance to be prepared by and at the expense of

the Purchaser. The draft thereof shall be submitted to the Vendor's Solicitor not less than seven working days, and the engrossment not less than four working days, before the closing date. The delivery of the said draft or engrossment shall not prejudice any outstanding Objection or Requisition validly made.

VACANT POSSESSION

21. Subject to any provision to the contrary in the Particulars or in the Conditions or implied by the nature of the transaction, the Purchaser shall be entitled to vacant possession of the subject property on completion of the sale.

LEASES

22. Where the subject property is sold subject to any lease, a copy of the same (or, if the provisions thereof have not been reduced to writing, such evidence of its nature and terms as the Vendor shall be able to supply) together with copies of any notices in the Vendor's possession served by or on the lessee shall, prior to the sale, be made available for inspection by the Purchaser or his Solicitor.

23. Unless the Special Conditions provide to the contrary, the Purchaser shall be entitled to assume that, at the date of sale, the Lessee named in any such Lease (as is referred to in Condition 22) is still the Lessee; that there has been no variation in the terms and condition of said Lease (other then such as may be evident from an inspection of the subject property or apparent from the Particulars or the documents furnished to the Purchaser prior to the sale), and that the said terms and conditions (save those pertaining to the actual state and condition of the subject property) have been complied with.

COMPLETION AND INTEREST

24. (a)   The sale shall be completed and the balance of the purchase price paid by the Purchaser on or before the closing date

    (b)   Completion shall take place at the Office of the Vendor's Solicitor

25. (a)   If by reason of any default on the part of the Purchaser, the purchase shall not have been completed on or before the later of (a) the closing date or (b) such subsequent date whereafter delay in completing shall not be attributable to default on the part of the Vendor

    (i)   the Purchaser shall pay interest to the Vendor on the balance of the purchase price remaining unpaid at the stipulated interest rate for the period between the closing date (or as the case may be such subsequent date as aforesaid) and the date of actual completion of the sale. Such interest shall accrue from day to day and shall be payable before and after any judgment and

    (ii)   the Vendor shall in addition to being entitled to receive such interest, have the right to take the rents and profits less the outgoings of the subject property up to the date of the actual completion of the sale

(b) If the Vendor by reason of this default shall not be able, ready and willing to complete the sale of the closing date he shall thereafter give to t he Purchaser at least five working days prior notice of a date upon which he shall be so able ready and willing and the Purchaser shall not before the expiration of that notice be deemed to be in default for the purpose of this Condition provided that no such notice shall be required if the Vendor is prevented from being able and ready to complete or to give said notice by reason of the act or default of the Purchaser.

26. The submission of an Apportionment Account made up to a particular date or other corresponding step taken in anticipation of competing the sale shall not per se preclude the Vendor from exercising his rights under the provisions of Condition 25 and in the event of such exercise the said Apportionment Account or the said other corresponding step shall (if appropriate) be deemed not to have been furnished or taken, and the Vendor shall be entitled to furnish a further Apportionment Account.

APPORTIONMENT AND POSSESSION

27. (a) Subject to the stipulations contained in the Conditions, the Purchaser, on paying the purchase price, shall be entitled to vacant possession of the subject property or (as the case may be) the rents and profits thereout with effect from the Apportionment Date.

(b) All rents, profits, rates, taxes, outgoings and moneys (including rent, outgoings and hypothecation) referable to the subject property shall for the purpose of this Condition, be apportioned (whether apportionable by law or not) on a day to day basis as at the Apportionment Date, up to which the liability for the entitlement to the same shall (subject to apportionment as aforesaid to accord with the position obtaining as to moneys paid or due at such date) be for the account of the Vendor and thereafter for that of the Purchaser provided that if completion shall have been delayed through the default of the Vendor the Purchaser may opt for apportionment under this Condition as at the closing date or at the date at which the Purchaser (if also in default) shall have ceased to have been so in default whichever shall be the later.

(c) In the implementation of this Condition the Vendor shall be regarded as being the owner of the subject property until midnight on such date as is appropriate for apportionment purposes.

(d) The balance of the purchase price shall (where appropriate) be adjusted upwards or downwards to accommodate apportionments calculated pursuant to this Condition and the expression "balance of the purchase price" where used in the Conditions shall be construed accordingly.

(e) To the extent that same shall be unknown at the Apportionment Date (or shall not then be readily ascertainable) amounts to be apportioned hereunder - including any amount apportionable pursuant to Condition 27(f) - shall be apportioned provisionally on a fair estimate thereof, and, upon ascertainment of the actual figure, a final apportionment shall be made, and the difference between it and the provisional apportionment shall be refunded by the Vendor or the Purchaser (as the case may be) to the other within ten working days of the liable party becoming aware of the amount of such difference.

(f)   Excise and kindred duties payable in respect of the subject property or any licence attached thereto shall be apportioned on a day to day basis as at the Apportionment Date up to which the liability for the same shall be for the account of the Vendor and thereafter for that of the Purchaser and Condition 27(c) shall apply for the purposes of such apportionment.

SECTION 45, LAND ACT 1965

28.   Where Section 45, Land Act, 1965 applies, the Purchaser shall, at his own expense, procure any such Certificate or Consent as may be necessary thereunder for the vesting of the subject property in him or his nominee and the sale is not conditional upon such consent being obtained.

COMPULSORY REGISTRATION

29. (a)   If all or any of the subject property isn unregistered land the registration of which was compulsory prior to the date of the sale the Vendor shall be obliged to procure such registration prior to completion of the sale.

(b)   If all or any of the subject property is unregistered land, the registration of which shall become compulsory at or subsequent to the date of sale, the Vendor shall not be under any obligation to procure such registration but shall at or prior to such completion furnish to the Purchaser a Map of the subject property complying with the requirements of the Land Registry as then recognised and further the Vendor shall, if so requested within two years after completion of the sale, by and at the expense of the Purchaser, supply any additional information, which he may reasonably be able to supply, and produce and furnish any documents in his possession that may be required to effect such registration.

SIGNING "IN TRUST" OR "AS AGENT"

30.   A Purchaser who signs the Memorandum "in Trust", "as Trustee" or "as Agent", or with any similar qualification or description without therein specifying the identity of the principal or other party for whom he so signs, shall be personally liable to complete the sale, and to fulfil all such further stipulations on the part of the Purchaser as are contained in the Conditions unless and until he shall have disclosed to the Vendor the name of his principal or other such party.

FAILURE TO PAY DEPOSIT

31.   The failure by the Purchaser to pay in full the deposit hereinbefore specified as payable by him shall constitute a breach of condition entitling the Vendor to

terminate the sale or to sue the Purchaser for damages or both but such entitlement shall be without prejudice to any rights otherwise available to the Vendor.

32. In case a cheque taken for the deposit (having been presented and whether or not it has been re-presented) shall not have been honoured, then and on that account the Vendor may (without prejudice to any rights otherwise available to him) elect either:

    (a)   to treat the Contract evidenced by the Memorandum, the Particulars and the Conditions as having been discharged by breach thereof on the Purchaser's part

        or

    (b)   to enforce payment of the deposit as a deposit by suing on the cheque or otherwise.

DIFFERENCES - ERRORS

33. (a)   In this Conditions "error" includes any omission, non-disclosure, discrepancy, difference, inaccuracy, mis-statement or mis-representation made in the Memorandum, the Particulars or the Conditions or in the course of any representation, response or negotiations leading to the sale, and whether in respect of measurements, quantities, descriptions or otherwise.

    (b)   The Purchaser shall be entitled to be compensated by the Vendor for any loss suffered by the Purchaser in his bargain relative to the sale as a result of an error made by or on behalf of the Vendor provided however that no compensation shall be payable for loss of trifling materiality unless attributable to recklessness or fraud on the part of the Vendor nor in respect of any matter of which the Purchaser shall be deemed to have had notice under Condition 16(a) nor in relation to any error in a location or similar plan furnished for identification only.

    (c)   Nothing in the Memorandum, the Particulars or the Conditions shall:

        (i)   entitle the Vendor to require the Purchaser to accept property which differs substantially from the property agreed to be sold whether in quantity, quality, tenure or otherwise, if the Purchaser would be prejudiced materially by reason of any such difference

            or

        (ii)   affect the right of the Purchaser to rescind or repudiate the sale where compensation for a claim attributable to a material error made by or on behalf of the Vendor cannot be reasonably assessed.

    (d)   Save as aforesaid, no error shall annul the sale or entitle the Vendor or Purchaser (as the case may be) to be discharged therefrom.

DOCUMENTS OF TITLE RELATING TO OTHER PROPERTY

34. (a)   Documents of title relating to other property as well as to the subject property shall be retained by the Vendor or other person entitled to the possession thereof.

   (b)   where the property is sold in lots, all documents of title relating to more than one lot shall be retained by the Vendor, until the completion of the sales of all the lots comprised in such documents, and shall then (unless they also relate to any property retained by the Vendor) be handed over to such of the Purchasers as the Vendor shall consider best entitled thereto.

   (c)   the Vendor shall give to the Purchaser (and where the property is sold in lots, to the Purchaser of each lot) certified copies of all documents retained under this Condition and pertinent to the title to be furnished (other than documents of record, of which plain copies will be given).

   (d)   subject as hereinafter provided, the Vendor shall give the usual statutory acknowledgement of the right of production and undertaking for safe custody of all documents (other than documents of record) retained by him under this Condition and pertinent to the title to be furnished. Such acknowledgement and undertaking shall be prepared by and at the expense of the Purchaser.

   (e)   if the Vendor is retaining any unregistered land held wholly or partly under the same title as the subject property, the Assurance shall be engrossed in duplicate by and at the expense of the Purchaser, who shall deliver to the Vendor the Counterpart thereof, same having been stamped and registered and (if appropriate) executed by the Purchaser.

DISCLOSURE OF NOTICES

35.   Where prior to the sale

   (a)   any closing, demolition or clearance Order
          or

   (b)   any notice (not being of the contents of the Development Plan other than an actual or proposed designation of all or any part of the subject property for compulsory acquisition).

Made or issued by or at the behest of a Competent Authority in respect of the subject property and affecting same at the date of sale has been notified or given to the Vendor (whether personally or by advertisement or posting on the subject property or in any other manner) or is otherwise known to the Vendor or where the subject property is at the date of sale affected by any award or grant which is or may be repayable by the Vendor's successor in title then if the Vendor fails to show

   (i)   that, before the sale, the Purchaser received notice or was aware of the matter in question
          or

(ii)   that same is no longer applicable or material

(iii)   that same does not prejudicially affect the value of the subject property

or

(iv)   that the subject thereof can and will be dealt with fully in the Apportionment Account

the Purchaser may by notice given to the Vendor rescind the sale.

DEVELOPMENT

36. (a)   Unless the Special Conditions contain a provision to the contrary, the Vendor warrants:

(1)   either

(i)   that there has been no development (which term includes material change of use) of, or execution of works on or to, the subject property since the 1stst day of October, 19674 for which Planning Permission or Building Bye-Law Approval was required by law.

or

(ii)   that all Planning Permissions and Building Bye-Law Approvals required by law for the development of, or the execution of works on or to, the subject property as at the date of sale, or for any change in the use thereof at that date were obtained (save in respect of matters of trifling materiality), and that, where implemented,. the conditions thereof and the conditions expressly notified with said Permissions by any Competent Authority in relation to and specifically addressed to such development or works were complied with substantially

and

(2)   that no claim for compensation has ever been made under Part III, Local Government (Planning and Development) Act, 1990

provided however that the foregoing warranty shall not extend to (and the Vendor shall not be required to establish) the obtaining of Approvals under the Building Bye-Laws or compliance with such Bye-Laws in respect of development or works executed prior to the 1st day of October, 1964.

(b)   The Vendor shall, with the copy documents to be delivered or sent in accordance with Condition 7, furnish to the Purchaser copies of all such Permissions and Approvals as are referred to in Condition 36(a) other than in the proviso thereto, and (where relevant) copies of all Fire Safety Certificates and (if available) Commencement Notices issued under Regulations made pursuant to the Building Control Act, 1990 and referable to the subject property.

(c) The Vendor shall, on or prior to completion of the sale, furnish to the Purchaser

   (i) written confirmation from the Local Authority of compliance with all conditions involving financial contributions or the furnishing of bonds in any such Permission or Approval (other than those referred to in the said proviso) or alternatively formal confirmation from the Local Authority that the roads and other services abutting on the subject property have been taken in charge by it without requirement for payment of moneys in respect of the same

   (ii) a Certificate or Opinion by an Architect or an Engineer (or other professionally qualified person competent so to certify or opine) confirming that, in relation to any such Permission or Approval (other than those referred to in the proviso aforesaid) the same relates to the subject property; that the development of the subject property has been carried out in substantial compliance therewith and that all conditions (other than financial conditions) thereof and all conditions expressly notified with said Permission by any Competent Authority and specifically directed to and materially affecting the subject property or any part of the same have been complied with substantially (and, in the event of the subject property forming part of a larger development, so far as was reasonably possible in the context of such development).

(d) Unless the Special Conditions contain a stipulation to the contrary, the Vendor warrants in all cases where the provisions of the Building Control Act, 1990 or of any Regulations from time to time made thereunder apply to the design or development of the subject property or any part of the same or any activities in connection therewith, that there has been substantial compliance with the said provisions in so far as they shall have pertained to such design development or activities and the Vendor shall, on or prior to completion of the sale, furnish to the Purchaser a Certificate or Opinion by an Architect or an Engineer (or other professionally qualified person competent so to certify or opine) confirming such substantial compliance as aforesaid.

RESCISSION

37. Upon rescission of the sale in accordance with any of the provisions herein or in the Special Conditions contained or otherwise:

(a) the Purchaser shall be entitled to a return of his deposit (save where it shall lawfully have been forfeited) but without interest thereon

(b) the Purchaser shall remit to the Vendor all documents in his possession belonging to the Vendor and the Purchaser shall at his expense (save where Special Conditions otherwise provide) procure the cancellation of any entry relating to the sale in any register.

38. If any such deposit as it to be returned pursuant to Condition 37 shall not have

been returned to the Purchaser within five working days from the date upon which the sale shall have been rescinded, the Purchaser shall be entitled to interest thereon at the stipulated interest rate from the expiration of the said period of five working days to the date upon which the deposit shall have been so returned.

39. The right to rescinded shall not be lost by reason only of any intermediate negotiations or attempt to comply with or to remove the issue giving rise to the exercise of such right

COMPLETION NOTICES

40. Save where time is of the essence in respect of the closing date, the following provisions shall apply:

(a) if the sale be not completed on or before the closing date either party may on or after that date (unless the sale shall first have been rescinded or become void) give to the other party notice to complete the sale in accordance with this condition, but such notice shall be effective only if the party giving it shall then either be able, ready and willing to complete the sale or is not so able, ready or willing by reason of the default or misconduct of the other party.

(b) upon service of such notice the party upon whom it shall have been served shall complete the sale within a period of twenty-eight after the date of such service (as defined in Condition 49 and excluding the date of service), and in respect of such period of time shall be the essence of the contract but without prejudice to any intermediate right of rescission by either party

(c) the recipient of any such notice shall give to the party serving the same reasonable advice of his readiness to complete

(d) if the Purchaser shall not comply with such a notice within the said period (or within any extension thereof which the Vendor may agree) he shall be deemed to have failed to comply with these Conditions in a material respect and the Vendor may enforce against the Purchaser, without further notice, such rights and remedies as may be available to the Vendor at law or in equality, or (without prejudice to such rights and remedies) may invoke and impose the provisions of Condition 41

(e) if the Vendor does not comply with such a notice within the said period (or within any extension thereof which the Purchaser may agree), then the Purchaser may elect either to enforce against the Vendor, without further notice, such rights and remedies as may be available to the Purchaser at law or in equality or (without prejudice to any right of the Purchaser to damages) to give notice to the Vendor requiring a return to the Purchaser of all moneys paid by him, whether by way of deposit or otherwise, on account of the purchase price. Condition 38 shall apply to all moneys so to be returned, the period of five working days therein being computed from the date of the giving of such last mentioned notice. If the Purchaser gives such a notice and all the said moneys and interest (if any) are remitted to him, the Purchaser shall no longer be entitled to specific performance of the sale, and shall return forthwith all documents in his possession belonging to the Vendor, and (at the Vendor's expense) procure the cancellation of any entry relating to the sale in any register

(f)   the party serving a notice under this Condition may, at the request of or with the consent of the other party, by written communication to the other party extend the term of such notice for one or more specified periods of time, and, in that case, the term of the notice shall be deemed to expire on the last day of such extended period or periods, and the notice shall operate as though such extended period or periods, had been specified in this Condition in lieu of the said period of twenty-eight days, and time shall be of the essence in relation to such extended period

(g)   the Vendor shall not be deemed to be other than able, ready and willing to complete for the purposes of this Condition

    (i)   by reason of the fact that the subject property has been mortgaged or charged, provided that the funds (including the deposit) receivable on completion shall (after allowing for all prior claims thereon) be sufficient to discharge the aggregate of all amounts payable in satisfaction of such mortgages and charges to the extent that they relate to the subject property

    or

    (ii)   by reason of being unable, not ready or unwilling at the date of services of such notice to deliver vacant possession of the subject property provided that (where it is a term of the sale that vacant possession thereof be given) the Vendor is, upon giving reasonable advice of the other party's intention to close the sale on a date within the said period of twenty - eight days or any extension thereof pursuant to Condition 40 (f), able, ready and willing to deliver vacant possession of the subject property on the date.

FORFEITURE OF DEPOSIT AND RESALE

41.   If the Purchaser shall fail in any material respect to comply with any of these Conditions, the Vendor (without prejudice to any rights or remedies available to him at law or in equity) shall be entitled to forfeit the deposit and shall be at liberty (without being obliged to tender an Assurance) to re-sell the subject property, with or without notice to the Purchaser, either by public auction or private treaty. In the event of the Vendor re-selling the subject property within one year after the closing date (or within one year computed from the expiration of any period by which the closing may have been extended pursuant to Condition 40) the deficiency (if any) arising on such re-sale and all costs and expenses attending the same or on any attempted re-sale shall (without prejudice to such damages to which the Vendor shall otherwise be

entitled) be made good to the Vendor by the Purchaser, who shall be allowed credit against same for the deposit so forfeited. Any increase in price obtained by the Vendor on any re-sale, whenever effected, shall belong to the Vendor.

DAMAGES FOR DEFAULT

42. Neither the Vendor not the Purchaser, in whose favour an order for specific performance has been made, shall be precluded from an award of damages at law or in equity, in the event of such order not being complied with.

RISK

43. Subject as hereinafter provided, the Vendor shall be liable for any loss or damage howsoever occasioned (other than by the Purchaser or his Agent) to the subject property (and the purchased chattels) between the date of sale and the actual completion of the sale BUT any such liability (including liability for consequential or resulting loss) shall not as to the amount thereof exceed the purchase price.

44. The liability imposed on the Vendor by Condition 43 shall not apply:

   (a) to inconsequential damage or insubstantial deterioration from reasonable wear and tear in the course of normal occupation and use, and not materially affecting value

   (b) to damage occasioned by operations reasonably undertaken by the Vendor in his removal from, and vacation of the subject property, provided that the same are so undertaken with reasonable care.

   (c) where any such loss or damage has resulted from a requirement restriction or obligation imposed by a Competent Authority after the date of sale.

45. Nothing in Conditions 43 and 44 shall affect:

   (a) the Purchaser's right to specific performance in an appropriate case

   (b) the Purchaser's right to rescind or repudiate the sale upon the Vendor's failure to deliver the subject property substantially in its condition at the date of sale (save where such failure shall have been occasioned by the Purchaser or his Agent)

   (c) the operation of the doctrine of conversion

   (d) the Purchaser's right to gains accruing to subject property (or the purchased chattels) after the date of sale

   (e) the Purchaser's right to effect on or after the date of sale his wown insurance against loss or damage in respect of the subject property or any part of the same (or the purchased chattels)

   (f) the rights and liabilities of parties other than the Vendor and the Purchaser

   (g) the rights and liabilities of the Purchaser on foot of any lease subsisting at the date of sale, or of any arrangement whereby the Purchaser shall prior to the actual completion of the sale have been allowed into occupation of the subject property or any part thereof (or into possession of the purchased chattels).

CHATTELS

46. Unless otherwise disclosed to the Purchaser prior to the sale the Vendor warrants that, at the actual completion of the sale, all the purchased chattels shall be his unencumbered property and that same shall not be subject to any lease, rental hire, hire-purchase or credit sale agreement or chattel mortgage.

INSPECTION

47. The Vendor shall accede to all such requests as may be made by the Purchaser for the inspection on a reasonable number of occasions and at reasonable times of the subject property (and the purchased chattels).

NON-MERGER

48. Notwithstanding delivery of the Assurance of the subject property to the Purchaser on foot of the sale, all obligations and provisions designed to survive completion of the sale and all warranties in the Conditions contained, which shall not have been implemented by the said Assurance, and which shall be capable of continuing or taking effect after such completion, shall enure and remain in full force and effect.

NOTICES

49. Unless otherwise expressly provided, any notice to be given or served on foot of the Conditions shall be in writing, and may (in addition to any other prescribed mode of service) be given:

(a)   by handing same to the intended recipient, and shall be deemed to have been delivered when so handed

(b)   by directing it to the intended recipient, and delivering it by hand, or sending same by prepaid post to:

    (i)   such address as shall have been advised by him to t he party serving the notice as being that required by the intended recipient for the service of notices,

       or

    (ii)   (failing such last mentioned advice) the address of the intended recipient as specified in the Memorandum,

       or

    (iii)   (in the event of the intended recipient being a Company) its Registered Office for the time being,

       or

    (iv)   the office of the Solicitor representing the intended recipient in relation to the sale

and any such notice shall e deemed to have been given or served, when delivered, at the time of delivery, and, when posted, at the expiration of three working days after the envelope containing the same, and properly addressed, was put in the post.

TIME LIMITS

50. Where the last day for taking any step on foot of the Conditions or any Notice served thereunder would, but for this provision, be a day other than a working day, such last day shall instead be the next following working day provided that for the purpose of this Condition the expression "working day" shall not be deemed to include (i) any Saturday, Sunday, Bank or Public Holiday nor (ii) any of the seven days immediately succeeding Christmas Day nor (iii) any day on which the registers or records wherein it shall be appropriate to make searches referable to the sale shall not be available to the public nor (iv) any day which shall be recognised by the Solicitors' Profession at large as being a day on which their offices are not open for business.

ARBITRATION

51. All differences and disputes between the Vendor and the Purchaser as to:
    (a)   whether a rent is or is not a rack rent for the purpose of Condition 10(c), or
    (b)   as to whether any interest is payable pursuant to Condition 25 or as to the rate or amount thereof or the date from which it shall be exigible, or
    (c)   the identification of the Apportionment Date, or the treatment or quantification of any item pursuant to the provisions for apportionment in the Conditions, or
    (d)   any issue on foot of Condition 33, including the applicability of said Condition, and the amount of compensation payable thereunder, or
    (e)   the materiality of any matter for the purpose of Condition 36(a), or
    (f)   the materiality of damage or any other question involving any of the provisions in Condition 43, 44 and 45, including the amount of compensation (if any) payable, or
    (g)   whether any particular item or thing is or is not included in the sale, or otherwise as to the nature or condition thereof

    shall be submitted to arbitration by a sole Arbitrator to be appointed (in the absence of agreement between the Vendor and the Purchaser upon such appointment and on the application of either of them) by the President (or other Officer endowed with the functions of such President) for the time being of the Law Society of Ireland or (in the event of the President or other Officer as aforesaid being unable or unwilling to make the appointment) by the next senior Officer of that Society who is so able and willing to make the appointment and such arbitration shall be governed by the Arbitration Acts, 1954 and 1980 provided however that if the Arbitrator shall relinquish his appointment or die, or if it shall become apparent that for any reason he shall be unable or shall have become unfit or unsuited (whether because of bias or otherwise) to complete his duties, or if he shall be removed from office by court Order, a substitute may be appointed in his place and in relation to any such appointment the procedures herein-before set forth shall be deemed to apply as though the substitution were an appointment de novo which said procedures may be repeated as many times as may be necessary.

Appendix III

OBJECTIONS AND REQUISITIONS ON TITLE

1996 Edition of Law Society Objections and Requisitions

OBJECTIONS AND REQUISITIONS ON TITLE

VENDOR:

PURCHASER:

PROPERTY:

YOUR REF: **OUR REF:**

1996 Edition of Law Society Objections and Requisitions

INDEX TO REQUISITIONS ON TITLE

Req	No Title	Page No
1.	Premises	821
2.	Services	821
3.	Easements and Rights	822
4.	Obligations/Privileges	822
5.	Forestry	823
6.	Fishing	823
7.	Sporting	823
8.	Possession	824
9.	Tenancies	824
10.	Housing (Private Rented Dwellings) Acts 1982-1983 (The Acts)	825
11.	Outgoings	826
12.	Notices	827
13.	Searches	829
14.	Incumbrances/Proceedings	830
15.	Voluntary Dispositions/Bankruptcy	830
16.	Taxation	831
17.	Non Resident Vendor	834
18.	Body Corporate Vendor	834
19.	Land Act 1965	836
20.	Unregistered Property	837
21.	Identity	838
22.	Registered Property	838
23.	Newly Erected Property	839
24.	Family Home Protection Act 1976 and Family Law Act 1995	840
25.	Family Law Act 1981 andFamily Law Act 1995	842
26.	Judicial Separation and Family Law Reform Act 1989 and Family Law Act 1995	842
27.	Local Government (Planning & Development) Act 1963	843
28.	Building Control Act 1990 and any Regulations or Instrument thereunder	846
29.	Fire Services Act 1981	847
30.	Safety Health and Welfare at Work (Construction) Regulations 1995	848
31.	Environmental	848
32.	Food Hygiene Regulations	849
33.	Leasehold/Fee Farm Grant Property	849
34.	Acquisitions of Fee Simple under the Landlord and Tenant (Ground Rent) Act 1967	850
35.	Local Government (Multi Storey Buildings) Act 1988	851
36.	New Flats/New Managed Properties	853
37.	Second Hand Flats/Second Hand Managed Properties	856
38.	Tax Based Incentives/Designated Areas	860
39.	Milk Quotas	861
40.	Licensing	862
41.	Restaurant/Hotel	866
42.	Special Restaurant Licence	867
43.	Dancing Music and Singing	869
44.	Completion	870

Please strike out and/or detach (where appropriate) Requisitions not Applicable

1. If these requisitions are used for the purpose of a mortgage "Vendor" shall read "Borrower" and "Purchaser" shall read "Lender"

2. In these Requisitions any reference to any Act shall include any extension amendment modification or re-enactment thereof and any regulation order or instrument made thereunder and for the time being in force.

OBJECTIONS ON TITLE	REPLIES

REQUISITIONS ON TITLE	REPLIES

Without prejudice to the foregoing objections (if any) the following Requisitions on Title are made:-

1. PREMISES

1. If any fixtures fittings or chattels included in the sale are the subject of any Lease, Rental, Hire Purchase Agreement or Chattel Mortgage furnish now the Agreement and on closing prove payment to date or (as the case may be) discharge thereof.

2. Which of the boundaries belong to the property and which are party.

3. In relation to the boundaries:-

    a. Furnish now any Agreements as to repair maintenance or otherwise.

    b. Are there are disputes with any adjoining owner.

4. Is the property registered under the National House Building Guarantee Scheme/HomeBond Scheme.

5. If so and if still in force furnish now Guarantee Certificate/Final Notice.

2. SERVICES

1. Is the property serviced with:-

    a. Drainage

    b. Water

    c. Electricity

    d. Telephone

    e. Gas

2. If applicable furnish letter(s) consenting to the transfer of the telephone line(s), instrument(s) and number(s) to the Purchaser.

REQUISITIONS ON TITLE	REPLIES

3. Have the services (including roads lanes footpaths sewers and drains) abutting or servicing the property been taken over by the Local Authority.

4. Furnish letter from the Local Authority or Solicitors Certificate based on an inspection of the Local Authority records or personal knowledge confirming the position.

5. If the services are not in charge furnish an Indemnity under Seal.

6. If an Indemnity has been given to the Vendor or his predecessor have it assigned to the Purchaser.

3. EASEMENTS AND RIGHTS

1.   a. Are there any pipes, drains, sewers, wires, cables or septic tank on under or over other property which serve the property in sale.
    b. If there are furnish now evidence of the easement grant or way-leave authorising same.
    c. What are the Vendor's rights and obligations in respect of the same.

2.   a. Is the property subject to any right of way water light air or drainage or to any other easement reservation covenant condition or restriction or to any right of any kind or
    b. Is the property subject to any liability to repair any road sewer drain or sea wall or to any other similar liability.
    c. If so, furnish now details of same.

4. OBLIGATIONS/PRIVILEGES

1. Is any road path drain wire cable pipe party wall or other facility (which is not in charge of the Local Authority) used in common with the owner or occupier of any other property.

REQUISITIONS ON TITLE	REPLIES

2. If so what are the Vendor's rights and obligations in respect of the aforementioned.

3. Furnish now any agreements in relation to such user.

5. FORESTRY

1. Is there any timber felling licence in existence.

2. If so furnish now any such licence.

3. Is there any unfulfilled condition requiring the planting or replanting of timber under the provisions of the Forestry Acts.

4. Give full details of such obligation.

5. Have any forestry grants been obtained.

6. If so furnish details and state whether any portion of the grant still remains payable.

6. FISHING

1. Furnish now details of any Fishing Licence or Right appurtenant to the property.

2. Is the property or any part thereof subject to any Licence or Right.

3. If granted by Deed furnish now a copy of such Deed.

4. Where any such Licence or Right (not granted by Deed) has not been exercised for twenty years furnish on closing affidavit to that effect.

7. SPORTING

1. Furnish now details of any Sporting Licence or Right appurtenant to the property.

2. Is the property or any part thereof subject to any Licence or Right.

3. If granted by Deed furnish now a copy of such Deed.

4. Where any such Licence or Right (not granted by Deed and not reserved to the Land Commission) in the case of:

REQUISITIONS ON TITLE	REPLIES

a. Section 18 of the Land Act 1965 has not exercised for twelve years furnish on closing affidavit to that effect.

b. Unregistered land has not been exercised for twenty years furnish on closing affidavit to that effect.

8. POSSESSION

Confirm that clear vacant possession of the entire property will be handed over at closing.

9. TENANCIES

1. a. Is the property or any part of it let.

    b. If so furnish now the Lease or Tenancy Agreement.

    c. If the Tenancy Agreement is not in writing state and prove the terms of the Tenancy.

    d. If the Tenant has completed a Renunciation under the Landlord & Tenant Act 1994 furnish now copy of same and original on closing.

2. When exactly did the tenant commence occupation of the property.

3. Furnish names of tenants, the rents payable and the gale days.

4. a. Was any security deposit paid by the Tenant at the commencement of tenancy

    b. If so the amount thereof should be handed to the Purchaser on closing.

5. a. If the property or any part of it is or was let, is it subject to any tenant's claim or future claim for compensation or otherwise.

    b. Is the Vendor or his Agent aware of any fact which will or may give rise to any such claim.

REQUISITIONS ON TITLE	REPLIES

6. a. Have any improvements been carried out by the tenant.
    b. If so furnish now details thereof.

7. On the closing hand over letters addressed to tenants notifying them of the sale and authorising payment of rents to the Purchaser.

8. If the tenancy is one to which the Housing (Miscellaneous Provisions) Act 1992 applies:-
    a. Have any Notices been served on the Vendor.
    b. If so, furnish now copies of same and evidence of compliance therewith.
    c. Confirm that the Tenant has been furnished with a rent book.
    d. Furnish certified copy Entry in the Register of the Housing Authority showing the property registered and any changes (as the case may be).

10. HOUSING (PRIVATE RENTED DWELLINGS) ACTS 1982-1983 (THE ACTS)

1. If the property or any part of it is a dwelling within the meaning of The Acts furnish now in respect of each tenant:-
    a. The date the tenant commenced to occupy the dwelling.
    b. The age and marital status of the tenant.
    c. The names and ages of those members of the tenant's family (within the meaning of The Acts) ordinarily residing in the dwelling.
    d. Particulars showing the basic rent of the dwelling pursuant to the Rent Restriction Acts 1960 to 1967.
    e. Copies of all notices served on or by the tenant.
    f. Copies of any orders determining the basic rent of the dwelling or any

REQUISITIONS ON TITLE	REPLIES

2. Confirm that the Vendor is the Landlord within the meaning of The Acts.

3. Furnish now:-
   a. Tenancy Agreement.
   b. Certificate of Registration with the Local Authority.
   c. Certificates of Registration of changes in terms of tenancy (if any) with the Local Authority.
   d. Certified copy Court Order or
   e. Certified copy Decision of Rent Tribunal or
   f. Certified copy Decision of Rent Officer

4. Has the rent of any tenancy been increased pursuant to Section 11(2) of the 1982 Act. If so vouch compliance therewith by furnishing Statutory Declaration of the Landlord or his Agent and Certificate of Registration.

5. Confirm that a Rent Book has been furnished to each tenant in compliance with the Regulations pursuant to the 1982 Act.

6. Has the Rent been paid to date.

7. a. Have any of the tenants made any improvements within the meaning of The Acts.
   b. If so have these improvements been taken into account in determining the rent.
   c. If so what proportion of the rent (if any) has been attributable to such improvements and how was this calculated.

11. OUTGOINGS
1. What is the Rateable Valuation of:
   a. Lands
   b. Buildings

REQUISITIONS ON TITLE	REPLIES

2. Has any work been carried out on the property which might result in the valuation being revised.

3. Has any notice or intimation been given of any change in the Rateable Valuation.

4. Give particulars of any remission of rates in force.

5.   a. Is there or has there been a separate water rate and/or refuse charge payable.
    b. If so, give full particulars naming the party to whom payable the basis of the charge and furnish now any Agreement or Contract which regulates such payment.

6. Give particulars of any other periodic or annual charge which affects the property or any part of it.

7. Furnish receipt to last accountable date in respect of all outgoings.

8. Furnish Apportionment Account together with vouchers necessary to vouch same.

9. Furnish on closing copy letter to Rating Authority notifying them of the change of ownership.

12. NOTICES

1.   a. Has any Notice, Certificate or Order been served upon or received by the Vendor or has the Vendor notice of any intention to serve any notice relating to the property or any part of it under the
Agricultural Credit Acts
Air Pollution Act
Building Control Act
Conveyancing Acts
Derelict Sites Acts

REQUISITIONS ON TITLE	REPLIES

Electricity Supply Acts
Environmental Agency Act
Fire Brigade Acts
Fire Services Acts
Forestry Acts
Gas Acts
Housing Acts
Housing (Private Rented Dwellings) Acts
Labourers Acts
Land Acts
Landlord and Tenants Acts
Local Government (Planning and Development)Acts
Local Government (Sanitary Services) Acts
Local Government (Sanitary Services) Acts
Mineral Development Acts
National Monuments Acts
Office Premises Act
Petroleum and other Minerals Development Acts
Public Health Acts
Registration of Title Act
Rent Restrictions Acts
Safety in Industry Acts
Succession Act
Water Pollution Act
Wildlife Act

or under any other Act or any Statutory Rule Order or Statutory Instrument.

b. Furnish now any Notice Certificate or Order so served or received.
c. Has the same been complied with.

REQUISITIONS ON TITLE	REPLIES

2.   a. Has the Vendor served any such Notice.

    b. If so furnish copy now.

3.   a. Has a Notice of intention to compulsorily acquire the property or to resume possession of the property or any part of it been served on the Vendor or his Agent by any Local or Statutory Authority or Body or person who has power to acquire the property compulsorily.

    b. If so furnish copy now.

13. SEARCHES

1. Give the Vendor's full name and present address.

2. Has the Vendor ever executed any document in relation to the property in the Irish equivalent or any other variant of his name.

3. Has the Vendor ever committed an act of bankruptcy or been adjudicated a bankrupt.

4. Purchaser will make Searches where necessary in the Registry of Deeds, Land Registry, Judgments (High Court Register of Judgments and Incumbrances affecting Real Estate) Bankruptcy Bills of Sale Sheriff's Revenue Sheriff's Office Companies Office and Planning Office and any acts appearing on any such Search must be explained and/or discharged (where applicable) by Vendor prior to or at closing.

5. Hand over now all Searches in Vendor's possession and furnish the Search provided for in the Contract with a full explanation (and discharge if applicable) of any Acts appearing therein.

REQUISITIONS ON TITLE	REPLIES

**14. INCUMBRANCES/
PROCEEDINGS**

1. Is the property subject to any:-

   a. Mortgage or Charge. If so, give full particulars. Evidence of Release or Discharge must be furnished on closing.
   b. Charge under the Public Health Acts as amended or extended.
   c. Rent charge.

2. a. Has the Vendor or his predecessor in title received any Grant in respect of the property
   b. If so furnish now particulars including the date of Grant approval.
   c. Is any part repayable.

3. Has any judgment been obtained against the Vendor which is capable of being registered as a Judgment Mortgage.

4. Is there any litigation pending or threatened or has any Court Order been made in relation to the property or any part of it or the use thereof or has any adverse claim thereto been made by any person.

5. a. Has any person other than the Vendor made any direct or indirect financial contribution or been the beneficiary of any agreement or arrangement whereby that person has acquired an interest in the property or any part of it.
   b. If so furnish now details of the interest acquired or claimed.

**15. VOLUNTARY DISPOSITIONS/
BANKRUPTCY**

If there is a voluntary disposition on Title furnish now in respect of each such disposition:-

REQUISITIONS ON TITLE	REPLIES

a. A Statutory Declaration from the Disponer that the disposition was made bona fide for the purpose of benefiting the Disponee and without fraudulent intent or if this is not within the reasonable procurement of the Vendor confirmation that the Vendor is not aware of any such fraudulent intent.

b. If the disposition was made within the past 5 years evidence by way of Statutory Declaration of the Disponer that at the date of the disposition the Disponer was solvent and able to meet his/her debts and liabilities without recourse to the property disposed of.

c. If the disposition was made within the past two years an insurance bond equal to the value of the property

d. A Bankruptcy Search against the Disponer.

16. TAXATION

1. a. On the death of any person on the title prior to the 1/4/1975 did any reversionary interest pass.

   b. If so was payment of Estate Duty arising on such passing deferred.

   c. If so, a certificate of the subsequent discharge of such duty must be furnished in any case where the reversionary interest fell into possession within six years of the date of this sale.

2. Furnish a certificate of absolute discharge from any Capital Acquisition Tax in respect of any gift or inheritance within the last twelve years or any gift within the meaning of Section 8 of the Capital Acquisitions Tax Act 1976.

REQUISITIONS ON TITLE	REPLIES

3. If there has been any taxable gift of the property comprised in the sale within the previous two years furnish now:

   a. Evidence by way of statutory declaration that the disponer is still alive.
   b. Term Assurance/Cash Deposit or other security to cover any additional Capital Acquisitions Tax which may arise by virtue of the death of the donor within two years from the date of the gift.

4. a. Was the property or any part thereof the subject of a discretionary trust as defined by the Finance Act 1984 on the 25th January 1984 or at any time thereafter.

   b. If so furnish now Certificate of Discharge from Capital Acquisitions Tax in relation thereto.

5. a. Has there been any death on the title after the 17th June 1993.
   b. If so furnish Certificate of Discharge from Probate Tax.

6. Where the title to the property or any part thereof depends on a claim of adverse possession furnish a Certificate of Discharge from Capital Acquisitions Tax pursuant to Section 146 of the Finance Act 1994.

7. If the consideration exceeds £100,000.00 either in this sale or in the aggregate of this and previous sales between the parties hereto furnish a Certificate under paragraph 11 of the Fourth Schedule to the Capital Gains Tax Act 1975

REQUISITIONS ON TITLE	REPLIES

8. In the event of such Certificate not being furnished on or prior to completion the Purchaser shall be bound to pay to the Revenue Commissioners 15% of the total consideration.

9. If the consideration is of such a kind that a monetary deduction cannot be made and the market value of the property exceeds £100,000.00 furnish a Certificate under paragraph 11(6) of the Fourth Schedule to the Capital Gains Tax Act 1975.

10. In the event of the Certificate referred to at 15.9 not being furnished the Purchaser shall be bound to give notice to the Revenue Commissioners of particulars of the transaction in accordance with paragraph 11(7) of the Fourth Schedule to the Capital Gains Tax Act 1975 as amended by Section 34 Finance Act 1982 and to enable the Purchaser to comply with Section 76 of the Finance Act 1995 the Vendor shall provide 15% of the estimated market value of the property to the Purchaser on closing.

11. Where the property in sale consists in whole or in part of residential property as defined in Section 95 of the Finance Act 1983 and the consideration exceeds the Residential Property Tax threshold furnish on or before closing:

   a. Certificate of Clearance from Residential Property Tax;
   b. Certificate of Discharge from Residential Property Tax where there has been a transfer between spouses after 17th June, 1993.

12. The Vendor must comply with the Finance Act 1909/10 as amended in relation to Particulars Delivered Stamp.

REQUISITIONS ON TITLE	REPLIES

17. NON RESIDENT VENDOR

1. If the Vendor is non-resident for tax purposes:

    a. Confirm that no direction has been served by the Revenue Commissioners under Section 21(2) Finance (Miscellaneous Provisions) Act 1968 as amended by Section 29 Finance Act 1981.

    b. On closing confirm in writing that no such direction has been served up to the time when the purchase monies are actually paid by the Purchaser

18. BODY CORPORATE VENDOR

1. Confirm that the Vendor is incorporated in the State.

2. Furnish now:-

    a. Certified copy Certificate of Incorporation together with Memorandum & Articles of Association Constitution or Rules evidencing the power to acquire hold mortgage or charge and dispose of property and the requirements for sealing documents.

    b. Copies of all existing mortgages charges debentures receiverships and winding up Notices.

3. Furnish on closing in relation to a Company:

    a. Certificate of Company Secretary that the Company has not executed any charges of any description which are not shown as registered in the Companies Registration Office.

REQUISITIONS ON TITLE	REPLIES

b. Certificate of Company Secretary that no Resolution to wind up the Company has been passed and that no Notice of a meeting at which it is proposed to wind up the Company has issued or been published and that no petition has been presented or is pending to wind up the Company or to place the Company in Receivership or to have a Receiver or an examiner appointed.

4. If the Company has issued a Debenture containing a Floating Charge, prove on closing that the Charge has not crystallised by way of letter from the Holder of the Floating Charge.

5. a. Does this transaction involve or form part of a larger transaction involving an arrangement within the meaning of Section 29(1)(a) and (b) of the Companies Act, 1990

   b. If so furnish relevant certificate of the Company Secretary.

   c. In respect of all transactions on title since the 1st day of February 1991 (including this transaction) involving such an arrangement furnish now a Resolution in General Meeting of the Company or its Holding Company as the case may be, approving the arrangement or alternatively a resolution in General Meeting of the Company or of its Holding Company as the case may be, in accordance with Section 29(3)(c) of the Act for the purpose of affirming the arrangement.

6. a. Does this transaction or any other transaction on title involve or form part of a larger transaction involving a loan quasi loan or credit transaction which is prohibited by Section 31 of the Companies Act 1990.

REQUISITIONS ON TITLE	REPLIES

b. If such transaction is not prohibited by reason of the exceptions contained in Sections 32 to 37 of the Act furnish Certificate of Company Secretary/Auditors to this effect and identifying the nature of the particular exception.

19. LAND ACT 1965

1. Furnish evidence of compliance with Section 45 of the Land Act 1965 in all appropriate cases

2. Was the ownership of the property vested in a Body Corporate and control of that Body Corporate transferred to a person who was not "a qualified person". If so

   (i) Was Notice served under Section 45(5) of the Land Act 1965 as amended.
   (ii) Has any action been taken on foot of any such Notice.

3 Furnish now copy of any Vesting Order made to provide for consolidation with the property sold.

4. Does the present transaction (or in the case of unregistered property any previous transaction) give rise to a letting sub-letting or subdivision of a holding which requires consent in writing under Section 12 of the Land Act 1965.

   a. If so furnish original letter consenting to the letting, sub-letting or subdivision of the property under Section 12 of the Land Act 1965 with the appropriate Map; and

   b. A letter from the Land Commission or its successors confirming that all relevant conditions in the Letter of Consent to subdivision have been complied with.

REQUISITIONS ON TITLE	REPLIES

In lieu of a. and b. above:-

    c. Confirm that the General Consent to subdivision pursuant to S.I. No. 13/77 applies to the present or any past sale.

    d. If the property is subject to a Land Purchase Annuity or Land Reclamation Annuity confirm that subdivisions (including the present sale) in excess of 2 hectares have not been effected under the General Consent procedure.

5. If any part of the holding of which the property forms part is situate within the boundary of a County Borough a Dublin County a Borough Urban District or Town confirm that the property is not subject to a Land Purchase Annuity.

20. UNREGISTERED PROPERTY

1. Furnish now a written Assent by the Personal Representative of any person on the title who died after 31st of May 1959.

2. If all or any of the property is unregistered land the registration of which was compulsory prior to the date of Contract procure such registration prior to completion of the sale

3. If all or any of the property is unregistered land the registration of which will become compulsory by virtue of this sale furnish now:

    a. A map of the property complying with the requirements of the Land Registry.

REQUISITIONS ON TITLE	REPLIES

   b. Vendor's undertaking that if requested to do so within two years from the completion of the sale he shall, at the Purchaser's expense supply any additional information which he may reasonably be able to supply and produce and furnish any documents in his possession that may be required to effect such registration.

4. Where may the originals of all title documents be inspected.

5. Which of them will be delivered to the Purchaser on completion.

6. If applicable who will give the Purchaser the usual statutory acknowledgement and undertaking for the production and safe custody of those documents not handed over.

21. IDENTITY
The identity of the property sold with that to which title is purported to be shown must be proved.

22. REGISTERED PROPERTY

1. Furnish now copies of the following:

   a. Certified copy Folio written up to date.
   b. Land Registry Map/File Plan
   c. Certificate of Redemption Value of any Land Purchase Annuity unless such annuity will be automatically removed.
   d. Draft Section 72 Declaration should any such burden affect the property.
   e. Draft Affidavit to convert possessory title to absolute where relevant.
   f. In the case of a transfer of part of a Folio a site map complying with Land Registry mapping requirements or a Land Registry Approved Scheme Map.

REQUISITIONS ON TITLE	REPLIES

2. Furnish on closing:

    a. Original Land Certificate or in the case of the transfer of part of a folio an undertaking to lodge it in the Land Registry immediately on completion and a letter consenting to its use for the purpose of the registration of the Purchaser's transfer.

    b. Where the Land Certificate has not issued confirmation that application has not been made for its issue.

    c. Land Registry Map/File Plan

    d. In the case of the transfer of part of a folio a site map complying with Land Registry Mapping requirements or a Land Registry Approved Scheme Map together with an undertaking by or on behalf of Vendor to discharge Land Registry mapping queries.

    e. Certificate of Redemption Value.

    f. Section 72 Declaration.

    g. If the title is possessory or qualified affidavit or sufficient evidence to enable the Purchaser to convert it to absolute.

3. Confirm that Vendor is the registered owner.

4. Have any dealings been registered on the Folio or are any dealings pending which are not shown on the Folio furnished.

23. NEWLY ERECTED PROPERTY

1. Furnish now

    a. Draft Assurance.

    b. Draft Site Map.

    c. Draft Statutory Declaration of Identity by the Vendor's Architect or other competent person confirming that the entire of the property as shown on the site map and the rights of way, easements and the services relating thereto form part of the lands to which the Vendor has shown title.

REQUISITIONS ON TITLE	REPLIES

d. Draft Indemnity in relation to roads footpaths sewers and all services.

e. Draft Indemnity in relation to defects.

f. Floor Area Certificate.

g. Particulars Delivered Form for completion by the Purchaser.

h HB10 HomeBond Scheme Guarantee Agreement.

2. At closing hand over:

a. Original Assurance duly completed assessed for stamp duty or adjudged exempt therefrom with Particulars Delivered Stamp impressed and a Certificate of Compliance with the building or other covenants endorsed thereon.

b. Memorial duly completed.

c. Architect's Statuary Declaration of Identity in accordance with 23.1.c.

d. Indemnity under Seal in relation to roads footpaths sewers and all services.

e. Indemnity under Seal in relation to defects.

f. Architect's Certificate confirming that all buildings have been erected within the confines of the site as per the Deed map.

g. HB10 Agreement under the HomeBond Scheme completed by the Vendor.

h. HB11 Notice under the HomeBond Scheme.

3. If the property is registered land furnish in addition certified copy of the Assurance.

24. FAMILY HOME PROTECTION ACT 1976 ("THE 1976 ACT") AND FAMILY LAW ACT 1995 ("THE 1995 ACT")

1. Is the property or any part thereof the Vendor's "family home" as defined in either the 1976 Act or 1995 Act.

REQUISITIONS ON TITLE	REPLIES

2. If the answer to 24.1 is in the affirmative furnish the prior written consent of the Vendor's spouse and verify the marriage by statutory declaration exhibiting therein copy civil marriage certificate and furnish draft Declaration and copy Exhibit now for approval.

3. If the answer to 24.1 is in the negative state the grounds relied upon and furnish now draft statutory declaration with exhibits for approval verifying these grounds.

4. In respect of all "conveyances" (as defined in the 1976 Act) of unregistered property made on or after the 12th July 1976 furnish spouses' prior written consents where appropriate together with verification of marriage by statutory declaration exhibiting therein copy civil marriage certificate or where consent is not necessary furnish evidence verifying same by way of statutory declaration.

5.   a. Did/does the property or any part thereof comprise the "family home" of any person other than the Vendor or previous owner.

    b. If so give the name of such person and give the nature of the "interest" (if any) in the property.

    c. In relation to any such person having an "interest" furnish the prior written consent of that person's spouse to any "conveyance" (as defined as aforesaid) of that person's interest in the property or any part thereof since 12th July 1976 and verify such spouse's marriage by statutory declaration exhibiting therein copy civil marriage certificate.

REQUISITIONS ON TITLE	REPLIES

d. If such person did not have an "interest" as above in the property or any part of it state the grounds relied upon and furnish now draft statutory declaration for approval verifying those grounds.

25. FAMILY LAW ACT 1981 ("THE 1981 ACT") AND THE FAMILY LAW ACT 1995 ("THE 1995 ACT")

1. Has there been any disposition of the property to which Sections 3 and 4 of the 1981 Act would apply.

2. If the answer to 25.1 is in the negative furnish statutory declaration verifying this fact on closing and furnish now draft Declaration for approval.

3. If such a disposition was made then the other party to the engagement and the donor must join in the Deed to release and assure his/her/their respective interest(s) in the property.

4. Confirm by way of Statutory Declaration that Section 5 of the 1981 Act (as amended by Section 48 of the 1995 Act) does not affect the property (if such is the case) and furnish now draft Declaration for approval.

26. JUDICIAL SEPARATION AND FAMILY LAW REFORM ACT 1989 ("THE 1989 ACT") AND FAMILY LAW ACT 1995 ("THE 1995 ACT")

1. Confirm by way of Statutory Declaration that no Application or Order has been made under the 1989 Act and that no order has been made under the 1995 Act.

REQUISITIONS ON TITLE	REPLIES

2. Confirm that this is not a "disposition" for the purposes of defeating a claim for "financial relief" (as defined in Section 29 of the 1989 Act) or "relief" (as defined in Section 35 of the 1995 Act).

3. If the Vendor acquired the property after 19/9/1989 confirm that he was a bona fide purchaser for value (other than marriage) without notice of any intention to defeat a claim for financial relief.

4. Furnish now draft Declaration for approval.

27. LOCAL GOVERNMENT (PLANNING & DEVELOPMENT) ACT 1963 ("THE PLANNING ACT")

1. Has there been in relation to the property any development (including change of use or exempted development) within the meaning of the Planning Act on or after the 1st October 1964.

2. In respect of all such developments furnish now (where applicable):
   a. Grant of Planning Permission or
   b. Outline Planning Permission and Grant of Approval.
   c. Building Bye Law Approval (if applicable).
   d. Evidence of Compliance with the financial conditions by way of letter/receipt from the Local Authority.
   e. Certificate/Opinion from an Architect/Engineer that the Permission/Approval relates to the property and that the development has been carried out in conformity with the Permission/Approval and with the Building Bye-Law Approval (if applicable) and that all conditions other than financial conditions have been complied with.

REQUISITIONS ON TITLE	REPLIES

f. In respect of exempted developments in each case the grounds upon which it is claimed that the development is an exempted development and certificate/opinion from an Architect/Engineer in support of such claim.

3. In respect of developments completed after the 1st November 1976 furnish now evidence by way of Statutory Declaration of a competent person that each development was completed prior to expiration of the Permission/Approval.

4. Is the property subject to:

    a. Any Special Amenity Area Preservation Conservation or any other order under the Planning Acts which affect the property or any part thereof.

    b. Any actual or proposed designation of all or any of the property whereby it would become liable to compulsory purchase or acquisition for any purpose under the Planning Acts.

5. Is there any unauthorised development as defined in the Planning Acts.

6. If there is any such unauthorised development furnish prior to closing:

    a. A retention permission for such development and

b. Satisfactory evidence of compliance from an Architect/Engineer with the conditions in the said permission and

c. If applicable satisfactory evidence from an Architect/Engineer that the development substantially complies with the Bye-Laws or with the Regulations made under the Building Control Act 1990.

REQUISITIONS ON TITLE	REPLIES

7. What is/are the present use/uses of the property.

8. Has the property been used for each of the uses aforesaid without material change continuously since the 1st day of October 1964.

9. Give particulars of any application for permission and/or approval under the Planning Acts and the Building Bye-laws and state the result thereof.

10 a. Has any agreement been entered into the Planning Authority pursuant to Section 38 of the 1963 Act restricting or regulating the development or use of the property.

   b. If so furnish now copy of same.

11. a. Has there been any application for or award of compensation under the Planning Acts.

   b. If so, furnish now copy of same.

   c. Has a statement of compensation been registered on the Planning Register under Section 9 of the 1990 Planning Act prohibiting development of the property under Section 10 of the said Act.

12. a. If any development was carried out prior to the 13th of December 1989 and Building Bye-Law Approval was either not obtained or not complied with furnish now Declaration that the development was completed prior to the 13th of December 1989 and that no Notice under Section 22 of the Building Control Act 1990 was served by the the Building Control Authority between the 1st June 1992 and the 1st of December 1992.

REQUISITIONS ON TITLE	REPLIES

b. Has there been any development carried out since the 13th of December 1989 with the benefit of Building Bye-Law Approval. If so furnish now copy of same and draft Engineer's/Architect's Opinion of Compliance.

13 Furnish now Statutory Declaration by a competent person evidencing user of the property from the 1st October 1964 to date.

28. BUILDING CONTROL ACT 1990 AND ANY REGULATIONS ORDER OR INSTRUMENT THEREUNDER (REFERRED TO COLLECTIVELY AS "THE REGULATIONS")

1. Is the property or any part thereof affected by any of the provisions of the Regulations.

2. If it is claimed that the property is not affected by the Regulations state why. Evidence by way of a Statutory Declaration of a competent person may be required to verify the reply.

3. If the property is affected by the Regulations furnish now a Certificate/ Opinion of Compliance by a competent person confirming that all necessary requirements of the Regulations have been met.

4. a. Has a Commencement Notice been given to the Building Control Authority in respect of the property.
   b. If so furnish now a copy of the same.

5. If the property is such that a Fire Safety Certificate is one of the requirements of the Regulations:

REQUISITIONS ON TITLE	REPLIES

a. A copy of the Fire Safety Certificate must be attached to and referred to in the Certificate of Compliance which should confirm that the works to the property have been carried out in accordance with the drawings and other particulars on foot of which the Fire Safety Certificate was obtained and with any conditions of the Fire Safety Certificate.

b. Confirm that no appeal was made by the Applicant for such Certificate against any of the conditions imposed by the Building Control Authority in such Fire Safety Certificate.

6. a. Has any Enforcement Notice under Section 8 of the Building Control Act been served.

b. If so, furnish now a copy of the Notice and a Certificate of Compliance made by a competent person.

7. If any application has been made to the District Court under Section 9 of the Building Control Act 1990 furnish details of the result of such application.

8. a. Has any application been made to the High Court under Section 12 of Building Control Act 1990.
b. If so furnish a copy of any Order made by the Court and evidence of any necessary compliance with such order by a Certificate of a competent person.

29. FIRE SERVICES ACT 1981 ("THE ACT")

1. a. Have any Notices been served under the Act.
   b. If so furnish now copies of same.
   c. Are there any proceedings pending under the Act.

REQUISITIONS ON TITLE	REPLIES

2. a. Has the property ever been inspected by the Fire Authority for the functional area within which the property is situate.

   b. If so what were its requirements.

3. Furnish Architect's/Engineer's Certificate of substantial Compliance with any such notices or requirements.

30. SAFETY HEALTH AND WELFARE AT WORK (CONSTRUCTION) REGULATIONS 1995 ("THE REGULATIONS")

1. Has any construction work (as defined in the Regulations) been undertaken by the Client (as defined in the Regulations) at or in the premises where the commencement stage (as defined in the Regulations) was subsequent to 1 March 1996.

2. If so furnish now copy Safety File containing the information required by the Regulations and furnish (if applicable) original Safety File on completion.

31. ENVIRONMENTAL

1. Has any notice certificate order requirement or recommendation been served upon or received by the Vendor or has the Vendor notice of any intention to serve any notice relating to the property or any part of it under or by virtue of or pursuant to the European Community Act 1972 by way of the implementation of directives for the control or prevention of pollution or preservation or improvement of the environment or any law relating to the Environment whether Irish Law European Community Law any common or customary law or legislation and any order rule regulation directive statutory instrument bye-law or any legislative measure thereunder; ("the Environmental Controls").

REQUISITIONS ON TITLE	REPLIES

2. Furnish now any notice certificate order requirement or recommendation so received.

3. Has the same been complied with?

4. Is the Vendor aware of any breach of the Environmental Controls in respect of the property.

5. If so give full particulars.

32. FOOD HYGIENE REGULATIONS

1. a. Is the use of the property one which requires to be registered with the Local Health Authority pursuant to the Food Hygiene Regulations 1950 as amended.
    b. If so furnish now evidence of such registration.
    c. Furnish evidence of compliance with any conditions or undertakings attached to such registration.

2. a. Has any notice been served by the Health Authority or has the Vendor or his agents any information of an intention to serve any such notice.
    b. If any such notices have been received furnish now full copies thereof stating whether same have been complied with either in full or in part.
    c. With regard to any such notices furnish details of any undertakings given in respect thereof.

33. LEASEHOLD/FEE FARM GRANT PROPERTY

1. Furnish evidence of the title to make the Lease/Fee Farm Grant.

2. Prove performance and observance of the covenants and conditions contained in the Lease/Fee Farm Grant.

3. Has any Notice affecting the property been served by the Lessor/Grantor.

REQUISITIONS ON TITLE	REPLIES

4. Has there been any breach, non observance or non-performance of any of the covenants conditions or stipulations contained in the Lease/Fee Farm Grant.

5. Produce for inspection and hand over at closing the last receipt for rent payable.

6. Furnish the name and address of the person to whom the rent is now payable and the åmount payable showing any deductions or adjustments together with copy letter to such person notifying them of the Assignment.

7. If the rent is nominal and has not been demanded in the case of a Lease for six years or a Fee Farm Grant for twelve years furnish now a draft of a Declaration to be completed by the Vendor on closing containing a statement that:

   a. No rent during that period has been demanded.
   b. No notices have been served upon him.
   c. There have been no breaches or non observance of the covenants and conditions contained in the Lease/ Fee Farm Grant.

8. Confirm that an allowance will be made in the appointment account in respect of any unpaid rent for the past six/twelve years.

9. Furnish the consent of the Landlord to the Assignment (if applicable) by way of endorsement on the Deed.

34. ACQUISITIONS OF FEE SIMPLE UNDER THE LANDLORD AND TENANT (GROUND RENT) ACT 1967

1. Has the Vendor taken any steps to acquire the Fee Simple.

2. If so what is the nature of the application i.e. is it by way of Vesting Certificate or otherwise.

REQUISITIONS ON TITLE	REPLIES

3. If it is by way of Vesting Certificate furnish copy thereof (if issued).

4. If the Vesting Certificate has not issued confirm whether the application for the vesting is being processed by way of consent or arbitration.

5. If the acquisition is by way of consent furnish the consent of the original applicant to the issue of the Vesting Certificate in the name of the Purchaser.

6. If the application is by way of arbitration furnish the consent of the original applicant to the continuation of the arbitration by the Land Registry on behalf of the Purchaser.

7. If the Vesting Certificate has not been registered arrange to have registration effected prior to completion.

8. If the Vendor has taken steps to acquire the Fee Simple and the acquisition is not by way of Vesting Certificate furnish details.

35. LOCAL GOVERNMENT (MULTI STOREY BUILDINGS) ACT 1988 ("THE 1988 ACT")

1. Is the property or any part of the property a multi-storey building within the meaning of the 1988 Act or does it form part of a development in which there is a multi-storey building with which it shares a common Management Company.

2. If so is it governed by:
   a. The Regulations as defined in Requisition 28 or
   b. The 1988 Act.

3. a. If the answer to 1 above is in the negative because the entire building was constructed prior to the 1st day of January 1950 furnish now a statutory declaration by a person who can prove satisfactorily that the building was so constructed.

851

REQUISITIONS ON TITLE	REPLIES

b. If the answer to 2b above is in the affirmative reply to Requisitions 4-9 below.

4. a. Has a notice been served by the local authority under section 2(2) of the 1988 Act.

    b. If so furnish now a copy of the same.

    c. Whether or not such notice has been served and the construction of the building was completed prior to the 14th November 1988 furnish now a certificate from a competent person in accordance with Section 3(a) or a declaration in accordance with Section 3(b) of the 1988 Act.

5. Where a Certificate has been submitted to the Local Authority pursuant to Section 3 of the 1988 Act:

    a. State whether or not the same is in accordance with the appropriate form provided for in the Regulations made and in force under the 1988 Act.

    b. Furnish now a copy of the said Certificate.

6. a. Has any work been carried out to the building which might nullify the effect of a Certificate furnished in accordance with Section 3 and require a further certificate in accordance with Section 5 of the 1988 Act.

    b. If so furnish now a certified copy of such certificate.

7. If the building is a multi-storey building the construction of which was not completed prior to the 14th of November 1988 furnish now a certified copy of the certificate in the prescribed form submitted to the Local Authority pursuant to Section 4 of the 1988 Act.

REQUISITIONS ON TITLE	REPLIES

8. Have any notices been served under the 1988 Act which have not been complied with.

9. Where any Certificate has been submitted to the Local Authority under the 1988 Act furnish a letter from the Local Authority confirming that the Certificate has been placed on the Register.

36. NEW FLATS/NEW MANAGED PROPERTIES (IN A DEVELOPMENT HEREINAFTER DESCRIBED AS "THE ESTATE")

1. Furnish now for perusal:
   a. Site Plan and Floor Plan showing the property coloured or outlined thereon.
   b. Certified copy Lease of the common areas to the Management Company (if applicable).
   c. Certified copy Contract for the sale of the reversionary interest to the Management Company.
   d. Certified copy of the Block Insurance Policy. The name of the Purchaser and, if requested, the interest of the Mortgagee must be noted thereon before completion and evidenced by letter from the Insurance company confirming that it will not cancel lapse or fail to renew the policy without first giving 15 days notice prior to cancellation to the Purchaser/Mortgagee.
   e. Certified copy Certificate of Incorporation and Memorandum and Articles of Association of the Management Company.

2. Confirm that on the completion of the Estate:

REQUISITIONS ON TITLE	REPLIES

a. All the Leases/Conveyances either granted or to be granted are or will be in a similar form to the Lease/Conveyance to the Purchaser. Certificate to this effect to be furnished on closing.

b. One Management Company will be responsible for the management of the external and/or internal common areas of the entire Estate and all the services relating thereto.

c. The service charge will be divided equally among the number of units in the Estate.

d. The only shareholders/members in the Management Company will be the unit owners.

e. Each of the unit owners will have equal shareholdings or voting rights.

3. Do/will any persons other than Purchasers (in particular the Developer or its nominees) hold shares or voting rights in the Management Company.

4. Is the Developer or the Management Company managing the Estate or has a firm of managing agents been engaged.

5. If a firm of managing agents has been engaged state:

   a. the name of the firm
   b. the terms of their engagements including (in particular) the amount of their charges.
   c. whether they are employed by the Developer or by the Management Company.

6. a. Are there Rules of the Management Company other than as set out in the Memorandum and Articles of Association.
   b. If so furnish now details of these Rules.

REQUISITIONS ON TITLE	REPLIES

7. a. Is it proposed to establish a sinking or reserve fund or has one already been established.

    b. If already established what is the present level of the fund and in whose name is it held.

8. a. Are the accounts of the Management Company available for the previous financial year.

    b. If so furnish now a copy of same.

9. What is the amount of the service charge currently payable.

10. Is the Vendor aware of any possible claim against the Management Company's funds.

11. Is the Vendor aware of any proposal by the Management Company to carry out any repair work or incur other expenditure which would substantially affect the charge payable at present.

12. Hand over on closing:

    a. Certified copy Folio showing the Management Company as registered owner or certified copy Deed of Assurance of the reversionary interest to the Management Company or, in lieu thereof, undertaking to furnish same.

    b. Share Certificate in or Certificate of Membership of the Management Company in the name of the Purchaser.

    c. Certified copy of the Block Insurance Policy with the Purchaser's and (if applicable) Mortgagee's name(s) noted thereon together with a certified copy of the receipt for the latest premium.

REQUISITIONS ON TITLE	REPLIES

13. Is the property a "qualifying" premises within the meaning of
    a. Section 23 of the Finance Act 1981;
    b. Section 29 of the Finance Act 1983;
    c. Section 27 of the Finance Act, 1988 (as extended).

14. If so furnish now:
    a. Floor area Certificate.
    b. Certificate from Minister for the Environment that the property conforms to the floor area limits and the required standard of construction.
    c. Builders Statement of the cost of construction and cost of site acquisition.
    d. Confirmation that the property has not ceased to be a qualifying premises within the meaning of the relevant Section.

15. Was the entire expenditure on the construction of the property incurred between:

    a. 28/1/1981 and 31/3/1984 or,
    b. 1/4/1984 and 31/3/1987 or,
    c. 1/1/1988 and 31/3/1992
       (or 31/7/1992 if foundations laid prior to 28/1/1992)

37. SECOND HAND FLATS/SECOND HAND MANAGED PROPERTIES (IN A DEVELOPMENT HEREINAFTER DESCRIBED AS "THE ESTATE")

1. Furnish now:
    a. Evidence by way of Companies Office Search that the Management Company is still registered in the Companies Office.
    b. Copy Folio showing Management Company as registered owner or,

REQUISITIONS ON TITLE	REPLIES

c. Copy Deed of Assurance of reversionary interest to the Management Company.

d. Certified copy of the Block Insurance Policy. The name of the purchaser and, if requested, the interest of mortgagee must be noted thereon before completion and evidenced by letter from the Insurance Company confirming that it will not cancel lapse or fail to renew the policy without first giving 15 days notice prior to cancellation to the Purchaser/ Mortgagee

e. Certified copy Certificate of Incorporation and Memorandum and Articles of Association of the Management Company.

2. If the Management Company is not the owner of the reversionary interest furnish now:

a. Copy Contract for Sale of the reversionary interest to the Management Company

b. Confirmation as to when it is anticipated the sale to the Management Company will be completed.

c. Evidence that the developer if a company is still registered in the Companies Office.

d. Developers' solicitors' undertaking to furnish 1b or 1c above.

3. Confirm that on the completion of the Estate:

a. One Management Company is or will be responsible for the management of the external and/or internal common areas of the entire Estate and all the services relating thereto.

REQUISITIONS ON TITLE	REPLIES

b. The only shareholders/members in the Management Company are/will be the unit owners.

c. Each of the unit owners has or will have equal shareholdings or voting rights.

d. The service charge is or will be divided equally amongst the number of the units in the Estate.

e. No persons other than unit owners (in particular, the Developer or its nominees) will hold shares or voting rights in the Management Company.

4. Who is at present managing the Estate.

5. If a firm of managing agents has been engaged state:

a. The name of the firm.

b. The terms of their engagement including (in particular) the amount of their charges.

c. Whether they are employed by the Developer or the Management Company.

6. a. Are there Rules of the Management Company other than as set out in the Memorandum and Articles of Association.

b. If so furnish now details of these Rules.

7. a. Has the Management Company put a sinking or reserve fund into effect.

b. If so what is the present level of the Fund and where and in whose name is it held.

8. Furnish now copy of the accounts of the Management Company for the previous financial year.

9. What is the amount of the service charge currently payable.

REQUISITIONS ON TITLE	REPLIES

10. Is the Vendor or the Management Company aware of any possible claim against the Management Company's Funds.

11. Is the Vendor aware of any proposal by the Management Company to carry out any repair work or incur other expenditure which would substantially affect the service charge payable at present.

12. Does the property qualify for Income Tax relief under
    a. Section 23 of the Finance Act 1981;
    b. Section 29 of the Finance Act 1983;
    c. Section 27 of the Finance Act 1988 (as extended).
    d. If so furnish now computation of the amount of the purchase consideration available for relief under Section 23 of the Finance Act 1981, Section 29 of the Finance Act 1983 or Section 27 of the Finance Act, 1988 (as extended) assuming compliance with the other conditions and evidence that the said amount shall be treated by the Revenue Commissioners as expenditure having been incurred in the construction of the property.

13. Confirm that the property has not ceased to be a "qualifying premises" within the meaning of the Section 23 of the Finance Act 1981 Section 29 of the Finance Act 1983 or Section 27 of the Finance Act 1988 (as extended).

14. State whether the entire expenditure on the construction of the property was incurred between:
    a. 28/1/1981 and 31/3/1984; or

REQUISITIONS ON TITLE	REPLIES

b. 1/4/1984 and 31/3/1987; or
c. 1/1/1988 and 31/3/1992
(or the 31/7/1992 if foundations laid before 28/1/1992)

15. Hand over on closing:
  a. Certified copy Folio showing Management Company as registered owner or
  b. Certified Copy Deed of Assurance of Reversionary Interest to the Management Company or
  c. Certified copy Contract for the Sale of the reversionary interest to the Management Company together with an assignment of the undertaking to furnish a certified copy of the aforesaid Deed/Folio.
  d. Share Certificate in or Certificate of Membership of the Management Company in the name of the Vendor.
  e. Share Transfer Form duly completed by Vendor (where applicable).
  f. Certified Copy of the Block Insurance Policy with the Purchaser's and (if applicable) Mortgagee's name(s) noted thereon together with a certified copy of the receipt for the latest premium.
  g. Receipt for latest payment of Service Charge.

38. TAX BASED INCENTIVES/ DESIGNATED AREAS

1. Is the property eligible for tax reliefs allowances or benefits.

2. If so under which of the Tax/Finance Acts is it so eligible.

3. Hand over on closing all documentation required on the part of the Vendor to transfer allowances to the Purchaser.

REQUISITIONS ON TITLE	REPLIES

39. MILK QUOTAS

In these Requisitions reference to the Regulations mean the European Communities (Milk Quotas) Regulations 1995 and any extension amendment modification or re-enactment thereof.

1. Is there a Milk Quota as defined in the Regulations attaching to the property.
2. If so furnish now a letter from the Vendor Co-Operative or Milk Purchaser certifying:

    a. The amount of the Vendor's Milk Quota in the current year.
    b. The amount of Milk supplied by the Vendor under his Quota for the current Quota Year up to the date of the Certificate.
    c. That the Quota is not a Slom 111 Quota.

3. Furnish now clarification as to whether the Vendor proposes filling any part of the unused Quota prior to the closing date and if so an estimate as to the amount proposed to be filled.
4. Furnish now evidence by way of Affidavit identifying the land to which the Milk Quota attaches including:

    a. Evidence to show that there was sufficient milk produced by the Vendor so as to identify "the land used for milk production" as defined by the Regulations or
    b. Exhibiting Certificate from the Minister identifying the land to which the Milk Quota attaches.

5. If part only of the Vendor's quota lands are being sold identify now by way of Map the lands to which the entire Quota attaches and confirm that the Quota has been apportioned between lands being sold and lands retained on a pro rata acreage basis.

REQUISITIONS ON TITLE	REPLIES

6. Furnish on closing:

   a. Transfer form in accordance with the First Schedule of the Regulations duly completed by the Vendor.

   b. An up-to-date letter from the Vendor Co-Operative or other Milk Purchaser certifying the amount of Quota filled by the Vendor in the current Quota year.

   c. The original of any Certificate of Retention or Certificate of Transfer issued by the Minister pursuant to the Regulations with the appropriate Maps attached thereto and confirmation that the Transfer was made within the time limit specified in the said Certificate.

7. a. If the ownership of the holding changed other than by way of inheritance since the 1st April 1994 has there been any reduction in the area of the holding since that date.

   b. If so furnish evidence to show that the Milk Quota attaching to the property disposed of from the holding is not included in the Milk Quota figure referred to in the Contract for Sale.

40. LICENSING

1. a. Is there a current licence attached to the property

   b. If so state fully and concisely the character of the licence and furnish a complete copy thereof (front and back).

REQUISITIONS ON TITLE	REPLIES

2. Is the licence a Publican's Licence (Ordinary) entitling the holder thereof to sell intoxicating liquor whether for consumption on or off the property during the ordinary hours of opening permitted by law.

3. Specify the Statute and Section(s) pursuant to which the licence was granted.

4. a. On what date was the licence first granted.
    b. If this information cannot be ascertained state whether the license was first granted prior to or subsequent to the 31st July 1902.

5. Does the license carry the benefit of any special or general exemptions.

6. a. Are there any conditions restrictions or qualifications attaching to the licence
    b. If so specify same in detail.

7. Is the property regularly open for the conduct of the Publican's business.

8. Furnish now plan of the property showing the exact extent of the property covered by the licence.

9. Are there any statutory provisions relating to the structural lay-out or user of the property non-compliance with which might affect the validity of the licence or the right to renew.

10. a. Has the property ever been altered or enlarged since the date upon which the same was first licensed.

    b. If so was an application made to the Court and an Order granted under Section 6 of the Licensing (Ireland) Act 1902 as amended by Section 24 of the Intoxicating Liquor Act 1960.

    c. If the answer to b. above is in the affirmative furnish copy Order now.

863

REQUISITIONS ON TITLE	REPLIES

11. a. Did the Applicant who was first granted the licence give any undertaking to the Court in relation to the conduct of the Licensed Premises or otherwise.
   b. If so give details.

12. a. Did any subsequent licensee for the time being give any undertakings to the Court or to any objectors upon any grant or renewal thereof.
   b. If so give details.

13. Is there any mortgage of any nature charge burden or equity affecting the property which would give any person other than the licensee either a legal or equitable interest in the licence.

14. Furnish details of all convictions against the licensee for the time being since the 4th July 1960 or since the date upon which the license was first granted whichever date is the later.

15. If it is contended that one or more of the convictions were not recordable on the licence pursuant to the provisions of Part (iii) of the Intoxicating Liquor Act 1927 state the reason(s).

16. Are there any convictions recorded on the license at present.

17. Are there any convictions recordable on the licence at this date.

18. a. If the property was sold to a bona fide purchaser for money or monies worth at any time since the 4th July 1960 or since the date upon which the licence was first granted, whichever date is the later, were Orders made under Section 30 of the Intoxicating Liquor Act 1927 directing that any offences recorded at the time of such transfer should cease to be recorded.

REQUISITIONS ON TITLE	REPLIES

b. If so give details in particular of the date or dates of such Orders.

19. Are there any Summonses pending against the Vendor for an alleged breach or breaches of the licensing laws.

20. Has the Vendor or his servants or agents committed any breach of the licensing laws in respect of which a Summons might issue against the Vendor.

21. Confirm that all the proper notices have been served for renewal of the licence if applicable.

22. Confirm that:

    a. The current licence will be endorsed by the Vendor and handed over to the Purchaser on closing.

    b. The Vendor will take all steps necessary including attendance at Court, if required to facilitate the transfer of the licence to the Purchaser.

23. a. Was compliance with any requirements of the Fire Authority outstanding at the last annual licensing sessions or has notice of any requirements been issued since that date.

    b. If so furnish Certificate from the Fire Authority confirming compliance therewith.

24. a. Has the Vendor served one calendar month's notice on the Fire Authority of his intention to apply for the renewal of a Licence at the next Annual Licensing Sessions.

    b. If so furnish copy and any reply received to such notice.

REQUISITIONS ON TITLE	REPLIES

41. RESTAURANT/HOTEL

1. a. Has the property an "Hotel Licence" attached thereto which issued pursuant to Section 2(2) of the Licensing (Ireland) Act 1902.

    b. If so confirm that there is no public bar on the property.

    c. If there is furnish now a copy of an order pursuant to Section 19 of the Intoxicating Liquor Act 1960 so authorising.

2. On what date was the property first certified by the Court as being suitable to receive an hotel licence.

3. State the number of apartments at present set apart and used exclusively as sleeping accommodation for travellers.

4. If the property was certified as an hotel either under the provisions of Section 42(1) of the Tourist Traffic Act 1952 or Section 20 of the Intoxicating Liquor Act 1960 furnish now the current Certificate of Registration from Bord Fáilte.

5. Has Bord Fáilte served any notice of additional requirements which must be complied with before the next annual licensing sessions.

6. a. Has any grant been paid to the licensee or any other person in respect of the property by Bord Fáilte.

    b. If so furnish details now.

7. a. Has the property been certified as being suitable to receive a full or limited Restaurant Certificate pursuant to the Intoxicating Liquor Act 1927.

REQUISITIONS ON TITLE	REPLIES

b. If so furnish now a copy of current certificate and confirm that the original will be furnished on closing.

42. SPECIAL RESTAURANT LICENCE

1. a. Is the Licence a Special Restaurant Licence issued pursuant to Sections 8 and 9 of the Intoxicating Liquor Act 1988.

    b. If so furnish now a complete copy of the current Licence.
    c. Confirm that the original current Licence will be endorsed by the Vendor and handed over to the Purchaser on completion.

2. On what date was the Licence first granted.

3. Furnish now a complete copy of the plans lodged in Court upon the grant of the Court Certificate authorising the issue of the Licence.

4. a. Have any alterations been made to the property from the position as shown in the said plans which might affect the validity of the Licence or might adversely affect the renewal thereof.

    b. If so give full particulars now.

5. a. Has the property been extended or enlarged from the position as shown Plans.
    b. If so give full particulars now.

6. Has any application been made and an Order granted by the Court consequent upon any such extension or enlargement.

REQUISITIONS ON TITLE	REPLIES

7. Confirm that the Vendor holds a current Bord Fáilte Certificate within the meaning of Section 8(2) of the Intoxicating Liquor Act 1988 in respect of the property and the Vendors Restaurant business carried on therein.

8. a. Furnish now a complete copy of such Bord Fáilte Certificate.

   b. Confirm that the original current Bord Fáilte Certificate will be endorsed by the Vendor and handed over to the Purchaser on completion.

9. a. Have any alterations been made to the property since the latest inspection thereof by or on behalf of Bord Fáilte in connection with the Bord Fáilte Certificate which might cause the Bord Fáilte Certificate to be cancelled or might adversely affect the renewal thereof.

   b. If so give full particulars.

10. a. Has Bord Fáilte any requirements in respect of the property which are still outstanding.

    b. If so furnish details now.

11. a. Confirm that the Vendor has not received and is not aware of any notice or intention on the part of Bord Fáilte to issue a notice threatening cancellation of the Bord Fáilte Certificate.

    b. If such notice has been received furnish now a complete copy thereof.

REQUISITIONS ON TITLE	REPLIES

12. a. Has the Vendor given any undertaking (formally or otherwise) to the Local Health Authority Bord Fáilte the Fire Authority the Gardaí the Courts or any other party for the purpose of obtaining the grant or renewal of the Licence or any registration certification withdrawal of objection or otherwise in connection with same.

    b. If so give now full particulars and confirm that such undertaking has been fully complied with.

13. Confirm that all proper notices have been served for the renewal of the Licence, if applicable.

14. Confirm that an application has been made for the renewal of the Bord Fáilte Certificate, if applicable.

43. DANCING MUSIC AND SINGING

1.   a. Is there a Public Dancing Licence attached to the property.
    b. If so furnish now a copy thereof and confirm that same will be handed over on closing.

2.   a. Is there a Music and Singing Licence attached to the property.
    b. If so furnish now a copy thereof and confirm that same will be handed over on closing endorsed by the Vendor.

3.   In respect of the licences referred to at 1 and 2:

    a. Did the applicant who was first granted the licence give any undertakings to the Court in relation to the conduct of the property or otherwise.

REQUISITIONS ON TITLE	REPLIES

b. If so furnish now details thereof.

c. Did the licence for the time being give any undertaking to the Court or to any objectors upon any grant or renewal thereof.

d. If so furnish now details thereof.

44. COMPLETION

Hand over on closing the following documents:

1. Such documents as arise from the foregoing requisitions

The right is reserved by the Purchaser to make any further objections or requisitions arising out of the above and the answers thereto and on the result of searches

Dated the   day of   19   Dated the   day of   19

Solicitor for Purchaser   Solicitor for Vendor

Appendix IV

LAND ACT, 1965, SECTION 45 (EXEMPTED "TOWNS")

Land Act, 1965, Section 45

Consent under section 45 is not required for the vesting of land situate in a County Borough, Borough, Urban District or "Town". The following list of what constitutes a "Town" for the purposes of the Act was prepared by Solicitor to the Land Commission (John Geraghty) and published in the Law Society's *Gazette*, December 1993. It has been updated to take account of the effect of the Local Government Act 1993 (which fixed the boundaries of the Counties of Dublin South, Fingal and Dun Laoghaire-Rathdown) and the Land Act 1965 (Additional Category of Qualified Person) Regulations 1994 (SI 67/1994).

Section 45, Land Act 1965 County Index to Exemption				
Counties	**County Boroughs**	**Boroughs**	**UDCs**	**Towns**
Carlow	-	-	Carlow	Muine Beag, Tullow
Cavan	-	-	Cavan	Bailieboro', Belturbet, Cootehill
Clare	-	-	Ennis Kilrush	Ennistymon, Kilkee, Shannon
Cork	Cork	-	Clonakilty Cobh Fermoy Kinsale Macroom Mallow Midleton Skibbereen Youghal	Bandon, Bantry, Blarney, Dunmanway, Kanturk, Millstreet, Mitchelstown, Passage West, Rathluirc (Charleville)
Donegal	-	-	Buncrana Bundoran Letterkenny	Ballybofey, Ballyshannon, Carndonagh, Donegal, Killybegs, Moville

Counties	County Boroughs	Boroughs	UDCs	Towns
Dublin	Dublin	-	-	Balbriggan Blanchardstown Clondalkin, Lucan-Doddsboro', Malahide, Rush, Skerries, Swords, Tallaght
Galway	Galway	-	Ballinasloe	Athenry, Clifden, Gort, Loughrea, Tuam
Kildare	-	-	Athy, Naas	Celbridge, Kildare, Leixlip, Maynooth, Monasterevin, Newbridge
Kilkenny	-	Kilkenny	-	Callan, Castlecomer/ Donaguile, Graigenamanagh/ Tinnahinch, Thomastown
Kerry	-	-	Killarney, Listowel, Tralee	Ballybunion, Cahirciveen, Castleisland, Dingle, Kenmare, Killorglin
Laois	-	-	-	Abbeyliex, Mountmellick, Mountrath, Portarlington, Portlaoise
Leitrim	-	-	-	Carrick-on-Shannon
Limerick	Limerick	-	-	Abbeyfeale, Killmallock, Newcastle West, Rathkeale
Longford	-	-	Longford	Granard
Louth	-	Drogheda	Dundalk	Ardee

Counties	County Boroughs	Boroughs	UDC's	Towns
Mayo	-	-	Ballina, Castlebar, Westport	Ballinrobe, Ballyhaunis, Claremorris, Swinford
Meath	-	-	Kells, Navan, Trim	-
Monaghan	-	-	Carrickmacross Castleblaney, Clones, Monaghan	Ballybay
Offaly	-	-	Birr, Tullamore	Banagher, Clara, Edenderry
Roscommon	-	-	-	Ballaghaderreen Boyle, Castlerea, Roscommon
Sligo	-	Sligo	-	-
Tipperary	-	Clonmel	Carrick-on-Suir, Cashel, Nenagh, Templemore, Thurles, Tipperary	Cahir, Fethard, Roscrea
Waterford	Waterford	-	Dungarvan	Lismore, Portlaw, Tramore
Westmeath	-	-	Athlone	Moate, Mullingar
Wexford	-	Wexford	Enniscorthy, New Ross	Gorey
Wicklow	-	-	Arklow, Bray Wicklow	Greystones/ Delgany, Rathdrum

Index

abstract of title, 1.33, 2.35, 14.43
  delivery, time for, 14.46-8
  English practice,1.33
  Irish practice, 14.43, 15.06
  photocopy, 1.33
  verification, 14.49-51
  waiver, 14.43.
accountants
  negligent misstatement, 5.27
accumulations, rule against
  wills, 19.58
ademption, doctrine of, 19.58
advancement
  wills, 19.66
adverse possession
  (*see also* **limitation of actions**,
  squatter)
  doctrine of, 1.15, 14.54
  good holding title, 14.12
  Land Act consent, 8.05
  leasehold property, 14.54, 14.81
  missing link, title, 14.61
  parliamentary conveyance heresy, 14.82
  tax clearance certificate, 1.15, 14.82,
  16.25
  tenant for life and remainderman, 14.81
agent
  (*see* **estate agent, house agent**)
agistment
  auctioneer, 2.35
  constructive notice, 9.23
  land, interest in, 6.09
  lettings, 1.13, 1.28, 6.09, 19.36, 18.05
  Statute of Frauds, 6.09
agreement
  (*see* **conditional contracts, contract,**
  contract for sale, lock-out
  agreements)
agriculture holdings, 16.31
  congested areas, 16.30
  subletting, etc, 16.30-5
agricultural land, 1.02, 1.13
  conveyancing, 1.15
    leasehold, 1.13
  enquiries, 5.18-9
  Land Act consent, 5.18, 16.30-5

  Land Purchase Acts, 1.02, 1.15, 16.30
  milk quota system, 1.14, 5.18
  title,
    compulsory registration, 1.02, 1.15
    investigation, 1.15
alienation
  family home, 16.62
***Allhusen v Whittell*, rule in**, 19.64
amalgamation schemes, 16.30
annuities
  (*see* **Land Purchase Acts**)
apartment
  (*see also* **Flat**)
  blocks, 16.95
appointment, power of
  root of title, 14.56
apportionment, 10.47
  date for,10.14, 20.05
  estimated, 20.10
  fee farm rents, 2.44
  financial charges, 2.44
  rates, 2.44, 20.05-7
  rents, 20.05-7
  rules, 19.64, 19.71
  service charges, 20.10
apportionment account, 9.28, 20.03-10,
  20.18
  agistment monies, 20.05
  agreements, 14.75
  annual outgoings, 1.08, 20.03-5
  conacre monies, 20.05
  deposit, 1.08,
  interest, 1.08, 20.09
  outgoings, 16.19
  purchase money, 1.08, 1.09, 20.08
  rates, 1.08, 16.19, 20.05-6
  rent, 1.08, 20.05
  residential property tax, 20.07
arbitration
  building agreements, 11.24
  compulsory purchase, 8.14
  conditions of sale, 10.66
  county registrar, 8.07, 8.10
  damage to property, 10.66
  interest, 10.66
  leasehold enfranchisement, 8.10

misdescription, 18.66
rent reviews, 19.34
arbitrator
appointment, 10.66, 11.24
specific performance, 10.66
architects,
certificate, 11.10, 11.16, 16.60,
16.76, 16.79
declaration, 16.60
negligent misstatement, 5.27
qualifications, 16.76
survey, 4.21
arrangement, deed of,
capital gains tax, 19.70
capital transfer tax, 19.70
assent, 19.69
(*see also* **personal representatives**)
conclusive, 15.19, 16.54
family homes, 16.62
own favour, 16.54
precedents, 19.69
requisitions on title, 15.19, 16.54
root of title, 14.56
title document, 14.66, 14.79
writing in, 17.02
assignment
registration, 20.34, 20.49
attorney, power of
execution of deed, 18.129, 18.131
family home consents, 16.69
auction
(*see also* **bidding, bids, sale**)
abortive, 2.28, 2.30
antiques, 2.24
bidding by vendor, 2.05, 2.14-8
binding contract, 6.14, 8.02
collateral contract, 2.20
conditions of sale, 2.16, 8.02,
conduct, 2.05-27
court sales, 8.13
damped sale, 2.24
dealers' rings, 2.24
highest bidder, 2.19
lots, sale in, 2.23
mock, 2.24
mortgage sale, 2.27

placard, 2.02
property, division of, 2.23
puffer, 2.14
reserve price 2.05, 2.14-8, 2.20, 2.27
solicitors' role, 1.07, 2.36-52, 8.02
terms of sale, 2.45-6
withdrawal of property, 2.05, 2.19-20
without reserve, 2.14, 2.20
works of art, 2.24
auctioneer
abortive auction, 2.07, 6.38
accounts, 2.04
agistment letting, 2.35
auction permits, 2.02
bankruptcy, 2.04, 2.26
bid, refusal of, 2.16, 2.23
bidding disputes, 2.23
certificate of qualification 2.02
clerk, 2.11, 6.40
client bank account, 2.04
commission, 2.04, 2.28-35
company, 2.02
conacre letting, 2.35
conditions of sale, 2.05
conduct of sale, 2.05-27
court sale, 2.27
remuneration, 2.27
custom of trade, 2.07
deceit, 5.24
deposit, 2.02, 2.03, 2.10, 10.29
lost, 2.26
receipt, 2.10, 2.26
disqualification, 2.02
duty of care, 2.12-3
expenses, 2.10, 2.27, 2.31
false statements, 2.13
fraudulent conduct, 2.13
guarantee bond, 2.02, 2.03
implied authority, 2.06-11, 6.91
delegate, to, 2.11, 6.40
employees, 2.09, 6.40
own property, 2.09
receive money, to, 2.10, 2.26
salesroom, 2.09, 6.38
sell, to, 2.07, 3.21

sign contract, to, 2.08-9, 6.38-4
insolvency, 2.26
instructions, 2.05
licences, 2.02
  excise duty, 2.02
  temporary, 2.02
negligence, 2.13
negligent misstatement, 2.13
nominee, 2.02
offence, conviction, 2.02
permit, 2.02
placard, 2.02
pre-contract negotiations, 1.05
private treaty sale, 2.07
puffing descriptions, 9.16, 9.29
remuneration, 2.27, 2.39, 8.13, 10.10
sale book, 6.16
stakeholder, 2.10, 2.26, 10.29
statutory regulation, 2.01-4
tax clearance certificate, 2.02
unauthorised acts, ratification, 2.07, 2.09
unincorporated association, 2.02
warrant of authority, breach of, 2.13
auditors
company, negligence, 5.27
assurance
  (*see also* **deed**), 10.43
Bain v Fothergill, **rule in**, 13.54, 13.79-80
application, 13.82-3
contract partially executed, 13.81, 13.83
fraud, 13.79, 13.84
Ireland, in, 13.81
rescission, 13.62
bank
bridging loan, 2.48, 3.44
deposit receipt, 10.32
executor and trustee, 19.67
title deeds,
  deposit, 2.43
  safekeeping, 2.43,
undertakings, 1.09, 2.43, 20.14
banker's draft, 20.24, 20.48

purchase money, 20.11, 20.21, 20.27, 20.29-32
redemption sum, 19.56
split, 19.56,
bankrupt
auctioneer, 2.04, 2.26
undischarged, 2.02
bankruptcy
act of, 12.28, 12.47
builder, 4.25, 11.17
disclaimers, 12.27
estate agent, 3.15
house agent, 3.15
purchaser, 11.18, 12.47-8
relation back, 12.28, 12.47
requisitions on title, 12.28, 15.46
search, 12.28
vendor, 12.27-8
bidder
disparaging remarks, 2.24
fraud on, 2.14, 2.24
highest, 2.19-20, 2.21, 2.22, 2.53, 8.02, 11.07
knock-out agreements, 2.24
misrepresentation, 2.24
potential, 2.54
prospective, 2.55
puffer, 2.14-5
secret agreements, 2.24
bidding, 2.21-5
disputes, 2.28
opening, 11.06-7
puffer, 2.14-5
re-opening, court sales, 2.15, 2.25, 11.06
solicitor, by, 2.55
vendor, by, 2.14-8
bids
accepted, 2.21-3
bogus, 2.24
communication, 2.21, 2.23
last undisputed, 2.23
offer and acceptance, 2.21
refusal, auctioneer, 2.21
retraction, 2.21

Birkenhead legislation, 1.27
boroughs, 16.44, 16.47
boundaries, 2.47, 9.14
  conclusive, 9.13
  county boroughs, etc, 16.47
  definition, 9.14
  Land Registry map, 9.13
  ownership, 9.14
  requisition on title, 16.07
  towns, 16.48
bridges, 16.100
builder
  (*see also* **NHBG Scheme,
  HomeBond Scheme**)
  bankruptcy, 11.17
  company search, 4.25, 11.17
  contract, 4.09
  deposit, booking, 3.15, 4.25, 10.23,
  11.17
  duty of care, 11.15
  duty to build properly, 11.15
  negligence, 4.11, 4.14-8
  nominees, 11.09, 11.11, 11.13
  sub-contractors, 11.15
  warranty,
    collateral, 11.14
    implied, 4.12-3
building
  (*see also* **multi-storey buildings,
  new buildings**)
  foundations, inspection of, 11.15
  materials, 11.15
  plans and specifications, 16.84-5
  safety file, 16.84-5
building agreements
  (see **building contracts**)
building bye-laws, 16.74, 16.79
  amnesty, 10.55, 10.69
building contracts, 4.19, 11.08-24
  (*see also* **HomeBond Scheme,
  NHBG Scheme**)
  agreement for sale, link, 11.11, 11.13
  arbitration, 11.24
  bankruptcy, 11.17, 11.18
  booking deposits, 11.17

collateral warranties, 4.19, 11.14
commercial developments 11.12,
11.13, 11.22
completion, 11.16, 11.23
defects, 11.21-2, 11.24
exemption clauses, 11.21
housing grants, 11.10, 16.60
implied warranty, 4.12-3, 11.15,
11.21
  express terms, 4.13
inflation, 11.16
insurance, 11.20
joint venture, 11.09
loan, subject to, 11.19
services, 11.15
stage payments, 11.09, 11.16-7
stamp duty, 11.10
standard form, 11.14
VAT, 11.11
building control, 1.22, 3.42, 16.79-82
  bye-law amnesty, 10.55, 10.69,
  16.77, 16.81
  certificate of compliance, 16.79-82,
  16.83
  competent person, 16.80
  enforcement notice, 16.80
  enquiries, 5.09, 5.12, 5.14
    pre-contract, 16.82
  regulations, 16.79, 16.80
  self-certification, 16.79
  substantial compliance, 16.80, 16,83
  warranty, 16.82
building regulations, 2.47, 3.43
  compliance, 16.74, 16.79
  national system, 16.79
building societies
  auctioneer, liability for, 3.14
  estate agent, liability for, 3.14
  survey, 3.40, 4.21-4, 5.06
    negligent, 4.23
    exclusion clause, 4.24
  undertakings to, 1.09, 2.43, 20.14,
  20.17
  valuations, 4.21-4
business property
  (see **commercial property**)

bye-laws
amnesty, 10.55, 10.69
cables
requisitions on title, 16.10
capital acquisitions tax
(*see also* **gift tax, inheritance tax**),
certificate of discharge, 16.25
charge on land, 16.25
capital gains tax, 2.49, 16.25
certificate of discharge, 16.25
disposal, settlement, 19.70
family arrangement, deed of, 19.70
non resident vendor, 16.26
requisitions on title, 16.25
capital money
receipt, 18.47
caretaker's agreement, 12.33, 12.43
caution
lodging, 6.66, 12.07, 12.52
caveat emptor, 4.03-4, 4.07-8
disclosure, duty of, 9.19
environment, 16.90
fitness for use, 4.08
habitability, 4.68
HomeBond Scheme, 4.25-8
new buildings, 4.09
particulars of sale, 9.08
patent defects, 9.22
physical defects, 4.03, 9.21
planning warranty, 16.75
principle, scope, 4.08-9
protection of purchaser, 4.20-8
inspection and survey, 4.21-4
title to property, 4.04
certificate for value, 18.108, 18.37,
18.40
certificate of title, 15.05
builder's contract, 11.09
lending institution, for, 11.09
mortgagee, 15.05
standard forms, 15.05
charge
floating, 6.09, 12.06, 16.27
registered, 19.55-6
requisition on title 16.22
severance, 16.69

chattels
fieri facias, 15.46
household, 16.62
appropriation, spouse's share, 19.60
mortgage, 9.15, 16.62
ownership, 1.03
physical delivery, 1.03
purchased, 9.15, 10.62, 16.06
requisition on title, 16.06
sale, included in, 9.15, 10.61
warranty, 9.15, 10.61, 16.06
cheque
(*see also* **banker's draft**)
deposit, for, 10.18, 10.24, 10.51
purchaser stopping, 10.18
Chesterfield's (Earl Of) Trusts, **Rule
In**, 19.64
children
family homes, 16.62
provision for, 19.60
trusts for, 19.62
Circuit Court
purchase price, lodgment, 8.18
closing
(*see also* **completion**)
date, 2.50, 3.48, 9.05, 10.14
closing order, 1.22
commercial property, 5.14-7, 11.12,
11.13, 11.22, 12.43
bare trust, 16.23
family home, 16.62
commission
(*see also* **fees**)
auctioneers', 2.04, 2.10, 2.28-35
amount, 2.31-3
effective cause, 2.29
entitlement, 2.28-30
payment, 2.34-5
contract or completion, 2.23-30
estate agents', 2.34, 3.18-32
amount, 3.31
entitlement, 3.19-30
payment, 3.32
house agents', 2.34, 3.18-32
amount, 3.31
entitlement, 3.19-30
payment, 3.32
IOU, 2.34

out-of-pocket expenses, 3.32
professional scale, 2.31
purchaser paying, 2.34, 3.32
quantum meruit, 2.30-1, 3.24
statutory scale, 2.31
Commissioners Of Public Works,
3.02
commorientes, 19.62
companies
(*see also* **corporations**)
articles of association, 16.27
auctioneer, 2.02
auditors, negligent misstatement,
5.27
capital gains, 16.26
certificate of incorporation, 5.12,
16.27
corporation tax, 16.26
debentures, 16.27
examiner, 16.27
floating charges, 16.27
income tax, 16.26
insolvent, 12.29, 12.48
Irish citizens, 16.37-8
liquidation, 12.29, 12.48
memorandum and articles, 5.12
receivership, 16.27
register, 4.25, 5.03, 11.17, 15.48
registration of deeds, 16.129-30
sealing requirements, 18.
search, 4.25, 15.48
section 29, 16.28
vendor, 16.27
winding-up, 16.27
compensation
agreement, 8.14
arbitration, 8.14, 8.22, 10.66
compulsory purchase, 8.14, 8.18
    assessment, 8.22, 1.48, 13.20
court, lodged in, 8.14, 8.18
development proposals, 8.22
Landlord and Tenant Acts, 16.16
misdescription, 9.32, 9.34, 9.45-6
not assessable, 9.48, 10.56
purchase price, abatement in, 5.26,
9.32, 9.34
statutory tenant, 6.12

completion, 1.09
(*see also* **completion notices**)
building agreement, 11.16, 11.23
closing date, 2.50, 3.48
date for, 1.08, 9.05, 10.14
documents, 16.108
interest charges, 9.05, 12.18-20
place for, 20.26
possession before, 12.32-4
post, by, 20.27
preparation for, 20.02-4
procedure, 20.29-35
    mortgage discharge, 20.32
purchaser's finance, 20.21
requisitions, outstanding, 20.23
searches, 20.22
unregistered land, 1.09
completion notices, 10.57, 13.19-24
abatement, qualification, 9.32, 9.46
able, ready and willing, 13.20-1
compensation, qualification, 9.32,
9.46, 13.20
forfeiture of deposit, 13.22
mortgage discharge, 13.20
rescission, 10.56
service, 13.19
two-edged sword, 13.20
vacant possession, 13.20
compulsory purchase, 1.23, 8.14-22
(*see also* **compensation**)
appeals, 8.17
deed poll, 8.18
entry on land, 8.19
housing authorities, 8.15
inquiry, 8.16
Land Commission, 8.20
notice to treat, 8.14, 8.18
notices, 8.14, 8.17
order, 1.22, 8.16-7
powers of, 1.22, 8.14
procedure, 1.23, 8.14
public authority activities, 1.23, 8.14
railways, 8.14
State bodies, 1.23, 8.14
vesting orders, 8.20-1

conacre
  auctioneer, 2.35
  land, interest in, 6.09
  lettings, 1.13, 1.28, 2.35
conditional contracts, 7.01-2
  (*see also* **subject to contract**)
  approval, subject to, 7.21
  condition,
    certainty, 7.15, 7.17
    precedent, 7.03
    subsequent, 7.03, 7.15, 7.16, 10.69
    waiver of benefit, 7.16
  conditions of sale, subject to, 7.13
  enquiries, subject to, 7.20
  exchange, subject to, 7.03, 7.07
  formal agreement, subject to, 7.11-2
  gazumping, 6.05
  general principles, 7.03-4
  illustrations, 7.05
  Land Act consent, subject to, 7.22,
  10.69
  licence, subject to, 7.22
  mortgage, subject to, 7.01, 7.14-5,
  10.67, 11.19
  planning permission, subject to, 1.21
  7.16-8, 10.32, 10.69
  reasonable endeavours, 7.18
  searches, subject to, 7.01, 7.20
  survey, subject to, 4.03, 7.01, 7.19
conditions of sale, 9.01, 9.03
  (*see also* **contract for sale, special
  conditions**)
  ambiguous, 10.04
  amendments, 10.06
  apportionment, 9.28, 10.14, 10.47
  arbitration, 10.66
  assurance, 10.43
  auctioneer's fees, 2.14-5, 2.34, 10.10
  auctions, 10.16
    bidding, 2.14, 8.02
    reserve price, 2.14-6, 2.27, 2.45
    right to bid, 2.16-7, 2.45
    withdrawal of property, 2.45
    without reserve, 2.16-8
  boundaries, 9.14, 16.07

building control, 10.55
bye-law amnesty, 10.55
chattels, warranty, 9.15, 10.61
clearance orders, 9.28
closed contract, 10.02
closing,
  date, 10.14
  order, 9.28
compensation, 9.45-6, 10.56
completion, 10.46
  date for, 2.50, 3.48, 9.05, 10.14
  notices, 10.56, 13.19-24
compulsory registration, 10.49
conflict, special conditions, 10.06,
10.67, 10.68
construction, 10.04, 10.06
  against vendor, 10.04, 14.07, 14.39
court sales, 8.13, 11.01-7
dangerous building notices, 9.28
definitions, 10.14
demolition order, 9.28
deposit, 2.10, 2.12, 2.26, 2.45, 10.16,
10.17-32, 10.51, 10.58, 13.31
documents of title, 9.39-41, 10.53
Documents Schedule, 9.03, 9.11,
9.24, 9.39-41
drafting, 9.02
duty of disclosure, 9.37-8, 9.44,
10.40
easements, 9.43
error, 9.44, 10.52
estate agent's commission, 2.34,
10.10
fences, 9.14
fixtures and fittings, 9.15
  warranty, 9.15, 10.61, 16.06
general, 9.01, 10.01, 10.13
headings, 10.15
hedges, 9.14
identity of property, 9.11, 10.39
inspection, 10.62
insurance, 3.46, 12.36-43
interest, 10.14, 10.46, 12.18-20
intermediate title, 10.37, 14.61
interpretation, 10.15

Land Act consent, 7.23, 10.12, 10.48
landlord's consent, 10.56
leases, 10.45
marginal notes, 10.15
merger, 10.63
misdescription, 5.21, 9.44
    remedies, 9.30, 9.36-48, 10.52
misleading, 9.37
misrepresentation, 5.21
notice of documents, 9.28, 9.39-41, 10.33
notices,
    disclosure of, 9.28, 10.54
objections, 9.38
open contract, 10.02
party walls, 9.14
planning legislation, 10.55, 16.74
    warranty, 16.75
possession before completion, 12.32-4
prior title, 10.36, 15.25
production of documents, 9.10-1, 10.53
register entries, cancellation, 6.65, 13.22, 13.23, 13,73
registered land, 9.02, 10.38, 14.31-2, 14.35-6
requisitions, 9.38, 10.12, 10.41, 10.56, 15.20-2
risk, 3.46, 12.36-43
rescission, 10.56
    compensation, 10.56
    completion notice, 10.56
    damage to property, 10.56
    landlord's, consent, 10.56
    misdescription, 9.47
    notices, non-disclosure, 10.56
    objections or requisition, 10.56
Schedule, 9.03
searches, 10.42, 15.43
signature, 10.50
solicitor,
    costs, 10.11
    selection, 10.08
standard forms, 10.03

statutory regulation, 10.07-11
tenancies, 9.42
time limits, 10.65
title to be deduced, 10.35, 15.04, 15.25-35
vacant possession, 10.44, 10.45, 16.15
vendor's duty of disclosure, 9.17, 9.19
consent
    (*see also* **Land Act consent**)
    landlord's, 18.15
consideration, 18.042
    leases, 19.25
Construction Industry Federation
    (*see also* **HomeBond Scheme, NHBG Scheme**)
    building agreement, 11.14
    structural guarantee scheme, 4.25
contract
    (*see also* **building contracts, exchange of contracts**)
    certainty, 6.02
    collateral, 2.20, 6.13
    consideration, 6.02
    draft, 6.15
    formation, 6.02-15
        auction, 6.14
    frustration, 12.37
    guarantee, 6.03
    legal capacity, 6.02
    legal relations, creation of, 6.02
        marriage, 6.03
    offer and acceptance, 6.02
    repudiatory breach, 13.04-9
    time of the essence, 2.50, 13.02, 13.12-24
    uberrimae fidei, 9.20
contract for sale
    (*see also* **exchange of contracts, memorandum of sale, part performance**),
    closed, 14.05
    closing date, 9.05, 13.10
    completion date, 6.25, 9.05

compulsory purchase, 8.14-22
court sales, 8.13, 11.01-7
date of, 6.63
deduction of title, 14.20-82
deposit, 6.18, 6.29, 6.61-2, 9.05
draft, 6.63
English law, 1.13
evidence in writing, 6.03, 6.05, 6.06,
6.14, 13.44
fixtures and fittings, 3.40, 9.15
formal, 9.02-3
formalities, 1.13-2
formation, 6.01-5
interest, 9.05, 12.18-20
negotiation of terms, 2.52, 3.50
notice to treat, 8.14, 8.18
open, 3.09, 4.04, 10.02
option to purchase, 8.03-6
parties, 6.20-1
parts of, 9.03
purchase price, 9.05
registered land, 6.06
registration, 6.64-6, 12.07
remedies for enforcement, 13.01
    election, 13.03-9
    general principles, 13.02
    time, 13.10-25
risk, 10.60, 12.36-43
signature, 6.62, 9.05, 10.50
witnesses, 9.05
statutory form, 6.05
time of the essence, 13.12-24
title page, 9.03
vacant possession, 6.18, 6.25
variation, oral, 6.14
void *ab initio*, 13.04, 13.66, 13.75
writing, 1.13
conversion, doctrine of, 6.11, 12.11-2
conveyance
    (*see also* **deed**)
    bargain and sale, 17.02
    building estates, 17.05
    cancellation, 5.23
    commencement, 18.07-8
    compulsory purchase, 17.09

construction, 17.13-26
date, 18.09-11
deed of grant, 17.02
definition, 18.82
delivery, 17.06
draft,
    furnishing, 17.01
drafting of, 17.02-3
    fee farm grantor's solicitor, 17.04
    lessor's solicitor, 17.04
    responsibility, 17.04-5
engrossment, 17.04-5, 17.06
execution by vendor, 17.06
fee farm grants, 19.46
feoffment, 17.02
forms, 17.02, 17.08-9
    vendor's, 17.05
fraudulent, 16.24
grantee himself, 18.85
jointly with another, 18.85
incumbrances, free from, 8.10
indenture, 18.07
lease and release, 17.02
leases, 19.23-36
matters of, 14.18
parcels clause, 17.23, 18.50
precedents, 17.08-9, 18.03
receipt clause, vendor's lien, 18.42-3
registered land, 17.03, 17.10, 18.04
sales, 19.02-22
standard form, 1.08
unsealed document, 17.02
voluntary, 14.67, 16.24
writing, no, 17.02
conveyancers
    abstract of title, 1.33
    bridging loans, advice, 2.48, 3.44
    caution, 1.04
    conservatism, 1.04
    flats, problems, 1.18
    tax laws, 1.24
conveyancing
    agricultural land, 1.13
    complexity of, 1.16-7
    controversy, recent, 1.02, 1.04

cost of, 1.02, 1.04
English practice, comparison, 1.26-33
family property, 1.25
flat schemes, 1.18, 19.12-3
freehold, 1.16
historical background, 1.11
Ireland, in, 1.11-33
land law, connection with, 1.01
leasehold, 1.13, 1.16, 1.28
modern developments, 1.20-5
monopoly, solicitors', 1.04
nature of, 1.01-10
planning law, impact of, 1.21-2
practice,
    changes in, 1.04
    improvements in, 1.04
procedures, 1.04
professional persons, 1.34-8
settlements, 1.27
simplification of, 1.02, 1.04, 1.07
statute law, 1.12
substantive land law, 1.27
transactions,
    stages, 1.05-9
two jurisdictions, 1.12
urban land, 1.16-9
Conveyancing Committee
auction deposits, 10.16
builders,
    contracts, 11.09
    searches, 11.17
    tax clearance certificates, 11.10
certificates,
    compliance, of, 16.76
    title, of, 15.05
Companies Act, 18.113
common seal, 1.35
conditions of sale, 9.01, 10.03
deduction of title, 9.24
family homes
    assents, 16.62
    consent on deed, 16.62
    guidelines, 16.61
    power of attorney, 16.69
    statutory declarations, 16.64-8, 16.72-3
    supporting evidence, 16.70
general conditions, 10.13, 10.68
lenders, acting for, 1.35
licensing regulations, 10.72
milk quotas, 10.72
mortgage, discharge of, 10.71
multi-storey buildings, 16.95-6
objections and requisitions form, 16.01-2
pre-contract enquiries, 5.06, 16.76, 16.95
pre-lease enquiries, 1.29, 5.12
pub, 10.72
restaurants, 10.72
risk, vendor retaining, 12.40-3
special conditions, 10.68
survey, 4.08, 4.22, 4.23
title documents, 9.24
urban areas, 16.44
vendor searches, 1.09, 5.03, 10.42, 15.43
co-owners
    (*see also* **joint tenants**)
    conveyance to, 18.91
co-ownership
    fragmentation, 1.02
    pyramid titles, 1.02
    trust for sale, statutory, 6.11
corporation tax, 1.26
    non-resident vendor, 16.26
corporations
    (*see also* **companies**)
    execution, 18.128
county boroughs, 16.44, 16.47
county registrar
    conveyance by, officer of court, 5.30
    freehold, acquisition of,
        arbitration, 8.07, 8.10
        price, 8.07, 8.10
        registers, 8.10
court
    approval, 11.07
    auctions, 2.27, 8.13

sales,
  bidding, 8.13, 11.01-7
  conditions of sale, 11.04
  conduct, 11.03
  forced, 11.02
  interest, 12.02
  maintenance of property, 12.23
  mode, 11.04
  reserve price, 11.04
  vacant possession, 11.03
  vendor, 2.24, 11.03
  written evidence, 6.08
  specific performance, 8.13
  vesting order, 8.13, 13.56
court order
  auctioneer's remuneration, 8.13
  sale, for, 8.13
    auctioneer's fees, 8.13
  specific performance, 13.56-8
covenants, 18.93-101
  (*see also* **restrictive covenants**)
  amenities, protecting, 8.12
  building, 16.60
  estates, 19.10
  creation, words of, 18.94
  enforcement, 19.12, 19.15-6
  estate scheme, 8.12
  execution by grantee, 18.95
  fee farm grants, 19.44
  flats, 19.15, 19.21-2
  indemnity, 18.98-9, 19.03, 19.31
  joint and several, 18.96-7
  leases, 19.29
  merger, 8.12
  mortgages, 19.53
  onerous, 9.25, 9.31, 9.39, 9.40
  recitals, 18.34
  usual, 9.39
covenants for title, 13.01, 17.25,
  18.100, 21.05-33
  assignment of leases, 19.31
  effect, 21.26-33
  enforceability, 21.21-5
  implied, 18.049, 19.31, 21.05, 21.07-
  20

  joint and several, 21.13
  magic phrase, 21.05
  merger, 10.63
  registered land, 21.06
Custom House Docks Area, 5.16
damages, 13.05, 13.75-87
  (*see also Bain v Fothergill,* **rule
  in**)
  alternative accommodation, 13.87
  assessment, 13.78
    date, 13.78
  bargain, loss of, 13.82, 13.84-6
  collateral warranty, 5.26, 13.76
  deceit, 5.24, 13.84
  delay, 13.10
  deposit, account of, 13.05, 13.01,
  13.78
  expenses, 13.78
    conveyancing, 13.85, 13.86-7
    out-of-pocket, 13.86
  fraudulent misrepresentation, 5.23,
  13.76
  Hadley v Baxendale, rule in, 13.77
  innocent misrepresentation, 6.68,
  12.75, 5.25, 13.76
  liquidated, 13.22
  measure, 13.05, 13.54
    contract, 13.87
    deceit, 5.24, 13.87
    Lord Cairns' Act, 13.54
    negligence, 5.24
    tort, 5.24
  merger, contract in conveyance,
  13.76
  misdescription, 5.26
  mitigation of loss, 13.06
  profit, loss of, 13.06, 13.78
  prospective profits, 13.85
  purchaser, 13.08, 13.79-87
  remoteness of damage, 13.22, 13.77,
  13.85
  resale, 13.78
  specific performance, in lieu, 13.04,
  13.54
  survey fees, 13.86

vendor, 13.77-8
warranty, breach of, 16.75
death duties
(*see also* **estate duty, legacy duty, succession duty**)
requisitions of title, 16.25
debentures, 6.09
deceit, 5.21, 5.24
damages, 5.24, 9.31
misdescription, 9.31
deduction of title, 14.20-82
(*see also* **abstract of title, root of title, title**)
closed contract, 14.05, 14.10
conveyance,
matters of, 14.18
sale, on, 14.62
copies of deeds, 14.43-8
documentary, 14.12, 14.82
Documents Schedule, 9.03, 9.11, 9.24, 9.39-41
equitable interests, 14.65
falsification of pedigree, 9.31
fee farm grants, 14.68-75
fraudulent concealment, 9.31
Land Registry,
folio, 15.06
map, 15.06
leases, 14.63, 14.68-76
length of title, 14.05, 14.54-67
missing links, 14.61, 14.82
mortgages, 14.64, 14.80
open contract, 3.09, 14.05
original deeds, 14.44
photocopying, 1.33, 9.24
possessory title, 14.12, 14.54, 14.58, 14.81-2
pre-contract, 1.07, 9.24
prima facie evidence, 1.07, 5.02, 14.02
registered land, 14.04, 14.13-4, 14.21-42
registered lease, copy, 14.31
restrictions, 14.05, 14.07, 14.38
root of title, 9.24

settlements and trusts for sale, 14.77-8
succession, 14.79
trusts, kept off title, 14.64
unregistered land, 14.04, 16.54
vendor's,
duty, 14.01
voluntary conveyances, 14.67
wills, 14.66
deed
(*see also* **conveyance, execution**)
acknowledgment and undertaking, 18.102-6
all estate clause, 18.82-3, 18.119
attestation, 18.133-6
certificates, 18.107-16
consideration, 18.42, 19.05, 19.25
construction, 17.14, 18.58-62, 18.78, 18.87
grantor, against, 17.21, 18.78
habendum, 18.87
operative, render, 17.26
contents, 18.01, 18.06
contradiction, 17.19
co-owners, 18.91
covenants, 18.93-101, 19.21-2
derogation from grant, 18.78, 18.80
exceptions and reservations, 18.73-81, 19.20
express provisions, 17.25
extrinsic evidence. 17.19
false description, 17.22
forgery, 18.10
form, 18.01
registered land, 18.04-5
unregistered land, 18.02-3
general words, 18.54, 18.57
grant, words of, 17.18, 18.48-9, 19.26, 19.41, 19.46
grantee's rights, 18.71-2, 19.19
habendum, 17.18, 18.42, 18.49, 18.50, 18.73, 18.82, 18.84-8, 19.03, 19.05, 19.41-2, 19.46, 19.49-50
intention of parties, 17.15
inter partes, 18.07-8, 18.23-4

land, description of, 18.51-62
maps or plans, 18.51, 18.53, 18.63-8, 19.09
  annexed, 17.23
memorial,
  execution, 18.136
  secondary evidence, 14.53
operative part, 17.18, 18.25, 18.38, 18.48
parcels clause, 17.23, 18.50-83, 19.09, 19.18
parties, 18.12
  description, 18.19-12
  format, 18.23-4
  necessary, 18.13-8
  nominees, 16.018
party, benefit, 18.13
poll, 18.07-8, 18.23-4
precedents, 18.02-3
proof, 14.51
receipt clause, 18.42-3, 19.05
recitals, 17.18, 18.05, 18.25-40, 19.24, 19.39, 19.48
  categories, 18.37-40
  effect, 18.27-36
registered land, 18.26
registration, 18.136, 20.42-4
schedules, 18.117
stamping, 18.108-12, 20.38-41
  insufficient, 15.13, 20.41
  presumed, 14.52, 15.13
supplemental, 18.39
tendendum, 18.84
testatum, 18.41, 19.31, 19.49
testimonium, 18.117-8
trusts, declaration of, 18.89-92
voluntary, 18.42
witnesses, 18.133-6
words,
  ordinary meaning, 17.16
  technical meaning, 17.17
delivery, 18.123-32, 19.56, 20.27
  (*see also* **escrows**)
  agents, 18.129
  corporations, 18.128

liquidators, 18.130
manner, 18.124
receivers, 18.131
deposit, 1.05
account, 13.05, 13.30-6
agent, 10.25
amount, 9.05, 10.19
auctioneer's, 2.10, 10.16, 10.29
bill of exchange, 2.10, 10.24
booking, 3.15, 4.25, 10.31, 11.17, 20.07
builder's, 3.15, 10.23, 10.25
cash, 2.10, 10.24
cheque, 2.10, 10.18, 10.24
condition precedent, 10.22
contract, under, 2.10, 2.26, 10.16-7, 10.51, 13.31
earnest money, 3.10
estate agent, 10.31
exchange of contracts, 6.15, 6.61-3
forfeiture, 10.18, 10.19, 10.26, 10.58, 13.03, 13.07, 13.08, 13.22, 13.30-3, 13.60
  penalty rules, 13.32-3
fundamental breach, 10.22
guarantee, 13.30
holder, capacity, 10.25-31
IOU, 2.10, 10.24
interest, 13.34, 13.85
investment, 10.32
joint names, in, 10.32
lien, purchaser's, 12.08, 12.44
lost,
  auctioneer, by, 2.26
  builder, 10.23, 10.25
  developer, 10.23, 10.25
  estate agent, by, 2,26, 10.23
  house agent, by, 2.26
  personal representative, 10.26
  vendor's responsibility, 2.26
open contract, 10.18
part payment, 10.18, 10.22, 10.31, 13.30
payment, 10.20-4
  how, 10.24

when, 10.21-2
whom, to, 10.23
pre-contract, 3.10-1, 10.23, 10.25,
10.31, 13.30,
recovery, 10.16, 10.51, 13.02, 13.23,
13.30, 13.34-6
return, 13.09, 13.85
security, 10.18, 10.19, 13.30-1
specific performance, 10.59
vendor, available to, 2.38
vendor's solicitor, payment to, 2.10,
2.26, 2.45, 10.23, 10.25, 10.28
designated areas, 5.16, 16.100
apartments, 16.98
developer
bankruptcy, 4.25
flat schemes, 1.17, 19.16
option to purchase, 8.03
development
(*see* **planning**)
disclaimer
liquidator, 12.29
Official Assignee, 12.28
disclosure
(*see also* **misdescription**)
agistment, 9.23
caveat emptor, 9.19
duty of, 9.17, 9.19
easements, 9.26, 9.43, 16.10
incumbrances, 9.26
insurance contracts, 9.20
latent defects, 9.24-7, 9.31-2, 9.38,
9.47
leases, 9.27, 9.40
notices, 9.27, 10.56
occupiers, 10.54
onerous covenants, 9.25, 9.31, 9.39,
9.40
occupiers, 9.23
patent defects, 9.22-3
physical defects, 9.41
restrictive covenants, 9.26
tenants, 9.23, 9.42
title rentcharges, 9.26
distress for rent, 2.31

ditch
(*see also* **hedge and ditch rule**),
9.14
meaning in Ireland, 18.62
requisitions on title, 16.07
documents
(*see* **documents of title**)
Documents Schedule, 7.03, 9.11, 9.24,
9.39-41
drainage, 3.55
public authority activities, 1.22
requisitions on title, 16.09
drains, 6.16
charge, taken in, 5.07, 16.09
requisition on title, 16.09
dwelling
(*see* **family home, HomeBond,
NHGB Scheme**)
EEC
Acquired Rights Directive, 5.15
environment, 16.86
establishment, right of, 16.29, 16.50
Land Act consents, 16,29
milk quotas, 16.101
safety, health, etc, 16.84
easements, 18.50, 18.71-2
appurtenant, 9.18
contracts for, 6.09
disclosure, 9.26, 9.43
particulars of sale, 9.18
quasi, 18.10
requisitions on title, 16.10
ejectment
caretaker's agreement, 12.33, 12.43
election
remedies, 13.02, 13.03-8
electricity
installations, 1.17
requisitions on title, 16.09
supply, 11.15, 16.09
engaged couples, 16.72
engineers
certificates, 16.76, 16.79, 16.95
chartered, 16.76
civil, 16.76, 16.79
electrical, 16.79

mechanical, 16.79
multi-storey buildings, 16.95
structural, 16.79
survey, 4.21
enquiries, 1.03, 4.02
 (*see also* **pre-contract enquiries,**
  searches)
 building control, 5.09
 drainage, 5.07
 easements, 5.07
 family homes, 5.08
 fixtures, 5.07
 insurance, 5.06
 Land Act consent, 5.08
 local authorities, 1.05, 5.06-7
 HomeBond Scheme, 5.07, 5.10
 planning, 5.06, 5.07
 residential property, 5.06-11
 roads, 5.06, 5.07
 services, 5.07
 survey, 5.06
equity
 delay defeats, 13.30
 puffer, 2.14-5
 redemption, clogs on, 19.52
escrows, 18.125-7, 20.12, 20.25
 corporations, 18.128
estate agent, 3.03
 agreements drawn up by, 6.63
 conduct of sale, 3.05-17
 deposit, 3.03, 10.31
  pre-contract, 2.10, 3.10-1, 3.14,
   10.03
 duty of care, 3.13-4, 5.27-8
 effective cause, 3.20, 3.22
 expenses, 3.05
 fees and commission, 3.18-32, 10.10
 guarantee bond, 3.15
 implied authority, 3.06-12
  delegate, to, 3.12
  receive money, to, 3.10-1
  sell, to, 3.07
  sign contract, to, 3.08-9
 instructions, 3.05
 licences, 3.02

negligent misstatement, 5.27-8
ostensible authority 3.11
pre-contract negotiations, 1.05
sole agent, 3.05, 3.20
sole right to sell, 3.05, 3.20
stakeholder, 3.16
statutory regulation, 3.01-4
warranty of authority, 1.35
estate duty, 1.27, 14.18, 14.49, 16.25
 reversionary interest, 16.25
estate scheme, 8.12
estoppel
 feeding, 18.33, 19.56
 recitals, 18.32-3
 tenancy by, 14.12
 tenant by, 14.82
exceptions, 18.50
 contra proferentem rule, 17.21
 implied, 18.80
 mines and minerals, 18.75
 pyramid title, 1.16
 quarries, 18.75
 registered land, 18.81
 reservations, distinction, 18.736
exchange of contracts, 1.32, 6.61-3
 advantages, 1.32, 6.63
 condition precedent, 6.62
 English practice, 1.32, 6.61, 6.63
 Irish practice, 1.32, 6.62-3
 post, by, 6.61, 6.63
 subject to contract, 6.61, 7.07, 7.08,
  7.11
execution, 18.119-32, 20.12
 (*see also* **delivery, escrows,**
  sealing, signature)
 agents, 18.129
 attestation, 18.133-6
 corporations, 18.128
 covenants, 18.95
 grantee, by, 18.77, 18.95
 liquidators, 18.130
 missing deed, 14.52
 proper, presumption, 17.24
 receivers, 18.131
 registered land, 18.132, 18.135

registration of deeds, 18.136
unregistered land, 18.133-4
wills, 19.58
executor, 19.67
sale, power of, 14.66
family homes, 6.31-60
(*see also* **spouse**)
alienation, 16.62
assents, 16.62
bankers' problems, 16.69
commercial use, 16.62
company property, 16.62
contract form, 9.06
conveyancing, definition, 3.39, 5.08,
16.62
court orders, 16.69
criminal offence, 5.09
definition, 16.62
disability, 16.69
enforceable agreement, 3.39, 5.08,
16.62
exceptions, 16.62
farm, 16.62
farmhouse, 16.62
future advances, 16.62, 16.69
full value, 16.62
good faith, 16.62, 16.65
household chattels, 16.62
joint deposits, 16.62
judgment mortgage, 16.62
lender's duty of care, 16.69
limitation period, 16.71
misrepresentation, 16.23
mortgagees, 15.01, 16.62
purchaser for value, 16.62
spouse's consent, 2.40, 2.47, 3.36,
4.06, 5.08, 9.06, 15.01, 16.23, 16.69
burden of proof, 16.62
contract only, 16.62
conveyance only, 16.62
desertion, 16.69
forms, 9.06, 16.09
general, 16.62, 16.69
independant legal advice, 16.23,
16.69

informed, 16.23, 16.67, 16.69
minor, 16.69
omission, 16.69
refusal, 16.69
severance, 16.69
statutory declarations, 16.64, 16.72
statutory sanction, 5.29
surety, 16.23
undue influence, 16.23
void conveyance, 16.23, 16.62,
16.70-1
farmers
establishment, right of, 16.29
home-made wills, 1.14
residence, rights of, 1.14
wills, failure to prove, 1.14
farmhouses
family homes, 16.62
farms
milk quotas, 16.101-3
time of essence, 13.15
fee farm grants, 1.17 14.68-75,
19.374-6
contracts for, 6.09
conversion, 14.11, 14.56
English conveyancing, 1.35
flats, 19.12, 19.15
leasehold law, 19.12
pyramid title, 1.17
reddendum, 19.43
sales, 19.02
series of, 1.17
fees
(*see also* **commission**)
auctioneers', 2.04, 2.28-35
amount, 2.31-3
court sales, 8.13
entitlement, 2.28-30
payment, 2.34-5
contract or completion, 3.23-30
estate agents', 3.18-32
amount, 3.31
entitlement, 3.19-30
payment, 3.32
house agents', 3.18-32

amount, 3.31
  entitlement, 3.19-30
  payment, 3.32
  purchaser's payment, 2.34, 3.32
fee simple
  acquisition of, 5.13, 16.94
  fee farm grantee, 1.16, 19.37
fences, 9.14, 16.07
  (*see also* **party fences**)
  ownership, 18.61
finance, 1.37, 5.14
  advice, 3.44-5
  bridging, 13.37, 20.18, 20.24
  deposit, 3.44
  insurance costs, 3.45, 5.12
  purchaser's, 20.18, 20.21
  search fees, 3.45
  solicitor's fees, 3.45
  stamp duty, 3.45
  survey fees, 3.45
fire
  authorities, 16.83
  certificates, 16.79, 16.80, 16.83
  enforcement notice, 16.80
  regulations, 16.79
fishing licence, 16.13
fittings, 3.40
  (*see also* **fixtures**)
  enquiries, 5.07
  warranty, 9.14
fixtures, 3.40, 9.15
  mortgaged premises, 6.10
  ornamental, 6.10
  requisitions on title, 16,60
  stamp duty, 9.15
  Statute of Frauds, 6.10
  tenants', 6.10
  trade, etc, 6.10
flats
  blocks, 16.97, 19.02, 19.11, 19.22
  common areas, 16.97
  common facilities. 1.18,19.11, 19.15-6, 19.19
  concurrent lease, 19.16
  covenants, 16.97, 19.15-6, 19.21-2

designated areas, 16.98
developer's responsibilities, 16.97, 19.16
fabric, 19.18
fee farm grants, 19.12, 19.15-6
freehold, 1.18, 19.12-3
HomeBond Scheme, 5.10, 5.11
insurance, 16.97-8
leasehold, 1.18, 19.12
maintenance and repair, 19.15, 19.20
management company, 19.16, 19.18
managing agents, 16.97
new, 16.97-8
sale, 19.11
schemes, 1.18,19.14-22
self-contained, 1.18, 19.15
service charges, 16.99
structure, 16.97
support, 1.18, 19.11, 19.19
walls, floors and ceilings, 19.18
floating charge, 6.09
  crystallisation, 12.06, 16.27
floor area certificates, 11.10, 16.60
food hygiene regulations, 16.91-2
  rescission, 9.47
footpaths
  taken in charge, 5.07, 16.09
  requisition on title, 16.09
forestry, 16.12
fraud, 21.05
  (see *also* **misrepresentation**)
  auctioneer, 5.24
  bidders' agreements, 2.24
  concealment, 9.31
  conveyances, 16.24
  court sales 2.25, 6.08, 9.30
  deceit, 5.21
  extrinsic evidence, 17.19
  latent defects, 9.31
  misdescription, 9.30
  part performance, 6.50
  proof, 5.23
  vendor, 2.24
Frauds, Statute of
  (*see also* **memorandum in writing**, **part performance**), 1.06, 6.03, 6.06-60, 7.03, 9.02
  action, 6.07-8
  agistment, 6.09

auctions, 8.02
building materials, 6.10
collateral contract, 6.13
conacre, 6.09
co-ownership, 6.11
court rules, 6.08
debentures, 6.09
defence, pleading, 6.07
easements, 6.09
farm implements, 6.13
fixtures, 6.10
floating charge, 6.09
fraud, 6.03
fructus industriales, 6.09
fructus naturales, 6.09
gazumping, 6.04, 6.05
goods, 6.09
grass, 6.09
grazing rights, 6.09
guarantee contracts, 6.03
land, 6.09-13
leases, 6.09
licences, 6.12
lock-out agreements, 6.04
lodgings, 6.12
marriage contracts, 6.03
meadowing, 6.09
mortgages, 6.09
object of, 6.03
option to purchase, 8.03
oral evidence, 6.03
pleading, 6.03, 6.07
pre-emption, right of, 8.04
replacement, 6.04, 6.05
residence, right of, 6.12
severance of agreement, 6.09, 6.13
shares, 6.10
signatures, 9.05
slag, 6.10
statutory tenant, 6.12
trees, 6,09
trust for sale, 6.11
undivided share, 6.11
waiver, 6.07
freehold
acquisition of, 8.07-12

buy out, 19.12
flying, 19.13
land, meaning of, 8.08
merger, 8.11
procedure, 8.08
purchase price, 8.10
gas
installations, 1.18
service, 6.09
supply, 11.15
gazumping, 6.04, 6.05
option to purchase, 6.05, 8.03
gift
engaged couples, 16.72
lapsed, wills, 19.58
witnesses, to, 19.58
gift tax
certificate of discharge, 16.25
settlements and trusts, 19.70
goods
sale of, 6.09
warranty, 9.15
grant
(see **deed**)
grazing rights
constructive notice, 9.23
Statute of Frauds, 6.09
ground rents
arbitration procedure, 16.94
consent procedure, 16,94
county registrar, 5.30
covenants, 1.17
information notice, 5.30
land, meaning of, 8.08
notice procedure, 8.08, 8.09
prohibition, 19.10
purchase
price, 8.10
scheme, 1.02, 1.17, 8.07-12, 16.94
vesting certificate, 8.08
habendum
(*see also* **deed**)
fee farm grants, 19.41-2
leases, 19.27
mortgages, 19.49-50

health authority, 16.91
hedge, 9.14
  meaning, 18.62
  requisition on title, 16.07
hedge and ditch rule, 18.62
heir-at-law
  sale, power of, 14.66
High Court
  auctioneer deposit, 2.02, 2.03
  authorised securities, 2.03
  compensation, lodged, 8.18
  CPOs, appeals, 8.17
highway
  (*see* **road**)
holiday cottages, 16.100
HomeBond Scheme, 4.25-8
  building agreements, 11.14, 11.17,
  11.21-2
  central heating system, 4.28
  commercial property, 11.17
  deposits, 3.15, 4.26, 11.17
  enquiries, 5.07, 5.10
  final notice, 16.60
  flats, 5.10
  Guarantee Agreement, 4.27, 16.60
  lift, 4.28
  non-structural defects, 4.28
  requisition on title, 16.08
  stage payments, 4.26
  swimming pool, 4.28
hotels
  fire certificates, 16.83
  licences, 5.17
  multi-storey building, 16.95
house
  (*see also* **dwelling**)
  definition, 3.01
  HomeBond Scheme, 4.25-8,
  new, 16.60
    housing estate, 16.60
  tax allowances, 16.100
house agent
  (*see also* **estate agent**)
  accounts, 3.03
  deposit,
    pre-contract, 2.10, 3.10

fees and commission, 3.18-32
implied authority, 3.12
  delegate, to, 3.06-12
  receive money, to, 3.10-1
  sell, to, 3.07
  sign contract. to, 3.08-9, 6.41
instructions, 3.05
negligent misstatement, 3.14
sole agent, 3.05, 3.11
sole right to sell, 3.05
statutory regulation, 3.01-4
housing
  compulsory purchase, 8.15
  estate, 16.60
  grants, 11.10, 16.60
  public authority activities, 1.22
***Howe v Lord Dartmouth,* rule in**, 19.64
  husband and wife
  joint tenants, 18.91
improvements
  Landlord and Tenant Acts, 16.16
  rent fixing, 16.18
income tax, 1.24
  non-resident vendor, 16.26
  wills, 19.62
incorporeal hereditaments
  land, 18.70
Incumbered Estates Court
  conveyance, 14.56
incumbrances, 19.02
  definition, 18.33
  disclosure, 9.26
  fraudulent concealment, 14.59, 14.61
  requisitions on title, 16.22-3
indemnity
  agreements, 14.75
  covenants, 18.98-9, 19.31
  defects, 16.60
  environmental, 16.90
  rentcharges, 19.31
  services, 16.60
industrial property
  (*see also* **commercial property**)
  tax allowances, 16.100
inheritance tax, 19.61
  certificate of discharge, 16.25

inspection
(*see also* **survey**)
purchased chattels, 10.62
reasonable, 10.62
insurance, 2.44, 3.46
block policy, 5.12, 16.97
bond, 15.24
building agreements. 16.20
double, 12.40
employers, 11.20
fire, 12.40
life, 3.47
mortgage, linked to, 3.47
public liability, 11.20
purchaser, 2.44, 2.46, 12.39-40
risk, passing of, 12.36-43
service charges, 5.12
uberrimae fidei, 9.20
vandals, 12.40
vendor, 12.38
interest
late completion, 2.50, 12.18-50, 20.10, 20.11
rates of, 2.27, 20.10
court, 12.20
stipulated, 10.14
vendor, 12.18-20
investigation of title, 1.02 1.07
(see also **certificate of title, title, requisitions on title, searches**)
agricultural land, 1.14
caveat emptor, 4.04
chain of title, 15.08-9
costs, 15.05
deeds,
execution, 15.11
registration, 15.14
stamping, 15.13
description of property, 15.10
equities note, 1.15, 14.38
exclusion, 15.04
incumbrances, 15.16
landlord's title, 5.12
mortgages, 15.05
agent, 15.05
non-lawyer, 15.03

parties' capacity, 15.15
post-contract, 9.24, 9.41
pre-contract, 9.24
prior title, 15.04
property description. 15.10
purchaser's duty, 15-01-2
pyramid title, 1.17
registered land, 15.07
registration of deeds, 15.14
restrictions. 13.34, 15.04
restrictive covenants, 1.17
technical words, 15.12
title,
documents, perusal, 15.06-16
unregistered land, 15.02, 15.08-16
Irish Auctioneers and Valuers Institute
compensation fund, 2.26, 3.17
scale of charges, 2.31
Irish Land Commission
(*see* **Land Commission**)
Irish land problem, 1.27
joint deposit
arbitration award, 9.34
receipt, 10.32
joint tenancy
severance, 6.32
joint tenants
family homes, 18.91
husband and wife, 18.91
memorandum of sale, 6.32
survivorship, right of, 18.91
judgment mortgages, 1.28
contract and completion, 12.02-6
enforcement, 12.09
family home, 16.62
limitation of action, 12.09
process of execution, 12.05
registration, 12.03, 12.09, 12.43, 15.45
requisition on title, 12.09
judgments
searches, 15.45
requisition on title, 16.22
keys
completion, handing over, 20.13, 20.25, 20.30

laches
  part performance, 6.52
  specific performance, 13.50
land
  (*see also* **agricultural land,
  registered land, urban land**)
  interest in, 6.09
  interests, overreaching, 18.017
  meaning of, 8.08
Land Act, 1.13
  consent, 5.08, 5.18, 7.22-3, 10.48,
  16.53-6, 18.114
  Irish citizen, 16.56
  qualified person, 5.18, 7.23, 16.50-6
  requisitions, 10.12, 16.29-56
  rescission, 10.48
  section 12, 16.30-5
  section 13, 16.36
  section 45, 16.37-56
    certificates, 16.50-6, 18.115
  special condition, 10.69
  sub-division, 5.18, 16.30-5
  urban area, 16.44-9
land certificate, 14.31-2
  copy, 14.31
  judgment mortgage, 9.02
  lodgment in Registry, 14.31-2, 16.59
  non-issue, 14.21, 14.31
  original, 16.59
  up-to-date, 9.02
Land Commission
  congestion, relief of, 16.30
  consent, 1.13, 5.08, 16.29-56
    certificate, 16.53-6
    qualified persons, 16.50-2
  house agent's licence, 3.02
  land certificate lodgment with, 14.31,
  14.32-3
  land purchase annuity, 1.13
  provisional list, 16.35
  subletting, etc., consent, 19.35
  urban area, certification, 1.13, 16.32,
  16.44-9
land law
  historical background, 1.11

  modern developments, 1.20
  substantive, 1.27-8
Land Purchase Acts, 14.13
  agricultural land, 1.02, 1.13, 1.15,
  1.28,
  annuities, 16.30, 16.32, 16.59
  conveyancing significance, 1.28
  registration, compulsory, 1.02, 1.15,
  1.69, 14.25
  urban land, 1.16, 16.30, 16.32, 16.37
Land Registry
  (*see also* **searches**) 1.07
  boundaries, 9.13, 16.07
  caution, contracts, 14.34
  compulsory registration, 1.09, 14.13-
  4, 14.22,
  file plan, 16.07, 16.58-9
  folio, 9.10, 14.33-5, 16.58-9, 18.55-6,
  map, 9.10, 9.13, 15.06, 16.07
    approved scheme, 16.58-9
  register, mirror of title, 1.14, 9.02,
  14.21, 14.24,14.27
  registration in, 20.44-6
  title, guaranteed, 9.02, 14.21
Landed Estates Court
  root of title, 14.56
landlord
  consent, 3.43, 14.75
  notice to, 20.47
landlord and tenant
  Acts, 16.16
  relation of, 1.17, 10.14
Law Reform Commission
  definitions, 17.17
  family homes, 16.70
  foreign company, 18.128
  interests of vendor and purchaser,
  12.02, 12.06
  passing of risk, 12.37
  power of attorney, 18.129
  words of limitation, 18.86
Law Society
  (*see also* **Conveyancing
  Committee**)
  building agreements, 11.14

auctioneers' contracts, 2.53
both parties, acting for, 1.34
company law committee, 16.28
milk quotas, 5.19
objections and requisitions form,
5.02, 5.05, 16.01
purchaser's protection clause, 7.14
standard form contracts, 1.06, 2.16,
2.21, 9.01-3, 9.36, 10.03,
lease combined with term of years,
1.28, 19.27
contracts for, 6.09
lease for lives renewable for ever,
1.28, 19.27
contracts for, 6.09
fee farm grants, conversion, 14.76
lives, 14.76
leases, 19.23
agricultural, 19.35-6
assignment, 6.09, 19.31
business, 19.34
concurrent, 19.16
conditions, 16.93
contracts for, 6.09
covenants, 16.93
definitions, 10.14
disclosure, 9.27
fee farm grants, 10.14
fieri facias, 15.46
forms, 19.24-30
future, prohibition, 19.10
grants, 6.09
long, 1.27,
proviso for re-entry, 19.30
reddendum, 19.28
series, 1.17
statutory powers, 19.33
sub, 19.32
surrender, 6.09
vendor's title, 16.93
lessor
consent, 14.75
solicitor's cost, 17.04
letters of administration
grant of, 14.66, 14.79

root of title, 14.56
licence
endorsements, 6.30
hotel, 5.17, 16.105
intoxicating liquor, 16.104-7
music and singing, 5.17, 16.107
public dancing, 5.17, 16.104
public houses, 5.17, 16.104
restaurant, 5.17, 16.105-6
Statute of Frauds, 6.12
licensed premises
time or the essence, 13.15
licensees
purchaser, 12.33
Licensing Acts
requisitions on title, 16.104-5
lien
common law, 12.13, 12.15-7, 12.44
equitable, 12.13, 12.5-7, 12.44
lender's, 12.16
purchaser's, 12.08, 12.44
relinquished, 12.17
solicitor's, 20.50
vendor's, 12.13, 12.15, 12.44, 18.45
light, rights of, 16.10
limitation of actions
(*see also* **adverse possession**)
constitutionality, 4.17
hidden defects, 4.17
period, 1.36
personal injuries, 4.17
property damage, 4.17
limitation, words of, 18.49, 18.86
assignments of leases, 19.31
registered land transfers, 18.05, 18.88
Limitations, Statute of, 13.10
liquidator
company, 11.07, 12.29
conveyance, joining in, 12.29
disclaimer, 12,29, 12,48
family homes, 16.70-1
lis pendens, 15.45
loans
(*see also* **lenders**)
approval, 7.14
bridging, 3.44, 10.71

mortgage, subject to, 7.14, 10.69
purchaser's protection clause, 7.14
local authorities
bye-laws, 16.74, 16.79
grants, 11.10, 16.60
registration of dwellings, 16.18
lock-out agreements, 6.04
maintenance
flats, 19.15, 19.20
vendor, 12.21-5
map
(*see also* **plan**)
boundaries, 9.12
construction of, 18.66-8
incorporation in deed, 9.12, 18.64-5
Land Registry, 9.12, 18.55, 18.69-70
ordnance, 18.55-6, 18.63, 18.69
title deeds, in, 18.51, 18.63-8
unreliability, 9.10, 9.12
matrimonial home
(*see also* **family homes**)
appropriation, spouse's share, 19.60
memorandum in writing, 6.06, 6.14-
31, 7.03, 9.02-3, 9.05-6, 10.01, 10.02
(see *also* **Frauds, Statute of**)
auctioneer, 2.15-6, 6.34, 6.38-40
clerk, 2.18, 6.40
authorised agents, 6.34-47
personal liability, 6.35
closing date, 9.05
contents, 6.17-26
contract,
precedes, 6.06, 6.14
subject to, 6.15
correspondence, 6.28
date of contract, 9.05
deposit, 6.18, 9.05
essential elements, 6.18, 6.25
extra terms, 6.19
family home consent, 9.06
form, 6.16-7
four "P"s, 6.18
house or estate agent, 6.41
intention of parties, 6.15
interest rate, 9.05

joinder of documents, 6.28-31
joint tenants, 6.30
leases, 6.18, 6.23, 6.26
names and addresses, 9.05
parol evidence, 6.22, 6.29-30
parties, 6.20-1
pre-emption, right of, 8.04
price, 6.24
property, 6.22-3
signature, 6.15, 6.18, 6.32-42
ratified 6.36
solicitor, 6.06, 6.42-7
correspondence, 6.15-6, 6.28, 6.47
personal liability, 6.35
wife, 6.37
writing, 6.27
memorandum of sale, 6.16
merger, 21.02-5
contract in conveyance, 10.63, 21.02
covenants, 8.12
title, for, 10.63
damages, 13.76
doctrine of, 21.03
freehold, acquisition of, 8.11
parties' intention, 10.63, 21.03
term of years, 19 05
title, adverse possession, 14.82.
milk quota, 16.101-2, 16.103
apportionment, 16.101-2
Common Agricultural Policy, 16.101
EC directives, 1.14, 16.101
enquiries, 5.19
special condition, 10.72
warranty, 16.101
minerals, 18.75
mines, 18.75
misdescription, 4.08, 5.21, 9.08, 10.52
(see also **disclosure**)
contractual, 9.30, 9.36-48
damages, 5.26
fact, of, 9.29
fraud, 9.31
general law, 9.29
insubstantial, 13.75
law, of, 9.29

minor errors, 9.34
opinion, of, 9.29
puffing advertisements, 9.29
remedies, 9.29-48, 13.03
specific performance, 9.34,
9.35,13.51, 13.53
substantial, 9.32-3, 13.51, 13.75
vendor,
  against, 9.35
misrepresentation, 4.08
agent, authorised, 5.22
auctioneer, 5.22, 5.24
estate agent, 5.22
fact, 5.23, 5.26
fraudulent, 5.23-5
house agent, 5.22
induced contract, 5.23, 5.26
innocent, 5.23, 5.26, 13.64
  damages in lieu, 5.26
law, 5.23, 5.26
non-disclosure, 5.23, 5.24, 13.65
opinion, 5.23, 5.26
post-completion, 5.23
pre-contract remedies, 5.21, 9.29
puffing advertisements, 5.23, 5.26,
9.29
rescission, 5.23, 5.26, 13.64
spouse's consent, 16.23
mistake
rescission, 13.66-7
month, 8.06
mortgagee
collateral advantage, 19.52
court sale, 2.27, 8.13
family homes, 15.01
leasing powers, 19.33
sale, power of, 19.02, 19.52
mortgages, 19.47-56
chattel, 16.62
contracts for, 6.09
discharge, 2.46, 10.71, 19.03, 19.07,
19.55-6
equitable, 16.62
freehold, 19.48-53
future advances, 16.62

leasehold, 19.54
redemption,
  proviso for, 19.47, 19.51
requisition on title, 16.22
satisfactory, 7.14
mortgagor
leasing powers, 19.33
multi-story buildings, 1.22, 3.42,
16.95-6
building regulations, 16.96
carparks, 16.100
certificate of compliance, 16.95-6
common management company,
16.95
enquiries, 5.12, 16.95
negligence
accountants, 15.05
architects, 1.38, 4.18, 5.23
auditors, 15.05
auctioneer, 1.38, 2.13, 5.27-8
beneficiary, disappointed, 1.37
builders, 1.37, 4.14-8
building inspector, 4.15
contributory, 1.36
conveyancing transactions, 1.36
economic loss, 1.36, 4.15-6, 11.22
engineers, 1.38, 4.18
estate agents, 1.38, 3.14, 5.27
expert opinion, 1.36
hand searches, 15.42
limitation period, 1.36, 4.17
local authority, 4.15, 4.18
property broker, 15.03
prospective purchaser, 1.38
proportionate liability, 15.05
solicitor, 1.35, 1.36, 5.28, 15.02,
15.37, 16.07
surveyor, 1.38, 4.18
undertakings, 1.37
valuations, 1.38
negligent misstatement, 5.27
accountants, 5.27
architects, 5.27
auctioneer, 2.13, 5.27-8
company auditors, 5.27

duty of care, 5.27
estate agent, 3.14, 5.27, 5.28
house agent, 3.14
lessors 5.27
letting agents, 5.27
personal responsibility, 5.28
preliminary enquiries, 5.27, 5.28
property broker, 5.28
special relationship, 5.27, 5.28
vendor, 5.28
vendor's solicitor, 5.27, 5.28
new buildings
  (*see also* **HomeBond Scheme,
  NHBG Scheme**)
  caveat emptor, 4.09, 4.11
  contract builder, 4.09, 4.11
  common law, 4.10-8
  implied warranty, 4.11-3
  spec builder, 4.09, 4.11
NHBG Scheme, 4.25-6
  deposits, 3.15, 4.25
notice, 4.02
  actual, 1.35
  agistment, 9.23
  constructive, 1.35, 9.22-3, 14.02,
  14.60, 14.71, 16.62, 18.45
  grazing, 9.23
  imputed, 4.02, 16.62
  occupiers, 9.23, 16.23
  registered land charges, 14.72
  tenants, 9.23
notice to quit
  disclosure, 9.27
objections to title, 15.17, 16.04
  (*see also* **requisitions on title**)
offer
  acceptance, and, 6.02
  bid at auction, 2.20-1, 8.02
  communication, 2.21
  written, oral acceptance, 6.14
office, 16.17
  blocks, 16.95
Official Assignee, 8.03-4
  auctioneer's client account, 2.04
  bankruptcy search, 15.47

disclaimer, 12.27, 12.47
  purchaser's bankruptcy, 12.47
  settlements, void, 16.24
  title, 12.28
  vendor's bankruptcy, 12.27
option to purchase
  developer, 8.03
  exercise
  gazumping, 6.05, 8.03
  landlord, 8.04
  pre-emption, right of, distinction,
  8.04
  purchase price, 8.06
  strict compliance, 8.05
ordnance survey
  registered land, 14.36, 18.55-6
particulars of sale, 2.51-2, 3.35, 9.01,
  9.03, 9.07-8
  (*see also* **disclosure,
  misdescription**)
  advertisements. 9.16
  auctions
    reserved price, 2.15
    right to bid, 2.15
    without reserve, 2.15
  easements, 9.18
  fixtures and fittings. 9.15
  legal description, 9.08, 9.17-8
  misdescription, 9.08
  physical description, 9.08, 9.09-16
  restrictive covenants, 9.18
parties
  address, 9.05, 18.20
  fee farm grants, 19.38
  memorandum, 6.20-1
  name, 18.19
  occupation, 18.20
  registered land, 18.22
part performance, 6.48-60, 13.44,
  13.54
  acts by plaintiff, 6.49
  alterations and improvements, 6.58
  conditions of operation, 6.49-54
  contract, reference to, 6.53
  conveyancing steps, 6.59-60

doctrine of, 6.03, 6.08, 6.48
equitable doctrine, 6.48, 6.51-2
estoppel licences, 6.12
exchange, contract for, 6.51
fraud by defendant, 6.50
illustrations, 6.55-60
laches, 6.52
land, contracts, 6.51
lease, contract for, 6.51
money, payment of, 6.59
parol evidence, 6.54
partnership agreement, 6.51
possession, 6.56-7
party fences, 2.47, 9.14
requisition on title, 16.007
party walls, 2.47, 9.14
flats, 19.18
ownership of. 18.61
requisitions on title, 16.07
pastoral holding, 1.13
Patman v Harland, **rule in**, 14.60,
14.71-3
abrogation, 14.72
perpetuities, rule against
easements and profits. 18.72. 18.79
options,
purchase, to, 8.04
renew lease, to, 8.04
reservations, 18.79
trustees' administrative powers,
18.90
trusts, 18.90
personal representatives
(*see* also **assents**)
family homes, 16.62
leasing powers, 19.33
sale, powers of, 14.66
plan
title deeds, in, 9.10, 9.12-3, 18.51,
18.63-8
planning
(*see also* **development**)
applications, 7.18
certificates of compliance, 16.76
conditions, 1.21, 16.75, 16.77

development, 1.21, 3.42
non-conforming, 16.77
unauthorised, 16.77
enquiries, 5.09, 5.14
legislation, 1.21, 10.55, 16.20, 16.74
permission, 1.21, 2.47, 3.42, 16.75
conditions, 7.16-8, 10.69
full, 7.17
outline, 7.17
register, 16.78
search, 16.78
substantial compliance, 16.75
unauthorised developments, 16.77
warranty, 16.75, 16.78
possession
(*see also* **adverse possession,**
vacant possession)
agistment, 6.09
completion, before, 12.32-4
conacre, 6.09
part performance, 6.48-60
purchaser, 20.13
precedents
books of, 1.08, 17.08-9, 18.08
pre-contract enquiries
(see **preliminary enquiries**)
pre-emption, right of, 8.04
crystallises, 8.04
option to purchase, distinction, 8.14
preliminary enquiries, 1.22, 1.29-30,
3.36, 3.49, 4.02, 16.01, 20.04
(see also **enquiries**)
Acquired Rights Directive, 5.15
agricultural land, 2.47, 5.18.19
caveat emptor, 4.02-5
check list, 1.22, 2.47, 5.06, 12.43
commercial property, 2.47, 5.14-7
due diligence, 5.14
employees, 5.15
England, in, 1.29
environment, 1.22, 3.36, 5.14, 16.89
family homes, 5.29
fee simple, acquisition of, 5.13
flats, 2.47
food hygiene regulations, 9.47, 16.92

HomeBond, 4.28
industrial property, 5.14
landlord's title, 5.12
licensed title, 2.47, 5.17, 16.103-7
milk quotas, 16.101
misrepresentation, 5.21-2
modern legislation, 1.29
multi-storey buildings, 2.47, 5.12
planning permission, 5.09, 5.14
pre-lease, 1.22, 5.12, 5.13
rack rent lease, 5.12
replies,
    inaccurate, 5.04, 5.20
    remedies, 5.20-30
service charges, 5.12
statutory sanction, 5.29-30
survey, 5.06
tax-based incentives, 5.26
price
    (*see also* **purchase money**)
    abatement, 5.26, 9.32
    deposit, part payment, 10.18, 10.22
    memorandum, 6.24
    reserve, 2.05
probate
    grant of, 14.66, 14.79
    root of title, 14.56
profits *à prendre*, 18.71-2
    contracts for, 6.09
    grants, 6.09
pub
    enquiries, 5.17
    fire certificate, 16.83
    special condition, 10.72
public auction
    (*see* **auction**)
public authority
    activities, 1.22
    charges, 4.05
    compulsory purchase, 1.23, 8.14
puffer, 2.14
purchase money
    abatement, 5.26, 9.32, 9.33
    apportionment account, 20.08
    investments, 2.49

joint deposit, 2.50
receipt, 20.33
stage payments, 10.31
unpaid, vendor's lien, 12.13, 12.15-7,
    12.44
purchaser
    alterations, 12.33
    bankruptcy, 11.18, 12.47-8
    beneficiary, 12.02
    caretaker's agreement, 12.33
    conversion, doctrine of, 12.25
    death, 12.46
    election of remedies, 13.09
    gains, 12.35
    improvements, 12.34
    insurance, 2.44, 2.46, 12.39-40
    interest charges, 2.27, 12.34, 12.45
    licence, 12.33
    lien, 12.08, 12.44
    losses, 12.36
    possession before completion, 12.32-
    4
    protection, 17.19-51
    ready, willing and able, 3.29-30
    rents and profits, 12.34
    repairs, 12.33, 12.34
    risk passing, 3.46, 13.36-43
    tenant at will, 12.33
    waiver, 12.32
pyramid titles, 1.17, 1.19
    fee farm grants, 14.68
    problems, 1.28
    registration of title, 14.24
rates
    apportionment, 16.19, 20.07
    ownership, change of, 20.37, 20.47
receipt
    capital money, 18.45, 18.47
    endorsed, building society, 17.02,
    19.55
    lien, 12.16
    outgoings, 16.19
    purchase money, 20.33
    solicitors, payment to, 18.46, 20.33
    subsequent purchaser, 18.45
    sufficient discharge, 18.44

receiver
execution of deed, 18.131
sale by, 12.06
recitals
civil proceedings, 18.03
construction, 18.35
covenants, creation of, 18.34
estoppel, 18.32-3, 19.56
fee farm grants, 19.39
introductory, 18.40, 18.85. 19.03
leases, 19.24
mortgages, 19.48
narrative, 18.38-9, 19.03, 19.31
pre-root documents, 18.29
trustee appointments, 18.30
trusts, 18.36
twenty years old, 14.51, 14.54, 18.28
rectification, 19.56, 21.39
conveyance, 17.07
mistake, 13.66, 21.35
parol evidence, 17.19
reddendum
fee farm grants, 19.43
leases, 19.28
refuse charge, 16.19
registered land, 12.49-52
(*see also* **land certificate, land
registry**)
adverse possession, 1.15, 14.82,
16.25
burdens,
lease, 14.23
unregistered, 14.27, 14.41-2, 16.23
caution, 6.66, 12.07, 12.52, 16.23
certificates, 18.116
charge, cancellation, 19.55-6
compulsory registration, 14.22. 18.10
conditions of sale, 9.02
contract for sale, 9.02
covenants for title, 21.06
equities,
cancellation, 14.26
note, 14.25-6, 14.38-40
subject to, 14.25, 14.38
filed plan, 16.58

folio, 14.30
official copies, 14.33-5, 16.58
indexes, 14.30
inhibition, 6.66
judgment mortgages, 12.05, 15.45
map, 14.30
official copies, 14.36, 16.58
mirror of title, 1.15, 9.12
occupiers, 16.23
parties' position, 12.49-52
purchaser's equity, 12.50
registers, inspection, 14.30
title registered, 14.23
class, 14.24. 14.37
guarantee, 9.02
perusal of, 15.07
transfer forms, 17.03, 18.24, 19.06
acknowledgment and undertaking,
18.16
all estate clause, 18.83
attestation, 18.135
commencement, 18.08
covenants, 18.101
date, 18.11
exceptions and reservations, 18.81
execution, 18.132
flats, 19.13
habendum, 18.88
maps or plans, 18.69-70
parcels, 18.55-7
parties' description. 18.22
receipt clause, 18.43
recitals, 18.26
sealing, 18.122, 18.132
section 72 declaration, 16.58, 16.59
testatum, 18.41
trusts, 18.92
unregistered rights, 12.50-1
words of grant, 18.48
registration, 18.44-8
equities note, 14.25-6, 14.38
pyramid titles, 14.24
title, of,
compulsory area, 1.02, 1.09, 14.22,
14.24

system, 1.02
voluntary, 1.16
Registry of Deeds, 1.27
(*see also* **searches**)
contract for sale, 6.65
deeds, registration of, 1.09, 6.65,
20.43
Index of Lands, 15.42
Index of Names, 15.42, 15.44
judgment mortgage, 5.45
memorial, 16.60, 20.43
copy, 14.53
execution, 14.53, 20.43
secondary evidence, 14.53
urban land, 1.16
relationship certificate, 18.109
remainderman
time running, 14.81
remedies
(*see also* **damages, rectification,
rescission, specific performance,
vendor and purchaser summons**)
contract, enforcement of, 13.01
election, 13.02, 13.03
purchaser, 13.08
vendor, 13.04-7
enquiries, inaccurate replies, 5.20-30
pre-completion, 13.01
pre-contract, 5.04, 5.20
post-completion, 13.01, 21.05-39
time, 13.10-25
rent
(see also **ground rents**)
apportionment, 8.08, 20.06
book, 16.17
fixing, 16.18
gross, 16.18
receipt
last, evidence, 14.75
registration, 16.18
review clauses, 19.34
rent officer, 16.18
rent tribunal, 16.18
rents and profits
investment property, 12.19
vendor, 12.14, 12.19

rentcharge
indemnity, 19.31
requisitions on title, 1.07, 1.29, 16.01-
2
(*see also* **objections to title, title**)
actual occupation, 16.23
assent,
furnishing, 16.54
go behind, 15.19
bankruptcy, 12.28, 16.24
bare trust, 16.23
beneficial interest, 16.23
body corporate vendor, 16.27
boundaries, 16.07
building control, 16.79-82
charges, 16.22
charitable organisation, 15.19
closed contract, 10.02
completion, 16.108
compulsory registration, 16.55
constructive notice, 16.23
conveyance, matters of, 15.28
definition, 10.14
description of land, 9.10
Designated Areas, 16.100
dwellings, 16.18
easements, 16.10
engaged couples, 16.72
environment, 1.22, 16.86-90
family homes, 16.23, 16.61-71
fee simple acquisitions, 16.94
fire services, 16.83
fishing, 16.13
expedition, 15.18
fixtures and fittings, 16.06
flats,
new, 16.97-8
second-hand, 16.99
food hygiene regulations, 9.47,
16.91-2
forestry, 16.12
fraudulent conveyances, 16.24
general principles, 15.18-9
HomeBond Scheme, 16.08, 16.80
identify, 16.60

improvements, 16.18
incumbrances, 16.22-3
intermediate title, 15.24
judgments, 16.22
judicial separation, 16.73
Land Act, 16.29-56
leasehold property, 16.93
licensing, 16.103-7
  dancing, 16.107
  hotels, 16.105
  music, 16.107
  pubs, 16.104
  restaurants, 16.105-6
  singing, 16.107
litigation, 16.07, 16.22
managed properties, 16.97-9
meaning, 5.02, 15.17
milk quotas, 16.101-2
mortgage, 16.22
mortgagee, 15.19
multi-storey buildings, 16.95-6
negligence, 15.02, 15.37, 16.07
newly erected property, 16.60
NHBG Scheme, 16.08
non-resident vendor, 16.26
notices, 9.47, 16.20
obligations, 16.11
open contract, 10.02
original deeds, 16.56
outgoings, 16.19
outstanding, 20.23
personal representative, 15.19
planning, 16.74-8
post-contract, 1.29, 4.06, 5.01-2, 9.47
possession, 16.15
premises, 16.06-8
privileges, 16.10
proceedings, 16.22-5
rates, 16.19
refuse charge, 16.19
registered land, 16.58-9
rejoinders, 15.38
rent, 16.18
replies, 15.34-8, 16.05, 16.07
rescission, 10.56

restrictions, 15.04
  contractual, 15.25-35
  statutory, 15.24
safety, etc at work, 16.84-5
searches, 16.21
services, 16.09
specific, 15.18
sporting, 16.14
spouse's consent, 16.23
stamping on deeds, 15.13
standard form, 15.17-8, 16.01-3
statutory provision, 15.19
taxation, 16.25, 16.100
tenancies, 16.16-7
tenant for life, 15.19
time for making, 15.20-2, 15.36
trusts, 15.19, 16.23
unregistered
  burdens, 14.41-2
  property, 16.54-6
vague, 15.18
voluntary dispositions, 16.24
waiver, 15.22, 15.29, 16.02
water charge, 16.19
rescission, 13.57-73, 21.34-8
common law, 13.58
compensation not assessable, 9.48
complete, failure to, 13.69-70
contractual right, 13.05, 13.70-74
  consent, 13.73-4
  notices, non-disclosure, 10.56,
  13.72
  requisitions on title, 13.34, 13.71
costs, indemnity, 13.07, 13.61
delay, 13.10, 13.17
deposit,
  forfeiture, 10.18, 10.19, 13.05,
  13.09, 13.57, 13.58, 13.60
duress, 13.48
equity, 13.58
fraud, 13.48, 13.58, 13.66, 21.35
fraudulent misrepresentation, 5.23,
13.64
grounds, 13.63-74
innocent misrepresentation, 13.56,
13.64, 21.36

Land Act consent, 10.48
meanings, confusion, 13.07, 13.57
misdescription, 9.31, 9.32, 9.47,
13.64-5
mistake, 13.48, 13.66-7, 21.37-8
non-disclosure, 13.65
post-completion, 21.34-8
recklessness, 15.31
repudiatory breach, 13.04-9
requisitions, 15.29-35
rent and profits, 13.60, 13.61
resale, 13.05, 13.61
restitutio in integrum, 13.59-62
purchaser, 13.62
vendor, 13.60-1
root of contract, 13.58, 13.66
status quo, return to, 13.05, 13.07,
13.09, 13.57, 13.58
time, 13.12
title, defect in, 13.68
trivial breach, 13.02
reservations, 18.50
contra proferentem rule, 17.21
exceptions, distinction, 18.73-4
execution of deed, grantee, 18.77,
18.119
implied, 18.78, 18.80
pyramid title, 1.17
registered land, 18.81
residence, right of, 1.15, 1.28
Statute of Frauds. 6.12
residential property tax
apportionment, 20.07
certificate of discharge, 16.25
restaurants
fire certificate, 16.83
food hygiene, 16.91-2
licences, 5.17, 10.72
special condition, 10.72
restrictive covenants, 14.73
disclosure, 9.26, 14.59
estate scheme, merger, 8.12
freehold,
enforceability, 19.10
registration, 14.60

particulars of sale, 9.18
relief against, 14.73
revenue certificates, 11.10, 18.108-12
Revenue Commissioners
auction permits, 2.02
auctioneer's licence, 2.02
building agreements, 11.10
house estate's licence, 3.02
non-resident vendor, 16.26
stamp duty
enforcement, 9.15
increase, 16.38-9
tax certificate, 14.18, 14.49, 16.25
reversionary interest, 16.25
risk, 10.60, 12.36
building agreement, 11.20
court sale, 11.07
vendor retaining, 12.25, 12.36-43
river
ownership, soil, 18.60
roads
building agreement, 11.15
charge, taken in, 5.07, 16.75
ownership, soil, 18.59
public authority activities, 1.22
requisition on title, 16.09
toll, 16.100
root of title, 14.28, 14.50, 14.56-8
deduction, 9.24
devise,
general, 14.56
specific, 14.56
fee farm grant, conversion, 14,11,
14.56
good, 14.55-7
Landed Estates Court conveyance,
14.56
new lease, statutory, 14.11
photocopy, draft contract, 14.02
powers of appointment, 14.56
special condition, 10.70
specified, 14.57
voluntary conveyance, 14.56
wills, 14.56

Royal Institute of Architects of Ireland
certificates of compliance, 16.77
safety
construction sites, 16.84
file, 16.84-5
sale
(*see also* **auction, contract for sale, court sales**)
conveyances, 19.02-22
goods, of, 9.15
new house, housing estate, 19.08-10
private treaty, 1.06, 10.17
statutory powers, 19.07
seal, 18.122
sealing, 18,122, 12.128
searches, 1.03, 1.07, 5.03, 15.39-48, 20.22
(*see also* **enquiries, preliminary enquiries**)
bankruptcy, 12.28
office, 15.47
companies register, 4.25, 5.03, 11.17, 15.48
England, 1.29
expense, 15.42
Judgments Office, 15.45
Land Registry, 4.04-5, 4.08, 5.03, 11.17, 14.30, 14.31, 15.40-1
hand, 15.41
official, 15.41
priority, 15.41
telegram, 15.41
telephone, 15.29, 15.41
local authorities, 1.29,
planning register, 5.06, 16.78
pre-contract, 1.29-30, 3.36, 4.02, 4.07
Registry of Deeds, 1.09, 1.16, 1.30, 3.36, 4.04-5, 5.03, 11.17, 14.64, 15.42-4, 16.21
common, 15.42
hand, 15.42
negative, 1.09, 15.42
requisitions on title, 16.21
Schedule, 5.03, 9.03, 10.42, 15.43

Sheriff's Office, 5.03, 5.46
vendor, 1.09, 5.03, 10.42, 16.21
septic tank, 16.10
services, 16.09
taken in charge, 16.11
service charges
apportionment, 20.10
flats, 16.99
Settled Land Acts, 19.33
settlements, 14.77, 19.70
creation, two documents, 14.77
sewerage
services, 11.15
sewers
charge, taken in, 5.07, 16.09
enquiries, 5.07
requisition on title, 16.09
sheriff
fieri facias, writ of, 15.46
shooting rights, 18.76
signature
agent, as, 6.35, 10.50
trust, in, 6.36, 10.50
Society of Chartered Surveyors
indemnity insurance, 2.26
solicitors
(*see also* **undertakings**)
accounts regulations, 10.26
authority,
to negotiate contract, 6.42-7
to sign contract, 6.42-7
bill of costs, 1.09, 20.37, 20.49
lien, 20.50
book deposit, 3.17
both parties, acting for, 1.34, 10.08
client accounts,
interest earned, 10.26
costs, 10.11
fees, 20.49
instructions, taking, 2.37-50, 3.34, 3.38
book, 6.16
negligence, 1.35, 1.36, 5.28, 14.45, 14.73, 15.02, 15.37, 16.07
officers of courts, 20.15
payments to, 18.46, 20.13

progress sheet, 2.37, 3.38
public auction sale, 2.37-50
role in conveyancing, 1.06-9, 2.36-52
solicitors financial services, 1.37
special conditions, 9.01, 10.01
bye-law amnesty, 10.55, 10.69,16.77
definitions, 10.68
general conditions
  amendments, 10.06, 10.68
  conflict, 10.06, 10.67, 10.68
Land Act consent, 10.69
landlord's consent, 10.69
milk quota, 10.72, 16.101
missing title documents, 10.70
mortgage,
  discharge, 10.71
  loan, 10.69
non-conforming development, 16.77
planning permission, 10.69
  warranty, 16.75
possessory title, 10.70
printed, 10.68
pubs, 10.72
restaurants, 10.72
root of title, 10.70
statutory restrictions, 10.67
time of essence, 13.19
title, deduction of, 10.70
VAT, 10.68
specific performance, 6.51-2, 13.37-56
  (*see also* **part performance**)
abatement in price, 9.32, 9.34, 13.53
acquiescence, 13.50
arbitrator, 10.66
bad title, 13.49, 13.52-3
building contracts, 13.41
clean hands, 13.43
compensation, 13.37, 13.51, 13.53
contract, breach of, 13.42
conversion, 12.12
conveyancing contracts, 13.39-41
court,
  sale, 8.13
  vesting order, 8.13
damages,

inadequate, 13.39
in default, 10.59, 13.03
in lieu, 13.05, 13.54
defences, 13.38, 13.41, 13.43-53
deposit, return of, 13.34-6
discretion, 10.38, 13.38
drunkenness, 13.48
equitable remedy, 13.38
exchange contracts, 13.40
fairness, lack of, 13.48-9
formalities, lack of, 13.44
fraudulent misrepresentation, 5.25
general principles, 13.38-42
hardship, 12.12, 13.48-9
improvident settlement, 13.48
incompleteness, 13,47
infant, 13.47
joint tenants, 6.30
laches, 13.50
law suit, 13.49, 13.52
leasehold repairing covenants, 13.41
lend money, contract to, 13.40
misdescription, 13.51, 13.53
misrepresentation, 5.25, 9.35
mutuality, 13.40, 13.41, 13.47
order, enforcement, 13.55-6
performance, supervision, 13.41
purchaser, 13.09, 13.37, 13.56
time, 13.10
title, lack of, 13.52-3
uncertainty, 13.45
undervalue, 13.48
vendor, 13.37, 13.40, 13.55
waiver, 13.53
sporting licences, 16.14
spouse
  (*see also* **family homes**)
consent, 2.40, 2.47, 3.36, 4.06, 5.08,
  9.06, 16.62-9
  court order, 16.69
  form, 9.06, 16.69, 18.115
  infant, 16.69
  prior, 16.62
  desertion, 16.69
legal right, 19.60

protection, 16.62
witness, 18.134
squatter
(*see also* **adverse possession**)
quality of title, 14.82
vacant possession, 10.44
stakeholder, 2.26
auctioneer, 2.26
deposit, 2.26, 2.45, 3.16, 10.25,
10.28, 13.34
estate agent, 3.16
interest,
account of, 2.10
principal, 10.26
solicitor, 2.10, 2.45
vendor,
liability, 2.10, 10.25-6
stamp duty, 1.31, 2.41, 3.110, 4.04
(*see also* **certificate for value**)
avoidance, 16.40
building agreements, 11.10
certificates, 9.15, 18.108-12, 20.40
condition of sale, 10.09
conveyances, 20.39-41
evasion, 9.15
evidence, 16.25, 20.38
fixtures and fittings, 9.15
floor area certificates, 11.10, 16.60
grant type houses, 11.10
increase in, 16.38-9
leases, 20.39
mortgages, 14.36
non-grant type, 11.10
PD stamp, 14.18, 14.49, 16.25, 20.41
penal, 16.39-43
penalty, 9.15
purchased chattels, 9.15
rates, 20.40
spouses, joint tenancy, 20.39
transactions, larger or series, 9.15,
18.108
Statute of Frauds
(*see* **Frauds, Statute of**)
Statute of Uses
(*see* **Uses, Statute of**)

statutory declaration
adverse possession, 14.12, 14.81
identity of property, 9.11, 16.57
lost deeds, 14.52
spouses, marriage, 16.64, 16.72
unregistered burdens, 14.41
verification of abstract, 14.49
statutory tenant, 6.12
streets, 6.12
(*see* **road**)
sub-division
general consent, 1.13, 16.34
land, of, 1.17
restrictions, 1.13, 16.03-5
subject to contract, 6.15, 7.06-13
conditions of sale, 7.13
denial of contract, 7.08, 7.10
exceptional cases, 7.08
exchange, 7.07, 7.08, 7.11
formal agreement, 7.11-2
intention, 7.06
solicitor's correspondence, 6.15,
6.47, 7.08, 7.09
title, 713
succession
(*see also* **wills**)
conversion, doctrine of, 6.11, 12.11-
12
succession duty, 1.27, 14.18, 14.49
support
flats, 1.18, 19.11, 19.19
mutual rights, party walls, 18.61
surrender
operation of law, 17.02
survey, 3.41, 4.03
conditional contract, 7.19
independent, 3.40, 4.06, 4.21-4, 5.06
lending institution, 3.40, 4.23-4, 5.06
negligent, 1.38, 4.18
valuer, 3.40
surveyor
negligent, 1.38, 4.18
qualified, 4.21
tax clearance certificates
builders, 11.10
conditions of sale, 10.43

taxation, 1.23-31
  (*see also* **capital acquisitions tax,
  capital gains tax, gift tax, income
  tax, inheritance tax, succession
  duty**).
  designated areas, 5.16
  estate planning, 1.23-31, 2.49
  incentives, 5.16
  settlements and trusts, 19.70
  wills, 19.61 -2
telephone line, 5.07
  requisition, 16.09
television cable, 5.07
Temple Bar area, 5.16
tenancies
  (*see also* **agricultural holdings**)
  compensation, 16.16
  disclosure, 9.42
  estoppel, 13.12
  new, 16.16
  office, 16.17
  periodic, 17.02
  renunciation, 16.17
tenant
  (*see also* **landlord and tenant**)
  estoppel, by, 14.82
  will, at, 12.33
tenant for life
  (*see also* **settlements**)
  dispossession, 14.81
  sale, powers of, 14.77, 18.42, 19.02
  statutory leases, 19.33
tenure, 9.07
testator
  (*see also* **wills**)
  disposition, freedom of, 19.60
  subsequent marriage, 19.58
timber rights, 18.76
time, 13.10-25
  chain transactions, 13.13
  clauses, 13.11
  completion notices, 13.19-24
  damages, 13.10
  essence, of the, 2.50, 13.03, 13.11-2,
  13.31
    delivery of abstract, 13.48

  equity, 13.11
  expressly, 13.13
  farm, 13.15
  hazardous property, 13.15
  implication, by, 13.14-5
  licensed premises, 13.15
  making, 13.16-24
  reasonable time, 13.17, 13.19
  rejoinders, 15.38
  rent reviews, 19.34
  requisitions on title, 15.20, 15.36
  residential property, 13.15
  two-edged sword, 13.13, 13.20
  unreasonable delay, 13.17, 13.19
  waiting period, 13.17-8
  waiver, 13.16, 13.25
  interest clause, 13.14
  notice, 13.12, 13.17-8
  rescission, 13.10
tithe rentcharge
  disclosure, 9.26, 14.45
  extinguished, 9.26
title
  (*see also* **abstract of title,
  certificate of title, deduction of
  title, investigation of title,
  pyramid titles, requisitions on
  title, root of title, title deeds, title
  documents**)
  acceptance, 15.49-53
    draft conveyance, delivery, 15.52
    possession, taking, 12.34, 15.53
    requisitions, failure to send, 15.51
  alterations, 12.34
  adverse possession, 14.12, 14.81
  bad, 13.52, 14.10, 14.17, 14.59,
  14.61, 15.17
  chain of, 14.61-7, 15.08-9
  closed contract, 14.05
  commencement, 14.57
  conveyance, matters of, 14.18
  defect, disclosure, 4.08
  delivery, 10.34, 14.46
  doubtful, 13.52, 14.10, 14.15-16,
  14.59

fraudulent concealment, 9.31
good, 14.10, 15.05, 15.17
  duty to show, 9.37
  holding, 13.34, 14.10, 14.12
gradations, 14.10
intermediate, 10.37, 14.61
length of, 14.05, 14.54-67
marketable, 14.10, 14.11
meanings, 14.09
open contract, 14.05
pedigree, falsification, 14.61
perusal, 15.06-16
possessory, 1.15, 10.70, 14.81-2,
  16.64
pre-root, 14.59, 14.24-5
prior, 10.36, 14.59, 15.04, 15.24-5
purchaser, force on, 14.10-1, 14.59,
  15.22
pyramid, 1.02, 1.17, 1.28
shortened, 14.69
special condition, 10.70
statutory period. 14.54-5
verification, 15.42, 20.29
waiver, 12.34, 14.19, 15.22
title deeds, 2.41-4, 3.35, 9.10,
  14.09,14.21
acknowledgment and undertaking,
  18.102-6
copies, 2.43, 14.43
deposit, 2.43
lost, 2.43, 14.52-3, 14.58
originals,
  checking copies, 20.27
  furnishing, 14.44, 16.56
photocopies, 14.43, 15.08
secondary evidence, 14.52-3, 14.58
title documents, 2.41-4, 9.10-11, 15.06,
  20.27
completion, 20.27
conclusive, 9.11
copies, 2.43, 14.43, 15.06
  certified or plain, 14.43
covenant for production, 18.102-6,
  19.31
fraudulent concealment. 14.61
inspection, 2.43, 6.23, 14.02, 20.27

Land Registry folio, 9.10
lost or mislaid, 2.43, 14.52-3, 14.58
memorials, 14.52-3
originals, 14.44, 16.56
other property, 10.53
perusal, 20.27
photocopies, 14.02, 14.43
pre-root title, 14.59
Schedule, 9.03, 9.11, 9.24
undertaking for safe-keeping. 2.43,
  18.102-6, 19.31
wills, 14.66
tort
  (*see also* **negligence**)
deceit, 5.21, 9.31
personal injuries, 4.14-18
town
boundaries, 16.47
definition, 16.44-8
non-municipal, 16.46
scheduled, 16.46
town and country planning
  (*see* **planning**)
trustees
administrative powers, 18.90
covenants for title, 15.19
joint tenants, 18.91
powers, 19.71
sale, statutory power, 14.65
settlement, of the, 15.15, 18.14
  receipt, 18.47
vendor, 12.02-29
vesting orders, 6.17
wills, 19.68
trusts, 2.20
charitable, 6.18
declaration of, 18.89-90
discretionary, 19.62
maintenance, etc., for, 19.62
recitals, 18.36
resulting, 18.42
title, kept off, 14.64, 15.19, 18.36,
  18.92
trusts for sale, 6.11
conveyancing difficulties, 14.68
statutory, 14.77-8

turbary, right of, 18.75
undertakings, 20.14-19
bank, to, 1.09, 2,43, 20.14, 20.17
building society, to, 2.43, 20.14, 20.17
discharge, 2.43, 20.14, 20.17, 20.37
honouring, 20.14-15
mortgage, discharge of, 10.71, 18.16, 18.103, 19.56, 20.14, 20.17, 20.37
mortgagee, to, 20.17
nature of, 20.15
note as to, 2.43
purchaser, to, 20.18
Registry of Deeds searches, 20.19, 20.37
requisitions, outstanding, 20.23
solicitors', 1.37, 20.15
statutory, 18.102-6
title deeds, 14.44, 18.103, 20.17
undue influence
spouse's consent, 16.23
urban areas, 1.13, 16.32, 16.44-9
uses
conveyance to, 18.85-6
reservations, 18.77
resulting, 15.12
Uses, Statute of, 18.77, 18.86, 18.90
vacant possession, 9.27, 10.44, 20.13
completion notice, 13.20
conditions of sale, 10.44
court sale, 11.03
leases, 9.27
requisitions on title, 16.15
rubbish, 10.44, 13.20
squatters, 10.44
tenant, 10.44
value
(*see also* **certificate for value**)
full, family homes, 16.62
valuer
lending institution, 3.40
survey, 3.40
VAT
building agreements, 11.11
landlord and tenant, 5.12

liability, 10.68
purchase price, in addition to, 10.68
special condition, 10.68
vendor
agricultural land, 12.22
bankruptcy, 12.27-9
bidding by, 2.14-18
wilful default, 12.18-19
court sales, 11.05, 12.33
death, 12.26
disclosure, duty of, 9.17, 9.19
election, 13.04
garden, 12.22
insolvency, 12.27-9
insurance, 12.38
interest, 12.18-20
investment property, 12.19
lease covenants, 12.22
lien, 12.13, 12.44
abandonment, 12.17
common law, 12.13, 12.55
equitable, 12.13, 12.15, 12.44
liquidation, 12.29
maintenance, duty of, 12.21-5
waiver, 12.24
misdescription, 9.35
non-resident, 16.25
possession, 12.13, 12.19, 12.21
remedies, election, 13.04-7
rents and profits, 12.14, 12.19
account, 12.14, 12.19, 12.21
resale, 13.04, 13.30, 13.31
risk, 12.25
tenancies, 12.22
title,
good, duty to show, 14.06-19
latent defects, disclosure, 14.02, 14.59, 14.61
patent defects, 14.59
trespassers, 12.22
trustee, 12.02-9
wilful default, 12.18-19
vendor and purchaser summons, 10.66, 13.02, 13.26-9, 13.16
waiver
abstract of title, 14.43

condition, benefit of, 6.07
covenant, breach of, 14.75
draft conveyance, delivery, 17.06
objection to title, 13.53, 14.19
possession, purchaser taking, 12.32-4
requisitions on title, delivery, 15.22,
15.29, 16.02
term of contract, 6.07
vendor's duty to maintain, 12.24
walls
  (*see also* **party walls**)
boundary, 9.14, 16.07
ownership, 18.61, 19.18
warranty
authority of, 1.35, 2.13
building contracts, implied, 4.22-3
building control, 16.80
chattels, 9.15, 10.61, 16.06
collateral, 4.08, 4.19, 5.26, 11.22
  builder, 4.13, 11.22
damages, 5.27
environmental, 16.90
fitness for use, 4.12, 11.22
fixtures and fittings, 9.14
furnished accommodation, 4.12
habitability, 4.12
milk quota, 16.101
planning 16.75, 16.78
sale of goods, 9.15
title, of, 19.05
water
charge, 16.19
requisition on title, 16.09, 16.19
services, 11.15, 16.09

way, rights of
requisition on title, 16.10
reservation, 18.76
wills, 19.57-68
  (*see also* **succession, testator**)
apportionment rules, 19.64
beneficiary, disappointed, 1.37
capacity, 19.58
construction, 19.58
contents, 19.59-68
equity, operate in, 14.56, 14.66
execution, 19.58
farmers, failure to prove, 1.15
form, 19.58
formalities, 19.58
grants, attached to, 14.66, 14.79
home-made, 1.15
signature, 6.33, 19.58
writing, 6.27
wires
requisitions on title, 16.10
witnesses, 18.133-6
gifts to, 19.58
registration of deeds, 18.136
spouse, 18.134
wills, 19.58
words
technical, 15.12
words of limitation
  (see **limitation, words of**)
working, 10.14
notices, 10.64
requisitions, 15.20
time limits, 10.65